1989

American Casebook Series
Hornbook Series and Basic Legal Texts
Nutshell Series

of

WEST PUBLISHING COMPANY
P.O. Box 64526
St. Paul, Minnesota 55164–0526

ACCOUNTING

Faris' Accounting and Law in a Nutshell, 377 pages, 1984 (Text)

Fiflis, Kripke and Foster's Teaching Materials on Accounting for Business Lawyers, 3rd Ed., 838 pages, 1984 (Casebook)

Siegel and Siegel's Accounting and Financial Disclosure: A Guide to Basic Concepts, 259 pages, 1983 (Text)

ADMINISTRATIVE LAW

Davis' Cases, Text and Problems on Administrative Law, 6th Ed., 683 pages, 1977 (Casebook)

Davis' Basic Text on Administrative Law, 3rd Ed., 617 pages, 1972 (Text)

Gellhorn and Boyer's Administrative Law and Process in a Nutshell, 2nd Ed., 445 pages, 1981 (Text)

Mashaw and Merrill's Cases and Materials on Administrative Law–The American Public Law System, 2nd Ed., 976 pages, 1985 (Casebook)

Robinson, Gellhorn and Bruff's The Administrative Process, 3rd Ed., 978 pages, 1986 (Casebook)

ADMIRALTY

Healy and Sharpe's Cases and Materials on Admiralty, 2nd Ed., 876 pages, 1986 (Casebook)

Maraist's Admiralty in a Nutshell, 390 pages, 1983 (Text)

Sohn and Gustafson's Law of the Sea in a Nutshell, 264 pages, 1984 (Text)

AGENCY—PARTNERSHIP

Fessler's Alternatives to Incorporation for Persons in Quest of Profit, 2nd Ed., 326 pages, 1986 (Casebook)

AGENCY—PARTNERSHIP—Cont'd

Henn's Cases and Materials on Agency, Partnership and Other Unincorporated Business Enterprises, 2nd Ed., 733 pages, 1985 (Casebook)

Reuschlein and Gregory's Hornbook on the Law of Agency and Partnership, 625 pages, 1979, with 1981 pocket part (Text)

Seavey, Reuschlein and Hall's Cases on Agency and Partnership, 599 pages, 1962 (Casebook)

Selected Corporation and Partnership Statutes and Forms, 555 pages, 1985

Steffen and Kerr's Cases and Materials on Agency-Partnership, 4th Ed., 859 pages, 1980 (Casebook)

Steffen's Agency-Partnership in a Nutshell, 364 pages, 1977 (Text)

AGRICULTURAL LAW

Meyer, Pedersen, Thorson and Davidson's Agricultural Law: Cases and Materials, 931 pages, 1985 (Casebook)

ALTERNATIVE DISPUTE RESOLUTION

Kanowitz' Cases and Materials on Alternative Dispute Resolution, 1024 pages, 1986 (Casebook)

AMERICAN INDIAN LAW

Canby's American Indian Law in a Nutshell, 288 pages, 1981 (Text)

Getches and Wilkinson's Cases on Federal Indian Law, 2nd Ed., approximately 870 pages, 1986 (Casebook)

ANTITRUST LAW

Gellhorn's Antitrust Law and Economics in a Nutshell, 3rd Ed., about 425 pages, 1987 (Text)

List current as of July, 1986

T7202—1g

I

LAW SCHOOL PUBLICATIONS—Continued

ANTITRUST LAW—Cont'd

Gifford and Raskind's Cases and Materials on Antitrust, 694 pages, 1983 with 1985 Supplement (Casebook)

Hovenkamp's Hornbook on Economics and Federal Antitrust Law, Student Ed., 414 pages, 1985 (Text)

Oppenheim, Weston and McCarthy's Cases and Comments on Federal Antitrust Laws, 4th Ed., 1168 pages, 1981 with 1985 Supplement (Casebook)

Posner and Easterbrook's Cases and Economic Notes on Antitrust, 2nd Ed., 1077 pages, 1981, with 1984–85 Supplement (Casebook)

Sullivan's Hornbook of the Law of Antitrust, 886 pages, 1977 (Text)

See also Regulated Industries, Trade Regulation

ART LAW

DuBoff's Art Law in a Nutshell, 335 pages, 1984 (Text)

BANKING LAW

Lovett's Banking and Financial Institutions in a Nutshell, 409 pages, 1984 (Text)

Symons and White's Teaching Materials on Banking Law, 2nd Ed., 993 pages, 1984 (Casebook)

BUSINESS PLANNING

Painter's Problems and Materials in Business Planning, 2nd Ed., 1008 pages, 1984 (Casebook)

Selected Securities and Business Planning Statutes, Rules and Forms, 470 pages, 1985

CIVIL PROCEDURE

Casad's Res Judicata in a Nutshell, 310 pages, 1976 (text)

Cound, Friedenthal, Miller and Sexton's Cases and Materials on Civil Procedure, 4th Ed., 1202 pages, 1985 with 1985 Supplement (Casebook)

Ehrenzweig, Louisell and Hazard's Jurisdiction in a Nutshell, 4th Ed., 232 pages, 1980 (Text)

Federal Rules of Civil-Appellate Procedure—West Law School Edition, about 550 pages, 1986

Friedenthal, Kane and Miller's Hornbook on Civil Procedure, 876 pages, 1985 (Text)

Kane's Civil Procedure in a Nutshell, 2nd Ed., 306 pages, 1986 (Text)

Koffler and Reppy's Hornbook on Common Law Pleading, 663 pages, 1969 (Text)

Marcus and Sherman's Complex Litigation—Cases and Materials on Advanced Civil Procedure, 846 pages, 1985 (Casebook)

Park's Computer-Aided Exercises on Civil Procedure, 2nd Ed., 167 pages, 1983 (Coursebook)

CIVIL PROCEDURE—Cont'd

Siegel's Hornbook on New York Practice, 1011 pages, 1978 with 1985 Pocket Part (Text)

See also Federal Jurisdiction and Procedure

CIVIL RIGHTS

Abernathy's Cases and Materials on Civil Rights, 660 pages, 1980 (Casebook)

Cohen's Cases on the Law of Deprivation of Liberty: A Study in Social Control, 755 pages, 1980 (Casebook)

Lockhart, Kamisar, Choper and Shiffrin's Cases on Constitutional Rights and Liberties, 6th Ed., about 1300 pages, 1986 with 1986 Supplement (Casebook)—reprint from Lockhart, et al. Cases on Constitutional Law, 6th Ed., 1986

Vieira's Civil Rights in a Nutshell, 279 pages, 1978 (Text)

COMMERCIAL LAW

Bailey's Secured Transactions in a Nutshell, 2nd Ed., 391 pages, 1981 (Text)

Epstein and Martin's Basic Uniform Commercial Code Teaching Materials, 2nd Ed., 667 pages, 1983 (Casebook)

Henson's Hornbook on Secured Transactions Under the U.C.C., 2nd Ed., 504 pages, 1979 with 1979 P.P. (Text)

Murray's Commercial Law, Problems and Materials, 366 pages, 1975 (Coursebook)

Nordstrom and Clovis' Problems and Materials on Commercial Paper, 458 pages, 1972 (Casebook)

Nordstrom, Murray and Clovis' Problems and Materials on Sales, 515 pages, 1982 (Casebook)

Nordstrom, Murray and Clovis' Problems and Materials on Secured Transactions, about 500 pages, 1987 (Casebook)

Selected Commercial Statutes, 1389 pages, 1985

Speidel, Summers and White's Teaching Materials on Commercial and Consumer Law, 3rd Ed., 1490 pages, 1981 (Casebook)

Stockton's Sales in a Nutshell, 2nd Ed., 370 pages, 1981 (Text)

Stone's Uniform Commercial Code in a Nutshell, 2nd Ed., 516 pages, 1984 (Text)

Uniform Commercial Code, Official Text with Comments, 994 pages, 1978

UCC Article 9, Reprint from 1962 Code, 128 pages, 1976

UCC Article 9, 1972 Amendments, 304 pages, 1978

Weber and Speidel's Commercial Paper in a Nutshell, 3rd Ed., 404 pages, 1982 (Text)

White and Summers' Hornbook on the Uniform Commercial Code, 2nd Ed., 1250 pages, 1980 (Text)

LAW SCHOOL PUBLICATIONS—Continued

COMMUNITY PROPERTY

Mennell's Community Property in a Nutshell, 447 pages, 1982 (Text)

Verrall and Bird's Cases and Materials on California Community Property, 4th Ed., 549 pages, 1983 (Casebook)

COMPARATIVE LAW

Barton, Gibbs, Li and Merryman's Law in Radically Different Cultures, 960 pages, 1983 (Casebook)

Glendon, Gordon and Osakive's Comparative Legal Traditions: Text, Materials and Cases on the Civil Law, Common Law, and Socialist Law Traditions, 1091 pages, 1985 (Casebook)

Glendon, Gordon, and Osakwe's Comparative Legal Traditions in a Nutshell, 402 pages, 1982 (Text)

Langbein's Comparative Criminal Procedure: Germany, 172 pages, 1977 (Casebook)

COMPUTERS AND LAW

Maggs and Sprowl's Computer Applications in the Law, about 300 pages, 1986 (Text)

Mason's An Introduction to the Use of Computers in Law, 223 pages, 1984 (Text)

CONFLICT OF LAWS

Cramton, Currie and Kay's Cases-Comments-Questions on Conflict of Laws, 3rd Ed., 1026 pages, 1981 (Casebook)

Scoles and Hay's Hornbook on Conflict of Laws, Student Ed., 1085 pages, 1982 with 1986 P.P. (Text)

Scoles and Weintraub's Cases and Materials on Conflict of Laws, 2nd Ed., 966 pages, 1972, with 1978 Supplement (Casebook)

Siegel's Conflicts in a Nutshell, 469 pages, 1982 (Text)

CONSTITUTIONAL LAW

Barron and Dienes' Constitutional Law in a Nutshell, about 400 pages, 1986 (Text)

Engdahl's Constitutional Power in a Nutshell: Federal and State, 411 pages, 1974 (Text)

Lockhart, Kamisar, Choper and Shiffrin's Cases-Comments-Questions on Constitutional Law, 6th Ed., 1601 pages, 1986 with 1986 Supplement (Casebook)

Lockhart, Kamisar, Choper and Shiffrin's Cases-Comments-Questions on the American Constitution, 6th Ed., about 1200 pages, 1986 with 1986 Supplement (Casebook)—abridgment of Lockhart, et al. Cases on Constitutional Law, 6th Ed., 1986

Manning's The Law of Church-State Relations in a Nutshell, 305 pages, 1981 (Text)

Miller's Presidential Power in a Nutshell, 328 pages, 1977 (Text)

CONSTITUTIONAL LAW—Cont'd

Nowak, Rotunda and Young's Hornbook on Constitutional Law, 3rd Ed., Student Ed., approximately 1100 pages, 1986 (Text)

Rotunda's Modern Constitutional Law: Cases and Notes, 2nd Ed., 1004 pages, 1985, with 1986 Supplement (Casebook)

Williams' Constitutional Analysis in a Nutshell, 388 pages, 1979 (Text)

See also Civil Rights

CONSUMER LAW

Epstein and Nickles' Consumer Law in a Nutshell, 2nd Ed., 418 pages, 1981 (Text)

McCall's Consumer Protection, Cases, Notes and Materials, 594 pages, 1977, with 1977 Statutory Supplement (Casebook)

Selected Commercial Statutes, 1389 pages, 1985

Spanogle and Rohner's Cases and Materials on Consumer Law, 693 pages, 1979, with 1982 Supplement (Casebook)

See also Commercial Law

CONTRACTS

Calamari & Perillo's Cases and Problems on Contracts, 1061 pages, 1978 (Casebook)

Calamari and Perillo's Hornbook on Contracts, 2nd Ed., 878 pages, 1977 (Text)

Corbin's Text on Contracts, One Volume Student Edition, 1224 pages, 1952 (Text)

Fessler and Loiseaux's Cases and Materials on Contracts, 837 pages, 1982 (Casebook)

Friedman's Contract Remedies in a Nutshell, 323 pages, 1981 (Text)

Fuller and Eisenberg's Cases on Basic Contract Law, 4th Ed., 1203 pages, 1981 (Casebook)

Hamilton, Rau and Weintraub's Cases and Materials on Contracts, 830 pages, 1984 (Casebook)

Jackson and Bollinger's Cases on Contract Law in Modern Society, 2nd Ed., 1329 pages, 1980 (Casebook)

Keyes' Government Contracts in a Nutshell, 423 pages, 1979 (Text)

Schaber and Rohwer's Contracts in a Nutshell, 2nd Ed., 425 pages, 1984 (Text)

COPYRIGHT

See Patent and Copyright Law

CORPORATIONS

Hamilton's Cases on Corporations—Including Partnerships and Limited Partnerships, 3rd Ed., 1213 pages, 1986 with 1986 Statutory Supplement (Casebook)

Hamilton's Law of Corporations in a Nutshell, 379 pages, 1980 (Text)

Henn's Teaching Materials on Corporations, 2nd Ed., about 1200 pages, 1986 (Casebook)

DOMESTIC RELATIONS

Clark's Cases and Problems on Domestic Relations, 3rd Ed., 1153 pages, 1980 (Casebook)

Clark's Hornbook on Domestic Relations, 754 pages, 1968 (Text)

Krause's Cases and Materials on Family Law, 2nd Ed., 1221 pages, 1983 with 1986 Supplement (Casebook)

Krause's Family Law in a Nutshell, 2nd Ed., 444 pages, 1986 (Text)

Krauskopf's Cases on Property Division at Marriage Dissolution, 250 pages, 1984 (Casebook)

ECONOMICS, LAW AND

Goetz' Cases and Materials on Law and Economics, 547 pages, 1984 (Casebook)

See also Antitrust, Regulated Industries

EDUCATION LAW

Alexander and Alexander's The Law of Schools, Students and Teachers in a Nutshell, 409 pages, 1984 (Text)

Morris' The Constitution and American Education, 2nd Ed., 992 pages, 1980 (Casebook)

EMPLOYMENT DISCRIMINATION

Jones, Murphy and Belton's Cases on Discrimination in Employment, about 930 pages, 1986 (Casebook)

Player's Cases and Materials on Employment Discrimination Law, 2nd Ed., 782 pages, 1984 (Casebook)

Player's Federal Law of Employment Discrimination in a Nutshell, 2nd Ed., 402 pages, 1981 (Text)

See also Women and the Law

ENERGY AND NATURAL RESOURCES LAW

Laitos' Cases and Materials on Natural Resources Law, 938 pages, 1985 (Casebook)

Rodgers' Cases and Materials on Energy and Natural Resources Law, 2nd Ed., 877 pages, 1983 (Casebook)

Selected Environmental Law Statutes, about 850 pages, 1986

Tomain's Energy Law in a Nutshell, 338 pages, 1981 (Text)

See also Environmental Law, Oil and Gas, Water Law

ENVIRONMENTAL LAW

Bonine and McGarity's Cases and Materials on the Law of Environment and Pollution, 1076 pages, 1984 (Casebook)

Findley and Farber's Cases and Materials on Environmental Law, 2nd Ed., 813 pages, 1985 (Casebook)

Findley and Farber's Environmental Law in a Nutshell, 343 pages, 1983 (Text)

ENVIRONMENTAL LAW—Cont'd

Rodgers' Hornbook on Environmental Law, 956 pages, 1977 with 1984 pocket part (Text)

Selected Environmental Law Statutes, about 950 pages, 1986

See also Energy Law, Natural Resources Law, Water Law

EQUITY

See Remedies

ESTATES

See Trusts and Estates

ESTATE PLANNING

Kurtz' Cases, Materials and Problems on Family Estate Planning, 853 pages, 1983 (Casebook)

Lynn's Introduction to Estate Planning, in a Nutshell, 3rd Ed., 370 pages, 1983 (Text)

See also Taxation

EVIDENCE

Broun and Meisenholder's Problems in Evidence, 2nd Ed., 304 pages, 1981 (Problem book)

Cleary and Strong's Cases, Materials and Problems on Evidence, 3rd Ed., 1143 pages, 1981 (Casebook)

Federal Rules of Evidence for United States Courts and Magistrates, 337 pages, 1984

Graham's Federal Rules of Evidence in a Nutshell, 429 pages, 1981 (Text)

Kimball's Programmed Materials on Problems in Evidence, 380 pages, 1978 (Problem book)

Lempert and Saltzburg's A Modern Approach to Evidence: Text, Problems, Transcripts and Cases, 2nd Ed., 1232 pages, 1983 (Casebook)

Lilly's Introduction to the Law of Evidence, 490 pages, 1978 (Text)

McCormick, Elliott and Sutton's Cases and Materials on Evidence, 5th Ed., 1212 pages, 1981 (Casebook)

McCormick's Hornbook on Evidence, 3rd Ed., Student Ed., 1156 pages, 1984 (Text)

Rothstein's Evidence, State and Federal Rules in a Nutshell, 2nd Ed., 514 pages, 1981 (Text)

Saltzburg's Evidence Supplement: Rules, Statutes, Commentary, 245 pages, 1980 (Casebook Supplement)

FEDERAL JURISDICTION AND PROCEDURE

Currie's Cases and Materials on Federal Courts, 3rd Ed., 1042 pages, 1982 with 1985 Supplement (Casebook)

Currie's Federal Jurisdiction in a Nutshell, 2nd Ed., 258 pages, 1981 (Text)

LAW SCHOOL PUBLICATIONS—Continued

**FEDERAL JURISDICTION AND PROCE-
DURE—Cont'd**

Federal Rules of Civil-Appellate Procedure—West Law School Edition, about 550 pages, 1986

Forrester and Moye's Cases and Materials on Federal Jurisdiction and Procedure, 3rd Ed., 917 pages, 1977 with 1985 Supplement (Casebook)

Redish's Cases, Comments and Questions on Federal Courts, 878 pages, 1983 with 1986 Supplement (Casebook)

Vetri and Merrill's Federal Courts, Problems and Materials, 2nd Ed., 232 pages, 1984 (Problem Book)

Wright's Hornbook on Federal Courts, 4th Ed., Student Ed., 870 pages, 1983 (Text)

FUTURE INTERESTS

See Trusts and Estates

IMMIGRATION LAW

Aleinikoff and Martin's Immigration Process and Policy, 1042 pages, 1985 (Casebook)

Weissbrodt's Immigration Law and Procedure in a Nutshell, 345 pages, 1984 (Text)

INDIAN LAW

See American Indian Law

INSURANCE

Dobbyn's Insurance Law in a Nutshell, 281 pages, 1981 (Text)

Keeton's Cases on Basic Insurance Law, 2nd Ed., 1086 pages, 1977

Keeton's Basic Text on Insurance Law, 712 pages, 1971 (Text)

Keeton's Case Supplement to Keeton's Basic Text on Insurance Law, 334 pages, 1978 (Casebook)

York and Whelan's Cases, Materials and Problems on Insurance Law, 715 pages, 1982, with 1985 Supplement (Casebook)

INTERNATIONAL LAW

Buergenthal and Maier's Public International Law in a Nutshell, 262 pages, 1985 (Text)

Folsom, Gordon and Spanogle's International Business Transactions – a Problem-Oriented Coursebook, 1160 pages, 1986 (Casebook)

Henkin, Pugh, Schachter and Smit's Cases and Materials on International Law, 2nd Ed., about 1200 pages, 1987 with Documents Supplement (Casebook)

Jackson and Davey's Legal Problems of International Economic Relations, 2nd Ed., about 1250 pages, 1986, with Documents Supplement (Casebook)

Kirgis' International Organizations in Their Legal Setting, 1016 pages, 1977, with 1981 Supplement (Casebook)

INTERNATIONAL LAW—Cont'd

Weston, Falk and D'Amato's International Law and World Order—A Problem Oriented Coursebook, 1195 pages, 1980, with Documents Supplement (Casebook)

Wilson's International Business Transactions in a Nutshell, 2nd Ed., 476 pages, 1984 (Text)

INTERVIEWING AND COUNSELING

Binder and Price's Interviewing and Counseling, 232 pages, 1977 (Text)

Shaffer's Interviewing and Counseling in a Nutshell, 353 pages, 1976 (Text)

INTRODUCTION TO LAW STUDY

Dobbyn's So You Want to go to Law School, Revised First Edition, 206 pages, 1976 (Text)

Hegland's Introduction to the Study and Practice of Law in a Nutshell, 418 pages, 1983 (Text)

Kinyon's Introduction to Law Study and Law Examinations in a Nutshell, 389 pages, 1971 (Text)

See also Legal Method and Legal System

JUDICIAL ADMINISTRATION

Nelson's Cases and Materials on Judicial Administration and the Administration of Justice, 1032 pages, 1974 (Casebook)

JURISPRUDENCE

Christie's Text and Readings on Jurisprudence—The Philosophy of Law, 1056 pages, 1973 (Casebook)

JUVENILE JUSTICE

Fox's Cases and Materials on Modern Juvenile Justice, 2nd Ed., 960 pages, 1981 (Casebook)

Fox's Juvenile Courts in a Nutshell, 3rd Ed., 291 pages, 1984 (Text)

LABOR LAW

Gorman's Basic Text on Labor Law—Unionization and Collective Bargaining, 914 pages, 1976 (Text)

Leslie's Labor Law in a Nutshell, 2nd Ed., 397 pages, 1986 (Text)

Nolan's Labor Arbitration Law and Practice in a Nutshell, 358 pages, 1979 (Text)

Oberer, Hanslowe, Andersen and Heinsz' Cases and Materials on Labor Law—Collective Bargaining in a Free Society, 3rd Ed., about 1200 pages, 1986 with Statutory Supplement (Casebook)

See also Employment Discrimination, Social Legislation

LAND FINANCE

See Real Estate Transactions

LAW SCHOOL PUBLICATIONS—Continued

LAND USE

Callies and Freilich's Cases and Materials on Land Use, 1233 pages, 1986 (Casebook)

Hagman's Cases on Public Planning and Control of Urban and Land Development, 2nd Ed., 1301 pages, 1980 (Casebook)

Hagman and Juergensmeyer's Hornbook on Urban Planning and Land Development Control Law, 2nd Ed., Student Edition, approximately 580 pages, 1986 (Text)

Wright and Gitelman's Cases and Materials on Land Use, 3rd Ed., 1300 pages, 1982 (Casebook)

Wright and Wright's Land Use in a Nutshell, 2nd Ed., 356 pages, 1985 (Text)

LEGAL HISTORY

Presser and Zainaldin's Cases on Law and American History, 855 pages, 1980 (Casebook)

See also Legal Method and Legal System

LEGAL METHOD AND LEGAL SYSTEM

Aldisert's Readings, Materials and Cases in the Judicial Process, 948 pages, 1976 (Casebook)

Berch and Berch's Introduction to Legal Method and Process, 550 pages, 1985 (Casebook)

Bodenheimer, Oakley and Love's Readings and Cases on an Introduction to the Anglo-American Legal System, 161 pages, 1980 (Casebook)

Davies and Lawry's Institutions and Methods of the Law—Introductory Teaching Materials, 547 pages, 1982 (Casebook)

Dvorkin, Himmelstein and Lesnick's Becoming a Lawyer: A Humanistic Perspective on Legal Education and Professionalism, 211 pages, 1981 (Text)

Greenberg's Judicial Process and Social Change, 666 pages, 1977 (Casebook)

Kelso and Kelso's Studying Law: An Introduction, 587 pages, 1984 (Coursebook)

Kempin's Historical Introduction to Anglo-American Law in a Nutshell, 2nd Ed., 280 pages, 1973 (Text)

Kimball's Historical Introduction to the Legal System, 610 pages, 1966 (Casebook)

Murphy's Cases and Materials on Introduction to Law—Legal Process and Procedure, 772 pages, 1977 (Casebook)

Reynolds' Judicial Process in a Nutshell, 292 pages, 1980 (Text)

See also Legal Research and Writing

LEGAL PROFESSION

Aronson, Devine and Fisch's Problems, Cases and Materials on Professional Responsibility, 745 pages, 1985 (Casebook)

Aronson and Weckstein's Professional Responsibility in a Nutshell, 399 pages, 1980 (Text)

LEGAL PROFESSION—Cont'd

Mellinkoff's The Conscience of a Lawyer, 304 pages, 1973 (Text)

Mellinkoff's Lawyers and the System of Justice, 983 pages, 1976 (Casebook)

Pirsig and Kirwin's Cases and Materials on Professional Responsibility, 4th Ed., 603 pages, 1984 (Casebook)

Schwartz and Wydick's Problems in Legal Ethics, 285 pages, 1983 (Casebook)

Selected Statutes, Rules and Standards on the Legal Profession, 276 pages, Revised 1984

Smith's Preventing Legal Malpractice, 142 pages, 1981 (Text)

Wolfram's Hornbook on Modern Legal Ethics, Student Edition, 1120 pages, 1986 (Text)

LEGAL RESEARCH AND WRITING

Cohen's Legal Research in a Nutshell, 4th Ed., 450 pages, 1985 (Text)

Cohen and Berring's How to Find the Law, 8th Ed., 790 pages, 1983. Problem book by Foster, Johnson and Kelly available (Casebook)

Cohen and Berring's Finding the Law, 8th Ed., Abridged Ed., 556 pages, 1984 (Casebook)

Dickerson's Materials on Legal Drafting, 425 pages, 1981 (Casebook)

Felsenfeld and Siegel's Writing Contracts in Plain English, 290 pages, 1981 (Text)

Gopen's Writing From a Legal Perspective, 225 pages, 1981 (Text)

Mellinkoff's Legal Writing—Sense and Nonsense, 242 pages, 1982 (Text)

Rombauer's Legal Problem Solving—Analysis, Research and Writing, 4th Ed., 424 pages, 1983 (Coursebook)

Squires and Rombauer's Legal Writing in a Nutshell, 294 pages, 1982 (Text)

Statsky's Legal Research, Writing and Analysis, 2nd Ed., 167 pages, 1982 (Coursebook)

Statsky and Wernet's Case Analysis and Fundamentals of Legal Writing, 2nd Ed., 441 pages, 1984 (Text)

Teply's Programmed Materials on Legal Research and Citation, 2nd Ed., 358 pages, 1986. Student Library Exercises available (Coursebook)

Weihofen's Legal Writing Style, 2nd Ed., 332 pages, 1980 (Text)

LEGISLATION

Davies' Legislative Law and Process in a Nutshell, 2nd Ed., 346 pages, 1986 (Text)

Nutting and Dickerson's Cases and Materials on Legislation, 5th Ed., 744 pages, 1978 (Casebook)

LAW SCHOOL PUBLICATIONS—Continued

LEGISLATION—Cont'd

Statsky's Legislative Analysis: How to Use Statutes and Regulations, 2nd Ed., 217 pages, 1984 (Text)

LOCAL GOVERNMENT

McCarthy's Local Government Law in a Nutshell, 2nd Ed., 404 pages, 1983 (Text)

Reynolds' Hornbook on Local Government Law, 860 pages, 1982 (Text)

Valente's Cases and Materials on Local Government Law, 2nd Ed., 980 pages, 1980 with 1982 Supplement (Casebook)

MASS COMMUNICATION LAW

Gillmor and Barron's Cases and Comment on Mass Communication Law, 4th Ed., 1076 pages, 1984 (Casebook)

Ginsburg's Regulation of Broadcasting: Law and Policy Towards Radio, Television and Cable Communications, 741 pages, 1979, with 1983 Supplement (Casebook)

Zuckman and Gayne's Mass Communications Law in a Nutshell, 2nd Ed., 473 pages, 1983 (Text)

MEDICINE, LAW AND

King's The Law of Medical Malpractice in a Nutshell, 2nd Ed., 342 pages, 1986 (Text)

Shapiro and Spece's Problems, Cases and Materials on Bioethics and Law, 892 pages, 1981 (Casebook)

Sharpe, Fiscina and Head's Cases on Law and Medicine, 882 pages, 1978 (Casebook)

MILITARY LAW

Shanor and Terrell's Military Law in a Nutshell, 378 pages, 1980 (Text)

MORTGAGES

See Real Estate Transactions

NATURAL RESOURCES LAW

See Energy and Natural Resources Law

NEGOTIATION

Edwards and White's Problems, Readings and Materials on the Lawyer as a Negotiator, 484 pages, 1977 (Casebook)

Williams' Legal Negotiation and Settlement, 207 pages, 1983 (Coursebook)

OFFICE PRACTICE

Hegland's Trial and Practice Skills in a Nutshell, 346 pages, 1978 (Text)

Strong and Clark's Law Office Management, 424 pages, 1974 (Casebook)

See also Computers and Law, Interviewing and Counseling, Negotiation

OIL AND GAS

Hemingway's Hornbook on Oil and Gas, 2nd Ed., Student Ed., 543 pages, 1983 with 1986 P.P. (Text)

OIL AND GAS—Cont'd

Kuntz, Lowe, Anderson and Smith's Cases and Materials on Oil and Gas Law, 857 pages, 1986 (Casebook)

Lowe's Oil and Gas Law in a Nutshell, 443 pages, 1983 (Text)

See also Energy and Natural Resources Law

PARTNERSHIP

See Agency—Partnership

PATENT AND COPYRIGHT LAW

Choate and Francis' Cases and Materials on Patent Law, 2nd Ed., 1110 pages, 1981 (Casebook)

Miller and Davis' Intellectual Property—Patents, Trademarks and Copyright in a Nutshell, 428 pages, 1983 (Text)

Nimmer's Cases on Copyright and Other Aspects of Entertainment Litigation, 3rd Ed., 1025 pages, 1985 (Casebook)

PRODUCTS LIABILITY

Noel and Phillips' Cases on Products Liability, 2nd Ed., 821 pages, 1982 (Casebook)

Noel and Phillips' Products Liability in a Nutshell, 2nd Ed., 341 pages, 1981 (Text)

PROPERTY

Bernhardt's Real Property in a Nutshell, 2nd Ed., 448 pages, 1981 (Text)

Boyer's Survey of the Law of Property, 766 pages, 1981 (Text)

Browder, Cunningham and Smith's Cases on Basic Property Law, 4th Ed., 1431 pages, 1984 (Casebook)

Bruce, Ely and Bostick's Cases and Materials on Modern Property Law, 1004 pages, 1984 (Casebook)

Burke's Personal Property in a Nutshell, 322 pages, 1983 (Text)

Cunningham, Stoebuck and Whitman's Hornbook on the Law of Property, Student Ed., 916 pages, 1984 (Text)

Donahue, Kauper and Martin's Cases on Property, 2nd Ed., 1362 pages, 1983 (Casebook)

Hill's Landlord and Tenant Law in a Nutshell, 2nd Ed., 311 pages, 1986 (Text)

Moynihan's Introduction to Real Property, 254 pages, 1962 (Text)

Uniform Land Transactions Act, Uniform Simplification of Land Transfers Act, Uniform Condominium Act, 1977 Official Text with Comments, 462 pages, 1978

See also Real Estate Transactions, Land Use

PSYCHIATRY, LAW AND

Reisner's Law and the Mental Health System, Civil and Criminal Aspects, 696 pages, 1985 (Casebooks)

LAW SCHOOL PUBLICATIONS—Continued

REAL ESTATE TRANSACTIONS

Bruce's Real Estate Finance in a Nutshell, 2nd Ed., 262 pages, 1985 (Text)

Maxwell, Riesenfeld, Hetland and Warren's Cases on California Security Transactions in Land, 3rd Ed., 728 pages, 1984 (Casebook)

Nelson and Whitman's Cases on Real Estate Transfer, Finance and Development, 2nd Ed., 1114 pages, 1981, with 1986 Supplement (Casebook)

Nelson and Whitman's Hornbook on Real Estate Finance Law, 2nd Ed., Student Ed., 941 pages, 1985 (Text)

Osborne's Cases and Materials on Secured Transactions, 559 pages, 1967 (Casebook)

REGULATED INDUSTRIES

Gellhorn and Pierce's Regulated Industries in a Nutshell, 394 pages, 1982 (Text)

Morgan, Harrison and Verkuil's Cases and Materials on Economic Regulation of Business, 2nd Ed., 666 pages, 1985 (Casebook)

See also Mass Communication Law, Banking Law

REMEDIES

Dobbs' Hornbook on Remedies, 1067 pages, 1973 (Text)

Dobbs' Problems in Remedies, 137 pages, 1974 (Problem book)

Dobbyn's Injunctions in a Nutshell, 264 pages, 1974 (Text)

Friedman's Contract Remedies in a Nutshell, 323 pages, 1981 (Text)

Leavell, Love and Nelson's Cases and Materials on Equitable Remedies and Restitution, 4th Ed., 1111 pages, 1986 (Casebook)

McCormick's Hornbook on Damages, 811 pages, 1935 (Text)

O'Connell's Remedies in a Nutshell, 2nd Ed., 320 pages, 1985 (Text)

York, Bauman and Rendleman's Cases and Materials on Remedies, 4th Ed., 1029 pages, 1985 (Casebook)

REVIEW MATERIALS

Ballantine's Problems

Black Letter Series

Smith's Review Series

West's Review Covering Multistate Subjects

SECURITIES REGULATION

Hazen's Hornbook on The Law of Securities Regulation, Student Ed., 739 pages, 1985 (Text)

Ratner's Securities Regulation: Materials for a Basic Course, 3rd Ed., 1000 pages, 1986 (Casebook)

Ratner's Securities Regulation in a Nutshell, 2nd Ed., 322 pages, 1982 (Text)

SECURITIES REGULATION—Cont'd

Selected Securities and Business Planning Statutes, Rules and Forms, 470 pages, 1985

SOCIAL LEGISLATION

Hood and Hardy's Workers' Compensation and Employee Protection Laws in a Nutshell, 274 pages, 1984 (Text)

LaFrance's Welfare Law: Structure and Entitlement in a Nutshell, 455 pages, 1979 (Text)

Malone, Plant and Little's Cases on Workers' Compensation and Employment Rights, 2nd Ed., 951 pages, 1980 (Casebook)

SPORTS LAW

Schubert, Smith and Trentadue's Sports Law, 395 pages, 1986 (Text)

TAXATION

Dodge's Cases and Materials on Federal Income Taxation, 820 pages, 1985 (Casebook)

Dodge's Federal Taxation of Estates, Trusts and Gifts: Principles and Planning, 771 pages, 1981 with 1982 Supplement (Casebook)

Garbis and Struntz' Cases and Materials on Tax Procedure and Tax Fraud, 829 pages, 1982 with 1984 Supplement (Casebook)

Gelfand and Salsich's State and Local Taxation and Finance in a Nutshell, 309 pages, 1986 (Text)

Gunn's Cases and Materials on Federal Income Taxation of Individuals, 785 pages, 1981 with 1985 Supplement (Casebook)

Hellerstein and Hellerstein's Cases on State and Local Taxation, 4th Ed., 1041 pages, 1978 with 1982 Supplement (Casebook)

Kahn and Gann's Corporate Taxation and Taxation of Partnerships and Partners, 2nd Ed., 1204 pages, 1985 (Casebook)

Kragen and McNulty's Cases and Materials on Federal Income Taxation: Individuals, Corporations, Partnerships, 4th Ed., 1287 pages, 1985 (Casebook)

McNulty's Federal Estate and Gift Taxation in a Nutshell, 3rd Ed., 509 pages, 1983 (Text)

McNulty's Federal Income Taxation of Individuals in a Nutshell, 3rd Ed., 487 pages, 1983 (Text)

Posin's Hornbook on Federal Income Taxation of Individuals, Student Ed., 491 pages, 1983 with 1985 pocket part (Text)

Selected Federal Taxation Statutes and Regulations, about 1400 pages, 1986

Solomon and Hesch's Cases on Federal Income Taxation of Individuals, about 800 pages, 1987 (Casebook)

LAW SCHOOL PUBLICATIONS—Continued

TAXATION—Cont'd

Sobeloff and Weidenbruch's Federal Income Taxation of Corporations and Stockholders in a Nutshell, 362 pages, 1981 (Text)

TORTS

Christie's Cases and Materials on the Law of Torts, 1264 pages, 1983 (Casebook)

Dobbs' Torts and Compensation—Personal Accountability and Social Responsibility for Injury, 955 pages, 1985 (Casebook)

Green, Pedrick, Rahl, Thode, Hawkins, Smith and Treece's Cases and Materials on Torts, 2nd Ed., 1360 pages, 1977 (Casebook)

Green, Pedrick, Rahl, Thode, Hawkins, Smith, and Treece's Advanced Torts: Injuries to Business, Political and Family Interests, 2nd Ed., 544 pages, 1977 (Casebook)—reprint from Green, et al. Cases and Materials on Torts, 2nd Ed., 1977

Keeton, Keeton, Sargentich and Steiner's Cases and Materials on Torts, and Accident Law, 1360 pages, 1983 (Casebook)

Kionka's Torts in a Nutshell: Injuries to Persons and Property, 434 pages, 1977 (Text)

Malone's Torts in a Nutshell: Injuries to Family, Social and Trade Relations, 358 pages, 1979 (Text)

Prosser and Keeton's Hornbook on Torts, 5th Ed., Student Ed., 1286 pages, 1984 (Text)

Shapo's Cases on Tort and Compensation Law, 1244 pages, 1976 (Casebook)

See also Products Liability

TRADE REGULATION

McManis' Unfair Trade Practices in a Nutshell, 444 pages, 1982 (Text)

Oppenheim, Weston, Maggs and Schechter's Cases and Materials on Unfair Trade Practices and Consumer Protection, 4th Ed., 1038 pages, 1983 with 1986 Supplement (Casebook)

See also Antitrust, Regulated Industries

TRIAL AND APPELLATE ADVOCACY

Appellate Advocacy, Handbook of, 2nd Ed., 182 pages, 1986 (Text)

Bergman's Trial Advocacy in a Nutshell, 402 pages, 1979 (Text)

Binder and Bergman's Fact Investigation: From Hypothesis to Proof, 354 pages, 1984 (Coursebook)

Goldberg's The First Trial (Where Do I Sit?, What Do I Say?) in a Nutshell, 396 pages, 1982 (Text)

Haydock, Herr and Stempel's, Fundamentals of Pre-Trial Litigation, 768 pages, 1985 (Casebook)

Hegland's Trial and Practice Skills in a Nutshell, 346 pages, 1978 (Text)

Hornstein's Appellate Advocacy in a Nutshell, 325 pages, 1984 (Text)

TRIAL AND APPELLATE ADVOCACY—Cont'd

Jeans' Handbook on Trial Advocacy, Student Ed., 473 pages, 1975 (Text)

Martineau's Cases and Materials on Appellate Practice and Procedure, about 550 pages, 1987 (Casebook)

McElhaney's Effective Litigation, 457 pages, 1974 (Casebook)

Nolan's Cases and Materials on Trial Practice, 518 pages, 1981 (Casebook)

Parnell and Shellhaas' Cases, Exercises and Problems for Trial Advocacy, 171 pages, 1982 (Coursebook)

Sonsteng, Haydock and Boyd's The Trialbook: A Total System for Preparation and Presentation of a Case, Student Ed., 404 pages, 1984 (Coursebook)

TRUSTS AND ESTATES

Atkinson's Hornbook on Wills, 2nd Ed., 975 pages, 1953 (Text)

Averill's Uniform Probate Code in a Nutshell, 425 pages, 1978 (Text)

Bogert's Hornbook on Trusts, 5th Ed., 726 pages, 1973 (Text)

Clark, Lusky and Murphy's Cases and Materials on Gratuitous Transfers, 3rd Ed., 970 pages, 1985 (Casebook)

Gulliver's Cases and Materials on Future Interests, 624 pages, 1959 (Casebook)

Gulliver's Introduction to the Law of Future Interests, 87 pages, 1959 (Casebook)—reprint from Gulliver's Cases and Materials on Future Interests, 1959

McGovern's Cases and Materials on Wills, Trusts and Future Interests: An Introduction to Estate Planning, 750 pages, 1983 (Casebook)

Mennell's Cases and Materials on California Decedent's Estates, 566 pages, 1973 (Casebook)

Mennell's Wills and Trusts in a Nutshell, 392 pages, 1979 (Text)

Powell's The Law of Future Interests in California, 91 pages, 1980 (Text)

Simes' Hornbook on Future Interests, 2nd Ed., 355 pages, 1966 (Text)

Turano and Radigan's Hornbook on New York Estate Administration, approximately 575 pages, 1986 (Text)

Uniform Probate Code, 5th Ed., Official Text With Comments, 384 pages, 1977

Waggoner's Future Interests in a Nutshell, 361 pages, 1981 (Text)

Waterbury's Materials on Trusts and Estates, 1039 pages, 1986 (Casebook)

WATER LAW

Getches' Water Law in a Nutshell, 439 pages, 1984 (Text)

CASES AND MATERIALS ON
DISCRIMINATION IN EMPLOYMENT
Fifth Edition

James E. Jones, Jr.
University of Wisconsin

William P. Murphy
University of North Carolina

Robert Belton
Vanderbilt University

for
THE LABOR LAW GROUP

AMERICAN CASEBOOK SERIES

WEST PUBLISHING CO.
ST. PAUL, MINN., 1987

Library of Congress Cataloging in Publication Data

Murphy, William P., 1919–
  Discrimination in employment.

  (American casebook series)
  Rev. ed. of: Discrimination in employment / prepared
by William P. Murphy, Julius G. Getman, James E.
Jones, Jr., for the Labor Law Group. 4th ed. 1979.
  Includes bibliographical references and index.
  1. Discrimination in employment—Law and legislation—
United States—Cases. I. Jones, James E. II. Belton,
Robert, 1935–   III. Title. IV. Series.

KF3464.A7M87 1986   344.73'01133   86–19096
                   347.3041133

ISBN 0-314-26129-X

Jones, Murphy & Belton Emply.Discrim. ACB

Foreword

The Labor Law Group is an association of law teachers, most of whom serve on faculties in the United States; others teach in Belgium, Canada, England and Israel.

At the December 1946 meeting of the Labor Law Roundtable of the Association of American Law Schools, Professor Willard Wirtz of Northwestern delivered a compelling paper criticizing the coursebooks on labor law then available. His remarks deeply impressed those present and the Roundtable Council organized a general conference on the teaching of the subject; that conference was held in Ann Arbor in 1947. Some of the conferees undertook to stay in touch, and to exchange proposals for sections of a hoped-for coursebook. The late Professor Robert E. Mathews, who as Roundtable Council chairman had obtained funding for the conference, served as coordinator. In 1948, a preliminary version became available in mimeographed form. It was used in 17 schools, and each user supplied comments and suggestions for change. In 1953, a hard-cover version was published under the title *Labor Relations and the Law*. The thirty-one "cooperating editors" were so convinced of the value of multi-campus collaboration that they gave up any individual claims to royalties. Instead, those royalties would be paid over to a trust fund, to be used to cover the expenses of multi-campus cooperative effort in producing future books. The Declaration of Trust memorializing this agreement was executed November 4, 1953, and remains the Group's charter. The hope that collaboration would continue to bear fruit has been fulfilled. Under Professor Mathews' continuing chairmanship the Group's members produced *Readings on Labor Law* in 1955, and *The Employment Relation and the Law* in 1957. A second edition of *Labor Relations and the Law* appeared in 1960, with Ben Aaron and Don Wollett as co-chairmen, a third edition in 1965, with Jerre Williams at the helm.

Toward the end of the 1960s the members of the Group, now chaired by Bill Murphy, decided that the labor law curriculum needed a thorough re-thinking. In June 1969 the Group sponsored a major conference at Boulder, Colorado, to which were invited both non-teaching practitioners and many teachers who were not Group members. At the conclusion of that conference, the Group decided to reshape its work substantially. Over the next year, specifics were hammered out at sessions in Chicago and Dallas: The Group would restructure itself into ten task forces, each of which would prepare a unit of no more than 200 pages on a discrete topic, such as employment discrimination or union-member relations. An individual teacher could then choose two, or three, of these units as the material around which to build a particular course.   This multi-unit approach dominated the Group's work throughout the 1970's, under Professor Murphy and his successors as chairman, Herb Sherman and Jim Jones.   As the decade progressed and teachers refined their views about what topics to include in the labor curriculum and how to address them some units were dropped from the series while others increased in length.

In 1984, the Group sponsored another general conference to discuss developments in the substance and teaching of labor and employment law, this time at Park City, Utah.   The discussions at that meeting and at a subsequent working session in St. Louis led to the conclusion that the Group should produce three conventional length coursebooks, one in each of the three areas that had emerged over the preceding decade as the building blocks of a sound basic labor law curriculum: union-management relations, employment discrimination, and the individual employment relation.   Other books, more compact in scope, are intended to encourage the teaching of courses beyond that bare minimum: books on comparative labor law, arbitration, industrial injury compensation, public sector bargaining, the union-member relationship, and the like.   There is a long range plan for a very different sort of coursebook, one that will address topics from each of the three core areas in a single volume.

At any one time, roughly twenty-five to thirty persons are actively engaged in the Group's work; this has proved a practical working limit, given problems of communication and logistics.   Coordination and editorial review of the multiple projects are the responsibility of the executive committee, who are also the successor trustees of the Group. Governance is by consensus; votes are taken only to elect trustees and to determine whom to invite to join the Group.   Since 1953, more than 70 persons have worked on Group projects; in keeping with the original agreement, none has ever received anything more than expenses.   Our goal is still that stated in the original Declaration of Trust: "to improve the training of law students . . . and to provide the best possible materials for such training."

THE EXECUTIVE COMMITTEE
ALVIN L. GOLDMAN
JAMES E. JONES, JR.
CORNELIUS J. PECK
ROBERT J. RABIN
ROBERT N. COVINGTON, CHAIRMAN

Editorial Policy Committee

The Labor Law Group

The Labor Law Group

Participating Members

Benjamin Aaron
University of California, Los Angeles

Reginald Alleyne
University of California, Los Angeles

Steven D. Anderman
University of Warwick

James B. Atleson
State University of New York, Buffalo

Robert Belton
Vanderbilt University

Roger Blanpain
University of Leuven

Robert N. Covington
Vanderbilt University

Matthew Finkin
Southern Methodist University

Alvin L. Goldman
University of Kentucky

James E. Jones, Jr.
University of Wisconsin

Thomas C. Kohler
Boston College

Mordehai Mironi
Tel Aviv University

Robert B. Moberly
University of Florida

Charles J. Morris
Southern Methodist University

William P. Murphy
University of North Carolina

Dennis R. Nolan
University of South Carolina

Cornelius J. Peck
University of Washington

Robert J. Rabin
Syracuse University

Mark A. Rothstein
West Virginia University

Ivan C. Rutledge
Mercer University

George Schatzki
University of Connecticut

Herbert L. Sherman, Jr.
University of Pittsburgh

Eileen Silverstein
University of Connecticut

Clyde W. Summers
University of Pennsylvania

Lea S. Vander Velde
University of Pennsylvania

Donald H. Wollett
University of the Pacific

Other Members

Harry W. Arthurs
York University

Alfred W. Blumrosen
Rutgers University

John E. Dunsford
St. Louis University

Julius G. Getman
University of Texas

The Honorable Joseph R. Grodin
Supreme Court of California

John Phillip Linn
University of Denver

Summary of Contents

Table of Contents

Statutory Appendix

*

Table of Cases

The principal cases are in bold type. Cases cited or discussed in the text are roman type. References are to pages. Cases cited in principal cases and within other quoted materials are not included.

*

CASES AND MATERIALS ON
DISCRIMINATION IN EMPLOYMENT
Fifth Edition

Chapter I

INTRODUCTION

A. PROLOGUE

In the fifteen years since the first edition of DISCRIMINATION IN EMPLOYMENT was prepared for the Labor Law Group, there have been many changes in the substantive law and the administrative structures which comprise this subject matter. Perhaps as significant, we may now refer to it as a bona fide area of substantive law. For many years it was a "piggy back" on labor law, constitutional law, or a portion of the then new field of poverty law. It was under that general heading that CASES ON RACIAL DISCRIMINATION IN EMPLOYMENT prepared by Michael I. Sovern was made available by West Publishing Company in 1969. It was possible to prepare a reasonably adequate unit on the subject of less than 300 pages—particularly as few if any schools devoted more than a portion of a course to the subject. Most labor relations law books started to include a section on EEO by the early 1970's and the commercial services started to publish the employment discrimination cases in separate volumes. We are now up to forty such volumes and there are more than a half dozen case books in one edition or another.

By 1983, 128 law schools were offering seminars or courses, or both, in this field. Many graduate business and industrial relations schools were also including employment discrimination in their course offerings.[1] In 1985, the Association of American Law Schools recognized a separate section on employment discrimination law.

This recognition and growth in the teaching of EEO is warranted by the increased caseload which indicates the extent to which legal resources are being devoted to this substantive area of law. At the end of the first decade of Title VII of the Civil Rights Act of 1964, we had twelve supreme court cases and less than 2,000 other reported EEO cases. In 1984, a computer search produced 132 supreme court cases,

---

1. See Jones & Ofria, "Employment Discrimination Law in American Law and Graduate Schools, a Census of Employment Discrimination Teachers," Bureau of National Affairs BNA Books, 1983.

1

2,226 court of appeals cases and 5,555 cases at the district court level for a total of 7,953 reported decisions. Perhaps more significant as an index of legal interest is the increase in employment discrimination cases filed in the U.S. district courts from 3,931 in 1975 to 5,477 in 1979 to 9,097 in 1983. There were 9,748 employment discrimination cases filed by June 30, 1984. By contrast, by that date there were only 9,637 labor cases which were pending in those courts.[2] Cases involving race and sex discrimination have dominated the statistics over the past twenty years. However, increasingly we are beginning to see age and handicap discrimination cases in the published reports as special aspects of law relating to those protected cases mature.

These figures clearly suggest the increasing importance of employment discrimination law. They do not, however, begin to tell the whole story as they do not reveal the extent to which employment discrimination matters occupy state and local administrative tribunals and courts. These proceedings, as well as those in the federal courts noted above, potentially involve lawyers. State and local jurisdictions are beginning to expand the protected classes to include marital status and sexual orientation and are beginning to consider comparable worth. It does not appear likely that interest in this area of law will decline in the near future.

B. SOME OBSERVATIONS ON THE HISTORY OF GOVERNMENTAL CIVIL RIGHTS ACTIVITIES *

1. THE PRESIDENTS

The story of modern efforts of government, particularly at the federal level, to establish equal employment opportunity begins with the issuance of Executive Order 8802[8] by President Roosevelt in 1941. Since the establishment by Roosevelt during World War II of the Fair Employment Practices Committee (FEPC) under the original executive order, every president has addressed equal employment opportunity with some policy. While there have been differences in emphasis under the various administrations, succeeding presidents, either through new executive initiatives of their own or by leaving in place policies inherited from their predecessors, have maintained a supportive posture of some form of equal employment opportunity.[9] The

---

2. Reports of the Proceedings of the Judicial Conference, Annual Report of the Director of the Administrative Office of the U.S. Courts, Washington, D.C. U.S. Government Printing Office, 1983, 1984.

* Excerpted from Jones, "Some Reflections on Title VII of the Civil Rights Act of 1964 at 20," 36 Mercer L.Rev. 813, 815–822 (Spring 1985). Reprinted by permission.

8. Exec. Order No. 8802, 3 C.F.R. 957 (1941).

9. See Jones, The Transformation of Fair Employment Policies Practices, Federal Policies and Worker Status Since the 30's at ch. 7 (1976); Jones, Twenty-One Years of Affirmative Action: The Maturation of the Administrative Enforcement Process Under Executive Order 11,246 as amended, 59 Chi.-Kent L.Rev. 67 (1982) and the various historical references there cited.

Reagan Administration in its first term kept in place the executive order programs which it inherited, despite great debate concerning whether the President would cancel the existing executive order program or substantially reduce its impact and effectiveness.

In 1961, President John F. Kennedy issued the historic Executive Order 10,925,[10] and Presidents Nixon, Ford, Carter, and Reagan, so far, have continued to operate under the substantive provisions of Executive Order 11,246 [11] as amended by Executive Order 11,375 [12] issued by President Lyndon Johnson. Carter's Reorganization Plan Number 1 of 1978 [13] consolidated enforcement in the United States Department of Labor rather than in contracting agencies and contributed to a more orderly administrative process in the enforcement of the program.

Although it would be overly complimentary to say that all of the administrations were aggressive in pursuing equality of employment opportunity during their tenures, it is fair to conclude that the changes which were initiated by presidential order, particularly from Johnson through Carter, were designed to expand and improve the president's programs. Although some of the defensive positions taken by members of the Reagan Administration have sought to characterize the Administration's proposals as promoting efficiency in line with the general philosophy of deregulation, the overall impression generated by administration pronouncements, both earlier and in the recent attacks upon affirmative action, can be fairly characterized as negative.

2. EARLY STATE ACTIVITIES

Between 1945 and 1949 eight fair employment practice measures were enacted into state law.[14] These early laws were passed in states with heavy concentrations of blacks. There is an obvious relationship between these facts as a matter of emerging political potential.

By 1966 there were at least twenty states that had some form of fair employment practice law and many also had laws on public accommodations, private housing, and other civil rights issues. Prior to the mid-1950's, however, the Congress of the United States was overwhelmingly negative regarding any kind of civil rights legislation. Remember that Congress, through the enactment of a series of limitations on appropriations, forced the Roosevelt FEPC operation out of business.[15] The Russell Rider,[16] which was passed in 1944, provided that no appropriations could be allotted to any agency established by executive order and in existence for more than one year if Congress had

10. Exec. Order No. 10,925, 3 C.F.R. 448 (1961).

11. Exec. Order No. 11,246, 3 C.F.R. 339 (1965), reprinted in 42 U.S.C. § 2000e, at 28 (1982).

12. Exec. Order No. 11,375, 3 C.F.R. 684, 32 Fed.Reg. 14,303 (1967).

13. Reorganization Plan No. 1, 3 C.F.R. 321 (1978).

14. See D. Lockard, Toward Equal Opportunity: A Study of State and Local Antidiscrimination Laws 22–24 (1968).

15. Id. at 19; see also P. Norgren & S. Hill, Toward Fair Employment (1964).

16. See Independent Offices Appropriation Act (Russell Amendment) 58 Stat. 387 (1944), amended by, 31 U.S.C. § 696 (1948).

not specifically appropriated the money for such agency or specifically authorized the expenditure of funds for it. The following year, in an effort to clarify the Rider, Congress enacted the Independent Offices Appropriation Act of 1945 [17] which made it clear that interdepartmental committees were not subject to the Russell Rider prohibition. This interagency exception enabled the subsequent executives to continue to operate little FEPC initiatives by using the device of at least two federal agencies plus representatives from the public.

During the mid-1950's, the Congress of the United States, led by the then Senate majority leader Lyndon Johnson, enacted some modern civil rights laws addressing, primarily, voter registration and the jurisdiction of federal courts in civil rights cases.[18] No doubt congressional response was due, at least in some part, to the increased activities of social protests, for example, the marches, the sit-ins, and the other demonstrations. It also seems beyond dispute that the increased potential of the newly enfranchised blacks for voting in the South, made possible by more effective federal voter registration laws, contributed to the rather rapid change of attitude in the Congress on civil rights issues. It is also probably fair to conclude that the demographic shifts brought about by World War II, the Korean police action, and other labor market forces which contributed to greater mobility of southern blacks from the rural areas to the cities of both the South and the North affected political climates at both the state and local levels. While it is difficult to link in a scientific fashion specific occurrences to particular responses, ordinary intuition strongly urges, if not compels, the conclusion that these factors were of critical significance in social change. As the federal government gradually proceeded to change its anti-civil-rights stance, the states continued to respond with pro-civil-rights legislation. These responses were further stimulated by the enactment of Title VII of the Civil Rights Act of 1964, which specifically encouraged the enactment of state and local fair employment practices laws.[19]

3. THE SUPREME COURT

As far back as 1944, in Steele v. Louisville & Nashville Railroad Co.[20] and its companion cases,[21] the Supreme Court gave impetus to a

---

17. 59 Stat. 134 (1945), amended by, 31 U.S.C. § 691 (1948).

18. Civil Rights Act of 1957, 71 Stat. 637 (1957) (current version at 42 U.S.C. § 1971 (1982)) (race, color, previous condition not to affect voting rights); 71 Stat. 634 (1957) (current version at 42 U.S.C. § 1975 (1982)) (establishment of Civil Rights Commission); 71 Stat. 638 (1957) (current version at 42 U.S.C. § 1995 (1982)) (right to trial by jury in federal courts); 71 Stat. 637 (1957) (current version at 28 U.S.C. § 1343 (1982)) (jurisdiction of federal district courts for recovery of damages

or equitable or other relief in civil rights cases); 71 Stat. 638 (1957) (current version at 28 U.S.C. § 1861 (1982)) (prescribing uniform qualifications for jurors in federal courts instead of making qualifications dependent on state laws).

19. See 42 U.S.C. 2000e–5 (1982).

20. 323 U.S. 192 (1944).

21. See Tunstall v. Brotherhood of Locomotive Firemen & Enginemen, 323 U.S. 210 (1944); see also Wallace Corp. v. NLRB, 323 U.S. 248 (1944).

general concept of fair employment. Although the decision in *Steele* was of limited effectiveness, it enunciated the proposition that trade unions operating under the Railway Labor Act owe black employees a duty "to represent non-union or minority union members of the craft without hostile discrimination, fairly, impartially, and in good faith." [22] While the concept was not an effective weapon against union discrimination in a practical sense,[23] it did set a tone of Supreme Court receptivity to the matter of fairness in employment. The duty-of-fair-representation cases were limited because of their *constitutional* basis. Unless there was a union operating under the authority of the federal law, employment discrimination was substantially beyond the scope of the Supreme Court's reach.

The Supreme Court, between 1948 and 1961, decided a series of constitutional cases involving civil rights which established a general legal framework of receptivity to the plight of the downtrodden. In Shelley v. Kraemer,[24] the Supreme Court adopted the view that the fourteenth amendment's equal protection clause prohibited the enforcement of racially-based restrictive covenants by state courts. In Hurd v. Hodge,[25] the Court found judicial enforcement of restrictive covenants by the District of Columbia courts violated the public policy expressed in statute. In the celebrated Brown v. Board of Education [26] and its companion case of Bolling v. Sharpe,[27] the Court held that the separate but equal doctrine, as applied in primary and secondary schools, was inherently unequal and violative of the fourteenth and the fifth amendments. Earlier cases such as Sweatt v. Painter [28] and McLaurin v. Oklahoma State Regents for Higher Education [29] had paved the way by establishing that segregation in professional education was violative of the Constitution. Other services provided by the state or state entities, such as housing and public transportation, were successfully attacked in the Supreme Court. In 1961, in Burton v. Wilmington Parking Authority,[30] the Supreme Court found that when governmental activity is so intertwined with private discrimination as to establish a symbiotic relationship, then private discrimination becomes state action subject to constitutional mandates of antidiscrimination.

This judicial activity at the Supreme Court level established a positive climate and contributed to the hope of minorities that equal justice under the law was indeed possible. The lifting of the various restrictions no doubt contributed to the willingness of activists to increase their efforts to secure genuine equality. A noted historian commented that:

22. 323 U.S. at 204.

23. See, Herring, The "Fair Representation" Doctrine: An Effective Weapon Against Union Racial Discrimination?, 24 Md.L.Rev. 113 (1964).

24. 334 U.S. 1 (1948).

25. 334 U.S. 24 (1948).

26. 347 U.S. 483 (1954).

27. 347 U.S. 497 (1954).

28. 339 U.S. 629 (1950).

29. 339 U.S. 637 (1950).

30. 365 U.S. 715 (1961).

The models of city ordinances and state laws and the increased political influence of civil rights advocates stimulated new action in the federal level. Civil rights acts were passed in 1957, 1960, and 1964—after almost complete federal inactivity in this area for more than three-quarters of a century. Strong leadership on the part of the executive and favorable judicial interpretation of old as well as new laws have made it clear that the war against the two worlds of race now enjoys the sanction of the law and its interpreters. In many respects this constitutes the most significant development in the struggle against racism in the present century.[31]

4. THE CIVIL RIGHTS ACT OF 1964

In 1964, the Congress of the United States enacted a comprehensive civil rights law. Title VII of that law addressed the problem of employment discrimination more comprehensively than that problem had ever been addressed by the federal government. Although it was far short of that hoped for, many hailed it as the beginning of a new day.[32] The law gave to the federal agency the power to investigate and conciliate, but gave it no enforcement authority. Enforcement of the law required the aggrieved plaintiff to secure a lawyer and to take the case to federal court. Congress adopted neither the administrative agency approach modeled after the National Labor Relations Act[33] nor an administrative enforcement mechanism modeled after the Fair Labor Standards Act of 1938.[34] The law was a curious blend of private enforcement and limited enforcement potential by the United States Justice Department. Despite these limitations, and to the surprise of some of us pessimists,[35] many good court decisions emerged in the early years.

5. CONGRESS ACTS AGAIN

After a comprehensive review of Title VII, Congress passed the Equal Employment Opportunity Act of 1972[36] in which it endorsed

31. Franklin, The Two Worlds of Race, 94 Daedalus 899, 919 (1965).

32. Michael Sovern provides a contemporaneous analysis of the new Title VII of the Civil Rights Act of 1964, as well as of other programs current at the time. He dubbed the EEOC the "poor and feeble thing with power to conciliate but not to compel." On the positive side, Congress at last had enacted a measure at the federal level and, despite its limitations, that was a substantial achievement. See generally M. Sovern, Legal Restraints on Racial Discrimination in Employment (1966).

33. 29 U.S.C. § 151 (1982).

34. Id. § 201.

35. The author was a senior federal lawyer in the United States Department of Labor, Office of the Solicitor, who was heavily involved in the legislative activities leading up to the enactment of the Civil Rights Act of 1964 (at least the employment title). Being an advocate of an exclusive federal commission with cease and desist powers, I was bitterly disappointed with the compromise which emerged from Congress. I expected the new Act to be strangled to death in litigation in hostile federal district courts in the South, and that it would take forever to get a meaningful body of law established as no case could be considered reliable precedent until the Supreme Court acted favorably upon it. The earlier courts' reception of the new law suggested that I was unduly pessimistic. This Article's examination of the Supreme Court's treatment of Title VII puts at issue the extent to which that pessimism was justified.

36. Equal Employment Opportunity Act of 1972, Pub.L. No. 92–261, 86 Stat.

lower court interpretations which it felt were consistent with its views, and made specific changes where it determined them to be necessary.[37] It expanded the coverage of Title VII by including state and local government employees in its protection and by including the federal employees, at least those in the executive branch. The Equal Employment Opportunity Act of 1972 reduced the number of employees necessary to bring an employer into coverage by that Act to fifteen, provided enforcement authority in the Equal Employment Opportunity Commission while retaining enforcement in the Justice Department against state and local entities, and retained the rights of private plaintiffs to pursue their cause in federal court. Thus, in a very short period of time, an even more positive response from the Congress of the United States can be seen.

The 1970's saw Congress address employment discrimination in a host of other laws. In 1972, Congress passed Title IX of the Higher Education Amendments of 1972[38] forbidding sex discrimination in educational institutions receiving federal funds. Congress passed the Vocational Rehabilitation Act of 1973[39] requiring federal contracts to provide employment opportunities to handicapped individuals. The Viet Nam Era Veterans' Readjustment Act of 1974[40] required federal contractors to promote employment opportunities for qualified disabled veterans and veterans of the Viet Nam era. Earlier, Congress had passed the Age Discrimination in Employment Act which was improved in the Age Discrimination Act of 1975.[41] In 1972, Congress passed the State and Local Fiscal Assistance Act which it amended in 1976 and 1980.[42]

6. THE CURRENT STATUS OF EEO LEGISLATION

We have an embarrassment of riches of supportive congressional action directed toward employment discrimination. No one seems to know at this writing the sum of all legislation, federal, state, and local, directed to the problem. This recitation of congressional action may not be complete, but it is apparent that Congress continues to act favorably. In 1982, Congress passed the Job Training Partnership Act[43] which explicitly adopted affirmative action obligations under the

103 (1972) (current version at 42 U.S.C. § 2000a (1982)).

37. See "Section by Section Analysis of H.R. 1746," accompanying the Equal Employment Opportunity Act of 1972, Conference Report, 118 Cong.Rec. 7166 (1972); S.Rep. No. 415, 92d Cong., 1st Sess. (1971); H.R.Rep. No. 238, 92d Cong., 1st Sess. (1971). See also the treatment of congressional intent as expressed in the legislative history in Franks v. Bowman Transp. Co., 424 U.S. 747, 762–70 (1976) (federal courts are empowered to fashion such relief, including retroactive seniority, as the particular circumstances require to make whole victims of discrimination); the dissenting opinion of Justice Marshall in International Bhd. of Teamsters v. United States, 431 U.S. 324, 381–94 (1977) (especially 391–94) (Section 703(h) of Title VII (codified at 42 U.S.C. § 2000e–2(h) (1976)) should not protect seniority systems which perpetuate past discrimination).

38. 20 U.S.C. § 1681 (1982).

39. 29 U.S.C. §§ 701, 793 (1982).

40. 38 U.S.C. §§ 2000, 2012 (1982).

41. 29 U.S.C. §§ 621–634 (1982) (as amended).

42. 31 U.S.C. § 6701 (1982).

43. 29 U.S.C. § 1501, § 1781 (1982).

executive order for certain employers. More modest protections of affirmative action are contained in legislation dealing with the restructuring of certain railroads in which hiring preferences pursuant to affirmative action plans are protected.[44] These laws, passed in the 1980's, were signed into law by President Reagan. Thus, despite the negative pronouncements of the current administration, Congress continues to behave in a highly positive fashion, albeit in more limited laws, and the President seems quietly to go along with those directions.

In June of 1983, most of the fifty states had a basic fair employment practice law covering race, color, religion, sex, age, and national origin. Some states cover additional categories of discrimination, such as handicap, marital status, equal pay, arrest records, and lie detectors. The District of Columbia and Puerto Rico, both federal entities, also have laws prohibiting discrimination. Alabama prohibited only handicapped discrimination, and Arkansas prohibited only age, handicap, and denials of equal pay. In July of 1983, Louisiana passed a law of general applicability prohibiting intentional discrimination on the basis of race, color, religion, sex, or national origin.[45] We do not know, and no one seems to have a record of, all the cities and other local entities of government, such as counties and independent school districts, that also may have acted in some way to support prohibitions on employment discrimination, including affirmative action.

This summary look at the positive contributions of entities of governments seems to establish rather convincingly that, by and large, the Presidents, the United States Congress, and the legislatures of the various states have provided, and continue to provide, positive support for the elimination of employment discrimination.

C. AN INVENTORY OF LAWS PROHIBITING EMPLOYMENT DISCRIMINATION

The source of antidiscrimination doctrine with which this book is most concerned is Title VII of the Civil Rights Act of 1964, 42 U.S.C. § 2000 et seq. In many settings, however, other sources may be turned to in addition to or instead of Title VII. The following list illustrates the variety of possibilities which counsel must consider:

44. See Rock Island Railroad Transition and Employee Assistance Act, 45 U.S.C. § 1004 (1982), amended by, 96 Stat. 2547 (1983); see also Milwaukee Railroad Restructuring Act, 45 U.S.C. § 907 (1982), amended by, 96 Stat. 2547 (1983); other laws such as the Federal Highway Aid Act, 23 U.S.C. § 105(f) (1982), amended by, 96 Stat. 2110 (1983) (10% set aside for socially and economically disadvantaged contractors); Part G of the Job Training Partnership Act, 29 U.S.C. §§ 1755, 1781 (1982), and §§ 1603(a)(1), 1691–92 of the same act; Foreign Service Act of 1980, 22 U.S.C. § 3905(b)(2) (1982), effective Feb. 15, 1981, also are supportive of equal employment and affirmative action initiatives.

45. Fair Employment Practices Manual (BNA) Vol. VII–A, at 451:102–104 (June 1983).

(1) The Federal Constitution

The Due Process Clause of the Fifth Amendment and the Due Process and Equal Protection Clauses of the Fourteenth Amendment have been interpreted to forbid invidious discrimination in government employment.

(2) The Early Civil Rights Acts

These statutes, now codified at 42 U.S.C. §§ 1981, 1983, and 1985 (insofar as they are relevant to the employment context), were long given a restrictive interpretation by the courts, but recent reinterpretations, such as that in the *Johnson* case, infra, make them important sources of antidiscrimination doctrine insofar as race and alienage are concerned. Whether they will be applied in sex, age, or other types of discrimination cases is less clear. Compare Cohen v. Illinois Institute of Technology, 524 F.2d 818 (7th Cir.1975), with McLellan v. Mississippi Power & Light Co., 545 F.2d 919 (5th Cir.1976). Enforcement is through litigation. The discriminatory act is treated as a type of economic tort. See Larson, The Development of Section 1981 as a Remedy for Racial Discrimination in Private Employment, 7 Harv.Civ. Rights—Civ.Lib.L.Rev. 56 (1972). See also The Expanding Scope of § 1981: Assault on Private Discrimination and a Cloud on Affirmative Action, 90 Harv.L.Rev. 412–52 (1977).

(3) The Civil Rights Act of 1964

This is the most important single source of antidiscrimination doctrine. Title VII forbids discrimination on the basis of race, color, creed, national origin, and sex (age is not mentioned) by employment agencies, labor organizations, and private and public employers. The statute creates the Equal Employment Opportunity Commission, which investigates complaints and seeks to negotiate settlements in cases in which discrimination is found by the EEOC to have occurred. If conciliation fails, either the EEOC or the individual may bring an action in federal court in the case of private employers, employment agencies, and labor organizations. The Attorney General rather than the EEOC brings the action in the case of state government employers. If federal employees are involved after October 1978, enforcement is through the EEOC rather than the Civil Service Commission, with the individual suits permitted following pursuit of the administrative remedy. Title VI forbids discrimination by recipients of federal financial assistance.

(4) Presidential Executive Orders

The major executive orders dealing with discrimination in employment are: Executive Order 11246 (discrimination on the basis of race, color, religion, sex, or national origin by federal contractors); Executive Order 11141 (age discrimination by contractors); Executive Order 11764 (making the Attorney General responsible for coordinating enforcement of Title VI of the Civil Rights Act of 1964 so far as recipients of federal financial assistance are concerned); and Executive Order 11478 (discrimination on the basis of race, color, religion, sex, or national origin in Federal Government employment).

(5) Equal Pay Act

This statute appears as Section 6(d) of the Fair Labor Standards Act. (29 U.S.C. Sec. 206(d)). It requires equal pay for equal work without regard to sex. The statute was administered by the Department of Labor until the enforcement of the statute was transferred to the EEOC by Reorganization Plan No. 1 of 1978.

(6) Age Discrimination in Employment Act

This statute (29 U.S.C. Sec. 621 et seq.) forbids employers (including the state and federal governments), labor organizations, and employment agencies to discriminate against individuals between the ages of 40 and 70 on the basis of age. Enforcement was through the Department of Labor until the Reorganization Plan No. 1 of 1978 transferred enforcement to the EEOC. Remedies include suits by the EEOC or by the discriminatee (except in the case of the Federal Government in which case enforcement is through the Civil Service Commission and the right of suit extends only to a discriminatee who has properly exhausted administrative remedies). A new statute, the Age Discrimination Act of 1975, applies to those employers receiving federal financial assistance.

(7) State Fair Employment Practice Laws

Most states and many local jurisdictions have fair employment practice laws applying to employers, unions, and employment agencies. Many states also provide that government agencies, political subdivisions, and contractors doing business with the state are obligated to provide equal employment opportunity.

State agencies process charges brought by claimants, and claims deferred to the agencies by the EEOC. As of fall 1978, the EEOC was deferring more than 60 percent of its job discrimination charges for initial action to 77 state and local fair employment practice agencies that have enforcement standards comparable to those of the EEOC.

State fair employment practice laws include bans against discrimination on the basis of sex, age, handicap, or marital status. When state laws extend beyond federal statutes, employers are bound by the more comprehensive requirements of state laws as well as the requirements of Title VII.

State laws often cover smaller employers. While Title VII applies to employers with 15 or more employees, state legislation may specify that an employer need have only one employee, or make no provision for the minimum number of employees needed to determine coverage.

(8) Labor Relations Laws

Both the Railway Labor Act (45 U.S.C. § 151 et seq.) and the National Labor Relations Act (29 U.S.C. § 151 et seq.) have been held to impose on labor organizations a duty to represent all members of relevant bargaining units fairly without regard to race, religion, national origin, and sex. This duty is enforceable by suit by a discriminatee. In addition, certain types of discriminatory acts by labor organizations or employers may constitute unfair labor practices, for which remedies are available through the administrative processes of the NLRB, or may constitute a basis for objecting to the selection of a labor organization as an exclusive bargaining representative. See generally Herring, The Fair Representation Doctrine: An Effective Weapon Against Union Racial Discrimination, 24 Md.L.Rev. 113 (1964); Leiken, The Current and Potential Equal Employment Role of the NLRB, 1971 Duke L.J. 833.

(9) Vocational Rehabilitation Act of 1973

Section 503 of this statute (29 U.S.C. § 793) requires federal contractors to take special steps to provide employment opportunities for handicapped individuals. Enforcement is through the Department of Labor.

(10) Vietnam Era Veterans Readjustment Act of 1974

38 U.S.C. § 2012 requires federal contractors to seek to promote employment opportunities for "qualified disabled veterans and veterans of the Vietnam era." Enforcement is through the Department of Labor. 38 U.S.C. § 2014 requires special consideration to be given such veterans in federal employment, with enforcement responsibility lodged in the Civil Service Commission.

(11) Title IX of the Higher Education Amendments of 1972

This Act, the principal section being 20 U.S.C. § 1681, forbids sex discrimination by educational institutions. It extends to matters other than employment and has received the greatest attention with respect to providing for rights of participation in physical education activities by women. The Act also amends Title IV of the Civil Rights Act of 1964 to include sex as a forbidden basis of discrimination. Administration is for the most part through the Department of Education.

(12) Collective Bargaining Agreements

Ninety-four per cent (94%) of collective bargaining agreements sampled by BNA in 1983 had guarantees against discrimination by the employer, the union or both. Ninety-one per cent (91%) of the clauses prohibit discrimination on the basis of race, creed, sex, national origin or age. BNA, Collective Bargaining Negotiations and Contracts, Vol. 2, 95:5.

Enforcement is through grievance procedures, often culminating in arbitration. Arbitrators' attitudes concerning their responsibilities and powers with regard to invidious discrimination vary. A good survey appears in M. Stone & E. Baderschneider, Arbitration of Discrimination Grievances (1974).

In an attempt to provide for better coordination of the federal efforts to combat discrimination, the Congress in 1972 established the Equal Employment Opportunity Coordinating Council (EEOCC). EEOCC is composed of the chief officers (or their delegates) of the Departments of Labor and Justice, the EEOC, the Civil Rights Commission, and the Civil Service Commission. EEOCC's success has thus far been limited, as illustrated by ongoing disagreement among the agencies with regard to uniform employee selection guidelines. The Reorganization Plan of 1978 abolished the Council and transferred its functions to the EEOC.

The bulk of the antidiscrimination laws listed have come into force within the past dozen or so years. Have they had any impact? No one simple answer to that query would be either honest or complete.

(13) Pregnancy Disability

In 1978 Congress amended Title VII of the Civil Rights Act of 1964 to prohibit sex discrimination on the basis of pregnancy. Section 701 of the statute was amended by adding a new subsection (K).

D. MAJOR FEDERAL ENFORCEMENT AGENCIES *

1. EQUAL EMPLOYMENT OPPORTUNITY COMMISSION

The purposes of the Equal Employment Opportunity Commission (EEOC) are to eliminate discrimination based on race, color, religion, sex, national origin, or age in hiring, promoting, firing, wages, testing, training, apprenticeship and all other conditions of employment. The Commission also promotes voluntary action programs by employers, unions and community organizations to make equal employment opportunity an actuality. EEOC also is responsible for all compliance and enforcement activities relating to equal employment opportunity among Federal employees and applicants, including handicap discrimination.

The Equal Employment Opportunity Commission was created by title VII of the Civil Rights Act of 1964 (78 Stat. 253; 42 U.S.C. 2000e), and became operational July 2, 1965. Title VII was amended by the Equal Employment Opportunity Act of 1972 (86 Stat. 103; 42 U.S.C. 2000e) and the Pregnancy Discrimination Act of 1978 (92 Stat. 2076; 42 U.S.C. 2000e).

* Source: U.S. Government Manual 1984/5, Office of the Federal Register, National Archives and Record Service, GSA.

Executive Order 12067 of June 30, 1978, effective July 1, 1978, abolished the Equal Employment Opportunity Coordinating Council, and transferred its duties to the Commission, with responsibility for providing coherence and direction to the Government's equal employment opportunity efforts. The Executive order also required that strong uniform enforcement standards be applied throughout the Government, standardized data collection procedures, joint training programs, the sharing of enforcement-related data among agencies, and the development of methods and priorities for complaint and compliance reviews.

Reorganization Plan No. 1 of 1978, effective May 6, 1978, transferred Federal equal employment functions from the Civil Service Commission to EEOC, effective on January 1, 1979. Functions transferred on January 1, 1979, included section 717 of title VII, which prohibits discrimination in employment in the Federal Government on the basis of race, color, religion, sex, or national origin; Executive Order No. 11478 of August 8, 1969, which set forth the U.S. policy of providing for equal employment opportunity in the Federal Government through affirmative action programs in Federal departments and agencies; Equal Pay Act of 1963 (EPA) (77 Stat. 56; 29 U.S.C. 206) in the Federal sector; and Age Discrimination in Employment Act of 1967 (ADEA) (81 Stat. 602; 29 U.S.C. 621) in the Federal sector. Also transferred was section 501 of the Rehabilitation Act of 1973 (87 Stat. 390; 29 U.S.C. 791), which pertains to employment discrimination against handicapped persons in the Federal Government.

On July 1, 1979, responsibility for enforcement in private industry as well as in State and local governments of the Equal Pay Act of 1963, which prohibits sex-based pay differences where the work performed is of equal skill, effort, and responsibility; and the Age Discrimination in Employment Act of 1967, which prohibits job discrimination against workers 40–70 years of age, was transferred from the Department of Labor to the Commission.

Under ADEA and EPA, the union, as an employer, is prohibited from discriminating against its employees or from causing an employer to discriminate. ADEA prohibits unions from discriminating against their members, while EPA does not.

The Commission operates through a 48-office field structure, which integrates legal and complaint processing functions.

Activities

Compliance Activities. The Commission's field offices receive written charges of job discrimination under title VII of the Civil Rights Act of 1964, as amended (78 Stat. 253; 42 U.S.C. 2000e), the Equal Pay Act of 1963 (77 Stat. 56; 29 U.S.C. 206), and the Age Discrimination in Employment Act of 1967 (81 Stat. 602; 29 U.S.C. 621). They also receive written or oral complaints under ADEA and EPA. These charges or complaints may be against public or private employers, labor organizations, joint labor-management and apprenticeship programs, and public or private employment agencies. Field offices may initiate investigations to find violations of ADEA and EPA. Members of the Commission also may initiate charges alleging that a violation of title VII has occurred. Section 501 of the Rehabilitation Act of 1973 (87 Stat. 390; 29 U.S.C. 791) covers Federal employees and applicants only.

Charges of title VII violations in private industry or State or local governments must be filed with the Commission within 180 days of the alleged violation, (or up to 300 days where a State or local fair employment practices agency initially was contacted), and the Commission is responsible for notifying persons so charged within 10 days of the receipt of a new charge. Before investigation, a charge must be deferred for 60 days to a local fair employment practices agency in States and municipalities where an agency with an enforceable fair employment practices law exists. The deferral period is 120 days for an agency which has been operating less than 1 year. Under a worksharing agreement executed between the Commission and State and local fair employment practices agencies, the Commission routinely will assume jurisdiction over certain charges of discrimination and proceed with its investigation rather than wait for the expiration of the deferral period.

The Commission has instituted new procedural regulations under title VII which encourage settlement of charges of discrimination prior to a determination by the agency on the merits of the charges. In addition, factfinding conferences may be required as part of the investigation and may assist in establishing the framework for a negotiated settlement. After an investigation, if there is reasonable cause to believe the charge is true, the district, area or local office attempts to remedy the alleged unlawful practices through the informal methods of conciliation, conference, and persuasion.

Unless an acceptable conciliation agreement has been secured, the Commission may, after 30 days from the date the charge was filed, bring suit in an appropriate Federal district court. The Attorney General brings suit when a State or local government, governmental agency or a political subdivision, is involved. If the Commission or the Attorney General does not proceed in this manner, at the conclusion of the administrative procedures, or earlier at the request of the charging party, a Notice of Right-to-Sue is issued which allows the charging party to proceed within 90 days in a Federal district court. In appropriate cases the Commission may intervene in such civil action if the case is of general public interest. The investigation and conciliation of charges having an industrywide or national impact are coordinated or conducted by the Office of Systemic Programs.

Under the provisions of title VII, section 706(f)(2), as amended by section 5 of the Equal Employment Opportunity Act of 1972 (86 Stat. 107; 42 U.S.C. 2000e–6), if it is concluded after a preliminary investigation that prompt judicial action is necessary to carry out the purposes of the act, the Commission or the Attorney General, in a case involving a State or local government, governmental agency or political subdivision, may bring an action for appropriate temporary or preliminary relief pending final disposition of a charge.

Complaints Against the Federal Government. Federal employees or applicants who want to file complaints of job discrimination based on race, color, national origin, sex, religion, age, or physical or mental handicap must first consult an equal employment opportunity counselor within their agency within 30 calendar days of the alleged act. If the complaint cannot be resolved informally, the person may file a formal complaint within 15 calendar days following the final interview with the counselor. (An individual who wishes to file a complaint under the Equal Pay Act of 1963 (77 Stat. 56; 29 U.S.C. 206) need not follow these procedures. Such complaints may be filed directly with the Commission—within 2 years of the alleged violation—and can be kept confidential. An individual may also elect to file suit under the Equal Pay Act of 1963 without prior resort to the agency or to EEOC.)

A complaint under the Age Discrimination in Employment Act of 1967 (81 Stat. 602; 29 U.S.C. 621) against a Federal agency or department must be filed in that agency or department with the agency or department head, director of equal employment opportunity, head of the field installation, equal employment opportunity officer, Federal women's program manager, or the Hispanic employment program manager (or any designee).

Charges or Complaints Under the Age Discrimination in Employment or Equal Pay Acts. An age discrimination charge must be filed with EEOC within 180 days of the alleged violation. This is extended to 300 days if a State has a statute prohibiting age discrimination and a mechanism for enforcement. The charging party may file suit after waiting 60 days for EEOC to attempt to eliminate the unlawful practice through informal methods of conciliation, conference, and persuasion. Should the Commission take legal action, an individual covered by such action may not file a private suit. If an individual files a complaint of age discrimination, his or her name will be kept confidential but the individual filing the complaint cannot bring a private suit unless he or she elects to file a charge first in accordance with the above requirements.

The Age Discrimination in Employment Act of 1967 (81 Stat. 602; 29 U.S.C. 621) and the Equal Pay Act of 1963 (77 Stat. 56; 29 U.S.C. 206) cover most employees or applicants in private industry and Federal, State, and local governments.

A lawsuit under the Equal Pay Act of 1963 may be filed by the Commission or by the complainant. There are no prerequisites to individual actions under this law. Back wages can be recovered for a period of up to 2 years prior to the filing of a suit, except in the case of willful violation, where 3 years backpay may be recovered. The name of the individual filing the complaint is kept confidential.

Other Activities. The Commission participates in the development of the employment discrimination law through the issuance of guidelines, publication of significant Commission decisions, and involvement in litigation brought under title VII and related statutes, and the Equal Pay Act of 1963 or the Age Discrimination in Employment Act of 1967.

The Commission has direct liaison with Federal, State, and local governments, employer and union organizations, trade associations, civil rights organizations, and other agencies and organizations concerned with employment of minority group members and women. The Commission engages in and contributes to the cost of research and other mutual interest projects with State and local agencies charged with the administration of fair employment practices laws. Furthermore, the Commission enters into worksharing agreements with the State and local agencies in order to avoid duplication of effort by identifying specific charges to be investigated by the respective agencies.

The Commission is also a major publisher of data on the employment status of minorities and women. Through six employment surveys (EEO-1 through EEO-6) covering private employers, apprenticeship programs, labor unions, State and local governments, elementary and secondary schools, and colleges and universities, the Commission tabulates and stores data on the ethnic, racial, and sex characteristics of employees at all job levels within the reported groups.

Research information thus collected is shared with selected Federal agencies, such as the Department of Health and Human Services, the Department of Labor, and others. It is also made available, in appropriate form, for public use.

Sources of Information

Library. Room 298, 2401 E Street NW., Washington, D.C. 20506. Phone, 202-634-6991.

2. DEPARTMENT OF JUSTICE

Civil Rights Division

The Civil Rights Division, headed by an Assistant Attorney General, was established in 1957 in response to the need to secure effective Federal enforcement of civil rights.

This Division is responsible for enforcing Federal civil rights laws which prohibit discrimination on the basis of race, national origin, religion, and in some instances, sex, or handicap in the areas of voting, education, employment, housing, credit, the use of public facilities and public accommodations, and in the administration of federally assisted programs. The congressional statutes enforced are, *inter alia*, the Civil

Rights Acts of 1957 (71 Stat. 634; 42 U.S.C. 1975), 1960 (74 Stat. 86; 42 U.S.C. 1971, 1974), 1964 (78 Stat. 241; 42 U.S.C. 2000a–h), 1968 (82 Stat. 73; 18 U.S.C. 245, 42 U.S.C. 3601–3619, 3631), the Voting Rights Act of 1965, as amended (79 Stat. 437; 42 U.S.C. 1971, 1973), the Equal Credit Opportunity Act, as amended in 1976 (90 Stat. 251; 15 U.S.C. 1691), and the Civil Rights of Institutionalized Persons Act of 1980 (94 Stat. 349; 42 U.S.C. 1997).

The Division also is responsible for the implementation of Executive Order 12250 of November 2, 1980, which requires coordination of efforts of Executive agencies and Departments to eliminate discrimination based on race, color, national origin, sex, religion, and handicap in programs receiving Federal financial assistance and discrimination based on handicap in federally conducted programs.

The Civil Rights Division also has the obligation to enforce specific criminal statutes including those concerning willful deprivation of constitutional rights under color of law or through conspiracy and violent interference with federally protected activities (18 U.S.C. 241, 242, 245).

The Civil Rights Division is divided into eight organizational units, each of which has jurisdiction over particular subject areas and related statutes. With the approval of the Assistant Attorney General and, where necessary, the Attorney General and Solicitor General, each litigating section undertakes or authorizes investigations, conducts negotiations, and initiates and conducts litigation. An appellate section handles most appeals and legislative matters.

For further information, contact the Executive Officer, Civil Rights Division, Department of Justice, Tenth Street and Pennsylvania Avenue NW., Washington, D.C. 20530. Phone, 202–633–4224.

3. DEPARTMENT OF LABOR
Federal Contract Compliance Programs

The Office of Federal Contract Compliance Programs is responsible for establishing policies and goals and providing leadership and coordination of the Government's program to achieve nondiscrimination in employment by Government contractors and subcontractors and in federally assisted construction programs.

The Office of Federal Contract Compliance Programs also is responsible for administering programs to assure affirmative action by government contractors to employ and advance in the employment of Vietnam-era veterans and handicapped workers; coordinating with the Equal Employment Opportunity Commission (EEOC) and the Department of Justice matters relating to title VII of the Civil Rights Act of 1964; and maintaining liaison with other agencies having civil rights and equal employment opportunity activities.

The Solicitor of Labor

The Solicitor has responsibility for all the legal activities of the Department, its legislative program, and serves as legal adviser to the Secretary and other officials of the Department.

The Solicitor, through a subordinate staff of attorneys in Washington and 16 field offices, directs a broad scale litigation effort pertaining to the many statutes administered by the Department including institution and prosecution of Civil Court actions under the Fair Labor Standards Act, as amended, the Employee Retirement Income Security Act of 1974, and the Migrant and Seasonal Agricultural Worker Protection Act. Attorneys also represent the Department in administrative hearings under various statutes, including the Occupational Safety and Health Act of 1970, the Federal Mine Safety and Health Act of 1977, and various government contract labor standards laws. The cited litigation is conducted independently under an agreement and delegation of authority from the Department of Justice. Litigation under several other acts is carried out in cooperation with the Department of Justice.

Appellate litigation is conducted by attorneys in the national headquarters, whereas the majority of trial litigation under the various statutes is carried out by attorneys under the direction of the regional solicitors who also serve as the legal advisers to the Department's officials in the field.

E. ECONOMIC CONSEQUENCES OF DISCRIMINATION: THE "PROBLEM" AND THE "PROGRESS" *

As we enter our third decade of experience under the Civil Rights Act of 1964, we continue to witness the proliferation of studies which attempt to analyze the economic consequences of discrimination. These studies provide a plethora of data to illustrate the "problem" associated with discrimination in employment, as well as evaluations of observable changes or trends in the employment conditions of the affected classes compared with those of a more favored group. These evaluations, in turn, have been expanded to include various analyses of the economic impact of equal employment opportunity, most particularly as related to the presence of affirmative action.

The nature of these studies has evolved along two broad categories. First, there are descriptive studies which focus on general labor market data (e.g., employment, unemployment, labor force participation, occupational distribution, etc.) across various demographic groups at the "macro" or economy-wide level of the U.S. labor force. Most, though not all, of these studies emphasize macro level trends without attempt-

---

* Portions of this section are taken from James E. Jones, Jr., "The Genesis and Present Status of Affirmative Action in Employment: Economic, Legal, and Political Realities," Iowa Law Review, Vol. 70, No. 4, May 1985, pp. 901–944.

ing to control for the influence of other variables. Secondly, there are econometric studies of the effectiveness of equal employment opportunity and affirmative action which emphasize employment and occupational distribution across race-sex groups at the firm level rather than economy-wide effects, and do attempt to control for other variables.

In an effort to offer the student as comprehensive review of the economic literature as feasible within a limited number of pages, we provide the following excerpts and summaries of selected studies published since the early 1960's. In selecting the particular studies, we attempt to identify some of the more influential studies which outline the relative employment conditions of affected classes at different points in time, and which provide the most comprehensive analysis of the economic impact associated with equal employment opportunity and affirmative action.

1. SELECTED STUDIES

(a) Descriptive Studies

The descriptive studies often emphasize comparisons between "majority group" members (usually white males) and "nonmajority" or "protected group" members on numerous employment related indices— wages, income, employment, labor force participation, occupational distribution (i.e., intermittant employment, involuntary parttime employment, overeducation, marginal jobs, etc.). In almost all the cases, blacks, Hispanics and females compare unfavorably with white males on the various measures. These employment disparities traditionally have been associated with discrimination against members of the protected group. Many of these studies also present changes over time on one or more of the various measures, and draw conclusions regarding the degree of the "problem" and the economic impact of equal employment opportunity combined with affirmative action efforts.

One of the earliest articles on point prior to the passage of the Civil Rights Act of 1964 was written by Matthew Kessler in 1963. The following excerpt from his article provides a general discussion of the economic status of nonwhite workers in the U.S. from the mid 1950's to the early 1960's.

(b) Economic Status of Non-White Workers, 1955–62

ECONOMIC STATUS OF NON–WHITE WORKERS, 1955–62 *

Matthew A. Kessler **

The gradual movement of nonwhite workers (over 90 percent of whom are Negroes) into higher skilled and better paying jobs has continued since the mid-1950's. However, despite these recent gains,

* Monthly Labor Review, July 1963.   ** Of the Division of Employment and Labor Force Analysis, Bureau of Labor Statistics.

large gaps continue to exist between white and nonwhite workers, as measured by most indicators of social and economic well-being.

Nonwhites continue to be concentrated in less-skilled jobs and are subject to more unemployment than whites. The jobless rates of nonwhites are still at least one and one-half times higher than for whites in every age-sex grouping, and for some age groupings are three times as high. Unemployment bears disproportionately on the nonwhite worker whatever his industry or occupation. Not only is he subject to more frequent spells of unemployment; once out of a job, he has tended to remain jobless for a longer period of time.

After achieving relatively substantial gains in money income during the early postwar period, nonwhite families have failed to keep pace with the rise in average income of white families since the mid-1950's, despite the continued shift of nonwhite workers into higher paying jobs.

During the past two decades, nonwhites have narrowed the educational gap that had historically existed between themselves and white persons, a development which has helped to foster their steady but slow movement up the occupational skill ladder. Since the mid-1950's, however, differences in the level of educational attainment between whites and nonwhites have remained essentially unchanged.

In a descriptive study, Herbert Hammerman utilizes a large body of data to examine with great precision the changes in the employment status of minorities and women as related to the affirmative action efforts between 1970 and 1980.

2. A DECADE OF NEW OPPORTUNITY: AFFIRMATIVE ACTION IN THE 70'S

A DECADE OF NEW OPPORTUNITY: AFFIRMATIVE ACTION IN THE 1970'S *

Herbert Hammerman

SUMMARY OF FINDINGS

In undertaking this study, we addressed the following questions:

—Do the data reveal significant change in the patterns of minority and female employment in the 1970s?

—If so, to what extent were such changes the result of affirmative action?

—Has affirmative action brought about fundamental changes in personnel practices and systems which traditionally had discriminated against minorities and women?

The answers briefly are that there *was* significant change, much of it was due to affirmative action, and appropriate changes in personnel

---

* The Potomac Institute, Inc., Washington, D.C. (October 1984). Reprinted by permission.

practices appear to have been made, at least among the larger employers in the nation.

We have found that at the end of the decade both minorities and women had greater employment in higher-paid jobs, where they had traditionally been under-represented, than at the beginning. This was true in all sectors that we examined—private employment, government employment in both the federal and the state and local spheres, to some extent in institutions of higher education (where data were not available for the early part of the decade), and in apprenticeships and union membership in the construction industry. We conclude also that the gains shown by the data were much greater than in previous decades, and for the first time represent a good start in the direction of equal employment opportunity, though not its final achievement. The achievements of equal employment opportunity have not yet neared the levels that would justify the dismantling of the governmental machinery that made them possible.

There can be no doubt that much of the change in employment patterns is attributable to affirmative action. As the 1960s drew to a close, employers found themselves increasingly in peril of heavy financial liabilities resulting from potential lawsuits brought under Title VII. Standardization of equal employment opportunity procedures became a necessary means of making required changes and providing good faith defenses. The fact that Revised Order No. 4, which set forth affirmative action procedures for government contractors, was issued in late 1971 during the Nixon administration would itself indicate that it was not strongly opposed by industry. The administration's action was assisted by an intensive educational program carried out by the National Association of Manufacturers. There is strong statistical evidence of the effectiveness of the affirmative action programs. The most striking is a recent study by the Office of Federal Contract Compliance (OFCCP) which revealed that between 1974 and 1980 minorities and women made significantly greater gains in establishments of federal government contractors than noncontractors.

It is also clear that industry has made substantial systemic changes in personnel practices to eliminate those which had stood in the way of effective equal employment opportunity. In some instances, companies like the American Telephone and Telegraph Company required judicially enforced consent decrees to make long overdue changes which, it would appear, they considered necessary at the time and for which they take credit today. In most instances, however, companies have been able to alter practices by making personnel management changes, including special training of supervisors, crediting EEO activities of supervisors, and developing professional staffs to monitor and oversee in-house equal opportunity programs. It is noteworthy that there has been relatively little opposition by industry to the affirmative action requirements of Executive Order 11246, which sets forth the EEO duties of federal contractors. In fact, those who would strip affirmative action of its numerical procedures clearly do not speak on behalf of most of big industry which sees it as "an essential management tool."

THE ECONOMIC SETTING

As an economic setting, the 1970s were an inauspicious time to inaugurate affirmative action. They witnessed a sharp contraction in the almost uninterrupted rate of economic growth of the preceding quarter of a century. Unemployment rates went up and after each rise stayed higher than they had been before. Poverty rates which had greatly declined in the 1960s stopped going down and were on the rise by 1981. The combination of economic stagnation and inflation, labelled "stagflation," kept real income from rising while monetary income moved up with prices. It was mainly the entrance of women into the labor force in unprecedented numbers, their labor force participation having increased from 42.0 percent in 1970 to 51.4 percent in 1980, that kept real family incomes from falling.

The economic climate was particularly harsh for blacks. The historical black-to-white unemployment ratio of 2 to 1 had declined to 1.8 to 1 by 1970; but, ten years later, it was up to 2.3 to 1. For black youth, unemployment rates were at catastrophic levels, above 40 percent by 1980, and were to go still higher. While there was virtually no change in the real income of white families between 1970 and 1980, the real income of black families declined almost 5 percent, reversing the earlier trend toward reducing the racial gap.

Some critics of affirmative action allude to these economic trends as evidence of the failure of affirmative action, where in fact the aggregate numbers tend to mask its success. Frequently the criticisms miss the point. Disaggregated, the data show that the percentage of black families *in the higher income brackets* actually increased in the course of the decade, as was also the case of white and Hispanic families. However, the proportion of black families in the low income brackets increased as well, again also true of white and Hispanic families. There were more families which were better off and more which were worse off in all groups. Also, there was an increase of families with female householders and no husband present among all groups. For blacks, this trend was particularly severe. In 1981 such female-householder families accounted for two-thirds of all black persons in poverty.

Affirmative action is a program developed to remedy discrimination in employment, not poverty, nor inadequate education. To the extent that it has been successful, therefore, its achievements have been made in the face of the countervailing effects of poverty, stagflation, and an increasing number of female householder families. It is thus fair to assume that the success of affirmative action would have been greater had those factors not been present.

The growth of female-householder families, has had a doubly negative effect on incomes, both as a result of the absence of another income, the husband's, and the low levels of female pay. The income of women working full-time and year-round was about three-fifths that of men in 1980, a ratio that had remained unchanged for two decades, but which did rise two to three percentage points in 1982. On the average, the incomes of women, whether white, black, or Hispanic, are lower than those of men, regardless of race or ethnicity. The factors of age and education have increased the incomes of men to a much greater extent than of women. Higher education has brought black males closer to the incomes of white males. While it has tended to bridge the racial gap among females, it has done little to bridge the male-female gap.

PRIVATE INDUSTRY EMPLOYMENT

Annual statistics published by the Equal Employment Opportunity Commission (EEOC), based upon that agency's EEO–1 surveys of private employers, reveal that minority groups and women made substantial employment gains between 1970 and 1980. The major increases were in the higher paid white-collar jobs (officials and managers, professionals, technicians, and sales workers), and, for male minorities, in the skilled crafts.

Black males improved their participation in all white-collar jobs, including clerical, and most substantially in the skilled crafts. The representation of black females increased in all but one of the nine job categories, that of service workers. Hispanics of both sexes improved their total labor force participation and their percentage of each job category.

While the representation of white women was virtually unchanged in the two job categories which traditionally have been their main source of employment, office and clerical workers and semiskilled operatives, it increased in all other jobs, exceptionally so in the white-collar jobs other than clerical. The statistics indicate that, when women entered the work force in increasing numbers in the 1970s, they did so substantially in the higher white-collar categories of jobs.

Comparisons of government contractors with noncontractors show that greater gains were made by contractors in the 1970s. In an analysis comparing data for two industry groups in which contractors predominate, i.e. manufacturing and a combination of transportation, communication, and public utilities, with an aggregate of all other surveyed industries, the Potomac Institute found a greater increase in minority and female representation in the contractor industries.

An OFCCP comparison of 77,000 establishments for 1974 and 1980, with an aggregate 1980 employment of 20.4 million, reveals substantially greater improvements in the representation of both minorities and women in establishments of government contractors compared with those of noncontractors. For minorities, there were greater increases in all but one job category, and most substantially in white-collar and skilled craft jobs. For women, contractor increases were greater in all job categories.

A further analysis was made of contractor establishments, separating those that had experienced compliance reviews by federal government agencies and those that had not been reviewed. In reviewed establishments, increases of minority representation were somewhat greater than in the unreviewed establishments in eight of the nine job categories. Increases in female representation were substantially greater in the four nonclerical white-collar jobs and in service jobs. Moreover, minority and female increases were substantially greater in both of the contractor groups than in the noncontractor group. Similar conclusions were reached by an independent scholar utilizing the tools of regression analysis on a similar data base.

APPRENTICESHIP AND UNION MEMBERSHIP IN CONSTRUCTION

The figures on minority apprentices show considerable increases from 1970 to 1979, the last year surveyed. More importantly, graduates from apprenticeship increased from little more than a trickle of minorities in 1970 to substantial proportions by 1979. Significantly, black representation among apprenticeship graduates in 1979 at 9.4 percent was as high as among apprentices, 9.6 percent, indicating a high degree of completion of the programs. These figures reflect substantial additions of minorities, particularly blacks against whom discrimination had been most blatant, to the permanent construction labor force. A study of minorities in construction in New York City revealed that, in the face of a sharp decline in total apprenticeship during the city's severe construction recession in the latter 1970s, the proportion of minorities increased steadily. Statistics on women in apprenticeship show a doubling in the number of female apprentices, increasing their proportions from 2.1 percent to 3.7 percent in one year (1978 to 1979).

Data on membership in referral unions in the building trades reveal that as late as 1970, blacks were virtually excluded from the mechanical trades, with only 1.8 percent of the membership. Hispanics, despite their lower general labor force participation, were better represented with 3.2 percent of the total. In the other skilled trades, excluding the less skilled laborers, the figures were somewhat higher, 4.8 percent for each. Reflecting the training programs and other affirmative action activities over the intervening nine-year period, the 1979 statistics show a marked increase to 4.3 percent for blacks and 4.2 percent for Hispanics in the mechanical trades. Black membership also increased, but less substantially in the other skilled trades. The data reveal clear but limited progress from a very low base of black participation, but the construction unions still had far to go to match black employment in skilled jobs in other industries.

GOVERNMENT EMPLOYMENT—FEDERAL

The federal government administers three broad compensation systems: the general schedule, mainly white collar and covering 60 percent of all federal employees; the wage systems, predominantly blue-collar jobs; and the postal service. Minority group employment was highest in the wage systems and lowest in the general schedule, but had its largest increase during the 1970s in the general schedule. There were greater proportions of minority groups, particularly blacks in the federal government than in private industry. Within all but the lowest of the 15 pay grades of the general schedule, minority groups and women had substantial increases in representation in the 1970s. Female participation rose 30 percent in the ten highest grades. Blacks more than doubled their 1970 representation in the six highest grades. Hispanics, sparse in 1970, had considerable percentage increases in all grades. Proportions of minorities and women remained thin in the highest grades. However, at the executive level, they rose rapidly in one year, 1979 to 1980, undoubtedly reflecting the strong emphasis on affirmative action in the late years of the decade.

GOVERNMENT EMPLOYMENT—STATE AND LOCAL

Great expansion of federal loan and grant programs to state and local governments during the 1970s and creation of federal agency staffs to administer EEO requirements brought increasing pressure to bear on such governments to comply with EEO requirements. Another factor has been the coverage of state and local governments by Title VII of the Civil Rights Act of 1964 after it was amended in 1972.

Statistics obtained by the EEOC on state and local governments show increased participation rates of all minority groups and women in virtually all of the eight job categories in the survey. For minorities, the figures in 1980 were slightly lower than in the federal government but considerably higher than in private industry. Female employment was greater than in the federal government and about the same as in industry. However, in white-collar jobs, state and local governments had a much greater female employment than both the federal government and industry.

The largest gains in the surveyed period were made by white females, particularly in the higher white-collar jobs. This reflected new work force participation since, as in other industries, their representation in clerical jobs remained unchanged. Minority women made gains in all white-collar jobs. Minority men gained most in protective service, mainly police and fire protection, and skilled craft jobs, and moderately in the higher white-collar categories.

EMPLOYMENT IN HIGHER EDUCATION

While women have almost one-half the total employment in institutions of higher education, they have little more than one-fourth of the faculty positions. Blacks and Hispanics are likewise much more poorly represented on faculties than in other positions. Surveys for 1975 and 1979 show decreases in the percentages of white and black males on faculties, and increases of Hispanic and Asian males and white and Asian females.

Considerably greater proportions of white male than minority male faculty members had tenure. Both white and minority males had greater tenure than either white or minority females. A similar pattern is found in the proportions of tenured faculty with full professorships: a smaller percentage of minority than white males and considerably smaller percentages of females, regardless of race and ethnicity.

Salary statistics also show white males with somewhat higher salaries than black and Hispanic males and much higher salaries than white, black, and Hispanic females. Sex differentials in salaries appear at all ranks and are greatest at the full professor level. However, most of the aggregate faculty differential is accounted for by the greater proportions of women in the lower paid faculty ranks.

EDUCATION AS EMPLOYMENT QUALIFICATION

There has been a great growth in secondary and higher education of both whites and blacks since World War II. In 1940, about two-fifths of all white persons age 25–29 and only one-eighth of all black persons in that age group had graduated high school. By 1979, the figures were about 87 percent of whites and 75 percent of blacks. While there was a small differential in favor of females of both races before the war, that seems to have been eliminated in the postwar era.

College enrollment increased spectacularly after the war, mainly in public institutions and in two-year community colleges. A major factor has been the enrollment of women, which increased from 41 percent to 51 percent of total enrollment in the 1970s. Enrollment of blacks increased considerably until the last half of the decade, when it started to decline, particularly in the case of male blacks. The main gains in the latter 1970s were made by white females at all levels of education. Proportionately, there were as many of them in graduate schools as in undergraduate schools. In contrast, there was a sharp decline in minority groups of both sexes after undergraduate school.

Figures on earned degrees show a much lower ratio of both women and blacks at the doctorate level. However, the percent of female doctorates almost doubled between 1971 and 1980. Information on degrees by field of study reveals emphasis by blacks and Hispanics on education, public affairs, psychology, social sciences, and, for Hispanics, language, in contrast to a greater emphasis by whites on business, engineering, physical sciences, and mathematics. While women continued high levels of specialization in traditional fields, such as education, library science, home economics, language, arts, and letters, the statistics show impressive increases in other fields, like business, physical sciences, engineering, and architecture.

In law, medical, and dental schools, total female enrollment rose sharply between 1971 and 1981: from 9 percent to 35 percent of law students; from 11 percent to 28 percent of medical students; and from 2 percent to 19 percent of dental students. Blacks and Hispanics also increased their representation, but to a smaller extent. From the midpoint of the ten-year period, from 1976 to 1981, there was a small decline in the percentage of blacks in each of the three types of professional schools.

Apparently, changing aspirations and self-image of women, notably white women, changing attitudes of admissions officers, and financial ability to bear increasing costs of higher and professional education account for the rapid gains made by women. On the other hand, the absence of financial ability seems to have hampered racial and ethnic minorities, particularly as economic recession increased in severity. Other suggested factors have been poor preparation of these minorities at the secondary school level in growing fields such as math and sciences, and difficulties in recruiting for higher education among poorly educated inner-city youth.

A conclusion that emerges from this study is that only those who are properly prepared by reason of education or training will benefit from the opportunities opened to women and minorities by affirmative action. Products of inferior education, school dropouts, the unskilled, recipients of diplomas that signify longevity or "life experiences" rather than academic achievement, and all the other unfortunates who are being shortchanged by society, among whose numbers minorities are so heavily concentrated, will never be able to measure up in their present circumstances to the work standards required to obtain and perform jobs competitively. Some proponents of "equality," fortunately in the minority, have suggested setting group quotas for employment of racial and ethnic minorities and women, regardless of qualification. No more certain way of destroying the concept of equal opportunity, and eventually American society, particularly in this emerging "hi-tech" era, can be envisioned. The solution is to enable every individual to compete on a truly equal basis by repairing and enhancing public education for all, meanwhile providing continuing remedial education for all those requiring it, providing training or retraining for skills of current currency, and continuing to work to eliminate every vestige of discrimination in all its manifold and ugly manifestations from American society.

Finally, labor economist Glen Cain notes that economics provides two broad definitions of discrimination in the labor market.[1] One is income inequality, which represents "long-lasting inequality in economic well-being among individuals based on their color, gender, or ethnic ties," and the other is earnings inequality, which represents economic discrimination as differences in pay or wage rates for comparable (i.e., equally productive) workers who differ only in group status.[2] He points out that the disparities on these two measures of discrimination are large and have persisted over time. More specifically, upon examining the progress since 1939 based on the first definition of economic

1. Glen Cain, "The Economics of Discrimination: Part I," Focus, Vol. 7, No. 2, (Summer 1984), University of Wisconsin-Madison, Institute for Research on Poverty, pp. 1–11.

2. Ibid., p. 2.

discrimination, Cain concludes that, "[w]hatever the reason, progress regarding the first type of economic discrimination, family income differences—and, by implication, differences in economic well-being—has been painfully slow." [3] Similarly, the earnings ratios for the major race-sex groups from 1939 to 1982 indicate that "the ratios are still so far short of unity in 1975–1982 that 'slow progress' is a fair and regrettable assessment." [4]

3. ECONOMETRIC STUDIES

The majority of econometric studies in this area of research have concentrated on the economic impact of affirmative action as associated with the federal government's contract compliance program. The assumption underlying these studies is that, if the program is administered effectively by the OFCCP, we should observe that the economic status of protected group members improves faster among federal contractors relative to noncontractors. The "micro" studies use data on employment and occupational distribution for all major race-sex groups at the firm level. Two variables in particular are emphasized: (1) some measure of change in the employment of protected group members relative to some measure of total employment at the firm, and changes in the occupational distribution of the major race-sex groups and (2) some measure of occupational distribution for protected group members.

Several econometric studies examine the impact of early OFCC enforcement efforts, using data from roughly 1966 to 1973 to determine the impact of contractor status on the relative position of protected group members.[5] There are four general findings of these studies. First, three of the four studies summarized here find an increase in the relative employment of black males that is greater by a sizeable, significant amount in the contractor sector; a representative estimate of this impact is that government contractors raise the employment of black males relative to white males 3.3 percent more than do noncontractors in the short run, which is equivalent to a 12.9 percent increase in the long run. Second, the results for females suggest that there is no positive impact for either white or minority females, especially for white females. Third, there is also no significant evidence of an increase in the relative occupational distribution of minorities or females. Fourth, the evidence is mixed, and generally negative, on

3. Ibid., p. 4.

4. Ibid., p. 5.

5. The studies summarized in this section include: George Burman, The Economics of Discrimination: The Impact of Public Policy, unpublished Ph.D. Thesis, Graduate School of Business, University of Chicago, 1977; Orley Ashenfelter and James Heckman, "Measuring the Effect of an Anti-Discrimination Program," in Evaluating the Labor Market Effects of Social Programs, Orley Ashenfelter and James Blum (eds.), Princeton, NJ: Industrial Relations Section, Princeton University, 1976: M. Goldstein and R. Smith, "The Estimated Impact of the Anti-Discrimination Program Aimed at Federal Contractors," Industrial and Labor Relations Review, Vol. 29, No. 4, July 1976, pp. 523–543; and James Heckman and Kenneth Wolpin, "Does the Contract Compliance Program Work: An Analysis of Chicago Data," Industrial and Labor Relations Review, Vol. 29, No. 4, July 1976, pp. 544–564.

whether compliance reviews are effective, i.e., related to changes in relative employment of protected group members or changes in their occupational status. It is important to remember, however, that the OFCCP did not start enforcing hiring goals for females until 1972; thus, any impact of OFCCP enforcement efforts would probably not be reflected in these studies, given the time period of the studies. More significantly, the goals and timetables obligation was not imposed upon most contractors until 1970–71.[6]

A more recent and comprehensive study of the impact of affirmative action is by Jonathan Leonard [7] of the National Bureau of Economic Research and the University of California at Berkeley. This study has several advantages over the early econometric studies just discussed, two of which in particular should be noted. First, it is a much more unified and comprehensive study of the impact of affirmative action than has heretofore been done. It examines not only the employment and occupational effects of affirmative action, but includes the impact on turnover and productivity, equal employment opportunity and trade unions, the interaction of residential and employment segregation, and the effectiveness of the OFCCP's compliance and enforcement efforts. Second, the study uses more recent data (the data are from 1974 and 1980) and thus it reflects more recent OFCCP efforts and the impact of those efforts over a longer period of time. The major findings and conclusions of the Leonard study include:

(1) Black male employment share increased relatively more in contractor establishments under the affirmative action obligation than in non-contractor establishments between 1974 and 1980. * * * This holds true * * * controlling for establishment size, growth industry, region, occupational structure, corporate structure, and past employment share. This appears to reflect changed establishment behavior, rather than the selection into contractor status of establishments with high or growing black male employment share.

(2) This positive employment impact has been relatively greater in the more highly skilled occupations, and has resulted in net occupational upgrading for black males.

(3) Compliance reviews have been an effective tool in promoting the employment of blacks.

(4) The impact of affirmative action on non-black minorities and on white females has been mixed. * * *

(5) Females and black males at a sample of reviewed establishments had a lower share of terminations relative to hires than other workers. The employment gains engendered by affirmative action do not seem to be transient.

6. Order No. 4, first issued by OFCC January 30, 1970; reissued September 30, 1972; codified at 41 C.F.R. 60–2, last amended at 44 Fed.Reg. 77000, December 28, 1979.

7. Jonathan S. Leonard, The Impact of Affirmative Action, U.S. Department of Labor, Washington, D.C., July 1983, released 1984.

(6) Economic growth is among the best policies for bringing minorities and females into the workforce. Minority and female employment shares increase fastest at growing establishments which can more easily accommodate the pressures of affirmative action. * * *

(7) Class action litigation under Title VII of the Civil Rights Act of 1964 has played a significant role in increasing black employment, and has had a relatively greater impact than affirmative action.

(8) The relative productivity of females and minority males has not significantly declined as their employment share has increased. * * *

(9) Black employment share grew faster in the union sector than in the non-union sector. * * *

(10) Distance from the ghetto is among the strongest determinants of the racial composition of the workforce. * * * Racial segregation in housing limits the potential of affirmative action to integrate the workplace. * * *

(11) The compliance review process, as part of the antidiscrimination effort, could be improved by targeting with greater frequency the establishments with the lowest proportion of minorities and females. * * *

(12) While the projections of minority and female employment given by establishments under affirmative action are inflated, they are significant. Establishments that set higher goals subsequently achieve more.

    The policy of affirmative action has had a short and turbulent history in this country. Of all the social programs that grew during the sixties, it has perhaps enjoyed the least measure of consensus. Its bureaucratic organization and body of regulations have undergone change at frequent intervals since its inception. While the targeting of enforcement could be improved, and while the impact of affirmative action on other groups is unclear, the evidence in this study is that affirmative action and Title VII have been successful in prompting the integration of blacks into the American workplace.

Chapter II

TITLE VII OF THE CIVIL RIGHTS ACT OF 1964

A. INTRODUCTION AND BACKGROUND

TITLE VII OF THE CIVIL RIGHTS ACT OF 1964: A DECADE OF PRIVATE ENFORCEMENT AND JUDICIAL DEVELOPMENTS *

Robert Belton

Title VII of the Civil Rights Act of 1964 established for the first time a comprehensive federal law to assure equality of employment opportunity in the private sector by making unlawful practices and devices that discriminate on the basis of race, sex, national origin, or religion. The enactment of Title VII on July 2, 1964, represented a twenty-year struggle by civil rights advocates. The prevailing attitude about Title VII, as finally enacted, was that, in effect, the civil rights movement had suffered a defeat. Congress had deleted the cease and desist provisions in earlier versions of the bill and had vested enforcement authority in the courts. Moreover, the Democratic Leadership Conference had agreed to a number of compromises to facilitate the passage of the 1964 Civil Rights Act.

* * *

Like many new laws, Title VII had more bones than flesh when first enacted. It had to be interpreted in numerous law suits before those protected would know what impact it would have on their right to equal employment. The following were some of the questions that had to be resolved: What constitutes proof of employment discrimination? What kinds of practices beyond the simple "white only" or "men only" policies are discriminatory? Does the Act reach present effects of past discriminatory practices even when such practices may have been eliminated prior to the effective date of the Act? If a seniority system facilitates some form of discrimination, under what circumstances would the system be illegal under the Act? What standards apply in determining whether a defendant has "intentionally" engaged in conduct made unlawful under the Act? Under what circumstances may an employer administer a "professionally developed ability" test? How should the rights of long term employees be reconciled with the rights of those protected by the Act who accrued little or no seniority because of exclusionary hiring practices? What are appropriate remedies for the various employment practices found to be unlawful?

The relatively short history of enforcement under the Act has spawned three generations of issues. The first generation embraced procedural problems including the following issues: What proceedings before the EEOC or other agencies are necessary before a complaint can be filed in federal court? May a plaintiff bring a class action on behalf of persons who have not filed charges with the EEOC? Is a jury trial required in Title VII cases by the seventh amendment to the Constitution? The second generation of issues included the definition of an unlawful employment practice and the type and quantum of proof necessary to establish a claim under the Act. In the third generation of issues the courts face the problems of formulating appropriate and effective remedies.

DISCRIMINATION AND AFFIRMATIVE ACTION: AN ANALYSIS OF COMPETING THEORIES OF EQUALITY AND *WEBER* *
59 N.C.L. Rev. 531 (1981)
Robert Belton

The primary purpose of Title VII was to improve the economic status of blacks as a group. Of all the civil rights legislation enacted prior to 1965, Title VII alone was aimed at the economic oppression of blacks, and few domestic problems have proved more tractable or received more scholarly attention than the depressed economic position of that group. The statutory language that Congress chose to carry out this purpose, however, provides a remedy that is not limited to blacks. Other groups, whether defined in terms of race, sex, ethnicity, or religion, also are given the protection of Title VII. Therefore, although it is clear that the primary purpose of Title VII was to provide a remedy for blacks, the effectuation of that purpose is inextricably linked to how the concept of "equality" (or "discrimination") should be construed in light of the broad statutory language used by Congress.

There are two basic concepts of equality that have been discussed in the cases and the literature. In most situations each yields a different outcome in the implementation of affirmative action. One conception of equality is *equal treatment*. It embraces the notion of color-blindness and focuses on fairness to the individual instead of fairness to the group of which he is a member. Under this view individual blacks should be treated "equally" by an employer in the sense that race should not be a factor in an employment decision. This conception of equality is often analogized to positions in a foot race: if race is eliminated as a factor in the employment decision, blacks will be on an equal footing with whites. An ambiguity exists, however, in the implementation of this view, because a pure application would prohibit consideration of race in *all* circumstances, even if the result is to perpetuate continuing effects of prior discrimination. Another application of this theory, one more consistent with decisions of the Supreme Court, would permit, and in some cases require, consideration of race in effectuating a remedy based upon a judicial, legislative, or administrative finding of unlawful discrimination against a group or an individual member of a group. The Supreme Court has found support for the equal treatment concept in section 703(a)(1) of Title VII, which makes it an unlawful employment practice for an employer to discriminate against *"any individual* * * * because of such *individual's* race." Claims of reverse discrimination such as Weber's are based on the equal treatment theory.

A second conception of equality is *equal opportunity* (or equal achievement). This view recognizes that race sometimes must be considered when distributing jobs among racial groups and requires those subject to Title VII to consider race in appropriate cases to ensure that discrimination is not perpetuated against protected classes. Only decisions that do not continue to disadvantage protected classes would be permitted. It is concerned also with both the quantity and quality (measured, for example, by income levels and status) of the jobs for which blacks are employed. Under this view of equality, jobs are to be distributed so that the relative economic position of blacks as a group is improved, making the economic status of blacks approximately equal to that of whites. Both the elimination of disproportionate underrepresentation of blacks in all levels of the actual work force of an employer and their overrepresentation in the unemployed ranks in the relevant labor market are the aims of this view of equality. Proponents of the second view of equality reject the equal treatment view as a spurious sort of equality because it fails to accommodate for the present and continuing effect of past discrimination. The Supreme Court has found statutory support in Title VII for the equal opportunity view of equality in section 703(a)(2), which provides that it is an unlawful employment practice for an employer to "limit, segregate, or classify his employees or applicants for employment in any way which would *deprive* or *tend to deprive* any individual of employment opportunity or otherwise *adversely affect* his status as an employee, because of such individual's race. * * *"

B. THEORIES OF DISCRIMINATION

1. DISPARATE IMPACT

GRIGGS v. DUKE POWER CO.

Supreme Court of the United States, 1971.
401 U.S. 424, 91 S.Ct. 849, 28 L.Ed.2d 158.

MR. CHIEF JUSTICE BURGER delivered the opinion of the Court.

We granted the writ in this case to resolve the question whether an employer is prohibited by the Civil Rights Act of 1964, Title VII, from requiring a high school education or passing of a standardized general intelligence test as a condition of employment in or transfer to jobs when (a) neither standard is shown to be significantly related to successful job performance, (b) both requirements operate to disqualify Negroes at a substantially higher rate than white applicants, and (c) the jobs in question formerly had been filled only by white employees as part of a longstanding practice of giving preference to whites.

Congress provided, in Title VII of the Civil Rights Act of 1964, for class actions for enforcement of provisions of the Act and this proceeding was brought by a group of incumbent Negro employees against Duke Power Company. All the petitioners are employed at the Company's Dan River Steam Station, a power generating facility located at Draper, North Carolina. At the time this action was instituted, the Company had 95 employees at the Dan River Station, 14 of whom were Negroes; 13 of these are petitioners here.

The District Court found that prior to July 2, 1965, the effective date of the Civil Rights Act of 1964, the Company openly discriminated on the basis of race in the hiring and assigning of employees at its Dan River plant. The plant was organized into five operating departments: (1) Labor, (2) Coal Handling, (3) Operations, (4) Maintenance, and (5) Laboratory and Test. Negroes were employed only in the Labor Department where the highest paying jobs paid less than the lowest paying jobs in the other four "operating" departments in which only whites were employed.[2] Promotions were normally made within each department on the basis of job seniority. Transferees into a department usually began in the lowest position.

In 1955 the Company instituted a policy of requiring a high school education for initial assignment to any department except Labor, and for transfer from the Coal Handling to any "inside" department (Operations, Maintenance, or Laboratory). When the Company abandoned its policy of restricting Negroes to the Labor Department in 1965, completion of high school also was made a prerequisite to transfer from Labor

---

2. A Negro was first assigned to a job in an operating department in August 1966, five months after charges had been filed with the Equal Employment Opportunity Commission. The employee, a high school graduate who had begun in the Labor Department in 1953, was promoted to a job in the Coal Handling Department.

to any other department. From the time the high school requirement was instituted to the time of trial, however, white employees hired before the time of the high school education requirement continued to perform satisfactorily and achieve promotions in the "operating" departments. Findings on this score are not challenged.

The Company added a further requirement for new employees on July 2, 1965, the date on which Title VII became effective. To qualify for placement in any but the Labor Department it became necessary to register satisfactory scores on two professionally prepared aptitude tests, as well as to have a high school education. Completion of high school alone continued to render employees eligible for transfer to the four desirable departments from which Negroes had been excluded if the incumbent had been employed prior to the time of the new requirement. In September 1965 the Company began to permit incumbent employees who lacked a high school education to qualify for transfer from Labor or Coal Handling to an "inside" job by passing two tests—the Wonderlic Personnel Test, which purports to measure general intelligence, and the Bennett Mechanical Comprehension Test. Neither was directed or intended to measure the ability to learn to perform a particular job or category of jobs. The requisite scores used for both initial hiring and transfer approximated the national median for high school graduates.[3]

The District Court had found that while the Company previously followed a policy of overt racial discrimination in a period prior to the Act, such conduct had ceased. The District Court also concluded that Title VII was intended to be prospective only and, consequently, the impact of prior inequities was beyond the reach of corrective action authorized by the Act.

The Court of Appeals was confronted with a question of first impression, as are we, concerning the meaning of Title VII. After careful analysis a majority of that court concluded that a subjective test of the employer's intent should govern, particularly in a close case, and that in this case there was no showing of a discriminatory purpose in the adoption of the diploma and test requirements. On this basis, the Court of Appeals concluded there was no violation of the Act.

The Court of Appeals reversed the District Court in part, rejecting the holding that residual discrimination arising from prior employment practices was insulated from remedial action.[4] The Court of Appeals

---

3. The test standards are thus more stringent than the high school requirement, since they would screen out approximately half of all high school graduates.

4. The Court of Appeals ruled that Negroes employed in the Labor Department at a time when there was no high school or test requirement for entrance into the higher paying departments could not now be made subject to those requirements, since whites hired contemporaneously into those departments were never subject to them. The Court of Appeals also required that the seniority rights of those Negroes be measured on a plantwide, rather than a departmental basis. However, the Court of Appeals denied relief to the Negro employees without a high school education or its equivalent who were hired into the Labor Department after institution of the educational requirement.

noted, however, that the District Court was correct in its conclusion that there was no showing of a racial purpose or invidious intent in the adoption of the high school diploma requirement or general intelligence test and that these standards had been applied fairly to whites and Negroes alike. It held that, in the absence of a discriminatory purpose, use of such requirements was permitted by the Act. In so doing, the Court of Appeals rejected the claim that because these two requirements operated to render ineligible a markedly disproportionate number of Negroes, they were unlawful under Title VII unless shown to be job related.[5] We granted the writ on these claims. 399 U.S. 926, 90 S.Ct. 2238, 26 L.Ed.2d 791.

The objective of Congress in the enactment of Title VII is plain from the language of the statute. It was to achieve equality of employment opportunities and remove barriers that have operated in the past to favor an identifiable group of white employees over other employees. Under the Act, practices, procedures, or tests neutral on their face, and even neutral in terms of intent, cannot be maintained if they operate to "freeze" the status quo of prior discriminatory employment practices.

The Court of Appeals' opinion, and the partial dissent, agreed that, on the record in the present case, "whites register far better on the Company's alternative requirements" than Negroes.[6] 420 F.2d 1225, 1239 n. 6. This consequence would appear to be directly traceable to race. Basic intelligence must have the means of articulation to manifest itself fairly in a testing process. Because they are Negroes, petitioners have long received inferior education in segregated schools and this Court expressly recognized these differences in Gaston County v. United States, 395 U.S. 285, 89 S.Ct. 1720, 23 L.Ed.2d 309 (1969). There, because of the inferior education received by Negroes in North Carolina, this Court barred the institution of a literacy test for voter registration on the ground that the test would abridge the right to vote indirectly on account of race. Congress did not intend by Title VII, however, to guarantee a job to every person regardless of qualifications. In short, the Act does not command that any person be hired simply because he was formerly the subject of discrimination, or because he is a member of a minority group. Discriminatory preference for any group, minority or majority, is precisely and only what Congress has

5. One member of that court disagreed with this aspect of the decision, maintaining, as do the petitioners in this Court, that Title VII prohibits the use of employment criteria that operate in a racially exclusionary fashion and do not measure skills or abilities necessary to performance of the jobs for which those criteria are used.

6. In North Carolina, 1960 census statistics show that, while 34% of white males had completed high school, only 12% of Negro males had done so. U.S. Bureau of the Census, U.S. Census of Population:

1960, Vol. 1, Characteristics of the Population, pt. 35, Table 47.

Similarly, with respect to standardized tests, the EEOC in one case found that use of a battery of tests, including the Wonderlic and Bennett tests used by the Company in the instant case, resulted in 58% of whites passing the tests, as compared with only 6% of the blacks. Decision of EEOC, CCH Empl.Prac. Guide, ¶ 17.304.53 (Dec. 2, 1966). See also Decision of EEOC 70–552, CCH Empl.Prac. Guide, ¶ 6139 (Feb. 19, 1970).

proscribed. What is required by Congress is the removal of artificial, arbitrary, and unnecessary barriers to employment when the barriers operate invidiously to discriminate on the basis of racial or other impermissible classification.

Congress has now provided that tests or criteria for employment or promotion may not provide equality of opportunity merely in the sense of the fabled offer of milk to the stork and the fox. On the contrary, Congress has now required that the posture and condition of the job-seeker be taken into account. It has—to resort again to the fable—provided that the vessel in which the milk is proffered be one all seekers can use. The Act proscribes not only overt discrimination but also practices that are fair in form, but discriminatory in operation. The touchstone is business necessity. If an employment practice which operates to exclude Negroes cannot be shown to be related to job performance, the practice is prohibited.

On the record before us, neither the high school completion requirement nor the general intelligence test is shown to bear a demonstrable relationship to successful performance of the jobs for which it was used. Both were adopted, as the Court of Appeals noted, without meaningful study of their relationship to job-performance ability. Rather, a vice president of the Company testified, the requirements were instituted on the Company's judgment that they generally would improve the overall quality of the work force.

The evidence, however, shows that employees who have not completed high school or taken the tests have continued to perform satisfactorily and make progress in departments for which the high school and test criteria are now used.[7] The promotion record of present employees who would not be able to meet the new criteria thus suggests the possibility that the requirements may not be needed even for the limited purpose of preserving the avowed policy of advancement within the Company. In the context of this case, it is unnecessary to reach the question whether testing requirements that take into account capability for the next succeeding position or related future promotion might be utilized upon a showing that such long-range requirements fulfill a genuine business need. In the present case the Company has made no such showing.

The Court of Appeals held that the Company had adopted the diploma and test requirements without any "intention to discriminate against Negro employees." 420 F.2d, at 1232. We do not suggest that either the District Court or the Court of Appeals erred in examining the employer's intent; but good intent or absence of discriminatory intent does not redeem employment procedures or testing mechanisms that operate as "built-in headwinds" for minority groups and are unrelated to measuring job capability.

7. For example, between July 2, 1965, and November 14, 1966, the percentage of white employees who were promoted but who were not high school graduates was nearly identical to the percentage of non-graduates in the entire white work force.

The Company's lack of discriminatory intent is suggested by special efforts to help the undereducated employees through Company financing of two-thirds the cost of tuition for high school training. But Congress directed the thrust of the Act to the *consequences* of employment practices, not simply the motivation. More than that, Congress has placed on the employer the burden of showing that any given requirement must have a manifest relationship to the employment in question.

The facts of this case demonstrate the inadequacy of broad and general testing devices as well as the infirmity of using diplomas or degrees as fixed measures of capability. History is filled with examples of men and women who rendered highly effective performance without the conventional badges of accomplishment in terms of certificates, diplomas, or degrees. Diplomas and tests are useful servants, but Congress has mandated the commonsense proposition that they are not to become masters of reality.

The Company contends that its general intelligence tests are specifically permitted by § 703(h) of the Act.[8] That section authorizes the use of "any professionally developed ability test" that is not "designed, intended *or used* to discriminate because of race * * *." (Emphasis added.)

The Equal Employment Opportunity Commission, having enforcement responsibility, has issued guidelines interpreting § 703(h) to permit only the use of job-related tests.[9] The administrative interpretation of the Act by the enforcing agency is entitled to great deference. See, e.g., United States v. City of Chicago, 400 U.S. 8, 91 S.Ct. 18, 27 L.Ed.2d 9 (1970); Udall v. Tallman, 380 U.S. 1, 85 S.Ct. 792, 13 L.Ed.2d 616 (1965); Power Reactor Development Co. v. Electricians, 367 U.S. 396, 81 S.Ct. 1529, 6 L.Ed.2d 924 (1961). Since the Act and its legislative history support the Commission's construction, this affords good reason to treat the guidelines as expressing the will of Congress.

Section 703(h) was not contained in the House version of the Civil Rights Act but was added in the Senate during extended debate. For a period, debate revolved around claims that the bill as proposed would

---

8. Section 703(h) applies only to tests. It has no applicability to the high school diploma requirement.

9. EEOC Guidelines on Employment Testing Procedures, issued August 24, 1966, provide:

"The Commission accordingly interprets 'professionally developed ability test' to mean a test which fairly measures the knowledge or skills required by the particular job or class of jobs which the applicant seeks, or which fairly affords the employer a chance to measure the applicant's ability to perform a particular job or class of jobs. The fact that a test was prepared by an individual or organization claiming expertise in test preparation does not, without more, justify its use within the meaning of Title VII."

The EEOC position has been elaborated in the new Guidelines on Employee Selection Procedures, 29 CFR § 1607, 35 Fed.Reg. 12333 (Aug. 1, 1970). These guidelines demand that employers using tests have available "data demonstrating that the test is predictive of or significantly correlated with important elements of work behavior which comprise or are relevant to the job or jobs for which candidates are being evaluated." Id., at § 1607.4(c).

prohibit all testing and force employers to hire unqualified persons simply because they were part of a group formerly subject to job discrimination.[10] Proponents of Title VII sought throughout the debate to assure the critics that the Act would have no effect on job-related tests. Senators Case of New Jersey and Clark of Pennsylvania, comanagers of the bill on the Senate floor, issued a memorandum explaining that the proposed Title VII "expressly protects the employer's right to insist that any prospective applicant, Negro or white, *must meet the applicable job qualifications.* Indeed, the very purpose of title VII is to promote hiring on the basis of job qualifications, rather than on the basis of race or color." 110 Cong.Rec. 7247.[11] (Emphasis added.) Despite these assurances, Senator Tower of Texas introduced an amendment authorizing "professionally developed ability tests." Proponents of Title VII opposed the amendment because, as written, it would permit an employer to give any test, "whether it was a good test or not, so long as it was professionally designed. Discrimination could actually exist under the guise of compliance with the statute." 110 Cong.Rec. 13504 (remarks of Sen. Case).

The amendment was defeated and two days later Senator Tower offered a substitute amendment which was adopted verbatim and is now the testing provision of § 703(h). Speaking for the supporters of Title VII, Senator Humphrey, who had vigorously opposed the first amendment, endorsed the substitute amendment, stating: "Senators on both sides of the aisle who were deeply interested in title VII have examined the text of this amendment and have found it to be in accord

10. The congressional discussion was prompted by the decision of a hearing examiner for the Illinois Fair Employment Commission in Myart v. Motorola Co. (The decision is reprinted at 110 Cong.Rec. 5662.) That case suggested that standardized tests on which whites performed better than Negroes could never be used. The decision was taken to mean that such tests could never be justified even if the needs of the business required them. A number of Senators feared that Title VII might produce a similar result. See remarks of Senators Ervin, 110 Cong.Rec. 5614–5616; Smathers, id., at 5999–6000; Holland, id., at 7012–7013; Hill, id., at 8447; Tower, id., at 9024; Talmadge, id., at 9025–9026; Fulbright, id., at 9599–9600; and Ellender, id., at 9600.

11. The Court of Appeals majority, in finding no requirement in Title VII that employment tests be job related, relied in part on a quotation from an earlier Clark-Case interpretative memorandum addressed to the question of the constitutionality of Title VII. The Senators said in that memorandum:

"There is no requirement in title VII that employers abandon bona fide quali-

fication tests where, because of differences in background and education, members of some groups are able to perform better on these tests than members of other groups. An employer may set his qualifications as high as he likes, he may test to determine which applicants have these qualifications, and he may hire, assign, and promote on the basis of test performance." 110 Cong.Rec. 7213.

However, nothing there stated conflicts with the later memorandum dealing specifically with the debate over employer testing, 110 Cong.Rec. 7247 (quoted from in the text above), in which Senators Clark and Case explained that tests which measure "applicable job qualifications" are permissible under Title VII. In the earlier memorandum Clark and Case assured the Senate that employers were not to be prohibited from using tests that determine *qualifications.* Certainly a reasonable interpretation of what the Senators meant, in light of the subsequent memorandum directed specifically at employer testing, was that nothing in the Act prevents employers from requiring that applicants be fit for the job.

with the intent and purpose of that title." 110 Cong.Rec. 13724. The amendment was then adopted.[12] From the sum of the legislative history relevant in this case, the conclusion is inescapable that the EEOC's construction of § 703(h) to require that employment tests be job related comports with congressional intent.

Nothing in the Act precludes the use of testing or measuring procedures; obviously they are useful. What Congress has forbidden is giving these devices and mechanisms controlling force unless they are demonstrably a reasonable measure of job performance. Congress has not commanded that the less qualified be preferred over the better qualified simply because of minority origins. Far from disparaging job qualifications as such, Congress has made such qualifications the controlling factor, so that race, religion, nationality, and sex become irrelevant. What Congress has commanded is that any tests used must measure the person for the job and not the person in the abstract.

The judgment of the Court of Appeals is, as to that portion of the judgment appealed from, reversed.

MR. JUSTICE BRENNAN took no part in the consideration or decision of this case.

Notes

1. The reference in *Griggs* to the stork and the fox is to the following Aesop fable:

A Fox one day invited a Stork to dinner, being disposed to divert himself at the expense of his guest, provided nothing for the entertainment but some thin soup in a shallow dish. This the Fox lapped up very readily, while the Stork, unable to gain a mouthfull with her long narrow bill, was as hungry at the end of dinner as at the beginning. The Fox meanwhile professed his regret at seeing his guest eat so sparingly. The Stork said little but begged that the Fox would do her the honor of returning her visit. Accordingly he agreed to dine with her on the following day. He arrived true to his appointment and the dinner was ordered forthwith. But when it was served up he found to his dismay that it was contained in a narrow necked vessel, down which the Stork readily thrust her long neck and bill, while the Fox was obliged to content himself with licking the neck of the jar.

2. The *Griggs* disparate treatment theory is based on the Court's construction of Section 702(a)(2) of Title VII. The Court did not explain its rationale for grounding the disparate impact theory on 702(a)(2) until

---

12. Senator Tower's original amendment provided in part that a test would be permissible "if * * * in the case of any individual, who is seeking employment with such employer, such test is designed to determine or predict whether such individual is suitable or trainable with respect to his employment in the particular business or enterprise involved * * *." 110 Cong.Rec. 13492. This language indicates that Senator Tower's aim was simply to make certain that job-related tests would be permitted. The opposition to the amendment was based on its loose wording which the proponents of Title VII feared would be susceptible of misinterpretation. The final amendment, which was acceptable to all sides, could hardly have required less of a job relation than the first.

eleven years later when it stated, in *Connecticut v. Teal*, 457 U.S. 440, 102 S.Ct. 2525, 73 L.Ed.2d 130 (1982):

> A disparate impact claim reflects the language of Section 703(a)(2) and Congress' basic objectives in enacting that statute: "to achieve equality of employment *opportunities* and remove barriers that have operated in the past to favor an identifiable group of white employees over other employees." When an employer uses a non-job-related barrier in order to deny a minority or woman applicant employment or promotion, and that barrier has a significant adverse effect on minorities or women, then the applicant has been deprived of an employment *opportunity* "because of * * * race, color, religion, sex, or national origin.

Id., 457 U.S. at 448, 102 S.Ct. at 2531 (emphasis in the original) (quoting *Griggs*, 401 U.S. at 429–30, 91 S.Ct. at 852–853). See Helfand & Pemberton, "The Continuing Vitality of Title VII Disparate Impact Analysis," 36 Mercer L. Rev. 939 (1985).

3. The disparate impact theory of discrimination has been used to challenge a wide range of employment practices other than the pen and paper tests and high school diploma requirements at issue in *Griggs* and *Albemarle Paper Co. v. Moody*. E.g., Dothard v. Rawlinson, 433 U.S. 321, 97 S.Ct. 2720, 53 L.Ed.2d 786 (1977) (sex discrimination—height and weight requirements); Gregory v. Litton Systems, Inc., 316 F.Supp. 401 (C.D.Cal. 1970), affirmed as modified, 472 F.2d 631 (9th Cir.1972) (race—arrest record history); Johnson v. Pike Corporation of America, 332 F.Supp. 490 (C.D.Cal. 1971) (race—garnishment proceedings); Green v. Missouri Pacific Railroad Co., 549 F.2d 1158 (8th Cir.1977) (race—record of criminal convictions); Chrisner v. Complete Auto Transit, Inc., 645 F.2d 1251 (6th Cir.1981) (race and sex—prior experience requirement).

4. In 1978 the Equal Employment Opportunity Commission, the Department of Justice, the Department of Labor, and the United States Civil Service Commission promulgated the Uniform Guidelines On Employee Selection Procedures ("Uniform Guidelines"), 29 C.F.R. Section 1607, et seq. (1981). The Uniform Guidelines adopts a broad definition of a selection procedure:

> Any measure, combination of measures, or procedure used as a basis for any employment decision. Selection procedures include the full range of assessment techniques from traditional paper and pencil tests, performance tests, training programs, or probationary periods and physical, educational, and work experience requirements through informal or casual interviews and unscored application forms.

29 C.F.R. Section 1607.16Q. An "employment decision" includes "tests and other selection procedures which are used as a basis for any employment decision", including but not limited to, "hiring, promotion, demotion, membership (for example, in a labor organization), referral, retention, * * * licensing and certification, to the extent that certification is covered by Federal equal employment law, [and] [o]ther selection decisions, such as selection for training or transfer * * * if they lead to any of the decisions listed above." Id. at Section 1607.2B.

ALBEMARLE PAPER CO. v. MOODY

Supreme Court of the United States, 1975.
422 U.S. 405, 95 S.Ct. 2362, 45 L.Ed.2d 280.

MR. JUSTICE STEWART delivered the opinion of the Court.

These consolidated cases raise two important questions under Title VII of the Civil Rights Act of 1964, 78 Stat. 253, as amended by the Equal Employment Opportunity Act of 1972, 86 Stat. 103, 42 U.S.C. § 2000e et seq. (1970 ed. and Supp. III): * * *. Second: What must an employer show to establish that pre-employment tests racially discriminatory in effect, though not in intent, are sufficiently "job-related" to survive challenge under Title VII?

I

The respondents—plaintiffs in the District Court—are a certified class of present and former Negro employees at a paper mill in Roanoke Rapids, N.C.; the petitioners—defendants in the District Court—are the plant's owner, the Albemarle Paper Co., and the plant employees' labor union, Halifax Local No. 425.

* * *

The court also refused to enjoin or limit Albemarle's testing program. Albemarle had required applicants for employment in the skilled lines of progression to have a high school diploma and to pass two tests, the Revised Beta Examination, allegedly a measure of non-verbal intelligence, and the Wonderlic Personnel Test (available in alternative Forms A and B), allegedly a measure of verbal facility. After this Court's decision in Griggs v. Duke Power Co., 401 U.S. 424, 91 S.Ct. 849, 28 L.Ed.2d 158 (1971), and on the eve of trial, Albemarle engaged an industrial psychologist to study the "job relatedness" of its testing program. His study compared the test scores of current employees with supervisorial judgments of their competence in ten job groupings selected from the middle or top of the plant's skilled lines of progression. The study showed a statistically significant correlation with supervisorial ratings in three job groupings for the Beta Test, in seven job groupings for either Form A or Form B of the Wonderlic Test, and in two job groupings for the required battery of both the Beta and the Wonderlic Tests. The respondents' experts challenged the reliability of these studies, but the court concluded:

> The personnel tests administered at the plant have undergone validation studies and have been proven to be job related. The defendants have carried the burden of proof in proving that these tests are "necessary for the safe and efficient operation of the business" and are, therefore, permitted by the Act. However, the high school education requirement used in conjunction with the testing requirements is unlawful in that the personnel tests alone are adequate to measure the mental ability and reading skills required for the job classifications.

* * *

As for the pre-employment tests, the Court of Appeals held, * * * that it was error

> to approve a validation study done without job analysis, to allow Albemarle to require tests for 6 lines of progression where there has been no validation study at all, and to allow Albemarle to require a person to pass two tests for entrance into 7 lines of progression when only one of those tests was validated for that line of progression.

In so holding the Court of Appeals "gave great deference" to the "Guidelines on Employee Selection Procedures," 29 CFR pt. 1607, which the EEOC has issued "as a workable set of standards for employers, unions and employment agencies in determining whether their selection procedures conform with the obligations contained in title VII * * *." 29 CFR § 1607.1(c).

We granted certiorari because of an evident Circuit conflict * * * and as to the showing required to establish the "job relatedness" of pre-employment tests.

* * *

III

In Griggs v. Duke Power Co., 401 U.S. 424, 91 S.Ct. 849, 28 L.Ed.2d 158 (1971), this Court unanimously held that Title VII forbids the use of employment tests that are discriminatory in effect unless the employer meets "the burden of showing that any given requirement [has] * * * a manifest relationship to the employment in question." Id., at 432, 91 S.Ct. at 854.[21] This burden arises, of course, only after the complaining party or class has made out a prima facie case of discrimination, i.e. has shown that the tests in question select applicants for hire or promotion in a racial pattern significantly different from that of the pool of applicants. See McDonnell Douglas Corp. v. Green, 411 U.S. 792, 802, 93 S.Ct. 1817, 1824, 36 L.Ed.2d 668 (1973). If an employer does then meet the burden of proving that its tests are "job related," it remains open to the complaining party to show that other tests or selection devices, without a similarly undesirable racial effect, would also serve the employer's legitimate interest in "efficient and trustworthy workmanship." Id., at 801, 93 S.Ct. at 1823. Such a showing would be evidence that the employer was using its tests merely as a "pretext" for discrimination. Id., at 804–805, 93 S.Ct. at 1825–1826. In the present case, however, we are concerned only with the question whether Albemarle has shown its tests to be job related.

The concept of job relatedness takes on meaning from the facts of the *Griggs* case.

* * *

Like the employer in *Griggs,* Albemarle uses two general ability tests, the Beta Examination, to test nonverbal intelligence, and the Wonderlic Test (Forms A and B), the purported measure of general verbal facility which was also involved in the *Griggs* case. Applicants for hire into various skilled lines of progression at the plant are required to score 100 on the Beta Exam and 18 on one of the Wonderlic Test's two alternative forms.[22]

The question of job relatedness must be viewed in the context of the plant's operation and the history of the testing program. The plant, which now employs about 650 persons, converts raw wood into paper products. It is organized into a number of functional departments, each with one or more distinct lines of progression, the theory being that workers can move up the line as they acquire the necessary skills. The number and structure of the lines have varied greatly over time. For many years, certain lines were themselves more skilled and paid higher wages than others, and until 1964 these skilled lines were expressly reserved for white workers. In 1968, many of the unskilled "Negro" lines were "end-tailed" onto skilled "white" lines, but it apparently remains true that at least the top jobs in certain lines require greater skills than the top jobs in other lines. In this sense, at least, it is still possible to speak of relatively skilled and relatively unskilled lines.

In the 1950's while the plant was being modernized with new and more sophisticated equipment, the Company introduced a high school diploma requirement for entry into the skilled lines. Though the Company soon concluded that this requirement did not improve the quality of the labor force, the requirement was continued until the District Court enjoined its use. In the late 1950's, the Company began using the Beta Examination and the Bennett Mechanical Comprehension Test (also involved in the *Griggs* case) to screen applicants for entry into the skilled lines. The Bennett Test was dropped several years later, but use of the Beta Test continued.[23]

The Company added the Wonderlic Tests in 1963, for the skilled lines, on the theory that a certain verbal intelligence was called for by the increasing sophistication of the plant's operations. The Company made no attempt to validate the test for job relatedness,[24] and simply adopted the national "norm" score of 18 as a cut-off point for new job

22. Albemarle has informed us that it has now reduced the cut-off score to 17 on the Wonderlic Test.

23. While the Company contends that the Bennett and Beta Tests were "locally validated" when they were introduced, no record of this validation was made. Plant officials could recall only the barest outlines of the alleged validation. Job relatedness cannot be proved through vague and unsubstantiated hearsay.

24. As explained by the responsible plant official, the Wonderlic Test was chosen in rather casual fashion:

"I had had experience with using the Wonderlic before, which is a short form Verbal Intelligence Test, and knew that it had, uh, probably more validation studies behind it than any other short

form Verbal Intelligence Test. So, after consultation we decided to institute the Wonderlic, in addition to the Beta, in view of the fact that the mill had changed quite a bit and it had become exceedingly more complex in operation * * * [W]e did not, uh, validate it, uh, locally, primarily, because of the, the expense of conducting such a validation, and there were some other considerations, such as, uh, we didn't know whether we would get the co-operation of the employees that we'd need to validate it against in taking the test, and we certainly have to have that, so, we used National Norms and on my suggestion after study of the Wonderlic and Norms had been established nationally for skilled jobs, we developed a, uh, cut-off score of eighteen (18)."

applicants.   After 1964, when it discontinued overt segregation in the lines of progression, the Company allowed Negro workers to transfer to the skilled lines if they could pass the Beta and Wonderlic Tests, but few succeeded in doing so.   Incumbents in the skilled lines, some of whom had been hired before adoption of the tests, were not required to pass them to retain their jobs or their promotion rights.   The record shows that a number of white incumbents in high-ranking job groups could not pass the tests.[25]

Because departmental reorganization continued up to the point of trial, and has indeed continued since that point, the details of the testing program are less than clear from the record.   The District Court found that, since 1963, the Beta and Wonderlic Tests have been used in 13 lines of progression, within eight departments.   Albemarle contends that at present the tests are used in only eight lines of progression, within four departments.

Four months before this case went to trial, Albemarle engaged an expert in industrial psychology to "validate" the job relatedness of its testing program.   He spent a half day at the plant and devised a "concurrent validation" study, which was conducted by plant officials, without his supervision.   The expert then subjected the results to statistical analysis.   The study dealt with 10 job groupings, selected from near the top of nine of the lines of progression.[26]   Jobs were grouped together solely by their proximity in the line of progression; no attempt was made to analyze jobs in terms of the particular skills they might require.   All, or nearly all, employees in the selected groups participated in the study—105 employees in all, but only four Negroes. Within each job grouping the study compared the test scores of each employee with an independent "ranking" of the employee, relative to each of his coworkers, made by two of the employee's supervisors.   The supervisors, who did not know the test scores, were asked to

> determine which ones they felt irrespective of the job that they were actually doing, but in their respective jobs, did a better job than the person they were rating against * * *.

For each job grouping, the expert computed the "Phi coefficient" of statistical correlation between the test scores and an average of the two supervisorial rankings.   Consonant with professional conventions, the expert regarded as "statistically significant" any correlation that could

25. In the course of a 1971 validation effort, see supra, at 2368 and infra, this page and 2378, test scores were accumulated for 105 incumbent employees (101 of whom were white) working in relatively high-ranking jobs. Some of these employees apparently took the tests for the first time as part of this study. The Company's expert testified that the test cut-off scores originally used to screen these incumbents for employment or promotion "couldn't have been * * * very high scores because some of these guys tested very low, as low as 8 in the Wonderlic test, and as low as 95 in the Beta. They couldn't have been using very high cut-off scores or they wouldn't have these low testing employees."

26. See the charts appended to this opinion. It should be noted that testing is no longer required for some of the job groups listed.

have occurred by change only five times, or fewer in 100 trials. On the basis of these results, the District Court found that "[t]he personnel test administered at the plant have undergone validation studies and have been proven to be job related." Like the Court of Appeals, we are constrained to disagree.

The EEOC has issued "Guidelines" for employers seeking to determine, through professional validation studies, whether their employment tests are job related. 29 CFR pt. 1607. These Guidelines draw upon and make reference to professional standards of test validation established by the American Psychological Association.[29] The EEOC Guidelines are not administrative regulations" promulgated pursuant to formal procedures established by the Congress. But, as this Court has heretofore noted, they do constitute "[t]he administrative interpretation of the Act by the enforcing agency," and consequently they are "entitled to great deference." Griggs v. Duke Power Co., 401 U.S., at 433–434, 91 S.Ct., at 854. See also Espinoza v. Farah Mfg. Co., 414 U.S. 86, 94, 94 S.Ct. 334, 339, 38 L.Ed.2d 287 (1973).

The message of these Guidelines is the same as that of the *Griggs* case—that discriminatory tests are impermissible unless shown, by professionally acceptable methods, to be "predictive of or significantly correlated with important elements of work behavior which comprise or are relevant to the job or jobs for which candidates are being evaluated." 29 CFR § 1607.4(c).

Measured against the Guidelines, Albemarle's validation study is materially defective in several respects:

(1) Even if it had been otherwise adequate, the study would not have "validated" the Beta and Wonderlic test battery for all of the skilled lines of progression for which the two tests are, apparently, now required. The study showed significant correlations for the Beta Exam in only three of the eight lines. Though the Wonderlic Test's Form A and Form B are in theory identical and interchangeable measures of verbal facility, significant correlations for one form but not for the other were obtained in four job groupings. In two job groupings neither form showed a significant correlation. Within some of the lines of progression, one form was found acceptable for some job groupings but not for others. Even if the study were otherwise reliable, this odd patchwork of results would not entitle Albemarle to impose its testing program under the Guidelines. A test may be used in jobs other than those for which it has been professionally validated only if there are "no significant differences" between the studied and unstudied jobs. 29 CFR § 1607.4(c)(2). The study in this case involved no analysis of the attributes of, or the particular skills needed in, the studied job groups.

29. American Psychological Association, Standards for Educational and Psychological Tests and Manuals (1966) (hereafter APA Standards). A volume of the same title, containing modifications, was issued in 1974. The EEOC Guidelines refer to the APA Standards at 29 CFR § 1607.5(a). Very similar guidelines have been issued by the Secretary of Labor for the use of federal contractors. 41 CFR § 60–3.1 et seq.

There is accordingly no basis for concluding that "no significant differences" exist among the lines of progression, or among distinct job groupings within the studied lines of progression. Indeed, the study's checkered results appear to compel the opposite conclusion.

(2) The study compared test scores with subjective supervisorial rankings. While they allow the use of supervisorial rankings in test validation, the Guidelines quite plainly contemplate that the rankings will be elicited with far more care than was demonstrated here.[30] Albemarle's supervisors were asked to rank employees by a "standard" that was extremely vague and fatally open to divergent interpretations. As previously noted, each "job grouping" contained a number of different jobs, and the supervisors were asked, in each grouping to

> determine which ones [employees] they felt irrespective of the job that they were actually doing, but in their respective jobs, did a better job than the person they were rating against *   *   *.

There is no way of knowing precisely what criteria of job performance the supervisors were considering, whether each of the supervisors was considering the same criteria or whether, indeed, any of the supervisors actually applied a focused and stable body of criteria of any kind.[32] There is, in short, simply no way to determine whether the criteria *actually* considered were sufficiently related to the Company's legitimate interest in job-specific ability to justify a testing system with a racially discriminatory impact.

(3) The Company's study focused, in most cases, on job groups near the top of the various lines of progression. In Griggs v. Duke Power Co., *supra,* the Court left open "the question whether testing requirements that take into account capability for the next succeeding position or related future promotion might be utilized upon a showing that such long-range requirements fulfill a genuine business need." 401 U.S., at 432, 91 S.Ct., at 854. The Guidelines take a sensible approach to this issue, and we now endorse it:

30. The Guidelines provide, at 29 CFR §§ 1607.5(b)(3) and (4):

"(3) The work behaviors or other criteria of employee adequacy which the test is intended to predict or identify must be fully described; and, additionally, in the case of rating techniques, the appraisal form(s) and instructions to the rater(s) must be included as a part of the validation evidence. Such criteria may include measures other than actual work proficiency, such as training time, supervisory ratings, regularity of attendance and tenure. Whatever criteria are used they must represent major or critical work behaviors as revealed by careful job analyses.

"(4) In view of the possibility of bias inherent in subjective evaluations, supervisory rating techniques should be carefully developed, and the ratings should be closely examined for evidence of bias. In addition, minorities might obtain unfairly low performance criterion scores for reasons other than supervisor's prejudice, as when, as new employees, they have had less opportunity to learn job skills. The general point is that all criteria need to be examined to insure freedom from factors which would unfairly depress the scores of minority groups."

32. It cannot escape notice that Albemarle's study was conducted by plant officials, without neutral, on-the-scene oversight, at a time when this litigation was about to come to trial. Studies so closely controlled by an interested party in litigation must be examined with great care.

If job progression structures and seniority provisions are so established that new employees will probably, within a reasonable period of time and in a great majority of cases, progress to a higher level, it may be considered that candidates are being evaluated for jobs at that higher level. However, where job progression is not so nearly automatic, or the time span is such that higher level jobs or employees' potential may be expected to change in significant ways, it shall be considered that candidates are being evaluated for a job at or near the entry level. 29 CFR § 1607.4(c)(1).

The fact that the best of those employees working near the top of a line of progression score well on a test does not necessarily mean that that test, or some particular cutoff score on the test, is a permissible measure of the minimal qualifications of new workers entering lower level jobs. In drawing any such conclusion, detailed consideration must be given to the normal speed of promotion, to the efficacy of on-the-job training in the scheme of promotion, and to the possible use of testing as a promotion device, rather than as a screen for entry into low-level jobs. The District Court made no findings on these issues. The issues take on special importance in a case, such as this one, where incumbent employees are permitted to work at even high-level jobs without passing the company's test battery. See 29 CFR § 1607.11.

(4) Albemarle's validation study dealt only with job-experienced, white workers; but the tests themselves are given to new job applicants, who are younger, largely inexperienced, and in many instances nonwhite. The APA Standards state that it is "essential" that

> [t]he validity of a test should be determined on subjects who are at the age or in the same educational or vocational situation as the persons for whom the test is recommended in practice. ¶ C 5.4.

The EEOC Guidelines likewise provide that "[d]ata must be generated and results separately reported for minority and nonminority groups wherever technically feasible." 29 CFR § 1607.5(b)(5). In the present case, such "differential validation" as to racial groups was very likely not "feasible," because years of discrimination at the plant have insured that nearly all of the upper level employees are white. But there has been no clear showing that differential validation was not feasible for lower level jobs. More importantly, the Guidelines provide:

> If it is not technically feasible to include minority employees in validation studies conducted on the present work force, the conduct of a validation study without minority candidates does not relieve any person of his subsequent obligation for validation when inclusion of minority candidates becomes technically feasible. 29 CFR § 1607.5(b) (1).

* * *

> * * * [E]vidence of satisfactory validity based on other groups will be regarded as only provisional compliance with these guidelines pending separate validation of the test for the minority group in question. 29 CFR § 1607.5(b)(5).

For all these reasons, we agree with the Court of Appeals that the District Court erred in concluding that Albemarle had proved the job relatedness of its testing program and that the respondents were consequently not entitled to equitable relief. The outright reversal by the Court of Appeals implied that an injunction should immediately issue against all use of testing at the plant. Because of the particular circumstances here, however, it appears that the more prudent course is to leave to the District Court the precise fashioning of the necessary relief in the first instance. During the appellate stages of this litigation, the plant has apparently been amending its departmental organization and the use made of its tests. The appropriate standard of proof for job relatedness has not been clarified until today. Similarly, the respondents have not until today been specifically apprised of their opportunity to present evidence that even validated tests might be a "pretext" for discrimination in light of alternative selection procedures available to the Company. We also note that the Guidelines authorize provisional use of tests, pending new validation efforts, in certain very limited circumstances. 29 CFR § 1607.9. Whether such circumstances now obtain is a matter best decided, in the first instance, by the District Court. That court will be free to take such new evidence, and to exercise such control of the Company's use and validation of employee selection procedures, as are warranted by the circumstances and by the controlling law.

Accordingly, the judgment is vacated, and these cases are remanded to the District Court for proceedings consistent with this opinion.

It is so ordered.

Judgment vacated and cases remanded.

MR. JUSTICE POWELL took no part in the consideration or decision of these cases.

*   *   *

MR. CHIEF JUSTICE BURGER, concurring in part and dissenting in part.

*   *   *

The Court's treatment of the testing issue is equally troubling. Its entire analysis is based upon a wooden application of EEOC Guidelines which, it says, are entitled to "great deference" as an administrative interpretation of Title VII under Griggs v. Duke Power Co., 401 U.S. 424, 91 S.Ct. 849, 28 L.Ed.2d 158 (1971). The Court's reliance upon *Griggs* is misplaced. There we were dealing with Guidelines which state that a test must be demonstrated to be job related before it can qualify for the exemption contained in § 703(h) of Title VII, 78 Stat. 257, 42 U.S.C. § 2000e–2(h), as a device not "designed, intended or used to discriminate *   *   *." Because this interpretation of specific statutory language was supported by both the Act and its legislative history, we observed that there was "good reason to treat the guidelines as expressing the will of Congress." 401 U.S., at 434, 91 S.Ct., at 855. See also Espinoza v. Farah Mfg. Co., 414 U.S. 86, 93–95, 94 S.Ct. 334, 339–340, 38 L.Ed.2d 287 (1973).

In contrast, the Guidelines upon which the Court now relies relate to methods for *proving* job relatedness; they interpret no section of Title VII and are nowhere referred to in its legislative history. Moreover, they are not federal regulations which have been submitted to public comment and scrutiny as required by the Administrative Procedure Act.[3] Thus, slavish adherence to the EEOC Guidelines regarding test validation should not be required; those provisions are, as their title suggests, guides entitled to the same weight as other well-founded testimony by experts in the field of employment testing.

The District Court so considered the Guidelines in this case and resolved any conflicts in favor of Albemarle's experts. For example, with respect to the question whether validating tests for persons at or near the top of a line of progression "is a permissible measure of the minimal qualifications of new workers," ante, at 2379–2380, the District Court found:

> The group tested was typical of employees in the skilled lines of progression. They were selected from the top and middle of various lines. Professional studies have shown that when tests are validated in such a narrow range of competence, there is a greater change that the test will validate even a broader range, that is, if job candidates as well as present employees are tested. 2 App. 490–491.

Unless this Court is prepared to hold that this and similar factual findings are clearly erroneous, the District Court's conclusion that Albemarle had sustained its burden of showing that its tests were job related is entitled to affirmance, if we follow traditional standards of review. At the very least, the case should be remanded to the Court of Appeals with instructions that it reconsider the testing issue, giving the District Court's findings of fact the deference to which they are entitled.

MR. JUSTICE BLACKMUN, concurring in the judgment.

* * *

I also agree with the decision of the Court to vacate the judgment of the Court of Appeals insofar as it appeared to require an injunction against all testing by Albemarle. I cannot join, however, in the Court's apparent view that absolute compliance with the EEOC Guidelines is a *sine qua non* of pre-employment test validation. The Guidelines, of course, deserve that deference normally due agency statements based on agency experience and expertise. Nevertheless, the Guidelines in question have never been subjected to the test of adversary comment. Nor are the theories on which the Guidelines are based beyond dispute. The simple truth is that pre-employment tests, like most attempts to

3. Such comment would not be a mere formality in light of the fact that many of the EEOC Guidelines are not universally accepted. For example, the Guideline relating to "differential validation," upon which the Court relies in this case, *ante*, at 2380, has been questioned by the American Psychological Association. See United States v. Georgia Power Co., 474 F.2d 906, 914 n. 8 (CA5 1973).

predict the future, will never be completely accurate. We should bear in mind that pre-employment testing, so long as it is fairly related to the job skills or work characteristics desired, possesses the potential of being an effective weapon in protecting equal employment opportunity because it has a unique capacity to measure all applicants objectively on a standardized basis. I fear that a too-rigid application of the EEOC Guidelines will leave the employer little choice, save an impossibly expensive and complex validation study, but to engage in a subjective quota system of employment selection. This, of course, is far from the intent of Title VII.

Notes

1. The differential validation theory discussed in *Moody* recognizes that a test may accurately predict the performance for one race but may underpredict for another race. The 1966 and 1970 EEOC Guidelines on Testing endorsed the differential validation theory under which employers were required to make separate validation studies for minorities and nonminorities. Compare United States v. City of Chicago, 549 F.2d 415, 433 (7th Cir.1977), cert. denied, 434 U.S. 875, 98 S.Ct. 225, 54 L.Ed.2d 155 (1977) (requiring differential validation) with Cormier v. P.P.G. Indus., Inc., 519 F.Supp. 211, 262 (W.D.La.1981) (rejecting requirement). The 1978 Uniform Guidelines eliminated the differential validation notion and replaced it with with a requirement of "unfairness studies." 29 C.F.R. Section 1607.14B(8).

2. There is no single method for validating an employment test for its relationship to job performance. Professional standards adopted by the American Psychological Association in its Standards for Educational and Psychological Tests and Manuals (1966) accept three basic methods of validation: "empirical" or "criterion" validity (demonstrated by identifying criteria that indicate successful job performance and then correlating test scores so identified); "construct" validity (demonstrated by examinations structured to measure the degree to which job applicants have identifiable characteristics that have been determined to be important in successful job performance); and "content" validity (demonstrated by tests whose content closely approximates tasks to be performed on the job by the applicant). See Uniform Guidelines, 29 C.F.R. Section 1607.5; Washington v. Davis, 426 U.S. 229, 247, n. 13, 96 S.Ct. 2040, 2051, n. 13, 48 L.Ed.2d 597 (1976).

WASHINGTON v. DAVIS

Supreme Court of the United States, 1976.
426 U.S. 229, 96 S.Ct. 2040, 48 L.Ed.2d 597.

MR. JUSTICE WHITE delivered the opinion of the Court.

This case involves the validity of a qualifying test administered to applicants for positions as police officers in the District of Columbia Metropolitan Police Department. The test was sustained by the District Court but invalidated by the Court of Appeals. We are in agreement with the District Court and hence reverse the judgment of the Court of Appeals.

I

This action began on April 10, 1970, when two Negro police officers filed suit against the then Commissioner of the District of Columbia, the Chief of the District's Metropolitan Police Department, and the Commissioners of the United States Civil Service Commission.[1] An amended complaint, filed December 10, alleged that the promotion policies of the Department were racially discriminatory and sought a declaratory judgment and an injunction. The respondents Harley and Sellers were permitted to intervene, their amended complaint asserting that their applications to become officers in the Department had been rejected, and that the Department's recruiting procedures discriminated on the basis of race against black applicants by a series of practices including, but not limited to, a written personnel test which excluded a disproportionately high number of Negro applicants. These practices were asserted to violate respondents' rights "under the due process clause of the Fifth Amendment to the United States Constitution, under 42 U.S.C. § 1981 and under D.C.Code § 1–320."[2] Defendants answered, and discovery and various other proceedings followed.[3] Respondents then filed a motion for partial summary judgment with respect to the recruiting phase of the case, seeking a declaration that the test administered to those applying to become police officers is

1. Under § 4–103 of the District of Columbia Code, appointments to the Metropolitan Police force were to be made by the Commissioner subject to the provisions of Title 5 of the United States Code relating to the classified civil service. The District of Columbia Council and the Office of Commissioner of the District of Columbia, established by Reorganization Plan No. 37 of 1967, were abolished as of January 2, 1975, and replaced by the Council of the District of Columbia and the Office of Mayor of the District of Columbia.

2. Title 42 U.S.C. § 1981 provides:

"All persons within the jurisdiction of the United States shall have the same right in every State and Territory to make and enforce contracts, to sue, be parties, give evidence, and to the full and equal benefit of all laws and proceedings for the security of persons and property as is enjoyed by white citizens, and shall be subject to like punishment, pains, penalties, taxes, licenses, and exactions of every kind, and to no other."

Section 1–320 of the District of Columbia Code (1973) provides:

"In any program of recruitment or hiring of individuals to fill positions in the government of the District of Columbia, no officer or employee of the government of the District of Columbia shall exclude or give preference to the residents of the

District of Columbia or any State of the United States on the basis of residence, religion, race, color, or national origin."

One of the provisions expressly made applicable to the Metropolitan Police force by § 4–103 is 5 U.S.C. § 3304(a), which provides:

"§ 3304. *Competitive service; examinations.*

"(a) The President may prescribe rules which shall provide, as nearly as conditions of good administration warrant, for—

"(1) open, competitive examinations for testing applicants for appointment in the competitive service which are practical in character and as far as possible relate to matters that fairly test the relative capacity and fitness of the applicants for the appointment sought; and

"(2) noncompetitive examinations when competent applicants do not compete after notice has been given of the existence of the vacancy."

The complaint asserted no claim under § 3304.

3. Those proceedings included a hearing on respondents' motion for an order designating the case as a class action. A ruling on the motion was held in abeyance and was never granted insofar as the record before us reveals.

"unlawfully discriminatory and thereby in violation of the due process clause of the Fifth Amendment * * *." No issue under any statute or regulation was raised by the motion. The District of Columbia defendants, petitioners here, and the federal parties also filed motions for summary judgment with respect to the recruiting aspects of the case, asserting that respondents were entitled to relief on neither constitutional nor statutory grounds.[4] The District Court granted petitioners' and denied respondents' motions. 348 F.Supp. 15 (DC1972).

According to the findings and conclusions of the District Court, to be accepted by the Department and to enter an intensive 17-week training program, the police recruit was required to satisfy certain physical and character standards, to be a high school graduate or its equivalent, and to receive a grade of at least 40 out of 80 on "Test 21," which is "an examination that is used generally throughout the federal service," which "was developed by the Civil Service Commission, not the Police Department," and which was "designed to test verbal ability, vocabulary, reading and comprehension." Id., at 16.

The validity of Test 21 was the sole issue before the court on the motions for summary judgment. The District Court noted that there was no claim of "an intentional discrimination or purposeful discriminatory acts" but only a claim that Test 21 bore no relationship to job performance and "has a highly discriminatory impact in screening out black candidates." Ibid. Respondents' evidence, the District Court said, warranted three conclusions: "(a) The number of black police officers, while substantial, is not proportionate to the population mix of the city. (b) A higher percentage of blacks fail the Test than whites. (c) The Test has not been validated to establish its reliability for measuring subsequent job performance." Ibid. This showing was deemed sufficient to shift the burden of proof to the defendants in the action, petitioners here; but the court nevertheless concluded that on the undisputed facts respondents were not entitled to relief. The District Court relied on several factors. Since August 1969, 44% of new police force recruits had been black; that figure also represented the proportion of blacks on the total force and was roughly equivalent to 20- to 29-year-old blacks in the 50-mile radius in which the recruiting efforts of the Police Department had been concentrated. It was undisputed that the Department had systematically and affirmatively sought to enroll black officers many of whom passed the test but failed to report for duty. The District Court rejected the assertion that Test 21 was culturally slanted to favor whites and was "satisfied that the undisputable facts prove the test to be reasonably and directly related to the requirements of the police recruit training program and that it is neither so designed nor operates [*sic*] to discriminate against otherwise qualified blacks." Id., at 17. It was thus not necessary to show that

4. In support of the motion, petitioners and the federal parties urged that they were in compliance with all applicable constitutional, statutory, and regulatory provisions, including the provisions of the Civil Service Act which since 1883 were said to have established a "job relatedness" standard for employment.

Test 21 was not only a useful indicator of training school performance but had also been validated in terms of job performance—"The lack of job performance validation does not defeat the Test, given its direct relationship to recruiting and the valid part it plays in this process." Ibid.   The District Court ultimately concluded that "[t]he proof is wholly lacking that a police officer qualifies on the color of his skin rather than ability" and that the Department "should not be required on this showing to lower standards or to abandon efforts to achieve excellence." [5]   Id., at 18.

Having lost on both constitutional and statutory issues in the District Court, respondents brought the case to the Court of Appeals claiming that their summary judgment motion, which rested on purely constitutional grounds, should have been granted.   The tendered constitutional issue was whether the use of Test 21 invidiously discriminated against Negroes and hence denied them due process of law contrary to the commands of the Fifth Amendment.   The Court of Appeals, addressing that issue, announced that it would be guided by Griggs v. Duke Power Co., 401 U.S. 424, 91 S.Ct. 849, 28 L.Ed.2d 158 (1971), a case involving the interpretation and application of Title VII of the Civil Rights Act of 1964, and held that the statutory standards elucidated in that case were to govern the due process question tendered in this one.[6] 168 U.S.App.D.C. 42, 512 F.2d 956 (1975).   The court went on to declare that lack of discriminatory intent in designing and administering Test 21 was irrelevant;   the critical fact was rather that a far greater proportion of blacks—four times as many—failed the test than did whites.   This disproportionate impact, standing alone and without regard to whether it indicated a discriminatory purpose, was held sufficient to establish a constitutional violation, absent proof by petitioners that the test was an adequate measure of job performance in addition to being an indicator of probable success in the training program, a burden which the court ruled petitioners had failed to discharge.   That the Department had made substantial efforts to recruit blacks was held beside the point and the fact that the racial distribution of recent hirings and of the Department itself might be roughly equivalent to the racial makeup of the surrounding community, broadly conceived, was put aside as a "comparison [not] material to this appeal."   Id., at 46 n. 24, 512 F.2d, at 960 n. 24.   The Court of Appeals, over a dissent, accordingly reversed the judgment of the

---

5. When summary judgment was granted, the case with respect to discriminatory promotions was still pending. The District Court, however, made the determination and direction authorized by Fed.Rule Civ. Proc. 54(b). The promotion issue was subsequently decided adversely to the original plaintiffs. Davis v. Washington, 352 F.Supp. 187 (DC 1972).

6. "Although appellants' complaint did not allege a violation of Title VII of the Civil Rights Act of 1964, which then was inapplicable to the Federal Government, decisions applying Title VII furnish additional instruction as to the legal standard governing the issues raised in this case. * * * The many decisions disposing of employment discrimination claims on constitutional grounds have made no distinction between the constitutional standard and the statutory standard under Title VII." 168 U.S.App.D.C. 42, 44 n. 2, 512 F.2d 956, 958 n. 2 (1975).

District Court and directed that respondents' motion for partial summary judgment be granted. We granted the petition for certiorari, 423 U.S. 820, 96 S.Ct. 33, 46 L.Ed.2d 37 (1975), filed by the District of Columbia officials.[7]

II

Because the Court of Appeals erroneously applied the legal standards applicable to Title VII cases in resolving the constitutional issue before it, we reverse its judgment in respondents' favor. Although the petition for certiorari did not present this ground for reversal,[8] our Rule 40(1)(d)(2) provides that we "may notice a plain error not presented";[9] and this is an appropriate occasion to invoke the Rule.

As the Court of Appeals understood Title VII,[10] employees or applicants proceeding under it need not concern themselves with the employer's possibly discriminatory purpose but instead may focus solely on the racially differential impact of the challenged hiring or promotion practices. This is not the constitutional rule. We have never held that the constitutional standard for adjudicating claims of invidious racial discrimination is identical to the standards applicable under Title VII, and we decline to do so today.

The central purpose of the Equal Protection Clause of the Fourteenth Amendment is the prevention of official conduct discriminating on the basis of race. It is also true that the Due Process Clause of the Fifth Amendment contains an equal protection component prohibiting the United States from invidiously discriminating between individuals or groups. Bolling v. Sharpe, 347 U.S. 497, 74 S.Ct. 693, 98 L.Ed. 884 (1954). But our cases have not embraced the proposition that a law or other official act, without regard to whether it reflects a racially

---

7. The Civil Service Commissioners, defendants in the District Court, did not petition for writ of certiorari but have filed a brief as respondents. See our Rule 21(4). We shall at times refer to them as the "federal parties."

8. Apparently not disputing the applicability of the *Griggs* and Title VII standards in resolving this case, petitioners presented issues going only to whether Griggs v. Duke Power Co., 401 U.S. 424, 91 S.Ct. 849, 28 L.Ed.2d 158 (1971), had been misapplied by the Court of Appeals.

9. See, e.g., Silber v. United States, 370 U.S. 717, 82 S.Ct. 1287, 8 L.Ed.2d 798 (1962); Carpenters v. United States, 330 U.S. 395, 412, 67 S.Ct. 775, 784, 91 L.Ed. 973, 987 (1947); Sibbach v. Wilson & Co., 312 U.S. 1, 16, 61 S.Ct. 422, 427, 85 L.Ed. 479, 486 (1941); Mahler v. Eby, 264 U.S. 32, 45, 44 S.Ct. 283, 288, 68 L.Ed. 549, 557 (1924); Weems v. United States, 217 U.S. 349, 362, 30 S.Ct. 544, 547, 54 L.Ed. 793, 796 (1910).

10. Although Title VII standards have dominated this case, the statute was not applicable to federal employees when the complaint was filed; and although the 1972 amendments extending the Title to reach Government employees were adopted prior to the District Court's judgment, the complaint was not amended to state a claim under that Title, nor did the case thereafter proceed as a Title VII case. Respondents' motion for partial summary judgment, filed after the 1972 amendments, rested solely on constitutional grounds; and the Court of Appeals ruled that the motion should have been granted.

At the oral argument before this Court, when respondents' counsel was asked whether "this is just a purely Title VII case as it comes to us from the Court of Appeals without any constitutional overtones," counsel responded: "My trouble honestly with that proposition is the procedural requirements to get into court under Title VII, and this case has not met them." Tr. of Oral Arg. 66.

discriminatory purpose, is unconstitutional *solely* because it has a racially disproportionate impact.

Almost 100 years ago, Strauder v. West Virginia, 100 U.S. 303, 25 L.Ed. 664 (1880), established that the exclusion of Negroes from grand and petit juries in criminal proceedings violated the Equal Protection Clause, but the fact that a particular jury or a series of juries does not statistically reflect the racial composition of the community does not in itself make out an invidious discrimination forbidden by the Clause. "A purpose to discriminate must be present which may be proven by systematic exclusion of eligible jurymen of the proscribed race or by unequal application of the law to such an extent as to show intentional discrimination." Akins v. Texas, 325 U.S. 398, 403–404, 65 S.Ct. 1276, 1279, 89 L.Ed. 1692, 1696 (1945). A defendant in a criminal case is entitled "to require that the State not deliberately and systematically deny to members of his race the right to participate as jurors in the administration of justice." Alexander v. Louisiana, 405 U.S. 625, 628– 629, 92 S.Ct. 1221, 1224, 31 L.Ed.2d 536 (1972). See also Carter v. Jury Comm'n, 396 U.S. 320, 335–337, 339, 90 S.Ct. 518, 526–528, 529, 24 L.Ed. 2d 549, 560–561, 562 (1970); Cassell v. Texas, 339 U.S. 282, 287–290, 70 S.Ct. 629, 631–633, 94 L.Ed. 839, 847–849 (1950); Patton v. Mississippi, 332 U.S. 463, 468–469, 68 S.Ct. 184, 187, 92 L.Ed. 76, 80 (1947).

The rule is the same in other contexts. Wright v. Rockefeller, 376 U.S. 52, 84 S.Ct. 603, 11 L.Ed.2d 512 (1964), upheld a New York congressional apportionment statute against claims that district lines had been racially gerrymandered. The challenged districts were made up predominantly of whites or of minority races, and their boundaries were irregularly drawn. The challengers did not prevail because they failed to prove that the New York Legislature "was either motivated by racial considerations or in fact drew the districts on racial lines"; the plaintiffs had not shown that the statute "was the product of a state contrivance to segregate on the basis of race or place of origin." Id., at 56, 58, 84 S.Ct., at 605, 11 L.Ed.2d, at 515. The dissenters were in agreement that the issue was whether the "boundaries * * * were purposefully drawn on racial lines." Id., at 67, 84 S.Ct., at 611, 11 L.Ed. 2d, at 522.

The school desegregation cases have also adhered to the basic equal protection principle that the invidious quality of a law claimed to be racially discriminatory must ultimately be traced to a racially discriminatory purpose. That there are both predominantly black and predominantly white schools in a community is not alone violative of the Equal Protection Clause. The essential element of *de jure* segregation is "a current condition of segregation resulting from intentional state action. Keyes v. School Dist. No. 1, 413 U.S. 189, 205, 93 S.Ct. 2686, 2696, 37 L.Ed.2d 548 (1973). The differentiating factor between *de jure* segregation and so-called *de facto* segregation * * * is *purpose* or *intent* to segregate." Id., at 208, 93 S.Ct., at 2696, 37 L.Ed.2d, at 561. See also id., at 199, 211, 213, 93 S.Ct. at 2692, 2698, 2699, 37 L.Ed.2d, at

558, 564, 566. The Court has also recently rejected allegations of racial discrimination based solely on the statistically disproportionate racial impact of various provisions of the Social Security Act because "[t]he acceptance of appellants' constitutional theory would render suspect each difference in treatment among the grant classes, however lacking in racial motivation and however otherwise rational the treatment might be." Jefferson v. Hackney, 406 U.S. 535, 548, 92 S.Ct. 1724, 1732, 32 L.Ed.2d 285, 297 (1972). And compare Hunter v. Erickson, 393 U.S. 385, 89 S.Ct. 557, 21 L.Ed.2d 616 (1969), with James v. Valtierra, 402 U.S. 137, 91 S.Ct. 1331, 28 L.Ed.2d 678 (1971).

This is not to say that the necessary discriminatory racial purpose must be express or appear on the face of the statute, or that a law's disproportionate impact is irrelevant in cases involving Constitution-based claims of racial discrimination. A statute, otherwise neutral on its face, must not be applied so as invidiously to discriminate on the basis of race. Yick Wo v. Hopkins, 118 U.S. 356, 6 S.Ct. 1064, 30 L.Ed. 220 (1886). It is also clear from the cases dealing with racial discrimination in the selection of juries that the systematic exclusion of Negroes is itself such an "unequal application of the law * * * as to show intentional discrimination." Akins v. Texas, supra, 325 U.S., at 404, 65 S.Ct., at 1279, 89 L.Ed., at 1696. Smith v. Texas, 311 U.S. 128, 61 S.Ct. 164, 85 L.Ed. 84 (1940); Pierre v. Louisiana, 306 U.S. 354, 59 S.Ct. 536, 83 L.Ed. 757 (1939); Neal v. Delaware, 103 U.S. 370, 26 L.Ed. 567 (1881). A prima facie case of discriminatory purpose may be proved as well by the absence of Negroes on a particular jury combined with the failure of the jury commissioners to be informed of eligible Negro jurors in a community, Hill v. Texas, 316 U.S. 400, 404, 62 S.Ct. 1159, 1161, 86 L.Ed. 1559, 1562 (1942), or with racially non-neutral selection procedures, Alexander v. Louisiana, supra; Avery v. Georgia, 345 U.S. 559, 73 S.Ct. 891, 97 L.Ed. 1244 (1953); Whitus v. Georgia, 385 U.S. 545, 87 S.Ct. 643, 17 L.Ed.2d 599 (1967). With a prima facie case made out, "the burden of proof shifts to the State to rebut the presumption of unconstitutional action by showing that permissible racially neutral selection criteria and procedures have produced the monochromatic result." Alexander, supra, 405 U.S., at 632, 92 S.Ct., at 1226, 31 L.Ed.2d, at 542. See also Turner v. Fouche, 396 U.S. 346, 361, 90 S.Ct. 532, 540, 24 L.Ed.2d 567, 579 (1970); Eubanks v. Louisiana, 356 U.S. 584, 587, 78 S.Ct. 970, 973, 2 L.Ed.2d 991, 994 (1958).

Necessarily, an invidious discriminatory purpose may often be inferred from the totality of the relevant facts, including the fact, if it is true, that the law bears more heavily on one race than another. It is also not infrequently true that the discriminatory impact—in the jury cases for example, the total or seriously disproportionate exclusion of Negroes from jury venires—may for all practical purposes demonstrate unconstitutionality because in various circumstances the discrimination is very difficult to explain on nonracial grounds. Nevertheless, we have not held that a law, neutral on its face and serving ends otherwise within the power of government to pursue, is invalid under the Equal

Protection Clause simply because it may affect a greater proportion of one race than of another. Disproportionate impact is not irrelevant, but it is not the sole touchstone of an invidious racial discrimination forbidden by the Constitution. Standing alone, it does not trigger the rule, McLaughlin v. Florida, 379 U.S. 184, 85 S.Ct. 283, 13 L.Ed.2d 222 (1964), that racial classifications are to be subjected to the strictest scrutiny and are justifiable only by the weightiest of considerations.

There are some indications to the contrary in our cases.

* * *

As an initial matter, we have difficulty understanding how a law establishing a racially neutral qualification for employment is nevertheless racially discriminatory and denies "any person * * * equal protection of the laws" simply because a greater proportion of Negroes fail to qualify than members of other racial or ethnic groups. Had respondents, along with all others who had failed Test 21, whether white or black, brought an action claiming that the test denied each of them equal protection of the laws as compared with those who had passed with high enough scores to qualify them as police recruits, it is most unlikely that their challenge would have been sustained. Test 21, which is administered generally to prospective Government employees, concededly seeks to ascertain whether those who take it have acquired a particular level of verbal skill; and it is untenable that the Constitution prevents the Government from seeking modestly to upgrade the communicative abilities of its employees rather than to be satisfied with some lower level of competence, particularly where the job requires special ability to communicate orally and in writing. Respondents, as Negroes, could no more successfully claim that the test denied them equal protection than could white applicants who also failed. The conclusion would not be different in the face of proof that more Negroes than whites had been disqualified by Test 21. That other Negroes also failed to score well would, alone, not demonstrate that respondents individually were being denied equal protection of the laws by the application of an otherwise valid qualifying test being administered to prospective police recruits.

Nor on the facts of the case before us would the disproportionate impact of Test 21 warrant the conclusion that it is a purposeful device to discriminate against Negroes and hence an infringement of the constitutional rights of respondents as well as other black applicants. As we have said, the test is neutral on its face and rationally may be said to serve a purpose the Government is constitutionally empowered to pursue. Even agreeing with the District Court that the differential racial effect of Test 21 called for further inquiry, we think the District Court correctly held that the affirmative efforts of the Metropolitan Police Department to recruit black officers, the changing racial composition of the recruit classes and of the force in general, and the relationship of the test to the training program negated any inference that the Department discriminated on the basis of race or that "a police officer qualifies on the color of his skin rather than ability." 348 F.Supp., at 18.

Under Title VII, Congress provided that when hiring and promotion practices disqualifying substantially disproportionate numbers of blacks are challenged, discriminatory purpose need not be proved, and that it is an insufficient response to demonstrate some rational basis for the challenged practices. It is necessary, in addition, that they be "validated" in terms of job performance in any one of several ways perhaps by ascertaining the minimum skill, ability, or potential necessary for the position at issue and determining whether the qualifying tests are appropriate for the selection of qualified applicants for the job in question. However this process proceeds, it involves a more probing judicial review of, and less deference to, the seemingly reasonable acts of administrators and executives than is appropriate under the Constitution where special racial impact, without discriminatory purpose, is claimed. We are not disposed to adopt this more rigorous standard for the purposes of applying the Fifth and the Fourteenth Amendments in cases such as this.

A rule that a statute designed to serve neutral ends is nevertheless invalid, absent compelling justification, if in practice it benefits or burdens one race more than another would be far-reaching and would raise serious questions about, and perhaps invalidate, a whole range of tax, welfare, public service, regulatory, and licensing statutes that may be more burdensome to the poor and to the average black than to the more affluent white.[14]

Given that rule, such consequences would perhaps be likely to follow. However, in our view, extension of the rule beyond those areas where it is already applicable by reason of statute, such as in the field of public employment, should await legislative prescription.

As we have indicated, it was error to direct summary judgment for respondents based on the Fifth Amendment.

III

We also hold that the Court of Appeals should have affirmed the judgment of the District Court granting the motions for summary judgment filed by petitioners and the federal parties. Respondents were entitled to relief on neither constitutional nor statutory grounds.

The submission of the defendants in the District Court was that Test 21 complied with all applicable statutory as well as constitutional

---

14. Goodman, De Facto School Segregation: A Constitutional and Empirical Analysis, 60 Calif.L.Rev. 275, 300 (1972), suggests that disproportionate-impact analysis might invalidate "tests and qualifications for voting, draft deferment, public employment, jury service, and other government-conferred benefits and opportunities * * *; [s]ales taxes, bail schedules, utility rates, bridge tolls, license fees, and other state-imposed charges." It has also been argued that minimum wage and usury laws as well as professional licensing requirements would require major modifications in light of the unequal-impact rule. Silverman, Equal Protection, Economic Legislation, and Racial Discrimination, 25 Vand.L.Rev. 1183 (1972). See also Demsetz, Minorities in the Market Place, 43 N.C.L.Rev. 271 (1965).

requirements; and they appear not to have disputed that under the statutes and regulations governing their conduct standards similar to those obtaining under Title VII had to be satisfied.[15] The District Court also assumed that Title VII standards were to control the case identified the determinative issue as whether Test 21 was sufficiently job related and proceeded to uphold use of the test because it was "directly related to a determination of whether the applicant possesses sufficient skills requisite to the demands of the curriculum a recruit must master at the police academy." 348 F.Supp., at 17. The Court of Appeals reversed because the relationship between Test 21 and training school success, if demonstrated at all, did not satisfy what it deemed to be the crucial requirement of a direct relationship between performance on Test 21 and performance on the policeman's job.

We agree with petitioners and the federal parties that this was error. The advisability of the police recruit training course informing the recruit about his upcoming job, acquainting him with its demands, and attempting to impart a modicum of required skills seems conceded. It is also apparent to us, as it was to the District Judge, that some minimum verbal and communicative skill would be very useful, if not essential, to satisfactory progress in the training regimen. Based on the evidence before him, the District Judge concluded that Test 21 was directly related to the requirements of the police training program and that a positive relationship between the test and training-course performance was sufficient to validate the former, wholly aside from its possible relationship to actual performance as a police officer. This conclusion of the District Judge that training-program validation may itself be sufficient is supported by regulations of the Civil Service Commission, by the opinion evidence placed before the District Judge, and by the current views of the Civil Service Commissioners who were parties to the case.[16] Nor is the conclusion foreclosed by either *Griggs*

---

15. In their memorandum supporting their motion for summary judgment, the federal parties argued:

"In *Griggs*, supra, the Supreme Court set a job-relationship standard for the private sector employers which has been a standard for federal employment since the passage of the Civil Service Act in 1883. In that act Congress has mandated that the federal government must use '* * * examinations for testing applicants for appointment * * * which * * * as far as possible relate to matters that fairly test the relative capacity and fitness of the applicants for the appointments sought.' 5 U.S.C. § 3304(a) (1). Defendants contend that they have been following the job-related standards of *Griggs*, supra, for the past eighty-eight years by virtue of the enactment of the Civil Service Act which guaranteed open and fair competition for jobs."

They went on to argue that the *Griggs* standard had been satisfied. In granting the motions for summary judgment filed by petitioners and the federal parties, the District Court necessarily decided adversely to respondents the statutory issues expressly or tacitly tendered by the parties.

16. See n. 17, infra. Current instructions of the Civil Service Commission on "Examining, Testing, Standards, and Employment Practices" provide in pertinent part:

"S2–2—Use of applicant appraisal procedures

a. *Policy.* The Commission's staff develops and uses applicant appraisal procedures to assess the knowledges, skills, and abilities of persons for jobs and not persons in the abstract.

or Albemarle Paper Co. v. Moody, 422 U.S. 405, 95 S.Ct. 2362, 45 L.Ed. 2d 280 (1975); and it seems to us the much more sensible construction of the job-relatedness requirement.

The District Court's accompanying conclusion that Test 21 was in fact directly related to the requirements of the police training program was supported by a validation study, as well as by other evidence of record; [17] and we are not convinced that this conclusion was erroneous.

The federal parties, whose views have somewhat changed since the decision of the Court of Appeals and who still insist that training-program validation is sufficient, now urge a remand to the District Court for the purpose of further inquiry into whether the training-program test scores, which were found to correlate with Test 21 scores, are themselves an appropriate measure of the trainee's mastership of the material taught in the course and whether the training program itself is sufficiently related to actual performance of the police officer's task. We think a remand is inappropriate. The District Court's judgment was warranted by the record before it, and we perceive no good reason to reopen it, particularly since we were informed at oral argument that although Test 21 is still being administered, the training program itself has undergone substantial modification in the course of this litigation. If there are now deficiencies in the recruiting practices under prevailing Title VII standards, those deficiencies are to be directly addressed in accordance with appropriate procedures mandated under that Title.

"(1) Appraisal procedures are designed to reflect real, reasonable, and necessary qualifications for effective job behavior.

"(2) An appraisal procedure must, among other requirements, have a demonstrable and rational relationship to important job-related performance objectives identified by management, such as:

"(a) Effective job performance;

"(b) Capability;

"(c) Success in training;

"(d) Reduced turnover; or

"(e) Job satisfaction." 37 Fed.Reg. 21557 (1972).

See also Equal Employment Opportunity Commission Guidelines on Employee Selection Procedures, 29 CFR § 1607.5(b)(3) (1975), discussed in Albemarle Paper Co. v. Moody, 422 U.S., at 430–435, 95 S.Ct. 2362, 2378–2380, 45 L.Ed.2d 280, 304–307.

17. The record includes a validation study of Test 21's relationship to performance in the recruit training program. The study was made by D.L. Futransky of the Standards Division, Bureau of Policies and Standards, United States Civil Service Commission. App. 99–109. Findings of the study included data "support[ing] the

conclusion that T[est] 21 is effective in selecting trainees who can learn the material that is taught at the Recruit School." Id., at 103. Opinion evidence, submitted by qualified experts examining the Futransky study and/or conducting their own research, affirmed the correlation between scores on Test 21 and success in the training program. E.g., Affidavit of Dr. Donald J. Schwartz (personnel research psychologist, United States Civil Service Commission), App. 178, 183 ("It is my opinion * * * that Test 21 has a significant positive correlation with success in the MPD Recruit School for both Blacks and whites and is therefore shown to be job related * * *"); affidavit of Diane E. Wilson (personnel research psychologist, United States Civil Service Commission), App. 185, 186 ("It is my opinion that there is a direct and rational relationship between the content and difficulty of Test 21 and successful completion of recruit school training")\,

The Court of Appeals was "willing to assume for purposes of this appeal that appellees have shown that Test 21 is predictive of further progress in Recruit School." 168 U.S.App.D.C., at 48, 512 F.2d, at 962.

The judgment of the Court of Appeals accordingly is reversed.

So ordered.

MR. JUSTICE STEWART joins Parts I and II of the Court's opinion.

MR. JUSTICE STEVENS, concurring.

While I agree with the Court's disposition of this case, I add these comments on the constitutional issue discussed in Part II and the statutory issue discussed in Part III of the Court's opinion.

The requirement of purposeful discrimination is a common thread running through the cases summarized in Part II. These cases include criminal convictions which were set aside because blacks were excluded from the grand jury, a reapportionment case in which political boundaries were obviously influenced to some extent by racial considerations, a school desegregation case, and a case involving the unequal administration of an ordinance purporting to prohibit the operation of laundries in frame buildings. Although it may be proper to use the same language to describe the constitutional claim in each of these contexts, the burden of proving a prima facie case may well involve differing evidentiary considerations. The extent of deference that one pays to the trial court's determination of the factual issue, and indeed, the extent to which one characterizes the intent issue as a question of fact or a question of law, will vary in different contexts.

Frequently the most probative evidence of intent will be objective evidence of what actually happened rather than evidence describing the subjective state of mind of the actor. For normally the actor is presumed to have intended the natural consequences of his deeds. This is particularly true in the case of governmental action which is frequently the product of compromise, of collective decisionmaking, and of mixed motivation. It is unrealistic, on the one hand, to require the victim of alleged discrimination to uncover the actual subjective intent of the decisionmaker or, conversely, to invalidate otherwise legitimate action simply because an improper motive affected the deliberation of a participant in the decisional process. A law conscripting clerics should not be invalidated because an atheist voted for it.

My point in making this observation is to suggest that the line between discriminatory purpose and discriminatory impact is not nearly as bright, and perhaps not quite as critical, as the reader of the Court's opinion might assume. I agree, of course, that a constitutional issue does not arise every time some disproportionate impact is shown. On the other hand, when the disproportion is as dramatic as in Gomillion v. Lightfoot, 364 U.S. 339, 81 S.Ct. 125, 5 L.Ed.2d 110 or Yick Wo v. Hopkins, 118 U.S. 356, 6 S.Ct. 1064, 30 L.Ed. 220 (1886), it really does not matter whether the standard is phrased in terms of purpose or effect. Therefore, although I accept the statement of the general rule in the Court's opinion, I am not yet prepared to indicate how that standard should be applied in the many cases which have formulated the governing standard in different language.

My agreement with the conclusion reached in Part II of the Court's opinion rests on a ground narrower than the Court describes. I do not rely at all on the evidence of good-faith efforts to recruit black police officers. In my judgment, neither those efforts nor the subjective good faith of the District administration, would save Test 21 if it were otherwise invalid.

There are two reasons why I am convinced that the challenge to Test 21 is insufficient. First, the test serves the neutral and legitimate purpose of requiring all applicants to meet a uniform minimum standard of literacy. Reading ability is manifestly relevant to the police function, there is no evidence that the required passing grade was set at an arbitrarily high level, and there is sufficient disparity among high schools and high school graduates to justify the use of a separate uniform test. Second, the same test is used throughout the federal service. The applicants for employment in the District of Columbia Police Department represent such a small fraction of the total number of persons who have taken the test that their experience is of minimal probative value in assessing the neutrality of the test itself. That evidence, without more, is not sufficient to overcome the presumption that a test which is this widely used by the Federal Government is in fact neutral in its effect as well as its "purpose" as that term is used in constitutional adjudication.

My study of the statutory issue leads me to the same conclusion reached by the Court in Part III of its opinion. Since the Court of Appeals set aside the portion of the District Court's summary judgment granting the defendants' motion, I agree that we cannot ignore the statutory claims even though as the Court makes clear, ante, at 238 n. 10, there is not Title VII question in this case. The actual statutory holdings are limited to 42 U.S.C. § 1981 and § 1–320 of the District of Columbia Code, to which regulations of the Equal Employment Opportunity Commission have no direct application.

The parties argued the case as though Title VII standards were applicable. In a general way those standards shed light on the issues, but there is sufficient individuality and complexity to that statute, and to the regulations promulgated under it, to make it inappropriate simply to transplant those standards in their entirety into a different statutory scheme having a different history. Moreover, the subject matter of this case—the validity of qualifications for the law enforcement profession—is one in which federal district judges have a greater expertise than in many others. I therefore do not regard this as a case in which the District Court was required to apply Title VII standards as strictly as would be necessary either in other contexts or in litigation actually arising under that statute.

The Court's specific holding on the job-relatedness question contains, I believe, two components. First, as a matter of law, it is permissible for the police department to use a test for the purpose of predicting ability to master a training program even if the test does not otherwise predict ability to perform on the job. I regard this as a reasonable proposition and not inconsistent with the Court's prior holdings, although some of its prior language obviously did not contemplate this precise problem. Second, as a matter of fact, the District Court's finding that there was a correlation between success on the test and success in the training program has sufficient evidentiary support to withstand attack under the "clearly erroneous" standard mandated by Fed.Rule Civ.Proc. 52(a). Whether or not we would have made the same finding of fact, the opinion evidence identified in n. 17 of the Court's opinion—and indeed the assumption made by the Court of Appeals quoted therein—is surely adequate to support the finding under the proper standard of appellate review.

On the understanding that nothing which I have said is inconsistent with the Court's reasoning, I join the opinion of the Court except to the extent that it expresses an opinion on the merits of the cases cited ante, at 2050, n. 12.

MR. JUSTICE BRENNAN, with whom MR. JUSTICE MARSHALL joins, dissenting.

The Court holds that the job qualification examination (Test 21) given by the District of Columbia Metropolitan Police Department does not unlawfully discriminate on the basis of race under either constitutional or statutory standards.

Initially, it seems to me that the Court should not pass on the statutory questions, because they are not presented by this case. The Court says that respondents' summary judgment motion "rested on purely constitutional grounds," ante, at 2046, and that "the Court of Appeals erroneously applied the legal standards applicable to Title VII cases in resolving the constitutional issue before it," ante, at 2046. There is a suggestion, however, that petitioners are entitled to prevail because they met the burden of proof imposed by 5 U.S.C. § 3304. Ante, at 2052 n. 15. As I understand the opinion, the Court therefore holds that Test 21 is job-related under § 3304, but not necessarily under Title VII. But that provision, by the Court's own analysis, is no more in the case than Title VII; respondents' "complaint asserted no claim under § 3304." Ante, at 2045 n. 2. Cf. ante, at 2046–2047 n. 10. If it was "plain error" for the Court of Appeals to apply a statutory standard to this case, as the Court asserts, ante, at 2046–2047, then it is unfortunate that the Court does not recognize that it is also plain error to address the statutory issues in Part III of its opinion.

Nevertheless, although it appears unnecessary to reach the statutory questions, I will accept the Court's conclusion that respondents were entitled to summary judgment if they were correct in their statutory arguments, and I would affirm the Court of Appeals because petitioners have failed to prove that Test 21 satisfies the applicable statutory standards. All parties' arguments and both lower court decisions were based on Title VII standards. In this context, I think it wrong to focus on § 3304 to the exclusion of the Title VII standards, particularly because the Civil Service Commission views the job-relatedness standards of Title VII and § 3304 as identical.[2] See also infra, at 2058–2059.

In applying a Title VII test,[3] both the District Court and the Court of Appeals held that respondents had offered sufficient evidence of discriminatory impact to shift to petitioners the burden of proving job relatedness. 348 F.Supp. 15, 16; 168 U.S.App.D.C. 42, 45–47, 512 F.2d 956, 959–961. The Court does not question these rulings, and the only issue before us is what petitioners were required to show and whether they carried their burden. The Court agrees with the District Court's conclusion that Test 21 was validated by a positive relationship between Test 21 scores and performance in police training courses. This result is based upon the Court's reading of the record, its interpretation of instructions governing testing practices issued by the Civil Service Commission (CSC), and "the current views of the Civil Service Commissioners who were parties to the case." We are also assured that today's result is not foreclosed by Griggs v. Duke Power Co., 401 U.S. 424, 91 S.Ct. 849, 28 L.Ed.2d 158 (1971), and Albemarle Paper Co. v. Moody, 422 U.S. 405, 95 S.Ct. 2362, 45 L.Ed.2d 280 (1975). Finally, the Court asserts that its conclusion is "the much more sensible construction of the job relatedness requirement." Ante, at 2053.

But the CSC instructions cited by the Court do not support the District Court's conclusion. More importantly, the brief filed in this Court by the CSC takes the position that petitioners did not satisfy the burden of proof imposed by the CSC guidelines. It also appears that longstanding regulations of the Equal Employment Opportunity Commission (EEOC)—previously endorsed by this Court—require a result contrary to that reached by the Court. Furthermore, the Court's conclusion is inconsistent with my understanding of the interpretation of Title VII in *Griggs* and *Albemarle*. I do not find this conclusion "much more sensible" and with all respect I suggest that today's decision has the potential of significantly weakening statutory safeguards against discrimination in employment.

I

On October 12, 1972, the CSC issued a supplement to the Federal Personnel Manual containing instructions for compliance with its general regulations concerning employment practices.[4] The provision cited

2. The only administrative authority relied on by the Court in support of its result is a regulation of the Civil Service Commission construing the civil service employment standards in Title 5 of the United States Code. Ante, at 2052–2053 n. 16. I note, however, that 5 U.S.C. § 3304 was brought into this case by the CSC, not by respondents, and the CSC's only reason for referring to that provision was to establish that petitioners had been "following the job-related standards of Griggs [v. Duke Power Co., 401 U.S. 424, 91 S.Ct. 849, 28 L.Ed.2d 158 (1971),] for the past eighty-eight years." Ante, at 2052 n. 15.

3. The provision in Title VII on which petitioners place principal reliance is 42 U.S.C. § 2000e–2(h). See Griggs v. Duke Power Co., supra, 401 U.S., at 433–436, 91 S.Ct., at 854–856, 28 L.Ed.2d, at 165–167.

4. See 5 CFR § 300.101 et seq. (1976). These instructions contain the "regulations" that the Court finds supportive of

by the Court requires that Test 21 "have a demonstrable and rational relationship to important job-related performance objectives identified by management." "Success in training" is one example of a possible objective. The statistical correlation established by the Futransky validity study, ante, at 2053 n. 17, was between applicants' scores on Test 21 and recruits' average scores on final examinations given during the police training course.

It is hornbook law that the Court accord deference to the construction of an administrative regulation when that construction is made by the administrative authority responsible for the regulation. E.g., Udall v. Tallman, 380 U.S. 1, 16, 85 S.Ct. 792, 801, 13 L.Ed.2d 616, 625 (1965). It is worthy of note, therefore, that the brief filed by the CSC in this case interprets the instructions in a manner directly contrary to the Court, despite the Court's claim that its result is supported by the Commissioners' "current views."

> Under Civil Service Commission regulations and current professional standards governing criterion-related test validation procedures, the job-relatedness of an entrance examination may be demonstrated by proof that scores on the examination predict properly measured success in job-relevant training (regardless of whether they predict success on the job itself).

> The documentary evidence submitted in the district court demonstrates that scores on Test 21 are predictive of Recruit School Final Averages. There is little evidence, however, concerning the relationship between the Recruit School tests and the substance of the training program, and between the substance of the training program and the post-training job of a police officer. *It cannot be determined, therefore, whether the Recruit School Final Averages are a proper measure of success in training and whether the training program is job-relevant.* Brief for CSC 14–15 (emphasis added).

The CSC maintains that a positive correlation between scores on entrance examinations and the criterion of success in training may establish the job relatedness of an entrance test—thus relieving an employer from the burden of providing a relationship to job performance after training—but only subject to certain limitations.

> Proof that scores on an entrance examination predict scores on training school achievement tests, however, does not, by itself, satisfy the burden of demonstrating the job-relatedness of the entrance examination. There must also be evidence—the nature of which will depend on the particular circumstances of the case—showing that the achievement test scores are an appropriate measure of the trainee's mastery of the material taught in the training program and that the training

the District Court's conclusion, which was reached under Title VII, but neither the instructions nor the general regulations are an interpretation of Title VII. The instructions were issued "under authority of sections 3301 and 3302 of title 5, United States Code, and E.O. 10577, 3 CFR 1954– 58 Comp., p. 218." 37 Fed.Reg. 21552 (1972). The pertinent regulations of the CSC in 5 CFR § 300.101 et seq. were promulgated pursuant to the same authorities, as well as 5 U.S.C. §§ 7151, 7154 and Exec.Order No. 11478, 3 CFR (1966–1970 Comp.) 803.

program imparts to a new employee knowledge, skills, or abilities required for performance of the post-training job. Id., at 24–25.

Applying its standards [5] the CSC concludes that none of the evidence presented in the District Court established "the appropriateness of using Recruit School Final Averages as the measure of training performance or the relationship of the Recruit School program to the job of a police officer." Id., at 30.[6]

The CSC's standards thus recognize that Test 21 can be validated by a correlation between Test 21 scores and recruits' averages on training examinations only if (1) the training averages predict job performance or (2) the averages are proved to measure performance in job-related training. There is no proof that the recruits' average is correlated with job performance after completion of training. See n. 10, infra. And although a positive relationship to the recruits' average might be sufficient to validate Test 21 if the average were proved to reflect mastery of material on the training curriculum that was in turn demonstrated to be relevant to job performance, the record is devoid of proof in this regard. First, there is no demonstration by petitioners that the training-course examinations measure comprehension of the training curriculum; indeed, these examinations do not even appear in the record. Furthermore, the Futransky study simply designated an average of 85 on the examination as a "good" performance and assumed that a recruit with such an average learned the material taught in the training course.[7] Without any further proof of the significance of a score of 85, and there is none in the record, I cannot agree that Test 21 is predictive of "success in training."

II

Today's decision is also at odds with EEOC regulations issued pursuant to explicit authorization in Title VII, 42 U.S.C. § 2000e–12(a). Although the dispute in this case is not within the EEOC's jurisdiction,

---

5. The CSC asserts that certain of its guidelines have some bearing on Test 21's job relatedness. Under the CSC instructions, " 'criterion-related' validity," see Douglas v. Hampton, 168 U.S.App.D.C. 62, 70 n. 60, 512 F.2d 976, 984 n. 60 (1975), can be established by demonstrating a correlation between entrance examination scores and "a criterion which is legitimately based on the needs of the Federal Government." ¶ S3–2(a)(2), 37 Fed.Reg. 21558 (1972). Further, to prove validity, statistical studies must demonstrate that Test 21, "to a significant degree, measures performance or qualifications requirements which are relevant to the job or jobs for which candidates are being evaluated." ¶ S3–3(a), 37 Fed.Reg. 21558 (1972). These provisions are ignored in the Court's opinion.

6. On this basis, the CSC argues that the case ought to be remanded to enable

petitioners to try to make such a demonstration, but this resolution seems to me inappropriate. Both lower courts recognized that petitioners had the burden of proof, and as this burden is yet unsatisfied, respondents are entitled to prevail.

7. The finding in the Futransky study on which the Court relies, ante, at 2053 n. 17, was that Test 21 "is effective in selecting trainees who can learn the material that is taught at the Recruit School," because it predicts averages over 85. On its face, this would appear to be an important finding, but the fact is that everyone learns the material included in the training course. The study noted that all recruits pass the training examinations; if a particular recruit has any difficulty, he is given assistance until he passes.

as I noted above, the proper construction of Title VII nevertheless is relevant. Moreover, the 1972 extension of Title VII to public employees gave the same substantive protection to those employees as had previously been accorded in the private sector, Morton v. Mancari, 417 U.S. 535, 546–547, 94 S.Ct. 2474, 2480–2481, 41 L.Ed.2d 290, 298–299 (1974), and it is therefore improper to maintain different standards in the public and private sectors. Chandler v. Roudebush, 425 U.S. 840, 864, 96 S.Ct. 1949, 1961, 48 L.Ed.2d 416, 433 (1976). See n. 2, supra.

As with an agency's regulations, the construction of a statute by the agency charged with its administration is entitled to great deference. Trafficante v. Metropolitan Life Ins. Co., 409 U.S. 205, 210, 93 S.Ct. 364, 367, 34 L.Ed.2d 415, 419 (1972); Udall v. Tallman, 380 U.S., at 16, 85 S.Ct., at 801, 13 L.Ed.2d at 625; Power Reactor Co. v. Electricians, 367 U.S. 396, 408, 81 S.Ct. 1529, 1535, 6 L.Ed.2d 924, 932 (1961). The deference due the pertinent EEOC regulations is enhanced by the fact that they were neither altered nor disapproved when Congress extensively amended Title VII in 1972.[8] Chemehuevi Tribe of Indians v. FPC, 420 U.S. 395, 410, 95 S.Ct. 1066, 1075, 43 L.Ed.2d 279, 290 (1975); Cammarano v. United States, 358 U.S. 498, 510, 79 S.Ct. 524, 531, 3 L.Ed.2d 462, 470 (1959); Allen v. Grand Central Aircraft Co., 347 U.S. 535, 547, 74 S.Ct. 745, 752, 98 L.Ed. 933, 943 (1954); Massachusetts Mut. Life Ins. Co. v. United States, 288 U.S. 269, 273, 53 S.Ct. 337, 339, 77 L.Ed. 739, 742 (1933). These principles were followed in *Albemarle*—where the Court explicitly endorsed various regulations no fewer than eight times in its opinion, 422 U.S., at 431–436, 95 S.Ct., at 2378–2381, 45 L.Ed.2d, at 304–307 [9]—and *Griggs*, 401 U.S., at 433–434, 91 S.Ct., at 854–855, 28 L.Ed.2d, at 165–166.

The EEOC regulations require that the validity of a job qualification test be proved by "empirical data demonstrating that the test is predictive of or significantly correlated with important elements of work behavior which comprise or are relevant to the job or jobs for which candidates are being evaluated." 29 CFR § 1607.4(c) (1975). This construction of Title VII was approved in *Albemarle*, where we quoted this provision and remarked that "[t]he message of these Guidelines is the same as that of the *Griggs* case." 422 U.S., at 431, 95 S.Ct., at 2378, 45 L.Ed.2d, at 304. The regulations also set forth minimum standards for validation and delineate the criteria that may be used for this purpose.

---

8. Still another factor mandates deference to the EEOC regulations. The House and Senate committees considering the 1972 amendments to Title VII recognized that discrimination in employment, including the use of testing devices, is a "complex and pervasive phenomenon." S.Rep. No. 92–415, p. 5 (1971); H.R.Rep. No. 92–238, p. 8 (1971); U.S.Code Cong. & Admin. News 1972, p. 2137. As a result, both committees noted the need to obtain "expert assistance" in this area. S.Rep. No. 92–415, supra, at 5; H.R.Rep. No. 92–238, supra, at 8.

9. Indeed, two Justices asserted that the Court relied too heavily on the EEOC guidelines. 422 U.S. 449, 95 S.Ct. 2389, 45 L.Ed.2d 316 (Blackmun, J., concurring in judgment); Id., at 451, 95 S.Ct., at 2387, 45 L.Ed.2d, at 317 (Burger, C.J., concurring in part and dissenting in part).

The work behaviors or other criteria of employee adequacy which the test is intended to predict or identify must be fully described; and, additionally, in the case of rating techniques, the appraisal form(s) and instructions to the rater(s) must be included as a part of the validation evidence. Such criteria may include measures other than actual work proficiency, such as training time, supervisory ratings, regularity of attendance and tenure. Whatever criteria are used they must represent major or critical work behaviors as revealed by careful job analyses. 29 CFR § 1607.5(b)(3) (1975).

This provision was also approved in *Albemarle*, 422 U.S., at 432, 95 S.Ct., at 2379, 45 L.Ed.2d, at 304, and n. 30.

If we measure the validity of Test 21 by this standard, which I submit we are bound to do, petitioners' proof is deficient in a number of ways similar to those noted above. First, the criterion of final training examination averages does not appear to be "fully described." Although the record contains some general discussion of the training curriculum, the examinations are not in the record, and there is no other evidence completely elucidating the subject matter tested by the training examinations. Without this required description we cannot determine whether the correlation with training examination averages is sufficiently related to petitioners' need to ascertain "job-specific ability." See *Albemarle*, 422 U.S., at 433, 95 S.Ct., at 2379, 45 L.Ed.2d, at 305. Second, the EEOC regulations do not expressly permit validation by correlation to training performance, unlike the CSC instructions. Among the specified criteria the closest to training performance is "training time." All recruits to the Metropolitan Police Department, however, go through the same training course in the same amount of time, including those who experience some difficulty. See n. 7, supra. Third, the final requirement of § 1607.5(b)(3) has not been met. There has been no job analysis establishing the significance of scores on training examinations, nor is there any other type of evidence showing that these scores are of "major or critical" importance.

Accordingly, EEOC regulations that have previously been approved by the Court set forth a construction of Title VII that is distinctly opposed to today's statutory result.

III

The Court also says that its conclusion is not foreclosed by *Griggs* and *Albemarle*, but today's result plainly conflicts with those cases. *Griggs* held that "[i]f an employment practice which operates to exclude Negroes cannot be shown to be *related to job performance*, the practice is prohibited." 401 U.S., at 431, 91 S.Ct., at 853, 28 L.Ed.2d, at 164 (emphasis added). Once a discriminatory impact is shown, the employer carries the burden of proving that the challenged practice "bear[s] a *demonstrable relationship to successful performance of the jobs* for which it was used." *Ibid.* (emphasis added). We observed further:

Nothing in the Act precludes the use of testing or measuring procedures; obviously they are useful. What Congress has forbidden is giving these devices and mechanisms controlling force unless they are demonstrably a reasonable measure of job performance. * * * What Congress has commanded is that any tests used must measure the person for the job and not the person in the abstract. Id., at 436, 91 S.Ct., at 856, 28 L.Ed.2d, at 167.

Albemarle read *Griggs* to require that a discriminatory test be validated through proof "by professionally acceptable methods" that it is " 'predictive of or significantly correlated with *important* elements of work behavior *which comprise or are relevant to the job or jobs* for which candidates are being evaluated.' " 422 U.S., at 431, 95 S.Ct., at 2378, 45 L.Ed.2d, at 304 (emphasis added), quoting 29 CFR § 1607.4(c) (1975). Further, we rejected the employer's attempt to validate a written test by proving that it was related to supervisors' job performance ratings, because there was no demonstration that the ratings accurately reflected job performance. We were unable "to determine whether the criteria *actually* considered were sufficiently related to the [employer's] legitimate interest in job-specific ability to justify a testing system with a racially discriminatory impact." 422 U.S., at 433, 95 S.Ct., at 2379, 45 L.Ed.2d, at 305 (emphasis in original). To me, therefore, these cases read Title VII as requiring proof of a significant relationship to job performance to establish the validity of a discriminatory test. See also McDonnell Douglas Corp. v. Green, 411 U.S. 792, 802, 93 S.Ct. 1817, 1824, 36 L.Ed.2d 668, 678 and n. 14 (1973). Petitioners do not maintain that there is a demonstrated correlation between Test 21 scores and job performance. Moreover, their validity study was unable to discern a significant positive relationship between training averages and job performance.[10] Thus, there is no proof of a correlation—either direct or indirect—between Test 21 and performance of the job of being a police officer.

It may well be that in some circumstances, proof of a relationship between a discriminatory qualification test and training performance is an acceptable substitute for establishing a relationship to job performance. But this question is not settled, and it should not be resolved by the minimal analysis in the Court's opinion. Moreover, it is particularly inappropriate to decide the question on this record. "Professionally acceptable methods" apparently recognize validation by proof of a correlation with training performance, rather than job performance, if (1) the training curriculum includes information proved to be important to job performance and (2) the standard used as a measure of training performance is shown to reflect the trainees' mastery of the material included in the training curriculum. See Brief for CSC 24–29; Brief for the Executive Committee of Division 14 of the American Psychological Assn. as Amicus Curiae 37–43. But no authority, whether professional,

---

10. Although the validity study found that Test 21 predicted job performance for white officers, but see *Albemarle*, 422 U.S., at 433, 95 S.Ct., at 2379, 45 L.Ed.2d, at 305, no similar relationship existed for black officers. The same finding was made as to the relationship between training examination averages and job performance. See id., at 435, 95 S.Ct., at 2380, 45 L.Ed.2d, at 306.

administrative, or judicial, has accepted the sufficiency of a correlation with training performance in the absence of such proof. For reasons that I have stated above, the record does not adequately establish either factor. As a result, the Court's conclusion cannot be squared with the focus on job performance in *Griggs* and *Albemarle*, even if this substitute showing is reconcilable with the holdings in those cases.

Today's reduced emphasis on a relationship to job performance is also inconsistent with clearly expressed congressional intent. A section-by-section analysis of the 1972 amendments to Title VII states as follows:

> In any area where the new law does not address itself, or in any areas where a specific contrary intention is not indicated, it was assumed that the present case law as developed by the courts would continue to govern the applicability and construction of Title VII. 118 Cong.Rec. 7166 (1972).

The pre-1972 judicial decisions dealing with standardized tests used as job qualification requirements uniformly follow the EEOC regulations discussed above and insist upon proof of a relationship to job performance to prove that a test is job related. Furthermore, the Court ignores Congress' explicit hostility toward the use of written tests as job-qualification requirements; Congress disapproved the CSC's "use of general ability tests which are not aimed at any direct relationship to specific jobs." H.R.Rep. No. 92–238, p. 24 (1971). See S.Rep. No. 92–415, pp. 14–15 (1971). Petitioners concede that Test 21 was devised by the CSC for general use and was not designed to be used by police departments.

Finally, it should be observed that every federal court, except the District Court in this case, presented with proof identical to that offered to validate Test 21 has reached a conclusion directly opposite to that of the Court today. Sound policy considerations support the view that, at a minimum, petitioners should have been required to prove that the police training examinations either measure job-related skills or predict job performance. Where employers try to validate written qualification tests by proving a correlation with written examinations in a training course, there is a substantial danger that people who have good verbal skills will achieve high scores on both tests due to verbal ability, rather than "job-specific ability." As a result, employers could validate any entrance examination that measures only verbal ability by giving another written test that measures verbal ability at the end of a training course. Any contention that the resulting correlation between examination scores would be evidence that the initial test is "job related" is plainly erroneous. It seems to me, however, that the Court's holding in this case can be read as endorsing this dubious proposition. Today's result will prove particularly unfortunate if it is extended to govern Title VII cases.

Accordingly, accepting the Court's assertion that it is necessary to reach the statutory issue, I would hold that petitioners have not met their burden of proof and affirm the judgment of the Court of Appeals.

Notes

1. In Village of Arlington Heights v. Metropolitan Housing Development Corp., 429 U.S. 252, 97 S.Ct. 555, 50 L.Ed.2d 450 (1977), the Court, in an opinion by Mr. Justice Powell, stated:

> *Davis* does not require a plaintiff to prove that the challenged action rested solely on racially discriminatory purposes. Rarely can it be said that a legislative or administrative body operating under a broad mandate made a decision motivated by a single concern, or even that a particular purpose was the "dominant" or "primary" one. In fact, it is because legislators and administrators are properly concerned with balancing numerous competing considerations that courts refrain from reviewing the merits of their decisions, absent a showing of arbitrariness or irrationality. But racial discrimination is not just another competing consideration. When there is proof that a discriminatory purpose has been a motivating factor in the decision, this judicial deference is no longer justified.

> Determining whether invidious discriminatory purpose was a motivating factor demands a sensitive inquiry into such circumstantial and direct evidence of intent as may be available. The impact of the official action—whether it "bears more heavily on one race than another" * * * may provide an important starting point. Sometimes a clear pattern, unexplainable on grounds other than race, emerges from the effect of the state action even when the governing legislation appears neutral on its face. Yick Wo v. Hopkins, 118 U.S. 356, 6 S.Ct. 1064, 30 L.Ed. 220 (1886); Guinn v. United States, 238 U.S. 347, 35 S.Ct. 926, 59 L.Ed. 1340 (1915); Lane v. Wilson, 307 U.S. 268, 59 S.Ct. 872, 83 L.Ed. 1281 (1939); Gomillion v. Lightfoot, 364 U.S. 339, 81 S.Ct. 125, 5 L.Ed.2d 110 (1960). The evidentiary inquiry is then relatively easy. But such cases are rare. Absent a pattern as stark as that in *Gomillion* or *Yick Wo,* impact alone is not determinative, and the Court must look to other evidence.

> The historical background of the decision is one evidentiary source, particularly if it reveals a series of official actions taken for invidious purposes. * * * The specific sequence of events leading up to the challenged decision also may shed some light on the decisionmaker's purpose. * * * Departures from the normal procedural sequence also might afford evidence that improper purposes are playing a role. Substantive departures too may be relevant, particularly if the factors usually considered important by the decisionmaker strongly favor a decision contrary to the one reached.

429 U.S. at 265–267, 97 S.Ct. at 563–564.

2. In Personnel Administrator Of Massachusetts v. Feeney, 442 U.S. 256, 99 S.Ct. 2282, 60 L.Ed.2d 870 (1979), the Court made the following observations in rejecting the claim by a female employee of the State who

challenged a veterans' preference statute on fourteenth amendment equal protection grounds: "Discriminatory intent is simply not amenable to calibration. It either is a factor that has influenced the legislative choice or it is not." 442 U.S. at 277, 99 S.Ct. at 2295 (citation omitted). "Discriminatory purpose * * * implies more than intent as volition or intent as awareness of consequences. * * * It implies that the decisionmaker, in this case a state legislature, selected or reaffirmed a particular course of action at least in part 'because of' not merely 'in spite of' its adverse effects upon an identifiable group." Id. at 279, 99 S.Ct. at 2296 (citations omitted).

2. DISPARATE TREATMENT

(a) Circumstantial Evidence Cases

INTERNATIONAL BROTHERHOOD OF TEAMSTERS v. UNITED STATES

Supreme Court of the United States, 1977.
431 U.S. 324, 97 S.Ct. 1843, 52 L.Ed.2d 396.

[The facts in the case are set out infra at pp. 96–97 and 220–225. Footnote 15 in the case is set out here because of the clear distinction that the Court made between the disparate impact and disparate treatment theories of discrimination].

"Disparate treatment" * * * is the most easily understood type of discrimination. The employer simply treats some people less favorably than others because of their race, color, sex, religion or national origin. Proof of discriminatory motive is critical, although it can in some situations be inferred from the mere fact of differences in treatment. * * * Undoubtedly disparate treatment was the most obvious evil Congress had in mind when it enacted Title VII. See, e.g., 110 Cong.Rec. 13088 (1964) (remarks of Sen. Humphrey) ("What the bill does * * * is simply to make it an illegal practice to use race as a factor in denying employment. It provides that men and women shall be employed on the basis of their qualifications, not as Catholic citizens, not as Protestant citizens, not as Jewish citizens, not as colored citizens, but as citizens of the United States").

Claims of disparate treatment may be distinguished from claims that stress "disparate impact." The latter involve employment practices that are facially neutral in their treatment of different groups but that in fact fall more harshly on one group than another and cannot be justified by business necessity. * * * Proof of discriminatory motive, we have held is not required under a disparate impact theory. Compare, e.g., Griggs v. Duke Power Co., * * * with McDonnell Douglas v. Green, 411 U.S. 792, 802–806. * * * See generally * * * Blumrosen, Strangers in Paradise: Griggs v. Duke Power Co., and the Concept of Employment Discrimination, 71 Mich.L.Rev. 59 (1972). Either theory may, of course, be applied to a particular set of facts.

McDONNELL DOUGLAS CORP. v. GREEN

Supreme Court of the United States, 1973.
411 U.S. 792, 93 S.Ct. 1817, 36 L.Ed.2d 668.

Mr. Justice Powell delivered the opinion of the Court.

The case before us raises significant questions as to the proper order and nature of proof in actions under Title VII of the Civil Rights Act of 1964, 78 Stat. 253, 42 U.S.C. § 2000e et seq.

Petitioner, McDonnell Douglas Corp., is an aerospace and aircraft manufacturer headquartered in St. Louis, Missouri, where it employs over 30,000 people. Respondent, a black citizen of St. Louis, worked for petitioner as a mechanic and laboratory technician from 1956 until August 28, 1964 when he was laid off in the course of a general reduction in petitioner's work force.

Respondent, a long-time activist in the civil rights movement, protested vigorously that his discharge and the general hiring practices of petitioner were racially motivated. As part of this protest, respondent and other members of the Congress on Racial Equality illegally stalled their cars on the main roads leading to petitioner's plant for the purpose of blocking access to it at the time of the morning shift change. The District Judge described the plan for, and respondent's participation in, the "stall-in" as follows:

> [F]ive teams, each consisting of four cars would 'tie up' five main access roads into McDonnell at the time of the morning rush hour. The drivers of the cars were instructed to line up next to each other completely blocking the intersections or roads. The drivers were also instructed to stop their cars, turn off the engines, pull the emergency brake, raise all windows, lock the doors, and remain in their cars until the police arrived. The plan was to have the cars remain in position for one hour.
>
> Acting under the "stall in" plan, plaintiff [respondent in the present action] drove his car onto Brown Road, a McDonnell access road, at approximately 7:00 a.m., at the start of the morning rush hour. Plaintiff was aware of the traffic problems that would result. He stopped his car with the intent to block traffic. The police arrived shortly and requested plaintiff to move his car. He refused to move his car voluntarily. Plaintiff's car was towed away by the police, and he was arrested for obstructing traffic. Plaintiff pleaded guilty to the charge of obstructing traffic and was fined. 318 F.Supp. 846.

On July 2, 1965, a "lock-in" took place wherein a chain and padlock were placed on the front door of a building to prevent the occupants, certain of petitioner's employees, from leaving. Though respondent apparently knew beforehand of the "lock-in," the full extent of his involvement remains uncertain.

Some three weeks following the "lock-in," on July 25, 1965, petitioner publicly advertised for qualified mechanics, respondent's trade, and respondent promptly applied for re-employment. Petitioner turned

down respondent, basing its rejection on respondent's participation in
the "stall-in" and "lock-in." Shortly thereafter, respondent filed a
formal complaint with the Equal Employment Opportunity Commission, claiming that petitioner had refused to rehire him because of his
race and persistent involvement in the civil rights movement, in
violation of §§ 703(a)(1) and 704(a) of the Civil Rights Act of 1964, 42
U.S.C. §§ 2000e–2(a)(1) and 2000e–3(a). The former section generally
prohibits racial discrimination in any employment decision while the
latter forbids discrimination against applicants or employees for attempting to protest or correct allegedly discriminatory conditions of
employment.

The Commission made no finding on respondent's allegation of
racial bias under § 703(a)(1), but it did find reasonable cause to believe
petitioner had violated § 704(a) by refusing to rehire respondent because of his civil rights activity. After the Commission unsuccessfully
attempted to conciliate the dispute, it advised respondent in March
1968, of his right to institute a civil action in federal court within 30
days.

On April 15, 1968, respondent brought the present action, claiming
initially a violation of § 704(a) and, in an amended complaint, a
violation of § 703(a)(1) as well. The District Court, 299 F.Supp. 1100,
dismissed the latter claim of racial discrimination in petitioner's hiring
procedures on the ground that the Commission had failed to make a
determination of reasonable cause to believe that a violation of that
section had been committed. The District Court also found that petitioner's refusal to rehire respondent was based solely on his participation in the illegal demonstrations and not on his legitimate civil rights
activities. The court concluded that nothing in Title VII or § 704
protected "such activity as employed by the plaintiff in the 'stall in' and
'lock in' demonstrations." 318 F.Supp., at 850.

On appeal, the Eighth Circuit affirmed that unlawful protests were
not protected activities under § 704(a), but reversed the dismissal of
respondent's § 703(a)(1) claim relating to racially discriminatory hiring
practices, holding that a prior Commission determination of reasonable
cause was not a jurisdictional prerequisite to raising a claim under ,hat
section in federal court. The court ordered the case remanded for trial
of respondent's claim under § 703(a)(1).

In remanding, the Court of Appeals attempted to set forth standards to govern the consideration of respondent's claim. The majority
noted that respondent had established a prima facie case of racial
discrimination; that petitioner's refusal to rehire respondent rested on
"subjective" criteria which carried little weight in rebutting charges of
discrimination; that, though respondent's participation in the unlawful
demonstrations might indicate a lack of a responsible attitude toward
performing work for that employer, respondent should be given the
opportunity to demonstrate that petitioner's reasons for refusing to
rehire him were mere pretext. In order to clarify the standards

governing the disposition of an action challenging employment discrimination, we granted certiorari, 409 U.S. 1036, 93 S.Ct. 522, 34 L.Ed.2d 485 (1972).

I

We agree with the Court of Appeals that absence of a Commission finding of reasonable cause cannot bar suit under an appropriate section of Title VII and that the District Judge erred in dismissing respondent's claim of racial discrimination under § 703(a)(1). Respondent satisfied the jurisdictional prerequisites to a federal action (i) by filing timely charges of employment discrimination with the Commission and (ii) by receiving and acting upon the Commission's statutory notice of the right to sue, 42 U.S.C. §§ 2000e–5(a) and 2000e–5(e). The Act does not restrict a complainant's right to sue to those charges as to which the Commission has made findings of reasonable cause, and we will not engraft on the statute a requirement which may inhibit the review of claims of employment discrimination in the federal courts. The Commission itself does not consider the absence of a "reasonable cause" determination as providing employer immunity from similar charges in a federal court, 29 CFR § 1601.30, and the courts of appeal have held that, in view of the large volume of complaints before the Commission and the nonadversary character of many of its proceedings, "court actions under Title VII are de novo proceedings and ∗ ∗ ∗ a Commission 'no reasonable cause' finding does not bar a lawsuit in the case." Robinson v. Lorillard Corp., 444 F.2d 791, 800 (CA4 1971); Beverly v. Lone Star Lead Construction Corp., 437 F.2d 1136 (CA5 1971); Flowers v. Local 6, Laborers International Union of North America, 431 F.2d 205 (CA7 1970); Fekete v. United States Steel Corp., 424 F.2d 331 (CA 3 1970).

Petitioner argues, as it did below, that respondent sustained no prejudice from the trial court's erroneous ruling because in fact the issue of racial discrimination in the refusal to re-employ "was tried thoroughly" in a trial lasting four days with "at least 80%" of the questions relating to the issue of "race." Petitioner, therefore, requests that the judgment below be vacated and the cause remanded with instructions that the judgment of the District Court be affirmed. We cannot agree that the dismissal of respondent's § 703(a)(1) claim was harmless error. It is not clear that the District Court's findings as to respondent's § 704(a) contentions involved the identical issues raised by his claim under § 703(a)(1). The former section relates solely to discrimination against an applicant or employee on account of his participation in legitimate civil rights activities or protests, while the latter section deals with the broader and centrally important question under the Act of whether for any reason, a racially discriminatory employment decision has been made. Moreover, respondent should have been accorded the right to prepare his case and plan the strategy of trial with the knowledge that the § 703(a)(1) cause of action was properly before the District Court. Accordingly, we remand the case for trial of respondent's claim of racial discrimination consistent with the views set forth below.

II

The critical issue before us concerns the order and allocation of proof in a private, non-class action challenging employment discrimination. The language of Title VII makes plain the purpose of Congress to assure equality of employment opportunities and to eliminate those discriminatory practices and devices which have fostered racially stratified job environments to the disadvantage of minority citizens. Griggs v. Duke Power Co., 401 U.S. 424, 429, 91 S.Ct. 849, 852, 28 L.Ed.2d 158 (1971); Castro v. Beecher, 459 F.2d 725 (CA1 1972); Chance v. Board of Examiners, 458 F.2d 1167 (CA2 1972); Quarles v. Philip Morris, Inc., 279 F.Supp. 505 (ED Va.1968). As noted in *Griggs*, supra:

> Congress did not intend by Title VII, however, to guarantee a job to every person regardless of qualifications. In short, the Act does not command that any person be hired simply because he was formerly the subject of discrimination, or because he is a member of a minority group. Discriminatory preference for any group, minority or majority, is precisely and only what Congress has proscribed. What is required by Congress is the removal of artificial, arbitrary, and unnecessary barriers to employment when the barriers operate invidiously to discriminate on the basis of racial or other impermissible classification. Id., 401 U.S., at 430–431, 91 S.Ct., at 853.

There are societal as well as personal interests on both sides of this equation. The broad, overriding interest, shared by employer, employee, and consumer, is efficient and trustworthy workmanship assured through fair and racially neutral employment and personnel decisions. In the implementation of such decisions, it is abundantly clear that Title VII tolerates no racial discrimination, subtle or otherwise.

In this case respondent, the complainant below, charges that he was denied employment "because of his involvement in civil rights activities" and "because of his race and color." [11] Petitioner denied discrimination of any kind, asserting that its failure to re-employ respondent was based upon and justified by his participation in the unlawful conduct against it. Thus, the issue at the trial on remand is framed by those opposing factual contentions. The two opinions of the Court of Appeals and the several opinions of the three judges of that court attempted, with a notable lack of harmony, to state the applicable rules as to burden of proof and how this shifts upon the making of a prima facie case. We now address this problem.

The complainant in a Title VII trial must carry the initial burden under the statute of establishing a prima facie case of racial discrimina-

---

11. The respondent initially charged petitioner in his complaint filed April 15, 1968, with discrimination because of his "involvement in civil rights activities." App. 7, 8. In his amended complaint, filed March 20, 1969, plaintiff broadened his charge to include denial of employment because of race in violation of § 703(a)(1). App. 27.

tion. This may be done by showing (i) that he belongs to a racial minority; (ii) that he applied and was qualified for a job for which the employer was seeking applicants; (iii) that, despite his qualifications, he was rejected; and (iv) that, after his rejection, the position remained open and the employer continued to seek applicants from persons of complainant's qualifications.[13] In the instant case, we agree with the Court of Appeals that respondent proved a prima facie case. 463 F.2d 337, 353. Petitioner sought mechanics, respondent's trade, and continued to do so after respondent's rejection. Petitioner, moreover, does not dispute respondent's qualifications[14] and acknowledges that his past work performance in petitioner's employ was "satisfactory."

The burden then must shift to the employer to articulate some legitimate, nondiscriminatory reason for the employee's rejection. We need not attempt in the instant case to detail every matter which fairly could be recognized as a reasonable basis for a refusal to hire. Here petitioner has assigned respondent's participation in unlawful conduct against it as the cause for his rejection. We think that this suffices to discharge petitioner's burden of proof at this stage and to meet respondent's prima facie case of discrimination.

The Court of Appeals intimated, however, that petitioner's stated reason for refusing to rehire respondent was a "subjective" rather than objective criterion which "carr[ies] little weight in rebutting charges of discrimination," 463 F.2d, at 343. This was among the statements which caused the dissenting judge to read the opinion as taking "the position that such unlawful acts as Green committed against McDonnell would not legally entitle McDonnell to refuse to hire him, even though no racial motivation was involved * * *." Id., at 355. Regardless of whether this was the intended import of the opinion, we think the court below seriously underestimated the rebuttal weight to which petitioner's reasons were entitled. Respondent admittedly had taken part in a carefully planned "stall-in," designed to tie up access to and egress from petitioner's plant at a peak traffic hour.[16] Nothing in Title VII compels an employer to absolve and rehire one who has engaged in such deliberate, unlawful activity against it.[17] In uphold-

13. The facts necessarily will vary in Title VII cases, and the specification above of the prima facie proof required from respondent is not necessarily applicable in every respect to differing factual situations.

14. We note that the issue of what may properly be used to test qualifications for employment is not present in this case. Where employers have instituted employment tests and qualifications with an exclusionary effect on minority applicants, such requirements must be "shown to bear a demonstrable relationship to successful performance of the jobs" for which they were used, Griggs v. Duke Power Co., 401 U.S. 424, 431, 91 S.Ct. 849, 853, 28 L.Ed.2d

158 (1971). Castro v. Beecher, 459 F.2d 725 (CA1 1972); Chance v. Board of Examiners, 458 F.2d 1167 (CA2 1972).

16. The trial judge noted that no personal injury or property damage resulted from the "stall-in" due "solely to the fact that law enforcement officials had obtained notice in advance of plaintiff's [here respondent's] demonstration and were at the scene to remove plaintiff's car from the highway." 318 F.Supp. 846, 851.

17. The unlawful activity in this case was directed specifically against petitioner. We need not consider or decide here whether, or under what circumstances, unlawful activity not directed against the

ing, under the National Labor Relations Act, the discharge of employees who had seized and forcibly retained an employer's factory buildings in an illegal sit-down strike, the Court noted pertinently:

> We are unable to conclude that Congress intended to compel employers to retain persons in their employ regardless of their unlawful conduct,—to invest those who go on strike with an immunity from discharge for acts of trespass or violence against the employer's property * * * Apart from the question of the constitutional validity of an enactment of that sort, it is enough to say that such a legislative intention should be found in some definite and unmistakable expression. NLRB v. Fansteel Corp., 306 U.S. 240, 255, 59 S.Ct. 490, 496, 83 L.Ed. 627 (1939).

Petitioner's reason for rejection thus suffices to meet the prima facie case, but the inquiry must not end here. While Title VII does not, without more, compel rehiring of respondent, neither does it permit petitioner to use respondent's conduct as a pretext for the sort of discrimination prohibited by § 703(a)(1). On remand, respondent must, as the Court of Appeals recognized, be afforded a fair opportunity to show that petitioner's stated reason for respondent's rejection was in fact pretext. Especially relevant to such a showing would be evidence that white employees involved in acts against petitioner of comparable seriousness to the "stall-in" were nevertheless retained or rehired. Petitioner may justifiably refuse to rehire one who was engaged in unlawful, disruptive acts against it, but only if this criterion is applied alike to members of all races.

Other evidence that may be relevant to any showing of pretext includes facts as to the petitioner's treatment of respondent during his prior term of employment; petitioner's reaction, if any, to respondent's legitimate civil rights activities; and petitioner's general policy and practice with respect to minority employment.[18] On the latter point, statistics as to petitioner's employment policy and practice may be helpful to a determination of whether petitioner's refusal to rehire respondent in this case conformed to a general pattern of discrimination against blacks. Jones v. Lee Way Motor Freight, Inc., 431 F.2d 245 (CA10 1970); Blumrosen, Strangers in Paradise: Griggs v. Duke Power Co., and the Concept of Employment Discrimination, 71 Mich.L.Rev. 59, 91–94 (1972).[19] In short, on the retrial respondent must be given a full

particular employer may be a legitimate justification for refusing to hire.

18. We are aware that some of the above factors were, indeed, considered by the District Judge in finding under § 704(a), that "defendant's [here petitioner's] reasons for refusing to rehire the plaintiff were motivated solely and simply by the plaintiff's participation in the 'stall in' and 'lock in' demonstrations." 318 F.Supp., at 850. We do not intimate that this finding must be overturned after consideration on remand of respondent's § 703(a)(1) claim. We do, however, insist that respondent under § 703(a)(1) must be given a full and fair opportunity to demonstrate by competent evidence that whatever the stated reasons for his rejection, the decision was in reality racially premised.

19. The District Court may, for example, determine, after reasonable discovery that "the [racial] composition of defendant's labor force is itself reflective of restrictive or exclusionary practices." See Blumrosen, supra, at 92. We caution that such general determinations, while helpful,

and fair opportunity to demonstrate by competent evidence that the presumptively valid reasons for his rejection were in fact a coverup for a racially discriminatory decision.

The court below appeared to rely upon Griggs v. Duke Power Co., supra, in which the Court stated: "If an employment practice which operates to exclude Negroes cannot be shown to be related to job performance, the practice is prohibited." 401 U.S., at 431, 91 S.Ct., at 853, 28 L.Ed.2d 158. But *Griggs* differs from the instant case in important respects. It dealt with standardized testing devices which, however neutral on their face, operated to exclude many blacks who were capable of performing effectively in the desired positions. *Griggs* was rightly concerned that childhood deficiencies in the education and background of minority citizens, resulting from forces beyond their control, not be allowed to work a cumulative and invidious burden on such citizens for the remainder of their lives. Id., at 430, 91 S.Ct., at 853. Respondent, however, appears in different clothing. He had engaged in a seriously disruptive act against the very one from whom he now seeks employment. And petitioner does not seek his exclusion on the basis of a testing device which overstates what is necessary for competent performance, or through some sweeping disqualification of all those with any past record of unlawful behavior, however remote, insubstantial, or unrelated to applicant's personal qualifications as an employee. Petitioner assertedly rejected respondent for unlawful conduct against it and, in the absence of proof of pretext or discriminatory application of such a reason, this cannot be thought the kind of "artificial, arbitrary, and unnecessary barriers to employment" which the Court found to be the intention of Congress to remove. Id., at 431, 91 S.Ct., at 853.[21]

III

In sum, respondent should have been allowed to pursue his claim under § 703(a)(1). If the evidence on retrial is substantially in accord with that before us in this case, we think that respondent carried his burden of establishing a prima facie case of racial discrimination and that petitioner successfully rebutted that case. But this does not end the matter. On retrial, respondent must be afforded a fair opportunity

may not be in and of themselves controlling as to an individualized hiring decision, particularly in the presence of an otherwise justifiable reason for refusing to rehire. See generally United States v. Bethlehem Steel Corp., 312 F.Supp. 977, 992 (WDNY 1970), order modified, 446 F.2d 652 (CA2 1971). Blumrosen, supra, n. 19, at 93.

21. It is, of course, a predictive evaluation, resistant to empirical proof, whether "an applicant's past participation in unlawful conduct directed at his prospective employer might indicate the applicant's lack of a responsible attitude toward per-

forming work for that employer." 463 F.2d, at 353. But in this case, given the seriousness and harmful potential of respondent's participation in the "stall-in" and the accompanying inconvenience to other employees, it cannot be said that petitioner's refusal to employ lacked a rational and neutral business justification. As the Court has noted elsewhere:

"Past conduct may well relate to present fitness; past loyalty may have a reasonable relationship to present and future trust." Garner v. Board of Public Works of Los Angeles, 341 U.S. 716, 720, 71 S.Ct. 909, 912, 95 L.Ed. 1317 (1951).

to demonstrate that petitioner's assigned reason for refusing to re-employ was a pretext or discriminatory in its application. If the District Judge so finds, he must order a prompt and appropriate remedy. In the absence of such a finding, petitioner's refusal to rehire must stand.

The cause is hereby remanded to the District Court for reconsideration in accordance with this opinion.

So ordered.

Remanded.

McDONALD v. SANTE FE TRAIL TRANSP. CO.

Supreme Court of the United States (1976).
427 U.S. 273, 96 S.Ct. 2574, 49 L.Ed.2d 493.

MR. JUSTICE MARSHALL delivered the opinion of the Court.

Petitioners, L.N. McDonald and Raymond L. Laird, brought this action in the United States District Court for the Southern District of Texas seeking relief against Santa Fe Trail Transportation Co. (Santa Fe) and International Brotherhood of Teamsters Local 988 (Local 988), which represented Santa Fe's Houston employees, for alleged violations of the Civil Rights Act of 1866, 42 U.S.C. § 1981, and of Title VII of the Civil Rights Act of 1964, 42 U.S.C. § 2000e et seq., in connection with their discharge from Santa Fe's employment. The District Court dismissed the complaint on the pleadings. The Court of Appeals for the Fifth Circuit affirmed. In determining whether the decisions of these courts were correct, we must decide, first, whether a complaint alleging that white employees charged with misappropriating property from their employer were dismissed from employment, while a black employee similarly charged was not dismissed, states a claim under Title VII.

*   *   *

I

Because the District Court dismissed this case on the pleadings, we take as true the material facts alleged in petitioners' complaint. Hospital Bldg. Co. v. Trustees of Rex Hospital, 425 U.S. 738, 740, 96 S.Ct. 1848, 1850, 48 L.Ed.2d 338 (1976). On September 26, 1970, petitioners, both white, and Charles Jackson, a Negro employee of Santa Fe, were jointly and severally charged with misappropriating 60 one-gallon cans of antifreeze which was part of a shipment Santa Fe was carrying for one of its customers. Six days later, petitioners were fired by Santa Fe, while Jackson was retained. A grievance was promptly filed with Local 988, pursuant to the collective-bargaining agreement between the two respondents, but grievance proceedings secured no relief. The following April, complaints were filed with the Equal Employment Opportunity Commission (EEOC) charging that Santa Fe had discriminated against both petitioners on the basis of their race in firing them, and that Local 988 had discriminated against McDonald on the basis of his race in failing properly to represent his interests in the grievance proceedings, all in violation of Title VII of the Civil Rights Act of 1964. Agency process proved equally unavailing for petitioners, however, and the EEOC notified them in July 1971 of their right under the Act to initiate a civil action in district court within 30 days. This suit followed, petitioners joining their § 1981 claim to their Title VII allegations.

* * *

We granted certiorari. 423 U.S. 923, 96 S.Ct. 264, 46 L.Ed.2d 248 (1975). We reverse.

II

Title VII of the Civil Rights Act of 1964 prohibits the discharge of "any individual" because of "such individual's race," § 703(a)(1), 42 U.S.C. § 2000e–2(a)(1). Its terms are not limited to discrimination against members of any particular race. Thus, although we were not there confronted with racial discrimination against whites, we described the Act in Griggs v. Duke Power Co., 401 U.S. 424, 431, 91 S.Ct. 849, 853, 28 L.Ed.2d 158 (1971), as prohibiting "[d]iscriminatory preference for *any* [racial] group, *minority or majority* " (emphasis added).[6] Similarly the EEOC, whose interpretations are entitled to great deference, id., at 433–434, 91 S.Ct., at 854–855, has consistently interpreted Title VII to proscribe racial discrimination in private employment against whites on the same terms as racial discrimination against non-whites, holding that to proceed otherwise would

> constitute a derogation of the Commission's Congressional mandate to eliminate all practices which operate to disadvantage the employment opportunities of any group protected by Title VII, including Caucasians. EEOC Decision No. 74–31, 7 FEP 1326, 1328, CCH EEOC Decisions ¶ 6404, p. 4084 (1973).

This conclusion is in accord with uncontradicted legislative history to the effect that Title VII was intended to "cover white men and white women and all Americans," 110 Cong.Rec. 2578 (1964) (remarks of Rep. Celler), and create an "obligation not to discriminate against whites," id., at 7218 (memorandum of Sen. Clark). See also id., at 7213 (memorandum of Sens. Clark and Case); id., at 8912 (remarks of Sen. Williams). We therefore hold today that Title VII prohibits racial discrimi-

---

6. Our discussion in McDonnell Douglas Corp. v. Green, 411 U.S. 792, 802, 93 S.Ct. 1817, 1824, 36 L.Ed.2d 596 (1973), of the means by which a Title VII litigant might make out a prima facie case of racial discrimination is not contrary. There we said that a complainant could establish a prima facie case by showing:

"(i) that he belongs to a racial minority; (ii) that he applied and was qualified for a job for which the employer was seeking applicants; (iii) that, despite his qualifications, he was rejected; and (iv) that, after his rejection, the position remained open and the employer continued to seek applicants from persons of complainant's qualifications." (Footnote omitted.) As we particularly noted, however, this "specification * * * of the prima facie proof required * * * is not necessarily applicable in every respect to differing factual situations." Id., at 802 n. 13. Requirement (i) of this sample pattern of proof was set out only to demonstrate how the racial character of the discrimination could be established in the most common sort of case, and not as an indication of any substantive limitation of Title VII's prohibition of racial discrimination.

nation against the white petitioners in this case upon the same standards as would be applicable were they Negroes and Jackson white.[8]

Respondents contend that, even though generally applicable to white persons, Title VII affords petitioners no protection in this case, because their dismissal was based upon their commission of a serious criminal offense against their employer. We think this argument is foreclosed by our decision in McDonnell Douglas Corp. v. Green, 411 U.S. 792, 93 S.Ct. 1817, 36 L.Ed.2d 668 (1973).

In *McDonnell Douglas,* a laid-off employee took part in an illegal "stall-in" designed to block traffic into his former employer's plant, and was arrested, convicted, and fined for obstructing traffic. At a later date, the former employee applied for an open position with the company, for which he was apparently otherwise qualified, but the employer turned down the application, assertedly because of the former employee's illegal activities against it. Charging that he was denied reemployment because he was a Negro, a claim the company denied, the former employee sued under Title VII. Reviewing the case on certiorari, we concluded that the rejected employee had adequately stated a claim under Title VII. See id., 411 U.S. at 801, 93 S.Ct. at 1823. Although agreeing with the employer that "[n]othing in Title VII compels an employer to absolve and rehire one who has engaged in such deliberate, unlawful activity against it," id., 411 U.S. at 803, 93 S.Ct. at 1825, we also recognized:

> [T]he inquiry must not end here. While Title VII does not, without more, compel rehiring of [the former employee], neither does it permit [the employer] to use [the former employee's] conduct as a pretext for the sort of discrimination prohibited by [the Act]. On remand, [the former employee] must * * * be afforded a fair opportunity to show that [the employer's] stated reason for [the former employee's] rejection was in fact pretext. Especially relevant to such a showing would be evidence that white employees involved in acts against [the employer] of comparable seriousness to the 'stall-in' were nevertheless retained or rehired. [The employer] may justifiably refuse to rehire one who was engaged in unlawful, disruptive acts against it, but only if

---

8. Local 988 explicitly concedes that it makes no difference that petitioners are white and Jackson Negro, rather than the other way around. Brief for Respondent Local 988, p. 7. Santa Fe, while conceding that "across-the-board discrimination in favor of minorities could never be condoned consistent with Title VII," contends nevertheless that "such discrimination * * * in isolated cases which cannot reasonably be said to burden whites as a class unduly," such as is alleged here, "may be acceptable." Brief for Respondent Santa Fe 20 (emphasis omitted). We cannot agree. There is no exception in the terms of the Act for isolated cases; on the contrary, "Title VII tolerates *no* racial discrimination, subtle or otherwise." McDonnell Douglas Corp. v. Green, supra, 411 U.S., at 801, 93 S.Ct. at 1824 (emphasis added).

Santa Fe disclaims that the actions challenged here were any part of an affirmative action program, see Brief for Respondent Santa Fe 19 n. 5, and we emphasize that we do not consider here the permissibility of such a program, whether judicially required or otherwise prompted. Cf. Brief for United States as *Amicus Curiae* 7 n. 5.

this criterion is applied alike to members of all races. Id., 411 U.S. at 804, 93 S.Ct. at 1825.[10]

We find this case indistinguishable from *McDonnell Douglas.* Fairly read, the complaint asserted that petitioners were discharged for their alleged participation in a misappropriation of cargo entrusted to Santa Fe, but that a fellow employee, likewise implicated, was not so disciplined, and that the reason for the discrepancy in discipline was that the favored employee is Negro while petitioners are white. See Conley v. Gibson, 355 U.S. 41, 45–46, 78 S.Ct. 99, 101–102, 2 L.Ed.2d 80 (1957).[11] While Santa Fe may decide that participation in a theft of cargo may render an employee unqualified for employment, this criterion must be "applied, alike to members of all races," and Title VII is violated if, as petitioners alleged, it was not.

We cannot accept respondents' argument that the principles of *McDonnell Douglas* are inapplicable where the discharge was based, as petitioners' complaint admitted, on participation in serious misconduct or crime directed against the employer. The Act prohibits *all* racial discrimination in employment, without exception for any group of particular employees, and while crime or other misconduct may be a legitimate basis for discharge, it is hardly one for racial discrimination. Indeed the Title VII plaintiff in *McDonnell Douglas* had been convicted for a nontrivial offense against his former employer. It may be that theft of property entrusted to an employer for carriage is a more compelling basis for discharge than obstruction of an employer's traffic arteries, but this does not diminish the illogic in retaining guilty employees of one color while discharging those of another color.

At this stage of the litigation the claim against Local 988 must go with the claim against Santa Fe, for in substance the complaint alleges that the union shirked its duty properly to represent McDonald, and instead "acquiesced and/or joined in" Santa Fe's alleged racial discrimination against him. Local 988 argues that as a matter of law it should

---

10. The use of the term "pretext" in this context does not mean, of course, that the Title VII plaintiff must show that he would have in any event been rejected or discharged solely on the basis of his race, without regard to the alleged deficiencies; as the closing sentence to the quoted passage makes clear, no more is required to be shown than that race was a "but for" cause. See also Albemarle Paper Co. v. Moody, 422 U.S. 405, 425, 95 S.Ct. 2362, 2375, 45 L.Ed.2d 280 (1975).

11. Santa Fe contends that petitioners were required to plead with "particularity" the degree of similarity between their culpability in the alleged theft and the involvement of the favored coemployee, Jackson. This assertion, apparently not made below, too narrowly constricts the role of the pleadings. Significantly, respondents themselves declined to plead any dissimi-

larities in the alleged misconduct of Jackson and petitioners, and did not amend their pleadings even after an interim order of the District Court indicated it regarded petitioners' allegations of racial discrimination as sufficient to raise the legal problem of dissimilar employment discipline of "equally guilty" employees of different races. App. 94. Of course, precise equivalence in culpability between employees is not the ultimate question: as we indicated in *McDonnell Douglas,* an allegation that other "employees involved in acts against [the employer] of *comparable seriousness* * * * were nevertheless retained * * *" is adequate to plead an inferential case that the employer's reliance on his discharged employee's misconduct as grounds for terminating him was merely a pretext. 411 U.S., at 804, 93 S.Ct., at 1825 (emphasis added).

not be subject to liability under Title VII in a situation, such as this, where some but not all culpable employees are ultimately discharged on account of joint misconduct, because in representing all the affected employees in their relations with the employer, the union may necessarily have to compromise by securing retention of only some. We reject the argument. The same reasons which prohibit an employer from discriminating on the basis of race among the culpable employees apply equally to the union; and whatever factors the mechanisms of compromise may legitimately take into account in mitigating discipline of some employees, under Title VII race may not be among them.

Thus, we conclude that the District Court erred in dismissing both petitioners' Title VII claims against Santa Fe, and petitioner McDonald's Title VII claim against Local 988.

FURNCO CONSTRUCTION CORP. v. WATERS

Supreme Court of the United States, 1978. •
438 U.S. 567, 98 S.Ct. 2943, 57 L.Ed.2d 957.

MR. JUSTICE REHNQUIST delivered the opinion of the Court.

Respondents are three black bricklayers who sought employment with petitioner Furnco Construction Corp. Two of the three were never offered employment. The third was employed only long after he initially applied. Upon adverse findings entered after a bench trial, the District Court for the Northern District of Illinois held that respondents had not proved a claim under either the "disparate treatment" theory of McDonnell Douglas Corp. v. Green, 411 U.S. 792, 93 S.Ct. 1817, 36 L.Ed.2d 668 (1973), or the "disparate impact" theory of Griggs v. Duke Power Co., 401 U.S. 424, 91 S.Ct. 849, 28 L.Ed.2d 158 (1971). The Court of Appeals for the Seventh Circuit, concluding that under *McDonnell Douglas* respondents had made out a prima facie case which had not been effectively rebutted, reversed the judgment of the District Court. 551 F.2d 1085 (1977). We granted certiorari to consider important questions raised by this case regarding the exact scope of the prima facie case under *McDonnell Douglas* and the nature of the evidence necessary to rebut such a case. 434 U.S. 996, 98 S.Ct. 632, 54 L.Ed.2d 490 (1977). Having concluded that the Court of Appeals erred in its treatment of the latter question, we reverse and remand to that court for further proceedings consistent with this opinion.

I

A few facts in this case are not in serious dispute. Petitioner Furnco, an employer within the meaning of §§ 701(b) and (h) of Title VII of the 1964 Civil Rights Act, 42 U.S.C. §§ 2000e(b) and (h) (1970 ed., Supp. V), specializes in refractory installation in steel mills and, more particularly, the rehabilitation or relining of blast furnaces with what is called in the trade "firebrick." Furnco does not, however, maintain a permanent force of bricklayers. Rather, it hires a superintendent for a specific job and then delegates to him the task of securing a competent work force. In August 1971, Furnco contracted with Interlake, Inc., to reline one of its blast furnaces. Joseph Dacies, who had been a job superintendent for Furnco since 1965, was placed in charge of the job and given the attendant hiring responsibilities. He did not accept applications at the jobsite, but instead hired only persons whom he knew to be experienced and competent in this type of work or persons who had been recommended to him as similarly skilled. He hired his first four bricklayers, all of whom were white, on two successive days in August, the 26th and 27th, and two in September, the 7th and 8th. On September 9 he hired the first black bricklayer. By September 13, he had hired 8 more bricklayers, 1 of whom was black; by September 17, 7 more had been employed, another of whom was black; and by September 23, 17 more were on the payroll, again with 1 black included in that number. From October 12 to 18, he hired 6 bricklayers, all of whom were black, including respondent Smith, who had worked for Dacies previously and had applied at the jobsite somewhat earlier. Respondents Samuels and Nemhard were not hired, though they were fully qualified and had also attempted to secure employment by appearing at the jobsite gate. Out of the total of 1,819 man-days worked on the Interlake job, 242, or 13.3%, were worked by black bricklayers.

Many of the remaining facts found by the District Court and the inferences to be drawn therefrom are in some dispute between the parties, but none was expressly found by the Court of Appeals to be clearly erroneous. The District Court elaborated at some length as to the "critical" necessity of insuring that only experienced and highly qualified fire-bricklayers were employed. Improper or untimely work would result in substantial losses both to Interlake, which was forced to shut down its furnace and lay off employees during the relining job, and to Furnco, which was paid for this work at a fixed price and for a fixed time period. In addition, not only might shoddy work slow this work process down, but it also might necessitate costly future maintenance work with its attendant loss of production and employee layoffs; diminish Furnco's reputation and ability to secure similar work in the future; and perhaps even create serious safety hazards, leading to explosions and the like. * * * These considerations justified Furnco's refusal to engage in on-the-job training or to hire at the gate, a hiring process which would not provide an adequate method of matching qualified applications to job requirements and assuring that the applicants are sufficiently skilled and capable. * * * Furthermore, there was no evidence that these policies and practices were a pretext to exclude black bricklayers or were otherwise illegitimate or had a disproportionate impact or effect on black bricklayers. * * * From late 1969 through late 1973, 5.7% of the bricklayers in the relevant labor force were minority group members, see 41 CFR § 60–11 et seq. (1977),[2] while, as mentioned before, 13.3% of the man-days on Furnco's Interlake job were worked by black bricklayers.

2. Respondents attempted to introduce a study conducted in late 1973 by the local union which matched members' names and race in an effort to show what percentage

Because of the above considerations and following the established practice in the industry, most of the firebricklayers hired by Dacies were persons known by him to be experienced and competent in this type of work. The others were hired after being recommended as skilled in this type of work by his general foreman, an employee (a black), another Furnco superintendent in the area, and Furnco's General Manager John Wright. Wright had not only instructed Dacies to employ, as far as possible, at least 16% black bricklayers, a policy due to Furnco's self-imposed affirmative-action plan to insure that black bricklayers were employed by Furnco in Cook County in numbers substantially in excess of their percentage in the local union,[3] but he had also recommended, in an effort to show good faith, that Dacies hire several specific bricklayers, who had previously filed a discrimination suit against Furnco, negotiations for the settlement of which had only recently broken down, see n. 3, supra.

From these factual findings, the District Court concluded that respondents had failed to make out a Title VII claim under the doctrine of Griggs v. Duke Power Co., 401 U.S. 424, 91 S.Ct. 849, 28 L.Ed.2d 158 (1971). Furnco's policy of not hiring at the gate was racially neutral on its face and there was no showing that it had a disproportionate impact or effect. * * * It also held that respondents had failed to prove a case of discrimination under McDonnell Douglas Corp. v. Green, 411 U.S. 792, 93 S.Ct. 1817, 36 L.Ed.2d 668 (1973). * * * It is not entirely clear whether the court thought respondents had failed to make out a prima facie case of discrimination under *McDonnell Douglas,* * * * but the court left no doubt that it thought Furnco's hiring practices and policies were justified as a "business necessity" in that they were required for the safe and efficient operation of Furnco's business, and were "not used as a pretext to exclude Negroes." Thus, even if a prima facie case had been made out, it had been effectively rebutted. * * *

Not only have Plaintiffs entirely failed to establish that Furnco's employment practices on the Interlake job discriminated against them

---

of the union membership was black. The study concluded that approximately 500 of the 3,800 union members were black. The District Court excluded this evidence because the study had been conducted two years after Furnco completed its job. App. to Pet. for Cert. A16 n. 1. The Court of Appeals thought rejection of this evidence was an abuse of discretion, but in dealing with the merits did not rely on the racial proportions in the labor force, so did not remand the case to permit introduction of that testimony. The Court of Appeals also noted that in any event respondents suffered no prejudice by the court's refusal to admit the study because it would not have demonstrated discrimination. The study showed that 13.7% of the membership of the union was black, while the evidence

demonstrated that 13.3% of the man-days were worked by black bricklayers, Furnco had set a goal of 16% black bricklayers, and 20% of the individuals hired were black. 551 F.2d 1085, 1090 (1977).

3. According to the District Court, this affirmative-action program was initiated by Furnco following a job performed in 1969–1970 from which charges of racial discrimination in hiring were filed by several black bricklayers. These claims are apparently still pending on appeal in the Illinois courts and the merits of a parallel federal action remain to be adjudicated. See App. to Pet. for Cert. A15; Batiste v. Furnco Construction Corp., 503 F.2d 447 (CA7 1974).

on the basis of race or constituted retaliatory conduct but Defendant has proven what it was not required to. By its cross-examination and direct evidence, Furnco has proven beyond all reasonable doubt that it did not engage in either racial discrimination or retaliatory conduct in its employment practices in regard to bricklayers on the Interlake job.

*   *   *

The Court of Appeals reversed, holding that respondents had made out a prima facie case under *McDonnell Douglas,* supra, 411 U.S. at 802, 93 S.Ct. 1817, which Furnco had not effectively rebutted. Because of the "historical inequality of treatment of black workers" [5] and the fact that the record failed to reveal that any white persons had applied at the gate, the Court of Appeals rejected Furnco's argument that discrimination had not been shown because a white appearing at the jobsite would have fared no better than respondents. That court also disagreed with Furnco's contention, which the District Court had adopted, that "the importance of selecting people whose capability had been demonstrated to defendant's brick superintendent is a 'legitimate, non-discriminatory reason' for defendant's refusal to consider plaintiffs." 551 F.2d, at 1088. Instead, the appellate court proceeded to devise what it thought would be an appropriate hiring procedure for Furnco, saying that "[i]t seems to us that there is a reasonable middle ground between immediate hiring decisions on the spot and seeking out employees from among those known to the superintendent." Ibid. This middle course, according to the Court of Appeals, was to take written applications, with inquiry as to qualifications and experience, and then check, evaluate, and compare those claims against the qualifications and experience of other bricklayers with whom the superintendent was already acquainted. We granted certiorari to consider whether the Court of Appeals had gone too far in substituting its own judgment as to proper hiring practices in the case of an employer which claimed the practices it had chosen did not violate Title VII.[6]

---

5. The court stated:

"The historical inequality of treatment of black workers seems to us to establish that it is *prima facie* racial discrimination to refuse to consider the qualifications of a black job seeker before hiring from an approved list containing only the names of white bricklayers. How else will qualified black applicants be able to overcome the racial imbalance in a particular craft, itself the result of past discrimination?" 551 F.2d at 1089.

6. The petition for certiorari set out three questions:

"1. Whether the Seventh Circuit, in reversing the judgment of the District Court, erred in finding as irrelevant to the issue of racial discrimination in hiring, statistics demonstrating that in hiring highly skilled bricklayers, the employer hired Negroes in a percentage far in excess of their statistical presence in the relevant labor force.

"2. Whether a court may find an employer guilty of racial discrimination in employment due to alleged disparate treatment in hiring without a finding of discriminatory intent or motive.

"3. Whether a hiring practice not shown to result in disparate impact or treatment of prospective minority employees and found by the District Court to be justified by business necessity and legitimate business reasons may be found to be racially discriminatory by the Court of Appeals merely because it is subjective and because the Court of Appeals substitutes its judgment for that of the District Court as to what constitutes legitimate business reasons." Pet. for Cert. 2.

II

A

We agree with the Court of Appeals that the proper approach was the analysis contained in *McDonnell Douglas,* supra.[7] We also think the Court of Appeals was justified in concluding that as a matter of law respondents made out a prima facie case of discrimination under *McDonnell Douglas.*

* * *

But *McDonnell Douglas* did make clear that a Title VII plaintiff carries the initial burden of showing actions taken by the employer from which one can infer, if such actions remain unexplained, that it is more likely than not that such actions were "based on a discriminatory criterion illegal under the Act." 431 U.S., at 358, 97 S.Ct., at 1866. See also id., at 335 n. 15, 97 S.Ct., at 1854. And here respondents carried that initial burden by proving they were members of a racial minority; they did everything within their power to apply for employment; Furnco has conceded that they were qualified in every respect for the jobs which were about to be open;[8] they were not offered employment, although Smith later was; and the employer continued to seek persons of similar qualifications.

B

We think the Court of Appeals went awry, however, in apparently equating a prima facie showing under *McDonnell Douglas* with an ultimate finding of fact as to discriminatory refusal to hire under Title VII; the two are quite different and that difference has a direct bearing on the proper resolution of this case. The Court of Appeals, as we read its opinion, thought Furnco's hiring procedures not only must be reasonably related to the achievement of some legitimate purpose, but also must be the method which allows the employer to consider the qualifications of the largest number of minority applicants. We think the imposition of that second requirement simply finds no support either in the nature of the prima facie case or the purpose of Title VII.

The central focus of the inquiry in a case such as this is always whether the employer is treating "some people less favorably than others because of their race, color, religion, sex, or national origin."

7. This case did not involve employment tests, which we dealt with in Griggs v. Duke Power Co., 401 U.S. 424, 91 S.Ct. 849, 28 L.Ed.2d 158 (1971), and in Albemarle Paper Co. v. Moody, 422 U.S. 405, 412–413, 95 S.Ct. 2362, 2369–2370, 45 L.Ed. 2d 280 (1975), or particularized requirements such as the height and weight specifications considered in Dothard v. Rawlinson, 433 U.S. 321, 329, 97 S.Ct. 2720, 2727, 53 L.Ed.2d 786 (1977), and it was not a "pattern or practice" case like Teamsters v. United States, 431 U.S. 324, 358, 97 S.Ct. 1843, 1866, 52 L.Ed.2d 396 (1977).

8. We note that this case does not raise any questions regarding exactly what sort of requirements an employer can impose upon any particular job. Furnco has conceded that for all its purposes respondents were qualified in every sense. Thus, with respect to the *McDonnell Douglas* prima facie case, the only question it places in issue is whether its refusal to consider respondents' applications at the gate was based upon legitimate, nondiscriminatory reasons and therefore permissible.

Teamsters v. United States, supra, at 335 n. 15, 97 S.Ct., at 1854. The method suggested in *McDonnell Douglas* for pursuing this inquiry, however, was never intended to be rigid, mechanized, or ritualistic. Rather, it is merely a sensible, orderly way to evaluate the evidence in light of common experience as it bears on the critical question of discrimination. A prima facie case under *McDonnell Douglas* raises an inference of discrimination only because we presume these acts, if otherwise unexplained, are more likely than not based on the consideration of impermissible factors. See Teamsters v. United States, supra, 431 U.S., at 358 n. 44, 97 S.Ct., at 1866. And we are willing to presume this largely because we know from our experience that more often than not people do not act in a totally arbitrary manner, without any underlying reasons, especially in a business setting. Thus, when all legitimate reasons for rejecting an applicant have been eliminated as possible reasons for the employer's actions, it is more likely than not the employer, who we generally assume acts only with *some* reason, based his decision on an impermissible consideration such as race.

When the prima facie case is understood in the light of the opinion in *McDonnell Douglas*, it is apparent that the burden which shifts to the employer is merely that of proving that he based his employment decision on a legitimate consideration, and not an illegitimate one such as race. To prove that, he need not prove that he pursued the course which would both enable him to achieve his own business goal *and* allow him to consider the *most* employment applications. Title VII prohibits him from having as a goal a work force selected by any proscribed discriminatory practice, but it does not impose a duty to adopt a hiring procedure that maximizes hiring of minority employees. To dispel the adverse inference from a prima facie showing under *McDonnell Douglas*, the employer need only "articulate some legitimate, nondiscriminatory reason for the employee's rejection." 411 U.S., at 802, 93 S.Ct., at 1824.

The dangers of embarking on a course such as that charted by the Court of Appeals here, where the court requires businesses to adopt what it perceives to be the "best" hiring procedures, are nowhere more evident than in the record of this very case. Not only does the record not reveal that the court's suggested hiring procedure would work satisfactorily, but also there is nothing in the record to indicate that it would be any less "haphazard, arbitrary, and subjective" than Furnco's method, which the Court of Appeals criticized as deficient for exactly those reasons. Courts are generally less competent than employers to restructure business practices, and unless mandated to do so by Congress they should not attempt it.

This is not to say, of course, that proof of a justification which is reasonably related to the achievement of some legitimate goal necessarily ends the inquiry. The plaintiff must be given the opportunity to introduce evidence that the proffered justification is merely a pretext for discrimination. And as we noted in *McDonnell Douglas*, supra, at

804–805, 93 S.Ct., at 1825–1826, this evidence might take a variety of forms. But the Court of Appeals, although stating its disagreement with the District Court's conclusion that the employer's hiring practices were a "legitimate, nondiscriminatory reason" for refusing to hire respondents, premised its disagreement on a view which we have discussed and rejected above. It did not conclude that the practices were a pretext for discrimination, but only that different practices would have enabled the employer to at least consider, and perhaps to hire, more minority employees. But courts may not impose such a remedy on an employer at least until a violation of Title VII has been proved, and here none had been under the reasoning of either the District Court or the Court of Appeals.

C

The Court of Appeals was also critical of petitioner's effort to employ statistics in this type of case. While the matter is not free from doubt, it appears that the court thought that once a *McDonnell Douglas* prima facie showing had been made out, statistics of a racially balanced work force were totally irrelevant to the question of motive. See 551 F.2d, at 1089. That would undoubtedly be a correct view of the matter if the *McDonnell Douglas* prima facie showing were the equivalent of an ultimate finding by the trier of fact that the original rejection of the applicant was racially motivated: A racially balanced work force cannot immunize an employer from liability for specific acts of discrimination. As we said in Teamsters v. United States, 431 U.S., at 341–342, 97 S.Ct., at 1857:

> [T]he District Court and the Court of Appeals found upon substantial evidence that the company had engaged in a course of discrimination that continued well after the effective date of Title VII. The company's later changes in its hiring and promotion policies could be of little comfort to the victims of the earlier post-Act discrimination, and could not erase its previous illegal conduct or its obligation to afford relief to those who suffered because of it.

See also Albemarle Paper Co. v. Moody, 422 U.S. 405, 412–413, 95 S.Ct. 2362, 2369–2370, 45 L.Ed.2d 280 (1975). It is clear beyond cavil that the obligation imposed by Title VII is to provide an equal opportunity for *each* applicant regardless of race, without regard to whether members of the applicant's race are already proportionately represented in the work force. See Griggs v. Duke Power Co., 401 U.S., at 430, 91 S.Ct., at 853; McDonald v. Santa Fe Trail Transportation Co., 427 U.S. 273, 279, 96 S.Ct. 2574, 2578, 49 L.Ed.2d 493 (1976).

A *McDonnell Douglas* prima facie showing is not the equivalent of a factual finding of discrimination, however. Rather, it is simply proof of actions taken by the employer from which we infer discriminatory animus because experience has proved that in the absence of any other explanation it is more likely than not that those actions were bottomed on impermissible considerations. When the prima facie showing is understood in this manner, the employer must be allowed some latitude to introduce evidence which bears on his motive. Proof that his work force was racially balanced or that it contained a disproportionately high percentage of minority employees is not wholly irrelevant on the issue of intent when that issue is yet to be decided. We cannot say that such proof would have absolutely no probative value in determining whether the otherwise unexplained rejection of the minority applicants was discriminatorily motivated. Thus, although we agree with the Court of Appeals that in this case such proof neither was nor could have been sufficient to *conclusively* demonstrate that Furnco's actions were not discriminatorily motivated, the District Court was entitled to *consider* the racial mix of the work force when trying to make the determination as to motivation. The Court of Appeals should likewise give similar consideration to the proffered statistical proof in any further proceedings in this case.

III

The parties also press upon the Court a large number of alternative theories of liability and defense, none of which were directly addressed by the Court of Appeals as we read its opinion. Given the present posture of this case, however, we think those matters which are still preserved for review are best decided by the Court of Appeals in the first instance. Accordingly, we declined to address them as an original matter here. The judgment of the Court of Appeals is reversed, and the case is remanded for further proceedings consistent with this opinion.

It is so ordered.

Mr. Justice Marshall, with whom Mr. Justice Brennan joins, concurring in part and dissenting in part.

* * *

There is nothing in today's opinion that is inconsistent with this approach or with our prior decisions. I must dissent, however, from the Court's apparent decision, see ante, at 2948, to foreclose on remand further litigation on the *Griggs* question of whether petitioner's hiring practices had a disparate impact. Respondents claim that petitioner's practice of hiring from a list of those who had previously worked for the foreman foreclosed Negroes from consideration for the vast majority of jobs. Although the foreman also hired a considerable number of Negroes through other methods, respondents assert that the use of other methods to augment the representation of Negroes in the work force does not answer whether the primary hiring practice is discriminatory.

It is clear that an employer cannot be relieved of responsibility for past discriminatory practices merely by undertaking affirmative action to obtain proportional representation in his work force. As the Court said in *Teamsters,* and reaffirms today, a "company's later changes in its hiring and promotion policies could be of little comfort to the victims of the earlier * * * discrimination, and could not erase its previous illegal conduct or its obligation to afford relief to those who suffered because of it." 431 U.S., at 341–342, 97 S.Ct., at 1857; ante, at 2951. Therefore, it is at least an open question whether the hiring of workers primarily from a list of past employees would, under *Griggs,* violate Title VII where the list contains no Negroes but the company uses additional methods of hiring to increase the numbers of Negroes hired.

The Court today apparently assumes that the Court of Appeals affirmed the District Court's findings that petitioner's hiring practice had no disparate impact. I cannot agree with that assumption. Because the Court of Appeals disposed of this case under the *McDonnell Douglas* analysis, it had no occasion to address those findings of the District Court pertaining to disparate impact. Although the Court of Appeals did discuss *Griggs* in its opinion, 551 F.2d 1085, 1089–1090 (1977), as I read that discussion the court was merely rejecting petitioner's argument that it could defeat respondents' *McDonnell Douglas* claim by showing that the work force had a large percentage of Negro members. I express no view on the issue of whether respondents' claim should prevail on the facts presented here since that question is not presently before us, but I believe that respondents' opportunity to make their claim should not be foreclosed by this Court.

Notes

1. The Supreme Court, in International Brotherhood Of Teamsters v. United States, 431 U.S. 324, 358, n. 44, 97 S.Ct. 1843, 1866, n. 44, 52 L.Ed.2d 396 (1977), stated:

> The *McDonnell Douglas* case involved an individual complainant seeking to prove one instance of unlawful discrimination. An employer's isolated decision to reject an applicant who belongs to a racial minority does not show that the rejection was racially based. Although the *McDonnell Douglas* formula does not require direct proof of discrimination, it does demand that the alleged discriminatee demonstrate at least that his rejection did not result from the two most common legitimate reasons on which an employer might rely to reject a job applicant: an absolute or relative lack of qualifications or the absence of a vacancy in the job sought. Elimination of these reasons for the refusal to hire is sufficient, absent other explanation, to create an inference that the decision was a discriminatory one.

2. The Court, in note 10 in McDonald v. Sante Fe Trail Transportation, equated the concept of "pretext" with the "but for" theory of causation. The lower courts have held, based in part on note 10, that a plaintiff must prove a causal connection between the adverse employment decision and discriminatory motivation of the defendant in order to establish liability. See also Lewis v. University of Pittsburgh, 725 F.2d 910 (3d Cir. 1983), cert. denied ___ U.S. ___, 105 S.Ct. 266, 83 L.Ed.2d 202 (1984) (discussing the relationship between the "but for", "substantial factor" and "a motivating factor" standards of causation). Bibbs v. Block, 778 F.2d 1318, 1320 (8th Cir.1985) (en banc), provided the following explanation on

the relationship between discriminatory motive and the pretext/causation element:

> In many Title VII cases, the proof proceeds on both sides on the premise that one motive only on the part of the employer—either an illegitimate one (e.g., race) or a legitimate one (e.g., ability to do the job)—has caused the adverse action of which the plaintiff complains. It is this type of case for which the familiar evidentiary framework of McDonnell Douglas v. Green * * * is designed. * * * Typically, the plaintiff will contend that one reason—race—was operative, the defendant will contend that another single reason—ability to do the job—motivated it, and the trier of fact will find one reason or the other (but not a combination) to be the true one. In such a case, the issues of motivation and causation are not distinctly separated, nor do they need to be. If the plaintiff shows the defendant's preferred reason to be pretext for race, the case is over. Liability is established. * * * The very showing that the defendant's asserted reason was a pretext for race is also a demonstration that but for his race plaintiff would have gotten the job. This is what pretext means: a *reason for the employment decision* is not the true reason.

Lewis v. Bloomsburg Mills, Inc., 773 F.2d 561, 571, n. 16 (4th Cir. 1985), is one of the few cases which discusses causation in the disparate impact cases:

> Causation is ordinarily not in issue in disparate impact cases because the claimant typically identifies and the employer concedes, at least conditionally, the existence of a facially neutral practice as the effective cause of any disparate impact shown. Reflecting this typical litigation pattern, courts sometimes speak as if identifying and proving such a practice as the effective cause is always an essential element of a claimant's "disparate impact" claim. See, e.g., EEOC v. Greyhound Lines, Inc., 635 F.2d 188, 193 (3d Cir.1980). This can cause confusion of doctrine. For while usual this, of course, is not the only possible litigation pattern out of which "disparate impact" cases may develop. Claimants, particularly class claimants, may well simply allege and offer proof of a significant discriminatory effect, knowing only that the effect is there, prepared to establish it either as intentional or merely the consequence of some policy or practice unknown or, if known, discounted as effective cause (i.e., to proceed alternatively on disparate treatment or disparate impact theories), depending upon the force of claimants' proof *and* upon the defensive stance yet to be assumed by the employer to that proof. A case may therefore well become effectively one of "disparate impact" only by virtue of the employer's defensive stand putting in issue for the first time an assertion that any disparate effect shown (or possibly conceded) is caused solely by a facially neutral practice or test.
>
> Where * * * such litigation pattern develops, the employer in effect has staked its case on the existence, the causal effect, and the business necessity of the practice, conceding at least conditionally the existence of the disparate impact and positively asserting the practice rather than any discriminatory intent as its business-necessitated

cause. In such case, the defense fails if either causation or necessity fails of proof, thereby leaving the disparate impact standing either unexplained or, if explained, unjustified. See generally, Wright v. Olin Corporation, 697 F.2d 1172 (4th Cir.1982); Wright v. National Archives and Records Service, 609 F.2d 702 (4th Cir.1979).

3. The lower courts, based on note 13 of *McDonnell Douglas,* have developed analogous models for the varying factual contexts in which claims of unlawful employment discrimination arise. In the discharge cases, for example, a plaintiff can establish a prima facie case by showing membership in a protected class, that plaintiff was satisfying the normal requirements of the job, discharge, and that after discharge (or demotion), the employer assigned another person to the plaintiff's job. See Taylor v. Jones, 653 F.2d 1193 (8th Cir.1981); Brown v. Tennessee, 701 F.2d 174 (6th Cir.1982) (failure to promote).

4. The courts are fairly uniform in holding that the fact that the employer selected or preferred a member of the same class to which the plaintiff belongs is not fatal to the establishment of a prima facie case. Jones v. Western Geophysical Co. of America, 669 F.2d 280, 284 (5th Cir. 1982) (replacement by member of same class may be evidence of pretext).

5. Where more than one person is considered for the same employment opportunity a plaintiff is not required to show that he or she is the best qualified to establish a prima facie case. E.g., Hawkins v. Anheuser-Busch, Inc., 697 F.2d 810, 813–814 (8th Cir.1983); Lynn v. Regents of Univ. of Calif., 656 F.2d 1337, 1342–1345 (9th Cir.1981), cert. denied 459 U.S. 823, 103 S.Ct. 53, 74 L.Ed.2d 59 (1982). See also Note, "Relative Qualifications and the Prima Facie Case in Title VII Litigation," 82 Colum.L.Rev. 553 (1982).

6. *Reverse Discrimination Claims.* As the Court noted, in note 8 of McDonald v. Sante Fe Trails, the employer expressly disclaimed any reliance on an affirmative action plan under which, for example, specific consideration of race or sex is a factor in the employment decision. Subsequent to United Steelworkers v. Weber, 443 U.S. 193, 99 S.Ct. 2721, 61 L.Ed.2d 480 (1979), the courts adopted a modification of the *McDonnell Douglas* analysis for the so-called reverse discrimination cases. For example, in Parker v. Baltimore and Ohio Railroad Co., 652 F.2d 1012, 1017 (D.C. Cir.1981), the court stated that it "has allowed majority plaintiffs to rely on the *McDonnell Douglas* criteria to prove a prima facie case of intentionally disparate treatment when background circumstances support a suspicion that the defendant is that unusual employer who discriminates against the majority." In Setser v. Novack Investment Co., 657 F.2d 962 (8th Cir.1981), the court held that the four-part *McDonnell Douglas* test will not necessarily show a prima facie violation. If a defendant produces evidence that an affirmative action plan satisfies the *Weber* standards, a plaintiff has the burden to show that some reason other than a remedial reason motivated the employer to adopt an affirmative action plan.

(b) *Pattern or Practice Cases*

INTERNATIONAL BROTHERHOOD OF TEAMSTERS v. UNITED STATES

Supreme Court of the United States, 1977.
431 U.S. 324, 97 S.Ct. 1843, 52 L.Ed.2d 396.

MR. JUSTICE STEWART delivered the opinion of the Court.

This litigation brings here several important questions under Title VII of the Civil Rights Act of 1964, 78 Stat. 253, as amended, 42 U.S.C. § 2000e et seq. (1970 ed. and Supp. V). The issues grow out of alleged unlawful employment practices engaged in by an employer and a union. The employer is a common carrier of motor freight with nationwide operations, and the union represents a large group of its employees. The District Court and the Court of Appeals held that the employer had violated Title VII by engaging in a pattern and practice of employment discrimination against Negroes and Spanish-surnamed Americans. * * *

* * *

I

The United States brought an action in a Tennessee federal court against the petitioner T.I.M.E.–D.C., Inc. (company), pursuant to § 707(a) of the Civil Rights Act of 1964, 42 U.S.C. § 2000e–6(a). The complaint charged that the company had followed discriminatory hiring, assignment, and promotion policies against Negroes at its terminal in Nashville, Tenn. The Government brought a second action against the company almost three years later in a Federal District Court in Texas, charging a pattern and practice of employment discrimination against Negroes and Spanish-surnamed persons throughout the company's transportation system. The petitioner International Brotherhood of Teamsters (union) was joined as a defendant in that suit. The two actions were consolidated for trial in the Northern District of Texas.

The central claim in both lawsuits was that the company had engaged in a pattern or practice of discriminating against minorities in hiring so-called line drivers. Those Negroes and Spanish-surnamed persons who had been hired, the Government alleged, were given lower paying, less desirable jobs as servicemen or local city drivers, and were thereafter discriminated against with respect to promotions and transfers. * * *

* * *

The cases went to trial and the District Court found that the Government had shown "by a preponderance of the evidence that T.I. M.E.–D.C. and its predecessor companies were engaged in a plan and practice of discrimination in violation of Title VII * * *."

* * *

A

Consideration of the question whether the company engaged in a pattern or practice of discriminatory hiring practices involves controlling legal principles that are relatively clear. The Government's theory of discrimination was simply that the company, in violation of § 703(a) of Title VII, regularly and purposefully treated Negroes and Spanish-surnamed Americans less favorably than white persons. The disparity in treatment allegedly involved the refusal to recruit, hire, transfer, or promote minority group members on an equal basis with white people, particularly with respect to line-driving positions. The ultimate factual issues are thus simply whether there was a pattern or practice of such disparate treatment and, if so, whether the differences were "racially premised." McDonnell Douglas Corp. v. Green, 411 U.S. 792, 805 n. 18, 93 S.Ct. 1817, 1825, 36 L.Ed.2d 668.

As the plaintiff, the Government bore the initial burden of making out a prima facie case of discrimination. Albemarle Paper Co. v. Moody, 422 U.S. 405, 425, 95 S.Ct. 2362, 2375, 45 L.Ed.2d 280; McDonnell Douglas Corp. v. Green, supra, 411 U.S., at 802, 93 S.Ct., at 1824. And, because it alleged a systemwide pattern or practice of resistance to the full enjoyment of Title VII rights, the Government ultimately had to prove more than the mere occurrence of isolated or "accidental" or sporadic discriminatory acts. It had to establish by a preponderance of the evidence that racial discrimination was the company's standard operating procedure—the regular rather than the unusual practice.[16]

We agree with the District Court and the Court of Appeals that the Government carried its burden of proof. As of March 31, 1971, shortly after the Government filed its complaint alleging systemwide discrimination, the company had 6,472 employees. Of these, 314 (5%) were Negroes and 257 (4%) were Spanish-surnamed Americans. Of the

---

16. The "pattern or practice" language in § 707(a) of Title VII, supra, at 1830 n. 1, was not intended as a term of art, and the words reflect only their usual meaning. Senator Humphrey explained:

"[A] pattern or practice would be present only where the denial of rights consists of something more than an isolated, sporadic incident, but is repeated, routine, or of a generalized nature. There would be a pattern or practice if, for example, a number of companies or persons in the same industry or line of business discriminated, if a chain of motels or restaurants practiced racial discrimination throughout all or a significant part of its system, or if a company repeatedly and regularly engaged in acts prohibited by the statute.

*   *   *   *   *

"The point is that single, insignificant, isolated acts of discrimination by a single business would not justify a finding of a pattern or practice * * *." 110 Cong. Rec. 14270 (1964).

This interpretation of "pattern or practice" appears throughout the legislative history of § 707(a), and is consistent with the understanding of the identical words as used in similar federal legislation. See 110 Cong.Rec. 12946 (1964) (remarks of Sen. Magnuson) (referring to § 206(a) of the Civil Rights Act of 1964, 42 U.S.C. § 2000a–5); 110 Cong.Rec. 13081 (1964) (remarks of Sen. Case); id., at 14239 (remarks of Sen. Humphrey); id., at 15895 (remarks of Rep. Celler). See also United States v. Jacksonville Terminal Co., 451 F.2d 418, 438, 441 (CA5); United States v. Ironworkers Local 86, 443 F.2d 544, 552 (CA9); United States v. West Peachtree Tenth Corp., 437 F.2d 221, 227 (CA5); United States v. Mayton, 335 F.2d 153, 158–159 (CA5).

1,828 line drivers, however, there were only 8 (0.4%) Negroes and 5 (0.3%) Spanish-surnamed persons, and all of the Negroes had been hired after the litigation had commenced. With one exception—a man who worked as a line driver at the Chicago terminal from 1950 to 1959—the company and its predecessors *did not employ a Negro on a regular basis as a line driver until 1969*. And, as the Government showed, even in 1971 there were terminals in areas of substantial Negro population where all of the company's line drivers were white.[17] A great majority of the Negroes (83%) and Spanish-surnamed Americans (78%) who did work for the company held the lower paying city operations and serviceman jobs,[18] whereas only 39% of the nonminority employees held jobs in those categories.

The Government bolstered its statistical evidence with the testimony of individuals who recounted over 40 specific instances of discrimination. Upon the basis of this testimony the District Court found that "[n]umerous qualified black and Spanish-surnamed American applicants who sought line driving jobs at the company over the years, either had their requests ignored, were given false or misleading information about requirements, opportunities, and application procedures, or were not considered and hired on the same basis that whites were considered and hired." Minority employees who wanted to transfer to line-driver jobs met with similar difficulties.[19]

The company's principal response to this evidence is that statistics can never in and of themselves prove the existence of a pattern or practice of discrimination, or even establish a prima facie case shifting to the employer the burden of rebutting the inference raised by the

17. In Atlanta, for instance, Negroes composed 22.35% of the population in the surrounding metropolitan area and 51.31% of the population in the city proper. The company's Atlanta terminal employed 57 line drivers. All were white. In Los Angeles, 10.84% of the greater metropolitan population and 17.88% of the city population were Negro. But at the company's two Los Angeles terminals there was not a single Negro among the 374 line drivers. The proof showed similar disparities in San Francisco, Denver, Nashville, Chicago, Dallas, and at several other terminals.

18. Although line-driver jobs pay more than other jobs, and the District Court found them to be "considered the most desirable of the driving jobs," it is by no means clear that all employees, even driver employees, would prefer to be line drivers. See infra, at 1871–1872, and n. 55. Of course, Title VII provides for equal opportunity to compete for any job, whether it is thought better or worse than another. See, e.g., United States v. Hayes Int'l Corp., 456 F.2d 112, 118 (CA5); United States v. National Lead Co., 438 F.2d 935, 939 (CA8).

19. Two examples are illustrative:

George Taylor, a Negro, worked for the company as a city driver in Los Angeles, beginning late in 1966. In 1968, after hearing that a white city driver had transferred to a line-driver job, he told the terminal manager that he also would like to consider line driving. The manager replied that there would be "a lot of problems on the road * * * with different people, Caucasian, et cetera," and stated: "I don't feel that the company is ready for this right now. * * * Give us a little time. It will come around, you know." Mr. Taylor made similar requests some months later and got similar responses. He was never offered a line-driving job or an application.

Feliberto Trujillo worked as a dockman at the company's Denver terminal. When he applied for a line-driver job in 1967, he was told by a personnel officer that he had one strike against him. He asked what that was and was told: "You're a Chicano, and as far as we know, there isn't a Chicano driver in the system."

figures. But, as even our brief summary of the evidence shows, this was not a case in which the Government relied on "statistics alone." The individuals who testified about their personal experiences with the company brought the cold numbers convincingly to life.

In any event, our cases make it unmistakably clear that "[s]tatistical analyses have served and will continue to serve an important role" in cases in which the existence of discrimination is a disputed issue. Mayor of Philadelphia v. Educational Equality League, 415 U.S. 605, 620, 94 S.Ct. 1323, 1333, 39 L.Ed.2d 630. See also McDonnell Douglas Corp. v. Green, 411 U.S., at 805, 93 S.Ct., at 1825. Cf. Washington v. Davis, 426 U.S. 229, 241–242, 96 S.Ct. 2040, 2048–2049, 48 L.Ed.2d 597. We have repeatedly approved the use of statistical proof, where it reached proportions comparable to those in this case, to establish a prima facie case of racial discrimination in jury selection cases, see, e.g., Turner v. Fouche, 396 U.S. 346, 90 S.Ct. 532, 24 L.Ed.2d 567; Hernandez v. Texas, 347 U.S. 475, 74 S.Ct. 667, 98 L.Ed. 866; Norris v. Alabama, 294 U.S. 587, 55 S.Ct. 579, 79 L.Ed. 1074. Statistics are equally competent in proving employment discrimination.[20] We

20. Petitioners argue that statistics, at least those comparing the racial composition of an employer's work force to the composition of the population at large, should never be given decisive weight in a Title VII case because to do so would conflict with § 703(j) of the Act, 42 U.S.C. § 2000e–2(j). That section provides:

"Nothing contained in this subchapter shall be interpreted to require any employer * * * to grant preferential treatment to any individual or to any group because of the race * * * or national origin of such individual or group on account of an imbalance which may exist with respect to the total number or percentage of persons of any race * * * or national origin employed by any employer * * * in comparison with the total number or percentage of persons of such race * * * or national origin in any community, State, section, or other area, or in the available work force in any community, State, section, or other area."

The argument fails in this case because the statistical evidence was not offered or used to support an erroneous theory that Title VII requires an employer's work force to be racially balanced. Statistics showing racial or ethnic imbalance are probative in a case such as this one only because such imbalance is often a telltale sign of purposeful discrimination; absent explanation, it is ordinarily to be expected that nondiscriminatory hiring practices will in time result in a work force more or less representative of the racial and ethnic composition of the population in the community from which employees are hired. Evidence of longlasting and gross disparity between the composition of a work force and that of the general population thus may be significant even though § 703(j) makes clear that Title VII imposes no requirement that a work force mirror the general population. See, e.g., United States v. Sheet Metal Workers Local 36, 416 F.2d 123, 127 n. 7 (CA8). Considerations such as small sample size may, of course, detract from the value of such evidence, see, e.g., Mayor of Philadelphia v. Educational Equality League, 415 U.S. 605, 620–621, 94 S.Ct. 1323, 1333, 39 L.Ed.2d 630, and evidence showing that the figures for the general population might not accurately reflect the pool of qualified job applicants would also be relevant. Ibid. See generally Schlei & Grossman, supra, n. 15, at 1161–1193.

"Since the passage of the Civil Rights Act of 1964, the courts have frequently relied upon statistical evidence to prove a violation. * * * In many cases the only available avenue of proof is the use of racial statistics to uncover clandestine and covert discrimination by the employer or union involved." United States v. Ironworkers Local 86, 443 F.2d, at 551. See also, e.g., Pettway v. American Cast Iron Pipe Co., 494 F.2d 211, 225 n. 34 (CA5); Brown v. Gaston County Dyeing Mach. Co., 457 F.2d 1377, 1382 (CA4); United States v. Jacksonville Terminal Co., 451 F.2d, at 442; Parham v. Southwestern Bell Tel. Co., 433 F.2d 421, 426 (CA8); Jones v. Lee Way

caution only that statistics are not irrefutable; they come in infinite variety and, like any other kind of evidence, they may be rebutted. In short, their usefulness depends on all of the surrounding facts and circumstances. See, e.g., Hester v. Southern R. Co., 497 F.2d 1374, 1379–1381 (CA5).

In addition to its general protest against the use of statistics in Title VII cases, the company claims that in this case the statistics revealing racial imbalance are misleading because they fail to take into account the company's particular business situation as of the effective date of Title VII. The company concedes that its line drivers were virtually all white in July 1965, but it claims that thereafter business conditions were such that its work force dropped. Its argument is that low personnel turnover, rather than post-Act discrimination, accounts for more recent statistical disparities. It points to substantial minority hiring in later years, especially after 1971, as showing that any pre-Act patterns of discrimination were broken.

The argument would be a forceful one if this were an employer who, at the time of suit, had done virtually no new hiring since the effective date of Title VII. But it is not. Although the company's total number of employees apparently dropped somewhat during the late 1960's, the record shows that many line drivers continued to be hired throughout this period, and that almost all of them were white.[21] To be sure, there were improvements in the company's hiring practices. The Court of Appeals commented that "T.I.M.E.–D.C.'s recent minority hiring progress stands as a laudable good faith effort to eradicate the effects of past discrimination in the area of hiring and initial assignment." [22] 517 F.2d, at 316. But the District Court and the Court of Appeals found upon substantial evidence that the company had engaged in a course of discrimination that continued well after the effective date of Title VII. The company's later changes in its hiring and promotion policies could be of little comfort to the victims of the earlier post-Act discrimination, and could not erase its previous illegal conduct or its obligation to afford relief to those who suffered because of it. Cf. Albemarle Paper Co. v. Moody, 422 U.S., at 413–423, 95 S.Ct., at 2369–2374.[23]

Motor Freight, Inc., 431 F.2d 245, 247 (CA10).

21. Between July 2, 1965, and January 1, 1969, hundreds of line drivers were hired systemwide, either from the outside or from the ranks of employees filling other jobs within the company. None was a Negro. Government Exhibit 204.

22. For example, in 1971 the company hired 116 new line drivers, of whom 16 were Negro or Spanish-surnamed Americans. Minority employees composed 7.1% of the company's systemwide work force in 1967 and 10.5% in 1972. Minority hiring increased greatly in 1972 and 1973, pre-

sumably due at least in part to the existence of the consent decree. See 517 F.2d, at 316 n. 31.

23. The company's narrower attacks upon the statistical evidence—that there was no precise delineation of the areas referred to in the general population statistics, that the Government did not demonstrate that minority populations were located close to terminals or that transportation was available, that the statistics failed to show what portion of the minority population was suited by age, health, or other qualifications to hold trucking jobs, etc.—are equally lacking in

The District Court and the Court of Appeals, on the basis of substantial evidence, held that the Government had proved a prima facie case of systematic and purposeful employment discrimination, continuing well beyond the effective date of Title VII. The company's attempts to rebut that conclusion were held to be inadequate.[24] For the reasons we have summarized, there is no warrant for this Court to disturb the findings of the District Court and the Court of Appeals on this basic issue.

*   *   *

Notes

Private plaintiffs may seek relief under the pattern and practice theory of discrimination. See, e.g., Franks v. Bowman Transportation Co., 424 U.S. 747, 96 S.Ct. 1251, 47 L.Ed.2d 444 (1976) (private class action Title VII case in which the plaintiffs alleged that the employer had engaged in a pervasive pattern of racial discrimination in various company policies, including hiring, transfer, and discharge of employees). The private plaintiff pattern and practice cases are generally brought as class actions under Rule 23 of the Federal Rules of Civil Procedure. Cooper v. Federal Reserve Bank of Richmond, 467 U.S. 867, 104 S.Ct. 2794, 81 L.Ed.2d 718 (1984), held that the elements of a prima facie case are the same in both private class action disparate treatment cases brought under Section 703(a)(1) and pattern or practice cases brought by the government under Section 717.

force. At best, these attacks go only to the accuracy of the comparison between the composition of the company's work force at various terminals and the general population of the surrounding communities. They detract little from the Government's further showing that Negroes and Spanish-surnamed Americans who were hired were overwhelmingly excluded from line-driver jobs. Such employees were willing to work, had access to the terminal, were healthy and of working age, and often were at least sufficiently qualified to hold city-driver jobs. Yet they became line drivers with far less frequency than whites. See, e.g., Pretrial Stipulation 14, summarized in 517 F.2d, at 312 n. 24 (of 2,919 whites who held driving jobs in 1971, 1,802 (62%) were line drivers and 1,117 (38%) were city drivers; of 180 Negroes and Spanish-surnamed Americans who held driving jobs, 13 (7%) were line drivers and 167 (93%) were city drivers).

In any event, fine tuning of the statistics could not have obscured the glaring absence of minority line drivers. As the Court of Appeals remarked, the company's inability to rebut the inference of discrimination came not from a misuse of statistics but from "the inexorable zero." Id., at 315.

24. The company's evidence, apart from the showing of recent changes in hiring and promotion policies, consisted mainly of general statements that it hired only the best qualified applicants. But "affirmations of good faith in making individual selections are insufficient to dispel a prima facie case of systematic exclusion." Alexander v. Louisiana, 405 U.S. 625, 632, 92 S.Ct. 1221, 1226, 31 L.Ed.2d 536.

The company also attempted to show that all of the witnesses who testified to specific instances of discrimination either were not discriminated against or suffered no injury. The Court of Appeals correctly ruled that the trial judge was not bound to accept this testimony and that it committed no error by relying instead on the other overpowering evidence in the case. 517 F.2d, at 315. The Court of Appeals was also correct in the view that individual proof concerning each class member's specific injury was appropriately left to proceedings to determine individual relief. In a suit brought by the Government under § 707(a) of the Act the District Court's initial concern is in deciding whether the Government has proved that the defendant has engaged in a pattern or practice of discriminatory conduct.

(c) Direct Evidence Cases

BELL v. BIRMINGHAM LINEN SERVICE

United States Court of Appeals for the Eleventh Circuit, 1983.
715 F.2d 1552, cert. denied, 467 U.S. 1204, 104 S.Ct. 2385,
81 L.Ed.2d 344 (1984).

TJOFLAT, CIRCUIT JUDGE:

Nora Bell brought this suit under Title VII of the Civil Rights Act of 1964, 42 U.S.C. § 2000e–2000e–17 (1976 & Supp. V 1981) alleging that Birmingham Linen Service declined to promote her, or "constructively demoted" her, because she was a woman. Following a non-jury trial, the district court concluded that Ms. Bell had failed to carry her burden of proving by a preponderance of the evidence that she was the victim of gender discrimination. The district court erred in applying the relevant legal principles; we therefore vacate the judgment and remand the case for additional factual findings under the correct legal standards.

I.

Birmingham Linen Service (BLS) operates an industrial laundry in Birmingham, Alabama. Nora Bell works as a presser in that laundry, and has worked for BLS some 23 years. Local 218 of the Laundry, Dry Cleaning, and Dye House Workers Union represents BLS' employees. A collective bargaining agreement between Local 218 and BLS governs the terms and conditions of employment of BLS' workers.

Article 18 of that agreement provides for a posting and bidding procedure to fill job vacancies within the collective bargaining unit. Under Article 18, both immediate job openings and trainee positions must be posted on the employee bulletin board for three working days so that bargaining unit employees may bid for them. Assignments to these jobs and training positions must be made from the bidding. A job will not be considered to be open, however, if a trainee has bid on the job previously and is willing to accept the new assignment. Thus, receipt of a trainee position is a steppingstone to filling a position that subsequently comes open.

We are hampered in our exposition of the events forming the background of this dispute because the district court failed to make findings concerning many of the basic, subsidiary facts which are unclear or disputed in the record. In March or April of 1977, Richard Day retired from his position as "washman" in BLS' washroom department.[1] On July 12, 1977, BLS' production manager, Gus Westbrook, posted a bid for an "extra washman" position.[2] Westbrook took down

---

1. It is undisputed that all washroom employees, including washmen, are men, and that no female has been employed in the washroom in over 30 years. It is also undisputed that washroom positions are among the highest paid positions in BLS' plant.

2. "Extra washman" is not a job listed in the collective bargaining agreement. The positions listed there are "washman" and "washman-trainee." Westbrook testified that the "extra washman" label for the job opening was a mistake, and that

the bid sheet on July 18, 1977. Four persons bid on the position: Nora Bell and three males, including Waddell Mason. Ms. Bell was the most senior employee who bid on the job. Westbrook awarded the position to Waddell Mason.

Bell complained to her union representative, Georgia Robinson, that she should have been awarded the extra washman position. Bell and Robinson went to see Westbrook to determine why Bell had not received the position. Westbrook apparently told them that Mason was more qualified. Bell and Robinson then met with plant manager Charles Jones on Friday, August 5, and complained that the job should have been awarded to Bell, the most senior bidder. After that meeting, BLS awarded the position to Ms. Bell. She was told to report to the washroom on Monday, August 8.

When Bell arrived in the washroom on August 8, Westbrook apparently told her that she would be performing "pulling" and "loading" functions.[3] Bell replied that the pulling and loading tasks were not part of the washman position upon which she had bid. Westbrook then offered Bell the apron that pullers wear to keep their clothing dry, and Bell refused to take the apron. Bell left the washroom to see plant manager Jones, who apparently told her to return to the washroom and talk with Westbrook.

Accompanied by union steward Robinson, Bell then met with Westbrook. Westbrook apparently told them that he gave Waddell Mason the job because he had experience in the washroom. He also stated, according to the testimony of both Bell and Robinson, that he would not put Nora Bell in the washroom because if he did, "every woman in the plant would want to go into the washroom." The district court, deciding the credibility of the evidence, specifically found that Westbrook made this statement, or a similar statement in substance, to Bell and Robinson.

Bell then left the washroom, and returned to her job as a presser. She left work that day, August 8, 1977, and filed both a grievance with her union and a charge of gender discrimination with the Equal Employment Opportunity Commission (EEOC). She filed a second, amended charge with the EEOC on September 13, 1978, alleging that Westbrook harassed and intimidated her in retaliation for filing the earlier charge.

* * *

After a two-day trial, the district court found that Bell did make out a prima facie case as to her promotion, or constructive demotion, claim under McDonnell Douglas v. Green, 411 U.S. 792, 93 S.Ct. 1817, 36 L.Ed.2d 668 (1973). The court found that a vacancy existed, that she

the posting should have read "washman-trainee."

3. As the terms imply, these functions involve loading linen into, and pulling linen out of, washing machines. Apparently, it is physically strenuous work and not an ordinary part of the "washman" function. Washmen sort the linen according to the type involved, determine the nature and degree of the soil, and then decide which formula and which chemicals should be used to clean the linen.

applied for it, that she was capable of being qualified for the job with reasonable training, and that the job was later filled by a male. The court further found that it was not necessary for a person to "pull and load" to train for the washman position, and that pulling and loading had not previously been a criterion for obtaining the job of washman.

Applying Texas Department of Community Affairs v. Burdine, 450 U.S. 248, 101 S.Ct. 1089, 67 L.Ed.2d 207 (1981), the court stated that a burden of production shifted to BLS to articulate a legitimate, nondiscriminatory reason for its refusal to place Bell in the washman position or its placing increased burdens on the job after Bell applied for the position. The court summarized BLS' position as being that Mason, the male who ultimately received the job, was already qualified for the job and had effectively been filling it. The court thus found that BLS satisfied its burden of production. The district court reasoned that BLS had rebutted the presumption of discrimination created by Bell's prima facie case; Bell therefore had to show that BLS' proffered reasons were mere pretext without substance, a task that merged with her ultimate burden of persuading the court she was the victim of intentional discrimination.

The court made additional findings, including, inter alia, that Westbrook had made the aforementioned sexist statement, that no female employee had worked in the washroom in over thirty years, and that it was not necessary to learn pulling and loading to be a washman. Citing Rohde v. K.O. Steel Castings, Inc., 649 F.2d 317 (5th Cir.Unit A 1981), the court concluded:

> [T]he real issue in this case, notwithstanding any comments made by Westbrook or the findings of the EEOC or the arbitration decision, is whether [BLS'] deliberate effort to place Mason in the position was motivated by matters relating to sex *or* whether this effort was motivated by Mason's prior experience and ability to perform the job without further training.

Record, vol. 1, at 92 (emphasis added).

The court found that the initial reason for posting the "extra washman" position on July 12, 1977, was to add a proper title to a position that Mason already occupied de facto, due to his incumbency in the washroom. Although this may have breached the collective bargaining agreement, the court concluded it did not reflect an intent to discriminate. It found that BLS' original intent was that the "extra washman" would perform other duties such as pulling and/or loading. The district court thus implicitly rejected its earlier suggestion that the pulling and loading requirements were placed on Bell to discourage her from taking the job. The court's ultimate conclusion was that the intent behind the whole procedure was to leave Mason in his same position but to change his job title. The complications that arose from the bid of a more senior employee, Bell, for the job related to possible violations of the collective bargaining agreement and not the civil rights laws. Concluding that Bell was not the victim of intentional discrimination, the district court entered judgment for BLS.

* * *

The Supreme Court, and this court, have stressed time and again that the four-part *McDonnell Douglas* test for establishing a prima facie case of disparate treatment is not intended to be a Procrustean bed within which all disparate treatment cases must be forced to lie. The Court in *McDonnell Douglas,* recognizing the wide variety of circumstances from which disparate treatment claims might arise, took pains to point out that its specification of the prima facie proof required of a Title VII plaintiff "is not necessarily applicable in every respect to differing factual situations." *McDonnell Douglas,* 411 U.S. at 802 n. 13, 93 S.Ct. at 1824 n. 13. The *Furnco* court reiterated that "[t]he method suggested in *McDonnell Douglas* for pursuing this inquiry [whether disparate treatment occurred] * * * was never intended to be rigid, mechanized, or ritualistic. Rather, it is merely a sensible, orderly way to evaluate the evidence in light of common experience as it bears on the critical question of discrimination." *Furnco,* 438 U.S. at 577, 98 S.Ct. at 2949.

The *McDonnell Douglas* method of establishing a prima facie case addresses two evidentiary problems common to most Title VII cases: (1) direct evidence of discriminatory intent will most likely be nonexistent or difficult to prove; and (2) the employer enjoys greater access to proof of its reasons for its own employment decisions.

* * *

It should be clear that the *McDonnell Douglas* method of proving a prima facie case pertains primarily, if not exclusively, to situations where direct evidence of discrimination is lacking. It would be illogical, indeed ironic, to hold a Title VII plaintiff presenting direct evidence of a defendant's intent to discriminate to a more stringent burden of proof, or to allow a defendant to meet that direct proof by merely articulating, but not proving, legitimate, nondiscriminatory reasons for its action.

Following these principles, this court has held that where a case of discrimination is proved by direct evidence, it is incorrect to rely on a *McDonnell Douglas* rebuttal. Lee v. Russell County Board of Education, 684 F.2d 769, 774 (11th Cir.1982). If the evidence consists of direct testimony that the defendant acted with a discriminatory motive, and the trier of fact accepts this testimony, the ultimate issue of discrimination is proved. Defendant cannot refute this evidence by mere articulation of other reasons; the legal standard changes dramatically:

> Once an [illegal] motive is proved to have been a significant or substantial factor in an employment decision, defendant can rebut only by *proving* by a preponderance of the evidence that the same decision would have been reached even absent the presence of that factor.

Id. (citing Mt. Healthy City School District v. Doyle, 429 U.S. 274, 287, 97 S.Ct. 568, 576, 50 L.Ed.2d 471) (emphasis added); accord Perryman v.

Johnson Products Co., 698 F.2d 1138, 1143 (11th Cir.1983); see Ramirez v. Sloss, 615 F.2d 163, 168 (5th Cir.1980).

The district court in this case specifically accepted as credible testimony indicating that BLS' decision-maker, Gus Westbrook, stated that he would not allow Bell into the washroom because if she were allowed in, all women would want to enter. This testimony is "highly probative evidence" of illegal discrimination. *Lee,* 684 F.2d at 775. Cf. Eastland v. TVA, 704 F.2d 613, 626 (11th Cir.1983) (testimony of selecting supervisor's racial bias, plus other evidence, defeated defendant's *McDonnell Douglas* rebuttal). The district court did not make any findings that Westbrook put aside his bias when he imposed the pulling and loading functions on Bell. Absent such a finding, it is impossible to conclude that BLS met its heavy burden of proving, under *Lee, Perryman,* and *Mt. Healthy,* that it would have reached the same decision without the presence of gender discrimination. This case must be remanded to the district court so that the court may evaluate the evidence under the *Mt. Healthy* standard.

The ultimate question in this case, the existence of discriminatory intent *vel non,* is a factual matter. See Pullman-Standard v. Swint, 456 U.S. 273, 289–90, 102 S.Ct. 1781, 1790–91, 72 L.Ed.2d 66 (1982). Bell urges us to reverse and remand this case for entry of judgment, since the district court's findings are infirm because of its erroneous view of the law and, in her view, "the record permits only one resolution of the factual issue." Id. at 292, 102 S.Ct. at 1792. We decline Bell's tempting invitation because we believe the district court's factual findings are inadequate to allow us to draw this conclusion.

To guide the district court, however, we emphasize those factors or reasons articulated by BLS which are *irrelevant,* as a matter of law, to the court's determination. The sole question before the district court on remand is whether Westbrook, and therefore BLS, imposed the pulling and loading tasks on Bell as a condition of the extra washman job in significant part because of her gender.[8] Mason's allegedly superior qualifications for the position have no bearing on the reasons BLS imposed the pulling and loading functions on Bell. For both logical and legal purposes, BLS abandoned its position that Mason deserved the job because of his superior qualifications when it agreed on August 5 that, notwithstanding anyone's qualifications, Bell would receive the posted vacancy.

Similarly, Westbrook's original intent, if any, simply to make official Mason's de facto occupancy of the position is irrelevant. When BLS agreed to give Bell the job on August 5—and all parties agree that this occurred—the only question for the district court to determine became: what was Westbrook's intent *at the time* he imposed the

---

8. It is undisputed in the trial record—as opposed to the EEOC proceedings—that Bell was offered the job, and that she left the position because Westbrook made pulling and loading a prerequisite to retaining the job.

pulling and loading functions on Bell? Did sexual bias play a significant role in this decision? [9]

We emphasize that under *Mt. Healthy,* and our cases applying *Mt. Healthy* in the Title VII context, BLS bears not a burden of production but a burden of persuasion. Unless the district court concludes that Westbrook's sexual bias had no relation whatsoever to his employment decision, BLS must establish by a preponderance of the evidence that it would have made the same decision in the absence of the illegal factor.[10]

Our careful scrutiny of the record reveals only one possible legitimate, nondiscriminatory reason for Westbrook's imposition of the pulling and loading functions on Bell: structural changes in the washroom that may have reduced BLS's need for washmen from two to one. These changes in equipment may have meant that BLS needed only one person to "fill in" for the absent washman on occasion, and for this reason posted the "extra washman" position with the intent that the occupant of the job pull and load in addition to wash.

However, the record evidence on this point is far from clear, to say the least. The district court, in order to credit BLS' explanation, must find as fact that the changes adverted to took place *prior* to July 12, 1977, the date the extra washman position was posted. To reiterate, given the evidence of direct discrimination, BLS bears the full burden of persuasion on this point. Unless the court finds that BLS established this by a preponderance of the evidence, it must enter judgment for Bell and grant appropriate relief.

9. In Whiting v. Jackson State Univ., 616 F.2d 116, 121 (5th Cir.1980), the former Fifth Circuit held "Title VII is not violated simply because an impermissible factor plays *some* part in the employer's decision. The forbidden taint need not be the sole basis for the action to warrant relief, but it must be a significant factor." (Emphasis in original.) Subsequently, this court has emphasized that this principle is "an extremely limited one: An insignificant [illegal] factor does not warrant relief, but significant reliance on an impermissible factor is a violation." *Lee,* 684 F.2d at 775 (citing Mt. Healthy v. Doyle, 429 U.S. at 287, 97 S.Ct. at 576).

The difficulty of proving discriminatory intent is well-known and, as indicated *supra* at 1556–1557, is an integral part of the rationale for the structure of the *McDonnell Douglas* analysis. Proof of significant reliance on discrimination as a basis for an employment decision, therefore, establishes a violation of Title VII.

This court has recently acknowledged the substantial criticism of the "but for" standard of causation in disparate treat-

ment cases. Lincoln v. Board of Regents, 697 F.2d at 938 n. 12. See Brodin, The Standard of Causation in the Mixed Motive Title VII Action: A Social Policy Perspective, 82 Colum.L.Rev. 292, 311–26 (1982). We acknowledge the practical difficulties presented to a trier-of-fact required to determine what would have occurred if the discrimination had not existed and not operated as a motivating factor. Id. at 320–21. Since the district court did not r.ake findings concerning the causal re' .tionship, if any, between the bias it found to exist and the action taken, it is unclear whether this case presents a "mixed motive" situation. We therefore have no occasion to reach the question of any possible modification of the *Mt. Healthy* standard in the Title VII context.

10. If the district court finds that Westbrook's bias played no role in his decision, it should clearly articulate the basis for its finding. This is necessary in light of the nature of the statement the court found that Westbrook had made and the highly probative character of testimony concerning direct decision-maker bias.

In making this finding, the district court should consider, inter alia, (1) the changing factual positions BLS has taken in the arbitration, EEOC, and judicial proceedings; (2) the evidence of the distribution of BLS' work force by sex among the various jobs in the plant, *see McDonnell Douglas*, 411 U.S. at 804–05, 93 S.Ct. at 1825; (3) BLS' breach of its collective bargaining agreement as it may or may not reflect on its motivation, see Loeb v. Textron, 600 F.2d at 1012 n. 6 (the more questionable the employer's reason, the more likely the reason is merely a pretext); and (4) the failure, if any, of BLS to follow objective standards in making its employment decision in this case, Harris v. Birmingham Board of Education, 712 F.2d 1377 at 1382, 1384 (11th Cir. Aug. 22, 1983); Watson v. National Linen Service, 686 F.2d 877, 881 (11th Cir.1982).

The judgment of the district court is Vacated and the case is Remanded for further proceedings consistent with this opinion.

Notes

In Trans-World Airlines, Inc. v. Thurston, 469 U.S. 111 , 105 S.Ct. 613, 83 L.Ed.2d 523 (1985), infra at p. 839, the Court, in an age discrimination case, held that the *McDonnell Douglas* test is inapplicable when the plaintiff presents direct evidence of discrimination.

(d) Mixed Motive Cases

BLALOCK v. METALS TRADES, INC.

United States Court of Appeals for the Sixth Circuit, 1985.
775 F.2d 703.

Before CONTIE, WELLFORD and MILBURN, CIRCUIT JUDGES.

CONTIE, CIRCUIT JUDGE.

Larry Blalock appeals the district court's judgment in favor of the defendant, Metals Trades, Inc. on Blalock's complaint alleging that Metals Trades discharged him on account of religious discrimination in violation of Title VII, 42 U.S.C. § 2000 et seq. For the reasons that follow, we reverse the judgment and remand the case to the district court for proceedings consistent with this opinion.

I.

Metals Trades is a closely held corporation principally owned by Wendall Woodward and Arnold Brewer. Woodward and Brewer each own 50 of the 101 shares of stock. The remaining share is owned by Woodward's brother, Evan. Wendall Woodward and Arnold Brewer jointly manage the business. Major decisions are made only after the two have reached an agreement. One area of sufficient importance to be subject to joint control is the hiring and firing of office personnel.

Woodward met Blalock through John Rothacker, a self-described "apostle." Rothacker testified that his mission as an apostle is to "establish the church" and to "establish Christians in the foundations of the faith as it is properly presented from the scriptures and the prophets and the apostles that wrote in the New Testament as well as the prophets of the Old." Woodward described Rothacker as his spiritual shepherd, but consistently maintained that although Rothacker "can give me advice * * * it's up to me to make up my mind how I have to handle it myself." Similarly, Rothacker testified that although "in spiritual matters" Woodward was "in submission" to Rothacker, he only offers advice in other areas and "the decisions ultimately reside with him [Woodward]." At the time of the events in question, Rothacker and Woodward regularly met in a prayer group. Members of the group introduced their personal problems to the group's discussion and prayers.

Blalock met Rothacker in 1972 or 1973 and became interested in his work.[1] Rothacker knew that Blalock had an engineering background and that he was interested in sales. In early 1974, Rothacker learned that Woodward was looking for a salesman with some engineering experience. Following a prayer meeting, Rothacker introduced Blalock and Woodward and suggested to Woodward that Blalock might fulfill his needs. In March 1974, Woodward hired Blalock.

It is undisputed that when Blalock began working for Metals Trades, he was told it was a "christian company."[2] Blalock assumed this meant that the company conducted its business with ethical standards consistent with biblical commands. Blalock did not believe that there were any specific religious requirements attendant to the job and Woodward testified that there were, in fact, no religious requirements. At the time, Blalock was eager to work for a christian company and requested and received permission to "witness" his faith to clients who expressed an interest in religious matters. Woodward was happy to have "a Christian, a good, moral, ethical man" working for Metals Trades.

Soon after Blalock started working at Metals Trades, he and Rothacker had a parting of the ways. The basis of their disagreement is undisputed. Blalock felt that Rothacker wanted him to submit to his authority, which he was unwilling to do. Rothacker, being an apostle, felt Blalock owed him a certain amount of obedience, which was not forthcoming. Blalock testified that during work hours Woodward relayed acrimonious messages and accusations from Rothacker to him. According to Blalock, Woodward also quoted bible verses to him, arguing that he was in doctrinal error in parting with Rothacker.

---

1. Rothacker testified that Blalock had sought training from him in the method of his ministry. Blalock testified that he only wanted to "observe" Rothacker. "He made some big claims for himself. I wanted to check them out."

does not contend that this action is barred by statutory, 42 U.S.C. § 2000e–1, or constitutional limitations, Dayton Christian Schools, Inc. v. Ohio Civil Rights Commission, 766 F.2d 932 (6th Cir.1985).

2. Although Metals Trades is described as a "christian company," Metals Trades

Woodward acknowledged that he may have passed on some information from Rothacker to Blalock, but he could not remember the content.

Arnold Brewer testified that he became disenchanted with Blalock soon after he started working at Metals Trades and Woodward confirmed Brewer's testimony. Woodward testified that he asked Brewer to give Blalock some more time. Brewer's specific complaints against Blalock were a perceived patronizing attitude, a habit of spending too much time agonizing over insignificant mechanical tolerances, leaving a mess on Brewer's desk and failing to call in to tell Metals Trades when he would be working.[3] Blalock testified, on the other hand, that Brewer asked him only two weeks before his discharge if he would consider working full time.

Blalock was fired in September 1974. Brewer had been unhappy with Blalock for some time and when Woodward reached a decision to fire Blalock, Brewer readily assented. Blalock and Woodward's versions of the actual firing are generally consistent. Woodward told Blalock he wanted to talk to him. Blalock asked if it concerned Rothacker and Woodward responded that it did. Blalock said he did not want to discuss it if it concerned Rothacker. According to Woodward, Blalock immediately left the room. Woodward admitted that he told Blalock "until he got things straightened with John [Rothacker], he was discharged." According to Blalock, he did not leave immediately, but instead stated that while he would discuss work matters, he would not talk about Rothacker. Blalock testified that although Woodward agreed to talk about work only, he never mentioned any work-related problems, but instead kept referring back to the biblical reference to "feigned obedience." After this went on for some time, according to Blalock, he told Woodward he was leaving. Blalock testified that at that point Woodward said, "consider yourself laid off * * * until the situation with you and John Rothacker is settled." Woodward testified, however, that his statement about Rothacker was "simply my reaction to his reaction" and that he never meant to condition employment on Blalock's relationship with Rothacker. Blalock subsequently telephoned Woodward in an attempt to recover his job. Blalock testified that he asked Woodward to talk only about their business relationship and leave religion out of it, but that Woodward refused to do so. Woodward's testimony was entirely consistent with this account.

Two letters from Woodward to the Ohio Civil Rights Commission were introduced into evidence. In the first, Woodward stated that "we were generally satisfied" with Blalock's performance of his sales duties. The letter expressed some displeasure, however, with Blalock's attitude and his engineering practices. A second letter states that Blalock was laid off because of the failure to notify Woodward which days he would be working and because Woodward asked him "a question and he refused to answer." Woodward testified that this referred to Blalock's

---

3. Blalock arranged to work three days out of each week. He was to tell Metals Trades which three days of the week he planned to work.

refusal to discuss Rothacker when he was discharged. The letter then states:

> Larry was hired with the full knowledge and understanding that Metals Trades is a Christian Company and our rule book is the word of God, or the Bible. He was in full accord and very excited. He said he wanted to work for a Christian Company and, being a salesman contacting new accounts, he wanted to witness to them; in which I encouraged him. Larry is a fine young man and he has my respect in many areas. I hated to lay him off as there are all too few men willing to commit themselves to Jesus—especially salesmen. Larry's problem is that he refuses to submit himself to those in authority over him and the Bible makes it clear that we are to be in submission. Larry was let go for strictly secular reasons but the root of his problem is spiritual, as the scriptures will show. * * *

The letter closed by quoting several biblical passages.

The district court accepted Blalock's contention that the precise analysis of Texas Department of Community Affairs v. Burdine, 450 U.S. 248, 101 S.Ct. 1089, 67 L.Ed.2d 207 (1981) and McDonnell Douglas Corp. v. Green, 411 U.S. 792, 93 S.Ct. 1817, 36 L.Ed.2d 668 (1973) does not apply in this case. "[T]his is a case in which the plaintiff has offered direct evidence that defendant intentionally discriminated against him." The court did "not agree, however, with plaintiff's assertion that he has proved his case by direct evidence that the defendant discharged him because of religious differences." The court found that

> [t]he personal relationship between plaintiff and Mr. Woodward that motivated Mr. Woodward to tolerate plaintiff's poor performance as an employee was rooted in their shared religious experience. When this personal relationship broke down, Mr. Woodward no longer felt motivated to close his eyes to plaintiff's attitudes and behavior as an employee.

The court held that "plaintiff has not proved that defendant fired him because of his religion or because of any particular religious beliefs he may have held" and that "there was no discriminatory intent in violation of Title VII." Further, "plaintiff has failed to prove that in terminating him, defendant intentionally discriminated against plaintiff because of his religion or religious beliefs." On appeal, Blalock contends first that the district court clearly erred in finding that Blalock had not established by direct evidence that Metals Trades acted with discriminatory intent, and, second, that, in light of its clearly erroneous findings, the district court erred in apportioning the burden of proof with respect to establishing the "cause" of Blalock's termination.

* * *

Prerequisite to examination of the district court's factual findings is a review of the legal standards applicable to this case. Two factors influence our determination of these standards: first, that plaintiff attempted to prove his case of discrimination by direct evidence, and, second, that the evidence suggests the possibility of dual motives for the discharge.

A.

First, we note, in agreement with the district court, that the *McDonnell Douglas* test and its shifting burdens are "inapplicable where the plaintiff presents direct evidence of discrimination." Trans World Airlines, Inc. v. Thurston, 469 U.S. 111, 105 S.Ct. 613, 622, 83 L.Ed.2d 523 (1985), citing International Brotherhood of Teamsters v. United States, 431 U.S. 324, 358 n. 44, 97 S.Ct. 1843, 1866 n. 44, 52 L.Ed.2d 396 (1977) ("the *McDonnell Douglas* formula does not require direct proof of discrimination"); Thompkins v. Morris Brown College, 752 F.2d 558, 563 (11th Cir.1985); Miles v. M.N.C. Corp., 750 F.2d 867, 875–76 (11th Cir.1985); Bell v. Birmingham Linen Service, 715 F.2d 1552, 1556 (11th Cir.1983), cert. denied, 467 U.S. 1204, 104 S.Ct. 2385, 81 L.Ed.2d 344 (1984) (*McDonnell Douglas* "is not intended to be a Procrustean bed within which all disparate treatment cases must be forced to lie."); Perryman v. Johnson Products Co., 698 F.2d 1138, 1143 (11th Cir.1983); Lee v. Russell County Board of Education, 684 F.2d 769, 774 (11th Cir.1982). Direct evidence and the *McDonnell Douglas* formulation are simply different evidentiary paths by which to resolve the ultimate issue of defendant's discriminatory intent. But see Zebedeo v. Martin E. Segal Co., 582 F.Supp. 1394, 1412 n. 7 (D.Conn. 1984). "Where the evidence for a prima facie case consists * * * of direct testimony that defendants acted with a discriminatory motivation, if the trier of fact believes the prima facie evidence the ultimate issue of discrimination is proved; no inference is required." *Lee,* 684 F.2d at 774; *Miles,* 750 F.2d at 875–76; *Perryman,* 698 F.2d at 1143.[5]

"When direct evidence of discrimination has been introduced, the lower court must, as an initial matter, specifically state whether or not it believes plaintiff's proffered direct evidence of discrimination." *Thompkins,* 752 F.2d at 564. The district court found that "there was no discriminatory intent in violation of Title VII."[6] Recognizing our

5. This distinction between direct and circumstantial evidence raises the issue of what constitutes "direct" evidence. Dybczak v. Tuskegee Institute, 737 F.2d 1524, 1528 (11th Cir.1984), cert. denied, ___ U.S. ___, 105 S.Ct. 1180, 84 L.Ed.2d 328 (1985) (statistics are not direct evidence); Johnson v. Allyn & Bacon, Inc., 731 F.2d 64, 69 n. 6 (1st Cir.), cert. denied, ___ U.S. ___, 105 S.Ct. 433, 83 L.Ed.2d 359 (1984) (statistical evidence is circumstantial); Clay v. Hyatt Regency Hotel, 724 F.2d 721, 724 (8th Cir.1984).

Of course, a plaintiff has no stake in characterizing his evidence as either circumstantial or direct, since our holding in Part B, infra, regarding the burden of proof, has been construed by other courts as applicable regardless of whether the evidence is circumstantial or direct. *Lee,* 684 F.2d at 774. However the evidence is characterized, the *McDonnell Douglas* formulation is applicable when it is helpful in resolving the ultimate issue of intentional discrimination.

6. We recognize that this statement could be construed as a conclusion that, even though there may have been some discriminatory intent, that intent did not cause the discharge, and, therefore, was not in violation of Title VII. Even if the district court so concluded, remand for consideration of the evidence in light of the burden of proof set out in Part B, infra, is required.

deferential standard of review, we respectfully disagree with this conclusion of the district court. This conclusion draws on other findings of fact made by the district court. The district court made a crucial finding, adequately supported by the record, which indicates that discrimination was at least a factor in Blalock's discharge. The district court held:

> The shared beliefs of plaintiff and Mr. Woodward was an aspect of their personal relationship with one another. In fact, it was in part because of this shared experience that *Mr. Woodward tolerated conduct and attitudes on the part of plaintiff that he may not have tolerated with any employee with whom he did not share such a personal relationship.*
>
> The personal relationship between plaintiff and Mr. Woodward that motivated Mr. Woodward to tolerate plaintiff's poor performance as an employee was rooted in their shared religious experience. *When this personal relationship broke down, Mr. Woodward no longer felt motivated to close his eyes to plaintiff's attitudes and behavior as an employee.* It was at this point that Mr. Woodward decided to capitulate to Mr. Brewer's position that plaintiff should be asked to leave their company.   *   *   *
>
> It is clear that Messrs. Woodward and Blalock voluntarily spun an entangled web of work, religion and personal relationships. It is not, therefore, surprising that a break in their religious ties caused the entire web, including their once positive relationship, to collapse. *Plaintiff could then no longer rely upon Mr. Woodward's enhanced tolerance to save his job.* Regardless of the fact that religion was an important aspect of the personal relationship between plaintiff and Mr. Woodward, plaintiff has not proved that defendant fired him because of his religion or because of any particular religious beliefs he may have held.

(emphasis added).

The district court adequately captured the situation that existed at Metals Trades, but simply drew the wrong conclusion as to the effect of the situation. It is no doubt true that "Woodward tolerated conduct and attitudes on the part of plaintiff that he may not have tolerated with an employee with whom he did not share such a personal relationship," and that it was only when "this relationship broke down [that] Woodward no longer felt motivated to close his eyes to plaintiff's attitudes and behavior." These findings, however, reveal that religion played a role in Blalock's discharge. The district court found that Woodward treated Blalock differently at different times depending upon Blalock's current religious views. This is the essence of discrimination. Woodward was willing to give special consideration to those persons who shared his religious views, but, when Blalock's religious views changed, Woodward no longer gave Blalock this special consideration.

In addition to the district court's own findings, other evidence in the record reveals that religious discrimination played at least a role in the employment decision. Blalock was not actually fired until he refused to discuss Rothacker. In a letter to the Ohio Civil Rights Commission, Woodward asserted that one reason for the discharge was Blalock's refusal to answer a question. Woodward testified, however, that this referred to Blalock's refusal to discuss his situation with Rothacker. Woodward admitted telling Blalock that he should consider himself discharged until he reconciled himself with Rothacker. When Blalock attempted to regain his job, Woodward refused to discuss the matter separately from religion. All of these factors make it very clear that Blalock's change in his religious views was at least a factor in the discharge.

The district court may have been lead astray by the fact that Woodward and Brewer found Blalock's work performance problematic at the time of discharge. There is certainly sufficient evidence in the record to support the conclusion that at the time of discharge Blalock was not meeting the level of work performance then expected of him. The problem is that this same level of performance was acceptable to Metals Trades until Blalock's and Woodward's religious differences became exacerbated. When an employer expresses an enhanced tolerance of an employee's performance because of his religion, but lowers its level of tolerance when the employee's previously agreeable religious views change, the employer has engaged in intentional differential treatment based on religion.[7]

B.

The district court's opinion fails to articulate the standard of causation required of Blalock, perhaps because of its conclusion that no discriminatory intent was implicated in the case. The Court has not held "that the Title VII plaintiff must show that he would have in any event been rejected or discharged solely on the basis of his race, without regard to the alleged deficiencies; * * * no more is required to be shown than that race was a 'but for' cause." McDonald v. Santa Fe Trail Transportation Co., 427 U.S. 273, 282 n. 10, 96 S.Ct. 2574, 2580 n. 10, 49 L.Ed.2d 493 (1976); Bibbs v. Block, 749 F.2d 508, 511 (8th Cir. 1984) (reh'g en banc granted, March 8, 1985); Jack v. Texaco Research Center, 743 F.2d 1129, 1131 (5th Cir.1984); Lewis v. University of Pittsburgh, 725 F.2d 910, 915 (3d Cir.1983), cert. denied, ___ U.S. ___, 105 S.Ct. 266, 83 L.Ed.2d 202 (1984); Sumler v. City of Winston-Salem, 448 F.Supp. 519, 528 (M.D.N.C.1978). This "but for" causation is

---

7. If it seems harsh to conclude that an employer discriminates by evaluating an employee under normal standards when the employer had previously evaluated the employee under more lenient standards, it should be pointed out that Metals Trades created a high potential for discrimination when it hired Blalock. That is, from what appears in the record, Woodward never had a great need for an employee with Blalock's background and it seems doubtful that Blalock ever would have been hired had he been, for example, a Moslem. Similarly, during the initial phase of Blalock's tenure at Metals Trades, other employees who did not share Woodward's religious views were apparently held to a higher standard of performance. Had one of them been discharged for misconduct of a severity comparable to that engaged in by Blalock, he or she would have had a potential claim of religious discrimination.

satisfied when the plaintiff establishes that the defendant's discriminatory intent more likely than not was the basis of the adverse employment action. *Burdine*, 450 U.S. at 256, 101 S.Ct. at 1095; *Furnco*, 438 U.S. at 577, 98 S.Ct. at 2949; *Bibbs*, 749 F.2d at 511. The Court, however, has not expressly explained causation requirements in a Title VII dual motive case.[8]

Blalock contends that the district court should have applied the causation analysis of Mt. Healthy School District Board of Education v. Doyle, 429 U.S. 274, 97 S.Ct. 568, 50 L.Ed.2d 471 (1977), a case in which the plaintiff alleged that he was terminated due to exercise of his First Amendment rights.

> A rule of causation which focuses solely on whether protected conduct played a part, "substantial" or otherwise, in a decision not to rehire, could place an employee in a better position as a result of the exercise of constitutionally protected conduct than he would have occupied had he done nothing. * * * The constitutional principle at stake is sufficiently vindicated if such an employee is placed in no worse a position than if he had not engaged in the conduct. A borderline or marginal candidate should not have the employment question resolved against him because of constitutionally protected conduct. But that same candidate ought not to be able, by engaging in such conduct, to prevent his employer from assessing his performance record and reaching a decision not to rehire on the basis of that record, simply because the protected conduct makes the employer more certain of the correctness of its decision.

429 U.S. at 285–86, 97 S.Ct. at 575. Further,

> the burden was properly placed upon respondent to show that his conduct was constitutionally protected, and that this conduct was a "substantial factor"—or to put it in other words, that it was a "motivating factor" in the Board's decision not to rehire him. Respondent having carried that burden, however, the District Court should have gone on to determine whether the Board had shown by a preponderance of the evidence that it would have reached the same decision as to respondent's reemployment even in the absence of the protected conduct.

Id. at 287, 97 S.Ct. at 576 (footnote omitted); Givhan v. Western Line Consolidated School District, 439 U.S. 410, 416–17, 99 S.Ct. 693, 697, 58 L.Ed.2d 619 (1979). The Court has applied this causation standard (sometimes called the "same decision" test) to Fourteenth Amendment claims, Village of Arlington Heights v. Metropolitan Housing Development Corp., 429 U.S. 252, 270 n. 21, 97 S.Ct. 555, 566 n. 21, 50 L.Ed.2d 450 (1977),[9] and more recently, to unfair labor practices, NLRB v.

---

8. The *McDonnell Douglas* test, while considering other reasons for the discharge as articulated by the defendant, is designed to ascertain the "true" reason for the discharge. "In a mixed-motive context such as this, the challenged employment decision presumably was motivated by *both* pretextual (unlawful) and nonpretextual (lawful) reasons." *Bibbs*, 749 F.2d at 511 n. 1.

9. Proof that discriminatory purpose in part motivated the decision would

Transportation Management Corp., 462 U.S. 393, 399–400, 103 S.Ct. 2469, 2473, 76 L.Ed.2d 667 (1983).[10] In *Transportation Management,* the Court explained that "[t]he employer is a wrongdoer; he has acted out of a motive that is declared illegitimate by the statute. It is fair that he bear the risk that the influence of legal and illegal motives cannot be separated, because he knowingly created the risk and because the risk was created not by innocent activity but by his own wrongdoing." Id. at 403, 103 S.Ct. at 2475. Further, we have applied the *Mt. Healthy* standard to an action under the Federal Coal Mine Health and Safety Act of 1969 after initially applying the *Burdine* test. Boich v. Federal Mine Safety & Health Review Commission, 704 F.2d 275, vacated, 719 F.2d 194 (6th Cir.1983).

The Court has implicitly, at least, approved application of the *Mt. Healthy* standards in Title VII cases. In East Texas Motor Freight System, Inc. v. Rodriguez, 431 U.S. 395, 97 S.Ct. 1891, 52 L.Ed.2d 453 (1977), the Court, citing *Mt. Healthy,* held that "[e]ven assuming, *arguendo,* that the company's failure even to consider the applications was discriminatory, the company was entitled to prove at trial that the respondents [plaintiffs] had not been injured because they were not qualified and would not have been hired in any event." Id. at 403 n. 9, 97 S.Ct. at 1897 n. 9. See Easley v. Anheuser-Busch, Inc., 758 F.2d 251, 262 (8th Cir.1985); King v. Trans World Airlines, 738 F.2d 255, 257–58 (8th Cir.1984).

Further, the Court's decisions in "pattern or practice" cases and class actions suggest that the burden of persuasion may in some cases properly be placed on the employer with respect to whether the same decision would have been reached even in the absence of discriminatory animus. In *Teamsters,* the Court held:

> By "demonstrating the existence of a discriminatory hiring pattern and practice" the plaintiffs had made out a prima facie case of discrimination against the individual class members; the burden therefore shifted to the employer "to prove that individuals who reapply were not in fact victims of previous hiring discrimination."
> * * * The *Franks* case thus illustrates another means by which a Title VII plaintiff's initial burden of proof can be met. The class there alleged a broad-based policy of employment discrimination; upon proof of that allegation there were reasonable grounds to infer that individual hiring decisions were made in pursuit of the discriminatory policy

have shifted to the Village the burden of establishing that the same decision would have resulted even had the impermissible purpose not been considered. If this were established, the complaining party in a case of this kind no longer fairly could attribute the injury complained of to improper consideration of a discriminatory purpose. In such circumstances, there would be no justification for judicial interference with the challenged decision.

Village of Arlington Heights, 429 U.S. at 270 n. 21, 97 S.Ct. at 566 n. 21. See also Hunter v. Underwood, ___ U.S. ___, 105 S.Ct. 1916, 1920, 85 L.Ed.2d 222 (1985).

10. "[P]roof that the discharge would have occurred in any event and for valid reasons amounted to an affirmative defense on which the employer carried the burden of proof by a preponderance of the evidence." *Transportation Management Corp.,* 462 U.S. at 400, 403, 103 S.Ct. at 2475.

and to require the employer to come forth with evidence dispelling that inference.

431 U.S. at 359, 97 S.Ct. at 1866 (footnote omitted). This shift is justified because "the finding of a pattern or practice changed the position of the employer to that of a proved wrongdoer." Id. at 359–60 n. 45, 97 S.Ct. at 1867 n. 45; Lee v. Washington County Board of Education, 625 F.2d 1235, 1239 (5th Cir.1980); Mims v. Wilson, 514 F.2d 106, 109–10 (5th Cir.1975).

Several decisions of our sister circuits have adopted the *Mt. Healthy* causation standard in dual motive Title VII cases. *Miles,* 750 F.2d at 876; Smith v. State of Georgia, 749 F.2d 683, 687 (11th Cir. 1985); Smallwood v. United Air Lines, Inc., 728 F.2d 614 (4th Cir.), cert. denied, ___ U.S. ___, 105 S.Ct. 120, 83 L.Ed.2d 62 (1984); *Bell,* 715 F.2d 1552 (11th Cir.1983); *Perryman,* 698 F.2d at 1143; Day v. Mathews, 530 F.2d 1083, 1085 (D.C.Cir.1976). But see Norcross v. Sneed, 755 F.2d 113, 118–119 (8th Cir.1985) (refused to apply *Mt. Healthy* to action under Rehabilitation Act of 1973, 29 U.S.C. § 794); Toney v. Block, 705 F.2d 1364 (D.C.Cir.1983). "Defendant cannot rebut this type of showing of discrimination [direct evidence of discriminatory motivation] simply by articulating or producing evidence of legitimate, nondiscriminatory reasons. * * * [D]efendant can rebut only by proving by a preponderance of the evidence that the same decision would have been reached even absent the presence of that factor." *Lee,* 684 F.2d at 774 (footnotes omitted). This is true whether the illegal motive is proven "by either circumstantial or direct evidence." Id.; *Zebedeo,* 582 F.Supp. at 1412 n. 7.[11]

We recently suggested approval of such a causation standard, noting that where there is "direct evidence of a facially discriminatory

11. This analysis is not inconsistent with the burden-shifting provisions of *Burdine.* League of United Latin American Citizens, Monterey Chapter 2055 v. City of Salinas Fire Department, 654 F.2d 557, 558–59 (9th Cir.1981). *Burdine* does not assume that the employer is a wrongdoer, and, therefore, only requires that the employer produce evidence relative to the reason for discharge. To the contrary, *Transportation Management, Mt. Healthy,* and the instant case all involve proven wrongdoers—those who acted at least in part based on discriminatory intent. Accordingly, to require the employer to prove that he would have reached the same decision even in the absence of consideration of impermissible factors does not, as rejected in *Burdine,* require an employer to prove, in the first instance, that its decision was lawful. 450 U.S. at 257, 101 S.Ct. at 1095. In *Transportation Management,* the Court noted that *Burdine* "is inapposite" to the dual motive issue. The Court held that, in *Burdine,*

the question was who had "[t]he ultimate burden of persuading the trier of fact that the defendant intentionally discriminated against the plaintiff * * *" 450 U.S. at 253, 101 S.Ct. at 1093. The Court discussed only the situation in which the issue is whether either illegal or legal motives, but not both, were the "true" motives behind the decision. It thus addressed the pretext case.

462 U.S. at 400 n. 5, 103 S.Ct. at 2473 n. 5. On the issue of discriminatory intent, the employer need only *produce* evidence of legitimate business purposes for the discharge to combat any inferences of discriminatory intent that might be drawn from plaintiff's proof. However, once plaintiff has established that the discharge was likely motivated by discriminatory animus, plaintiff has established his case, and it is defendant's burden to *prove* that the discharge would have occurred despite the proven discriminatory animus.

policy, the burden of persuasion would shift to the defendant to justify its actions by whatever means available." Lujan v. Franklin County Board of Education, 766 F.2d 917, 929 n. 16 (6th Cir.1985), citing *Bell,* 715 F.2d 1552. See also EEOC v. Maxwell Co., 726 F.2d 282, 283–84 (6th Cir.1984).

The Eighth Circuit has rejected the *Mt. Healthy* causation standard finding that

> [r]ather than requiring proof that race was a "substantial" or "determining" factor in the decision, we find that a plaintiff proves his claim of unlawful discrimination by showing that "a discriminatory reason more likely [than not] motivated the employer." *Burdine,* 450 U.S. at 256, 101 S.Ct. at 1095 * * * Nothing more is required of a plaintiff to establish liability under Title VII. Once the trier of fact has found that race was a factor influencing the decision, we find it error to attempt to quantify race as a minor factor. * * *

> We find it inherently inconsistent to say that race was a discernable factor in the decision, but the same decision would have been made absent racial considerations. Thus, we think that once race is shown to be a causative factor in the employment decision, it is clearly erroneous to find that racial considerations did not affect the outcome of the decision.

Bibbs, 749 F.2d at 511–12. The court apparently relied on *Burdine* in refusing to shift the burden of proof to defendant. Id. at 513.

For two reasons, we decline to follow *Bibbs.* First, the court in *Bibbs* assumed that the *Mt. Healthy* standard places a greater burden on a plaintiff than does *Burdine.* We disagree. Under *Mt. Healthy,* a plaintiff must show by a preponderance of the evidence that his race or religion was a "motivating factor" in the employer's decision to discharge him. Under *Burdine,* a plaintiff must show that the discharge was more likely than not motivated by race or religion. We discern no meaningful difference in these burdens. Second, the court in *Bibbs* indicated that if race was a motivating factor in the employer's decision, it would be "inherently inconsistent" to find that the same decision would have been made even in the absence of the unlawful motivation. We likewise disagree. Certainly, in some fact situations, a finding that an employment decision was motivated by discriminatory animus would effectively preclude an employer from contending that the same decision would have been made regardless of the employer's motivation. However, as the cases reveal, employment decisions are often complex, and, where dozens of factors are involved in evaluation of an employee, the fact that one such factor is impermissible does not necessarily preclude the contention that the adverse employment action would have been taken regardless of the impermissible factor. Of course, the fact that plaintiff's case has already been established before the burden shifts, emphasizes the difficulty of the employer's burden.

Beyond this, we leave further elucidation of how an employer can meet his burden to the concrete facts of future cases.[12]

Accordingly, we hold that in order to prove a violation of Title VII, a plaintiff need demonstrate by a preponderance of the evidence that the employer's decision to take an adverse employment action was more likely than not motivated by a criterion proscribed by the statute. Upon such proof, the employer has the burden to prove that the adverse employment action would have been taken even in the absence of the impermissible motivation, and that, therefore, the discriminatory animus was not the cause of the adverse employment action.

(e) Subjective Criteria Cases

GRIFFIN v. CARLIN

United States Court of Appeals for the Eleventh Circuit, 1985.
755 F.2d 1516.

TUTTLE, SENIOR CIRCUIT JUDGE:

Ernest Griffin and 21 other black employees and former employees of the United States Postal Service at Jacksonville, Florida, appeal from a decision of the district court finding no classwide or individual discrimination under Title VII of the Civil Rights Act of 1964, as amended, 42 U.S.C. § 2000e–16. Appellants contend that the district court erred in excluding their challenge to written tests used in the promotion process, in excluding all disparate impact claims, and in finding no disparate treatment in promotions, awards, discipline, and details. On cross-appeal, the Postal Service argues that the district court erred in allowing a third-party complaint to serve as the administrative basis for this suit and in certifying this suit as a class action.

On August 29, 1971, Griffin filed with the United States Civil Service Commission a complaint under the third-party complaint procedure authorized by then-current regulations of the Commission and of the Postal Service. 5 C.F.R. § 713.204(d)(6) (1971); 39 C.F.R. § 747.5(a) (1971). The complaint stated:

> Please accept this letter as a third party discrimination complaint against Postmaster J.E. Workman of the Jacksonville, Florida Post Office. This discriminatory complaint is based on race since qualified blacks were and are still being systematically excluded in training and development and opportunities for advancements.

The Postal Service investigated the complaint and found no discrimination.

---

12. We recognize, however, that "[h]aving injured respondent [plaintiff] solely on the basis of an unlawful classification, petitioner [employer] cannot now hypothesize that it might have employed lawful means of achieving the same result." *Regents of University of California v. Bakke,* 438 U.S. 265, 320 n. 54, 98 S.Ct. 2733, 2764 n. 54, 57 L.Ed.2d 750 (1978). Consideration of an employer's other grounds for discharge should not "result in fictitious recasting of past conduct." *Id.*

On July 7, 1972, plaintiffs filed a class action suit in federal district court challenging defendant's use of discriminatory assignment and promotion methods and other discriminatory employment practices. On January 9, 1973, the district court entered an order authorizing plaintiffs to proceed as representatives of a class and dismissing that portion of the plaintiffs' complaint which challenged the use of written tests in the promotion process. The dismissal was based on the court's finding that plaintiffs had failed to exhaust administrative remedies as to the testing issue.

In 1976, plaintiff Griffin was fired from the Postal Service. He appealed the discharge under the then-existing regulatory scheme to the United States Civil Service Commission. In that appeal, he raised the claim that he had been discriminated against because of his race and that the action was part of a pattern and practice of racial discrimination and reprisal against those persons challenging discrimination. Griffin timely filed a supplemental complaint in the present action raising those claims. On the district court's order, a consolidated amended complaint was filed on November 12, 1981. This complaint again alleged discrimination against blacks in defendant's assignment and promotion methods and other employment practices.

On September 8, 1982, the district court dismissed plaintiffs' disparate impact claims on the grounds that plaintiffs' pleadings had failed to put defendants on notice as to which employment practices would be challenged on this theory and that only objective, facially neutral employment practices could be challenged on a disparate impact theory. Thus, the case proceeded to trial on a disparate treatment theory.

The Jacksonville Post Office employed an average of 1,880 persons during the period covered by this lawsuit. Approximately 32 percent of these employees were black. The employees included clerks, mail handlers, city carriers, window clerks, and motor vehicle operators.

The Jacksonville Post Office promotes persons to supervisory positions almost entirely from within its work force. The process for promotion to initial supervisory positions has undergone some changes during the period covered by the lawsuit. In 1968, the Post Office used two written examinations, one for vehicle services and one for the post office branch. In order to be placed on the supervisory register and be eligible for promotion, employees had to attain a particular score on the examination. The top 15 percent of the employees on the register were placed in the "zone of consideration" and were notified of supervisory vacancies. In 1972, the zone of consideration standard was eliminated and persons who had attained a passing score on the examination were evaluated and graded by their supervisors. Those receiving an "A" rating were eligible for immediate promotion. In 1976, the examination was eliminated and employees were instead required to complete a training program as a precondition for promotion. In 1978, the Postal Service initiated the Profile Assessment System for Supervisors (PASS) which made eligibility for the supervisory registers dependent on both supervisory assessment and self-assessment. No written examination was used under the PASS program. Under all of these promotion systems, promotion advisory boards interviewed and recommended eligible candidates for promotion, and the final selection was made by the Postmaster.

Both plaintiffs and defendants relied heavily on statistical data. Plaintiffs' statistics showed that blacks are far more likely to hold jobs at level 4 or lower and far less likely to hold jobs at or above level 7, the initial supervisory level.[2] According to plaintiffs, the probabilities that the grade distributions shown in their tables would occur by chance are one in 10,000. Plaintiffs' statistics showed that while 35 percent of the work force is black, blacks held only 5 percent of all supervisory jobs in 1969 and only 21 percent in 1981. These statistics also indicated that blacks were promoted to supervisory positions in numbers far lower than expected from 1964 through 1976. Plaintiffs contend that the key to the under-representation of blacks in supervisory positions is their under-representation on the supervisory registers. Their statistics indicated that the probabilities that the number of blacks on the registers could have occurred by chance ranged from 15 in one hundred trillion in 1968 to 67 in 100,000 in 1977.[3]

2.

Year	Race	Levels 1–6	Levels 7 & Above	% at 7+
1969	Black	720	10	1%
	Other	1181	171	13%
1970	Black	711	12	2%
	Other	1133	171	13%
1971	Black	666	11	2%
	Other	1134	166	13%
1972	Black	647	11	2%
	Other	1068	166	13%
1973	Black	756	17	2%
	Other	1230	162	12%
1974	Black	753	23	3%
	Other	1221	177	13%
1975	Black	744	27	4%
	Other	1213	185	13%
1976	Black	725	28	4%
	Other	1159	186	14%
1977	Black	712	28	4%
	Other	1122	181	14%
1978	Black	702	43	6%
	Other	1103	183	14%
1979	Black	680	68	9%
	Other	1106	227	17%
1980	Black	734	51	6%
	Other	1189	195	14%
1981	Black	728	46	6%
	Other	1225	185	13%

Source: Table 12, Plaintiffs' Exhibit # 1.

3.

Register	Craft		Registers		Probability	
	White	Black	White	Black		
1968	1084	583	86	3	.1481	D–12*
1970	1070	580	123	16	.4160	D–10
1973	1053	617	216	49	.1206	D–11

Plaintiffs' statistics were based on the use of the entire craft work force of the Jacksonville Post Office as the applicant pool for supervisory positions. The government contends that the appropriate pool is those individuals on the supervisory registers. Using this pool, the government's statistics showed no evidence of systemic discrimination against blacks seeking supervisory positions.

Plaintiffs' statistics showed a consistent statistically significant over-disciplining of blacks in comparison to their numbers in the relevant work force. Blacks, who constitute 35 percent of the work force, received between 52 and 67 percent of the discipline.[4] The government concedes that blacks are disciplined more often than whites, but argues that factors other than race explain the disparity. Defendants' statistics illustrated that black employees at the Jacksonville Post Office are, on the average, younger than white employees and take more time off from work. The Postal Service statistics also demonstrated that, controlling for the number of previous offenses, black employees did not receive more severe punishment than white employees.

In finding no discrimination, the district court held that plaintiffs' statistical tables had negligible probative value. This finding was based in part on the court's determination that plaintiffs' expert had failed to control for relevant variables, such as the fact that promotions

	Craft		Registers		Probability	
Register	White	Black	White	Black		
1974	1055	652	155	71	.1399	D–01
1975	982	627	230	84	.3246	D–06
May '77	949	641	81	26	.2436	D–03
Dec. '77	949	641	89	32	.6700	D–03
1978 PM	933	611	14	5	.1708	
Vab	933	611	16	9	.4413	
CS	933	611	105	59	.1811	
MP	933	611	116	93	.9492	

* D–12 indicates that in the number to the left the decimal point should be followed by 12 zeroes, and so on.

Source: Table 2, Plaintiffs' Exhibit # 1.

4.

Incidences of Disciplinary Action by Race, Percentage of Discipline and Year.

Year	Black		Other		Total	Probability
	#	%	#	%		
1969	66	54%	57	46%	123	.001
1970	77	66%	39	34%	116	.001
1971	63	65%	34	35%	97	.001
1972	51	65%	28	35%	79	.001
1973	38	55%	31	45%	69	.001
1974	100	51%	98	49%	198	.001
1975	324	64%	182	36%	36	.001
1976	161	56%	124	44%	285	.001
1977	22	67%	11	33%	33	.001
1978	204	58%	144	41%	348	.001
1979	154	55%	124	45%	278	.001
1980	178	52%	165	48%	343	.001
1981	305	52%	285	48%	590	.001

Source: Table 9.1, Plaintiffs' Exhibit # 1.

were made only from those on the supervisory registers. In addition, the court noted that defendants were able to point out errors in many of plaintiffs' tables, that many of plaintiffs' tables provided no raw data, and that the credibility of plaintiffs' expert was undercut by his presentation at the last minute of a substantially new statistical report. The court found the report prepared by defendant's expert to be a reliable and credible analysis of the promotion practices at the Post Office. The court also found that, based upon the government's statistics, it is likely that there were different characteristics, patterns of conduct, or reactions to circumstance which explain the different levels of discipline.

Appellants introduced the testimony of 24 black class members to bring their statistical evidence to life. The district court concluded that appellants had not produced a single witness who had demonstrated a claim of discrimination. The court found that many of plaintiffs' witnesses were not believable, that others were mistaken that they were eligible for promotion, that others were not as qualified as the employee selected, that some of the promotions challenged had gone to black employees, and that there were other non-discriminatory reasons to explain the other alleged instances of discrimination.

* * *

II. DISMISSAL OF DISPARATE IMPACT CLAIMS

In the court below plaintiffs sought to rely on a disparate impact theory as well as on a disparate treatment theory. Plaintiffs sought to apply the disparate impact theory both to the final results of the multi-component promotion process and to several component parts of that process, including promotion advisory boards, awards, and discipline. In its order of September 8, 1982, the district court granted defendant's motion to dismiss all claims by plaintiff based on a disparate impact theory. The court found that disparate impact analysis is appropriate only to challenge objective, facially neutral employment practices, and not to challenge either the cumulative effect of employment practices or subjective decision-making. The court further found that plaintiffs' pleadings had failed to put defendants on notice as to which employment practices would be challenged on a disparate impact theory.

The district court relied on *Pouncy v. Prudential Insurance Company of America,* 668 F.2d 795 (5th Cir.1982), and on *Harris v. Ford Motor Co.,* 651 F.2d 609 (8th Cir.1981). In *Harris,* the Eighth Circuit held that a subjective decision-making system cannot alone form the foundation for a disparate impact case. Id. at 611. In *Pouncy,* the Fifth Circuit stated:

> The discriminatory impact model of proof in an employment discrimination case is not, however, the appropriate vehicle from which to launch a wide ranging attack on the cumulative effect of a company's employment practices. * * * We require proof that a specific practice results in a discriminatory impact on a class in an employer's work force in order to allocate fairly the parties' respective

burdens of proof at trial. * * * Identification by the aggrieved party of the specific employment practice responsible for the disparate impact is necessary so that the employer can respond by offering proof of its legitimacy.

Id. at 800–01.

A recent Eleventh Circuit decision referred to the *Pouncy* case and indicated that use of the disparate impact model to attack the excessive subjectivity of a personnel system is "troublesome." The court stated, however:

> Former Fifth Circuit precedent, however, indicates that subjective selection and promotion procedures may be attacked under the disparate impact theory. See Johnson v. Uncle Ben's, Inc., 628 F.2d 419, 426–27 (5th Cir.1980), vacated, 451 U.S. 902, 101 S.Ct. 1967, 68 L.Ed.2d 290 (1981), modified and aff'd in part, rev'd in part, 657 F.2d 750 (5th Cir.1981), cert. denied, 459 U.S. 967, 103 S.Ct. 293, 74 L.Ed.2d 277 (1982).

Eastland v. Tennessee Valley Authority, 704 F.2d 613, 619–20 (11th Cir. 1983), cert. denied sub nom., James v. Tennessee Valley Authority, ___ U.S. ___, 104 S.Ct. 1415, 79 L.Ed.2d 741 (1984). In *Eastland,* the Court declined to decide whether the prior Fifth Circuit case law was distinguishable because the Court found that plaintiffs had failed to prove discrimination under the disparate impact theory.

In this case the issues of whether the disparate impact model can be used to challenge the final results of a multi-component selection process and whether the disparate impact model can be used to challenge subjective elements of a selection process are squarely before us. We find that we are bound by former Fifth Circuit precedent to allow disparate impact challenges to the end result of multi-component selection procedures and to subjective selection procedures.[5] Further, we hold that even if these prior Fifth Circuit cases were not binding, use of the disparate impact theory to challenge the end result of multi-component selection processes and to challenge subjective elements of those processes is appropriate. We therefore reverse the order of the district court dismissing plaintiffs' disparate impact claims.

Several decisions of the former Fifth Circuit, binding on this panel, applied a disparate impact analysis to the end result of multi-component selection processes containing subjective elements. For example, in Johnson v. Uncle Ben's, Inc., 628 F.2d 419, 426–27 (5th Cir.1980), vacated, 451 U.S. 902, 101 S.Ct. 1967, 68 L.Ed.2d 290 (1981), modified and aff'd in part, rev'd in part, 657 F.2d 750 (5th Cir.1981), cert. denied, 459 U.S. 967, 103 S.Ct. 293, 74 L.Ed.2d 277 (1982), the court applied a disparate impact analysis to a promotion system based on the use of subjective supervisory evaluations. See also, Crawford v. Western Electric Co., Inc., 614 F.2d 1300, 1318 (5th Cir.1980) (applying disparate

5. Fifth Circuit decisions prior to October 1, 1981, are binding in this Circuit and cannot be overruled except by the court acting en banc. Bonner v. City of Prichard, 661 F.2d 1206, 1207 (11th Cir.1981).

impact analysis to index review system involving subjective elements); Rowe v. General Motors Corp., 457 F.2d 348, 354–55 (5th Cir.1972) (applying disparate impact analysis to promotion system involving foreman's recommendations).

Even if we were not bound by these decisions to allow application of disparate impact analysis to the end result of a multi-component promotion process and to processes involving subjective elements, we would still be inclined not to follow the decision of the current Fifth Circuit in *Pouncy*.[6] The Supreme Court first articulated the disparate impact model of discrimination, under which proof of discriminatory intent is not necessary, in Griggs v. Duke Power Co., 401 U.S. 424, 91 S.Ct. 849, 28 L.Ed.2d 158 (1971). In *Griggs,* the Court indicated that Title VII requires "the removal of artificial, arbitrary, and unnecessary barriers to employment" which "operate as 'built-in headwinds' for minority groups and are unrelated to measuring job capability." Id. at 431–32, 91 S.Ct. at 853–54. The Court in *Griggs* did not differentiate between objective and subjective barriers, and, in fact, the Court made frequent references to "practices" and "procedures," terms that clearly encompass more than isolated, objective components of the overall process.[7]

In the recent case of Connecticut v. Teal, 457 U.S. 440, 102 S.Ct. 2525, 73 L.Ed.2d 130 (1982), the Supreme Court held that the "bottom line" result of a promotional process could not be used as a defense to a disparate impact challenge to a particular selection procedure used in that promotion process. The Court emphasized the holding in *Griggs* that Title VII requires the elimination of "artificial, arbitrary, and

6. We note that while many subsequent Fifth Circuit cases have followed *Pouncy, see e.g., Carroll v. Sears, Roebuck & Co.,* 708 F.2d 183, 188 (5th Cir.1983) ("The use of subjective criteria to evaluate employees in hiring and job placement decisions is not within the category of facially neutral procedures to which the category of facially neutral procedures to which the disparate impact model is applied."), at least one post-*Pouncy* Fifth Circuit decision has applied disparate impact analysis to a subjective promotional system. Page v. U.S. Industries, Inc., 726 F.2d 1038 (5th Cir.1984). In *Page,* the Court noted the *Pouncy* decision but stated:

It is clear that a promotional system which is based upon subjective selection criteria is not discriminatory per se. Consequently, such a system can be facially neutral but yet be discriminatorily applied so that it impacts adversely on one group. In using a disparate impact analysis, the district court pointed out that many of this Court's decisions examine the classwide impact of a subjective promotional system. See, e.g.,

James v. Stockham Valves & Fittings Co., 559 F.2d 310 (5th Cir.1977), cert. denied, 434 U.S. 1034, 98 S.Ct. 767, 54 L.Ed.2d 781 (1978); Rowe v. General Motors Corp., 457 F.2d 348 (5th Cir.1972). We agree with the district court's assessment that the subjective promotional system in this case indeed may have had a classwide impact. Thus, we examine the defendant's promotional system under the disparate impact model as well.

Id. at 1046. We note also the recent decision of the D.C. Circuit in Segar v. Smith, 738 F.2d 1249, 1288 n. 34 (D.C.Cir.1984) ("Though these practices arguably encompass some subjective judgments as to agents' performance, we find that disparate impact appropriately applies to them.")

7. E.g., 401 U.S. at 430, 91 S.Ct. at 853 ("practices, procedures, or tests"); id. at 431, 91 S.Ct. at 853 ("practices"); id. at 432, 91 S.Ct. at 854 ("employment procedures or testing mechanisms"); id. ("any given requirement").

unnecessary barriers to employment," and again did not differentiate between objective and subjective criteria nor give any indication that a disparate impact challenge could not be made to a promotional system as a whole. See 457 U.S. at 448–452, 102 S.Ct. at 2532–2534. The Court noted the legislative history of the 1972 amendments to Title VII, 86 Stat. 103–113, which extended Title VII to federal government employees. The Court pointed out that Congress recognized and endorsed the disparate impact analysis employed in *Griggs*. The Court specifically cited the Senate Report (S.Rep.No. 92–415, p. 5 (1971)), which stated:

> Employment discrimination as viewed today is a * * * complex and pervasive phenomenon. Experts familiar with the subject now generally describe the problem in terms of 'systems' and 'effects' rather than simply intentional wrongs.

Connecticut v. Teal, 457 U.S. 440, 447 n. 8, 102 S.Ct. 2525, 2531 n. 8, 73 L.Ed.2d 130. The dissenters in *Teal*, while disagreeing with the Court's conclusion that the bottom line could not be used as a defense, clearly indicated their understanding that disparate impact challenges could be made to the total selection process. The dissenters stated that "our disparate-impact cases consistently have considered whether the result of an employer's *total selection process* had an adverse impact upon the protected group." Id. at 458, 102 S.Ct. at 2537 (Powell, J., dissenting) (emphasis in original).

We have repeatedly held that subjective practices such as interviews and supervisory recommendations are capable of operating as barriers to minority advancement. See, e.g., Johnson, 628 F.2d at 426; Rowe, 457 F.2d at 359; Miles v. M.N.C. Corp., 750 F.2d 867, 871 (11th Cir. Jan. 13, 1985). Exclusion of such subjective practices from the reach of the disparate impact model of analysis is likely to encourage employers to use subjective, rather than objective, selection criteria. Rather than validate education and other objective criteria, employers could simply take such criteria into account in subjective interviews or review panel decisions. It could not have been the intent of Congress to provide employers with an incentive to use such devices rather than validated objective criteria.

Likewise, limiting the disparate impact model to situations in which a single component of the process results in an adverse impact completely exempts the situation in which an adverse impact is caused by the interaction of two or more components. This problem was recognized in the recent Eighth Circuit decision in Gilbert v. City of Little Rock, Ark., 722 F.2d 1390 (8th Cir.1983), cert. denied, ___ U.S. ___, 104 S.Ct. 2347, 80 L.Ed.2d 820 (1984). The Court there held that the district court's finding of no discrimination under a disparate impact theory was incorrect because "the district court neglected to adequately consider the interrelationship of the component factors and, more specifically, whether the oral interview and performance appraisal factors * * * had a disparate impact. * * *" Id. at 1397–98.

Finally, we note that the Uniform Guidelines on Employee Selection Procedures, 29 C.F.R. § 1607, developed by the four federal agencies with responsibility for enforcing Title VII, interpret the disparate impact model to apply to all selection procedures, whether objective or subjective. The Guidelines define the selection procedures to which a disparate impact analysis applies as follows:

> Any measure, combination of measures, or procedure used as a basis for any employment decision. Selection procedures include the full range of assessment techniques from traditional paper and pencil tests, performance tests, training programs, or probationary periods and physical, educational, and work experience requirements through informal or casual interviews and unscored application forms.

29 C.F.R. § 1607.16(Q).

We therefore reverse the order of the district court dismissing plaintiffs' disparate impact claims and remand to that Court for consideration of the plaintiffs' disparate impact challenges to the final result of the defendants' overall promotion process and to specific components of that process whether subjective or objective.

Notes

The courts of appeals are split on the issue of the applicability of disparate impact analysis to subjective selection procedures. The Fourth, Fifth, Eighth, and Tenth Circuits have held that disparate impact analysis applies only to objective employee selection criteria. EEOC v. Federal Reserve Bank of Richmond, 698 F.2d 633 (4th Cir.1983); Pouncy v. Prudential Insurance Co. of America, 668 F.2d 795 (5th Cir.1982); Talley v. United States Postal Service, 720 F.2d 505 (8th Cir.1983); Harris v. Ford Motor Co., 651 F.2d 609 (8th Cir.1981); Mortensen v. Callaway, 672 F.2d 822 (10th Cir. 1982). The Sixth and District of Columbia Circuits have upheld the use of disparate impact in the subjective criteria cases. Rowe v. Cleveland Pnuematic Co., Numerical Controls, Inc., 690 F.2d 88 (6th Cir.1982); Segar v. Smith, 738 F.2d 1249 (D.C.Cir.1984).

C. ORDER AND ALLOCATION OF THE BURDENS OF PROOF

TEXAS DEPARTMENT OF COMMUNITY AFFAIRS v. BURDINE

Supreme Court of the United States, 1981.
450 U.S. 248, 101 S.Ct. 1089, 67 L.Ed.2d 207.

JUSTICE POWELL delivered the opinion of the Court.

This case requires us to address again the nature of the evidentiary burden placed upon the defendant in an employment discrimination suit brought under Title VII of the Civil Rights Act of 1964, 42 U.S.C. § 2000e et seq. The narrow question presented is whether, after the plaintiff has proved a prima facie case of discriminatory treatment, the burden shifts to the defendant to persuade the court by a preponderance of the evidence that legitimate, non-discriminatory reasons for the challenged employment action existed.

I

Petitioner, the Texas Department of Community Affairs (TDCA), hired respondent, a female, in January 1972, for the position of accounting clerk in the Public Service Careers Division (PSC). PSC provided training and employment opportunities in the public sector for unskilled workers. When hired, respondent possessed several years' experience in employment training. She was promoted to Field Services Coordinator in July 1972. Her supervisor resigned in November of that year, and respondent was assigned additional duties. Although she applied for the supervisor's position of Project Director, the position remained vacant for six months.

PSC was funded completely by the United States Department of Labor. The Department was seriously concerned about inefficiencies at PSC. In February 1973, the Department notified the Executive Director of TDCA, B.R. Fuller, that it would terminate PSC the following month. TDCA officials, assisted by respondent, persuaded the Department to continue funding the program, conditioned upon PSC's reforming its operations. Among the agreed conditions were the appointment of a permanent Project Director and a complete reorganization of the PSC staff.

After consulting with personnel within TDCA, Fuller hired a male from another division of the agency as Project Director. In reducing the PSC staff, he fired respondent along with two other employees, and retained another male, Walz, as the only professional employee in the division. It is undisputed that respondent had maintained her application for the position of Project Director and had requested to remain with TDCA. Respondent soon was rehired by TDCA and assigned to another division of the agency. She received the exact salary paid to the Project Director at PSC, and the subsequent promotions she has received have kept her salary and responsibility commensurate with what she would have received had she been appointed Project Director.

Respondent filed this suit in the United States District Court for the Western District of Texas. She alleged that the failure to promote and the subsequent decision to terminate her had been predicated on gender discrimination in violation of Title VII. After a bench trial, the District Court held that neither decision was based on gender discrimination. The court relied on the testimony of Fuller that the employment decisions necessitated by the commands of the Department of Labor were based on consultation among trusted advisers and a nondiscriminatory evaluation of the relative qualifications of the individuals involved. He testified that the three individuals terminated did not work well together, and that TDCA thought that eliminating this problem would improve PSC's efficiency. The court accepted this explanation as rational and, in effect, found no evidence that the decisions not to promote and to terminate respondent were prompted by gender discrimination.

The Court of Appeals for the Fifth Circuit reversed in part. 608 F.2d 563 (1979). The court held that the District Court's "implicit evidentiary finding" that the male hired as Project Director was better qualified for that position than respondent was not clearly erroneous. Accordingly, the court affirmed the District Court's finding that respondent was not discriminated against when she was not promoted. The Court of Appeals, however, reversed the District Court's finding that Fuller's testimony sufficiently had rebutted respondent's prima facie case of gender discrimination in the decision to terminate her employment at PSC. The court reaffirmed its previously announced views that the defendant in a Title VII case bears the burden of proving by a preponderance of the evidence the existence of legitimate nondiscriminatory reasons for the employment action and that the defendant also must prove by objective evidence that those hired or promoted were better qualified than the plaintiff. The court found that Fuller's testimony did not carry either of these evidentiary burdens. It, therefore, reversed the judgment of the District Court and remanded the case for computation of backpay. Because the decision of the Court of Appeals as to the burden of proof borne by the defendant conflicts with interpretations of our precedents adopted by other Courts of Appeals, we granted certiorari. 447 U.S. 920, 100 S.Ct. 3009, 65 L.Ed.2d 1112 (1980). We now vacate the Fifth Circuit's decision and remand for application of the correct standard.

II

In McDonnell Douglas Corp. v. Green, 411 U.S. 792, 93 S.Ct. 1817, 36 L.Ed.2d 668 (1973), we set forth the basic allocation of burdens and order of presentation of proof in a Title VII case alleging discriminatory treatment.[5] First, the plaintiff has the burden of proving by the preponderance of the evidence a prima facie case of discrimination. Second, if the plaintiff succeeds in proving the prima facie case, the burden shifts to the defendant "to articulate some legitimate, nondiscriminatory reason for the employee's rejection." Id., at 802, 93 S.Ct. at 1824. Third, should the defendant carry this burden, the plaintiff must then have an opportunity to prove by a preponderance of the evidence that the legitimate reasons offered by the defendant were not its true reasons, but were a pretext for discrimination. Id., at 804, 93 S.Ct., at 1825.

The nature of the burden that shifts to the defendant should be understood in light of the plaintiff's ultimate and intermediate burdens. The ultimate burden of persuading the trier of fact that the defendant

---

5. We have recognized that the factual issues, and therefore the character of the evidence presented, differ when the plaintiff claims that a facially neutral employment policy has a discriminatory impact on protected classes. See *McDonnell Douglas,* 411 U.S., at 802, n. 14, 93 S.Ct., at 1824 n. 14; Teamsters v. United States, 431 U.S. 324, 335–336, and n. 15, 97 S.Ct. 1843, 1854–1855, n. 15, 52 L.Ed.2d 396 (1977).

intentionally discriminated against the plaintiff remains at all times with the plaintiff. See Board of Trustees of Keene State College v. Sweeney, 439 U.S. 24, 25, n. 2, 99 S.Ct. 295, 296, n. 2, 58 L.Ed.2d 216 (1978); id., at 29, 99 S.Ct., at 297 (STEVENS, J., dissenting). See generally 9 J. Wigmore, Evidence § 2489 (3d ed. 1940) (the burden of persuasion "never shifts"). The *McDonnell Douglas* division of intermediate evidentiary burdens serves to bring the litigants and the court expeditiously and fairly to this ultimate question.

The burden of establishing a prima facie case of disparate treatment is not onerous. The plaintiff must prove by a preponderance of the evidence that she applied for an available position for which she was qualified, but was rejected under circumstances which give rise to an inference of unlawful discrimination.[6] The prima facie case serves an important function in the litigation: it eliminates the most common nondiscriminatory reasons for the plaintiff's rejection. See Teamsters v. United States, 431 U.S. 324, 358, and n. 44, 97 S.Ct. 1843, 1866, n. 44, 52 L.Ed.2d 396 (1977). As the Court explained in Furnco Construction Corp. v. Waters, 438 U.S. 567, 577, 98 S.Ct. 2943, 2949, 57 L.Ed.2d 957 (1978), the prima facie case "raises an inference of discrimination only because we presume these acts, if otherwise unexplained, are more likely than not based on the consideration of impermissible factors." Establishment of the prima facie case in effect creates a presumption that the employer unlawfully discriminated against the employee. If the trier of fact believes the plaintiff's evidence, and if the employer is silent in the face of the presumption, the court must enter judgment for the plaintiff because no issue of fact remains in the case.[7]

The burden that shifts to the defendant, therefore, is to rebut the presumption of discrimination by producing evidence that the plaintiff was rejected, or someone else was preferred, for a legitimate, nondiscriminatory reason. The defendant need not persuade the court that it was actually motivated by the proffered reasons. See *Sweeney*, supra,

6. In *McDonnell Douglas*, supra, we described an appropriate model for a prima facie case of racial discrimination. The plaintiff must show: "(i) that he belongs to a racial minority; (ii) that he applied and was qualified for a job for which the employer was seeking applicants; (iii) that, despite his qualifications, he was rejected; and (iv) that, after his rejection, the position remained open and the employer continued to seek applicants from persons of complainant's qualifications." 411 U.S., at 802, 93 S.Ct., at 1824.

We added, however, that this standard is not inflexible, as "[t]he facts necessarily will vary in Title VII cases, and the specification above of the prima facie proof required from respondent is not necessarily applicable in every respect in differing factual situations." Id., at 802, n. 13, 93 S.Ct., at 1824 n. 13.

In the instant case, it is not seriously contested that respondent has proved a prima facie case. She showed that she was a qualified woman who sought an available position, but the position was left open for several months before she finally was rejected in favor of a male, Walz, who had been under her supervision.

7. The phrase "prima facie case" not only may denote the establishment of a legally mandatory, rebuttable presumption, but also may be used by courts to describe the plaintiff's burden of producing enough evidence to permit the trier of fact to infer the fact at issue. 9 J. Wigmore, Evidence § 2494 (3d ed. 1940). *McDonnell Douglas* should have made it apparent that in the Title VII context we use "prima facie case" in the former sense.

at 25, 99 S.Ct., at 296. It is sufficient if the defendant's evidence raises a genuine issue of fact as to whether it discriminated against the plaintiff.[8] To accomplish this, the defendant must clearly set forth, through the introduction of admissible evidence, the reasons for the plaintiff's rejection.[9] The explanation provided must be legally sufficient to justify a judgment for the defendant. If the defendant carries this burden of production, the presumption raised by the prima facie case is rebutted,[10] and the factual inquiry proceeds to a new level of specificity. Placing this burden of production on the defendant thus serves simultaneously to meet the plaintiff's prima facie case by presenting a legitimate reason for the action and to frame the factual issue with sufficient clarity so that the plaintiff will have a full and fair opportunity to demonstrate pretext. The sufficiency of the defendant's evidence should be evaluated by the extent to which it fulfills these functions.

The plaintiff retains the burden of persuasion. She now must have the opportunity to demonstrate that the proffered reason was not the true reason for the employment decision. This burden now merges with the ultimate burden of persuading the court that she has been the victim of intentional discrimination. She may succeed in this either directly by persuading the court that a discriminatory reason more likely motivated the employer or indirectly by showing that the employer's proffered explanation is unworthy of credence. See *McDonnell Douglas,* 411 U.S., at 804–805, 93 S.Ct., at 1825–1826.

III

In reversing the judgment of the District Court that the discharge of respondent from PSC was unrelated to her sex, the Court of Appeals

8. This evidentiary relationship between the presumption created by a prima facie case and the consequential burden of production placed on the defendant is a traditional feature of the common law. "The word 'presumption' properly used refers only to a device for allocating the production burden." F. James & G. Hazard, Civil Procedure § 7.9, p. 255 (2d ed. 1977) (footnote omitted). See Fed.Rule Evid. 301. See generally 9 J. Wigmore, Evidence § 2491 (3d ed. 1940). Cf. J. Maguire, Evidence, Common Sense and Common Law 185–186 (1947). Usually, assessing the burden of production helps the judge determine whether the litigants have created an issue of fact to be decided by the jury. In a Title VII case, the allocation of burdens and the creation of a presumption by the establishment of a prima facie case is intended progressively to sharpen the inquiry into the elusive factual question of intentional discrimination.

9. An articulation not admitted into evidence will not suffice. Thus, the defendant cannot meet its burden merely through an answer to the complaint or by argument of counsel.

10. See generally J. Thayer, Preliminary Treatise on Evidence 346 (1898). In saying that the presumption drops from the case, we do not imply that the trier of fact no longer may consider evidence previously introduced by the plaintiff to establish a prima facie case. A satisfactory explanation by the defendant destroys the legally mandatory inference of discrimination arising from the plaintiff's initial evidence. Nonetheless, this evidence and inferences properly drawn therefrom may be considered by the trier of fact on the issue of whether the defendant's explanation is pretextual. Indeed, there may be some cases where the plaintiff's initial evidence, combined with effective cross-examination of the defendant, will suffice to discredit the defendant's explanation.

adhered to two rules it had developed to elaborate the defendant's burden of proof. First, the defendant must prove by a preponderance of the evidence that legitimate, nondiscriminatory reasons for the discharge existed. 608 F.2d, at 567. See Turner v. Texas Instruments, Inc., 555 F.2d 1251, 1255 (CA5 1977). Second, to satisfy this burden, the defendant "must prove that those he hired * * * were somehow *better* qualified than was plaintiff; in other words, comparative evidence is needed." 608 F.2d, at 567 (emphasis in original). See East v. Romine, Inc., 518 F.2d 332, 339–340 (CA5 1975).

A

The Court of Appeals has misconstrued the nature of the burden that *McDonnell Douglas* and its progeny place on the defendant. See Part II, supra. We stated in *Sweeney* that "the employer's burden is satisfied if he simply 'explains what he has done' or 'produc[es] evidence of legitimate nondiscriminatory reasons.'" 439 U.S., at 25, n. 2, 99 S.Ct., at 296, n. 2, quoting id., at 28, 29, 99 S.Ct., at 297–298 (STEVENS, J., dissenting). It is plain that the Court of Appeals required much more: it placed on the defendant the burden of persuading the court that it had convincing, objective reasons for preferring the chosen applicant above the plaintiff.[11]

The Court of Appeals distinguished *Sweeney* on the ground that the case held only that the defendant did not have the burden of proving the absence of discriminatory intent. But this distinction slights the rationale of *Sweeney* and of our other cases. We have stated consistently that the employee's prima facie case of discrimination will be rebutted if the employer articulates lawful reasons for the action; that is, to satisfy this intermediate burden, the employer need only produce admissible evidence which would allow the trier of fact rationally to conclude that the employment decision had not been motivated by discriminatory animus. The Court of Appeals would require the defendant to introduce evidence which, in the absence of any evidence of pretext, would *persuade* the trier of fact that the employment action was lawful. This exceeds what properly can be demanded to satisfy a burden of production.

The court placed the burden of persuasion on the defendant apparently because it feared that "[i]f an employer need only *articulate* —not

---

11. The court reviewed the defendant's evidence and explained its deficiency:

"Defendant failed to introduce comparative factual data concerning Burdine and Walz. Fuller merely testified that he discharged and retained personnel in the spring shakeup at TDCA primarily on the recommendations of subordinates and that he considered Walz qualified for the position he was retained to do. Fuller failed to specify any objective criteria on which he based the decision to discharge Burdine and retain Walz. He stated only that the action was in the best interest of the program and that there had been some friction within the department that might be alleviated by Burdine's discharge. Nothing in the record indicates whether he examined Walz' ability to work well with others. This court in *East* found such unsubstantiated assertions of 'qualification' and 'prior work record' insufficient absent data that will allow a true *comparison* of the individuals hired and rejected." 608 F.2d, at 568.

prove—a legitimate, nondiscriminatory reason for his action, he may compose fictitious, but legitimate, reasons for his actions." Turner v. Texas Instruments, Inc., supra, at 1255 (emphasis in original). We do not believe, however, that limiting the defendant's evidentiary obligation to a burden of production will unduly hinder the plaintiff. First, as noted above, the defendant's explanation of its legitimate reasons must be clear and reasonably specific. Supra, at 1094. See Loeb v. Textron, Inc., 600 F.2d 1003, 1011–1012, n. 5 (CA1 1979). This obligation arises both from the necessity of rebutting the inference of discrimination arising from the prima facie case and from the requirement that the plaintiff be afforded "a full and fair opportunity" to demonstrate pretext. Second, although the defendant does not bear a formal burden of persuasion, the defendant nevertheless retains an incentive to persuade the trier of fact that the employment decision was lawful. Thus, the defendant normally will attempt to prove the factual basis for its explanation. Third, the liberal discovery rules applicable to any civil suit in federal court are supplemented in a Title VII suit by the plaintiff's access to the Equal Employment Opportunity Commission's investigatory files concerning her complaint. See EEOC v. Associated Dry Goods Corp., 449 U.S. 590, 101 S.Ct. 817, 66 L.Ed.2d 762 (1981). Given these factors, we are unpersuaded that the plaintiff will find it particularly difficult to prove that a proffered explanation lacking a factual basis is a pretext. We remain confident that the *McDonnell Douglas* framework permits the plaintiff meriting relief to demonstrate intentional discrimination.

B

The Court of Appeals also erred in requiring the defendant to prove by objective evidence that the person hired or promoted was more qualified than the plaintiff. *McDonnell Douglas* teaches that it is the plaintiff's task to demonstrate that similarly situated employees were not treated equally. 411 U.S., at 804, 93 S.Ct., at 1825. The Court of Appeals' rule would require the employer to show that the plaintiff's objective qualifications were inferior to those of the person selected. If it cannot, a court would, in effect, conclude that it has discriminated.

The court's procedural rule harbors a substantive error. Title VII prohibits all discrimination in employment based upon race, sex, and national origin. "The broad, overriding interest, shared by employer, employee, and consumer, is efficient and trustworthy workmanship assured through fair and * * * neutral employment and personnel decisions." *McDonnell Douglas,* supra, at 801, 93 S.Ct., at 1823. Title VII, however, does not demand that an employer give preferential treatment to minorities or women. 42 U.S.C. § 2000e–2(j). See Steelworkers v. Weber, 443 U.S. 193, 205–206, 99 S.Ct. 2721, 2728–2729, 61 L.Ed.2d 480 (1979). The statute was not intended to "diminish traditional management prerogatives." Id., at 207, 99 S.Ct., at 2729. It does not require the employer to restructure his employment practices to maximize the number of minorities and women hired. Furnco Construction Corp. v. Waters, 438 U.S. 567, 577–578, 98 S.Ct. 2943, 2949–2950, 57 L.Ed.2d 957 (1978).

The views of the Court of Appeals can be read, we think, as requiring the employer to hire the minority or female applicant whenever that person's objective qualifications were equal to those of a white male applicant. But Title VII does not obligate an employer to accord this preference. Rather, the employer has discretion to choose among equally qualified candidates, provided the decision is not based upon unlawful criteria. The fact that a court may think that the employer misjudged the qualifications of the applicants does not in itself expose him to Title VII liability, although this may be probative of whether the employer's reasons are pretexts for discrimination. Loeb v. Textron, Inc., supra, at 1012, n. 6; see Lieberman v. Gant, 630 F.2d 60, 65 (CA2 1980).

IV

In summary, the Court of Appeals erred by requiring the defendant to prove by a preponderance of the evidence the existence of nondiscriminatory reasons for terminating the respondent and that the person retained in her stead had superior objective qualifications for the position.[12] When the plaintiff has proved a prima facie case of discrimination, the defendant bears only the burden of explaining clearly the nondiscriminatory reasons for its actions. The judgment of the Court of Appeals is vacated, and the case is remanded for further proceedings consistent with this opinion.

It is so ordered.

Notes

1. Rule 41(b) of the Federal Rules of Civil Procedure provides that a defendant may, without waiving his or her right to offer evidence, move for dismissal on the ground that plaintiff has shown no right to relief at the close of plaintiff's case-in-chief. When a defendant establishes its legitimate nondiscriminatory reason in the context of plaintiff's case-in-chief, either through adverse witnesses, express statements of the plaintiff, or documentary evidence, a Rule 41(b) dismissal is procedurally proper. McDaniel v. Temple Independent School Dist., 770 F.2d 1340, 1366, n. 3 (5th Cir.1985).

2. The Supreme Court has not addressed the question whether a defendant in a disparate impact case bears the burden of production or burden of persuasion on the *Griggs* business' necessity or job-relatedness defense. See *Burdine*, n. 5. Several lower courts have held that the defendant bears the burden of persuasion rather than the *Burdine* burden of production on these elements. Nash v. Consolidated City of Jacksonville,

---

12. Because the Court of Appeals applied the wrong legal standard to the evidence, we have no occasion to decide whether it erred in not reviewing the District Court's finding of no intentional discrimination under the "clearly erroneous" standard of Federal Rule of Civil Procedure 52(a). Addressing this issue in this case would be inappropriate because the District Court made no findings on the intermediate questions posed by *McDonnell Douglas*.

Duval County, 763 F.2d 1393, 1397 (11th Cir.1985); Lewis v. Bloomsburg Mills, Inc., 773 F.2d 561, 571–72 (4th Cir.1985).

3. For a comprehensive treatment of the order and allocation of the burdens of proof in employment discrimination law, see Belton, "Burden of Pleading and Proof in Discrimination Cases: Toward a Theory of Procedural Justice," 34 Vand.L.Rev. 1205 (1981).

UNITED STATES POSTAL SERVICE BOARD OF GOVERNORS v. AIKENS

Supreme Court of the United States, 1983.
460 U.S. 711, 103 S.Ct. 1478, 75 L.Ed.2d 403.

JUSTICE REHNQUIST delivered the opinion of the Court.

Respondent Louis Aikens filed suit under Title VII of the Civil Rights Act of 1964, as amended, 42 U.S.C. § 2000e *et seq.,* claiming that petitioner, the United States Postal Service, discriminated against him on account of his race. Aikens, who is black, claimed that the Postal Service had discriminatorily refused to promote him to higher positions in the Washington, D.C. Post Office where he had been employed since 1937. After a bench trial, the District Court entered judgment in favor of the Postal Service, but the Court of Appeals reversed. 642 F.2d 514 (CADC 1980). We vacated the Court of Appeals' judgment and remanded for reconsideration in light of Texas Department of Community Affairs v. Burdine, 450 U.S. 248, 101 S.Ct. 1089, 67 L.Ed.2d 207 (1981). 453 U.S. 902, 101 S.Ct. 3135, 69 L.Ed.2d 989 (1981).

On remand, the Court of Appeals reaffirmed its earlier holding that the District Court had erred in requiring Aikens to offer direct proof of discriminatory intent. It also held that the District Court erred in requiring Aikens to show, as part of his *prima facie* case, that he was "as qualified or more qualified" than the people who were promoted. 665 F.2d 1057, 1058, 1059 (CADC 1981) *(Per Curiam)*. We granted certiorari. 455 U.S. 1015, 102 S.Ct. 1707, 72 L.Ed.2d 132 (1982).

The Postal Service argues that an employee who has shown only that he was black, that he applied for a promotion for which he possessed the minimum qualifications, and that the employer selected a nonminority applicant has not established a *"prima facie"* case of employment discrimination under Title VII. Aikens argues that he submitted sufficient evidence that the Postal Service discriminated against him to warrant a finding of a *prima facie* case.[2] Because this

2. Aikens showed that white persons were consistently promoted and detailed over him and all other black persons between 1966 and 1974. Aikens has been rated as "an outstanding supervisor whose management abilities are far above average." App. 8. There was no derogatory or negative information in his Personnel Folder. He had more supervisory seniority and training and development courses than all but one of the white persons who were promoted above him. He has a Masters Degree and has completed three years of residence towards a Ph.D. Aikens had substantially more education than the white employees who were advanced ahead of him: of the 12, only two had any education beyond high school and none had a college degree. He introduced testimony that the person responsible for the promotion decisions at issue had made numerous derogatory comments about blacks in gen-

case was fully tried on the merits, it is surprising to find the parties
and the Court of Appeals still addressing the question whether Aikens
made out a *prima facie* case. We think that by framing the issue in
these terms, they have unnecessarily evaded the ultimate question of
discrimination *vel non.*[3]

By establishing a *prima facie* case, the plaintiff in a Title VII action
creates a rebuttable "presumption that the employer unlawfully discriminated against" him. Texas Department of Community Affairs v.
Burdine, 450 U.S. 248, 254, 101 S.Ct. 1089, 1094, 67 L.Ed.2d 207 (1981).
See McDonnell Douglas Corp. v. Green, 411 U.S. 792, 93 S.Ct. 1817, 36
L.Ed.2d 668 (1973). To rebut this presumption, "the defendant must
clearly set forth, through the introduction of admissible evidence, the
reasons for the plaintiff's rejection. *Burdine,* supra, 450 U.S., at 255,
101 S.Ct., at 1094. In other words, the defendant must "produc[e]
evidence that the plaintiff was rejected, or someone else was preferred,
for a legitimate, nondiscriminatory reason." Id., at 254, 101 S.Ct., at
1094.

But when the defendant fails to persuade the district court to
dismiss the action for lack of a *prima facie* case,[4] and responds to the
plaintiff's proof by offering evidence of the reason for the plaintiff's
rejection, the fact finder must then decide whether the rejection was
discriminatory within the meaning of Title VII. At this stage, the
McDonnell-Burdine presumption "drops from the case," id., at 255, n.
10, 101 S.Ct., at 1095, n. 10, and "the factual inquiry proceeds to a new
level of specificity." Id., at 255, 101 S.Ct., at 1095. After Aikens
presented his evidence to the District Court in this case, the Postal
Service's witnesses testified that he was not promoted because he had
turned down several lateral transfers that would have broadened his
Postal Service experience. See Tr. 311–313, 318–320, 325; Pet.App.
53a. The District Court was then in a position to decide the ultimate
factual issue in the case.

The "factual inquiry" in a Title VII case is "whether the defendant
intentionally discriminated against the plaintiff." *Burdine,* supra, at
253, 101 S.Ct., at 1093. In other words, is "the employer * * *
treating 'some people less favorably than others because of their race,
color, religion, sex, or national origin.'" Furnco Construction Corp. v.

---

eral and Aikens in particular. If the District Court were to find, on the basis of this
evidence, that the Postal Service did discriminate against Aikens, we do not believe that this would be reversible error.

3. As in any lawsuit, the plaintiff may
prove his case by direct or circumstantial
evidence. The trier of fact should consider
all the evidence, giving it whatever weight
and credence it deserves. Thus, we agree
with the Court of Appeals that the District
Court should not have required Aikens to
submit direct evidence of discriminatory
intent. See International Brotherhood of

Teamsters v. United States, 431 U.S. 324,
358 n. 44, 97 S.Ct. 1843, 1866 n. 44, 52
L.Ed.2d 396 (1977) ("[T]he *McDonnell
Douglas* formula does not require direct
proof of discrimination").

4. It appears that at one point in the
trial the District Court decided that Aikens
had made out a *prima facie* case. When
Aikens concluded his case in chief, the
Postal Service moved to dismiss on the
ground that there was no *prima facie* case.
Tr. 256. The District Court denied this
motion. Tr. 259. See Pet.App. 47a.

Waters, 438 U.S. 567, 577, 98 S.Ct. 2943, 2949, 57 L.Ed.2d 957 (1978), quoting Int'l Brotherhood of Teamsters v. United States, 431 U.S. 324, 335, n. 15, 97 S.Ct. 1843, 1854, n. 15, 52 L.Ed.2d 396 (1977). The *prima facie* case method established in *McDonnell Douglas* was "never intended to be rigid, mechanized, or ritualistic. Rather, it is merely a sensible, orderly way to evaluate the evidence in light of common experience as it bears on the critical question of discrimination." *Furnco*, supra, 438 U.S., at 577, 98 S.Ct., at 2949. Where the defendant has done everything that would be required of him if the plaintiff had properly made out a *prima facie* case, whether the plaintiff really did so is no longer relevant. The district court has before it all the evidence it needs to decide whether "the defendant intentionally discriminated against the plaintiff." *Burdine*, supra, 450 U.S., at 253, 101 S.Ct., at 1093.

On the state of the record at the close of the evidence, the District Court in this case should have proceeded to this specific question directly, just as district courts decide disputed questions of fact in other civil litigation.[5] As we stated in *Burdine:*

> The plaintiff retains the burden of persuasion. [H]e may succeed in this either directly by persuading the court that a discriminatory reason more likely motivated the employer or indirectly by showing that the employer's proffered explanation is unworthy of credence. 450 U.S., at 256, 101 S.Ct., at 1095.

In short, the district court must decide which party's explanation of the employer's motivation it believes.

All courts have recognized that the question facing triers of fact in discrimination cases is both sensitive and difficult. The prohibitions against discrimination contained in the Civil Rights Act of 1964 reflect an important national policy. There will seldom be "eyewitness" testimony as to the employer's mental processes. But none of this means that trial courts or reviewing courts should treat discrimination differently from other ultimate questions of fact. Nor should they make their inquiry even more difficult by applying legal rules which were devised to govern "the allocation of burdens and order of presentation of proof," *Burdine*, supra, at 252, 101 S.Ct., at 1093, in deciding this ultimate question. The law often obliges finders of fact to inquire into a person's state of mind. As Lord Justice Bowen said in treating this problem in an action for misrepresentation nearly a century ago:

> The state of a man's mind is as much a fact as the state of his digestion. It is true that it is very difficult to prove what the state of a man's mind at a particular time is, but if it can be ascertained it is as much as fact as anything else. Eddington v. Fitzmaurice, 29 Ch.Div. 459, 483 (1885).

---

5. Of course, the plaintiff must have an adequate "opportunity to demonstrate that the proffered reason was not the true reason for the employment decision," but rather a pretext. *Burdine*, supra, at 256, 101 S.Ct. at 1095. There is no suggestion in this case that Aikens did not have such an opportunity.

The District Court erroneously thought that respondent was required to submit direct evidence of discriminatory intent, see n. 3, supra, and erroneously focused on the question of *prima facie* case rather than directly on the question of discrimination. Thus we cannot be certain that its findings of fact in favor of the Postal Service were not influenced by its mistaken view of the law. We accordingly vacate the judgment of the Court of Appeals, and remand the case to the District Court so that it may decide on the basis of the evidence before it whether the Postal Service discriminated against Aikens.

It is so ordered.

JUSTICE MARSHALL concurs in the judgment.

JUSTICE BLACKMUN, with whom JUSTICE BRENNAN joins, concurring.

* * *

ANDERSON v. CITY OF BESSEMER
Supreme Court of the United States, 1985.
470 U.S. 564, 105 S.Ct. 1504, 84 L.Ed.2d 518.

JUSTICE WHITE delivered the opinion of the Court.

In Pullman-Standard v. Swint, 456 U.S. 273, 102 S.Ct. 1781, 72 L.Ed.2d 66 (1982), we held that a District Court's finding of discriminatory intent in an action brought under Title VII of the Civil Rights Act of 1964, 78 Stat. 253, as amended, 42 U.S.C. § 2000e et seq., is a factual finding that may be overturned on appeal only if it is clearly erroneous. In this case, the Court of Appeals for the Fourth Circuit concluded that there was clear error in a District Court's finding of discrimination and reversed. Because our reading of the record convinces us that the Court of Appeals misapprehended and misapplied the clearly-erroneous standard, we reverse.

I

Early in 1975, officials of respondent City of Bessemer City, North Carolina, set about to hire a new Recreation Director for the city. Although the duties that went with the position were not precisely delineated, the new Recreation Director was to be responsible for managing all of the city's recreational facilities and for developing recreational programs—athletic and otherwise—to serve the needs of the city's residents. A five-member committee selected by the Mayor was responsible for choosing the Recreation Director. Of the five members, four were men; the one woman on the committee, Mrs. Auddie Boone, served as the chairperson.

Eight persons applied for the position of Recreation Director. Petitioner, at the time a 39-year-old schoolteacher with college degrees in social studies and education, was the only woman among the eight. The selection committee reviewed the resumes submitted by the applicants and briefly interviewed each of the jobseekers. Following the interviews, the committee offered the position to Mr. Donald Kincaid, a 24-year-old who had recently graduated from college with a degree in physical education. All four men on the committee voted to offer the job to Mr. Kincaid; Mrs. Boone voted for petitioner.

Believing that the committee had passed over her in favor of a less qualified candidate solely because she was a woman, petitioner filed discrimination charges with the Charlotte District Office of the Equal Employment Opportunity Commission. In July 1980 (five years after petitioner filed the charges), the EEOC's District Director found that there was reasonable cause to believe that petitioner's charges were true and invited the parties to attempt a resolution of petitioner's grievance through conciliation proceedings. The EEOC's efforts proved unsuccessful, and in due course, petitioner received a right-to-sue letter.

Petitioner then filed this Title VII action in the United States District Court for the Western District of North Carolina. After a 2-day trial during which the court heard testimony from petitioner, Mr. Kincaid, and the five members of the selection committee, the court issued a brief memorandum of decision setting forth its finding that petitioner was entitled to judgment because she had been denied the position of Recreation Director on account of her sex. In addition to laying out the rationale for this finding, the memorandum requested that petitioner's counsel submit proposed findings of fact and conclusions of law expanding upon those set forth in the memorandum. Petitioner's counsel complied with this request by submitting a lengthy set of proposed findings (App. 11a–34a); the court then requested and received a response setting forth in detail respondent's objections to the proposed findings (id., at 36a–47a)—objections that were, in turn, answered by petitioner's counsel in a somewhat less lengthly reply (id., at 48a–54a). After receiving these submissions, the court issued its own findings of fact and conclusions of law. 557 F.Supp. 412, 413–419 (1983).

As set forth in the formal findings of fact and conclusions of law, the court's finding that petitioner had been denied employment by respondent because of her sex rested on a number of subsidiary findings. First, the court found that at the time the selection committee made its choice, petitioner had been better qualified than Mr. Kincaid to perform the range of duties demanded by the position. The court based this finding on petitioner's experience as a classroom teacher responsible for supervising schoolchildren in recreational and athletic activities, her employment as a hospital recreation director in the late 1950's, her extensive involvement in a variety of civic organizations, her knowledge of sports acquired both as a high school athlete and as a mother of children involved in organized athletics, her skills as a public speaker, her experience in handling money (gained in the course of her community activities and in her work as a bookkeeper for a group of physicians), and her knowledge of music, dance, and crafts. The court found that Mr. Kincaid's principal qualifications were his experience as a student teacher and as a coach in a local youth basketball league, his extensive knowledge of team and individual sports, acquired as a result of his lifelong involvement in athletics, and his formal training as a physical education major in college. Noting that the position of Recreation Director involved more than the management of athletic programs, the court concluded that petitioner's greater breadth of experience made her better qualified for the position.

Second, the court found that the male committee members had in fact been biased against petitioner because she was a woman. The court based this finding in part on the testimony of one of the committee members that he believed it would have been "real hard" for a woman to handle the job and that he would not want his wife to have to perform the duties of the Recreation Director. The finding of bias found additional support in evidence that another male committee member had told Mr. Kincaid, the successful applicant, of the vacancy and had also solicited applications from three other men, but had not attempted to recruit any women for the job.

Also critical to the court's inference of bias was its finding that petitioner, alone among the applicants for the job, had been asked whether she realized the job would involve night work and travel and whether her husband approved of her applying for the job. The court's finding that the committee had pursued this line of inquiry only with petitioner was based on the testimony of petitioner that these questions had been asked of her and the testimony of Mrs. Boone that similar questions had not been asked of the other applicants. Although Mrs. Boone also testified that during Mr. Kincaid's interview, she had made a "comment" to him regarding the reaction of his new bride to his taking the position of Recreation Director, the court concluded that this comment was not a serious inquiry, but merely a "facetious" remark prompted by Mrs. Boone's annoyance that only petitioner had been questioned about her spouse's reaction. The court also declined to credit the testimony of one of the male committee members that Mr. Kincaid had been asked about his wife's feelings "in a way" and the testimony of another committeeman that all applicants had been questioned regarding their willingness to work at night and their families' reaction to night work. The court concluded that the finding that only petitioner had been seriously questioned about her family's reaction suggested that the male committee members believed women had special family responsibilities that made certain forms of employment inappropriate.

Finally, the court found that the reasons offered by the male committee members for their choice of Mr. Kincaid were pretextual. The court rejected the proposition that Mr. Kincaid's degree in physical education justified his choice, as the evidence suggested that where male candidates were concerned, the committee valued experience more highly than formal training in physical education.[1] The court

---

1. The evidence established that the committee members had initially favored a third candidate, Bert Broadway, and had decided not to hire him only because he stated that he was unwilling to move to Bessemer City. Mr. Broadway had two years of experience as a community recrea-

also rejected the claim of one of the committeemen that Mr. Kincaid had been hired because of the superiority of the recreational programs he planned to implement if selected for the job. The court credited the testimony of one of the other committeemen who had voted for Mr. Kincaid that the programs outlined by petitioner and Mr. Kincaid were substantially identical.

On the basis of its findings that petitioner was the most qualified candidate, that the committee had been biased against hiring a woman, and that the committee's explanations for its choice of Mr. Kincaid were pretextual, the court concluded that petitioner had met her burden of establishing that she had been denied the position of Recreation Director because of her sex. Petitioner having conceded that ordering the city to hire her would be an inappropriate remedy under the circumstances, the court awarded petitioner backpay in the amount of $30,397.00 and attorney's fees of $16,971.59.

The Fourth Circuit reversed the District Court's finding of discrimination. 717 F.2d 149 (1983). In the view of the Court of Appeals, three of the District Court's crucial findings were clearly erroneous: the finding that petitioner was the most qualified candidate, the finding that petitioner had been asked questions that other applicants were spared, and the finding that the male committee members were biased against hiring a woman. Having rejected these findings, the Court of Appeals concluded that the District Court had erred in finding that petitioner had been discriminated against on account of her sex.

II

We must deal at the outset with the Fourth Circuit's suggestion that "close scrutiny of the record in this case [was] justified by the manner in which the opinion was prepared," id., at 156—that is, by the District Court's adoption of petitioner's proposed findings of fact and conclusions of law. The court recalled that the Fourth Circuit had on many occasions condemned the practice of announcing a decision and leaving it to the prevailing party to write the findings of fact and conclusions of law. See, e.g., Cuthbertson v. Biggers Bros., Inc., 702 F.2d 454 (1983); EEOC v. Federal Reserve Bank of Richmond, 698 F.2d 633 (1983); Chicopee Mfg. Corp. v. Kendall Co., 288 F.2d 719 (1961). The court rejected petitioner's contention that the procedure followed by the trial judge in this case was proper because the judge had given respondent an opportunity to object to the proposed findings and had not adopted petitioner's findings verbatim. According to the court, the vice of the procedure lay in the trial court's solicitation of findings after it had already announced its decision and in the court's adoption of the "substance" of petitioner's proposed findings.

We, too, have criticized courts for their verbatim adoption of findings of fact prepared by prevailing parties, particularly when those

tion director; but like petitioner, he lacked a college degree in physical education.

findings have taken the form of conclusory statements unsupported by citation to the record. See, e.g., United States v. El Paso Natural Gas Co., 376 U.S. 651, 656–657, 84 S.Ct. 1044, 1047–1048, 12 L.Ed.2d 12 (1964); United States v. Marine Bancorporation, 418 U.S. 602, 615, n. 13, 94 S.Ct. 2856, 2866, n. 13, 41 L.Ed.2d 978 (1974). We are also aware of the potential for overreaching and exaggeration on the part of attorneys preparing findings of fact when they have already been informed that the judge has decided in their favor. See J. Wright, The Nonjury Trial—Preparing Findings of Fact, Conclusions of Law, and Opinions, Seminars for Newly Appointed United States District Judges 159, 166 (1962). Nonetheless, our previous discussions of the subject suggest that even when the trial judge adopts proposed findings verbatim, the findings are those of the court and may be reversed only if clearly erroneous. United States v. Marine Bancorporation, supra, at 615, n. 13, 94 S.Ct., at 2866, n. 13; United States v. El Paso Natural Gas Co., supra, 376 U.S., at 656–657, 84 S.Ct., at 1047–1048.

In any event, the District Court in this case does not appear to have uncritically accepted findings prepared without judicial guidance by the prevailing party. The court itself provided the framework for the proposed findings when it issued its preliminary memorandum, which set forth its essential findings and directed petitioner's counsel to submit a more detailed set of findings consistent with them. Further, respondent was provided and availed itself of the opportunity to respond at length to the proposed findings. Nor did the District Court simply adopt petitioner's proposed findings: the findings it ultimately issued—and particularly the crucial findings regarding petitioner's qualifications, the questioning to which petitioner was subjected, and bias on the part of the committeemen—vary considerably in organization and content from those submitted by petitioner's counsel. Under these circumstances, we see no reason to doubt that the findings issued by the District Court represent the judge's own considered conclusions. There is no reason to subject those findings to a more stringent appellate review than is called for by the applicable rules.

III

Because a finding of intentional discrimination is a finding of fact, the standard governing appellate review of a district court's finding of discrimination is that set forth in Federal Rule of Civil Procedure 52(a): "Findings of fact shall not be set aside unless clearly erroneous, and due regard shall be given to the opportunity of the trial court to judge of the credibility of the witnesses." The question before us, then, is whether the Court of Appeals erred in holding the District Court's finding of discrimination to be clearly erroneous.

Although the meaning of the phrase "clearly erroneous" is not immediately apparent, certain general principles governing the exercise of the appellate court's power to overturn findings of a district court may be derived from our cases. The foremost of these principles, as the Fourth Circuit itself recognized, is that "a finding is 'clearly erroneous' when although there is evidence to support it, the reviewing court on the entire evidence is left with the definite and firm conviction that a mistake has been committed." United States v. United States Gypsum Co., 333 U.S. 364, 395, 68 S.Ct. 525, 542, 92 L.Ed. 746 (1948). This standard plainly does not entitle a reviewing court to reverse the finding of the trier of fact simply because it is convinced that it would have decided the case differently. The reviewing court oversteps the bounds of its duty under Rule 52 if it undertakes to duplicate the role of the lower court. "In applying the clearly erroneous standard to the findings of a district court sitting without a jury, appellate courts must constantly have in mind that their function is not to decide factual issues *de novo*." Zenith Radio Corp. v. Hazeltine Research, Inc., 395 U.S. 100, 123, 89 S.Ct. 1562, 1576, 23 L.Ed.2d 129 (1969). If the district court's account of the evidence is plausible in light of the record viewed in its entirety, the court of appeals may not reverse it even though convinced that had it been sitting as the trier of fact, it would have weighed the evidence differently. Where there are two permissible views of the evidence, the factfinder's choice between them cannot be clearly erroneous. United States v. Yellow Cab Co., 338 U.S. 338, 342, 70 S.Ct. 177, 179, 94 L.Ed. 150 (1949); see also Inwood Laboratories, Inc. v. Ives Laboratories, Inc., 456 U.S. 844, 102 S.Ct. 2182, 72 L.Ed.2d 606 (1982).

This is so even when the district court's findings do not rest on credibility determinations, but are based instead on physical or documentary evidence or inferences from other facts. To be sure, various Courts of Appeals have on occasion asserted the theory that an appellate court may exercise de novo review over findings not based on credibility determinations. See, e.g., Orvis v. Higgins, 180 F.2d 537 (CA2 1950); Lydle v. United States, 635 F.2d 763, 765, n. 1 (CA6 1981); Swanson v. Baker Industries, Inc., 615 F.2d 479, 483 (CA8 1980). This theory has an impressive genealogy, having first been articulated in an opinion written by Judge Frank and subscribed to by Judge Augustus Hand, see Orvis v. Higgins, supra, but it is impossible to trace the theory's lineage back to the text of Rule 52, which states straightforwardly that "findings of fact shall not be set aside unless clearly erroneous." That the Rule goes on to emphasize the special deference to be paid credibility determinations does not alter its clear command: Rule 52 "does not make exceptions or purport to exclude certain categories of factual findings from the obligation of a court of appeals to accept a district court's findings unless clearly erroneous." Pullman-Standard v. Swint, 456 U.S., at 287, 102 S.Ct., at 1789.

The rationale for deference to the original finder of fact is not limited to the superiority of the trial judge's position to make determinations of credibility. The trial judge's major role is the determination of fact, and with experience in fulfilling that role comes expertise. Duplication of the trial judge's efforts in the court of appeals would very likely contribute only negligibly to the accuracy of fact determination at a huge cost in diversion of judicial resources. In addition, the parties to a case on appeal have already been forced to concentrate their energies and resources on persuading the trial judge that their account of the facts is the correct one; requiring them to persuade three more judges at the appellate level is requiring too much. As the Court has stated in a different context, the trial on the merits should be "the 'main event' * * * rather than a 'tryout on the road.'" Wainwright v. Sykes, 433 U.S. 72, 90, 97 S.Ct. 2497, 2508, 53 L.Ed.2d 594 (1977). For these reasons, review of factual findings under the clearly-erroneous standard—with its deference to the trier of fact—is the rule, not the exception.

When findings are based on determinations regarding the credibility of witnesses, Rule 52 demands even greater deference to the trial court's findings; for only the trial judge can be aware of the variations in demeanor and tone of voice that bear so heavily on the listener's understanding of and belief in what is said. See Wainwright v. Witt, 469 U.S. ___, 105 S.Ct. 844, 83 L.Ed.2d 841 (1985). This is not to suggest that the trial judge may insulate his findings from review by denominating them credibility determinations, for factors other than demeanor and inflection go into the decision whether or not to believe a witness. Documents or objective evidence may contradict the witness' story; or the story itself may be so internally inconsistent or implausible on its face that a reasonable factfinder would not credit it. Where such factors are present, the court of appeals may well find clear error even in a finding purportedly based on a credibility determination. See, e.g., United States v. United States Gypsum Co., supra, 333 U.S. at 396, 68 S.Ct., at 542. But when a trial judge's finding is based on his decision to credit the testimony of one of two or more witnesses, each of whom has told a coherent and facially plausible story that is not contradicted by extrinsic evidence, that finding, if not internally inconsistent, can virtually never be clear error. Cf. United States v. Aluminum Co. of America, 148 F.2d 416, 433 (CA2 1945); Orvis v. Higgins, supra, at 539–540.

IV

Application of the foregoing principles to the facts of the case lays bare the errors committed by the Fourth Circuit in its employment of the clearly-erroneous standard. In detecting clear error in the District Court's finding that petitioner was better qualified than Mr. Kincaid, the Fourth Circuit improperly conducted what amounted to a *de novo* weighing of the evidence in the record. The District Court's finding was based on essentially undisputed evidence regarding the respective backgrounds of petitioner and Mr. Kincaid and the duties that went with the position of Recreation Director. The District Court, after considering the evidence, concluded that the position of Recreation Director in Bessemer City carried with it broad responsibilities for creating and managing a recreation program involving not only athletics, but also other activities for citizens of all ages and interests. The court determined that petitioner's more varied educational and employment background and her extensive involvement in a variety of civic activities left her better qualified to implement such a rounded program than Mr. Kincaid, whose background was more narrowly focused on athletics.

The Fourth Circuit, reading the same record, concluded that the basic duty of the Recreation Director was to implement an athletic program, and that the essential qualification for a successful applicant would be either education or experience specifically related to athletics.[2] Accordingly, it seemed evident to the Court of Appeals that Mr. Kincaid was in fact better qualified than petitioner.

Based on our own reading of the record, we cannot say that either interpretation of the facts is illogical or implausible. Each has support in inferences that may be drawn from the facts in the record; and if either interpretation had been drawn by a district court on the record before us, we would not be inclined to find it clearly erroneous. The question we must answer, however, is not whether the Fourth Circuit's interpretation of the facts was clearly erroneous, but whether the District Court's finding was clearly erroneous. See McAllister v. United States, 348 U.S. 19, 20–21, 75 S.Ct. 6, 7–8, 99 L.Ed. 20 (1954). The District Court determined that petitioner was better qualified, and, as we have stated above, such a finding is entitled to deference notwithstanding that it is not based on credibility determinations. When the record is examined in light of the appropriately deferential standard, it is apparent that it contains nothing that mandates a finding that the District Court's conclusion was clearly erroneous.

Somewhat different concerns are raised by the Fourth Circuit's treatment of the District Court's finding that petitioner, alone among the applicants for the position of Recreation Director, was asked questions regarding her spouse's feelings about her application for the position. Here the error of the Court of Appeals was its failure to give due regard to the ability of the District Court to interpret and discern the credibility of oral testimony. The Court of Appeals rested its rejection of the District Court's finding of differential treatment on its own interpretation of testimony by Mrs. Boone—the very witness whose testimony, in the view of the District Court, supported the finding. In the eyes of the Fourth Circuit, Mrs. Boone's testimony that she had made a "comment" to Mr. Kincaid about the feelings of his wife (a comment judged "facetious" by the District Court) conclusively established that Mr. Kincaid, and perhaps other male applicants as well, had been questioned about the feelings of his spouse.

2. The Fourth Circuit thus saw no inconsistency between the statement of the male committee members that they preferred Bert Broadway because of his experience and their claim that they had selected Mr. Kincaid over petitioner because of his formal training. See n. 1, supra. In the view of the Court of Appeals, this demonstrated only that Mr. Broadway had relevant experience and Mr. Kincaid had relevant education, while petitioner had neither.

Mrs. Boone's testimony on this point, which is set forth in the margin,[3] is certainly not free from ambiguity. But Mrs. Boone several times stated that other candidates had not been questioned about the reaction of their wives—at least, "not in the same context" as had petitioner. And even after recalling and calling to the attention of the court that she had made a comment on the subject to Mr. Kincaid, Mrs. Boone denied that she had "asked" Mr. Kincaid about his wife's reaction. Mrs. Boone's testimony on these matters is not inconsistent with the theory that her remark was not a serious inquiry into whether Mr. Kincaid's wife approved of his applying for the position. Whether the judge's interpretation is actually correct is impossible to tell from the paper record, but it is easy to imagine that the tone of voice in which the witness related her comment, coupled with her immediate denial that she had questioned Mr. Kincaid on the subject, might have conclusively established that the remark was a facetious one. We therefore cannot agree that the judge's conclusion that the remark was facetious was clearly erroneous.

Once the trial court's characterization of Mrs. Boone's remark is accepted, it is apparent that the finding that the male candidates were not seriously questioned about the feelings of their wives cannot be deemed clearly erroneous. The trial judge was faced with the testimony of three witnesses, one of whom (Mrs. Boone) stated that none of the other candidates had been so questioned, one of whom (a male committee member) testified that Mr. Kincaid had been asked such a question "in a way," and one of whom (another committeeman) testified that all the candidates had been subjected to similar questioning. None of these accounts is implausible on its face, and none is contradicted by

---

3. "Q: Did the committee members ask that same kind of question of the other applicants?

"A: Not that I recall."

"Q: Do you deny that the other applicants, aside from the plaintiff, were asked about the prospect of working at night in that position?

"A: Not to my knowledge.

"Q: Are you saying they were not asked that?

"A: They were not asked, not in the context that they were asked of Phyllis. I don't know whether they were worried because Jim wasn't going to get his supper or what. You know, that goes both ways.

"Q: Did you tell Phyllis Anderson that Donnie Kincaid was not asked about night work?

"A: He wasn't asked about night work.

"Q: That answers one question. Now, let's answer the other one. Did you tell Phyllis Anderson that, that Donnie Kincaid was not asked about night work?

"A: Yes, after the interviews—I think the next day or sometime, and I know—may I answer something?

"Q: If it's a question that has been asked; otherwise, no. It's up to the Judge to say.

"A: You asked if there was any question asked about—I think Donnie was just married, and I think I made the comment to him personally—and your new bride won't mind.

"Q: So, you asked him yourself about his own wife's reaction?

"A: No, no.

"Q: That is what you just said.

"Mr. Gibson: Objection, Your Honor.

"[The] Court: Sustained. You don't have to rephrase the answer."

App. 108a, 120a–121a.

any reliable extrinsic evidence. Under these circumstances, the trial court's decision to credit Mrs. Boone was not clearly erroneous.

The Fourth Circuit's refusal to accept the District Court's finding that the committee members were biased against hiring a woman was based to a large extent on its rejection of the finding that petitioner had been subjected to questioning that the other applicants were spared. Given that that finding was not clearly erroneous, the finding of bias cannot be termed erroneous: it finds support not only in the treatment of petitioner in her interview, but also in the testimony of one committee member that he believed it would have been difficult for a woman to perform the job and in the evidence that another member solicited applications for the position only from men.[4]

Our determination that the findings of the District Court regarding petitioner's qualifications, the conduct of her interview, and the bias of the male committee members were not clearly erroneous leads us to conclude that the court's finding that petitioner was discriminated against on account of her sex was also not clearly erroneous. The District Court's findings regarding petitioner's superior qualifications and the bias of the selection committee are sufficient to support the inference that petitioner was denied the position of Recreation Director on account of her sex. Accordingly, we hold that the Fourth Circuit erred in denying petitioner relief under Title VII.

In so holding, we do not assert that our knowledge of what happened 10 years ago in Bessemer City is superior to that of the Court of Appeals; nor do we claim to have greater insight than the Court of Appeals into the state of mind of the men on the selection committee who rejected petitioner for the position of Recreation Director. Even the trial judge, who has heard the witnesses directly and who is more closely in touch than the appeals court with the milieu out of which the controversy before him arises, cannot always be confident that he "knows" what happened. Often, he can only determine whether the plaintiff has succeeded in presenting an account of the facts that is more likely to be true than not. Our task—and the task of appellate tribunals generally—is more limited still: we must determine whether the trial judge's conclusions are clearly erroneous. On the record before us, we cannot say that they are. Accordingly, the judgment of the Court of Appeals is

Reversed.

4. The Fourth Circuit's suggestion that any inference of bias was dispelled by the fact that each of the male committee members was married to a woman who had worked at some point in the marriage is insufficient to establish that the finding of bias was clearly erroneous. Although we decline to hold that a man's attitude toward his wife's employment is irrelevant to the question whether he may be found to have a bias against working women, any relevance the factor may have in a particular case is a matter for the district court to weigh in its consideration of bias, not the court of appeals.

JUSTICE POWELL, concurring.

*   *   *

JUSTICE BLACKMUN, concurring in the judgment.

I would like to join the Court's opinion, for I think its judgment is correct, and I agree with most of what the Court says. I, however, do not join the broad dictum, * * * to the effect that the same result is to be reached when the District Court's findings are based wholly on documentary evidence and do not rest at all on credibility determinations. In the past, I have joined at least one opinion that, generally, is to the opposite effect. See United States v. Mississippi Valley Barge Line Co., 285 F.2d 381, 388 (CA8 1960). See also Ralston Purina Co. v. General Foods Corp., 442 F.2d 389, 391 (CA8 1971); Frito-Lay, Inc. v. So Good Potato Chip Co., 540 F.2d 927, 930 (CA8 1976); Swanson v. Baker Industries, Inc., 615 F.2d 479, 483 (CA8 1980).

While the Court may be correct in its dictum today, certainly this case does not require us to decide the question. The record contains far more than documentary evidence, as the Court's opinion so adequately discloses. In a case that requires resolution of the question, I might eventually be persuaded that the Court's approach is wise. I prefer, however, to wait for a case where the issue must be resolved and where it has been briefed and argued by the parties, rather than to address the issue by edict without these customary safeguards.

I therefore join the Court only in its judgment and not in its opinion.

Notes

1. In Pullman-Standard v. Swint, 456 U.S. 273, 102 S.Ct. 1781, 72 L.Ed.2d 66 (1982), the Court held that a finding of intent to discriminate is a pure question of fact subject to the clearly erroneous rule of Rule 52(a) of the Federal Rules of Civil Procedure.

2. A court of appeals in reviewing the findings of fact in the discrimination cases is likely to (1) consider all of the evidence in the light most favorable to the party winning in the district court; (2) assume all conflicts in the evidence were decided in favor of the winning party; (3) assume as proven all facts which the winning party's evidence tended to prove; (4) give the winning party all favorable inferences which reasonably can be drawn from the evidence; and (5) affirm the factual findings of the district court if reasonable men could disagree. See Gilkerson v. Toastmaster, Inc., 770 F.2d 133, 136 (8th Cir.1985). Also, a court of appeals will not "ramsack the record" looking for clearly erroneous factual mistakes. Casillas v. United States Navy, 735 F.2d 338, 342–43 (9th Cir.1984).

D. STATISTICAL EVIDENCE

HAZELWOOD SCHOOL DISTRICT v. UNITED STATES

Supreme Court of the United States, 1977.
433 U.S. 299, 97 S.Ct. 2736, 53 L.Ed.2d 768.

MR. JUSTICE STEWART delivered the opinion of the Court.

The petitioner Hazelwood School District covers 78 square miles in the northern part of St. Louis County, Mo. In 1973 the Attorney General brought this lawsuit against Hazelwood and various of its officials, alleging that they were engaged in a "pattern or practice" of employment discrimination in violation of Title VII of the Civil Rights Act of 1964, 78 Stat. 253, as amended, 42 U.S.C. § 2000e et seq. (1970 ed. and Supp. V). The complaint asked for an injunction requiring Hazelwood to cease its discriminatory practices, to take affirmative steps to obtain qualified Negro faculty members, and to offer employment and give backpay to victims of past illegal discrimination.

Hazelwood was formed from 13 rural school districts between 1949 and 1951 by a process of annexation. By the 1967–1968 school year, 17,550 students were enrolled in the district, of whom only 59 were Negro; the number of Negro pupils increased to 576 of 25,166 in 1972–1973, a total of just over 2%.

From the beginning, Hazelwood followed relatively unstructured procedures in hiring its teachers. Every person requesting an application for a teaching position was sent one, and completed applications were submitted to a central personnel office, where they were kept on file.[2] During the early 1960's the personnel office notified all applicants whenever a teaching position became available, but as the number of applications on file increased in the late 1960's and early 1970's, this practice was no longer considered feasible. The personnel office thus began the practice of selecting anywhere from 3 to 10 applicants for interviews at the school where the vacancy existed. The personnel office did not substantively screen the applicants in determining which of them to send for interviews, other than to ascertain that each applicant, if selected, would be eligible for state certification by the time he began the job. Generally, those who had most recently submitted applications were most likely to be chosen for interviews.[3]

Interviews were conducted by a department chairman, program coordinator, or the principal at the school where the teaching vacancy existed. Although those conducting the interviews did fill out forms rating the applicants in a number of respects, it is undisputed that each school principal possessed virtually unlimited discretion in hiring

---

2. Before 1954 Hazelwood's application forms required designation of race, and those forms were in use as late as the 1962–1963 school year.

3. Applicants with student or substitute teaching experience at Hazelwood were given preference if their performance had been satisfactory.

teachers for his school. The only general guidance given to the principals was to hire the "most competent" person available, and such intangibles as "personality, disposition, appearance, poise, voice, articulation, and ability to deal with people" counted heavily. The principal's choice was routinely honored by Hazelwood's Superintendent and the Board of Education.

In the early 1960's Hazelwood found it necessary to recruit new teachers, and for that purpose members of its staff visited a number of colleges and universities in Missouri and bordering States. All the institutions visited were predominantly white, and Hazelwood did not seriously recruit at either of the two predominantly Negro four-year colleges in Missouri.[4] As a buyer's market began to develop for public school teachers, Hazelwood curtailed its recruiting efforts. For the 1971–1972 school year, 8,127 persons applied for only 234 teaching vacancies; for the 1972–1973 school year, there were 2,373 applications for 282 vacancies. A number of the applicants who were not hired were Negroes.

Hazelwood hired its first Negro teacher in 1969. The number of Negro faculty members gradually increased in successive years: 6 of 957 in the 1970 school year; 16 of 1,107 by the end of the 1972 school year; 22 of 1,231 in the 1973 school year. By comparison, according to 1970 census figures, of more than 19,000 teachers employed in that year in the St. Louis area, 15.4% were Negro. That percentage figure included the St. Louis City School District, which in recent years has followed a policy of attempting to maintain a 50% Negro teaching staff. Apart from that school district, 5.7% of the teachers in the county were Negro in 1970.

Drawing upon these historic facts, the Government mounted its "pattern or practice" attack in the District Court upon four different fronts. It adduced evidence of (1) a history of alleged racially discriminatory practices, (2) statistical disparities in hiring, (3) the standardless and largely subjective hiring procedures, and (4) specific instances of alleged discrimination against 55 unsuccessful Negro applicants for teaching jobs. Hazelwood offered virtually no additional evidence in response, relying instead on evidence introduced by the Government, perceived deficiencies in the Government's case, and its own officially promulgated policy "to hire all teachers on the basis of training, preparation and recommendations, regardless of race, color or creed."[6]

The District Court ruled that the Government had failed to establish a pattern or practice of discrimination. The court was unpersuaded by the alleged history of discrimination, noting that no dual

---

4. One of those two schools was never visited even though it was located in nearby St. Louis. The second was briefly visited on one occasion, but no potential applicant was interviewed.

6. The defendants offered only one witness, who testified to the total number of teachers who had applied and were hired for jobs in the 1971–1972 and 1972–1973 school years. They introduced several exhibits consisting of a policy manual, policy book, staff handbook, and historical summary of Hazelwood's formation and relatively brief existence.

school system had ever existed in Hazelwood. The statistics showing that relatively small numbers of Negroes were employed as teachers were found nonprobative, on the ground that the percentage of Negro pupils in Hazelwood was similarly small. The court found nothing illegal or suspect in the teacher-hiring procedures that Hazelwood had followed. Finally, the court reviewed the evidence in the 55 cases of alleged individual discrimination, and after stating that the burden of proving intentional discrimination was on the Government, it found that this burden had not been sustained in a single instance. Hence, the court entered judgment for the defendants. 892 F.Supp. 1276 (ED Mo.).

The Court of Appeals for the Eighth Circuit reversed. 534 F.2d 805. After suggesting that the District Court had assigned inadequate weight to evidence of discriminatory conduct on the part of Hazelwood before the effective date of Title VII, the Court of Appeals rejected the trial court's analysis of the statistical data as resting on an irrelevant comparison of Negro teachers to Negro pupils in Hazelwood. The proper comparison, in the appellate court's view, was one between Negro teachers in Hazelwood and Negro teachers in the relevant labor market area. Selecting St. Louis County and St. Louis City as the relevant area, the Court of Appeals compared the 1970 census figures, showing that 15.4% of teachers in that area were Negro, to the racial composition of Hazelwood's teaching staff. In the 1972–1973 and 1973–1974 school years, only 1.4% and 1.8%, respectively, of Hazelwood's teachers were Negroes. This statistical disparity, particularly when viewed against the background of the teacher-hiring procedures that Hazelwood had followed, was held to constitute a prima facie case of a pattern or practice of racial discrimination.

In addition, the Court of Appeals reasoned that the trial court had erred in failing to measure the 55 instances in which Negro applicants were denied jobs against the four-part standard for establishing a prima facie case of individual discrimination set out in this Court's opinion in McDonnell Douglas Corp. v. Green, 411 U.S. 792, 802, 93 S.Ct. 1817, 1824, 36 L.Ed.2d 668. Applying that standard, the appellate court found 16 cases of individual discrimination, which "buttressed" the statistical proof. Because Hazelwood had not rebutted the Government's prima facie case of a pattern or practice of racial discrimination, the Court of Appeals directed judgment for the Government and prescribed the remedial order to be entered.

We granted certiorari, 429 U.S. 1037, 97 S.Ct. 730, 50 L.Ed.2d 747 to consider a substantial question affecting the enforcement of a pervasive federal law.

The petitioners primarily attack the judgment of the Court of Appeals for its reliance on "undifferentiated work force statistics to find an unrebutted prima facie case of employment discrimination." The question they raise, in short, is whether a basic component in the Court of Appeals' finding of a pattern or practice of discrimination—the comparatively small percentage of Negro employees in Hazelwood's teaching staff—was lacking in probative force.

This Court's recent consideration in International Brotherhood of Teamsters v. United States, 431 U.S. 324, 97 S.Ct. 1843, 52 L.Ed.2d 396 of the role of statistics in pattern-or-practice suits under Title VII provides substantial guidance in evaluating the arguments advanced by the petitioners. In that case we stated that it is the Government's burden to "establish by a preponderance of the evidence that racial discrimination was the [employer's] standard operating procedure—the regular rather than the unusual practice." Id., at 336, 97 S.Ct., at 1855. We also noted that statistics can be an important source of proof in employment discrimination cases, since

> absent explanation, it is ordinarily to be expected that nondiscriminatory hiring practices will in time result in a work force more or less representative of the racial and ethnic composition of the population in the community from which employees are hired. Evidence of long-lasting and gross disparity between the composition of a work force and that of the general population thus may be significant even though § 703(j) makes clear that Title VII imposes no requirement that a work force mirror the general population. Id., at 340 n. 20, 97 S.Ct., at 1856 n. 20.

See also Village of Arlington Heights v. Metropolitan Housing Development Corp., 429 U.S. 252, 266, 97 S.Ct. 555, 564, 50 L.Ed.2d 450; Washington v. Davis, 426 U.S. 229, 241–242, 96 S.Ct. 2040, 2048–2049, 48 L.Ed.2d 597. Where gross statistical disparities can be shown, they alone may in a proper case constitute prima facie proof of a pattern or practice of discrimination. *Teamsters,* supra, 431 U.S. at 339, 97 S.Ct., at 1856.

There can be no doubt, in light of the *Teamsters* case, that the District Court's comparison of Hazelwood's teacher work force to its student population fundamentally misconceived the role of statistics in employment discrimination cases. The Court of Appeals was correct in the view that a proper comparison was between the racial composition of Hazelwood's teaching staff and the racial composition of the qualified public school teacher population in the relevant labor market.[13] See

---

13. In *Teamsters,* the comparison between the percentage of Negroes on the employer's work force and the percentage in the general area-wide population was highly probative, because the job skill there involved—the ability to drive a truck—is one that many persons possess or can fairly readily acquire. When special qualifications are required to fill particular jobs, comparisons to the general population (rather than to the smaller group of individuals who possess the necessary qualifications) may have little probative value. The comparative statistics introduced by the Government in the District Court, however, were properly limited to public school teachers, and therefore this is not a case like Mayor v. Educational Equality League, 415 U.S. 605, 94 S.Ct. 1323, 39 L.Ed.2d 630, in which the racial-composition comparisons failed to take into account special qualifications for the position in question. Id., at 620–621, 94 S.Ct., at 1333–1334.

Although the petitioners concede as a general matter the probative force of the comparative work-force statistics, they object to the Court of Appeals' heavy reliance on these data on the ground that applicant-flow data, showing the actual percentage of white and Negro applicants for teaching

Teamsters, supra, at 337–338, and n. 17, 97 S.Ct., at 1855, and n. 17. The percentage of Negroes on Hazelwood's teaching staff in 1972–1973 was 1.4% and in 1973–1974 it was 1.8%. By contrast, the percentage of qualified Negro teachers in the area was, according to the 1970 census, at least 5.7%.[14] Although these differences were on their face substantial, the Court of Appeals erred in substituting its judgment for that of the District Court and holding that the Government had conclusively proved its "pattern or practice" lawsuit.

The Court of Appeals totally disregarded the possibility that this prima facie statistical proof in the record might at the trial court level be rebutted by statistics dealing with Hazelwood's hiring after it became subject to Title VII. Racial discrimination by public employers was not made illegal under Title VII until March 24, 1972. A public employer who from that date forward made all its employment decisions in a wholly nondiscriminatory way would not violate Title VII even if it had formerly maintained an all-white work force by purposefully excluding Negroes.[15] For this reason, the Court cautioned in the *Teamsters* opinion that once a prima facie case has been established by statistical work-force disparities, the employer must be given an opportunity to show that "the claimed discriminatory pattern is a product of pre-Act hiring rather than unlawful post-Act discrimination." 431 U.S., at 360, 97 S.Ct., at 1867.

positions at Hazelwood, would be firmer proof. As we have noted, see n. 5, supra, there was no clear evidence of such statistics. We leave it to the District Court on remand to determine whether competent proof of those data can be adduced. If so, it would, of course, be very relevant. Cf. Dothard v. Rawlinson, 433 U.S., 321, 330, 97 S.Ct. 2720, 2727, 53 L.Ed.2d 786.

14. As is discussed below, the Government contends that a comparative figure of 15.4%, rather than 5.7%, is the appropriate one. See infra, at 2743–2744. But even assuming, *arguendo,* that the 5.7% figure urged by the petitioners is correct, the disparity between that figure and the percentage of Negroes on Hazelwood's teaching staff would be more than fourfold for the 1972–1973 school year, and threefold for the 1973–1974 school year. A precise method of measuring the significance of such statistical disparities was explained in Castaneda v. Partida, 430 U.S. 482, 496–497, n. 17, 97 S.Ct. 1272, 1281, n. 17, 51 L.Ed.2d 498, n. 17. It involves calculation of the "standard deviation" as a measure of predicted fluctuations from the expected value of a sample. Using the 5.7% figure as the basis for calculating the expected value, the expected number of Negroes on the Hazelwood teaching staff would be roughly 63 in 1972–1973 and 70 in 1973–1974. The observed number in those years

was 16 and 22, respectively. The difference between the observed and expected values was more than six standard deviations in 1972–1973 and more than five standard deviations in 1973–1974. The Court in *Castaneda* noted that "[a]s a general rule for such large samples, if the difference between the expected value and the observed number is greater than two or three standard deviations," then the hypothesis that teachers were hired without regard to race would be suspect. 430 U.S., at 497 n. 17, 97 S.Ct., at 1281 n. 17.

15. This is not to say that evidence of pre-Act discrimination can never have any probative force. Proof that an employer engaged in racial discrimination prior to the effective date of Title VII might in some circumstances support the inference that such discrimination continued, particularly where relevant aspects of the decisionmaking process had undergone little change. Cf. Fed.Rule Evid. 406; Village of Arlington Heights v. Metropolitan Housing Development Corp., 429 U.S. 252, 267, 97 S.Ct. 555, 564, 50 L.Ed.2d 450; 1 J. Wigmore, Evidence § 92 (3d ed. 1940); 2 *id.,* 302–305, 371, 375. And, of course, a public employer even before the extension of Title VII in 1972 was subject to the command of the Fourteenth Amendment not to engage in purposeful racial discrimination.

The record in this case showed that for the 1972–1973 school year, Hazelwood hired 282 new teachers, 10 of whom (3.5%) were Negroes; for the following school year it hired 128 new teachers, 3 of whom (4.1%) were Negroes. Over the two-year period, Negroes constituted a total of 15 of the 405 new teachers hired (3.7%). Although the Court of Appeals briefly mentioned these data in reciting the facts, it wholly ignored them in discussing whether the Government had shown a pattern or practice of discrimination. And it gave no consideration at all to the possibility that post-Act data as to the number of Negroes hired compared to the total number of Negro applicants might tell a totally different story.[16]

What the hiring figures prove obviously depends upon the figures to which they are compared. The Court of Appeals accepted the Government's argument that the relevant comparison was to the labor market area of St. Louis County and the city of St. Louis, in which, according to the 1970 census, 15.4% of all teachers were Negro. The propriety of that comparison was vigorously disputed by the petitioners, who urged that because the city of St. Louis has made special attempts to maintain a 50% Negro teaching staff, inclusion of that school district in the relevant market area distorts the comparison. Were that argument accepted, the percentage of Negro teachers in the relevant labor market area (St. Louis County alone) as shown in the 1970 census would be 5.7% rather than 15.4%.

The difference between these figures may well be important; the disparity between 3.7% (the percentage of Negro teachers hired by Hazelwood in 1972–1973 and 1973–1974) and 5.7% may be sufficiently small to weaken the Government's other proof, while the disparity between 3.7% and 15.4% may be sufficiently large to reinforce it.[17]   In

16. See n. 13, supra, and n. 21, infra. But cf. *Teamsters,* 431 U.S., at 364–367, 97 S.Ct., at 1868–1869.

17. Indeed, under the statistical methodology explained in Castaneda v. Partida, supra, 430 U.S., at 496–497, n. 17, 97 S.Ct. 1272, at 1281, n. 17, 51 L.Ed.2d 498 n. 17, involving the calculation of the standard deviation as a measure of predicted fluctuations, the difference between using 15.4% and 5.7% as the areawide figure would be significant. If the 15.4% figure is taken as the basis for comparison, the expected number of Negro teachers hired by Hazelwood in 1972–1973 would be 43 (rather than the actual figure of 10) of a total of 282, a difference of more than five standard deviations; the expected number of 1973–1974 would be 19 (rather than the actual figure 5) of a total of 123, a difference of more than three standard deviations. For the two years combined, the difference between the observed number of 15 Negro teachers hired (of a total of 405) would vary from the expected number of 62 by more than six standard deviations. Because a fluctuation of more than two or three standard deviations would undercut the hypothesis that decisions were being made randomly with respect to race, 430 U.S., at 497 n. 17, 97 S.Ct., at 1281 n. 17, each of these statistical comparisons would reinforce rather than rebut the Government's other proof. If, however, the 5.7% areawide figure is used, the expected number of Negro teachers hired in 1972–1973 would be roughly 16, less than two standard deviations from the observed number of 10; for 1973–1974, the expected value would be roughly seven, less than one standard deviation from the observed value of 5; and for the two years combined, the expected value of 23 would be less than two standard deviations from the observed total of 15. A more precise method of analyzing these statistics confirms the results of the standard deviation analysis. See F. Mosteller, R. Rourke, & G. Thomas, Probability with Statistical Applications 494 (2d ed. 1970).

determining which of the two figures—or, very possibly, what intermediate figure—provides the most accurate basis for comparison to the hiring figures at Hazelwood, it will be necessary to evaluate such considerations as (i) whether the racially based hiring policies of the St. Louis City School District were in effect as far back as 1970, the year in which the census figures were taken; [18] (ii) to what extent those policies have changed the racial composition of that district's teaching staff from what it would otherwise have been; (iii) to what extent St. Louis' recruitment policies have diverted to the city, teachers who might otherwise have applied to Hazelwood; [19] (iv) to what extent Negro teachers employed by the city would prefer employment in other districts such as Hazelwood; and (v) what the experience in other school districts in St. Louis County indicates about the validity of excluding the City School District from the relevant labor market.

It is thus clear that a determination of the appropriate comparative figures in this case will depend upon further evaluation by the trial court. As this Court admonished in *Teamsters:* "[S]tatistics * * * come in infinite variety * * *. [T]heir usefulness depends on all of the surrounding facts and circumstances." 431 U.S., at 340, 97 S.Ct., at 1856–1857. Only the trial court is in a position to make the appropriate determination after further findings. And only after such a determination is made can a foundation be established for deciding whether or not Hazelwood engaged in a pattern or practice of racial discrimination in its employment practices in violation of the law.[20]

We hold, therefore, that the Court of Appeals erred in disregarding the post-Act hiring statistics in the record, and that it should have remanded the case to the District Court for further findings as to the relevant labor market area and for an ultimate determination of whether Hazelwood engaged in a pattern or practice of employment discrimination after March 24, 1972.[21] Accordingly, the judgment is vacated, and the case is remanded to the District Court for further proceedings consistent with this opinion.

These observations are not intended to suggest that precise calculations of statistical significance are necessary in employing statistical proof, but merely to highlight the importance of the choice of the relevant labor market area.

18. In 1970 Negroes constituted only 42% of the faculty in St. Louis city schools, which could indicate either that the city's policy was not yet in effect or simply that its goal had not yet been achieved.

19. The petitioners observe, for example, that Harris Teachers College in St. Louis, whose 1973 graduating class was 60% Negro, is operated by the city. It is the petitioners' contention that the city's public elementary and secondary schools occupy an advantageous position in the recruitment of Harris graduates.

20. Because the District Court focused on a comparison between the percentage of Negro teachers and Negro pupils in Hazelwood, it did not undertake an evaluation of the relevant labor market, and its casual dictum that the inclusion of the city of St. Louis "distorted" the labor market statistics was not based upon valid criteria. 392 F.Supp. 1276, 1287 (ED Mo.).

21. It will also be open to the District Court on remand to determine whether sufficiently reliable applicant-flow data are available to permit consideration of the petitioners' argument that those data may undercut a statistical analysis dependent upon hirings alone.

It is so ordered.

MR. JUSTICE BRENNAN, concurring.

I join the Court's opinion.

* * *

In the present case, the District Court had adopted a wholly inappropriate legal standard of discrimination, and therefore did not evaluate the factual record before it in a meaningful way. This remand in effect orders it to do so. It is my understanding, as apparently it is MR. JUSTICE STEVENS', post, at 2747 n. 5, that the statistical inquiry mentioned by the Court, ante, at 2743 n. 17, and accompanying text, can be of no help to the Hazelwood School Board in rebutting the Government's evidence of discrimination. Indeed, even if the relative comparison market is found to be 5.7% rather than 15.4% black, the applicable statistical analysis at most will not serve to bolster the Government's case. This obviously is of no aid to Hazelwood in meeting *its* burden of proof. Nonetheless I think that the remand directed by the Court is appropriate and will allow the parties to address these figures and calculations with greater care and precision. I also agree that given the misapplication of governing legal principles by the District Court. Hazelwood reasonably should be given the opportunity to come forward with more focused and specific applicant-flow data in the hope of answering the Government's prima facie case. If, as presently seems likely, reliable applicant data are found to be lacking, the conclusion reached by my Brother Stevens will inevitably be forthcoming.

MR. JUSTICE STEVENS, dissenting.

* * *

* * * In this case, since neither party complains that any relevant evidence was excluded, our task is to decide (1) whether the Government's evidence established a prima facie case; and (2), if so, whether the remaining evidence is sufficient to carry Hazelwood's burden of rebutting that prima facie case.

I

The first question is clearly answered by the Government's statistical evidence, its historical evidence, and its evidence relating to specific acts of discrimination.

One-third of the teachers hired by Hazelwood resided in the city of St. Louis at the time of their initial employment. As Mr. Justice Clark explained in his opinion for the Court of Appeals, it was therefore appropriate to treat the city, as well as the county, as part of the relevant labor market.[2] In that market, 15% of the teachers were

---

2. "We accept the Government's contention that St. Louis City and County is the relevant labor market area for our consideration. The relevant labor market area is that area from which the employer draws its employees. United States v. Ironworkers Local 86, 443 F.2d 544, 551 n. 19 (9th Cir.1971). Of the 176 teachers hired by Hazelwood between October, 1972, and September, 1973, approximately 80 percent resided in St. Louis City and County at the time of their initial employment.

black. In the Hazelwood District at the time of trial less than 2% of the teachers were black. An even more telling statistic is that after Title VII became applicable to it, only 3.7% of the new teachers hired by Hazelwood were black. Proof of these gross disparities was in itself sufficient to make out a *prima facie* case of discrimination. See International Brotherhood of Teamsters v. United States, 431 U.S. 324, 339, 97 S.Ct. 1843, 1856, 52 L.Ed.2d 396 (1977); Castaneda v. Partida, 430 U.S. 482, 494–498, 97 S.Ct. 1272, 1280–1282, 51 L.Ed.2d 498.

As a matter of history, Hazelwood employed no black teachers until 1969. Both before and after the 1972 amendment making the statute applicable to public school districts, petitioner used a standardless and largely subjective hiring procedure. Since "relevant aspects of the decisionmaking process had undergone little change," it is proper to infer that the pre-Act policy of preferring white teachers continued to influence Hazelwood's hiring practices.[3]

The inference of discrimination was corroborated by post-Act evidence that Hazelwood had refused to hire 16 qualified black applicants for racial reasons. Taking the Government's evidence as a whole, there can be no doubt about the sufficiency of its *prima facie* case.

II

Hazelwood "offered virtually no additional evidence in response," ante, at 2739. It challenges the Government's statistical analysis by claiming that the city of St. Louis should be excluded from the relevant market and pointing out that only 5.7% of the teachers in the county (excluding the city) were black. It further argues that the city's policy of trying to maintain a 50% black teaching staff diverted teachers from the county to the city. There are two separate reasons why these arguments are insufficient: they are not supported by the evidence; even if true, they do not overcome the Government's case.

Approximately one-third of the teachers hired during this period resided in the City of St. Louis and 40 percent resided in areas of St. Louis County other than the Hazelwood District." 534 F.2d 805, 811–812, n. 7 (1976).

It is noteworthy that in the Court of Appeals, Chief Judge Gibson, in dissent, though urging—as Hazelwood had in the District Court—that the labor market was even broader than the Government contended, id., at 821, did not question the propriety of including the city in the same market as the county, see Defendants' Brief and Memorandum in Support of Its Proposed Findings of Fact and Conclusions of Law, filed on Aug. 21, 1974, in Civ. Act. No. 73–C–553(A) (ED Mo.). In this Court, petitioners had abandoned any argument similar to that made below.

3. Proof that an employer engaged in racial discrimination prior to the effective date of the Act creates the inference that such discrimination continued "particularly where relevant aspects of the decisionmaking process [have] undergone little change. Cf. Fed.Rule Evid. 406; Village of Arlington Heights v. Metropolitan Housing Development Corp., 429 U.S. 252, 267, 97 S.Ct. 555, 50 L.Ed.2d 450; 1 J. Wigmore, Evidence § 92 (3d ed. 1940); 2 id., §§ 302–305, 371, 375. And, of course, a public employer even before the extension of Title VII in 1972 was subject to the command of the Fourteenth Amendment not to engage in purposeful racial discrimination." Ante, at 2742–2743, n. 15.

Since Hazelwood's hiring before 1972 was so clearly discriminatory, there is some irony in its claim that "Hazelwood continued [after 1972] to select its teachers on the same careful basis that it had relied on before in staffing its growing system." Brief for Petitioners 29–30.

The petitioners offered no evidence concerning wage differentials, commuting problems, or the relative advantages of teaching in an inner-city school as opposed to a suburban school. Without any such evidence in the record, it is difficult to understand why the simple fact that the city was the source of a third of Hazelwood's faculty should not be sufficient to demonstrate that it is a part of the relevant market. The city's policy of attempting to maintain a 50/50 ratio clearly does not undermine that conclusion, particularly when the record reveals no shortage of qualified black applicants in either Hazelwood or other suburban school districts.[4] Surely not *all* of the 2,000 black teachers employed by the city were unavailable for employment in Hazelwood at the time of their initial hire.

But even if it were proper to exclude the city of St. Louis from the market, the statistical evidence would still tend to prove discrimination. With the city excluded, 5.7% of the teachers in the remaining market were black. On the basis of a random selection, one would therefore expect 5.7% of the 405 teachers hired by Hazelwood in the 1972–1973 and 1973–1974 school years to have been black. But instead of 23 black teachers, Hazelwood hired only 15, less than two-thirds of the expected number. Without the benefit of expert testimony, I would hesitate to infer that the disparity between 23 and 15 is great enough, in itself, to prove discrimination.[5] It is perfectly clear, however, that whatever probative force this disparity has, it tends to prove discrimination and does absolutely nothing in the way of carrying Hazelwood's burden of overcoming the Government's *prima facie* case.

Absolute precision in the analysis of market data is too much to expect. We may fairly assume that a nondiscriminatory selection process would have resulted in the hiring of somewhere between the 15% suggested by the Government and the 5.7% suggested by petitioners, or perhaps 30 or 40 black teachers, instead of the 15 actually hired.[6] On that assumption, the Court of Appeals' determination that there were 16 individual cases of discriminatory refusal to hire black applicants in the post-1972 period seems remarkably accurate.

In sum, the Government is entitled to prevail on the present record. It proved a prima facie case, which Hazelwood failed to rebut. Why, then, should we burden a busy federal court with another trial? Hazelwood had an opportunity to offer evidence to dispute the 16

---

4. "Had there been evidence obtainable to contradict and disprove the testimony offered by [the Government], it cannot be assumed that the State would have refrained from introducing it." Pierre v. Louisiana, 306 U.S. 354, 361–362, 59 S.Ct. 536, 540, 83 L.Ed. 757.

5. After I had drafted this opinion, one of my law clerks advised me that, given the size of the two-year sample, there is only about a 5% likelihood that a disparity this large would be produced by a random se-

lection from the labor pool. If his calculation (which was made using the method described in H. Blalock, Social Statistics 151–173 (1972)) is correct, it is easy to understand why Hazelwood offered no expert testimony.

6. Some of the other school districts in the county have a 10% ratio of blacks on their faculties. See Plaintiff's Exhibit 54 in Civ. Act. No. 73–C–553(A) (ED Mo.1975); Brief for United States 30 n. 30.

examples of racially motivated refusals to hire; but as the Court notes, the Court of Appeals has already "held that none of the 16 prima facie cases of individual discrimination had been rebutted by the petitioners. See 534 F.2d 805, 814 (CA8)." Ante, at 2740 n. 10. Hazelwood also had an opportunity to offer any evidence it could muster to show a change in hiring practices or to contradict the fair inference to be drawn from the statistical evidence. Instead, it "offered virtually no additional evidence in response," ante, at 2739.

Perhaps "a totally different story" might be told by other statistical evidence that was never presented, ante, at 2742. No lawsuit has ever been tried in which the losing party could not have pointed to a similar possibility.[7] It is always possible to imagine more evidence which could have been offered, but at some point litigation must come to an end.[8]

Rather than depart from well-established rules of procedure, I would affirm the judgment of the Court of Appeals.[9] Since that judgment reflected a correct appraisal of the record, I see no reason to prolong this litigation with a remand neither side requested.[10]

7. Since Hazelwood failed to offer any "applicant-flow data" at the trial, and since it does not now claim to have any newly discovered evidence, I am puzzled by Mr. Justice Brennan's explanation of the justification for a remand. Indeed, after the first trial was concluded, Hazelwood emphasized the fact that no evidence of this kind had been presented; it introduced no such evidence itself. It stated: 'There is absolutely no evidence in this case that provides any basis for making a comparison between black applicants and white applicants and their treatment by the Hazelwood School District relative to hiring or not being hired for a teaching position." Defendants' Brief and Memorandum in Support of Its Proposed Findings of Fact and Conclusions of Law, supra, n. 2, at 22.

8. My analysis of this case is somewhat similar to Mr. Justice Rehnquist's analysis in Dothard v. Rawlinson:

"If the defendants in a Title VII suit believe there to be any reason to discredit plaintiffs' statistics that does not appear on their face, the opportunity to challenge them is available to the defendants just as in any other lawsuit. They may endeavor to impeach the reliability of the statistical evidence, they may offer rebutting evidence, they may disparage in arguments or in briefs the probative weight which the plaintiffs' evidence should be accorded. Since I agree with the Court that appellants made virtually no such effort, * * * I also agree with it that the District Court cannot be said to have erred as a matter of law in finding that a *prima facie* case had been made out in the instant case." 433 U.S. 321, at 338–339, 97 S.Ct. 2720, 2731, 53 L.Ed.2d 786 (concurring opinion).

9. It is interesting to compare the disposition in this case with that in Castaneda v. Partida, 430 U.S. 482, 97 S.Ct. 1272, 51 L.Ed.2d 498. In *Castaneda*, as in this case, "[i]nexplicably, the State introduced practically no evidence," id., at 498, 97 S.Ct., at 1282. But in *Castaneda*, unlike the present case, the Court affirmed the finding of discrimination, rather than giving the State a second chance at trying its case. (It should be noted that the *Castaneda* Court expressly stated that it was possible that the statistical discrepancy could have been explained by the State. Id., at 499, 97 S.Ct., at 1282.)

10. Hazelwood's brief asks only for a remand "for reconsideration of the alleged individual cases of discrimination * * *." Brief for Petitioners 78. Hazelwood explains: "[The question raised in its petition for certiorari is] a question of law. It is a question of what sort of evidentiary showing satisfies Title VII. * * * The question is whether on the evidence of record an unrebutted *prima facie* case was established." Reply Brief for Petitioners 2.

BAZEMORE v. FRIDAY

Supreme Court of the United States, 1986.
___ U.S. ___, 106 S.Ct. 3000, ___L.Ed.2d ___.

PER CURIAM.

These cases present several issues arising out of petitioners' action against respondents for alleged racial discrimination in employment and provision of services by the North Carolina Agricultural Extension Service (Extension Service).

The District Court, * * * after a lengthy trial, entered judgment for respondents in all respects, finding that petitioners had not carried their burden of demonstrating that respondents had engaged in a pattern or practice of racial discrimination. * * * The Court of Appeals affirmed. 751 F.2d 662 (CA4 1984). We hold, for the reasons stated in the opinion of JUSTICE BRENNAN, that the Court of Appeals erred in holding that under Title VII of the Civil Rights Act of 1964, as amended, the Extension Service had no duty to eradicate salary disparities between white and black workers that had their origin prior to the date Title VII was made applicable to public employers; that the Court of Appeals erred in disregarding petitioners' statistical analysis because it reflected pre-Title VII salary disparities, and in holding that petitioners' regressions were unacceptable as evidence of discrimination; that the Court of Appeals erred in ignoring evidence presented by petitioners in addition to their multiple regression analyses; [and] that, on remand, the Court of Appeals should examine all of the evidence in the record relating to salary disparities under the clearly erroneous standard * * *. [The opinion for the Court by JUSTICE WHITE on another issue omitted].

* * *

JUSTICE BRENNAN for a unanimous Court, concurring in part.

I

A

The purpose of North Carolina's agricultural extension program, administered through the North Carolina Agricultural Extension Service (Extension Service), is to aid in the dissemination, of "useful and practical information on subjects relating to agriculture and home economics." * * *

* * *

Prior to August 1, 1965, the Extension Service was divided into two branches: a white branch and a "Negro branch." Only the "Negro branch" had a formal racial designation. The "Negro branch" was composed entirely of black personnel and served only black farmers, homemakers and youth. The white branch employed no blacks, but did on occasion serve blacks. On August 1, 1965, in response to the Civil Rights Act of 1964, the State merged the two branches of the Extension Service into a single organization. However, as the District Court subsequently found, "[the] unification and integration of the Extension Service did not result immediately in the elimination of some disparities which had existed between the salaries of white personnel and black personnel * * *."

* * *

We granted certiorari, 474 U.S. ___, 106 S.Ct. 379, 88 L.Ed.2d 333 (1985).[4]

II

The first issue we must decide is whether the Court of Appeals erred in upholding the District Court's finding that petitioners had not proved by a preponderance of the evidence that the respondents had discriminated against black Extension Service employees in violation of Title VII by paying them less than whites employed in the same positions. The Court of Appeals reasoned that the Extension Service was under no obligation to eliminate any salary disparity between blacks and whites that had its origin prior to 1972 when Title VII became applicable to public employers such as the Extension Service. It also reasoned that factors, other than those included in the petitioners' multiple regression analyses, affected salary, and that therefore those regression analyses were incapable of sustaining a finding in favor of petitioners.

A

Both the Court of Appeals and the District Court found that before the black and white Extension Service branches were merged in 1965, the Extension Service maintained two separate, racially-segregated branches and paid black employees less than white employees. * * * The Court of Appeals also acknowledged that after the merger of the Extension Service, "[s]ome pre-existing salary disparities continued to linger on," and that these disparities continued after Title VII became applicable to the Extension Service in March 1972 and after this suit was filed. * * * Indeed, the Court of Appeals noted that "the Extension Service admits that, while it had made some adjustments to try to get rid of the salary disparity resulting on account of pre-Act discrimination, it has not made all the adjustments necessary to get rid of all such disparity." * * * The court interpreted petitioners' claim on appeal to be that "the pre-Act discriminatory difference in salaries should have been affirmatively eliminated but has not." 751 F.2d at 670. Relying on our cases in Hazelwood School District v.

---

4. The question presented in the Federal Government's petition is whether black state employees establish a claim under § 703(a) of the 1964 Civil Rights Act, 42 U.S.C. 2000e–2(a), by identifying current salary disparities between themselves and white employees holding the same jobs, when such disparities result from a State policy before 1965 of paying blacks lower salaries than whites.

The private petitioners presented the same question as that presented by the Federal Government, and * * * additional questions:

(1) May a regression analysis be treated as probative evidence of discrimination where the analysis does not incorporate every conceivable relevant variable?

* * *

United States, 433 U.S. 299, 97 S.Ct. 2736, 53 L.Ed.2d 768 (1977), and United Air Lines, Inc. v. Evans, 431 U.S. 553, 97 S.Ct. 1885, 52 L.Ed.2d 571 (1977), it concluded, "[w]e do not think this is the law." 751 F.2d, at 670.

The error of the Court of Appeals with respect to salary disparities created prior to 1972 and perpetuated thereafter is too obvious to warrant extended discussion: that the Extension Service discriminated with respect to salaries *prior* to the time it was covered by Title VII does not excuse perpetuating that discrimination *after* the Extension Service became covered by Title VII. To hold otherwise would have the effect of exempting from liability those employers who were historically the greatest offenders of the rights of blacks. A pattern or practice that would have constituted a violation of Title VII, but for the fact that the statute had not yet become effective, became a violation upon Title VII's effective date, and to the extent an employer continued to engage in that act or practice, he is liable under that statute. While recovery may not be permitted for pre-1972 acts of discrimination, to the extent that this discrimination was perpetuated after 1972, liability may be imposed.

Each week's pay check that delivers less to a black than to a similarly situated white is a wrong actionable under Title VII, regardless of the fact that this pattern was begun prior to the effective date of Title VII. The Court of Appeals plainly erred in holding that the pre-Act discriminatory difference in salaries did not have to be eliminated.[6]

* * *

6. Neither *Hazelwood* nor *Evans* suggest any different rule, and indeed support the result here. In *Evans*, respondent, a female flight attendant, was forced to resign in 1968 from her position due to her employer's policy forbidding female flight attendants to marry. Respondent there never brought an action with respect to this forced resignation. In 1972 she was rehired by the airline as a new hire, and given seniority only from that date. Although her claim with respect to the 1968 resignation was time barred, respondent filed suit claiming that the airline was guilty of a present, continuing violation of Title VII because the seniority system treats her less favorably than males who were hired after her termination in 1968 and prior to her re-employment. Further, she claimed that the seniority system gave present effect to the past, illegal forced retirement and thereby perpetuates the consequences of forbidden discrimination. Respondent had made no allegation that the seniority system itself was intentionally designed to discriminate. Because a lawsuit on the forced resignation was time barred, however, it was to be treated as an act occurring before the statute was passed, and therefore it had "no present legal consequences," 431 U.S., at 558, 97 S.Ct. at 1889, even though "[i]t may constitute relevant background evidence in a proceeding in which the status of a current practice is at issue." Ibid. The "critical question," the Court declared, "is whether any *present violation* exists." Ibid. (emphasis added). Because the employer was not engaged in discriminatory practices at the time the respondent in *Evans* brought suit, there simply was no violation of Title VII.

In *Hazelwood*, the Attorney General brought suit against the Hazelwood School District and various of its officials claiming that they were engaged in a pattern or practice of discriminatory hiring in violation of Title VII. We vacated the decision of the Court of Appeals that directed judgment for the Government, because that decision did not take into account the possibility that the prima facie statistical proof in the record "might at the trial court level be rebutted by statistics dealing with Hazelwood's hiring after it became subject to Title VII." We explained that "[a] public employer who from [1972] forward made all its employment decisions in a wholly nondiscriminatory way would not

B

We now turn to the issue of whether the Court of Appeals erred in upholding the District Court's refusal to accept the petitioners' expert statistical evidence as proof of discimination by a preponderance of the evidence.

* * *

At trial, petitioners relied heavily on multiple regression analyses designed to demonstrate that blacks were paid less than similarly situated whites. The United States' expert prepared multiple regression analyses relating to salaries for the years 1974, 1975, and 1981. Certain of these regressions used four independent variables—race, education, tenure, and job title. Petitioners selected these variables based on discovery testimony by an Extension Service official that four factors were determinative of salary: education, tenure, job title, and job performance. * * * In addition, regressions done by the Extension Service itself for 1971 included the variables race, sex, education, and experience; and another in 1974 used the variables race, education, and tenure to check for disparities between the salaries of blacks and whites. * * *

The regressions purported to demonstrate that in 1974 the average black employee earned $331 less per year than a white employee with the same job title, education, and tenure, * * * and that in 1975 the disparity was $395. * * * The regression for 1981 showed a smaller disparity which lacked statistical significance.

The Court of Appeals stated that the

> "district court refused to accept plaintiffs' expert testimony as proof of discrimination by a preponderance of the evidence because the plaintiffs' expert had not included a number of variable factors the court considered relevant, among them being the across the board and percentage pay increases which varied from county to county. The district court was, of course, correct in this analysis." 751 F.2d, at 672.

The Court of Appeals thought the District Court correct for essentially two reasons: First, the Court of Appeals rejected petitioners' regression analysis because it "contained salary figures which reflect the effect of pre-Act discrimination, a consideration not actionable under Title VII * * *." Ibid. (footnote omitted). Second, the court believed that "[a]n appropriate regression analysis of salary should * * * include *all* measurable variables thought to have an effect on salary level." Ibid. In particular, the court found that the failure to consider county to county differences in salary increases was signifi-

violate Title VII even if it had formerly maintained an all-white work force by purposefully excluding Negroes." 433 U.S., at 309, 97 S.Ct., at 2742.

Here, however, petitioners are alleging that in continuing to pay blacks less than similarly situated whites, respondents have *not* from the date of the act forward "made all [their] employment decisions in a wholly nondiscriminatory way." Ibid. Our holding in no sense gives legal effect to the pre-1972 actions, but, consistent with *Evans* and *Hazelwood*, focuses on the present salary structure, which is illegal if it is a mere continuation of the pre-1965 discriminatory pay structure.

cant. It concluded, noting that "both experts omitted from their respective analysis variables which ought to be reasonably viewed as determinants of salary. As a result, the regression analysis presented here must be considered unacceptable as evidence of discrimination." Ibid. The Court of Appeals' treatment of the statistical evidence in this case was erroneous in important respects.

1

The Court of Appeals erred in stating that petitioners' regression analyses were "unacceptable as evidence of discrimination," because they did not include "all measurable variables thought to have an effect on salary level." The court's view of the evidentiary value of the regression analyses was plainly incorrect. While the omission of variables from a regression analysis may render the analysis less probative than it otherwise might be, it can hardly be said, absent some other infirmity, that an analysis which accounts for the major factors "must be considered unacceptable as evidence of discrimination." Ibid. Normally, failure to include variables will affect the analysis' probativeness, not its admissibility.

Importantly, it is clear that a regression analysis that includes less than "all measurable variables" may serve to prove a plaintiff's case. A plaintiff in a Title VII suit need not prove discrimination with scientific certainty; rather, his or her burden is to prove discrimination by a preponderance of the evidence. Texas Department of Community Affairs v. Burdine, 450 U.S. 248, 252, 101 S.Ct. 1089, 1093, 67 L.Ed.2d 207 (1981). Whether, in fact, such a regression analysis does carry the plaintiffs' ultimate burden will depend in a given case on the factual context of each case in light of all the evidence presented by both the plaintiff and the defendant. However, as long as the court may fairly conclude, in light of all the evidence, that it is more likely than not that impermissible discrimination exists, the plaintiff is entitled to prevail.

* * *

Petitioners also presented evidence of pre-Act salary discrimination, and of respondents' ineffectual attempts to eradicate it. For example, the petitioners submitted evidence, and the District Court found, that blacks were paid less than whites in comparable positions prior to the merger of the black and white services in 1965. Moreover, in 1971, the respondents acknowledged that substantial salary differences between blacks and whites existed. In addition, evidence was offered tc show that the efforts by the Extension Service to equalize those salaries in 1971 were insufficient to accomplish the goal. As we made clear in Hazelwood School District v. United States, 433 U.S., at 309–310, n. 15, 97 S.Ct. at 2742–43, n. 15 "[p]roof that an employer engaged in racial discrimination prior to the effective date of Title VII might in some circumstances support the inference that such discrimination continued, particularly where relevant aspects of the decision-making process had undergone little change."

Further, petitioners presented evidence to rebut respondents' contention that county to county variations in contributions to salary explain the established disparity between black and white salaries. The United States presented evidence, which it claims respondents did not rebut, establishing that black employees were not located disproportionately in the counties that contributed only a small amount to Extension Service salaries. * * * Absent a disproportionate concentration of blacks in such counties, it is difficult, if not impossible, to understand how the fact that some counties contribute less to salaries than others could explain disparities between black and white salaries. In addition, the United States presented an exhibit based on 1973 data for 23 counties showing 29 black employees who were earning less than whites in the same county who had comparable or lower positions and tenure. * * *

Finally, and there was some overlap here with evidence used to discredit the county to county variation theory, the petitioners presented evidence consisting of individual comparisons between salaries of blacks and whites similarly situated. * * * Witness testimony, claimed by petitioners to be unrebutted, also confirmed the continued existence of such disparities. * * *

Setting out the range of persuasive evidence offered by the petitioners demonstrates the error of the Court of Appeals in focusing solely on the characteristics of the regression analysis. Although we think that consideration of the evidence makes a strong case for finding the District Court's conclusion clearly erroneous, we leave that task to the Court of Appeals on remand which must make such a determination based on the "entire evidence" in the record. United States v. United States Gypsum Co., 333 U.S. 364, 68 S.Ct. 525, 92 L.Ed. 746 (1948).

* * *

Notes

Measurements of Impact. The courts have used a variety of standards to determine whether the impact of an employment practice has a significant adverse effect on a protected class. Gross disparity alone, in some instances, may be sufficient. For example, in International Brotherhood Of Teamsters v. United States, 431 U.S. 324, 342, n. 23, 97 S.Ct. 1843, 1858, n. 23, 52 L.Ed.2d 396 (1977), the Court noted that the employer's inability to rebut the inference of discrimination was not the result of the misuse of statistics but from the "inexorable zero". The Uniform Guidelines adopts a "four-fifths" rule:

> A selection rate for any race, sex, or ethnic group which is less than four-fifths ($\frac{4}{5}$) (or eighty percent) of the rate for the group with the highest rate will generally be regarded by Federal enforcement agencies as evidence of adverse impact, while a greater than four-fifths rate will generally not be regarded by Federal enforcement agencies as evidence of adverse impact.

29 C.F.R. Section 1607.4D. Some courts have adopted this rule. E.g., Firefighters Institute for Racial Equality v. St. Louis, 616 F.2d 350, 356–57

(8th Cir.1980), cert. denied 452 U.S. 938, 101 S.Ct. 3079, 69 L.Ed.2d 951 (1981). Brotherhood v. City of Omaha, 39 FEP Cases 152 (D.Neb. Sept. 5, 1985). But see Clady v. County of Los Angeles, 770 F.2d 1421 (9th Cir.1985) (rejecting a rigid adherence to the "80%" rule); Shoben, Differential Pass-Fail Rates in Employment Testing: Statistical Proof Under Title VII, 91 Harv.L.Rev. 793, 805 (1978) (criticizing rule as ill-conceived on the ground that it produces an anomalous result because it fails to take account of differences in sampling sizes).

One of the most widely accepted and used measurements of "substantial" or "significant" statistical disparity is the standard deviation theory. Standard deviation is a professionally accepted statistical method designed to determine whether observed differences and expected differences occurred by chance, or whether a factor other than chance can be relied upon to explain the differences. The Supreme Court sanctioned the use of the standard deviation theory in *Hazelwood*.

Multiple regression analysis is one of the more complex statistical models used in discrimination cases to determine the presence or absence of significant disparate impact. See Coates v. Johnson & Johnson, 756 F.2d 524 (7th Cir.1985); Finkelstein, The Judicial Reception of Multiple Regression Studies in Race and Sex Discrimination Cases, 80 Colum.L.Rev. 736 (1980).

The literature on the subject is rich on expository and critical commentary. For a sampling, see, D. Baldus & J. Cole, Statistical Proof of Discrimination (1980) (bibliography); Shoben, Probing the Discriminatory Effect of Employee Selection Procedures with Disparate Impact Analysis Under Title VII, 56 Tex.L.Rev. 1 (1977).

DOTHARD v. RAWLINSON

Supreme Court of the United States, 1977.
433 U.S. 321, 97 S.Ct. 2720, 53 L.Ed.2d 786.

MR. JUSTICE STEWART delivered the opinion of the Court.

Appellee Dianne Rawlinson sought employment with the Alabama Board of Corrections as a prison guard, called in Alabama a "correctional counselor." After her application was rejected, she brought this class suit under Title VII of the Civil Rights Act of 1964, 78 Stat. 253, as amended, 42 U.S.C. § 2000e *et seq.* (1970 ed. and Supp. V), and under 42 U.S.C. § 1983, alleging that she had been denied employment because of her sex in violation of federal law. A three-judge Federal District Court for the Middle District of Alabama decided in her favor. Mieth v. Dothard, 418 F.Supp. 1169. We noted probable jurisdiction of this appeal from the District Court's judgment. 429 U.S. 976, 97 S.Ct. 483, 50 L.Ed.2d 583.

I

At the time she applied for a position as correctional counselor trainee, Rawlinson was a 22-year-old college graduate whose major course of study had been correctional psychology. She was refused employment because she failed to meet the minimum 120-pound weight requirement established by an Alabama statute. The statute also establishes a height minimum of 5 feet 2 inches.[2]

After her application was rejected because of her weight, Rawlinson filed a charge with the Equal Employment Opportunity Commission, and ultimately received a right-to-sue letter. She then filed a complaint in the District Court on behalf of herself and other similarly situated women, challenging the statutory height and weight minima as violative of Title VII and the Equal Protection Clause of the Fourteenth Amendment.

* * *

II

In enacting Title VII, Congress required "the removal of artificial, arbitrary, and unnecessary barriers to employment when the barriers operate invidiously to discriminate on the basis of racial or other impermissible classification." Griggs v. Duke Power Co., 401 U.S. 424, 431, 91 S.Ct. 849, 853, 28 L.Ed.2d 158. The District Court found that the minimum statutory height and weight requirements that applicants for employment as correctional counselors must meet constitute the sort of arbitrary barrier to equal employment opportunity that Title VII forbids. The appellants assert that the District Court erred both in finding that the height and weight standards discriminate against women, and in its refusal to find that, even if they do, these standards are justified as "job related."

A

The gist of the claim that the statutory height and weight requirements discriminate against women does not involve an assertion of purposeful discriminatory motive. It is asserted, rather, that these facially neutral qualification standards work in fact disproportionately to exclude women from eligibility for employment by the Alabama Board of Corrections. We dealt in Griggs v. Duke Power Co., supra and Albemarle Paper Co. v. Moody, 422 U.S. 405, 95 S.Ct. 2362, 45 L.Ed.2d 280, with similar allegations that facially neutral employment standards disproportionately excluded Negroes from employment, and those cases guide our approach here.

Those cases make clear that to establish a *prima facie* case of discrimination, a plaintiff need only show that the facially neutral standards in question select applicants for hire in a significantly discriminatory pattern. Once it is thus shown that the employment standards are discriminatory in effect, the employer must meet "the

---

2. The statute establishes minimum physical standards for all law enforcement officers. In pertinent part, it provides:

"(d) *Physical qualifications.*—The applicant shall be not less than five feet two inches nor more than six feet ten inches in height, shall weigh not less than 120 pounds nor more than 300 pounds and shall be certified by a li- censed physician designated as satisfactory by the appointing authority as in good health and physically fit for the performance of his duties as a law-enforcement officer. The commission may for good cause shown permit variances from the physical qualifications prescribed in this subdivision." Ala.Code, Tit. 55, § 373(109) (Supp.1973).

burden of showing that any given requirement [has] * * * a manifest relationship to the employment in question." Griggs v. Duke Power Co., supra, at 432, 91 S.Ct., at 854. If the employer proves that the challenged requirements are job related, the plaintiff may then show that other selection devices without a similar discriminatory effect would also "serve the employer's legitimate interest in 'efficient and trustworthy workmanship.'" Albemarle Paper Co. v. Moody, supra, at 425, 95 S.Ct., at 2375, quoting McDonnell Douglas Corp. v. Green, 411 U.S. 792, 801, 93 S.Ct. 1817, 1823, 36 L.Ed.2d 668.

Although women 14 years of age or older compose 52.75% of the Alabama population and 36.89% of its total labor force, they hold only 12.9% of its correctional counselor positions. In considering the effect of the minimum height and weight standards on this disparity in rate of hiring between the sexes, the District Court found that the 5'2"-requirement would operate to exclude 33.29% of the women in the United States between the ages of 18–79, while excluding only 1.28% of men between the same ages. The 120-pound weight restriction would exclude 22.29% of the women and 2.35% of the men in this age group. When the height and weight restrictions are combined, Alabama's statutory standards would exclude 41.13% of the female population while excluding less than 1% of the male population.[12] Accordingly, the District Court found that Rawlinson had made out a prima facie case of unlawful sex discrimination.

The appellants argue that a showing of disproportionate impact on women based on generalized national statistics should not suffice to establish a prima facie case. They point in particular to Rawlinson's failure to adduce comparative statistics concerning actual applicants for correctional counselor positions in Alabama. There is no requirement, however, that a statistical showing of disproportionate impact must always be based on analysis of the characteristics of actual applicants. See Griggs v. Duke Power Co., supra, 401 U.S., at 430, 91 S.Ct., at 853. The application process might itself not adequately reflect the actual potential applicant pool, since otherwise qualified people might be discouraged from applying because of a self-recognized inability to meet the very standards challenged as being discriminatory. See International Brotherhood of Teamsters v. United States, 431 U.S. 324, 365–367, 97 S.Ct. 1843, 1869–1871, 52 L.Ed.2d 396. A potential applicant could easily determine her height and weight and conclude that to make an application would be futile. Moreover, reliance on

---

12. Affirmatively stated, approximately 99.76% of the men and 58.87% of the women meet both these physical qualifications. From the separate statistics on height and weight of males it would appear that after adding the two together and allowing for some overlap the result would be to exclude between 2.35% and 3.63% of males from meeting Alabama's statutory height and weight minima. None of the parties has challenged the accuracy of the District Court's computations on this score, however, and the discrepancy is in any event insignificant in light of the gross disparity between the female and male exclusions. Even under revised computations the disparity would greatly exceed the 34% to 12% disparity that served to invalidate the high school diploma requirement in the *Griggs* case. 401 U.S., at 430, 91 S.Ct., at 853.

general population demographic data was not misplaced where there was no reason to suppose that physical height and weight characteristics of Alabama men and women differ markedly from those of the national population.

For these reasons, we cannot say that the District Court was wrong in holding that the statutory height and weight standards had a discriminatory impact on women applicants. The plaintiffs in a case such as this are not required to exhaust every possible source of evidence, if the evidence actually presented on its face conspicuously demonstrates a job requirement's grossly discriminatory impact. If the employer discerns fallacies or deficiencies in the data offered by the plaintiff, he is free to adduce countervailing evidence of his own. In this case no such effort was made.[13]

B

We turn, therefore, to the appellants' argument that they have rebutted the prima facie case of discrimination by showing that the height and weight requirements are job related. These requirements, they say, have a relationship to strength, a sufficient but unspecified amount of which is essential to effective job performance as a correctional counselor. In the District Court, however, the appellants produced no evidence correlating the height and weight requirements with the requisite amount of strength thought essential to good job performance. Indeed, they failed to offer evidence of any kind in specific justification of the statutory standards.[14]

If the job-related quality that the appellants identify is bona fide, their purpose could be achieved by adopting and validating a test for applicants that measures strength directly. Such a test, fairly administered, would fully satisfy the standards of Title VII because it would be one that "measure[s] the person for the job and not the person in the abstract." Griggs v. Duke Power Co., 401 U.S., at 436, 91 S.Ct., at 856.

13. The height and weight statute contains a waiver provision that the appellants urge saves it from attack under Title VII. See n. 2, supra. The District Court noted that a valid waiver provision might indeed have that effect, but found that applicants were not informed of the waiver provision, and that the Board of Corrections had never requested a waiver from the Alabama Peace Officers' Standards and Training Commission. The court therefore correctly concluded that the waiver provision as administered failed to overcome the discriminatory effect of the statute's basic provisions.

14. In what is perhaps a variation on their constitutional challenge to the validity of Title VII itself, see n. 1, supra, the appellants contend that the establishment of the minimum height and weight standards by statute requires that they be giv-

en greater deference than is typically given private employer-established job qualifications. The relevant legislative history of the 1972 amendments extending Title VII to the States as employers does not, however, support such a result. Instead, Congress expressly indicated the intent that the same Title VII principles be applied to governmental and private employers alike. See H.R.Rep. No. 92–238, p. 17 (1971); S.Rep. No. 92–415, p. 10 (1971); U.S.Code Cong. & Admin.News 1972, p. 2137. See also Schaeffer v. San Diego Yellow Cabs, 462 F.2d 1002 (CA9). Thus for both private and public employers, "[t]he touchstone is business necessity," Griggs, 401 U.S., at 431, 91 S.Ct., at 853; a discriminatory employment practice must be shown to be necessary to safe and efficient job performance to survive a Title VII challenge.

But nothing in the present record even approaches such a measurement.

For the reasons we have discussed, the District Court was not in error in holding that Title VII of the Civil Rights Act of 1964, as amended, prohibits application of the statutory height and weight requirements to Rawlinson and the class she represents.

* * *

Mr. Justice Rehnquist, with whom The Chief Justice and Mr. Justice Blackmun join, concurring in the result and concurring in part.

I agree with, and join, Parts I and III of the Court's opinion in this case and with its judgment. While I also agree with the Court's conclusion in Part II of its opinion, holding that the District Court was "not in error" in holding the statutory height and weight requirements in this case to be invalidated by Title VII, * * * the issues with which that Part deals are bound to arise so frequently that I feel obliged to separately state the reasons for my agreement with its result. I view affirmance of the District Court in this respect as essentially dictated by the peculiarly limited factual and legal justifications offered below by appellants on behalf of the statutory requirements. For that reason, I do not believe—and do not read the Court's opinion as holding—that all or even many of the height and weight requirements imposed by States on applicants for a multitude of law enforcement agency jobs are pretermitted by today's decision.

I agree that the statistics relied upon in this case are sufficient, absent rebuttal, to sustain a finding of a *prima facie* violation of § 703(a)(2), in that they reveal a significant discrepancy between the numbers of men, as opposed to women, who are automatically disqualified by reason of the height and weight requirements. The fact that these statistics are national figures of height and weight, as opposed to statewide or pool-of-labor-force statistics, does not seem to me to require us to hold that the District Court erred as a matter of law in admitting them into evidence. See Hamling v. United States, 418 U.S. 87, 108, 124–125, 94 S.Ct. 2887, 2902, 2911–2912, 41 L.Ed.2d 590 (1974); cf. Zenith Radio Corp. v. Hazeltine, 395 U.S. 100, 123–125, 89 S.Ct. 1562, 1576–1578, 23 L.Ed.2d 129 (1969). It is for the District Court, in the first instance, to determine whether these statistics appear sufficiently probative of the ultimate fact in issue—whether a given job qualification requirement has a disparate impact on some group protected by Title VII. Hazelwood School District v. United States, 433 U.S., 299, at 312–313, 97 S.Ct. 2736, at 2744, 53 L.Ed.2d 768; see Hamling v. United States, supra, 418 U.S., at 108, 124–125, 94 S.Ct., at 2902, 2911–2912; Mayor v. Educational Equality League, 415 U.S. 605, 621 n. 20, 94 S.Ct. 1323, 1333, 39 L.Ed.2d 630 (1974); see also McAllister v. United States, 348 U.S. 19, 75 S.Ct. 6, 99 L.Ed. 20 (1954); United States v. Yellow Cab Co., 338 U.S. 338, 340–342, 70 S.Ct. 177, 178–179, 94 L.Ed. 150 (1949). In making this determination, such statistics are to be considered in light of all other relevant facts and circumstances. Cf. Teamsters v.

United States, 431 U.S. 324, 340, 97 S.Ct. 1843, 1857, 52 L.Ed.2d 396 (1977). The statistics relied on here do not suffer from the obvious lack of relevancy of the statistics relied on by the District Court in Hazelwood School District v. United States, 433 U.S., at 308, 97 S.Ct., at 2742. A reviewing court cannot say as a matter of law that they are irrelevant to the contested issue or so lacking in reliability as to be inadmissible.

If the defendants in a Title VII suit believe there to be any reason to discredit plaintiffs' statistics that does not appear on their face, the opportunity to challenge them is available to the defendants just as in any other lawsuit. They may endeavor to impeach the reliability of the statistical evidence, they may offer rebutting evidence, or they may disparage in arguments or in briefs the probative weight which the plaintiffs' evidence should be accorded. Since I agree with the Court that appellants made virtually no such effort, ante, at 2727–2728, I also agree with it that the District Court cannot be said to have erred as a matter of law in finding that a prima facie case had been made out in the instant case.

While the District Court's conclusion is by no means *required* by the proffered evidence, I am unable to conclude that the District Court's finding in that respect was clearly erroneous. In other cases there could be different evidence which could lead a district court to conclude that height and weight are in fact an accurate enough predictor of strength to justify, under all the circumstances, such minima. Should the height and weight requirements be found to advance the job-related qualification of strength sufficiently to rebut the prima facie case, then, under our cases, the burden would shift back to appellee Rawlinson to demonstrate that other tests, *without* such disparate effect, would also meet that concern. Albemarle Paper Co. v. Moody, 422 U.S. 405, 425, 95 S.Ct. 2362, 2375, 45 L.Ed.2d 280 (1975). But, here, the District Court permissibly concluded that appellants had not shown enough of a nexus even to rebut the inference.

Appellants, in order to rebut the prima facie case under the statute, had the burden placed on them to advance job-related reasons for the qualification. McDonnell Douglas Corp. v. Green, 411 U.S. 792, 802, 93 S.Ct. 1817, 1824, 36 L.Ed.2d 668 (1973). This burden could be shouldered by offering evidence or by making legal arguments not dependent on any new evidence. The District Court was confronted, however, with only one suggested job-related reason for the qualification—that of strength. Appellants argued only the job-relatedness of actual physical strength; they did not urge that an equally job-related qualification for prison guards is the *appearance* of strength. As the Court notes, the primary job of correctional counselor in Alabama prisons "is to maintain security and control of the inmates * * *," ante, at 2725, a function that I at least would imagine is aided by the psychological impact on prisoners of the presence of tall and heavy guards. If the appearance of strength had been urged upon the District

Court here as a reason for the height and weight minima, I think that the District Court would surely have been entitled to reach a different result than it did. For, even if not perfectly correlated, I would think that Title VII would not preclude a State from saying that anyone under 5'2" or 120 pounds, no matter how strong in fact, does not have a sufficient appearance of strength to be a prison guard.

But once the burden has been placed on the defendant, it is then up to the defendant to articulate the asserted job-related reasons underlying the use of the minima. McDonnell Douglas Corp. v. Green, supra, at 802, 93 S.Ct., at 1824; Griggs v. Duke Power Co., 401 U.S. 424, 431, 91 S.Ct. 849, 853, 28 L.Ed.2d 158 (1971); Albemarle Paper Co. v. Moody, supra, 422 U.S., at 425, 95 S.Ct., at 2375. Because of this burden, a reviewing court is not ordinarily justified in relying on arguments in favor of a job qualification that were not first presented to the trial court. Cf. United States v. Arnold, Schwinn & Co., 388 U.S. 365, 374 n. 5, 87 S.Ct. 1856, 1863, 18 L.Ed.2d 1249 (1967); Thomas v. Taylor, 224 U.S. 73, 84, 32 S.Ct. 403, 406, 56 L.Ed. 673 (1912); Bell v. Bruen, 1 How. 169, 187, 11 L.Ed. 89 (1843). As appellants did not even present the "appearance of strength" contention to the District Court as an asserted job-related reason for the qualification requirements, I agree that their burden was not met. The District Court's holding thus did not deal with the question of whether such an assertion could or did rebut appellee Rawlinson's *prima facie* case.

CONNECTICUT v. TEAL

Supreme Court of the United States, 1982.
457 U.S. 440, 102 S.Ct. 2525, 73 L.Ed.2d 130.

JUSTICE BRENNAN delivered the opinion of the Court.

We consider here whether an employer sued for violation of Title VII of the Civil Rights Act of 1964 may assert a "bottom-line" theory of defense. Under that theory, as asserted in this case, an employer's acts of racial discrimination in promotions—effected by an examination having disparate impact—would not render the employer liable for the racial discrimination suffered by employees barred from promotion if the "bottom-line" result of the promotional process was an appropriate racial balance. We hold that the "bottom line" does not preclude respondent employees from establishing a prima facie case, nor does it provide petitioner employer with a defense to such a case.

I

Four of the respondents, Winnie Teal, Rose Walker, Edith Latney, and Grace Clark, are black employees of the Department of Income Maintenance of the State of Connecticut. Each was promoted provisionally to the position of Welfare Eligibility Supervisor and served in that capacity for almost two years. To attain permanent status as supervisors, however, respondents had to participate in a selection process that required, as the first step, a passing score on a written examination. This written test was administered on December 2, 1978, to 329 candidates. Of these candidates, 48 identified themselves as black and 259 identified themselves as white. The results of the examination were announced in March 1979. With the passing score set at 65,[3] 54.17 percent of the identified black candidates passed. This was approximately 68 percent of the passing rate for the identified white candidates.[4] The four respondents were among the blacks who failed the examination, and they were thus excluded from further consideration for permanent supervisory positions. In April 1979, respondents instituted this action in the United States District Court for the District of Connecticut against petitioners, the State of Connecticut, two state agencies, and two state officials. Respondents alleged, *inter alia*, that petitioners violated Title VII by imposing, as an absolute condition for consideration for promotion, that applicants pass a written test that excluded blacks in disproportionate numbers and that was not job related.

More than a year after this action was instituted, and approximately one month before trial, petitioners made promotions from the eligibility list generated by the written examination. In choosing persons from that list, petitioners considered past work performance, recommendations of the candidates' supervisors and, to a lesser extent, seniority. Petitioners then applied what the Court of Appeals characterized as an affirmative-action program in order to ensure a significant number of minority supervisors. Forty-six persons were promoted to permanent supervisory positions, 11 of whom were black and 35 of whom were white. The overall result of the selection process was that, of the 48 identified black candidates who participated in the selection process, 22.9 percent were promoted and of the 259 identified white candidates, 13.5 percent were promoted.[6] It is this "bottom-line" result, more favorable to blacks than to whites, that petitioners urge should be adjudged to be a complete defense to respondents' suit.

3. The mean score on the examination was 70.4 percent. However, because the black candidates had a mean score 6.7 percentage points lower than the white candidates, the passing score was set at 65, apparently in an attempt to lessen the disparate impact of the examination. See id., at 135, and n. 4.

4. The following table shows the passing rates of various candidate groups:

Candidate Group	Number	No. Receiving Passing Score	Passing Rate (%)
Black	48	26	54.17
Hispanic	4	3	75.00
Indian	3	2	66.67
White	259	206	79.54
Unidentified	15	9	60.00
Total	329	246	74.77

Petitioners do not contest the District Court's implicit finding that the examination itself resulted in disparate impact under the "eighty percent rule" of the Uniform Guidelines on Employee Selection Procedures adopted by the Equal Employment Opportunity Commission. See App. to Pet. for Cert. 18a, 23a, and n. 2. Those guidelines provide that a selection rate that "is less than [80 percent] of the rate for the group with the highest rate will generally be regarded * * * as evidence of adverse impact." 29 CFR § 1607.4D (1981).

6. The actual promotion rate of blacks was thus close to 170 percent that of the actual promotion rate of whites.

After trial, the District Court entered judgment for petitioners. The court treated respondents' claim as one of disparate impact under Griggs v. Duke Power Co., 401 U.S. 424, 91 S.Ct. 849, 28 L.Ed.2d 158 (1971), Albemarle Paper Co. v. Moody, 422 U.S. 405, 95 S.Ct. 2362, 45 L.Ed.2d 280 (1975), and Dothard v. Rawlinson, 433 U.S. 321, 97 S.Ct. 2720, 53 L.Ed.2d 786 (1977). However, the court found that, although the comparative passing rates for the examination indicated a prima facie case of adverse impact upon minorities, the result of the entire hiring process reflected no such adverse impact. Holding that these "bottom-line" percentages precluded the finding of a Title VII violation, the court held that the employer was not required to demonstrate that the promotional examination was job related. The United States Court of Appeals for the Second Circuit reversed, holding that the District Court erred in ruling that the results of the written examination alone were insufficient to support a prima facie case of disparate impact in violation of Title VII. 645 F.2d 133 (1981). The Court of Appeals stated that where "an identifiable pass-fail barrier denies an employment opportunity to a disproportionately large number of minorities and prevents them from proceeding to the next step in the selection process," that barrier must be shown to be job related. Id., at 138. We granted certiorari, 454 U.S. 813, 102 S.Ct. 89, 70 L.Ed.2d 82 (1981), and now affirm.

II

A

We must first decide whether an examination that bars a disparate number of black employees from consideration for promotion, and that has not been shown to be job related, presents a claim cognizable under Title VII. Section 703(a)(2) of Title VII provides in pertinent part:

It shall be an unlawful employment practice for an employer—

* * *

(2) to limit, segregate, or classify his employees or applicants for employment in any way which would deprive or tend to deprive any individual of employment opportunities or otherwise adversely affect his status as an employee, because of such individual's race, color, religion, sex, or national origin. 78 Stat. 255, as amended, 42 U.S.C. § 2000e-2(a)(2).

Respondents base their claim on our construction of this provision in Griggs v. Duke Power Co., supra. Prior to the enactment of Title VII, the Duke Power Co. restricted its black employees to the labor department. Beginning in 1965, the company required all employees who desired a transfer out of the labor department to have either a high school diploma or to achieve a passing grade on two professionally prepared aptitude tests. New employees seeking positions in any department other than labor had to possess both a high school diploma and a passing grade on these two examinations. Although these requirements applied equally to white and black employees and applicants, they barred employment opportunities to a disproportionate number of blacks. While there was no showing that the employer had a racial purpose or invidious intent in adopting these requirements, this Court held that they were invalid because they had a disparate impact and were not shown to be related to job performance:

> [Title VII] proscribes not only overt discrimination but also practices that are fair in form, but discriminatory in operation. The touchstone is business necessity. If an employment practice which operates to exclude Negroes cannot be shown to be related to job performance, the practice is prohibited. 401 U.S., at 431, 91 S.Ct., at 853.

* * *

Petitioners' examination, which barred promotion and had a discriminatory impact on black employees, clearly falls within the literal language of § 703(a)(2), as interpreted by *Griggs*. The statute speaks, not in terms of jobs and promotions, but in terms of *limitations* and *classifications* that would deprive any individual of employment *opportunities*.[9] A disparate-impact claim reflects the language of § 703(a)(2) and Congress' basic objectives in enacting that statute: "to achieve equality of employment *opportunities* and remove barriers that have operated in the past to favor an identifiable group of white employees over other employees." 401 U.S., at 429–430, 91 S.Ct., at 852–853 (emphasis added). When an employer uses a nonjob-related barrier in order to deny a minority or woman applicant employment or promotion, and that barrier has a significant adverse effect on minorities or women, then the applicant has been deprived of an employment *opportunity* "because of * * * race, color, religion, sex, or national origin." In other words, § 703(a)(2) prohibits discriminatory "artificial, arbitrary, and unnecessary barriers to employment," 401 U.S., at 431, 91 S.Ct., at 853, that "limit * * * or classify * * * applicants for employment * * * in any way which would deprive or tend to deprive any individual of employment *opportunities*." (Emphasis added.)

Relying on § 703(a)(2), *Griggs* explicitly focused on employment "practices, procedures, or tests," 401 U.S., at 430, 91 S.Ct., at 853, that deny equal employment "opportunity," id., at 431, 91 S.Ct., at 853. We concluded that Title VII prohibits "procedures or testing mechanisms that operate as 'built-in headwinds' for minority groups." Id., at 432, 91 S.Ct., at 854. We found that Congress' primary purpose was the prophylactic one of achieving equality of employment "opportunities" and removing "barriers" to such equality. Id., at 429–430, 91 S.Ct., at 852–853. See Albemarle Paper Co. v. Moody, 422 U.S., at 417, 95 S.Ct., at 2371. The examination given to respondents in this case surely constituted such a practice and created such a barrier.

9. In contrast, the language of § 703(a)(1), 42 U.S.C. § 2000e–2(a)(1), if it were the only protection given to employees and applicants under Title VII, might support petitioners' exclusive focus on the overall result. That subsection makes it an unlawful employment practice "to fail or refuse to hire or to discharge any individual, or otherwise to discriminate against any individual with respect to his compensation, terms, conditions or privileges of employment, because of such individual's race, color, religion, sex, or national origin."

Our conclusion that § 703(a)(2) encompasses respondents' claim is reinforced by the terms of Congress' 1972 extension of the protections of Title VII to state and municipal employees. See n. 8, supra. Although Congress did not explicitly consider the viability of the defense offered by the state employer in this case, the 1972 amendments to Title VII do reflect Congress' intent to provide state and municipal employees with the protection that Title VII, as interpreted by *Griggs,* had provided to employees in the private sector: equality of *opportunity* and the elimination of discriminatory *barriers* to professional development. The Committee Reports and the floor debates stressed the need for equality of opportunity for minority applicants seeking to obtain governmental positions. E.g., S.Rep. No. 92–415, p. 10 (1971); 118 Cong.Rec. 1815 (1972) (remarks of Sen. Williams). Congress voiced its concern about the widespread use by state and local governmental agencies of "invalid selection techniques" that had a discriminatory impact. S.Rep. No. 92–415, supra, at 10; H.R.Rep. No. 92–238, p. 17 (1971); 117 Cong.Rec. 31961 (1971) (remarks of Rep. Perkins).

The decisions of this Court following *Griggs* also support respondents' claim. In considering claims of disparate impact under § 703(a)(2) this Court has consistently focused on employment and promotion requirements that create a discriminatory bar to *opportunities.* This Court has never read § 703(a)(2) as requiring the focus to be placed instead on the overall number of minority or female applicants actually hired or promoted. Thus Dothard v. Rawlinson, 433 U.S. 321, 97 S.Ct. 2720, 53 L.Ed.2d 786 (1977), found that minimum statutory height and weight requirements for correctional counselors were the sort of arbitrary barrier to equal employment opportunity for women forbidden by Title VII. Although we noted in passing that women constituted 36.89 percent of the labor force and only 12.9 percent of correctional counselor positions, our focus was not on this "bottom line." We focused instead on the disparate effect that the minimum height and weight standards had on applicants: classifying far more women than men as ineligible for employment. Id., at 329–330, and n. 12, 97 S.Ct., at 2726–2727, and n. 12. Similarly, in Albemarle Paper Co. v. Moody, supra, the action was remanded to allow the employer to attempt to show that the tests that he had given to his employees for promotion were job related. We did not suggest that by promoting a sufficient number of the black employees who passed the examination, the employer could avoid this burden. See 422 U.S., at 436, 95 S.Ct., at 2380. See also New York Transit Authority v. Beazer, 440 U.S. 568, 584, 99 S.Ct. 1355, 1365, 59 L.Ed.2d 587 (1979) ("A prima facie violation of the Act may be established by statistical evidence showing that an employment *practice* has the effect of denying members of one race equal access to employment *opportunities* ") (emphasis added).

In short, the District Court's dismissal of respondents' claim cannot be supported on the basis that respondents failed to establish a prima facie case of employment discrimination under the terms of § 703(a)(2). The suggestion that disparate impact should be measured only at the bottom line ignores the fact that Title VII guarantees these individual respondents the *opportunity* to compete equally with white workers on the basis of job-related criteria. Title VII strives to achieve equality of opportunity by rooting out "artificial, arbitrary, and unnecessary" employer-created barriers to professional development that have a discriminatory impact upon individuals. Therefore, respondents' rights under § 703(a)(2) have been violated, unless petitioners can demonstrate that the examination given was not an artificial, arbitrary, or unnecessary barrier, because it measured skills related to effective performance in the role of Welfare Eligibility Supervisor.

B

The United States, in its brief as *amicus curiae,* apparently recognizes that respondents' claim in this case falls within the affirmative commands of Title VII. But it seeks to support the District Court's judgment in this case by relying on the defenses provided to the employer in § 703(h).[11] Section 703(h) provides in pertinent part:

> 'Notwithstanding any other provision of this subchapter, it shall not be an unlawful employment practice for an employer * * * to give and to act upon the results of any professionally developed ability test provided that such test, its administration or action upon the results is not designed, intended or used to discriminate because of race, color, religion, sex or national origin." 78 Stat. 257, as amended, 42 U.S.C. § 2000e–2(h).

The Government argues that the test administered by the petitioners was not "used to discriminate" because it did not actually deprive disproportionate numbers of blacks of promotions. But the Government's reliance on § 703(h) as offering the employer some special haven for discriminatory tests is misplaced. We considered the relevance of this provision in *Griggs.* After examining the legislative history of § 703(h), we concluded that Congress, in adding § 703(h), intended only to make clear that tests that were *job related* would be permissible despite their disparate impact. 401 U.S., at 433–436, 91 S.Ct., at 854–856. As the Court recently confirmed, § 703(h), which was introduced as an amendment to Title VII on the Senate floor, "did not alter the meaning of Title VII, but 'merely clarifie[d] its present intent and effect.'" American Tobacco Co. v. Patterson, 456 U.S. 63, 73, n. 11, 102 S.Ct. 1534, 1539, n. 11, 71 L.Ed.2d 748 (1982), quoting 110 Cong.Rec. 12723 (1964) (remarks of Sen. Humphrey). A nonjob-related test that has a disparate racial impact, and is used to "limit" or "classify" employees, is "used to discriminate" within the meaning of Title VII, whether or not it was "designed or intended" to have this effect and despite an employer's efforts to compensate for its discriminatory effect. See *Griggs,* 401 U.S., at 433, 91 S.Ct., at 854.

---

11. The Government's brief is submitted by the Department of Justice, which shares responsibility for federal enforcement of Title VII with the Equal Employment Opportunity Commission (EEOC). The EEOC declined to join this brief. See Brief for United States as *Amicus Curiae* 1, and n.

In sum, respondents' claim of disparate impact from the examination, a pass-fail barrier to employment opportunity, states a prima facie case of employment discrimination under § 703(a)(2), despite their employer's nondiscriminatory "bottom line," and that "bottom line" is no defense to this prima facie case under § 703(h).

III

Having determined that respondents' claim comes within the terms of Title VII, we must address the suggestion of petitioners and some *amici curiae* that we recognize an exception, either in the nature of an additional burden on plaintiffs seeking to establish a prima facie case or in the nature of an affirmative defense, for cases in which an employer has compensated for a discriminatory pass-fail barrier by hiring or promoting a sufficient number of black employees to reach a nondiscriminatory "bottom line." We reject this suggestion, which is in essence nothing more than a request that we redefine the protections guaranteed by Title VII.[12]

Section 703(a)(2) prohibits practices that would deprive or tend to deprive *"any individual* of employment opportunities." The principal focus of the statute is the protection of the individual employee, rather than the protection of the minority group as a whole. Indeed, the entire statute and its legislative history are replete with references to protection for the individual employee. See, e.g., §§ 703(a)(1), (b), (c), 704(a), 78 Stat. 255–257, as amended, 42 U.S.C. §§ 2000e–2(a)(1), (b), (c), 2000e–3(a); 110 Cong.Rec. 7213 (1964) (interpretive memorandum of Sens. Clark and Case) ("discrimination is prohibited as to any individual"); id., at 8921 (remarks of Sen. Williams) ("Every man must be

---

12. Petitioners suggest that we should defer to the EEOC Guidelines in this regard. But there is nothing in the Guidelines to which we might defer that would aid petitioners in this case. The most support petitioners could conceivably muster from the Uniform Guidelines on Employee Selection Procedures, 29 CFR pt. 1607 (1981) (now issued jointly by the EEOC, the Office of Personnel Management, the De-·partment of Labor, and the Department of Justice, see 29 CFR § 1607.1A (1981)), is *neutrality* on the question whether a discriminatory barrier that does not result in a discriminatory overall result constitutes a violation of Title VII. Section 1607.4C of the Guidelines, relied upon by petitioners, states that as a matter of *"administrative and prosecutorial discretion, in usual circumstances,"* the agencies will not take enforcement action based upon the disparate impact of any component of a selection process if the total selection process results in no adverse impact. (Emphasis added.) The agencies made clear that the "guidelines do not address the underlying ques-

tion of law," and that an individual "who is denied the job because of a particular component in a procedure which otherwise meets the 'bottom line' standard * * * retains the right to proceed through the appropriate agencies, and into Federal court." 43 Fed.Reg. 38291 (1978). See 29 CFR § 1607.16I (1981). In addition, in a publication entitled Adoption of Questions and Answers to Clarify and Provide a Common Interpretation of the Uniform Guidelines on Employee Selection Procedures, the agencies stated:

"Since the [bottom-line] concept is not a rule of law, it does not affect the discharge by the EEOC of its statutory responsibilities to investigate charges of discrimination, render an administrative finding on its investigation, and engage in voluntary conciliation efforts. Similarly, with respect to the other issuing agencies, the bottom line concept applies not to the processing of individual charges, but to the initiation of enforcement action." 44 Fed.Reg. 12000 (1979).

judged according to his ability. In that respect, all men are to have an equal opportunity to be considered for a particular job").

In suggesting that the "bottom line" may be a defense to a claim of discrimination against an individual employee, petitioners and *amici* appear to confuse unlawful discrimination with discriminatory intent. The Court has stated that a nondiscriminatory "bottom line" and an employer's good-faith efforts to achieve a nondiscriminatory work force, might in some cases assist an employer in rebutting the inference that particular action had been intentionally discriminatory: "Proof that [a] work force was racially balanced or that it contained a disproportionately high percentage of minority employees is not wholly irrelevant on the issue of intent when that issue is yet to be decided." Furnco Construction Corp. v. Waters, 438 U.S. 567, 580, 98 S.Ct. 2943, 2951, 57 L.Ed.2d 957 (1978). See also Teamsters v. United States, 431 U.S. 324, 340, n. 20, 97 S.Ct. 1843, 1856–1857, n. 20, 52 L.Ed.2d 396 (1977). But resolution of the factual question of intent is not what is at issue in this case. Rather, petitioners seek simply to justify discrimination against respondents on the basis of their favorable treatment of other members of respondents' racial group. Under Title VII, "[a] racially balanced work force cannot immunize an employer from liability for specific acts of discrimination." Furnco Construction Corp. v. Waters, 438 U.S., at 579, 98 S.Ct., at 2950–2951.

> It is clear beyond cavil that the obligation imposed by Title VII is to provide an equal opportunity for *each* applicant regardless of race, without regard to whether members of the applicant's race are already proportionately represented in the work force. See Griggs v. Duke Power Co., 401 U.S., at 430 [91 S.Ct., at 853]; McDonald v. Santa Fe Trail Transportation Co., 427 U.S. 273, 279 [96 S.Ct. 2574, 2578, 49 L.Ed.2d 493] (1976)." Ibid. (emphasis in original).

It is clear that Congress never intended to give an employer license to discriminate against some employees on the basis of race or sex merely because he favorably treats other members of the employees' group. We recognized in Los Angeles Dept. of Water & Power v. Manhart, 435 U.S. 702, 98 S.Ct. 1370, 55 L.Ed.2d 657 (1978), that fairness to the class of women employees as a whole could not justify unfairness to the individual female employee because the "statute's focus on the individual is unambiguous." Id., at 708, 98 S.Ct., at 1375. Similarly, in Phillips v. Martin Marietta Corp., 400 U.S. 542, 91 S.Ct. 496, 27 L.Ed.2d 613 (1971) (*per curiam*), we recognized that a rule barring employment of all married *women* with preschool children, if not a bona fide occupational qualification under § 703(e), violated Title VII, even though female applicants without preschool children were hired in sufficient numbers that they constituted 75 to 80 percent of the persons employed in the position plaintiff sought.

Petitioners point out that *Furnco, Manhart,* and *Phillips* involved facially discriminatory policies, while the claim in the instant case is one of discrimination from a facially neutral policy. The fact remains, however, that irrespective of the form taken by the discriminatory practice, an employer's treatment of other members of the plaintiffs' group can be "of little comfort to the victims of * * * discrimination." Teamsters v. United States, supra, 431 U.S., at 342, 97 S.Ct., at 1858. Title VII does not permit the victim of a facially discriminatory policy to be told that he has not been wronged because other persons of his or her race or sex were hired. That answer is no more satisfactory when it is given to victims of a policy that is facially neutral but practically discriminatory. Every *individual* employee is protected against both discriminatory treatment and "practices that are fair in form, but discriminatory in operation." Griggs v. Duke Power Co., 401 U.S., at 431, 91 S.Ct., at 853. Requirements and tests that have a discriminatory impact are merely some of the more subtle, but also the more pervasive, of the "practices and devices which have fostered racially stratified job environments to the disadvantage of minority citizens." McDonnell Douglas Corp. v. Green, 411 U.S., at 800, 93 S.Ct., at 1823.

IV

In sum, petitioners' nondiscriminatory "bottom line" is no answer, under the terms of Title VII, to respondents' prima facie claim of employment discrimination. Accordingly, the judgment of the Court of Appeals for the Second Circuit is affirmed, and this case is remanded to the District Court for further proceedings consistent with this opinion.

It is so ordered.

JUSTICE POWELL, with whom THE CHIEF JUSTICE, JUSTICE REHNQUIST, and JUSTICE O'CONNOR join, dissenting.

In past decisions, this Court has been sensitive to the critical difference between cases proving discrimination under Title VII, 42 U.S.C. § 2000e et seq. (1976 ed. and Supp. IV), by a showing of disparate treatment or discriminatory intent and those proving such discrimination by a showing of disparate impact. Because today's decision blurs that distinction and results in a holding inconsistent with the very nature of disparate-impact claims, I dissent.

I

Section 703(a)(2) of Title VII, 42 U.S.C. § 2000e–2(a)(2), provides that it is an unlawful employment practice for an employer to

> limit, segregate, or classify his employees or applicants for employment in any way which would deprive or tend to deprive any individual of employment opportunities or otherwise adversely affect his status as an employee, because of such individual's race, color, religion, sex, or national origin.

Although this language suggests that discrimination occurs only on an individual basis, in Griggs v. Duke Power Co., 401 U.S. 424, 432, 91 S.Ct. 849, 854, 28 L.Ed.2d 158 (1971), the Court held that discriminatory intent on the part of the employer against an individual need not be shown when "employment procedures or testing mechanisms * * * operate as 'built-in headwinds' for minority groups and are unrelated to measuring job capability." Thus, the Court held that the "disparate impact" of an employer's practices on a racial group can violate § 703(a)(2) of Title VII. In *Griggs* and each subsequent disparate-impact case, however, the Court has considered, not whether the claimant as an individual had been classified in a manner impermissible under § 703(a)(2), but whether an employer's procedures have had an adverse impact on the protected *group* to which the individual belongs.

Thus, while disparate-*treatment* cases focus on the way in which an individual has been treated, disparate-*impact* cases are concerned with the protected group. This key distinction was explained in Furnco Construction Corp. v. Waters, 438 U.S. 567, 581–582, 98 S.Ct. 2943, 2952, 57 L.Ed.2d 957 (1978) (MARSHALL, J., concurring in part):

> It is well established under Title VII that claims of employment discrimination because of race may arise in two different ways. Teamsters v. United States, 431 U.S. 324, 335–336, n. 15 [97 S.Ct. 1843, 1854–1855, n. 15, 52 L.Ed.2d 396 (1977). An individual may allege that he has been subjected to "disparate treatment" because of his race, or that he has been the victim of a facially neutral practice having a "disparate impact" on his racial group.

In keeping with this distinction, our disparate-impact cases consistently have considered whether the result of an employer's *total selection process* had an adverse impact upon the protected group. If this case were decided by reference to the total process—as our cases suggest that it should be—the result would be clear. Here 22.9% of the blacks who entered the selection process were ultimately promoted, compared with only 13.5% of the whites. To say that this selection process had an unfavorable "disparate impact" on blacks is to ignore reality.

The Court, disregarding the distinction drawn by our cases, repeatedly asserts that Title VII was designed to protect individual, not group, rights. It emphasizes that some individual blacks were eliminated by the disparate impact of the preliminary test. But this argument confuses the *aim* of Title VII with the legal theories through which its aims were intended to be vindicated. It is true that the aim of Title VII is to protect individuals, not groups. But in advancing this commendable objective, Title VII jurisprudence has recognized two distinct methods of proof. In one set of cases—those involving direct proof of discriminatory intent—the plaintiff seeks to establish direct, intentional discrimination against him. In that type of case, the individual is at the forefront throughout the entire presentation of evidence. In disparate-impact cases, by contrast, the plaintiff seeks to carry his burden of proof by way of *inference*—by showing that an employer's selection process results in the rejection of a disproportionate number of members of a protected group to which he belongs. From such a showing a fair inference then may be drawn that the rejected applicant, as a member of that disproportionately excluded group, was himself a victim of that process' " 'built-in headwinds.' " *Griggs,* supra, at 432, 91 S.Ct., at 854. But this method of proof—which actually *defines* disparate-impact theory under Title VII—invites the plaintiff to prove discrimination by reference to the group rather than to the allegedly affected individual. There can be no violation of Title VII on the basis of disparate impact in the absence of disparate impact on a *group.*

In this case respondent black employees seek to benefit from a conflation of "discriminatory treatment" and "disparate impact" theories. But they cannot have it both ways. Having undertaken to prove discrimination by reference to one set of group figures (used at a preliminary point in the selection process), these respondents then claim that *non*discrimination cannot be proved by viewing the impact of the entire process on the group as a whole. The fallacy of this reasoning—accepted by the Court—is transparent. It is to confuse the individualistic *aim* of Title VII with the methods of proof by which Title VII rights may be vindicated. The respondents, as individuals, are entitled to the full personal protection of Title VII. But, having undertaken to prove a violation of their rights by reference to group figures, respondents cannot deny petitioners the opportunity to rebut their evidence by introducing figures of the same kind. Having pleaded a disparate-impact case, the plaintiff cannot deny the defendant the opportunity to show that there was no disparate impact. As the Court of Appeals for the Third Circuit noted in EEOC v. Greyhound Lines, Inc., 635 F.2d 188, 192 (1980):

> [N]o violation of Title VII can be grounded on the disparate impact theory without proof that the questioned policy or practice has had a disproportionate impact on the employer's workforce. This conclusion should be as obvious as it is tautological: there can be no disparate impact unless there is [an ultimate] disparate impact.

Where, under a facially neutral employment process, there has been no adverse effect on the group—and certainly there has been none here—Title VII has not been infringed.

II

The Court's position is no stronger in case authority than it is in logic. None of the cases relied upon by the Court controls the outcome of this case. Indeed, the disparate-impact cases do not even support the propositions for which they are cited. For example, the Court cites Dothard v. Rawlinson, 433 U.S. 321, 97 S.Ct. 2720, 53 L.Ed.2d 786 (1977) (holding impermissible minimum statutory height and weight requirements for correctional counselors), and observes that "[a]lthough we noted in passing that women constituted 36.89 percent of the labor force and only 12.9 percent of correctional counselor positions, our focus was not on this 'bottom line.' We focused instead on the disparate effect that the minimum height and weight standards had on applicants: classifying far more women than men as ineligible for employment." Ante, at 2533. In *Dothard,* however, the Court was not considering a case in which there was any difference between the discriminatory effect of the employment standard and the number of minority members actually hired. The *Dothard* Court itself stated:

> [T]o establish a prima facie case of discrimination, a plaintiff need only show that the facially neutral standards in question *select* applicants *for hire* in a discriminatory pattern. Once it is shown that *the employment standards* are discriminatory in effect, the employer must meet "the burden of showing that any given requirement [has] * * * a manifest relationship to the employment in question." 433 U.S., at 329, 97 S.Ct., at 2726–2727 (emphasis added).

The *Dothard* Court did not decide today's case. It addressed only a case in which the challenged standards had a discriminatory impact at the bottom line—the hiring decision. And the *Dothard* Court's "focus," referred to by the Court, is of no help in deciding the instant case.[6]

The Court concedes that the other major cases on which it relies, *Furnco, Los Angeles Dept. of Water & Power v. Manhart,* 435 U.S. 702, 98 S.Ct. 1370, 55 L.Ed.2d 657 (1978), and *Phillips v. Martin Marietta Corp.,* 400 U.S. 542, 91 S.Ct. 496, 27 L.Ed.2d 613 (1971) (*per curiam*) "involved facially discriminatory policies, while the claim in the instant case is one of discrimination from a facially neutral policy." Ante, at 2535. The Court nevertheless applies the principles derived from those cases to the case at bar. It does so by reiterating the view that Title VII protects *individuals,* not *groups,* and therefore that the manner in which an employer has treated other members of a group cannot defeat the claim of an individual who has suffered as a result of even a facially neutral policy. As appealing as this sounds, it confuses the distinction—uniformly recognized until today—between disparate *impact* and disparate *treatment.* See, supra, at 2537. Our cases, cited above, have made clear that discriminatory-impact claims cannot be based on how an individual is treated in isolation from the treatment of other members of the group. Such claims necessarily are based on whether

---

6. The Court cites language from two other disparate-impact cases. The Court notes that in Albemarle Paper Co. v. Moody, 422 U.S. 405, 95 S.Ct. 2362, 45 L.Ed.2d 280 (1975), the Court "remanded to allow the employer to attempt to show that the tests * * * given * * * for promotion were job related." *Ante,* at 2533. But the fact that the Court did so without suggesting "that by promoting a sufficient number of black employees who passed the examination, the employer could avoid this burden," ibid., can hardly be precedent for the negative of that proposition when the issue was neither presented in the facts of the case nor addressed by the Court.

Similarly, New York Transit Authority v. Beazer, 440 U.S. 568, 99 S.Ct. 1355, 59 L.Ed.2d 587 (1979), provides little support despite the language quoted by the Court. See ante, at 2533, quoting 440 U.S., at 584,

99 S.Ct., at 1365 (" 'A prima facie violation of the Act may be established by statistical evidence showing that an employment *practice* has the effect of denying members of one race equal access to employment *opportunities.*' ") (emphasis added by the Court). In *Beazer,* the Court ruled that the statistical evidence actually presented was insufficient to establish a prima facie case of discrimination, and in doing so it indicated that it would have found statistical evidence of the number of applicants *and* employees in a methadone program quite probative. See id., at 585, 99 S.Ct., at 1365. *Beazer* therefore does not justify the Court's speculation that the number of blacks and Hispanics actually employed were irrelevant to whether a case of disparate impact had been established under Title VII.

the group fares less well than other groups under a policy, practice, or test. Indeed, if only one minority member has taken a test, a disparate-impact claim cannot be made, regardless of whether the test is an initial step in the selection process or one of several factors considered by the employer in making an employment decision.

III

Today's decision takes a long and unhappy step in the direction of confusion. Title VII does not require that employers adopt merit hiring or the procedures most likely to permit the greatest number of minority members to be considered for or to qualify for jobs and promotions. See Texas Dept. of Community Affairs v. Burdine, 450 U.S. 248, 258–259, 101 S.Ct. 1089, 1096–1097, 67 L.Ed.2d 207 (1981); *Furnco*, 438 U.S., at 578, 98 S.Ct., at 2950. Employers need not develop tests that accurately reflect the skills of every individual candidate; there are few if any tests that do so. Yet the Court seems unaware of this practical reality, and perhaps oblivious to the likely consequences of its decision. By its holding today, the Court may force employers either to eliminate tests or rely on expensive, job-related, testing procedures, the validity of which may or may not be sustained if challenged. For state and local governmental employers with limited funds, the practical effect of today's decision may well be the adoption of simple quota hiring.[8] This arbitrary method of employment is itself unfair to individual applicants, whether or not they are members of minority groups. And it is not likely to produce a competent work force. Moreover, the Court's decision actually may result in employers employing *fewer* minority members. As Judge Newman noted in Brown v. New Haven Civil Service Board, 474 F.Supp. 1256, 1263 (Conn.1979):

> [A]s private parties are permitted under Title VII itself to adopt voluntary affirmative action plans, * * * Title VII should not be construed to prohibit a municipality's using a hiring process that results in a percentage of minority policemen approximating their percentage of the local population, instead of relying on the expectation that a validated job-related testing procedure will produce an equivalent result, yet with the risk that it might lead to substantially less minority hiring.

Finding today's decision unfortunate in both its analytical approach and its likely consequences, I dissent.

8. Another possibility is that employers may integrate consideration of test results into one overall hiring decision based on that "factor" *and* additional factors. Such a process would not, even under the Court's reasoning, result in a finding of discrimination on the basis of disparate impact unless the actual hiring decisions had a disparate impact on the minority group. But if employers integrate test results into a single-step decision, they will be free to select *only* the number of minority candidates proportional to their representation in the work force. If petitioners had used this approach, they would have been able to hire substantially fewer blacks without liability on the basis of disparate impact. The Court hardly could have intended to encourage this.

E. THE BUSINESS NECESSITY DEFENSE

CONTRERAS v. CITY OF LOS ANGELES

United States Court of Appeals for the Ninth Circuit, 1981.
656 F.2d 1276, cert. denied 455 U.S. 1021, 102 S.Ct. 1719,
72 L.Ed.2d 140 (1982).

WALLACE, CIRCUIT JUDGE:

Certain former and present city workers (appellants) appeal from the district court's judgment that they are entitled to no relief under Title VII of the Civil Rights Act of 1964, 42 U.S.C. § 2000e et seq., and 42 U.S.C. § 1981, for having lost their jobs by failing allegedly discriminatory civil service examinations. We affirm.

I

Contreras, E. Gonzalez, Mock, and Zavala (accountants) were employed by the City of Los Angeles (City) as Senior Accountants in the Training and Job Development Division of the Mayor's office. Maria Gonzalez (Gonzalez) was employed in the same division as an Auditor. Each had served efficiently in his or her position for more than one and one-half years, having been originally hired on the basis of oral interviews at a time when the Mayor's office was not subject to the stringent hiring requirements of the City's civil service rules and regulations.

In early 1976, when the City transferred the function of the Training and Job Development Division to the newly created Community Development Department, the senior accountant and auditor positions previously assigned to the Mayor's office became subject to the City's civil service commission. Consequently, appellants were required to pass written examinations before assuming senior accountant and auditor status in the new department. The City Council, in an effort to avoid possible inequities to appellants and others employed in the Mayor's office, proposed an amendment to the city charter exempting the employees from the examination requirement. Unfortunately for appellants, that amendment was defeated by the electorate in November 1976.

Prior to the rejection of the amendment, accountants took and failed the senior accountant examination. Gonzalez passed the auditor examination but scored too low to be employed as an auditor in the new office. Although accountants thus became ineligible for their former senior accountant positions, each of them scored high enough to be employed at his former salary as regular civil service labor-market analysts. Gonzalez took a position with the State of California, but maintains her standing in this litigation by asserting a continuing interest in returning to her former auditor position.

Following voter rejection of the exempting amendment, appellants commenced this action in district court, claiming that the City's examinations unlawfully discriminated against Spanish-surnamed applicants.

They requested that the district court enjoin the City from using the discriminatory examinations, order the City to develop examinations that accurately predict job performance, and order the City to retain appellants in their former positions until the new examinations are developed.

II

* * *

In this case the district judge accepted evidence probative of all three stages of the Title VII inquiry. After doing so, he ruled that appellants had failed to establish a prima facie case of discriminatory impact upon Spanish-surnamed applicants, that the City had proven the senior accountant and auditor examinations to be job related, and that appellants had failed to prove the existence of a non-discriminatory alternative that would select qualified employees with the same degree of accuracy as the written examination. We must first determine whether the district court's finding that appellants failed to present a prima facie case of discrimination is clearly erroneous.

* * *

We conclude that the district court's finding that accountants failed to establish a prima facie case of discrimination was not clearly erroneous. In doing so we recognize the discriminatory implications of the disparate examination statistics and the expert testimony concerning their reliability. On the other hand, the City's expert testimony, the small statistical base, and the impeachment of the statistics by evidence of the accountants' failure to study, all convince us that the district court's conclusion was not an unreasonable interpretation of the evidence presented. "[W]here the evidence would support a conclusion either way but * * * the trial court has decided it to weigh more heavily for the defendant[,] [s]uch a choice between two permissible views of the weight of evidence is not 'clearly erroneous.'" * * *.

B. THE AUDITOR EXAMINATION

Gonzalez also relied upon statistical evidence in attempting to prove the discriminatory impact of the auditor examination: 6 of 23 or 26.1 percent of the Spanish-surnamed applicants passed the examination, while 23 of 36 or 63.9 percent of the white applicants passed. The mean score of Spanish-surnamed applicants, 57.3, was more than 10 points below the 67.4 mean score of white applicants. The district judge expressly found that this evidence indicated a statistical adverse impact on Spanish-surnamed auditor applicants. Although Gonzalez passed the auditor examination, she failed to secure her desired position because she did not score highly enough. She relies upon the disproportionate pass rate to contend that she lost her job through an unlawfully discriminatory examination.

The district judge ruled that Gonzalez did not establish a prima facie case of discriminatory impact. He did so by combining the distribution of scores on the auditor examination with the results of a separate, senior auditor examination, on which Spanish-surnamed applicants performed better than any other ethnic group. Because 75 of the 125 questions on the senior auditor examination also appeared on the 100-question auditor examination, the district judge concluded that the auditor examination could not have discriminated against Spanish-surnamed applicants. The district judge also relied upon the fact that Gonzalez was denied employment not solely on the basis of her written examination score, but also on the basis of an oral interview score.

The district judge erred in concluding that Gonzalez failed to establish a prima facie case of discriminatory impact. The City did not rebut the statistical evidence produced by Gonzalez. Moreover, the district judge's reason for concluding that Gonzalez failed in her proof—the combined results of the senior auditor and auditor examinations—did not validly refute the clear import of Gonzalez' evidence. The senior auditor results were taken from an extremely small sample size, since only 9 Spanish-surnamed applicants took the test. It was clear error for the district court to conclude that these statistically insignificant results of the senior auditor examination permitted disregard of the statistical results of the auditor examination, particularly when there was no evidence that the Spanish-surnamed senior auditor applicants performed well on the same questions that the Spanish-surnamed auditor applicants failed. Indeed, the City's expert witness testified that it is not sound statistical procedure to combine the results of two separate examinations.

Nor does the fact that Gonzalez was denied employment on the basis of a combined oral interview and written examination score support the district court's ruling that Gonzalez failed in her proof. Gonzalez' written examination score, although high enough to pass, was lower than the average passing score. Her oral interview score, on the other hand, was well above average. Thus, it was her written examination score that most substantially impaired her chances of obtaining the auditor position.

Statistical disparities alone may constitute prima facie proof of discrimination. New York Transit Authority v. Beazer, 440 U.S. 568, 584, 99 S.Ct. 1355, 1365, 59 L.Ed.2d 587 (1979); Hazelwood School District v. United States, 433 U.S. 299, 307–08, 97 S.Ct. 2736, 2741–42, 53 L.Ed.2d 768 (1977). * * * Although the prima facie case requirement is not automatically satisfied by statistical evidence of adverse impact, we hold that a prima facie case is established when such evidence of discriminatory impact is completely uncontroverted. Accordingly, we reverse the district court's ruling that Gonzalez failed to establish prima facie discrimination. We must therefore determine whether the City met its burden of proving that the auditor examination was job related.

III

A. The Employer's Burden of Proof Under Title VII

The allocation of proof in Title VII cases is well established. Once a plaintiff has met his or her burden of proving a prima facie case of discriminatory impact, the employer bears some burden of justifying the business practice in terms of business need. If this burden is met, the plaintiff then assumes the burden of proving the availability of an effective business alternative with less disparate racial impact.[5] Despite this well-established procedure, courts differ on just what an employer must prove to discharge its burden. See Comment, The Business Necessity Defense to Disparate-Impact Liability Under Title VII, 46 U.Chi.L.Rev. 911, 912 (1979). Indeed, cases within this circuit might be read to differ on the weight of the employer's burden. Compare Craig v. County of Los Angeles, 626 F.2d 659 (9th Cir.1980), and deLaurier v. San Diego Unified School District, 588 F.2d 674 (9th Cir.1978), with Blake v. City of Los Angeles, 595 F.2d 1367 (9th Cir. 1979), and deLaurier v. San Diego Unified School District, supra, 588 F.2d at 685–92 (Hufstedler, J., dissenting). The question before us is: what must an employer show to meet its burden of proving that pre-employment test, having a disproportionate, adverse impact on a racial minority, are sufficiently justified by business need to survive a Title VII challenge?

In Craig v. County of Los Angeles, supra, we recently concluded that an employer must prove such tests to be "significantly job-related." 626 F.2d at 662. We stated that our standard for proof of job-relatedness was articulated by the Supreme Court:

> [D]iscriminatory tests are impermissible unless shown, by professionally accepted methods, to be 'predictive of or significantly correlated with important elements of work behavior which comprise or are

---

5. The purpose of the procedure, as the Supreme Court recently spelled out, is ultimately to focus the court's attention on the issue of discrimination. "In a Title VII case, the allocation of burdens * * * is intended progressively to sharpen the inquiry into the elusive factual question of intentional discrimination." Texas Department of Community Affairs v. Burdine, 450 U.S. 248, 255 n. 8, 101 S.Ct. 1089, 1094, n. 8, 67 L.Ed.2d 207 (1981).

This formulation was written in a disparate treatment case. In a disparate impact case the dialectic of the allocation of burdens sharpens the inquiry down to a factual question of discrimination, but not necessarily intentional discrimination in the sense of discrimination that is conscious and purposeful.

In the disparate impact case, the plaintiff will recover if the disparate impact stems from decisions or practices that cannot be given a genuine business justification. A practice that is unjustifiable in race and sex neutral business terms is not always the product of intentional discrimination. The decision makers may simply have missed a less discriminatory option. In such an event we could speak of "negligent discrimination."

The chief point, however, and one that *Burdine* makes clear, is that Title VII does not ultimately focus on ideal social distributions of persons of various races and both sexes. Instead it is concerned with combating culpable discrimination. In disparate impact cases, culpable discrimination takes the form of business decisions that have a discriminatory impact and are not justified by their job-relatedness.

relevant to the job or jobs for which candidates are being evaluated.'
29 C.F.R. § 1607.4(c).

626 F.2d at 662, quoting Albemarle Paper Co. v. Moody, supra, 422 U.S.
at 431, 95 S.Ct. at 2378. We went on to state that an employer "must
demonstrate a significant relation between the challenged selection
device or criteria and the important elements of the job or training
program, not merely some 'rational basis' for the challenged practice.
However, the employer need not establish a perfect positive correlation
between the selection criteria and the important elements of work."
626 F.2d at 664 (citation and footnote omitted).

The employer's burden in *Craig* comports with that applied in
deLaurier v. San Diego Unified School District, supra, 588 F.2d 674, a
case decided almost two years earlier. In *deLaurier* we applied a
standard "commonly referred to as the 'business necessity' or 'job
relatedness' defense * * *." Id. at 678. Although we stated that the
employment practice in question must be shown to be " 'necessary to
safe and efficient job performance,' " id. at 678, quoting Dothard v.
Rawlinson, supra, 433 U.S. at 331 n. 14, 97 S.Ct. at 2728 n. 14, our
application of this language to the facts demonstrated that the employer's burden is met with less than proof of absolute business necessity.
The school district in *deLaurier* attempted to justify its mandatory
maternity leave policy with evidence that teaching ability declines as
the date of delivery approaches, and that the school district needs
advance notice to procure long-term teacher substitutes. 588 F.2d at
678 n. 8. The school district did not thereby prove that its maternity
leave policy, which required teachers to stop work at the start of their
ninth month of pregnancy, was necessarily required for successful
operation of the schools. See id. at 687–91 (Hufstedler, J., dissenting).
Nonetheless, we upheld the maternity leave policy as a job-related
employment practice. Id. at 678–79. We treated "job related" and
"business necessity" as interchangeable terms, neither of which required proof that the challenged policy was absolutely necessary for
operation of the business.

Gonzalez refers us to Blake v. City of Los Angeles, supra, 595 F.2d
1367, a case decided six months after *deLaurier*. *Blake* might be
interpreted as adopting a much more demanding employer burden of
proof than that required in *deLaurier*. In *Blake* we stated that an
employer must prove not only that his screening device is job related;
he must further prove it " 'necessary to safe and efficient job performance * * *.' " Id. at 1376, quoting, again, the phrase from Dothard v.
Rawlinson, supra, 433 U.S. at 332 n. 14, 97 S.Ct. 2728 n. 14. Although
both *deLaurier* and *Blake* quoted this language, it could be argued
persuasively that *Blake* applied it more nearly literally than did *de-
Laurier*. *deLaurier* essentially applied a job-relatedness standard.
Blake defined "job-related," quite properly, as "the capacity of selection
devices to measure traits that are important to successful job performance." 595 F.2d at 1377. *Blake* also stated, however, that " 'job-

relatedness' is relevant only for the purpose of trying to prove that the characteristics which the various tests select are directly related to the business necessity." Id. This formulation might seem to suggest that business necessity is something over and above job relatedness—that is, over and above what is "important to successful job performance." Id. On such a reading, *Blake*'s use of the *Dothard* expression "necessary" would clearly mean something different from that expression's use in *Craig* and *deLaurier*. Thus, in order to determine the test to be applied to the auditor's examination given Gonzalez, we must first harmonize our cases.

Because it is the language from *Dothard* that is at the root of the issue before us, our effort to harmonize our cases must be guided by the Supreme Court's interpretation of that language. Before turning to the Supreme Court cases, we identify the issue in more detail.

The *Craig* test, by permitting job-related employment practices, views Title VII, as far as this case is concerned, as prohibiting only race-related employment criteria. The test maximizes employer freedom, restricting it only when employment decisions are made wholly or partially on the basis of race. It mandates employer color-blindness, but otherwise respects an employer's right to seek maximum employee productivity and efficiency. Thus, the *Craig/deLaurier* test tolerates a disparate impact on racial minorities so long as that impact is only an incidental product of criteria that genuinely predict or significantly correlate with successful job performance, and does not result from criteria that make race a factor in employment decisions.

The interpretation of *Blake* referred to above, on the other hand, views Title VII as much more restrictive of employer decision-making. That reading would not tolerate a disparate impact on racial minorities that results from job-related criteria. So understood, *Blake* would allow disparately impacting criteria only when forbidding them would seriously damage the business, that is, when they are "necessary" to operation of the business. Such a test would thus minimize an employer's freedom, permitting him to employ disproportionately-impacting criteria only if he can prove them necessary to the functioning of his enterprise. That such criteria are effective predictors of employee performance is insufficient under this view of Title VII. Thus, such a test would prohibit some pre-employment screening devices permitted by the *Craig/deLaurier* test: devices that actually predict employee performance, but that cannot be proven necessary to the operation of the business.

In determining whether Title VII requires application of the employer's burden of proof set forth in *Craig* and *deLaurier* or some other level of proof, we are not free to invoke our perception of ideal social policy. Rather, we must ascertain Congress' intent in enacting Title VII. Because the face of the statute does not clearly resolve the question before us, we look for guidance to the legislative history of

Title VII, * * * and to interpretative pronouncements by the Supreme Court.

Congress' primary objective in passing Title VII was to eliminate race-related employment criteria. * * * Critics of the legislation were concerned that Title VII would intolerably burden employers and would force them to abandon employee selection practices based on productivity and efficiency. See Griggs v. Duke Power Co., 401 U.S. 424 at 434 & n. 10, 91 S.Ct. 849 at 855 & n. 10, 28 L.Ed.2d 158. However, "[p]roponents of Title VII sought throughout the debate to assure the critics that the Act would have no effect on job-related tests." Id. at 434, 91 S.Ct. at 855. * * * Senators Clark and Case assured the critics that "[a]n employer may set his qualifications as high as he likes * * *," id. at 7213, and Senator Humphrey stated that "[t]he employer will outline the qualifications to be met for the job. The employer, not the Government will establish the standards." Id. at 13088.

By enacting Title VII, "[d]iscriminatory preference for any group, minority or majority, is precisely and only what Congress has proscribed." Griggs v. Duke Power Co., supra, 401 U.S. at 431, 91 S.Ct. at 853. The legislative history, of Title VII clearly reveals that Congress was concerned about preserving employer freedom, and that it acted to mandate employer color-blindness with as little intrusion into the free enterprise system as possible. See Developments in the Law—Employment Discrimination and Title VII of the Civil Rights Act of 1964, 84 Harv.L.Rev. 1109, 1113–19 (1971); Comment, The Business Necessity Defense to Disparate-Impact Liability Under Title VII, 46 U.Chi.L.Rev. 911, 926–30 (1979); Note, Business Necessity under Title VII of the Civil Rights Act of 1964: A No-Alternative Approach, 84 Yale L.J. 98, 102–06 (1974). The question of preferential treatment has recently provided an occasion for the Supreme Court to state its understanding that Title VII "was not intended to 'diminish traditional management prerogatives.'" Texas Department of Community Affairs v. Burdine, 450 U.S. 248, 259, 101 S.Ct. 1089, 1096, 67 L.Ed.2d 207 (1981), quoting United Steelworkers of America v. Weber, 443 U.S. 193, 207, 99 S.Ct. 2721, 2729, 61 L.Ed.2d 480 (1979).

Therefore, we conclude that the employer's burden of proof required by *Craig* and *deLaurier* is more consistent with Congress' Title VII intent than the employer's burden of proof required by the interpretation of *Blake* suggested above. Our review of Supreme Court case law reinforces this conclusion.

The Supreme Court first considered an employer's duty under Title VII in Griggs v. Duke Power Co., supra, 401 U.S. 424, 91 S.Ct. at 850, and concluded that "Congress has placed on the employer the burden of showing that any given requirement must have a manifest relationship to the employment in question." Id. at 432, 91 S.Ct. at 854. *Griggs* suggests that the Court perceived "business necessity" to be the same standard as "job-related," and viewed both as requiring only that an employer prove that his employment practices are legitimately related to job performance:

> The Act proscribes not only overt discrimination but also practices that are fair in form, but discriminatory in operation. The touchstone is business necessity. If an employment practice which operates to exclude Negroes cannot be shown to be related to job performance, the practice is prohibited.

Id. at 431, 91 S.Ct. at 853.

Four years after the *Griggs* decision, the Supreme Court answered the very question considered by us today: "What must an employer show to establish that pre-employment tests racially discriminatory in effect, though not in intent, are sufficiently 'job related' to survive challenge under Title VII?" Albemarle Paper Co. v. Moody, supra, 422 U.S. at 408, 95 S.Ct. at 2367. The employer in *Albemarle* attempted to justify its use of aptitude tests that disproportionately excluded blacks by employing an expert to "validate" the tests in terms of job-relatedness. Various defects in the validation study convinced the Supreme Court that the employer had failed to satisfy its burden of proof. 422 U.S. at 431–36, 95 S.Ct. at 2378–80. Significantly, however, the Court did not interpret Title VII as requiring employer proof of a strong form of "business necessity." Indeed, the Court in *Albemarle* never used the term "business necessity." Rather, the Court "clarified" the "standard of proof for job relatedness," id. at 436, 95 S.Ct. at 2380, by articulating a standard that is "the same as that of the *Griggs* case—that discriminatory tests are impermissible unless shown, by professionally acceptable methods, to be 'predictive of or significantly correlated with important elements of work behavior which comprise or are relevant to the job or jobs for which the candidates are being evaluated.' " Id. at 431, 95 S.Ct. at 2378, quoting 29 C.F.R. § 1607.4(c). It was this articulation of an employer's Title VII burden that we relied upon in *Craig.* 626 F.2d at 662.

We now turn to the troublesome Supreme Court language that appears in Dothard v. Rawlinson, supra, 433 U.S. 321, 97 S.Ct. at 2723. *Dothard* invalidated a height and weight requirement for prison guards that disproportionately excluded women applicants and was not proven to be "job-related." 433 U.S. at 332, 97 S.Ct. at 2728. In doing so, the Court required employer proof identical to that required in its earlier cases: "the employer must meet 'the burden of showing that any given requirement [has] * * * a manifest relationship to the employment in question.' " Id. at 329, 97 S.Ct. at 2727, quoting Griggs v. Duke Power Co., supra, 401 U.S. at 432, 91 S.Ct. at 854. Although the holding tracks prior Supreme Court cases, an unnecessary footnote contains the few words that cause our present difficulty: "a discriminatory employment practice must be shown to be necessary to safe and efficient job performance to survive a Title VII challenge." 433 U.S. at 332 n. 14, 97 S.Ct. at 2728 n. 14. This footnote formulation is belied by the broader standard applied in the *Dothard* text. See id. at 329, 331–32, 97 S.Ct. at 2726, 2727–28.

Since *Dothard,* the Court has indicated that the *Griggs/Albemarle* standard, rather than the *Dothard* footnote, controls Title VII inquiries. In New York Transit Authority v. Beazer, 440 U.S. 568, 99 S.Ct. 1355, 59 L.Ed.2d 587 (1979), the plaintiffs challenged a Transit Authority (TA) refusal to hire narcotics users, specifically methadone users. The Court stated:

> Respondents recognize, and the findings of the District Court establish, that TA's legitimate employment goals of safety and efficiency require that exclusion of all users of illegal narcotics, barbiturates, and amphetamines, and of a majority of all methadone users. The District Court also held that those goals require the exclusion of all methadone users from the 25% of its positions that are "safety sensitive." Finally, the District Court noted that those goals are significantly served by—*even if they do not require*—TA's rule as it applies to all methadone users including those who are seeking employment in nonsafety-sensitive positions. *The record thus demonstrates that TA's rule bears a "manifest relationship to the employment in question."* Griggs v. Duke Power Co., 401 U.S. 424, 432, 91 S.Ct. 849, 854, 28 L.Ed. 2d 158. See Albemarle Paper Co. v. Moody, 422 U.S. 405, 425, 95 S.Ct. 2362, 2375, 45 L.Ed.2d 280.

Id. 440 U.S. at 587 n. 31, 99 S.Ct. at 1366 n. 31 (emphasis added) (citations omitted). Thus, the Court's most recent application of the employer's Title VII burden of proof not only follows the standards set forth in *Griggs* and *Albemarle,* but implicitly approves employment practices that significantly serve, but are neither required by nor necessary to, the employer's legitimate business interests.

We conclude that any employer burden of proof that could be suggested by the possible strong reading of *Blake*'s "business necessity" language would be inconsistent with Supreme Court case law and the Congressional intent underlying Title VII. Accordingly, we reject that interpretation of *Blake.* We interpret *Blake* in line with our precedents decided before (*deLaurier*) and after (*Craig*) that case. We hold that discriminatory tests are impermissible unless shown, by professionally accepted methods, to be predictive of or significantly correlated with important elements of work behavior that comprise or are relevant to the job or jobs for which candidates are being evaluated.[6]

B. VALIDATION OF THE AUDITOR EXAMINATION

The district court made two conclusions of law relevant to the validation issue:

6. In Harris v. Pan American World Airways, Inc., 649 F.2d 670 (9th Cir.1980), our court again quoted the *Blake* standard. Id. at 675. It was, however, unnecessary to the disposition of that case to examine the possibility of conflict between *Blake* and *Craig.* Therefore our court did not reach the question we now consider, and *Harriss* does not compel any particular result here.

4. The Defendants may demonstrate that a test is job related by any competent evidence. Washington v. Davis, 426 U.S. 229 [96 S.Ct. 2040, 48 L.Ed.2d 597] (1976); see also, Blake v. City of Los Angeles, [435 F.Supp. 55 (C.D.Cal.1977)] * * *.

6. There is no magic in any validating procedure, and the Defendants need only supply competent and relevant evidence upon the issue of the job-relatedness of their employment standards. Washington v. Davis, 426 U.S. 229 (1976) at 247 n. 13 [96 S.Ct. 2040 at 2051 n. 13, 48 L.Ed.2d 597].

These conclusions would be error if they implied that the evidence need not show that the screening device was validated "by professionally acceptable methods" to be " 'predictive of or significantly correlated with important elements of work behavior which comprise or are relevant to the job or jobs for which candidates are being evaluated.' " Albemarle Paper Co. v. Moody, supra, 422 U.S. at 431, 95 S.Ct. at 2378, quoting 29 C.F.R. § 1607.4(c).

* * * Footnote 13 of Washington v. Davis discusses three different standards adopted by the American Psychological Association, and itself cites *Albemarle* and 29 C.F.R. § 1607.[7] * * *

* * * Title VII requires no single method of examination validation, but only that the method chosen be professionally acceptable. See Albemarle Paper Co. v. Moody, supra, 422 U.S. at 431, 95 S.Ct. at 2378. To this end, the Equal Employment Opportunity Commission (EEOC) has issued guidelines defining minimum standards for professionally acceptable validation studies. See 29 C.F.R. § 1607.14 (1979). These standards are not mandatory, but they are "entitled to great deference," Griggs v. Duke Power Co., supra, 401 U.S. at 434, 91 S.Ct. at 855, and an employer who disregards them must articulate some cogent reason for doing so and generally bears a heavier than usual burden of proving job relatedness. United States v. City of Chicago, 549 F.2d 415, 430 (7th Cir.1977); United States v. Georgia Power Co., 474 F.2d 906, 913 (5th Cir.1973).

7. Footnote 13 reads as follows:

It appears beyond doubt by now that there is no single method for appropriately validating employment tests for their relationship to job performance. Professional standards developed by the American Psychological Association in its Standards for Educational and Psychological Tests and Manuals (1966), accept three basic methods of validation: "empirical" or "criterion" validity (demonstrated by identifying criteria that indicate successful job performance and then correlating test scores and the criteria so identified); "construct" validity (demonstrated by examinations structured to measure the degree to which job applicants have identifiable characteristics that have been determined to be important in successful job performance); and "content" validity (demonstrated by tests whose content closely approximates tasks to be performed on the job by the applicant). These standards have been relied upon by the Equal Employment Opportunity Commission in fashioning its Guidelines on Employee Selection Procedures, 29 CFR pt. 1607 (1975), and have been judicially noted in cases where validation of employment tests has been in issue. See, e.g., Albemarle Paper Co. v. Moody, 422 U.S. 405, 431, 95 S.Ct. 2362, 2378, 45 L.Ed.2d 280 (1975); Douglas v. Hampton, 168 U.S.App.D.C., at 70, 512 F.2d, at 964; Vulcan Society v. Civil Service Comm'n, 490 F.2d 387, 394 (CA2 1973).

In *Craig*, we established a three-step procedure for validation of examinations used to select employees from among a group of applicants:

> The employer must first specify the particular trait or characteristic which the selection device is being used to identify or measure. The employer must then determine that that particular trait or characteristic is an important element of work behavior. Finally, the employer must demonstrate by "professionally acceptable methods" that the selection device is "predictive of or significantly correlated" with the element of work behavior identified in the second step.

Craig v. County of Los Angeles, 626 F.2d 659, 662 (9th Cir.1980), quoting Albemarle Paper Co. v. Moody, supra, 422 U.S. at 431, 95 S.Ct. at 2378. Applying the *Craig* procedure to the facts of this case, we conclude that the City successfully validated the auditor examination in terms of job-relatedness.

The City's validation of the auditor examination consisted of two phases: a job-analysis phase and an examination-review phase. In the job-analysis phase, a number of auditors and auditor supervisors employed in various civil service positions throughout the city were organized as a group of job experts for the purpose of determining what skill, knowledge, and ability was essential to the position of auditor. These job experts held four meetings. At the first meeting, they compiled a list of the tasks performed by City-employed auditors. At the second meeting, they determined what skills, knowledge, and ability are required to perform those tasks. At the third meeting, these skills, knowledge, and ability, known as job "elements," were ranked by the job experts on the basis of their importance to the job of auditor. Each job expert ranked the elements himself or herself, without the help of other experts, and the results were averaged to produce a final ranking. From the results of this final ranking, a City personnel analyst compiled a list of elements "critical" to the position of auditor. By definition, these critical elements were the various skills, knowledge, or ability sufficiently essential to the job of auditor to be tested on the auditor examination. At the fourth meeting, the job experts weighted the critical elements according to their relative importance to the auditor position. Again, the weighting was done on an individual basis, the final weighting being an average of all of the job experts' results. Standard deviation analysis was performed on this average, and on the average produced at the third meeting, to protect against one expert skewing the results by extreme rankings or weightings. The final product of these meetings, a compilation of elements critical to the position of auditor, weighted according to their relative importance, was used by the City's examining division to create the 100-question auditor examination.

The examination review phase of the City's validation study occurred after the applicants had taken the examination. In this phase, a new group of job experts was selected from among civil service auditors and supervisors employed by the City. These experts individually reviewed each question and decided if it tested one of the critical elements identified in the first phase. Only if five of the seven job experts agreed that a question tested a critical element was the question considered job related. As a result of this procedure, all but five questions were determined to be job related.

This validation study satisfies our three-step procedure set forth in Craig v. County of Los Angeles, supra, 626 F.2d at 662. First, the initial meetings during the job-analysis phase determined which characteristics or traits were important elements of the auditor position. Third, the examination-review phase demonstrated that the auditor examination was significantly correlated with those elements of work behavior identified in the job-analysis phase.

* * *

V

In summary, we conclude that accountants failed to establish a prima facie case of discriminatory impact by the senior accountant examination. Gonzalez, although successfully establishing a prima facie case of discriminatory impact by the auditor examination, failed to prove that a less discriminatory alternative was available to the City. Thus, the City's proof that its auditor examination was job related entitles it to judgment. Accordingly, we affirm the district court's decision that appellants are entitled to no relief under Title VII.

Affirmed.

TANG, CIRCUIT JUDGE, specially concurring in part and dissenting in part.

I

I write separately for two reasons. First, although I agree with the majority that the Title VII disparate impact business necessity defense requires only that the employer "demonstrate a significant relation between the challenged selection device or criteria and the important elements of the job or training program * * *," ante, at 1277–1279, quoting Craig v. County of Los Angeles, 626 F.2d 659, 664 (9th Cir. 1980), I cannot sanction its assertion that we must "harmonize" Blake v. City of Los Angeles, 595 F.2d 1367 (9th Cir.1979) cert. denied, 446 U.S. 928, 100 S.Ct. 1865, 64 L.Ed.2d 281 (1980), with our other precedents before determining which test to apply to the auditor's examination. See ante, at 1276–1277. Until today, there was no confusion in this circuit concerning the appropriate test to apply in the business necessity defense. Second, I dissent from the majority's conclusion that 'the district court properly found the City's evidence sufficient to meet its burden on the business necessity defense. See ante, at 1282–1283. Because the lower court applied the wrong legal standard at the business necessity stage of the proof process, its findings cannot be reviewed under the clearly erroneous standard. Therefore, rather than deferring to the lower court's findings, I would remand the case for a reevaluation and an introduction of evidence in light of the proper legal standard.

* * *

The *Blake* court did not demand an "absolutely necessary" relationship; rather it required a close or direct relationship. *Blake* did not, as the majority implies, ignore the Supreme Court's *Albemarle* decision; it expressly relied upon *Albemarle* in formulating the job relatedness standard. See id. at 1378, citing Albemarle v. Moody, supra, 422 U.S. at 431, 95 S.Ct. at 2378. Although *Blake* assertedly relied upon dictum in *Dothard*, ante, at 1279–1282, the language cited in *Blake* is probably a holding.[2] At any rate, because *de Laurier* expressly adopted the same formulation in construing and applying the business necessity defense, the majority's criticism is patently underinclusive. See *de Laurier*, 588 F.2d at 678, quoting Dothard v. Rawlinson, 433 U.S. at 331 n. 14, 97 S.Ct. at 2728 n. 14.

2. Footnote 14 of *Dothard* provides:

In what is perhaps a variation on their constitutional challenge to the validity of Title VII itself, see n. 1, supra, the appellants contend that the establishment of the minimum height and weight standards by statute requires that they be given greater deference than is typically given private employer-established job qualifications. The relevant legislative history of the 1972 amendments extending Title VII to the States as employers does not, however, support such a result. Instead, Congress expressly indicated the intent that the same Title VII principles be applied to governmental and private employers alike. See H.R.Rep. No. 92–238, p. 17 (1971); S.Rep. No. 92–415, p. 10 (1971); U.S.Code Cong. & Admin.News 1972, p. 2137. See also Schaeffer v. San Diego Yellow Cabs, 462 F.2d 1002 (CA9). Thus for both private and public employers, "[t]he touchstone is business necessity," *Griggs*, 401 U.S. at 431, 91 S.Ct. at 853; a discriminatory employment practice must be shown to be necessary to safe and efficient job performance to survive a Title VII challenge.

Dothard v. Rawlinson, 433 U.S. at 331 n. 14, 97 S.Ct. at 2728 n. 14. Because the Court expressly rejected the employer's argument that governmental entities were entitled to greater deference than private employers, the Court appears to have rendered a holding. Subsequent cases have cited this passage in *Dothard*, clearly proceeding under the assumption that the language is controlling precedent. See United States v. Miami, 614 F.2d 1322, 1366 n. 27 (5th Cir.1980), reh. granted, 625 F.2d 1310 (5th Cir.1980); Boyd v. Ozark Airlines, Inc.,

568 F.2d 50, 54 n. 3 (8th Cir.1977); Liberies v. Daniel, 477 F.Supp. 504, 508 (N.D.Ill. 1979).

Even if we were to assume that the employers in *Dothard* failed to properly raise the public/private distinction at trial, an assumption open to serious question, see *Dothard*, 433 U.S. at 323 n. 1, 97 S.Ct. at 2724 n. 1, two considerations indicate that the Court's language would still constitute a holding. First, whether an appellate court will review an issue not properly raised at trial is a matter committed to its discretion. Singleton v. Wulff, 428 U.S. 106, 120, 96 S.Ct. 2868, 2872, 49 L.Ed.2d 826 (1972); Reliance Finance Corp. v. Miller, 557 F.2d 674, 682–83 (9th Cir.1977). Because the Court affirmatively exercised its discretion and reviewed the public/private distinction in *Dothard*, its pronouncement is a holding. A second, purely definitional ground independently preserves the language's status as holding. Even if the Court had disposed of the issue on the basis of the employer's failure to raise it at trial, the fact that the Court concurrently confronted and resolved the question on a substantive ground precludes the dictum characterization suggested by the majority opinion. See Union Pacific Railroad Co. v. Mason City and Fort Dodge Co., 199 U.S. 160, 166, 26 S.Ct. 19, 20, 50 L.Ed. 134 (1905) (a district ruling or any question fairly arising in a trial is not obiter dictum, and when the judgment rests upon two grounds, either being sufficient to sustain it, and the appellate court sustains it on both grounds, the ruling on neither is *obiter* but each is the ruling of the court and of equal validity with the other); Railroad Companies v. Schutte, 103 U.S. 118, 143, 26 L.Ed. 327 (1880) (same).

* * *

Blake's retention of the *de Laurier* business necessity defense and its rejection of the absolute necessity standard is perhaps best illustrated by comparing the language in *Blake* with the wording used in cases that do require an absolutely necessary relationship between the job practice and the business need. When courts require strict necessity, specific, unmistakable language is employed: "Necessity connotes an *irresistible demand* * * *. [A practice] must *not only directly foster* safety and efficiency * * *, but also must *be essential* to those goals." United States v. Bethlehem Steel Corporation, 446 F.2d 652, 662 (2nd Cir.1971) (emphasis added). See, e.g., Kirby v. Colony Furniture Co., Inc., 613 F.2d 696, 705 n. 6 (8th Cir.1980); Green v. Missouri Pacific Railroad Company, 523 F.2d 1290, 1295–98 (8th Cir.1975); Rock v. Norfolk & W. Ry. Co., 473 F.2d 1344, 1349 (4th Cir.), cert. denied 412 U.S. 933, 93 S.Ct. 2754, 37 L.Ed.2d 161 (1973); United States v. St. Louis-San Francisco Ry. Co., 464 F.2d 301, 308 (8th Cir.) (en banc), cert. denied, 409 U.S. 1107, 93 S.Ct. 900, 34 L.Ed.2d 687 (1972); United States v. Jacksonville Terminal Co., 451 F.2d 418, 451 (5th Cir.1971), cert. denied, 406 U.S. 906, 92 S.Ct. 1607, 31 L.Ed.2d 815 (1972). Similar language is simply not present in *Blake*. On the contrary, the court in *Blake* specifically required that the practice be "directly related to the business necessity." *Blake*, 595 F.2d at 1377. By demanding that the practice do more than "directly foster" the business need, the circuit cases cited above expressly reject the "directly related" standard established in *Blake*. Hence, *Blake*'s language is fundamentally irreconcilable with decisions that require an absolutely necessary relationship.

(2)

ALLOCATION OF BURDEN OF PROOF REGARDING LESS
DISCRIMINATORY ALTERNATIVES

It might be argued that, if *Blake* did require absolute necessity between the employment practice and business need, it would subtly shift the plaintiff's burden of proving the availability of less discriminatory alternatives into the defendant's business necessity defense because no less discriminatory alternatives could exist if the practice were absolutely necessary to the business need. It could be argued further that, by implicitly requiring proof of the absence of less discriminatory alternatives, the employer is burdened with an unduly onerous task: proof of a negative.[4] Indeed, these concerns probably constitute the

---

4. Proof of a negative in Title VII cases would not necessarily be onerous. For instance, it might not be impractical to require the employer to make a preliminary demonstration of the absence of less discriminatory alternatives under a relaxed burden of proof followed by a more thorough presentation of proof by the plaintiff. See Bernardt, Griggs v. Duke Power Co.: The Implications for Private and Public Employers, 50 Texas L.Rev. 901, 914–15 (1972). Our duty in Title VII cases, however, is to discern Congressional intent, not to speculate about the degree of difficulty in proving negative propositions. Since the statute at issue is silent, administrative considerations are instructive. See Griggs v. Duke Power Co., 401 U.S. 424, 433–34, 91 S.Ct. 849, 854–55, 28 L.Ed.2d 158 (1971) (though not formal regulations, guidelines are entitled to great deference).

unarticulated predicate to the majority's perception of intracircuit discord.

The court in Robinson v. Lorillard Corporation, 444 F.2d 791, 798 n. 7 (4th Cir.1971), made these same arguments yet the question underlying the assertions—whether proof of an absolutely necessary relationship between the job practice and business need subsumes the proof of alternatives issue—was neither explored nor proven. Although there may be an immediate intuitive appeal in the *Robinson* view, the more probable interpretation of the language in *Dothard* suggests that the Court's definition of "necessary" excludes any consideration of less discriminatory alternatives in the employer's burden of proof.

If we assume that the words "necessary to safe and efficient job performance" refer to the means/end relationship between the job practice and business need (an assumption the majority and I seem to agree upon, see ante, at 1274–1277), the *Dothard* Court appears to have required simply that the means—the job practice—efficiently maximize the end—the business need. Since the end in issue at this stage of the proof process, i.e., the employer's business purpose, is economic and not necessarily coextensive with interests sought to be protected by less discriminatory alternatives, see ante, at 1277–1279 (legitimacy of employer goals of efficiency and productivity), it is entirely possible to find an optimal or "necessary" advancement of business need, thereby fulfilling the employer's burden, and a corresponding substantial infringement upon employee rights. See Albemarle Paper Co. v. Moody, 422 U.S. at 431–32, 95 S.Ct. at 2378, (test may significantly predict work behavior and still be discriminatory). Consequently, the distinction between an absolutely necessary relationship and a reasonably necessary relationship, rather than indicating the degree to which a less discriminatory alternatives analysis is implicated in the business necessity defense, is exclusively concerned with the measure of efficiency between the job practice and business need. The existence or nonexistence of less discriminatory alternatives is neither definitionally nor operationally material to an analysis that solely concerns itself with the substantiality of this means/end relationship.

As late as 1973 the EEOC Guidelines required that the employer establish the nonexistence of less discriminatory alternatives. 29 C.F.R. § 1607.3 (1973). Although the Guidelines might have influenced some courts to place the alternatives burden on the plaintiff, the Guidelines were apparently so rigid that even the EEOC did not apply them strictly. See Developments in the Law—Employment Discrimination and Title VII of the Civil Rights Act of 1964, 84 Harv.L.Rev. 1109, 1157 & n. 232 (1971). Since then, the regulations have been rewritten. Although, as a whole, the most recent guideline is somewhat equivocal, it now appears to place the alternative burden on the plaintiff:

> Whenever the user is shown an alternative selection procedure with evidence of less adverse impact and substantial evidence of validity for the same job in similar circumstances, the user should investigate it to determine the appropriateness of using or validating it in accord with these guidelines.

29 C.F.R. § 1607.3 (1979). This allocation, of course, is consistent with Albemarle v. Moody, 422 U.S. at 431–32, 95 S.Ct. at 2378, *Blake,* 595 F.2d at 1383 and *de Laurier,* 588 F.2d at 681.

Although an examination of less discriminatory alternatives could overlap with proof offered at the business necessity stage, the overlay would in no sense be an inevitable product of requiring a "necessary" relationship between the job practice and business need. Indeed, the Court suggested as much in *Dothard* when it asserted that the employer's business need, strong prison guards, "could be achieved by [alternatively] adopting and validating a test for applicants that *measures strength directly*. Such a test, *fairly administered,* would fully satisfy the standards of Title VII * * *." Dothard v. Rawlinson, 433 U.S. at 332, 97 S.Ct. at 2728 (footnote omitted) (emphasis added). The Court offered this *alternative* test as evidence of the relative inefficiency of testing employed by the institution, not as evidence of the existence of less discriminatory alternatives. This latter concern is parenthetically indicated by the requirement that the strength test be "fairly administered." Proof of fair administration would entail an examination of less discriminatory alternatives to the optimally efficient business need test and, therefore, constitute an element of the plaintiff's burden.

Several cases seem to support the propositions that: (1) by focusing solely upon the degree of efficiency between job practice and business need, the "necessary" language in *Dothard* excludes consideration of less discriminatory alternatives as part of the employer's proof; and (2) any discussion of alternatives during judicial review of the employer's burden of proof centers on more efficient alternatives, and not, necessarily, on less discriminatory alternatives. See Albemarle Paper Co. v. Moody, 422 U.S. at 432, 95 S.Ct. at 2378 (study's failure to analyze particular skills needed in job precluded a finding of significant correlation); Craig v. County of Los Angeles, 626 F.2d at 668 (county's test failed to consider alternative fact that, by virtue of cultural rapport, Mexican-American police officer would be more efficient in dealing with Mexican-American constituency); *Blake,* 595 F.2d at 1376 (fact that police department functioned successfully without previous regulation indicated that the rule was not necessary to efficient operation).

Of course, the more obvious evidence that the Court in *Dothard* did not intend that the word "necessary" subsume consideration of less discriminatory alternatives is the likelihood that the Court would not, within a period of only two years, implicitly contradict the allocation scheme announced in *Albemarle.* Therefore, the predicate to the possible criticism of *Blake* discussed here—that the word "necessary" effects a subtle shift in burdens—must be regarded with some caution.

Even if we work under the assumption that an "absolutely necessary" standard shifts the burden of proving alternatives,[5] however, it is

---

5. Although *Blake* cites and quotes *Robinson,* 444 F.2d at 791, a case that obscured the proper distinction between burdens of proof, see *Robinson,* 444 F.2d at 793, *Blake* does so only in response to the trial court's erroneous construction of the same quotation of the "good faith issue." See *Blake,* 595 F.2d at 1376; Blake v. City of Los Angeles, 435 F.Supp. 55, 61–62 (C.D. Cal.1977). *Blake* does not countenance or follow *Robinson's* rather loose description of the allocation issue. Compare *Blake,* 595 F.2d at 1383 (establishing a clear separation of the business necessity defense from proof of less discriminatory alternatives), with *de Laurier,* 588 F.2d at 691

clear that *Blake* does not employ the subtle technique attributed to it by the majority. First, as is demonstrated in the preceding section *Blake* does not require absolute necessity. Second, as shown below, *Blake* implicitly acknowledged the danger of a *sub silentio* shift in burdens by expressly segregating the "alternatives" discussion from its business necessity analysis. Finally, *Blake* is directly contrary to the *de Laurier* dissent and entirely consistent with the *de Laurier* majority on the issue of proving alternatives.

Quite apart from its content, the organization of the *Blake* opinion indicates that the court followed the precedent of *de Laurier* and *Albemarle*. The discussions of the business necessity defense and the plaintiff's proof of less discriminatory alternatives are plainly demarcated by separate subtitles. *Blake*, 595 F.2d at 1375, 1383. By structurally dissociating these two burdens, *Blake* implies that, under a reasonable necessity standard, the plaintiff's burden is not subtly shifted into the business necessity defense. Cases that require absolute necessity stand in direct contrast.[6]

The comparison between *Blake* and the *de Laurier* dissent is most important on the issue of proof of less discriminatory alternatives: *Blake* directly conflicts with the allocation advocated in the *de Laurier* dissent. In discussing the issue of alternatives, the *de Laurier* dissent, unlike *Blake*, drastically blurred and probably ignored the distinction between the business necessity defense and the plaintiff's burden of showing less discriminatory alternatives:

> Even if the district court's findings were unavailable, the business necessity conclusion cannot be sustained because the district court completely failed to consider the existence of less burdensome alternatives, such as individualized decision-making, that would serve the legitimate interests of the school district as well as the mandatory leave policy. The evidence presented by both parties, and the court's own findings of fact, strongly suggest the availability of such alternatives, and *Dothard requires that they be considered in establishing the business necessity defense.*

de Laurier, 588 F.2d at 691 (Hufstedler, J., dissenting) (emphasis added). Although the *de Laurier* dissent is wrong in its construction of *Dothard*, our subsequent reliance on *Dothard* in *Blake* was fortified by the correct interpretation and an express citation to *Albemarle*: "Even if an employer meets his burden of demonstrating business necessity, Title VII plaintiffs may prevail if they show that alternative selection

(Hufstedler, J., dissenting) (blurring the distinction between proof of business necessity and less discriminatory alternatives).

6. Cases requiring that the employer establish the absence of less burdensome alternatives indiscriminately merge their discussion of the two burdens. See Kirby v. Colony Furniture Co., Inc., 613 F.2d 696, 705 n. 6 (8th Cir.1980); Green v. Missouri Pacific Railroad Co., 523 F.2d 1290, 1295–98 (8th Cir.1975); United States v. St. Louis-San Francisco Railway Company, 464 F.2d 301, 308 (8th Cir.) (en banc), cert. denied, 409 U.S. 1107, 93 S.Ct. 900, 34 L.Ed.2d 687 (1972); United States v. Jacksonville Terminal Co., 451 F.2d 418, 451 (5th Cir.1971), cert. denied, 406 U.S. 906, 92 S.Ct. 1607, 31 L.Ed.2d 815 (1972); Robinson v. Lorillard, 444 F.2d 791, 798 & n. 7 (4th Cir.1971).

devices are available that would serve the employer's legitimate interests without discriminatory effects." (*Albemarle*, supra, 422 U.S. at
425, 95 S.Ct. at 2375). *Blake*, 595 F.2d at 1367. Thus, *Blake* unmistakably rejects the *de Laurier* dissent's analysis on the proof of alternatives
issue. Contrary to the *de Laurier* dissent, *Blake* assigns to the plaintiff
the burden of demonstrating less burdensome alternatives, thereby
correctly applying the *de Laurier* majority standard.

B.

An analysis of *Blake* and a comparison between it and the *de
Laurier* majority indicates that the same degree of necessity is demanded in both cases—reasonable necessity. Moreover, those circuits that
have adopted a strict or absolute necessity approach to the business
necessity defense expressly indicate the use of the more exacting
standard by employing words such as "irresistible" and "essential" in
expressing the degree of necessity required and discard the "directly
foster" standard as too lenient. *Blake*, on the other hand, adopts a
"directly related to" standard that is substantively indistinguishable
from the "directly foster" test. Thus, *Blake* eschews the more demanding tests of other circuits and, consistent with *de Laurier*, adopts an
intermediate standard requiring more than a rational relationship but
less than an absolutely necessary connection. This standard fully
comports with our decisions, including that announced today by the
majority. See ante, at 1275–1277 (requiring more than a rational
relationship).

An examination of the *Blake* decision also contradicts any claim
that it either sanctions or encourages a *sub silentio* shift in the burden
of showing the availability of less burdensome alternatives. By requiring less than absolute necessity and by separating the discussion and
application of the business necessity defense from the analysis of less
burdensome alternatives, *Blake* precludes any subtle shift in burden of
proof, even if such a shift were possible. Moreover, *Blake* clearly
disavows the *de Laurier* dissent's allocation of proof on the alternatives
issue. *Blake*, therefore, correctly observes the *de Laurier* majority's
precedent on the issue of proving less discriminatory alternatives.

There is no intracircuit discord over the business necessity defense.
The *Craig* decision, a purported foil to the *Blake* analysis, see ante, at
1276–1277, directly cites the *Blake* formulation of the business necessity defense, 626 F.2d at 662 (citing with approval the page at which
Blake quotes the contested *Dothard* language), and characterizes the
job relatedness standard as "rigorous" immediately after praising the
"instructive" benefits of *Blake*. 626 F.2d at 666. Compare *Blake*, 595
F.2d at 1377 (business necessity defense is narrow), with *Craig*, 626 F.2d
at 656 (job relatedness standards are rigorous). Moreover, in Harriss v.
Pan American World Airways, Inc., 649 F.2d 670 at 675 (9th Cir. as
corrected Dec. 30, 1980), we again affirmed *Blake*'s formulation of the
business necessity defense and quoted *Dothard* and *Blake* for the
proposition that "a discriminatory employment practice must be shown

to be necessary to safe and efficient job performance." *Harriss,* slip op. at 675. Indeed, *Harriss* relied on *Blake* in order to *hold* that the defendant's evidence was "sufficiently compelling." Id. at 675. The majority opinion today, not *Craig,* is the first decision to suggest that there might be a conflict in the development of this circuit's business necessity standards. As a matter of precedent, therefore, *Craig* has validated *Blake's* status in this circuit.[7]

*   *   *

Notes

1. Robinson v. Lorillard Corp., 444 F.2d 791, 789 (4th Cir.1971), petition for certiorari dismissed, 404 U.S. 1006, 92 S.Ct. 573, 30 L.Ed.2d 655 (1971), adopted a test of business necessity which, at one time, was the leading test:

> Collectively these cases [Griggs v. Duke Power Co.; Local 189, United Papermakers and Paperworkers v. United States, 416 F.2d 980 (5th Cir.1969), cert. denied, 397 U.S. 919, 90 S.Ct. 926, 25 L.Ed.2d 100 (1970)] conclusively establish that the applicable test is not merely whether there exists a business purpose for adhering to a challenged practice. The test is whether there exists an overriding legitimate business purpose such that the practice is necessary to the safe and efficient operation of the business. Thus, the business purpose must be sufficiently compelling to override any racial impact; the challenged practice must effectively carry out the business purpose it is alleged to serve; and there must be available no acceptable alternative policies or practices which would better accomplish the business purpose advanced, or accomplish it equally well with a lesser differential impact.

7. The majority quotes the Supreme Court's recent *disparate treatment* decision in Texas Department of Community Affairs v. Burdine, 450 U.S. 248, 101 S.Ct. 1089, 67 L.Ed.2d 207 (1981), for the proposition that "[i]n a Title VII case, the allocation of burdens * * * is intended progressively to sharpen the inquiry into the elusive factual question of *intentional* discrimination." Ante at 1275 n. 5, quoting *Burdine,* 450 U.S. at 255, 101 S.Ct. at 1094 (emphasis added). It also suggests that Title VII is "concerned with combating *culpable* discrimination" and that "[i]n disparate impact cases, *culpable* discrimination takes the form of business decisions that have a discriminatory impact and are not justified by their job-relatedness." Ante at 1275 n. 5 (emphasis added). Despite the majority's protestations to the contrary, see ante at 1275 n. 5 the cumulative effect of its quotation of *Burdine* and its requirement of "culpable discrimination" is the insertion of a subtle intent requirement into disparate impact litigation.

It is black-letter law that intent is irrelevant in disparate impact cases. International Brotherhood of Teamsters v. United States, 431 U.S. 324, 334–35 n. 15 (1977); Griggs v. Duke Power Co., 401 U.S. 424, 432, (1971); Williams v. Colorado Springs, Colorado School District # 11, (and Colorado Springs Teachers Association), 641 F.2d 835, 839–40 (9th Cir.1981); Golden v. International Association of Firefighters, 633 F.2d 817, 821 (9th Cir.1980); Ensley Branch of N.A.A.C.P. v. Seibels, 616 F.2d 812, 823 n. 27 (5th Cir.1980); Crawford v. Western Electric Co., Inc., 614 F.2d 1300, 1309 (5th Cir.1980); Kirby v. Colony Furniture Co., Inc., 613 F.2d 696–704 (8th Cir. 1980). By intimating that procedures in disparate impact litigation are designed to focus on intent, the majority today ignores a decade of precedent. Accordingly, I dissent from the majority's dictum and its reference to "culpable discrimination."

2. Spurlock v. United Airlines, Inc., 475 F.2d 216 (10th Cir.1972), a race discrimination case, dealt with whether certain requirements for airline flight officer, including a college degree, were job-related within the meaning of Griggs v. Duke Power. The Tenth Circuit adopted a sliding scale approach in upholding the validity of the defendant's job criteria:

> When a job requires a small amount of skill and training and the consequences of hiring an unqualified applicant are insignificant, the courts should examine closely any pre-employment standard or criterion which discriminates against minorities. In such a case, the defendant should have a heavy burden to demonstrate to the court's satisfaction that his employment criteria are job-related. On the other hand, when the job clearly requires a high degree of skill and the economic and human risks involved in hiring an unqualified applicant are great, the employer bears a correspondingly lighter burden to show that his employment criteria are job-related. Cf. 29 C.F.R. Sec. 1607.–5(c)(2)(iii). * * * The courts, therefore, should proceed with great caution before requiring an employer to lower his pre-employment standards for such a job.

475 F.2d at 219. Other courts of appeals have expressly approved the *Spurlock* sliding scale approach. See Davis v. City of Dallas, 777 F.2d 205 (5th Cir.1985) (collecting cases).

F. SENIORITY

1. LAYOFFS, RECALLS, AND PROMOTIONS—THE CRITICAL PROBLEMS OF SENIORITY AND CIVIL RIGHTS

The critical role of seniority in determining who should work and its priority position in trade union ideology insured that efforts would be made by its supporters to immunize it from the emerging EEO law and the attempts of civil rights advocates to curb its effect. It is no wonder that the AFL–CIO's legislative support of the Civil Rights Act of 1964 included efforts to insure that precious seniority rights would not be adversely affected by the new civil rights. That the trade union objectives in this regard were less than clearly successful is attested to by two factors: (1) the ambiguity of §§ 703(h) and (j) of the Civil Rights Act of 1964, and (2) extensive litigation of seniority issues.

The cases which are included in this chapter illustrate the evolution of EEO seniority law. Before turning to these cases, examine the following excerpt, which shows the conflict between civil rights objectives and the effects of seniority systems.

LAST HIRED, FIRST FIRED—LAYOFFS AND CIVIL RIGHTS
U.S. Commission on Civil Rights, February 1977

Layoffs in the United States economy are generally based on seniority, or "the last hired, first fired" principle. Seniority involves a set of rules which gives workers with longer years of continuous service a prior claim to a job over others with fewer years of service. What is referred to here is "competitive status seniority" as opposed to "benefit seniority." Competitive status seniority determines priorities for promotion, job security, shift preference, and other employment advantages. By contrast, benefit seniority, earned without regard to the status of other employees, determines the eligibility for certain types of fringe benefits, such as paid vacations or sick leave.

In applying competitive status seniority, companies differ as to the unit within which seniority operates. In some, length of service may be measured by total length of employment with employer ("plant" or "mill" seniority). In others, length of service in a department ("department" seniority) or length of service in a job ("job" seniority) are the units used for applying seniority.

By itself a seniority system is racially and sexually nondiscriminatory. It applies equally to whites and nonwhites, men and women, allocating jobs on the length of service in the unit in which seniority operates. Indeed, it is the "facially neutral" feature that gave rise to its introduction. Unions demanded the establishment of the seniority system to replace the foreman's complete authority over promotion and layoff. Seniority is one of the union organizer's principal and more effective appeals in unionizing a plant's work force.

For union officials or nonunion employers, the length-of-service seniority rule is an objective internal device for allocating job opportunities among members. It helps to immunize the union or the employers from the criticisms of disgruntled employees denied promotion or laid off. Yet seniority systems have been significant instruments of racial and sex discrimination, as part III of this report will demonstrate.

A 1975 survey of major collective bargaining agreements in the United States found that 90 percent contained layoff provisions; in 85 percent of these contracts, seniority was a factor. More than 42 percent of the agreements provided for layoffs based on seniority alone, and 30 percent provided for seniority as the "determining factor" in layoffs (i.e., more senior employees are retained during a reduction in force only if they are qualified for available jobs). Other factors are given equal consideration with seniority in less than 1 percent of the contracts. Seniority is the sole or determining factor in at least two-thirds of the contracts in all manufacturing industries except printing and in most nonmanufacturing industries except maritime, services, construction, and insurance and finance.

Most agreements also provide for eventual loss of seniority and recall rights in a long layoff. Seniority retention periods may last from 6 months or less to 5 years; one year is the most common term.

Always a vital concern, seniority becomes decisive during periods of economic downturn when jobs are scarce. In an industrial or other employment setting, a worker's place in the seniority "pecking order" can mean the difference between having a job and being unemployed.

The implications of the "last in, first out" rule for new workers, whether minorities, women, or youth generally, are obvious. The disproportionately high rates of job loss among minorities have already been noted. In some areas where minorities represented only 10 to 12 percent of the work force, they accounted for 60 to 70 percent of those being laid off in 1974. Many companies which had only recently hired significant numbers of minority and women employees have laid off workers. A Business Week survey of companies that have undergone layoffs failed to find a single employer who refrained from using the "last in, first out" approach in order to retain minority or women workers.

For example, at the Norton Company, an abrasives manufacturer in Worcester, Mass., the percentage of minority workers on the firm's total work force dropped from 3.7 percent in 1973 (up from 1.9 percent in 1971) to 2.7 percent in 1974—"a countrywide pattern that varies only in timing and degree." Elsewhere:

> A Pittsburgh-based conglomerate that recently followed seniority in laying off 15 percent of its 30,000 member work force reports that 26 percent of its black employees and an even larger percentage of its women lost their jobs. In the auto industry * * * layoffs of 215,000 out of 750,000 production workers have removed large numbers of minority workers from some plants and all women from others.

Layoffs of employees by State and local government agencies have also been based on "last in, first out," with disparate effects on minorities and women. For example, layoffs in mid-1975 of 371 female officers appointed since January 1973 by the New York City Police Department ended their brief tenure with the previously overwhelmingly male police force. Over half of all Hispanic city workers in New York lost their jobs between July 1974 and November 1975. In a number of school districts in California and the Southwest, Mexican American teachers were disproportionately threatened by layoffs because of their low seniority. Some 300 Asian American employees of the California Department of Transportation faced layoffs in September 1975. A spokesperson for these workers described the problems created for this minority group:

> There is an extraordinary multiplying effect when Asians are laid off * * * not only does it affect their families so much more by creating unmanageable financial hardships, but you have to consider how much harder it is for them to find new jobs. Asians aren't as mobile as Caucasians, many have a language difficulty, [and] recent affirmative action policies have been so delayed that few have the seniority to hold on to positions. * * *

While seniority does generally determine which employees are to be laid off first, it is not uniformly or always given exclusive weight. In 11 percent of labor contracts, seniority is a secondary factor to be considered only when factors such as ability and physical fitness are equal. Forty-six percent of the contracts allow for exceptions from seniority in layoffs, and union representatives are given superseniority for layoff purposes in more than three-fourths of these provisions. About 19 percent of layoff provisions in manufacturing contracts afford similar protection to specially skilled employees whom management desires to retain. Still other contracts exclude older or handicapped workers from the seniority provisions for layoffs.

Some agreements provide for payment of supplemental unemployment benefits (SUB) to buttress unemployment compensation for job losers. Contracts providing such plans differ as to the amount a worker can receive and the duration of such payments.

These are the mechanics of layoffs by seniority. The Commission wishes to stress the fact that while seniority usually determines who is to be laid off first, there are various exceptions to "last hired, first fired"—applied to groups or categories of workers. [Footnotes omitted.]

2. PHASE I—THE PRESENT EFFECTS OF PAST DISCRIMINATION AS A VIOLATION OF TITLE VII

TITLE VII, SENIORITY AND THE SUPREME COURT: CLARIFICATION OR RETREAT? *

26 Kansas Law Review, 1, 3–25 (1977)
James E. Jones, Jr.

* * *

I. SENIORITY UNDER TITLE VII AT THE PRE-*Bowman* THRESHHOLD

Seniority as a fundamental right enjoys a position in trade union values second, perhaps, only to union antipathy to the labor injunction. Although courts have consistently held that seniority is not an indefeasible right, but rather an expectation that owes its legal status to collective bargaining agreements which the parties may alter, union members perceive seniority as a vested right and no amount of preachment seems to affect this misconception. It is no wonder, then, that the AFL–CIO in its support of equal employment legislation would make herculean efforts to insure that the workers' perceptions of seniority were not destroyed by a civil rights act that labor supported.

The fruits of that effort are contained in Title VII of the Civil Rights Act of 1964, as amended, although it is clear from the ambiguous language of the statute that seniority was not as securely protected as union advocates contend was intended. The legislative history of the relevant provisions of Title VII of the Civil Rights Act has been argued and reargued and, in my opinion, the history clouds rather than clarifies the language of the statute. The unsurprising ambiguity of a statute seeking to regulate that controversial subject guaranteed early

and sustained litigation over the power of the courts to affect seniority
rights under Title VII.

A.   INDUSTRIAL SENIORITY

Quarles v. Philip Morris, Inc. was the first post-1964 case of major
significance dealing with the seniority issue. *Quarles'* interpretation of
Title VII to permit judicial invasion of "job" or "departmental" seniority systems found to be discriminatory has been generally followed in
subsequent cases. In the Philip Morris plants involved in *Quarles*, the
company had frozen Blacks into jobs in the most undesirable departments in the plant, first, by hiring and placing them in those departments, and second, by making seniority dependent upon the amount of
time that the individual had worked in the department rather than in
the plant as a whole. Any transfers between departments that were
permitted would result in loss of seniority in its most valuable aspect—
that relating to the competitive status that governs promotion as well
as protection against layoffs. Some of the Black employees who transferred were permitted to bump back into their prior departments and
retain their seniority in the event that there were layoffs, but not all
Black employees had these rights.

In his seminal opinion, Judge Butzner of the United States District
Court for the Eastern District of Virginia defined a "bona fide seniority
system" under Title VII, which would be entitled to protection under
the statute, to exclude systems that perpetuated the present effects of
past discrimination. The court, in addressing the seniority system,
concluded:

> Obviously one characteristic of a *bona fide* seniority system must be a
> lack of discrimination. Nothing in Section 703(h), or in its legislative
> history, suggests that a racially discriminatory seniority system estab-
> lished before the act is a *bona fide* seniority system under the act.
> * * * The court holds a departmental seniority system that has its
> genesis in racial discrimination is not a *bona fide* seniority system.

The court also pointed out:

> First, it [the legislative history] contains no express statement about
> departmental seniority. Nearly all of the references are clearly to
> employment seniority. None of the excerpts upon which the company
> and the union rely suggests that as a result of past discrimination a
> Negro is to have employment opportunities inferior to those of a white
> person who has less employment seniority. * * * [T]he legislative
> history indicates that a discriminatory seniority system established
> before the act cannot be held lawful under the act. The history leads
> the court to conclude that Congress did not intend to require "reverse
> discrimination"; that is, the act does not require that Negroes be
> preferred over white employees who possess employment seniority. It
> is also apparent that Congress did not intend to freeze an entire
> generation of Negro employees into discriminatory patterns that exist-
> ed before the act.

The remedy in *Quarles* was the establishment of a system in which an employee transferred from one department to another would carry to the new department seniority established as of the date on which the employee was hired. *Quarles*, while not without its critics, was an odds-on candidate for the most significant lower court case of the first decade of Title VII of the Civil Rights Act. The opinion clearly declared that present effects of past discrimination are subject to the reach of the law, which was a major conceptual contribution. *Quarles* also interpreted the new statute to protect only bona fide seniority systems. Both concepts attracted substantial judicial followings.

In Local 189, United Papermakers & Paperworkers v. United States, the first seniority case to come before a federal appellate court under Title VII, considerable weight was added to the interpretation of *Quarles*. Although defendant company, Crown Zellerbach, Corp., utilized a job seniority rather than a departmental seniority system, the fundamental aspects of the cases were sufficiently congruent for the cases to fit comfortably within the same legal principles. The Fifth Circuit stated:

> Title VII of the Civil Rights Act of 1964 prohibits discrimination in all aspects of employment. In this case we deal with one of the most perplexing issues troubling the Courts on Title VII: how to reconcile equal employment opportunity *today* with seniority expectations based on *yesterday's* built-in racial discrimination. May an employer continue to award formerly "white jobs" on the basis of seniority attained in other formerly white jobs, or must the employer consider the employee's experience in formerly "Negro jobs" as an equivalent measure of seniority? We affirm the decision of the district court. We hold that Crown Zellerbach's job seniority system in effect at its Bogalusa Paper Mill prior to February 1, 1968, was unlawful because by carrying forward the effects of former discriminatory practices the system results in present and future discrimination. When a Negro applicant has the qualifications to handle a particular job, the Act requires that Negro seniority be equated with white seniority.

The concepts from these two seminal cases quickly became the conventional wisdom in Title VII cases involving departmental or related types of seniority.

Had the Fifth Circuit stopped with validation of the principles of *Quarles*, it might have faced less of a dilemma in fashioning an appropriate remedy when Franks v. Bowman Transportation Co. came before it for review. In seeking to confine the impact of *Local 189*, however, Judge Wisdom, speaking for the court, tacked on some dicta that became as persuasive in subsequent decisions as the holding of the case itself. The court said:

> No doubt, Congress, to prevent "reverse discrimination" meant to protect certain rights that could not have existed but for previous racial discrimination. For example a Negro who had been rejected by an employer on racial grounds before passage of the Act could not, after being hired, claim to outrank whites who had been hired before

him but after his original rejection, even though the Negro might have had senior status but for the past discrimination. As the court pointed out in *Quarles*, the treatment of "job" or "department seniority" raises problems different from those discussed in the Senate debates: "a department seniority system that has its genesis in racial discrimination is not a bona fide seniority system." * * *

It is one thing for legislation to require the creation of *fictional* seniority for newly hired Negroes, and quite another thing for it to require that time *actually worked* in Negro jobs be given equal status with time worked in white jobs.

The court concluded, in agreement with *Quarles*, that Congress exempted from the antidiscrimination requirement only those seniority rights that gave white workers preference over junior Negroes.

Thus, the dicta in *Local 189* defined the Title VII concept of preferential treatment as not permitting grants of retroactive seniority or bumping privileges to injured Black employees. The conclusion that plant-wide seniority could be asserted only with respect to job vacancies and not with respect to presently filled jobs, which would result in displacing incumbent white employees, was held to apply even if the new Black employees had actually suffered pre-Act discrimination in the form of rejection of their job applications because of race. The court decided that it was not the policy of Title VII to make incumbent white employees suffer for the past discriminatory acts of their employer. Generally speaking, this limited view of the scope of the court's remedial authority in seniority cases in *industrial employment* represented the prevailing view when *Bowman* was decided by the Supreme Court.

B. Construction Union Seniority

The Fifth Circuit decided *Local 189* with no apparent recognition that it was inconsistent in principle with its previous decision in Local 53, International Heat & Frost Insulators v. Vogler, a case involving a construction union seniority system. The court made no persuasive arguments distinguishing *Local 53* except to say that the facts did not mesh completely with those of *Local 189*. In discussing the controlling difference between the nepotism rule of *Local 53* and the seniority situation of *Local 189* as they related to business necessity, the court found neither situation met the business necessity test.

Local 53 was an appeal from a temporary injunction that prohibited the union's admitted discrimination in membership policies, referrals for employment, and training. The union was the exclusive representative for workers engaged in the asbestos and insulation trades in southeastern Louisiana, including the metropolitan areas of New Orleans and Baton Rouge, and in some counties in Mississippi. It effectively controlled employment and training opportunities in the area and in practice, although not by contract, operated a referral system. In order to be admitted into the union at the top journeyman mechanic's rate, applicants were required to be physically fit citizens under thirty years of age, to obtain written recommendations from three members, and to obtain the approval of the majority of the members voting by secret ballot at a union meeting. Additionally, the applicant had to have four years of experience as an improver or helper-member of the union. Improver membership, however, was restricted to sons or close relatives living in the households of members. The district court found that the union had engaged in a pattern or practice of race and national origin discrimination in pursuing its exclusionary and nepotistic policies and granted the injunction. The injunction required the union to cease the discrimination, prohibited the use of members' endorsements or family relations or elections as criteria for membership, and ordered four individuals admitted to the union and nine others referred to work. The referrals were to be chronological—alternating one white and one Black—until objective membership criteria were developed under the supervision of the court.

In sustaining the preliminary injunction, the Fifth Circuit dismissed the following union arguments: (1) The injunction had retrospective effect and penalized the union for pre-Act discrimination in violation of congressional intent; (2) the injunction violated the Act's prohibition against preferential racial treatment and established a quota system to correct racial imbalance; or, (3) the injunction was inconsistent with federal labor legislation and exceeded the district court's discretion under Title VII. The Fifth Circuit asserted that the district court was fully empowered to eliminate the present effects of past discrimination, citing the district court opinion in *Local 189* and *Quarles*. By requiring alternating Black-white referrals the court necessarily affected the seniority of the members of Local 53 and the court was well aware of this effect. The Fifth Circuit distinguished United States v. Sheet Metal Workers Local 36, saying: "Regardless of the validity of the referral seniority systems involved there, [in the Sheet Metal Workers case] they are not analogous to the exclusion of negroes from an all white union by a system of nepotism." The Court expressed no opinion regarding whether the referral seniority system in the Sheet Metal Workers case "would constitute an abuse of discretion by retroactively penalizing pre-Act discrimination, by destroying 'vested' seniority rights or by giving preferential treatment to negroes."

Subsequent to *Local 53,* the Eighth Circuit reversed the lower court's decision in United States v. Sheet Metal Workers Local 36 and remanded it to the district court for drastic modifications in the referral system affecting the seniority of incumbent white workers. The Eighth Circuit's relief was substantially broader than had previously been utilized, for it extended to individuals who might not have been personally injured by the union's discriminatory refusal to admit or refer Blacks. The court stated:

> We recognize that each of the cases cited in note 15 to support our position can be distinguished on the grounds that in each case, a number of known members of the minority group had been discrimi-

nated against after the passage of the Civil Rights Act. Here, we do not have such evidence but we do not believe it is necessary. The record does show that qualified Negro tradesmen have been and continue to be residents of the area. It further shows that they were acutely aware of the Local's policies toward minority groups. It is also clear that they knew that even if they were permitted to use the referral system and became members of the union, they would have to work for at least a year before they could move into a priority group which would assure them reasonably full employment. In light of this knowledge, it is unreasonable to expect any Negro tradesman working for a Negro contractor or a nonconstruction white employer would seek to use the referral system or to join either Local.

On remand, the court directed that if the Local wished to retain its referral system, it would have to modify it not only to eliminate discriminatory residency requirements, but also experience requirements under the collective bargaining agreement since Blacks had been denied the opportunity to obtain experience. The court directed that Blacks with five or more years of experience in the construction industry who wanted to register for employment were to be permitted to do so, and were to be placed in the highest priority group for referral. If they passed a fair journeyman's examination, they were to have continuing rights of referral from the highest priority group. Blacks who did not have the requisite construction experience on the date of the opinion, but who acquired it within five years, were to be given the same opportunities. Blacks with nonconstruction experience would be given an opportunity to take the journeyman's examination, and if they passed, they were to be put in the highest category if they had been *residents of the area* for five years. Other arrangements were made to slot Blacks with less comparable experience into the referral categories appropriate to their years of relevant experience.

The court was acutely aware that its disposition of the matter did indeed affect seniority rights, but asserted that no white craftsman was deprived of any bona fide seniority rights nor would any be ousted from the priority group for which he had satisfied the eligibility requirements. The court asserted that its remedy made it possible for qualified Blacks who had been deprived of the opportunity to gain experience in the construction industry or to gain experience under the collective bargaining agreement to be placed in the group where they would have an equal opportunity to be referred for work.

In 1972 Vogler v. McCarty, Inc. was back before the Fifth Circuit. It is clear in this case that the Court was aware that it was adjusting the seniority system of Local 53. In working out the referral system under the court's order in the earlier case, the district court had set up separate hiring books and maintained them for four categories of employees: (1) white mechanics, (2) Black mechanics, (3) white improvers, and (4) Black improvers. The union alternated referrals between white and Black workers on a one-to-one basis. The white mechanics were divided into "A" books and "B" books. The workers listed in the

"A" book were those with more than five years experience in the trade, while those in the "B" book had less than five years of such experience. Referral preferences were given to workers listed in the "A" book. Because of the influx of Blacks into the trade and the depressed economy, it was necessary to rearrange the lists of white employees because some white mechanics were losing their eligibility for hospitalization and pension benefits. In response to this, three lists of white mechanics, based upon different periods of experience, were substituted for the two previous lists. This system resulted in more employment for more experienced white employees at the expense of less experienced white employees, but provided for stable employment for at least some white workers. The Black workers, because of the required one-white-one-Black referral system, were unaffected by the change.

The court, rejecting arguments that Title VII did not provide discretionary authority in the district courts to rearrange the seniority of white workers, asserted that:

> Adequate protection of Negro rights under Title VII may necessitate, as in the instant case, some adjustment of the rights of white employees. The Court must be free to deal equitably with conflicting interests of white employees in order to shape remedies that will most effectively protect and redress the rights of the Negro victims of discrimination.

* * *

C. Early Conclusions

The cases discussed above illustrate the prevailing views of the limits and scope of the power of the judicial system to affect seniority systems under Title VII during the period in question. It is also apparent, from the foregoing analysis, that views of judicial power differed seemingly on the basis of whether *an industrial seniority system* or the functional equivalent of *seniority in construction unions* was before the court. This result is remarkable for there is nothing in Title VII that suggests that there is one rule for industrial unions and a different rule for construction unions with regard to seniority, and typically in labor law when industrial situations do not fit the construction model, Congress has made specific accommodation for the uniqueness of construction problems. This difference in approach to the seniority issue by the courts had not yet been resolved or harmonized when the Supreme Court addressed Franks v. Bowman Transportation Co.

The proliferation in recent years of cases in which seniority issues are implicated prevents any meaningful analysis of all of those cases and all of the variations in how the courts handled them. In my opinion, the discussions of the four major cases from the industrial and construction situations illustrate the dominant themes that were prevailing at the time *Bowman* was taken to the Supreme Court. The point sought to be made by this dual analysis is to underscore the conflict. The courts found no impediment to revising referral union seniority systems, and giving to plaintiffs, with or without demonstration of personal injury, referral rights equivalent to industrial "fictional seniority," even though in construction unions referral rights are the most significant aspects of competitive status seniority. This posture, then, was the curious state of the law on seniority, or perhaps the muddled state would be a better term, when *Bowman* and its contemporaries landed on the Supreme Court docket.

II. SENIORITY IN THE SUPREME COURT IN OCTOBER TERM, 1975–1976

In order that we may have a frame of reference against which to evaluate the implications of the Supreme Court's decision in Franks v. Bowman Transportation Co. we need first to examine the cases pending before the Supreme Court contemporaneously with *Bowman*, and then to search the disposition of those cases by the Supreme Court after *Bowman* for such implications as might appear. The departmental seniority and job seniority cases had settled into a generally predictable pattern for the incumbent Black following the *Quarles* and *Local 189* analyses. The presiding seniority issue in the Supreme Court at October Term 1975, concerned the problems of layoffs. It is curious that even in the Fifth Circuit the promotion cases that have been suggested as providing a bridge to challenging plantwide seniority cases have not received the same attention as the layoff cases. Perhaps this result is dictated by economic conditions.

A. SENIORITY CASES PENDING BEFORE THE COURT

The Waters v. Wisconsin Steel Works case was the first contemporary of *Bowman* to seek Supreme Court review. Wisconsin Steel Works is an International Harvester plant in Chicago that hired its first Black bricklayers in its bricklaying department in 1964. Waters, one of the five Blacks hired, had applied to the company earlier and had been turned down. A change in the steelmaking process motivated the company to cut back in its bricklaying department, and by March 1965 more than thirty bricklayers had been laid off, including all five of the Blacks. Plaintiff Waters and three others had been laid off pursuant to the last hired, first fired seniority system, even before completing their three month probationary period. The company viewed the cutback as permanent and, along with the union, changed the collective bargaining agreement to provide severance pay for long-service bricklayers. The contract provided, however, that by opting for severance pay, the two-year right to recall under the contract was forfeited. A number of the white bricklayers with long service accepted the severance pay option. When it turned out the company's estimate of its long term labor needs was wrong, the severance pay agreement was amended to permit recall of the white bricklayers. Several white workers who had accepted severance pay were returned to work with Wisconsin Steel Works, despite the pendency of reapplication by Waters and an application by Samuels, a new Black applicant. Waters, who had no recall right because of his failure to complete the probationary period, was later rehired for two months in 1967.

Plaintiffs filed a complaint with the Equal Employment Opportunity Commission (EEOC) challenging the company's hiring and layoff policies as discriminatory under Title VII. At first, the Commission found no probable cause, but subsequent evidence, particularly the severance agreement, caused the Commission to change its mind and determine that plaintiffs did have cause to sue. The district court found that both the seniority system and the severance agreement violated Title VII and 42 U.S.C. § 1981. The Seventh Circuit Court of Appeals, however, reversed on the seniority system, but affirmed the illegality of the severance agreement as it applied to Waters. While agreeing with the lower court that the company had discriminated in hiring prior to 1964, the Seventh Circuit nevertheless held that the last hired, first fired seniority system was not itself racially discriminatory, nor did it have the effect of perpetuating prior racial discrimination in violation of Title VII. The court found the seniority system to be bona fide and supported by the distinction between departmental and plant-wide seniority that emerged from the dicta in *Local 189.* The court felt that to alter these rights earned by length of service would be placing the burden of past discrimination created by the employer upon the shoulders of the innocent white employees. In addition, the Court held that the seniority system that it determined to be acceptable under Title VII was lawful under 42 U.S.C. § 1981. This determination was made in the face of the uniformly affirmed position that the equal employment provisions of Title VII do not supercede the provisions of section 1981. Moreover, the remedies fashioned by Congress in Title VII were not intended to preempt the general remedial language of the older law.

Meanwhile, the Third Circuit Court of Appeals was faced with a rather novel procedural situation in 1974 in Jersey Central Power & Light Co. v. IBEW Local 327. The Jersey Central Power and Light Company was anticipating layoffs and brought an action against the unions representing its employees and the EEOC for declaratory judgment to resolve an apparent conflict between obligations imposed by an EEOC conciliation agreement and the collective bargaining agreement. The company also sought to broaden the declaratory judgment to include its obligation under Title VII and under Executive Order No. 11,246, but the district court apparently excluded consideration of these broader laws and restricted its consideration to construing what the judge called two contracts.

The EEOC conciliation agreement provided for a five year affirmative action hiring program to increase the percentages of minorities and women in Jersey Central's work force. The collective bargaining agreement provided for layoffs in inverse order of employment date. Obviously, if the collective bargaining agreement operated in the normal last hired, first fired procedure, there would be substantial decrease in the percentage of minorities and females remaining in Jersey Central's work force if the planned layoffs came about. In viewing the potential conflict between these two agreements, the lower court ruled that to the extent the terms of the contracts were inconsistent, the EEOC agreement should prevail. To carry this out, the court ordered the use of three seniority lists—one for minorities, one for women, and one for other employees. Layoffs were to be apportioned among them so that when they were completed the percentages that had been achieved by the affirmative action plan would be maintained.

The Third Circuit Court of Appeals reversed and held that the collective bargaining agreement controlled the order of layoffs despite the disproportionate impact on minorities and female workers. While the court agreed that the controversy was a matter of contract law, the court interpreted the conciliation agreement of the EEOC as not being in conflict with or frustrated by the collective bargaining agreement. In its view, the conciliation agreement was directed solely to hiring and explicitly incorporated the collective bargaining agreement for other aspects of employment. The court went on to consider whether the seniority clause was invalid as contrary to public policy and to delineate the type of evidence the district court could entertain on remand or in a related case. The majority held that a seniority clause providing for layoffs by reverse order of seniority was not contrary to public policy and welfare, and consequently was not subject to modification by court decree. Moreover, the court, relying on *Waters* and *Local 189* for support, concluded that "Congress intended to bar proof of the 'perpetuating' effect of a plant-wide seniority system as it regarded such systems as 'bona fide'" although it recognized that these systems might well perpetuate past discriminatory practices. "[T]he only evidence probative in a challenge to a plant-wide seniority system would be evidence directed to its *bona fide* character; that is, evidence directed either to the neutrality of the seniority system or evidence directed to ascertaining an intent or design to disguise discrimination."

* * *

Before turning to the discussion of *Bowman,* a brief mention of Meadows v. Ford Motor Co. is appropriate. Dolores Marie Meadows brought a class action under Title VII of the Civil Rights Act of 1964 for back pay and injunctive relief, alleging sex discrimination in hiring. The district court granted partial summary judgment in finding defendant liable, but denied back pay and retroactive seniority. Plaintiffs established that between April 1971 and April 1973 the Ford Motor Company, at its new truck plant near Louisville, Kentucky, had hired nine hundred men. On the basis of a 150-pound weight requirement for production job eligibility, however, the company had hired no women. On review, the Sixth Circuit held that both back pay and date of application seniority would be permissible remedies under Title VII. Rejecting the argument that the equitable discretion of the court was somehow restricted, the court declared that "[i]f eligibility and discriminatory refusal are established, then back pay should be fully awarded, including compensation for fringe benefits then enjoyed by employees." On the seniority issue, the court recognized that there were even greater problems involved in an award of retroactive job seniority than in determining matters of back pay and other fringe benefits. The court opined as follows:

> Seniority is a system of job security calling for a reduction of work forces in periods of low production by layoff first of those employees with the most recent dates of hire. It is justified among workers by the concept that the older workers in point of service have earned their retention of jobs by the length of prior services for the particular employer. From the employer's point of view, it is justified by the fact that it means retention of the most experienced and presumably most skilled of the work force. Obviously, the grant of fully retroactive seniority would collide with both of these principles.

The court noted that while the burden of retroactive pay would fall upon the party who violated the law, the burden of retroactive seniority for layoff purposes would be borne by other workers who were innocent of any wrongdoing. The court determined, however, that there was no provision to be found in the statute that prohibited retroactive seniority, and held that the remedy for the wrong of discriminatory refusal to hire lay in the first instance with the district judge.

* * *

It was significant at the time, with so many cases following the lead of the Fifth Circuit in *Local 189*, that this court declared its disagreement with the limited view of the equitable powers of the district courts. The *Meadows* case was pending certiorari when *Bowman* was decided.

B. FRANKS v. BOWMAN TRANSPORTATION CO.

In Franks v. Bowman Transp. Co., petitioner Franks brought a class action against his former employer, the Bowman Transportation Company, and his local and international unions, alleging racially discriminatory employment practices in violation of Title VII. Petitioner Lee intervened, alleging racially discriminatory hiring and discharge of over-the-road (OTR) truck drivers. The district court found discriminatory practices in hiring, transfer, and discharge of employees, and also found that these practices were perpetuated in the company's collective bargaining agreement with the union. The court permanently enjoined the discriminatory practices and ordered Bowman to notify the class of Black nonemployee applicants for OTR positions (Class 3), and the class of Black employees who had applied for transfer to OTR positions (Class 4) of their priority rights for consideration for these jobs. The court did not grant other specific relief requested.

The Court of Appeals for the Fifth Circuit held that the district court had exercised its discretion under an erroneous view of the law insofar as it failed to award back pay to the unnamed class members of both Classes 3 and 4, and vacated the judgment in that respect. The judgment was reversed insofar as it failed to award any seniority remedy to members of Class 4 (the employees who sought and obtained priority consideration for transfer to OTR positions after the judgment of the district court). In respect to unnamed members of Class 3 (nonemployee Black applicants who applied for and were denied OTR positions prior to January 1, 1972) the court of appeals affirmed the denial of any form of seniority relief. The only issue before the Supreme Court was the question of retroactive seniority status from the date of application for Class 3 members, none of which involved years prior to 1970.

Reversing the court of appeals, the Supreme Court held that seniority relief for Class 3 members was not barred by section 703(h) of Title VII. The court of appeals had reasoned that a discriminatory refusal to hire did not affect the bona fides of a seniority system, and that differences in the benefits and conditions of employment that a seniority system accorded to older and newer employees was protected as a lawful employment practice by section 703(h).

"Significantly, neither Bowman nor the unions undertake to defend the Court of Appeals' judgment on that ground. It is clearly erroneous." The Court noted that the petitioners were challenging the hiring system, rather than the seniority system, as being racially discriminatory and were seeking the seniority status they would have achieved absent discriminatory refusal to hire. The Court concluded that the legislative history indicated that section 703(h) was a definitional section directed toward defining what is and what is not illegal in instances in which post-Act operation of a seniority system is challenged. The court also held that the section was not intended to modify or restrict relief otherwise appropriate under the remedial provisions of Title VII when a discriminatory practice, such as the refusal to hire, was found. The Supreme Court held, therefore, that the court of appeals erred in concluding as a matter of law that section 703(h) barred the award of seniority relief to the unnamed Class 3 members.

Having determined that section 703(h) did not provide protection per se for seniority systems once an illegally discriminatory practice had occurred after the effective date of the Act, the Court went on to declare that an award of the seniority relief requested in this case was appropriate under the remedial provisions of Title VII, specifically section 706(g). In the prior Term, in Albemarle Paper Co. v. Moody, the Court had determined that federal courts have broad discretion under Title VII to fashion the most complete relief possible to restore persons to the positions they would have been in but for the discrimination. To effectuate this

> "make whole" objective, Congress in Section 706(g) vested broad equitable discretion in the federal courts to "order such affirmative action as may be appropriate, which may include, but is not limited to, reinstatement or hiring of employees, with or without back pay * * *, or any other equitable relief as the court deems appropriate.

The Court noted that at Bowman Transportation Company seniority computed from the departmental date of hire determined the order of layoff, recall, and job assignment and, therefore, the earnings of the OTR drivers. Seniority computed from the company's date of hire determined vacation and pension benefits. Therefore, the award of retroactive seniority was necessary to provide make-whole relief for the class members who applied for jobs with Bowman as well as for the Class 4 employees who applied for transfers. The Court held that there was no basis in Title VII or its legislative history for upholding the court of appeals' distinction between the two classes.

The Court recognized that an award of seniority status is not required in all circumstances but is subject to the sound equitable discretion of the district court. Denial of seniority relief is permissible, however, only if the statutory purposes of elimination of discrimination and providing complete relief are not frustrated. Moreover, seniority relief may not be denied on the grounds that the class-based relief is not appropriate; that there is no evidence each of the class members *was* an actual victim of racial discrimination, or; that the award will conflict with the economic interests of other employees or will deprive employees of vested rights under the collective bargaining agreement. Whether or not individual members of the class are entitled to seniority relief would be determined when those persons reapply for the OTR positions; at that point evidence that particular individuals were not victims of racial discrimination would be material. The petitioners had carried the burden of demonstrating the existence of the discriminatory hiring patterns and practices of the respondents; the burden would therefore be upon the respondents to prove that individuals who reapply were not *in-fact victims* of previous hiring discrimination.

Significantly, the Supreme Court declared that

[D]enial of seniority relief to identifiable victims of racial discrimination on the sole ground that such relief diminishes the expectations of other, arguably innocent, employees would if applied generally frustrate the central "make-whole" objective of Title VII. These conflicting interests of other employees will, of course, always be present in instances where some scarce employment benefit is distributed among employees on the basis of their status in the seniority hierarchy. But, as we have said, there is nothing in the language of Title VII, or in its legislative history, to show that Congress intended generally to bar this form of relief to victims of illegal discrimination, and the experience under its remedial model in the National Labor Relations Act points to the contrary. Accordingly, we find untenable the conclusion that this form of relief may be denied merely because the interests of other employees may thereby be affected.

* * *

Almost with the back of its hand, the Court dismisses the court of appeals' reasoning regarding the effect of discriminatory refusals *to hire* on the bona fides of a seniority system. This teaching is highly significant since the Court also lays to rest the view of the Fifth Circuit that a seniority system that was plant-wide was protected under section 703(h) as being "not an unlawful employment practice." If the disparate impact of seniority systems is removed from the scope of the law by declaration that these systems are not *in law* discriminatory, plaintiffs affected thereby will be foreclosed from attacking them, and all of the new legal concepts that have emerged through other Title VII cases will avail them nothing. The consequences test of Griggs v. Duke Power Co., which shifts the burden to the respondent once disparate impact has been shown and imposes the higher burden of business necessity upon him, would never have come into play for these insulated practices. This result was not foreshadowed in *Bowman.* It awaited United States v. International Brotherhood of Teamsters, discussed below. [Footnotes omitted.]

* * *

3. PHASE II—THE NEW LAW OF SENIORITY

INTERNATIONAL BRO. OF TEAMSTERS v. UNITED STATES

The Supreme Court of the United States, 1977.
431 U.S. 324, 97 S.Ct. 1843, 52 L.Ed.2d 396.

MR. JUSTICE STEWART delivered the opinion of the Court.

This litigation brings here several important questions under Title VII of the Civil Rights Act of 1964, 78 Stat. 253, as amended, 42 U.S.C. § 2000e et seq. (1970 ed. and Supp. V). The issues grow out of alleged unlawful employment practices engaged in by an employer and a union. The employer is a common carrier of motor freight with nationwide operations, and the union represents a large group of its employees. The District Court and the Court of Appeals held that the employer had violated Title VII by engaging in a pattern and practice of employment discrimination against Negroes and Spanish-surnamed Americans, and that the union had violated the Act by agreeing with the employer to create and maintain a seniority system that perpetuated the effects of past racial and ethnic discrimination. In addition to the basic questions presented by these two rulings, other subsidiary issues must be resolved if violations of Title VII occurred—issues concerning the nature of the relief to which aggrieved individuals may be entitled.

I

The United States brought an action in a Tennessee federal court against the petitioner T.I.M.E.–D.C., Inc. (the company) pursuant to § 707(a) of the Civil Rights Act of 1964, 42 U.S.C. § 2000e–6(a).[1] The

1. At the time of suit the statute provided as follows:

"(a) Whenever the Attorney General has reasonable cause to believe that any person or group of persons is engaged in a pattern or practice of resistance to the full enjoyment of any of the rights secured by this subchapter, and that the pattern or practice is of such a nature and is intended to deny the full exercise of the rights herein described, the Attorney General may bring a civil action in

complaint charged that the company had followed discriminatory hiring, assignment, and promotion policies against Negroes at its terminal in Nashville, Tenn.[2] The Government brought a second action against the company almost three years later in a federal district court in Texas, charging a pattern and practice of employment discrimination against Negroes and Spanish-surnamed persons throughout the company's transportation system. The petitioner International Brotherhood of Teamsters (the union) was joined as a defendant in that suit. The two actions were consolidated for trial in the Northern District of Texas.

The central claim in both lawsuits was that the company had engaged in a pattern or practice of discriminating against minorities in hiring so-called line drivers. Those Negroes and Spanish-surnamed persons who had been hired, the Government alleged, were given lower paying, less desirable jobs as servicemen or local city drivers, and were thereafter discriminated against with respect to promotions and transfers.[3] In this connection the complaint also challenged the seniority system established by the collective-bargaining agreements between the employer and the union. The Government sought a general injunctive remedy and specific "make whole" relief for all individual discriminatees, which would allow them an opportunity to transfer to line-driver jobs with full company seniority for all purposes.

The cases went to trial[4] and the District Court found that the Government had shown "by a preponderance of the evidence that T.I.

the appropriate district court of the United States by filing with it a complaint (1) signed by him (or in his absence the Acting Attorney General), (2) setting forth facts pertaining to such pattern or practice, and (3) requesting such relief, including an application for a permanent or temporary injunction, restraining order or other order against the person or persons responsible for such pattern or practice, as he deems necessary to insure the full enjoyment of the rights herein described."

Section 707 was amended by § 5 of the Equal Employment Opportunity Act of 1972, 86 Stat. 107, 42 U.S.C. § 2000e–6(c) (Supp. V), to give the Equal Employment Opportunity Commission, rather than the Attorney General, the authority to bring "pattern or practice" suits under that section against private-sector employers. In 1974, an order was entered in this action substituting the EEOC for the United States but retaining the United States as a party for purposes of jurisdiction, appealability, and related matters. See 42 U.S.C. § 2000e–6(d) (Supp. V).

2. The named defendant in this suit was T.I.M.E. Freight, Inc., a predecessor of T.I.M.E.–D.C., Inc. T.I.M.E.–D.C., Inc., is a

nationwide system produced by 10 mergers over a 17-year period. See United States v. T.I.M.E.–D.C., Inc., 517 F.2d 299, 304, and n. 6 (CA5). It currently has 51 terminals and operates in 26 States and three Canadian provinces.

3. *Line drivers,* also known as over-the-road drivers, engage in long-distance hauling between company terminals. They compose a separate bargaining unit at T.I. M.E.–D.C. Other distinct bargaining units include *servicemen,* who service trucks, unhook tractors and trailers, and perform similar tasks; and *city operations,* composed of dockmen, hostlers, and city drivers who pick up and deliver freight within the immediate area of a particular terminal. All of these employees were represented by the petitioner International Brotherhood of Teamsters.

4. Following the receipt of evidence, but before decision, the Government and the company consented to the entry of a Decree in Partial Resolution of Suit. The consent decree did not constitute an adjudication on the merits. The company agreed, however, to undertake a minority recruiting program; to accept applications from all Negroes and Spanish-surnamed Americans who inquired about employ-

M.E.–D.C. and its predecessor companies were engaged in a plan and practice of discrimination in violation of Title VII * * *." [5] The court further found that the seniority system contained in the collective-bargaining contracts between the company and the union violated Title VII because it "operate[d] to impede the free transfer of minority groups into and within the company." Both the company and the union were enjoined from committing further violations of Title VII.

With respect to individual relief the court accepted the Government's basic contention that the "affected class" of discriminatees included all Negro and Spanish-surnamed incumbent employees who had been hired to fill city operations or serviceman jobs at every terminal that had a line-driver operation.[6] All of these employees, whether hired before or after the effective date of Title VII, thereby became entitled to preference over all other applicants with respect to consideration for future vacancies in line-driver jobs.[7] Finding that members of the affected class had been injured in different degrees, the court created three subclasses. Thirty persons who had produced "the most convincing evidence of discrimination and harm" were found to have suffered "severe injury." The court ordered that they be offered the opportunity to fill line-driver jobs with competitive seniority dating back to July 2, 1965, the effective date of Title VII.[8] A second subclass

ment, whether or not vacancies existed, and to keep such applications on file and notify applicants of job openings; to keep specific employment and recruiting records open to inspection by the Government and to submit quarterly reports to the District Court; and to adhere to certain uniform employment qualifications respecting hiring and promotion to line driver and other jobs.

The decree further provided that future job vacancies at any T.I.M.E.–D.C. terminal would be filled first "[b]y those persons who may be found by the Court, if any, to be individual or class discriminatees suffering the present effects of past discrimination because of race or national origin prohibited by Title VII of the Civil Rights Act of 1964." Any remaining vacancies could be filled by "any other persons," but the company obligated itself to hire one Negro or Spanish-surnamed person for every white person hired at any terminal until the percentage of minority workers at that terminal equaled the percentage of minority group members in the population of the metropolitan area surrounding the terminal. Finally, the company agreed to pay $89,500 in full settlement of any backpay obligations. Of this sum, individual payments not exceeding $1,500 were to be paid to "alleged individual and class discriminatees" identified by the Government.

The Decree in Partial Resolution of Suit narrowed the scope of the litigation, but the District Court still had to determine whether unlawful discrimination had occurred. If so, the Court had to identify the actual discriminatees entitled to fill future job vacancies under the decree. The validity of the collective-bargaining contract's seniority system also remained for decision, as did the question whether any discriminatees should be awarded additional equitable relief such as retroactive seniority.

5. The District Court's Memorandum Decision in United States v. T.I.M.E.–D.C., Inc., Civ. No. 5–868 (Oct. 19, 1972), is not officially reported. It is unofficially reported at 6 FEP Cases 690 and 6 EPD ¶ 8979.

6. The Government did not seek relief for Negroes and Spanish-surnamed Americans hired at a particular terminal after the date on which that terminal first employed a minority group member as a line driver.

7. See supra, at 1851–1852, n. 4.

8. If an employee in this class had joined the company after July 2, 1965, then the date of his initial employment rather than the effective date of Title VII was to determine his competitive seniority.

included four persons who were "very possibly the objects of discrimination" and who "were likely harmed," but as to whom there had been no specific evidence of discrimination and injury. The court decreed that these persons were entitled to fill vacancies in line-driving jobs with competitive seniority as of January 14, 1971, the date on which the Government had filed its system-wide lawsuit. Finally, there were over 300 remaining members of the affected class as to whom there was "no evidence to show that these individuals were either harmed or not harmed individually." The court ordered that they be considered for line-driver jobs [9] ahead of any applicants from the general public but behind the two other subclasses. Those in the third subclass received no retroactive seniority; their competitive seniority as line drivers would begin with the date they were hired as line drivers. The court further decreed that the right of any class member to fill a line-driver vacancy was subject to the prior recall rights of laid-off line drivers, which under the collective-bargaining agreements then in effect extended for three years.[10]

The Court of Appeals for the Fifth Circuit agreed with the basic conclusions of the District Court: that the company had engaged in a pattern or practice of employment discrimination and that the seniority system in the collective-bargaining agreements violated Title VII as applied to victims of prior discrimination. United States v. T.I.M.E.-D.C., Inc., 517 F.2d 299. The appellate court held, however, that the relief ordered by the District Court was inadequate. Rejecting the District Court's attempt to trisect the affected class, the Court of Appeals held that all Negro and Spanish-surnamed incumbent employees were entitled to bid for future line-driver jobs on the basis of their company seniority, and that once a class member had filled a job, he could use his full company seniority—even if it predated the effective date of Title VII—for all purposes, including bidding and layoff. This award of retroactive seniority was to be limited only by a "qualification date" formula, under which seniority could not be awarded for periods prior to the date when (1) a line-driving position was vacant,[11] *and* (2)

9. As with the other subclasses, there were a few individuals in the third group who were found to have been discriminated against with respect to jobs other than line driver. There is no need to discuss them separately in this opinion.

10. This provision of the decree was qualified in one significant respect. Under the Southern Conference Area Over-the-Road Supplemental Agreement between the employer and the union, line drivers employed at terminals in certain southern States work under a "modified" seniority system. Under the modified system an employee's seniority is not confined strictly to his home terminal. If he is laid off at his home terminal he can move to another terminal covered by the Agreement and retain his seniority, either by filling a va-

cancy at the other terminal or by "bumping" a junior line driver out of his job if there is no vacancy. The modified system also requires that any new vacancy at a covered terminal be offered to laid-off line drivers at all other covered terminals before it is filled by any other person. The District Court's final decree, as amended slightly by the Court of Appeals, 517 F.2d, at 323, altered this system by requiring that any vacancy be offered to all members of all three subclasses before it may be filled by laid-off line drivers from other terminals.

11. Although the opinion of the Court of Appeals in this case did not specifically mention the requirement that a vacancy exist, it is clear from earlier and later opinions of that court that this require-

the class member met (or would have met, given the opportunity) the qualifications for employment as a line driver.[12]   Finally, the Court of Appeals modified that part of the District Court's decree that had subjected the rights of class members to fill future vacancies to the recall rights of laid-off employees.   Holding that the three-year priority in favor of laid-off workers "would unduly impede the eradication of past discrimination," id., at 322, the Court of Appeals ordered that class members be allowed to compete for vacancies with laid-off employees on the basis of the class members' retroactive seniority.   Laid-off line drivers would retain their prior recall rights with respect only to "purely temporary" vacancies.   Ibid.[13]

The Court of Appeals remanded the case to the District Court to hold the evidentiary hearings necessary to apply these remedial principles.   We granted both the company's and the union's petitions for certiorari to consider the significant questions presented under the Civil Rights Act of 1964, 425 U.S. 990, 96 S.Ct. 2200, 48 L.Ed.2d 814.

II

In this Court the company and the union contend that their conduct did not violate Title VII in any respect, asserting first that the evidence introduced at trial was insufficient to show that the company engaged in a "pattern or practice" of employment discrimination.   The union further contends that the seniority system contained in the collective-bargaining agreements in no way violated Title VII.   If these contentions are correct, it is unnecessary, of course, to reach any of the issues concerning remedies that so occupied the attention of the Court of Appeals.

A

Consideration of the question whether the company engaged in a pattern or practice of discriminatory hiring practices involves controlling legal principles that are relatively clear.   The Government's theory of discrimination was simply that the company, in violation of § 703(a) of Title VII,[14] regularly and purposefully treated Negroes and

ment is a part of the Fifth Circuit's "qualification date" formula.   See, e.g., Rodriquez v. East Texas Motor Freight, 505 F.2d 40, 63 n. 29 (CA5), rev'd on other grounds, 431 U.S. 395, 97 S.Ct. 1891, 52 L.Ed.2d 453, cited in United States v. T.I.M.E.–D.C., 517 F.2d, at 318 n. 35; Sagers v. Yellow Freight System, Inc., 529 F.2d 721, 731–734 (CA5 1976).

12.   For example, if a class member began his tenure with the company on January 1, 1966, at which time he was qualified as a line driver and a line-driving vacancy existed, his competitive seniority upon becoming a line driver would date back to January 1, 1966.   If he became qualified or if a vacancy opened up only at a later date, then that later date would be used.

13.   The Court of Appeals also approved (with slight modification) the part of the District Court's order that allowed class members to fill vacancies at a particular terminal ahead of line drivers laid off at other terminals.   See supra, at 1853, n. 10.

14.   Section 703(a) of Title VII, 42 U.S.C. § 2000e–2(a) (1970 ed. and Supp. V), provides:

"(a) It shall be an unlawful employment practice for an employer—

"(1) to fail or refuse to hire or to discharge any individual, or otherwise to discriminate against any individual with respect to his compensation, terms, conditions, or privileges of employment, be-

Spanish-surnamed Americans less favorably than white persons. The disparity in treatment allegedly involved the refusal to recruit, hire, transfer, or promote minority group members on an equal basis with white people, particularly with respect to line-driving positions. The ultimate factual issues are thus simply whether there was a pattern or practice of such disparate treatment and, if so, whether the differences were "racially premised." McDonnell Douglas Corp. v. Green, 411 U.S. 792, 805 n. 18, 93 S.Ct. 1817, 1825, 36 L.Ed.2d 668.[15]

As the plaintiff, the Government bore the initial burden of making out a prima facie case of discrimination. Albemarle Paper Co. v. Moody, 422 U.S. 405, 425, 95 S.Ct. 2362, 2375, 45 L.Ed.2d 280; McDonnell Douglas Corp. v. Green, supra, 411 U.S., at 802, 93 S.Ct., at 1824. And, because it alleged a systemwide pattern or practice of resistance to the full enjoyment of Title VII rights, the Government ultimately had to prove more than the mere occurrence of isolated or "accidental" or sporadic discriminatory acts. It had to establish by a preponderance of the evidence that racial discrimination was the company's standard operating procedure—the regular rather than the unusual practice.[16]

cause of such individual's race, color, religion, sex, or national origin; or

"(2) to limit, segregate, or classify his employees or applicants for employment in any way which would deprive or tend to deprive any individual of employment opportunities or otherwise adversely affect his status as an employee, because of such individual's race, color, religion, sex, or national origin."

15. "Disparate treatment" such as alleged in the present case is the most easily understood type of discrimination. The employer simply treats some people less favorably than others because of their race, color, religion, sex, or national origin. Proof of discriminatory motive is critical, although it can in some situations be inferred from the mere fact of differences in treatment. See, e.g., Village of Arlington Heights v. Metropolitan Housing Dev. Corp., 429 U.S. 252, 265–266, 97 S.Ct. 555, 563–565, 50 L.Ed.2d 450. Undoubtedly disparate treatment was the most obvious evil Congress had in mind when it enacted Title VII. See, e.g., 110 Cong.Rec. 13088 (1964) (remarks of Sen. Humphrey) ("What the bill does * * * is simply to make it an illegal practice to use race as a factor in denying employment. It provides that men and women shall be employed on the basis of their qualifications, not as Catholic citizens, not as protestant citizens, not as Jewish citizens, not as colored citizens, but as citizens of the United States").

Claims of disparate treatment may be distinguished from claims that stress "disparate impact." The latter involve employment practices that are facially neutral in their treatment of different groups but that in fact fall more harshly on one group than another and cannot be justified by business necessity. See infra, at 1861. Proof of discriminatory motive, we have held, is not required under a disparate impact theory. Compare, e.g., Griggs v. Duke Power Co., 401 U.S. 424, 430–432, 91 S.Ct. 849, 853–854, 28 L.Ed.2d 158, with McDonnell Douglas Corp. v. Green, 411 U.S. 792, 802–806, 93 S.Ct. 1817, 1824–1826, 36 L.Ed.2d 668. See generally Schlei & Grossman, Employment Discrimination Law 1–12 (1976); Blumrosen, Strangers in Paradise: Griggs v. Duke Power Co. and the Concept of Employment Discrimination, 71 Mich.L.Rev. 59 (1972). Either theory may, of course, be applied to a particular set of facts.

16. The "pattern or practice" language in § 707(a) of Title VII, supra, at 1830 n. 1, was not intended as a term of art, and the words reflect only their usual meaning. Senator Humphrey explained:

"[A] pattern or practice would be present only where the denial of rights consists of something more than an isolated, sporadic incident, but is repeated, routine, or of a generalized nature. There would be a pattern or practice if, for example, a number of companies or persons in the same industry or line of business discriminated, if a chain of motels or restaurants practiced racial discrimination throughout all or a significant part of its system, or if a company

We agree with the District Court and the Court of Appeals that the Government carried its burden of proof. As of March 31, 1971, shortly after the Government filed its complaint alleging system-wide discrimination, the company had 6,472 employees. Of these, 314 (5%) were Negroes and 257 (4%) were Spanish-surnamed Americans. Of the 1,828 line drivers, however, there were only 8 (0.4%) Negroes and 5 (0.3%) Spanish-surnamed persons, and all of the Negroes had been hired after the litigation had commenced. With one exception—a man who worked as a line driver at the Chicago terminal from 1950 to 1959—the company and its predecessors *did not employ a Negro on a regular basis as a line driver until 1969.* And, as the Government showed, even in 1971 there were terminals in areas of substantial Negro population where all of the company's line drivers were white.[17] A great majority of the Negroes (83%) and Spanish-surnamed Americans (78%) who did work for the company held the lower-paying city operations and serviceman jobs,[18] whereas only 39% of the nonminority employees held jobs in those categories.

The Government bolstered its statistical evidence with the testimony of individuals who recounted over 40 specific instances of discrimination. Upon the basis of this testimony the District Court found that "[n]umerous qualified black and Spanish-surnamed American applicants who sought line-driving jobs at the company over the years had their requests ignored, were given false or misleading information about requirements, opportunities, and application procedures, or were not considered and hired on the same basis that whites were considered

repeatedly and regularly engaged in acts prohibited by the statute.

*   *   *   *   *

"The point is that single, insignificant, isolated acts of discrimination by a single business would not justify a finding of a pattern or practice * * *." 110 Cong. Rec. 14270 (1964).

This interpretation of "pattern or practice" appears throughout the legislative history of § 707(a), and is consistent with the understanding of the identical words as used in similar federal legislation. See id., at 12946 (remarks of Sen. Magnuson) (referring to § 206(a) of the Civil Rights Act of 1964, 42 U.S.C. § 2000a–5(a)); id., at 13081 (remarks of Sen. Case); id., at 14239 (remarks of Sen. Humphrey); id., at 15895 (remarks of Rep. Celler). See also United States v. Jacksonville Terminal Co., 451 F.2d 418, 438, 441 (CA5); United States v. Ironworkers Local 86, 443 F.2d 544, 552 (CA9); United States v. West Peachtree Tenth Corp., 437 F.2d 221, 227 (CA5); United States v. Mayton, 335 F.2d 153, 158–159 (CA5).

17. In Atlanta, for instance, Negroes composed 22.35% of the population in the surrounding metropolitan area and 51.31% of the population in the city proper. The company's Atlanta terminal employed 57 line drivers. All were white. In Los Angeles, 10.84% of the greater metropolitan population and 17.88% of the city population were Negro. But at the company's two Los Angeles terminals there was not a single Negro among the 374 line drivers. The proof showed similar disparities in San Francisco, Denver, Nashville, Chicago, Dallas, and at several other terminals.

18. Although line-driver jobs pay more than other jobs, and the District Court found them to be "considered the most desirable of the driving-jobs," it is by no means clear that all employees, even driver employees, would prefer to be line drivers. See infra, at 1871–1872, and n. 55. Of course, Title VII provides for equal opportunity to compete for *any* job, whether it is thought better or worse than another. See, e.g., United States v. Hayes Internat'l Corp., 456 F.2d 112, 118 (CA5); United States v. National Lead Co., 438 F.2d 935, 939 (CA8).

and hired." Minority employees who wanted to transfer to line-driver jobs met with similar difficulties.[19]

The company's principal response to this evidence is that statistics can never in and of themselves prove the existence of a pattern or practice of discrimination, or even establish a prima facie case shifting to the employer the burden of rebutting the inference raised by the figures. But, as even our brief summary of the evidence shows, this was not a case in which the Government relied on "statistics alone." The individuals who testified about their personal experiences with the company brought the cold numbers convincingly to life.

In any event, our cases make it unmistakably clear that "[s]tatistical analyses have served and will continue to serve an important role" in cases in which the existence of discrimination is a disputed issue. Mayor of Philadelphia v. Educational Equality League, 415 U.S. 605, 620, 94 S.Ct. 1323, 1333, 39 L.Ed.2d 630. See also McDonnell Douglas Corp. v. Green, supra, 411 U.S., at 805, 93 S.Ct., at 1825. Cf. Washington v. Davis, 426 U.S. 229, 241–242, 96 S.Ct. 2040, 2048–2049, 48 L.Ed.2d 597. We have repeatedly approved the use of statistical proof, where it reached proportions comparable to those in this case, to establish a prima facie case of racial discrimination in jury selection cases, see, e.g., Turner v. Fouche, 396 U.S. 346, 90 S.Ct. 532, 24 L.Ed.2d 567; Hernandez v. Texas, 347 U.S. 475, 74 S.Ct. 667, 98 L.Ed. 866; Norris v. Alabama, 294 U.S. 587, 55 S.Ct. 579, 79 L.Ed. 1074. Statistics are equally competent in proving employment discrimination.[20] We

---

19. Two examples are illustrative:

George Taylor, a Negro, worked for the company as a city driver in Los Angeles, beginning late in 1966. In 1968, after hearing that a white city driver had transferred to a line-driver job, he told the terminal manager that he also would like to consider line driving. The manager replied that there would be "a lot of problems on the road * * * with different people, Caucasian, et cetera," and stated "I don't feel the company is ready for this right now. * * * Give us a little time. It will come around, you know." Mr. Taylor made similar requests some months later and got similar responses. He was never offered a line-driving job or an application.

Feliberto Trujillo worked as a dockman at the company's Denver terminal. When he applied for a line-driver job in 1967, he was told by a personnel officer that he had one strike against him. He asked what that was and was told: "You're a Chicano, and as far as we know, there isn't a Chicano driver in the system."

20. Petitioners argue that statistics, at least those comparing the racial composition of an employer's work force to the composition of the population at large, should never be given decisive weight in a Title VII case because to do so would conflict with § 703(j) of the Act, 42 U.S.C. § 2000e–2(j). That section provides:

"Nothing contained in this subchapter shall be interpreted to require any employer * * * to grant preferential treatment to any individual or to any group because of the race * * * or national origin of such individual or group on account of an imbalance which may exist with respect to the total number or percentage of persons of any race * * * or national origin employed by any employer * * * in comparison with the total number or percentage of persons of such race * * * or national origin in any community, State, section, or other area, or in the available work force in any community, State, section, or other area."

The argument fails in this case because the statistical evidence was not offered or used to support an erroneous theory that Title VII requires an employer's work force to be racially balanced. Statistics showing racial or ethnic imbalance are probative in a case such as this one only because such imbalance is often a telltale sign of purposeful discrimination; absent explana-

caution only that statistics are not irrefutable; they come in infinite variety and, like any other kind of evidence, they may be rebutted. In short, their usefulness depends on all of the surrounding facts and circumstances. See, e.g., Hester v. Southern R. Co., 497 F.2d 1374, 1379–1381 (CA5).

In addition to its general protest against the use of statistics in Title VII cases, the company claims that in this case the statistics revealing racial imbalance are misleading because they fail to take into account the company's particular business situation as of the effective date of Title VII. The company concedes that its line drivers were virtually all white in July 1965, but it claims that thereafter business conditions were such that its work force dropped. Its argument is that low personnel turnover, rather than post-Act discrimination, accounts for more recent statistical disparities. It points to substantial minority hiring in later years, especially after 1971, as showing that any pre-Act patterns of discrimination were broken.

The argument would be a forceful one if this were an employer who, at the time of suit, had done virtually no new hiring since the effective date of Title VII. But it is not. Although the company's total number of employees apparently dropped somewhat during the late 1960's, the record shows that many line drivers continued to be hired throughout this period, and that almost all of them were white.[21] To be sure, there were improvements in the company's hiring practices. The Court of Appeals commented that "T.I.M.E.–D.C.'s recent minority hiring progress stands as a laudable good faith effort to eradicate the effects of past discrimination in the area of hiring and initial assignment."[22] 517 F.2d, at 316. But the District Court and the Court of

tion, it is ordinarily to be expected that nondiscriminatory hiring practices will in time result in a work force more or less representative of the racial and ethnic composition of the population in the community from which employees are hired. Evidence of longlasting and gross disparity between the composition of a work force and that of the general population thus may be significant even though § 703(j) makes clear that Title VII imposes no requirement that a work force mirror the general population. See, e.g., United States v. Sheet Metal Workers Local 36, 416 F.2d 123, 127 n. 7 (CA8). Considerations such as small sample size may, of course, detract from the value of such evidence, see, e.g., Mayor of Philadelphia v. Educational Equality League, 415 U.S. 605, 620–621, 94 S.Ct. 1323, 1333, 39 L.Ed.2d 630, and evidence showing that the figures for the general population might not accurately reflect the pool of qualified job applicants would also be relevant. Ibid. See generally Schlei & Grossman, Employment Discrimination Law, 1161–1193 (1976).

"Since the passage of the Civil Rights Act of 1964, the courts have frequently relied upon statistical evidence to prove a violation. * * * In many cases the only available avenue of proof is the use of racial statistics to uncover clandestine and covert discrimination by the employer or union involved." United States v. Ironworkers Local 86, 443 F.2d 544, 551 (CA9). See also, e.g., Pettway v. American Cast Iron Pipe Co., 494 F.2d 211, 225 n. 34 (CA5); Brown v. Gaston County Dyeing Mach. Co., 457 F.2d 1377, 1382 (CA4); United States v. Jacksonville Terminal Co., 451 F.2d 418, 442 (CA5); Parham v. Southwestern Bell Tel. Co., 433 F.2d 421, 426 (CA8); Jones v. Lee Way Motor Freight, Inc., 431 F.2d 245, 247 (CA10).

21. Between July 2, 1965, and January 1, 1969, hundreds of line drivers were hired systemwide, either from the outside or from the ranks of employees filling other jobs within the company. None was a Negro. Government Exh. 204.

22. For example, in 1971 the company hired 116 new line drivers, of whom 16

Appeals found upon substantial evidence that the company had engaged in a course of discrimination that continued well after the effective date of Title VII. The company's later changes in its hiring and promotion policies could be little comfort to the victims of the earlier post-Act discrimination, and could not erase its previous illegal conduct or its obligation to afford relief to those who suffered because of it. Cf. Albemarle Paper Co. v. Moody, supra, 422 U.S., at 413–423, 95 S.Ct., at 2369–2374.[23]

The District Court and the Court of Appeals, on the basis of substantial evidence, held that the Government had proved a *prima facie* case of systematic and purposeful employment discrimination, continuing well beyond the effective date of Title VII. The company's attempts to rebut that conclusion were held to be inadequate.[24]

*   *   *

were Negro or Spanish-surnamed Americans. Minority employees composed 7.1% of the company's systemwide work force in 1967 and 10.5% in 1972. Minority hiring increased greatly in 1972 and 1973, presumably due at least in part to the existence of the consent decree. See 517 F.2d, at 316 n. 31.

23. The company's narrower attacks upon the statistical evidence—that there was no precise delineation of the areas referred to in the general population statistics, that the Government did not demonstrate that minority populations were located close to terminals or that transportation was available, that the statistics failed to show what portion of the minority population was suited by age, health, or other qualifications to hold trucking jobs, etc.—are equally lacking in force. At best, these attacks go only to the accuracy of the comparison between the composition of the company's work force at various terminals and the general population of the surrounding communities. They detract little from the Government's further showing that Negroes and Spanish-surnamed Americans who were hired were overwhelmingly excluded from line-driver jobs. Such employees were willing to work, had access to the terminal, were healthy and of working age, and often were at least sufficiently qualified to hold city-driver jobs. Yet they became line drivers with far less frequency than whites. See, e.g., Pre-trial Stipulation 14, summarized at 517 F.2d, at 312 n. 24 (of 2,919 whites who held driving jobs in 1971, 1,802 (62%) were line drivers and 1,117 (38%) were city drivers; of 180 Negroes and Spanish-surnamed Americans who held driving jobs, 13 (7%) were line drivers and 167 (93%) were city drivers).

In any event, fine tuning of the statistics could not have obscured the glaring absence of minority line drivers. As the Court of Appeals remarked, the company's inability to rebut the inference of discrimination came not from a misuse of statistics but from "the inexorable zero." 517 F.2d at 315.

24. The company's evidence, apart from the showing of recent changes in hiring and promotion policies, consisted mainly of general statements that it hired only the best qualified applicants. But "affirmations of good faith in making individual selections are insufficient to dispel a prima facie case of systematic exclusion." Alexander v. Louisiana, 405 U.S. 625, 632, 92 S.Ct. 1221, 1226, 31 L.Ed.2d 536.

The company also attempted to show that all of the witnesses who testified to specific instances of discrimination either were not discriminated against or suffered no injury. The Court of Appeals correctly ruled that the trial judge was not bound to accept this testimony and that it committed no error by relying instead on the other overpowering evidence in the case. 517 F.2d, at 315. The Court of Appeals was also correct in the view that individual proof concerning each class member's specific injury was appropriately left to proceedings to determine individual relief. In a suit brought by the Government under § 707(a) of the Act the District Court's initial concern is in deciding whether the Government has proved that the defendant has engaged in a pattern or practice of discriminatory conduct. See infra, at 1865–1868.

B

The District Court and the Court of Appeals also found that the seniority system contained in the collective-bargaining agreements between the company and the union operated to violate Title VII of the Act.

For purposes of calculating benefits, such as vacations, pensions, and other fringe benefits, an employee's seniority under this system runs from the date he joins the company, and takes into account his total service in all jobs and bargaining units. For competitive purposes, however, such as determining the order in which employees may bid for particular jobs, are laid off, or are recalled from layoff, it is bargaining-unit seniority that controls. Thus, a line driver's seniority, for purposes of bidding for particular runs [25] and protection against layoff, takes into account only the length of time he has been a line driver at a particular terminal.[26] The practical effect is that a city driver or serviceman who transfers to a line-driver job must forfeit all the competitive seniority he has accumulated in his previous bargaining unit and start at the bottom of the line-drivers' "board."

The vice of this arrangement, as found by the District Court and the Court of Appeals, was that it "locked" minority workers into inferior jobs and perpetuated prior discrimination by discouraging transfers to jobs as line drivers. While the disincentive applied to all workers, including whites, it was Negroes and Spanish-surnamed persons who, those courts found, suffered the most because many of them had been denied the equal opportunity to become line drivers when they were initially hired, whereas whites either had not sought or were refused line-driver positions for reasons unrelated to their race or national origin.

The linchpin of the theory embraced by the District Court and the Court of Appeals was that a discriminatee who must forfeit his competitive seniority in order finally to obtain a line-driver job will never be able to "catch up" to the seniority level of his contemporary who was not subject to discrimination.[27] Accordingly, this continued, built-in disadvantage to the prior discriminatee who transfers to a line-driver job was held to constitute a continuing violation of Title VII, for which

---

25. Certain long-distance runs, for a variety of reasons, are more desirable than others. The best runs are chosen by the line drivers at the top of the "board"—a list of drivers arranged in order of their bargaining-unit seniority.

26. Both bargaining-unit seniority and company seniority rights are generally limited to service at one particular terminal, except as modified by the Southern Conference Area Over-the-Road Supplemental Agreement. See supra, at 1833, n. 10.

27. An example would be a Negro who was qualified to be a line driver in 1958 but who, because of his race, was assigned instead a job as a city driver, and is allowed to become a line driver only in 1971. Because he loses his competitive seniority when he transfers jobs, he is forever junior to white line drivers hired between 1958 and 1970. The whites, rather than the Negro, will henceforth enjoy the preferable runs and the greater protection against layoff. Although the original discrimination occurred in 1958—before the effective date of Title VII—the seniority system operates to carry the effects of the earlier discrimination into the present.

both the employer and the union who jointly created and maintain the seniority system were liable.

The union, while acknowledging that the seniority system may in some sense perpetuate the effects of prior discrimination, asserts that the system is immunized from a finding of illegality by reason of § 703(h) of Title VII, 42 U.S.C. § 2000e–2(h), which provides in part:

> Notwithstanding any other provision of this subchapter, it shall not be an unlawful employment practice for an employer to apply different standards of compensation, or different terms, conditions, or privileges of employment pursuant to a bona fide seniority * * * system, * * * provided that such differences are not the result of an intention to discriminate because of race * * * or national origin * * *.

It argues that the seniority system in this case is "bona fide" within the meaning of § 703(h) when judged in light of its history, intent, application, and all of the circumstances under which it was created and is maintained. More specifically, the union claims that the central purpose of § 703(h) is to ensure that mere perpetuation of *pre-Act* discrimination is not unlawful under Title VII. And, whether or not § 703(h) immunizes the perpetuation of *post-Act* discrimination, the union claims that the seniority system in this case has no such effect. Its position in this Court, as has been its position throughout this litigation, is that the seniority system presents no hurdle to post-Act discriminatees who seek retroactive seniority to the date they would have become line drivers but for the company's discrimination. Indeed, the union asserts that under its collective-bargaining agreements the union will itself take up the cause of the post-Act victim and attempt, through grievance procedures, to gain for him full "make whole" relief, including appropriate seniority.

The Government responds that a seniority system that perpetuates the effects of prior discrimination—pre- or post-Act—can never be "bona fide" under § 703(h); at a minimum Title VII prohibits those applications of a seniority system that perpetuate the effects on incumbent employees of prior discriminatory job assignments.

The issues thus joined are open ones in this Court.[28] We considered § 703(h) in Franks v. Bowman Transportation Co., 424 U.S. 747, 96

---

28. Concededly, the view that § 703(h) does not immunize seniority systems that perpetuate the effects of prior discrimination has much support. It was apparently first adopted in Quarles v. Philip Morris, Inc., 279 F.Supp. 505 (ED Va.). The court there held that "a departmental seniority system *that has its genesis in racial discrimination* is not a *bona fide* seniority system." Id., at 517 (first emphasis added). The *Quarles* view has since enjoyed whole-sale adoption in the Courts of Appeals. See, e.g., Local 189, United Paperworkers v. United States, 416 F.2d 980, 987–988 (CA5); United States v. Sheet Metal Workers Local 36, 416 F.2d 123, 133–134, n. 20 (CA8); United States v. Bethlehem Steel Corp., 446 F.2d 652, 658–659 (CA2); United States v. Chesapeake & Ohio R. Co., 471 F.2d 582, 587–588 (CA4). Insofar as the result in *Quarles* and in the cases that followed it depended upon findings that the seniority systems were themselves "racially discriminatory" or had their "genesis in racial discrimination," 279 F.Supp., at 517, the decisions can be viewed as resting upon the proposition that a seniority system that perpetuates the effects of pre-Act

S.Ct. 1251, 47 L.Ed.2d 444, but there decided only that § 703(h) does not bar the award of retroactive seniority to job applicants who seek relief from an employer's post-Act hiring discrimination. We stated that "the thrust of [§ 703(h)] is directed toward defining what is and what is not an illegal discriminatory practice in instances in which the post-Act operation of a seniority system is challenged as perpetuating the effects of discrimination occurring prior to the effective date of the Act." 424 U.S., at 761, 96 S.Ct., at 1263. Beyond noting the general purpose of the statute, however, we did not undertake the task of statutory construction required in this case.

(1)

Because the company discriminated both before and after the enactment of Title VII, the seniority system is said to have operated to perpetuate the effects of both pre- and post-Act discrimination. Post-Act discriminatees, however, may obtain full "make whole" relief, including retroactive seniority under Franks v. Bowman, supra, without attacking the legality of the seniority system as applied to them. *Franks* made clear and the union acknowledges that retroactive seniority may be awarded as relief from an employer's discriminatory hiring and assignment policies even if the seniority system agreement itself makes no provision for such relief.[29] 424 U.S., at 778–779, 96 S.Ct., at 1271. Here the Government has proved that the company engaged in a post-Act pattern of discriminatory hiring, assignment, transfer and promotion policies. Any Negro or Spanish-surnamed American injured by those policies may receive all appropriate relief as a direct remedy for this discrimination.[30]

discrimination cannot be bona fide if an intent to discriminate entered into its very adoption.

29. Article 38 of the National Master Freight Agreement between T.I.M.E.–D.C. and the International Brotherhood of Teamsters in effect as of the date of the systemwide lawsuit provided:

"The Employer and the Union agree not to discriminate against any individual with respect to his hiring, compensation, terms or conditions of employment because of such individual's race, color, religion, sex, or national origin, nor will they limit, segregate or classify employees in any way to deprive any individual employee of employment opportunities because of his race, color, religion, sex, or national origin."

Any discrimination by the company would apparently be a grievable breach of this provision of the contract.

30. The legality of the seniority system insofar as it perpetuates post-Act discrimi-

nation nonetheless remains at issue in this case, in light of the injunction entered against the union. See supra, at 1852. Our decision today in United Air Lines v. Evans, 431 U.S. 553, 97 S.Ct. 1885, 51 L.Ed. 2d 571, is largely dispositive of this issue. *Evans* holds that the operation of a seniority system is not unlawful under Title VII even though it perpetuates post-Act discrimination that has not been the subject of a timely charge by the discriminatee. Here, of course, the Government has sued to remedy the post-Act discrimination directly, and there is no claim that any relief would be time-barred. But this is simply an additional reason not to hold the seniority system unlawful, since such a holding would in no way enlarge the relief to be awarded. See Franks v. Bowman, 424 U.S., at 778–779, 96 S.Ct. at 1271. Section 703(h) on its face immunizes all bona fide seniority systems, and does not distinguish between the perpetuation of pre- and post-Act discrimination.

(2)

What remains for review is the judgment that the seniority system unlawfully perpetuated the effects of *pre-Act* discrimination. We must decide, in short, whether § 703(h) validates otherwise bona fide seniority systems that afford no constructive seniority to victims discriminated against prior to the effective date of Title VII, and it is to that issue that we now turn.

The primary purpose of Title VII was "to assure equality of employment opportunities and to eliminate those discriminatory practices and devices which have fostered racially stratified job environments to the disadvantage of minority citizens. McDonnell Douglas Corp. v. Green, supra, 411 U.S., at 800, 93 S.Ct., at 1823.[31] See also Albemarle Paper Co. v. Moody, supra, 422 U.S., at 417–418, 95 S.Ct., at 2371–2372; Alexander v. Gardner-Denver Co., 415 U.S. 36, 44, 94 S.Ct. 1011, 1017, 39 L.Ed.2d 147. Griggs v. Duke Power Co., supra, 401 U.S., at 429–431, 91 S.Ct., at 852–853. To achieve this purpose, Congress "proscribe[d] not only overt discrimination but also practices that are fair in form, but discriminatory in operation." *Griggs*, 401 U.S., at 431, 91 S.Ct., at 853. Thus, the Court has repeatedly held that a prima facie Title VII violation may be established by policies or practices that are neutral on their face and in intent but that nonetheless discriminate in effect against a particular group. General Electric Co. v. Gilbert, 429 U.S. 125, 137, 97 S.Ct. 401, 408, 50 L.Ed.2d 343; Washington v. Davis, 426 U.S. 229, 246–247, 96 S.Ct. 2040, 2050–2051, 48 L.Ed.2d 597; Albemarle Paper Co. v. Moody, supra, 422 U.S., at 422, 425, 95 S.Ct., at 2374, 2375; McDonnell Douglas Corp. v. Green, supra, 411 U.S., at 802 n. 14, 93 S.Ct., at 1824; Griggs v. Duke Power Co., supra.

One kind of practice "fair in form, but discriminatory in operation" is that which perpetuates the effects of prior discrimination.[32] As the Court held in *Griggs*, supra: "Under the Act, practices, procedures, or tests neutral on their face, and even neutral in terms of intent, cannot be maintained if they operate to 'freeze' the status quo of prior discriminatory employment practices." 401 U.S., at 430, 91 S.Ct., at 853.

---

31. We also noted in *McDonnell Douglas* that:

"There are societal as well as personal interests on both sides of the [employer-employee] equation. The broad, overriding interest, shared by employer, employee, and consumer, is efficient and trustworthy workmanship assured through fair and racially neutral employment and personnel decisions. In the implementation of such decisions, it is abundantly clear that Title VII tolerates no racial discrimination, subtle or otherwise." 411 U.S., at 801, 93 S.Ct., at 1823.

32. Local 53 Asbestos Workers v. Vogler, 407 F.2d 1047 (CA5), provides an apt illustration. There a union had a policy of excluding persons not related to present members by blood or marriage. When in 1966 suit was brought to challenge this policy, all of the union's members were white, largely as a result of pre-Act, intentional racial discrimination. The court observed: "While the nepotism requirement is applicable to black and white alike and is not on its face discriminatory, in a completely white union the present effect of its continued application is to forever deny to negroes and Mexican-Americans any real opportunity for membership." 407 F.2d, at 1054.

* * *

Were it not for § 703(h), the seniority system in this case would seem to fall under the *Griggs* rationale. The heart of the system is its allocation of the choicest jobs, the greatest protection against layoffs, and other advantages to those employees who have been line drivers for the longest time. Where, because of the employer's prior intentional discrimination, the line drivers with the longest tenure are without exception white, the advantages of the seniority system flow disproportionately to them and away from Negro and Spanish-surnamed employees who might by now have enjoyed those advantages had not the employer discriminated before the passage of the Act. This disproportionate distribution of advantages does in a very real sense "operate to 'freeze' the status quo of prior discriminatory employment practices." Ibid. But both the literal terms of § 703(h) and the legislative history of Title VII demonstrate that Congress considered this very effect of many seniority systems extended a measure of immunity to them.

* * *

In sum, the unmistakable purpose of § 703(h) was to make clear that the routine application of a bona fide seniority system would not be unlawful under Title VII. As the legislative history shows, this was the intended result even where the employer's pre-Act discrimination resulted in whites having greater existing seniority rights than Negroes. Although a seniority system inevitably tends to perpetuate the effects of pre-Act discrimination in such cases, the congressional judgment was that Title VII should not outlaw the use of existing seniority lists and thereby destroy or water down the vested seniority rights of employees simply because their employer had engaged in discrimination prior to the passage of the Act.

To be sure, § 703(h) does not immunize all seniority systems. It refers only to "bona fide" systems, and a proviso requires that any differences in treatment not be "the result of an intention to discriminate because of race * * * or national origin * * *." But our reading of the legislative history compels us to reject the Government's broad argument that no seniority system that tends to perpetuate pre-Act discrimination can be "bona fide." To accept the argument would require us to hold that a seniority system becomes illegal simply because it allows the full exercise of the pre-Act seniority rights of employees of a company that discriminated before Title VII was enacted. It would place an affirmative obligation on the parties to the seniority agreement to subordinate those rights in favor of the claims of pre-Act discriminatees without seniority. The consequence would be a perversion of the congressional purpose. We cannot accept the invitation to disembowel § 703(h) by reading the words "bona fide" as the Government would have us do.[38] Accordingly, we hold that an other-

38. For the same reason, we reject the contention that the proviso in § 703(h), which bars differences in treatment resulting from "an intention to discriminate," applies to any application of a seniority system that may perpetuate past discrimination. In this regard the language of the Justice Department memorandum intro-

wise neutral, legitimate seniority system does not become unlawful under Title VII simply because it may perpetuate pre-Act discrimination. Congress did not intend to make it illegal for employees with vested seniority rights to continue to exercise those rights, even at the expense of pre-Act discriminatees.[39]

That conclusion is inescapable even in a case, such as this one, where the pre-Act discriminatees are incumbent employees who accumulated seniority in other bargaining units. Although there seems to be no explicit reference in the legislative history to pre-Act discriminatees already employed in less desirable jobs, there can be no rational basis for distinguishing their claims from those of persons initially denied *any* job but hired later with less seniority than they might have had in the absence of pre-Act discrimination.[40] We rejected any such distinction in *Franks*, finding that it had "no support anywhere in Title VII or its legislative history," 424 U.S., at 768, 96 S.Ct., at 1266. As discussed above, Congress in 1964 made clear that a seniority system is not unlawful because it honors employees' existing rights, even where the employer has engaged in pre-Act discriminatory hiring or promotion practices. It would be as contrary to that mandate to forbid the exercise of seniority rights with respect to discriminatees who held inferior jobs as with respect to later-hired minority employees

duced at the legislative hearings, see supra, at 1862, is especially pertinent: "It is perfectly clear that when a worker is laid off or denied a chance for promotion because he is 'low man on the totem pole' he is not being discriminated against because of his race * * *. Any differences in treatment based on established seniority rights would not be based on race and would not be forbidden by the title." 110 Cong.Rec. 7207 (1964).

39. The legislative history of the 1972 amendments to Title VII, summarized and discussed in *Franks*, supra, 424 U.S., at 764–765, n. 21, 96 S.Ct., at 1264; *id.,* at 796–797, n. 18, 96 S.Ct., at 1263 (opinion of Powell, J.), in no way points to a different result. As the discussion in *Franks* indicates, that history is itself susceptible of different readings. The few broad references to perpetuation of pre-Act discrimination or "*de facto* segregated job ladders," see e.g., S.Rep. No. 92–415, pp. 5, 9 (1971); H.R.Rep. No. 92–238, pp. 8, 17 (1971), U.S. Code Cong. & Admin.News 1972, p. 2137, did not address the specific issue presented by this case. And the assumption of the authors of the Conference Report that "the present case law as developed by the courts would continue to govern the applicability and construction of Title VII," see *Franks*, supra, at 765 n. 21, 96 S.Ct., at 1264, of course does not foreclose our consideration of that issue. More importantly, the section of Title VII that we construe here,

§ 703(h), was enacted in 1964, not 1972. The views of members of a later Congress, concerning different sections of Title VII, enacted after this litigation was commenced, are entitled to little if any weight. It is the intent of the Congress that enacted § 703(h) in 1964, unmistakable in this case, that controls.

40. That Title VII did not proscribe the denial of fictional seniority to pre-Act discriminatees who got *no* job was recognized even in Quarles v. Philip Morris, Inc., 279 F.Supp. 505 (ED Va.), and its progeny. *Quarles* stressed the fact that the references in the legislative history were to employment seniority rather than departmental seniority. 279 F.Supp., at 516. In Local 189, United Paperworkers v. United States, 416 F.2d 980 (CA5), another leading case in this area, the court observed:

"No doubt, Congress, to prevent 'reverse discrimination' meant to protect certain seniority rights that could not have existed but for previous racial discrimination. For example a Negro who had been rejected by an employer on racial grounds before passage of the Act could not, after being hired, claim to outrank whites who had been hired before him but after his original rejection, even though the Negro might have had senior status but for the past discrimination." 416 F.2d, at 994.

who previously were denied any job. If anything, the latter group is the more disadvantaged. As in *Franks*, " '[i]t would indeed be surprising if Congress gave a remedy for the one [group] which it denied for the other.' " Id., quoting Phelps Dodge Corp. v. NLRB, 313 U.S. 177, 187, 61 S.Ct. 845, 849, 85 L.Ed. 1271.[41]

(3)

The seniority system in this case is entirely bona fide. It applies equally to all races and ethnic groups. To the extent that it "locks" employees into nonline-driver jobs, it does so for all. The city drivers and servicemen who are discouraged from transferring to line-driver jobs are not all Negroes or Spanish-surnamed Americans; to the contrary, the overwhelming majority are white. The placing of line drivers in a separate bargaining unit from other employees is rational in accord with the industry practice, and consistent with NLRB precedents.[42] It is conceded that the seniority system did not have its genesis in racial discrimination, and that it was negotiated and has been maintained free from any illegal purpose. In these circumstances, the single fact that the system extends no retroactive seniority to pre-Act discriminatees does not make it unlawful.

Because the seniority system was protected by § 703(h), the union's conduct in agreeing to and maintaining the system did not violate Title VII. On remand, the District Court's injunction against the union must be vacated.[43]

III

Our conclusion that the seniority system does not violate Title VII will necessarily affect the remedy granted to individual employees on remand of this litigation to the District Court. Those employees who suffered only pre-Act discrimination are not entitled to relief, and no person may be given retroactive seniority to a date earlier than the effective date of the Act. Several other questions relating to the

41. In addition, there is no reason to suppose that Congress intended in 1964 to extend less protection to legitimate departmental seniority systems than to plant-wide seniority systems. Then as now, seniority was measured in a number of ways, including length of time with the employer, in a particular plant, in a department, in a job, or in a line of progression. See Aaron, Reflections on the Legal Nature and Enforceability of Seniority Rights, 75 Harv.L.Rev. 1532, 1534 (1962); Cooper & Sobel, Seniority and Testing under Fair Employment Laws: A General Approach to Objective Criteria of Hiring and Promotion, 82 Harv.L.Rev. 1598, 1602 (1969). The legislative history contains no suggestion that any one system was preferred.

42. See Georgia Highway Express, 150 N.L.R.B. 1649, 1651: "The Board has long held that local drivers and over-the-road drivers constitute separate appropriate units where they are shown to be clearly defined, homogeneous, and functionally distinct groups with separate interests which can effectively be represented separately for bargaining purposes. * * * In view of the different duties and functions, separate supervision, and different bases of payment, it is clear that the over-the-road drivers have divergent interests from those of the employees in the [city operations] unit * * * and should not be included in that unit."

43. The union will properly remain in this litigation as a defendant so that full relief may be awarded the victims of the employer's post-Act discrimination. Fed. Rule Civ.Proc. 19(a). See EEOC v. MacMillan Bloedel Containers, Inc., 503 F.2d 1086, 1095 (CA6).

appropriate measure of individual relief remain, however, for our consideration.

[The Court's discussion of the relief to be afforded victims of post act discrimination and the concurring and dissenting opinions of Justices Marshall and Brennan are omitted.]

UNITED AIRLINES, INC. v. EVANS
431 U.S. 553, 97 S.Ct. 1885, 52 L.Ed.2d 571 (1977).

Ms. Evans was employed by United Airlines as a flight attendant from November 1966 to February 1968. During this period of employment, United maintained a policy of refusing to allow its female flight attendants to be married. When she married in 1968, she was forced to resign. The policy was subsequently declared in violation of Title VII in Sprogis v. United Air Lines, Inc., 444 F.2d 1194 (7th Cir.1971), cert. denied 404 U.S. 991, 92 S.Ct. 536, 30 L.Ed.2d 543 (1971). However Ms. Evans was not a party to that case and did not file a charge with the EEOC within 90 days of her separation in 1968. Consequently, a claim based on her discriminatory forced resignation was time barred.

In November of 1968, United entered into a new collective bargaining agreement which ended the preexisting no marriage rule and provided for reinstatement of certain employees who had been terminated pursuant to that rule. Ms. Evans was not covered by the agreement and after repeated effort was rehired as a new employee in 1972. For seniority purposes she was treated as though she had no prior service.

She filed the timely charge with EEOC in 1973 alleging a continued discrimination against her on the basis of sex and eventually brought an action in the district court. The district court concluded that her failure to file a charge within 90 days of her separation caused her claim to be time barred and foreclosed any relief under Title VII. A divided panel of the Court of Appeals initially affirmed and then after the Supreme Court's decision in Franks v. Bowman Transportation Company, 424 U.S. 747, 96 S.Ct. 1251, 47 L.Ed.2d 444 (1976), the court granted the petition for rehearing and unanimously reversed. The Supreme Court granted cert. and held that the complaint was properly dismissed.

The Court held that United did not commit a present, continuing violation of Title VII by refusing to credit Ms. Evans, after rehiring her in 1972, with her pre-1972 seniority. Despite the fact that each time seniority credit was used to affect her current employment she was disadvantaged by loss of time occasioned by her forced resignation under a policy subsequently declared illegal under Title VII, the Court concluded that this did not constitute a continuing violation. The Court ruled that absent any allegation that United's seniority system, which was neutral in its operation, discriminated against former female employees or victims of past discrimination plaintiff could not make out a case based on the operation of the neutral seniority system. The court held that Section 703(h) of Title VII barred Ms. Evans claim absent any attack on the bona fides of the seniority system or any charge that the system was intentionally designed to discriminate because of race, color, religion, sex, or national origin. The court held that "The statute does not foreclose attacks on the current operation of seniority systems which are subject to challenge as discriminatory. But such a challenge to a neutral system may not be predicated on the mere fact that a past event which has no present legal significance has affected the calculation of seniority credit, even if the past event might at one time have justified a valid claim against the employer."

Justices Marshall and Brennan dissented concluding, among other things, that treating the employee as a new employee even though she was wrongfully forced to resign was a continuing violation.

4. PHASE III—SENIORITY UNDER TITLE VII AFTER TEAM-STERS

Justice Marshall, with whom Justice Brennan joined, concurred in part and dissented, bitterly, in part from the *Teamsters* decision. The dissenters pointed out that without a single dissent, six courts of appeals in over thirty cases had taken the opposite view of § 703(h) regarding seniority systems that perpetuated the effects of prior discrimination and two other courts of appeals had indicated their agreement, also without dissent. (431 U.S. at 378, 379, 97 S.Ct. at 1876, 1877.) Further, the overwhelming weight of scholarly opinion was in accord with this view. (431 U.S. at 380 n. 5, 97 S.Ct. at 1877, n. 5.) Additionally, the dissenters asserted that when Congress enacted the Equal Employment Opportunity Act of 1972 amending Title VII, it was made clear that it approved of the lower court decisions invalidating seniority systems that perpetuated discrimination. They contended, as well, that both the Senate and the House reports expressly approved the perpetuation principle as applied to seniority systems. (431 U.S. at 391–393, 97 S.Ct. at 1883–1884.)

It seems clear that the Supreme Court in *Teamsters* rejected the present effects of past discrimination theory where those consequences are telescoped into the future by a bona fide seniority system. However, the case focused attention for future litigation on the issue of determining the bona fides of the seniority system. Thus, the focus of post-*Teamsters* seniority litigation is directed to what may be termed the "bona fide seniority system exception" which would make seniority systems vulnerable if it can be established that they were designed, maintained or manipulated as a result of an intention to discriminate. Of course, if it can be established that the policy or practice which is under attack is not a seniority system, then it can be contended that the rule established in *Teamsters* is not applicable. The question of what constitutes a seniority system reached the court in California Brewers Association v. Bryant.

California Brewers Association v. Bryant, 444 U.S. 598, 100 S.Ct. 814, 63 L.Ed.2d 55 (1980).

Justice Stewart begins the opinion for the Court by setting forth the rule of *Duke* that Title VII makes unlawful practices, procedures, or tests that operate to freeze the status quo of prior discriminatory employment practices. Griggs v. Duke Power Company, 401 U.S. 424, 430, 91 S.Ct. 849, 853, 28 L.Ed.2d 158 (1971). To this he adds the interpretation of the Supreme Court of Section 703(h) which emerged in International Brotherhood of Teamsters v. United States, 431 U.S. 324, 352, 97 S.Ct. 1843, 1863, 52 L.Ed.2d 396 (1977) that the unmistakable purpose of Section 703(h) was to make clear that the routine application of a bona fide seniority system would not be unlawful under Title VII even where the employer's pre-Act discrimination resulted in whites having greater existing seniority rights than blacks. The *Bryant* case concerned the application of Section 703(h) to a particular clause in a California Brewery Industry collective bargaining agreement that accorded greater benefit to "permanent" than to "temporary" employees. The clause in question provides that a temporary employee must work at least 45 weeks in a single calendar year before he can become a permanent employee. Permanent status and time and grade determined the order in which one worked and who would be laid off first. The Ninth Circuit concluded that the provision had an adverse impact on black employees and kept them from becoming permanent. It found that the probationary system did not allow employment rights to increase as length of service increased with the effect that fewer senior employees could acquire greater rights. As employee rights did not automatically accrue with time, the court concluded that the 45 week requirement was not a part of a seniority system. It stated: "The 45 week rule is simply a classification device to determine who enters the permanent employee seniority line and this function does not make the rule a part of the seniority system. Otherwise, any hiring policy, (e.g., an academic degree requirement) or classification device (e.g., merit promotion) would become a part of a seniority system merely because it affects who enters the seniority line."

The Supreme Court disagreed. It asserted: "Title VII does not define the term 'seniority system', and no comprehensive definition of the phrase emerges from the legislative history of Section 703(h). Moreover, our cases have not purported to delineate the contours of its meaning. It is appropriate, therefore, to begin with the commonly accepted notions about 'seniority' in industrial relations, and to consider those concepts in the context of Title VII and this country's labor policy." * * *

" * * * Congress passed the Civil Rights Act of 1964 against the backdrop of this Nation's longstanding labor policy of leaving to the chosen representatives of employers and employees the freedom through collective bargaining to establish conditions of employment applicable to a particular business or industrial environment. See generally Steelworkers v. Weber, 443 U.S. 193, 99 S.Ct. 2721, 61 L.Ed.2d 480. It does not behoove a court to second-guess either that process or its products. Porter Co. v. NLRB, 397 U.S. 99, 90 S.Ct. 821, 25 L.Ed.2d 146. Seniority systems, reflecting as they do, not only the give and take of free collective bargaining, but also the specific characteristics of a particular business or industry, inevitably come in all sizes and shapes. See Ford Motor Co. v. Huffman, 345 U.S. 330, 73 S.Ct. 681, 97 L.Ed. 1048; Aeronautical Lodge v. Campbell, 337 U.S. 521, 69 S.Ct. 1287, 93 L.Ed. 1513. As we made clear in the *Teamsters* case, seniority may be "measured in a number of ways" and the legislative history of § 703(h) does not suggest that it was enacted to prefer any particular variety of seniority system over any other. 431 U.S., at 355, n. 41, 97 S.Ct., at 1865.

What has been said does not mean that § 703(h) is to be given a scope that risks swallowing up Title VII's otherwise broad prohibition of "practices, procedures, or tests" that disproportionately affect members of those groups that the Act protects. Significant freedom must be afforded employers and unions to create differing seniority systems. But that freedom must not be allowed to sweep within the ambit of § 703(h) employment rules that depart fundamentally from commonly accepted notions concerning the acceptable contours of a seniority system, simply because those rules are dubbed "seniority" provisions or have some nexus to an arrangement that concededly operates on the basis of seniority. There can be no doubt, for instance, that a threshold requirement for entering a seniority track that took the form of an educational prerequisite would not be part of a "seniority system" within the intendment of § 703(h). * * *

For the reasons stated, the judgment before us is vacated, and the case is remanded to the Court of Appeals for the Ninth Circuit for further proceedings consistent with this opinion.

It is so ordered.

MR. JUSTICE POWELL and MR. JUSTICE STEVENS took no part in the consideration or decision of this case.

MR. JUSTICE MARSHALL, with whom MR. JUSTICE BRENNAN and MR. JUSTICE BLACKMUN join, dissenting.

Notes

1. On the issue of bona fide merit systems see Guardians Association v. Civil Service Commission, 633 F.2d 232 (2d Cir.1980). That case was reviewed by the Supreme Court in Guardians Association v. Civil Service Commission of the City of New York, 463 U.S. 582, 103 S.Ct. 3221, 77 L.Ed. 2d 866 (1983). However the Supreme Court decision does not address the issue of bona fide merit system but rather is limited to whether private plaintiffs in the case needed to prove discriminatory intent to establish a violation of Title VI of the Civil Rights Act of 1964 and the regulations promulgated thereunder.

2. For a discussion of a multiplicity of seniority systems and problems see Weiner, "Seniority Systems Under *Teamsters* and *Bryant*," Vol. 6 Employee Relations Law Journal pp. 437, 457; see also Hillman, "Seniority Systems and Allocation of the Burden of Proving Bona Fides," 54 St. John's Law Review 706 (1980); Note, "The New Definition of Seniority System Violations Under Title VII: He Who Seeks Equity * * *," 56 Texas Law Review 301 (1975).

AMERICAN TOBACCO CO. v. PATTERSON

The Supreme Court of the United States, 1982.
456 U.S. 63, 102 S.Ct. 1534, 71 L.Ed.2d 748.

JUSTICE WHITE delivered the opinion of the Court.

Under Griggs v. Duke Power Co., 401 U.S. 424, 91 S.Ct. 849, 28 L.Ed.2d 158 (1971), a prima facie violation of Title VII of the Civil Rights Act of 1964, 78 Stat. 253, as amended, 42 U.S.C. § 2000e et seq. (1976 ed. and Supp.IV), "may be established by policies or practices that are neutral on their face and in intent but that nonetheless discriminate in effect against a particular group." Teamsters v. United States, 431 U.S. 324, 349, 97 S.Ct. 1843, 1861, 52 L.Ed.2d 396 (1977). A seniority system "would seem to fall under the *Griggs* rationale" if it were not for § 703(h) of the Civil Rights Act. * * * Under § 703(h), the fact that a seniority system has a discriminatory impact is not alone sufficient to invalidate the system; actual intent to discriminate must be proved. The Court of Appeals in this case, however, held that § 703(h) does not apply to seniority systems adopted after the effective date of the Civil Rights Act. We granted the petition for certiorari to address the validity of this construction of the section. 452 U.S. 937, 101 S.Ct. 3078, 69 L.Ed.2d 951 (1982).

* * *

On its face § 703(h) makes no distinction between pre- and post-Act seniority systems, just as it does not distinguish between pre- and post-Act merit systems or pre- and post-Act ability tests. The section does not take the form of a saving clause or a grandfather clause designed to exclude existing practices from the operation of a new rule. Other sections of Title VII enacted by the same Congress contain grandfather clauses, see § 701(b), 78 Stat. 253, as amended, 42 U.S.C. § 2000e–(b), a difference which increases our reluctance to transform a provision that we have previously described as "defining what is and what is not an illegal discriminatory practice * * *," Franks v. Bowman Transportation Co., 424 U.S. 747, 761, 96 S.Ct. 1251, 1262, 47 L.Ed.2d 444 (1976), from a definitional clause into a grandfather clause.

* * *

III

Although the plain language of § 703(h) makes no distinction between pre-Act and post-Act seniority systems, the court below found support for its distinction between the two in the legislative history. Such an interpretation misreads the legislative history.

We have not been informed of and have not found a single statement anywhere in the legislative history saying that § 703(h) does not protect seniority systems adopted or modified after the effective date of Title VII. Nor does the legislative history reveal that Congress intended to distinguish between adoption and application of a bona fide seniority system.

* * *

IV

Our prior decisions have emphasized that "seniority systems are afforded special treatment under Title VII itself," Trans World Airlines, Inc. v. Hardison, 432 U.S. 63, 81, 97 S.Ct. 2264, 2275, 53 L.Ed.2d 113 (1977), and have refused to narrow § 703(h) by reading into it limitations not contained in the statutory language. In Teamsters v. United States, supra, we held that § 703(h) exempts from Title VII the disparate impact of a bona fide seniority system even if the differential treatment is the result of pre-Act racially discriminatory employment practices. Similarly, by holding that "[a] discriminatory act which is not made the basis for a timely charge is the legal equivalent of a discriminatory act which occurred before the statute was passed." United Air Lines, Inc. v. Evans, 431 U.S. 553, 558, 97 S.Ct. 1885, 1889, 52 L.Ed.2d 571 (1977), the Court interpreted § 703(h) to immunize seniority systems which perpetuate post-Act discrimination. Thus taken together, *Teamsters* and *Evans* stand for the proposition stated in *Teamsters* that "[s]ection 703(h) on its face immunizes *all* bona fide seniority systems, and does not distinguish between the perpetuation of pre- and post-Act" discriminatory impact. *Teamsters,* 431 U.S., at 348, n. 30, 97 S.Ct., at 1861, n. 30 (emphasis added).[16] Section 703(h) makes no distinction between seniority systems adopted before its effective date and those adopted after its effective date. Consistent with our prior decisions, we decline respondents' invitation to read such a distinction into the statute.

Seniority provisions are of "overriding importance" in collective bargaining, Humphrey v. Moore, 375 U.S. 335, 346, 84 S.Ct. 363, 370, 11 L.Ed.2d 370 (1964), and they "are universally included in these con-

---

16. Nowhere in Teamsters v. United States does the Court indicate when the seniority system at issue there was adopted, and examination of the record illustrates the difficulty of fixing an adoption date. Article V of the National Motor Freight Agreement of 1964 contains a seniority provision subject to modification by area agreements and local union riders. See Brief for Petitioner Teamsters, O.T. 1976, No. 75–636, pp. 24–25. However, National Motor Freight Agreements are of 3-year duration, and the 1970 Agreement was in effect when the complaint was filed. If a seniority system ceases to exist when the collective-bargaining agreement which creates it lapses, then the seniority system in *Teamsters* was adopted post-Title VII. On the other hand, if in practice the seniority system was continuously in effect from 1964, it can be argued that its adoption predates Title VII. However, *Teamsters* places no importance on the date the seniority system was adopted, and we follow *Teamsters* by refusing to distinguish among seniority systems based on date of adoption. Given the difficulty of determining when one seniority system ends and another begins and the lack of legislative guidance, we think it highly unlikely Congress intended for courts to distinguish between pre-Act and post-Act seniority systems.

tracts." Trans World Airlines, Inc. v. Hardison, supra, 432 U.S. at 79, 97 S.Ct., at 2274. See also Aaron, Reflections on the Legal Nature and Enforceability of Seniority Rights, 75 Harv.L.Rev. 1532, 1534 (1962). The collective-bargaining process "lies at the core of our national labor policy. * * *" Trans World Airlines, Inc. v. Hardison, supra, 432 U.S., at 79, 97 S.Ct. at 2274. See, e.g., 29 U.S.C. § 151. Congress was well aware in 1964 that the overall purpose of Title VII, to eliminate discrimination in employment, inevitably would, on occasion, conflict with the policy favoring minimal supervision by courts and other governmental agencies over the substantive terms of collective-bargaining agreements. California Brewers Assn. v. Bryant, 444 U.S. 598, 608, 100 S.Ct. 814, 820, 63 L.Ed.2d 55 (1980). Section 703(h) represents the balance Congress struck between the two policies, and it is not this Court's function to upset that balance.

Because a construction of § 703(h) limiting its application to seniority systems in place prior to the effective date of the statute would be contrary to its plain language, inconsistent with our prior cases, and would run counter to the national labor policy, we vacate the judgment below and remand for further proceedings consistent with this opinion.

So ordered.

JUSTICE BRENNAN, with whom JUSTICE MARSHALL and JUSTICE BLACK-MUN join, dissenting.

PULLMAN–STANDARD, A DIVISION OF PULLMAN, INC. v. SWINT

The Supreme Court of the United States, 1982.
456 U.S. 273, 102 S.Ct. 1781, 72 L.Ed.2d 66.

JUSTICE WHITE delivered the opinion of the Court.

Respondents were black employees at the Bessemer, Ala., plant of petitioner Pullman-Standard (the Company), a manufacturer of railway freight cars and parts. They brought suit against the Company and the union petitioners—the United Steelworkers of America, AFL–CIO–CLC, and its Local 1466 (collectively USW)—alleging violations of Title VII of the Civil Rights Act of 1964, as amended, 78 Stat. 253, 42 U.S.C. § 2000e et seq. (1976 ed. and Supp.IV), and 42 U.S.C. § 1981.[1] As they come here, these cases involve only the validity, under Title VII, of a seniority system maintained by the Company and USW. The District Court found "that the differences in terms, conditions or privileges of employment resulting [from the seniority system] are 'not the result of an intention to discriminate' because of race or color," App. to Pet. for Cert. in No. 80–1190, p. A–147 (hereinafter App.), and held, therefore,

---

1. In their original complaint, besides challenging the seniority system discussed in this opinion, plaintiffs also alleged discrimination in job assignments and promotions and the failure to post publicly a list of changes in assignments. These were all brought as "class" issues. Two charges of individual discrimination were also brought. The Court of Appeals held that the Company had violated Title VII in making job assignments and in selecting foremen. In granting certiorari, we declined to review those aspects of the decision.

that the system satisfied the requirements of § 703(h) of the Act. The Court of Appeals for the Fifth Circuit reversed:

> Because we find that the differences in the terms, conditions and standards of employment for black workers and white workers at Pullman-Standard resulted from an intent to discriminate because of race, we hold that the system is not legally valid under section 703(h) of Title VII, 42 U.S.C. 2000e–2(h). 624 F.2d 525, 533–534 (1980).

We granted the petitions for certiorari filed by USW and by the Company, 451 U.S. 906, 101 S.Ct. 1972, 68 L.Ed.2d 293 (1981), limited to the first question presented in each petition: whether a court of appeals is bound by the "clearly erroneous" rule of Federal Rule of Civil Procedure 52(a) in reviewing a district court's findings of fact, arrived at after a lengthy trial, as to the motivation of the parties who negotiated a seniority system; and whether the court below applied wrong legal criteria in determining the bona fides of the seniority system. We conclude that the Court of Appeals erred in the course of its review and accordingly reverse its judgment and remand for further proceedings.

* * *

Section 703(h), 78 Stat. 257, as set forth in 42 U.S.C. § 2000e–2(h), provides in pertinent part:

> Notwithstanding any other provision of this subchapter, it shall not be an unlawful employment practice for an employer to apply different standards of compensation, or different terms, conditions, or privileges of employment pursuant to a bona fide seniority * * * system * * * provided that such differences are not the result of an intention to discriminate because of race.

Under this section, a showing of disparate impact is insufficient to invalidate a seniority system, even though the result may be to perpetuate pre-Act discrimination. In Trans World Airlines, Inc. v. Hardison, 432 U.S. 63, 82, 97 S.Ct. 2264, 2275, 53 L.Ed.2d 113 (1977), we summarized the effect of § 703(h) as follows: "[A]bsent a discriminatory purpose, the operation of a seniority system cannot be an unlawful employment practice even if the system has some discriminatory consequences." Thus, any challenge to a seniority system under Title VII will require a trial on the issue of discriminatory intent: Was the system adopted because of its racially discriminatory impact?

This is precisely what happened in these cases. Following our decision in *Teamsters*, the District Court held a new trial on the limited question of whether the seniority system was "instituted or maintained contrary to Section 703(h) of the new Civil Rights Act of 1964." App. A–125. That court concluded, as we noted above and will discuss below, that the system was adopted and maintained for purposes wholly independent of any discriminatory intent. The Court of Appeals for the Fifth Circuit reversed.

II

Petitioners submit that the Court of Appeals failed to comply with the command of Rule 52(a) that the findings of fact of a district court may not be set aside unless clearly erroneous.

* * *

The District Court approached the question of discriminatory intent in the manner suggested by the Fifth Circuit in James v. Stockham Valves & Fittings Co., 559 F.2d 310 (1977). There, the Court of Appeals stated that under *Teamsters* "the totality of the circumstances in the development and maintenance of the system is relevant to examining that issue." 559 F.2d, at 352. There were, in its view, however, four particular factors that a court should focus on.[8]

First, a court must determine whether the system "operates to discourage all employees equally from transferring between seniority units." Ibid. The District Court held that the system here "was facially neutral and * * * was applied equally to all races and ethnic groups."

* * *

Second, a court must examine the rationality of the departmental structure, upon which the seniority system relies, in light of the general industry practice. *James,* supra, at 352. The District Court found that linking seniority to "departmental age" was "the modal form of agreements generally, as well as with manufacturers of railroad equipment in particular."

* * *

Third, a court had to consider "whether the seniority system had its genesis in racial discrimination," *James,* supra, at 352, by which it meant the relationship between the system and other racially discriminatory practices. Although finding ample discrimination by the Company in its employment practices and some discriminatory practices by the union,[11] the District Court concluded that the seniority system was in no way related to the discriminatory practices:

---

8. The Fifth Circuit relied upon the following passage in *Teamsters,* 431 U.S., at 355–356, 97 S.Ct., at 1864–1865:

"The seniority system in this litigation is entirely bona fide. It applies equally to all races and ethnic groups. To the extent that it 'locks' employees into non-line-driver jobs, it does so for all. * * * The placing of line drivers in a separate bargaining unit from other employees is rational, in accord with the industry practice, and consistent with National Labor Relation Board precedents. It is conceded that that seniority system did not have its genesis in racial discrimination, and that it was negotiated and has been maintained free from any illegal purpose."

This passage was of course not meant to be an exhaustive list of all the factors that a district court might or should consider in making a finding of discriminatory intent.

11. With respect to USW, the District Court found that "[u]nion meetings were conducted with different sides of the hall for white and black members, and social functions of the union were also segregated." App. A–142. It also found, however, that "[w]hile possessing some of the trappings taken from an otherwise segregated society, the USW local was one of the few institutions in the area which did not function in fact to foster and maintain segregation; rather, it served a joint interest of white and black workers which had a

The seniority system * * * had its genesis * * * at a period when racial segregation was certainly being practiced; but this system was not itself the product of this bias. The system rather came about as a result of colorblind objectives of a union which—unlike most structures and institutions of the era—was not an arm of a segregated society. Nor did it foster the discrimination * * * which was being practiced by custom in the plant. App. A–144.

Finally, a court must consider "whether the system was negotiated and has been maintained free from any illegal purpose." *James*, supra, at 352. Stating that it had "carefully considered the detailed record of negotiation sessions and contracts which span a period of some thirty-five years," App. A–146, the court found that the system was untainted by any discriminatory purpose. Thus, although the District Court focused on particular factors in carrying out the analysis required by § 703(h), it also looked to the entire record and to the "totality of the system under attack." Id., at A–147.

The Court of Appeals addressed each of the four factors of the *James* test and reached the opposite conclusion.

* * *

In connection with its assertion that it was convinced that a mistake had been made, the Court of Appeals, in a footnote, referred to the clearly-erroneous standard of Rule 52(a). Id., at 533, n. 6.[14] It pointed out, however, that if findings "are made under an erroneous view of controlling legal principles, the clearly-erroneous rule does not apply, and the findings may not stand." Ibid. Finally, quoting from East v. Romine, Inc., 518 F.2d 332, 339 (CA5 1975), the Court of Appeals repeated the following view of its appellate function in Title VII cases where purposeful discrimination is at issue:

> 'Although discrimination *vel non* is essentially a question of fact it is, at the same time, the ultimate issue for resolution in this case, being expressly proscribed by 42 U.S.C.A. § 2000e–2(a). As such, a finding of discrimination or nondiscrimination is a finding of ultimate fact. [Cites omitted.] In reviewing the district court's findings, there-fore, we will proceed to make an independent determination of appellant's allegations of discrimination, though bound by findings of subsidiary fact which are themselves not clearly erroneous.' 624 F.2d, at 533, n. 6.

* * *

Rule 52(a) broadly requires that findings of fact not be set aside unless clearly erroneous. It does not make exceptions or purport to

higher priority than racial considerations." Id., at A–143.

14. In United States v. United States Gypsum Co., 333 U.S. 364, 395, 68 S.Ct. 525, 541, 92 L.Ed. 746 (1948), this Court characterized the clearly-erroneous standard as follows:

"A finding is 'clearly erroneous' when although there is evidence to support it, the reviewing court on the entire evidence is left with the definite and firm conviction that a mistake has been committed."

We note that the Court of Appeals quoted this passage at the conclusion of its analysis of the District Court opinion. Supra, at 1787.

exclude certain categories of factual findings from the obligation of a court of appeals to accept a district court's findings unless clearly erroneous. It does not divide facts into categories; in particular, it does not divide findings of fact into those that deal with "ultimate" and those that deal with "subsidiary" facts.

The Rule does not apply to conclusions of law. The Court of Appeals, therefore, was quite right in saying that if a district court's findings rest on an erroneous view of the law, they may be set aside on that basis. But here the District Court was not faulted for misunderstanding or applying an erroneous definition of intentional discrimination.[17] It was reversed for arriving at what the Court of Appeals thought was an erroneous finding as to whether the differential impact of the seniority system reflected an intent to discriminate on account of race. That question, as we see it, is a pure question of fact, subject to Rule 52(a)'s clearly-erroneous standard. It is not a question of law and not a mixed question of law and fact.

* * * Differentials among employees that result from a seniority system are not unlawful employment practices unless the product of an intent to discriminate. It would make no sense, therefore, to say that the intent to discriminate required by § 703(h) may be presumed from such an impact. As § 703(h) was construed in *Teamsters,* there must be a finding of actual intent to discriminate on racial grounds on the part of those who negotiated or maintained the system. That finding appears to us to be a pure question of fact.

This is not to say that discriminatory impact is not part of the evidence to be considered by the trial court in reaching a finding on whether there was such a discriminatory intent as a factual matter.[18] We do assert, however, that under § 703(h) discriminatory intent is a finding of fact to be made by the trial court; it is not a question of law and not a mixed question of law and fact of the kind that in some cases may allow an appellate court to review the facts to see if they satisfy some legal concept of discriminatory intent.[19] Discriminatory intent

17. As we noted above, the Court of Appeals did at certain points purport to correct what it viewed as legal errors on the part of the District Court. The presence of such legal errors may justify a remand by the Court of Appeals to the District Court for additional factfinding under the correct legal standard. Infra, at 1791–1792.

18. See, e.g., Furnco Construction Corp. v. Waters, 438 U.S. 567, 580, 98 S.Ct. 2943, 2951, 57 L.Ed.2d 957 (1978): "Proof that [an employer's] work force was racially balanced or, that it contained a disproportionately high percentage of minority employees is not wholly irrelevant on the issue of intent when that issue is yet to be decided."

19. We need not, therefore, address the much-mooted issue of the applicability of the Rule 52(a) standard to mixed questions of law and fact—i.e., questions in which the historical facts are admitted or established, the rule of law is undisputed, and the issue is whether the facts satisfy the statutory standard, or to put it another way, whether the rule of law as applied to the established facts is or is not violated. There is substantial authority in the Circuits on both sides of this question. Compare United States ex rel. Johnson v. Johnson, 531 F.2d 169, 174, n. 12 (CA3 1976); Stafos v. Jarvis, 477 F.2d 369, 372 (CA10 1973); and Johnson v. Salisbury, 448 F.2d 374, 377 (CA6 1971), with Rogers v. Bates, 431 F.2d 16, 18 (CA8 1970); and Pennsylvania Casualty Co. v. McCoy, 167 F.2d

here means actual motive; it is not a legal presumption to be drawn
from a factual showing of something less than actual motive. Thus, a
court of appeals may only reverse a district court's finding on discriminatory intent if it concludes that the finding is clearly erroneous under
Rule 52(a). Insofar as the Fifth Circuit assumed otherwise, it erred.

* * * It follows that when a district court's finding on such an
ultimate fact is set aside for an error of law, the court of appeals is not
relieved of the usual requirement of remanding for further proceedings
to the tribunal charged with the task of factfinding in the first instance.

Accordingly, the judgment of the Court of Appeals is reversed, and
the cases are remanded to that court for further proceedings consistent
with this opinion.

So ordered.

JUSTICE STEVENS, concurring in part.

Except to the extent that the Court's preliminary comments on the
burden of sustaining "any challenge to a seniority system under Title
VII," ante, at 1784, are inconsistent with the views I expressed separately in American Tobacco Co. v. Patterson, 456 U.S. 63, 86, 102 S.Ct.
1534, 1547, 71 L.Ed.2d 748, I join the Court's opinion.

JUSTICE MARSHALL, with whom JUSTICE BLACKMUN joins except as to
Part I, dissenting.

Notes

The dissenting opinion of Justices Marshall, with whom Justice
Blackman joined except as to part 1, asserts that the Supreme Court
implicitly acknowledges that proof of the four factors approved by the Fifth
Circuit in James v. Stockham Valves & Fittings Co., supra, satisfies the
requirements of *Teamsters*. The majority of the Court indicates that the
James factors are nothing more than a summary of the criteria examined
by the Supreme Court in International Brotherhood of Teamsters v. United
States, 431 U.S. 324, at 355–356, 97 S.Ct. 1843 at 1864–1865, 52 L.Ed.2d 396.
It should be noted that the Court indicates that the four factors were not
the only way to demonstrate the existence of discriminatory intent.

As could be expected, post-*Teamsters* seniority cases reflect lawyer's
efforts to establish the necessary factors to come within the exception to
Teamsters. It is reasoned that if the plaintiff could demonstrate that the
seniority systems under attack were not bona fide, then the measure of
immunity granted such systems by the ruling of *Teamsters* would not be
applicable. The applicable law would be pre-*Teamsters* interpretations.

132, 133 (CA5 1948). There is also support
in decisions of this Court for the proposition that conclusions on mixed questions of
law and fact are independently reviewable
by an appellate court, e.g., Bogardus v.
Commissioner, 302 U.S. 34, 39, 58 S.Ct. 61,
64, 82 L.Ed. 32 (1937); Helvering v. Tex-
Penn Oil Co., 300 U.S. 481, 491, 57 S.Ct.
569, 573, 81 L.Ed. 755 (1937); Helvering v.
Rankin, 295 U.S. 123, 131, 55 S.Ct. 732,
736, 79 L.Ed. 1343 (1935). But cf., Commissioner v. Duberstein, 363 U.S. 278, 289, 80
S.Ct. 1190, 1198, 4 L.Ed.2d 1218 (1960);
Commissioner v. Heininger, 320 U.S. 467,
475, 64 S.Ct. 249, 254, 88 L.Ed. 171 (1943).

Wattleton et al. v. International Brotherhood of Boiler Makers, etc., 686 F.2d 586 (7th Cir.1982), cert. denied 459 U.S. 1208, 103 S.Ct. 1199, 75 L.Ed.2d 442 (1983) is an illustration of a post-*Teamsters* seniority case.

WATTLETON v. INTERNATIONAL BROTH. OF BOILER MAKERS, ETC.

United States Court of Appeals for the Seventh Circuit, (1982).
686 F.2d 586.

LEIGHTON, DISTRICT JUDGE.

In this appeal by a local union of blacksmiths, we are asked to resolve two issues. First, whether the district court's findings of fact concerning the seniority system contained in the union's collective bargaining agreements with the Ladish Company of Cudahy, Wisconsin are clearly erroneous. Second, whether the district court erred in concluding that the seniority system in question is not bona fide within the meaning of Section 703(h) of Title VII because it was negotiated and maintained for the purpose, and with the intent and effect, of discriminating against Negroes employed by Ladish.

We hold that the district court's findings are not clearly erroneous; they are supported by substantial evidence in the record. And, in our judgment, the court was correct in concluding that the union's seniority system is not bona fide within the meaning of Section 703(h) of Title VII. Therefore, we affirm the district court. The following is a summary of its findings.

I

The Ladish Company is a major employer in the Milwaukee, Wisconsin area, the plant here involved being in Cudahy, a Milwaukee suburb. The company produces and finishes metal products; it does significant contractual work for federal agencies and has been in production since 1927. Ladish is a unionized employer; and during the time relevant to this case, it has had collective bargaining agreements with seven unions. However, the only one in this appeal is the appellant, Local # 1509 of the International Brotherhood of Boiler Makers, Iron Ship Builders, Blacksmiths, Forgers and Helpers (hereafter referred to as the Blacksmiths).

Prior to World War II, few Negroes lived in the Milwaukee area. But in the post-war period, they began to migrate from the Deep South and settled in and around the city where their population increased steadily. They were limited in the purchasing of homes and the renting of apartments to areas of Milwaukee where living arrangements were substandard; and at the same time, there were racially discriminatory practices against Negroes in employment opportunities, in the location of schools, and in everyday social contacts. And at Ladish's Cudahy plant, no Negroes were employed prior to 1948; but their number in the workforce increased as the years progressed into the '50's.

The minimum ability requirements for the greatest majority of jobs in the Ladish plant were simple literacy and good health. Although the company sought skilled craftsmen to fill certain of the journeyman jobs and apprenticeable trades, most of its employees at the entry level were hired with little, if any, skills; consequently, most of them learned while on the job. The Negroes hired between 1948 and 1968 were neither less skilled, less qualified, nor less apt to learn job skills than were the Caucasians hired during the same period. All Negroes, however, were assigned jobs in the Machinists' unit, assignments that were solely made by Ladish, intentionally and based on race. The jobs to which the Negroes were assigned were mainly as grinders and truckers: the dirtiest, lowest paid, and least desirable.

During the same period, Caucasians hired by Ladish were assigned jobs in the Blacksmiths' bargaining unit, and under the jurisdiction of other union locals. It was Ladish's policy to allow inter-bargaining unit transfers by all of its employees during the period in question; but the seniority system maintained by the Blacksmiths and the other unions discouraged transfers by employees who had been with the company for a significant period of time because the result subjected an employee to possible layoff, or forced him to accept the least desirable job in his new unit. At various times from August 1949, Caucasian employees of Ladish transferred from jobs within the jurisdiction of other bargaining units to those within the jurisdiction of the Blacksmiths, all of them, for a period at least, utilizing their carryover seniority for layoff and recall purposes. However, no Negro employee succeeded in effecting such a transfer despite existing advantages in jobs under the Blacksmiths.

In 1973 and 1974, the Office of Federal Contract Compliance (OFCC) conducted an audit of Ladish's Cudahy facility which included an analysis of the company's then existing workforce. In response to OFCC requests, and in compliance with its obligations as a federal contractor, Ladish prepared detailed information concerning its employees. It listed all of Cudahy's hourly employees hired from August 1948 to December 1967, the distribution of those hirings by bargaining units, a list of those minorities the company hired prior to January 1, 1968 who were still employed in 1974, and a distribution of the company's hirings by bargaining unit. The audit eventually focused on whether Ladish's then existing workforce had an "affected class"; that is, a class consisting of employees who by virtue of past hiring discrimination, and by the nature of the limited seniority carryover provisions of the pertinent collective bargaining agreements, were in a position that they continued to suffer the present effects of past racially discriminatory acts. Based on its audit, its examination of documents and evidence furnished by Ladish, OFCC concluded that an affected class existed at Ladish, consisting of all Negroes who were hired by the company prior to January 22, 1968, and who were placed by Ladish in jobs under the jurisdiction of the Machinists.

II

Shortly after the OFCC reached the conclusion that Ladish had an affected class of Negro employees who had suffered employment discrimination, the first of 18 Negroes employed by Ladish filed a charge of employment discrimination with the Milwaukee office of the Equal Employment Opportunity Commission, naming as respondents the Ladish Company and the seven unions with which it had collective bargaining agreements. He alleged that:

> Prior to 1968, Ladish Company maintained a segregated hiring policy wherein all Black workers were hired into Union contracted Machinists jobs, which were the lowest paying jobs available at the Company. Such a policy has led to a current and continuing system of discrimination in seniority, wages and promotion. As a Black employee, I and others similarly situated, have been discriminated against as a result of Ladish's past policies of segregated hiring and resultant seniority and salary system. The affiliated Unions have contributed to this discrimination via the Union Contract.

On various dates thereafter, EEOC letters telling the complainants of their right to sue in the appropriate United States district court were issued; and on December 29, 1975, this suit was filed by 11 Negro employees of Ladish, on their behalf and on behalf of all others similarly situated. Later, seven other Negro employees filed similar EEOC charges, received letters concerning their right to sue; and on May 3, 1977, filed a motion for leave to intervene as plaintiffs in the suit. This was allowed; and on February 12, 1980, the district court granted, in part, plaintiffs' motion to certify the class.

* * *

On the same date, the court granted a motion that severed the issue of liability from those of damages and remedies, in the event liability was established at trial. Then, at a conference held on November 3, 1980, plaintiffs, the Ladish Company, and four of the seven unions, informed the district judge that they were prepared to settle the case as to them.[1] They reported agreement to a proposed consent decree, and requested a hearing.

* * *

The effect of the settlement was to remove the Ladish Company and the four unions from the suit. This having been done, the remaining issues between plaintiffs, the remaining union locals: the Machinists,[2] the Die Sinkers,[3] and the Blacksmiths, were set for trial. They were heard to the court on plaintiffs' contention that (1) Ladish, with the full knowledge, cooperation and complicity of the three unions,

---

1. The unions were (1) International Federation of Professional and Technical Engineers, Local # 92 (IFPTE); (2) International Brotherhood of Firemen and Oilers, Local # 125 (IBFO); (3) International Brotherhood of Electrical Workers, Local # 494 (IBEW); and (4) Associated Unions of America, Local # 500 (AUA).

2. The International Association of Machinists and Aerospace Workers, District No. 10, Local # 1862 (Machinists).

3. International Die Sinkers Conference and Milwaukee Die Sinkers, Lodge # 140 (Die Sinkers).

maintained a policy and practice of hiring Negroes and assigning them to the dirtiest, lowest paying, and least desirable jobs within the jurisdiction of the Machinists; (2) Ladish, with the acquiescence of the three unions, maintained a policy of refusing to promote and transfer Negroes to better paying and more desirable jobs within their jurisdictions; (3) the three unions, by reason of seniority systems in their respective collective bargaining agreements, perpetuated the initial discrimination against Negroes because their seniority systems prevented them from transferring to better paying and more desirable jobs with full carryover seniority within the respective jurisdictions; and (4) that the Machinists' bargaining unit failed to properly and fairly represent its Negro members.

After hearing evidence, the district court made findings of fact and reached conclusions of law published in Wattleton v. Ladish Co., 520 F.Supp. 1329 (E.D.Wis.1981). It found that during the period in question, all persons who were hired by Ladish and given jobs in the Machinists' and Die Sinkers' bargaining unit were accepted without regard to race or national origin, 520 F.Supp. at 1338; and that the Machinists did not fail to properly and fairly represent their Negro members. 520 F.Supp. at 1347. But as to the Blacksmiths, the district court weighed the credibility of four Negroes who testified about their work experience at Ladish, reviewed the record, and found that no Negro employee in the Cudahy plant transferred to a job under the jurisdiction of the Blacksmiths because its members, expressing its policy, made it clear to Ladish, and to the Negroes, that the local union would not accept them into its bargaining unit, 520 F.Supp. at 1341; that the OFCC determinations, the testimony of Ladish's Negro employees, and the operation of the challenged systems were persuasive evidence that the seniority provisions had perpetuated the effects of prior discriminatory practices and have carried their effects into the present, 520 F.Supp. at 1341; that the challenged seniority systems in the separate bargaining units were rational, in conformance with industry practice, and with the provisions of the National Relations Act, 520 F.Supp. at 1342; and that because they were originally negotiated at a time when Negroes were not employed at Ladish, the seniority systems of the three unions, including the Blacksmiths', did not have their genesis in racial discrimination. 520 F.Supp. at 1343.

Having made these findings, the court then turned to the question whether the challenged seniority systems, after their genesis, were thereafter negotiated and maintained free from any illegal purpose. 520 F.Supp. at 1343. It found that there being no evidence to the contrary, the Negro plaintiffs had not established that the seniority systems which existed under the collective bargaining agreements between Ladish, the Machinists, and the Die Sinkers were maintained with a purpose and intent to discriminate against them. 520 F.Supp. at 1346. But tracing the history of the Ladish-Blacksmiths' collective bargaining agreements, as it had in those between Ladish and the other two unions, the district court found that while the Blacksmiths' seniority system under examination was essentially the same as the one contained in the original agreement, the provisions had not been carried forward unchanged. In fact, there had been three changes, and all of them "coincided with the time Ladish first began to hire blacks in 1948 * * * or with times of a steady increase in the hiring of blacks at Ladish." 520 F.Supp. at 1345.

The first change was included in the agreement effective August 22, 1949 to September 30, 1951 and provided that plantwide seniority would carry over to jobs under the jurisdiction of the Blacksmiths for purposes of layoff. This difference benefitted only Caucasians who, without difficulty, transferred into the Blacksmiths' bargaining unit; no Negro was successful in making such a transfer. The second was elimination, in the same collective bargaining agreement, of a nondiscrimination clause that was not again included in an agreement between Ladish and the Blacksmiths until passage of Title VII in 1964. The third was inclusion in the August 22, 1949 agreement of a provision regarding interbargaining unit transfers which stated that:

> Permanent inter-bargaining unit transfers will be made by agreement between Management and the Bargaining Committee of the unit to which the employee is being transferred.

The district court found that on August 22, 1949 "and thereafter, [this provision] gave the Blacksmiths virtual veto power over interbargaining unit transfers." 520 F.Supp. at 1345.

Based on the evidence that showed these three changes, the evidence relating to the feelings of individual blacksmiths toward transfers by Negroes to jobs in their unit, the evidence which showed that Caucasians transferred to jobs under the Blacksmiths with full carryover seniority while at the same time Negroes were discouraged from doing so; and having drawn reasonable inferences therefrom, the district court found "that the challenged seniority system contained in the Ladish-Blacksmiths' collective bargaining agreement, inter alia, was negotiated and maintained with a purpose of preventing only blacks from entering into jobs under the jurisdiction of the Blacksmiths." * * * 520 F.Supp. at 1346; and, "that the seniority systems negotiated between Ladish and the Blacksmiths have and were intended to have a disparate impact on black workers at Ladish." 520 F.Supp. at 1347. Therefore, the court concluded that "the seniority system of the Blacksmiths is not bona fide within the meaning of 703(h) of Title VII." In this appeal, the Blacksmiths contend that the district court's findings are clearly erroneous; and that there was error in the conclusion reached.

III

A

Rule 52(a), Fed.R.Civ.P., broadly requires that in a non-jury case the district court's "[f]indings of fact shall not be set aside unless clearly erroneous, and due regard shall be given to the opportunity of the trial court to judge the credibility of the witnesses [sic]." Pullman-Standard v. Swint, __ U.S. __, 102 S.Ct. 1781, 1789, 72 L.Ed.2d 66 (1982).

* * *

Neither our examination of the record nor any point raised in this appeal leaves us with a definite and firm conviction that a mistake was committed by the district court in its factual findings; we cannot say that they are clearly erroneous. Culbertson v. Jno. McCall Coal Company, Inc., 495 F.2d 1403, 1405 (4th Cir.1974); Davis v. Murphy, 587 F.2d 362, 364 (7th Cir.1978). Therefore, we turn to the question whether the court erred in concluding that the Blacksmiths' seniority system is not bona fide within the meaning of Section 703(h), Title VII.

B

Title VII of the Civil Rights Act of 1964 makes unlawful practices, procedures, or tests that "operate to 'freeze' the status quo of prior discriminatory employment practices." Griggs v. Duke Power Co., 401 U.S. 424, 430, 91 S.Ct. 849, 853, 28 L.Ed.2d 158 (1971). To this rule, Section 703(h) of the Act, 42 U.S.C. § 2000e–2(h) provides an exception:

> [I]t shall not be an unlawful employment practice for an employer to apply different standards of compensation, or different terms, conditions, or privileges of employment pursuant to a bona fide seniority * * * system, * * * provided that such differences are not the result of an intention to discriminate because of race * * *

California Brewers Ass'n v. Bryant, 444 U.S. 598, 600, 100 S.Ct. 814, 816, 63 L.Ed.2d 55 (1980). This exception extends not only to Title VII actions, but also bars section 1981 claims. Pettway v. American Cast Iron Pipe Co., 576 F.2d 1157, 1191–1192 (5th Cir.1978). It applies to seniority systems with a disparate racial impact only when "differences in treatment [are] not the result of an intention to discriminate because of race." International Bro. of Teamsters v. United States, 431 U.S. 324, 353, 97 S.Ct. 1843, 1863, 52 L.Ed.2d 396 (1977); Terrell v. United States Pipe & Foundry Co., 644 F.2d 1112, 1118 (5th Cir.1981). Accordingly, it has been held that provisions for seniority rights "designed or operated to discriminate on an illegal basis is not a 'bona fide' system." Acha v. Beame, 570 F.2d 57, 64 (2nd Cir.1978); and see United Airlines, Inc. v. Evans, 431 U.S. 553, 559, 97 S.Ct. 1885, 1889, 52 L.Ed.2d 571 (1977).

Section 703(c)(1) of Title VII, 42 U.S.C. § 2000e–2(c)(1), provides that:

> It shall be an unlawful employment practice for a labor organization—
>
> > to exclude * * * from its membership, or otherwise to discriminate against, any individual because of his race, color, religion, sex, or national origin; * * *.

Thus, it is clearly a violation of this section for a union, international or local, to maintain a seniority system for the purpose of excluding Negroes from membership because of their race; and certainly, such a system is not protected by the exception in section 703(f) of Title VII. Hameed v. Intern. Ass'n of Bridge, etc., 637 F.2d 506 (8th Cir.1980); Glus v. G.C. Murphy Co., 629 F.2d 248 (3rd Cir.1980); Freeman v. Motor Convoy, Inc., 409 F.Supp. 1100 (N.D.Ga.1975); United States by Clark v. United Papermakers & Paperworkers, 282 F.Supp. 39 (E.D.La.1968). Therefore, after findings that the Blacksmiths negotiated and maintained their seniority system for the illegal purpose, and with the intent and effect, of discriminating against Negroes because of their race, the district court could only conclude that the system is not bona fide within the meaning of section 703(h) of Title VII. International Bro. of Teamsters v. United States, 431 U.S. 324, 346, 97 S.Ct. 1843, 1860, 52 L.Ed.2d 396 (1977); Sears v. Atchison, Topeka & Santa Fe Ry. Co., 454 F.Supp. 158, 179 (D.Kan.1978); rev'd on other grounds, 645 F.2d 1365 (10th Cir.1981). For these reasons, the judgment of the district court is affirmed.

Notes

1. The real significance of the *Wattleton* case lies in the remedy granted by the court below with regard to seniority. The following is the pertinent excerpt from the decision of the district court:

WATTLETON v. LADISH CO.

United States District Court, Eastern District of Wisconsin, 1981.
520 F.Supp. 1329.

* * *

"Having found a violation of Title VII with respect to the seniority system implemented by Ladish and the Blacksmiths, the Court concludes that all class members in this action should be granted an opportunity to transfer from their jobs within the jurisdiction of the Machinists to job vacancies within the jurisdiction of the Blacksmiths with full carryover seniority for all purposes. The Court has reviewed the terms of the consent decree previously entered between plaintiffs, Ladish, and four union defendants (not including the Blacksmiths). The Court determines that the seniority carryover relief established in the consent decree to which Ladish has already agreed would constitute reasonable and proper relief in this proceeding against the Blacksmiths. That is, those individuals who have indicated, pursuant to the consent decree, that they desire to transfer to jobs within the jurisdiction of the Blacksmiths shall be given an opportunity to do so as vacancies arise under the terms of the consent decree. This procedure will allow blacks to transfer from their present positions to jobs within the jurisdiction of the Blacksmiths with full carryover seniority to be exercised in the Blacksmiths' unit for all pertinent purposes and thereby obtain their "rightful place." Local 189, United Papermakers and Paperworkers, AFL–CIO, CLC v. United States, 416 F.2d 980 (5th Cir.1969), cert. denied 397 U.S. 919, 90 S.Ct. 926, 25 L.Ed.2d 100 (1970); United States v. N. L. Industries, Inc., 479 F.2d 354 (8th Cir.1973).

"Plaintiffs are also entitled to monetary compensation for the loss they have suffered as a result of the discrimination of the defendant Blacksmiths. Class members will be entitled to back pay with appropriate interest and to front pay to compensate them for any monetary loss sustained as a result of discrimination. Albemarle Paper Co. v. Moody, 422 U.S. 405, 95 S.Ct. 2362, 45 L.Ed.2d 280 (1975); Franks v. Bowman Transportation Co., 424 U.S. 747, 96 S.Ct. 1251, 47 L.Ed.2d 444 (1976). The back pay period will begin December 30, 1969, the appropriate limitation period in Wisconsin under § 1981. * * *"

2. There have been a number of other post-*Teamster* cases in which the bona fides of the seniority system have been successfully challenged; Sears v. Atchison Topeka & Santa Fe Railroad Co., 645 F.2d 1365 (10th Cir. 1981); Terrell v. United States Pipe & Foundry Co., 644 F.2d 1112 (5th Cir. 1981); Scarlett v. Seaboard Coast Line Railroad, 676 F.2d 1043 (5th Cir. 1982).

The issue is still alive in Swint v. Pullman Standard, which is on remand from the Supreme Court (456 U.S. 273, 292–293, 102 S.Ct. 1781, 1792, 72 L.Ed.2d 66 (1982), discussed supra, remanded 692 F.2d 1031 (5th Cir.1982).

3. It should be noted, to the extent that these cases involve the seniority of affected class members accumulated prior to July 2, 1965, the mere passage of time makes it unlikely that any meaningful relief will be forthcoming. The original complaint in *Swint* was filed in 1971. Increasingly affected class members are either retiring or dying. Delay in the disposition of these cases can in the ultimate sense be justice denied.

G. SEX DISCRIMINATION

1. EMPLOYMENT

HISHON v. KING & SPALDING

Supreme Court of the United States, 1984.
467 U.S. 69, 104 S.Ct. 2229, 81 L.Ed.2d 59.

CHIEF JUSTICE BURGER delivered the opinion of the Court.

We granted certiorari to determine whether the District Court properly dismissed a Title VII complaint alleging that a law partnership discriminated against petitioner, a woman lawyer employed as an associate, when it failed to invite her to become a partner.

I

A

In 1972 petitioner Elizabeth Anderson Hishon accepted a position as an associate with respondent, a large Atlanta law firm established as a general partnership. When this suit was filed in 1980, the firm had more than 50 partners and employed approximately 50 attorneys as associates. Up to that time, no woman had ever served as a partner at the firm.

Petitioner alleges that the prospect of partnership was an important factor in her initial decision to accept employment with respondent. She alleges that respondent used the possibility of ultimate partnership as a recruiting device to induce petitioner and other young lawyers to become associates at the firm. According to the complaint, respondent represented that advancement to partnership after five or six years was "a matter of course" for associates "who receive[d] satisfactory evaluations" and that associates were promoted to partnership "on a fair and equal basis." Petitioner alleges that she relied on these representations when she accepted employment with respondent. The complaint further alleges that respondent's promise to consider her on a "fair and equal basis" created a binding employment contract.

In May 1978 the partnership considered and rejected Hishon for admission to the partnership; one year later, the partners again declined to invite her to become a partner. Once an associate is passed over for partnership at respondent's firm, the associate is notified to begin seeking employment elsewhere. Petitioner's employment as an associate terminated on December 31, 1979.

B

Hishon filed a charge with the Equal Employment Opportunity Commission on November 19, 1979, claiming that respondent had discriminated against her on the basis of her sex in violation of Title VII of the Civil Rights Act of 1964, 78 Stat. 241, as amended, 42 U.S.C. §§ 2000e *et seq.* (1976 ed. and Supp. V). Ten days later the Commission issued a notice of right to sue, and on February 27, 1980, Hishon brought this action in the United States District Court for the Northern District of Georgia. She sought declaratory and injunctive relief, back pay, and compensatory damages "in lieu of reinstatement and promotion to partnership." This, of course, negates any claim for specific performance of the contract alleged.

The District Court dismissed the complaint on the ground that Title VII was inapplicable to the selection of partners by a partnership.

A divided panel of the United States Court of Appeals for the Eleventh Circuit affirmed. 678 F.2d 1022 (1982). We granted certiorari.

II

At this stage of the litigation, we must accept petitioner's allegations as true. A court may dismiss a complaint only if it is clear that no relief could be granted under any set of facts that could be proved consistent with the allegations. Conley v. Gibson, 355 U.S. 41, 45–46 (1957). The issue before us is whether petitioner's allegations state a claim under Title VII, the relevant portion of which provides as follows:

(a) *It shall be an unlawful employment practice for an employer—*

(1) to fail or refuse to hire or to discharge any individual, or otherwise *to discriminate against any individual with respect to his* compensation, *terms, conditions, or privileges of employment, because of such individual's* race, color, religion, *sex,* or national origin. 42 U.S.C. § 2000e–2(a) (emphasis added).

A

Petitioner alleges that respondent is an "employer" to whom Title VII is addressed.[3] She then asserts that consideration for partnership was one of the "terms, conditions, or privileges of employment" as an associate with respondent. See § 2000e–2(a)(1). If this is correct, respondent could not base an adverse partnership decision on "race, color, religion, sex, or national origin."

Once a contractual relationship of employment is established, the provisions of Title VII attach and govern certain aspects of that relationship. In the context of Title VII, the contract of employment may be written or oral, formal or informal; an informal contract of employment may arise by the simple act of handing a job applicant a shovel and providing a workplace. The contractual relationship of employment triggers the provision of Title VII governing "terms, conditions, or privileges of employment." Title VII in turn forbids discrimination on the basis of "race, color, religion, sex, or national origin."

Because the underlying employment relationship is contractual, it follows that the "terms, conditions, or privileges of employment" clearly include benefits that are part of an employment contract. Here, petitioner in essence alleges that respondent made a contract to consider her for partnership.[6] Indeed, this promise was allegedly a key contractual provision which induced her to accept employment. If the evidence at trial establishes that the parties contracted to have petitioner considered for partnership, that promise clearly was a term, condition, or privilege of her employment. Title VII would then bind respondents to consider petitioner for partnership as the statute provides, i.e., without regard to petitioner's sex. The contract she alleges would lead to the same result.

Petitioner's claim that a contract was made, however, is not the only allegation that would qualify respondent's consideration of petitioner for partnership as a term, condition, or privilege of employment. An employer may provide its employees with many benefits that it is under no obligation to furnish by any express or implied contract. Such a benefit, though not a contractual *right* of employment, may qualify as a "privileg[e]" of employment under Title VII. A benefit

---

3. The statute defines an "employer" as a "person engaged in an industry affecting commerce who has fifteen or more employees for each working day in each of twenty or more calendar weeks in the current or preceding calendar year," § 2000e(b), and a "person" is explicitly defined to include "partnerships," § 2000e(a) (1976 ed., Supp. V). The complaint alleges that respondent's partnership satisfies these requirements. Joint-Appendix (J.A.) 6.

6. Petitioner not only alleges that respondent promised to consider her for partnership, but also that it promised to consider her on a "fair and equal basis." This latter promise is not necessary to petitioner's Title VII claim. Even if the employment contract did not afford a basis for an implied condition that the ultimate decision would be fairly made on the merits, Title VII itself, would impose such a requirement. If the promised consideration for partnership is a term, condition, or privilege of employment, then the partnership decision must be without regard to "race, color, religion, sex, or national origin."

that is part and parcel of the employment relationship may not be doled out in a discriminatory fashion, even if the employer would be free under the employment contract simply not to provide the benefit at all. Those benefits that comprise the "incidents of employment," S.Rep. No. 867, 88th Cong., 2d Sess. 11 (1964),[7] or that form "an aspect of the relationship between the employer and employees," Allied Chemical & Alkali Workers v. Pittsburgh Plate Glass Co., 404 U.S. 157, 178, 92 S.Ct. 383, 397, 30 L.Ed.2d 341 (1971),[8] may not be afforded in a manner contrary to Title VII.

Several allegations in petitioner's complaint would support the conclusion that the opportunity to become a partner was part and parcel of an associate's status as an employee at respondent's firm, independent of any allegation that such an opportunity was included in associates' employment contracts. Petitioner alleges that respondent's associates could regularly expect to be considered for partnership at the end of their "apprenticeships," and it appears that lawyers outside the firm were not routinely so considered.[9] Thus, the benefit of partnership consideration was allegedly linked directly with an associate's status as an employee, and this linkage was far more than coincidental: petitioner alleges that respondent explicitly used the prospect of ultimate partnership to induce young lawyers to join the firm. Indeed, the importance of the partnership decision to a lawyer's status as an associate is underscored by the allegation that associates' employment is terminated if they are not elected to become partners. These allegations, if proved at trial, would suffice to show that partnership consideration was a term, condition, or privilege of an associate's employment at respondent's firm, and accordingly that partnership consideration must be without regard to sex.

B

Respondent contends that advancement to partnership may never qualify as a term, condition, or privilege of employment for purposes of Title VII. First, respondent asserts that elevation to partnership

7. Senate Report 867 concerned S. 1937, which the Senate postponed indefinitely after it amended a House version of what ultimately became the Civil Rights Act of 1964. See 110 Cong.Rec. 14,602 (1964). The report is relevant here because S. 1937 contained language similar to that ultimately found in the Civil Rights Act. It guaranteed "equal employment opportunity," which was defined to "include all the compensation, terms, conditions, and privileges of employment." S.Rep. No. 867, 88th Cong., 2d Sess. 24 (1964).

8. *Allied Chemical* pertains to Section 8(d) of the National Labor Relations Act (NLRA), which describes the obligation of employers and unions to meet and confer regarding "wages, hours, and other terms and conditions of employment." 49 Stat. 452, as added, 29 U.S.C. § 158(d). The meaning of this analogous language sheds light on the Title VII provision at issue here. We have drawn analogies to the NLRA in other Title VII contexts, see Franks v. Bowman Transportation Co., 424 U.S. 747, 768–770, 96 S.Ct. 1251, 1266–1267, 47 L.Ed.2d 444 (1976), and have noted that certain sections of Title VII were expressly patterned after the NLRA, see Albemarle Paper Co. v. Moody, 422 U.S. 405, 419, 95 S.Ct. 2362, 2372, 45 L.Ed.2d 280 (1975).

9. Respondent's own submissions indicate that most of respondent's partners in fact were selected from the ranks of associates who had spent their entire prepartnership legal careers (excluding judicial clerkships) with the firm. See J.A. 45.

entails a change in status from an "employee" to an "employer." However, even if respondent is correct that a partnership invitation is not itself an offer of employment, Title VII would nonetheless apply and preclude discrimination on the basis of sex. The benefit a plaintiff is denied need not *be* employment to fall within Title VII's protection; it need only be a term, condition, or privilege *of* employment. It is also of no consequence that employment as an associate necessarily ends when an associate becomes a partner. A benefit need not accrue before a person's employment is completed to be a term, condition, or privilege of that employment relationship. Pension benefits, for example, qualify as terms, conditions, or privileges of employment even though they are received only after employment terminates. Arizona Governing Committee for Tax Deferred Annuity & Deferred Compensation Plans v. Norris, ___ U.S. ___, ___, 103 S.Ct. 3492, ___ (1983). Accordingly, nothing in the change in status that advancement to partnership might entail means that partnership consideration falls outside the terms of the statute. See Lucido v. Cravath, Swaine & Moore, 425 F.Supp. 123, 128–129 (SDNY 1977).

Second, respondent argues that Title VII categorically exempts partnership decisions from scrutiny. However, respondent points to nothing in the statute or the legislative history that would support such a *per se* exemption.[10] When Congress wanted to grant an employer complete immunity, it expressly did so.[11]

Third, respondent argues that application of Title VII in this case would infringe constitutional rights of expression or association. Although we have recognized that the activities of lawyers may make a "distinctive contribution ∗ ∗ ∗ to the ideas and beliefs of our society," NAACP v. Button, 371 U.S. 415, 431, 83 S.Ct. 328, 337, 9 L.Ed.2d 405 (1963), respondent has not shown how its ability to fulfill such a function would be inhibited by a requirement that it consider petitioner for partnership on her merits. Moreover, as we have held in another context, "[i]nvidious private discrimination may be characterized as a form of exercising freedom of association protected by the First Amend-

---

10. The only legislative history respondent offers to support its position is Senator Cotton's defense of an unsuccessful amendment to limit Title VII to businesses with 100 or more employees. In this connection the Senator stated: "[W]hen a small businessman who employs 30 or 25 or 26 persons selects an employee, he comes very close to selecting a partner; and when a businessman selects a partner, he comes dangerously close to the situation he faces when he selects a wife." 110 Cong.Rec. 13,085 (1964); accord 118 Cong. Rec. 1524, 2391 (1972).

Because Senator Cotton's amendment failed, it is unclear to what extent Congress shared his concerns about selecting partners. In any event, his views hardly

conflict with our narrow holding today: that in appropriate circumstances partnership consideration may qualify as a term, condition, or privilege of a person's employment with an employer large enough to be covered by Title VII.

11. For example, Congress expressly exempted Indian tribes and certain agencies of the District of Columbia, 42 U.S.C. § 2000e(b)(1), small businesses and bona fide private membership clubs, § 2000e(b) (2), and certain employees of religious organizations, § 2000e–1. Congress initially exempted certain employees of educational institutions, § 702, 78 Stat. 255 (1964), but later revoked that exemption, Equal Employment Opportunity Act of 1972, § 3, 86 Stat. 103.

ment, but it has never been accorded affirmative constitutional protections." Norwood v. Harrison, 413 U.S. 455, 470, 93 S.Ct. 2804, 2813, 37 L.Ed.2d 723 (1973). There is no constitutional right, for example, to discriminate in the selection of who may attend a private school or join a labor union. Runyon v. McCrary, 427 U.S. 160, 96 S.Ct. 2586, 49 L.Ed.2d 415 (1976); Railway Mail Association v. Corsi, 326 U.S. 88, 93–94, 65 S.Ct. 1483, 1487–1488, 89 L.Ed. 2072 (1945).

III

We conclude that petitioner's complaint states a claim cognizable under Title VII. Petitioner therefore is entitled to her day in court to prove her allegations. The judgment of the Court of Appeals is reversed, and the case is remanded for further proceedings consistent with this opinion.

It is so ordered.

JUSTICE POWELL, concurring.

I join the Court's opinion holding that petitioner's complaint alleges a violation of Title VII and that the motion to dismiss should not have been granted. Petitioner's complaint avers that the law firm violated its promise that she would be considered for partnership on a "fair and equal basis" within the time span that associates generally are so considered.[1] Petitioner is entitled to the opportunity to prove these averments.

I write to make clear my understanding that the Court's opinion should not be read as extending Title VII to the management of a law firm by its partners. The reasoning of the Court's opinion does not require that the relationship among partners be characterized as an "employment" relationship to which Title VII would apply. The relationship among law partners differs markedly from that between employer and employee—including that between the partnership and its associates.[2] The judgmental and sensitive decisions that must be made among the partners embrace a wide range of subjects.[3] The essence of the law partnership is the common conduct of a shared enterprise. The

---

1. Law firms normally require a period of associateship as a prerequisite to being eligible to "make" partner. This need not be an inflexible period, as firms may vary from the norm and admit to partnership earlier than, or subsequent to, the customary period of service. Also, as the complaint recognizes, many firms make annual evaluations of the performances of associates, and usually are free to terminate employment on the basis of these evaluations.

2. Of course, an employer may not evade the strictures of Title VII simply by labeling its employees as "partners." Law partnerships usually have many of the characteristics that I describe generally here.

3. These decisions concern such matters as participation in profits and other types of compensation; work assignments; approval of commitments in bar association, civic or political activities; questions of billing; acceptance of new clients; questions of conflicts of interest; retirement programs; and expansion policies. Such decisions may affect each partner of the firm. Divisions of partnership profits, unlike shareholders' rights to dividends, involve judgments as to each partner's contribution to the reputation and success of the firm. This is true whether the partner's participation in profits is measured in terms of points or percentages, combinations of salaries and points, salaries and bonuses, and possibly in other ways.

relationship among law partners contemplates that decisions important to the partnership normally will be made by common agreement, see, e.g., Memorandum of Agreement, King & Spalding, App. 153–164 (Respondent's partnership agreement), or consent among the partners.

Respondent contends that for these reasons application of Title VII to the decision whether to admit petitioner to the firm implicates the constitutional right to association. But here it is alleged that respondent as an employer is obligated by contract to consider petitioner for partnership on equal terms without regard to sex. I agree that enforcement of this obligation, voluntarily assumed, would impair no right of association.[4]

In admission decisions made by law firms, it is now widely recognized—as it should be—that in fact neither race nor sex is relevant. The qualities of mind, capacity to reason logically, ability to work under pressure, leadership and the like are unrelated to race or sex. This is demonstrated by the success of women and minorities in law schools, in the practice of law, on the bench, and in positions of community, state and national leadership. Law firms—and, of course, society—are the better for these changes.

2. PENSIONS

CITY OF LOS ANGELES, DEPT. OF WATER v. MANHART

Supreme Court of the United States, 1978.
435 U.S. 702, 98 S.Ct. 1370, 55 L.Ed.2d 657.

MR. JUSTICE STEVENS delivered the opinion of the Court.

As a class, women live longer than men. For this reason, the Los Angeles Department of Water and Power required its female employees

---

4. The Court's opinion properly reminds us that "invidious private discrimination * * * has never been afforded affirmative constitutional protections." Op., at 2235. This is not to say, however, that enforcement of laws that ban discrimination will always be without cost to other values, including constitutional rights. Such laws may impede the exercise of personal judgment in choosing one's associates or colleagues. See generally, Fallon, To Each According to His Ability, From None According to His Race: The Concept of Merit in the Law of Antidiscrimination, 60 Boston Univ.L.Rev. 815, 844–860 (1980). Impediments to the exercise of one's right to choose one's associates can violate the right of association protected by the First and Fourteenth Amendments. Cf. NAACP v. Button, 371 U.S. 415, 83 S.Ct. 328, 9 L.Ed.2d 405 (1963); NAACP v. Alabama, 357 U.S. 449, 78 S.Ct. 1163, 2 L.Ed.2d 1488 (1958).

With respect to laws that prevent discrimination, much depends upon the standards by which the courts examine private decisions that are an exercise of the right of association. For example, the courts of appeals generally have acknowledged that respect for academic freedom requires some deference to the judgment of schools and universities as to the qualifications of professors, particularly those considered for tenured positions. Lieberman v. Gant, 630 F.2d 60, 67–68 (CA2 1980); Kunda v. Muhlenberg College, 621 F.2d 532, 547–548 (CA3 1980). Cf. Regents of the University of California v. Bakke, 438 U.S. 265, 311–315, 98 S.Ct. 2733, 2759–2761, 57 L.Ed.2d 750 (1978) (opinion of Justice Powell). The present case, before us on a motion to dismiss for lack of subject matter jurisdiction, does not present such an issue.

to make larger contributions to its pension fund than its male employees. We granted certiorari to decide whether this practice discriminated against individual female employees because of their sex in violation of § 703(a)(1) of the Civil Rights Act of 1964, as amended.[1]

For many years the Department has administered retirement, disability, and death-benefit programs for its employees. Upon retirement each employee is eligible for a monthly retirement benefit computed as a fraction of his or her salary multiplied by years of service. The monthly benefits for men and women of the same age, seniority, and salary are equal. Benefits are funded entirely by contributions from the employees and the Department, augmented by the income earned on those contributions. No private insurance company is involved in the administration or payment of benefits.

Based on a study of mortality tables and its own experience, the Department determined that its 2,000 female employees, on the average, will live a few years longer than its 10,000 male employees. The cost of a pension for the average retired female is greater than for the average male retiree because more monthly payments must be made to the average woman. The Department therefore required female employees to make monthly contributions to the fund which were 14.84% higher than the contributions required of comparable male employees.[4] Because employee contributions were withheld from paychecks a female employee took home less pay than a male employee earning the same salary.[5]

Since the effective date of the Equal Employment Opportunity Act of 1972, the Department has been an employer within the meaning of Title VII of the Civil Rights Act of 1964. See 42 U.S.C. § 2000e (1970 ed., Supp.V). In 1973, respondents brought this suit in the United States District Court for the Central District of California on behalf of a class of women employed or formerly employed by the Department. They prayed for an injunction and restitution of excess contributions.

While this action was pending, the California Legislature enacted a law prohibiting certain municipal agencies from requiring female employees to make higher pension fund contributions than males. The Department therefore amended its plan, effective January 1, 1975. The current plan draws no distinction, either in contributions or in benefits, on the basis of sex. On a motion for summary judgment, the District Court held that the contribution differential violated § 703(a)

1. The section provides:

"It shall be an unlawful employment practice for an employer—

"(1) to fail or refuse to hire or to discharge any individual, or otherwise to discriminate against any individual with respect to his compensation, terms, conditions, or privileges of employment, because of such individual's race, color, religion, sex, or national origin * * *" 78 Stat. 255, 42 U.S.C. § 2000e–2(a)(1).

4. The Department contributes an amount equal to 110% of all employee contributions.

5. The significance of the disparity is illustrated by the record of one woman whose contributions to the fund (including interest on the amount withheld each month) amounted to $18,171.40; a similarly situated male would have contributed only $12,843.53.

(1) and ordered a refund of all excess contributions made before the amendment of the plan. The United States Court of Appeals for the Ninth Circuit affirmed.[10]

The Department and various *amici curiae* contend that: (1) the differential in take-home pay between men and women was not discrimination within the meaning of § 703(a)(1) because it was offset by a difference in the value of the pension benefits provided to the two classes of employees; (2) the differential was based on a factor "other than sex" within the meaning of the Equal Pay Act of 1963 and was therefore protected by the so-called Bennett Amendment; (3) the rationale of General Electric Co. v. Gilbert, 429 U.S. 125, 97 S.Ct. 401, 50 L.Ed.2d 343, requires reversal; and (4) in any event, the retroactive monetary recovery is unjustified. We consider these contentions in turn.

I

There are both real and fictional differences between women and men. It is true that the average man is taller than the average woman; it is not true that the average woman driver is more accident prone than the average man.[12] Before the Civil Rights Act of 1964 was enacted, an employer could fashion his personnel policies on the basis of assumptions about the differences between men and women, whether or not the assumptions were valid.

It is now well recognized that employment decisions cannot be predicated on mere "stereotyped" impressions about the characteristics of males or females.[13] Myths and purely habitual assumptions about a woman's inability to perform certain kinds of work are no longer acceptable reasons for refusing to employ qualified individuals, or for paying them less. This case does not, however, involve a fictional difference between men and women. It involves a generalization that the parties accept as unquestionably true: Women, as a class, do live longer than men. The Department treated its women employees differently from its men employees because the two classes are in fact different. It is equally true, however, that all individuals in the respective classes do not share the characteristic that differentiates the average class representatives. Many women do not live as long as the average man and many men outlive the average woman. The question,

---

10. 553 F.2d 581 (1976). Two weeks after the Ninth Circuit decision, this Court decided General Electric Co. v. Gilbert, 429 U.S. 125, 97 S.Ct. 401, 50 L.Ed.2d 343. In response to a petition for rehearing, a majority of the Ninth Circuit panel concluded that its original decision did not conflict with *Gilbert*. 553 F.2d, at 592 (1977). Judge Kilkenny dissented. Id., at 594.

12. See Developments in the Law, Employment Discrimination and Title VII of the Civil Rights Act of 1964, 84 Harv.L. Rev. 1109, 1174 (1971).

13. "In forbidding employers to discriminate against individuals because of their sex, Congress intended to strike at the entire spectrum of disparate treatment of men and women resulting from sex stereotypes. Section 703(a)(1) subjects to scrutiny and eliminates such irrational impediments to job opportunities and enjoyment which have plagued women in the past." Sprogis v. United Air Lines, Inc., 444 F.2d 1194, 1198 (CA7 1971).

therefore, is whether the existence or nonexistence of "discrimination" is to be determined by comparison of class characteristics or individual characteristics. A "stereotyped" answer to that question may not be the same as the answer that the language and purpose of the statute command.

The statute makes it unlawful "to discriminate against any *individual* with respect to his compensation, terms, conditions, or privileges of employment, because of such *individual's* race, color, religion, sex, or national origin." 42 U.S.C. § 2000e–2(a)(1) (emphasis added). The statute's focus on the individual is unambiguous. It precludes treatment of individuals as simply components of a racial, religious, sexual, or national class. If height is required for a job, a tall woman may not be refused employment merely because, on the average, women are too short. Even a true generalization about the class is an insufficient reason for disqualifying an individual to whom the generalization does not apply.

That proposition is of critical importance in this case because there is no assurance that any individual woman working for the Department will actually fit the generalization on which the Department's policy is based. Many of those individuals will not live as long as the average man. While they were working, those individuals received smaller paychecks because of their sex, but they will receive no compensating advantage when they retire.

It is true, of course, that while contributions are being collected from the employees, the Department cannot know which individuals will predecease the average woman. Therefore, unless women as a class are assessed an extra charge, they will be subsidized, to some extent, by the class of male employees.[14] It follows, according to the Department, that fairness to its class of male employees justifies the extra assessment against all of its female employees.

But the question of fairness to various classes affected by the statute is essentially a matter of policy for the legislature to address. Congress has decided that classifications based on sex, like those based on national origin or race, are unlawful. Actuarial studies could unquestionably identify differences in life expectancy based on race or national origin, as well as sex.[15] But a statute that was designed to make race irrelevant in the employment market, see Griggs v. Duke Power Co., 401 U.S. 424, 436, 91 S.Ct. 849, 856, 28 L.Ed.2d 158, could

---

14. The size of the subsidy involved in this case is open to doubt, because the Department's plan provides for survivors' benefits. Since female spouses of male employees are likely to have greater life expectancies than the male spouses of female employees, whatever benefits men lose in "primary" coverage for themselves, they may regain in "secondary" coverage for their wives.

15. For example, the life expectancy of a white baby in 1973 was 72.2 years; a nonwhite baby could expect to live 65.9 years, a difference of 6.3 years. See Public Health Service, IIA Vital Statistics of the United States, 1973, Table 5–3.

not reasonably be construed to permit a take-home-pay differential based on a racial classification.[16]

Even if the statutory language were less clear, the basic policy of the statute requires that we focus on fairness to individuals rather than fairness to classes. Practices that classify employees in terms of religion, race, or sex tend to preserve traditional assumptions about groups rather than thoughtful scrutiny of individuals. The generalization involved in this case illustrates the point. Separate mortality tables are easily interpreted as reflecting innate differences between the sexes; but a significant part of the longevity differential may be explained by the social fact that men are heavier smokers than women.[17]

Finally, there is no reason to believe that Congress intended a special definition of discrimination in the context of employee group insurance coverage. It is true that insurance is concerned with events that are individually unpredictable, but that is characteristic of many employment decisions. Individual risks, like individual performance, may not be predicted by resort to classifications proscribed by Title VII. Indeed, the fact that this case involves a group insurance program highlights a basic flaw in the Department's fairness argument. For when insurance risks are grouped, the better risks always subsidize the poorer risks. Healthy persons subsidize medical benefits for the less healthy; unmarried workers subsidize the pensions of married workers;[18] persons who eat, drink, or smoke to excess may subsidize pension benefits for persons whose habits are more temperate. Treating different classes of risks as though they were the same for purposes of group insurance is a common practice that has never been considered inherently unfair. To insure the flabby and the fit as though they were equivalent risks may be more common than treating men and women alike;[19] but nothing more than habit makes one "subsidy" seem less fair than the other.[20]

16. Fortifying this conclusion is the fact that some States have banned higher life insurance rates for blacks since the 19th century. See generally M. James, The Metropolitan Life—A Study in Business Growth 338–339 (1947).

17. See R. Retherford, The Changing Sex Differential in Mortality 71–82 (1975). Other social causes, such as drinking or eating habits—perhaps even the lingering effects of past employment discrimination—may also affect the mortality differential.

18. A study of life expectancy in the United States for 1949–1951 showed that 20-year-old men could expect to live to 60.6 years of age if they were divorced. If married, they could expect to reach 70.9 years of age, a difference of more than 10 years. Id., at 93.

19. The record indicates, however, that the Department has funded its death-benefit plan by equal contributions from male and female employees. A death benefit—unlike a pension benefit—has less value for persons with longer life expectancies. Under the Department's concept of fairness, then, this neutral funding of death benefits is unfair to women as a class.

20. A variation on the Department's fairness theme is the suggestion that a gender-neutral pension plan would itself violate Title VII because of its disproportionately heavy impact on male employees. Cf. Griggs v. Duke Power Co., 401 U.S. 424, 91 S.Ct. 849, 28 L.Ed.2d 158. This suggestion has no force in the sex discrimination context because each retiree's total pension benefits are ultimately determined by his *actual life span;* any differential in benefits paid to men and women in the aggre-

An employment practice that requires 2,000 individuals to contribute more money into a fund than 10,000 other employees simply because each of them is a woman, rather than a man, is in direct conflict with both the language and the policy of the Act. Such a practice does not pass the simple test of whether the evidence shows "treatment of a person in a manner which but for that person's sex would be different." [21]   It constitutes discrimination and is unlawful unless exempted by the Equal Pay Act of 1963 or some other affirmative justification.

II

Shortly before the enactment of Title VII in 1964, Senator Bennett proposed an amendment providing that a compensation differential based on sex would not be unlawful if it was authorized by the Equal Pay Act, which had been passed a year earlier.[22]   The Equal Pay Act requires employers to pay members of both sexes the same wages for equivalent work, except when the differential is pursuant to one of four specified exceptions.[23]   The Department contends that the fourth excep-

gate is thus "based on [a] factor other than sex," and consequently immune from challenge under the Equal Pay Act, 29 U.S.C. § 206(d); cf. n. 24, infra.   Even under Title VII itself—assuming disparate-impact analysis applies to fringe benefits, cf. Nashville Gas Co. v. Satty, 434 U.S. 136, 144–145, 98 S.Ct. 347, 352, 54 L.Ed.2d 356—the male employees would not prevail.   Even a completely neutral practice will inevitably have *some* disproportionate impact on one group or another.   *Griggs* does not imply, and this Court has never held, that discrimination must always be inferred from such consequences.

21. Developments in the Law, supra 1170; see also Sprogis v. United Air Lines, Inc., 444 F.2d, at 1205 (Stevens, J., dissenting).

22. The Bennett Amendment became part of § 703(h), which provides in part:

"It shall not be unlawful employment practice under this title for any employer to differentiate upon the basis of sex in determining the amount of the wages or compensation paid or to be paid to employees of such employer if such differentiation is authorized by the provisions of section 6(d) of the Fair Labor Standards Act of 1938, as amended (29 U.S.C. § 206(d))."   78 Stat. 257, 42 U.S.C. § 2000e–2(h).

23. The Equal Pay Act provides, in part:

"No employer having employees subject to any provisions of this section shall

discriminate, within any establishment in which such employees are employed, between employees on the basis of sex by paying wages to employees in such establishment at a rate less than the rate at which he pays wages to employees of the opposite sex in such establishment for equal work on jobs the performance of which requires equal skill, effort, and responsibility, and which are performed under similar working conditions, except where such payment is made pursuant to (i) a seniority system; (ii) a merit system; (iii) a system which measures earnings by quantity or quality of production; or (iv) a differential based on any other factor other than sex: Provided, That an employer who is paying a wage rate differential in violation of this subsection shall not, in order to comply with the provisions of this subsection, reduce the wage rate of any employee."   77 Stat. 56, 29 U.S.C. § 206(d).

We need not decide whether retirement benefits or contributions to benefit plans are "wages" under the Act, because the Bennett Amendment extends the Act's four exceptions to all forms of "compensation" covered by Title VII.   See n. 22, supra. The Department's pension benefits, and the contributions that maintain them, are "compensation" under Title VII.   Cf. Peters v. Missouri-Pacific R. Co., 483 F.2d 490, 492 n. 3 (CA5 1973), cert. denied, 414 U.S. 1002, 94 S.Ct. 356, 38 L.Ed.2d 238.

tion applies here. That exception authorizes a "differential based on any other factor other than sex."

The Department argues that the different contributions exacted from men and women were based on the factor of longevity rather than sex. It is plain, however, that any individual's life expectancy is based on a number of factors, of which sex is only one. The record contains no evidence that any factor other than the employee's sex was taken into account in calculating the 14.84% differential between the respective contributions by men and women. We agree with Judge Duniway's observation that one cannot "say that an actuarial distinction based entirely on sex is 'based on any other factor other than sex.' Sex is exactly what it is based on." 553 F.2d 581, 588 (1976).[24]

We are also unpersuaded by the Department's reliance on a colloquy between Senator Randolph and Senator Humphrey during the debate on the Civil Rights Act of 1964. Commenting on the Bennett Amendment, Senator Humphrey expressed his understanding that it would allow many differences in the treatment of men and women under industrial benefit plans, including earlier retirement options for women. Though he did not address differences in employee contributions based on sex, Senator Humphrey apparently assumed that the 1964 Act would have little, if any, impact on existing pension plans. His statement cannot, however, fairly be made the sole guide to interpreting the Equal Pay Act, which had been adopted a year earlier; and it is the 1963 statute, with its exceptions, on which the Department ultimately relies. We conclude that Senator Humphrey's isolated comment on the Senate floor cannot change the effect of the plain language of the statute itself.[26]

---

24. The Department's argument is specious because its contribution schedule distinguished only imperfectly between long-lived and short-lived employees, while distinguishing precisely between male and female employees. In contrast, an entirely gender-neutral system of contributions and benefits would result in differing retirement benefits precisely "based on" longevity, for retirees with long lives would always receive more money than comparable employees with short lives. Such a plan would also distinguish in a crude way between male and female pensioners, because of the difference in their average life spans. It is this sort of disparity—and not an explicitly gender-based differential—that the Equal Pay Act intended to authorize.

26. The administrative constructions of this provision look in two directions. The Wage and Hour Administrator, who is charged with enforcing the Equal Pay Act, has never expressly approved different *employee* contribution rates, but he has said that either equal employer contributions or equal benefits will satisfy the Act. 29 CFR § 800.116(d) (1977). At the same time, he has stated that a wage differential based on differences in the average costs of employing men and women is not based on a "'factor other than sex.'" 29 CFR § 800.151 (1977). The Administrator's reasons for the second ruling are illuminating:

"To group employees solely on the basis of sex for purposes of comparison of costs necessarily rests on the assumption that the sex factor alone may justify the wage differential—an assumption plainly contrary to the terms and purpose of the Equal Pay Act. Wage differentials so based would serve only to perpetuate and promote the very discrimination at which the Act is directed, because in any grouping by sex of the employees to which the cost data relates, the group cost experience is necessarily assessed against an individual of one sex without regard to whether it costs an employer more or less to employ such individual than a particular individual of the opposite sex under similar working conditions

III

The Department argues that reversal is required by General Electric Co. v. Gilbert, 429 U.S. 125, 97 S.Ct. 401, 50 L.Ed.2d 343. We are satisfied, however, that neither the holding nor the reasoning of *Gilbert* is controlling.

In *Gilbert* the Court held that the exclusion of pregnancy from an employer's disability benefit plan did not constitute sex discrimination within the meaning of Title VII. Relying on the reasoning in Geduldig v. Aiello, 417 U.S. 484, 94 S.Ct. 2485, 41 L.Ed.2d 256, the Court first held that the General Electric plan did not involve "discrimination based upon gender as such." [27] The two groups of potential recipients which that case concerned were pregnant women and nonpregnant persons. " 'While the first group is exclusively female, the second includes members of both sexes.' " 429 U.S., at 135, 97 S.Ct., at 407. In contrast, each of the two groups of employees involved in this case is composed entirely and exclusively of members of the same sex. On its face, this plan discriminates on the basis of sex whereas the General Electric plan discriminated on the basis of a special physical disability.

In *Gilbert* the Court did note that the plan as actually administered had provided more favorable benefits to women as a class than to men as a class. This evidence supported the conclusion that not only had plaintiffs failed to establish a prima facie case by proving that the plan was discriminatory on its face, but they had also failed to prove any discriminatory effect.

In this case, however, the Department argues that the absence of a discriminatory effect on women as a class justifies an employment practice which, on its face, discriminated against individual employees because of their sex. But even if the Department's actuarial evidence is sufficient to prevent plaintiffs from establishing a prima facie case on the theory that the effect of the practice on women as a class was discriminatory, that the evidence does not defeat the claim that the

in jobs requiring equal skill, effort, and responsibility." Ibid. To the extent that they conflict, we find that the reasoning of § 800.151 has more "power to persuade" than the *ipse dixit* of § 800.116. Cf. Skidmore v. Swift & Co., 323 U.S. 134, 140, 65 S.Ct. 161, 164, 89 L.Ed. 124.

27. Quoting from the *Geduldig* opinion, the Court stated:

" '[T]his case is thus a far cry from cases like Reed v. Reed, 404 U.S. 71, [92 S.Ct. 251, 30 L.Ed.2d 225] (1971), and Frontiero v. Richardson, 411 U.S. 677 [93 S.Ct. 1764, 36 L.Ed.2d 583] (1973), involving discrimination based upon gender as

such. The California insurance program does not exclude anyone from benefit eligibility because of gender but merely removes one physical condition—pregnancy—from the list of compensable disabilities.' " 429 U.S., at 134, 97 S.Ct., at 407.

After further quotation, the Court added:

"The quoted language from *Geduldig* leaves no doubt that our reason for rejecting appellee's equal protection claim in that case was that the exclusion of pregnancy from coverage under California's disability-benefits plan was not in itself discrimination based on sex." Id., at 135, 97 S.Ct., at 407.

practice, on its face, discriminated against every individual woman employed by the Department.[30]

In essence, the Department is arguing that the prima facie showing of discrimination based on evidence of different contributions for the respective sexes is rebutted by its demonstration that there is a like difference in the cost of providing benefits for the respective classes. That argument might prevail if Title VII, contained a cost justification defense comparable to the affirmative defense available in a price discrimination suit.[31] But neither Congress nor the courts have recognized such a defense under Title VII.[32]

Although we conclude that the Department's practice violated Title VII, we do not suggest that the statute was intended to revolutionize the insurance and pension industries. All that is at issue today is a requirement that men and women make unequal contributions to an employer-operated pension fund. Nothing in our holding implies that it would be unlawful for an employer to set aside equal retirement contributions for each employee and let each retiree purchase the largest benefit which his or her accumulated contributions could command in the open market.[33] Nor does it call into question the insur-

30. Some *amici* suggest that the Department's discrimination is justified by business necessity. They argue that, if no gender distinction is drawn, many male employees will withdraw from the plan, or even the Department, because they can get a better pension plan in the private market. But the Department has long required equal contributions to its death-benefit plan, see n. 19, supra, and since 1975 it has required equal contributions to its pension plan. Yet the Department points to no "adverse selection" by the affected employees, presumably because an employee who wants to leave the plan must also leave his job, and few workers will quit because one of their fringe benefits could theoretically be obtained at a marginally lower price on the open market. In short, there has been no showing that sex distinctions are reasonably necessary to the normal operation of the Department's retirement plan.

31. See 15 U.S.C. § 13(a) (1976 ed.). Under the Robinson-Patman Act, proof of cost differences justifies otherwise illegal price discrimination; it does not negate the existence of the discrimination itself. See FTC v. Morton Salt Co., 334 U.S. 37, 44–45, 68 S.Ct. 822, 827–828, 92 L.Ed. 1196. So here, even if the contribution differential were based on a sound and well-recognized business practice, it would nevertheless be discriminatory, and the defendant would be forced to assert an affirmative defense to escape liability.

32. Defenses under Title VII and the Equal Pay Act are considerably narrower. See, e.g., n. 30, supra. A broad cost-differential defense was proposed and rejected when the Equal Pay Act became law. Representative Findley offered an amendment to the Equal Pay Act that would have expressly authorized a wage differential tied to the "ascertainable and specific added cost resulting from employment of the opposite sex." 109 Cong.Rec. 9217 (1963). He pointed out that the employment of women might be more costly because of such matters as higher turnover and state laws restricting women's hours. Id., at 9205. The Equal Pay Act's supporters responded that any cost differences could be handled by focusing on the factors other than sex which actually caused the differences, such as absenteeism or number of hours worked. The amendment was rejected as largely redundant for that reason. Id., at 9217.

The Senate Report, on the other hand, does seem to assume that the statute may recognize a very limited cost defense, based on "all of the elements of the employment costs of both men and women." S.Rep. No. 176, 88th Cong., 1st Sess., 4 (1963). It is difficult to find language in the statute supporting even this limited defense; in any event, no defense based on the *total* cost of employing men and women was attempted in this case.

33. Title VII and the Equal Pay Act primarily govern relations between em-

ance industry practice of considering the composition of an employer's work force in determining the probable cost of a retirement or death benefit plan.[34] Finally, we recognize that in a case of this kind it may be necessary to take special care in fashioning appropriate relief.

IV

The Department challenges the District Court's award of retroactive relief to the entire class of female employees and retirees. Title VII does not require a district court to grant any retroactive relief. A court that finds unlawful discrimination "may enjoin [the discrimination] * * * and order such affirmative action as may be appropriate, which may include, but is not limited to, reinstatement * * * with or without back pay * * * or any other equitable relief as the court deems appropriate." 42 U.S.C. § 2000e–5(g) (1970 ed., Supp. V). To the point of redundancy, the statute stresses that retroactive relief "may" be awarded if it is "appropriate."

In Albemarle Paper Co. v. Moody, 422 U.S. 405, 95 S.Ct. 2362, 45 L.Ed.2d 280, the Court reviewed the scope of a district court's discretion to fashion appropriate remedies for a Title VII violation and concluded that "backpay should be denied only for reasons which, if applied generally, would not frustrate the central statutory purposes of eradicating discrimination throughout the economy and making persons whole for injuries suffered through past discrimination." Id., at 421, 95 S.Ct., at 2373. Applying that standard, the Court ruled that an award of backpay should not be conditioned on a showing of bad faith. Id., at 422–423, 95 S.Ct., at 2373–2374. But the Albemarle Court also held that backpay was not to be awarded automatically in every case.[35]

The Albemarle presumption in favor of retroactive liability can seldom be overcome, but it does not make meaningless the district courts' duty to determine that such relief is appropriate. For several

ployees and their employer, not between employees and third parties. We do not suggest, of course, that an employer can avoid his responsibilities by delegating discriminatory programs to corporate shells. Title VII applies to "any agent" of a covered employer, 42 U.S.C. § 2000e(b) (1970 ed., Supp. V), and the Equal Pay Act applies to "any person acting directly or indirectly in the interest of an employer in relation to an employee." 29 U.S.C. § 203(d). In this case, for example, the Department could not deny that the administrative board was its agent after it successfully argued that the two were so inseparable that both shared the city's immunity from suit under 42 U.S.C. § 1983.

34. Title VII bans discrimination against an "individual" because of "such individual's" sex. 42 U.S.C. § 2000e–2(a) (1). The Equal Pay Act prohibits discrimination "within any establishment," and discrimination is defined as "paying wages to employees * * * at a rate less than the rate at which [the employer] pays wages to employees of the opposite sex" for equal work. 29 U.S.C. § 206(d)(1). Neither of these provisions makes it unlawful to determine the funding requirements for an establishment's benefit plan by considering the composition of the entire force.

35. Specifically, the Court held that a defendant prejudiced by his reliance on a plaintiff's initial waiver of any backpay claims could be absolved of backpay liability by a district court. 422 U.S., at 424, 95 S.Ct., at 2374. The Court reserved the question whether reliance of a different kind—on state "protective" laws requiring sex differentiation—would also save a defendant from liability. Id., at 423 n. 18, 95 S.Ct., at 2374.

reasons, we conclude that the District Court gave insufficient attention
to the equitable nature of Title VII remedies.[36]   Although we now have
no doubt about the application of the statute in this case, we must
recognize that conscientious and intelligent administrators of pension
funds, who did not have the benefit of the extensive briefs and arguments presented to us, may well have assumed that a program like the
Department's was entirely lawful.   The courts had been silent on the
question, and the administrative agencies had conflicting views.[37]   The
Department's failure to act more swiftly is a sign, not of its recalcitrance, but of the problem's complexity.   As commentators have noted,
pension administrators could reasonably have thought it unfair—or
even illegal—to make male employees shoulder more than their "actuarial share" of the pension burden.[38]   There is no reason to believe that
the threat of a backpay award is needed to cause other administrators
to amend their practices to conform to this decision.

36. According to the District Court, the
defendant's liability for contributions did
not begin until April 5, 1972, the day the
Equal Employment Opportunity Commission issued an interpretation casting doubt
on some varieties of pension fund discrimination. See 37 Fed.Reg. 6835–6837. Even
assuming that the EEOC's decision should
have put the defendants on notice that
they were acting illegally, the date chosen
by the District Court was too early. The
court should have taken into account the
difficulty of amending a major pension
plan, a task that cannot be accomplished
overnight. Moreover, it should not have
given conclusive weight to the EEOC
guideline. See General Electric Co. v. Gilbert, 429 U.S., at 141, 97 S.Ct., at 411. The
Wage and Hour Administrator, whose rulings also provide a defense in sex discrimination cases, 29 U.S.C. § 259, refused to
follow the EEOC. See n. 37, infra.

Further doubt about the District Court's
equitable sensitivity to the impact of a
refund order is raised by the court's decision to award the full difference between
the contributions made by male employees
and those made by female employees.
This may give the victims of the discrimination more than their due. If an undifferentiated actuarial table had been employed in 1972, the contributions of women
employees would no doubt have been lower
than they were, but they would not have
been as low as the contributions actually
made by men in that period. The District
Court should at least have considered ordering a refund of only the difference between contributions made by women and
the contributions they would have made
under an actuarially sound and nondiscriminatory plan.

37. As noted earlier, n. 26, supra, the
position of the Wage and Hour Administrator has been somewhat confusing. His
general rule rejected differences in average
cost as a defense, but his more specific rule
lent some support to the Department's
view by simply requiring an employer to
equalize either his contributions or employee benefits. Compare 29 CFR § 800.151
(1977) with § 800.116(d). The EEOC requires equal benefits. See 29 CFR
§§ 1604.9(e) and (f) (1977). Two other
agencies with responsibility for equal opportunity in employment adhere to the
Wage and Hour Administrator's position.
See 41 CFR § 60.20.3(c) (1977) (Office of
Federal Contract Compliance); 45 CFR
§ 86.56(b)(2) (1976) (Dept. of Health, Education, and Welfare). See also 40 Fed.Reg.
24135 (1975) (HEW).

38. "If an employer establishes a pension plan, the charges of discrimination
will be reversed: if he chooses a money
purchase formula, women can complain
that they receive less per month. While
the employer and the insurance company
are quick to point out that women as a
group actually receive more when equal
contributions are made—because of the
long-term effect of compound interest—
women employees still complain of discrimination. If the employer chooses the defined benefit formula, his male employees
can allege discrimination because he contributes more for women as a group than
for men as a group. The employer is in a
dilemma: he is damned in the discrimination context no matter what he does."
Note, Sex Discrimination and Sex-Based
Mortality Tables, 53 B.U.L.Rev. 624, 633–
634 (1973) (footnotes omitted).

Nor can we ignore the potential impact which changes in rules affecting insurance and pension plans may have on the economy. Fifty million Americans participate in retirement plans other than Social Security. The assets held in trust for these employees are vast and growing—more than $400 billion was reserved for retirement benefits at the end of 1976 and reserves are increasing by almost $50 billion a year.[39] These plans, like other forms of insurance depend on the accumulation of large sums to cover contingencies. The amounts set aside are determined by a painstaking assessment of the insurer's likely liability. Risks that the insurer foresees will be included in the calculation of liability, and the rates or contributions charged will reflect that calculation. The occurrence of major unforeseen contingencies, however, jeopardizes the insurer's solvency and, ultimately, the insureds' benefits. Drastic changes in the legal rules governing pension and insurance funds, like other unforeseen events, can have this effect. Consequently, the rules that apply to these funds should not be applied retroactively unless the legislature has plainly commanded that result.[40] The EEOC itself has recognized that the administrators of retirement plans must be given time to adjust gradually to Title VII's demands.[41] Courts have also shown sensitivity to the special dangers of retroactive Title VII awards in this field. See Rosen v. Public Serv. Elec. & Gas Co., 328 F.Supp. 454, 466–468 (DCNJ 1971).

There can be no doubt that the prohibition against sex-differentiated employee contributions represents a marked departure from past practice. Although Title VII was enacted in 1964, this is apparently the first litigation challenging contribution differences based on valid actuarial tables. Retroactive liability could be devastating for a pension fund. The harm would fall in large part on innocent third parties. If, as the courts below apparently contemplated, the plaintiffs' contributions are recovered from the pension fund,[43] the administrators of the

39. American Council of Life Insurance, Pension Facts 1977, pp. 20–23.

40. In 1974, Congress underlined the importance of making only gradual and prospective changes in the rules that govern pension plans. In that year, Congress passed a bill regulating employee retirement programs. Employee Retirement Income Security Act of 1974, 88 Stat. 829. The bill paid careful attention to the problem of retroactivity. It set a wide variety of effective dates for different provisions of the new law; some of the rules will not be fully effective until 1984, a decade after the law was enacted. See, e.g., in 1970 ed., Supp. V of 29 U.S.C. § 1061(a) (Sept. 2, 1974); § 1031(b)(1) (Jan. 1, 1975); § 1086(b) (Dec. 31, 1975); § 1114(c)(4) (June 30, 1977); § 1381(c)(1) (Jan. 1, 1978); § 1061(c) (Dec. 31, 1980); § 1114(c) (June 30, 1984).

41. In February 1968, the EEOC issued guidelines disapproving differences in male and female retirement ages. In September of the same year, EEOC's general counsel gave an opinion that retirement plans could set gradual schedules for complying with the guidelines and that the judgment of the parties about how speedily to comply "would carry considerable weight." See Chastang v. Flynn & Emrich Co., 541 F.2d 1040, 1045 (CA4 1976).

43. The Court of Appeals plainly expected the plan to pay the award, for it noted that imposing retroactive liability "might leave the plan somewhat underfunded." 553 F.2d, at 592. After making this observation, the Court of Appeals suggested a series of possible solutions to the problem—the benefits of all retired workers could be lowered, the burden on current employees could be increased, or the Department could decide to contribute enough to offset the plan's unexpected loss. Ibid.

fund will be forced to meet unchanged obligations with diminished assets.[44] If the reserve proves inadequate, either the expectations of all retired employees will be disappointed or current employees will be forced to pay not only for their own future security but also for the unanticipated reduction in the contributions of past employees.

Without qualifying the force of the *Albemarle* presumption in favor of retroactive relief, we conclude that it was error to grant such relief in this case. Accordingly, although we agree with the Court of Appeals' analysis of the statute, we vacate its judgment and remand the case for further proceedings consistent with this opinion.

It is so ordered.

MR. JUSTICE BRENNAN took no part in the consideration or decision of this case.

MR. JUSTICE BLACKMUN, concurring in part and concurring in the judgment.

MR. CHIEF JUSTICE BURGER, with whom MR. JUSTICE REHNQUIST joins, concurring in part and dissenting in part.

I join Part IV of the Court's opinion; as to Parts I, II, and III, I dissent.

Gender-based actuarial tables have been in use since at least 1843, and their statistical validity has been repeatedly verified. The vast life insurance, annuity, and pension plan industry is based on these tables. As the Court recognizes, ante, at 1375, it is a fact that "women, as a class, do live longer than men." It is equally true that employers cannot know in advance when individual members of the classes will die. Ante, at 1375. Yet, if they are to operate economically workable group pension programs, it is only rational to permit them to rely on statistically sound and proved disparities in longevity between men and women. Indeed, it seems to me irrational to assume Congress intended to outlaw use of the fact that, for whatever reasons or combination of reasons, women as a class outlive men.

The Court's conclusion that the language of the civil rights statute is clear, admitting of no advertence to the legislative history, such as there was, is not soundly based. An effect upon pension plans so revolutionary and discriminatory—this time favorable to women at the expense of men—should not be read into the statute without either a clear statement of that intent in the statute, or some reliable indication in the legislative history that this was Congress' purpose. The Court's casual dismissal of Senator Humphrey's apparent assumption that the "Act would have little, if any, impact on existing pension plans," is to dismiss a significant manifestation of what impact on industrial benefit

---

44. Two commentators urging the illegality of gender-based pension plans noted the danger of "staggering damage awards," and they proposed as one cure the exercise of judicial "discretion [to] refuse a backpay award because of the hardship it would work on an employer who had acted in good faith * * *." Bernstein & Williams, Title VII and the Problem of Sex Classifications in Pension Programs, 74 Colum.L.Rev. 1203, 1226, 1227 (1974).

plans was contemplated. It is reasonably clear there was no intention to abrogate an employer's right, in this narrow and limited context, to treat women differently from men in the face of historical reliance on mortality experience statistics.

The reality of differences in human mortality is what mortality experience tables reflect. The difference is the added longevity of women. All the reasons why women statistically outlive men are not clear. But categorizing people on the basis of sex, the one acknowledged immutable difference between men and women, is to take into account all of the unknown reasons, whether biologically or culturally based, or both, which give women a significantly greater life expectancy than men. It is therefore true as the Court says, "that any individual's life expectancy is based on a number of factors, of which sex is only one." But it is not true that by seizing upon the only constant, "measurable" factor, no others were taken into account. All other factors, whether known but variable—or unknown—are the elements which automatically account for the actuarial disparity. And all are accounted for when the constant factor is used as a basis for determining the costs and benefits of a group pension plan.

Here, of course, petitioners are discriminating in take-home pay between men and women. Cf. General Electric Co. v. Gilbert, 429 U.S. 125, 97 S.Ct. 401, 50 L.Ed.2d 343 (1976); Nashville Gas Co. v. Satty, 434 U.S. 136, 98 S.Ct. 347, 54 L.Ed.2d 356 (1977). The practice of petitioners, however, falls squarely under the exemption provided by the Equal Pay Act of 1963, 29 U.S.C. § 206(d), incorporated into Title VII by the so-called Bennett Amendment, 78 Stat. 257, now 42 U.S.C. § 2000e–2(h). That exemption tells us that an employer may not discriminate between employees on the basis of sex by paying one sex lesser compensation that the other "except where such payment is made pursuant to * * * a differential based on any other factor other than sex * * *." The "other factor other than sex" is longevity; sex is the umbrella-constant under which all of the elements leading to differences in longevity are grouped and assimilated, and the only objective feature upon which an employer—or anyone else, including insurance companies—may reliably base a cost differential for the "risk" being insured.

This is in no sense a failure to treat women as "individuals" in violation of the statute, as the Court holds. It is to treat them as individually as it is possible to do in the face of the unknowable length of each individual life. Individually, every woman has the same statistical possibility of outliving men. This is the essence of basing decisions on reliable statistics when individual determinations are infeasible or, as here, impossible.

Of course, women cannot be disqualified from, for example, heavy labor just because the generality of women are thought not as strong as men—a proposition which perhaps may sometimes be statistically demonstrable, but will remain individually refutable. When, however, it is impossible to tailor a program such as a pension plan to the individual, nothing should prevent application of reliable statistical facts to the individual, for whom the facts cannot be disproved until long after planning, funding, and operating the program have been undertaken.

I find it anomalous, if not contradictory, that the Court's opinion tells us, in effect, *ante,* at 1380, and n. 33, that the holding is not really a barrier to responding to the complaints of men employees, as a group. The Court states that employers may give their employees precisely the same dollar amount and require them to secure their own annuities directly from an insurer, who, of course, is under no compulsion to ignore 135 years of accumulated, recorded longevity experience.

MR. JUSTICE MARSHALL, concurring in part and dissenting in part.

I agree that Title VII of the Civil Rights Act of 1964, as amended, forbids petitioners' practice of requiring female employees to make larger contributions to a pension fund than do male employees. I therefore join all of the Court's opinion except Part IV.

ARIZONA GOVERNING COMMITTEE v. NORRIS

Supreme Court of the United States, 1983.
463 U.S. 1073, 103 S.Ct. 3492, 77 L.Ed.2d 1236.

PER CURIAM.

Petitioners in this case administer a deferred compensation plan for employees of the State of Arizona. The respondent class consists of all female employees who are enrolled in the plan or will enroll in the plan in the future. Certiorari was granted to decide whether Title VII of the Civil Rights Act of 1964, as amended, 42 U.S.C. § 2000e et seq., prohibits an employer from offering its employees the option of receiving retirement benefits from one of several companies selected by the employer, all of which pay a woman lower monthly retirement benefits than a man who has made the same contributions; and whether, if so, the relief awarded by the District Court was proper. The Court holds that this practice does constitute discrimination on the basis of sex in violation of Title VII, and that all retirement benefits derived from contributions made after the decision today must be calculated without regard to the sex of the beneficiary. This position is expressed in Parts I, II, and III of the opinion of JUSTICE MARSHALL, post, p. 3494, which are joined by JUSTICE BRENNAN, JUSTICE WHITE, JUSTICE STEVENS, and JUSTICE O'CONNOR. The Court further holds that benefits derived from contributions made prior to this decision may be calculated as provided by the existing terms of the Arizona plan. This position is expressed in Part III of the opinion of JUSTICE POWELL, post, p. 3504, which is joined by THE CHIEF JUSTICE, JUSTICE BLACKMUN, JUSTICE REHNQUIST, and JUSTICE O'CONNOR. Accordingly, the judgment of the Court of Appeals is affirmed in part, reversed in part, and the case is remanded for further proceedings consistent with this opinion. The Clerk is directed to issue the judgment August 1, 1983.

It is so ordered.

JUSTICE MARSHALL, with whom JUSTICE BRENNAN, JUSTICE WHITE, JUSTICE STEVENS, and JUSTICE O'CONNOR join as to Parts I, II, and III, concurring in the judgment in part, and with whom JUSTICE BRENNAN, JUSTICE WHITE, and JUSTICE STEVENS join as to Part IV.

In Los Angeles Dept. of Water & Power v. Manhart, 435 U.S. 702, 98 S.Ct. 1370, 55 L.Ed.2d 657 (1978), this Court held that Title VII of the Civil Rights Act of 1964 prohibits an employer from requiring women to make larger contributions in order to obtain the same monthly pension benefits as men. The question presented by this case is whether Title VII also prohibits an employer from offering its employees the option of receiving retirement benefits from one of several companies selected by the employer, all of which pay a woman lower monthly benefits than a man who has made the same contributions.

I

A

Since 1974 the State of Arizona has offered its employees the opportunity to enroll in a deferred compensation plan administered by the Arizona Governing Committee for Tax Deferred Annuity and Deferred Compensation Plans (Governing Committee). Ariz.Rev.Stat.Ann. § 38–871 et seq.; Ariz.Regs. 2–9–01 et seq. Employees who participate in the plan may thereby postpone the receipt of a portion of their wages until retirement. By doing so, they postpone paying federal income tax on the amounts deferred until after retirement, when they receive those amounts and any earnings thereon.

After inviting private companies to submit bids outlining the investment opportunities that they were willing to offer State employees, the State selected several companies to participate in its deferred compensation plan. Many of the companies selected offer three basic retirement options: (1) a single lump-sum payment upon retirement, (2) periodic payments of a fixed sum for a fixed period of time, and (3) monthly annuity payments for the remainder of the employee's life. When an employee decides to take part in the deferred compensation plan, he must designate the company in which he wishes to invest his deferred wages. Employees must choose one of the companies selected by the State to participate in the plan; they are not free to invest their deferred compensation in any other way. At the time an employee enrolls in the plan, he may also select one of the payout options offered by the company that he has chosen, but when he reaches retirement age he is free to switch to one of the company's other options. If at retirement the employee decides to receive a lump-sum payment, he may also purchase any of the options then being offered by the other companies participating in the plan. Many employees find an annuity contract to be the most attractive option, since receipt of a lump sum upon retirement requires payment of taxes on the entire sum in one year, and the choice of a fixed sum for a fixed period requires an employee to speculate as to how long he will live.

Once an employee chooses the company in which he wishes to invest and decides the amount of compensation to be deferred each month, the State is responsible for withholding the appropriate sums from the employee's wages and channelling those sums to the company designated by the employee. The State bears the cost of making the necessary payroll deductions and of giving employees time off to attend group meetings to learn about the plan, but it does not contribute any monies to supplement the employees' deferred wages.

For an employee who elects to receive a monthly annuity following retirement, the amount of the employee's monthly benefits depends upon the amount of compensation that the employee deferred (and any earnings thereon), the employee's age at retirement, and the employee's sex. All of the companies selected by the State to participate in the plan use sex-based mortality tables to calculate monthly retirement benefits. App. 12. Under these tables a man receives larger monthly payments than a woman who deferred the same amount of compensation and retired at the same age, because the tables classify annuitants on the basis of sex and women on average live longer than men.[2] Sex is the only factor that the tables use to classify individuals of the same age; the tables do not incorporate other factors correlating with longevity such as smoking habits, alcohol consumption, weight, medical history, or family history. App. 13.

As of August 18, 1978, 1,675 of the State's approximately 35,000 employees were participating in the deferred compensation plan. Of these 1,675 participating employees, 681 were women, and 572 women had elected some form of future annuity option. As of the same date, 10 women participating in the plan had retired, and four of those 10 had chosen a life-time annuity. App. 6.

B

On May 3, 1975, respondent Nathalie Norris, an employee in the Arizona Department of Economic Security, elected to participate in the plan. She requested that her deferred compensation be invested in the Lincoln National Life Insurance Company's fixed annuity contract. Shortly thereafter Arizona approved respondent's request and began withholding $199.50 from her salary each month.

On April 25, 1978, after exhausting administrative remedies, respondent brought suit in the United States District Court for the

---

2. Different insurance companies participating in the plan use different means of classifying individuals on the basis of sex. Several companies use separate tables for men and women. Another company uses a single actuarial table based on male mortality rates, but calculates the annuities to be paid to women by using a six-year "setback," i.e., by treating a woman as if she were a man six years younger and had the life expectancy of a man that age. App. 12.

District of Arizona against the State, the Governing Committee, and several individual members of the Committee. Respondent alleged that the defendants were violating § 703(a) of Title VII of the Civil Rights Act of 1964, 78 Stat. 255, as amended, 42 U.S.C. § 2000e–2(a), by administering an annuity plan that discriminates on the basis of sex. Respondent requested that the District Court certify a class under Fed. Rules Civ.Proc. 23(b)(2) consisting of all female employees of the State of Arizona "who are enrolled or will in the future enroll in the State Deferred Compensation Plan." Complaint ¶ V.

On March 13, 1980, the District Court certified a class action and granted summary judgment for the plaintiff class, holding that the State's plan violates Title VII, 486 F.Supp. 645. The court directed petitioners to cease using sex-based actuarial tables and to pay retired female employees benefits equal to those paid to similarly situated men. The United States Court of Appeals for the Ninth Circuit affirmed, with one judge dissenting. 671 F.2d 330 (1982). We granted certiorari to decide whether the Arizona plan violates Title VII and whether, if so, the relief ordered by the District Court was proper. ___ U.S. ___, 103 S.Ct. 205, 74 L.Ed.2d 164 (1982).

II

We consider first whether petitioners would have violated Title VII if they had run the entire deferred compensation plan themselves, without the participation of any insurance companies. Title VII makes it an unlawful employment practice "to discriminate against any individual with respect to his compensation, terms, conditions, or privileges of employment, because of such individual's race, color, religion, sex or national origin." 42 U.S.C. § 2000e–2(a)(1). There is no question that the opportunity to participate in a deferred compensation plan constitutes a "conditio[n] or privileg[e] of employment," and that retirement benefits constitute a form of "compensation." The issue we must decide is whether it is discrimination "because of * * * sex" to pay a retired woman lower monthly benefits than a man who deferred the same amount of compensation.

We have no hesitation in holding, as have all but one of the lower courts that have considered the question, that the classification of employees on the basis of sex is no more permissible at the pay-out stage of a retirement plan than at the pay-in stage.[10] We reject petitioners' contention that the Arizona plan does not discriminate on

10. It is irrelevant that female employees in *Manhart* were required to participate in the pension plan, whereas participation in the Arizona deferred compensation plan is voluntary. Title VII forbids all discrimination concerning "compensation, terms, conditions, or privileges of employment," not just discrimination concerning those aspects of the employment relationship as to which the employee has no choice. It is likewise irrelevant that the Arizona plan includes two options—the lump-sum option and the fixed-sum-for-a-fixed-period option—that are provided on equal terms to men and women. An employer that offers one fringe benefit on a discriminatory basis cannot escape liability because he also offers other benefits on a nondiscriminatory basis. Cf. Mississippi University for Women v. Hogan, ___ U.S. ___, ___, n. 8, 102 S.Ct. 3331, 3336, n. 8, 73 L.Ed.2d 1090 (1982).

the basis of sex because a woman and a man who defer the same amount of compensation will obtain upon retirement annuity policies having approximately the same present actuarial value.[11]   Arizona has simply offered its employees a choice among different levels of annuity benefits, any one of which, if offered alone, would be equivalent to the plan at issue in *Manhart*, where the employer determined both the monthly contributions employees were required to make and the level of benefits that they were paid.   If a woman participating in the Arizona plan wishes to obtain monthly benefits equal to those obtained by a man, she must make greater monthly contributions than he, just as the female employees in *Manhart* had to make greater contributions to obtain equal benefits.   For any particular level of benefits that a woman might wish to receive, she will have to make greater monthly contributions to obtain that level of benefits than a man would have to make.   The fact that Arizona has offered a range of discriminatory benefit levels, rather than only one such level, obviously provides no basis whatsoever for distinguishing *Manhart*.

In asserting that the Arizona plan is non-discriminatory because a man and a woman who have made equal contributions will obtain annuity policies of roughly equal present actuarial value, petitioners incorrectly assume that Title VII permits an employer to classify employees on the basis of sex in predicting their longevity.   Otherwise there would be no basis for postulating that a woman's annuity policy has the same present actuarial value as the policy of a similarly situated man even though her policy provides lower monthly benefits.[12]   This underlying assumption—that sex may properly be used to predict longevity—is flatly inconsistent with the basic teaching of *Manhart*: that Title VII requires employers to treat their employees as *individuals*, not "as simply components of a racial, religious, sexual, or national class."   435 U.S., at 708, 98 S.Ct., at 1375.   *Manhart* squarely rejected the notion that, because women as a class live longer than men, an employer may adopt a retirement plan that treats every individual woman less favorably than every individual man.   Id., at 716–717, 98 S.Ct., at 1379–1380.

* * *

We conclude that it is just as much discrimination "because of
* * * sex" to pay a woman lower benefits when she has made the

---

11. The present actuarial value of an annuity policy is determined by multiplying the present value (in this case, the value at the time of the employee's retirement) of each monthly payment promised by the probability, which is supplied by an actuarial table, that the annuitant will live to receive that payment.   An annuity policy issued to a retired female employee under a sex-based retirement plan will have roughly the same present actuarial value as a policy issued to a similarly situated

man, since the lower value of each monthly payment she is promised is offset by the likelihood that she will live longer and therefore receive more payments.

12. See Spirt v. Teachers Ins. & Annuity Ass'n., supra, 691 F.2d, at 1061–1062; Brilmayer, Hekeler, Laycock & Sullivan, Sex Discrimination in Employer-Sponsored Insurance Plans: A Legal and Demographic Analysis, 47 U.Chi.L.Rev. 505, 512–514 (1980).

same contributions as a man as it is to make her pay larger contributions to obtain the same benefits.

III

Since petitioners plainly would have violated Title VII if they had run the entire deferred compensation plan themselves, the only remaining question as to liability is whether their conduct is beyond the reach of the statute because it is the companies chosen by petitioners to participate in the plan that calculate and pay the retirement benefits.

Title VII "primarily govern[s] relations between employees and their employer, not between employees and third parties." [16] *Manhart,* 435 U.S., at 718, n. 33, 98 S.Ct., at 1380, n. 33. Recognizing this limitation on the reach of the statute, we noted in *Manhart* that

> Nothing in our holding implies that it would be unlawful for an employer to set aside equal retirement contributions for each employee and let each retiree purchase the largest benefits which his or her accumulated contributions could command in the open market. Id. 435 U.S., at 717–718, 98 S.Ct., at 1379–1380 (footnote omitted).

Relying on this caveat, petitioners contend that they have not violated Title VII because the life annuities offered by the companies participating in the Arizona plan reflect what is available in the open market. Petitioners cite a statement in the stipulation of facts entered into in the District Court that "[a]ll tables presently in use provide a larger sum to a male than to a female of equal age, account value and any guaranteed payment period." App. 10.[17]

It is no defense that all annuities immediately available in the open market may have been based on sex-segregated actuarial tables. In context it is reasonably clear that the stipulation on which petitioners rely means only that all the tables used by the companies taking part in the Arizona plan are based on sex, but our conclusion does not depend upon whether petitioner's construction of the stipulation is accepted or rejected. It is irrelevant whether any other insurers offered annuities on a sex-neutral basis, since the State did not simply set aside retirement contributions and let employees purchase annuities on the open market. On the contrary, the State provided the opportunity to obtain an annuity as part of its own deferred compensation plan. It invited insurance companies to submit bids outlining the terms on which they would supply retirement benefits [19] and selected

---

16. The statute applies to employers and "any agent" of an employer. 42 U.S.C. § 2000e(b).

17. Petitioners also emphasize that an employee participating in the Arizona plan can elect to receive a lump-sum payment upon retirement and then "purchase the largest benefits which his or her accumulated contributions could command in the open market." The fact that the lump-sum option permits this has no bearing, however, on whether petitioners have discriminated because of sex in offering an annuity option to its employees. As we have pointed out above, ante, at note 10, it is no defense to discrimination in the provision of a fringe benefit that another fringe benefit is provided on a nondiscriminatory basis.

19. The State's contract procurement documents asked the bidders to quote annuity rates for men and women.

the companies that were permitted to participate in the plan. Once the State selected these companies, it entered into contracts with them governing the terms on which benefits were to be provided to employees. Employees enrolling in the plan could obtain retirement benefits only from one of those companies, and no employee could be contacted by a company except as permitted by the State. Ariz.Regs. 2–9–06.A, 2–9–20.A.

Under these circumstances there can be no serious question that petitioners are legally responsible for the discriminatory terms on which annuities are offered by the companies chosen to participate in the plan. Having created a plan whereby employees can obtain the advantages of using deferred compensation to purchase an annuity only if they invest in one of the companies specifically selected by the State, the State cannot disclaim responsibility for the discriminatory features of the insurers' options. Since employers are ultimately responsible for the "compensation, terms, conditions, [and] privileges of employment" provided to employees, an employer that adopts a fringe-benefit scheme that discriminates among its employees on the basis of race, religion, sex, or national origin violates Title VII regardless of whether third parties are also involved in the discrimination.[21] In this case the State of Arizona was itself a party to contracts concerning the annuities to be offered by the insurance companies, and it is well established that both parties to a discriminatory contract are liable for any discriminatory provisions the contract contains, regardless of which party initially suggested inclusion of the discriminatory provisions. It would be inconsistent with the broad remedial purposes of Title VII to hold that an employer who adopts a discriminatory fringe benefit plan can avoid liability on the ground that he could not find a third party willing to

21. An analogy may usefully be drawn to our decision in Ford Motor Co. v. NLRB, 441 U.S. 488, 99 S.Ct. 1842, 60 L.Ed.2d 420 (1979). The employer in that case provided in-plant food services to its employees under a contract with an independent caterer. We held that the prices charged for the food constituted "terms and conditions of employment" under the National Labor Relations Act (NLRA) and were therefore mandatory subjects for collective bargaining. We specifically rejected the employer's argument that, because the food was provided by a third party, the prices did not implicate " 'an aspect of the relationship between the employer and employees.' " Id., 441 U.S., at 501, 99 S.Ct., at 1851, quoting Allied Chemical & Alkali Workers v. Pittsburgh Plate Glass Co., 404 U.S. 157, 176, 92 S.Ct. 383, 396, 30 L.Ed.2d 341 (1971). We emphasized that the selection of an independent contractor to provide the food did not change the fact that "the matter of in-plant food prices and services is an aspect of the relationship between Ford and its own employees." 441 U.S., at 501, 99 S.Ct., at 1851.

Just as the issue in *Ford* was whether the employer had refused to bargain with respect to "terms and conditions of employment," 29 U.S.C. § 158(d), the issue here is whether petitioners have discriminated against female employees with respect to "compensation, terms, conditions or privileges of employment." Even more so than in-plant food prices, retirement benefits are matters "of deep concern" to employees, id., 441 U.S., at 498, 99 S.Ct., at 1849, and plainly constitute an aspect of the employment relationship. Indeed, in *Ford* we specifically compared in-plant food services to "other kinds of benefits, such as health insurance, implicating outside suppliers." Id., 441 U.S., at 503, n. 15, 99 S.Ct., at 1852, n. 15. We do not think it makes any more difference here than it did in *Ford* that the employer engaged third parties to provide a particular benefit rather than directly providing the benefit itself.

treat his employees on a nondiscriminatory basis.[24] An employer who confronts such a situation must either supply the fringe benefit himself, without the assistance of any third party, or not provide it at all.

JUSTICE POWELL, with whom THE CHIEF JUSTICE, JUSTICE BLACKMUN, and JUSTICE REHNQUIST join as to Parts I and II, dissenting in part and with whom THE CHIEF JUSTICE, JUSTICE BLACKMUN, JUSTICE REHNQUIST, and JUSTICE O'CONNOR join as to Part III, concurring in part.

The Court today holds that an employer may not offer its employees life annuities from a private insurance company that uses actuarially sound, sex-based mortality tables. This holding will have a far-reaching effect on the operation of insurance and pension plans. Employers may be forced to discontinue offering life annuities, or potentially disruptive changes may be required in long-established methods of calculating insurance and pensions.[1] Either course will work a major change in the way the cost of insurance is determined—to the probable detriment of *all* employees. This is contrary to our explicit recognition in Los Angeles Dept. of Water & Power v. Manhart, 435 U.S. 702, 717, 98 S.Ct. 1370, 1380, 55 L.Ed.2d 657 (1978), that Title VII "was [not] intended to revolutionize the insurance and pension industries."

I

The State of Arizona provides its employees with a voluntary pension plan that allows them to defer receipt of a portion of their compensation until retirement. If an employee chooses to participate, an amount designated by the employee is withheld from each paycheck and invested by the State on the employee's behalf. When an employee retires, he or she may receive the amount that has accrued in one of three ways. The employee may withdraw the total amount accrued, arrange for periodic payments of a fixed sum for a fixed time, or use the accrued amount to purchase a life annuity.

24. Such a result would be particularly anomalous where, as here, the employer made no effort to determine whether third parties would provide the benefit on a neutral basis. Contrast The Chronicle of Higher Education, note 15, supra, at 25–26 (explaining how the University of Minnesota obtained agreements from two insurance companies to use sex-neutral annuity tables to calculate annuity benefits for its employees). Far from bargaining for sex-neutral treatment of its employees, Arizona asked companies seeking to participate in its plan to list their annuity rates for men and women separately.

1. The cost of continuing to provide annuities may become prohibitive. The *minimum* additional cost necessary to equalize benefits prospectively would range from $85 to $93 million each year for at least

the next 15 years. United States Department of Labor, Cost Study of the Impact of an Equal Benefits Rule on Pension Benefits 4 (1983) (hereinafter Department of Labor Cost Study). This minimum cost assumes that employers will be free to use the least costly method of adjusting benefits. This assumption may be unfounded. If employers are required to "top up" benefits—i.e., calculate women's benefits at the rate applicable to men rather than apply a unisex rate to both men and women—the cost of providing purely prospective benefits would range from $428 to $676 million each year for at least the next 15 years. Department of Labor Cost Study 31. No one seriously suggests that these costs will not be passed on—in large part—to the annuity beneficiaries or, in the case of state and local governments, to the public.

There is no contention that the State's plan discriminates between men and women when an employee contributes to the fund. The plan is voluntary and each employee may contribute as much as he or she chooses. Nor does anyone contend that either of the first two methods of repaying the accrued amount at retirement is discriminatory. Thus, if Arizona had adopted the same contribution plan but provided only the first two repayment options, there would be no dispute that its plan complied with Title VII of the Civil Rights Act of 1964, as amended, 42 U.S.C. § 2000e et seq. The first two options, however, have disadvantages. If an employee chooses to take a lump-sum payment, the tax liability will be substantial. The second option ameliorates the tax problem by spreading the receipt of the accrued amount over a fixed period of time. This option, however, does not guard against the possibility that the finite number of payments selected by the employee will fail to provide income for the remainder of his or her life.

The third option—the purchase of a life annuity—resolves both of these problems. It reduces an employee's tax liability by spreading the payments out over time, and it guarantees that the employee will receive a stream of payments for life. State law prevents Arizona from accepting the financial uncertainty of funding life annuities. Ariz.Rev. Stat.Ann. § 38–871(C)(1) (1983). But to achieve tax benefits under federal law, the life annuity must be purchased from a company designated by the retirement plan. Rev.Rul. 72–25, 1972–1 Cum.Bull. 127; Rev.Rul. 68–99, 1968–1 Cum.Bull 193. Accordingly, Arizona contracts with private insurance companies to make life annuities available to its employees. The companies that underwrite the life annuities, as do the vast majority of private insurance companies in the United States, use sex-based mortality tables. Thus, the only effect of Arizona's third option is to allow its employees to purchase at a tax saving the same annuities they otherwise would purchase on the open market.

The Court holds that Arizona's voluntary plan violates Title VII. In the majority's view, Title VII requires an employer to follow one of three courses. An employer must provide unisex annuities itself, contract with insurance companies to provide such annuities, or provide no annuities to its employees. Ante, at 3502 (MARSHALL, J., concurring in the judgment in part). The first option is largely illusory. Most employers do not have either the financial resources or administrative ability to underwrite annuities. Or, as in this case, state law may prevent an employer from providing annuities. If unisex annuities are available, an employer may contract with private insurance companies to provide them. It is stipulated, however, that the insurance companies with which Arizona contracts do not provide unisex annuities, nor do insurance companies generally underwrite them. The insurance industry either is prevented by state law from doing so or it views unisex mortality tables as actuarially unsound. An employer, of course, may choose the third option. It simply may decline to offer its employees the right to purchase annuities at a substantial tax saving. It is difficult to see the virtue in such a compelled choice.

II

As indicated above, the consequences of the Court's holding are unlikely to be beneficial. If the cost to employers of offering unisex annuities is prohibitive or if insurance carriers choose not to write such annuities, employees will be denied the opportunity to purchase life annuities—concededly the most advantageous pension plan—at lower cost.[4] If, alternatively, insurance carriers and employers choose to offer these annuities, the heavy cost burden of equalizing benefits probably will be passed on to current employees. There is no evidence that Congress intended Title VII to work such a change. Nor does *Manhart* support such a sweeping reading of this statute. That case expressly recognized the limited reach of its holding—a limitation grounded in the legislative history of Title VII and the inapplicability of Title VII's policies to the insurance industry.

A

We were careful in *Manhart* to make clear that the question before us was narrow. We stated: "All that is at issue today is a requirement that men and women make unequal contributions to an *employer-operated* pension fund." 435 U.S., at 717, 98 S.Ct., at 1380 (emphasis added). And our holding was limited expressly to the precise issue before us. We stated that "[a]lthough we conclude that the Department's practice violated Title VII, we do not suggest that the statute was intended to revolutionize the insurance and pension industries." Ibid.

The Court in *Manhart* had good reason for recognizing the narrow reach of Title VII in the particular area of the insurance industry. Congress has chosen to leave the primary responsibility for regulating the insurance industry to the respective States. See McCarran-Ferguson Act, 59 Stat. 33, as amended, 15 U.S.C. § 1011 et seq. This Act reflects the long-held view that the "continued regulation * * * by the several States of the business of insurance is in the public interest." 15 U.S.C. § 1011; see SEC v. National Securities, Inc., 393 U.S. 453, 458–459, 89 S.Ct. 564, 567–568, 21 L.Ed.2d 668 (1969). Given the consistent policy of entrusting insurance regulation to the States, the majority is not justified in assuming that Congress intended in 1964 to require the industry to change long-standing actuarial methods, approved over decades by state insurance commissions.

Nothing in the language of Title VII supports this preemption of state jurisdiction. Nor has the majority identified any evidence in the legislative history that Congress considered the widespread use of sex-

---

4. This is precisely what has happened in this case. Faced with the liability resulting from the Court of Appeals' judgment, the State of Arizona discontinued making life annuities available to its employees. Tr. of Oral Arg. 8. Any employee who now wishes to have the security provided by a life annuity must withdraw his or her accrued retirement savings from the state pension plan, pay federal income tax on the amount withdrawn, and then use the remainder to purchase an annuity on the open market—which most likely will be sex-based. The adverse effect of today's holding apparently will fall primarily on the State's employees.

based mortality tables to be discriminatory or that it intended to modify its previous grant by the McCarran-Ferguson Act of exclusive jurisdiction to the States to regulate the terms of protection offered by insurance companies.

B

As neither the language of the statute nor the legislative history supports its holding, the majority is compelled to rely on its perception of the policy expressed in Title VII. The policy, of course, is broadly to proscribe discrimination in employment practices. But the statute itself focuses specifically on the individual and "precludes treatment of individuals as simply components of a racial, religious, sexual or national class." This specific focus has little relevance to the business of insurance. Insurance and life annuities exist because it is impossible to measure accurately how long any one individual will live. Insurance companies cannot make individual determinations of life expectancy; they must consider instead the life expectancy of identifiable groups. Given a sufficiently large group of people, an insurance company can predict with considerable reliability the rate and frequency of deaths within the group based on the past mortality experience of similar groups. Title VII's concern for the effect of employment practices on the individual thus is simply inapplicable to the actuarial predictions that must be made in writing insurance and annuities.

C

The accuracy with which an insurance company predicts the rate of mortality depends on its ability to identify groups with similar mortality rates. The writing of annuities thus requires that an insurance company group individuals according to attributes that have a significant correlation with mortality. The most accurate classification system would be to identify all attributes that have some verifiable correlation with mortality and divide people into groups accordingly, but the administrative cost of such an undertaking would be prohibitive. Instead of identifying all relevant attributes, most insurance companies classify individuals according to criteria that provide both an accurate and efficient measure of longevity, including a person's age and sex. These particular criteria are readily identifiable, stable, and easily verifiable. See Benston, The Economics of Gender Discrimination in Employee Fringe Benefits: *Manhart* Revisited, 49 U.Chi.L.Rev. 489, 499–501 (1982).

It is this practice—the use of a sex-based group classification—that the majority ultimately condemns. The policies underlying Title VII, rather than supporting the majority's decision, strongly suggest—at least for me—the opposite conclusion. This remedial statute was enacted to eradicate the types of discrimination in employment that then were pervasive in our society. The entire thrust of Title VII is directed against *discrimination* —disparate treatment on the basis of race or sex that intentionally or arbitrarily affects an individual. But as JUSTICE BLACKMUN has stated, life expectancy is a "nonstigmatizing factor that demonstrably differentiates females from males and that is not measurable on an individual basis. * * * [T]here is nothing arbitrary, irrational, or 'discriminatory' about recognizing the objective and accepted * * * disparity in female-male life expectancies in computing rates for retirement plans." *Manhart*, 435 U.S., at 724, 98 S.Ct., at 1383 (opinion concurring in part and concurring in the judgment). Explicit sexual classifications, to be sure, require close examination, but they are not automatically invalid.[8] Sex-based mortality tables reflect objective actuarial experience. Because their use does not entail discrimination in any normal understanding of that term,[9] a court should hesitate to invalidate this long-approved practice on the basis of its own policy judgment.

Congress may choose to forbid the use of any sexual classifications in insurance, but nothing suggests that it intended to do so in Title VII. And certainly the policy underlying Title VII provides no warrant for extending the reach of the statute beyond Congress' intent.

3. PREGNANCY

NEWPORT NEWS SHIPBUILDING AND DRY DOCK COMPANY v. EEOC

Supreme Court of the United States, 1983.
462 U.S. 669, 103 S.Ct. 2622, 77 L.Ed.2d 89.

JUSTICE STEVENS delivered the opinion of the Court.

In 1978 Congress decided to overrule our decision in General Electric Co. v. Gilbert, 429 U.S. 125, 97 S.Ct. 401, 50 L.Ed.2d 343 (1976), by amending Title VII of the Civil Rights Act of 1964 "to prohibit sex discrimination on the basis of pregnancy." [1] On the effective date of the act, petitioner amended its health insurance plan to provide its female employees with hospitalization benefits for pregnancy-related conditions to the same extent as for other medical conditions. The plan continued, however, to provide less favorable pregnancy benefits for

---

8. Title VII does not preclude the use of all sex classifications, and there is no reason for assuming that Congress intended to do so in this instance. See n. 7, supra.

9. Indeed, if employers and insurance carriers offer annuities based on unisex mortality tables, men as a class will receive less aggregate benefits than similarly situated women.

1. Pub.L. 95–555, 92 Stat. 2076 (quoting title of 1978 Act). The new statute (the Pregnancy Discrimination Act) amended the "Definitions" section of Title VII, 42 U.S.C. § 2000e (1976), to add a new subsection (k) reading in pertinent part as follows:

"The terms 'because of sex' or 'on the basis of sex' include, but are not limited to, because of or on the basis of pregnancy, childbirth, or related medical conditions; and women affected by pregnancy, childbirth, or related medical conditions shall be treated the same for all employment-related purposes, including receipt of benefits under fringe benefit programs, as other persons not so affected but similar in their ability or inability to work, and nothing in section 2000e–2(h) of this title shall be interpreted to permit otherwise. * * *"

spouses of male employees. The question presented is whether the amended plan complies with the amended statute.

Petitioner's plan provides hospitalization and medical-surgical coverage for a defined category of employees [3] and a defined category of dependents. Dependents covered by the plan include employees' spouses, 'unmarried children between 14 days and 19 years of age, and some older dependent children.[4] Prior to April 29, 1979, the scope of the plan's coverage for eligible dependents was identical to its coverage for employees. All covered males, whether employees or dependents, were treated alike for purposes of hospitalization coverage. All covered females, whether employees or dependents, also were treated alike. Moreover, with one relevant exception, the coverage for males and females was identical. The exception was a limitation on hospital coverage for pregnancy that did not apply to any other hospital confinement.[6]

After the plan was amended in 1979, it provided the same hospitalization coverage for male and female employees themselves for all medical conditions, but it differentiated between female employees and spouses of male employees in its provision of pregnancy-related benefits.[7] In a booklet describing the plan, petitioner explained the amendment that gave rise to this litigation in this way:

> B. Effective April 29, 1979, maternity benefits for female employees will be paid the same as any other hospital confinement as described in question 16. This applies only to deliveries beginning on April 29, 1979 and thereafter.
>
> C. Maternity benefits for the wife of a male employee will continue to be paid as described in part "A" of this question. App. to Pet. for Cert. 37a.

In turn, Part A stated, "The Basic Plan pays up to $500 of the hospital charges and 100% of reasonable and customary for delivery and anesthesiologist charges." Ibid. As the Court of Appeals observed, "To the extent that the hospital charges in connection with an uncomplicated

---

3. On the first day following three months of continuous service, every active, full-time, production, maintenance, technical, and clerical area bargaining unit employee becomes a plan participant. App. to Pet. for Cert. 29a.

4. For example, unmarried children up to age 23 who are full-time college students solely dependent on an employee and certain mentally or physically handicapped children are also covered. Id., at 30a.

6. For hospitalization caused by uncomplicated pregnancy, petitioner's plan paid 100% of the reasonable and customary physicians' charges for delivery and anesthesiology, and up to $500 of other hospital charges. For all other hospital confinement, the plan paid in full for a semi-

private room for up to 120 days and for surgical procedures; covered the first $750 of reasonable and customary charges for hospital services (including general nursing care, x-ray examinations, and drugs) and other necessary services during hospitalization; and paid 80 percent of the charges exceeding $750 for such services up to a maximum of 120 days. Id., at 31a–32a (question 16); see id., at 44a–45a (same differentiation for coverage after the employee's termination).

7. Thus, as the EEOC found after its investigation, "the record reveals that the present disparate impact on male employees had its genesis in the gender-based distinction accorded to female employees in the past." App. 37.

delivery may exceed $500, therefore, a male employee receives less complete coverage of spousal disabilities than does a female employee." 667 F.2d 448, 449 (CA4 1982).

After the passage of the Pregnancy Discrimination Act, and before the amendment to petitioner's plan became effective, the Equal Opportunity Employment Commission issued "interpretive guidelines" in the form of questions and answers.[8] Two of those questions, numbers 21 and 22, made it clear that the EEOC would consider petitioner's amended plan unlawful. Number 21 read as follows:

> 21. Q. Must an employer provide health insurance coverage for the medical expenses of pregnancy-related conditions of the spouses of male employees? Of the dependents of all employees?
>
> A. Where an employer provides no coverage for dependents, the employer is not required to institute such coverage. However, if an employer's insurance program covers the medical expenses of spouses of female employees, then it must equally cover the medical expenses of spouses of male employees, including those arising from pregnancy-related conditions.
>
> But the insurance does not have to cover the pregnancy-related conditions of non-spouse dependents as long as it excludes the pregnancy-related conditions of such non-spouse dependents of male and female employees equally." 44 Fed.Reg. 23804, 23807 (April 20, 1979).[9]

On September 20, 1979, one of petitioner's male employees filed a charge with the EEOC alleging that petitioner had unlawfully refused to provide full insurance coverage for his wife's hospitalization caused by pregnancy; a month later the United Steelworkers filed a similar charge on behalf of other individuals. App. 15–18. Petitioner then commenced an action in the United States District Court for the Eastern District of Virginia, challenging the Commission's guidelines

8. Interim interpretive guidelines were published for comment in the Federal Register on March 9, 1979. 44 Fed.Reg. 13278–13281. Final guidelines were published in the Federal Register on April 20, 1979. Id., at 23804–23808. The EEOC explained, "It is the Commission's desire * * * that all interested parties be made aware of the EEOC's view of their rights and obligations in advance of April 29, 1979, so that they may be in compliance by that date." Id., at 23804. The questions and answers are reprinted as an appendix to 28 CFR § 1604 (1982).

9. Question 22 is equally clear. It reads:

"22. Q. Must an employer provide the same level of health insurance coverage for the pregnancy-related medical conditions of the spouses of male employees as it provides for its female employees?

"A. No. It is not necessary to provide the same level of coverage for the pregnancy-related medical conditions of spouses of male employees as for female employees. However, where the employer provides coverage for the medical conditions of the spouses of its employees, then the level of coverage for pregnancy-related medical conditions of the spouses of male employees must be the same as the level of coverage for all other medical conditions of the spouses of female employees. For example, if the employer covers employees for 100 percent of reasonable and customary expenses sustained for a medical condition, but only covers dependent spouses for 50 percent of reasonable and customary expenses for their medical conditions, the pregnancy-related expenses of the male employee's spouse must be covered at the 50 percent level." 44 Fed.Reg., at 23807–23808.

and seeking both declaratory and injunctive relief. The complaint named the EEOC, the male employee, and the United Steelworkers of America as defendants. App. 5–14. Later the EEOC filed a civil action against petitioner alleging discrimination on the basis of sex against male employees in the company's provision of hospitalization benefits. App. 28–31. Concluding that the benefits of the new Act extended only to female employees, and not to spouses of male employees, the District Court held that petitioner's plan was lawful and enjoined enforcement of the EEOC guidelines relating to pregnancy benefits for employees' spouses. 510 F.Supp. 66 (1981). It also dismissed the EEOC's complaint. App. to Pet. for Cert. 21a. The two cases were consolidated on appeal.

A divided panel of the United States Court of Appeals for the Fourth Circuit reversed, reasoning that since "the company's health insurance plan contains a distinction based on pregnancy that results in less complete medical coverage for male employees with spouses than for female employees with spouses, it is impermissible under the statute." 667 F.2d 448, 451 (1982). After rehearing the case en banc, 682 F.2d 113, the court reaffirmed the conclusion of the panel over the dissent of three judges who believed the statute was intended to protect female employees "in their ability or inability to work," and not to protect spouses of male employees. App. to Pet. for Cert. 1a. Because the important question presented by the case had been decided differently by the United States Court of Appeals for the Ninth Circuit, EEOC v. Lockheed Missiles and Space Co., 680 F.2d 1243 (1982), we granted certiorari. ___ U.S. ___, 103 S.Ct. 487 (1982).

Ultimately the question we must decide is whether petitioner has discriminated against its male employees with respect to their compensation, terms, conditions, or privileges of employment because of their sex within the meaning of § 703(a)(1) of Title VII.[11] Although the Pregnancy Discrimination Act has clarified the meaning of certain terms in this section, neither that Act nor the underlying statute contains a definition of the word "discriminate." In order to decide whether petitioner's plan discriminates against male employees because of *their* sex, we must therefore go beyond the bare statutory language. Accordingly, we shall consider whether Congress, by enacting the Pregnancy Discrimination Act, not only overturned the specific holding in General Electric v. Gilbert, supra, but also rejected the test

---

11. Section 703(a), 42 U.S.C. § 2000e–2(a) (1976), provides in pertinent part:

"(a) It shall be an unlawful employment practice for an employer—

"(1) to fail or refuse to hire or discharge any individual, or otherwise to discriminate against any individual with respect to his compensation, terms, conditions, or privileges of employment, because of such individual's race, color, religion, sex, or national origin; * * *."

Although the 1978 Act makes clear that this language should be construed to prohibit discrimination against a female employee on the basis of her own pregnancy, it did not remove or limit Title VII's prohibition of discrimination on the basis of the sex of the employee—male or female—which was already present in the Act. As we explain infra, petitioner's plan discriminates against male employees on the basis of their sex.

of discrimination employed by the Court in that case. We believe it did. Under the proper test petitioner's plan is unlawful, because the protection it affords to married male employees is less comprehensive than the protection it affords to married female employees.

I

At issue in General Electric v. Gilbert was the legality of a disability plan that provided the company's employees with weekly compensation during periods of disability resulting from nonoccupational causes. Because the plan excluded disabilities arising from pregnancy, the District Court and the Court of Appeals concluded that it discriminated against female employees because of their sex. This Court reversed.

After noting that Title VII does not define the term "discrimination," the Court applied an analysis derived from cases construing the Equal Protection Clause of the Fourteenth Amendment to the Constitution. 429 U.S., at 133, 97 S.Ct., at 406. The *Gilbert* opinion quoted at length from a footnote in Geduldig v. Aiello, 417 U.S. 484, 94 S.Ct. 2485, (1974), a case which had upheld the constitutionality of excluding pregnancy coverage under California's disability insurance plan.[12] "Since it is a finding of sex-based discrimination that must trigger, in a case such as this, the finding of an unlawful employment practice under § 703(a)(1)," the Court added, "*Geduldig* is precisely in point in its holding that an exclusion of pregnancy from a disability-benefits plan providing general coverage is not a gender-based discrimination at all." 429 U.S., at 136, 97 S.Ct., at 408.

The dissenters in *Gilbert* took issue with the majority's assumption "that the Fourteenth Amendment standard of discrimination is coterminous with that applicable to Title VII." Id., at 154, n. 6, 97 S.Ct., at 417, n. 6 (BRENNAN, J., dissenting); id., at 160–161, 97 S.Ct., at 420 (STEVENS, J, dissenting).[13] As a matter of statutory interpretation, the

12. " 'While it is true that only women can become pregnant, it does not follow that every legislative classification concerning pregnancy is a sex-based classification like those considered in Reed [v. Reed, 404 U.S. 71, 92 S.Ct. 251, 30 L.Ed.2d 225], supra, and *Frontiero*, supra. Normal pregnancy is an objectively identifiable physical condition with unique characteristics. Absent a showing that distinctions involving pregnancy are mere pretexts designed to effect an invidious discrimination against the members of one sex or the other, lawmakers are constitutionally free to include or exclude pregnancy from the coverage of legislation such as this on any reasonable basis, just as with respect to any other physical condition.

" 'The lack of identity between the excluded disability and gender as such under this insurance program becomes clear upon the most cursory analysis. The program divides potential recipients into two groups—pregnant women and nonpregnant persons. While the first group is exclusively female, the second includes members of both sexes.' Id., at 496–497, n. 20 [94 S.Ct., at 2492, n. 20]." 429 U.S., at 134–135, 97 S.Ct., at 407.

The principal emphasis in the text of the *Geduldig* opinion, unlike the quoted footnote, was on the reasonableness of the State's cost justifications for the classification in its insurance program. See n. 13, infra.

13. As the text of the *Geduldig* opinion makes clear, in evaluating the constitutionality of California's insurance program, the Court focused on the "non-invidious" character of the State's legitimate fiscal interest in excluding pregnancy coverage.

dissenters rejected the Court's holding that the plan's exclusion of disabilities caused by pregnancy did not constitute discrimination based on sex. As Justice Brennan explained, it was facially discriminatory for the company to devise "a policy that, but for pregnancy, offers protection for all risks, even those that are 'unique to' men or heavily male dominated." Id., at 160, 97 S.Ct., at 420. It was inaccurate to describe the program as dividing potential recipients into two groups, pregnant women and non-pregnant persons, because insurance programs "deal with future *risks* rather than historic facts." Rather, the appropriate classification was "between persons who face a risk of pregnancy and those who do not." Id., at 161–162, n. 5, 97 S.Ct., at 421, n. 5 (STEVENS, J., dissenting). The company's plan, which was intended to provide employees with protection against the risk of uncompensated unemployment caused by physical disability, discriminated on the basis of sex by giving men protection for all categories of risk but giving women only partial protection. Thus, the dissenters asserted that the statute had been violated because conditions of employment for females were less favorable than for similarly situated males.

When Congress amended Title VII in 1978, it unambiguously expressed its disapproval of both the holding and the reasoning of the Court in the *Gilbert* decision. It incorporated a new subsection in the "definitions" applicable "[f]or the purposes of this subchapter." 42 U.S.C. § 2000e–2 (1976 ed., Supp. V.). The first clause of the Act states, quite simply: "The terms 'because of sex' or 'on the basis of sex' include, but are not limited to, because of or on the basis of pregnancy, childbirth, or related medical conditions." § 2000e–(k).[14] The House Report stated, "It is the Committee's view that the dissenting Justices correctly interpreted the Act." Similarly, the Senate Report quoted passages from the two dissenting opinions, stating that they "correctly express both the principle and the meaning of title VII."[16] Proponents of the bill repeatedly emphasized that the Supreme Court had erroneously interpreted Congressional intent and that amending legislation was necessary to reestablish the principles of Title VII law as they had been understood prior to the *Gilbert* decision. Many of them expressly agreed with the views of the dissenting Justices.[17]

417 U.S., at 496, 94 S.Ct., at 2491. This justification was not relevant to the statutory issue presented in *Gilbert*. See n. 25, infra.

14. The meaning of the first clause is not limited by the specific language in the second clause, which explains the application of the general principle to women employees.

16. S.Rep. No. 95–331, 95th Cong., 1st Sess. 2–3 (1977), Leg.Hist. at 39–40.

17. S.Rep. No. 95–331, supra n. 16, at 7–8 ("the bill is merely reestablishing the law as it was understood prior to *Gilbert* by the EEOC and by the lower courts"); H.R.Rep.

No. 95–948, 95th Cong., 2d Sess. 8 (1978) (same); 123 Cong.Rec. 10582 (1977) (remarks of Rep. Hawkins) ("H.R. 5055 does not really add anything to title VII as I and, I believe, most of my colleagues in Congress when title VII was enacted in 1964 and amended in 1972, understood the prohibition against sex discrimination in employment. For, it seems only commonsense, that since only women can become pregnant, discrimination against pregnant people is necessarily discrimination against women, and that forbidding discrimination based on sex therefore clearly forbids discrimination based on pregnancy."); id., at 29387 (remarks of Sen. Williams) ("this bill

As petitioner argues, congressional discussion focused on the needs of female members of the work force rather than spouses of male employees. This does not create a "negative inference" limiting the scope of the act to the specific problem that motivated its enactment. See United States v. Turkette, 452 U.S. 576, 591, 101 S.Ct. 2524, 2532, 69 L.Ed.2d 246 (1981). Cf. McDonald v. Santa Fe Trail Transp. Co., 427 U.S. 273, 285–296, 96 S.Ct. 2574, 2581–2586, 49 L.Ed.2d 493 (1976).[18] Congress apparently assumed that existing plans that included benefits for dependents typically provided no less pregnancy-related coverage for the wives of male employees than they did for female employees.[19] When the question of differential coverage for dependents was addressed in the Senate Report, the Committee indicated that it should be resolved "on the basis of existing title VII principles." [20] The legislative

is simply corrective legislation, designed to restore the law with respect to pregnant women employees to the point where it was last year, before the Supreme Court's decision in *Gilbert* * * * "); id., at 29647; id., at 29655 (remarks of Sen. Javits) ("What we are doing is leaving the situation the way it was before the Supreme Court decided the Gilbert case last year."); 124 Cong.Rec. 21436 (1978) (remarks of Rep. Sarasin) ("This bill would restore the interpretation of title VII prior to that decision").

18. In *McDonald*, the Court held that 42 U.S.C. § 1981 (1976), which gives "all persons within the jurisdiction of the United States * * * the same right in every State and Territory to make and enforce contracts * * * as is enjoyed by white citizens," protects whites against discrimination on the basis of race even though the "immediate impetus for the bill was the necessity for further relief of the constitutionally emancipated former Negro slaves." 427 U.S., at 289, 96 S.Ct., at 2583.

19. This, of course, was true of petitioner's plan prior to the enactment of the statute. See p. 2624, supra. See S.Rep. No. 95–331, supra n. 15, at 6, Leg.Hist. at 43 ("Presumably because plans which provide comprehensive medical coverage for spouses of women employees but not spouses of male employees are rare, we are not aware of any Title VII litigation concerning such plans. It is certainly not this committee's desire to encourage the institution of such plans."); 123 Cong.Rec. 29,663 (1977) (remarks of Senator Cranston); Brief for the Equal Employment Opportunity Commission 31–33, n. 31.

20. "Questions were raised in the committee's deliberations regarding how this bill would affect medical coverage for dependents of employees, as opposed to employees themselves. In this context it

must be remembered that the basic purpose of this bill is to protect women employees, it does not alter the basic principles of title VII law as regards sex discrimination. Rather, this legislation clarifies the definition of sex discrimination for title VII purposes. Therefore the question in regard to dependents' benefits would be determined on the basis of existing title VII principles." Leg.Hist. at 42–43; S.Rep. No. 95–331, supra n. 16, at 6.

This statement does not imply that the new statutory definition has no applicability; it merely acknowledges that the new definition does not itself resolve the question.

The dissent quotes extensive excerpts from an exchange on the Senate floor between Senators Hatch and Williams. Post, at 2635. Taken in context, this colloquy clearly deals only with the second clause of the bill, see n. 14, supra, and Senator Williams, the principal sponsor of the legislation, addressed only the bill's effect on income maintenance plans. Leg.Hist. at 80. Senator Williams first stated, in response to Senator Hatch, "With regard to more maintenance plans for pregnancy-related disabilities, I do not see how this language could be misunderstood." Upon further inquiry from Senator Hatch, he replied, "If there is any ambiguity, with regard to income maintenance plans, I cannot see it." At the end of the same response, he stated, "It is narrowly drawn and would not give any employee the right to obtain income maintenance as a result of the pregnancy of someone who is not an employee." Ibid. These comments, which clearly limited the scope of Senator Williams' responses, are omitted from the dissent's lengthy quotation, post, at 2635.

Other omitted portions of the colloquy make clear that it was logical to discuss the pregnancies of employees' spouses in

context makes it clear that Congress was not thereby referring to the view of Title VII reflected in this Court's *Gilbert* opinion. Proponents of the legislation stressed throughout the debates that Congress had always intended to protect *all* individuals from sex discrimination in employment—including but not limited to pregnant women workers.[21] Against this background we review the terms of the amended statute to decide whether petitioner has unlawfully discriminated against its male employees.

II

Section 703(a) makes it an unlawful employment practice for an employer to "discriminate against any individual with respect to his compensation, terms, conditions, or privileges of employment, because of such individual's race, color, religion, sex, or national origin. * * *" 42 U.S.C. § 2002e–2(a) (1976). Health insurance and other fringe benefits are "compensation, terms, conditions, or privileges of employment." Male as well as female employees are protected against discrimination. Thus, if a private employer were to provide complete health insurance coverage for the dependents of its female employees, and no coverage at all for the dependents of its male employees, it would violate Title VII.[22] Such a practice would not pass the simple

connection with income maintenance plans. Senator Hatch asked, "what about the status of a woman coworker who is not pregnant but rides with a pregnant woman and cannot get to work once the pregnant female commences her maternity leave or the employed mother who stays home to nurse her pregnant daughter?" The reference to spouses of male employees must be understood in light of these hypothetical questions; it seems to address the situation in which a male employee wishes to take time off from work because his wife is pregnant.

21. See, e.g., 123 Cong.Rec. 7539 (1977) (remarks of Sen. Williams) ("the Court has ignored the congressional intent in enacting title VII of the Civil Rights Act—that intent was to protect all individuals from unjust employment discrimination, including pregnant workers"); id., at 29385, 29652. In light of statements such as these, it would be anomalous to hold that Congress provided that an employee's pregnancy is sex-based, while a spouse's pregnancy is gender-neutral.

During the course of the Senate debate on the Pregnancy Discrimination Act, Senator Bayh and Senator Cranston both expressed the belief that the new act would prohibit the exclusion of pregnancy coverage for spouses if spouses were otherwise fully covered by an insurance plan. See 123 Cong.Rec. 29642, 29663 (1977). Because our holding relies on the 1978 legis-

lation only to the extent that it unequivocally rejected the *Gilbert* decision, and ultimately we rely on our understanding of general Title VII principles, we attach no more significance to these two statements than to the many other comments by both Senators and Congressmen disapproving the Court's reasoning and conclusion in *Gilbert.* See n. 17, supra.

22. Consistently since 1970 the EEOC has considered it unlawful under Title VII for an employer to provide different insurance coverage for spouses of male and female employees. See Guidelines On Discrimination Because of Sex, 29 CFR 1604.9(d); Commission Decision No. 70–510, 1973 E.E.O.C. Dec. (CCH) ¶ 6132 (Feb. 4, 1970) (accident and sickness insurance); Commission Decision No. 70–513, 1973 E.E.O.C. Dec. (CCH) ¶ 6114 (Feb. 4, 1970) (death benefits to surviving spouse); Commission Decision No. 70–660, 1973 E.E.O.C. Dec. (CCH) ¶ 6133 (Mar. 24, 1970) (health insurance); Commission Decision No. 71–1100, 1973 E.E.O.C. Dec. (CCH) ¶ 6197 (Dec. 31, 1970) (group insurance).

Similarly, in our Equal Protection Clause cases we have repeatedly held that, if the spouses of female employees receive less favorable treatment in the provision of benefits, the practice discriminates not only against the spouses but also against the female employees on the basis of sex. Frontiero v. Richardson, 411 U.S. 677, 688, 93 S.Ct. 1764, 1771, 36 L.Ed.2d 583 (1973)

test of Title VII discrimination that we enunciated in Los Angeles Department of Water & Power v. Manhart, 435 U.S. 702, 711, 98 S.Ct. 1370, 1377, 55 L.Ed.2d 657 (1978), for it would treat a male employee with dependents "in a manner which but for that person's sex would be different." [23] The same result would be reached even if the magnitude of the discrimination were smaller. For example, a plan that provided complete hospitalization coverage for the spouses of female employees but did not cover spouses of male employees when they had broken bones would violate Title VII by discriminating against male employees.

Petitioner's practice is just as unlawful. Its plan provides limited pregnancy-related benefits for employees' wives, and affords more extensive coverage for employees' spouses for all other medical conditions requiring hospitalization. Thus the husbands of female employees receive a specified level of hospitalization coverage for all conditions; the wives of male employees receive such coverage except for pregnancy-related conditions. [24] Although *Gilbert* concluded that an otherwise inclusive plan that singled out pregnancy-related benefits for exclusion was nondiscriminatory on its face, because only women can become pregnant, Congress has unequivocally rejected that reasoning. The 1978 Act makes clear that it is discriminatory to treat pregnancy-related conditions less favorably than other medical conditions. Thus petitioner's plan unlawfully gives married male employees a benefit package for their dependents that is less inclusive than the dependency coverage provided to married female employees.

(opinion of Brennan, J.) (increased quarters allowances and medical and dental benefits); id., at 691 (Powell, J., concurring in the judgment); Weinberger v. Wiesenfeld, 420 U.S. 636, 645, 95 S.Ct. 1225, 1231, 43 L.Ed.2d 514 (1975) (Social Security benefits for surviving spouses); see also id., at 654–655, 95 S.Ct., at 1236 (Powell, J., concurring); Califano v. Goldfarb, 430 U.S. 199, 207–208, 97 S.Ct. 1021, 1027, 51 L.Ed.2d 270 (1977) (opinion of Brennan, J.) (Social Security benefits for surviving spouses); Wengler v. Druggists Mutual Ins. Co., 446 U.S. 142, 147, 100 S.Ct. 1540, 1543, 64 L.Ed.2d 107 (1980) (workers' compensation death benefits for surviving spouses).

23. The *Manhart* case was decided several months before the Pregnancy Discrimination Act was passed. Although it was not expressly discussed in the legislative history, it set forth some of the "existing title VII principles" on which Congress relied. Cf. Cannon v. University of Chicago, 441 U.S. 677, 696–698, 99 S.Ct. 1946, 1957–1958, 60 L.Ed.2d 560 (1979). In *Manhart* the Court struck down the employer's policy of requiring female employees to make larger contributions to its pension fund

than male employees, because women as a class tend to live longer than men.

"An employment practice that requires 2,000 individuals to contribute more money into a fund than 10,000 other employees simply because each of them is a woman, rather than a man, is in direct conflict with both the language and the policy of the Act. Such a practice does not pass the simple test of whether the evidence shows 'treatment of a person in a manner which but for that person's sex would be different.' It constitutes discrimination and is unlawful unless exempted by the Equal Pay Act of 1963 or some other affirmative justification." 435 U.S., at 711, 98 S.Ct., at 1377. The internal quotation was from Developments in the Law, Employment Discrimination and Title VII of the Civil Rights Act of 1964, 84 Harv.L.Rev. 1109, 1170 (1971).

24. This policy is analogous to the exclusion of broken bones for the wives of male employees, except that both employees' wives and employees' husbands may suffer broken bones, but only employees' wives can become pregnant.

There is no merit to petitioner's argument that the prohibitions of Title VII do not extend to discrimination against pregnant spouses because the statute applies only to discrimination in employment. A two-step analysis demonstrates the fallacy in this contention. The Pregnancy Discrimination Act has now made clear that, for all Title VII purposes, discrimination based on a woman's pregnancy is, on its face, discrimination because of her sex. And since the sex of the spouse is always the opposite of the sex of the employee, it follows inexorably that discrimination against female spouses in the provision of fringe benefits is also discrimination against male employees. Cf. Wengler v. Druggists Mutual Ins. Co., 446 U.S. 142, 147, 100 S.Ct. 1540, 1543, 64 L.Ed.2d 107 (1980).[25] By making clear that an employer could not discriminate on the basis of an employee's pregnancy, Congress did not erase the original prohibition against discrimination on the basis of an employee's sex.

In short, Congress' rejection of the premises of General Electric v. Gilbert forecloses any claim that an insurance program excluding pregnancy coverage for female beneficiaries and providing complete coverage to similarly situated male beneficiaries does not discriminate on the basis of sex. Petitioner's plan is the mirror image of the plan at issue in *Gilbert*. The pregnancy limitation in this case violates Title VII by discriminating against male employees.[26]

The judgment of the Court of Appeals is

Affirmed.

JUSTICE REHNQUIST, with whom JUSTICE POWELL joins, dissenting.

In General Electric Co. v. Gilbert, 429 U.S. 125, 97 S.Ct. 401, 50 L.Ed.2d 343 (1976), we held that an exclusion of pregnancy from a disability-benefits plan is not discrimination "because of [an] individual's * * * sex" within the meaning of Title VII of the Civil Rights Act

25. See n. 22, supra. This reasoning does not require that a medical insurance plan treat the pregnancies of employees' wives the same as the pregnancies of female employees. For example, as the EEOC recognizes, see n. 9, supra (Question 22), an employer might provide full coverage for employees and no coverage at all for dependents. Similarly, a disability plan covering employees' children may exclude or limit maternity benefits. Although the distinction between pregnancy and other conditions is, according to the 1978 Act, discrimination "on the basis of sex," the exclusion affects male and female *employees* equally since both may have pregnant dependent daughters. The EEOC's guidelines permit differential treatment of the pregnancies of dependents who are not spouses. See 44 Fed.Reg. 23804, 23805, 23807 (1979).

26. Because the 1978 Act expressly states that exclusion of pregnancy coverage

is gender-based discrimination on its face, it eliminates any need to consider the average monetary value of the plan's coverage to male and female employees. Cf. *Gilbert*, 429 U.S., at 137–140, 97 S.Ct., at 408–410.

The cost of providing complete health insurance coverage for the dependents of male employees, including pregnant wives, might exceed the cost of providing such coverage for the dependents of female employees. But although that type of cost differential may properly be analyzed in passing on the constitutionality of a State's health insurance plan, see Geduldig v. Aiello, supra, no such justification is recognized under Title VII once discrimination has been shown. *Manhart*, supra, 435 U.S., at 716–717, 98 S.Ct., at 1379; 29 CFR § 1604.9(e) (1982) ("It shall not be a defense under Title VII to a charge of sex discrimination in benefits that the cost of such benefits is greater with respect to one sex than the other.")

of 1964, § 703(a)(I), 78 Stat. 255, 42 U.S.C. § 2000e–2(a)(1).[1] In our view, therefore, Title VII was not violated by an employer's disability plan that provided all employees with non-occupational sickness and accident benefits, but excluded from the plan's coverage disabilities arising from pregnancy. Under our decision in *Gilbert*, petitioner's otherwise inclusive benefits plan that excludes pregnancy benefits for a male employee's spouse clearly would not violate Title VII. For a different result to obtain, *Gilbert* would have to be judicially overruled by this Court or Congress would have to legislatively overrule our decision in its entirety by amending Title VII.

Today, the Court purports to find the latter by relying on the Pregnancy Discrimination Act of 1978, Pub.L. 95–555, 92 Stat. 2076, 42 U.S.C. § 2000e(k), a statute that plainly speaks only of female employees affected by pregnancy and says nothing about spouses of male employees.[2] Congress, of course, was free to legislatively overrule *Gilbert* in whole or in part, and there is no question but what the Pregnancy Discrimination Act manifests congressional dissatisfaction with the result we reached in *Gilbert*. But I think the Court reads far more into the Pregnancy Discrimination Act than Congress put there, and that therefore it is the Court, and not Congress, which is now overruling *Gilbert*.

In a case presenting a relatively simple question of statutory construction, the Court pays virtually no attention to the language of the Pregnancy Discrimination Act or the legislative history pertaining to that language. The Act provides in relevant part:

> The terms "because of sex" or "on the basis of sex" include, but are not limited to, because of or on the basis of pregnancy, childbirth, or related medical conditions; and women affected by pregnancy, childbirth, or related medical conditions shall be treated the same for all employment-related purposes, including receipt of benefits under fringe benefit programs, as other persons not so affected but similar in their ability or inability to work. * * *

Pub.L. 95–555, 92 Stat. 2076, 42 U.S.C. § 2000e(k).

The Court recognizes that this provision is merely definitional and that "[u]ltimately the question we must decide is whether petitioner has discriminated against its male employees * * * because of their sex within the meaning of § 703(a)(1)" of Title VII. Ante, at 2626. Section 703(a)(1) provides in part:

> It shall be an unlawful employment practice for an employer * * * to fail or refuse to hire or to discharge any individual, or otherwise to

---

1. In *Gilbert* the Court did leave open the possibility of a violation where there is a showing "that distinctions involving pregnancy are mere pretexts designed to effect an invidious discrimination against members of one sex or the other." 429 U.S. 125, 135, 97 S.Ct. 401, 407, 50 L.Ed.2d 343 (1976) (quoting Geduldig v. Aiello, 417 U.S. 484, 496–497 n. 20, 94 S.Ct. 2485, 2491–2492 n. 20, 41 L.Ed.2d 256 (1974)).

2. By referring to "female employees," I do not intend to imply that the Pregnancy Discrimination Act does not also apply to "female applicants for employment." I simply use the former reference as a matter of convenience.

discriminate against any individual with respect to his compensation, terms, conditions, or privileges of employment, because of such individual's race, color, religion, sex, or national origin. * * * 42 U.S.C. § 2000e–2(a)(1).

It is undisputed that in § 703(a)(1) the word "individual" refers to an employee or applicant for employment. As modified by the first clause of the definitional provision of the Pregnancy Discrimination Act, the proscription in § 703(a)(1) is for discrimination "against any individual * * * *because of such individual's* * * * *pregnancy,* childbirth, or related medical conditions." This can only be read as referring to the pregnancy of an employee.

That this result was not inadvertent on the part of Congress is made very evident by the second clause of the Act, language that the Court essentially ignores in its opinion. When Congress in this clause further explained the proscription it was creating by saying that "women affected by pregnancy * * * shall be treated the same * * * as other persons not so affected but *similar in their ability or inability to work*" it could only have been referring to *female employees.* The Court of Appeals below stands alone in thinking otherwise.[3]

The Court concedes that this is a correct reading of the second clause. Ante at 2628 n. 14. Then in an apparent effort to escape the impact of this provision, the Court asserts that "[t]he meaning of the first clause is not limited by the specific language in the second clause." Ante, at 2628 n. 14. I do not disagree. But this conclusion does not help the Court, for as explained above, when the definitional provision of the first clause is inserted in § 703(a)(1), it says the very same thing: the proscription added to Title VII applies only to female employees.

The plain language of the Pregnancy Discrimination Act leaves little room for the Court's conclusion that the Act was intended to extend beyond female employees. The Court concedes that "congressional discussion focused on the needs of female members of the work force rather than spouses of male employees." Ante, at 2629. In fact, the singular focus of discussion on the problems of the *pregnant worker* is striking.

When introducing the Senate Report on the bill that later became the Pregnancy Discrimination Act, its principal sponsor, Senator Williams, explained:

3. See EEOC v. Joslyn Manufacturing & Supply Co., 706 F.2d 1469, 1479 (CA7, 1983); EEOC v. Lockheed Missiles & Space Co., 680 F.2d 1243, 1245 (CA9 1982).

The Court of Appeals' majority, responding to the dissent's reliance on this language, excused the import of the language by saying: "The statutory reference to 'ability or inability to work' denotes disability and does not suggest that the spouse must be an employee of the employer providing the coverage. In fact, the statute says 'as other persons not so affected'; it does not say 'as other *employees* not so affected.'" 667 F.2d 448, 450–451 (CA4 1982); App. to Petn. for Cert. al. This conclusion obviously does not comport with a common-sense understanding of the language. The logical explanation for Congress' reference to "persons" rather than "employees" is that Congress intended that the amendment should also apply to applicants for employment.

Because of the Supreme Court's decision in the *Gilbert* case, this legislation is necessary to provide fundamental protection against sex discrimination for our Nation's 42 million *working women*. This protection will go a long way toward insuring that American women are permitted to assume their rightful place in our Nation's economy.

In addition to providing protection to *working women* with regard to fringe benefit programs, such as health and disability insurance programs, this legislation will prohibit other employment policies which adversely affect *pregnant workers*. 124 Cong.Rec. S18,977 (daily ed. Oct. 13, 1978) (emphasis added).[4]

As indicated by the examples in the margin, the Congressional Record is overflowing with similar statements by individual members of Congress expressing their intention to insure with the Pregnancy Discrimination Act that working women are not treated differently because of pregnancy. Consistent with these views, all three committee reports on the bills that led to the Pregnancy Discrimination Act expressly state that the Act would require employers to treat pregnant employees the same as "other employees." [6]

The Court tries to avoid the impact of this legislative history by saying that it "does not create a 'negative inference' limiting the scope of the act to the specific problem that motivated its enactment." Ante, at 2629. This reasoning might have some force if the legislative history was silent on an arguably related issue. But the legislative history is not silent. The Senate Report provides:

Questions were raised in the committee's deliberations regarding how this bill would affect medical coverage for dependents of employees, as opposed to employees themselves. In this context it must be remembered that the basic purpose of this bill is to protect women employees, it does not alter the basic principles of title VII law as regards sex discrimination. * * * [T]he question in regard to dependents' benefits would be determined on the basis of existing title VII principles. * * * *[T]he question of whether an employer who does cover dependents, either with or without additional cost to the employ-*

---

4. Reprinted in Senate Committee on Labor and Human Resources, 96th Cong., 2d Sess., Legislative History of the Pregnancy Discrimination Act of 1978, at 200–201 [hereinafter referred to as "Leg.Hist."]. In the foreword to the official printing of the Act's legislative history, Senator Williams further described the purpose of the Act, saying:

"The Act provides an essential protection for working women. The number of women in the labor force has increased dramatically in recent years. Most of these women are working or seeking work because of the economic need to support themselves or their families. It is expected that this trend of increasing participation by women in the workforce will continue in the future and that an increasing proportion of working women will be those who are mothers. It is essential that these women and their children be fully protected against the harmful effects of unjust employment discrimination on the basis of pregnancy." Leg.Hist., at iii.

6. See Report of the Senate Committee on Human Resources, S.Rep. No. 33, 95th Cong., 1st Sess. (1977), Leg.Hist., at 38–53; Report of the House Committee on Education and Labor, H.R.Rep. No. 948, 95th Cong., 2d Sess. (1978), Leg.Hist., at 147–164; Report of the Committee of Conference, H.R.Rep. No. 1786, 95th Cong., 2d Sess. (1978), Leg.Hist., at 194–198.

ee, may exclude conditions related to pregnancy from that coverage is a different matter. Presumably because plans which provide comprehensive medical coverage for spouses of women employees but not spouses of male employees are rare, we are not aware of any title VII litigation concerning such plans. It is certainly not this committee's desire to encourage the institution of such plans. If such plans should be instituted in the future, the question would remain whether, under title VII, the affected employees were discriminated against on the basis of their sex as regards the extent of coverage for their dependents. S.Rep. No. 331, 95th Cong., 1st Sess. 5–6 (1977), Leg.Hist., at 42–43 (emphasis added).

This plainly disclaims any intention to deal with the issue presented in this case. Where Congress says that it would not want "to encourage" plans such as petitioner's, it cannot plausibly be argued that Congress has intended "to prohibit" such plans. Senator Williams was questioned on this point by Senator Hatch during discussions on the floor and his answers are to the same effect.

MR. HATCH: ∗ ∗ ∗ The phrase "women affected by pregnancy, childbirth or related medical conditions," ∗ ∗ ∗ appears to be overly broad, and is not limited in terms of employment. It does not even require that the person so affected be pregnant.

Indeed under the present language of the bill, it is arguable that spouses of male employees are covered by this civil rights amendment. ∗ ∗ ∗

Could the sponsors clarify exactly whom that phrase intends to cover?

∗   ∗   ∗   ∗   ∗   ∗   ∗   ∗   ∗

MR. WILLIAMS: ∗ ∗ ∗ I do not see how one can read into this any pregnancy other than that pregnancy that relates to the employee, and if there is any ambiguity, *let it be clear here and now that this is very precise. It deals with a woman, a woman who is an employee,* an employee in a work situation where all disabilities are covered under a company plan that provides income maintenance in the event of medical disability; that her particular period of disability, when she cannot work because of childbirth or anything related to childbirth is excluded. ∗ ∗ ∗

∗   ∗   ∗   ∗   ∗   ∗   ∗   ∗   ∗

MR. HATCH: So the Senator is satisfied that, though the committee language I brought up, "woman affected by pregnancy" seems to be ambiguous, what it means is that *this act only applies to the particular woman who is actually pregnant, who is an employee and has become pregnant after her employment?*

∗   ∗   ∗   ∗   ∗   ∗   ∗   ∗   ∗

MR. WILLIAMS: *"Exactly."* 123 Cong.Rec. S15,038–39 (daily ed. Sept. 16, 1977), Leg.Hist., at 80 (emphasis added).

It seems to me that analysis of this case should end here. Under our decision in General Electric Co. v. Gilbert petitioner's exclusion of pregnancy benefits for male employee's spouses would not offend Title VII. Nothing in the Pregnancy Discrimination Act was intended to reach beyond female employees. Thus, *Gilbert* controls and requires that we reverse the Court of Appeals. But it is here, at what should be the stopping place, that the Court begins. The Court says:

> Although the Pregnancy Discrimination Act has clarified the meaning of certain terms in this section, neither that Act nor the underlying statute contains a definition of the word "discriminate." In order to decide whether petitioner's plan discriminates against male employees because of *their* sex, we must therefore go beyond the bare statutory language. Accordingly, we shall consider whether Congress, by enacting the Pregnancy Discrimination Act, not only overturned the specific holding in General Electric v. Gilbert, supra, but also rejected the test of discrimination employed by the Court in that case. We believe it did." Ante, at 2627.

It would seem that the Court has refuted its own argument by recognizing that the Pregnancy Discrimination Act only clarifies the meaning of the phrases "because of sex" and "on the basis of sex," and says nothing concerning the definition of the word "discriminate." [8] Instead the Court proceeds to try and explain that while Congress said one thing, it did another.

The crux of the Court's reasoning is that even though the Pregnancy Discrimination Act redefines the phrases "because of sex" and "on the basis of sex" only to include discrimination against female employees affected by pregnancy, Congress also expressed its view that in *Gilbert* "the Supreme Court ∗ ∗ ∗ erroneously interpreted Congressional intent." Ante, at 2628. See also ante, at 2631. Somehow the Court then concludes that this renders all of *Gilbert* obsolete.

In support of its argument, the Court points to a few passages in congressional reports and several statements by various members of the 95th Congress to the effect that the Court in *Gilbert* had, when it construed Title VII, misperceived the intent of the 88th Congress. Ante, at 2629 and n. 17. The Court also points out that "[m]any of [the members of 95th Congress] expressly agreed with the views of the dissenting Justices." Ante, at 2629. Certainly *various members of Congress* said as much. But the fact remains that *Congress as a body* has not expressed these sweeping views in the Pregnancy Discrimination Act.

Under our decision in General Electric Co. v. Gilbert, petitioner's exclusion of pregnancy benefits for male employee's spouses would not violate Title VII. Since nothing in the Pregnancy Discrimination Act even arguably reaches beyond female employees affected by pregnancy, *Gilbert* requires that we reverse the Court of Appeals. Because the Court concludes otherwise, I dissent.

---

8. The Court also concedes at one point that the Senate Report on the Pregnancy Discrimination Act "acknowledges that the new definition [in the Act] does not itself resolve the question" presented in this case. Ante, at 2629 n. 20.

Note

Gilbert was a 703(a)(1) case. In Nashville Gas Co. v. Satty, 434 U.S. 136, 98 S.Ct. 347, 54 L.Ed.2d 356 (1977) the Court, per Justice Rehnquist, used Section 703(a)(2) to invalidate the employer's exclusion of pregnancy leave from the general practice of recognizing the seniority of employees returning from leave because of disease or any disability. Females returning from pregnancy leave had no right to return to their former job, and were divested of their prior accumulated seniority, which adversely affected their reemployment opportunity. The Court viewed the seniority policy as neutral, since under Gilbert the decision not to treat pregnancy as a disease or disability for purposes of seniority was not on its face discriminatory. Adverting to the disparate impact rationale of Griggs, the Court concluded that the employer "has imposed on women a substantial burden that men need not suffer" and stated that the holding in Gilbert "does not allow us to read 703(a)(2) to permit an employer to burden female employees in such a way as to deprive them of employment opportunities because of their different roles." The employer offered no proof of business necessity.

WRIGHT v. OLIN CORPORATION

United States Court of Appeals for the Fourth Circuit, 1982.
697 F.2d 1172.

PHILLIPS, CIRCUIT JUDGE.

III

We turn now to the claim related to Olin's "fetal vulnerability" program.

A

The details of this program's initiation and of its operation were established without dispute at trial. In February 1978, after some four years of planning, Olin adopted its "female employment and fetal vulnerability" program which created 3 job classifications. 1) Restricted jobs are those which "may require contact with and exposure to known or suspected abortifacient or teratogenic agents." Fertile women are excluded from such jobs. Any woman age 5 through 63 is assumed to be fertile and can be placed in a restricted job only after consulting with Olin's medical doctors to confirm the woman cannot bear children and will sustain no other adverse physiological effects from the environment. 2) Controlled jobs may require very limited contact with the harmful chemicals. Pregnant women may work at such jobs only after individual case-by-case evaluations. Non-pregnant women may work in controlled jobs after signing a form stating that they recognize that the job presents "some risk, although slight." Olin encourages women in controlled jobs to bid for other jobs if they intend to become pregnant. 3) Unrestricted jobs are those which do "not present a hazard to the pregnant female or the fetus." They are open to all women.

There are approximately 265 job classifications in Olin's Pisgah Forest plant. At the beginning of the fetal vulnerability program, twelve jobs were placed in the restricted category and a significant number were classified as controlled jobs. At least five of the eleven lines of progression in the film division are affected by the policy. As required under OSHA regulations, Olin orally warns its male employees about lead exposure at the Pisgah plant, but the warnings are much less formal than the written warnings to women. No actual restrictions are placed on male employees.

The only evidence going to the purpose and the felt necessity for the program was provided by the oral testimony of three Olin employees. Dr. O'Connell, Corporate Director of Health Affairs, and a medical doctor, testified that Olin's Department of Hygiene and Toxicology reviewed the medical literature and concluded that the program was necessary, essentially to protect the unborn fetuses of pregnant women employees from the damaging toxic effects of certain chemicals, principally lead, used in the manufacturing process to which the women were exposed. A further consideration, apparently secondary, was the danger from the same source to the pregnant employee herself. Dr. O'Connell could not name the articles or journals which supported this medical conclusion.

Fletcher Roberts, Director of Safety Loss Prevention at Pisgah Forest, not a medically trained person, testified that the company had measured the actual exposure levels at the Pisgah plant and had rejected alternatives, such as substituting non-toxic materials or improving ventilation or personal protective equipment, as being infeasible. The third witness, Dr. Ryan, Group Medical Director at the Pisgah Forest plant, testified that though he had not been consulted during the program's development and was not familiar with any research done before its implementation, he agreed with the "basic policy." None of these witnesses was qualified or testified as an expert in any relevant scientific or medical field.

Relying directly upon the testimony of these three witnesses, the district court made critical findings of fact against the claimants. The central finding was "that the policy was instituted for sound medical and humane reasons * * * not * * * with the intent or purpose to discriminate against females because of their sex * * * [but with] the purpose * * * to protect the unborn fetus." On this basis the court concluded as a matter of law that the policy "does not discriminate against females in violation of Title VII."

This appeal of course challenges these specific rulings, and our review properly centers upon them.

B

The first problem is to put the rulings in the proper conceptual framework for analysis. The parties are in hopeless conflict on this fundamental point. Because that conflict reveals the essence of the problem, we summarize the opposing contentions in some detail.

Olin contends that the proper analytical framework is that developed for assessing claims of disparate treatment in McDonnell Douglas v. Green, 411 U.S. 792, 93 S.Ct. 1817, 36 L.Ed.2d 668 (1973), and its progeny. Within that framework, the argument runs, the district court's rulings are supportable under principles most recently explained in Texas Department of Community Affairs v. Burdine, 450 U.S. 248, 101 S.Ct. 1089, 67 L.Ed.2d 207 (1981). Under *Burdine*, says Olin, the purpose of the program as "articulated" by its witnesses sufficed as a "legitimate nondiscriminatory reason" to rebut any *prima facie* case of sex discrimination established by proof of the program's existence and intended operation. Because this reason was not then proven by the claimants to have been pretextual, the district court properly determined that intentional discrimination had not been established under the *Burdine* analysis. This determination, says Olin, properly disposed of the claim without need to assess it under other theories.

On the other hand, claimants contend that the undisputed evidence of the program's intended operation, with its manifestly adverse effect upon the employment opportunities of women only, established a *prima facie* case of overt, intentional discrimination. To such proof, say claimants, the *McDonnell Douglas* proof scheme, concerned as it is only with inferential proof of covert intention, simply does not apply. Evidence of such an overtly intended discriminatory effect may not be rebutted by any amount of proof of gender-neutral or even benign purpose or motivation underlying it. A *prima facie* case of this kind may only be overcome by establishment of the narrow, statutory b.f.o.q. defense specially provided by § 703(a) of Title VII, 42 U.S.C. § 2000e–2(a). Here that justification defense, an affirmative one as to which the defendant-employer had the burden of persuasion, was not established in evidence. Hence, say claimants, the district court erred as a matter of law in failing to find Olin in violation of Title VII on this claim.

Alternatively,[17] claimants contend that if the fetal vulnerability program is construed—as arguably they concede it might be—as a "facially-neutral" policy based upon the potential for pregnancy, mere proof of its existence and implementation established a *prima facie* case of disparate impact under Griggs v. Duke Power Co., 401 U.S. 424, 91 S.Ct. 849, 28 L.Ed.2d 158 (1971), and its progeny, particularly Nashville Gas Co. v. Satty, 434 U.S. 136, 98 S.Ct. 347, 54 L.Ed.2d 356 (1977). Such a *prima facie* case may only be overcome by establishment of the judicially developed business necessity defense. This justification defense, like the b.f.o.q. defense an affirmative one as to which the defendant-employer bore the burden of persuasion, they argue was not

---

17. Actually, the claimants suggest that disparate impact/business necessity theory might apply until enactment of the "pregnancy amendment" to Title VII, 42 U.S.C. § 2000e(k), effective October 31, 1978, and overt act/b.f.o.q. theory thereafter, on the basis that as of the enactment date the program became "overtly" one of sex discrimination. Without regard to whether that would make any difference on the facts of this case, we reject it as conceptually unsound for reasons that will appear.

established on the evidence here. Hence, say claimants, on this alternative theory as well, the district court erred as a matter of law in failing to find Olin in violation of Title VII.

In any event, claimants contend, the district court erred as a matter of law, and Olin persists in the error on appeal, in treating this claim as one properly assessed only as one of covert "disparate treatment" which was sufficiently rebutted and not re-established by proof of pretext under the *McDonnell Douglas* proof scheme. For this reason, the argument runs, the district court's rejection of this claim on that basis without assessing it under other theories reflects a misapprehension and misapplication of controlling legal principle. Claimants urge that this requires at least a vacation of this portion of the judgment and a remand for new trial under properly applicable principles.

Faced with these conflicting and alternatively advanced contentions, we note at the outset that the problem of fitting the fetal vulnerability program into the appropriate theory of claim and defense as developed in Title VII litigation is one of first impression with this court and—we are advised—with any court of appeals. We therefore approach it as an open one.

We must start by conceding that the fact situation it presents does not fit with absolute precision into any of the developed theories. It differs in some respects—either in its claim or defense elements—from each of the paradigmatic fact situations with which the different theories have been centrally concerned. This of course accounts for the conflict on the point between the parties.

That there would be such fact situations in Title VII litigation has always been recognized by the Supreme Court as it has developed and applied the different theories. The Court has continually admonished,[18] and indeed demonstrated in its own decisions,[19] that these theories were not expected nor intended to operate with rigid precision with respect to the infinite variety of factual patterns that would emerge in Title VII litigation.

Furthermore, as is well established, it is often appropriate to assess particular Title VII claims and defenses alternatively under different theories. See, e.g., Furnco Construction Corp. v. Waters, 438 U.S. 567, 98 S.Ct. 2943, 57 L.Ed.2d 957 (1978); Wright v. National Archives & Records Service, 609 F.2d 702 (4th Cir.1979) (en banc). This simply reflects the general procedural principle that in Title VII litigation, as in other civil cases, parties may not be forced to elect between theories but may, within substantive limits, advance and are entitled to have

18. See, e.g., Furnco Construction Corp. v. Waters, 438 U.S. 567, 575–77, 98 S.Ct. 2943, 2948–49, 57 L.Ed.2d 957 (1978); International Brotherhood of Teamsters v. United States, 431 U.S. 324, 358–60, 97 S.Ct. 1843, 1866–67, 52 L.Ed.2d 396 (1977).

19. See, e.g., New York City Transit Authority v. Beazer, 440 U.S. 568, 99 S.Ct.

1355, 59 L.Ed.2d 587 (1979) ("pretext" proof proper as rebuttal in disparate impact case); Albemarle Paper Co. v. Moody, 422 U.S. 405, 95 S.Ct. 2362, 45 L.Ed.2d 280 (1975) (same).

considered alternative and even inconsistent theories. See Fed.R.Civ.P. 8(e)(2).

Where, as here, a particular fact situation might arguably be assessed under different theories, and where the different theories might yield different results, a choice between the different theories may of course finally be forced upon the courts. In such a case, the proper course is to seek guidance in the general principles underlying Title VII which the special theories of claim and defense were all designed to serve, and to stay as near as may be within developed doctrine for the sake of maintaining its stability and predictability.

With these points in mind, the *McDonnell Douglas* disparate treatment proof scheme [20] is immediately revealed to be wholly inappropriate for resolving the legal and factual theories of claim and defense centered on the fetal vulnerability program. Turning to the overt sex-discrimination/b.f.o.q. theory of claim and defense and the disparate impact/business necessity theory, we conclude that the latter is best suited for a principled application of Title VII doctrine to the fetal vulnerability program.[21]

20. That proof scheme was essentially developed for the recurring factual situation in which the claim is simply that an employer has, though covertly, treated the claimant "less favorably than others because of * * * race, religion, sex or national origin," International Brotherhood of Teamsters v. United States, 431 U.S. 324, 335 n. 15, 97 S.Ct. 1843, 1854 n. 15, 52 L.Ed.2d 396 (1977), and the employer's only proffered defense is simply one of denial and rebuttal: "race or sex had nothing to do with it, there was another legitimate reason." See *Burdine,* 450 U.S. at 254–55, 257–58, 101 S.Ct. at 1094, 1995–96. The special feature of this proof scheme in its threshold presumption to aid proof of the claimed intent to "treat less favorably" that is provided precisely because that intent is denied, is not manifest, and can only be proved circumstantially. See Furnco Construction Corp. v. Waters, 438 U.S. 567, 576–77, 98 S.Ct. 2943, 2949–50, 57 L.Ed.2d 957 (rationale of proof scheme).

Neither the factual claim nor the factual defense centered here upon the fetal vulnerability program logically invokes that special theory of claim and defense. Here the claim is that the intention to "treat less favorably" is manifest in the very nature of the program and the factual defense is not truly aimed at rebutting this indisputable fact but at justifying it on the basis that the purpose behind it was benign in relation to the claimants' sex. To force such a claim and defense into that special proof scheme would torture its logical foundations. More importantly, treat-

ing this as the exclusive theory upon which liability might be based would subvert the settled alternative principle that employer policies or practices that manifestly disfavor women employees in relation to comparably situated males constitute violations of Title VII irrespective of specific intent or motive, unless those policies or practices are affirmatively justified under one of the developed business-related defenses. See Griggs v. Duke Power Co., 401 U.S. 424, 91 S.Ct. 849, 28 L.Ed.2d 158 (1971). That is to say, it would deny claimants' right to have their claim assessed, at least alternatively, under disparate impact theory.

21. The inappropriateness of applying the overt discrimination/b.f.o.q. theory of claim and defense—or, more accurately, of treating it as the exclusively applicable, hence dispositive, theory—is that, properly applied, it would prevent the employer from asserting a justification defense which under developed Title VII doctrine it is entitled to present.

Properly applied, this statutory defense is a narrow one, see Dothard v. Rawlinson, 433 U.S. 321, 334, 97 S.Ct. 2720, 2729, 53 L.Ed.2d 786 (1977), under which a concededly discriminatory occupational qualification is shown to be justified because related to the very ability of the disqualified person to perform the job, or, as this court has put it, to be "necessary to the essence of [the] business." Arritt v. Grisell, 567 F.2d 1267, 1271 (4th Cir.1977). As such, it was obviously designed as a necessary, narrow exception to the otherwise flat prohibi-

The factual claim and defense actually advanced here by the parties find their closest parallel in the paradigmatic fact pattern out of which this theory of claim and defense evolved. That pattern involves "employment practices that are facially neutral in their treatment of different groups but that in fact fall more harshly on one group than another and cannot be justified by business necessity." *Teamsters,* 431 U.S. at 336 n. 15, 97 S.Ct. at 1855 n. 15.

While the "facial neutrality" of Olin's fetal vulnerability program might be subject to logical dispute, the dispute would involve mere semantic quibbling having no relevance to the underlying substantive principle that gave rise to this theory. That principle, one of profound importance in the evolution of Title VII doctrine, has as its critical feature the consequences of employment policies rather than the "neutrality" with which the policies happen to be formally expressed. Its essence is that disproportionate consequences of an employment practice, even if unintended or indeed benignly motivated, may, like intentional invidiously discriminatory employer actions, constitute violations of Title VII. See id.

While the principle was first recognized in a context where as a matter of formal expression the challenged practice happened to be "facially neutral" in the most obvious sense of the term, see Griggs v. Duke Power Co., 401 U.S. 424, 91 S.Ct. 849, 28 L.Ed.2d 158 (1971) (hiring test), it has long been applied as well to policies whose "facial neutrality" was only superficial in view of the palpable correlation between the gender of employees and its manifest consequences. See Nashville Gas Co. v. Satty, 434 U.S. 136, 98 S.Ct. 347, 54 L.Ed.2d 356 (1977) (no seniority accumulated during maternity leave).

That is exactly the situation here, where a policy, though literally expressed in gender-neutral terms, has as its obvious and indisputably intended consequence the imposing upon women workers of a "substantial burden that men need not suffer." Id. at 142, 98 S.Ct. at 351. As

tion against the most obvious form of employment discrimination—an overt qualification such as "males only." But nothing in the statutory exception itself or in Title VII in general suggested that this defense defined the full reach of business justification defenses under Title VII— whether to overt or other forms of discrimination—and the *Griggs* Court's recognition of the obviously wider business necessity defense soon confirmed that this was not the case.

An employer may of course in particular litigation still invoke only the narrow b.f.o.q. defense. Almost invariably this is the litigation pattern when the claim is of overt discrimination by means of occupational qualification. But this merely reflects specific litigation choices and the invariability of this factual pattern in the world of employment relations, rather than any general constraints of substantive doctrine. While the loose equation— overt discrimination/only b.f.o.q. defense— is therefore properly descriptive of a paradigmatic litigation pattern, it is not an accurate statement of any inherent constraints in Title VII doctrine.

In this case, where the defendant-employer has not attempted to present a classic b.f.o.q. defense, it may not properly be forced to do so. We therefore reject claimant's suggestion that because the claim of violation here is arguably one of "overt" discrimination, the employer is confined to a b.f.o.q. defense that obviously cannot be established and indeed is not advanced. Instead defendant is entitled to have considered—though not necessarily to have accepted—the defense actually advanced under the wider scope of the business necessity theory.

the *Satty* Court unhesitatingly applied disparate impact theory to the factual situation there presented, so should it be applied here to the generally comparable situation.

C

With the disparate impact/business necessity theory of claim and defense identified as the appropriate one to apply in resolution of the fetal vulnerability issue, the next problem is the proper way to apply it at this point in the litigation.

So far as the record reveals, its possible applicability was not considered by the district court. As earlier indicated, a plausible assumption is that the court accepted Olin's argument that the case was properly assessed only as one of covert disparate treatment and on that basis found the claimants' proof insufficient to prove the requisite intent to discriminate against women. On that view of the case, there was of course no reason to consider whether any justification defense might also have been established.

As our earlier discussion has anticipated, we hold this assessment to be erroneous as a matter of law. Controlling legal principles were misapplied in several critical respects. Most importantly, the assessment failed to take into account that irrespective of Olin's specific intent or motive in adopting and implementing this employment policy, the policy's indisputably adverse effect upon women's employment opportunities while not touching those of men constituted a violation of § 703(a)(2) of Title VII, Nashville Gas Co. v. Satty, 434 U.S. at 142, 98 S.Ct. at 351, unless the policy could be objectively justified under the business necessity theory of defense.

We therefore hold, in line with our earlier discussion of this theory of recovery, that the evidence of the existence and operation of the fetal vulnerability program established as a matter of law a *prima facie* case of Title VII violation. That leaves the question of how the relevant business necessity defense should now be applied at this stage in the litigation.

Claimants urge that we should apply it on this appeal—though presumably the application would be one of the first instance—and hold as a matter of law that the defense was not established on the evidence. Since Olin as defendant had the burden and the opportunity to attempt to establish it, this could be done. But we are not disposed to take this course.

Though the evidence adduced on trial would not suffice to support a finding of business necessity as we think it should be applied to this particular employment policy, we do not think it would be fair to resolve the case by our first instance application of the defense on the present record. In view of the course of proceedings below, the fact that the fetal vulnerability issue is one of first impression, and the need to adapt the business necessity defense to some of its unique and previously unencountered aspects, we think the proper course is to remand for further proceedings confined solely to that issue and on the basis of guidance now to be given.

D

It remains to adapt the business necessity defense—in both its substantive and procedural aspects—to the unique circumstances presented by this employment practice. As *amici* in particular press upon us, the underlying legal and social problem presented is one of complexity and mounting importance in the proper administration of the national policies against employment discrimination as expressed in Title VII.[24]

Briefly put, the legal problem is whether and, if so, on what basis, employment practices avowedly designed to protect the unborn fetuses of women workers from workplace dangers can be justified on that basis despite their disproportionate adverse impact upon women's employment opportunities. The social implications of this problem and of any answers given to it are obviously important ones of national policy that might well be, but have not been, addressed narrowly and specifically by Congress. In the absence of such a specific congressional expression, the judicial task is not to devise that policy but to divine probable congressional intention. This may only be done by looking to the broader statutory framework and to authoritative judicial interpretations of that framework.

A threshold question is whether under any circumstances the protection of workers' unborn children can properly be considered such a "necessity." The answer is not implicit in the term. Neither, it must be confessed, is it plainly given in the decisional law elaborating the concept of "business necessity" since its original recognition and application in *Griggs*.

That original application, in a challenge to the use of intelligence tests and diploma requirements, was to the most obviously job-related "necessity" of being able effectively to perform the job in question. Since *Griggs*, the necessity contemplated has been held to run as well to considerations of workplace safety. In our own frequently cited and applied formulation in Robinson v. Lorillard Corp., 444 F.2d 791 (4th Cir.), cert. dismissed, 404 U.S. 1006, 92 S.Ct. 573, 30 L.Ed.2d 665 (1971), Judge Sobeloff put it that the "test is whether there exists an overriding legitimate business purpose such that the practice is necessary to the *safe* and efficient operation of the business." 444 F.2d at 798

---

24. Though, as indicated, the question is apparently one of first impression at the court of appeals level, we are advised that the practice is spreading and that it has been presented in a number of cases, some pending, some settled by consent decrees, in the district courts. The legal, social and economic implications of the problems have drawn a considerable body of scholarly comment. See, e.g., Williams, Firing the Woman to Protect the Fetus: The Reconciliation of Fetal Protection with Employment Opportunity Goals Under Title VII, 69 Geo.L.J. 641 (1981) (legal/social); Finneran, Title VII and Restrictions on Employment of Fertile Women, 31 Lab.L.J. 223 (1980) (appropriate legal theory); McGarity & Schroeder, Risk-Oriented Employment Screening, 59 Tex.L.Rev. 999 (1981) (legal/economic).

(emphasis added). And the Supreme Court has since also put it that the necessity runs to "safe and efficient job performance." Dothard v. Rawlinson, 433 U.S. 321, 332 n. 14, 97 S.Ct. 2720, 2728 n. 14, 53 L.Ed.2d 786 (1977) (emphasis added).

But the question of whose safety may properly be considered a matter of "business necessity" remains an open one. The logical possibilities include women workers themselves, customers—particularly personal service customers—of the business, and others—including fellow workers—legitimately exposed under the circumstances of the particular business to any of its workplace hazards. We are of course concerned here only with the last of these. But the developed judicial view respecting the other two categories is an obvious starting point, since they have been the subject of specific applications whereas the last has not.

Though the safety of women workers themselves might be thought the most obvious subject of necessary—hence legally justifiable—restrictions on their employment opportunities, the opposite of course has been held. Among the most obvious targets of the sex-discrimination prohibitions of Title VII were those stereotypical assumptions about women workers' special societal role and physical and emotional vulnerabilities which had generated both "protective" laws and private practices restricting their employment opportunities. Rooting out those restrictions has required that they not now be routinely justified under any of the business-related defenses. Accordingly, the general view when these defenses have been raised by employers has been that they must be rejected because "it is the purpose of Title VII to allow the individual woman to make [the] choice for herself." Dothard v. Rawlinson, 433 U.S. at 335, 97 S.Ct. at 2729 (b.f.o.q. defense); see Burwell v. Eastern Air Lines, Inc., 633 F.2d 361, 371 (4th Cir.1980) (en banc) (business necessity defense), cert. denied, 450 U.S. 965, 101 S.Ct. 1480, 67 L.Ed.2d 613 (1981).

The same overriding consideration does not, of course, apply to the safety of others than the women workers themselves. And when that other is a customer required by the very nature of the business to be exposed to certain hazards related to its operation by employees, then the "safety and efficiency" of the operation is in effect an indivisible concern rather than two distinct ones. In such cases, the safety of the customer has been recognized to be of such overriding business necessity that the legal defense should in appropriate circumstances be available. See, e.g., Burwell (airline passenger safety justifies, as business necessity, policy of mandatory leave for pregnant stewardesses); cf. New York City Transit Authority v. Beazer, 440 U.S. 568, 99 S.Ct. 1355, 59 L.Ed.2d 587 (1979) (transit authority passenger safety justifies, as sufficiently "job-related," policy excluding methadone users from hire).

For purposes of our analysis, the legitimacy of an employer's purpose to protect by discriminatory means the safety of the unborn children of workers would appear to lie conceptually somewhere between a purpose to protect the safety of workers themselves and a purpose to protect that of customers exposed in the normal course to workplace hazards. In attempting to find the more appropriate analogy as between these two objects of safety concerns, it may be helpful to think of unborn children of workers as a special category—though one with quite unique characteristics—of all invitees and licensees legitimately on business premises and exposed to any of its associated hazards. Certainly the safety of unborn children of workers would seem no less a matter of legitimate business concern than the safety of the traditional business licensee or invitee upon an employer's premises.

Of such licensees and invitees, it cannot be said—as it can of the workers themselves—that in matters touching their exposure to workplace hazards they, rather than the employer, should have the absolute right of choice as against the right of the employer to guard against it by measures impinging on protected worker interests. On the other hand, it cannot be said of such licensees and invitees—as it can of business customers being served in the workplace—that their safety is so much an aspect of the efficient operation of the business that its protection constitutes a manifest necessity of the business.

Viewing the problem in this focused way in attempting to divine probable legislative intent, we believe the safety of unborn children is more appropriately analogized to the safety of personal service customers of the business. The business necessity to provide for customer safety is obviously one of more "overriding" importance, see *Lorillard*, 444 F.2d at 798, than is the necessity to provide for business "visitor" safety. But we cannot believe that Congress meant by Title VII absolutely to deprive employers of the right to provide any protection for licensees and invitees legitimately and necessarily upon their premises by any policy having a disparate impact upon certain workers. See *Beazer*, 440 U.S. at 587 & n. 31, 99 S.Ct. at 1366 & n. 31. Especially do we think it unlikely that Congress could have intended such a consequence—given the business imperatives of good labor relations—when the "visitors" protected are members, or potential members, of workers' families.

On this basis we hold that under appropriate circumstances an employer may, as a matter of business necessity, impose otherwise impermissible restrictions on employment opportunity that are reasonably required to protect the health of unborn children of women workers against hazards of the workplace.[26]

26. We do not think that a general basis for the "business necessity" asserted here need be sought in other considerations than the general societal interest—reflected in many national laws imposing legal obligations upon business enterprises—in having those enterprises operated in ways protective of the health of workers and their families, consumers, and environmental neighbors. E.g., 15 U.S.C. §§ 2051–2083 (Consumer Product Safety Act); 21 U.S.C. §§ 301–392 (Federal Food, Drug and Cosmetic Act); 29 U.S.C. §§ 651–678 (Occupational Safety and Health Act).

For this reason it is irrelevant that, as claimants point out, the mere purpose to avoid potential liability and consequent ec-

Having determined that the business necessity defense may under appropriate circumstances be an available one in the instant case, we turn now to the problem of how—substantively and procedurally—the defense, as adapted to the program here in issue, may be established in proof. The following principles, drawn from developed business necessity doctrine, we hold to be controlling.

1. The burden of persuasion is upon the employer to prove that significant risks of harm to the unborn children of women workers from their exposure during pregnancy to toxic hazards in the workplace make necessary, for the safety of the unborn children, that fertile women workers, though not men workers,[27] be appropriately restricted from exposure to those hazards and that its program of restriction is effective for the purpose. See *Lorillard*, 444 F.2d at 798 (necessity and effectiveness criteria stated).

2. This burden may not be carried by proof alone that the employer subjectively and in good faith believed its program to be necessary and effective for the purpose. Irrespective of the employer's subjective belief and motivation, the significance of the risk, the extent of its confinement to the unborn children of women as opposed to men workers, the consequent necessity of protective measures confined to women workers, and the effectiveness of the actual program for the intended purposes must be established by independent, objective evidence. See Dothard v. Rawlinson, 433 U.S. at 333, 97 S.Ct. at 2728 (objective basis rather than subjective assumptions required to establish b.f.o.q. defense); *Burwell*, 633 F.2d at 367 n. 6 (objective proof required to establish business necessity).

3. While proof of these essential elements of the defense need not be solely by means of expert opinion evidence, the essentially scientific nature of the dispositive issues requires that findings and conclusions establishing the defense be supported by the opinion evidence of qualified experts in the relevant scientific fields.[28]

onomic loss may not suffice, standing alone, to establish a business necessity defense. See Los Angeles Dept. of Water & Power v. Manhart, 435 U.S. 702, 716–17, 98 S.Ct. 1370, 1379–80, 55 L.Ed.2d 657 (1978).

That providing workplace safety is in general a matter of "business necessity" does not, of course, establish that in particular cases a specific safety-related "necessity" is sufficiently "compelling" to "override" conflicting private interests protected by Title VII. See *Lorillard*, 444 F.2d at 798. That is precisely the issue here.

27. Showing that the risk sought to be avoided is, on the best available scientific data, substantially confined to the exposure of women workers is critical to showing the program's effectiveness. It is not effective for the stated purpose of protecting offspring of exposed workers from toxic hazards if it is underinclusive for the purpose. Of course, if it were equally inclusive of men and women, it could not violate Title VII, even if it were wholly ineffective in protecting against the actual risks from exposure of either or both sexes.

28. The evidence given by the three witnesses for Olin on trial would obviously not suffice objectively to validate the necessity and effectiveness of the program. Their testimony went only to establish their own good faith belief, based upon manifestly inadequate data which, in any event, they were not appropriately qualified as experts to evaluate.

On this appeal, opposing *amici* have invited our attention to a considerable body of scientific data and studies bearing upon all the points here identified as critical to the issues of necessity and effectiveness.

4. To establish the requisite degree and cast of the risk of harm, it is not necessary to prove the existence of a general consensus on the points within the qualified scientific community. It suffices to show that within that community there is so considerable a body of opinion that significant risk exists, and that it is substantially confined to women workers, that an informed employer could not responsibly fail to act on the assumption that this opinion might be the accurate one. See *Burwell,* 633 F.2d at 373 (employer's discriminatory protective policy properly judged by contemporaneously available information, not on basis of hypotheses requiring unreasonable experimentation nor on ultimate validation of assumptions).

5. Proof of the requisite degree and cast of the risk of harm and of effectiveness of the challenged program to avoid it establishes the business necessity defense *prima facie.*

6. This *prima facie* defense may, however, be rebutted, see Albemarle Paper Co. v. Moody, 422 U.S. 405, 425, 95 S.Ct. 2362, 2375, 45 L.Ed.2d 280 (1974), by proof that there are "acceptable alternative policies or practices which would better accomplish the business purpose * * * [of protecting against the risk of harm], or accomplish it equally well with a lesser differential * * * impact [between women and men workers]." *Lorillard,* 444 F.2d at 798; see *Dothard,* 433 U.S. at 329, 97 S.Ct. at 2726; *Albemarle Paper,* 422 U.S. at 425, 95 S.Ct. at 2375.[29]

7. Such rebutting evidence to the *prima facie* defense, if accepted, may have either of two effects, both resulting in employer liability, but with possibly different remedial consequences. See *Burwell,* 633 F.2d at 372 n. 18 (dual relevance of rebutting proof intimated).

By showing an "acceptable alternative" that would accomplish the protective purpose "equally well with lesser differential impact," the evidence would at least negate *prima facie* proof of the business

Expressing no opinion upon its admissibility in detail if properly offered on trial, we merely note that that is where it must be considered in the first instance.

29. This court's formulation of the "business necessity" defense in *Lorillard* clearly contemplated that proof of "no acceptable alternatives" should be part of the defendant employer's burden in establishing the defense. See 444 F.2d at 798. While the Supreme Court has never expressly repudiated this aspect of *Lorillard,* its subsequent decisions in *Beazer, Dothard* and *Albemarle Paper* have so clearly indicated that proof of "acceptable alternatives" is claimant's burden in "rebuttal," that we must consider *Lorillard's* formulation to that extent no longer authoritative.

Proof burden aside, we of course express no opinion as to whether any "acceptable

alternatives" may here be shown. The most obvious possibilities—as suggested on appeal by *amici* associated in interest with claimants—would involve reduction of workplace hazards to the point that no, or less stringent, restrictions were necessary to give adequate protection; imposing equal restrictions on men and women workers; imposing less stringent restrictions on women without reduction of hazards; or various combinations of these. Whether any alternatives such as these or others are "acceptable," in terms of their effectiveness and their economic and technological feasibility, is a factual/legal issue to be addressed by the district court in the first instance on the basis of any evidence adduced upon it in further proceedings.

necessity of the specific program by having demonstrated an "unnecessary" degree of overkill in it.

While this would require a finding of liability, any resulting remedial decree should only vindicate, in both prospective and monetary relief aspects, the claimant's rights as they would exist under the "acceptable alternative" policy.[30]

But it is possible that the "rebuttal" evidence might suffice, either alone or in conjunction with other evidence, to carry the claimants' retained burden of persuasion that behind the proven but *prima facie* justified disparate impact of the program there lay in fact a discriminatory intent; that the program in effect involved "disparate treatment." This would result from proof that in view of the demonstrated degree of overkill in the challenged program, the purpose advanced for it had now been revealed to be all along a mere "pretext." See *Beazer,* 440 U.S. at 587, 99 S.Ct. at 1366; *Albemarle Paper,* 422 U.S. at 425, 95 S.Ct. at 2375.

---

30. By this we reject the possible implication from the Supreme Court's decisions in *Albemarle Paper* and *Beazer* that the only possible effect of such rebutting evidence is to show discriminatory intent by proof of "pretext." We are aware that the question is an arguable one upon which there is a difference of scholarly and judicial opinion. As to the former, compare, e.g., Furnish, A Path Through the Maze: Disparate Impact and Disparate Treatment Under Title VII of the Civil Rights Act of 1964 After Beazer and Burdine, 23 B.C.L. Rev. 419, 423–25 (1982) (may have dual relevance, to prove pretext or to "undercut" defense), with Note, Rebutting the Griggs Prima Facie Case Under Title VII: Limiting Judicial Review of Less Restrictive Alternatives, 1981 U.Ill.L.Rev. 181, 207–10 (1981) (only relevant to prove pretext). As to the latter, there appears to be little beyond a few decisions making assumptions running both ways. Compare, e.g., Blake v. City of Los Angeles, 595 F.2d 1367, 1383 (9th Cir.1979) (dictum: dual relevance assumed), cert. denied, 446 U.S. 928, 100 S.Ct. 1865, 64 L.Ed.2d 281 (1980), with Harless v. Duck, 14 Fair Empl.Prac. Cas. 1616, 1625 (N.D.Ohio 1977) (only relevant to prove pretext).

Our interpretation of the critical Supreme Court decisions is that they establish two things: (1) that the defendant-employer's burden to prove business necessity in justification of a disparate impact does not include proof of "no acceptable alternatives," the burden instead being upon claimants in rebuttal to prove that acceptable alternatives exist, see supra note 29; and (2) that such rebuttal evidence

may prove a disparate treatment violation notwithstanding that claimant's proof initially went only to establish disparate impact, see infra note 31.

In the absence of a definitive statement to that effect by the Supreme Court, we do not believe that the Court intended also to deny the opportunity of a claimant to establish the right to a remedy designed to create a "lesser differential impact," see *Lorillard,* 444 F.2d at 798, justified at the lesser but not the extant level by business necessity. We observe in this connection that in *Dothard* the Court did not advert to pretext as the object of rebuttal proof. 433 U.S. at 329, 97 S.Ct. at 2726.

We do not understand Furnco Construction Corp. v. Waters, 438 U.S. 567, 98 S.Ct. 2943, 57 L.Ed.2d 957 (1978), to be to the contrary. That decision held that a court may not impose upon an employer a remedy requiring it to adopt the "best" practices available for the enhancement of minority employment opportunities, because courts are "generally less competent than employers to restructure business practices." Id. at 578, 98 S.Ct. at 2950. But this was on the basis that no Title VII violation had been proven in the particular case, either of disparate impact or disparate treatment. Id.

Here disparate impact has been proven *prima facie,* and the question is merely whether under the flexible remedial powers conferred by Title VII, a remedy designed to minimize but not completely remove the burden of a proven disparate impact may be imposed.

Upon such a determination, with liability now established for a disparate treatment violation, any resulting remedial decree should of course vindicate claimants' rights wholly freed of any restrictive policy.[31]

IV

The judgment is affirmed in all respects save that portion denying relief to claimants on their "fetal vulnerability" claim. As to that portion, the judgment is vacated and the case is remanded for further proceedings consistent with this opinion.

Notes

On remand the Company satisfied the District Court that the Circuit Court's business necessity requirements were met. 585 F.Supp. 1447 (W.D. N.C.1984).

For different analyses and results in cases involving the discharge of pregnant X-ray technicians, see Zuniga v. Kleberg County Hospital, 692 F.2d 986 (5th Cir.1982) and Hayes v. Shelby Memorial Hospital, 726 F.2d 1543 (11th Cir.1984).

4. HARASSMENT

MERITOR SAVINGS BANK, FSB v. VINSON ET AL.

Supreme Court of the United States, 1986.
___ U.S. ___, 106 S.Ct. 2399, 91 L.Ed.2d 49.

JUSTICE REHNQUIST delivered the opinion of the Court.

This case presents important questions concerning claims of workplace "sexual harassment" brought under Title VII of the Civil Rights Act of 1964, 78 Stat. 253, as amended, 42 U.S.C. § 2000e et seq.

I

In 1974, respondent Mechelle Vinson met Sidney Taylor, a vice president of what is now petitioner Meritor Savings Bank (the bank) and manager of one of its branch offices. When respondent asked whether she might obtain employment at the bank, Taylor gave her an application, which she completed and returned the next day; later that same day Taylor called her to say that she had been hired. With Taylor as her supervisor, respondent started as a teller-trainee, and thereafter was promoted to teller, head teller, and assistant branch manager. She worked at the same branch for four years, and it is undisputed that her advancement there was based on merit alone. In September 1978, respondent notified Taylor that she was taking sick

---

31. The Supreme Court's recognition in *Albemarle Paper* and *Beazer* that following *prima facie* proof and *prima facie* avoidance of a disparate impact claim, a claimant can yet prove discriminatory treatment by showing "pretext" in the challenged practice simply reaffirms the Court's consistent admonition that both theories may appropriately be applied as alternative bases of recovery on the same set of facts. See *Teamsters,* 431 U.S. at 336 n. 15, 97 S.Ct. at 1855 n. 15.

leave for an indefinite period. On November 1, 1978, the bank discharged her for excessive use of that leave.

Respondent brought this action against Taylor and the bank, claiming that during her four years at the bank she had "constantly been subjected to sexual harassment" by Taylor in violation of Title VII. She sought injunctive relief, compensatory and punitive damages against Taylor and the bank, and attorney's fees.

At the 11-day bench trial, the parties presented conflicting testimony about Taylor's behavior during respondent's employment.* Respondent testified that during her probationary period as a teller-trainee, Taylor treated her in a fatherly way and made no sexual advances. Shortly thereafter, however, he invited her out to dinner and, during the course of the meal, suggested that they go to a motel to have sexual relations. At first she refused, but out of what she described as fear of losing her job she eventually agreed. According to respondent, Taylor thereafter made repeated demands upon her for sexual favors, usually at the branch, both during and after business hours; she estimated that over the next several years she had intercourse with him some 40 or 50 times. In addition, respondent testified that Taylor fondled her in front of other employees, followed her into the women's restroom when she went there alone, exposed himself to her, and even forcibly raped her on several occasions. These activities ceased after 1977, respondent stated, when she started going with a steady boyfriend.

Respondent also testified that Taylor touched and fondled other women employees of the bank, and she attempted to call witnesses to support this charge. But while some supporting testimony apparently was admitted without objection, the District Court did not allow her "to present wholesale evidence of a pattern and practice relating to sexual advances to other female employees in her case in chief, but advised her that she might well be able to present such evidence in rebuttal to the defendants' cases." Vinson v. Taylor, 22 EPD ¶ 30708, pp. 14688–14689, 23 FEP Cases 37, 38, 39, n. 1 (D DC 1980). Respondent did not offer such evidence in rebuttal. Finally, respondent testified that because she was afraid of Taylor she never reported his harassment to any of his supervisors and never attempted to use the bank's complaint procedure.

Taylor denied respondent's allegations of sexual activity, testifying that he never fondled her, never made suggestive remarks to her, never engaged in sexual intercourse with her and never asked her to do so. He contended instead that respondent made her accusations in response to a business-related dispute. The bank also denied respondent's allegations and asserted that any sexual harassment by Taylor was unknown to the bank and engaged in without its consent or approval.

---

* Like the Court of Appeals, this Court was not provided a complete transcript of the trial. We therefore rely largely on the District Court's opinion for the summary of the relevant testimony.

The District Court denied relief, but did not resolve the conflicting testimony about the existence of a sexual relationship between respondent and Taylor. It found instead that

> "If [respondent] and Taylor did engage in an intimate or sexual relationship during the time of [respondent's] employment with [the bank], that relationship was a voluntary one having nothing to do with her continued employment at [the bank] or her advancement or promotions at that institution." Id., at 42 (footnote omitted).

The court ultimately found that respondent "was not the victim of sexual harassment and was not the victim of sexual discrimination" while employed at the bank. Id., 43.

Although it concluded that respondent had not proved a violation of Title VII, the District Court nevertheless went on to address the bank's liability. After noting the bank's express policy against discrimination, and finding that neither respondent nor any other employee had ever lodged a complaint about sexual harassment by Taylor, the court ultimately concluded that "the bank was without notice and cannot be held liable for the alleged actions of Taylor." Id., at 42.

The Court of Appeals for the District of Columbia Circuit reversed. 243 U.S.App.D.C. 323, 753 F.2d 141 (1985). Relying on its earlier holding in Bundy v. Jackson, 205 U.S.App.D.C. 444, 641 F.2d 934 (1981), decided after the trial in this case, the court stated that a violation of Title VII may be predicated on either of two types of sexual harassment: harassment that involves the conditioning of concrete employment benefits on sexual favors, and harassment that, while not affecting economic benefits, creates a hostile or offensive working environment. The court drew additional support for this position from the Equal Employment Opportunity Commission's Guidelines on Discrimination Because of Sex, 29 CFR § 1604.11(a) (1985), which set out these two types of sexual harassment claims. Believing that "Vinson's grievance was clearly of the [hostile environment] type," 243 U.S.App.D.C., at 327, 753 F.2d, at 145, and that the District Court had not considered whether a violation of this type had occurred, the court concluded that a remand was necessary.

The court further concluded that the District Court's finding that any sexual relationship between respondent and Taylor "was a voluntary one" did not obviate the need for a remand. "[U]ncertain as to precisely what the [district] court meant" by this finding, the Court of Appeals held that if the evidence otherwise showed that "Taylor made Vinson's toleration of sexual harassment a condition of her employment," her voluntariness "had no materiality whatsoever." Id., at 328, 753 F.2d, at 146. The court then surmised that the District Court's finding of voluntariness might have been based on "the voluminous testimony regarding respondent's dress and personal fantasies," testimony that the Court of Appeals believed "had no place in this litigation." Id., at 328, 336, 753 F.2d, at 146, n. 36.

As to the bank's liability, the Court of Appeals held that an employer is absolutely liable for sexual harassment practiced by supervisory personnel, whether or not the employer knew or should have known about the misconduct. The court relied chiefly on Title VII's definition of "employer" to include "any agent of such a person," 42 U.S.C. § 2000e(b), as well as on the EEOC guidelines. The court held that a supervisor is an "agent" of his employer for Title VII purposes, even if he lacks authority to hire, fire, or promote, since "the mere existence—or even the appearance—of a significant degree of influence in vital job decisions gives any supervisor the opportunity to impose on employees." 243 U.S.App.D.C., at 332, 753 F.2d, at 150.

In accordance with the foregoing, the Court of Appeals reversed the judgment of the District Court and remanded the case for further proceedings. A subsequent suggestion for rehearing en banc was denied, with three judges dissenting. 245 U.S.App.D.C. 1330, 760 F.2d 1330 (1985). We granted certiorari, 474 U.S. ___, 106 S.Ct. 57, 88 L.Ed.2d 46 (1985), and now affirm but for different reasons.

II

Title VII of the Civil Rights Act of 1964 makes it "an unlawful employment practice for an employer * * * to discriminate against any individual with respect to his compensation, terms, conditions, or privileges of employment, because of such individual's race, color, religion, sex, or national origin." 42 U.S.C. § 2000e–2(a)(1). The prohibition against discrimination based on sex was added to Title VII at the last minute on the floor of the House of Representatives. 110 Cong.Rec. 2577–2584 (1964). The principal argument in opposition to the amendment was that "sex discrimination" was sufficiently different from other types of discrimination that it ought to receive separate legislative treatment. See id., at 2577 (Statement of Rep. Celler quoting letter from United States Department of Labor); id., at 2584 (statement of Rep. Green). This argument was defeated, the bill quickly passed as amended, and we are left with little legislative history to guide us in interpreting the Act's prohibition against discrimination based on "sex."

Respondent argues, and the Court of Appeals held, that unwelcome sexual advances that create an offensive or hostile working environment violate Title VII. Without question, when a supervisor sexually harasses a subordinate because of the subordinate's sex, that supervisor "discriminate[s]" on the basis of sex. Petitioner apparently does not challenge this proposition. It contends instead that in prohibiting discrimination with respect to "compensation, terms, conditions, or privileges" of employment, Congress was concerned with what petitioner describes as "tangible loss" of "an economic character," not "purely psychological aspects of the workplace environment." Brief for Petitioner 30–31, 34. In support of this claim petitioner observes that in both the legislative history of Title VII and this Court's Title VII decisions, the focus has been on tangible, economic barriers erected by discrimination.

We reject petitioner's view. First, the language of Title VII is not limited to "economic" or "tangible" discrimination. The phrase "terms, conditions, or privileges of employment" evinces a congressional intent " 'to strike at the entire spectrum of disparate treatment of men and women' " in employment. Los Angeles Department of Water and Power v. Manhart, 435 U.S. 702, 707, n. 13, 98 S.Ct. 1370, 1375, n. 13, 55 L.Ed.2d 657 (1978), quoting Sprogis v. United Air Lines, Inc., 444 F.2d 1194, 1198 (CA7 1971). Petitioner has pointed to nothing in the Act to suggest that Congress contemplated the limitation urged here.

Second, in 1980 the EEOC issued guidelines specifying that "sexual harassment," as there defined, is a form of sex discrimination prohibited by Title VII. As an "administrative interpretation of the Act by the enforcing agency," Griggs v. Duke Power Co., 401 U.S. 424, 433–434, 91 S.Ct. 849, 855, 28 L.Ed.2d 158 (1971), these guidelines, " 'while not controlling upon the courts by reason of their authority, do constitute a body of experience and informed judgment to which courts and litigants may properly resort for guidance,' " General Electric Co. v. Gilbert, 429 U.S. 125, 141–142, 97 S.Ct. 401, 410–11, 50 L.Ed.2d 343 (1976), quoting Skidmore v. Swift & Co., 323 U.S. 134, 140, 65 S.Ct. 161, 164, 89 L.Ed. 124 (1944). The EEOC guidelines fully support the view that harassment leading to noneconomic injury can violate Title VII.

In defining "sexual harassment," the guidelines first describe the kinds of workplace conduct that may be actionable under Title VII. These include "[u]nwelcome sexual advances, requests for sexual favors, and other verbal or physical conduct of a sexual nature." 29 CFR § 1604.11(a) (1985). Relevant to the charges at issue in this case, the guidelines provide that such sexual misconduct constitutes prohibited "sexual harassment," whether or not it is directly linked to the grant or denial of an economic *quid pro quo*, where "such conduct has the purpose or effect of unreasonably interfering with an individual's work performance or creating an intimidating, hostile, or offensive working environment." § 1604.11(a)(3).

In concluding that so-called "hostile environment" (i.e., non *quid pro quo*) harassment violates Title VII, the EEOC drew upon a substantial body of judicial decisions and EEOC precedent holding that Title VII affords employees the right to work in an environment free from discriminatory intimidation, ridicule, and insult. See generally 45 Fed.Reg. 74676 (1980). Rogers v. EEOC, 454 F.2d 234 (CA5 1971), cert. denied, 406 U.S. 957, 92 S.Ct. 2058, 32 L.Ed.2d 343 (1972), was apparently the first case to recognize a cause of action based upon a discriminatory work environment. In *Rogers*, the Court of Appeals for the Fifth Circuit held that a Hispanic complainant could establish a Title VII violation by demonstrating that her employer created an offensive work environment for employees by giving discriminatory service to its

Hispanic clientele. The court explained that an employee's protections under Title VII extend beyond the economic aspects of employment:

> "[T]he phrase 'terms, conditions or privileges of employment' in [Title VII] is an expansive concept which sweeps within its protective ambit the practice of creating a working environment heavily charged with ethnic or racial discrimination. * * * One can readily envision working environments so heavily polluted with discrimination as to destroy completely the emotional and psychological stability of minority group workers * * *." 454 F.2d, at 238.

Courts applied this principle to harassment based on race, e.g., Firefighters Institute for Racial Equality v. St. Louis, 549 F.2d 506, 514–515 (CA8), cert. denied sub nom. Banta v. United States, 178 U.S.App.D.C. 91, 98, 434 U.S. 819, 98 S.Ct. 60, 54 L.Ed.2d 76 (1977); Gray v. Greyhound Lines, East, 178 U.S.App.D.C. 91, 98, 545 F.2d 169, 176 (1976), religion, e.g., Compston v. Borden, Inc., 424 F.Supp. 157 (SD Ohio 1976), and national origin, e.g., Cariddi v. Kansas City Chiefs Football Club, 568 F.2d 87, 88 (CA8 1977). Nothing in Title VII suggests that a hostile environment based on discriminatory sexual harassment should not be likewise prohibited. The guidelines thus appropriately drew from, and were fully consistent with, the existing caselaw.

Since the guidelines were issued, courts have uniformly held, and we agree, that a plaintiff may establish a violation of Title VII by proving that discrimination based on sex has created a hostile or abusive work environment. As the Court of Appeals for the Eleventh Circuit wrote in Henson v. Dundee, 682 F.2d 897, 902 (1982):

> "Sexual harassment which creates a hostile or offensive environment for members of one sex is every bit the arbitrary barrier to sexual equality at the workplace that racial harassment is to racial equality. Surely, a requirement that a man or woman run a gauntlet of sexual abuse in return for the privilege of being allowed to work and make a living can be as demeaning and disconcerting as the harshest of racial epithets."

Accord, Katz v. Dole, 709 F.2d 251, 254–255 (CA4 1983); Bundy v. Jackson, 205 U.S.App.D.C. 444, 641 F.2d, at 934–944 (1981); Zabkowicz v. West Bend Co., 589 F.Supp. 780 (ED Wisc. 1984).

Of course, as the courts in both *Rogers* and *Henson* recognized, not all workplace conduct that may be described as "harassment" affects a "term, condition, or privilege" of employment within the meaning of Title VII. See Rogers v. EEOC, supra, at 238 ("mere utterance of an ethnic or racial epithet which engenders offensive feelings in an employee" would not affect the conditions of employment to sufficiently significant degree to violate Title VII); *Henson*, supra, at 904 (quoting same). For sexual harassment to be actionable, it must be sufficiently severe or pervasive "to alter the conditions of [the victim's] employment and create an abusive working environment." Ibid. Respondent's allegations in this case—which include not only pervasive harassment but also criminal conduct of the most serious nature—are plainly sufficient to state a claim for "hostile environment" sexual harassment.

The question remains, however, whether the District Court's ultimate finding that respondent "was not the victim of sexual harassment," 22 EPD ¶ 30708, at 14692–14693, 23 FEP Cases, at 43, effectively disposed of respondent's claim. The Court of Appeals recognized, we think correctly, that this ultimate finding was likely based on one or both of two erroneous views of the law. First, the District Court apparently believed that a claim for sexual harassment will not lie absent an *economic* effect on the complainant's employment. See ibid. ("It is without question that sexual harassment of female employees in which they are asked or required to submit to sexual demands as a *condition to obtain employment or to maintain employment or to obtain promotions* falls within protection of Title VII.") (emphasis added). Since it appears that the District Court made its findings without ever considering the "hostile environment" theory of sexual harassment, the Court of Appeals' decision to remand was correct.

Second, the District Court's conclusion that no actionable harassment occurred might have rested on its earlier "finding" that "[i]f [respondent] and Taylor did engage in an intimate or sexual relationship * * * that relationship was a voluntary one." Id., at 14692, 23 FEP Cases, at 42. But the fact that sex-related conduct was "voluntary," in the sense that the complainant was not forced to participate against her will, is not a defense to a sexual harassment suit brought under Title VII. The gravamen of any sexual harassment claim is that the alleged sexual advances were "unwelcome." 29 CFR § 1604.11(a) (1985). While the question whether particular conduct was indeed unwelcome presents difficult problems of proof and turns largely on credibility determinations committed to the trier of fact, the District Court in this case erroneously focused on the "voluntariness" of respondent's participation in the claimed sexual episodes. The correct inquiry is whether respondent by her conduct indicated that the alleged sexual advances were unwelcome, not whether her actual participation in sexual intercourse was voluntary.

Petitioner contends that even if this case must be remanded to the District Court, the Court of Appeals erred in one of the terms of its remand. Specifically, the Court of Appeals stated that testimony about respondent's "dress and personal fantasies," 243 U.S.App.D.C. at 328, n. 36, 753 F.2d, at 146, n. 36, which the District Court apparently admitted into evidence, "had no place in this litigation." Ibid. The apparent ground for this conclusion was that respondent's voluntariness *vel non* in submitting to Taylor's advances was immaterial to her sexual harassment claim. While "voluntariness" in the sense of consent is not a defense to such a claim, it does not follow that a complainant's sexually provocative speech or dress is irrelevant as a matter of law in determining whether he or she found particular sexual advances unwelcome. To the contrary, such evidence is obviously relevant. The EEOC guidelines emphasize that the trier of fact must determine the existence of sexual harassment in light of "the record as a whole" and "the totality of circumstances, such as the nature of the sexual advances and the context in which the alleged incidents occurred." 29 CFR § 1604.11(b) (1985). Respondent's claim that any marginal relevance of the evidence in question was outweighed by the potential for unfair prejudice is the sort of argument properly addressed to the District Court. In this case the District Court concluded that the evidence should be admitted, and the Court of Appeals' contrary conclusion was based upon the erroneous, categorical view that testimony about provocative dress and publicly expressed sexual fantasies "had no place in this litigation." 243 U.S.App.D.C., at 328, n. 36, 753 F.2d, at 146, n. 36. While the District Court must carefully weigh the applicable considerations in deciding whether to admit evidence of this kind, there is no *per se* rule against its admissibility.

III

Although the District Court concluded that respondent had not proved a violation of Title VII, it nevertheless went on to consider the question of the bank's liability. Finding that "the bank was without notice" of Taylor's alleged conduct, and that notice to Taylor was not the equivalent of notice to the bank, the court concluded that the bank therefore could not be held liable for Taylor's alleged actions. The Court of Appeals took the opposite view, holding that an employer is strictly liable for a hostile environment created by a supervisor's sexual advances, even though the employer neither knew nor reasonably could have known of the alleged misconduct. The court held that a supervisor, whether or not he possesses the authority to hire, fire, or promote, is necessarily an "agent" of his employer for all Title VII purposes, since "even the appearance" of such authority may enable him to impose himself on his subordinates.

The parties and *amici* suggest several different standards for employer liability. Respondent, not surprisingly, defends the position of the Court of Appeals. Noting that Title VII's definition of "employer" includes any "agent" of the employer, she also argues that "so long as the circumstance is work-related, the supervisor is the employer and the employer is the supervisor." Brief for Respondent 27. Notice to Taylor that the advances were unwelcome, therefore, was notice to the bank.

Petitioner argues that respondent's failure to use its established grievance procedure, or to otherwise put it on notice of the alleged misconduct, insulates petitioner from liability for Taylor's wrongdoing. A contrary rule would be unfair, petitioner argues, since in a hostile environment harassment case the employer often will have no reason to know about, or opportunity to cure, the alleged wrongdoing.

The EEOC, in its brief as *amicus curiae,* contends that courts formulating employer liability rules should draw from traditional agency principles. Examination of those principles has led the EEOC to the view that where a supervisor exercises the authority actually delegated to him by his employer, by making or threatening to make decisions affecting the employment status of his subordinates, such actions are properly imputed to the employer whose delegation of authority empowered the supervisor to undertake them. Brief for United States and Equal Employment Opportunity Commission as *Amicus Curiae* 22. Thus, the courts have consistently held employers liable for the discriminatory discharges of employees by supervisory personnel, whether or not the employer knew, should have known, or approved of the supervisor's actions. E.g., Anderson v. Methodist Evangelical Hospital, Inc., 464 F.2d 723, 725 (CA6 1972).

The EEOC suggests that when a sexual harassment claim rests exclusively on a "hostile environment" theory, however, the usual basis for a finding of agency will often disappear. In that case, the EEOC believes, agency principles lead to

> "a rule that asks whether a victim of sexual harassment had reasonably available an avenue of complaint regarding such harassment, and, if available and utilized, whether that procedure was reasonably responsive to the employee's complaint. If the employer has an expressed policy against sexual harassment and has implemented a procedure specifically designed to resolve sexual harassment claims, and if the victim does not take advantage of that procedure, the employer should be shielded from liability absent actual knowledge of the sexually hostile environment (obtained, e.g., by the filing of a charge with the EEOC or a comparable state agency). In all other cases, the employer will be liable if it has actual knowledge of the harassment or if, considering all the facts of the case, the victim in question had no reasonably available avenue for making his or her complaint known to appropriate management officials." Brief for United States and Equal Opportunity Employment Commission as *Amici Curiae* 26.

As respondent points out, this suggested rule is in some tension with the EEOC guidelines, which hold an employer liable for the acts of its agents without regard to notice. 29 CFR § 1604.11(c) (1985). The guidelines do require, however, an "examin[ation of] the circumstances of the particular employment relationship and the job [f]unctions performed by the individual in determining whether an individual acts in either a supervisory or agency capacity." Ibid.

This debate over the appropriate standard for employer liability has a rather abstract quality about it given the state of the record in this case. We do not know at this stage whether Taylor made any sexual advances toward respondent at all, let alone whether those advances were unwelcome, whether they were sufficiently pervasive to constitute a condition of employment, or whether they were "so pervasive and so long continuing ∗ ∗ ∗ that the employer must have become conscious of [them]," Taylor v. Jones, 653 F.2d 1193, 1197–1199

(CA8 1981) (holding employer liable for racially hostile working environment based on constructive knowledge).

We therefore decline the parties' invitation to issue a definitive rule on employer liability, but we do agree with the EEOC that Congress wanted courts to look to agency principles for guidance in this area. While such common-law principles may not be transferable in all their particulars to Title VII, Congress' decision to define ."employer" to include any "agent" of an employer, 42 U.S.C. § 2000e(b), surely evinces an intent to place some limits on the acts of employees for which employers under Title VII are to be held responsible. For this reason, we hold that the Court of Appeals erred in concluding that employers are always automatically liable for sexual harassment by their supervisors. See generally Restatement (Second) of Agency §§ 219–237 (1958). For the same reason, absence of notice to an employer does not necessarily insulate that employer from liability. Ibid.

Finally, we reject petitioner's view that the mere existence of a grievance procedure and a policy against discrimination, coupled with respondent's failure to invoke that procedure, must insulate petitioner from liability. While those facts are plainly relevant, the situation before us demonstrates why they are not necessarily dispositive. Petitioner's general nondiscrimination policy did not address sexual harassment in particular, and thus did not alert employees to their employer's interest in correcting that form of discrimination. App. 25. Moreover, the bank's grievance procedure apparently required an employee to complain first to her supervisor, in this case Taylor. Since Taylor was the alleged perpetrator, it is not altogether surprising that respondent failed to invoke the procedure and report her grievance to him. Petitioner's contention that respondent's failure should insulate it from liability might be substantially stronger if its procedures were better calculated to encourage victims of harassment to come forward.

IV

In sum, we hold that a claim of "hostile environment" sex discrimination is actionable under Title VII, that the District Court's findings were insufficient to dispose of respondent's hostile environment claim, and that the District Court did not err in admitting testimony about respondent's sexually provocative speech and dress. As to employer liability, we conclude that the Court of Appeals was wrong to entirely disregard agency principles and impose absolute liability on employers for the acts of their supervisors, regardless of the circumstances of a particular case.

Accordingly, the judgment of the Court of Appeals reversing the judgment of the District Court is affirmed, and the case is remanded for further proceedings consistent with this opinion.

It is so ordered.

JUSTICE MARSHALL, with whom JUSTICE BRENNAN, JUSTICE BLACKMUN, and JUSTICE STEVENS, join, concurring in the judgment.

I fully agree with the Court's conclusion that workplace sexual harassment is illegal, and violates Title VII. Part III of the Court's opinion, however, leaves open the circumstances in which an employer is responsible under Title VII for such conduct. Because I believe that question to be properly before us, I write separately.

The issue the Court declines to resolve is addressed in the EEOC Guidelines on Discrimination Because of Sex, which are entitled to great deference. See Griggs v. Duke Power Co., 401 U.S. 424, 433–434, 91 S.Ct. 849, 854–55, 28 L.Ed.2d 158 (1971) (EEOC Guidelines on Employment Testing Procedures of 1966); see also ante, at ——. The Guidelines explain:

> "Applying general Title VII principles, an employer * * * is responsible for its acts and those of its agents and supervisory employees with respect to sexual harassment regardless of whether the specific acts complained of were authorized or even forbidden by the employer and regardless of whether the employer knew or should have known of their occurrence. The Commission will examine the circumstances of the particular employment relationship and the job functions performed by the individual in determining whether an individual acts in either a supervisory or agency capacity.

> "With respect to conduct between fellow employees, an employer is responsible for acts of sexual harassment in the workplace where the employer (or its agents or supervisory employees) knows or should have known of the conduct, unless it can show that it took immediate and appropriate corrective action." 29 CFR §§ 1604.11(c), (d) (1985).

The Commission, in issuing the Guidelines, explained that its rule was "in keeping with the general standard of employer liability with respect to agents and supervisory employees. * * * [T]he Commission and the courts have held for years that an employer is liable if a supervisor or an agent violates the Title VII, regardless of knowledge or any other mitigating factor." 45 Fed.Reg. 74676 (1980). I would adopt the standard set out by the Commission.

An employer can act only through individual supervisors and employees; discrimination is rarely carried out pursuant to a formal vote of a corporation's board of directors. Although an employer may sometimes adopt company-wide discriminatory policies violative of Title VII, acts that may constitute Title VII violations are generally effected through the actions of individuals, and often an individual may take such a step even in defiance of company policy. Nonetheless, Title VII remedies, such as reinstatement and backpay, generally run against the employer as an entity.[1] The question thus arises as to the circumstances under which an employer will be held liable under Title VII for the acts of its employees.

The answer supplied by general Title VII law, like that supplied by federal labor law, is that the act of a supervisory employee or agent is imputed to the employer.[2] Thus, for example, when a supervisor discriminatorily fires or refuses to promote a black employee, that act is, without more, considered the act of the employer. The courts do not stop to consider whether the employer otherwise had "notice" of the action, or even whether the supervisor had actual authority to act as he did. E.g., Flowers v. Crouch-Walker Corp., 552 F.2d 1277, 1282 (CA7 1977); Young v. Southwestern Savings and Loan Assn., 509 F.2d 140 (CA5 1975); Anderson v. Methodist Evangelical Hospital, Inc., 464 F.2d 723 (CA6 1972). Following that approach, every Court of Appeals that has considered the issue has held that sexual harassment by supervisory personnel is automatically imputed to the employer when the harassment results in tangible job detriment to the subordinate employee. See Horn v. Duke Homes, Inc., Div. of Windsor Mobile Homes, 755 F.2d 599, 604–606 (CA7 1985); Vinson v. Taylor, 243 U.S.App.D.C. 323, 329–334, 753 F.2d 141, 147–152 (1985); Craig v. Y&Y Snacks, Inc., 721 F.2d 77, 80–81 (CA3 1983); Katz v. Dole, 709 F.2d 251, 255, n. 6 (CA4 1983); Henson v. City of Dundee, 682 F.2d 897, 910 (CA11 1982); Miller v. Bank of America, 600 F.2d 211, 213 (CA9 1979).

The brief filed by the Solicitor General on behalf of the EEOC in this case suggests that a different rule should apply when a supervisor's harassment "merely" results in a discriminatory work environment. The Solicitor General concedes that sexual harassment that affects tangible job benefits is an exercise of authority delegated to the supervisor by the employer, and thus gives rise to employer liability. But, departing from the EEOC Guidelines, he argues that the case of a supervisor merely creating a discriminatory work environment is different because the supervisor "is not exercising, or threatening to exercise, actual or apparent authority to make personnel decisions affecting the victim." Brief for United States and EEOC as *Amici Curiae* 24. In the latter situation, he concludes, some further notice requirement should therefore be necessary.

The Solicitor General's position is untenable. A supervisor's responsibilities do not begin and end with the power to hire, fire, and discipline employees, or with the power to recommend such actions. Rather, a supervisor is charged with the day-to-day supervision of the

---

1. The remedial provisions of Title VII were largely modeled on those of the National Labor Relations Act (NLRA). See Albemarle Paper Co. v. Moody, 422 U.S. 405, 419, and n. 11, 95 S.Ct. 2362, 2372, and n. 11 (1975); see also Franks v. Bowman Transportation Co., 424 U.S. 747, 768–770, 96 S.Ct. 1251, 1266–67, 47 L.Ed.2d 444 (1976).

2. For NLRA cases, see, e.g., Graves Trucking, Inc. v. NLRB, 692 F.2d 470 (CA7 1982); NLRB v. Kaiser Agricultural Chemical, Division of Kaiser Aluminum & Chemical Corp., 473 F.2d 374, 384 (CA5 1973); Amalgamated Clothing Workers of America v. NLRB, 124 U.S.App.D.C. 365, 377, 365 F.2d 898, 909 (1966).

work environment and with ensuring a safe, productive, workplace. There is no reason why abuse of the latter authority should have different consequences than abuse of the former. In both cases it is the authority vested in the supervisor by the employer that enables him to commit the wrong: it is precisely because the supervisor is understood to be clothed with the employer's authority that he is able to impose unwelcome sexual conduct on subordinates. There is therefore no justification for a special rule, to be applied *only* in "hostile environment" cases, that sexual harassment does not create employer liability until the employee suffering the discrimination notifies other supervisors. No such requirement appears in the statute, and no such requirement can coherently be drawn from the law of agency.

Agency principles and the goals of Title VII law make appropriate some limitation on the liability of employers for the acts of supervisors. Where, for example, a supervisor has no authority over an employee, because the two work in wholly different parts of the employer's business, it may be improper to find strict employer liability. See 29 CFR § 1604.11(c) (1985). Those considerations, however, do not justify the creation of a special "notice" rule in hostile environment cases.

Further, nothing would be gained by crafting such a rule. In the "pure" hostile environment case, where an employee files an EEOC complaint alleging sexual harassment in the workplace, the employee seeks not money damages but injunctive relief. See Bundy v. Jackson, 205 U.S.App.D.C. 444, 446, 641 F.2d 934, 936, n. 12 (1981). Under Title VII, the EEOC must notify an employer of charges made against it within 10 days after receipt of the complaint. 42 U.S.C. § 2000e–5(b). If the charges appear to be based on "reasonable cause," the EEOC must attempt to eliminate the offending practice through "informal methods of conference, conciliation, and persuasion." Ibid. An employer whose internal procedures assertedly would have redressed the discrimination can avoid injunctive relief by employing these procedures after receiving notice of the complaint or during the conciliation period. Cf. Brief for United States and EEOC as *Amici Curiae* 26. Where a complainant, on the other hand, seeks backpay on the theory that a hostile work environment effected a constructive termination, the existence of an internal complaint procedure may be a factor in determining not the employer's liability but the remedies available against it. Where a complainant without good reason bypassed an internal complaint procedure she knew to be effective, a court may be reluctant to find constructive termination and thus to award reinstatement or backpay.

I therefore reject the Solicitor General's position. I would apply in this case the same rules we apply in all other Title VII cases, and hold that sexual harassment by a supervisor of an employee under his supervision, leading to a discriminatory work environment, should be imputed to the employer for Title VII purposes regardless of whether the employee gave "notice" of the offense.

JUSTICE STEVENS, concurring.

Because I do not see any inconsistency between the two opinions, and because I believe the question of statutory construction that JUSTICE MARSHALL has answered is fairly presented by the record, I join both the Court's opinion and JUSTICE MARSHALL'S opinion.

Notes

King v. Palmer, 778 F.2d 878 (D.C.Cir.1985). Plaintiff Mabel King applied for a promotion to supervisory nurse at the District of Columbia jail. The promotion was awarded to Norma Grant. The promoting supervisor was Dr. Francis Smith, Chief Medical Officer. In King's Title VII suit, there was evidence of a sexual relationship between Smith and Grant, e.g., kisses, hugs, and other amorous behavior. Defendants asserted that Grant was promoted because of superior qualifications. The District Court found that the relationship between Smith and Grant had been a substantial factor in Grant's promotion, that King had made out a prima facie case, and that defendants' rebuttal was "unsupported by testimony the Court finds credible" and "clearly pretextual." The Court nevertheless entered judgment for defendants because plaintiff had not proved by direct evidence that the sexual relationship had ever been consummated.

The Court of Appeals reversed. Invoking *Burdine,* the Court rejected the lower court's requirement that discrimination be proved by direct evidence, and stated that an unrebutted prima facie case requires judgment for the plaintiff. The Court specifically rejected the District Court's "inexplicable distinction between sexual intercourse and other (arguably lesser) forms of sexual conduct . . .. We cannot even imagine how a court could begin to make qualitative distinctions between different forms of sexual encounters. A requirement of proof of intercourse might have the advantage of any "bright line" test, but it would establish a patently absurd legal principle. We therefore refuse to require a plaintiff who has provided clear evidence of sexual conduct to do more and demonstrate directly that the relationship had been consummated." The Court left open the case where plaintiff showed only that the candidate selected for promotion was more "attractive" to the selecting officials.

5. SEXUAL PREFERENCE

DeSANTIS v. PACIFIC TELEPHONE AND TELEGRAPH CO., INC.

United States Court of Appeals, for the Ninth Circuit, 1979.
608 F.2d 327.

CHOY, CIRCUIT JUDGE:

Male and female homosexuals brought three separate federal district court actions claiming that their employers or former employers discriminated against them in employment decisions because of their homosexuality. They alleged that such discrimination violated Title VII of the Civil Rights Act of 1964, 42 U.S.C. § 2000e et seq., and 42 U.S.C. § 1985(3). The district courts dismissed the complaints as failing to state claims under either statute. Plaintiffs below appealed. Because of the similarity of issues involved, this court consolidated the appeals at the request of counsel for appellants. We affirm.

II.   TITLE VII CLAIM

Appellants argue first that the district courts erred in holding that Title VII does not prohibit discrimination on the basis of sexual preference. They claim that in prohibiting certain employment discrimination on the basis of "sex," Congress meant to include discrimination on the basis of sexual orientation. They add that in a trial they could establish that discrimination against homosexuals disproportionately effects men and that this disproportionate impact and correlation between discrimination on the basis of sexual preference and discrimination on the basis of "sex" requires that sexual preference be considered a subcategory of the "sex" category of Title VII. See 42 U.S.C. § 2000e–2.

A.   CONGRESSIONAL INTENT IN PROHIBITING "SEX" DISCRIMINATION

In Holloway v. Arthur Andersen & Co., 566 F.2d 659 (9th Cir.1977), plaintiff argued that her employer had discriminated against her because she was undergoing a sex transformation and that this discrimination violated Title VII's prohibition on sex discrimination. This court rejected that claim, writing:

> The cases interpreting Title VII sex discrimination provisions agree that they were intended to place women on an equal footing with men. [Citations omitted.]
>
> Giving the statute its plain meaning, this court concludes that Congress had only the traditional notions of "sex" in mind. Later legislative activity makes this narrow definition even more evident. Several bills have been introduced to *amend* the Civil Rights Act to prohibit discrimination against "sexual preference." None have [*sic*] been enacted into law.
>
> Congress has not shown any intent other than to restrict the term "sex" to its traditional meaning. Therefore, this court will not expand Title VII's application in the absence of Congressional mandate. The manifest purpose of Title VII's prohibition against sex discrimination in employment is to ensure that men and women are treated equally, absent a bona fide relationship between the qualifications for the job and the person's sex.

Id. at 662–63 (footnotes omitted); see Baker v. California Land Title Co., 507 F.2d 895, 896 & n. 2 (9th Cir.1974), cert. denied, 422 U.S. 1046, 95 S.Ct. 2664, 45 L.Ed.2d 699 (1975); Rosenfeld v. Southern Pacific Co., 444 F.2d 1219, 1225 (9th Cir.1971).

Following *Holloway,* we conclude that Title VII's prohibition of "sex" discrimination applies only to discrimination on the basis of gender and should not be judicially extended to include sexual preference such as homosexuality. See Smith v. Liberty Mutual Insurance Co., 569 F.2d 325, 326–27 (5th Cir.1978); Holloway, 566 F.2d at 662–63; Voyles v. Ralph K. Davies Medical Center, 403 F.Supp. 456, 456–57 (N.D.Cal.1975), aff'd without published opinion, 570 F.2d 354 (9th Cir. 1978).[3]

---

3. Based on a similar reading of the legislative history and the principle that "words used in statutes are to be given their ordinary meaning," the EEOC has concluded "that when Congress used the word sex in Title VII it was referring to a person's gender" and not to "sexual prac-

B.　Disproportionate Impact

Appellants argue that recent decisions dealing with disproportionate impact require that discrimination against homosexuals fall within the purview of Title VII.　They contend that these recent decisions, like Griggs v. Duke Power Co., 401 U.S. 424, 91 S.Ct. 849, 28 L.Ed.2d 158 (1971), establish that any employment criterion that affects one sex more than the other violates Title VII.　They quote from *Griggs:*

> What is required by Congress [under Title VII] is the removal of artificial, arbitrary, and unnecessary barriers to employment when the barriers operate invidiously to discriminate on the basis of racial or other impermissible classifications.

401 U.S. at 431, 91 S.Ct. at 853.　They claim that in a trial they could prove that discrimination against homosexuals disproportionately affects men both because of the greater incidence of homosexuality in the male population and because of the greater likelihood of an employer's discovering male homosexuals compared to female homosexuals.

Assuming that appellants can otherwise satisfy the requirement of *Griggs,* we do not believe that *Griggs* can be applied to extend Title VII protection to homosexuals.　In finding that the disproportionate impact of educational tests on blacks violated Title VII, the Supreme Court in *Griggs* sought to effectuate a major congressional purpose in enacting Title VII: protection of blacks from employment discrimination.　For as the Supreme Court noted in Philbrook v. Goldgett, 421 U.S. 707, 95 S.Ct. 1893, 44 L.Ed.2d 525 (1975), in construing a statute, "[o]ur objective * * * is to ascertain the congressional intent and give effect to the legislative will."　Id. at 713, 95 S.Ct. at 1898.

The *Holloway* court noted that in passing Title VII Congress did not intend to protect sexual orientation and has repeatedly refused to extend such protection.　See part IIA supra.　Appellants now ask us to employ the disproportionate impact decisions as an artifice to "bootstrap" Title VII protection for homosexuals under the guise of protecting men generally.

This we are not free to do.　Adoption of this bootstrap device would frustrate congressional objectives as explicated in *Holloway,* not effectuate congressional goals as in *Griggs.*　It would achieve by judicial "construction" what Congress did not do and has consistently refused to do on many occasions.　It would violate the rule that our duty in construing a statute is to "ascertain * * * and give effect to the legislative will."　*Philbrook,* 421 U.S. at 713, 95 S.Ct. at 1898.　We conclude that the *Griggs* disproportionate impact theory may not be applied to extend Title VII protection to homosexuals.[4]

C.　Differences in Employment Criteria

Appellants next contend that recent decisions have held that an employer generally may not use different employment criteria for men and women.　They claim that if a male employee prefers males as

---

tices."　EEOC Dec. No. 76–75, [1976] Emp. Prac.Guide (CCH) ¶ 6495, at 4266.

　4.　Appellants do not contend that any prior decision of any federal court has applied the disproportionate impact analysis

to extend Title VII protection to homosexuals.　Recent cases have typically applied the analysis to protect racial minority groups and women.

sexual partners, he will be treated differently from a female who prefers male partners. They conclude that the employer thus uses different employment criteria for men and women and violates the Supreme Court's warning in Phillips v. Martin-Marietta Corp., 400 U.S. 542, 91 S.Ct. 496, 27 L.Ed.2d 613 (1971):

> The Court of Appeals therefore erred in reading this section as permitting one hiring policy for women and another for men * * *.

Id. at 544, 91 S.Ct. at 497.

We must again reject appellants' efforts to "bootstrap" Title VII protection for homosexuals. While we do not express approval of an employment policy that differentiates according to sexual preference, we note that whether dealing with men or women the employer is using the same criterion: it will not hire or promote a person who prefers sexual partners of the same sex. Thus this policy does not involve different decisional criteria for the sexes.

D. INTERFERENCE WITH ASSOCIATION

Appellants argue that the EEOC has held that discrimination against an employee because of the race of the employee's friends may constitute discrimination based on race in violation of Title VII. See EEOC Dec. No. 71–1902, [1972] Empl.Prac.Guide (CCH) ¶ 6281; EEOC Dec. No. 71–969, [1972] Empl.Prac.Guide (CCH) ¶ 6193. They contend that analogously discrimination because of the sex of the employees' sexual partner should constitute discrimination based on sex.

Appellants, however, have not alleged that appellees have policies of discriminating against employees because of the gender of their friends. That is, they do not claim that the appellees will terminate anyone with a male (or female) friend. They claim instead that the appellees discriminate against employees who have a certain type of relationship—i.e., homosexual relationship—with certain friends. As noted earlier, that relationship is not protected by Title VII. See part IIA supra. Thus, assuming that it would violate Title VII for an employer to discriminate against employees because of the gender of their friends, appellants' claims do not fall within this purported rule.

E. EFFEMINACY

Appellant Strailey contends that he was terminated by the Happy Times Nursery School because that school felt that it was inappropriate for a male teacher to wear an earring to school. He claims that the school's reliance on a stereotype—that a male should have a virile rather than an effeminate appearance—violates Title VII.

In *Holloway* this court noted that Congress intended Title VII's ban on sex discrimination in employment to prevent discrimination because of gender, not because of sexual orientation or preference. See part IIA supra. Recently the Fifth Circuit similarly read the legislative history of Title VII and concluded that Title VII thus does not protect against discrimination because of effeminacy. Smith v. Liberty Mutual Insurance Co., 569 F.2d at 326–27. We agree and hold that discrimination because of effeminacy, like discrimination because of homosexuality (part IIA supra) or transsexualism (*Holloway*), does not fall within the purview of Title VII.

E. CONCLUSION AS TO TITLE VII CLAIM

Having determined that appellants' allegations do not implicate Title VII's prohibition on sex discrimination, we affirm the district court's dismissals of the Title VII claims.

SNEED, CIRCUIT JUDGE (concurring and dissenting):

I concur in the majority's opinion save subpart B of Part II thereof.

I, respectfully dissent from subpart B which holds that male homosexuals have not stated a Title VII claim under the disproportionate impact theories of Griggs v. Duke Power Co., 401 U.S. 424, 91 S.Ct. 849, 28 L.Ed.2d 158 (1971). My position is not foreclosed by our holding, with which I agree, that Title VII does not afford protection to homosexuals, male or female. The male appellants' complaint, as I understand it, is based on the contention that the use of homosexuality as a disqualification for employment, which for *Griggs'* purposes must be treated as a facially neutral criterion, impacts disproportionately on *males* because of the greater visibility of male homosexuals and a higher incidence of homosexuality among males than females.

To establish such a claim will be difficult because the male appellants must prove that as a result of the appellee's practices there exists discrimination against males *qua* males. That is, to establish a prima facie case under *Griggs* it will not be sufficient to show that appellees have employed a disproportionately large number of female *homosexuals* and a disproportionately small number of male *homosexuals.* Rather it will be necessary to establish that the use of homosexuality as a bar to employment disproportionately impacts on *males,* a class that enjoys Title VII protection. Such a showing perhaps could be made were male homosexuals a very large proportion of the total applicable male population.

My point of difference with the majority is merely that the male appellants in their *Griggs* claim are not using that case "as an artifice to 'bootstrap' Title VII protection for homosexuals under the guise of protecting men generally." (p. 2011). Their claim, if established properly, would in fact protect males generally. I would permit them to try to make their case and not dismiss it on the pleadings.

6. COMPENSATION

CORNING GLASS WORKS v. BRENNAN
Supreme Court of the United States, 1974.
417 U.S. 188, 94 S.Ct. 2223, 41 L.Ed.2d 1.

MR. JUSTICE MARSHALL delivered the opinion of the Court.

These cases arise under the Equal Pay Act of 1963, 77 Stat. 56, § 3, 29 U.S.C. § 206(d)(1),[1] which added to § 6 of the Fair Labor Standards

---

1. "No employer having employees subject to any provisions of this section shall discriminate, within any establishment in which such employees are employed, between employees on the basis of sex by paying wages to employees in such establishment at a rate less than the rate at which he pays wages to employees of the opposite sex in such establishment for equal work on jobs the performance of which requires equal skill, effort, and responsibility, and which are performed under similar working conditions, except where such payment is made pursuant to (i) a seniority system; (ii) a merit system; (iii) a system which measures earnings by

Act of 1938 the principle of equal pay for equal work regardless of sex. The principal question posed is whether Corning Glass Works violated the Act by paying a higher base wage to male night shift inspectors than it paid to female inspectors performing the same tasks on the day shift, where the higher wage was paid in addition to a separate night shift differential paid to all employees for night work. In No. 73–29, the Court of Appeals for the Second Circuit, in a case involving several Corning plants in Corning, New York, held that this practice violated the Act. 474 F.2d 226 (1973). In No. 73–695, the Court of Appeals for the Third Circuit, in a case involving a Corning plant in Wellsboro, Pennsylvania, reached the opposite conclusion. 480 F.2d 1254 (1973). We granted certiorari and consolidated the cases to resolve this unusually direct conflict between two circuits. 414 U.S. 1110, 94 S.Ct. 839, 38 L.Ed.2d 737 (1973). Finding ourselves in substantial agreement with the analysis of the Second Circuit, we affirm in No. 73–29 and reverse in No. 73–695.

I

Prior to 1925, Corning operated its plants in Wellsboro and Corning only during the day, and all inspection work was performed by women. Between 1925 and 1930, the company began to introduce automatic production equipment which made it desirable to institute a night shift. During this period, however, both New York and Pennsylvania law prohibited women from working at night.[2] As a result, in order to fill inspector positions on the new night shift, the company had to recruit male employees from among its male dayworkers. The male employees so transferred demanded and received wages substantially higher than those paid to women inspectors engaged on the two day shifts.[3] During this same period, however, no plant-wide shift differential existed and male employees working at night, other than inspectors, received the same wages as their day shift counterparts. Thus a situation developed where the night inspectors were all male,[4] the day inspectors all female, and the male inspectors received significantly higher wages.

quantity or quality of production; or (iv) a differential based on any other factor other than sex: Provided, That an employer who is paying a wage rate differential in violation of this subsection shall not, in order to comply with the provisions of this subsection, reduce the wage rate of any employee."

2. New York prohibited the employment of women between 10 p.m. and 6 a.m. See 1927 N.Y.Laws, c. 453; 1930 N.Y.Laws, c. 868. Pennsylvania also prohibited them from working between 10 p.m. and 6 a.m. See Act of July 25, 1913, Act No. 466, Pa. Laws 1913.

3. Higher wages were demanded in part because the men had been earning more money on their day shift jobs than women were paid for inspection work. Thus, at the time of the creation of the new night shift, female day shift inspectors received

wages ranging from 20 to 30 cents per hour. Most of the men designated to fill the newly created night shift positions had been working in the blowing room where the lowest wage rate was 48 cents per hour and where additional incentive pay could be earned. As night shift inspectors these men received 53 cents per hour. There is also some evidence in the record that additional compensation was necessary because the men viewed inspection jobs as "demeaning" and as "women's work."

4. A temporary exception was made during World War II when manpower shortages caused Corning to be permitted to employ women on the steady night shift inspection jobs at both locations. It appears that women night inspectors during this period were paid the same higher night shift wages earned by the men.

In 1944, Corning plants at both locations were organized by a labor union and a collective-bargaining agreement was negotiated for all production and maintenance employees. This agreement for the first time established a plant-wide shift differential,[5] but this change did not eliminate the higher base wage paid to male night inspectors. Rather, the shift differential was superimposed on the existing difference in base wages between male night inspectors and female day inspectors.

Prior to June 11, 1964, the effective date of the Equal Pay Act, the law in both Pennsylvania and New York was amended to permit women to work at night. It was not until some time after the effective date of the Act, however, that Corning initiated efforts to eliminate the differential rates for male and female inspectors. Beginning in June 1966, Corning started to open up jobs on the night shift to women. Previously separate male and female seniority lists were consolidated and women became eligible to exercise their seniority, on the same basis as men, to bid for the higher paid night inspection jobs as vacancies occurred.

On January 20, 1969, a new collective-bargaining agreement went into effect, establishing a new "job evaluation" system for setting wage rates. The new agreement abolished for the future the separate base wages for day and night shift inspectors and imposed a uniform base wage for inspectors exceeding the wage rate for the night shift previously in effect. All inspectors hired after January 20, 1969, were to receive the same base wage, whatever their sex or shift. The collective-bargaining agreement further provided, however, for a higher "red circle" rate for employees hired prior to January 20, 1969, when working as inspectors on the night shift. This "red circle" rate served essentially to perpetuate the differential in base wages between day and night inspectors.

The Secretary of Labor brought these cases to enjoin Corning from violating the Equal Pay Act and to collect back wages allegedly due female employees because of past violations. Three distinct questions are presented: (1) Did Corning ever violate the Equal Pay Act by paying male night shift inspectors more than female day shift inspectors? (2) If so, did Corning cure its violation of the Act in 1966 by permitting women to work as night shift inspectors? (3) Finally, if the violation was not remedied in 1966, did Corning cure its violation in 1969 by equalizing day and night inspector wage rates but establishing higher "red circle" rates for existing employees working on the night shift?

II

Congress' purpose in enacting the Equal Pay Act was to remedy what was perceived to be a serious and endemic problem of employment discrimination in private industry—the fact that the wage structure of "many segments of American industry has been based on an ancient but outmoded belief that a man, because of his role in society, should be

---

5. The shift differential was originally three cents an hour for the afternoon shift and five cents an hour for the night shift. It has been increased to 10 and 16 cents per hour respectively.

paid more than a woman even though his duties are the same." S.Rep. No. 176, 88th Cong., 1st Sess., 1 (1963). The solution adopted was quite simple in principle: to require that "equal work will be rewarded by equal wages." Ibid.

The Act's basic structure and operation are similarly straightforward. In order to make out a case under the Act, the Secretary must show that an employer pays different wages to employees of opposite sexes "for equal work on jobs the performance of which requires equal skill, effort, and responsibility, and which are performed under similar working conditions." Although the Act is silent on this point, its legislative history makes plain that the Secretary has the burden of proof on this issue, as both of the courts below recognized.

The Act also establishes four exceptions—three specific and one a general catchall provision—where different payment to employees of opposite sexes "is made pursuant to (i) a seniority system; (ii) a merit system; (iii) a system which measures earnings by quantity or quality of production; or (iv) a differential based on any other factor other than sex." Again, while the Act is silent on this question, its structure and history also suggest that once the Secretary has carried his burden of showing that the employer pays workers of one sex more than workers of the opposite sex for equal work, the burden shifts to the employer to show that the differential is justified under one of the Act's four exceptions. All of the many lower courts that have considered this question have so held, and this view is consistent with the general rule that the application of an exemption under the Fair Labor Standards Act is a matter of affirmative defense on which the employer has the burden of proof.

The contentions of the parties in this case reflect the Act's underlying framework. Corning argues that the Secretary has failed to prove that Corning ever violated the Act because day shift work is not "performed under similar working conditions" as night shift work. The Secretary maintains that day shift and night shift work are performed under "similar working conditions" within the meaning of the Act. Although the Secretary recognizes that higher wages may be paid for night shift work, the Secretary contends that such a shift differential would be based upon a "factor other than sex" within the catch-all exception to the Act and that Corning has failed to carry its burden of proof that its higher base wage for male night inspectors was in fact based on any factor other than sex.

The courts below relied in part on conflicting statements in the legislative history having some bearing on this question of statutory construction. The Third Circuit found particularly significant a statement of Congressman Goodell, a sponsor of the Equal Pay bill, who, in the course of explaining the bill on the floor of the House, commented that "standing as opposed to sitting, pleasantness or unpleasantness of surroundings, periodic rest periods, hours of work, *difference in shift,* all would logically fall within the working condition factor." 109 Cong. Rec. 9209 (1963) (emphasis added). The Second Circuit, in contrast, relied on a statement from the House Committee Report which, in describing the broad general exception for differentials "based on any other factor other than sex," stated: "Thus, among other things, shift differentials ∗ ∗ ∗ would also be excluded. ∗ ∗ ∗" H.R.Rep. No. 309, 88th Cong., 1st Sess., 3 (1963). U.S.Code Cong. & Admin.News 1963, pp. 687, 689.

We agree with Judge Friendly, however, that in this case a better understanding of the phrase "performed under similar working conditions" can be obtained from a consideration of the way in which Congress arrived at the statutory language than from trying to reconcile or establish preferences between the conflicting interpretations of the Act by individual legislators or the committee reports. As Mr. Justice Frankfurter remarked in an earlier case involving interpretation of the Fair Labor Standards Act, "regard for the specific history of the legislative process that culminated in the Act now before us affords more solid ground for giving it appropriate meaning." United States v. Universal C.I.T. Credit Corp., 344 U.S. 218, 222, 73 S.Ct. 227, 230, 97 L.Ed. 260 (1952).

The most notable feature of the history of the Equal Pay Act is that Congress recognized early in the legislative process that the concept of equal pay for equal work was more readily stated in principle than reduced to statutory language which would be meaningful to employers and workable across the broad range of industries covered by the Act. As originally introduced, the Equal Pay bill required equal pay for "equal work on jobs the performance of which requires equal skills." There were only two exceptions—for differentials "made pursuant to a seniority or merit increase system which does not discriminate on the basis of sex. ∗ ∗ ∗"

In both the House and Senate committee hearings, witnesses were highly critical of the Act's definition of equal work and of its exemptions. Many noted that most of American industry used formal, systematic job evaluation plans to establish equitable wage structures in their plants.[15] Such systems, as explained coincidentally by a representative of Corning Glass Works who testified at both hearings, took into consideration four separate factors in determining job value— skill, effort, responsibility and working conditions—and each of these four components was further systematically divided into various subcomponents. Under a job evaluation plan, point values are assigned to each of the subcomponents of a given job, resulting in a total point figure representing a relatively objective measure of the job's value.

In comparison to the rather complex job evaluation plans used by industry, the definition of equal work used in the first drafts of the Equal Pay bill was criticized as unduly vague and incomplete. Industry representatives feared that as a result of the bill's definition of

---

15. See, e.g., Hearings On Equal Pay Act of 1963 before the Subcommittee on Labor of the Senate Committee on Labor and Public Welfare, 88th Cong., 1st Sess., 26, 73, 79, 124, 140, 178 (1963) (hereinafter Senate Hearings); Hearings on Equal Pay Act before the Special Subcommittee on Labor of the House Committee on Education and Labor, 88th Cong., 1st Sess., 145–146 (1963) (hereinafter House Hearings).

equal work, the Secretary of Labor would be cast in the position of second-guessing the validity of a company's job evaluation system. They repeatedly urged that the bill be amended to include an exception for job classification systems, or otherwise to incorporate the language of job evaluation into the bill. Thus Corning's own representative testified:

> Job evaluation is an accepted and tested method of attaining equity in wage relationship.
>
> A great part of industry is committed to job evaluation by past practice and by contractual agreement as the basis for wage administration.
>
> "Skill" alone, as a criterion, fails to recognize other aspects of the job situation that affect job worth.
>
> We sincerely hope that this committee in passing legislation to eliminate wage differences based on sex alone, will recognize in its language the general role of job evaluation in establishing equitable rate relationship.

We think it plain that in amending the bill's definition of equal work to its present form, the Congress acted in direct response to these pleas. Spokesmen for the amended bill stated, for example, during the House debates:

> The concept of equal pay for jobs demanding equal skill has been expanded to require also equal effort, responsibility, and similar working conditions. These factors are the core of all job classification systems. They form a legitimate basis for differentials in pay.

Indeed, the most telling evidence of congressional intent is the fact that the Act's amended definition of equal work incorporated the specific language of the job evaluation plan described at the hearings by Corning's own representative—that is, the concepts of "skill," "effort," "responsibility," and "working conditions."

Congress' intent, as manifested in this history, was to use these terms to incorporate into the new federal Act the well-defined and well-accepted principles of job evaluation so as to ensure that wage differentials based upon bona fide job evaluation plans would be outside the purview of the Act. The House Report emphasized:

> This language recognizes that there are many factors which may be used to measure the relationships between jobs and which establish a valid basis for a difference in pay. These factors will be found in a majority of the job classification systems. Thus, it is anticipated that a bona fide job classification program that does not discriminate on the basis of sex will serve as a valid defense to a charge of discrimination. H.R.Rep. No. 309, supra, at 3, U.S.Code Cong. & Admin.News, 1963, pp. 688, 689.

It is in this light that the phrase "working conditions" must be understood, for where Congress has used technical words or terms of art, "it [is] proper to explain them by reference to the art or science to which they [are] appropriate." Greenleaf v. Goodrich, 101 U.S. 278, 284 (1880). This principle is particularly salutary where, as here, the legislative history reveals that Congress incorporated words having a special meaning within the field regulated by the statute so as to overcome objections by industry representatives that statutory definitions were vague and incomplete.

While a layman might well assume that time of day worked reflects one aspect of a job's "working conditions," the term has a different and much more specific meaning in the language of industrial relations. As Corning's own representative testified at the hearings, the element of working conditions encompasses two subfactors: "surroundings" and "hazards." "Surroundings" measures the elements, such as toxic chemicals or fumes, regularly encountered by a worker, their intensity, and their frequency. "Hazards" takes into account the physical hazards regularly encountered, their frequency, and the severity of injury they can cause. This definition of "working conditions" is not only manifested in Corning's own job evaluation plans but is also well accepted across a wide range of American industry.

Nowhere in any of these definitions is time of day worked mentioned as a relevant criterion. The fact of the matter is that the concept of "working conditions," as used in the specialized language of job evaluation systems, simply does not encompass shift differentials. Indeed, while Corning now argues that night inspection work is not equal to day inspection work, all of its own job evaluation plans, including the one now in effect, have consistently treated them as equal in all respects, including working conditions.[22] And Corning's Manager of Job Evaluation testified in No. 73–29 that time of day worked was not considered to be a "working condition." Significantly, it is not the Secretary in this case who is trying to look behind Corning's bona fide job evaluation system to require equal pay for jobs which Corning has historically viewed as unequal work. Rather, it is Corning which asks us to differentiate between jobs which the company itself has always equated. We agree with the Second Circuit that the inspection work at issue in this case, whether performed during the day or night, is "equal work" as that term is defined in the Act.

22. Pursuant to its 1944 collective-bargaining agreement, Corning adopted a job classification system developed by its consultants, labeled the SJ & H plan, which evaluated inspector jobs on the basis of "general schooling," "training period," "manual skill," "versatility," "job knowledge," "responsibility," and "working conditions." Under this evaluation, the inspector jobs, regardless of shift, were found equal in all respects, including "working conditions," which were defined as the "surrounding conditions (wet, heat, cold, dust, grease, noises, etc.) and physical hazards (bruises, cuts, heavy lifting, fumes, slippery floors, machines, chemicals, gases, bodily injuries, etc.) to which employees are unavoidably subjected while performing the duties."

A new plan, put into effect in 1963–1964 and called the CGW plan, also found no significant differences in the duties performed by men and women inspectors and awarded the same point values for skill, effort, responsibility, and working conditions, regardless of shift.

This does not mean, of course, that there is no room in the Equal Pay Act for nondiscriminatory shift differentials. Work on a steady night shift no doubt has psychological and physiological impacts making it less attractive than work on a day shift. The Act contemplates that a male night worker may receive a higher wage than a female day worker, just as it contemplates that a male employee with 20 years' seniority can receive a higher wage than a woman with two years' seniority. Factors such as these play a role under the Act's four exceptions—the seniority differential under the specific seniority exception, the shift differential under the catch-all exception for differentials "based on any other factor other than sex." [25]

The question remains, however, whether Corning carried its burden of proving that the higher rate paid for night inspection work, until 1966 performed solely by men, was in fact intended to serve as compensation for night work, or rather constituted an added payment based upon sex. We agree that the record amply supports the District Court's conclusion that Corning had not sustained its burden of proof. As its history revealed, "the higher night rate was in large part the product of the generally higher wage level of male workers and the need to compensate them for performing what were regarded as demeaning tasks." 474 F.2d, at 233. The differential in base wages originated at a time when no other night employees received higher pay than corresponding day workers, and it was maintained long after the company instituted a separate plant-wide shift differential which was thought to compensate adequately for the additional burdens of night work. The differential arose simply because men would not work at the low rates paid women inspectors, and it reflected a job market in which Corning could pay women less than men for the same work. That the company took advantage of such a situation may be understandable as a matter of economics, but its differential nevertheless became illegal once Congress enacted into law the principle of equal pay for equal work.

III

We now must consider whether Corning continued to remain in violation of the Act after 1966 when, without changing the base wage rates for day and night inspectors, it began to permit women to bid for jobs on the night shift as vacancies occurred. It is evident that this was more than a token gesture to end discrimination, as turnover in the night shift inspection jobs was rapid. The record in No. 73–29 shows, for example, that during the two-year period after June 1, 1966, the date women were first permitted to bid for night inspection jobs, women took 152 of the 278 openings, and women with very little seniority were able to obtain positions on the night shift. Relying on these facts, the company argues that it ceased discriminating against women in 1966, and was no longer in violation of the Equal Pay Act.

25. An administrative interpretation by the Wage and Hour Administrator recognizes the legitimacy of night shift differentials shown to be based on a factor other than sex. See 29 CFR § 800.145 (1973).

But the issue before us is not whether the company, in some abstract sense, can be said to have treated men the same as women after 1966. Rather, the question is whether the company remedied the specific violation of the Act which the Secretary proved. We agree with the Second Circuit, as well as with all other circuits that have had occasion to consider this issue, that the company could not cure its violation except by equalizing the base wages of female day inspectors with the higher rates paid the night inspectors. This result is implicit in the Act's language, its statement of purpose, and its legislative history.

As the Second Circuit noted, Congress enacted the Equal Pay Act "[r]ecognizing the weaker bargaining position of many women and believing that discrimination in wage rates represented unfair employer exploitation of this source of cheap labor." 474 F.2d, at 234. In response to evidence of the many families dependent on the income of working women, Congress included in the Act's statement of purpose a finding that "the existence . . . of wage differentials based on sex * * * depresses wages and living standards for employees necessary for their health and efficiency." Pub.L. 88–38, § 2(a)(1), 77 Stat. 56 (1963). And Congress declared it to be the policy of the Act to correct this condition. § 2(b).

To achieve this end, Congress required that employers pay equal pay for equal work and then specified:

> Provided, That an employer who is paying a wage rate differential in violation of this subsection shall not, in order to comply with the provisions of this subsection, reduce the wage rate of any employee. 29 U.S.C. § 206(d)(1).

The purpose of this proviso was to ensure that to remedy violations of the Act, "[t]he lower wage rate must be increased to the level of the higher." H.R.Rep. No. 309, supra, at 3, U.S.Code Cong. & Admin.News, 1963, p. 688. Comments of individual legislators are all consistent with this view. Representative Dwyer remarked, for example, "The objective of equal pay legislation * * * is not to drag down men workers to the wage levels of women, but to raise women to the levels enjoyed by men in cases where discrimination is still practiced." Representative Griffin also thought it clear that "[t]he only way a violation could be remedied under the bill * * * is for the lower wages to be raised to the higher."

By proving that after the effective date of the Equal Pay Act, Corning paid female day inspectors less than male night inspectors for equal work, the Secretary implicitly demonstrated that the wages of female day shift inspectors were unlawfully depressed and that the fair wage for inspection work was the base wage paid to male inspectors on the night shift. The whole purpose of the Act was to require that these depressed wages be raised, in part as a matter of simple justice to the employees themselves, but also as a matter of market economics, since Congress recognized as well that discrimination in wages on the basis of sex "constitutes an unfair method of competition." Pub.L. 88–38, supra, § 2(a)(5).

We agree with Judge Friendly that

> In light of this apparent congressional understanding, we cannot hold that Corning, by allowing some—or even many—women to move into the higher paid night jobs, achieved full compliance with the Act. Corning's action still left the inspectors on the day shift—virtually all women—earning a lower base wage than the night shift inspectors because of a differential initially based on sex and still not justified by any other consideration; in effect, Corning was still taking advantage of the availability of female labor to fill its day shift at a differentially low wage rate not justified by any factor other than sex. 474 F.2d, at 235.

The Equal Pay Act is broadly remedial, and it should be construed and applied so as to fulfill the underlying purposes which Congress sought to achieve. If, as the Secretary proved, the work performed by women on the day shift was equal to that performed by men on the night shift, the company became obligated to pay the women the same base wage as their male counterparts on the effective date of the Act. To permit the company to escape that obligation by agreeing to allow some women to work on the night shift at a higher rate of pay as vacancies occurred would frustrate, not serve, Congress' ends.

The company's final contention—that it cured its violation of the Act when a new collective-bargaining agreement went into effect on January 20, 1969—need not detain us long. While the new agreement provided for equal base wages for night or day inspectors hired after that date, it continued to provide unequal base wages for employees hired before that date, a discrimination likely to continue for some time into the future because of a large number of laid-off employees who had to be offered re-employment before new inspectors could be hired. After considering the rather complex method in which the new wage rates for employees hired prior to January 1969 were calculated and the company's stated purpose behind the provisions of the new agreement, the District Court in No. 73–29 concluded that the lower base wage for day inspectors was a direct product of the company's failure to equalize the base wages for male and female inspectors as of the effective date of the Act. We agree it is clear from the record that had the company equalized the base-wage rates of male and female inspectors on the effective date of the Act, as the law required, the day inspectors in 1969 would have been entitled to the same higher "red circle" rate the company provided for night inspectors. We therefore conclude that on the facts of this case, the company's continued discrimination in base wages between night and day workers, though phrased in terms of a neutral factor other than sex, nevertheless operated to perpetuate the effects of the company's prior illegal practice of paying women less than men for equal work. Cf. Griggs v. Duke Power Co., 401 U.S. 424, 430, 91 S.Ct. 849, 853, 28 L.Ed.2d 158 (1971).

The judgment in No. 73–29 is affirmed. The judgment in No. 73–695 is reversed and the case remanded to the Court of Appeals for further proceedings consistent with this opinion.

It is so ordered.

MR. JUSTICE STEWART took no part in the consideration or decision of these cases.

THE CHIEF JUSTICE, MR. JUSTICE BLACKMUN, and MR. JUSTICE REHNQUIST dissent and would affirm the judgment of the Court of Appeals for the Third Circuit and reverse the judgment of the Court of Appeals for the Second Circuit for the reasons stated by Judge Adams in his opinion for the Court of Appeals in Brennan v. Corning Glass Works, 480 F.2d 1254 (CA 3 1973).

THOMPSON v. SAWYER

United States Court of Appeals for the District of Columbia, 1982.
678 F.2d 257.

MIKVA, CIRCUIT JUDGE:

I. THE APPLICABLE STATUTES

The Equal Pay Act prohibits payment of unequal wages for equal work on grounds of sex, unless the difference is justified by one of four enumerated defenses: a seniority system, a merit system, a system that measures pay by quality or quantity of production, or any other factor not based on sex. 29 U.S.C. § 206(d) (1976). It was passed in 1963, as an amendment to the Fair Labor Standards Act (FLSA), Pub.L. No. 88–38, 77 Stat. 56. Under the Equal Pay Act, employees have access to the recovery provided by the FLSA, including unpaid wages and an additional equal amount as "liquidated damages," 29 U.S.C. § 216(b), (c) (Supp. III 1979). Recovery is limited normally to two years, but extended to three years for a willful violation, id. § 255 (1976). In 1974, the definition of "employer" in the FLSA was amended to include public agencies, id. § 203(d) (1976), thus allowing federal employees to sue under the Equal Pay Act.

Although allegations of large-scale sexual discrimination are likely to involve complaints under both the Equal Pay Act and Title VII, the interrelationships between the statutes have proved troublesome. The same employment situation may give rise to a claim for relief under either statute. Plaintiffs may recover under both statutes provided each is separately satisfied and the plaintiff does not recover doubly for the same wrong. E.g., Laffey v. Northwest Airlines, 567 F.2d 429, 445 (D.C.Cir.1976), cert. denied, 434 U.S. 1086, 98 S.Ct. 1281, 55 L.Ed.2d 792 (1978). For example, a plaintiff may recover under the Equal Pay Act for unequal pay for equal work, and obtain additional recovery under Title VII for discriminatory denial of training or promotion opportunities.

B. LIABILITY UNDER THE EQUAL PAY ACT

An employer violates the Equal Pay Act by paying unequal wages for "equal work on jobs the performance of which requires equal skill, effort, and responsibility and which are performed under similar working conditions." 29 U.S.C. § 206(d)(1) (1976). Determination that an Equal Pay Act violation has occurred involves both a legal and a factual problem. The legal issue is the standard of equality to be applied under the Act. The factual issue is whether the jobs in question met the standard, and the burden of proof is on plaintiffs to show that they did. Corning Glass Works v. Brennan, 417 U.S. 188, 94 S.Ct. 2223, 41 L.Ed.2d 1 (1974); Laffey v. Northwest Airlines, Inc., 567 F.2d 429, 448 (D.C.Cir.1976). Once plaintiffs meet their burden, the burden then shifts to defendants to show that the pay differential was justified under one of the exceptions to the Act, Corning Glass, 417 U.S. at 205, 94 S.Ct. at 2233; *Laffey,* 567 F.2d at 448. With respect to plaintiffs' burden, GPO alleges both that the trial judge employed the wrong legal standard and that his finding that plaintiffs had met their burden for operators of the Smyth sewing machine was clearly erroneous. GPO also claims to have rebutted plaintiffs' case by showing that traditional industry classifications and training requirements justified the differential. The plaintiffs contend that they met their burden not only as to the Grade 4 bindery workers, but with respect to other bindery workers whose Equal Pay case was unsuccessful in the district court: The oversewer and Singer machine operators, handworkers, and passport inspectors.

1. *The Legal Standard.* Like most legislation, the Equal Pay Act of 1963 was a compromise. Congress for several years had considered competing versions of what ultimately became the Act. Some versions sought to prohibit unequal pay for *comparable* work; this approach had been used during World War II by the National War Labor Board. S.Rep. No. 176, 88th Cong., 1st Sess. 3 (1963) [hereinafter, *Senate Report*]. Other versions sought only to prohibit unequal pay for *equal* work. "Equality" prevailed, in the main to avoid imposing job comparisons on employers. See, e.g., 108 Cong.Rec. 9196 (1963) (Remarks of Rep. Frelinghuysen); id. at 9209 (Remarks of Rep. Goodell).

Although passing the more limited statute, Congress recognized the disputatious nature of the term "equality." Sponsors of more extensive versions of the bill were careful to emphasize that "equality" did not mean "identity": "it is not the intent of the Senate that jobs must be identical. Such a conclusion would obviously be ridiculous." Id. at 9761 (Remarks of Sen. McNamara). Sponsors in the House, although anxious to emphasize the limited nature of the bill, also used language short of absolute identity:

> I think it is important that we have clear legislative history at this point. Last year when the House changed the word 'comparable' to 'equal' the clear intention was to narrow the whole concept ∗ ∗ ∗ the

jobs involved should be virtually identical, * * * very much alike or closely related to each other.

Id. at 9197 (Remarks of Rep. Goodell). The legislative history thus contains ammunition both for those who would insist on a very narrow reading of "equality," and for those who would urge a more expansive understanding of the term.[9]

Congress did not, however, leave interpretation of the diffuse term "equal" completely unchannelled. It wrote four aspects of equal work into the statute itself: equal skill, effort, responsibility, and working conditions. These factors are commonly used in job evaluation as practiced by industrial engineers, and Congress clearly intended the statute to be interpreted in light of this body of expertise.[10]

In applying the term "equal work," courts have been led by the legislative history toward a "substantially equal" test, a middle course between a requirement that the jobs in question be "exactly alike" and a requirement that they be merely "comparable." [11] This middle path was adopted by implication by the Supreme Court in its only full-scale treatment of the Equal Pay Act, Corning Glass Works v. Brennan, 417 U.S. 188, 94 S.Ct. 2223, 41 L.Ed.2d 1 (1974). In addition to normal shift differentials, Corning paid a higher base wage to male inspectors on the night shift than to female inspectors on the day shift. The differential was a relic of the days when it was necessary to recruit men to work at night because women were prohibited from doing so by state statutes. In finding a violation of the Equal Pay Act, the Court interpreted the statutory factor of "working conditions" in light of its meaning in job evaluation plans, which generally confine the meaning of "working conditions" to job surroundings and hazards, id. at 202, 94 S.Ct. at 2231. Because night work and day work are different in one respect—the time of performance—*Corning Glass* implicitly rejected an Equal Pay Act standard of virtual identity, although the case did not explicitly formulate an Equal Pay Act test.

Laffey v. Northwest Airlines, Inc., 567 F.2d 429 (D.C.Cir.1976), the leading Equal Pay Act case in this circuit, adopted the "substantially equal" test in reliance on *Corning Glass.* Our discussion of the test read in full:

> For "[it] is now well settled that jobs need not be identical in every respect before the Equal Pay Act is applicable"; [citing *Corning Glass*] the phrase "equal work" does not mean that the jobs must be identical,

9. Compare Angelo v. Bacharach Instrument Co., 555 F.2d 1164, 1174 (3d Cir. 1977) (quoting remarks of Rep. Frelinghuysen and Rep. Goodell) with Shultz v. Wheaton Glass Co., 421 F.2d 259, 265 (3d Cir.), cert. denied, 398 U.S. 905, 90 S.Ct. 1696, 26 L.Ed.2d 64 (1970) (quoting Senate and House Reports in support of "substantially equal" standard).

10. *Senate Report* at 3; H.R.Rep. No. 309, 88th Cong., 1st Sess. 3 (1963) [herein-

after, House Report]; Corning Glass Works v. Brennan, 417 U.S. 188, 201, 94 S.Ct. 2223, 2231, 41 L.Ed.2d 1 (1974). See generally Murphy, Female Wage Discrimination: A Study of the Equal Pay Act 1963– 1970, 39 U.Cin.L.Rev. 615 (1970).

11. Sullivan, The Equal Pay Act of 1963: Making and Breaking a Prima Facie Case, 31 Ark.L.Rev. 545 (1978).

but merely that they must be "substantially equal." A wage differential is justified only if it compensates for an appreciable variation in skill, effort or responsibility between otherwise comparable job work activities.

567 F.2d at 449 (citations omitted). The "substantially equal" test has now been adopted by every other circuit to pass on the question. Judge Richey employed this test in the case at bar, J.A. 195, and we reaffirm our approval of it.

This case, however, presents a difficult and largely unexplored problem in the interpretation of the Equal Pay Act: whether work may be substantially equal, in spite of the fact that it is performed on different machines.[13] Bindery worker Grade 4s work on the Smyth sewing machine; bookbinders do not. GPO contends that this fact is sufficient as a matter of law to preclude the finding of an Equal Pay violation. Judge Richey concluded that it was not, and that work on the Smyth was sufficiently like the work performed by bookbinders on other machines as to allow relief under the Act. J.A. 195.

In determining that work on different machines could be "substantially equal," Judge Richey was guided by Department of Labor regulations:

> [T]he performance of jobs on different machines or equipment would not necessarily result in a determination that the work so performed is unequal within the meaning of the statute if the equal pay provisions otherwise apply.

29 C.F.R. § 800.123 (1980). This court has paid substantial deference to Department of Labor regulations in interpreting the Act, see *Laffey*, 567 F.2d at 449,[14] and we continue to do so.

---

13. Very few cases have raised this question. In Hodgson v. Daisy Manufacturing Co., 317 F.Supp. 538 (W.D.Ark. 1970), aff'd in part and rev'd on other grounds in part, 445 F.2d 823 (8th Cir. 1971), the court found a violation where male gun assemblers were paid higher wages for assembling larger gun barrels with somewhat larger but slower presses than those employed by the women assemblers. See also Ridgway v. United Hospitals-Miller Division, 563 F.2d 923 (8th Cir. 1977) (job of female surgical assistant in ophthalmology substantially equal to job of male surgical assistant in urology, since both involved similar work with delicate instruments); Usery v. Allegheny County Institution Dist., 544 F.2d 148 (3d Cir. 1976), cert. denied, 430 U.S. 946, 97 S.Ct. 1582, 51 L.Ed.2d 793 (1977), (jobs of beauticians and barbers substantially equal, even though the former used different tools such as curlers and hair irons). In Angelo v. Bacharach Instrument Co., 555 F.2d 1164 (3d Cir.1977), the court held that female light assemblers had not carried their burden of showing their jobs were substantially equal to those of male heavy assemblers. In *Angelo*, however, the jobs were performed in different plant divisions and involved assembly of instruments as different as small gas detectors and large diesel fuel pumps. Id. at 1167.

14. The Department of Labor was not given rulemaking power under the Equal Pay Act. *House Report* at 3; 109 Cong. Rec. 9209 (remarks of Rep. Goodell). These regulations are the Department's official interpretations of the Act, 29 C.F.R. § 800.1 (1980), and thus not entitled to the special deference given interpretation by agencies with rule-making power. Nonetheless, the Department of Labor is entitled to deference as the agency charged by Congress with enforcing the Equal Pay Act. See Federal Election Comm'n v. Democratic Senatorial Campaign Comm., 454 U.S. 27, 37, 102 S.Ct. 38, 44, 70 L.Ed.2d 23 (1981).

Congress never specifically considered whether work performed on different machines might be equal for purposes of the Equal Pay Act.[15] To refuse to find work "equal" merely because it is performed on different machines, however, would be to insist on the requirement of exact identity declared "obviously ridiculous" by Senator McNamara and rejected by all of the courts treating the subject. See supra at 271, 272 n. 12. The result would be largely to foreclose application of the Act whenever machines are involved—an evisceration of the Act clearly at odds with Congress' broad remedial goals. See *Senate Report* at 1; *House Report* at 2. For example, different typewriters, power saws or automobiles are *different* machines.

Moreover, the very fact that Congress chose to channel the term "equality" by the language of job evaluation programs presupposes a recognition that jobs can be substantially equal even though performed with different equipment or machines. Job evaluation plans focus on experience, skill, surroundings, and responsibility and clearly contemplate assigning common classifications to work on related, albeit different machines.[16] Along these lines, in the congressional debates Representative Goodell presented guidelines for the interpretation of job content that emphasized that jobs be "normally related" and "fall within closely related job classifications"—both descriptions that apply easily to different components of a single productive process. Of course, work on different machines can differ radically; Representative Goodell used the example that driving a truck would not be equal to piloting a tug boat. 109 Cong.Rec. 9209 (1963). The question in every Equal Pay Act case is simply whether the jobs in question are sufficiently related and sufficiently similar in skill, effort, responsibility, and working conditions, as to be substantially equal.

2. *The Facts of This Case and the Standard of Review.* The trial judge's findings of fact in an equal pay case are like any other finding

---

15. Neither the Senate nor the House Hearings considered the application of the Equal Pay Act to jobs performed on different machines. Indeed, the hearings contain almost no discussion of the Act's implications for most jobs in heavy industry—apparently because of the assumption that women held very few such jobs similar to those held by men. See, e.g., Hearings on H.R. 3861, 4269 & Related Bills Before the Special Subcomm. on Labor of the Comm. on Education & Labor, 88th Cong., 1st Sess. 38 (1963) (statement of Esther Peterson) ("The occupation of operatives included 3.4 million women and 8.7 million men in 1962, but relatively few of these workers appeared to be doing similar work.") [hereinafter *House Hearings*]. Examples of similar work in industry that were discussed included selector, packer, and bench assembler. See, e.g., Hearings on S. 882 and S. 910 Before the Subcomm.

on Labor of the Comm. on Labor & Public Welfare, 88th Cong., 1st Sess. 94 (1963) (statement of Minnie Miles). Indeed, the only mention of work on different machines in the entire hearings was Representative Thompson's observation that large and small punch presses would involve different effort, but might become equal if automation altered the operation of heavy presses. *House Hearings* at 168.

16. See, e.g., D. Belcher, Compensation Administration 172–73 (1974) (example of steel industry plan classifying various machine jobs together); Dictionary of Occupational Titles 574–76 and Appendix (1977) (classifying together various bindery machine operations). For a criticism of the sex bias of certain job evaluation plans, see National Academy of Sciences, Job Evaluation: An Analytic Review (1979).

of fact; they may be overturned on appeal only if clearly erroneous. Fed.R.Civ.P. 52(a); see, e.g., United States v. United States Gypsum Co., 333 U.S. 364, 395, 68 S.Ct. 525, 541, 92 L.Ed. 746 (1948); *Laffey,* 567 F.2d at 453; Kinsey v. First Regional Securities, Inc., 557 F.2d 830, 835–36 (D.C.Cir.1977); Causey v. Ford Motor Co., 516 F.2d 416, 420 (5th Cir. 1975). Judge Richey did not err in finding that GPO violated the Equal Pay Act with respect to bindery workers operating the Smyth sewing machine but not with respect to other bindery worker machine operators, handworkers, and passport inspectors.

a. *Bindery Work Operators of the Smyth Sewing Machine.* The Smyth sewing machine is a multi-needle machine for sewing groups of pages ("signatures") together into what we would recognize as the "inside" of a book. The operator of the Smyth chooses the number of needles required for a particular job and sets thread and bobbin tension for each needle. She also sets the needles to position stitching properly along the spine of the book and sets guides to position signatures as they are sewn together. She is responsible for routine maintenance tasks such as changing needles and oiling and cleaning the machines. In operating the machine, she opens signatures and places them on a "pusher." Because the operator does not control the pace of the pusher, considerable dexterity is required to feed at the proper rate. The Smyth also runs paste along the spine of the book to ensure additional strength; the Smyth operator must coordinate a cutter at the proper moment when the "inside" of a particular book is sewn together. Tr. Mar. 8, 1979, at 55–65.

In finding that plaintiffs had met their Equal Pay Act burden to prove substantial equality between the jobs of the Smyth operators and bookbinders, Judge Richey relied heavily upon the testimony of plaintiffs' expert witness, James O'Connell, that operation of the Smyth is substantially equal to operation of many bookbinder machines. J.A. 186. He viewed O'Connell's testimony as buttressed by the testimony of plaintiffs' other expert, Bertram Gottlieb, and the testimony of journeymen bindery workers, bookbinders, and GPO officials. J.A. 166–72, 176–79, 186–87. Judge Richey discounted the testimony of defendant's expert Irwin Lazarus, upon finding flaws both in his methodology and its execution. J.A. 173–76. While GPO sought to question Mr. O'Connell's qualifications as an expert, Tr. Mar. 15, 1979, at 263–305, Mr. O'Connell was the personnel management specialist chosen by the Civil Service Commission to review GPO job classifications after plaintiffs filed their administrative complaint. GPO is hard pressed to attack the credentials of the expert assigned by the government to this case. In any event, it is not for us to second-guess reasonable judgments by the trial judge with regard to the weight to be accorded expert testimony.

Because he had been assigned to investigate the administrative complaint of Smyth operators, Mr. O'Connell compared the job of operating the Smyth to a wide range of bookbinder jobs. He initially determined that the Smyth's creation of a book's "inside," and book-binder tasks such as folding and cutting signatures, making a book cover ("case") and "casing" the inside into the cover, were an integral part of the same productive process. Id. at 21. He noted their physical and organizational proximity and that they involved similar functions: gluing, stitching, cutting, and putting together the parts of a book. Within the process, Mr. O'Connell observed the Smyth and twenty-five bookbinder machine operations, to determine whether they involved similar difficulty, responsibility, and qualifications. Id. at 9, 70. He characterized the Smyth operation as more like many bookbinder jobs than the latter were like each other. The Smyth, he concluded, "was in the middle range of difficulty, responsibility and qualification require-ments of bookbinder machine operations." Id. at 20.

Cross-examination did elicit the admission that Mr. O'Connell had given similar "effort" ratings to the Smyth and a cloth cutter that required loading 100-lb. bolts in order to position them for cutting. Id. at 109. There is dispute about the extent to which different kinds and amounts of effort may be compared for purposes of a finding of "equality" under the Equal Pay Act.[17] The Department of Labor regulations define "effort" to include both mental and physical exer-tion, and allow effort of different kinds to be balanced in application of the Act, 29 C.F.R. § 800.127 (1980). To illustrate, the regulations suggest that the effort of a male checker who sometimes carries heavy packages may be equated with the effort of a female checker who sometimes performs fill-in work requiring greater dexterity, whereas a regular additional task of lifting from an assembly line could justify a wage differential. Id. § 800.218. GPO, disputing this approach, con-tends that jobs are substantially equal only if they involve effort of the same kind.[18]

17. On fact situations quite similar to each other, courts have disagreed about whether unequal pay violated the Act. Compare Shultz v. American Can Co.—Dixie Products, 424 F.2d 356 (3d Cir.1970) (work substantially equal even though night shift operators required to load paper onto machines for between 7 and 33 min-utes per eight hour shift) with Wirtz v. Dennison Mfg. Co., 265 F.Supp. 787 (D.Mass.1967) (additional tasks of loading and machine repair on night shift war-ranted wage differential even though these tasks occupied less than 10% of working time). Also compare Brennan v. Board of Education of Jersey City, 374 F.Supp. 817 (D.N.J.1974) (male and female custodial jobs substantially equal even though addi-tional male tasks included snow shoveling and buffing while additional female tasks included scouring down bathrooms and washing down furniture) with Usery v. Co-lumbia University, 568 F.2d 953 (2d Cir. 1977) (not error to find heavy cleaning

required greater effort on the part of male custodians). Courts also have disagreed about whether different kinds of effort may be compared. Compare Hodgson v. Daisy Manufacturing Co., 317 F.Supp. 538 (W.D.Ark.1970), aff'd in part and rev'd in part on other grounds, 445 F.2d 823 (8th Cir.1971) (physical effort required in press-ing larger gun barrels may be weighed against mental effort required in pressing smaller barrels) with Angelo v. Bacharach Instrument Co., 555 F.2d 1164 (3d Cir.1977) (improper to compare physical and mental effort). Commentators tend to conclude that different kinds and amounts of effort may be balanced under the Equal Pay Act. E.g., Johnson, The Equal Pay Act of 1963: A Practical Analysis, 24 Drake L.Rev. 570, 587 (1975); Sullivan, supra note 13, at 568.

18. GPO Brief at 23. As GPO objects both to comparisons of different types of effort and to balancing effort against other Equal Pay Act factors, we note that GPO's

We need not reach this troublesome issue of how effort is to be defined. Cross-examination did not raise similar questions about the other bookbinders' machines to which plaintiffs' experts favorably compared the Smyth. To prove a violation under the Equal Pay Act, plaintiffs need only show their jobs were equal to the jobs of *some* bookbinders, but treated unequally. Plaintiffs need not show that their jobs were substantially similar to all, or even most bookbinder jobs. Id. § 800.238; *Laffey,* 567 F.2d at 450; Shultz v. Wheaton Glass Co., 421 F.2d 259, 264 (3d Cir.), cert. denied, 398 U.S. 905, 90 S.Ct. 1696, 26 L.Ed. 2d 64 (1970); Elisburg, Equal Pay in the United States: the Development and Implementation of the Equal Pay Act of 1963, 29 Lab.L.J. 195 (1978). For purposes of an Equal Pay Act violation, it is irrelevant that GPO classifies the bookbinder jobs that resemble plaintiffs' together with other jobs that do not. The testimony of the plaintiffs' expert witnesses supports a finding that the Smyth operators' jobs were substantially equal to the jobs of some bookbinders. Operators of the Smyth sewing machine, therefore, carried their burden of establishing a *prima facie* case of an Equal Pay Act violation by GPO.

GPO makes two other objections to the plaintiffs' *prima facie* showing. First, GPO contends that bookbinders have supervisory authority over bindery workers with whom they work and thus more responsibility than Smyth operators. The trial judge's finding that bookbinders do not have supervisory authority, however, J.A. 188–89, is securely based in the trial record. For example, a Bindery superintendent, Kenneth Kingsbury, testified that bookbinders neither disciplined the bindery workers with whom they worked, nor were held accountable for their mistakes. Tr. Mar. 13, 1979, at 13–14. Moreover, quite a number of the bookbinders' machines to which the Smyth was compared favorably were operated by a single bookbinder, and thus presented no opportunity for direction of the work of others.

Second, GPO alleges that the plaintiffs' experts mistakenly compared single *operations* rather than entire jobs. Judge Richey, however, found explicitly that rotation among operations was not required of bookbinders. J.A. 176. His finding is amply supported by the trial testimony. Mr. Kingsbury testified that bookbinders normally had a regular assignment and that operators of major machines rarely changed assignments. Id. at 15–25. Assignments were cemented by seniority, and it was not unusual for bookbinders to spend entire careers in the same section of the Bindery. Id. at 16, 32. Mr. Kingsbury admitted that GPO had not formally studied the need for back-up rotation and had kept no formal statistics on bookbinder assignments. Id. at 17, 59. Ammi Potter, Mr. Kingsbury's successor as Bindery Supervisor, also testified that GPO had not evaluated whether it could operate with bookbinders who operated only one machine, Tr.

own expert witness used a job evaluation plan that assigned "points" to job factors such as experience or physical demand and summed the results. The summation explicitly weighed different aspects of a job against each other. GPO's objections, therefore, undercut the presentation of its own witness.

Mar. 14, 1979, at 25–27. While it appears that as GPO's work force contracts, rotation may become more important, id. at 29–30, the record does not show that Judge Richey erred in concluding that rotation was not a necessary part of all bookbinders' jobs during the time the alleged violations of the Equal Pay Act took place.

We conclude that the plaintiffs succeeded in proving a *prima facie* case of an Equal Pay Act violation with respect to the Smyth operators. Once the plaintiffs have made out such a *prima facie* case, the burden shifts to the defendants to show that their payment of unequal wages was justified under one of the exceptions enumerated in the statute: "(i) a seniority system; (ii) a merit system; (iii) a system which measures earning by quantity or quality of production; or (iv) a differential based on any other factor other than sex." 29 U.S.C. § 206(d)(1) (1976); *Corning Glass*, 417 U.S. 188, 94 S.Ct. 2223, 41 L.Ed. 2d 1. Judge Richey found that GPO's "only defense is that the bookbinder's job involves a four year apprenticeship requirement in the form of a training program that has traditionally excluded women" and that the burden had not been met. J.A. 187. In this appeal, GPO contends that traditional industry patterns of classification and training are a differential based on a factor other than sex, and hence a defense to the Equal Pay Act charge.

Traditional industry practice was certainly the kind of difference contemplated as a factor "other than sex" under the Equal Pay Act. As Representative Goodell remarked, "Differences in pay that are based upon historical and widely accepted differences in job content will not be challenged, *if not based on sex*." 109 Cong.Rec. 9209 (1963) (emphasis added). Traditional industry practice may reveal continuing fealty to sexual discrimination, however, and if so does not shield employers against the charge of an Equal Pay Act violation. E.g., *Corning Glass*, 417 U.S. at 205, 94 S.Ct. at 2233; *Laffey*, 567 F.2d at 451. For example, the "traditions" of paying women less than men, or of assigning different labelling to female and male jobs, no matter how hoary, are not defenses to the Equal Pay Act. To hold otherwise would protect the most egregious forms of discrimination, merely because, like Faulkner's Dilsey, they have endured.

The differences in machine assignments and training opportunities found at GPO were certainly longstanding in the binding industry. The record amply reveals, however, that these differences constituted a continuing structure of sexual discrimination. See supra pp. 265–266. The history of the binding industry, therefore, does not provide GPO with a defense to the Equal Pay Act violation charged here. We affirm Judge Richey's conclusion that GPO failed to rebut the plaintiffs' *prima facie* case that GPO violated the Equal Pay Act with respect to the Smyth operators.

C. The Remedy Under the Equal Pay Act

An employer who violates the Equal Pay Act is subject to the remedial provisions of the Equal Pay Act's statutory parent, the FLSA.

For relief purposes, the FLSA does not distinguish between wages that were sexually discriminatory and wages that were deficient for other reasons, such as a failure to reach the current minimum. 29 U.S.C. § 206(b) (Supp. III 1979). The remedial provisions of the FLSA originally were simple: an employer was doubly liable to affected employees: for unpaid wages and an additional, equal amount in liquidated damages. 29 U.S.C. § 216(b), (c) (Supp. III 1979). In the original FLSA both awards were mandatory. Pub.L. No. 718, 52 Stat. 1069 (1938). Concerned that this remedial provision was sometimes unjustly harsh, Congress amended the FLSA by two provisions relevant here, Portal to Portal Pay Act of 1947 (Portal Act), Pub.L. No. 49, 61 Stat. 84 (1947). First, the Portal Act limited FLSA recovery to two years, or three years in the event of a willful violation. 29 U.S.C. § 255(a) (1976). For a named plaintiff, this period is calculated from the date suit was filed; for others, it is calculated from the date they "opted into" the lawsuit, id. § 216(c) (Supp. III 1979). Second, awards of liquidated damages are no longer mandatory. If the employer convinces the court that he paid the deficient compensation in good faith and had reasonable grounds for believing he was in compliance with the FLSA, the court has discretion to forego any or all of the allowable award of liquidated damages. Id. § 260 (1976).

KOUBA v. ALLSTATE INSURANCE COMPANY

United States Court of Appeals for the Ninth Circuit, 1982.
691 F.2d 873.

CHOY, CIRCUIT JUDGE:

This appeal calls into question the scope of the "factor other than sex" exception to the Equal Pay Act of 1963 as incorporated into Title VII of the Civil Rights Act of 1964, 42 U.S.C. § 2000e, et seq., by the Bennett Amendment. Because the district court misconstrued the exception, we reverse and remand.

I

Allstate Insurance Co. computes the minimum salary guaranteed to a new sales agent on the basis of ability, education, experience, and prior salary. During an 8-to-13 week training period, the agent receives only the minimum. Afterwards, Allstate pays the greater of the minimum and the commissions earned from sales. A result of this practice is that, on the average, female agents make less than their male counterparts.

Lola Kouba, representing a class of all female agents, argued below that the use of prior salary caused the wage differential and thus constitutes unlawful sex discrimination. Allstate responded that prior salary is a "factor other than sex" within the meaning of the statutory exception. The district court entered summary judgment against Allstate, reasoning that (1) because so many employers paid discriminatory salaries in the past, the court would presume that a female agent's prior salary was based on her gender unless Allstate presented evidence to rebut that presumption, and (2) absent such a showing (which Allstate did not attempt to make), prior salary is not a factor other than sex.

II

The Equal Pay Act prohibits differential payments between male and female employees doing equal work except when made pursuant to any of three specific compensation systems or "any other factor other than sex." These exceptions are affirmative defenses which the employer must plead and prove. Corning Glass Works v. Brennan, 417 U.S. 188, 196–97, 94 S.Ct. 2223, 2229, 41 L.Ed.2d 1 (1974) (claim brought under the Equal Pay Act).

Because Kouba brought her claim under Title VII rather than directly under the Equal Pay Act,[3] Allstate contends that the standard Title VII rules govern the allocation of evidentiary burdens. It cites Texas Department of Community Affairs v. Burdine, 450 U.S. 248, 253, 101 S.Ct. 1089, 1091, 67 L.Ed.2d 207 (1981), for the proposition that under Title VII an employee alleging sex discrimination bears the burden of persuasion at all times as to all issues, and concludes that Kouba failed to carry the burden of showing that the wage differential did not result from a factor other than sex.[4]

Allstate misallocates the burden. In County of Washington v. Gunther, 452 U.S. 161, 170–71, 101 S.Ct. 2242, 2248–49, 68 L.Ed.2d 751 (1981), the Supreme Court recognized that very different principles govern the standard structure of Title VII litigation, including burdens of proof, and the structure of Title VII litigation implicating the "factor other than sex" exception to an equal-pay claim (though the Court reserved judgment on specifically how to structure an equal-pay claim under Title VII). Accordingly, we have held that even under Title VII, the employer bears the burden of showing that the wage differential resulted from a factor other than sex. Piva v. Xerox Corp., 654 F.2d 591, 598–601 (9th Cir.1981); Gunther v. County of Washington, 623 F.2d 1303, 1319 (9th Cir.1979) (supplemental opinion denying rehearing), aff'd, 452 U.S. 161, 101 S.Ct. 2242, 68 L.Ed.2d 751 (1981). Nothing in *Burdine* converts this affirmative defense, which the employer must plead and prove under *Corning Glass,* into an element of the cause of action, which the employee must show does not exist.

III

In an effort to carry its burden, Allstate asserts that if its use of prior salary caused the wage differential,[5] prior salary constitutes a

---

3. Her apparent reasons for bringing a Title VII action were the uncertainty at that time how the Equal Pay Act affected Title VII and the apparently less-demanding class-consent requirements under Title VII, Kuhn v. Philadelphia Electric Co., 475 F.Supp. 324, 326 (E.D.Pa.1979).

4. Allstate does not dispute that otherwise Kouba established a prima facie case. Thus, for purposes of this appeal, we assume that she has.

5. Allstate questions whether its use of prior salary caused the wage differential.

factor other than sex. An obstacle to evaluating Allstate's contention is the ambiguous statutory language. The parties proffer a variety of possible interpretations of the term "factor other than sex."

A

We can discard at the outset three interpretations manifestly incompatible with the Equal Pay Act. At one extreme are two that would tolerate all but the most blatant discrimination. Kouba asserts that Allstate wrongly reads "factor other than sex" to mean any factor that either does not refer on its face to an employee's gender or does not result in all women having lower salaries than all men. Since an employer could easily manipulate factors having a close correlation to gender as a guise to pay female employees discriminatorily low salaries, it would contravene the Act to allow their use simply because they also are facially neutral or do not produce complete segregation. Not surprisingly, Allstate denies relying on either reading of the exception.

At the other extreme is an interpretation that would deny employers the opportunity to use clearly acceptable factors. Kouba insists that in order to give the Act its full remedial force, employers cannot use any factor that perpetuates historic sex discrimination. The court below adopted a variation of this interpretation: the employer must demonstrate that it made a reasonable attempt to satisfy itself that the factor causing the wage differential was not the product of sex discrimination. Kouba v. Allstate Insurance Co., 523 F.Supp. 148, 162 (E.D.Cal. 1981). But while Congress fashioned the Equal Pay Act to help cure long-standing societal ills, it also intended to exempt factors such as training and experience that may reflect opportunities denied to women in the past. H.R.Rep. No. 309, 88th Cong., 1st Sess. 3, reprinted in 1963 U.S.Code Cong. & Ad.News 687, 689. See, e.g., Strecker v. Grand Forks County Social Service Board, 640 F.2d 96, 100 (8th Cir. 1981); Horner v. Mary Institute, 613 F.2d 706, 714 (8th Cir.1980); EEOC v. Aetna Insurance Co., 616 F.2d 719, 726 & n. 10 (4th Cir.1980); EEOC v. New York Times Broadcasting Service, Inc., 542 F.2d 356, 359–60 (6th Cir.1976). Neither Kouba's interpretation nor the district court's variation can accommodate practices that Congress and the courts have approved.

B

All three interpretations miss the mark in large part because they do not focus on the reason for the employer's use of the factor. The Equal Pay Act concerns business practices. It would be nonsensical to sanction the use of a factor that rests on some consideration unrelated to business. An employer thus cannot use a factor which causes a wage differential between male and female employees absent an acceptable business reason.[6] Conversely, a factor used to effectuate some business policy is not prohibited simply because a wage differential results.

We leave that issue for the district court on remand.

6. Not every reason making economic sense is acceptable. See Corning Glass

Even with a business-related requirement, an employer might assert some business reason as a pretext for a discriminatory objective. This possibility is especially great with a factor like prior salary which can easily be used to capitalize on the unfairly low salaries historically paid to women. See Futran v. RING Radio Co., 501 F.Supp. 734, 739 n. 2 (N.D.Ga.1980) (expressing concern that the use of prior salary would perpetuate the traditionally lower salaries paid women); Neely v. MARTA, 24 F.E.P. Cases 1610, 1611 (N.D.Ga.1980) (same). The ability of courts to protect against such abuse is somewhat limited, however. The Equal Pay Act entrusts employers, not judges, with making the often uncertain decision of how to accomplish business objectives. See County of Washington v. Gunther, 452 U.S. at 170–71, 101 S.Ct. at 2248–49. We have found no authority giving guidance on the proper judicial inquiry absent direct evidence of discriminatory intent. A pragmatic standard, which protects against abuse yet accommodates employer discretion, is that the employer must use the factor reasonably in light of the employer's stated purpose as well as its other practices. The specific relevant considerations will of course vary with the situation. In Part IV of this opinion, we outline how the court below should apply this test to the business reasons given by Allstate for its use of prior salary.

C

Relying on recent Supreme Court precedent, Kouba would limit the category of business reasons acceptable under the exception to those that measure the value of an employee's job performance to his or her employer. In County of Washington v. Gunther, 452 U.S. at 170–71 n. 11, 101 S.Ct. at 2248–49 n. 11, the Court reported that Congress added the exception "because of a concern that bona fide job evaluation systems used by American businesses would otherwise be disrupted." In Corning Glass Works v. Brennan, 417 U.S. at 199, 94 S.Ct. at 2230, the Court explained that these systems "took into consideration four separate factors in determining job value—skill, effort, responsibility and working conditions—and each of these four components was further systematically divided into various subcomponents." Our study of the legislative history of the Equal Pay Act confirms that Congress discussed only factors that reflect job value.

In drafting the Act, however, Congress did not limit the exception to job-evaluation systems. Instead, it excepted "any other factor other than sex" and thus created a "broad general exception." H.R.Rep. No. 309, 88th Cong., 1st Sess. 3, reprinted in 1963 U.S.Code Cong. & Ad. News 687, 689. While a concern about job-evaluation systems served as the impetus for creating the exception, Congress did not limit the exception to that concern.

Works v. Brennan, 417 U.S. at 205, 94 S.Ct. at 2233. This appeal does not, however, require us to compile a complete list of unacceptable factors or even formulate a standard to distinguish them from acceptable ones. We leave those tasks for another day.

Other language in the Act supports this conclusion. The statutory definition of equal work incorporates the four factors listed in *Corning Glass* as the standard components in job-evaluation systems. (The Act refers to "equal work on jobs the performance of which requires equal skill, effort, and responsibility, and which are performed under similar working conditions.") It would render the "factor other than sex" exception surplusage to limit the exception to the same four factors. And while we might be able to distinguish other factors that also reflect job value, the scope of the exception would be exceedingly narrow if limited to other apparently uncommon factors. The broad language of the exception belies such limitation.

Accordingly, no court or other authority has inferred a job-evaluation requirement. We, too, reject that limitation on the "factor other than sex" exception.

IV

Allstate provides two business reasons for its use of prior salary that the district court must evaluate on remand.[7] We will discuss each explanation in turn without attempting to establish a comprehensive framework for its evaluation. The district court should mold its inquiry to the particular facts that unfold at trial.

A

Allstate asserts that it ties the guaranteed monthly minimum to prior salary as part of a sales-incentive program. If the monthly minimum far exceeds the amount that the agent earned previously, the agent might become complacent and not fulfill his or her selling potential. By limiting the monthly minimum according to prior salary, Allstate hopes to motivate the agent to make sales, earn commissions, and thus improve his or her financial position. Presumably, Allstate cannot set a uniform monthly minimum so low that it motivates all sales agents, because then prospective agents with substantially higher prior salaries might not risk taking a job with Allstate.

This reasoning does not explain Allstate's use of prior salary during the initial training period. Because the agents cannot earn commissions at that time, there is no potential reward to motivate them to make sales.

When commissions become available, we wonder whether Allstate adjusts the guaranteed minimum regularly and whether most agents earn commission-based salaries. On remand, the district court should

---

7. A third reason given by Allstate is that an individual with a higher prior salary can demand more in the marketplace. Courts disagree whether market demand can ever justify a wage differential. Compare, e.g., Horner v. Mary Institute, 613 F.2d 706, 714 (8th Cir.1980) (allowing it in limited situations), with Futran v. RING Radio Co., 501 F.Supp. 734, 739 (N.D.Ga. 1980) (disallowing it always). We need not rule whether Congress intended to prohibit the use of market demand. Because Allstate did not present any evidence to support its use of prior salary in response to market demand, the district court properly disposed of that reason on summary judgment.

inquire into these and other issues that relate to the reasonableness of the use of prior salary in the incentive program.

B

Reasoning that salary corresponds roughly to an employee's ability, Allstate also claims that it uses prior salary to predict a new employee's performance as a sales agent. Relevant considerations in evaluating the reasonableness of this practice include (1) whether the employer also uses other available predictors of the new employee's performance, (2) whether the employer attributes less significance to prior salary once the employee has proven himself or herself on the job, and (3) whether the employer relies more heavily on salary when the prior job resembles the job of sales agent.

V

In conclusion, the Equal Pay Act does not impose a strict prohibition against the use of prior salary. Thus while we share the district court's fear that an employer might manipulate its use of prior salary to underpay female employees, the court must find that the business reasons given by Allstate do not reasonably explain its use of that factor before finding a violation of the Act.

Reversed and remanded.

COUNTY OF WASHINGTON v. GUNTHER

Supreme Court of the United States, 1981.
452 U.S. 161, 101 S.Ct. 2242, 68 L.Ed.2d 751.

JUSTICE BRENNAN delivered the opinion of the Court.

The question presented is whether § 703(h) of Title VII of the Civil Rights Act of 1964, 78 Stat. 257, 42 U.S.C. § 2000e–2(h), restricts Title VII's prohibition of sex-based wage discrimination to claims of equal pay for equal work.

I

This case arises over the payment by petitioner, County of Washington, Or., of substantially lower wages to female guards in the female section of the county jail than it paid to male guards in the male section of the jail.[1] Respondents are four women who were employed to guard female prisoners and to carry out certain other functions in the jail.[2] In January 1974, the county eliminated the female section of the

1. Prior to February 1, 1973, the female guards were paid between $476 and $606 per month, while the male guards were paid between $668 and $853. Effective February 1, 1973, the female guards were paid between $525 and $668, while salaries for male guards ranged from $701 to $940. 20 FEP Cases 788, 789 (Or.1976).

2. Oregon requires that female inmates be guarded solely by women, Or.Rev.Stat.

§§ 137.350, 137.360 (1979), and the District Court opinion indicates that women had not been employed to guard male prisoners. 20 FEP Cases, at 789, 792 nn. 8, 9. For purposes of this litigation, respondents concede that gender is a bona fide occupational qualification for some of the female guard positions. See 42 U.S.C. § 2000e–2(e)(1); Dothard v. Rawlinson, 433 U.S. 321, 97 S.Ct. 2720, 53 L.Ed.2d 786 (1977).

jail, transferred the female prisoners to the jail of a nearby county, and discharged respondents.   20 FEP Cases 788, 790 (Or.1976).

Respondents filed suit against petitioners in Federal District Court under Title VII, 42 U.S.C. § 2000e et seq., seeking backpay and other relief.[3]   They alleged that they were paid unequal wages for work substantially equal to that performed by male guards, and in the alternative, that part of the pay differential was attributable to intentional sex discrimination.   The latter allegation was based on a claim that, because of intentional discrimination, the county set the pay scale for female guards, but not for male guards, at a level lower than that warranted by its own survey of outside markets and the worth of the jobs.

After trial, the District Court found that the male guards supervised more than 10 times as many prisoners per guard as did the female guards, and that the females devoted much of their time to less valuable clerical duties.   It therefore held that respondents' jobs were not substantially equal to those of the male guards, and that respondents were thus not entitled to equal pay.   The Court of Appeals affirmed on that issue, and respondents do not seek review of the ruling.

The District Court also dismissed respondents' claim that the discrepancy in pay between the male and female guards was attributable in part to intentional sex discrimination.   It held as a matter of law that a sex-based wage discrimination claim cannot be brought under Title VII unless it would satisfy the equal work standard of the Equal Pay Act of 1963, 29 U.S.C. § 206(d).   The court therefore permitted no additional evidence on this claim, and made no findings on whether petitioner county's pay scales for female guards resulted from intentional sex discrimination.

The Court of Appeals reversed, holding that persons alleging sex discrimination "are not precluded from suing under Title VII to protest * * * discriminatory compensation practices" merely because their jobs were not equal to higher paying jobs held by members of the opposite sex.   602 F.2d 882, 891 (CA9 1979), supplemental opinion on denial of rehearing, 9 Cir., 623 F.2d 1303, 1313, 1317 (1980).   The court remanded to the District Court with instructions to take evidence on respondents' claim that part of the difference between their rate of pay and that of the male guards is attributable to sex discrimination.   We granted certiorari, 449 U.S. 950, 101 S.Ct. 352, 66 L.Ed.2d 213 (1980), and now affirm.

We emphasize at the outset the narrowness of the question before us in this case.   Respondents' claim is not based on the controversial

---

3. Respondents could not sue under the Equal Pay Act because the Equal Pay Act did not apply to municipal employees until passage of the Fair Labor Standards Amendments of 1974, 88 Stat. 55, 58–62.   Title VII has applied to such employees since passage of the Equal Employment Opportunity Act of 1972, § 2(1), 86 Stat. 103.

concept of "comparable worth,"[6] under which plaintiffs might claim increased compensation on the basis of a comparison of the intrinsic worth or difficulty of their job with that of other jobs in the same organization or community.[7] Rather, respondents seek to prove, by direct evidence, that their wages were depressed because of intentional sex discrimination, consisting of setting the wage scale for female guards, but not for male guards, at a level lower than its own survey of outside markets and the worth of the jobs warranted. The narrow question in this case is whether such a claim is precluded by the last sentence of § 703(h) of Title VII, called the "Bennett Amendment."[8]

II

Title VII makes it an unlawful employment practice for an employer "to discriminate against any individual with respect to his compensation, terms, conditions, or privileges of employment, because of such individual's * * * sex * * *" 42 U.S.C. § 2000e–2(a). The Bennett Amendment to Title VII, however provides:

> It shall not be an unlawful employment practice under this subchapter for any employer to differentiate upon the basis of sex in determining the amount of the wages or compensation paid or to be paid to employees of such employer if such differentiation is authorized by the provisions of section 206(d) of title 29. 42 U.S.C. § 2000e–2(h).

To discover what practices are exempted from Title VII's prohibitions by the Bennett Amendment, we must turn to § 206(d)—the Equal Pay Act—which provides in relevant part:

> No employer having employees subject to any provisions of this section shall discriminate, within any establishment in which such employees are employed, between employees on the basis of sex by paying wages to employees in such establishment at a rate less than the rate at which he pays wages to employees of the opposite sex in such establishment for equal work on jobs the performance of which

6. The concept of "comparable worth" has been the subject of much scholarly debate, as to both its elements and its merits as a legal or economic principle. See e.g., E. Livernash, Comparable Worth: Issues and Alternatives (1980); Blumrosen, Wage Discrimination, Job Segregation, and Title VII of the Civil Rights Act of 1964, 12 U.Mich.J.L.Ref. 397 (1979); Nelson, Opton, & Wilson, Wage Discrimination and the "Comparable Worth" Theory in Perspective, 13 U.Mich.J.L.Ref. 231 (1980). The Equal Employment Opportunity Commission has conducted hearings on the question, see BNA Daily Labor Report Nos. 83–85 (Apr. 28–30, 1980), and has commissioned a study of job evaluation systems, see D. Treiman, Job Evaluation; An Analytic Review (1979) (interim report).

7. Respondents thus distinguish Lemons v. City and County of Denver, 620 F.2d

228 (CA10), cert. denied, 449 U.S. 888, 101 S.Ct. 244, 66 L.Ed.2d 114 (1980), on the ground that the plaintiffs, nurses employed by a public hospital, sought increased compensation on the basis of a comparison with compensation paid to employees of comparable value—other than nurses—in the community, without direct proof of intentional discrimination.

8. We are not called upon in this case to decide whether respondents have stated a prima facie case of sex discrimination under Title VII, cf. Christensen v. Iowa, 563 F.2d 353 (CA8 1977), or to lay down standards for the further conduct of this litigation. The sole issue we decide is whether respondents' failure to satisfy the equal work standard of the Equal Pay Act in itself precludes their proceeding under Title VII.

requires equal skill, effort, and responsibility, and which are performed under similar working conditions, except where such payment is made pursuant to (i) a seniority system; (ii) a merit system; (iii) a system which measures earnings by quantity or quality of production; or (iv) a differential based on any other factor other than sex. 77 Stat. 56, 29 U.S.C. § 206(d)(1).

On its face, the Equal Pay Act contains three restrictions pertinent to this case. First, its coverage is limited to those employers subject to the Fair Labor Standards Act. S.Rep. No. 176, 88th Cong., 1st Sess., 2 (1963). Thus, the Act does not apply, for example, to certain businesses engaged in retail sales, fishing, agriculture, and newspaper publishing. See 29 U.S.C. §§ 203(s), 213(a) (1976 ed. and Supp. III). Second, the Act is restricted to cases involving "equal work on jobs the performance of which requires equal skill, effort, and responsibility, and which are performed under similar working conditions." 29 U.S.C. § 206(d)(1). Third, the Act's four affirmative defenses exempt any wage differentials attributable to seniority, merit, quantity or quality of production, or "any other factor other than sex." Ibid.

Petitioners argue that the purpose of the Bennett Amendment was to restrict Title VII sex-based wage discrimination claims to those that could also be brought under the Equal Pay Act, and thus that claims not arising from "equal work" are precluded. Respondents, in contrast, argue that the Bennett Amendment was designed merely to incorporate the four affirmative defenses of the Equal Pay Act into Title VII for sex-based wage discrimination claims. Respondents thus contend that claims for sex-based wage discrimination can be brought under Title VII even though no member of the opposite sex holds an equal but higher paying job, provided that the challenged wage rate is not based on seniority, merit, quantity or quality of production, or "any other factor other than sex." The Court of Appeals found respondents' interpretation the "more persuasive." 623 F.2d, at 1311. While recognizing that the language and legislative history of the provision are not unambiguous, we conclude that the Court of Appeals was correct.

A

The language of the Bennett Amendment suggests an intention to incorporate only the affirmative defenses of the Equal Pay Act into Title VII. The Amendment bars sex-based wage discrimination claims under Title VII where the pay differential is "authorized" by the Equal Pay Act. Although the word "authorize" sometimes means simply "to permit," it ordinarily denotes affirmative enabling action. Black's Law Dictionary 122 (5th ed. 1979) defines "authorize" as "[t]o empower; to give a right or authority to act." [9] Cf. 18 U.S.C. § 1905 (prohibiting the release by federal employees of certain information "to any extent not authorized by law"); 28 U.S.C. § 1343 (1976 ed., Supp. III) (granting

9. Similarly, Webster's Third New International Dictionary 147 (1976) states that the word "authorize" "indicates en- dowing formally with a power or right to act, usu. with discretionary privileges." (Examples deleted.)

district courts jurisdiction over "any civil action authorized by law"). The question, then, is what wage practices have been affirmatively authorized by the Equal Pay Act.

The Equal Pay Act is divided into two parts: a definition of the violation, followed by four affirmative defenses. The first part can hardly be said to "authorize" anything at all: it is purely prohibitory. The second part, however, in essence "authorizes" employers to differentiate in pay on the basis of seniority, merit, quantity or quality of production, or any other factor other than sex, even though such differentiation might otherwise violate the Act. It is to these provisions, therefore, that the Bennett Amendment must refer.

Petitioners argue that this construction of the Bennett Amendment would render it superfluous. See United States v. Menasche, 348 U.S. 528, 538–539, 75 S.Ct. 513, 519–520, 99 L.Ed. 615 (1955). Petitioners claim that the first three affirmative defenses are simply redundant of the provisions elsewhere in § 703(h) of Title VII that already exempt bona fide seniority and merit systems and systems measuring earnings by quantity or quality of production,[10] and that the fourth defense— "any other factor other than sex"—is implicit in Title VII's general prohibition of sex-based discrimination.

We cannot agree. The Bennett Amendment was offered as a "technical amendment" designed to resolve any potential conflicts between Title VII and the Equal Pay Act. Thus, with respect to the first three defenses, the Bennett Amendment has the effect of guaranteeing that courts and administrative agencies adopt a consistent interpretation of like provisions in both statutes. Otherwise, they might develop inconsistent bodies of case law interpreting two sets of nearly identical language.

More importantly, incorporation of the fourth affirmative defense could have significant consequences for Title VII litigation. Title VII's prohibition of discriminatory employment practices was intended to be broadly inclusive, proscribing "not only overt discrimination but also practices that are fair in form, but discriminatory in operation." Griggs v. Duke Power Co., 401 U.S. 424, 431, 91 S.Ct. 849, 853, 28 L.Ed. 2d 158 (1971). The structure of Title VII litigation, including presumptions, burdens of proof, and defenses, has been designed to reflect this approach. The fourth affirmative defense of the Equal Pay Act, however, was designed differently, to confine the application of the Act to wage differentials attributable to sex discrimination. H.R.Rep. No. 309, 88th Cong., 1st Sess., 3 (1963), U.S.Code Cong. & Admin.News 1963, p.

---

10. Section 703(h), as set forth in 42 U.S.C. § 2000e–2(h), provides in relevant part:

"Notwithstanding any other provision of this subchapter, it shall not be an unlawful employment practice for an employer to apply different standards of compensation, or different terms, conditions, or privileges of employment pursuant to a bona fide seniority or merit system, or a system which measures earnings by quantity or quality of production * * * provided that such differences are not the result of an intention to discriminate because of * * * sex * * *." (Emphasis added.)

687. Equal Pay Act litigation, therefore, has been structured to permit employers to defend against charges of discrimination where their pay differentials are based on a bona fide use of "other factors other than sex." [11]   Under the Equal Pay Act, the courts and administrative agencies are not permitted to "substitute their judgment for the judgment of the employer * * * who [has] established and applied a bona fide job rating system," so long as it does not discriminate on the basis of sex.   109 Cong.Rec. 9209 (1963) (statement of Rep. Goodell, principal exponent of the Act).   Although we do not decide in this case how sex-based wage discrimination litigation under Title VII should be structured to accommodate the fourth affirmative defense of the Equal Pay Act, see n. 8, supra, we consider it clear that the Bennett Amendment, under this interpretation, is not rendered superfluous.

We therefore conclude that only differentials attributable to the four affirmative defenses of the Equal Pay Act are "authorized" by that Act within the meaning of § 703(h) of Title VII.

B

The legislative background of the Bennett Amendment is fully consistent with this interpretation.

Title VII was the second bill relating to employment discrimination to be enacted by the 88th Congress.   Earlier, the same Congress passed the Equal Pay Act "to remedy what was perceived to be a serious and endemic problem of [sex-based] employment discrimination in private industry," Corning Glass Works v. Brennan, 417 U.S. 188, 195, 94 S.Ct. 2223, 2228, 41 L.Ed.2d 1 (1974).   Any possible inconsistency between the Equal Pay Act and Title VII did not surface until late in the debate over Title VII in the House of Representatives, because, until then, Title VII extended only to discrimination based on race, color, religion, or national origin, see H.R.Rep. No. 914, 88th Cong., 1st Sess., 10 (1963), U.S.Code Cong. & Admin.News 1964, p. 2355, while the Equal Pay Act applied only to sex discrimination.   Just two days before voting on Title VII, the House of Representatives amended the bill to proscribe sex discrimination, but did not discuss the implications of the overlapping jurisdiction of Title VII, as amended, and the Equal Pay Act.   See 110 Cong.Rec. 2577–2584 (1964).   The Senate took up consideration of the House version of the Civil Rights bill without reference to any committee.   Thus, neither House of Congress had the opportunity to undertake formal analysis of the relation between the two statutes.

11. The legislative history of the Equal Pay Act was examined by this Court in Corning Glass Works v. Brennan, 417 U.S. 188, 198–201, 94 S.Ct. 2223, 2229–2231, 41 L.Ed.2d 1 (1974).   The Court observed that earlier versions of the Equal Pay bill were amended to define equal work and to add the fourth affirmative defense because of a concern that bona fide job-evaluation systems used by American businesses would otherwise be disrupted.   Id., at 199–201, 94 S.Ct., at 2230–2231.   This concern is evident in the remarks of many legislators.   Representative Griffin, for example, explained that the fourth affirmative defense is a "broad principle," which "makes clear and explicitly states that a differential based on any factor or factors other than sex would not violate this legislation."   109 Cong.Rec. 9203 (1963).

Several Senators expressed concern that insufficient attention had been paid to possible inconsistencies between the statutes. See id., at 7217 (statement of Sen. Clark); id., at 13647 (statement of Sen. Bennett). In an attempt to rectify the problem, Senator Bennett proposed his amendment. Id., at 13310. The Senate leadership approved the proposal as a "technical amendment" to the Civil Rights bill, and it was taken up on the floor on June 12, 1964, after cloture had been invoked. The Amendment engendered no controversy, and passed without recorded vote. The entire discussion comprised a few short statements:

Mr. BENNETT. Mr. President, after many years of yearning by members of the fair sex in this country, and after very careful study by the appropriate committees of Congress, last year Congress passed the so-called Equal Pay Act, which became effective only yesterday.

By this time, programs have been established for the effective administration of this act. Now, when the civil rights bill is under consideration, in which the word "sex" has been inserted in many places, I do not believe sufficient attention may have been paid to possible conflicts between the wholesale insertion of the word "sex" in the bill and in the Equal Pay Act.

The purpose of my amendment is to provide that in the event of conflicts, the provisions of the Equal Pay Act shall not be nullified.

I understand that the leadership in charge of the bill have agreed to the amendment as a proper technical correction of the bill. If they will confirm that understand [*sic*], I shall ask that the amendment be voted on without asking for the yeas and nays.

"Mr. HUMPHREY. The amendment of the Senator from Utah is helpful. I believe it is needed. I thank him for his thoughtfulness. The amendment is fully acceptable.

Mr. DIRKSEN. Mr. President, I yield myself 1 minute.

We were aware of the conflict that might develop, because the Equal Pay Act was an amendment to the Fair Labor Standards Act. The Fair Labor Standards Act carries out certain exceptions.

All that the pending amendment does is recognize those exceptions, that are carried in the basic act.

Therefore, this amendment is necessary, in the interest of clarification. Id., at 13647.

As this discussion shows, Senator Bennett proposed the Amendment because of a general concern that insufficient attention had been paid to the relation between the Equal Pay Act and Title VII, rather than because of a *specific* potential conflict between the statutes.[13] His

---

13. The dissent finds it "obvious" that the "principal way" the Equal Pay Act might have been "nullified" by enactment of Title VII is that the "equal pay for equal work standard" would not apply under Title VII. Post, at 2260. There is however, no support for this conclusion in the legislative history: not one Senator or Congressman discussing the Bennett Amendment during the debates over Title VII so much as mentioned the "equal pay for equal work" standard. Rather, Senator Bennett's expressed concern was for preserving the "programs" that had "been established for the effective administration" of the Equal Pay Act. 110 Cong.Rec. 13647

explanation that the Amendment assured that the provisions of the Equal Pay Act "shall not be nullified" in the event of conflict with Title VII may be read as referring to the affirmative defenses of the Act. Indeed, his emphasis on the "technical" nature of the Amendment and his concern for not disrupting the "effective administration" of the Equal Pay Act are more compatible with an interpretation of the Amendment as incorporating the Act's affirmative defenses, as administratively interpreted, than as engrafting all the restrictive features of the Equal Pay Act onto Title VII.[14]

Senator Dirksen's comment that all that the Bennett Amendment does is to "recognize" the exceptions carried in the Fair Labor Standards Act, suggests that the Bennett Amendment was necessary because of the exceptions to coverage in the Fair Labor Standards Act, which made the Equal Pay Act applicable to a narrower class of employers than was Title VII. See supra, at 2247. The Bennett Amendment clarified that the standards of the Equal Pay Act would govern even those wage discrimination cases where only Title VII would otherwise apply. So understood, Senator Dirksen's remarks are not inconsistent with our interpretation.

Although there was no debate on the Bennett Amendment in the House of Representatives when the Senate version of the Act returned for final approval, Representative Celler explained each of the Senate's amendments immediately prior to the vote. He stated that the Bennett Amendment "[p]rovides that compliance with the Fair Labor Standards Act as amended satisfies the requirement of the title barring discrimination because of sex. * * *" 110 Cong.Rec. 15896 (1964). If taken literally, this explanation would restrict Title VII's coverage of sex discrimination more severely than even petitioners suggest: not only would it confine *wage discrimination* claims to those actionable under the Equal Pay Act, but it would block *all other* sex discrimination claims as well. We can only conclude that Representative Celler's explanation was not intended to be precise, and does not provide a solution to the present problem.

Thus, although the few references by Members of Congress to the Bennett Amendment do not explicitly confirm that its purpose was to incorporate into Title VII the four affirmative defenses of the Equal

(1964). This suggests that the focus of congressional concern was on administrative interpretation and enforcement procedures, rather than on the "equal work" limitation.

14. The argument in the dissent that under our interpretation, the Equal Pay Act would be impliedly repealed and rendered a nullity, post, at 2260, is mistaken. Not only might the substantive provisions of the Equal Pay Act's affirmative defenses affect the outcome of some Title VII sex-based wage discrimination cases, see supra, at 2248–2249, but the procedural charac-

teristics of the Equal Pay Act also remain significant. For example, the statute of limitations for backpay relief is more generous under the Equal Pay Act than under Title VII, and the Equal Pay Act, unlike Title VII, has no requirement of filing administrative complaints and awaiting administrative conciliation efforts. Given these advantages, many plaintiffs will prefer to sue under the Equal Pay Act rather than Title VII. See B. Babcock, A. Freedman, E. Norton, & S. Ross, Sex Discrimination and the Law 507 (1975).

Pay Act in sex-based wage discrimination cases, they are broadly consistent with such a reading, and do not support an alternative reading.

C

The interpretations of the Bennett Amendment by the agency entrusted with administration of Title VII—the Equal Employment Opportunity Commission—do not provide much guidance in this case. Cf. Griggs v. Duke Power Co., 401 U.S., at 433–434, 91 S.Ct., at 854–855. The Commission's 1965 Guidelines on Discrimination Because of Sex stated that "the standards of 'equal pay for equal work' set forth in the Equal Pay Act for determining what is unlawful discrimination in compensation are applicable to Title VII." 29 CFR § 1604.7(a) (1966). In 1972, the EEOC deleted this portion of the Guideline, see 37 Fed.Reg. 6837 (1972). Although the original Guideline may be read to support petitioners' argument that no claim of sex discrimination in compensation may be brought under Title VII except where the Equal Pay Act's "equal work" standard is met, EEOC practice under this Guideline was considerably less than steadfast.

The restrictive interpretation suggested by the 1965 Guideline was followed in several opinion letters in the following years. During the same period, however, EEOC decisions frequently adopted the opposite position. For example, a reasonable-cause determination issued by the Commission in 1968 stated that "the existence of separate and different wage rate schedules for male employees on the one hand, and female employees on the other doing reasonably comparable work, establishes discriminatory wage rates based solely on the sex of the workers." Harrington v. Piccadilly Cafeteria, Case No. AU 7–3–173 (Apr. 25, 1968).

The current Guideline does not purport to explain whether the equal work standard of the Equal Pay Act has any application to Title VII, see 29 CFR § 1604.8 (1980), but the EEOC now supports respondents' position in its capacity as *amicus curiae*. In light of this history, we feel no hesitation in adopting what seems to us the most persuasive interpretation of the Amendment, in lieu of that once espoused, but not consistently followed, by the Commission.

D

Our interpretation of the Bennett Amendment draws additional support from the remedial purposes of Title VII and the Equal Pay Act. Section 703(a) of Title VII makes it unlawful for an employer "to fail or refuse to hire or to discharge any individual, or *otherwise to discriminate* against any individual with respect to his compensation, terms, conditions, or privileges of employment" because of such individual's sex. 42 U.S.C. § 2000e–2(a) (emphasis added). As Congress itself has indicated, a "broad approach" to the definition of equal employment opportunity is essential to overcoming and undoing the effect of discrimination. S.Rep. No. 867, 88th Cong., 2d Sess., 12 (1964). We must therefore avoid interpretations of Title VII that deprive victims of discrimination of a remedy, without clear congressional mandate.

Under petitioners' reading of the Bennett Amendment, only those sex-based wage discrimination claims that satisfy the "equal work" standard of the Equal Pay Act could be brought under Title VII. In practical terms, this means that a woman who is discriminatorily underpaid could obtain no relief—no matter how egregious the discrimination might be—unless her employer also employed a man in an equal job in the same establishment, at a higher rate of pay. Thus, if an employer hired a woman for a unique position in the company and then admitted that her salary would have been higher had she been male, the woman would be unable to obtain legal redress under petitioners' interpretation. Similarly, if an employer used a transparently sex-biased system for wage determination, women holding jobs not equal to those held by men would be denied the right to prove that the system is a pretext for discrimination. Moreover, to cite an example arising from a recent case, Los Angeles Dept. of Water & Power v. Manhart, 435 U.S. 702, 98 S.Ct. 1370, 55 L.Ed.2d 657 (1978), if the employer required its female workers to pay more into its pension program than male workers were required to pay, the only women who could bring a Title VII action under petitioners' interpretation would be those who could establish that a man performed equal work: a female auditor thus might have a cause of action while a female secretary might not. Congress surely did not intend the Bennett Amendment to insulate such blatantly discriminatory practices from judicial redress under Title VII.

Moreover, petitioners' interpretation would have other far-reaching consequences. Since it rests on the proposition that any wage differentials not prohibited by the Equal Pay Act are "authorized" by it, petitioners' interpretation would lead to the conclusion that discriminatory compensation by employers not covered by the Fair Labor Standards Act is "authorized"—since not prohibited—by the Equal Pay Act. Thus it would deny Title VII protection against sex-based wage discrimination by those employers not subject to the Fair Labor Standards Act but covered by Title VII. See supra, at 2247. There is no persuasive evidence that Congress intended such a result, and the EEOC has rejected it since at least 1965. See 29 CFR § 1604.7 (1966). Indeed, petitioners themselves apparently acknowledge that Congress intended Title VII's broader coverage to apply to equal pay claims under Title VII, thus impliedly admitting the fallacy in their own argument. Brief for Petitioners 48.

Petitioners' reading is thus flatly inconsistent with our past interpretations of Title VII as "prohibit[ing] all practices in whatever form which create inequality in employment opportunity due to discrimination on the basis of race, religion, sex, or national origin." Franks v. Bowman Transportation Co., 424 U.S. 747, 763, 96 S.Ct. 1251, 1263 (1976). As we said in Los Angeles Dept. of Water & Power v. Manhart, supra, at 707, n. 13, 98 S.Ct., at 1375, n. 13: "In forbidding employers to discriminate against individuals because of their sex, Congress intended to strike at the *entire spectrum* of disparate treatment of men and women resulting from sex stereotypes." (Emphasis added.) We must therefore reject petitioners' interpretation of the Bennett Amendment.

III

Petitioners argue strenuously that the approach of the Court of Appeals places "the pay structure of virtually every employer and the entire economy *   *   * at risk and subject to scrutiny by the federal courts." Brief for Petitioners 99–100. They raise the specter that "Title VII plaintiffs could draw any type of comparison imaginable concerning job duties and pay between any job predominantly performed by women and any job predominantly performed by men." Id., at 101. But whatever the merit of petitioners' arguments in other contexts, they are inapplicable here, for claims based on the type of job comparisons petitioners describe are manifestly different from respondents' claim. Respondents contend that the County of Washington evaluated the worth of their jobs; that the county determined that they should be paid approximately 95% as much as the male correctional officers; that it paid them only about 70% as much, while paying the male officers the full evaluated worth of their jobs; and that the failure of the county to pay respondents the full evaluated worth of their jobs can be proved to be attributable to intentional sex discrimination. Thus, respondents' suit does not require a court to make its own subjective assessment of the value of the male and female guard jobs, or to attempt by statistical technique or other method to quantify the effect of sex discrimination on the wage rates.

We do not decide in this case the precise contours of lawsuits challenging sex discrimination in compensation under Title VII. It is sufficient to note that respondents' claims of discriminatory undercompensation are not barred by § 703(h) of Title VII merely because respondents do not perform work equal to that of male jail guards. The judgment of the Court of Appeals is therefore

Affirmed.

JUSTICE REHNQUIST, with whom THE CHIEF JUSTICE, JUSTICE STEWART, and JUSTICE POWELL join, dissenting.

The Court today holds a plaintiff may state a claim of sex-based wage discrimination under Title VII without even establishing that she has performed "equal or substantially equal work" to that of males as defined in the Equal Pay Act. Because I believe that the legislative history of both the Equal Pay Act of 1963 and Title VII clearly establishes that there can be no Title VII claim of sex-based wage discrimination without proof of "equal work," I dissent.

Because the decision does not rest on any reasoned statement of logic or principle, it provides little guidance to employers or lower courts as to what types of compensation practices might now violate

Title VII. The Court correctly emphasizes that its decision is narrow, and indeed one searches the Court's opinion in vain for a hint as to what pleadings or proof other than that adduced in this particular case, see ante, at 2253–2254, would be sufficient to state a claim of sex-based wage discrimination under Title VII. To paraphrase Justice Jackson, the Court today does not and apparently cannot enunciate any legal criteria by which suits under Title VII will be adjudicated and it lays "down no rule other than our passing impression to guide ourselves or our successors." Bob-Lo Excursion Co. v. Michigan, 333 U.S. 28, 45, 68 S.Ct. 358, 366, 92 L.Ed. 455 (1948). All we know is that Title VII provides a remedy when, as here, plaintiffs seek to show by *direct* evidence that their employer *intentionally* depressed their wages. And, for reasons that go largely unexplained, we also know that a Title VII remedy may not be available to plaintiffs who allege theories different than that alleged here, such as the so-called "comparable worth" theory. One has the sense that the decision today will be treated like a restricted railroad ticket, "good for this day and train only." Smith v. Allwright, 321 U.S. 649, 669, 64 S.Ct. 757, 768, 88 L.Ed. 987 (1944) (Roberts, J., dissenting).

In the end, however, the flaw with today's decision is not so much that it is so narrowly written as to be virtually meaningless, but rather that its legal analysis is wrong. The Court is obviously more interested in the consequences of its decision than in discerning the intention of Congress. In reaching its desired result, the Court conveniently and persistently ignores relevant legislative history and instead relies wholly on what it believes Congress *should* have enacted.

II

THE EQUAL PAY ACT

The starting point for any discussion of sex-based wage discrimination claims must be the Equal Pay Act of 1963, enacted as an amendment to the Fair Labor Standards Act of 1938, 29 U.S.C. §§ 201–219 (1976 ed., Supp. III). It was there that Congress, after 18 months of careful and exhaustive study, specifically addressed the problem of sex-based wage discrimination. The Equal Pay Act states that employers shall not discriminate on the basis of sex by paying different wages for jobs that require equal skill, effort, and responsibility. In adopting the "equal pay for equal work" formula, Congress carefully considered and ultimately rejected the "equal pay for comparable worth" standard advanced by respondents and several *amici*. As the legislative history of the Equal Pay Act amply demonstrates, Congress realized that the adoption of the comparable-worth doctrine would ignore the economic realities of supply and demand and would involve both governmental agencies and courts in the impossible task of ascertaining the worth of comparable work, an area in which they have little expertise.

Thus, the legislative history of the Equal Pay Act clearly reveals that Congress was unwilling to give either the Federal Government or the courts broad authority to determine comparable wage rates. Congress recognized that the adoption of such a theory would ignore economic realities and would result in major restructuring of the American economy. Instead, Congress concluded that governmental intervention to equalize wage differentials was to be undertaken only within one circumstance: when men's and women's jobs were identical or nearly so, hence unarguably of equal worth. It defies common sense to believe that the same Congress—which, after 18 months of hearings and debates, had decided in 1963 upon the extent of federal involvement it desired in the area of wage rate claims—intended *sub silentio* to reject all of this work and to abandon the limitations of the equal work approach just one year later, when it enacted Title VII.

TITLE VII

Congress enacted the Civil Rights Act of 1964, 42 U.S.C. § 2000a et seq., one year after passing the Equal Pay Act. Title VII prohibits discrimination in employment on the basis of race, color, national origin, religion, and sex. 42 U.S.C. § 2000e–2(a)(1). The question is whether Congress intended to completely turn its back on the "equal work" standard enacted in the Equal Pay Act of 1963 when it adopted Title VII only one year later.

The Court answers that question in the affirmative, concluding that Title VII must be read more broadly than the Equal Pay Act. In so holding, the majority wholly ignores this Court's repeated adherence to the doctrine of *in pari materia,* namely, that "[w]here there is no clear intention otherwise, a specific statute will not be controlled or nullified by a general one, regardless of the priority of enactment." Radzanower v. Touche Ross & Co., 426 U.S. 148, 153, 96 S.Ct. 1989, 1992, 48 L.Ed.2d 540 (1976), citing Morton v. Mancari, 417 U.S. 535, 550–551, 94 S.Ct. 2474, 2482–2483, 41 L.Ed.2d 290 (1974).

When those principles are applied to this case, there can be no doubt that the Equal Pay Act and Title VII should be construed *in pari materia.* The Equal Pay Act is the more specific piece of legislation, dealing solely with sex-based wage discrimination, and was the product of exhaustive congressional study. Title VII, by contrast, is a general antidiscrimination provision, passed with virtually no consideration of the specific problem of sex-based wage discrimination. See General Electric Co. v. Gilbert, 429 U.S. 125, 143, 97 S.Ct. 401, 411, 50 L.Ed.2d 343 (1976) (the legislative history of the sex discrimination amendment is "notable primarily for its brevity").[4] Most significantly, there is

---

4. Indeed, Title VII was originally intended to protect the rights of Negroes. On the final day of consideration by the entire House, Representative Smith added an amendment to prohibit sex discrimination. It has been speculated that the amendment was added as an attempt to thwart passage of Title VII. The amendment was passed by the House that same day, and the entire bill was approved two days later and sent to the Senate without any consideration of the effect of the amendment on the Equal Pay Act. The attenuated history of the sex amendment to Title VII makes it difficult to believe that Congress thereby intended to wholly abandon the carefully crafted equal work standard of the Equal Pay Act.

absolutely nothing in the legislative history of Title VII which reveals an intent by Congress to repeal by implication the provisions of the Equal Pay Act. Quite the contrary, what little legislative history there is on the subject—such as the comments of Senators Clark and Bennett and Representative Celler, and the contemporaneous interpretation of the EEOC—indicates that Congress intended to incorporate the substantive standards of the Equal Pay Act into Title VII so that sex-based wage discrimination claims would be governed by the equal work standard of the Equal Pay Act and by that standard alone. See discussion infra, at 2258–2262.

In order to reach the result it so desperately desires, the Court neatly solves the problem of this contrary legislative history by simply giving it "no weight."

The Court blithely ignores all of this legislative history and chooses to interpret the Bennett Amendment as incorporating only the Equal Pay Act's four affirmative defenses, and not the equal work requirement. That argument does not survive scrutiny. In the first place, the language of the Amendment draws no distinction between the Equal Pay Act's standard for liability—equal pay for equal work—and the Act's defenses. Nor does any Senator or Congressman even come close to suggesting that the Amendment incorporates the Equal Pay Act's affirmative defenses into Title VII, but not the equal work standard itself. Quite the contrary, the concern was that Title VII would render the Equal Pay Act a nullity. It is only too obvious that reading just the four affirmative defenses of the Equal Pay Act into Title VII does not protect the careful draftsmanship of the Equal Pay Act. We must examine statutory words in a manner that " 'reconstitute[s] the gamut of values current at the time when the words were uttered.' " National Woodwork Manufacturers Assn. v. NLRB, 386 U.S. 612, 620, 87 S.Ct. 1250, 1255, 18 L.Ed.2d 357 (1967) (quoting L. Hand, J.). In this case, it stands Congress' concern on its head to suppose that Congress sought to incorporate the affirmative defenses, but not the equal work standard. It would be surprising if Congress in 1964 sought to reverse its decision in 1963 to require a showing of "equal work" as a predicate to an equal pay claim and at the same time carefully preserve the four affirmative defenses.

Moreover, even on its own terms the Court's argument is unpersuasive. The Equal Pay Act contains four statutory defenses: different compensation is permissible if the differential is made by way of (1) a seniority system, (2) a merit system, (3) a system which measures earnings by quantity or quality of production, or (4) is based on any other factor other than sex. 29 U.S.C. § 206(d)(1). The flaw in interpreting the Bennett Amendment as incorporating only the four defenses of the Equal Pay Act into Title VII is that Title VII, even without the Bennett Amendment, contains those very same defenses. The opening sentence of § 703(h) protects differentials and compensation based on seniority, merit, or quantity or quality of production.

These are three of the four EPA defenses. The fourth EPA defense, "a factor other than sex," is already implicit in Title VII because the statute's prohibition of sex discrimination applies only if there is discrimination on the basis of sex. Under the Court's interpretation, the Bennett Amendment, the second sentence of § 703(h), is mere surplusage. United States v. Menasche, 348 U.S. 528, 538–539, 75 S.Ct. 513, 519–520, 99 L.Ed. 615 (1955) ("It is our duty 'to give effect, if possible, to every clause and word of a statute,' Montclair v. Ramsdell, 107 U.S. 147, 152 [2 S.Ct. 391, 394, 27 L.Ed. 431], rather than emasculate an entire section") The Court's answer to this argument is curious. It suggests that repetition ensures that the provisions would be consistently interpreted by the courts. Ante, at 2248. But that answer only speaks to the purpose for incorporating the defenses in each statute, not for stating the defenses twice in the same statute. Courts are not quite as dense as the majority assumes.

In sum, Title VII and the Equal Pay Act, read together, provide a balanced approach to resolving sex-based wage discrimination claims. Title VII guarantees that qualified female employees will have access to all jobs, and the Equal Pay Act assures that men and women performing the same work will be paid equally. Congress intended to remedy wage discrimination through the Equal Pay Act standards, whether suit is brought under that statute or under Title VII. What emerges is that Title VII would have been construed *in pari materia* even without the Bennett Amendment, and that the Amendment serves simply to insure that the equal work standard would be the standard by which all wage compensation claims would be judged.

IV

Even though today's opinion reaches what I believe to be the wrong result, its narrow holding is perhaps its saving feature. The opinion does not endorse to so-called "comparable worth" theory: though the Court does not indicate how a plaintiff might establish a prima facie case under Title VII, the Court does suggest that allegations of unequal pay for unequal, but comparable, work will not state a claim on which relief may be granted. The Court, for example, repeatedly emphasizes that this is not a case where plaintiffs ask the court to compare the value of dissimilar jobs or to quantify the effect of sex discrimination on wage rates. Ante, at 2246, 2253–2254. Indeed, the Court relates, without criticism, respondents' contention that Lemons v. City and County of Denver, 620 F.2d 228 (CA10), cert. denied, 449 U.S. 888, 101 S.Ct. 244, 66 L.Ed.2d 114 (1980), is distinguishable. Ante, at 2246, n. 7. There the court found that Title VII did not provide a remedy to nurses who sought increased compensation based on a comparison of their jobs to dissimilar jobs of "comparable" value in the community. See also Christensen v. Iowa, 563 F.2d 353 (CA8 1977) (no prima facie case under Title VII when plaintiffs, women clerical employees of a university, sought to compare their wages to the employees in the physical plant).

Given that implied repeals of legislation are disfavored, TVA v. Hill, 437 U.S. 153, 189, 98 S.Ct. 2279, 2299, 57 L.Ed.2d 117 (1978), we should not be surprised that the Court disassociates itself from the entire notion of "comparable worth." In enacting the Equal Pay Act in 1963, Congress specifically prohibited the courts from comparing the wage rates of dissimilar jobs: there can only be a comparison of wage rates where jobs are "equal or substantially equal." Because the legislative history of Title VII does not reveal an intent to overrule that determination, the courts should strive to harmonize the intent of Congress in enacting the Equal Pay Act with its intent in enacting Title VII. Where, as here, the policy of prior legislation is clearly expressed, the Court should not "transfuse the successor statute with a gloss of its own choosing." De Sylva v. Ballentine, 351 U.S. 570, 579, 76 S.Ct. 974, 979, 100 L.Ed.2d 1415 (1956).

Because there are no logical underpinnings to the Court's opinion, all we may conclude is that even absent a showing of equal work there is a cause of action under Title VII where there is direct evidence that an employer has *intentionally* depressed a woman's salary because she is a woman. The decision today does not approve a cause of action based on a *comparison* of the wage rates of dissimilar jobs.

For the foregoing reasons, however, I believe that even that narrow holding cannot be supported by the legislative history of the Equal Pay Act and Title VII. This is simply a case where the Court has superimposed upon Title VII a "gloss of its own choosing."

AMERICAN FEDERATION OF STATE, COUNTY, AND MUNICIPAL EMPLOYEES v. STATE OF WASHINGTON

United States Court of Appeals for the Ninth Circuit, 1985.
770 F.2d 1401.

KENNEDY, CIRCUIT JUDGE:

In this class action affecting approximately 15,500 of its employees, the State of Washington was sued in the United States District Court for the Western District of Washington. The class comprises state employees who have worked or do work in job categories that are or have been at least seventy percent female. The action was commenced for the class members by two unions, the American Federation of State, County, and Municipal Employees (AFSCME) and the Washington Federation of State Employees (WFSE). In all of the proceedings to date and in the opinion that follows, the plaintiffs are referred to as AFSCME. The district court found the State discriminated on the basis of sex in violation of Title VII of the Civil Rights Act of 1964, 42 U.S.C. § 2000e–2(a) (1982), by compensating employees in jobs where females predominate at lower rates than employees in jobs where males predominate, if these jobs, though dissimilar, were identified by certain studies to be of comparable worth. The State appeals. We conclude a violation of Title VII was not established here, and we reverse.

The State of Washington has required salaries of state employees to reflect prevailing market rates. See Wash.Rev.Code Ann. § 28B.16.100(16) (1983) (effective March 29, 1979); State Civil Service Law, ch. 1, § 16, 1961 Wash.Laws 7, 17. Throughout the period in question, comprehensive biennial salary surveys were conducted to assess prevailing market rates. The surveys involved approximately 2,700 employers in the public and private sectors. The results were reported to state personnel boards, which conducted hearings before employee representatives and agencies and made salary recommendations to the State Budget Director. The Director submitted a proposed budget to the Governor, who in turn presented it to the state legislature. Salaries were fixed by enactment of the budget.

In 1974 the State commissioned a study by management consultant Norman Willis to determine whether a wage disparity existed between employees in jobs held predominantly by women and jobs held predominantly by men. The study examined sixty-two classifications in which at least seventy percent of the employees were women, and fifty-nine job classifications in which at least seventy percent of the employees were men. It found a wage disparity of about twenty percent, to the disadvantage of employees in jobs held mostly by women, for jobs considered of comparable worth. Comparable worth was calculated by evaluating jobs under four criteria: knowledge and skills, mental demands, accountability, and working conditions. A maximum number of points was allotted to each category: 280 for knowledge and skills, 140 for mental demands, 160 for accountability, and 20 for working conditions. Every job was assigned a numerical value under each of the four criteria. The State of Washington conducted similar studies in 1976 and 1980, and in 1983 the State enacted legislation providing for a compensation scheme based on comparable worth. The scheme is to take effect over a ten-year period. Act of June 15, 1983, ch. 75, 1983 Wash.Laws 1st Ex.Sess. 2071.

AFSCME filed charges with the Equal Employment Opportunity Commission (EEOC) in 1981, alleging the State's compensation system violated Title VII's prohibition against sex discrimination in employment. The EEOC having taken no action, the United States Department of Justice issued notices of right to sue, expressing no opinion on the merits of the claims. In 1982 AFSCME brought this action in the district court, seeking immediate implementation of a system of compensation based on comparable worth. The district court ruled in favor of AFSCME and ordered injunctive relief and back pay. Its findings of fact, conclusions of law, and opinion are reported. American Federation of State, County, and Municipal Employees v. Washington, 578 F.Supp. 846 (W.D.Wash.1983) (*AFSCME I*).

AFSCME alleges sex-based wage discrimination throughout the state system, but its explanation and proof of the violation is, in essence, Washington's failure as early as 1979 to adopt and implement at once a comparable worth compensation program. The trial court adopted this theory as well. *AFSCME I,* 578 F.Supp. at 865–71. The comparable worth theory, as developed in the case before us, postulates that sex-based wage discrimination exists if employees in job classifications occupied primarily by women are paid less than employees in job classifications filled primarily by men, if the jobs are of equal value to the employer, though otherwise dissimilar. See, e.g., Jacobs, Comparable Worth, Case & Com., March-April 1985, at 12; Bellak, Comparable Worth: A Practitioner's View, in 1 Comparable Worth: Issue for the 80's, at 75 (United States Commission on Civil Rights, June 6–7, 1984); Northrup, Comparable Worth and Realistic Wage Setting, in 1 Comparable Worth: Issue for the 80's, at 93 (United States Commission on Civil Rights, June 6–7, 1984), see also American Nurses' Association v. Illinois, 606 F.Supp. 1313, 1315 (N.D.Ill.1985) (mem.). We must determine whether comparable worth, as presented in this case, affords AFSCME a basis for recovery under Title VII.

Section 703(a) of Title VII states in pertinent part:

It shall be an unlawful employment practice for an employer—

(1) * * * to discriminate against any individual with respect to his compensation, terms, conditions, or privileges of employment, because of such individual's * * * sex * * * or

(2) to limit, segregate, or classify his employees or applicants for employment in any way *which would deprive or tend to deprive any individual of employment opportunities* * * * because of such individual's * * * sex * * *.

42 U.S.C. § 2000e–2(a) (1982) (emphasis added).

The Bennett Amendment to Title VII, designed to relate Title VII to the Equal Pay Act [1], see County of Washington v. Gunther, 452 U.S. 161, 173–76, 101 S.Ct. 2242, 2249–51, 68 L.Ed.2d 751 (1981), and eliminate any potential inconsistencies between the two statutes, provides:

It shall not be an unlawful employment practice under this subchapter for any employer to differentiate upon the basis of sex in determining the amount of the wages or compensation paid or to be paid to employees of such employer if such differentiation is authorized by the provisions of section 206(d) of title 29.

42 U.S.C. § 2000e–2(h) (1982). It is evident from the legislative history of the Equal Pay Act that Congress, after explicit consideration, rejected proposals that would have prohibited lower wages for comparable work, as contrasted with equal work. See 109 Cong.Rec. 9197–9208

---

1. The Equal Pay Act provides in relevant part:

No employer * * * shall discriminate * * * between employees on the basis of sex by paying wages to employees in such establishment at a rate less than the rate at which he pays wages to employees of the opposite sex in such establishment for equal work on jobs the performance of which requires equal skill, effort, and responsibility, and which are performed under similar working conditions, except where such payment is made pursuant to (i) a seniority system; (ii) a merit system; (iii) a system which measures earnings by quantity or quality of production; or (iv) a differential based on any factor other than sex.

29 U.S.C. § 200(d)(1) (1982).

(Remarks of Rep. Goodell), 9196 (Remarks of Rep. Frelinghuysen), 9197–98 (Remarks of Reps. Griffin and Thompson) (1963). The legislative history of the Civil Rights Act of 1964 and the Bennett Amendment, however, is inconclusive regarding the intended coverage of Title VII's prohibition against sex discrimination, and contains no explicit discussion of compensation for either comparable or equal work. See generally General Electric Co. v. Gilbert, 429 U.S. 125, 143, 97 S.Ct. 401, 411, 50 L.Ed.2d 343 (1976) ("[t]he legislative history of Title VII's prohibition of sex discrimination is notable primarily for its brevity"). The Supreme Court in *Gunther,* stressing the broad remedial purposes of Title VII, construed the Bennett Amendment to incorporate into Title VII the four affirmative defenses of the Equal Pay Act, but not to limit discrimination suits involving pay to the cause of action provided in the Equal Pay Act. 452 U.S. at 168–71, 101 S.Ct. at 2247–49. The Court noted, however, that the case before it did not involve the concept of comparable worth, id. at 166, 101 S.Ct. at 2246, and declined to define "the precise contours of lawsuits challenging sex discrimination in compensation under Title VII." Id. at 181, 101 S.Ct. at 2254.

In the instant case, the district court found a violation of Title VII, premised upon both the disparate impact and the disparate treatment theories of discrimination. *AFSCME I,* 578 F.Supp. at 864. Under the disparate impact theory, discrimination may be established by showing that a facially neutral employment practice, not justified by business necessity, has a disproportionately adverse impact upon members of a group protected under Title VII. See Dothard v. Rawlinson, 433 U.S. 321, 328–29, 97 S.Ct. 2720, 2726–27, 53 L.Ed.2d 786 (1977); Griggs v. Duke Power Co., 401 U.S. 424, 430–31, 91 S.Ct. 849, 853–54, 28 L.Ed.2d 158 (1971). Proof of an employer's intent to discriminate in adopting a particular practice is not required in a disparate impact case. International Brotherhood of Teamsters v. United States, 431 U.S. 324, 335 n. 15, 97 S.Ct. 1843, 1854 n. 15, 52 L.Ed.2d 396 (1977); Spaulding v. University of Washington, 740 F.2d 686, 705 (9th Cir.), cert. denied, ___ U.S. ___, 105 S.Ct. 511, 83 L.Ed.2d 401 (1984). The theory is based in part on the rationale that where a practice is specific and focused we can address whether it is a pretext for discrimination in light of the employer's explanation for the practice. Under the disparate treatment theory, in contrast, an employer's intent or motive in adopting a challenged policy is an essential element of liability for a violation of Title VII. *Teamsters,* 431 U.S. at 335 n. 15, 97 S.Ct. at 1854 n. 15 (proof of discriminatory motive is critical to establish a prima facie case of discrimination in a treatment case); *Spaulding,* 740 F.2d at 700; Heagney v. University of Washington, 642 F.2d 1157, 1163 (9th Cir. 1981). It is insufficient for a plaintiff alleging discrimination under the disparate treatment theory to show the employer was merely aware of the adverse consequences the policy would have on a protected group. See Personnel Administrator of Massachusetts v. Feeney, 442 U.S. 256, 279, 99 S.Ct. 2282, 2296, 60 L.Ed.2d 870 (1979) (discriminatory purpose implies more than awareness of consequences). The plaintiff must show the employer chose the particular policy because of its effect on members of a protected class. Id. (discriminatory intent implies selection of a particular course of action "at least in part 'because of,' not merely 'in spite of,' its adverse effects upon an identifiable group"); *Teamsters,* 431 U.S. at 335 n. 15, 97 S.Ct. at 1854 n. 15 (plaintiff must allege the employer "treats some people less favorably than others because of their race, color, religion, sex, or national origin"). We consider each theory of liability in turn. Though there are both questions of fact and law in the district court's opinion, the result we reach is the same under either the clearly erroneous or the *de novo* standard of review. See *Spaulding,* 740 F.2d at 699. We begin by reviewing the district court's judgment in favor of AFSCME under the disparate impact theory.

The trial court erred in ruling that liability was established under a disparate impact analysis. The precedents do not permit the case to proceed upon that premise. AFSCME's disparate impact argument is based on the contention that the State of Washington's practice of taking prevailing market rates into account in setting wages has an adverse impact on women, who, historically, have received lower wages than men in the labor market. Disparate impact analysis is confined to cases that challenge a specific, clearly delineated employment practice applied at a single point in the job selection process. Atonio v. Wards Cove Packing Co., 768 F.2d 1120, 1130 (9th Cir.1985); see also *Dothard,* 433 U.S. at 328–29, 97 S.Ct. at 2726–27 (height and weight requirement disproportionately excluded women); *Griggs,* 401 U.S. at 430–31, 91 S.Ct. at 853–54 (requirement of high school diploma or satisfactory performance on standardized tests disproportionately affected minorities); Harriss v. Pan American World Airways, Inc., 649 F.2d 670, 674 (9th Cir.1980) (policy mandating maternity leave immediately upon learning of pregnancy had an adverse impact on women); Gregory v. Litton Systems, 472 F.2d 631, 632 (9th Cir.1972) (policy excluding applicants with arrest records adversely affected minorities). The instant case does not involve an employment practice that yields to disparate impact analysis. As we noted in an earlier case, the decision to base compensation on the competitive market, rather than on a theory of comparable worth, involves the assessment of a number of complex factors not easily ascertainable, an assessment too multifaceted to be appropriate for disparate impact analysis. *Spaulding,* 740 F.2d at 708. In the case before us, the compensation system in question resulted from surveys, agency hearings, administrative recommendations, budget proposals, executive actions, and legislative enactments. A compensation system that is responsive to supply and demand and other market forces is not the type of specific, clearly delineated employment policy contemplated by *Dothard* and *Griggs;* such a compensation system, the result of a complex of market forces, does not constitute a single practice that suffices to support a claim under disparate impact theory. See *Spaulding,* 740 F.2d at 708; see also *Atonio,* at 1129 (broad scale attacks against a wide range of ill-defined employment practices are inappropriate for disparate impact analysis); Pouncy v. Prudential Insurance Co., 668 F.2d 795, 800–01 (5th Cir.1982) (disparate impact model is ill-suited for application to wide-ranging challenges to general compensation policies). Such cases are controlled by disparate treatment analysis. Under these principles and precedents, we must reverse the district court's determination of liability under the disparate impact theory of discrimination.

We consider next the allegations of disparate treatment. Under the disparate treatment theory, AFSCME was required to prove a prima facie case of sex discrimination by a preponderance of the evidence. Texas Department of Community Affairs v. Burdine, 450 U.S. 248, 252–53, 101 S.Ct. 1089, 1093–94, 67 L.Ed.2d 207 (1981); Furnco Construction Corp. v. Waters, 438 U.S. 567, 576, 98 S.Ct. 2943, 2949, 57 L.Ed.2d 957 (1978); McDonnell Douglas Corp. v. Green, 411 U.S. 792, 802, 93 S.Ct. 1817, 1824, 36 L.Ed.2d 668 (1973); *Spaulding*, 740 F.2d at 700. As previously noted, liability for disparate treatment hinges upon proof of discriminatory intent. *Teamsters*, 431 U.S. at 335 n. 15, 97 S.Ct. at 1854 n. 15; *Spaulding*, 740 F.2d at 700; *Heagney*, 642 F.2d at 1163. In an appropriate case, the necessary discriminatory animus may be inferred from circumstantial evidence. *Furnco*, 438 U.S. at 579–80, 98 S.Ct. at 2950–51 (discriminatory intent may be inferred from the actions of an employer where "experience has proved that in the absence of any other explanation it is more likely than not that those actions were bottomed on impermissible considerations"); *Teamsters*, 431 U.S. at 335 n. 15, 97 S.Ct. at 1854 n. 15. Our review of the record, however, indicates failure by AFSCME to establish the requisite element of intent by either circumstantial or direct evidence.

AFSCME contends discriminatory motive may be inferred from the Willis study, which finds the State's practice of setting salaries in reliance on market rates creates a sex-based wage disparity for jobs deemed of comparable worth. AFSCME argues from the study that the market reflects a historical pattern of lower wages to employees in positions staffed predominantly by women; and it contends the State of Washington perpetuates that disparity, in violation of Title VII, by using market rates in the compensation system. The inference of discriminatory motive which AFSCME seeks to draw from the State's participation in the market system fails, as the State did not create the market disparity and has not been shown to have been motivated by impermissible sex-based considerations in setting salaries.

The requirement of intent is linked at least in part to culpability, see *Spaulding* at 708; Contreras v. City of Los Angeles, 656 F.2d 1267, 1275 n. 5 (9th Cir.1981), cert. denied, 455 U.S. 1021, 102 S.Ct. 1719, 72 L.Ed.2d 140 (1982). That concept would be undermined if we were to hold that payment of wages according to prevailing rates in the public and private sectors is an act that, in itself, supports the inference of a purpose to discriminate. Neither law nor logic deems the free market system a suspect enterprise. Economic reality is that the value of a particular job to an employer is but one factor influencing the rate of compensation for that job. Other considerations may include the availability of workers willing to do the job and the effectiveness of collective bargaining in a particular industry. Christensen v. Iowa, 563 F.2d 353, 356 (8th Cir.1977). We recognized in *Spaulding* that employers may be constrained by market forces to set salaries under prevailing wage rates for different job classifications, 740 F.2d at 708. We find nothing in the language of Title VII or its legislative history to indicate Congress intended to abrogate fundamental economic principles such as the laws of supply and demand or to prevent employers from competing in the labor market. See Lemons v. Denver, 620 F.2d 228, 229 (10th Cir.), cert. denied, 449 U.S. 888, 101 S.Ct. 244, 66 L.Ed.2d 114 (1980); *Christensen,* 563 F.2d at 356.

While the Washington legislature may have the discretion to enact a comparable worth plan if it chooses to do so, Title VII does not obligate it to eliminate an economic inequality that it did not create. See *Lemons,* 620 F.2d at 229 (this type of wage disparity, generated by market forces, was not sought to be remedied by the Civil Rights Act and is not within the scope of the equal protection clause); *Christensen,* 563 F.2d at 355–56 (same); Briggs v. Madison, 536 F.Supp. 435, 447 (W.D.Wis.1982) (same). Title VII was enacted to ensure equal opportunity in employment to covered individuals, McDonnell Douglas, 411 U.S. at 800, 93 S.Ct. at 1823; *Christensen,* 563 F.2d at 356, and the State of Washington is not charged here with barring access to particular job classifications on the basis of sex. See *Lemons,* 620 F.2d at 230; *Christensen,* 563 F.2d at 356.

We have recognized that in certain cases an inference of intent may be drawn from statistical evidence. *Spaulding,* 740 F.2d at 703; Lynn v. Regents of the University of California, 656 F.2d 1337, 1342 (9th Cir.1981), cert. denied, 459 U.S. 823, 103 S.Ct. 53, 74 L.Ed.2d 59 (1982); accord, *Teamsters,* 431 U.S. at 339–40, 97 S.Ct. at 1856–57. We have admonished, however, that statistics must be relied on with caution. *Spaulding,* 740 F.2d at 703. Though the comparability of wage rates in dissimilar jobs may be relevant to a determination of discriminatory animus, id. at 700–01, job evaluation studies and comparable worth statistics alone are insufficient to establish the requisite inference of discriminatory motive critical to the disparate treatment theory. Id. at 703 (circumstantial statistical evidence alone is insufficient to establish an inference of discriminatory intent in a disparate treatment case). The weight to be accorded such statistics is determined by the existence of independent corroborative evidence of discrimination. *Teamsters,* 431 U.S. at 339–40, 97 S.Ct. at 1856–57 (statistics are most useful when supplemented with testimony of specific incidents of discrimination); *Spaulding,* 740 F.2d at 703; White v. City of San Diego, 605 F.2d 455, 460 (9th Cir.1979); United States v. Iron Workers Local 86, 443 F.2d 544, 551 (9th Cir.), cert. denied, 404 U.S. 984, 92 S.Ct. 447, 30 L.Ed.2d 367 (1971). We conclude the independent evidence of discrimination presented by AFSCME is insufficient to support an inference of the requisite discriminatory motive under the disparate treatment theory.

AFSCME offered proof of isolated incidents of sex segregation as evidence of a history of sex-based wage discrimination. The evidence is discussed in *AFSCME I*, 578 F.Supp. at 860, and consists of "help wanted" advertisements restricting various jobs to members of a particular sex. These advertisements were often placed in separate "help wanted—male" and "help wanted—female" columns in state newspapers between 1960 and 1973, though most were discontinued when Title VII became applicable to the states in 1972. At trial, AFSCME called expert witnesses to testify that a causal relationship exists between sex segregation practices and sex-based wage discrimination, and that the effects of sex segregation practices may persist even after the practices are discontinued. However, none of the individually named plaintiffs in the action ever testified regarding specific incidents of discrimination. The isolated incidents alleged by AFSCME are insufficient to corroborate the results of the Willis study and do not justify an inference of discriminatory motive by the State in the setting of salaries for its system as a whole. Given the scope of the alleged intentional act, and given the attempt to show the core principle of the State's market-based compensation system was adopted or maintained with a discriminatory purpose, more is required to support the finding of liability than these isolated acts, which had only an indirect relation to the compensation principle itself.

We also reject AFSCME's contention that, having commissioned the Willis study, the State of Washington was committed to implement a new system of compensation based on comparable worth as defined by the study. Whether comparable worth is a feasible approach to employee compensation is a matter of debate. See generally Comparable Worth: Issue for the 80's (United States Commission on Civil Rights, Vols. 1 and 2, June 6–7, 1984); Vieira, Comparable Worth and the Gunther Case: The New Drive for Equal Pay, 18 U.C.D.L.Rev. 449 (1985); Levit & Mahoney, The Future of Comparable Worth Theory, 56 U.Colo.L.Rev. 99 (1984); Comment, The Comparable Worth Dilemma: Are Apples and Oranges Ripe for Comparison?, 37 Baylor L.Rev. 227 (1985). Assuming, however, that like other job evaluation studies it may be useful as a diagnostic tool, we reject a rule that would penalize rather than commend employers for their effort and innovation in undertaking such a study. See *American Nurses' Association*, 606 F.Supp. at 1317–18 (a rule requiring implementation of results of job evaluation studies would deter employers from conducting such studies). The results of comparable worth studies will vary depending on the number and types of factors measured and the maximum number of points allotted to each factor. A study that indicates a particular wage structure might be more equitable should not categorically bind the employer who commissioned it. The employer should also be able to take into account market conditions, bargaining demands, and the possibility that another study will yield different results. Id. at 1318.

Cf. *Gunther,* 452 U.S. at 180–81, 101 S.Ct. at 2253–54 (once an employer decided to adopt a particular job evaluation system, it could not be applied inconsistently).

We hold there was a failure to establish a violation of Title VII under the disparate treatment theory of discrimination, and reverse the district court on this aspect of the case as well. The State of Washington's initial reliance on a free market system in which employees in male-dominated jobs are compensated at a higher rate than employees in dissimilar female-dominated jobs is not in and of itself a violation of Title VII, notwithstanding that the Willis study deemed the positions of comparable worth. Absent a showing of discriminatory motive, which has not been made here, the law does not permit the federal courts to interfere in the market-based system for the compensation of Washington's employees.

Certain procedural errors were committed by the district court, including misallocating the burdens of proof and precluding the State from presenting much of its evidence. Though these errors complicate our review of the record unnecessarily, they need not be addressed, given our disposition on the merits of the case.

Reversed.

7. BONA FIDE OCCUPATIONAL QUALIFICATION

DIAZ v. PAN AMERICAN WORLD AIRWAYS, INC.

United States Court of Appeals for the Fifth Circuit, 1971.
442 F.2d 385.

TUTTLE, CIRCUIT JUDGE:

This appeal presents the important question of whether Pan American Airlines' refusal to hire appellant and his class of males solely on the basis of their sex violates § 703(a)(1) of Title VII of the 1964 Civil Rights Act. Because we feel that being a female is not a "bona fide occupational qualification" for the job of flight cabin attendant, appellee's refusal to hire appellant's class solely because of their sex, does constitute a violation of the Act.

The facts in this case are not in dispute. Celio Diaz applied for a job as flight cabin attendant with Pan American Airlines in 1967. He was rejected because Pan Am had a policy of restricting its hiring for that position to females. He then filed charges with the Equal Employment Opportunity Commission (EEOC) alleging that Pan Am had unlawfully discriminated against him on the grounds of sex. The Commission found probable cause to believe his charge, but was unable to resolve the matter through conciliation with Pan Am. Diaz next filed a class action in the United States District Court for the Southern District of Florida on behalf of himself and others similarly situated, alleging that Pan Am had violated Section 703 of the 1964 Civil Rights

Act by refusing to employ him on the basis of his sex; he sought an injunction and damages.

Pan Am admitted that it had a policy of restricting its hiring for the cabin attendant position to females. Thus, both parties stipulated that the primary issue for the District Court was whether, for the job of flight cabin attendant, being a female is a "bona fide occupational qualification (hereafter BFOQ) reasonably necessary to the normal operation" of Pan American's business.

The trial court found that being a female was a BFOQ, D.C., 311 F.Supp. 559. Before discussing its findings in detail, however, it is necessary to set forth the framework within which we view this case.

Section 703(a) of the 1964 Civil Rights Act provides, in part:

(a) It shall be an unlawful employment practice for an employer—

> (1) to fail or refuse to hire or to discharge any individual, or otherwise to discriminate against any individual with respect to his compensation, terms, conditions, or privileges of employment, because of such individual's race, color, religion, sex or national origin * * *.

The scope of this section is qualified by § 703(e) which states:

(e) Notwithstanding any other provision of this subchapter,

> (1) it shall not be an unlawful employment practice for an employer to hire and employ employees * * * on the basis of his religion, sex, or national origin in those certain instances where religion, sex, or national origin is a bona fide occupational qualification reasonably necessary to the normal operation of that particular business or enterprise * * *.

Since it has been admitted that appellee has discriminated on the basis of sex, the result in this case, turns, in effect, on the construction given to this exception.

We note, at the outset, that there is little legislative history to guide our interpretation. The amendment adding the word "sex" to "race, color, religion and national origin" was adopted one day before House passage of the Civil Rights Act. It was added on the floor and engendered little relevant debate. In attempting to read Congress' intent in these circumstances, however, it is reasonable to assume, from a reading of the statute itself, that one of Congress' main goals was to provide equal access to the job market for both men and women. Indeed, as this court in Weeks v. Southern Bell Telephone and Telegraph Co., 5 Cir., 408 F.2d 228 at 235 clearly stated, the purpose of the Act was to provide a foundation in the law for the principle of nondiscrimination. Construing the statute as embodying such a principle is based on the assumption that Congress sought a formula that would not only achieve the optimum use of our labor resources but, and more importantly, would enable individuals to develop as individuals.

Attainment of this goal, however, is, as stated above, limited by the bona fide occupational qualification exception in section 703(e). In construing this provision, we feel, as did the court in *Weeks,* supra, that it would be totally anomalous to do so in a manner that would, in effect, permit the exception to swallow the rule. Thus, we adopt the EEOC guidelines which state that "the Commission believes that the bona fide occupational qualification as to sex should be interpreted narrowly." 29 CFR 1604.1(a) Indeed, close scrutiny of the language of this exception compels this result. As one commentator has noted:

> The sentence contains several restrictive adjectives and phrases: it applies only "*in those certain instances*" where there are "*bona fide*" qualifications "*reasonably necessary*" to the operation of that "*particular*" enterprise. The care with which Congress has chosen the words to emphasize the function and to limit the scope of the exception indicates that it had no intention of opening the kind of enormous gap in the law which would exist if [for example] an employer could legitimately discriminate against a group solely because his employees, customers, or clients discriminated against that group. Absent much more explicit language, such a broad exception should not be assumed for it would largely emasculate the act. (emphasis added) 65 Mich.L. Rev. (1966).

Thus, it is with this orientation that we now examine the trial court's decision. Its conclusion was based upon (1) its view of Pan Am's history of the use of flight attendants; (2) passenger preference; (3) basic psychological reasons for the preference; and (4) the actualities of the hiring process.

Having reviewed the evidence submitted by Pan American regarding its own experience with both female and male cabin attendants it had hired over the years, the trial court found that Pan Am's current hiring policy was the result of a pragmatic process, "representing a judgment made upon adequate evidence acquired through Pan Am's considerable experience, and designed to yield under Pan Am's current operating conditions better *average* performance for its passengers than would a policy of mixed male and female hiring." (emphasis added) The performance of female attendants was *better* in the sense that they were *superior* in such non-mechanical aspects of the job as "providing reassurance to anxious passengers, giving courteous personalized service and, in general, making flights as pleasurable as possible within the limitations imposed by aircraft operations."

The trial court also found that Pan Am's passengers overwhelmingly preferred to be served by female stewardesses. Moreover, on the basis of the expert testimony of a psychiatrist, the court found that an airplane cabin represents a unique environment in which an air carrier is required to take account of the special psychological needs of its passengers. These psychological needs are better attended to by females. This is not to say that there are no males who would not have the necessary qualities to perform these non-mechanical functions, but the trial court found that the actualities of the hiring process would make it more difficult to find these few males. Indeed, "the admission of men to the hiring process, in the present state of the art of employment selection, would have increased the number of unsatisfactory employees hired, and reduced the average levels of performance of Pan Am's complement of flight attendants. * * * " In what appears to be a summation of the difficulties which the trial court found would follow from admitting males to this job the court said "that to eliminate the female sex qualification would simply eliminate the *best* available tool for screening out applicants *likely* to be unsatisfactory and thus reduce the *average* level of performance." (emphasis added)

Because of the narrow reading we give to section 703(e), we do not feel that these findings justify the discrimination practiced by Pan Am.

We begin with the proposition that the use of the word "necessary" in section 703(e) requires that we apply a business *necessity* test, not a business *convenience* test. That is to say, discrimination based on sex is valid only when the *essence* of the business operation would be undermined by not hiring members of one sex exclusively.

The primary function of an airline is to transport passengers safely from one point to another. While a pleasant environment, enhanced by the obvious cosmetic effect that female stewardesses provide as well as, according to the finding of the trial court, their apparent ability to perform the non-mechanical functions of the job in a more effective manner than most men, may all be important, they are tangential to the essence of the business involved. No one has suggested that having male stewards will so seriously affect the operation of an airline as to jeopardize or even minimize its ability to provide safe transportation from one place to another. Indeed the record discloses that many airlines including Pan Am have utilized both men and women flight cabin attendants in the past and Pan Am, even at the time of this suit, has 283 male stewards employed on some of its foreign flights.

We do not mean to imply, of course, that Pan Am cannot take into consideration the ability of *individuals* to perform the non-mechanical functions of the job. What we hold is that because the non-mechanical aspects of the job of flight cabin attendant are not "reasonably necessary to the normal operation" of Pan Am's business, Pan Am cannot exclude *all* males simply because *most* males may not perform adequately.

Appellees argue, however, that in so doing they have complied with the rule in *Weeks*. In that case, the court stated:

> We conclude that the principle of nondiscrimination requires that we hold that in order to rely on the bona fide occupational qualification exception an employer has the burden of proving that he had reasonable cause to believe, that is, a factual basis for believing, that all or substantially all women would be unable to perform safely and efficiently the duties of the job involved. Id. 408 F.2d at 235

We do not agree that in this case "all or substantially all men" have been shown to be inadequate and, in any event, in *Weeks*, the job that most women supposedly could not do was necessary to the normal operation of the business. Indeed, the inability of switchman to perform his or her job could cause the telephone system to break down. This is of an entirely different magnitude than a male steward who is perhaps not as soothing on a flight as a female stewardess.

Appellees also argue, and the trial court found, that because of the actualities of the hiring process, "the b.._' ...unable initial test for determining whether a particular applicant for employment is likely to have the personality characteristics conducive to high-level perform- ance of the flight attendant's job as currently defined is consequently the applicant's biological sex." Indeed, the trial court found that it was simply not practicable to find the few males that would perform properly.

We do not feel that this alone justifies discriminating against all males. Since, as stated above, the basis of exclusion is the ability to perform non-mechanical functions which we find to be tangential to what is "reasonably *necessary*" for the business involved, the exclusion of *all* males because this is the *best* way to select the kind of personnel Pan Am desires simply cannot be justified. Before sex discrimination can be practiced, it must not only be shown that it is impracticable to find the men that possess the abilities that most women possess, but that the abilities are *necessary* to the business, not merely tangential.

Similarly, we do not feel that the fact that Pan Am's passengers prefer female stewardesses should alter our judgment. On this subject, EEOC guidelines state that a BFOQ ought not be based on "the refusal to hire an individual because of the preferences of co-workers, the employer, clients or customers. * * *" 29 CFR § 1604.1(iii).

As the Supreme Court stated in Griggs v. Duke Power Co., 400 U.S. 424, 91 S.Ct. 849, 28 L.Ed.2d 158 (1971), "the administration interpreta- tion of the Act by the enforcing agency is entitled to great deference. See also, United States v. City of Chicago, 400 U.S. 8, 91 S.Ct. 18, 27 L.Ed.2d 9 (1970); Udall v. Tallman, 380 U.S. 1, 85 S.Ct. 792, 13 L.Ed.2d 616 (1965); Power Reactor Development Co. v. Electricians, 367 U.S. 396, 81 S.Ct. 1529, 6 L.Ed.2d 924 (1961). While we recognize that the public's expectation of finding one sex in a particular role may cause some initial difficulty, it would be totally anomalous if we were to allow the preferences and prejudices of the customers to determine whether the sex discrimination was valid. Indeed, it was, to a large extent, these very prejudices the Act was meant to overcome. Thus, we feel that customer preference may be taken into account only when it is based on the company's inability to perform the primary function or service it offers.

Of course, Pan Am argues that the customers' preferences are not based on "stereotyped thinking," but the ability of women stewardesses to better provide the non-mechanical aspects of the job. Again, as stated above, since these aspects are tangential to the business, the fact that customers prefer them cannot justify sex discrimination.

The judgment is reversed and the case is remanded for proceedings not inconsistent with this opinion.

ON PETITION FOR REHEARING AND PETITION FOR
REHEARING EN BANC

PER CURIAM:

The Petition for Rehearing is denied and no member of this panel
nor Judge in regular active service on the Court having requested that
the Court be polled on rehearing en banc, (Rule 35 Federal Rules of
Appellate Procedure; Local Fifth Circuit Rule 12) the Petition for
Rehearing En Banc is denied.

DOTHARD v. RAWLINSON

Supreme Court of the United States, 1977.
433 U.S. 321, 97 S.Ct. 2720, 53 L.Ed.2d 786.

(This is a continuation of the case on page 162).

MR. JUSTICE STEWART.

Unlike the statutory height and weight requirements, Regulation
204 explicitly discriminates against women on the basis of their sex. In
defense of this overt discrimination the appellants rely on § 703(e) of
Title VII, 42 U.S.C. § 2000e–2(e), which permits sex-based discrimination "in those certain instances where * * * sex * * * is a bona fide
occupational qualification reasonably necessary to the normal operation of that particular business or enterprise."

The District Court rejected the bona-fide-occupational-qualification
(bfoq) defense, relying on the virtually uniform view of the federal
courts that § 703(e) provides only the narrowest of exceptions to the
general rule requiring equality of employment opportunities. This
view has been variously formulated. In Diaz v. Pan American World
Airways, 442 F.2d 385, 388, the Court of Appeals for the Fifth Circuit
held that "discrimination based on sex is valid only when the essence of
the business operation would be undermined by not hiring members of
one sex exclusively." (Emphasis in original.) In an earlier case, Weeks
v. Southern Bell Telephone and Telegraph Co., 5 Cir., 408 F.2d 228, 235,
the same court said that an employer could rely on the bfoq exception
only by proving "that he had reasonable cause to believe, that is, a
factual basis for believing, that all or substantially all women would be
unable to perform safely and efficiently the duties of the job involved."
See also Phillips v. Martin Marietta Corp., 400 U.S. 542, 91 S.Ct. 496, 27
L.Ed.2d 613. But whatever the verbal formulation, the federal courts
have agreed that it is impermissible under Title VII to refuse to hire an
individual woman or man on the basis of stereotyped characterizations
of the sexes, and the District Court in the present case held in effect
that Regulation 204 is based on just such stereotypical assumptions.

We are persuaded—by the restrictive language of § 703(e), the
relevant legislative history, and the consistent interpretation of the
Equal Employment Opportunity Commission [19]—that the bfoq exception

---

19. The EEOC issued guidelines on sex
discrimination in 1965 reflecting its position that "the bona fide occupational qualification as to sex should be interpreted

was in fact meant to be an extremely narrow exception to the general prohibition of discrimination on the basis of sex. In the particular factual circumstances of this case, however, we conclude that the District Court erred in rejecting the State's contention that Regulation 204 falls within the narrow ambit of the bfoq exception.

The environment in Alabama's penitentiaries is a peculiarly inhospitable one for human beings of whatever sex. Indeed, a Federal District Court has held that the conditions of confinement in the prisons of the State, characterized by "rampant violence" and a "jungle atmosphere," are constitutionally intolerable. Pugh v. Locke, 406 F.Supp. 318, 325 (MD Ala.). The record in the present case shows that because of inadequate staff and facilities, no attempt is made in the four maximum-security male penitentiaries to classify or segregate inmates according to their offense or level of dangerousness—a procedure that, according to expert testimony, is essential to effective penological administration. Consequently, the estimated 20% of the male prisoners who are sex offenders are scattered throughout the penitentiaries' dormitory facilities.

In this environment of violence and disorganization, it would be an oversimplification to characterize Regulation 204 as an exercise in "romantic paternalism." Cf. Frontiero v. Richardson, 411 U.S. 677, 684, 93 S.Ct. 1764, 1769, 36 L.Ed.2d 583. In the usual case, the argument that a particular job is too dangerous for women may appropriately be met by the rejoinder that it is the purpose of Title VII to allow the individual woman to make that choice for herself.[21] More is at stake in this case, however, than an individual woman's decision to weigh and accept the risks of employment in a "contact" position in a maximum-security male prison.

The essence of a correctional counselor's job is to maintain prison security. A woman's relative ability to maintain order in a male, maximum-security, unclassified penitentiary of the type Alabama now runs could be directly reduced by her womanhood. There is a basis in fact for expecting that sex offenders who have criminally assaulted women in the past would be moved to do so again if access to women were established within the prison. There would also be a real risk that other inmates, deprived of a normal heterosexual environment, would assault women guards because they were women.[22] In a prison system where violence is the order of the day, where inmate access to guards is facilitated by dormitory living arrangements, where every

narrowly." 29 CFR § 1604.2(a). It has adhered to that principle consistently, and its construction of the statute can accordingly be given weight. See Griggs v. Duke Power Co., 401 U.S., at 434, 91 S.Ct., at 855; McDonald v. Santa Fe Trail Transportation Co., 427 U.S. 273, 279–280, 96 S.Ct. 2574, 2577–2578, 49 L.Ed.2d 493.

21. See, e.g., Weeks v. Southern Bell Telephone & Telegraph Co., 408 F.2d 228, 232–236 (CA5); Bowe v. Colgate-Palmolive Co., supra, 416 F.2d, at 717–718; Rosenfeld v. Southern Pacific Co., supra.

22. The record contains evidence of an attack on a female clerical worker in an Alabama prison, and of an incident involving a woman student who was taken hostage during a visit to one of the maximum-security institutions.

institution is understaffed, and where a substantial portion of the inmate population is composed of sex offenders mixed at random with other prisoners, there are few visible deterrents to inmate assaults on women custodians.

Appellee Rawlinson's own expert testified that dormitory housing for aggressive inmates poses a greater security problem than single-cell lockups, and further testified that it would be unwise to use women as guards in a prison where even 10% of the inmates had been convicted of sex crimes and were not segregated from the other prisoners.[23] The likelihood that inmates would assault a woman because she was a woman would pose a real threat not only to the victim of the assault but also to the basic control of the penitentiary and protection of its inmates and the other security personnel. The employee's very womanhood would thus directly undermine her capacity to provide the security that is the essence of a correctional counselor's responsibility.

There was substantial testimony from experts on both sides of this litigation that the use of women as guards in "contact" positions under the existing conditions in Alabama maximum-security male penitentiaries would pose a substantial security problem, directly linked to the sex of the prison guard. On the basis of that evidence, we conclude that the District Court was in error in ruling that being male is not a bona fide occupational qualification for the job of correctional counselor in a "contact" position in an Alabama male maximum-security penitentiary.

The judgment is accordingly affirmed in part and reversed in part, and the case is remanded to the District Court for further proceedings consistent with this opinion.

It is so ordered.

MR. JUSTICE MARSHALL, with whom MR. JUSTICE BRENNAN joins, concurring in part and dissenting in part.

The Court is unquestionably correct when it holds "that the bfoq exception was in fact meant to be an extremely narrow exception to the general prohibition of discrimination on the basis of sex." Ante, at 2729. See Phillips v. Martin Marietta Corp., 400 U.S. 542, 544, 91 S.Ct. 496, 497, 27 L.Ed.2d 613 (1971) (Marshall, J., concurring). I must, however, respectfully disagree with the Court's application of the bfoq exception in this case.

The Court properly rejects two proffered justifications for denying women jobs as prison guards. It is simply irrelevant here that a guard's occupation is dangerous and that some women might be unable to protect themselves adequately. Those themes permeate the testimo-

---

23. Alabama's penitentiaries are evidently not typical. Appellee Rawlinson's two experts testified that in a normal, relatively stable maximum-security prison—characterized by control over the inmates, reasonable living conditions, and segregation of dangerous offenders—women guards could be used effectively and beneficially. Similarly, an *amicus* brief filed by the State of California attests to that State's success in using women guards in all-male penitentiaries.

ny of the state officials below, but as the Court holds, "the argument that a particular job is too dangerous for women" is refuted by the "purpose of Title VII to allow the individual woman to make that choice for herself." Ante, at 2729, 2730. Some women, like some men, undoubtedly are not qualified and do not wish to serve as prison guards, but that does not justify the exclusion of all women from this employment opportunity. Thus, "[i]n the usual case," ibid., the Court's interpretation of the bfoq exception would mandate hiring qualified women for guard jobs in maximum-security institutions. The highly successful experiences of other States allowing such job opportunities, see briefs for the States of California and Washington, as *amici curiae*, confirm that absolute disqualification of women is not, in the words of Title VII, "reasonably necessary to the normal operation" of a maximum security prison.

What would otherwise be considered unlawful discrimination against women is justified by the Court, however, on the basis of the "barbaric and inhumane" conditions in Alabama prisons, conditions so bad that state officials have conceded that they violate the Constitution. See Pugh v. Locke, 406 F.Supp. 318, 329, 331 (MD Ala.1976). To me, this analysis sounds distressingly like saying two wrongs make a right. It is refuted by the plain words of § 703(e). The statute requires that a bfoq be "reasonably necessary to the normal operation of that particular business or enterprise." But no governmental "business" may operate "normally" in violation of the Constitution. Every action of government is constrained by constitutional limitations. While those limits may be violated more frequently than we would wish, no one disputes that the "normal operation" of all government functions takes place within them. A prison system operating in blatant violation of the Eighth Amendment is an exception that should be remedied with all possible speed, as Judge Johnson's comprehensive order in Puch v. Locke, supra, is designed to do. In the meantime, the existence of such violations should not be legitimatized by calling them "normal." Nor should the Court accept them as justifying conduct that would otherwise violate a statute intended to remedy age-old discrimination.

The Court's error in statutory construction is less objectionable, however, than the attitude it displays toward women. Though the Court recognizes that possible harm to women guards is an unacceptable reason for disqualifying women, it relies instead on an equally speculative threat to prison discipline supposedly generated by the sexuality of female guards. There is simply no evidence in the record to show that women guards would create any danger to security in Alabama prisons significantly greater than that which already exists. All of the dangers—with one exception discussed below—are inherent in a prison setting, whatever the gender of the guards.

The Court first sees women guards as a threat to security because "there are few visible deterrents to inmate assaults on women custodians." Ante, at 2730. In fact, any prison guard is constantly subject to the threat of attack by inmates, and "invisible" deterrents are the guard's only real protection. No prison guard relies primarily on his or her ability to ward off an inmate attack to maintain order. Guards are typically unarmed and sheer numbers of inmates could overcome the normal complement. Rather, like all other law enforcement officers, prison guards must rely primarily on the moral authority of their office and the threat of future punishment for miscreants. As one expert testified below, common sense, fairness, and mental and emotional stability are the qualities a guard needs to cope with the dangers of the job. App. 81. Well qualified and properly trained women, no less than men, have these psychological weapons at their disposal.

The particular severity of discipline problems in the Alabama maximum-security prisons is also no justification for the discrimination sanctioned by the Court. The District Court found in Pugh v. Locke, supra, that guards "must spend all their time attempting to maintain control or to protect themselves." 406 F.Supp., at 325. If male guards face an impossible situation, it is difficult to see how women could make the problem worse, unless one relies on precisely the type of generalized bias against women that the Court agrees Title VII was intended to outlaw. For example, much of the testimony of appellants' witnesses ignores individual differences among members of each sex and reads like "ancient canards about the proper role of women." Phillips v. Martin Marietta Corp., 400 U.S., at 545, 91 S.Ct., at 498. The witnesses claimed that women guards are not strict disciplinarians; that they are physically less capable of protecting themselves and subduing unruly inmates; that inmates take advantage of them as they did their mothers, while male guards are strong father figures who easily maintain discipline, and so on.[2] Yet the record shows that the presence of

---

2. See, e.g., App. 111–112, 117–118, 144, 147, 151–153, 263–264, 290–292, 301–302. The State Commissioner of Corrections summed up these prejudices in his testimony:

"Q Would a male that is 5'6", 140 lbs., be able to perform the job of Correctional Counselor in an all male institution?

*   *   *   *   *

"A Well, if he qualifies otherwise, yes.

"Q But a female 5'6", 140 lbs., would not be able to perform all the duties?

"A No.

"Q What do you use as a basis for that opinion?

"A The innate intention between a male and a female. The physical capabilities, the emotions that go into the psychic make-up of a female vs. the psychic make-up of a male. The attitude of the rural type inmate we have vs. that

of a woman. The superior feeling that a man has, historically, over that of a female." Id., at 153.

Strikingly similar sentiments were expressed a century ago by a Justice of this Court in a case long since discredited:

"I am not prepared to say that it is one of [women's] fundamental rights and privileges to be admitted into every office and position, including those which require highly special qualifications and demanding special responsibilities. * * * [I]n my opinion, in view of the particular characteristics, destiny, and mission of woman, it is within the province of the legislature to ordain what offices, positions, and callings shall be filled and discharged by men, and shall receive the benefit of those energies and responsibilities, and that decision and firmness which are presumed to predominate in the sterner sex." Bradwell v. Illinois, 16 Wall. 130, 139, 142, 21 L.Ed. 442 (1873) (Bradley, J., concurring).

women guards has not led to a single incident amounting to a serious breach of security in any Alabama institution.[3] And, in any event, "[g]uards rarely enter the cell blocks and dormitories," Pugh v. Locke, 406 F.Supp., at 325, where the danger of inmate attacks is the greatest.

It appears that the real disqualifying factor in the Court's view is "[t]he employee's very womanhood." Ante, at 2730. The Court refers to the large number of sex offenders in Alabama prisons, and to "[t]he likelihood that inmates would assault a woman because she was a woman." Ibid. In short, the fundamental justification for the decision is that women as guards will generate sexual assaults. With all respect, this rationale regrettably perpetuates one of the most insidious of the old myths about women—that women, wittingly or not, are seductive sexual objects. The effect of the decision, made I am sure with the best of intentions, is to punish women because their very presence might provoke sexual assaults. It is women who are made to pay the price in lost job opportunities for the threat of depraved conduct by prison inmates. Once again, "[t]he pedestal upon which women have been placed has * * *, upon closer inspection, been revealed as a cage." Sail'er Inn, Inc. v. Kirby, 5 Cal.3d 1, 20, 95 Cal. Rptr. 329, 341, 485 P.2d 529, 541 (1971). It is particularly ironic that the cage is erected here in response to feared misbehavior by imprisoned criminals.[4]

The Court points to no evidence in the record to support the asserted "likelihood that inmates would assault a woman because she was a woman." Ante, at 2730. Perhaps the Court relies upon common sense, or "innate recognition." Brief for Appellants 51. But the danger in this emotionally laden context is that common sense will be used to mask the " 'romantic paternalism' " and persisting discriminatory attitudes that the Court properly eschews. Ante, at 2729. To me, the only matter of innate recognition is that the incidence of sexually motivated attacks on guards will be minute compared to the "likelihood that inmates will assault" a *guard* because he or she is a *guard*.

The proper response to inevitable attacks on both female and male guards is not to limit the employment opportunities of law-abiding women who wish to contribute to their community, but to take swift and sure punitive action against the inmate offenders. Presumably, one of the goals of the Alabama prison system is the eradication of inmates' antisocial behavior patterns so that prisoners will be able to live one day in free society. Sex offenders can begin this process by

3. The Court refers to two incidents involving potentially dangerous attacks on women in prisons. Ante, at 2730 n. 22. But these did not involve trained corrections officers; one victim was a clerical worker and the other a student visiting on a tour.

4. The irony is multiplied by the fact that enormous staff increases are required by the District Court's order in Pugh v. Locke, 406 F.Supp. 318 (M.D.Ala.1976). This necessary hiring would be a perfect opportunity for appellants to remedy their past discrimination against women, but instead the Court's decision permits that policy to continue. Moreover, once conditions are improved in accordance with the *Pugh* order, the problems that the Court perceives with women guards will be substantially alleviated.

learning to relate to women guards in a socially acceptable manner. To deprive women of job opportunities because of the threatened behavior of convicted criminals is to turn our social priorities upside down.[5]

Although I do not countenance the sex discrimination condoned by the majority, it is fortunate that the Court's decision is carefully limited to the facts before it. I trust the lower courts will recognize that the decision was impelled by the shockingly inhuman conditions in Alabama prisons, and thus that the "extremely narrow [bfoq] exception" recognized here, ante, at 2729, will not be allowed "to swallow the rule" against sex discrimination. See Phillips v. Martin Marietta Corp., 400 U.S., at 545, 91 S.Ct., at 498. Expansion of today's decision beyond its narrow factual basis would erect a serious roadblock to economic equality for women.

WILSON v. SOUTHWEST AIRLINES CO.

517 F.Supp. 292, 1981.

Patrick E. Higginbotham, District Judge.

This case presents the important question whether femininity, or more accurately female sex appeal, is a bona fide occupational qualification ("BFOQ") for the jobs of flight attendant and ticket agent with Southwest Airlines.

From the personality description suggested by The Bloom Agency, Southwest developed its now famous "Love" personality. Southwest projects an image of feminine spirit, fun and sex appeal. Its ads promise to provide "tender loving care" to its predominantly male, business passengers. The first advertisements run by the airline featured the slogan, "AT LAST THERE IS SOMEBODY ELSE UP THERE WHO LOVES YOU." Variations on this theme have continued through newspaper, billboard, magazine and television advertisements during the past ten years.[4] Bloom's "Love" campaign was given a boost

---

5. The appellants argue that restrictions on employment of women are also justified by consideration of inmates' privacy. It is strange indeed to hear state officials who have for years been violating the most basic principles of human decency in the operation of their prisons suddenly become concerned about inmate privacy. It is stranger still that these same officials allow women guards in contact positions in a number of nonmaximum-security institutions, but strive to protect inmates' privacy in the prisons where personal freedom is most severely restricted. I have no doubt on this record that appellants' professed concern is nothing but a feeble excuse for discrimination.

As the District Court suggested, it may well be possible, once a constitutionally adequate staff is available, to rearrange work assignments so that legitimate inmate privacy concerns are respected without denying jobs to women. Finally, if women guards behave in a professional manner at all times, they will engender reciprocal respect from inmates, who will recognize that their privacy is being invaded no more than if a woman doctor examines them. The suggestion implicit in the privacy argument that such behavior is unlikely on either side is an insult to the professionalism of guards and the dignity of inmates.

4. Unabashed allusions to love and sex pervade all aspects of Southwest's public image. Its T.V. commercials feature attractive attendants in fitted outfits, catering to male passengers while an alluring feminine voice promises inflight love. On board, attendants in hot-pants (skirts

in 1974–1975 when the last of Southwest's competitors moved its operations to the new Dallas/Fort Worth Regional Airport, leaving Southwest as the only heavy carrier flying out of Dallas' convenient and fortuitously named, Love Field.

Over the years, Southwest gained national and international attention as the "love airline." Southwest Airlines' stock is traded on the New York Stock Exchange under the ticker symbol "LUV". During 1977 when Southwest opened five additional markets in Texas, the love theme was expanded to "WE'RE SPREADING LOVE ALL OVER TEXAS."

As an integral part of its youthful, feminine image, Southwest has employed only females in the high customer contact positions of ticket agent and flight attendant. From the start, Southwest's attractive personnel, dressed in high boots and hot-pants, generated public interest and "free ink." Their sex appeal has been used to attract male customers to the airline. Southwest's flight attendants, and to a lesser degree its ticket agents, have been featured in newspaper, magazine, billboard and television advertisements during the past ten years. Some attendants assist in promotional events for other businesses and civic organizations. Southwest flight attendants and ticket agents are featured in the company's in-flight magazine and have received notice in numerous other national and international publications. The airline also encourages its attendants to entertain the passengers and maintain an atmosphere of informality and "fun" during flights. According to Southwest, its female flight attendants have come to "personify" Southwest's public image.

Less certain, however, is Southwest's assertion that its females-only hiring policy is necessary for the continued success of its image and its business. Based on two onboard surveys, one conducted in October, 1979, before this suit was filed, and another in August, 1980, when the suit was pending, Southwest contends its attractive flight attendants are the "largest single component" of its success. In the 1979 survey, however, of the attributes considered most important by passengers, the category "courteous and attentive hostesses" ranked fifth in importance behind (1) on time departures, (2) frequently scheduled departures, (3) friendly and helpful reservations and ground personnel, and (4) convenient departure times, Defendant's Exh. 1 at 2 (¶ 17) and 39 (Question 14). Apparently, one of the remaining eight alternative categories, "attractive hostesses," was not selected with sufficient frequency to warrant being included in the reported survey results.

In evaluating Southwest's BFOQ defense, therefore, the Court proceeds on the basis that "love," while important, is not everything in the relationship between Defendant and its passengers. Still, it is proper to infer from the airline's competitive successes that Southwest's

---

are now optional) serve "love bites" (toasted almonds) and "love potions" (cocktails). Even Southwest's ticketing system features a "quickie machine" to provide "instant gratification."

overall "love image" has enhanced its ability to attract passengers. To the extent the airline has successfully feminized its image and made attractive females an integral part of its public face, it also follows that femininity and sex appeal are qualities related to successful job performance by Southwest's flight attendants and ticket agents. The strength of this relationship has not been proved. It is with this factual orientation that the Court turns to examine Southwest's BFOQ defense.

Diaz and its progeny establish that to recognize a BFOQ for jobs requiring multiple abilities, some sex-linked and some sex-neutral, the sex-linked aspects of the job must predominate. Only then will an employer have satisfied *Weeks'* requirement that sex be so essential to successful job performance that a member of the opposite sex could not perform the job. An illustration of such dominance in sex cases is the exception recognized by the EEOC for authenticity and genuineness. Supra at note 20. In the example given in § 1604.2(a)(2), that of an actor or actress, the primary function of the position, its essence, is to fulfill the audience's expectation and desire for a particular role, characterized by particular physical or emotional traits. Generally, a male could not supply the authenticity required to perform a female role. Similarly, in jobs where sex or vicarious sexual recreation is the primary service provided, e.g. a social escort or topless dancer, the job automatically calls for one sex exclusively; the employee's sex and the service provided are inseparable. Thus, being female has been deemed a BFOQ for the position of a Playboy Bunny, female sexuality being reasonably necessary to perform the dominant purpose of the job which is forthrightly to titillate and entice male customers. See St. Cross v. Playboy Club, Appeal No. 773, Case No. CFS 22618–70 (New York Human Rights Appeal Board, 1971) (dicta); Weber v. Playboy Club, Appeal No. 774, Case No. CFS 22619–70 (New York Human Rights Appeal Board, 1971) (dicta). One court has also suggested, without holding, that the authenticity exception would give rise to a BFOQ for Chinese nationality where necessary to maintain the authentic atmosphere of an ethnic Chinese restaurant, Utility Workers v. Southern California Edison, 320 F.Supp. 1262, 1265 (C.D.Cal.1970).[22] Consistent with the language of *Diaz*, customer preference for one sex only in such a case would logically be so strong that the employer's ability to perform the primary function or service offered would be undermined by not hiring members of the authentic sex or group exclusively.[23]

---

22. Similarly, in Avigliano v. Sumitomo Shoji America, Inc., 638 F.2d 552 (2nd Cir. 1981), the Second Circuit remanded for a determination whether being of Japanese nationality was a BFOQ for management positions in a Japanese firm's U.S. subsidiary.

23. Customer preference may also give rise to a BFOQ for one sex where the preference is based upon a desire for sexual privacy. The privacy right has been recognized in a variety of situations, in-cluding disrobing, sleeping, or performing bodily functions in the presence of the opposite sex. See, e.g. Fesel v. Masonic Home of Delaware, Inc., 428 F.Supp. 573 (D.Del., 1977); Mieth v. Dothard, 418 F.Supp. 1169, 1184–85 (M.D.Ala.1976) (three-judge District Court) aff'd in part, rev'd in part sub nom. Dothard v. Rawlinson, 433 U.S. 321, 97 S.Ct. 2720, 53 L.Ed.2d 786 (1977); Reynolds v. Wise, 375 F.Supp. 145, 151 (N.D.Tex.1973); EEOC, Toward

The Court is aware of only one decision where sex was held to be a BFOQ for an occupation not providing primarily sex oriented services. In Fernandez v. Wynn Oil Co., 20 FEP Cases 1162 (C.D.Cal.1979), the court approved restricting to males the job of international marketing director for a company with extensive overseas operations. The position involved primarily attracting and transacting business with Latin American and Southeast Asian customers who would not feel comfortable doing business with a woman. The court found that the customers' attitudes, customs, and mores relating to the proper business roles of the sexes created formidable obstacles to successful job performance by a woman. South American distributors and customers, for example, would have been offended by a woman conducting business meetings in her hotel room. Applying the *Diaz* test, the court concluded that hiring a female as international marketing director "would have totally subverted any business [defendant] hoped to accomplish in those areas of the world." Id. at 1165.[24] Because hiring a male was *necessary* to the Defendant's ability to continue its foreign operations, sex was deemed a BFOQ for the marketing position.

APPLICATION OF THE BONA FIDE OCCUPATIONAL QUALIFICATION TO SOUTHWEST AIRLINES

Applying the first level test for a BFOQ, with its legal gloss, to Southwest's particular operations results in the conclusion that being female is not a qualification required to perform successfully the jobs of flight attendant and ticket agent with Southwest. Like any other airline, Southwest's primary function is to transport passengers safely and quickly from one point to another.[25] See, e.g., *Diaz,* supra, 442 F.2d at 388. To do this, Southwest employs ticket agents whose primary job duties are to ticket passengers and check baggage, and flight attendants, whose primary duties are to assist passengers during boarding and deboarding, to instruct passengers in the location and use of aircraft safety equipment, and to serve passengers cocktails and snacks during the airline's short commuter flights. Mechanical, non-sex-linked duties dominate both these occupations. Indeed, on Southwest's short-haul commuter flights there is time for little else. That South-

---

Job Equality for Women 5 (1969). See also, Sirota, supra, note 12, at 1060–65.

24. In reaching its conclusion, the court followed *Diaz* in adopting a very narrow standard for weighing customer preference, stating:

Customer preferences should not be bootstrapped to the level of business necessity. The only occasion where customer preference will rise to the dignity of a bona fide occupational qualification is where no customer will do business with a member of one sex either because it would destroy the essence of the business or would create serious safety and efficiency problems.

Id. at 1165.

25. Southwest's argument that its primary function is "to make a profit," not to transport passengers, must be rejected. Without doubt the goal of every business is to make a profit. For purposes of BFOQ analysis, however, the business "essence" inquiry focuses on the particular service provided and the job tasks and functions involved, not the business goal. If an employer could justify employment discrimination merely on the grounds that it is necessary to make a profit, Title VII would be nullified in short order.

west's female personnel may perform their mechanical duties "with love" does not change the result. "Love" is the manner of job performance, not the job performed.

While possession of female allure and sex appeal have been made qualifications for Southwest's contact personnel by virtue of the "love" campaign, the functions served by employee sexuality in Southwest's operations are not dominant ones. According to Southwest, female sex appeal serves two purposes: (1) attracting and entertaining male passengers and (2) fulfilling customer expectations for female service engendered by Southwest's advertising which features female personnel. As in *Diaz*, these non-mechanical, sex-linked job functions are only "tangential" to the essence of the occupations and business involved. Southwest is not a business where vicarious sex entertainment is the primary service provided. Accordingly, the ability of the airline to perform its primary business function, the transportation of passengers, would not be jeopardized by hiring males.

Southwest does not face the situation anticipated in *Diaz* [26] and encountered in *Fernandez* where an established customer preference for one sex is so strong that the business would be undermined if employees of the opposite sex were hired. Southwest's claim that its customers prefer females rests primarily upon inferences drawn from the airline's success after adopting its female personality. But according to Southwest's own surveys, that success is attributable to many factors. There is no competent proof that Southwest's popularity derives directly from its females-only policy to the exclusion of other factors like dissatisfaction with rival airlines and Southwest's use of convenient Love and Hobby Fields. Nor is there competent proof that the customer preference for females is so strong that Defendant's male passengers would cease doing business with Southwest as was the case in *Fernandez*. In short, Southwest has failed in its proof to satisfy *Diaz's* business necessity requirement, without which customer preference may not give rise to a BFOQ for sex.

Southwest contends, nevertheless, that its females-only policy is reasonably necessary to the continued success of its "love" marketing campaign. Airline management testified that Southwest's customers will be disappointed if they find male employees after seeing only female personnel advertised. As a matter of law, this argument fails to support a BFOQ for sex. The court in *Diaz* emphasized that its test was one of business *necessity,* not business *convenience. Diaz,* supra, 442 F.2d at 388; Fernandez v. Wynn Oil Co., supra, 20 FEP at 1164. In Weeks v. Southern Bell Telephone and Telegraph Co., supra, 408 F.2d at 234–35, the Fifth Circuit expressly disapproved of the broad construction of the BFOQ exception in Bowe v. Colgate Palmolive Co., 272 F.Supp. 332, 362 (S.D.Ind.1967) aff'd in part and rev'd in part 416 F.2d

---

26. To reiterate, the Fifth Circuit in *Diaz,* supra, 442 F.2d at 389, announced that " * * * customer preference may be taken into account only when it is based on the company's inability to perform the primary function or service it offers."

711 (7th Cir.1969) which would have permitted sex discrimination where sex was "rationally related to an end which [the employer] has a right to achieve—production, profit, or business reputation."

It is also relevant that Southwest's female image was adopted at its discretion, to promote a business unrelated to sex. Contrary to the unyielding South American preference for males encountered by the Defendant company in *Fernandez,* Southwest exploited, indeed nurtured, the very customer preference for females it now cites to justify discriminating against males. See note 21, supra. Moreover, the fact that a vibrant marketing campaign was necessary to distinguish Southwest in its early years does not lead to the conclusion that sex discrimination was then, or is now, a business *necessity.* Southwest's claim that its female image will be tarnished by hiring males is, in any case, speculative at best.

The few cases on point support the conclusion that sex does not become a BFOQ merely because an employer chooses to exploit female sexuality as a marketing tool, or to better insure profitability. In Guardian Capital Corp. v. New York State Division of Human Rights, 46 App.Div.2d 832, 360 N.Y.S.2d 937 (1974) app. dismissed 48 A.D.2d 753, 368 N.Y.S.2d 594 (1975) for example, the court prohibited an employer from firing male waiters to hire sexually attractive waitresses in an attempt to change the appeal of the business and boost sales. Similarly, in University Parking, Inc. v. Hotel and Restaurant Employees & Bartenders' Int'l Un., 71–2 Lab.Arb.Awards 5360 (1971) (Peck, Arb.), the arbitrator denied an employer's right to replace three waitresses with waiters in order to "upgrade" his business and respond to customer desires for "classier" French service.[27] Merely because Southwest's female image was established in "good faith" [28] and has become its trademark does not distinguish Defendant's conduct from the discriminatory business decisions disapproved of in these cases.

Neither, in the final analysis, does Southwest's "battle-for-inches" with its competitors rise to the level of business *necessity.* *Diaz's* necessity test focuses on the company's ability "to perform the primary function or service it offers," not its ability to compete. *Diaz,* supra, 442 F.2d at 389. As one court has noted in the context of racial discrimination, "[t]he expense involved in changing from a discriminatory system * * * [fails to constitute] a business necessity that would justify the continuation of * * * discrimination." Bush v. Lone Star Steel Co., 373 F.Supp. 526, 533 (E.D.Tex.1974); see also Robinson v. Lorillard Corp., 444 F.2d 791, 799 n. 8 (4th Cir.) cert. dismissed 404 U.S.

---

27. The EEOC reached the same result in EEOC Decision No. YSF–9–058 1973 EEOC Dec. 4125 (1969).

28. Under Title VII, it is immaterial that Southwest's feminized marketing strategy was conceived and implemented in "good faith," not in a desire to discriminate against males. Even in cases of unintentional discrimination, the absence of bad motive or intent does not redeem employment practices with forbidden discriminatory consequences. See Griggs v. Duke Power Co., 401 U.S. 424, 432, 91 S.Ct. 849, 854, 28 L.Ed.2d 158 (1971); Vuyanich v. Republic National Bank, 78 F.R.D. 352, 358 (N.D.Tex.1978).

1006, 92 S.Ct. 573, 30 L.Ed.2d 655 (1971) ("dollar cost alone is not determinative"). Similarly, a potential loss of profits or possible loss of competitive advantage following a shift to non-discriminatory hiring does not establish business necessity under *Diaz*. To hold otherwise would permit employers within the same industry to establish different hiring standards based on the financial condition of their respective businesses. A rule prohibiting only financially successful enterprises from discriminating under Title VII, while allowing their less successful competitors to ignore the law, has no merit.

Southwest, however, has failed to establish by competent proof that revenue loss would result directly from hiring males. Analogous to the holding in Guardian Capital Corp. v. New York State Division of Human Rights, supra, 360 N.Y.S.2d at 938–39, an employer's mere "beforehand belief" that sex discrimination is a financial imperative, alone, does not establish a BFOQ for sex.

CONCLUSION

In rejecting Southwest's BFOQ defense, this court follows Justice Marshall's admonition that the BFOQ exception should not be permitted to "swallow the rule." See Phillips v. Martin Marietta Corp., 400 U.S. 542, 545, 91 S.Ct. 496, 498, 27 L.Ed.2d 613 (1971) (Marshall, J. concurring). Southwest's position knows no principled limit. Recognition of a sex BFOQ for Southwest's public contact personnel based on the airline's "love" campaign opens the door for other employers freely to discriminate by tacking on sex or sex appeal as a qualification for any public contact position where customers preferred employees of a particular sex.[29] In order not to undermine Congress' purpose to prevent employers from "refusing to hire an individual based on stereotyped characterizations of the sexes," see Phillips v. Martin Marietta Corp., supra, 400 U.S. at 545, 91 S.Ct. at 498, a BFOQ for sex must be denied where sex is merely useful for attracting customers of the opposite sex, but where hiring both sexes will not alter or undermine the essential function of the employer's business. Rejecting a wider BFOQ for sex does not eliminate the commercial exploitation of sex appeal. It only requires, consistent with the purposes of Title VII, that employer's exploit the attractiveness and allure of a sexually integrated workforce. Neither Southwest, nor the traveling public, will suffer from such a rule. More to the point, it is my judgment that this is what Congress intended.

One final observation is called for. This case has serious underpinnings, but it also has disquieting strains. These strains, and they were only that, warn that in our quest for non-racist, non-sexist goals, the demand for equal rights can be pushed to silly extremes. The rule of law in this country is so firmly embedded in our ethical regimen that little can stand up to its force—except literalistic insistence upon one's rights. And such inability to absorb the minor indignities suffered

29. See Note: "Developments in the Law—Employment Discrimination and Title VII of the Civil Rights Act of 1964," 84 Harv.L.Rev. 1109, 1185 (1971).

daily by us all without running to court may stop it dead in its tracks. We do not have such a case here—only warning signs rumbling from the facts.

H. RELIGION

TRANS WORLD AIRLINES, INC. v. HARDISON

Supreme Court of the United States, 1977.
432 U.S. 63, 97 S.Ct. 2264, 53 L.Ed.2d 113.

MR. JUSTICE WHITE delivered the opinion of the Court.

Section 703(a)(1) of the Civil Rights Act of 1964, Title VII, makes it an unlawful employment practice for an employer to discriminate against an employee or a prospective employee on the basis of his or her religion. At the time of the events involved here, a guideline of the Equal Employment Opportunity Commission (EEOC), required, as the Act itself now does, that an employer, short of "undue hardship," make "reasonable accommodations" to the religious needs of its employees. The issue in this case is the extent of the employer's obligation under Title VII to accommodate an employee whose religious beliefs prohibit him from working on Saturdays.

I

We summarize briefly the facts found by the District Court.

Petitioner Trans World Airlines (TWA) operates a large maintenance and overhaul base in Kansas City, Mo. On June 5, 1967, respondent Larry G. Hardison was hired by TWA to work as a clerk in the Stores Department at its Kansas City base. Because of its essential role in the Kansas City operation, the Stores Department must operate 24 hours per day, 365 days per year, and whenever an employee's job in that department is not filled, an employee must be shifted from another department, or a supervisor must cover the job, even if the work in other areas may suffer.

Hardison, like other employees at the Kansas City base, was subject to a seniority system contained in a collective-bargaining agreement [1] that TWA maintains with petitioner International Association of Machinists and Aerospace Workers (IAM). The seniority system is implemented by the union steward through a system of bidding by employees for particular shift assignments as they become available. The most senior employees have first choice for job and shift assignments, and the most junior employees are required to work when the

---

1. The TWA–IAM agreement provides in pertinent part:

"The principle of seniority shall apply in the application of this Agreement in all reductions or increases of force, preference of shift assignment, vacation period selection, in bidding for vacancies or new jobs, and in all promotions, demotions, or transfers involving classifications covered by this Agreement.

"Except as hereafter provided in this paragraph, seniority shall apply in selection of shifts and days off within a classification within a department * * *." App. 214.

union steward is unable to find enough people willing to work at a particular time or in a particular job to fill TWA's needs.

In the spring of 1968 Hardison began to study the religion known as the Worldwide Church of God. One of the tenets of that religion is that one must observe the Sabbath by refraining from performing any work from sunset on Friday until sunset on Saturday. The religion also proscribes work on certain specified religious holidays.

When Hardison informed Everett Kussman, the manager of the Stores Department, of his religious conviction regarding observance of the Sabbath, Kussman agreed that the union steward should seek a job swap for Hardison or a change of days off; that Hardison would have his religious holidays off whenever possible if Hardison agreed to work the traditional holidays when asked; and that Kussman would try to find Hardison another job that would be more compatible with his religious beliefs. The problem was temporarily solved when Hardison transferred to the 11 p.m.–7 a.m. shift. Working this shift permitted Hardison to observe his Sabbath.

The problem soon reappeared when Hardison bid for and received a transfer from Building 1, where he had been employed, to Building 2, where he would work the day shift. The two buildings had entirely separate seniority lists; and while in Building 1 Hardison had sufficient seniority to observe the Sabbath regularly, he was second from the bottom on the Building 2 seniority list.

In Building 2 Hardison was asked to work Saturdays when a fellow employee went on vacation. TWA agreed to permit the union to seek a change of work assignments for Hardison, but the union was not willing to violate the seniority provisions set out in the collective-bargaining contract, and Hardison had insufficient seniority to bid for a shift having Saturdays off.

A proposal that Hardison work only four days a week was rejected by the company. Hardison's job was essential and on weekends he was the only available person on his shift to perform it. To leave the position empty would have impaired supply shop functions, which were critical to airline operations; to fill Hardison's position with a supervisor or an employee from another area would simply have undermanned another operation; and to employ someone not regularly assigned to work Saturdays would have required TWA to pay premium wages.

When an accommodation was not reached, Hardison refused to report for work on Saturdays. A transfer to the twilight shift proved unavailing since that scheduled still required Hardison to work past sundown on Fridays. After a hearing, Hardison was discharged on grounds of insubordination for refusing to work during his designated shift.

Hardison, having first invoked the administrative remedy provided by Title VII, brought this action for injunctive relief in the United States District Court against TWA and IAM, claiming that his discharge by TWA constituted religious discrimination in violation of Title VII, 42 U.S.C. § 2000e–2(a)(1). He also charged that the union had discriminated against him by failing to represent him adequately in his dispute with TWA and by depriving him of his right to exercise his religious beliefs. Hardison's claim of religious discrimination rested on 1967 EEOC guidelines requiring employers "to make reasonable accommodations to the religious needs of employees" whenever such accommodation would not work an "undue hardship," 29 CFR § 1605.1 (1968), and on similar language adopted by Congress in the 1972 amendments to Title VII, 42 U.S.C. § 2000e(j) (1970 ed., Supp. V).

After a bench trial, the District Court ruled in favor of the defendants. Turning first to the claim against the union, the District Court ruled that although the 1967 EEOC guidelines were applicable to unions, the union's duty to accommodate Hardison's belief did not require it to ignore its seniority system as Hardison appeared to claim. As for Hardison's claim against TWA, the District Court rejected at the outset TWA's contention that requiring it in any way to accommodate the religious needs of its employees would constitute an unconstitutional establishment of religion. As the District Court construed the Act, however, TWA had satisfied its "reasonable accommodations" obligation, and any further accommodation would have worked an undue hardship on the company.

The Court of Appeals for the Eighth Circuit reversed the judgment for TWA. It agreed with the District Court's constitutional ruling, but held that TWA had not satisfied its duty to accommodate. Because it did not appear that Hardison had attacked directly the judgment in favor of the union, the Court of Appeals affirmed that judgment without ruling on its substantive merits.

In separate petitions for certiorari TWA and IAM contended that adequate steps had been taken to accommodate Hardison's religious observances and that to construe the statute to require further efforts at accommodation would create an establishment of religion contrary to the First Amendment of the Constitution. TWA also contended that the Court of Appeals improperly ignored the District Court's findings of fact.

We granted both petitions for certiorari. Because we agree with petitioners that their conduct was not a violation of Title VII, we need not reach the other questions presented.

The Court of Appeals found that TWA had committed an unlawful employment practice under § 703(a)(1) of the Act, 42 U.S.C. § 2000e–2(a)(1), which provides:

(a) It shall be an unlawful employment practice for an employer—

(1) to fail to refuse to hire or to discharge any individual, or otherwise to discriminate against any individual with respect to his compensation, terms, conditions, or privileges of employment, because of such individual's race, color, religion, sex, or national origin.

The emphasis of both the language and the legislative history of the statute is on eliminating discrimination in employment; similarly situated employees are not to be treated differently solely because they differ with respect to race, color, religion, sex, or national origin. This is true regardless of whether the discrimination is directed against majorities or minorities. McDonald v. Santa Fe Trail Transportation Co., 427 U.S. 273, 280, 96 S.Ct. 2574, 2578, 49 L.Ed.2d 493 (1976). See Griggs v. Duke Power Co., 401 U.S. 424, 431, 91 S.Ct. 849, 853, 28 L.Ed. 2d 158 (1971).

The prohibition against religious discrimination soon raised the question of whether it was impermissible under § 703(a)(1) to discharge or refuse to hire a person who for religious reasons refused to work during the employer's normal work-week. In 1966 an EEOC guideline dealing with this problem declared that an employer had an obligation under the statute "to accommodate to the reasonable religious needs of employees * * * where such accommodation can be made without serious inconvenience to the conduct of the business." 29 CFR § 1605.1 (1967).

In 1967 the EEOC amended its guidelines to require employers "to make reasonable accommodations to the religious needs of employees and prospective employees where such accommodations can be made without undue hardship on the conduct of the employer's business." The EEOC did not suggest what sort of accommodations are "reasonable" or when hardship to an employer becomes "undue."

This question—the extent of the required accommodation—remained unsettled when this Court, in Dewey v. Reynolds Metals Co., 402 U.S. 689, 91 S.Ct. 2186, 29 L.Ed.2d 267 (1971), affirmed by an equally divided Court the Sixth Circuit's decision in 429 F.2d 324 (1970). The discharge of an employee who for religious reasons had refused to work on Sundays was there held by the Court of Appeals not to be an unlawful employment practice because the manner in which the employer allocated Sunday work assignments was discriminatory in neither its purpose nor effect; and consistent with the 1967 EEOC guidelines, the employer had made a reasonable accommodation of the employee's beliefs by giving him the opportunity to secure a replacement for his Sunday work.

In part "to resolve by legislation" some of the issues raised in *Dewey,* 118 Cong.Rec. 706 (1972) (remarks of Sen. Randolph), Congress included the following definition of religion in its 1972 amendments to Title VII:

> The term "religion" includes all aspects of religious observance and practice, as well as belief, unless an employer demonstrates that he is unable to reasonably accommodate to an employee's or prospective employee's religious observance or practice without undue hardship on the conduct of the employer's business.

The intent and effect of this definition was to make it an unlawful employment practice under § 703(a)(1) for an employer not to make reasonable accommodations, short of undue hardship, for the religious practices of his employees and prospective employees. But like the EEOC guidelines, the statute provides no guidance for determining the degree of accommodation that is required of an employer. The brief legislative history of § 701(j) is likewise of little assistance in this regard.[9] The proponent of the measure, Senator Jennings Randolph, expressed his general desire "to assure that freedom from religious discrimination in the employment of workers is for all time guaranteed by law," 118 Cong.Rec. 705 (1972) but he made no attempt to define the precise circumstances under which the "reasonable accommodation" requirement would be applied.

In brief, the employer's statutory obligation to make reasonable accommodation for the religious observances of its employees, short of incurring an undue hardship, is clear, but the reach of that obligation has never been spelled out by Congress or by EEOC guidelines. With this in mind, we turn to a consideration of whether TWA has met its obligation under Title VII to accommodate the religious observances of its employees.

III

The Court of Appeals held that TWA had not made reasonable efforts to accommodate Hardison's religious needs under the 1967 EEOC guidelines in effect at the time the relevant events occurred. In its view, TWA had rejected three reasonable alternatives, any one of which would have satisfied its obligation without undue hardship. First, within the framework of the seniority system, TWA could have permitted Hardison to work a four-day week, utilizing in his place a supervisor or another worker on duty elsewhere. That this would have caused other shop functions to suffer was insufficient to amount to undue hardship in the opinion of the Court of Appeals. Second— according to the Court of Appeals, also within the bounds of the collective-bargaining contract—the company could have filled Hardison's Saturday shift from other available personnel competent to do the job, of which the court said there were at least 200. That this would have involved premium overtime pay was not deemed an undue hardship. Third, TWA could have arranged a "swap between Hardison and another employee either for another shift or for the Sabbath days." In response to the assertion that this would have involved a breach of the seniority provisions of the contract, the court noted that it had not been settled in the courts whether the required statutory accommodation to religious needs stopped short of transgressing seniority rules, but found it unnecessary to decide the issue because, as the Court of Appeals saw the record, TWA had not sought, and the union had therefore not declined to entertain, a possible variance from the seniority provisions

---

9. Section 701(j) was added to the 1972 amendments on the floor of the Senate. The legislative history of the measure consists chiefly of a brief floor debate in the Senate, contained in less than two pages of the Congressional Record and consisting principally of the views of the proponent of the measure, Senator Jennings Randolph. 118 Cong.Rec. 705–706 (1972).

of the collective-bargaining agreement. The company had simply left the entire matter to the union steward who the Court of Appeals said "likewise did nothing."

We disagree with the Court of Appeals in all relevant respects. It is our view that TWA made reasonable efforts to accommodate and that each of the Court of Appeals' suggested alternatives would have been an undue hardship within the meaning of the statute as construed by the EEOC guidelines.

A

It might be inferred from the Court of Appeals' opinion and from the brief of the EEOC in this Court that TWA's efforts to accommodate were no more than negligible. The findings of the District Court, supported by the record, are to the contrary. In summarizing its more detailed findings, the District Court observed:

> TWA established as a matter of fact that it did take appropriate action to accommodate as required by Title VII. It held several meetings with plaintiff at which it attempted to find a solution to plaintiff's problems. It did accommodate plaintiff's observance of his special religious holidays. It authorized the union steward to search for someone who would swap shifts, which apparently was normal procedure.

It is also true that TWA itself attempted without success to find Hardison another job. The District Court's view was that TWA had done all that could reasonably be expected within the bounds of the seniority system.

The Court of Appeals observed, however, that the possibility of a variance from the seniority system was never really posed to the union. This is contrary to the District Court's findings and to the record. The District Court found that when TWA first learned of Hardison's religious observances in April 1968, it agreed to permit the union's steward to seek a swap of shifts or days off but that "the steward reported that he was unable to work out scheduling changes and that he understood that no one was willing to swap days with plaintiff". Later, in March 1969, at a meeting held just two days before Hardison first failed to report for his Saturday shift, TWA again "offered to accommodate plaintiff's religious observance by agreeing to any trade of shifts or change of sections that plaintiff and the union could work out * * *. Any shift or change was impossible within the seniority framework and the union was not willing to violate the seniority provisions set out in the contract to make a shift or change." As the record shows, Hardison himself testified that Kussman was willing, but the union was not, to work out a shift or job trade with another employee.

We shall say more about the seniority system, but at this juncture it appears to us that the system itself represented a significant accommodation to the needs, both religious and secular, of all of TWA's employees. As will become apparent, the seniority system represents a neutral way of minimizing the number of occasions when an employee must work on a day that he would prefer to have off. Additionally, recognizing that weekend work schedules are the least popular, the company made further accommodation by reducing its work force to a bare minimum on those days.

B

We are also convinced, contrary to the Court of Appeals, that TWA itself cannot be faulted for having failed to work out a shift or job swap for Hardison. Both the union and TWA had agreed to the seniority system; the union was unwilling to entertain a variance over the objections of men senior to Hardison; and for TWA to have arranged unilaterally for a swap would have amounted to a breach of the collective-bargaining agreement.

(1)

Hardison and the EEOC insist that the statutory obligation to accommodate religious needs takes precedence over both the collective-bargaining contract and the seniority rights of TWA's other employees. We agree that neither a collective-bargaining contract nor a seniority system may be employed to violate the statute, but we do not believe that the duty to accommodate requires TWA to take steps inconsistent with the otherwise valid agreement. Collective bargaining, aimed at effecting workable and enforceable agreements between management and labor, lies at the core of our national labor policy, and seniority provisions are universally included in these contracts. Without a clear and express indication from Congress, we cannot agree with Hardison and the EEOC that an agreed-upon seniority system must give way when necessary to accommodate religious observances. The issue is important and warrants some discussion.

Any employer who, like TWA, conducts an around-the-clock operation is presented with the choice of allocating work schedules either in accordance with the preferences of its employees or by involuntary assignment. Insofar as the varying shift preferences of its employees complement each other, TWA could meet its manpower needs through voluntary work scheduling. In the present case, for example, Hardison's supervisor foresaw little difficulty in giving Hardison his religious holidays off since they fell on days that most other employees preferred to work, while Hardison was willing to work on the traditional holidays that most other employees preferred to have off.

Whenever there are not enough employees who choose to work a particular shift, however, some employees must be assigned to that shift even though it is not their first choice. Such was evidently the case with regard to Saturday work; even though TWA cut back its weekend work force to a skeleton crew, not enough employees chose those days off to staff the Stores Department through voluntary scheduling. In these circumstances, TWA and IAM agreed to give first preference to employees who had worked in a particular department the longest.

Had TWA nevertheless circumvented the the seniority system by relieving Hardison of Saturday work and ordering a senior employee to replace him, it would have denied the latter his shift preference so that Hardison could be given his. The senior employee would also have been deprived of his contractual rights under the collective-bargaining agreement.

It was essential to TWA's business to require Saturday and Sunday work from at least a few employees even though most employees preferred those days off. Allocating the burdens of weekend work was a matter for collective bargaining. In considering criteria to govern this allocation, TWA and the union had two alternatives: adopt a neutral system, such as seniority, a lottery, or rotating shifts; or allocate days off in accordance with the religious needs of its employees. TWA would have had to adopt the latter in order to assure Hardison and others like him of getting the days off necessary for strict observance of their religion, but it could have done so only at the expense of others who had strong, but perhaps nonreligious, reasons for not working on weekends. There were no volunteers to relieve Hardison on Saturdays, and to give Hardison Saturdays off, TWA would have had to deprive another employee of his shift preference at least in part because he did not adhere to a religion that observed the Saturday Sabbath.

Title VII does not contemplate such unequal treatment. The repeated, unequivocal emphasis of both the language and the legislative history of Title VII is on eliminating discrimination in employment, and such discrimination is proscribed when it is directed against majorities as well as minorities. See supra, at 2270–2271. Indeed, the foundation of Hardison's claim is that TWA and IAM engaged in religious *discrimination* in violation of § 703(a)(1) when they failed to arrange for him to have Saturdays off. It would be anomalous to conclude that by "reasonable accommodation" Congress meant that an employer must deny the shift and job preference of some employees, as well as deprive them of their contractual rights, in order to accommodate or prefer the religious needs of others, and we conclude that Title VII does not require an employer to go that far.

(2)

Our conclusion is supported by the fact that seniority systems are afforded special treatment under Title VII itself. Section 703(h) provides in pertinent part:

> Notwithstanding any other provision of this subchapter, it shall not be an unlawful employment practice for an employer to apply different standards of compensation, or different terms, conditions, or privileges of employment pursuant to a bona fide seniority or merit system * * * provided that such differences are not the result of an

intention to discriminate because of race, color, religion, sex, or national origin * * *. 42 U.S.C. § 2000e–2(h).

"[T]he unmistakable purpose of § 703(h) was to make clear that the routine application of a bona fide seniority system would not be unlawful under Title VII." International Brotherhood of Teamsters v. United States, 431 U.S. 324, 352, 97 S.Ct. 1843, 1863, 52 L.Ed.2d 396 (1977). See also United Air Lines, Inc. v. Evans, 431 U.S. 553, 97 S.Ct. 1885, 52 L.Ed.2d 571 (1977). Section 703(h) is "a definitional provision; as with the other provisions of § 703, subsection (h) delineates which employment practices are illegal and thereby prohibited and which are not." Franks v. Bowman Transportation Co., 424 U.S. 747, 758, 96 S.Ct. 1251, 1261, 47 L.Ed.2d 444 (1976). Thus, absent a discriminatory purpose, the operation of a seniority system cannot be an unlawful employment practice even if the system has some discriminatory consequences.

There has been no suggestion of discriminatory intent in this case. "The seniority system was not designed with the intention to discriminate against religion nor did it act to lock members of any religion into a pattern wherein their freedom to exercise their religion was limited. It was coincidental that in plaintiff's case the seniority system acted to compound his problems in exercising his religion." The Court of Appeals' conclusion that TWA was not limited by the terms of its seniority system was in substance nothing more than a ruling that operation of the seniority system was itself an unlawful employment practice even though no discriminatory purpose had been shown. That ruling is plainly inconsistent with the dictates of § 703(h), both on its face and as interpreted in the recent decisions of this Court.

As we have said, TWA was not required by Title VII to carve out a special exception to its seniority system in order to help Hardison to meet his religious obligations.

C

The Court of Appeals also suggested that TWA could have permitted Hardison to work a four-day week if necessary in order to avoid working on his Sabbath. Recognizing that this might have left TWA short-handed on the one shift each week that Hardison did not work, the court still concluded that TWA would suffer no undue hardship if it were required to replace Hardison either with supervisory personnel or with qualified personnel from other departments. Alternatively, the Court of Appeals suggested that TWA could have replaced Hardison on his Saturday shift with other available employees through the payment of premium wages. Both of these alternatives would involve costs to TWA, either in the form of lost efficiency in other jobs or higher wages.

To require TWA to bear more than a *de minimis* cost in order to give Hardison Saturdays off is an undue hardship.[15] Like abandon-

---

15. The dissent argues that "the costs to TWA of either paying overtime or not   replacing respondent would [not] have been more than *de minimis*." Post, at

ment of the seniority system, to require TWA to bear additional costs when no such costs are incurred to give other employees the days off that they want would involve unequal treatment of employees on the basis of their religion. By suggesting that TWA should incur certain costs in order to give Hardison Saturdays off the Court of Appeals would in effect require TWA to finance an additional Saturday off and then to choose the employee who will enjoy it on the basis of his religious beliefs. While incurring extra costs to secure a replacement for Hardison might remove the necessity of compelling another employee to work involuntarily in Hardison's place, it would not change the fact that the privilege of having Saturdays off would be allocated according to religious beliefs.

As we have seen, the paramount concern of Congress in enacting Title VII was the elimination of discrimination in employment. In the absence of clear statutory language or legislative history to the contrary, we will not readily construe the statute to require an employer to discriminate against some employees in order to enable others to observe their Sabbath.

MR. JUSTICE MARSHALL, with whom MR. JUSTICE BRENNAN joins, dissenting.

Today's decision deals a fatal blow to all efforts under Title VII to accommodate work requirements to religious practices. The Court holds, in essence, that although the EEOC regulations and the Act state that an employer must make reasonable adjustments in his work demands to take account of religious observances, the regulation and Act do not really mean what they say. An employer, the Court concludes, need not grant even the most minor special privilege to religious observers to enable them to follow their faith. As a question of social policy, this result is deeply troubling, for a society that truly values religious pluralism cannot compel adherents of minority religions to make the cruel choice of surrendering their religion or their job. And as a matter of law today's result is intolerable, for the Court adopts the very position that Congress expressly rejected in 1972, as if we were free to disregard congressional choices that a majority of this Court thinks unwise. I therefore dissent.

I

With respect to each of the proposed accommodations to respondent Hardison's religious observances that the Court discusses, it ultimately notes that the accommodation would have required "unequal treatment," ante, at 2275, 2277, in favor of the religious observer. That is quite true. But if an accommodation can be rejected simply because it

2281 n. 6. This ignores, however, the express finding of the District Court that "[b]oth of these solutions would have created an undue burden on the conduct of TWA's business", 375 F.Supp., at 891, and it fails to take account of the likelihood that a company as large as TWA may have many employees whose religious observances, like Hardison's prohibit them from working on Saturdays or Sundays.

involves preferential treatment, then the regulation and the statute, while brimming with "sound and fury," ultimately "signif[y] nothing."

The accommodation issue by definition arises only when a neutral rule of general applicability conflicts with the religious practices of a particular employee. In some of the reported cases, the rule in question has governed work attire; in other cases it has required attendance at some religious function; in still other instances, it has compelled membership in a union; and in the largest class of cases, it has concerned work schedules. What all these cases have in common is an employee who could comply with the rule only by violating what the employee views as a religious commandment. In each instance, the question is whether the employee is to be exempt from the rule's demands. To do so will always result in a privilege being "allocated according to religious beliefs," ante, at 2277, unless the employer gratuitously decides to repeal the rule *in toto*. What the statute says, in plain words, is that such allocations are required unless "undue hardship" would result.

The Court's interpretation of the statute, by effectively nullifying it, has the singular advantage of making consideration of petitioners' constitutional challenge unnecessary. The Court does not even rationalize its construction on this ground, however, nor could it, since "resort to an alternative construction to avoid deciding a constitutional question is appropriate only when such a course is 'fairly possible' or when the statute provides a 'fair alternative' construction." Swain v. Pressley, 430 U.S. 372, 378, n. 11, 97 S.Ct. 1224, 1228, 51 L.Ed.2d 411 (1977). Moreover, while important constitutional questions would be posed by interpreting the law to compel employers (or fellow employees) to incur substantial costs to aid the religious observer,[3] not all accommodations are costly, and the constitutionality of the statute is not placed in serious doubt simply because it sometimes requires an exemption from a work rule.

II

Once it is determined that the duty to accommodate sometimes requires that an employee be exempted from an otherwise valid work requirement, the only remaining question is whether this is such a case: Did TWA prove that it exhausted all reasonable accommodations, and that the only remaining alternatives would have caused undue hardship on TWA's business? To pose the question is to answer it, for all that the District Court found TWA had done to accommodate respondent's Sabbath observance was that it "held several meetings with [respondent] * * * [and] authorized the union steward to search for someone who would swap shifts." 375 F.Supp. 877, 890–891 (WD

---

3. Because of the view I take of the facts, see Part II, infra, I find it unnecessary to decide how much cost an employer must bear before he incurs "undue hardship." I also leave for another day the merits of any constitutional objections that could be raised if the law were construed to require employers (or employees) to assume significant costs in accommodating.

Mo.1974). To conclude that TWA, one of the largest air carriers in the Nation, would have suffered undue hardship had it done anything more defies both reason and common sense.

The Court implicitly assumes that the only means of accommodation open to TWA were to compel an unwilling employee to replace Hardison; to pay premium wages to a voluntary substitute; or to employ one less person during respondent's Sabbath shift. Based on this assumption, the Court seemingly finds that each alternative would have involved undue hardship not only because Hardison would have been given a special privilege, but also because either another employee would have been deprived of rights under the collective-bargaining agreement, ante, at 2274–2275, or because "more than a de minimis cost," ante, at 2277, would have been imposed on TWA. But the Court's myopic view of the available options is not supported by either the District Court's findings or the evidence adduced at trial. Thus, the Court's conclusion cannot withstand analysis, even assuming that its rejection of the alternatives it does discuss is justifiable.

To begin with, the record simply does not support the Court's assertion, made without accompanying citations, that "[t]here were no volunteers to relieve Hardison on Saturdays." Everett Kussman, the manager of the department in which respondent worked, testified that he had made no effort to find volunteers, and the union stipulated that its steward had not done so either, id., at 158. Thus, contrary to the Court's assumption, there may have been one or more employees who, for reasons of either sympathy or personal convenience, willingly would have substituted for respondent on Saturdays until respondent could either regain the non-Saturday shift he had held for the three preceding months or transfer back to his old department where he had sufficient seniority to avoid Saturday work. Alternatively, there may have been an employee who preferred respondent's Thursday-Monday daytime shift to his own; in fact, respondent testified that he had informed Kussman and the union steward that the clerk on the Sunday-Thursday night shift (the "graveyard" shift) was dissatisfied with his hours. Id., at 70. Thus, respondent's religious observance might have been accommodated by a simple trade of days or shifts without necessarily depriving any employee of his or her contractual rights and without imposing significant costs on TWA. Of course, it is also possible that no trade—or none consistent with the seniority system—could have been arranged. But the burden under the EEOC regulation is on TWA to establish that a reasonable accommodation was not possible. 29 CFR § 1605.1(c) (1976). Because it failed either to explore the possibility of a voluntary trade or to assure that its delegate, the union steward, did so, TWA was unable to meet its burden.

Nor was a voluntary trade the only option open to TWA that the Court ignores; to the contrary, at least two other options are apparent from the record. First, TWA could have paid overtime to a voluntary replacement for respondent—assuming that someone would have been willing to work Saturdays for premium pay—and passed on the cost to respondent. In fact, one accommodation Hardison suggested would have done just that by requiring Hardison to work overtime when needed at regular pay. Under this plan, the total overtime cost to the employer—and the total number of overtime hours available for other employees—would not have reflected Hardison's Sabbath absences. Alternatively, TWA could have transferred respondent back to his previous department where he had accumulated substantial seniority, as respondent also suggested. Admittedly, both options would have violated the collective-bargaining agreement; the former because the agreement required that employees working over 40 hours per week receive premium pay, and the latter because the agreement prohibited employees from transferring departments more than once every six months. But neither accommodation would have deprived any other employee of rights under the contract or violated the seniority system in any way. Plainly an employer cannot avoid his duty to accommodate by signing a contract that precludes all reasonable accommodations; even the Court appears to concede as much, ante, at 2274. Thus I do not believe it can be even seriously argued that TWA would have suffered "undue hardship" to its business had it required respondent to pay the extra costs of his replacement, or had it transferred respondent to his former department.

What makes today's decision most tragic, however, is not that respondent Hardison has been needlessly deprived of his livelihood simply because he chose to follow the dictates of his conscience. Nor is the tragedy exhausted by the impact it will have on thousands of Americans like Hardison who could be forced to live on welfare as the price they must pay for worshiping their God. The ultimate tragedy is that despite Congress' best efforts, one of this Nation's pillars of strength—our hospitality to religious diversity—has been seriously eroded. All Americans will be a little poorer until today's decision is erased.

I respectfully dissent.

Notes

1. In Estate of Thornton v. Caldor, Inc., 472 U.S. ___, 105 S.Ct. 2914, 86 L.Ed.2d 557 (1985) the Supreme Court invalidated, on First Amendment establishment grounds, a Connecticut statute prohibiting employers from requiring an employee to work on any particular day of the week which was observed by the employee as a Sabbath. The Court emphasized the mandatory, absolute and unqualified right of the employee, and the disregard of any burden or inconvenience imposed upon the employer or fellow workers. In a concurring opinion, Justice O'Connor, joined by Justice Marshall, distinguished the Connecticut statute from the employee's reasonable duty to accommodate required by Title VII.

2. Numerous cases have arisen concerning the duty to accommodate when employees, working under a collective bargaining agreement which requires union membership, have refused to join the union because of religious conviction. See. e.g. Tooley v. Martin-Marietta Corp., 648 F.2d 1239 (9th Cir.1981), cert. denied 454 U.S. 1098, 102 S.Ct. 671, 70 L.Ed.2d 639 (1981), holding that the employee and union were required by section 701(g) to permit the employees to pay an amount equal to union dues to a mutually acceptable charity.

A new section 19 was added to the National Labor Relations Act in 1980, expanding a 1974 provision which applied only to health care employees. Under the new provision employees who have religious objection to union membership are exempted from financial support but may be required by the collective agreement to contribute an amount equal to union dues and initiation fees to a non-religious charitable fund which may be designated in the agreement or, if not, chosen by the employee.

PHILBROOK v. ANSONIA BOARD OF EDUCATION

United States Court of Appeals, for the Second Circuit, 1985.
757 F.2d 476.

OAKES, CIRCUIT JUDGE:

Ronald Philbrook, a high school teacher in Ansonia, Connecticut, appeals from a judgment of the United States District Court for the District of Connecticut, Thomas F. Murphy, Judge, after a bench trial, finding that he failed to prove his claim of religious discrimination in employment against the Ansonia Board of Education (the "school board") and the Ansonia Federation of Teachers, Local 1012 (the "union"). Philbrook, a member of the Worldwide Church of God, claims that the school board's leave policies violate Title VII of the Civil Rights Act of 1964, and the free exercise clause of the First Amendment. Reaching only the statutory issue, we reverse and remand.

BACKGROUND

Appellant has taught typing and business at Ansonia High School since 1962. Some time later he began studying and observing the teachings of the Worldwide Church of God. In February, 1968, he was baptized into the church, of which he remains a member. The tenets of the church require members to refrain from secular employment on certain designated holy days each year. These holy days are determined with reference to the Hebrew calendar. Thus they often fall on different days in different years. Several of these holy days usually fall during a school week. Appellant estimated that if he is to observe the required holy days he will have to miss approximately six school days each year.

The school board's leave policies, as outlined in collective bargaining agreements with the union, have changed over time.

While none of these early agreements expressly stated that personal business leave could not be used for religious observance, it appears that the school board interpreted these categories as exclusive. Later contracts makes the exclusivity explicit. The 1969–1970 contract again allowed three days for personal business and three days for religious holidays, but the latter were no longer part of annual leave. Moreover, it stated that "[n]o annual leave, including accumulated days, shall be used for absence due to Religious Holidays in excess of 3 days per year." The 1970–1971 contract added a provision stating that personal business leave days could not be used for any of a number of enumerated activities, including "[a]ny religious activity."

The next modification of the restrictions on personal business leave is evinced by the agreement for 1978 through 1982. The contract still provided for three days, but only one was at the teacher's discretion. The other two would be authorized only after the teacher gave the reason for his or her absence. The current agreement, in effect until 1985, contains the same leave provisions.

From 1967 through 1976, appellant took unauthorized absences for religious holidays in excess of three days per year, for which the school board docked appellant's salary. Although some of the contracts during this period appear to leave the reason for personal business absences to the teacher's discretion, appellant claims to have taken no personal business leave on church holy days. In 1976, however, appellant stopped taking unauthorized leaves for religious reasons, claiming that his family could not sustain the financial strain of the docked salary. He began to schedule required hospital visits on church holy days, and on several occasions he worked on a holy day.

Appellant claims to have sought relief from both school authorities and the union. The school board has always allowed appellant to take unpaid leave for religious holy days, but appellant has repeatedly suggested two other arrangements. On the one hand, appellant has asked that the school board allow personal business leave to be used for religious observance. On the other hand, appellant has offered to pay the full cost of a substitute instead of being docked the larger pro rata salary deduction for observing religious holy days in excess of the three allotted by contract.[3] Moreover, he has agreed to supervise the substitute and to make up for days missed by doing meaningful school work at other times. The school board has consistently rejected both proposals.

DISCUSSION

APPELLANT'S PRIMA FACIE CASE

In this case of first impression, we begin by examining Title VII's prohibition against religious discrimination. Under Title VII, an employer cannot discriminate against any employee on the basis of the employee's religious beliefs unless the employer shows that he cannot "reasonably accommodate" the employee's religious needs without "un-

---

3. In 1984, it cost $30 per day to hire a substitute, while the school board would have docked appellant over $130 for one unauthorized absence.

due hardship on the conduct of the employer's business." The parties
assume and we agree that Title VII requires the plaintiff to make out a
prima facie case of discrimination, after which the burden shifts onto
the employer to show that it cannot reasonably accommodate the
plaintiff without undue hardship on the conduct of the employer's
business. See, e.g., Turpen v. Missouri-Kansas-Texas Railroad Co., 736
F.2d 1022, 1026 (5th Cir.1984); Anderson v. General Dynamics Convair
Aerospace Division, 589 F.2d 397, 401 (9th Cir.1978), cert. denied, 442
U.S. 921, 99 S.Ct. 2848, 61 L.Ed.2d 290 (1979). While the district court
omitted to apply this burden of proof sequence or to make the findings
required under it, necessitating remand, we state the guidelines for the
case on remand.

We first adopt the approach to plaintiff's *prima facie* case taken by
several courts of appeal:

> A plaintiff in a [Title VII] case makes out a *prima facie* case of
> religious discrimination by proving: (1) he or she has a bona fide
> religious belief that conflicts with an employment requirement; (2) he
> or she informed the employer of this belief; (3) he or she was disci-
> plined for failure to comply with the conflicting employment require-
> ment.

On the record before us plaintiff has almost certainly satisfied this
prima facie standard.

We reject the school board's invitation to hold that appellant has
failed to establish the sincerity of his religious beliefs. The district
court expressly declined to make any such finding. In fact, on the
record below, we would be inclined to reverse a finding of insincerity as
clearly erroneous.

Turning to the remaining requirements of plaintiff's prima facie
showing, appellant gave unrebutted testimony that he informed the
school board and the union of his need to be absent on religious holy
days, although it is not clear when the union became aware of appellant's needs. On remand, such a finding might be necessary to determine the amount of back pay appellant is entitled to receive, assuming
that issue is reached. In addition, it seems clear that appellant
suffered a detriment from the conflict between his religious practices
and the employment requirements. The district court placed much
reliance on the fact that appellant was not forced into a choice between
his job and his religious beliefs, but we hold that such a choice cannot
be distinguished from the choice here between giving up a portion of his
salary and his religious beliefs. While we acknowledge that some
courts have stated that discharge was required to make a *prima facie*
showing of discrimination, see, e.g., *Brown*, 601 F.2d at 959, Title VII
prohibits not only discrimination in hiring and firing but also discrimination "with respect to compensation, terms, conditions or privileges."

"REASONABLE ACCOMMODATION" AND "UNDUE HARDSHIP"

The crucial issues in this case remaining for determination involve
interpreting the meaning of and relationship between the terms "rea-

sonable accommodation" and "undue hardship." The central precedent, of course is Trans World Airlines, Inc. v. Hardison, 432 U.S. 63, 97 S.Ct. 2264, 53 L.Ed.2d 113 (1977), the only case in which the Supreme Court has addressed "reasonable accommodation" and "undue hardship" under Title VII.

Hardison did not sound a death knell to the employer's duty to accommodate under Title VII. In *Anderson,* 589 F.2d at 402, the Ninth Circuit rejected a union's argument that any hypothetical hardship constitutes "undue hardship," noting that "[u]ndue means something greater than hardship. Undue hardship cannot be proved by assumptions nor by opinions based on hypothetical facts." Similarly, the *Brown* court held that speculative costs to the employer could not discharge its burden of proving undue hardship. 601 F.2d at 961.

The school board argues that we should find that its longstanding accommodation of three days of paid leave and additional days of unpaid leave for religious observance constitutes a reasonable accommodation and thus satisfies its duty to accommodate, citing the Tenth Circuit's decision in Pinsker v. Joint District No. 28J, 735 F.2d 388, 391 (10th Cir.1984). The *Pinsker* court held that a policy allowing two days of paid leave for religious reasons and additional days of unpaid leave satisfied the duty to accommodate. We presume that Ansonia's leave policy is also "reasonable." And if Title VII's duty to accommodate were to be defined without reference to undue hardship, we would hold that the school board has satisfied its burden. The duty to accommodate, however, cannot be defined without reference to undue hardship. In many circumstances, more than one accommodation could be called "reasonable." Where the employer and the employee each propose a reasonable accommodation, Title VII requires the employer to accept the proposal the employee prefers unless that accommodation causes undue hardship on the employer's conduct of his business.

Although the courts interpreting Title VII's duty to accommodate have never expressly articulated this point, their analyses are consistent with this approach. In most cases, the court is called upon to assess only the employee's proposal; the court does not have to assess the propriety of the employer's offering one accommodation but rejecting the employee's proposed accommodation. Nevertheless, the Fifth Circuit in *Turpen* did state, as we have suggested above, that the reasonableness and undue hardship questions were "interlocking." Previously, in Brener v. Diagnostic Center Hospital, 671 F.2d 141 (5th Cir.1982), the Fifth Circuit had interpreted the duty to accommodate in the same way we do today. The *Brener* court analyzed the reasonableness of the employer's proposed accommodation, id. at 145–46, but went on to examine the employee's proposed accommodations to determine whether any did not cause the employer undue hardship. The implication is that, even if the employer proposes a reasonable accommodation it has not satisfied its duty to accommodate unless the employee's suggested accommodations would lead to greater than de minimis cost.

The EEOC's recent guidelines on religious discrimination—while not dispositive of the interpretation of Title VII, see *Gilbert,* 429 U.S. at 140–42, 97 S.Ct. at 410–11—also support the approach we above suggest. See 29 C.F.R. § 1605.2(c)(2) (1984).[7]

As noted, appellant has offered two proposed accommodations—the use of personal business leave for religious observance and the payment of the cost of a substitute in exchange for not being docked salary for religious leave in excess of three days. On remand the district court must determine whether accepting either of appellant's proposed accommodations would cause undue hardship. We note, however, that on the record before us it appears that neither of the accommodations would lead to greater than de minimis costs.

Appellant clearly prefers that the school board allow him to use personal business leave for religious holy days. The critical factual question concerning this proposal is the past and current scope of the personal business leave provisions. As noted earlier, from 1968 through 1977 three personal business days could be taken at the teacher's discretion, and from 1977 to the present, at least one could be taken at the teacher's discretion. This leaves in the air whether any such day may be taken for any reason except those specifically mentioned, such as religious reasons. Thus, the question is open whether they are usable for various secular purposes, including activities not inconsistent with religious observance. The provision does include the words "legitimate and necessary," but left unsaid is whether leaving the reason to the teacher's discretion abrogates this limiting language. Appellant claims that the provision allows attendance at charity meetings, while the school board argues that its scope is much more narrow. One of the appellant's exhibits at trial—entitled "Teacher Absence Report"—indicates that many teachers have taken at least one personal business day a year and some more than one. It also appears that personal business days are taken more frequently than religious holy days. The presence of a contract provision that allows leave for limited secular activities, such as sick leave or leave for court appearances, does not show that additional paid leave for religious observance in lieu of personal business leave would not cause undue hardship. Employers and unions must be free to outline specific types of paid leaves in a

---

7. Section 1605.2(c)(2) provides:

(2) When there is more than one method of accommodation available which would not cause undue hardship, the Commission will determine whether the accommodation offered is reasonable by examining:

(i) The alternatives for accommodation considered by the employer or labor organization; and

(ii) The alternatives for accommodation, if any, actually offered to the individual requiring accommodation. Some alternatives for accommodating religious practices might disadvantage the individual with respect to his or her employment opportunities [*sic*], such as compensation, terms, conditions, or privileges of employment. Therefore, when there is more than one means of accommodation which would not cause undue hardship, the employer or labor organization must offer the alternative which least disadvantages the individual with respect to his or her employment opportunities.

contract without the threat of being charged with religious discrimination. But if the personal business leave provision is as broad as appellant claims, it becomes difficult to believe that dropping the religious exception causes undue hardship.[8]

Even if the district court finds that the personal business accommodation would lead to undue hardship—or if the school board and the union were to agree to take the personal business leave provisions out of the contract altogether—the district court must assess the cost of accepting appellant's substitute proposal. Appellant has offered to pay for a substitute and even to work on other days to make up for the time missed. While there is some testimony below concerning the cost of using substitutes, the court never focused on the cost of appellant's proposed accommodation. The Superintendent of Schools testified that it is difficult to find certified substitutes, especially those qualified to teach typing and business; that the quality of learning with a substitute is low; that substitutes often have difficulty keeping discipline; and that when substitutes teach classroom equipment is often damaged. Yet several questions still must be addressed. Because presumably appellant would know about his upcoming religious holy days well in advance, it is possible that he can work out an arrangement that avoids the traditional problems of finding a qualified substitute at the last minute. While we recognize the difficulty of discipline in a high school classroom, it may also be that discipline and teaching difficulties can be avoided in a business course by having appellant closely supervise the substitute.

On the record before us, we decline to accept the school board's argument that the substitute accommodation as a matter of law poses greater than de minimis costs. This case thus might well be distinguishable from *Hardison*. The *Hardison* Court held that a need for premium pay or a loss of efficiency can cause undue hardship. Under the proposed substitute accommodation, the school board would not be paying premium wages. Appellant is not asking to have his religious activities subsidized, as the school board claims. Appellant has offered to pay the cost of the substitute and to make up for time off: appellant does not ask for payment for time when he is not working. Moreover, we are not ready to hold that the school board has shown that there will be a greater than de minimis loss in efficiency. The *Hardison* Court held that using a supervisor or an employee from another area amounted to a greater than de minimis cost because it left other operations undermanned. The same problems may not arise under the substitute accommodation. One would suppose that the school system

---

8. On remand, the district court must make findings about the use of personal business leave from 1968 through the present. Appellant does not only seek prospective relief; he also seeks back pay.

In its brief on appeal, the school board seems to assume that the burden is on appellant to show that the personal business accommodation would not cause undue hardship. It is not: once appellant has made out a *prima facie* case, the school board has the burden of showing that an accommodation *would* cause undue hardship.

has the ability to find qualified substitutes. If appellant communicates with the substitute before and after the days he must miss, there may well be no appreciable loss in the quality of education, where the number of additional substitute days appears to be three.[10] Cf. *Turpen,* 736 F.2d at 1028 & n. 6 (holding that it was not clearly erroneous for the district court to find that a substitute accommodation caused undue hardship when there was no built-in system for substitution).

The school board also suggests that accommodating appellant would constitute preferential treatment. We disagree. While we acknowledge the cautionary language of the Supreme Court in *Hardison,* we do not interpret *Hardison* as vitiating the employer's duty to accommodate. Appellant's proposal for the use of personal business leave for religious observance is not one seeking preferential treatment. He is asking the school board and the union to change its leave policy as applied to everyone. Nor would his substitute accommodation allocate a privilege "according to religious beliefs." *Hardison,* 432 U.S. at 85, 97 S.Ct. at 2277. Appellant has asked to be treated differently; he has not asked for privileged treatment. In exchange for additional days off, he is willing to make up for time off *and* pay for the substitute. Differential treatment cannot be equated with privileged treatment. Accepting the school board's argument would "preclude all forms of accommodation and defeat the very purpose behind § 2000e(j)." *Brown,* 601 F.2d at 962.[11]

---

10. 29 C.F.R. § 1605.2(d)(1)(i) advocates the use of "voluntary substitutes" as an example of reasonable accommodation without undue hardship:

(i) Voluntary Substitutes and "Swaps"

Reasonable accommodation without undue hardship is generally possible where a voluntary substitute with substantially similar qualifications is available. One means of substitution is the voluntary swap. In a number of cases, the securing of a substitute has been left entirely up to the individual seeking the accommodation. The Commission believes that the obligation to accommodate requires that employers and labor organizations facilitate the securing of a voluntary substitute with substantially similar qualifications. Some means of doing this which employers and labor organizations should consider are: to publicize policies regarding accommodation and voluntary substitution; to promote an atmosphere in which such substitutions are favorably regarded; to provide a central file, bulletin board or other means for matching voluntary substitutes with positions for which substitutes are needed.

11. Perhaps *Hardison* may be read as equating "undue hardship" with preferen-

tial treatment. That is to say, accepting an accommodation that would lead to greater than de minimis costs to the employer constitutes under *Hardison* preferential treatment when looked at from the perspective of the employees. Yet accepting a proposal that would not cause undue hardship, does not constitute preferential treatment. We need not reach this question, however.

Moreover, in light of our remand, we do not address the hypothetical question whether accepting either of appellant's proposed accommodations constitutes an unconstitutional establishment of religion. We do note, however, that several courts of appeals have held that Title VII's duty to accommodate does not run afoul of the First Amendment. See McDaniel v. Essex International, Inc., 696 F.2d 34, 37 (6th Cir. 1982); Tooley v. Martin-Marietta Corp., 648 F.2d 1239, 1244–46 (9th Cir.), cert. denied, 454 U.S. 1098, 102 S.Ct. 671, 70 L.Ed. 2d 639 (1981); Nottelson v. Smith Steel Workers, 643 F.2d 445, 453–55 (7th Cir.), cert. denied, 454 U.S. 1046, 102 S.Ct. 587, 70 L.Ed.2d 488 (1981); Hardison v. Trans World Airlines, Inc., 527 F.2d 33, 43–44 (8th Cir.1975), rev'd on other grounds, 432 U.S. 63, 97 S.Ct. 2264, 53 L.Ed.2d 113 (1977).

UNION LIABILITY

Finally, we reject the union's argument that we find it not liable for any religious discrimination on the record before us. Title VII places a duty on unions not "to cause or attempt to cause an employer to discriminate against an individual." 42 U.S.C. § 2000e–2(c)(3). We have stated previously that a union's liability depends on its "responsibility for the discrimination." EEOC v. Enterprise Association Steamfitters Local No. 638, 542 F.2d 579, 586 (2d Cir.1976), cert. denied, 430 U.S. 911, 97 S.Ct. 1186, 51 L.Ed.2d 588 (1977). This conclusion is consistent with that of other courts. See, e.g., Hardison v. Trans World Airlines, Inc., 527 F.2d 33, 42–43 (8th Cir.1975), rev'd on other grounds, 432 U.S. 63, 97 S.Ct. 2264, 53 L.Ed.2d 113 (1977). In *Hardison*, the Eighth Circuit wrote that "the union may be held liable if it purposefully acts or refuses to act in a manner which prevents or obstructs a reasonable accommodation by the employer so as to cause the employer to discriminate." Id. at 42. In this case, various union officers testified that they had proposed changes in the collective bargaining agreement's leave policies, but all were rejected. Appellant claims that the union never really pushed for these changes. The union did join appellant in seeking arbitration on appellant's leave policy grievance, but, at the same time, it appears that the union declined to enter into an EEOC conciliation agreement with appellant. Clearly, any further discussion of the issue must await a more detailed development of the facts.

Judgment reversed and remanded for proceedings not inconsistent with the foregoing.

POLLACK, SENIOR DISTRICT JUDGE (dissenting):

The issue in this case is whether the School Board should be forced to pay a teacher for not working. There is no indication that the School Board, the Union, or the collective bargaining agreement intended to discriminate against anyone, including plaintiff, on the basis of religion. The School Board and Union, and the membership of the latter, adopted a facially neutral policy giving each employee three days of paid religious leave and three days of paid secular personal leave, which were not to be interchangeable. If an employee wished to take additional religious leave, he was privileged to do so at his own cost without suffering any impact on his employment status.

The majority views the School Board's policy as one that facially discriminates on the basis of religion because it "affords some teachers all the leave they need for religious reasons but does not extend that benefit to members of religious groups that have more than three holy days per year." However, neither case law nor the legislative history of the statute support the majority's expansive position that an employer "discriminates" within the meaning of Title VII if he refuses to give an employee more than three paid religious days when the employee desires more paid leave.

The legislative history makes it clear that Title VII was not concerned with the "no work-no pay" situation. Rather, as the Senate Floor managers explained, the statute was concerned with discriminatory practices, i.e., the situation where an employer

> refuse[d] to hire or to discharge any individual or otherwise to discriminate against him with respect to compensation or terms or conditions of employment because of such individual's race, color, religion, sex, or national origin *in such a way as to deprive them of employment opportunities or otherwise affect adversely their employment status.*

110 Cong.Rec. 7212 (1964) (April 8, 1964) (Interpretative Memorandum of Title VII submitted by Senators Case and Clark) (emphasis added).

Moreover, the nature of the discrimination that lies at the base of Title VII matters was starkly explained in language that admits of no confusion. The Senate sponsors stated that:

> To discriminate is to make distinctions or differences in the treatment of employees * * *

Id. at 7218.

The leave policy at issue here does not make distinctions between employees or deny plaintiff the opportunity to pursue his employment and yet have time off to observe his religious holy days. This is not a case where plaintiff is denied employment because his religious beliefs preclude him from working on certain days. See, e.g., Reid v. Memphis Publishing Co., 468 F.2d 346 (6th Cir.1972). Nor is plaintiff subject to discharge because his religion forbids him to work on these days. See, e.g., Brown v. General Motors Corp., 601 F.2d 956 (8th Cir.1979). Likewise, the policy has no adverse impact on plaintiff's opportunities for advancement; plaintiff has not been denied a promotion because of his religious beliefs. See, e.g., Haring v. Blumenthal, 471 F.Supp. 1172 (S.D.N.Y.1979).

The School Board's policy neither deprives the plaintiff of employment opportunities nor adversely affects his employment status. As Judge Murphy succinctly stated, "[P]laintiff could go without let or hindrance whenever and wherever he wished" (Op. at 13)—but at his own expense. Since the policy does not "discriminate" within Title VII's use and meaning of that term, the statute may not be invoked against the School Board.

It is also clear that the Board has agreeably and reasonably accommodated the plaintiff. Recently, in Pinsker v. Joint District No. 28J, 735 F.2d 388 (10th Cir.1984), the Tenth Circuit held that a school board made a reasonable accommodation by permitting a teacher to take unpaid leave for religious observance. In *Pinsker,* teachers had a pool of 12 days of paid leave, of which two could be used for "special leave" purposes including religious observance. Plaintiff argued that Title VII required the Board to adopt a leave policy that was less burdensome to religious practices. The court disagreed, stating that the statute does not require employers to "accommodate the employee's

practices in such a way that spares the employee any cost whatsoever."
Id. at 390–91.

In *Pinsker,* the court also held that

> [d]efendant's policy and practices jeopardized neither [plaintiff's] job
> nor his observation of religious holidays. Because teachers are likely
> to have not only different religions but also different degrees of
> devotion to their religions, a school district cannot be expected to
> negotiate leave policies broad enough to suit every employee's religious
> needs perfectly.

Id. at 391.

The neutral leave policy challenged here is embodied in a valid
collective bargaining agreement. "Collective bargaining, aimed at effecting workable and enforceable agreements between management and
labor, lies at the core of our national labor policy * * *" Trans
World Airlines, Inc. v. Hardison, 432 U.S. 63, 79, 97 S.Ct. 2264, 2274, 53
L.Ed.2d 113 (1977). Where, as here, the agreement neither impairs
employment status nor imposes any artificial, arbitrary, and unnecessary barriers to employment, then, as the Supreme Court stated in
Hardison, "we do not believe that the duty to accommodate requires
[the employer] to take steps inconsistent with the otherwise valid
[collective bargaining agreement]." Id. Paid leave from employment is
neither contractually nor Constitutionally mandated.

Since the School Board's leave policy does not discriminate on the
basis of religion, plaintiff failed—as early as the close of his case—to
make out a prima facie case. Consequently, the judgment of dismissal
should be affirmed.

FELDSTEIN v. THE CHRISTIAN
SCIENCE MONITOR

United States District Court for the District of Massachusetts, 1983.
555 F.Supp. 974.

MAZZONE, DISTRICT JUDGE.

This matter arises from a suit brought under Title VII of the Civil
Rights Act of 1964, 42 U.S.C. § 2000e et seq., by the plaintiff, Mark
Feldstein, against the defendants, the Christian Science Monitor (the
Monitor), the First Church of Christ, Scientist (the Church), and the
Christian Science Publishing Society (the Publishing Society). The
matter is before the Court on defendants' motion for summary judgment. The defendants bring their motion on several grounds: first,
that the Monitor is a religious activity of a religious organization and is
therefore entitled to discriminate in its employment practices in favor
of co-religionists; second, that as a result of the Monitor's status, this
Court is prohibited from inquiring into the presence or absence of a
religious character in particular jobs; and finally, that the plaintiff's
constitutional challenges to Title VII's treatment of religious activity,

and specifically his challenge to the 1972 amendment to section 702 of the Act, 42 U.S.C. § 2000e–1, are without merit.

The undisputed facts in the case are as follows. In January of 1979, Feldstein inquired at the Monitor whether there would be job openings on its news reporting staff upon his graduation from college in June. At that time, Feldstein was a college student interested in pursuing a career in journalism. Upon making his inquiry, Feldstein was instructed to contact the Personnel Department of the Church, where he was asked if he was a member of the Christian Scientist Church. He indicated that he was not, and was informed that he would stand little, if any, chance of becoming employed by the Monitor as a reporter, as only Christian Scientists were hired except in the rare circumstance that no qualified member of the Church was available. Feldstein nevertheless requested and obtained an employment application for a reporter's position.

The employment application, used for positions throughout the Church, contains several questions relating to religious practice, including "Are you * * * a member of the Mother Church? A branch Church member? Class taught?"; "Are you free from the use of liquor, tobacco, drugs, medicine?"; "Do you subscribe to the Christian Science periodicals?"; "Are you a daily student of the lesson-sermon?"; and inquiries directed to the applicant's present and past religious affiliation. References are sought from "two Christian Scientists who can comment on your character and your practice of Christian Science." The application closes with the following statement:

> The First Church of Christ, Scientist, may by law apply the test of religious qualifications to its employment policies. Those who meet this requirement and are otherwise qualified will be hired, promoted and transferred without regard to their race, national origin, sex, color or age.

Feldstein filed his application with the Church in March of 1979, together with a copy of his *curriculum vitae,* letters of recommendation, and a portfolio of newspaper articles that he had written. In April, he was notified by a Church Personnel Representative that his application for employment as a reporter had been rejected. Feldstein has alleged, and the record would seem to support, that his application for employment was not given a full consideration because he was not a Christian Scientist.

Title VII of the Civil Rights Act of 1964 was originally passed as an expression of Congress' laudable intention to eliminate all forms of unjustified discrimination in employment, whether such discrimination be based on race, color, religion, sex, or national origin. This posed a sharp question under the Establishment Clause of the First Amendment to the United States Constitution as to whether Congress could properly regulate the employment practices, and specifically the preference for co-religionists, of religious organizations in matters related to their religious activities. As a result, the original Title VII contained an exemption from the operation of Title VII's proscriptions with respect to the employment of co-religionists to perform work related to the employer's religious activity. Church-affiliated educational institutions were also permitted to hire on the basis of religion.

In 1972, a number of amendments to Title VII were proposed in an effort to alter and expand the existing exemption for religious organizations. The most sweeping of these, introduced by Senator Sam Ervin, proposed to remove religious organizations entirely from the requirements of Title VII. Concern was expressed by Senator Ervin that unless the amendment was passed, an unconstitutional encroachment on the operations of religious organizations by the government would result:

> It is impossible to separate the religious and non-religious activities of a religious corporation or religious association or religious educational institution or religious society from its other activities * * * Congress does not keep the states—that is, the Government's—hands out of religion by enacting a bill which says that the Government can regulate and control the employment practices of all of the religious groups in this country * * * in respect to all of their employees who are not strictly engaged in carrying out the religious affairs of those institutions.

Legislative History of the Equal Employment Opportunity Act of 1972, 1212 and 1223 (1972).

Of the two goals initially sought by Senator Ervin and others in the efforts to amend the religious organization exemption in Title VII—permitting religious organizations to discriminate in employment on any grounds, and not merely on the basis of religion; and expanding the exemption to include non-religious as well as religious activities of religious groups—only one was ultimately achieved. Title VII was amended to eliminate the qualification that only religious activities of religious organizations would be exempt from suit based on religious discrimination. Section 2000e–1 provides, as a result of the 1972 amendment:

> This subchapter shall not apply * * * to a religious corporation, association, educational institution, or society with respect to the employment of individuals of a particular religion to perform work connected with the carrying on by such corporation, association, educational institution or society of its activities.

42 U.S.C. § 2000e–1.

It is clear that the disposition of this matter turns on two key issues: first, whether the Monitor is a religious activity of a religious organization and therefore within the limited exemption provided by Congress in the Civil Rights Act of 1964; and second, if it is not a religious activity of a religious organization, whether the 1972 amendment to Title VII excluding from the scope of Title VII *all* activities of whatever nature of a religious organization is constitutional in light of the requirements of the Free Exercise and Establishment clauses of the First Amendment.

It is self-evident, as well as uncontested, that the First Church of Christ, Scientist is a religious organization. The status of the Christian Science Publishing Society and of the Monitor is less clear. The plaintiff has argued that the Monitor is a highly regarded and impartial newspaper carrying news stories, articles, features, columns and editorials that are secular in nature and content. The defendants take exception to this characterization of the Monitor and make reference to a number of facts in support of their position that the newspaper is a religious activity of a religious organization and therefore exempt from regulation under Title VII.

According to the uncontroverted affidavit of Michael West, Treasurer of the Christian Science Church and Trustee of the Christian Science Publishing Society, the Monitor is published by the Christian Science Publishing Society, an organ of the Christian Science Church. Both the Publishing Society and the Monitor were founded by Mary Baker Eddy, the founder of the Christian Science faith. The deed of trust of the Publishing Society declares as its purpose "more effectually promoting and extending the religion of Christian Science." According to the by-laws of the Church, it is the "privilege and duty" of every member of the Church to subscribe to periodicals published by the Church, including the Monitor. The Board of Trustees of the Church is directed to "conduct the business of the Christian Science Publishing Society on a strictly Christian basis, for the promotion of the interests of Christian Science." The Board of Directors of the Church is charged with the duty to keep Church periodicals "ably edited and * * * abreast of the times," and elects the editors and manager of the Publishing Society. The by-laws specifically provide that no-one who is not acceptable to the Board shall in any manner be connected with the publishing efforts of the Church. The Board of Directors is responsible for the editorial content of the Monitor and review on a daily basis material appearing in the Monitor.

The Church organization is also involved with the operation of the Monitor in a financial capacity. The by-laws require that the Church provide a "suitable building" for the Monitor's operations. The Church routinely subsidizes the Monitor, which otherwise would run at a significant loss. The Monitor elects, on religious grounds, not to carry advertisements for a number of products, including liquor, tobacco, drugs, medicines, vitamins, and energy stimulants. Advertising policy is formulated in part by Monitor Advertising Information Committees appointed by the Publishing Society on recommendation of local branch churches. Circulation is developed through Christian Science Reading Rooms, and by Church members who act without compensation as circulation representatives.

The plaintiff does not contest that the Christian Science Church is intimately involved with the management, the day-to-day operations and the financial affairs of the Monitor. Paragraph 5 of his complaint states in part:

> Defendant First Church of Christ, Scientist is a non-incorporated religious association * * * Control of the Church is vested in a Board of Directors who serve in accordance with terms set out in the *Church Manual.* Pursuant to the *Church Manual, the Board has ultimate authority for and responsibility over the policy and operations of the Monitor.*

> *   *   *   *   *   *   *   *   *

> Defendant Christian Science Publishing Society * * * is in the business of publishing and does publish a number of publications including the *Monitor. Control over the daily operations of the Publishing Society, including those daily operations involved in publishing the Monitor, is vested in a Board of Trustees which in turn is directly accountable to the Board of Directors of the Church.*

Plaintiff's Complaint, ¶ 5 (emphasis supplied).

Numerous administrative bodies have considered the status of the Monitor and have determined that it is a religious activity, including the Equal Employment Opportunity Commission (finding it had no jurisdiction over the Monitor), the Internal Revenue Service (finding in 1977 that the Monitor is "merely a department of the First Church of Christ, Scientist" and in 1955 that the Publishing Society is "operated exclusively for religious purposes"), the Department of National Revenue of Canada, the state income tax administrators for Illinois and Massachusetts, and the District of Columbia unemployment compensation board. The District of Columbia board noted:

> The question has been raised as to whether or not the operation of the Christian Science Monitor should unclass the Society as an exclusively religious organization. From the information submitted it would appear that the primary purpose of the Monitor is a missionary one to try and interest individuals in Christian Science. In addition, the Monitor carries a religious message each day. It is believed, that as its primary purpose is religious, that any other purpose would appear purely * * * ancillary.

Certainly it is true that "not every enterprise cloaking itself in the name of religion can claim the Constitutional protection conferred by that status." Van Schaick v. Church of Scientology of California, Inc., 535 F.Supp. 1125, 1144 (D.Mass.1982) quoting Founding Church of Scientology v. United States, 409 F.2d 1146, 1160 (D.C.Cir.1969). Similarly, not every endeavour that is affiliated, however tenuously, with a recognized religious body may qualify as a religious activity of that body and come within the scope of the protection from governmental involvement that is afforded by the First Amendment. At the same time, however, a religious activity of a religious organization does not lose that special status merely because it holds some interest for persons not members of the faith, or occupies a position of respect in the secular world at large. Though "the 'wall between church and state' is not absolute." I am nevertheless unwilling to involve the federal court in what is ultimately an internal administrative matter of a religious activity.

While fully crediting the plaintiff's statements that the Monitor holds itself out as an objective and unbiased reporter of world news and events, I cannot ignore the close and significant relationship existing between the Christian Science Church, the Publishing Society and the Monitor; or the declared purpose, both at the time of its founding and until the present, of the Monitor to promulgate and advance the tenets of Christian Science. I find the conclusion inescapable that the Monitor is itself a religious activity of a religious organization, albeit one with a recognized position and an established reputation in the secular community.

Having concluded that the Monitor is a religious activity of a religious organization, I find that the constitutionality of that part of section 702 of Title VII, 42 U.S.C. § 2000e–1, that extends the exemption provided for religious organizations to *all* their activities, secular and religious, is simply not here implicated. However, were it to be, I would have grave doubts as to its ability to pass constitutional muster under the Establishment clause of the First Amendment. It is not mandated under the Constitution that Congress prohibit discrimination on grounds of religion in private sector employment. However, having elected to do so in the Civil Rights Act of 1964, the Congress *is* under a constitutional obligation to do so in a way that neither favors nor disfavors secular, private sector enterprises that may be conducted by religious organizations.

> The exemption presently afforded by Title VII, 42 U.S.C. § 2000e–1, is a remarkably clumsy accommodation of religious freedom with the compelling interests of the state, providing on the one hand far too broad a shield for the secular activities of religiously affiliated entities with not the remotest claim to first amendment protection while on the other hand permitting intrusions into wholly religious functions.

Equal Employment Opportunity Commission v. Southwestern Baptist Theological Seminary, 485 F.Supp. 255, 260 (N.D.Tex.1980); see King's Garden, Inc. v. F.C.C., 498 F.2d 51, 55–57 (D.C.Cir.), cert. denied 419 U.S. 996, 95 S.Ct. 309, 42 L.Ed.2d 269 (1974). It is well established that the expression of a preference for all religions is as constitutionally infirm as a preference for, or a discrimination against, a particular religion. See Committee for Public Education v. Nyquist, 413 U.S. 756, 771, 93 S.Ct. 2955, 2964, 37 L.Ed.2d 948 (1973) and cases cited therein. Either would fly in the face of the terms and requirements of the First Amendment.

Because I find that the Monitor is a religious activity of a religious organization, I find that it is permissible for the Monitor to apply a test of religious affiliation to candidates for employment. Therefore, I find as a matter of law that the defendants have not committed an unlawful employment practice under the Civil Rights Act of 1964. The defendants' motion for summary judgment is granted and the complaint is dismissed.

So Ordered.

I. NATIONAL ORIGIN

EREBIA v. CHRYSLER PLASTIC PRODUCTS CORPORATION

United States Court of Appeals, for the Sixth Circuit, 1985.
772 F.2d 1250.

PHILLIPS, SENIOR CIRCUIT JUDGE.

This case involves a claim under 42 U.S.C. § 1981 alleging that defendant-appellant Chrysler Plastic Products Corporation was responsible for a hostile work environment where plaintiff-appellee Federico Erebia was subjected to ethnic slurs. The jury returned a verdict in favor of plaintiff, awarding $10,000 in compensatory damages and $30,000 in punitive damages. Defendant appeals.

Plaintiff Erebia testified in his own behalf and was his only witness. He testified he had lived in Mexico from age two until twenty-two, returning to the United States in 1957. His parents were Mexican. He had been employed by Chrysler Plastic Products Corporation for eighteen years beginning November 8, 1965. At the time of trial he was an Inspection Supervisor. During much of his employment he has worked in the evenings as a supervisor in the calendar department, where ingredients are rolled into a film for production. He testified that he had worked in other departments as well.

Due to the statute of limitations period, plaintiff testified only to events occurring after February 3, 1977. He testified that after this date he had many problems with hourly employees. He testified that an hourly employee, Rolland Forney, who had a mailman classification, "kept calling me names, and it got to the point where, you know, you can only take so much. They're going to have to start answering because I have never got any backing from the company as far as for discipline." Erebia was called "a wet bag [sic], tomato picker." Plaintiff testified that Rolland Forney refused to follow his instructions "everyday * * * on a daily basis" from 1977 until 1980 when Forney was laid off. Forney would refuse to follow instructions, as he told plaintiff, because "I was Mexican and he was white."

Plaintiff referred to Marv Keegan, a production superintendent, as "my boss." Plaintiff complained to Keegan about the situation on virtually a daily basis. Keegan did nothing in response except to advise Erebia to "build up a case."

Plaintiff testified that an hourly employee in the laminating department under his supervision, Wilbur Wood, also directed racial slurs at him. Plaintiff stated: "He mainly told me to go back to Mexico, there was some white person that could be doing my job instead of a

Mexican." Wood refused to follow plaintiff's directions almost every day from April of 1980 to the end of July the same year, when Erebia was laid off.

Plaintiff stated that he constantly kept seeing his boss, Keegan, about the problem and approached the general foreman, Jim Lilje, as well. The managers did nothing in response. Erebia discussed the problems on two occasions with personnel manager Jack Lenz. Plaintiff testified: "His advice was that I was a hot headed Mexican, that I should put a deaf ear to it, that it was nothing but shop talk to me." Plaintiff replied that "everybody was just too much to be ignored."

At a second meeting with Lenz in the summer of 1977, plaintiff explained that the employees refused to abide by his instructions and abused him constantly. He was told that he should take the slurs and abuse "like nothing." Erebia was "highly upset" about the abuses and failure to follow instructions and the poor backing of management. He criticized management. Lenz became upset and made the statement, "I'll hurt you economically."

On cross-examination, Erebia admitted that he engaged in "shop talk" and that it was common in his employment to use profanity. He also admitted that he had called an hourly employee a "gringo" after the employee had called him a "wet back." Plaintiff admitted that he had, in December of 1977, told the husband of a plant worker, a Mr. Baum, that he should go back to Germany and he was a "queer communist."

Plaintiff testified that "shop talk" is an exchange that is acceptable to both parties involved and would not encompass conversations to which someone objects. He testified that he had not used any slurs where anyone objected. He stated that he knew of no cases other than his own where racial slurs were directed to supervisors by hourly employees.

The defense did not call as witnesses any of the individuals plaintiff said had slurred him. Nor did it call any of the management employees plaintiff testified had failed to respond to his complaints.

II

We turn first to appellant Chrysler's contention that there was insufficient evidence to support the jury's verdict that Chrysler intentionally discriminated against plaintiff by maintaining a discriminatory working environment. The cause of action for hostile work environment was first recognized in Rogers v. EEOC, 454 F.2d 234 (5th Cir. 1971), cert. denied, 406 U.S. 957, 92 S.Ct. 2058, 32 L.Ed.2d 343 (1972). That case, like many cases following it, was decided under Section 703 of Title VII, 42 U.S.C. § 2000e–2(a), which makes it unlawful to discriminate with respect to terms, conditions, or privileges of employment.

Although Title VII clearly applies to national origin discrimination, section 1981 is not so specific. Appellant has not maintained, however, that section 1981 does not cover the charges Erebia has brought in this case. Although courts have had some difficulty with cases alleging only national origin discrimination under section 1981, where there are allegations that discrimination against Hispanics is of a racial character a cause of action under section 1981 has been recognized. See Gonzalez v. Standford Applied Engineering, Inc., 597 F.2d 1298, 1300 (9th Cir.1979) (per curiam) (dismissal of section 1981 claim brought by a Mexican-American was improper because "prejudice towards those of Mexican descent having a skin color not characteristically Caucasian must be said to be racial prejudice under § 1981"); Manzanares v. Safeway Stores, Inc., 593 F.2d 968, 971 (10th Cir.1979) (reversing dismissal of a section 1981 action brought by a Mexican-American and holding that racial discrimination is not to be limited to the technical or restrictive meaning). In the present case section 1981 clearly applies because the slurs Erebia testified about were of a racial character. Erebia reported statements such as "I was Mexican and he was white" and "some white person could be doing my job instead of a Mexican."

In Rogers v. EEOC, supra, 454 F.2d 234, 238 (5th Cir.1971), cert. denied, 406 U.S. 957, 92 S.Ct. 2058, 32 L.Ed.2d 343 (1972), Judge Goldberg held that an employee of Spanish origin surnamed American had a cause of action against an employer for "the practice of creating a working environment heavily charged with ethnic or racial discrimination." He stressed that while the simple utterance of a racial epithet would be insufficient to assert a cause of action, an action under Title VII would lie where a working environment is "so heavily polluted with discrimination as to destroy completely the emotional and psychological stability of minority group members."

Courts addressing claims of hostile working environment have emphasized that incidents of racial slurs must be more than sporadic and that the plaintiff must demonstrate that management failed to take adequate steps to remedy the situation.

In a case such as this where the trier of fact has found a hostile work environment and the employer's responsibility by its refusal to address the problem, the case comes to this Court in a different posture from a claim denied in the District Court. It is the function of the jury to consider credibility and other factors at play in plaintiff's claim. The jury determination will not be overturned lightly. Chrysler maintains that this case should be reversed merely because it arguably comes within the circumstances of cases upholding a denial of a claim on appeal under a clearly erroneous or substantial evidence review. Our task, however, is to determine whether the jury verdict is supported by substantial evidence.

In the present case, we find that the jury's verdict was supported by substantial evidence. Plaintiff's uncontested testimony was that he was subjected to slurs from February 1977 to July of 1982. His uncontested testimony was that he reported the slurs regularly during that period to three different managers who at best did nothing in response or, at worst called him a "hot-headed Mexican" or threatened him with economic harm. There is clearly substantial evidence on both the elements of repeated slurs and management's tolerance and condonation of the situation.

Chrysler emphasizes that this action was brought under section 1981 and not Title VII. A claim under section 1981 requires proof of intentional or purposeful discrimination. General Building Contractors Association, Inc. v. Pennsylvania, 458 U.S. 375, 391, 102 S.Ct. 3141, 3150, 73 L.Ed.2d 835 (1982).

The jury's finding of intentional discrimination by Chrysler management is supported by substantial evidence. Management was aware of plaintiff's many complaints of harassment and condoned the situation by taking no steps to improve conditions and by seeking to intimidate plaintiff. No showing that it received complaints from white supervisors of harassment by minorities and responded differently is required. However, we observe that management, through Ferguson, did investigate a complaint presented to him by a white employee against Erebia in regard to the incident with Baum. There was no investigation of plaintiff's complaints, ostensibly because they were not presented to Ferguson. The fact that plaintiff's complaints were not relayed to Ferguson is the substance of plaintiff's complaint—lack of response by management.

III

Appellant challenges the jury's award of $10,000 compensatory damages arguing there was insufficient proof of actual injury such as emotional distress, embarrassment, or humiliation. Courts have allowed recovery under section 1981 for emotional distress, but there must be sufficient evidence to support the award.

In the present case, plaintiff's only proof of emotional harm consisted of his statements that he was "highly upset" about the slurs and that "you can only take so much." His conduct in complaining to management on a regular basis also demonstrated a high level of concern. This proof, however, is insufficient to support the verdict for compensatory damages * * *.

We reject appellee's contention that there was insufficient evidence to support the punitive damages award. As noted in Rodgers, "punitive damages may stand independently of compensatory." The issues of willfulness underlying the punitive damages award are separate from issues relating to compensatory damages. The jury awarded punitive damages based on instructions requiring it to find the defendant's actions were "wanton or oppressively done." The court stated that a "failure to act is wantonly done if done in reckless or callous disregard of or indifference to the rights of one or more persons, including the injured person."

The jury's award for punitive damages was supported by substantial evidence. Plaintiff testified that he continuously brought the problem of racial slurs to the attention of his supervisors and that they failed to take any action to rectify the situation. It is significant that Chrysler did not introduce as rebuttal witnesses any of the employees named by Erebia as having bombarded him repeatedly with ethnic slurs on virtually a daily basis. Neither were the supervisors to whom Erebia testified that he made complaints and asked for relief over and over again called as witnesses. Malice may be inferred from conduct and surrounding circumstances. Additionally, the jury could find malice in Lenz's threat that he would hurt plaintiff economically for pursuing his complaints of harassment. Because the award is supported by substantial evidence, the court did not abuse its discretion in denying the motion for a new trial. Accordingly, the punitive damages award must stand.

CORNELIA G. KENNEDY, CIRCUIT JUDGE, dissenting.

I agree with the majority that persons of Mexican ancestry are entitled to the protection of section 1981 where, as here, they are discriminated against based on some perceived racial differences, as opposed to mere national origin discrimination. I do not agree, however, that the evidence of discrimination in this case is sufficient to support a section 1981 violation.

The court in Johnson v. Bunny Bread Co., 646 F.2d 1250, 1297 (8th Cir.1981), articulated the applicable standard as follows: "Unquestionably, a working environment dominated by racial slurs constitutes a violation of Title VII. This is not to say, however, that all racial slurs rise to the level of Title VII violations. In this area, we deal with degrees." Racial remarks by a single subordinate do not create a working environment dominated by racial slurs. Racial harassment directed at an employee by a single supervisor can sufficiently poison the employee's working atmosphere, since a supervisor can dominate the workplace with respect to his subordinate. The attitudes of a number of co-employees can also control one's working atmosphere. But here we have the weakest case of all—a foreman claiming that a single one of his subordinates has, by—using racial epithets, "dominated" the foreman's working environment.

The degree of racial hostility found to constitute a racially charged working atmosphere in other cases has been considerably greater and more widespread than that faced by Erebia.

A § 1981 violation requires a finding of intentional discrimination on the part of the employer. Intent may be inferred from the employer's tolerance of racial harassment "sufficiently pervasive as to alter the conditions of employment and create an abusive working environment," Henson v. City of Dundee, 682 F.2d 897, 904 (11th Cir.1982). An employer free of discriminatory motives would not tolerate disruption of the workplace by racial harassment. Such an inference is not proper where, under the circumstances, a nondiscriminatory employer would not be expected to take further action. Here the employer's actions are fully consistent with the inference that Erebia's supervisors merely expected their foreman to handle a problem with his subordinate by himself. Erebia's immediate supervisor repeatedly told him to "build a case." Specific times, places, and witnesses would be needed to discharge or suspend a union employee. There is no evidence that Erebia, an experienced foreman, did build his case. The personnel manager, Lenz, advised Erebia that he should ignore verbal abuse from subordinates and not pay any attention to shop talk. The later of Erebia's two complaints to Lenz was in the summer of 1977, five and one-half years before suit was filed. An inference of intent to discriminate, proper when management tolerates racial harassment by supervisors or co-employees, is not necessarily proper when management tolerates a racially-based disciplinary problem a foreman has with a subordinate. The racially charged hostile working atmosphere referred to in Title VII cases is thus needed to supply the intent element as well as the discrimination element of a § 1981 claim.

GARCIA v. GLOOR

United States Court of Appeals for the Fifth Circuit, 1980.
618 F.2d 264.

ALVIN B. RUBIN, CIRCUIT JUDGE:

IT IS ORDERED that this court's opinion reported at 609 F.2d 156 (5th Cir.1980) be withdrawn and the following is substituted:

Invoking Title VII, the Equal Employment Opportunity Act, 42 U.S.C. § 2000e–2 [EEO Act], Hector Garcia, a native-born American of Mexican descent, challenges as discriminatory his employer's rule that prohibits employees engaged in sales work from speaking Spanish on the job. Because the group of employees Mr. Garcia sought to represent was not numerous enough to constitute a class, we affirm the trial court's denial of class action certification. We conclude that the "speak-only-English" rule, as it was applied to Mr. Garcia by his employer, does not discriminate on the basis of national origin. We therefore affirm the district court's judgment that Mr. Garcia's discharge for violating the rule was not unlawful.

I.

Hector Garcia, who was twenty-four years of age at the time of trial, completed the first semester of the tenth grade in Texas public schools. He speaks both English and Spanish. His grandparents were immigrants from Mexico; he is native-born, but he has always spoken Spanish in his own household.

In 1975, he was employed as a salesman by Gloor Lumber and Supply, Inc., in Brownsville, Texas. His duties included stocking his department and keeping it in order, assisting other department salespersons and selling lumber, hardware and supplies. He had received compliments from management on his work and in May 1975 had received a bonus of $250. However, there was also evidence that Mr. Garcia was not a satisfactory employee, that management's compliments were bestowed as incentives to better performance when, on occasion, his work showed some improvement and that a bonus was awarded to all employees at year-end without regard to merit.

Gloor had a rule prohibiting employees from speaking Spanish on the job unless they were communicating with Spanish-speaking customers. Most of Gloor's employees were bilingual, but some who worked outside in the lumber yard did not speak English. The rule did not apply to those employees. It also did not apply to conversation during work breaks.

Mr. Garcia testified that, because Spanish is his primary language, he found the English-only rule difficult to follow. He testified that on June 10, 1975 he was asked a question by another Mexican-American employee about an item requested by a customer and he responded in Spanish that the article was not available. Alton Gloor, an officer and stockholder of Gloor, overheard the conversation. Thereafter Mr. Garcia was discharged.

Mr. Gloor testified, and the district court found as a fact, that Mr. Garcia's discharge was for a combination of deficiencies—failure to keep his inventory current, failure to replenish the stock on display from stored merchandise, failure to keep his area clean and failure to respond to numerous reprimands—as well as for violation of the English-only rule. The court also found that the English-only policy was not strictly enforced but that Mr. Garcia had violated it "at every opportunity since the time of his hiring according to his own testimony."

In addition to offering this evidence to justify firing Mr. Garcia, Mr. Gloor testified that there were business reasons for the language policy: English-speaking customers objected to communications between employees that they could not understand; pamphlets and trade literature were in English and were not available in Spanish, so it was important for employees to be fluent in English apart from conversations with English-speaking customers; if employees who normally spoke Spanish off the job were required to speak English on the job at all times and not only when waiting on English-speaking customers, they would improve their English; and the rule would permit supervisors, who did not speak Spanish, better to oversee the work of subordinates. The district court found that these were valid business reasons and that they, rather than discrimination, were the motive for the rule.

An expert witness called by the plaintiff testified that the Spanish language is the most important aspect of ethnic identification for Mexican-Americans, and it is to them what skin color is to others. Consequently, Mr. Garcia contends, with support from the Equal Employment Opportunity Commission [EEOC], that the rule violates the EEO Act and the Civil Rights Acts, 42 U.S.C. §§ 1981 and 1985(c).

Of the eight salesmen employed by Gloor in 1975, seven were Hispanic, a matter perhaps of business necessity, because 75% of the population in its business area is of Hispanic background and many of

Gloor's customers wish to be waited on by a salesman who speaks Spanish. Of its 39 employees, 31 were Hispanic, and a Hispanic sat on the Board of Directors. There is no contention that Gloor discriminated against Hispanic-Americans in any other way.

The narrow issue is whether the English-only rule as applied to Mr. Garcia imposed a discriminatory condition of employment.

III.

Although the trial judge concluded that Mr. Garcia was fired for a number of reasons, including deliberately speaking Spanish on the job in purposeful violation of Gloor's rule, the judge made no finding concerning the substantiality of the language violation in contributing to the matrix of motive. Perhaps under the evidence he could not, once the omelet had been cooked, determine what each egg had contributed to it.

Employer action does not violate Title VII merely because a reprobated reason plays some part in the employer's decision, see Rogers v. Equal Employment Opportunity Commission, D.C.Cir.1977, 551 F.2d 456; yet the forbidden taint need not be the sole basis for the action in order to condemn it. The record would support a finding that Mr. Garcia's use of Spanish was a significant factor and, therefore, rather than remand for a determination by the trial court, we will assume for present purposes that it was. We turn then to the issue that appears to both parties and the several amici to be at the core of the case.

In interpreting the statute [1] we start with its plain words without pausing to consider whether a statute differently framed would yield results more consonant with fairness and reason. The statute forbids discrimination in employment on the basis of national origin. Neither the statute nor common understanding equates national origin with the language that one chooses to speak.[2] Language may be used as a covert basis for national origin discrimination, but the English-only rule was not applied to Garcia by Gloor either to this end or with this result.

Mr. Garcia argues that it is discriminatory to prohibit employees from speaking a foreign language on the basis of a thesis that, if an employee whose most familiar language is not English is denied the right to converse in that language, he is denied a privilege of employment enjoyed by employees most comfortable in English; this, necessarily, discriminates against him on the basis of national origin because national origin influences or determines his language preference.

1. While the EEOC has considered in specific instances whether a policy prohibiting the speaking of Spanish in normal interoffice contacts discriminates on the basis of national origin, [1972] Empl.Prac. Guide (CCH) ¶ 6293; [1972] Empl.Prac. Guide (CCH) ¶ 6173, it has adopted neither a regulation stating a standard for testing such language rules nor any general policy, presumed to be derived from the stat-ute, prohibiting them. We therefore approach the problem on the basis of the statute itself and the case law.

2. The statute's legislative history concerning the meaning of "national origin" is "quite meager." See Espinoza v. Farah Mfg. Co., 1973, 414 U.S. 86, 88, 94 S.Ct. 334, 337, 38 L.Ed.2d 287, 291.

Whether or not this argument might have a tenable basis if made on behalf of all employees who are bilingual or if invoked against a rule that forbade all use of any language but English we need not consider. Mr. Garcia was fully bilingual. He chose deliberately to speak Spanish instead of English while actually at work. He was permitted to speak the language he preferred during work breaks.

No authority cited to us gives a person a right to speak any particular language while at work; unless imposed by statute, the rules of the workplace are made by collective bargaining or, in its absence, by the employer. An employer's failure to forbid employees to speak English does not grant them a privilege. The refusal to hire applicants who cannot speak English might be discriminatory if the jobs they seek can be performed without knowledge of that language, but the obverse is not correct: if the employer engages a bilingual person, that person is granted neither right nor privilege by the statute to use the language of his personal preference. Mr. Garcia was bilingual. Off the job, when he spoke one language or another, he exercised a preference. He was hired by Gloor precisely because he was bilingual, and, apart from the contested rule, his preference in language was restricted to some extent by the nature of his employment. On the job, in addressing English-speaking customers, he was obliged to use English; in serving Spanish-speaking patrons, he was required to speak Spanish. The English-only rule went a step further and restricted his preference while he was on the job and not serving a customer.

Let us assume that, as contended by Mr. Garcia, there was no genuine business need for the rule and that its adoption by Gloor was arbitrary. The EEO Act does not prohibit all arbitrary employment practices. It does not forbid employers to hire only persons born under a certain sign of the zodiac or persons having long hair or short hair or no hair at all. It is directed only at specific impermissible bases of discrimination—race, color, religion, sex, or national origin. National origin must not be confused with ethnic or sociocultural traits or an unrelated status, such as citizenship or alienage, Espinoza v. Farah Manufacturing Co., 1973, 414 U.S. 86, 94 S.Ct. 334, 38 L.Ed.2d 287, or poverty, Ybarra v. City of Los Altos Hills, 9 Cir.1974, 503 F.2d 250, 253, or with activities not connected with national origin, such as labor agitation, Balderas v. La Casita Farms, Inc., 5 Cir. 1974, 500 F.2d 195, 198.

Save for religion, the discriminations on which the Act focuses its laser of prohibition are those that are either beyond the victim's power to alter, see Willingham v. Macon Telegraph Publishing Co., 5 Cir. 1975, (en banc), 507 F.2d 1084 (employer's grooming code that required different hair lengths for males and females held not to constitute sex discrimination), or that impose a burden on an employee on one of the prohibited bases. No one can change his place of birth (national origin), the place of birth of his forebears (national origin), his race or fundamental sexual characteristics. As this court said in *Willingham,*

"Equal employment *opportunity* may be secured only when employers are barred from discriminating against employees on the basis of immutable characteristics, such as race and national origin. * * * But a hiring policy that distinguishes on some other ground, such as grooming codes or length of hair, is related more closely to the employer's choice of how to run his business than to equality of employment opportunity." 507 F.2d at 1091 (emphasis in original).

The argument is made that the rule is discriminatory in impact, even if that result was not intentional, because it was likely to be violated only by Hispanic-Americans and that, therefore, they have a higher risk of incurring penalties. The disparate impact test has been applied to hiring criteria, Griggs v. Duke Power Co., 1971, 401 U.S. 424, 91 S.Ct. 849, 28 L.Ed.2d 158, and to on-the-job policies, Nashville Gas Co. v. Satty, 1977, 434 U.S. 136, 98 S.Ct. 347, 54 L.Ed.2d 356. It forbids the use of any employment criterion, even one neutral on its face and not intended to be discriminatory, if, in fact, the criterion causes discrimination as measured by the impact on a person or group entitled to equal opportunity. However, there is no disparate impact if the rule is one that the affected employee can readily observe and nonobservance is a matter of individual preference. Mr. Garcia could readily comply with the speak-English-only rule; as to him nonobservance was a matter of choice. In similar fashion, an employer might, without business necessity, adopt a rule forbidding smoking on the job. The Act would not condemn that rule merely because it is shown that most of the employees of one race smoke, most of the employees of another do not and it is more likely that a member of the race more addicted to tobacco would be disciplined.

We do not denigrate the importance of a person's language of preference or other aspects of his national, ethnic or racial self-identification. Differences in language and other cultural attributes may not be used as a fulcrum for discrimination. However, the English-only rule, as applied by Gloor to Mr. Garcia, did not forbid cultural expression to persons for whom compliance with it might impose hardship. While Title VII forbids the imposition of burdensome terms and conditions of employment as well as those that produce an atmosphere of racial and ethnic oppression, see Rogers v. Equal Employment Opportunity Commission, 5 Cir.1971, 454 F.2d 234, 238–39, cert. denied, 1972, 406 U.S. 957, 92 S.Ct. 2058, 32 L.Ed.2d 343, the evidence does not support a finding that the English-only rule had this effect on Mr. Garcia.

The EEO Act does not support an interpretation that equates the language an employee prefers to use with his national origin. To a person who speaks only one tongue or to a person who has difficulty using another language than the one spoken in his home, language might well be an immutable characteristic like skin color, sex or place of birth. However, the language a person who is multi-lingual elects to speak at a particular time is by definition a matter of choice. No claim is made that Garcia and the other employees engaged in sales were unable to speak English. Indeed, it is conceded that all could do so and that this ability was an occupational qualification because of the requirement that they wait on customers who spoke only English or who used that language by choice. Nor are we confronted with a case where an employee inadvertently slipped into using a more familiar tongue.

The rule was confined to the work place and work hours. It did not apply to conversations during breaks or other employee free-time. There is no evidence that Gloor forbade speaking Spanish to discriminate in employment or that the effect of doing so was invidious to Hispanic Americans. We do not consider rules that turn on the language used in an employee's home, the one he chooses to speak when not at work or the tongue spoken by his parents or grandparents. In some circumstances, the ability to speak or the speaking of a language other than English might be equated with national origin, but this case concerns only a requirement that persons capable of speaking English do so while on duty.

That this rule prevents some employees, like Mr. Garcia, from exercising a preference to converse in Spanish does not convert it into discrimination based on national origin. Reduced to its simplest, the claim is "others like to speak English on the job and do so without penalty. Speaking Spanish is very important to me and is inherent in my ancestral national origin. Therefore, I should be permitted to speak it and the denial to me of that preference so important to my self-identity is statutorily forbidden." The argument thus reduces itself to a contention that the statute commands employers to permit employees to speak the tongue they prefer. We do not think the statute permits that interpretation, whether the preference be slight or strong or even one closely related to self-identity.

Mr. Garcia and the EEOC would have us adopt a standard that the employer's business needs must be accomplished in the manner that appears to us to be the least restrictive. The statute does not give the judiciary such latitude in the absence of discrimination. Judges, who have neither business experience nor the problem of meeting the employees' payroll, do not have the power to preempt an employer's business judgment by imposing a solution that appears less restrictive. See Furnco Construction Corp. v. Waters, 1978, 438 U.S. 567, 98 S.Ct. 2943, 57 L.Ed.2d 957.

Notes

1. *Aliens.* The Supreme Court's only Title VII encounter with national origin was Espinoza v. Farah Manufacturing Co., 414 U.S. 86, 94 S.Ct. 334, 38 L.Ed.2d 287 (1973). At issue was the Company's longstanding policy against the employment of aliens. The Court equated national origin with ancestry, and rejected the argument that refusal to hire because of non-citizenship constituted discrimination on the basis of nation-

al origin. The Court relied heavily on the historical practices of denying federal employment to aliens. The Court recognized that refusal to hire because of alienage could be a pretext for national origin discrimination, but found this not to be the case here, since 96% of the employees at the plant were citizens of Mexican ancestry.

Guerra v. Manchester Terminal Corp., 498 F.2d 641 (5th Cir.1974) held that 42 U.S.C. Section 1981 was applicable to aliens under the "all persons" coverage.

In Hampton v. Wong, 426 U.S. 88, 96 S.Ct. 1895, 48 L.Ed.2d 495 (1976) the Supreme Court invalidated the exclusion of aliens from the federal service by Civil Service Commission regulation, but recognized that there were national interests which would justify the exclusion if it were directed by either Congress or the President. President Ford promptly issued Executive Order 11935 (see Reference Supplement).

As to state laws disqualifying aliens from employment or licensing, the Supreme court has invalidated under the Equal Protection Clause state laws which prohibited aliens, e.g., from holding classified civil service jobs, Sugarman v. Dougall, 413 U.S. 634, 93 S.Ct. 2842, 37 L.Ed.2d 853 (1973), and practicing law, In re Griffiths, 413 U.S. 717, 93 S.Ct. 2851, 37 L.Ed.2d 910 (1973). But the Court has also recognized that some state functions are so related to the operation of the state as a political and governmental entity as to permit the confinement of such positions to citizens. Thus, the court has upheld state laws denying aliens the right to serve in the state police force, Foley v. Connelie, 435 U.S. 291, 98 S.Ct. 1067, 55 L.Ed.2d 287 (1978), to become probation officers, Cabell v. Chavez-Salido, 454 U.S. 432, 102 S.Ct. 735, 70 L.Ed.2d 677 (1982), and to teach in the public schools, Ambach v. Norwich, 441 U.S. 68, 99 S.Ct. 1589, 60 L.Ed.2d 49 (1979): The "governmental function" umbrella is not broad enough, however, to include a notary public. Bernal v. Fainter, 467 U.S. 216, 104 S.Ct. 2312, 81 L.Ed.2d 175 (1984).

2. *Indians.* Note the exclusion of Indian tribes from the definition of "employer" in Section 701(b) of Title VII. Note also the exemption in Section 703(1) for businesses or enterprises on or near an Indian reservation.

At issue in Morton v. Mancari, 417 U.S. 535, 94 S.Ct. 2474, 41 L.Ed.2d 290 (1974) was the policy of granting preference to qualified Indians for positions in the Bureau of Indian Affairs. The Court noted that "the federal policy of according some hiring preference to Indians in the Indian service dates at least as far back as 1834" and discussed the reasons for the policy. The conclusion was that the historic policy had not been rendered invalid, under a theory of implied repeal, by the 1972 extension of Title VII to federal employment.

J. RETALIATION

PAYNE v. McLEMORE'S WHOLESALE & RETAIL STORES

United States Court of Appeals for the Fifth Circuit, 1981.
654 F.2d 1130, cert. denied 455 U.S. 1000, 102 S.Ct. 1630,
71 L.Ed.2d 866 (1982).

SAM D. JOHNSON, CIRCUIT JUDGE:

This is a Title VII action alleging that in early 1971, defendant McLemore's Wholesale & Retail Stores, Inc. failed to rehire plaintiff Charles Payne because of his participation in activities protected by section 704(a) of the Civil Rights Act of 1964. 42 U.S.C.A. § 2000e–3(a).

* * *

Plaintiff began his employment with defendant about May or June of 1966. Plaintiff originally worked in McLemore's fertilizer plant. The operation of the plant was seasonal in nature since the demand for fertilizer was dependent upon the farmers' planting seasons. During the first two years of plaintiff's employment with defendant, he was laid off for three months each year during the seasonal decline in work. In later years, during the off-season plaintiff was not laid off, but was instead shifted to positions in other parts of the defendant's operations. As a result, during his employment with McLemore's, plaintiff worked as a fertilizer plant operator, a truck driver, a warehouse worker, a dock worker, and a farm store porter.

In November 1970, plaintiff was once again laid off due to the seasonal business decline. Two other black employees and two white employees were laid off at the same time. About a month later, plaintiff became involved in the formation and organization of the Franklin Parish Improvement Organization, a nonprofit civil rights organization. The formation of the Improvement Organization was precipitated by an incident involving two black children who were turned away from a public swimming pool. The organization was interested in improving social conditions of blacks in Franklin Parish, and it focused especially on the need to get blacks hired in retail stores in money-handling and supervisory positions in order to improve the treatment that blacks received while shopping in stores. Shortly after its formation, the members of the organization decided to boycott several retail businesses, including those of defendant in Winnsboro. Plaintiff organized and implemented the boycott and was actively involved in picketing McLemore's Jitney Jungle Food Stores. Defendant knew of plaintiff's involvement in the boycott and picketing. Moreover, the boycott and picketing were effective and defendant's business suffered as a result.

In previous years when he had been laid off, plaintiff had always gone back to work for defendant when the work picked back up. In the year of the boycott, however, he was not recalled or rehired.[3] In February 1971, plaintiff filed a charge of discrimination against McLemore's with the Equal Employment Opportunity Commission (EEOC). The charge alleged that plaintiff was not called back to work because he had attended a civil rights meeting.

*   *   *

On June 17, 1976, plaintiff filed this action in federal district court alleging that defendant's failure to rehire plaintiff was a result of plaintiff's race and his civil rights activity. In its answer, McLemore's denied that it had committed any discriminatory actions, and asserted that the reason the plaintiff was not rehired was because he failed to reapply for a position with McLemore's after he was laid off. The district court held that plaintiff did reapply for his job, but that he was not rehired because of his participation in boycotting and picketing activities. The court further found that participation in the boycott and picketing was protected activity under section 704(a) of Title VII; in other words, the district court concluded that the boycott and picketing were in opposition to an unlawful employment practice of the defendant. The court awarded plaintiff back pay, costs, and attorney's fees totalling $16,260.90.

The opposition clause of section 704(a) of Title VII provides protection against retaliation for employees who oppose unlawful employment practices committed by an employer. (Section 704(a) also contains a participation clause that protects employees against retaliation for their participation in the procedures established by Title VII to enforce its provisions. The participation clause is not involved in this lawsuit.) The opposition clause of section 704(a) provides:

> It shall be an unlawful employment practice for an employer to discriminate against any of his employees or applicants for employment * * * *because he has opposed any practice made an unlawful employment practice by this subchapter* * * *.

42 U.S.C.A. § 2000e–3(a) (emphasis added).

In this case, plaintiff contends that he was not rehired in retaliation for his boycott and picketing activities which were, according to plaintiff, in opposition to unlawful employment practices committed by McLemore's. Plaintiff asserted that the unlawful employment practices his boycott and picketing activities were intended to protest were McLemore's discrimination against blacks in hiring and promotion— specifically, McLemore's failure to employ blacks in money-handling, clerking, or supervisory positions. In demonstrating his contentions at trial, plaintiff had the initial burden of establishing a prima facie case

---

3. Of the four other employees who were laid off at the same time as plaintiff, only one was rehired—a black employee who was not involved in the boycott or picketing by the Franklin Parish Improvement Organization. Both plaintiff and Russell Brass (the other black employee who was laid off and not rehired) were involved in the boycott and picketing. According to defendant, the employee who was rehired was the only one of the five employees who were laid off that reapplied for a job.

of discrimination. McDonnell Douglas Corp. v. Green, 411 U.S. 792, 802, 93 S.Ct. 1817, 1824, 36 L.Ed.2d 668 (1973). The burden then shifted to the defendant to articulate a legitimate, nondiscriminatory reason for the failure to rehire the plaintiff. Id. See Texas Department of Community Affairs v. Burdine, 450 U.S. 248, 101 S.Ct. 1089, 1093, 67 L.Ed.2d 207 (1981). Finally, if the defendant carried his burden, the plaintiff was entitled to an opportunity to show that the defendant's stated reason for its failure to rehire plaintiff was in fact pretextual. *McDonnell Douglas,* 411 U.S. at 804, 93 S.Ct. at 1825; *Burdine,* 101 S.Ct. at 1093. See Whatley v. Metropolitan Atlanta Rapid Transit Authority, 632 F.2d 1325, 1327–28 (5th Cir.1980) (participation clause case).

"To establish a prima facie case under [section 704(a)] the plaintiff must establish (1) statutorily protected expression, (2) an adverse employment action, and (3) a causal link between the protected expression and the adverse action." Smalley v. City of Eatonville, 640 F.2d 765, 769 (5th Cir.1981); *Whatley,* 632 F.2d at 1328. The first element of the prima facie case—statutorily protected expression—requires conduct by the plaintiff that is in opposition to an unlawful employment practice of the defendant. Thus, for the plaintiff to prove that he engaged in statutorily protected expression, he must show that the boycott and picketing activity in which he participated was in opposition to conduct by McLemore's that was made unlawful by Title VII. According to the plaintiff, the purpose of the boycott and picketing was to oppose McLemore's discrimination against blacks in hiring and promotion. Plaintiff's complaint stated that the Franklin Parish Improvement Organization "engaged in the peaceful boycotting of Winnsboro stores, among them McLemore's Jitney Jungle Food Stores, which had refused to employ blacks except in a few menial positions."

* * * Testimony was offered at trial indicating that McLemore's discriminated against blacks in employment opportunities and that the boycott and picketing were in opposition to the failure of blacks to be given clerking, money-handling, and supervisory jobs in McLemore's enterprises, as well as in other enterprises in Winnsboro, Louisiana.

* * * Thus, there is substantial evidence to support the district court finding that the purpose of the boycott and picketing was to oppose defendant's discrimination against blacks in certain employment opportunities [7]—an unlawful employment practice under section 703(a)(1).

7. Defendant claims that plaintiff did not engage in the boycott and picketing to oppose unlawful employment practices of McLemore's. Instead, it is McLemore's contention that the boycott and picketing were conducted to publicize the issues of integration of public facilities and common courtesy to blacks. To support this allegation, defendant points to the incident that initiated the formation of the Franklin Parish Improvement Organization—two black children being turned away from the town's segregated public swimming pool. In addition, McLemore's points to testimony of Russell Brass, who stated at trial that, "[I]f a white lady was waiting on [a black customer] * * * and another white lady would come by then the * * * [saleslady] would * * * tell the black that they had to wait." 1st Supp. Record

Defendant argues, however, that plaintiff failed to establish his prima facie case because he failed to prove that defendant had committed any unlawful employment practices. Plaintiff responds that he was not required to prove the actual existence of those unlawful employment practices; instead, he asserts that it was sufficient to establish a *prima facie* case if he had a *reasonable belief* that defendant had engaged in the unlawful employment practices. We agree with plaintiff and conclude that it was not fatal to plaintiff's section 704(a) case that he failed to prove, under the *McDonnell Douglas* criteria for proving an unlawful employment practice under section 703(a)(1), that McLemore's discriminated against blacks in retail store employment opportunities.

The Ninth Circuit was apparently the first appellate court to decide whether the opposition clause of section 704(a) required proof of actual discrimination. Sias v. City Demonstration Agency, 588 F.2d 692 (9th Cir.1978). * * * The Sias court quoted extensively from Hearth v. Metropolitan Transit Commission, 436 F.Supp. 685 (D.Minn. 1977), which held that "as long as the employee had a reasonable belief that what was being opposed constituted discrimination under Title VII, the claim of retaliation does not hinge upon a showing that the employer was in fact in violation of Title VII." Id. at 688. The *Hearth* court went on to state:

> But this Court believes that appropriate informal opposition to perceived discrimination must not be chilled by the fear of retaliatory action in the event the alleged wrongdoing does not exist. It should not be necessary for an employee to resort immediately to the EEOC or similar State agencies in order to bring complaints of discrimination to the attention of the employer with some measure of protection. The resolution of such charges without governmental prodding should be encouraged.

> The statutory language does not compel a contrary result. The elimination of discrimination in employment is the purpose behind Title VII and the statute is entitled to a liberal interpretation. When an employee reasonably believes that discrimination exists, opposition thereto is opposition to an employment practice made unlawful by Title VII even if the employee turns out to be mistaken as to the facts.

Id. at 688–89 (footnote omitted), quoted in *Sias*, 588 F.2d at 695. The Seventh Circuit has also adopted this position. Berg v. La Crosse Cooler Co., 612 F.2d 1041 (7th Cir.1980). In *Berg*, the plaintiff was discharged when she challenged her employer's failure to provide pregnancy benefits as sex-based discrimination. After she was fired, the United States Supreme Court ruled that a disability benefits plan does not violate Title VII because of its failure to cover pregnancy

at 85. Although the Improvement Organization was, in part, occasioned by the position of blacks in Winnsboro in general, and although the boycott and picketing may have been to some extent a protest of this position, the district court's conclusion that the boycott and picketing activity was in opposition to unlawful employment practices of McLemore's is supported by substantial evidence.

related disabilities.　General Electric Co. v. Gilbert, 429 U.S. 125, 97 S.Ct. 401, 50 L.Ed.2d 343 (1976).　The Seventh Circuit held that where the employee opposed a practice that she reasonably believed was an unlawful employment practice under Title VII, her opposition was protected from retaliatory discharge even where the practice was later determined not be an unlawful employment practice.　The court concluded that to interpret the opposition clause to require proof of an actual unlawful employment practice

> undermines Title VII's central purpose, the elimination of employment discrimination by informal means; destroys one of the chief means of achieving that purpose, the frank and nondisruptive exchange of ideas between employers and employees; and serves no redeeming statutory or policy purposes of its own.　Section 2000e–3(a) plays a central role in effectuating these objectives.　By protecting employees from retaliation, it is designed to encourage employees to call to their employers' attention discriminatory practices of which the employer may be unaware or which might result in protracted litigation to determine their legality if they are not voluntarily changed.

612 F.2d at 1045.

The Fifth Circuit has not heretofore directly addressed the issue whether proof of an actual unlawful employment practice is necessary under the opposition clause, or whether an employee is protected from retaliation under the opposition clause if the employee reasonably believes that the employer is engaged in unlawful employment practices.　To the extent that earlier Fifth Circuit cases provide guidance to this Court, however, they indicate that the reasonable belief test of the Seventh and Ninth Circuits comports with the decisions of this Circuit and the policies underlying Title VII.　In Pettway v. American Cast Iron Pipe Co., 411 F.2d 998 (5th Cir.1969), this Court held that an employee was protected by the participation clause of section 704(a) from discharge in retaliation for filing a charge with the EEOC, regardless of the truth or falsity of the contents of the charge.　The Court stated that:

> There can be no doubt about the purpose of § 704(a).　In unmistakable language it is to protect the employee who utilizes the tools provided by Congress to protect his rights.　The Act will be frustrated if the employer may unilaterally determine the truth or falsity of charges and take independent action.

Id. at 1004–05.　Thus, the Court held that where the communication with the EEOC satisfied the requirements of a "charge," the charging party could not be discharged for the writing and the court could not "either sustain any employer disciplinary action or deny relief because of the presence of * * * malicious material."　Id. at 1007.[9]

---

9. Although this Court considers the reasoning of the *Pettway* decision to support the reasonable belief test in opposition clause cases, at least one district court has viewed the *Pettway* case quite differently.

The district court in EEOC v. C & D Sportswear Corp., 398 F.Supp. 300 (M.D. Ga.1975), held that "baseless accusations" were protected "only as a means of protecting access to the Commission."　Id. at 305.

* * *

To effectuate the policies of Title VII and to avoid the chilling effect that would otherwise arise, we are compelled to conclude that a plaintiff can establish a prima facie case of retaliatory discharge under the opposition clause of section 704(a) if he shows that he had a reasonable belief that the employer was engaged in unlawful employment practices.[11] While the district court made no explicit finding that plaintiff's opposition was based upon a reasonable belief that McLemore's hiring and promotional policies violated Title VII, such a finding is implicit and is sufficiently supported by evidence in the record.

Thus, that court concluded that the result in *Pettway* was limited to actions under the participation clause, and did not apply to actions under the opposition clause. The *C & D Sportswear* court held:

> Accordingly, the only reasonable interpretation to be placed on Section 704(a) is that where accusations are made in the context of charges before the EEOC, the truth or falsity of that accusation is a matter to be determined by the EEOC, and thereafter by the courts. However, where accusations are made outside the procedures set forth by Congress that accusation is made at the accuser's peril. In order to be protected, it must be established that the accusation is well-founded. If it is, there is, in fact, an unlawful employment practice and he has the right, protected by Section 704(a), to oppose it. However, where there is no underlying unlawful employment practice the employee has no right to make that accusation in derogation of the procedures provided by statute.

Id. at 306. We find the reasoning of the *C & D Sportswear* district court unpersuasive and the result unjustifiably restrictive. In *C & D Sportswear,* an employee called the president of the company a racist and was discharged for making that accusation. The district court reasoned that

> access to the EEOC must be protected. On the other hand, accusations of racism ought not to be made lightly. Unfounded accusations might well incite racism where none had previously existed. Were employees free to make unfounded accusations of racism against their employers and fellow employees, racial discord, disruption, and disharmony would likely ensue. This would be wholly contrary to Congress' intention that race be removed, as far as possible, as an issue in employment.

Id. at 305–06. While unfounded, inflammatory accusations of racism might, on balance, be found to provide the employer with a legitimate, nondiscriminatory reason for discharging an employee, this would neither require nor suggest that all unfounded accusations should be totally unprotected by the opposition clause of section 704(a). It is as important to protect an employee's right to oppose perceived discrimination by appropriate, informal means as it is to protect his right of access to the EEOC. An employee who engages in opposition activity should not be required to act at his own peril if it turns out that no unlawful employment practice actually exists, as long as the employee holds a reasonable belief that the unlawful employment practices do exist.

11. The First Circuit has adopted a somewhat different test than have the Seventh and Ninth Circuits. The First Circuit has not explicitly decided whether a section 704(a) plaintiff must "demonstrate that he harbored a 'reasonable belief' of discriminatory employer behavior" or whether the plaintiff must show that he harbored a " 'conscientiously held belief' of such misconduct." Monteiro v. Poole Silver Co., 615 F.2d 4, 8 (1st Cir.1980) (footnote omitted). The *Monteiro* court found that "[u]nder either standard—the employer's conduct being nondiscriminatory in fact—the plaintiff must show that his so-called opposition was in response to some *honestly held,* if mistaken, feeling that discriminatory practices existed." Id. (emphasis added) (footnote omitted). Thus, according to that court, if a reasonable person might have believed that the employer was engaged in unlawful employment practices, but the plaintiff actually did not in good faith hold such a belief, then the plaintiff's opposition conduct is unprotected. Id. at 8 n. 6. We need not decide here whether it is necessary to adopt a good faith requirement in addition to the reasonable belief requirement since, in the case before this Court, the plaintiff believed—reasonably and in good faith— that McLemore's was engaged in unlawful employment practices, and plaintiff's opposition conduct was in response to this belief.

Thus, plaintiff established that he reasonably believed that defendant McLemore's discriminated against blacks in employment opportunities. Moreover, plaintiff showed that his boycott and picketing activities were in opposition to this unlawful employment practice. Defendant's failure to rehire the plaintiff was undoubtedly an adverse employment action. Finally, there was evidence to support an inference that defendant's failure to rehire plaintiff was causally related to plaintiff's boycott and picketing activities.[13] Thus, plaintiff successfully established a prima facie case, thereby raising an inference of unlawful discrimination under section 704(a). The burden then shifted to the defendant to "rebut the presumption of discrimination by producing evidence" of a legitimate, nondiscriminatory reason for its failure to rehire plaintiff. *Burdine,* 101 S.Ct. at 1094.

Defendant McLemore's steadfastly maintained at trial that the *only* reason plaintiff was not rehired was because he failed to reapply for a position with defendant. This comprised the full and complete extent of the rebuttal evidence presented by the agents of the defendant in an effort to articulate a legitimate, nondiscriminatory reason for the failure to rehire the plaintiff.

* * *

This reason—the failure to reapply—would, if believed, be legally sufficient to justify a judgment for the defendant. Thus, the defendant carried its rebuttal burden at trial.

After the defendant has an opportunity to rebut plaintiff's prima facie case, the plaintiff has a corresponding opportunity to show that the defendant's proffered explanation was in fact pretextual. Here, plaintiff presented substantial evidence that he did reapply for a job with McLemore's. The trial court found "as a fact that Mr. Payne did reapply for his position with the defendant corporation." Record, vol. 2, at 313. There is, therefore, substantial evidence in the record to support the district court's conclusion that the defendant's explanation for its failure to rehire the plaintiff was merely pretextual. The district court further found that members of McLemore's knew of plaintiff's participation in the boycott and picketing, and that there was a causal relationship between defendant's failure to rehire plaintiff and plaintiff's participation in the protest activity. There is also substantial evidence in the record to support the district court's conclusion in this regard. Thus, on the facts and arguments presented to the trial court, that court correctly held that the defendant's failure to rehire the plaintiff violated section 704(a); that is, that the defendant's stated reason for not rehiring the plaintiff (the plaintiff's failure to reapply for a job) was merely pretextual and that the defendant's actual reason for

13. An inference that defendant's failure to rehire the plaintiff was caused by plaintiff's participation in the boycott and picketing activity was proper in view of the existence of evidence that the employer was aware of the plaintiff's activities and that, within a relatively short time after those activities took place, the adverse employment consequence occurred. The defendant was then entitled to an opportunity to introduce evidence to rebut this inference.

not rehiring the plaintiff was the plaintiff's participation in activities in opposition to unlawful employment practices of the defendant.

Now on appeal, for the first time, defendant contends that even if plaintiff's activity was in opposition to unlawful employment practices of defendant, plaintiff's actions were not protected by section 704(a) because the *form* of plaintiff's opposition was not covered by the statute. It is well-established that not all activity in opposition to unlawful employment practices is protected by section 704(a). Hochstadt v. Worcester Foundation for Experimental Biology, 545 F.2d 222, 229–34 (1st Cir.1976). Certain conduct—for example, illegal acts of opposition or unreasonably hostile or aggressive conduct—may provide a legitimate, independent, and nondiscriminatory basis for an employee's discharge. Id. at 229. "There may arise instances where the employee's conduct in protest of an unlawful employment practice so interferes with the performance of his job that it renders him ineffective in the position for which he was employed. In such a case, his conduct, or form of opposition, is not covered by § 704(a)." Rosser v. Laborers' International Union, Local 438, 616 F.2d 221, 223 (5th Cir.), cert. denied, 449 U.S. 887, 101 S.Ct. 241, 66 L.Ed.2d 112 (1980). In order to determine when such a situation exists, the court must engage in a balancing test: "[T]he courts have required that the employee conduct be reasonable in light of the circumstances, and have held that 'the employer's right to run his business must be balanced against the rights of the employee to express his grievances and promote his own welfare.'" Jefferies v. Harris County Community Action Association, 615 F.2d 1025, 1036 (5th Cir.1980) (quoting Hochstadt, 545 F.2d at 233).

It appears that a number of cases have assumed that it is part of defendant's rebuttal burden to show that the form of plaintiff's opposition was unprotected by the statute. See, e.g., Rosser, 616 F.2d at 223–24; Jefferies, 615 F.2d at 1035–37; *Hochstadt,* 545 F.2d at 229–34. If the defendant took an adverse employment action against the plaintiff because of opposition conduct by the plaintiff that was outside the protection of the statute, then the defendant may have had a legitimate, nondiscriminatory reason to justify its actions. Thus, in the case before this Court, if the *form* of plaintiff's activities placed them outside the protection of section 704(a), then the defendant may have had a legitimate, nondiscriminatory reason for its failure to rehire the plaintiff. However, if the form of plaintiff's activities was the nondiscriminatory reason for the defendant's failure to rehire the plaintiff, it was the defendant's responsibility to introduce evidence to that effect at trial.

* * * Here, the defendant failed to offer any evidence at trial that its legitimate and nondiscriminatory reason for not rehiring the plaintiff was that plaintiff had engaged in hostile, unprotected activity that was detrimental to the employer's interests. With respect to the defendant's burden of rebutting plaintiff's *prima facie* case, the *Burdine* Court stated that: "An articulation not admitted into evidence will not suffice. Thus, the defendant cannot meet its burden merely through an answer to the complaint or by argument of counsel." 101 S.Ct. at 1094 n. 9. If the defendant cannot meet its rebuttal burden by answer to the complaint or by argument of counsel at trial, the defendant undoubtedly cannot meet its rebuttal burden solely by argument of counsel for the first time on *appeal.*

* * *

While a finding of discrimination is an ultimate fact subject to plenary review, we are bound to the subsidiary facts as found by the district court unless they are clearly erroneous. See Thompson v. Leland Police Department, 633 F.2d 1111, 1112 (5th Cir.1980). Here, the district court's findings of subsidiary fact are not clearly erroneous, and there are sufficient subsidiary facts to support the ultimate finding that McLemore's failure to rehire plaintiff constituted discriminatory action under section 704(a). Since plaintiff made out his prima facie case of discrimination under section 704(a), and since the only explanation offered by the defendant for its failure to rehire plaintiff was correctly determined to be pretextual, the judgment of the district court for plaintiff is

Affirmed.

Notes

1. A constructive discharge is a form of retaliation which most courts recognize as actionable under Title VII. A constructive discharge consists of acts of discrimination in violation of Title VII which make working conditions so intolerable that a reasonable employee would be forced to resign. Goss v. Exxon Office Systems Co., 747 F.2d 885 (3d Cir.1984). The courts of appeals disagree on the substantive standard for a finding of constructive discharge. Some courts require a finding that the alleged retaliation must be an intentional course of conduct calculated to force the plaintiff to resign. E.g., Johnson v. Bunny Bread Co., 646 F.2d 1250 (8th Cir.1981); Muller v. United States Steel Corp., 509 F.2d 923 (10th Cir.), cert. denied, 423 U.S. 825, 96 S.Ct. 39, 46 L.Ed.2d 41 (1975). Other courts have adopted an objective standard, requiring no more than a finding that the conduct complained of has the foreseeable result of making working conditions so unpleasant or difficult that a reasonable person in the employee's shoes would resign. E.g., Held v. Gulf Oil Co., 684 F.2d 427 (6th Cir.1982); Bourque v. Powell Electrical Mfg. Co., 617 F.2d 61 (5th Cir.1980).

2. A preliminary injunction is a form of relief that an employee subject to alleged unlawful retaliation may seek after a charge of discrimination has been filed with the EEOC but before the administrative process has been exhausted. A preliminary injunction is designed, in part, to preserve the status quo pending a hearing on the merits. Most courts of appeals have upheld jurisdiction of district courts to grant relief prior to the exhaustion of administrative remedies but have limited preliminary relief to a narrow class of cases in which the employer retaliates against an employee for filing a charge of discrimination with the EEOC. See Bailey v. Delta Air Lines, Inc., 722 F.2d 942 (1st Cir.1983) (collecting cases).

3. The Court, in Sampson v. Murray, 415 U.S. 61, 94 S.Ct. 937, 39 L.Ed.2d 166 (1974), established a stringent irreparable injury standard for a preliminary injunction:

> Even under the traditional standards of [irreparable injury], it seems clear that the temporary loss of income, ultimately to be recovered, does not usually constitute irreparable injury. In [Virginia Petroleum Jobbers Ass'n. v. FPC, 104 U.S.App.D.C. 106, 259 F.2d 921 (1958)] the court stated:
>
>> The key word in this consideration is *irreparable.* Mere injuries, however substantial in terms of money, time and energy necessarily expended in the absence of a stay, are not enough. The possibility that adequate compensatory or other corrective relief will be available at a later date, in the ordinary course of litigation, weighs heavily against a claim of irreparable injury.

415 U.S. at 90, 94 S.Ct. at 952–953. After holding that even a satisfactory showing of loss of income and damage to reputation are not enough to demonstrate irreparable injury, the Court stated:

> We recognize that cases may arise in which the circumstances surrounding an employee's discharge, together with the resultant effect on the employee, may so far depart from the normal situation that irreparable injury might be found. Such extraordinary cases are hard to define in advance of their occurrence. We have held that an insufficiency of savings or difficulties of immediately obtaining other employment—external factors common to most discharged employees and not attributable to any unusual actions relating to the dischrage itself—will not support a finding of irreparable injury, however severely they may affect a particular individual. But we do not wish to be understood as foreclosing relief in the genuinely extraordinary situation.

415 U.S. at 92 & n. 68, 94 S.Ct. at 953 & n. 68.

Sampson was not a Title VII case but the lower courts have applied its stringent irreparable injury standard to cases in which preliminary relief is sought under Title VII. See, e.g., Steward v. United States Immigration and Naturalization Service, 762 F.2d 193 (2d Cir.1985).

4. The EEOC is granted specific statutory authority to seek preliminary relief when, after a charge has been filed, it "concludes on the basis of a preliminary investigation that prompt judicial action is necessary to carry out the purposes of" Title VII. 42 U.S.C. Section 2000e(5)(f)(2). See EEOC v. Chrysler Corp., 733 F.2d 1183 (6th Cir.1984). The courts of appeals are divided on the question whether the EEOC must meet the same stringent standard of irreparable injury that is applicable to preliminary injunction claims brought by private parties. See EEOC v. Anchor Hocking Corp., 666 F.2d 1037 (6th Cir.1981) (irreparable injury will not be presumed); United States v. Hayes International Corp., 415 F.2d 1038 (5th Cir.1969) (irreparable injury will be presumed from the very fact that the statute has been violated).

K. EXHAUSTION OF ADMINISTRATIVE REMEDIES

1. BASIC REQUIREMENTS

An individual seeking relief under Title VII must exhaust administrative remedies before seeking judicial relief. The Supreme Court has held that a plaintiff (or charging party) must satisfy only two requirements before filing suit in federal court pursuant to Section 706(5)(f)(1), 42 U.S.C. Section 2000e–(5)(f)(1): (1) timely file a charge with the EEOC and (2) timely file a complaint in federal court within ninety days of receipt of notice of right to sue from the EEOC. McDonnell Douglas Corp v. Green, 411 U.S. 792, 798, 93 S.Ct. 1817, 1822, 36 L.Ed.2d 668 (1973); Alexander v. Gardner-Denver Co., 415 U.S. 36, 47, 94 S.Ct. 1011, 1019, 39 L.Ed.2d 147 (1974). If these two requirements have been satisfied, jurisdiction of the federal court is not defeated even though the EEOC has not complied with or completed all of the duties imposed upon it in other sections of Title VII, e.g., failure of the EEOC to serve a copy of the charge on respondent, Russell v. American Tobacco Co., 528 F.2d 357, 365 (4th Cir.1975), cert. denied 425 U.S. 935, 96 S.Ct. 1666, 48 L.Ed.2d 176 (1976); failure of EEOC to find reasonable cause to believe that an unlawful employment practice has been committed, Robinson v. Lorillard Corp., 444 F.2d 791 (4th Cir.1971), cert. dismissed, 406 U.S. 1006, 95 S.Ct. 573, 30 L.Ed.2d 655 (1971); EEOC's failure to attempt conciliation, Dent v. St. Louis-San Francisco Ry. Co., 406 F.2d 399 (5th Cir.1969), cert. denied, 403 U.S. 912, 91 S.Ct. 2219, 29 L.Ed.2d 689 (1971); and failure of the EEOC to issue notice of right to sue when plaintiff is entitled to it, Perdue v. Roy Stone Transfer Corp., 690 F.2d 1091 (4th Cir.1982).

2. TIMELY FILING WITH THE EEOC

The time within which to file a charge with the EEOC depends on whether the claim arises in a deferral or nondeferral jurisdiction. A deferral jurisdiction is one which has a state or local agency authorized to grant or seek relief from employment discrimination or to institute criminal proceedings against such practices. 42 U.S.C. Section 2000e– 5(c). A non-deferral jurisdiction is one which does not satisfy the requirements of Section 2000e–5(c). The EEOC designates deferral jurisdictions as "706 Agencies" and periodically updates its list of agencies which falls within its designation. See 29 C.F.R. Sections 1607.70–1607.75. Title VII provides that, with respect to a claim arising in a deferral jurisdiction, a person alleging unlawful discrimination shall file a charge with the EEOC within 300 days after the alleged unlawful employment practice has occurred, but a charge may not be filed with the EEOC before the expiration of sixty days after proceedings have been commenced under state or local law, unless such proceedings have been earlier terminated. Sections 2000e–5(c) and 5(e). With respect to a claim arising in non-deferral jurisdictions, Title VII provides that a charge shall be filed within one hundred and eighty days after the alleged unlawful employment practice has occurred. The Court held, in New York Gaslight Club, Inc. v. Carey, 447 U.S. 54, 65, 100 S.Ct. 2024, 2031, 64 L.Ed.2d 723 (1980), that initial resort to state or local agencies in deferral jurisdictions is mandated and recourse to federal court is appropriate only when state law does not provide for relief. The EEOC cannot properly proceed with a charge if resort to a state or local agency is mandated in the first instance. The EEOC may, however, refer the charge to a state or local agency on behalf of a charging party, defer its own action on the charge, and then assume jurisdiction over the charge when appropriate deference to the state or local agency has been satisfied. See Love v. Pullman Co., 404 U.S. 522, 92 S.Ct. 616, 30 L.Ed.2d 679 (1972).

In Delaware State College v. Ricks, 449 U.S. 250, 101 S.Ct. 498, 66 L.Ed.2d 431 (1980), the Supreme Court held that a determination whether a charge has been timely filed with the EEOC requires a court to identify precisely the date on which the unlawful employment practice occurred. In *Ricks,* the plaintiff, a black college faculty member, had received notice in March 1974 that he would not receive tenure and, at the same time the college gave him a terminal contract. Under the terminal contract the plaintiff would be allowed to continue as a faculty member only until the end of the 1974–75 academic year, or June 3, 1975. Ricks filed a grievance pursuant to the college grievance policy but the committee almost immediately recommended that his grievance be denied. Ricks filed his charge with the EEOC on April 4, 1975 but the EEOC could not assume jurisdiction over the charge until April 28, 1975 because the claim arose in a deferral state. The Supreme Court considered three different reference points in determining whether Ricks had filed a timely charge with the EEOC: (1) the date when the college decided to terminate Ricks; (2) the date the college gave Ricks actual notice of its decision to terminate him; and (3) the date Ricks' discharge became effective pursuant to the terminal contract. The Court found that Ricks had not filed a timely charge because the precise unlawful employment practice "occurred" within the meaning of Title VII in March 1974:

> [T]he only alleged discrimination occurred—and the filing limitations period therefore commenced—at the time the tenure decision was made and communicated to Ricks. That is so even though one of the *effects* of the denial of tenure—the eventual loss of a teaching position—did not occur until later. * * * "[T]he proper focus is upon the time of the *discriminatory acts,* not upon the time at which the *consequences* of the act becomes most painful." Abramson v. University of Hawaii, 594 F.2d 202, 209 (9th Cir.1979) (emphasis added); see United Air Lines v. Evans, * * * 431 U.S. at 558, 97 S.Ct. at 1889. * * *. It is simply insufficient for Ricks to allege that his termination "gives present effect to the past illegal act and therefore perpetuates the consequences of forbidden discrimination." Id. 431 U.S. at 557, 97 S.Ct. at 1888. The emphasis is not upon the effects of an

earlier employment decision; rather it "is [upon] whether any present *violation* exist."

449 U.S. at 258, 101 S.Ct. at 504 (some citations omitted; emphasis of the Court). The policy reason on which the Court relied was that periods of limitations reflect a value judgment concerning the point at which the interests in favor of protecting valid claims are outweighed by the interests in prohibiting stale claims.

3. THE CONTINUING VIOLATION THEORY AND TIMELY FILING

The Court, in *Ricks*, rejected also the plaintiff's argument based on the continuing violation theory. The continuing violation theory has its doctrinal foundation in the development of the present effects of past discrimination, a theory of discrimination used extensively in the seniority discrimination cases prior to *Teamsters*. The Supreme Court rejected the continued reliance on the "continuing violation" theory in United Air Lines, Inc. v. Evans, 431 U.S. 553, 97 S.Ct. 1885, 52 L.Ed.2d 591 (1977). If the claim is based on the continuing impact of a past, discrete act of discrimination, then the rule of *Ricks* and *Evans* is applicable; if, however, the implementation of a policy can be deemed to be renewed each day it is in effect, then the time begins to run anew each day the policy is in effect. See Hall v. Ledex, Inc., 669 F.2d 397 (6th Cir.1982) (equal pay case).

4. TIMELY FILING IN DEFERRAL JURISDICTIONS

Mohasco Corp. v. Silver, 447 U.S. 807, 100 S.Ct. 2486, 65 L.Ed.2d 532 (1980), involved the question whether Congress intended the term "filed" to have the same meaning in subsections (c) and (d) of Section 706. 42 U.S.C. Sections 2000e–5(c) and (d). The plaintiff, claiming that he had been discharged on August 29, 1975 because of religious discrimination, first filed his charge with the EEOC on June 15, 1976—291 days after his discharge. The EEOC, in turn, referred the charge to the state agency—the New York State Division of Human Rights—since the claim arose in a deferral jurisdiction. EEOC assumed jurisdiction over the charge 357 days after the plaintiff's discharge. The district court dismissed plaintiff's complaint on the ground that it had not been filed within the 300-day limitations period of Section 706(c), and the Supreme Court affirmed. The Court held, relying in substantial part on the legislative history of the 1972 amendments to Title VII, that the word "filed" as used in Sections 706(c) and (d) has the same meaning. Among the arguments that the Court specifically rejected were (1) the term "filed" as used in Section 706(c) merely requires the EEOC to postpone any action on a charge arising in a deferral jurisdiction for at least sixty days; (2) it would be unfair to lay persons who often proceed without counsel not to allow the full 300 days in which to file a charge in a deferral jurisdiction; and (3) that a less literal reading of Title VII would be more consistent with the policy of deferring to state agencies. Under *Mohasco*, then, a complainant, as a general rule, has only 240 days within which to file a charge with the EEOC when the claim arises in a deferral jurisdiction.

In footnotes 16 and 19 of *Mohasco,* the Court addressed an issue which had divided the lower courts: whether, in a deferral jurisdiction, the 300 days rule applies when no charge has been filed with the state or local agency within 180 days of the occurrence of the allegedly unlawful employment practice. The Court stated that a complainant in a deferral state need only file his charge within 240 days of the alleged discriminatory employment practice in order to preserve his rights under Title VII, but if the complainant files the charge later than 240 days but not more than 300 days, his right to seek relief under Title VII is preserved if the state agency completes its consideration of the charge prior to the end of the 300 days.

An issue which the Supreme Court has not addressed is whether the 300 day limitations period applies if a charge has not been timely filed with a state or local agency, as provided under state or local law. In his dissenting opinion in Delaware State College v. Ricks, 449 U.S. 250, 260, n. 13, 101 S.Ct. 498, 505, n. 13, 66 L.Ed.2d 431 (1980), Justice Stevens stated that a plaintiff would arguably have had to timely file with the state or local agency, but the majority found it unnecessary to decide the issue.

5. TIMELY FILING AND EQUITABLE CONSIDERATIONS

In Zipes v. Trans World Airlines, Inc., 455 U.S. 385, 102 S.Ct. 1127, 71 L.Ed.2d 234 (1982), the Court held that filing a timely charge with the EEOC is not a jurisdictional prerequisite but a requirement, like a statute of limitations, that is subject to waiver, estoppel, and equitable tolling. The Court thus clarified some loose language that it had used in several earlier cases in which it referred to the timely filing requirement as "jurisdictional."

One of the leading cases on equitable tolling is Reeb v. Economic Opportunity Atlanta, Inc., 516 F.2d 924 (5th Cir.1975). Plaintiff had been informed upon her termination that defendant did not have sufficient funds to continue her position. She believed the defendant because her position had been terminated on a prior occasion for the same reason. She did not file a charge with the EEOC within the then applicable limitations period—ninety days—of her latest termination. The plaintiff learned about six months later that she had been terminated so the position could be awarded to an allegedly less qualified male. She then promptly filed a charge with the EEOC. The district court dismissed for lack of jurisdiction. The court of appeals reversed:

> In these circumstances we apply the familiar equitable modification to statutes of limitations: the statute does not begin to run until the facts which would support cause of action are apparent or should be apparent to a person with a reasonably prudent regard for his rights. A corollary of this principle, often found in the cases where wrongful concealment of facts is alleged, is that a party responsible for

> such wrongful concealment is estopped from asserting a statute of
> limitations as a defense. * * * "No man may take advantage of his
> own wrong."

Id. at 930 (quoting Glus v. Brooklyn Eastern District Terminal, 359 U.S.
231, 232–33, 79 S.Ct. 760, 761–762, 3 L.Ed.2d 770 (1959)).

In Leake v. University of Cincinnati, 605 F.2d 255 (6th Cir.1979),
the court held that defendant waived its right to seek dismissal for
plaintiff's failure to timely file a charge when it expressly told the
plaintiff that it would not assert the defense in an effort to obtain more
time to conduct its own investigation of the charge. The Sixth Circuit
also found that a charge had been timely filed, in Morgan v. Washington Mfg. Co., 660 F.2d 710 (6th Cir.1981), when the plaintiff first wrote
a letter to President Carter within two months after her discharge; the
White House, in turn, forwarded the letter to the Department of Labor;
and the Department of Labor finally referred the letter to the EEOC
shortly after the 180 days had expired.

The *Zipes'* liberal tolling, estoppel, and waiver rules may not apply
when the plaintiff is represented by counsel at all stages of the
proceedings. See Leite v. Kennecott Corp., 31 FEP Cases 390 (D.Mass.
1983).

6. STATE JUDICIAL REMEDIES AND RES JUDICATA

Mohasco supports the proposition that prior resort to state and
local administrative remedies is a prerequisite to seeking judicial relief
under Title VII. Assuming that a plaintiff has otherwise satisfied the
timely filing requirements, a plaintiff is entitled to a trial *de novo* in
federal court. The issue in Kremer v. Chemical Construction Corp., 456
U.S. 461, 102 S.Ct. 1883, 72 L.Ed.2d 762 (1982), was whether a federal
court is required to give preclusive or res judicata effect to a state court
judgment when a plaintiff in an employment discrimination case seeks
state judicial review after first exhausting state administrative remedies. Kremer, a Jewish immigrant from Poland, worked for the Chemical Construction Corporation until 1975, when he was laid off. Claiming that his layoff was based on unlawful national origin and religious
considerations, Kremer first filed a charge of discrimination with the
EEOC. The EEOC, in turn, deferred action on the charge and referred
the charge to the state agency which had authority to grant relief. The
state agency investigated the charge and found it to be meritless.
Kremer then sought judicial review and the state appellate court
unanimously affirmed the decision of the state agency. The EEOC
eventually reviewed the charge but made a no cause finding. Kremer,
after receiving his notice of right to sue, filed suit in federal court. The
lower federal courts dismissed Kremer's complaint on the ground of res
judicata and the Supreme Court, in a 5–4 decision, affirmed. Relying
on 28 U.S.C. Section 1738, which requires the federal courts to grant
full faith and credit to state court judgments, the Court held that the
principles of res judicata apply unless Title VII partially repealed

Section 1738. The Court found nothing in the language of Title VII nor its legislative history supported either an expressed or implied rule against the applicability of Section 1973 to employment discrimination litigation. The Court thus held that Kremer's Title VII claim was barred under the principles of res judicata. Justice Blackmun, joined by Justices Brennan and Marshall, commenting on the practical implication of *Kremer,* stated:

> The lesson of the Court's ruling is: An unsuccessful state discrimination complainant should not seek state judicial review. If a discrimination complainant pursues state judicial review and loses—a likely result given the deferential standard of review in state courts—he forfeits his right to seek redress in federal court. If, however, he simply bypasses the state courts, he can proceed to the EEOC and ultimately to federal court. Instead of a deferential review of an agency record, he will receive in federal court a *de novo* hearing accompanied by procedural aids such as broad discovery rules and the ability to subpoena witnesses.

456 U.S. at 504, 102 S.Ct. at 1909 (1982). A critical discussion of the range of issues raised by *Kremer* is found in Catania, "Access to the Federal Courts for Title VII Claimants in the Post-Kremer Era: Keeping the Doors Open," 16 Loy. (Chicago). U.L.J. 209 (1985).

In Marrese v. American Academy of Orthopaedic Surgeons, 470 U.S. 373, 105 S.Ct. 1327, 84 L.Ed.2d 274 (1985), the Court interpreted *Kremer* to mean that "absent an exception to [the full faith and credit statute, 28 U.S.C. Sec. 1738], state law determines at least the preclusive effect of a prior state judgment in a subsequent action involving a claim within the exclusive jurisdiction of the federal courts." ___ U.S. at ___, 105 S.Ct. at 1352. Under *Marrese,* the first task of the federal court is to determine the preclusive effect of issues that were decided in the state litigation. Only if the court finds that state law would bar relitigation is it then necessary to consider if an exception to Section 1738 applies.

In University of Tennessee v. Elliott, ___ U.S. ___, 106 S.Ct. 3220, ___ L.Ed.2d ___ (1986), the plaintiff, after being informed that he would be discharged for inadequate work performance and misconduct on the job first sought relief under the state's administrative procedure act. Prior to the administrative hearing, the plaintiff filed suit in federal court seeking relief under Title VII and other civil rights statutes, claiming that his proposed discharge was racially motivated. The federal court initially entered a TRO restraining the University from discharging the plaintiff but later iifted the order permitting the administrative proceeding to go forward. The administrative law judge held that it did not have jurisdiction to adjudicate the plaintiff's civil rights claims but did allow him to present, as an affirmative defense, evidence that his proposed discharge was racially motivated. The administrative law judge ruled against the plaintiff, finding, *inter alia*, that the proposed dismissal was not racially motivated. The plaintiff did not seek judicial review of the administrative decision but instead returned to federal court to pursue his civil rights claims. The district court dismissed all of the claims on the ground res judicata. The Supreme Court held, based on the language and legislative history of Title VII and the Court's analysis in *Kremer*, that Congress did not intend unreviewed state administrative proceedings to have preclusive effect on Title VII claims. After noting that 28 U.S.C. Section 1738 does not apply to administrative decisions unreviewed in state courts, the Court also rejected defendant's invitation to adopt a common law rule of preclusion for Title VII claims. The Court held, however, that findings of a state administrative agency may bar a plaintiff from relitigating a discrimination claim under the Reconstruction-era Civil Rights Acts, e.g., 42 U.S.C. Sections 1983 and 1981, when the agency acts in a quasi-judicial capacity.

Trujillo v. County of Santa Clara, 766 F.2d 1368 (9th Cir.1985), held that *Kremer* applies when the defendant rather than the plaintiff seeks further review of the administrative decision in state court.

Kremer does not apply when the state has deprived the plaintiff of a property interest in violation of the due process clause of the fourteenth amendment. In Logan v. Zimmerman Brush Co., 455 U.S. 422, 102 S.Ct. 1148, 71 L.Ed.2d 265 (1982), the plaintiff filed a charge of discrimination under the Illinois equal employment law. State law required the Illinois Fair Employment Practices Commission to hold a fact finding conference within 120 days after a claimant filed a charge. The claimant was not granted a hearing on the merits and the claimant appealed. The state highest court held that it did not have jurisdiction to hear the appeal because it deemed the requirement of a fact finding hearing within 120 days to be mandatory. The Supreme Court reversed holding that the state had deprived the claimant of property right without due process of law.

7. ELECTION OF REMEDIES, WAIVER, AND TOLLING

In Alexander v. Gardner-Denver Co., 415 U.S. 36, 94 S.Ct. 1011, 39 L.Ed.2d 147 (1974), the Court held that an employee's statutory right to a trial *de novo* under Title VII is not defeated by prior submission of his or her claim to final arbitration under a nondiscriminatory clause of a collective bargaining agreement. The Court rejected several arguments in support of a contrary rule. First, the Court ruled that the doctrine of election of remedies is inapplicable to foreclose de novo review because the distinctly separate nature of contractual and statutory rights is not vitiated merely because both were violated as a result of the same factual occurrence. Second, the Court held that the plaintiff had not waived his rights under Title VII by first pursuing the grievance-arbitration route because rights conferred under a collective bargaining agreement and Title VII spring from different sources and serve different policy concerns: contractual rights may be relinquished by a union as the collective bargaining agent to obtain economic benefits for bargaining unit members; rights conferred by Title VII, on the other hand, represent a congressional command that each employee be free from discriminatory practices on an individual basis.

In footnote 21, the Court held that an arbitral decision may be admitted into evidence and accorded such weight as the trial court deems appropriate:

> We adopt no standards as to the weight to be accorded an arbitral decision, since this must be determined in the court's discretion with regard to the facts and circumstances of each case. Relevant factors include the existence of provisions in the collective bargaining agreement that conform substantially with Title VII, the degree of procedural fairness in the arbitral forum, adequacy of the record with respect to the issue of discrimination, and the special competence of particular arbitrators. When an arbitral determination gives full consideration to an employees's Title VII rights, a court may properly accord it great weight. This is especially true where the issue is solely one of fact, specifically addressed by the parties and decided by the arbitrator on the basis of an adequate record. But courts should ever be mindful that Congress, in enacting Title VII, thought it necessary to provide a judicial forum for the ultimate resolution of discriminatory employment claims. It is the duty of courts to assure the full availability of this forum.

415 U.S. at 60, n. 21, 94 S.Ct. at 1025, n. 21.

Resort to the grievance arbitration procedure does not toll the running of the limitations period within which a person claiming to be aggrieved must file a charge with the EEOC. International Union of Electrical, Radio and Machine Workers, Local 790 v. Robbins & Myers, Inc., 429 U.S. 229, 97 S.Ct. 441, 50 L.Ed.2d 427 (1976).

8. TIMELY FILING IN FEDERAL COURT AFTER RECEIPT OF STATUTORY NOTICE

Section 706(f)(1), 42 U.S.C. 2000e–5(f)(1), provides that a complaint must be filed in the appropriate federal district court within ninety days after receipt of the notice of right to sue from the EEOC. The courts have held that the ninety days do not begin to run until the complaining party has received actual notice. In Franks v. Bowman Transportation Co., 495 F.2d 398, 401–406 (5th Cir.1974), modified on other grounds 424 U.S. 747, 96 S.Ct. 1251, 47 L.Ed.2d 444 (1976), the EEOC sent the statutory notice but the plaintiff's nine year old son received and eventually lost it. Approximately one year later the plaintiff requested a right to sue letter not knowing that his son had lost the first one. The court held that the complaint had been timely filed within ninety days of the receipt of the second letter and rejected defendant's argument that the plaintiff should be deemed to have received the first one under a constructive receipt theory. However, in Bell v. Eagle Motor Lines, Inc., 693 F.2d 1086 (11th Cir.1982), the court relied upon the constructive receipt doctrine when the plaintiff filed his complaint more than ninety days after his wife had received the statutory notice.

The doctrine of laches may bar suit if an aggrieved party unreasonably delays requesting the right to sue notice or the notice is returned to the EEOC because the plaintiff failed to provide the EEOC with a current address and the defendant is prejudiced by the plaintiff's conduct.

A special set of problems arises when the plaintiff is represented by counsel at any time during the course of the administrative process or before the time runs after receipt of notice of right to sue. If an attorney has been designated as the agent of a plaintiff to receive the notice, the ninety days begins to run upon receipt of the notice by the attorney. See Perez v. Dana Corp., 545 F.Supp. 950 (E.D.Pa.1982).

9. WHAT CONSTITUTES A COMPLAINT

In Baldwin County Welcome Center v. Brown, 466 U.S. 147, 104 S.Ct. 1723, 80 L.Ed.2d 196 (1984), the Court held that the filing of the notice of right to sue does not toll the running of the ninety days filing requirement because the statutory notice, standing alone, fails to satisfy Rule 8(a) of the Federal Rules of Civil Procedure. Rule 8(a) states that a complaint must state the basis of jurisdiction, set forth a short, plain statement of the facts and a prayer for relief. *Baldwin* puts an end to the rule that had been approved by a number of lower courts holding that the mere filing of the right to sue notice by a layman tolls the running of the ninety days limitations rule. The Court arguably carved out exceptions to the *Baldwin* rule in those situations in which the plaintiff has received inadequate notice from the EEOC; or a motion for the appointment of counsel has been filed within the limitations period along with the statutory notice; or the court itself has led a plaintiff to believe that everything necessary to preserve jurisdiction has been done; or the defendant has engaged in affirmative conduct which caused the plaintiff to delay filing his or her complaint. 466 U.S. at 151, 104 S.Ct. at 1725–26.

10. THE RELATIONSHIP BETWEEN THE SCOPE OF THE CHARGE AND SCOPE OF THE COMPLAINT

As a general rule a plaintiff may allege in a judicial complaint only those claims that were made in the EEOC charge. Also, the general rule requires that only those respondents named in the EEOC charge can be named as defendants in the lawsuit. The courts have adopted the "like and related" rule to determine which claims can be asserted in a lawsuit when a particular claim has not been clearly set out as such in the EEOC charge. The "like and related" doctrine, which has its doctrinal foundations in Sanchez v. Standard Brands, Inc., 431 F.2d 455 (5th Cir.1970), holds that a plaintiff may raise as a claim in the judicial complaint any kind of discrimination like or related to the allegations contained in the EEOC charge and which the EEOC could be expected to investigate during the pendency of the charge before the EEOC. In *Sanchez*, the plaintiff, a black female, had specifically checked the box on the EEOC charge form marked "Race or Color", but she had not checked the box marked "Sex." She had stated in the "Explanation" section of the form that the employer's agent had "accused me of being the [leader] of the girls on the floor." The Fifth Circuit found the statement in the explanation section sufficient to state a claim for sex discrimination in addition to the claim for race discrimination. Most courts of appeals have followed the *Sanchez* rule. See Babrocky v. Jewel Food Co. & Retail Meatcutters, 773 F.2d 857 (7th Cir.1985).

L. CLASS ACTIONS

1. INTRODUCTION AND HISTORICAL DEVELOPMENTS

Many employment discrimination cases are brought as class actions pursuant to Rule 23 of the Federal Rules of Civil Procedure. Rule 23, in pertinent part, provides:

(a) *Prerequisites to a Class Action.* One or more members of a class may sue or be sued as representative parties on behalf of all only if (1) the class is so numerous that joinder of all members is impracticable, (2) there are questions of law or fact common to the class, (3) the claims or defenses of the representative parties are typical of the claims or defenses of the class, and (4) the representative parties will fairly and adequately protect the interest of the class.

(b) *Class Actions Maintainable.* An action may be maintained as a class action if the prerequisites of subdivision (a) are satisfied and in addition:

(1) The prosecution of separate actions by or against individual members of the class would create a risk of

(A) inconsistent or varying adjudications with respect to individual members of the class which would establish incompatible standards of conduct for the party opposing the class, or

(B) adjudications with respect to individual members of the class which would as a practical matter be dispositive of the interests of other members not parties to the adjudications or substantially impair or impede their ability to protect their interests; or

(2) the party opposing the class has acted or refused to act on grounds generally applicable to the class, thereby making appropriate final injunctive relief or corresponding declaratory relief with respect to the class as a whole; or

(3) the court finds that the questions of law or fact common to the members of the class predominate over any questions affecting only individual members, and that a class action is superior to other available methods for the fair and efficient adjudication of the controversy. * * *

(c) *Determination by Order Whether Class Action to be Maintained.* * * *

(1) As soon as practicable after the commencement of an action brought as a class action, the court shall determine by order whether it is to be so maintained. An order under this subdivision may be conditional, and may be altered or amended before the decision on the merits.

Subdivision (b)(2) was specifically added in the 1966 revisions of Rule 23 to provide for class action in civil rights cases. Advisory Committee's Notes, 39 F.R.D. 98, 102 (1966). Most employment discrimination cases are certified under (b)(2), but the question whether (b)(2) or (b)(3) is the proper subdivision is not free from doubt. See Wetzel v. Liberty Mutual Insurance Co., 508 F.2d 239 (3d Cir.1975), cert. denied 421 U.S. 1011, 95 S.Ct. 2415, 44 L.Ed.2d 679 (1975).

Prior to the Supreme Court's decision in East Texas Motor Freight Systems, Inc. v. Rodriguez, 431 U.S. 395, 97 S.Ct. 1891, 52 L.Ed.2d 453 (1977), the lower courts had liberally construed Rule 23 to allow broad based class actions in which a single plaintiff or group of plaintiffs could seek relief from a broad range of allegedly discriminatory employment practices. In Hall v. Werthan Bag Corp., 251 F.Supp. 184 (M.D. Tenn.1966), one of the first cases to reject the argument that class actions may not be brought to enforce rights created by Title VII, the court stated:

> Race discrimination is by definition a class discrimination. If it exists, it applies throughout the class. This does not mean, however, that the effects of the discrimination will always be felt equally by all the members of the racial class. For example, if an employer's racially discriminatory preferences are merely one of several factors which enter into employment decisions, the unlawful preferences may or may not be controlling in regard to the hiring or promotion of a particular member of the racial class. But although the actual effects of a discriminatory policy may thus vary throughout the class, the existence of the discriminatory policy threatens the entire class. And whether the Damoclean threat of a racially discriminatory policy hangs over the racial class is a question of fact common to all members of the class.

Id. at 186. The reasoning in *Hall* formed the doctrinal foundations for the development of the "across-the-board" theory of class actions in employment discrimination litigation. Johnson v. Georgia Highway Express, Inc., 417 F.2d 1122 (5th Cir.1969), was one of the leading court of appeals decisions which adopted the "across-the-board" class action theory. *Johnson* held that a plaintiff who alleged "across-the-board" discrimination could represent all persons, however situated, who were affected by an employer's or union's discriminatory practices. For example, an employee whose individual discrimination claim was based on circumstances surrounding his or her discharge could represent all individuals claiming discrimination in hiring, promotion, working conditions, and wages. See also Senter v. General Motors Co., 532 F.2d 511 (6th Cir.1976), cert. denied 429 U.S. 870, 97 S.Ct. 182, 50 L.Ed.2d 150 (1976); Rich v. Martin Marietta Corp., 522 F.2d 333 (10th Cir.1975).

2. CLASS ACTIONS IN THE SUPREME COURT

The Supreme Court first addressed the "across-the-board" theory in class actions in 1977 in East Texas Motor Freight System v. Rodriguez, 431 U.S. 395, 97 S.Ct. 1891, 52 L.Ed.2d 453 (1977). The plaintiff, three Mexican-Americans, were employed as city drivers. They had been refused an intra-company transfer under a no-transfer policy which prohibited movement of employees between city drivers jobs and over-the-road drivers jobs. They brought a Title VII class action challenging the legality of the no-transfer policy and the seniority system under the disparate treatment theory and sought to represent a class of all Mexican-Americans and blacks employed as city drivers. The proposed class included, among others, individuals who had been discriminated against in initial assignment as city drivers. The plaintiffs stipulated that they had not been victims of initial job assignments. Also they had not moved for class certification prior to trial. The trial court denied class certification but the court of appeals reversed, holding that the failure of the plaintiffs to move for class certification before trial was irrelevant. The court of appeals then certified the action as a proper class action under Rule 23.

A unanimous Supreme Court vacated and remanded. The Court found that class certification was inappropriate on two grounds: First, the plaintiffs themselves were found not to be adequate representatives of the class they sought to represent; second, the requisite class had been too broadly defined. The Court deemed the failure of the plaintiffs to move for class certification prior to trial and the district court's finding that they had not been the victims of unlawful employment discrimination to be fatal in satisfying the adequacy of representation requirement of Rule 23. The Court questioned the vitality of the across-the-board approach to class action theory when it held that class action treatment was inappropriate because the plaintiffs were not members of a class they sought to represent and a class action could be brought only by persons "possess[ing] the same interest and suffer[ing] the same injury" as class members. Since the plaintiffs had stipulated that they had suffered no discrimination with respect to their initial job assignments, the Court found that "they were hardly in a position to mount a classwide attack on the no-transfer rule * * * on the ground that [it] perpetuated past discrimination and locked minorities into less desirable jobs to which they had been discriminatorily assigned."

Lower courts split on the issue whether *Rodriquez* sounded the death knell for across-the-board class actions. Some court held that it did. E.g., Hill v. Western Electric Co., Inc., 596 F.2d 99, 101–102 (4th Cir.1979), cert. denied 444 U.S. 929, 100 S.Ct. 271, 62 L.Ed.2d 186 (1979). Other courts, however, continued to certify class actions under the across-the-board theory. E.g., Satterwhite v. Greenville, 578 F.2d 987, 993, n. 8 (5th Cir.1978), vacated on other grounds 445 U.S. 940, 100 S.Ct. 1334, 63 L.Ed.2d 773 (1980).

In General Telephone Company of the Southwest v. Falcon, 457 U.S. 147, 102 S.Ct. 2364, 72 L.Ed.2d 740 (1982), the issue before the Court was whether the plaintiff, a Mexican-American, who claimed that he was denied a promotion on the basis of national origin, could represent a class composed of Mexican-Americans "persons who are employed, or might be employed by GENERAL TELEPHONE COMPA-

NY, at its place of business located in Irving, Texas, who have been or who continue to be or might be adversely affected by the practices" complained of in the complaint. 457 U.S. at 157, 102 S.Ct. at 2367. Reversing the lower court and speaking directly to the across-the-board theory, the Court stated that,

> We cannot disagree with the proposition underlying the across-the-board rule—that racial discrimination is by definition class discrimination. But the allegation that such discrimination has occurred neither demonstrates whether a class action may be maintained in accordance with Rule 23 nor defines the class that may be certified. Conceptually, there is a wide gap between (a) an individual's claim that he has been denied a promotion on discriminatory grounds, and his otherwise unsupported allegation that the company has a policy of discrimination, and (b) the existence of a class of persons who have suffered the same injury as that individual, such that the individual's claim and the class claim will share common questions of law or fact and that the individual's claim will be typical of the class claim. For the [plaintiff] to bridge that gap, he must prove much more than the validity of his own claim. Even though evidence that he was passed over for promotion when several less deserving whites were advanced may support the conclusion that respondent was denied the promotion because of his national origin, such evidence would not necessarily justify the additional inferences (1) that this discriminatory treatment is typical of petitioner's promotion practices, (2) that petitioner's promotion practices are motivated by a policy of ethnic discrimination that pervades petitioner's Irving division, or (3) that this policy of ethnic discrimination is reflected in the petitioner's other employment practices, such as hiring, in the same way it is manifested in the promotion practices. These additional inferences demonstrate the tenuous character of any presumption that the class claims are "fairly encompassed" with respondent's claim.

457 U.S. at 157–58, 105 S.Ct. at 2370–71. In a critical footnote the Court stated:

> If petitioner used a biased testing procedure to evaluate both applicants for employment and incumbent employees, a class action on behalf of every applicant or employee who might have been prejudiced by the test clearly would satisfy the commonality and typicality requirements of Rule 23(a). Significant proof that an employer operated under a general policy of discrimination conceivably could justify a class of both applicants and employees if the discrimination manifested itself in hiring and promotion practices in the same general fashion, such as through an entirely subjective decisionmaking process. In this regard it is noteworthy that Title VII prohibits discriminatory employment *practices,* not an abstract policy of discrimination. * * *

457 U.S. at 159, n. 15, 102 S.Ct. 2371, n. 15. Although lower courts, after *Falcon,* have generally abandoned the earlier liberality with which class actions were certified, note 15 has been seen as a "window" for broad class certification in a limited class of cases. E.g., Richardson v. Byrd, 709 F.2d 1016 (5th Cir.1983).

3. CLASS ACTION CERTIFICATION PROCEDURES

The courts, pursuant to Rule 23(c)(1), usually conduct a class certification hearing at an earlier stage in the case. Some courts have adopted local rules establishing procedures and timetables for plaintiffs who seek to pursue a class action. The plaintiff has the burden of proving that all of the criteria for class certification are satisfied. See, e.g., Shelton v. Pargo, Inc., 582 F.2d 1298 (4th Cir.1978). An order denying class certification is, as a general rule, not immediately appealable. Gardner v. Westinghouse Broadcasting Co., 437 U.S. 478, 98 S.Ct. 2451, 57 L.Ed.2d 364 (1978). Putative class members may intervene to appeal the denial of class certification after the merits of the case have been decided. United Airlines, Inc. v. McDonald, 432 U.S. 385, 97 S.Ct. 2464, 53 L.Ed.2d 423 (1977).

4. INDIVIDUAL RIGHTS AND CLASS ACTIONS

Each member of a properly certified class need not have exhausted his or her administrative remedies before the EEOC as long as one of the named plaintiffs has satisfied the exhaustion requirement. Albemarle Paper Co. v. Moody, 422 U.S. 405, 414, n. 8, 95 S.Ct. 2362, 2370, n. 8, 45 L.Ed.2d 280 (1975).

In Crown, Cork & Seal Co., Inc. v. Parker, 462 U.S. 345, 103 S.Ct. 2392, 76 L.Ed.2d 628 (1983), the Court considered the issue whether the filing of a class action tolls the applicable limitations period and thus permits all class members of the putative class to file individual claims in the event class certification is denied, provided the individual actions are filed within the time remaining in the limitations period. Relying, in part, on its earlier decisions in American Pipe & Const. Co. v. Utah, 414 U.S. 538, 94 S.Ct. 756, 38 L.Ed.2d 713 (1974), and Eisen v. Carlisle & Jacquelin, 417 U.S. 156, 94 S.Ct. 2140, 40 L.Ed.2d 732 (1974), the Court held that the commencement of a class action suspends the applicable limitations period as to all putative class members who would have been parties had the suit been certified as a class action. Once certification has been denied, putative class members have the option to either file their own suit or intervene in the pending action.

Courts have discretion whether to allow individuals who have not filed their own charges with the EEOC to intervene after class certification is denied. Wheeler v. American Home Products Corp., 582 F.2d 891 (5th Cir.1977).

Cooper v. Federal Reserve Bank of Richmond, 467 U.S. 867, 104 S.Ct. 2794, 81 L.Ed.2d 718 (1984), involved the issue whether a judgment in a class action, after a ruling on the merits that an employer did not engage in a general pattern of discrimination against a class, precludes a class member from maintaining a subsequent action alleging an individual claim of discrimination against the same employer. The Court held a decision that an employer did not engage in classwide discrimination is not res judicata as to particular individual members of the class who subsequently seek relief from individual acts of discrimination. The Court acknowledged that a class action judgment is ordinarily binding upon all members of the class but based its decision on what it deemed to be a crucial distinction between class actions and individual claims of discrimination:

> The crucial difference between an individual's claim of discrimination and a class action alleging a general pattern or practice of discrimination is manifest. The inquiry regarding an individual's claim is the reason for a particular employment decision, while "at the liability stage of a pattern-or-practice trial the focus often will not be on individual hiring decisions, but on the pattern of discriminatory decisionmaking."

467 U.S. at 876, 104 S.Ct. at 2800 (citing *Teamsters v. United States,* 431 U.S. 324, 360, n. 46, 97 S.Ct. 1843, 1867, n. 46, 52 L.Ed.2d 396 (1977)). The court of appeals had based its decision on the *claim* preclusion branch of res judicata. The Supreme Court based its decision on the *issue* preclusion branch of res judicata when it held that "[a] judgment in favor of either side is conclusive in a subsequent action between on any issue actually litigated and determined." 467 U.S. at 874, 104 S.Ct. at 2799.

M.   FEDERAL GOVERNMENT EMPLOYEES

Employees of the federal government, like employees of state and local governments, were not covered under Title VII, as originally enacted in 1984. Congress extended coverage to federal, state, and local government under the 1972 amendments to Title VII. Section 701(a), 42 U.S.C. Section 2000e–(a) ("person" includes governments, governmental agencies, and political subdivisions; Section 717, 42 U.S.C. Section 716 (federal government).

1.   ADMINISTRATIVE ENFORCEMENT OF FEDERAL EMPLOYEE CLAIMS

Under the 1972 amendments to Title VII, Congress vested administrative enforcement of employment discrimination claims against the federal government and its agencies in the Civil Service Commission. Thus, a federal employee had to exhaust administrative remedies before the Civil Service Commission. The Reorganization Plan of 1978 transferred jurisdiction over actions brought under Section 717 of Title VII to the EEOC, but the effective date of the transfer was delayed until January 1, 1979 to coincide with the effective date of the Civil Service Reform Act of 1978.

The Civil Service Reform Act, Pub.L. No. 95–454, 5 U.S.C. Sections 1101 et seq. (Supp. IV 1980), abolished the Civil Service Commission and separated its functions into two new agencies—the Office of Personnel and Management (OPM) and the Merit Systems Protections Board (MSPB). The Civil Service Reform Act established two categories of cases to determine appropriate exhaustion of administrative requirements in claims of federal employees. The EEOC was given administrative jurisdiction over so-called "pure" claims of employment discrimination. If the claim involved both unlawful employment discrimination and other allegations, it is termed a "mixed-claim". Federal employees may seek *de novo* review in federal court under Section 717 after exhaustion of administrative remedies before the EEOC in the "pure" cases and the MSPB in the "mixed-claim" cases. In the "mixed-claim" cases, an aggrieved individual is not required to (but may) obtain appellate review in the courts of appeals or the Court of Claims. 5 U.S.C. Sections 7703(b)(1) and (b)(2); Doyal v. Marsh, 777 F.2d 1526 (11th Cir.1985).

2. RIGHT TO TRIAL DE NOVO

In Chandler v. Roudebush, 425 U.S. 840, 96 S.Ct. 1949, 48 L.Ed.2d 416 (1976), the Court rejected the government's argument that federal employees are not entitled to a trial *de novo* in federal court under Section 717. Construing the language in 717, which provides that actions against the federal government are to be governed by the "provisions of section 706(f) through (k), as applicable", the Court held that federal employees, like employees in the private sector, are entitled to a trial *de novo* in federal court after timely exhausting administrative remedies.

3. TITLE VII AS THE EXCLUSIVE REMEDY FOR FEDERAL EMPLOYEES

The plaintiffs in Brown v. General Services Administration, 425 U.S. 820, 96 S.Ct. 1961, 48 L.Ed.2d 402 (1976) sued the federal government in a discrimination case basing jurisdiction on both Title VII and the Civil Rights Act of 1866, 42 U.S.C. Section 1981. The Court held that Title VII provides the exclusive and pre-emptive remedy for unlawful employment discrimination claims by federal employees.

N. EEOC ENFORCEMENT AND LITIGATION

1. PREREQUISITES TO PATTERN OR PRACTICE CASES

The 1972 amendments to Title VII authorizes the EEOC to file pattern or practice suits in federal courts under Section 717. 42 U.S.C. Section 2000e–6. In Occidental Life Insurance Co. v. EEOC, 432 U.S. 355, 97 S.Ct. 2447, 53 L.Ed.2d 402 (1977), the Court held that the EEOC is not required to file a pattern or practice case in federal court within the 180 day provision of Section 706(f)(1), 42 U.S.C. Section 2000e–5(f)(1). The Court based its decision on the procedural protection a defendant has under the administrative enforcement scheme and the inherent power of a federal court, under the doctrine of laches, to fashion an equitable remedy when inordinate delay by the EEOC in filing suit results in prejudice to a defendant. Thus, for example, the court in EEOC v. Westinghouse Electric Co., 592 F.2d 484 (8th Cir. 1979), affirmed a dismissal of a portion of a case relating to claims arising before 1971 on the grounds of inordinate delay, destruction of records by the defendant, turnover of supervisory personnel, and the erosion of the memory of certain potential witnesses for the defendant.

2. DIRECT SUITS BY THE EEOC

Section 706, 42 U.S.C. Section 20000–5, sets out a number of procedural steps that the EEOC is to take before it brings a pattern or practice suit. These steps include receipt of timely charge, service of notice of the charge on the respondent within ten days, deferral to an appropriate state or local agency, investigation of the charge, a determination of whether there is reasonable cause to believe an unlawful employment practice has been committed, and an attempt to conciliate if reasonable cause is found. As a general rule the EEOC must have discharged its statutory duties in satisfying these steps before it can file a pattern or practice suit in federal court. As an alternative to dismissal for failure to satisfy its statutory obligations, a court may stay further proceedings pending completion of EEOC's statutory obligations. EEOC v. Klinger Electric Corp., 636 F.2d 104 (5th Cir.1981) (*per curiam*).

The EEOC does not have to comply with the requirements of Rule 23 of the Federal Rules of Civil Procedure to obtain relief on behalf of a class. General Telephone Co. v. EEOC, 446 U.S. 318, 100 S.Ct. 1698, 64 L.Ed.2d 319 (1980).

3. INTERVENTION IN PRIVATE CASES

The EEOC may intervene in private lawsuits pursuant to Sections 705(g)(6) and 706(f)(1), 42 U.S.C. Sections 2000e–4(g)(6) and 2000e–5(f)(1). Section 706(f)(1) provides for the method of intervention: upon timely application, the court may, in its discretion, permit the EEOC to intervene in a civil action upon certification that the case is of general public importance. The EEOC thus must satisfy three prerequisites to intervene in a private lawsuit: certification that the case is of general public importance; file a timely application for intervention; and obtain permission of the district court.

In Harris v. Amoco Production Co., 768 F.2d 669 (5th Cir.1985), four black employees brought a class action alleging that the employer discriminated against blacks in the areas of initial job assignment, promotion, and compensation. The EEOC then intervened in the action, but after its intervention, the private plaintiffs, before the case was certified as a class action, settled their case with the employer. The district court then dismissed the entire case. In reversing the dismissal of the case as to EEOC's complaint in intervention, the court of appeals held that (1) the EEOC's claim should not have been dismissed even though the private plaintiffs had settled their case and even though the EEOC had not satisfied the requirements for a direct action in its own name; and (2) that the rule of General Telephone Co. v. EEOC, supra, applies even when the EEOC seeks to intervene in a pending action. The Sixth Circuit, in Horn v. Eltra Corp., 686 F.2d 439

(6th Cir.1982), unlike the Fifth Circuit, held that the settlement of the private action was sufficient to revoke EEOC's status as an intervenor.

The EEOC may not expand the scope of the claims when it intervenes in a private civil action unless the EEOC has complied with its statutory obligation with respect to the additional claims it seeks to press. Johnson v. Nekoosa-Edwards Paper Co., 558 F.2d 841 (8th Cir. 1977), cert. denied 434 U.S. 920, 98 S.Ct. 394, 54 L.Ed.2d 276 (1977).

Under Section 706(f)(1), a private plaintiff may intervene in a suit as a matter of right if the EEOC first files suit. The courts are split on whether the EEOC is limited to intervention or can file an action in its own name when a private plaintiff is the first to file suit in federal court. See, e.g., EEOC v. Kimberly-Clark Corp., 511 F.2d 1352 (6th Cir. 1975), cert. denied 423 U.S. 994, 96 S.Ct. 420, 46 L.Ed.2d 368 (1975) (private action cuts off right of EEOC to file suit in its own name).

O. RELIEF

1. THE MAKE–WHOLE AND RIGHTFUL PLACE THEORIES

ALBEMARLE PAPER CO. v. MOODY

Supreme Court of the United States, 1975.
422 U.S. 405, 95 S.Ct. 2362, 45 L.Ed.2d 280.

Mr. Justice Stewart delivered the opinion of the Court.

These consolidated cases raise two important questions under Title VII of the Civil Rights Act of 1964, 78 Stat. 253, as amended by the Equal Employment Opportunity Act of 1972, 86 Stat. 103, 42 U.S.C. § 2000e et seq. (1970 ed. and Supp. III): First: When employees or applicants for employment have lost the opportunity to earn wages because an employer has engaged in an unlawful discriminatory employment practice, what standards should a federal district court follow in deciding whether to award or deny backpay? * * *

* * *

I

* * *

The respondents assured the court that the suit involved no claim for any monetary awards on a class basis, but in June 1970, after several years of discovery, the respondents moved to add a class demand for backpay. The court ruled that this issue would be considered at trial.

At the trial, in July and August 1971, the major issues were the plant's seniority system, its program of employment testing, and the question of backpay. In its opinion of November 9, 1971, the court found that the petitioners had "strictly segregated" the plant's departmental "lines of progression" prior to January 1, 1964, reserving the higher paying and more skilled lines for whites. The "racial identifiability" of whole lines of progression persisted until 1968, when the lines were reorganized under a new collective-bargaining agreement.

The court found, however, that this reorganization left Negro employees " 'locked' in the lower paying job classifications." The formerly "Negro" lines of progression had been merely tacked on to the bottom of the formerly "white" lines, and promotions, demotions, and layoffs continued to be governed—where skills were "relatively equal"—by a system of "job seniority." Because of the plant's previous history of overt segregation, only whites had seniority in the higher job categories. Accordingly, the court ordered the petitioners to implement a system of "plantwide" seniority.

The court refused, however, to award backpay to the plaintiff class for losses suffered under the "job seniority" program.[3] The court explained:

> In the instant case there was no evidence of bad faith noncompliance with the Act. It appears that the company as early as 1964 began active recruitment of blacks for its Maintenance Apprentice Program. Certain lines of progression were merged on its own initiative, and as judicial decisions expanded the then existing interpretations of the Act, the defendants took steps to correct the abuses without delay. * * *

> In addition, an award of back pay is an equitable remedy. * * * The plaintiffs' claim for back pay was filed nearly five years after the institution of this action. It was not prayed for in the pleadings. Although neither party can be charged with deliberate dilatory tactics in bringing this cause to trial, it is apparent that the defendants would be substantially prejudiced by the granting of such affirmative relief. The defendants might have chosen to exercise unusual zeal in having this court determine their rights at an earlier date had they known that back pay would be at issue.

* * *

We granted certiorari because of an evident Circuit conflict as to the standards governing awards of backpay.

* * *

II

Whether a particular member of the plaintiff class should have been awarded any backpay and, if so, how much, are questions not involved in this review. The equities of individual cases were never reached. Though at least some of the members of the plaintiff class obviously suffered a loss of wage opportunities on account of Albemarle's unlawfully discriminatory system of job seniority, the District Court decided that *no* backpay should be awarded to *anyone* in the class. The court declined to make such an award on two stated grounds: the lack of "evidence of bad faith non-compliance with the Act," and the fact that "the defendants would be substantially

---

3. Under Title VII backpay liability exists only for practices occurring after the effective date of the Act, July 2, 1965, and accrues only from a date two years prior to the filing of a charge with the EEOC. See 42 U.S.C. § 2000e–5(g) (1970 ed., Supp. III). Thus no award was possible with regard to the plant's pre-1964 policy of "strict segregation."

prejudiced" by an award of backpay that was demanded contrary to an earlier representation and late in the progress of the litigation. Relying directly on Newman v. Piggie Park Enterprises, 390 U.S. 400, 88 S.Ct. 964, 19 L.Ed.2d 1263 (1968), the Court of Appeals reversed, holding that backpay could be denied only in "special circumstances." The petitioners argue that the Court of Appeals was in error—that a district court has virtually unfettered discretion to award or deny backpay, and that there was no abuse of that discretion here.[8]

Piggie Park Enterprises, supra, is not directly in point. The Court held there that attorneys' fees should "ordinarily" be awarded—i.e., in all but "special circumstances"—to plaintiffs successful in obtaining injunctions against discrimination in public accommodations, under Title II of the Civil Rights Act of 1964. While the Act appears to leave Title II fee awards to the district court's discretion, 42 U.S.C. § 2000a–3(b), the court determined that the great public interest in having injunctive actions brought could be vindicated only if successful plaintiffs, acting as "private attorneys general," were awarded attorneys' fees in all but very unusual circumstances. There is, of course, an equally strong public interest in having injunctive actions brought under Title VII, to eradicate discriminatory employment practices. But this interest can be vindicated by applying the *Piggie Park* standard to the *attorneys' fees* provision of Title VII, 42 U.S.C. § 2000e–5(k), see Northcross v. Memphis Board of Education, 412 U.S. 427, 428, 93 S.Ct. 2201, 2202, 37 L.Ed.2d 48 (1973). For guidance as to the granting and denial of *backpay,* one must, therefore, look elsewhere.

The petitioners contend that the statutory scheme provides no guidance, beyond indicating that backpay awards are within the district

---

8. The petitioners also contend that no backpay can be awarded to those unnamed parties in the plaintiff class who have not themselves filed charges with the EEOC. We reject this contention. The Courts of Appeals that have confronted the issue are unanimous in recognizing that backpay may be awarded on a class basis under Title VII without exhaustion of administrative procedures by the unnamed class members. See, e.g., Rosen v. Public Service Electric & Gas Co., 409 F.2d 775, 780 (CA3 1969), and 477 F.2d 90, 95–96 (CA3 1973); Robinson v. Lorillard Corp., 444 F.2d 791, 802 (CA4 1971); United States v. Georgia Power Co., 474 F.2d 906, 919–921 (CA5 1973); Head v. Timken Roller Bearing Co., supra, at 876; Bowe v. Colgate-Palmolive Co., 416 F.2d 711, 719–721 (CA7 1969); United States v. N.L. Industries, Inc., 479 F.2d 354, 378–379 (CA8 1973). The Congress plainly ratified this construction of the Act in the course of enacting the Equal Employment Opportunity Act of 1972, Pub.L. 92–261, 86 Stat. 103. The House of Representative passed a bill, H.R.

1746, 92d Cong., 1st Sess., that would have barred, in § 3(e), an award of backpay to any individual who "neither filed a charge [with the EEOC] nor was named in a charge or amendment thereto." But the Senate Committee on Labor and Public Welfare recommended, instead, the re-enactment of the backpay provision without such a limitation, and cited with approval several cases holding that backpay was awardable to class members who had not personally filed, nor been named in, charges to the EEOC, S.Rep.No. 92–415, p. 27 (1971). See also 118 Cong.Rec. 4942 (1972). The Senate passed a bill without the House's limitation, id., at 4944, and the Conference Committee adopted the Senate position. A Section-by-Section Analysis of the Conference Committee's resolution notes that "[a] provision limiting class actions was contained in the House bill and specifically rejected by the Conference Committee," id., at 7168, 7565. The Conference Committee bill was accepted by both Chambers. Id., at 7170, 7573.

court's discretion. We disagree. It is true that backpay is not an automatic or mandatory remedy; like all other remedies under the Act, it is one which the courts "may" invoke.[9] The scheme implicitly recognizes that there may be cases calling for one remedy but not another, and—owing to the structure of the federal judiciary—these choices are, of course, left in the first instance to the district courts. However, such discretionary choices are not left to a court's "inclination, but to its judgment; and its judgment is to be guided by sound legal principles." United States v. Burr, 25 F.Cas.No.14,692d, pp. 30, 35 (CC Va.1807) (Marshall, C.J.). The power to award backpay was bestowed by Congress, as part of a complex legislative design directed at a historic evil of national proportions. A court must exercise this power "in light of the large objectives of the Act," Hecht Co. v. Bowles, 321 U.S. 321, 331, 64 S.Ct. 587, 592, 88 L.Ed. 754 (1944). That the court's discretion is equitable in nature, see Curtis v. Loether, 415 U.S. 189, 197, 94 S.Ct. 1005, 1010, 39 L.Ed.2d 260 (1974), hardly means that it is unfettered by meaningful standards or shielded from thorough appellate review. In Mitchell v. Robert DeMario Jewelry, 361 U.S. 288, 292, 80 S.Ct. 332, 335, 4 L.Ed.2d 323 (1960), this Court held, in the face of a silent statute, that district courts enjoyed the "historic power of equity" to award lost wages to workmen unlawfully discriminated against under § 17 of the Fair Labor Standards Act of 1938, 52 Stat. 1069, as amended, 29 U.S.C. § 217 (1958 ed). The Court simultaneously noted that "the statutory purposes [leave] little room for the exercise of discretion not to order reimbursement." 361 U.S., at 296, 80 S.Ct. at 337.

It is true that "[e]quity eschews mechanical rules * * * [and] depends on flexibility." Holmberg v. Armbrecht, 327 U.S. 392, 396, 66 S.Ct. 582, 584, 90 L.Ed. 743 (1946). But when Congress invokes the Chancellor's conscience to further transcendant legislative purposes, what is required is the principled application of standards consistent with those purposes and not "equity [which] varies like the Chancellor's

9. Title 42 U.S.C. § 2000e–5(g) (1970 ed., Supp. III) provides:

"If the court finds that the respondent has intentionally engaged in or is intentionally engaging in an unlawful employment practice charged in the complaint, the court may enjoin the respondent from engaging in such unlawful employment practice, and order such affirmative action as may be appropriate, which may include, but is not limited to, reinstatement or hiring of employees, with or without back pay (payable by the employer, employment agency, or labor organization, as the case may be, responsible for the unlawful employment practice), or any other equitable relief as the court deems appropriate. Back pay liability shall not accrue from a date more than two years prior to the filing of a charge with the Commission. Interim earnings or amounts earnable with reasonable diligence by the person or persons discriminated against shall operate to reduce the back pay otherwise allowable. No order of the court shall require the admission or reinstatement of an individual as a member of a union, or the hiring, reinstatement, or promotion of an individual as an employee, or the payment to him of any back pay, if such individual was refused admission, suspended, or expelled, or was refused employment or advancement or was suspended or discharged for any reason other than discrimination on account of race, color, religion, sex, or national origin or in violation of section 2000e–3(a) of this title."

foot." [10] Important national goals would be frustrated by a regime of
discretion that "produce[d] different results for breaches of duty in
situations that cannot be differentiated in policy." Moragne v. States
Marine Lines, 398 U.S. 375, 405, 90 S.Ct. 1772, 1790, 26 L.Ed.2d 339
(1970).

The District Court's decision must therefore be measured against
the purposes which inform Title VII. As the Court observed in Griggs
v. Duke Power Co., 401 U.S., at 429–430, 91 S.Ct., at 853, the primary
objective was a prophylactic one:

> It was to achieve equality of employment opportunities and remove
> barriers that have operated in the past to favor an identifiable group of
> white employees over other employees.

Backpay has an obvious connection with this purpose. If employers
faced only the prospect of an injunctive order, they would have little
incentive to shun practices of dubious legality. It is the reasonably
certain prospect of a backpay award that "provide[s] the spur or
catalyst which causes employers and unions to self-examine and to self-
evaluate their employment practices and to endeavor to eliminate, so
far as possible, the last vestiges of an unfortunate and ignominious page
in this country's history." United States v. N.L. Industries, Inc., 8 Cir.,
479 F.2d at 354, 379 (CA8 1973).

It is also the purpose of Title VII to make persons whole for
injuries suffered on account of unlawful employment discrimination.
This is shown by the very fact that Congress took care to arm the
courts with full equitable powers. For it is the historic purpose of
equity to "secur[e] complete justice," Brown v. Swann, 10 Pet. 497, 503,
9 L.Ed. 508 (1836); see also Porter v. Warner Holding Co., 328 U.S. 395,
397–398, 66 S.Ct. 1086, 1088–1089, 90 L.Ed. 1332 (1946). "[W]here
federally protected rights have been invaded, it has been the rule from
the beginning that courts will be alert to adjust their remedies so as to
grant the necessary relief." Bell v. Hood, 327 U.S. 678, 684, 66 S.Ct.
773, 777, 90 L.Ed. 939 (1946). Title VII deals with legal injuries of an
economic character occasioned by racial or other antiminority discrimination. The terms "complete justice" and "necessary relief" have
acquired a clear meaning in such circumstances. Where racial discrimination is concerned, "the [district] court has not merely the power but
the duty to render a decree which will so far as possible eliminate the
discriminatory effects of the past as well as bar like discrimination in
the future." Louisiana v. United States, 380 U.S. 145, 154, 85 S.Ct. 817,
822, 13 L.Ed.2d 709 (1965). And where a legal injury is of an economic
character,

> [t]he general rule is, that when a wrong has been done, and the law
> gives a remedy, the compensation shall be equal to the injury. The
> latter is the standard by which the former is to be measured. The

---

10. Eldon, L.C., in Gee v. Pritchard, 2
Swans. *403, *414, 36 Eng.Rep. 670, 674
(1818).

injured party is to be placed, as near as may be, in the situation he would have occupied if the wrong had not been committed. Wicker v. Hoppock, 6 Wall. 94, 99, 18 L.Ed. 752 (1867).

The "make whole" purpose of Title VII is made evident by the legislative history. The backpay provision was expressly modeled on the backpay provision of the National Labor Relations Act.[11] Under that Act, "[m]aking the workers whole for losses suffered on account of an unfair labor practice is part of the vindication of the public policy which the Board enforces." Phelps Dodge Corp. v. NLRB, 313 U.S. 177, 197, 61 S.Ct. 845, 854, 85 L.Ed. 1271 (1941). See also Nathanson v. NLRB, 344 U.S. 25, 27, 73 S.Ct. 80, 82, 97 L.Ed. 23; NLRB v. J.H. Rutter-Rex Mfg. Co., 396 U.S. 258, 263, 90 S.Ct. 417, 420, 24 L.Ed.2d 405 (1969). We may assume that Congress was aware that the Board, since its inception, has awarded backpay as a matter of course—not randomly or in the exercise of a standardless discretion, and not merely where employer violations are peculiarly deliberate, egregious, or inexcusable.[12] Furthermore, in passing the Equal Employment Opportunity Act of 1972, Congress considered several bills to limit the judicial power to award backpay. These limiting efforts were rejected, and the backpay provision was re-enacted substantially in its original form.[13] A Section-by-Section Analysis introduced by Senator Williams to accom-

---

11. Section 10(c) of the NLRA, 49 Stat. 454, as amended, 29 U.S.C. § 160(c), provides that when the Labor Board has found that a person has committed an "unfair labor practice," the Board "shall issue" an order "requiring such person to cease and desist from such unfair labor practice, and to take such affirmative action including reinstatement of employees with or without back pay, as will effectuate the policies of this subchapter." The backpay provision of Title VII provides that when the court has found "an unlawful employment practice," it "may enjoin" the practice "and order such affirmative action as may be appropriate, which may include, but is not limited to, reinstatement or hiring of employees, with or without back pay * * *." 42 U.S.C. § 2000e–5(g) (1970 ed., Supp. III). The framers of Title VII stated that they were using the NLRA provision as a model. 110 Cong.Rec. 6549 (1964) (remarks of Sen. Humphrey); id., at 7214 (interpretative memorandum by Sens. Clark and Case). In early versions of the Title VII provision on remedies, it was stated that a court "may" issue injunctions, but "shall" order appropriate affirmative action. This anomaly was removed by Substitute Amendment No. 656, 110 Cong.Rec. 12814, 12819 (1964). The framers regarded this as merely a "minor language change," id., at 12723–12724 (remarks of Sen. Humphrey). We can find here no intent to back away from the NLRA model or to denigrate in any way the status of backpay relief.

12. "The finding of an unfair labor practice and discriminatory discharge is presumptive proof that some back pay is owed by the employer," NLRB v. Mastro Plastics Corp., 354 F.2d 170, 178 (CA2 1965). While the backpay decision rests in the NLRB's discretion, and not with the courts, NLRB v. J.H. Rutter-Rex Mfg. Co., 396 U.S. 258, 263, 90 S.Ct. 417, 420, 24 L.Ed.2d 405 (1969), the Board has from its inception pursued "a practically uniform policy with respect to these orders requiring affirmative action." NLRB, First Annual Report 124 (1936).

"[I]n all but a few cases involving discriminatory discharges, discriminatory refusals to employ or reinstate, or discriminatory demotions in violation of section 8(3), the Board has ordered the employer to offer reinstatement to the employee discriminated against and to make whole such employee for any loss of pay that he has suffered by reason of the discrimination." NLRB Annual Report, Second p. 148 (1937).

13. As to the unsuccessful effort to restrict class actions for backpay, see n. 8, supra. In addition, the Senate rejected an amendment which would have required a jury trial in Title VII cases involving backpay, 118 Cong.Rec. 4917, 4919–4920 (1972) (remarks of Sens. Ervin and Javits),

pany the Conference Committee Report on the 1972 Act strongly reaffirmed the "make whole" purpose of Title VII:

> The provisions of this subsection are intended to give the courts wide discretion exercising their equitable powers to fashion the most complete relief possible. In dealing with the present section 706(g) the courts have stressed that the scope of relief under that section of the Act is intended to make the victims of unlawful discrimination whole, and that the attainment of this objective rests not only upon the elimination of the particular unlawful employment practice complained of, but also requires that persons aggrieved by the consequences and effects of the unlawful employment practice be, so far as possible, restored to a position where they would have been were it not for the unlawful discrimination. 118 Cong.Rec. 7168 (1972).

As this makes clear, Congress' purpose in vesting a variety of "discretionary" powers in the courts was not to limit appellate review of trial courts, or to invite inconsistency and caprice, but rather to make possible the "fashion[ing] [of] the most complete relief possible."

It follows that, given a finding of unlawful discrimination, backpay should be denied only for reasons which, if applied generally, would not frustrate the central statutory purposes of eradicating discrimination throughout the economy and making persons whole for injuries suffered through past discrimination.[14] The courts of appeals must maintain a consistent and principled application of the backpay provision, consonant with the twin statutory objectives, while at the same time recognizing that the trial court will often have the keener appreciation of those facts and circumstances peculiar to particular cases.

The District Court's stated grounds for denying backpay in this case must be tested against these standards. The first ground was that Albemarle's breach of Title VII had not been in "bad faith."[15] This is not a sufficient reason for denying backpay. Where an employer *has* shown bad faith—by maintaining a practice which he knew to be illegal or of highly questionable legality—he can make no claims whatsoever on the Chancellor's conscience. But, under Title VII, the mere absence of bad faith simply opens the door to equity; it does not depress the scales in the employer's favor. If backpay were awardable only upon a showing of bad faith, the remedy would become a punishment for moral turpitude, rather than a compensation for workers' injuries. This

---

and rejected a provision that would have limited backpay liability to a date two years prior to filing a complaint in court. Compare H.R. 1746, which passed the House, with the successful Conference Committee bill, analyzed at 118 Cong.Rec. 7168 (1972), which adopted a substantially more liberal limitation, i.e., a date two years prior to filing a charge with the EEOC. See 42 U.S.C. § 2000e–5(g) (1970 ed., Supp. III).

14. It is necessary, therefore, that if a district court does decline to award backpay, it carefully articulate its reasons.

15. The District Court thought that the breach of Title VII had not been in "bad faith" because judicial decisions had only recently focused directly on the discriminatory impact of seniority systems. The court also noted that Albemarle had taken some steps to recruit black workers into one of its departments and to eliminate strict segregation through the 1968 departmental merger.

would read the "make whole" purpose right out of Title VII, for a worker's injury is no less real simply because his employer did not inflict it in "bad faith." [16] Title VII is not concerned with the employer's "good intent or absence of discriminatory intent" for "Congress directed the thrust of the Act to the *consequences* of employment practices, not simply the motivation." Griggs v. Duke Power Co., 401 U.S., at 432, 91 S.Ct., at 854. See also Watson v. City of Memphis, 373 U.S. 526, 535, 83 S.Ct. 1314, 1319–1320, 10 L.Ed.2d 529 (1963); Wright v. Council of City of Emporia, 407 U.S. 451, 461–462, 92 S.Ct. 2196, 2202–2203, 33 L.Ed.2d 51 (1972).[17] To condition the awarding of backpay on a showing of "bad faith" would be to open an enormous chasm between injunctive and backpay relief under Title VII. There is nothing on the face of the statute or in its legislative history that justifies the creation of drastic and categorical distinctions between those two remedies.[18]

The District Court also grounded its denial of backpay on the fact that the respondents initially disclaimed any interest in backpay, first asserting their claim five years after the complaint was filed. The court concluded that the petitioners had been "prejudiced" by this conduct. The Court of Appeals reversed on the ground "that the broad aims of Title VII require that the issue of back pay be fully developed and determined even though it was not raised until the post-trial stage of litigation," 474 F.2d, at 141.

It is true that Title VII contains no legal bar to raising backpay claims after the complaint for injunctive relief has been filed, or indeed after a trial on that complaint has been had. Furthermore, Fed.Rule Civ.Proc. 54(c) directs that

> every final judgment shall grant the relief to which the party in whose favor it is rendered is entitled, even if the party has not demanded such relief in his pleadings.

16. The backpay remedy of the NLRA on which the Title VII remedy was modeled, see n. 11, supra, is fully available even where the "unfair labor practice" was committed in good faith. See, e.g., NLRB v. J.H. Rutter-Rex Mfg. Co., 396 U.S., at 265, 90 S.Ct. 417, 421, 24 L.Ed.2d 405; American Machinery Corp. v. NLRB, 5 Cir., 424 F.2d 1321, 1328–1330 (CA5 1970); Laidlaw Corp. v. NLRB, 7 Cir., 414 F.2d 99, 107 (CA7 1969).

17. Title VII itself recognizes a complete, but very narrow, immunity for employer conduct shown to have been undertaken "in good faith, in conformity with, and in reliance on any written interpretation or opinion of the [Equal Employment Opportunity] Commission." 42 U.S.C. § 2000e–12(b). It is not for the courts to upset this legislative choice to recognize only a narrowly defined "good faith" defense.

18. We note that some courts have denied backpay, and limited their judgments to declaratory relief, in cases where the employer discriminated on sexual grounds in reliance on state "female protective" statutes that were inconsistent with Title VII. See, e.g., Kober v. Westinghouse Electric Corp., 3 Cir., 480 F.2d 240 (CA3 1973); LeBlanc v. Southern Bell Telephone & Telegraph Co., 5 Cir., 460 F.2d 1228 (CA5 1972); Manning v. General Motors Corp., 466 F.2d 812 (CA6 1972); Rosenfeld v. Southern Pacific Co., 9 Cir., 444 F.2d 1219 (CA9 1971). There is no occasion in this case to decide whether these decisions were correct. As to the effect of Title VII on state statutes inconsistent with it, see 42 U.S.C. § 2000e–7.

But a party may not be "entitled" to relief if its conduct of the cause has improperly and substantially prejudiced the other party. The respondents here were not merely tardy, but also inconsistent, in demanding backpay. To deny backpay because a *particular* cause has been prosecuted in an eccentric fashion, prejudicial to the other party, does not offend the broad purposes of Title VII. This is not to say, however, that the District Court's ruling was necessarily correct. Whether the petitioners were in fact prejudiced, and whether the respondents' trial conduct was excusable, are questions that will be open to review by the Court of Appeals, if the District Court, on remand, decides again to decline to make any award of backpay.[20] But the standard of review will be the familiar one of whether the District Court was "clearly erroneous" in its factual findings and whether it "abused" its traditional discretion to locate "a just result" in light of the circumstances peculiar to the case, Langnes v. Green, 282 U.S. 531, 541, 51 S.Ct. 243, 247, 75 L.Ed. 520 (1931). On these issues of procedural regularity and prejudice, the "broad aims of Title VII" provide no ready solution.

* * *

Backpay in Title VII cases is generally computed, with respect to each affected employee or group of employees, by determining the amount of compensation lost as a direct result of the employer's discriminatory decision not to hire or promote. In litigation such as this, where the plaintiff class is limited to present and former employees of petitioner company who were denied promotions into the more lucrative positions because of their race, there is no need to make additional findings and offsetting computations for wages earned in alternative employment during the relevant period.

The information needed in order to compute backpay for non-promotion is contained in the personnel records and pay schedules normally maintained by an employer, some under compulsion of law. These data include the time at which an employee in the favored group was promoted over an otherwise more senior member of the disfavored class, and the wage differential that the promotion entailed. Rarely, if ever, could an employer plausibly invoke the doctrine of laches on the usual ground that the passage of time has put beyond reach evidence or testimony necessary to his case.

The prejudice on which the District Court relied here was, indeed, of a different and more speculative variety. The court made no findings of fact relevant to the subject, but found it "apparent" that prejudice would accrue because "[t]he defendants might have chosen to exercise unusual zeal in having this court determine their rights at an earlier date had they known that back pay would be at issue." 2 App. 498. This indulgent speculation is clearly not an adequate basis on which to deny the successful Title VII complainant compensatory

---

20. The District Court's stated grounds for denying backpay were, apparently, cumulative rather than independent. The District Court may, of course, reconsider its backpay determination in light of our ruling on the "good faith" question.

backpay and surely even less of a reason for penalizing the members of the class that he represents. In posing as an issue on remand "[w]hether the petitioners were *in fact* prejudiced," ante, at 2375 (emphasis added), the Court recognizes as much.

Although on the record now before us I have no doubt that respondents' tardiness in asserting their claim to backpay was excusable in light of the uncertain state of the law during the first years of this litigation, I agree that the District Court should be the first to pass upon the issues as the Court has posed them. Doubtful though I remain about their ability to do so, petitioners are entitled at least to an opportunity to prove that respondents' delay prejudiced their defense so substantially as to make an award of compensatory relief oppressive.

MR. JUSTICE REHNQUIST, concurring.

* * *

But precisely to the extent that an award of backpay is thought to flow as a matter of course from a finding of wrongdoing, and thereby becomes virtually indistinguishable from an award for damages, the question (not raised by any of the parties, and therefore quite properly not discussed in the Court's opinion), of whether either side may demand a jury trial under the Seventh Amendment becomes critical. We said in Curtis v. Loether, 415 U.S. 189, 197, 94 S.Ct. 1005, 1010, 39 L.Ed.2d 260 (1974), in explaining the difference between the provision for damages under § 812 of the Civil Rights Act of 1968, 82 Stat. 88, 42 U.S.C. § 3612, and the authorization for the award of backpay which we treat here:

> In Title VII cases, also, the courts have relied on the fact that the decision whether to award back-pay is committed to the discretion of the trial judge. There is no comparable discretion here: if a plaintiff proves unlawful discrimination and actual damages, he is entitled to judgment for that amount. * * * Whatever may be the merit of the "equitable" characterization in Title VII cases, there is surely no basis for characterizing the award of compensatory and punitive damages here as equitable relief. (Footnote omitted.)

In *Curtis,* supra, the Court further quoted the description of the Seventh Amendment in Mr. Justice Story's opinion for this Court in Parsons v. Bedford, 3 Pet. 433, 447, 7 L.Ed. 732 (1830), to the effect that:

> In a just sense, the amendment then may well be construed to embrace all suits which are not of equity and admiralty jurisdiction, whatever may be the peculiar form which they may assume to settle legal rights.

To the extent, then, that the District Court retains substantial discretion as to whether or not to award backpay notwithstanding a finding of unlawful discrimination, the nature of the jurisdiction which the court exercises is equitable, and under our cases neither party may demand a jury trial. To the extent that discretion is replaced by awards which follow as a matter of course from a finding of wrongdoing, the action of the court in making such awards could not be fairly characterized as equitable in character, and would quite arguably be subject to the provisions of the Seventh Amendment.

* * *

I agree, nonetheless, with the Court that the District Court should not have denied backpay in this litigation simply on the ground that Albemarle's breach of Title VII had not been in "bad faith." Good faith is a necessary condition for obtaining equitable consideration, but in view of the narrower "good faith" defense created by statute, 42 U.S.C. § 2000e–12(b), it is not for this Court to expand such a defense beyond those situations to which Congress had made it applicable. I do not read the Court's opinion to say, however, that the facts upon which the District Court based its conclusion, ante, at 2374 n. 15, would not have supported a finding that the conduct of Albemarle was reasonable under the circumstances as well as being simply in good faith. Nor do I read the Court's opinion to say that such a combination of factors might not, in appropriate circumstances, be an adequate basis for denial of backpay. See Schaeffer v. San Diego Yellow Cabs, Inc., 462 F.2d 1002, 1006 (CA9 1972); United States v. Georgia Power Co., 474 F.2d 906, 922 (CA5 1973).

* * *

Mr. CHIEF JUSTICE BURGER, concurring in part and dissenting in part.

I agree with the Court's opinion insofar as it holds that the availability of backpay is a matter which Title VII commits to the sound equitable discretion of the trial court. I cannot agree with the Court's application of that principle in this case, or with its method of reviewing the District Court's findings regarding Albemarle's testing policy.

With respect to the backpay issue, it must be emphasized that Albemarle was not held liable for practicing overt racial discrimination. It is undisputed that it voluntarily discontinued such practices prior to the effective date of Title VII and that the statute does not—and could not—apply to acts occurring before its passage. The basis of Albemarle's liability was that its seniority system perpetuated the effects of past discrimination and, as the District Court pointed out, the law regarding an employer's obligation to cure such effects was unclear for a considerable period of time. Moreover, the District Court's finding that Albemarle did not act in bad faith was not simply a determination that it thought its seniority system was legal but, rather, a finding that both prior to and after the filing of this lawsuit it took steps to integrate minorities into its labor force and to promptly fulfill its obligations under the law as it developed.[1]

---

1. The District Court concluded that Albemarle was entirely justified in maintaining some type of seniority system which insured that its employees would have "a certain degree of training and experience."

Its findings regarding the absence of bad faith were as follows:

"It appears that the company as early as 1964 began active recruitment of blacks for its Maintenance Apprentice

In light of this background, the Court's suggestion that the district Court "conditioned" awards of backpay upon a showing of bad faith, ante, at 2374, is incorrect. Moreover, the District Court's findings on this point cannot be disregarded as irrelevant. As the Court's opinion notes, one of Congress' major purposes in giving district courts discretion to award backpay in Title VII actions was to encourage employers and unions "'to self-examine and to self-evaluate their employment practices and to endeavor to eliminate, so far as possible, the last vestiges of an unfortunate and ignominious page in this country's history.'" Ante, at 2372. By the same token, if employers are to be assessed backpay even where they have attempted in good faith to conform to the law, they will have little incentive to eliminate marginal practices until bound by a court judgment. Plainly, then, the District Court's findings relate to "reasons which, if applied generally, would not frustrate the central statutory purposes * * *." Ante, at 2373. Because respondents waited five years before changing their original position disclaiming backpay and belatedly seeking it, thus suggesting that a desire to be "made whole" was not a major reason for their pursuit of this litigation, I cannot say that the District Court abused its discretion by denying that remedy.[2]

* * *

MR. JUSTICE BLACKMUN, concurring in the judgment.

I concur in the judgment of the Court, but I do not agree with all that is said in the Court's opinion.

The statutory authority for making awards of backpay in Title VII cases is cast in language that emphasizes flexibility and discretion in fashioning an appropriate remedy:

> If the court finds that the respondent has intentionally engaged in or is intentionally engaging in an unlawful employment practice charged in the complaint, the court may enjoin the respondent from engaging in such unlawful employment practice, and order such affirmative action *as may be appropriate, which may include,* but is not limited to, reinstatement or hiring of employees, *with or without* back pay * * * or any other equitable relief as the court deems appropriate. 78 Stat. 261, as amended, 86 Stat. 107, 42 U.S.C. § 2000e–5(g) (1970 ed., Supp. III) (emphasis added).

Despite this statutory emphasis on discretion, the Court of Appeals in this case reasoned by analogy to Newman v. Piggie Park Enterprises, 390 U.S. 400, 88 S.Ct. 964, 19 L.Ed.2d 1263 (1968), that once a violation of Title VII had been established, "[back pay] should ordinarily be awarded * * * unless special circumstances would render such an award unjust." 474 F.2d 134, 142 (CA4 1973). Today the Court rejects

Program. Certain lines of progression were merged on its own initiative, and as judicial decisions expanded the then existing interpretations of the Act, the defendants took steps to correct the abuses without delay." 2 App. 498.

2. As the Court points out, ante, at 2375 n. 20, the District Court's reasons for denying backpay were cumulative. It did not favor one policy of Title VII to the exclusion of all others, as I fear this Court is now doing.

the "special circumstances" test adopted by the Court of Appeals and holds that the power to award backpay is a discretionary power, the exercise of which must be measured against "the purposes which inform Title VII." Ante, at 2370–2371. With this much of the Court's opinion I agree. The Court goes on to suggest, however, that an employer's good faith is never a sufficient reason for refusing to award backpay. Ante, at 2373–2374. With this suggestion I do not agree. Instead, I believe that the employer's good faith may be a very relevant factor for a court to consider in exercising its discretionary power to fashion an appropriate affirmative action order. Thus, to take a not uncommon example, an employer charged with sex discrimination may defend on the ground that the challenged conduct was *required* by a State's "female protective" labor statute. See, e.g., Kober v. Westinghouse Electric Corp., 480 F.2d 240 (CA3 1973); Manning v. General Motors, 466 F.2d 812 (CA6 1972), cert. denied, 410 U.S. 946, 93 S.Ct. 1366, 35 L.Ed.2d 613 (1973); Schaeffer v. San Diego Yellow Cabs, Inc., 462 F.2d 1002 (CA9 1972); LeBlanc v. Southern Bell Telephone & Telegraph Co., 460 F.2d 1228 (CA5), cert. denied, 409 U.S. 990, 93 S.Ct. 320, 34 L.Ed.2d 257 (1972). In such a case, the employer may be thrust onto the horns of a dilemma: either he must violate Title VII or he must violate a presumptively valid state law. Even though good-faith reliance on the state statute may not exonerate an employer from a finding that he has intentionally violated Title VII, see, e.g., Kober v. Westinghouse Electric Corp., supra; cf., ante, at 2374 nn. 17–18, surely the employer's good-faith effort to comply with Title VII to the extent possible under state law is a relevant consideration in considering whether to award backpay. Although backpay in such a case would serve the statutory purpose of making the discriminatee whole, it would do so at the expense of an employer who had no alternative under state law and who derived no economic benefit from the challenged conduct.

Notes

1. *Back Pay.* The courts have held that back pay should completely redress the economic injury a plaintiff has suffered as a result of unlawful discrimination. The award thus include the salary and wages, including raises, which a discriminatee would have received but for discrimination, and appropriate adjustments for sick leave, vacation pay, pension benefits and other fringe benefits. See Rasimas v. Michigan Department of Mental Health, 714 F.2d 614, 626–67 (6th Cir.1983), cert. denied 466 U.S. 950, 104 S.Ct. 2151, 80 L.Ed.2d 537 (1984); Pettway v. American Cast Iron Pipe Co., 494 F.2d 211, 253–45 (5th Cir.1974). District courts have discretion whether to award prejudgment interest and, if awarded, the applicable rate—simple or compound. See EEOC v. Wooster Brush Co., 727 F.2d 566 (6th Cir.1984). Post-judgment interest is now mandatory under the federal interest rate statute. 28 U.S.C. Section 1961, as amended in 1982.

2. *The Collateral Source Doctrine.* The collateral source doctrine holds that funds received from a source other than, for example, wages and salaries a discriminatee would normally receive from an employer, should

be deducted from the back pay award. Funds which arguably fall within the collateral source doctrine in the employment discrimination cases include, for example, unemployment compensation, welfare assistance, and other forms of social security. The courts of appeals are split on whether funds received from a collateral source should be deducted from the back pay award. Compare, e.g., *Rasimas,* supra with Kauffman v. Sidereal Corp., 695 F.2d 343 (9th Cir.1982). The courts which hold that funds from a collateral source should not be deducted have placed heavy reliance on NLRB v. Gullet Gin, 340 U.S. 361, 364, 71 S.Ct. 337, 339–340, 95 L.Ed. 337 (1951). *Gullet Gin,* an NLRB case, held that the reduction of a back pay award under the collateral source doctrine should be left to the discretion of the district court.

3. *The Mitigation Doctrine.* Section 706(g) of Title VII, which imposes a duty to mitigate damages, states, in pertinent part that, "Interim earnings or amounts earnable with reasonable diligence by the person or persons discriminated against shall operate to reduce the back pay otherwise allowable." The Supreme Court addressed the mitigation doctrine in Ford Motor Co. v. EEOC, 458 U.S. 219, 102 S.Ct. 3057, 73 L.Ed.2d 721 (1982). The issue in the case was whether a defendant's offer of jobs to discriminatees after earlier rejections for employment on the basis of unlawful discrimination, but without the full measure of relief (here seniority relief), cuts off the defendant's liability for back pay from the date of the offer. The Court held that, under the facts of the case, the discriminatees had failed to mitigate damages in the rejection of the defendant's offer of employment and were not entitled to back pay from the date of rejection.

The finding that a discriminatee has or has not exercised reasonable diligence is an issue of fact subject to the clearly erroneous rule of Rule 52(a) of the Federal Rules of Civil Procedure. The defendant has the burden of proof on the issue whether a discriminatee has failed to exercise reasonable diligence to mitigate damages. See *Rasimas,* supra.

4. *The Moody Special Circumstances Doctrine.* Factors which constitute special circumstances to preclude an award of back pay are exceedingly rare. Among the arguments which have been rejected as supporting a finding of special circumstances are good faith effort to comply with federal law, *Moody,* supra; and difficulty in calculating back pay, Pettway v. American Cast Iron Pipe Co., 494 F.2d 211, 253–254 (5th Cir.1974). The Supreme Court found special circumstances sufficient to deny back pay to a class of females in City of Los Angeles, Department of Water and Power v. Manhart, supra, p. 262. The one category of cases in which the courts have found special circumstances involves sex discrimination claims when a defendant has relied, in good faith, on state female protective legislation. See cases cited in *Moody,* supra note 18.

5. For a comprehensive treatment of the range of issues dealing with back pay, see "Special Project—Back Pay in Employment Discrimination Cases," 35 Vand.L.Rev. 893 (1982).

6. As originally enacted in 1964, Title VII was a Commerce Power statute which applied only to private employment. The 1972 amendments to Title VII extended coverage to state and local governments. In Fitzpat-

rick v. Bitzer, 427 U.S. 445, 96 S.Ct. 2666, 49 L.Ed.2d 614 (1976) the Supreme Court stated that "There is no dispute that in enacting the 1972 Amendments to Title VII to extend coverage to the States as employers, Congress exercised its power under section 5 of the Fourteenth Amendment." The question at issue in *Fitzpatrick* was whether the State could invoke the Eleventh Amendment to immunize itself from liability for the back wage payments provided as a remedy for Title VII violations. In general, the Eleventh Amendment does provide state immunity from monetary damages unless the state has waived the immunity. In *Fitzpatrick,* the Court stated:

> But we think that the Eleventh Amendment, and the principle of state sovereignty which it embodies, see Hans v. Louisiana, 134 U.S. 1, 10 S.Ct. 504, 33 L.Ed. 842 (1890), are necessarily limited by the enforcement provisions of section 5 of the Fourteenth Amendment. * * * We think that Congress may, in determining what is "appropriate legislation" for the purpose of enforcing the provisions of the Fourteenth Amendment, provide for private suits against States or state officials which are constitutionally impermissible in other contexts.

427 U.S. at 456, 96 S.Ct. at 2671.

Fitzpatrick recognizes the principle that Congress has the power to override Eleventh Amendment immunity from monetary damage. It is frequently a separate question whether Congress has in fact done so in a particular statute. For the Supreme Court's resolution of this question under the Vocational Rehabilitation Act of 1973, see Atascadero State Hospital v. Scanlon, infra Chapter 7, p. 956.

FRANKS v. BOWMAN TRANSPORTATION CO., INC.

Supreme Court of the United States, 1976.
424 U.S. 747, 96 S.Ct. 1251, 47 L.Ed.2d 444.

MR. JUSTICE BRENNAN delivered the opinion of the Court.

This case presents the question whether identifiable applicants who were denied employment because of race after the effective date and in violation of Title VII of the Civil Rights Act of 1964, 78 Stat. 253, as amended, 42 U.S.C. § 2000e et seq. (1970 ed. and Supp. IV), may be awarded seniority status retroactive to the dates of their employment applications.

Petitioner Franks brought this class action in the United States District Court for the Northern District of Georgia against his former employer, respondent Bowman Transportation Co., and his unions, the International Union of District 50, Allied and Technical Workers of the United States and Canada, and its local, No. 13600, alleging various racially discriminatory employment practices in violation of Title VII. Petitioner Lee intervened on behalf of himself and others similarly situated alleging racially discriminatory hiring and discharge policies limited to Bowman's employment of over-the-road (OTR) truck drivers. Following trial, the District Court found that Bowman had engaged in a pattern of racial discrimination in various company policies, including the hiring, transfer, and discharge of employees, and found further that the discriminatory practices were perpetrated in Bowman's collective-bargaining agreement with the unions. The District Court certified the action as a proper class action under Fed.Rule Civ.Proc. 23(b)(2), and of import to the issues before this Court, found that petitioner Lee represented all black applicants who sought to be hired or to transfer to OTR driving positions prior to January 1, 1972. In its final order and decree, the District Court subdivided the class represented by petitioner Lee into a class of black nonemployee applicants for OTR positions prior to January 1, 1972 (class 3), and a class of black employees who applied for transfer to OTR positions prior to the same date (class 4).

In its final judgment entered July 14, 1972, the District Court permanently enjoined the respondents from perpetuating the discriminatory practices found to exist, and, in regard to the black applicants for OTR positions, ordered Bowman to notify the members of both subclasses within 30 days of their right to priority consideration for such jobs. The District Court declined, however, to grant to the unnamed members of classes 3 and 4 any other specific relief sought, which included an award of backpay and seniority status retroactive to the date of individual application for an OTR position.

On petitioners' appeal to the Court of Appeals for the Fifth Circuit, raising for the most part claimed inadequacy of the relief ordered respecting unnamed members of the various subclasses involved, the Court of Appeals affirmed in part, reversed in part, and vacated in part. 495 F.2d 398 (1974). The Court of Appeals held that the District Court had exercised its discretion under an erroneous view of law insofar as it failed to award backpay to the unnamed class members of both classes 3 and 4, and vacated the judgment in that respect. The judgment was reversed insofar as it failed to award any seniority remedy to the members of class 4 who after the judgment of the District Court sought and obtained priority consideration for transfer to OTR positions. As respects unnamed members of class 3—nonemployee black applicants who applied for and were denied OTR positions prior to January 1, 1972—the Court of Appeals affirmed the District Court's denial of any form of seniority relief. Only this last aspect of the Court of Appeals' judgment is before us for review under our grant of the petition for certiorari. 420 U.S. 989, 95 S.Ct. 1421, 43 L.Ed.2d 669 (1975).

* * *

II

In affirming the District Court's denial of seniority relief to the class 3 group of discriminatees, the Court of Appeals held that the relief was barred by § 703(h) of Title VII, 42 U.S.C. § 2000e–2(h). We disagree. Section 703(h) provides in pertinent part:

> Notwithstanding any other provision of this title, it shall not be an unlawful employment practice for an employer to apply different standards of compensation, or different terms, conditions, or privileges

of employment pursuant to a bona fide seniority or merit system * * * provided that such differences are not the result of an intention to discriminate because of race, color, religion, sex, or national origin * * *.

The Court of Appeals reasoned that a discriminatory refusal to hire "does not affect the bona fides of the seniority system. Thus, the differences in the benefits and conditions of employment which a seniority system accords to older and newer employees is protected [by § 703(h)] as 'not an unlawful employment practice". 495 F.2d, at 417. Significantly, neither Bowman nor the unions undertake to defend the Court of Appeals' judgment on that ground. It is clearly erroneous.

The black applicants for OTR positions composing class 3 are limited to those whose applications were put in evidence at the trial.[10] The underlying legal wrong affecting them is not the alleged operation of a racially discriminatory seniority system but of a racially discriminatory hiring system. Petitioners do not ask for modification or elimination of the existing seniority system, but only an award of the seniority status they would have individually enjoyed under the present system but for the illegal discriminatory refusal to hire. It is this context that must shape our determination as to the meaning and effect of § 703(h).

On its face, § 703(h) appears to be only a definitional provision; as with the other provisions of § 703, subsection (h) delineates which employment practices are illegal and thereby prohibited and which are not.[11] Section 703(h) certainly does not expressly purport to qualify or proscribe relief otherwise appropriate under the remedial provisions of Title VII, § 706(g), 42 U.S.C. § 2000e–5(g), in circumstances where an illegal discriminatory act or practice is found. Further, the legislative history of § 703(h) plainly negates its reading as limiting or qualifying the relief authorized under § 706(g). The initial bill reported by the House Judiciary Committee as H.R. 7152[12] and passed by the full House on February 10, 1964,[13] did not contain § 703(h). Neither the House bill nor the majority Judiciary Committee Report[14] even mentioned the problem of seniority. That subject thereafter surfaced during the debate of the bill in the Senate. This debate prompted

---

10. By its terms, the judgment of the District Court runs to all black applicants for OTR positions prior to January 1, 1972, and is not qualified by a limitation that the discriminatory refusal to hire must have taken place after the effective date of the Act. However, only post-Act victims of racial discrimination are members of class 3. Title VII's prohibition on racial discrimination in hiring became effective on July 2, 1965, one year after the date of its enactment. Pub.L. 88–352, §§ 716(a)–(b), 78 Stat. 266. Petitioners sought relief in this case for identifiable applicants for OTR positions "whose applications were put in evidence at the trial." App. 20a.

There were 206 unhired black applicants prior to January 1, 1972, whose written applications are summarized in the record and none of the applications relates to years prior to 1970. Id., at 52a, Table VA.

11. See Last Hired, First Fired Seniority, Layoffs, and Title VII: Questions of Liability and Remedy, 11 Col.J.L. & Soc. Prob. 343, 376, 378 (1975).

12. See H.R.Rep. No. 914, 88th Cong., 1st Sess., U.S.Code Cong. & Admin.News 1964, p. 2355 (1963).

13. 110 Cong.Rec. 2804 (1964).

14. H.R.Rep. No. 914, supra.

Senators Clark and Case to respond to criticism that Title VII would destroy existing seniority systems by placing an interpretive memorandum in the Congressional Record. The memorandum stated: "Title VII would have no effect on established seniority rights. Its effect is prospective and not retrospective." 110 Cong.Rec. 7213 (1964).[15] Senator Clark also placed in the Congressional Record a Justice Department statement concerning Title VII which stated: "[I]t has been asserted that Title VII would undermine vested rights of seniority. This is not correct. Title VII would have no effect on seniority rights existing at the time it takes effect." Id., at 7207.[16] Several weeks thereafter,

15. The full text of the memorandum pertaining to seniority states:

"Title VII would have no effect on established seniority rights. Its effect is prospective and not retrospective. Thus, for example, if a business has been discriminating in the past and as a result has an all-white working force, when the title comes into effect the employer's obligation would be simply to fill future vacancies on a nondiscriminatory basis. He would not be obliged—or indeed, permitted—to fire whites in order to hire Negroes, or to prefer Negroes for future vacancies, or, once Negroes are hired, to give them special seniority rights at the expense of the white workers hired earlier. (However, where waiting lists for employment or training are, prior to the effective date of the title, maintained on a discriminatory basis, the use of such lists after the title takes effect may be held an unlawful subterfuge to accomplish discrimination.)"

16. The full text of the statement pertinent to seniority reads:

"First, it has been asserted that title VII would undermine vested rights of seniority. This is not correct. Title VII would have no effect on seniority rights existing at the time it takes effect. If, for example, a collective bargaining contract provides that in the event of layoffs, those who were hired last must be laid off first, such a provision would not be affected in the least by title VII. This would be true even in the case where owing to discrimination prior to the effective date of the title, white workers had more seniority than Negroes. Title VII is directed at discrimination based on race, color, religion, sex, or national origin. It is perfectly clear that when a worker is laid off or denied a chance for promotion because under established seniority rules he is 'low man on the totem pole' he is not being discriminated against because of his race. Of course, if the seniority rule itself is discriminatory,

it would be unlawful under title VII. If a rule were to state that all Negroes must be laid off before any white man, such a rule could not serve as the basis for a discharge subsequent to the effective date of the title. I do not know how anyone could quarrel with such a result. But, in the ordinary case, assuming that seniority rights were built up over a period of time during which Negroes were not hired, these rights would not be set aside by the taking effect of title VII. Employers and labor organizations would simply be under a duty not to discriminate against Negroes because of their race. Any differences in treatment based on established seniority rights would not be based on race and would not be forbidden by the title." 110 Cong. Rec. 7207 (1964).

Senator Clark also introduced into the Congressional Record a set of answers to a series of questions propounded by Senator Dirksen. Two of these questions and answers are pertinent to the issue of seniority:

"Question. Would the same situation prevail in respect to promotions, when that management function is governed by a labor contract calling for promotions on the basis of seniority? What of dismissals? Normally, labor contracts call for 'last hired, first fired.' If the last hired are Negroes, is the employer discriminating if his contract requires they be first fired and the remaining employees are white?

"Answer. Seniority rights are in no way affected by the bill. If under a 'last hired, first fired' agreement a Negro happens to be the 'last hired,' he can still be 'first fired' as long as it is done because of his status as 'last hired' and not because of his race.

"Question. If an employer is directed to abolish his employment list because of discrimination what happens to seniority?

following several informal conferences among the Senate leadership, the House leadership, the Attorney General and others, see Vaas, Title VII: Legislative History, 7 B.C.Ind. & Com.L.Rev. 431, 445 (1966), a compromise substitute bill prepared by Senators Mansfield and Dirksen, Senate majority and minority leaders respectively, containing § 703(h) was introduced on the Senate floor.[17] Although the Mansfield-Dirksen substitute bill, and hence § 703(h), was not the subject of a committee report, see generally Vaas, supra, Senator Humphrey, one of the informal conferees, later stated during debate on the substitute that § 703(h) was not designed to alter the meaning of Title VII generally but rather "merely clarifies its present intent and effect." 110 Cong. Rec. 12723 (1964). Accordingly, whatever the exact meaning and scope of § 703(h) in light of its unusual legislative history and the absence of the usual legislative materials, see Vaas, supra, at 457–458, it is apparent that the thrust of the section is directed toward defining what is and what is not an illegal discriminatory practice in instances in which the post-Act operation of a seniority system is challenged as perpetuating the effects of discrimination occurring prior to the effective date of the Act. There is no indication in the legislative materials that § 703(h) was intended to modify or restrict relief otherwise appropriate once an illegal discriminatory practice occurring after the effective date of the Act is proved—as in the instant case, a discriminatory refusal to hire. This accords with the apparently unanimous view of commentators, see Cooper & Sobol, Seniority and Testing Under Fair Employment Laws: A General Approach to Objective Criteria of Hiring and Promotion, 82 Harv.L.Rev. 1598, 1632 (1969); Stacy, Title VII Seniority Remedies in a Time of Economic Downturn, 28 Vand.L.Rev. 487, 506 (1975).[18] We therefore hold that the Court of Appeals erred in concluding that, as a matter of law, § 703(h) barred the award of seniority relief to the unnamed class 3 members.

III

There remains the question whether an award of seniority relief is appropriate under the remedial provisions of Title VII, specifically, § 706(g).[19]

"Answer. The bill is not retroactive, and it will not require an employer to change existing seniority lists." Id., at 7217.

17. Id., at 11926, 11931.

18. Cf. Gould, Employment Security, Seniority and Race: The Role of Title VII of the Civil Rights Act of 1964, 13 How.L.J. 1, 8–9, and n. 32 (1967); see also Jurinko v. Edwin L. Wiegand Co., 477 F.2d 1038 (C.A.3), vacated and remanded on other grounds, 414 U.S. 970, 94 S.Ct. 293, 38 L.Ed.2d 214 (1973), wherein the court awarded back seniority in a case of discriminatory hiring after the effective date of Title VII without any discussion of the impact of § 703(h) on the propriety of such a remedy.

19. Section 706(g) of Title VII, 42 U.S.C. § 2000e–5(g) (1970 ed., Supp. IV), provides:

"If the court finds that the respondent has intentionally engaged in or is intentionally engaging in an unlawful employment practice charged in the complaint, the court may enjoin the respondent from engaging in such unlawful employment practice, and order such affirmative action as may be appropriate, which may include, but is not limited to, reinstatement or hiring of employees, with or without back pay (payable by the employer, employment agency, or labor organization, as the case may be, responsible for the unlawful employment practice), or any other equitable relief as the court deems appropriate. Back pay liability shall not accrue from a date

We begin by repeating the observation of earlier decisions that in enacting Title VII of the Civil Rights Act of 1964, Congress intended to prohibit all practices in whatever form which create inequality in employment opportunity due to discrimination on the basis of race, religion, sex, or national origin, Alexander v. Gardner-Denver Co., 415 U.S. 36, 44, 94 S.Ct. 1011, 1017, 39 L.Ed.2d 147, 155 (1974); McDonnell Douglas Corp. v. Green, 411 U.S. 792, 800, 93 S.Ct. 1817, 1823, 36 L.Ed. 2d 668, 676 (1973); Griggs v. Duke Power Co., 401 U.S. 424, 429–430, 91 S.Ct. 849, 852–853, 28 L.Ed.2d 158, 163–164 (1971), and ordained that its policy of outlawing such discrimination should have the "highest priority," *Alexander,* supra, 415 U.S., at 47, 94 S.Ct. at 1019, 39 L.Ed.2d at 158; Newman v. Piggie Park Enterprises, Inc., 390 U.S. 400, 402, 88 S.Ct. 964, 966, 19 L.Ed.2d 1263, 1265 (1968). Last Term's Albemarle Paper Co. v. Moody, 422 U.S. 405, 95 S.Ct. 2362, 45 L.Ed.2d 280 (1975), consistently with the congressional plan, held that one of the central purposes of Title VII is "to make persons whole for injuries suffered on account of unlawful employment discrimination." Id., at 418, 95 S.Ct., at 2372, 45 L.Ed.2d, at 297. To effectuate this "make whole" objective, Congress in § 706(g) vested broad equitable discretion in the federal courts to "order such affirmative action as may be appropriate, which may include, but is not limited to, reinstatement or hiring of employees, with or without back pay * * *, or any other equitable relief as the court deems appropriate." The legislative history supporting the 1972 amendments of § 706(g) of Title VII affirms the breadth of this discretion. "The provisions of [§ 706(g)] are intended to give the courts wide discretion exercising their equitable powers to fashion the most complete relief possible. * * * [T]he Act is intended to make the victims of unlawful employment discrimination whole, and * * * the attainment of this objective * * * requires that persons aggrieved by the consequences and effects of the unlawful employment practice be, so far as possible, restored to a position where they would have been were it not for the unlawful discrimination." Section-by-Section Analysis of H.R. 1746, accompanying the Equal Employment Opportunity Act of 1972—Conference Report, 118 Cong.Rec. 7166, 7168 (1972). This is emphatic confirmation that federal courts are empowered to fashion such relief as the particular circumstances of a case may require to effect restitution, making whole insofar as possible the victims of racial discrimination in hiring.[21] Adequate relief may be well be denied in

more than two years prior to the filing of a charge with the Commission. Interim earnings or amounts earnable with reasonable diligence by the person or persons discriminated against shall operate to reduce the back pay otherwise allowable. No order of the court shall require the admission or reinstatement of an individual as a member of a union, or the hiring, reinstatement, or promotion of an individual as an employee, or the payment to him of any back pay, if such individual was refused admission, suspended, or expelled, or was refused employment or advancement or was suspended or discharged for any reason other than discrimination on account of race, color, religion, sex, or national origin or in violation of section 2000e–3(a) of this title."

21. It is true that backpay is the only remedy specifically mentioned in § 706(g). But to draw from this fact and other sections of the statute, post, at 1276–1278, any implicit statement by Congress that seniority relief is a prohibited, or at least less available, form of remedy is not warranted. Indeed, any such contention necessarily disregards the extensive legislative history

the absence of a seniority remedy slotting the victim in that position in the seniority system that would have been his had he been hired at the time of his application. It can hardly be questioned that ordinarily such relief will be necessary to achieve the "make-whole" purposes of the Act.

Seniority systems and the entitlements conferred by credits earned thereunder are of vast and increasing importance in the economic employment system of this Nation. S. Slichter, J. Healy, & E. Livernash, The Impact of Collective Bargaining on Management 104–115 (1960). Seniority principles are increasingly used to allocate entitlements to scarce benefits among competing employees ("competitive status" seniority) and to compute noncompetitive benefits earned under the contract of employment ("benefit" seniority). Ibid. We have already said about "competitive status" seniority that it "has become of overriding importance, and one of its major functions is to determine who gets or who keeps an available job." Humphrey v. Moore, 375 U.S. 335, 346–347, 84 S.Ct. 363, 370, 11 L.Ed.2d 370, 380 (1964). "More than any other provision of the collective[-bargaining] agreement * * * seniority affects the economic security of the individual employee covered by its terms." Aaron, Reflections on the Legal Nature and

underlying the 1972 amendments to Title VII. The 1972 amendments added the phrase speaking to "other equitable relief" in § 706(g). The Senate Report manifested an explicit concern with the "earnings gap" presently existing between black and white employees in American society. S.Rep. No. 92–415, p. 6 (1971). The Reports of both Houses of Congress indicated that "rightful place" was the intended objective of Title VII and the relief accorded thereunder. Ibid.; H.R.Rep. No. 92–238, p. 4 (1971), U.S.Code Cong. & Admin.News 1972, p. 2137. As indicated, infra, at 1265–1266, and n. 28, rightful-place seniority, implicating an employee's *future* earnings, job security, and advancement prospects, is absolutely essential to obtaining this congressionally mandated goal.

The legislative history underlying the 1972 amendments completely answers the argument that Congress somehow intended seniority relief to be less available in pursuit of this goal. In explaining the need for the 1972 amendments, the Senate Report stated:

"Employment discrimination as viewed today is a * * * complex and pervasive phenomenon. Experts familiar with the subject now generally describe the problem in terms of 'systems' and 'effects' rather than simply intentional wrongs, and the literature on the subject is replete with discussions of, for example, the mechanics of seniority and lines of progression, perpetuation of the present effect of pre-act discriminatory

practices through various institutional devices, and testing and validation requirements." S.Rep. No. 92–415, supra, at 5. See also H.R.Rep. No. 92–238, supra, at 8. In the context of this express reference to seniority, the Reports of both Houses cite with approval decisions of the lower federal courts which granted forms of retroactive "rightful place" seniority relief. S.Rep. No. 92–415, supra, at 5 n. 1; H.R.Rep. No. 92–238, supra, at 8 n. 2. (The dissent, post, at 1279 n. 18, would distinguish these lower federal court decisions as not involving instances of discriminatory *hiring*. Obviously, however, the concern of the entire thrust of the dissent—the impact of rightful-place seniority upon the expectations of other employees—is in no way a function of the specific type of illegal discriminatory practice upon which the judgment of liability is predicated.) Thereafter, in language that could hardly be more explicit, the analysis accompanying the Conference Report stated:

"In any area where the new law does not address itself, or in any areas where a specific contrary intention is not indicated, it was assumed *that the present case law as developed by the courts would continue to govern the applicability and construction of Title VII.*" Section-By-Section Analysis of H.R.1746, accompanying The Equal Employment Opportunity Act of 1972—Conference Report, 118 Cong.Rec. 7166 (1972) (emphasis added).

Enforceability of Seniority Rights, 75 Harv.L.Rev. 1532, 1535 (1962). "Competitive status" seniority also often plays a broader role in modern employment systems, particularly systems operated under collective-bargaining agreements:

> Included among the benefits, options, and safeguards affected by competitive status seniority, are not only promotion and layoff, but also transfer, demotion, rest days, shift assignments, prerogative in scheduling vacation, order of layoff, possibilities of lateral transfer to avoid layoff, 'bumping' possibilities in the face of layoff, order of recall, training opportunities, working conditions, length of layoff endured without reducing seniority, length of layoff recall rights will withstand, overtime opportunities, parking privileges, and, in one plant, a pre-ferred place in the punch-out line. Stacy, 28 Vand.L.Rev., supra, at 490 (footnotes omitted).

Seniority standing in employment with respondent Bowman, computed from the departmental date of hire, determines the order of layoff and recall of employees. Further, job assignments for OTR drivers are posted for competitive bidding and seniority is used to determine the highest bidder. As OTR drivers are paid on a per-mile basis, earnings are therefore to some extent a function of seniority. Additionally, seniority computed from the company date of hire determines the length of an employee's vacation and pension benefits. Obviously merely to require Bowman to hire the class 3 victim of discrimination falls far short of a "make whole" remedy.[27] A concomitant award of the seniority credit he presumptively would have earned but for the wrongful treatment would also seem necessary in the absence of justification for denying that relief. Without an award of seniority dating from the time when he was discriminatorily refused employment, an individual who applies for and obtains employment as an OTR driver pursuant to the District Court's order will never obtain his rightful place in the hierarchy of seniority according to which these various employment benefits are distributed. He will perpetually remain subordinate to persons who, but for the illegal discrimination, would have been in respect to entitlement to these benefits his inferiors.[28]

27. Further, at least in regard to "benefit"-type seniority such as length of vacation leave and pension benefits in the instant case, any general bar to the award of retroactive seniority for victims of illegal hiring discrimination serves to undermine the mutually reinforcing effect of the dual purposes of Title VII; it reduces the restitution required of an employer at such time as he is called upon to account for his discriminatory actions perpetrated in violation of the law. See Albemarle Paper Co. v. Moody, 422 U.S. 405, 417–418, 95 S.Ct. 2362, 2371–2372, 45 L.Ed.2d 280, 296–297 (1975).

28. Accordingly, it is clear that the seniority remedy which petitioners seek does not concern only the "make-whole" purposes of Title VII. The dissent errs in treating the issue of seniority relief as implicating only the "make whole" objective of Title VII and in stating that "Title VII's 'primary objective' of eradicating discrimination is not served at all * * *." Post, at 1275. Nothing could be further from reality—the issue of seniority relief cuts to the very heart of Title VII's primary objective of eradicating present and future discrimination in a way that backpay, for example, can never do. "[S]eniority, after all, is a right which a worker exercises in each job movement in the future, rather than a simple one-time payment for the past." Poplin, Fair Employment in a Depressed Economy: The Layoff Problem, 23 U.C.L.A.L.Rev. 177, 225 (1975).

The Court of Appeals apparently followed this reasoning in holding that the District Court erred in not granting seniority relief to class 4 Bowman employees who were discriminatorily refused transfer to OTR positions. Yet the class 3 discriminatees in the absence of a comparable seniority award would also remain subordinated in the seniority system to the class 4 discriminatees. The distinction plainly finds no support anywhere in Title VII or its legislative history. Settled law dealing with the related "twin" areas of discriminatory hiring and discharges violative of the National Labor Relations Act, 49 Stat. 449, as amended, 29 U.S.C. § 151 et seq., provides a persuasive analogy. "[I]t would indeed be surprising if Congress gave a remedy for the one which it denied for the other." Phelps Dodge Corp. v. NLRB, 313 U.S. 177, 187, 61 S.Ct. 845, 849, 85 L.Ed. 1271, 1279 (1941). For courts to differentiate without justification between the classes of discriminatees "would be a differentiation not only without substance but in defiance of that against which the prohibition of discrimination is directed." Id., at 188, 61 S.Ct., at 850, 85 L.Ed., at 1280.

Similarly, decisions construing the remedial section of the National Labor Relations Act, § 10(c), 29 U.S.C. § 160(c)—the model for § 706(g), *Albemarle Paper*, 422 U.S., at 419, 95 S.Ct., at 2372, 45 L.Ed.2d, at 297 [29]—make clear that remedies constituting authorized "affirmative action" include an award of seniority status, for the thrust of "affirmative action" redressing the wrong incurred by an unfair labor practice is to make "the employees whole, and thus restor[e] the economic status quo that would have obtained but for the company's wrongful [act]." NLRB v. Rutter-Rex Mfg. Co., 396 U.S. 258, 263, 90 S.Ct. 417, 420, 24 L.Ed.2d 405, 411 (1969). The task of the NLRB in applying § 10(c) is "to take measures designed to recreate the conditions and relationships that would have been had there been no unfair labor practice." Carpenters v. NLRB, 365 U.S. 651, 657, 81 S.Ct. 875, 879, 6 L.Ed.2d 1, 5 (1961) (Harlan, J., concurring). And the NLRB has often required that the hiring of employees who have been discriminatorily refused employment be accompanied by an award of seniority equivalent to that which they would have enjoyed but for the illegal conduct. See, e.g., In re Phelps Dodge Corp., 19 N.L.R.B. 547, 600, and n. 39, 603–604 (1940), modified on other grounds, 313 U.S. 177, 61 S.Ct. 845, 85 L.Ed. 1271 (1941) (ordering persons discriminatorily refused employment hired "without prejudice to their seniority or other rights and privileges"); In re Nevada Consolidated Copper Corp., 26 N.L.R.B. 1182, 1235 (1940), enforced, 316 U.S. 105, 62 S.Ct. 960, 86 L.Ed. 1305 (1942) (ordering

---

29. To the extent that there is a difference in the wording of the respective provisions, § 706(g) grants, if anything, broader discretionary powers than those granted the National Labor Relations Board. Section 10(c) of the NLRA authorizes "such affirmative action including reinstatement of employees with or without back pay, as will effectuate the policies of this sub-chapter," 29 U.S.C. § 160(c), whereas § 706(g) as amended in 1972 authorizes "such affirmative action as may be appropriate, which may include, *but is not limited to*, reinstatement *or hiring* of employees, with or without back pay * * *, *or any other equitable relief as the court deems appropriate*." 42 U.S.C. § 2000e–5(g) (1970 ed., Supp. IV) (emphasis added).

persons discriminatorily refused employment hired with "any seniority or other rights and privileges they would have acquired, had the respondent not unlawfully discriminated against them"). Plainly the "affirmative action" injunction of § 706(g) has no lesser reach in the district courts. "Where racial discrimination is concerned, 'the [district] court has not merely the power but the duty to render a decree which will so far as possible eliminate the discriminatory effects of the past as well as bar like discrimination in the future.'" *Albemarle Paper,* supra, 422 U.S., at 418, 95 S.Ct., at 2372, 45 L.Ed.2d at 297.

IV

We are not to be understood as holding that an award of seniority status is requisite in all circumstances. The fashioning of appropriate remedies invokes the sound equitable discretion of the district courts. Respondent Bowman attempts to justify the District Court's denial of seniority relief for petitioners as an exercise of equitable discretion, but the record is its own refutation of the argument.

Albemarle Paper, supra, at 416, 95 S.Ct., at 2371, 45 L.Ed.2d, at 296, made clear that discretion imports not the court's "'inclination, but * * * its judgment; and its judgment is to be guided by sound legal principles.'" Discretion is vested not for purposes of "limit[ing] appellate review of trial courts, or * * * invit[ing] inconsistency and caprice," but rather to allow the most complete achievement of the objectives of Title VII that is attainable under the facts and circumstances of the specific case. 422 U.S., at 421, 95 S.Ct., at 2373, 45 L.Ed. 2d, at 298. Accordingly, the District Court's denial of any form of seniority remedy must be reviewed in terms of its effect on the attainment of the Act's objectives under the circumstances presented by this record. No less than with the denial of the remedy of backpay, the denial of seniority relief to victims of illegal racial discrimination in hiring is permissible "only for reasons which, if applied generally, would not frustrate the central statutory purposes of eradicating discrimination throughout the economy and making persons whole for injuries suffered through past discrimination." Ibid.

The District Court stated two reasons for its denial of seniority relief for the unnamed class members.[30] The first was that those individuals had not filed administrative charges under the provisions of Title VII with the Equal Employment Opportunity Commission and therefore class relief of this sort was not appropriate. We rejected this justification for denial of class-based relief in the context of backpay awards in *Albemarle Paper,* and for the same reasons reject it here. This justification for denying class-based relief in Title VII suits has been unanimously rejected by the courts of appeals, and Congress

30. Since the Court of Appeals concluded that an award of retroactive seniority to the unnamed members of class 3 was barred by § 703(h), a conclusion which we today reject, the court did not address specifically the District Court's stated reasons for refusing the relief. The Court of Appeals also stated, however, that the District Court did not "abuse its discretion" in refusing such relief, 495 F.2d 398, 418 (1974), and we may therefore appropriately review the validity of the District Court's reasons.

ratified that construction by the 1972 amendments. *Albemarle Paper,* supra, at 414 n. 8, 95 S.Ct., at 2370, 45 L.Ed.2d, at 294.

The second reason stated by the District Court was that such claims "presuppose a vacancy, qualification, and performance by every member. There is no evidence on which to base these multiple conclusions." Pet. for Cert. A54. The Court of Appeals rejected this reason insofar as it was the basis of the District Court's denial of backpay, and of its denial of retroactive seniority relief to the unnamed members of class 4. We hold that it is also an improper reason for denying seniority relief to the unnamed members of class 3.

We read the District Court's reference to the lack of evidence regarding a "vacancy, qualification, and performance" for every individual member of the class as an expression of concern that some of the unnamed class members (unhired black applicants whose employment applications were summarized in the record) may not in fact have been actual victims of racial discrimination. That factor will become material however only when those persons reapply for OTR positions pursuant to the hiring relief ordered by the District Court. Generalizations concerning such individually applicable evidence cannot serve as a justification for the denial of relief to the entire class. Rather, at such time as individual class members seek positions as OTR drivers, positions for which they are presumptively entitled to priority hiring consideration under the District Court's order,[31] evidence that particular individuals were not in fact victims of racial discrimination will be material. But petitioners here have carried their burden of demonstrating the existence of a discriminatory hiring pattern and practice by the respondents and, therefore, the burden will be upon respondents to prove that individuals who reapply were not in fact victims of previous hiring discrimination. Cf. McDonnell Douglas Corp. v. Green, 411 U.S. 792, 802, 93 S.Ct. 1817, 1824, 36 L.Ed.2d 668, 677 (1973); Baxter v. Savannah Sugar Rfg. Corp., 495 F.2d 437, 443–444 (C.A. 5), cert. denied, 419 U.S. 1033, 95 S.Ct. 515, 42 L.Ed.2d 308 (1974).[32] Only if this burden is met may retroactive seniority—if otherwise deter-

---

31. The District Court order is silent as to whether applicants for OTR positions who were previously discriminatorily refused employment must be presently qualified for those positions in order to be eligible for priority hiring under that order. The Court of Appeals, however, made it plain that they must be. Id., at 417. We agree.

32. Thus Bowman may attempt to prove that a given individual member of class 3 was not in fact discriminatorily refused employment as an OTR driver in order to defeat the individual's claim to seniority relief as well as any other remedy ordered for the class generally. Evidence of a lack of vacancies in OTR positions at the time the individual application was filed, or evidence indicating the individual's lack of qualification for the OTR positions—under nondiscriminatory standards *actually applied* by Bowman to individuals who were in fact hired—would of course be relevant. It is true, of course, that obtaining the third category of evidence with which the District Court was concerned—what the individual discriminatee's job performance would have been but for the discrimination—presents great difficulty. No reason appears, however, why the victim rather than the perpetrator of the illegal act should bear the burden of proof on this issue.

mined to be an appropriate form of relief under the circumstances of the particular case—be denied individual class members.

Respondent Bowman raises an alternative theory of justification. Bowman argues that an award of retroactive seniority to the class of discriminatees will conflict with the economic interests of other Bowman employees. Accordingly, it is argued, the District Court acted within its discretion in denying this form of relief as an attempt to accommodate the competing interests of the various groups of employees.[33]

We reject this argument for two reasons. First, the District Court made no mention of such considerations in its order denying the seniority relief. As we noted in *Albemarle Paper*, 422 U.S., at 421 n. 14, 95 S.Ct., at 2373, 45 L.Ed.2d, at 299, if the district court declines, due to the peculiar circumstances of the particular case, to award relief generally appropriate under Title VII, "[i]t is necessary * * * that * * * it carefully articulate its reasons" for so doing. Second, and more fundamentally, it is apparent that denial of seniority relief to identifiable victims of racial discrimination on the sole ground that such relief diminishes the expectations of other, arguably innocent, employees would if applied generally frustrate the central "make whole" objective of Title VII. These conflicting interests of other employees will, of course, always be present in instances where some scarce employment benefit is distributed among employees on the basis of their status in the seniority hierarchy. But, as we have said, there is nothing in the language of Title VII, or in its legislative history, to show that Congress intended generally to bar this form of relief to victims of illegal discrimination, and the experience under its remedial model in the National Labor Relations Act points to the contrary.[34]

33. Even by its terms, this argument could apply only to the award of retroactive seniority for purposes of "competitive status" benefits. It has no application to a retroactive award for purposes of "benefit" seniority—extent of vacation leave and pension benefits. Indeed, the decision concerning the propriety of this latter type of seniority relief is analogous, if not identical, to the decision concerning an award of backpay to an individual discriminatee hired pursuant to an order redressing previous employment discrimination.

34. With all respect, the dissent does not adequately treat with and fails to distinguish, post, at 1279–1281, the standard practice of the National Labor Relations Board granting retroactive seniority relief under the National Labor Relations Act to persons discriminatorily discharged or refused employment in violation of the Act. The Court in Phelps Dodge Corp. v. NLRB, 313 U.S. 177, 196, 61 S.Ct. 845, 853, 85 L.Ed. 1271, 1284 (1941), of course, made reference to "restricted judicial review" as

that case arose in the context of review of the policy determinations of an independent administrative agency, which are traditionally accorded a wide-ranging discretion under accepted principles of judicial review. "Because the relation of remedy to policy is peculiarly a matter for administrative competence, courts must not enter the allowable area of the Board's discretion." Id., at 194, 61 S.Ct., at 852, 85 L.Ed., at 1283. As we made clear in *Albemarle Paper*, however, the pertinent point is that in utilizing the NLRA as the remedial model for Title VII, reference must be made to actual operation and experience as it has evolved in administrating the Act. E.g., "We may assume that Congress was aware that the Board, since its inception, has awarded backpay as a matter of course." 422 U.S., at 419–420, 95 S.Ct., at 2372, 45 L.Ed.2d, at 298. "[T]he Board has from its inception pursued 'a practically uniform policy with respect to these orders requiring affirmative action.'" Id., at 2373 n. 12.

Accordingly, we find untenable the conclusion that this form of relief may be denied merely because the interests of other employees may thereby be affected. "If relief under Title VII can be denied merely because the majority group of employees, who have not suffered discrimination, will be unhappy about it, there will be little hope of correcting the wrongs to which the Act is directed." United States v. Bethlehem Steel Corp., 446 F.2d 652, 663 (C.A.2 1971).[35]

With reference to the problems of fairness or equity respecting the conflicting interests of the various groups of employees, the relief which petitioners seek is only seniority status retroactive to the date of individual application, rather than some form of arguably more complete relief.[36] No claim is asserted that nondiscriminatee employees holding OTR positions they would not have obtained but for the illegal discrimination should be deprived of the seniority status they have earned. It is therefore clear that even if the seniority relief petitioners seek is awarded, most if not all discriminatees who actually obtain OTR jobs under the court order will not truly be restored to the actual seniority that would have existed in the absence of the illegal discrimination. Rather, most discriminatees even under an award of retroactive seniority status will still remain subordinated in the hierarchy to a position inferior to that of a greater total number of employees than would have been the case in the absence of discrimination. Therefore,

The dissent has cited no case, and our research discloses none, wherein the Board has ordered hiring relief and yet withheld the remedy of retroactive seniority status. Indeed, the Court of Appeals for the First Circuit has noted that a Board order requiring hiring relief "without prejudice to * * * seniority and other rights and privileges" is "language * * * in the standard form which has long been in use by the Board." NLRB v. Draper Corp., 159 F.2d 294, 296–297, and n. 1 (1947). The Board "routinely awards both back pay and retroactive seniority in hiring discrimination cases." Poplin, supra, n. 28, at 223. See also Edwards & Zaretsky, Preferential Remedies for Employment Discrimination, 74 Mich.L.Rev. 1, 45 n. 224 (1975) (a "common remedy"); Last Hired, First Fired Seniority, Layoffs and Title VII, supra, n. 11, at 377 ("traditionally and uniformly required"). This also is a "presumption" in favor of this form of seniority relief. If victims of racial discrimination are under Title VII to be treated differently and awarded less protection than victims of unfair labor practice discrimination under the NLRA, some persuasive justification for such disparate treatment should appear. That no justification exists doubtless explains the position of every union participate in the proceedings before the Court in the instant case arguing for the conclusion we have reached.

35. See also Vogler v. McCarty, Inc., 451 F.2d 1236, 1238–1239 (C.A. 5 1971):

"Adequate protection of Negro rights under Title VII may necessitate, as in the instant case, some adjustment of the rights of white employees. The Court must be free to deal equitably with conflicting interests of white employees in order to shape remedies that will most effectively protect and redress the rights of the Negro victims of discrimination."

36. Another countervailing factor in assessing the expected impact on the interests of other employees actually occasioned by an award of the seniority relief sought is that it is not probable in instances of class-based relief that all of the victims of the past racial discrimination in hiring will actually apply for and obtain the prerequisite hiring relief. Indeed, in the instant case, there appear in the record the rejected applications of 166 black applicants who claimed at the time of application to have had the necessary job qualifications. However, the Court was informed at oral argument that only a small number of those individuals have to this date actually been hired pursuant to the District Court's order ("five, six, seven, something in that order"), Tr. of Oral Arg. 23, although ongoing litigation may ultimately determine more who desire the hiring relief and are eligible for it. Id., at 15.

the relief which petitioners seek, while a more complete form of relief than that which the District Court accorded, in no sense constitutes "complete relief." [37] Rather, the burden of the past discrimination in hiring is with respect to competitive status benefits divided among discriminatee and nondiscriminatee employees under the form of relief sought. The dissent criticizes the Court's result as not sufficiently cognizant that it will "directly implicate the rights and expectations of perfectly innocent employees." Post, at 1276. We are of the view, however, that the result which we reach today—which, standing alone,[38] establishes that a sharing of the burden of the past discrimination is presumptively necessary—is entirely consistent with any fair characterization of equity jurisdiction,[39] particularly when considered in light of our traditional view that "[a]ttainment of a great national policy * * * must not be confined within narrow canons for equitable relief deemed suitable by chancellors in ordinary private controversies." Phelps Dodge Corp. v. NLRB, 313 U.S., at 188, 61 S.Ct., at 850, 85 L.Ed., at 1280.

Certainly there is no argument that the award of retroactive seniority to the victims of hiring discrimination in any way deprives other employees of indefeasibly vested rights conferred by the employment contract. This Court has long held that employee expectations arising from a seniority system agreement may be modified by statutes furthering a strong public policy interest.[40] Tilton v. Missouri Pacific R. Co., 376 U.S. 169, 84 S.Ct. 595, 11 L.Ed.2d 590 (1964) (construing §§ 9(c)(1) and 9(c)(2) of the Universal Military Training and Service Act, 1948, 50 U.S.C. App. §§ 459(c)(1) and (2), which provided that a re-

37. In no way can the remedy established as presumptively necessary be characterized as "total restitution," post, at 1277, n. 9, or as deriving from an "absolutist conception of 'make whole'" relief. Post, at 1277.

38. In arguing that an award of the seniority relief established as presumptively necessary does nothing to place the burden of the past discrimination on the wrongdoer in most cases—the employer—the dissent of necessity addresses issues not presently before the Court. Further remedial action by the district courts, having the effect of shifting to the employer the burden of the past discrimination in respect of competitive-status benefits, raises such issues as the possibility of an injunctive "hold harmless" remedy respecting all affected employees in a layoff situation, Brief for Local 862, United Automobile Workers, as *Amicus Curiae;* the possibility of an award of monetary damages (sometimes designated "front pay") in favor of each employee and discriminatee otherwise bearing some of the burden of the past discrimination, ibid., and the propriety of such further remedial action in instances wherein the union has been adjudged a participant in the illegal conduct. Brief for United States et al. as *Amici Curiae.* Such issues are not presented by the record before us, and we intimate no view regarding them.

39. " 'The qualities of mercy and practicality have made equity the instrument for nice adjustment and reconciliation between the public interest and private needs as well as between competing private claims.' " " 'Moreover, * * * equitable remedies are a special blend of what is necessary, what is fair, and what is workable * * *.

" 'In equity, as nowhere else, courts eschew rigid absolutes and look to the practical realities and necessities inescapably involved in reconciling competing interests * * *' " Post, at 1276.

40. "[C]laims under Title VII involve the vindication of a major public interest * * *." Section-By-Section Analysis of H.R. 1746, accompanying the Equal Employment Opportunity Act of 1972—Conference Report, 118 Cong.Rec. 7166, 7168 (1972).

employed returning veteran should enjoy the seniority status he would have acquired but for his absence in military service); Fishgold v. Sullivan Drydock & Repair Corp., 328 U.S. 275, 66 S.Ct. 1105, 90 L.Ed. 1230 (1946) (construing the comparable provision of the Selective Training and Service Act of 1940). The Court has also held that a collective-bargaining agreement may go further, enhancing the seniority status of certain employees for purposes of furthering public policy interests beyond what is required by statute, even though this will to some extent be detrimental to the expectations acquired by other employees under the previous seniority agreement. Ford Motor Co. v. Huffman, 345 U.S. 330, 73 S.Ct. 681, 97 L.Ed. 1048 (1953). And the ability of the union and employer voluntarily to modify the seniority system to the end of ameliorating the effects of past racial discrimination, a national policy objective of the "highest priority," is certainly no less than in other areas of public policy interests. Pellicer v. Brotherhood of Ry. & S.S. Clerks, 217 F.2d 205 (C.A.5 1954), cert. denied, 349 U.S. 912, 75 S.Ct. 601, 99 L.Ed. 1246 (1955). See also Cooper & Sobol, 82 Harv.L. Rev. at 1605.

V

In holding that class-based seniority relief for identifiable victims of illegal hiring discrimination is a form of relief generally appropriate under § 706(g), we do not in any way modify our previously expressed view that the statutory scheme of Title VII "implicitly recognizes that there may be cases calling for one remedy but not another, and—owing to the structure of the federal judiciary—these choices are, of course, left in the first instance to the district courts." *Albemarle Paper,* 422 U.S., at 416, 95 S.Ct., at 2370, 45 L.Ed.2d at 295. Circumstances peculiar to the individual case may, of course, justify the modification or withholding of seniority relief for reasons that would not if applied generally undermine the purposes of Title VII.[41] In the instant case it appears that all new hirees establish seniority only upon completion of a 45-day probationary period, although upon completion seniority is retroactive to the date of hire. Certainly any seniority relief ultimately awarded by the District Court could properly be cognizant of this fact. *Amici* and the respondent union point out that there may be circumstances where an award of full seniority should be deferred until completion of a training or apprenticeship program, or other preliminaries required of all new hirees. We do not undertake to delineate all such possible circumstances here. Any enumeration must await partic-

41. Accordingly, to no "significant extent" do we "[strip] the district courts of [their] equity powers." Post, at 1274. Rather our holding is that in exercising their equitable powers, district courts should take as their starting point the presumption in favor of rightful-place seniority relief, and proceed with further legal analysis from that point; and that such relief may not be denied on the abstract basis of adverse impact upon interests of other employees but rather only on the basis of unusual adverse impact arising from facts and circumstances that would not be generally found in Title VII cases. To hold otherwise would be to shield "inconsisten[t] and capri[cious]" denial of such relief from "thorough appellate review." *Albemarle Paper,* 422 U.S., at 421, 416, 95 S.Ct., at 2373, 2371, 45 L.Ed.2d, at 299, 296.

ular cases and be determined in light of the trial courts' "keener appreciation" of peculiar facts and circumstances. *Albemarle Paper,* supra, at 421–422, 95 S.Ct., at 2373, 45 L.Ed.2d, at 299.

Accordingly, the judgment of the Court of Appeals affirming the District Court's denial of seniority relief to class 3 is reversed, and the case is remanded to the District Court for further proceedings consistent with this opinion.

It is so ordered.

Reversed and remanded.

MR. JUSTICE STEVENS took no part in the consideration or decision of this case.

MR. CHIEF JUSTICE BURGER, concurring in part and dissenting in part.

I agree generally with Mr. Justice Powell, but I would stress that although retroactive benefit-type seniority relief may sometimes be appropriate and equitable, competitive-type seniority relief at the expense of wholly innocent employees can rarely, if ever, be equitable if that term retains traditional meaning. More equitable would be a monetary award to the person suffering the discrimination. An award such as "front pay" could replace the need for competitive-type seniority relief. See, ante, at 1270, n. 38. Such monetary relief would serve the dual purpose of deterring wrongdoing by the employer or union—or both—as well as protecting the rights of innocent employees. In every respect an innocent employee is comparable to a "holder-in-due-course" of negotiable paper or a bona fide purchaser of property without notice of any defect in the seller's title. In this setting I cannot join in judicial approval of "robbing Peter to pay Paul."

I would stress that the Court today does not foreclose claims of employees who might be injured by this holding from securing equitable relief on their own behalf.

MR. JUSTICE POWELL, with whom MR. JUSTICE REHNQUIST joins, concurring in part and dissenting in part.

*   *   *

Although I am in accord with much of the Court's discussion in Parts III and IV, I cannot accept as correct its basic interpretation of § 706(g) as virtually requiring a district court, in determining appropriate equitable relief in a case of this kind, to ignore entirely the equities that may exist in favor of innocent employees. Its holding recognizes no meaningful distinction, in terms of the equitable relief to be granted, between "benefit"-type seniority and "competitive"-type seniority. The Court reaches this result by taking an absolutist view of the "make whole" objective of Title VII, while rendering largely meaningless the discretionary authority vested in district courts by § 706(g) to weigh the equities of the situation. Accordingly, I dissent from Parts III and IV.

*   *   *

II

When a district court orders an award of backpay or retroactive seniority, it exercises equity powers expressly conferred upon it by Congress. The operative language of § 706(g) states that upon a finding of an unlawful employment practice the district court may enjoin the practice and, further, may

> order such affirmative action as may be appropriate, which may include, but is not limited to, reinstatement or hiring of employees, with or without back pay (payable by the employer, employment agency, or labor organization, as the case may be, responsible for the unlawful employment practice), or any other equitable relief as the court deems appropriate. 42 U.S.C. 2000e–5(g) (1970 ed., Supp. IV).

The last phrase speaking to "other equitable relief" was added by a 1972 amendment, Pub.L. No. 92–261, 86 Stat. 103. As noted in *Albemarle,* supra, at 420–421, 95 S.Ct., at 2372–2373, 45 L.Ed.2d, at 298–299, and again by the Court today, ante, at 1264–1265, a Section-by-Section Analysis accompanying the Conference Report on that amendment stated that it was Congress' intention in § 706(g) "to give the courts wide discretion exercising their equitable powers to fashion the most complete relief possible." 118 Cong.Rec. 7168 (1972).

The expansive language of § 706(g) and the 1972 legislative history support a general directive to district courts to grant "make whole" relief liberally and not refuse it arbitrarily. There is nothing in either of those sources, however, to suggest that rectifying economic losses from past wrongs requires the district courts to disregard normal equitable considerations. Indeed, such a requirement is belied by the language of the statute itself, which speaks of "such affirmative action as may be appropriate" and such "equitable relief as the court deems appropriate." The Section-by-Section Analysis similarly recognized that in fashioning "the most complete relief possible" the court still is to exercise "equitable powers." But in holding that a district court in the usual case should order full retroactive seniority as a remedy for a discriminatory refusal to hire without regard to the effect upon innocent employees hired in the interim, the Court to a significant extent strips the district courts of the equity powers vested in them by Congress.

III

A

In *Albemarle Paper* the Court read Title VII as creating a presumption in favor of backpay. Rather than limiting the power of district courts to do equity, the presumption insures that complete equity normally will be accomplished. Backpay forces the employer[4] to account for economic benefits that he wrongfully has denied the victim

---

4. In an appropriate case, of course, Title VII remedies may be ordered against a wrongdoing union as well as the employer.

of discrimination. The statutory purposes and equitable principles converge, for requiring payment of wrongfully withheld wages deters further wrongdoing at the same time that their restitution to the victim helps make him whole.

Similarly, to the extent that the Court today finds a like presumption in favor of granting *benefit*-type seniority, it is recognizing that normally this relief also will be equitable. As the Court notes, ante, at 773 n. 33, this type of seniority, which determines pension rights, length of vacations, size of insurance coverage and unemployment benefits, and the like, is analogous to backpay in that its retroactive grant serves "the mutually reinforcing effect of the dual purposes of Title VII," ante, at 767 n. 27. Benefit-type seniority, like backpay, serves to work complete equity by penalizing the wrongdoer economically at the same time that it tends to make whole the one who was wronged.

But the Court fails to recognize that a retroactive grant of *competitive*-type seniority invokes wholly different considerations. This is the type of seniority that determines an employee's preferential rights to various economic advantages at the expense of other employees. These normally include the order of layoff and recall of employees, job and trip assignments, and consideration for promotion.

It is true, of course, that the retroactive grant of competitive-type seniority does go a step further in "making whole" the discrimination victim, and therefore arguably furthers one of the objectives of Title VII. But apart from extending the make-whole concept to its outer limits, there is no similarity between this drastic relief and the granting of backpay and benefit-type seniority. First, a retroactive grant of competitive-type seniority usually does not directly affect the employer at all. It causes only a rearrangement of employees along the seniority ladder without any resulting increase in cost.[5] Thus, Title VII's "primary objective" of eradicating discrimination is not served at all,[6] for the employer is not deterred from the practice.

---

5. This certainly would be true in this case, as conceded by counsel for Bowman at oral argument. There the following exchange took place:

"QUESTION: How is Bowman injured by this action?

"MR. PATE [Counsel for Bowman]: By seniority? By the grant of this remedy?

"QUESTION: Either way.

"MR. PATE: It is not injured either way and the company, apart from the general interest of all of us in the importance of the question, has no specific tangible interest in it in this case as to whether seniority is granted to this group or not. That is correct." Tr. of Oral Arg. 42. In a supplemental memorandum filed after oral argument, petitioners referred to this statement by Bowman's counsel and suggested that he apparently was referring to the competitive aspects of seniority, such as which employees were to get the best job assignments, since Bowman certainly *would* be economically disadvantaged by the benefit-type seniority, such as seniority-related increases in backpay. I agree that in the context Bowman's counsel spoke, he was referring to the company's lack of a tangible interest, in whether or not competitive-type seniority was granted.

6. The Court in *Albemarle* noted that this primary objective had been recognized in Griggs v. Duke Power Co., 401 U.S. 424, 91 S.Ct. 849, 28 L.Ed.2d 158 (1971). See 422 U.S., at 417, 95 S.Ct., at 2371, 45 L.Ed.

The second, and in my view controlling, distinction between these types of relief is the impact on other workers. As noted above, the granting of backpay and of benefit-type seniority furthers the prophylactic and make-whole objectives of the statute without penalizing other workers. But competitive seniority benefits, as the term implies, directly implicate the rights and expectations of perfectly innocent employees.[7] The economic benefits awarded discrimination victims would be derived not at the expense of the employer but at the expense of other workers. Putting it differently, those disadvantaged—sometimes to the extent of losing their jobs entirely—are not the wrongdoers who have no claim to the Chancellor's conscience, but rather are innocent third parties.

As noted above in Part II, Congress in § 706(g) expressly referred to "appropriate" affirmative action and "other equitable relief as the court deems appropriate." And the 1972 Section-by-Section Analysis still recognized that the touchstone of any relief is equity. Congress could not have been more explicit in leaving the relief to the equitable discretion of the court, to be determined in light of all relevant facts and circumstances. Congress did underscore "backpay" by specific reference in § 706(g), but no mention is made of the granting of other benefits upon ordering reinstatement or hiring. The entire question of retroactive seniority was thus deliberately left to the discretion of the district court, a discretion to be exercised in accordance with equitable principles.

> The essence of equity jurisdiction has been the power of the Chancellor to do equity and to mould each decree to the necessities of the particular case. Flexibility rather than rigidity has distinguished it. The qualities of mercy and practicality have made equity the instrument for nice adjustment and reconciliation between the public interest and private needs as well as between competing private claims. Hecht Co. v. Bowles, 321 U.S. 321, 329–330, 64 S.Ct. 587, 592, 88 L.Ed. 754 (1944). "Moreover, * * * equitable remedies are a special blend of what is necessary, what is fair, and what is workable. * * *" Lemon v. Kurtzman, 411 U.S. 192, 200, 93 S.Ct. 1463, 1469, 36 L.Ed.2d 151, 161 (1973) (opinion of Burger, C.J.).

2d, at 296; see also supra, at 1273. In *Griggs,* the Court found this objective to be "plain from the language of the statute." 401 U.S., at 429, 91 S.Ct., at 853, 28 L.Ed. 2d, at 163. In creating a presumption in favor of a retroactive grant of competitive-type seniority the Court thus exalts the make-whole purpose, not only above fundamental principles of equity, but also above the primary objective of the statute recently found to be plain on its face.

7. Some commentators have suggested that the expectations of incumbents somehow may be illegitimate because they result from past discrimination against others. Cooper & Sobol, Seniority and Testing under Fair Employment Laws: A General Approach to Objective Criteria of Hiring and Promotion, 82 Harv.L.Rev. 1598, 1605–1606 (1969). Such reasoning is badly flawed. Absent some showing of collusion, the incumbent employee was not a party to the discrimination by the employer. Acceptance of the job when offered hardly makes one an accessory to a discriminatory failure to hire someone else. Moreover, the incumbent's expectancy does not result from discrimination against others, but is based on his own efforts and satisfactory performance.

In equity, as nowhere else, courts eschew rigid absolutes and look to the practical realities and necessities inescapably involved in reconciling competing interests * * *. Id., at 201, 93 S.Ct., at 1469, 36 L.Ed.2d 161.

The decision whether to grant competitive-type seniority relief therefore requires a district court to consider and weigh competing equities. In any proper exercise of the balancing process, a court must consider both the claims of the discrimination victims and the claims of incumbent employees who, if competitive seniority rights are awarded retroactively to others, will lose economic advantages earned through satisfactory and often long service.[8] If, as the Court today holds, the district court may not weigh these equities much of the language of § 706(g) is rendered meaningless. We cannot assume that Congress intended either that the statutory language be ignored or that the earned benefits of incumbent employees be wiped out by a presumption created by this Court.[9]

B

The Court's concern to effectuate an absolutist conception of "make whole" should be tempered by a recognition that a retroactive grant of competitive-type seniority touches upon other congressional concerns expressed in Title VII. Two sections of the Act, although not speaking directly to the issue, indicate that this remedy, unlike backpay and benefit-type seniority, should not be granted automatically.

The first section, § 703(h), has been discussed in the Court's opinion. As there noted, the "thrust" of that section is the validation of seniority plans in existence on the effective date of Title VII. The

---

8. The Court argues that a retroactive grant of competitive-type seniority always is equitable because it "divides the burden" of past discrimination between incumbents and victims. Ante, at 1270. Aside from its opacity, this argument is flawed by what seems to be a misperception of the nature of Title VII relief. Specific relief necessarily focuses upon the individual victim, not upon some "class" of victims. A grant of full retroactive seniority to an individual victim of Bowman's discriminatory hiring practices will place that person exactly where he would have been had he been hired when he first applied. The question for a district court should be whether it is equitable to place that individual in that position despite the impact upon all incumbents hired after the date of his unsuccessful application. Any additional effect upon the entire work force—incumbents and the newly enfranchised victims alike—of similar relief to still *earlier* victims of the discrimination, raises distinctly different issues from the equity, vis-á-vis incumbents, of granting retroactive seniority to each victim.

9. Indeed, the 1972 amendment process which produced the Section-by-Section Analysis containing the statement of the Act's "make whole" purpose, also resulted in an addition to § 706(g) itself clearly showing congressional recognition that total restitution to victims of discrimination is not a feasible goal. As originally enacted, § 706(g) contained simply an authorization to district courts to order reinstatement with or without backpay, with no limitation on how much backpay the courts could order. In 1972, however, the Congress added a limitation restricting the courts to an award to a date two years prior to the filing of a charge with EEOC. While it is true that Congress at the same time rejected an even more restrictive limitation, see Albemarle Paper Co. v. Moody, supra, 422 U.S., at 420 n. 13, 95 S.Ct., at 2373, 45 L.Ed.2d, at 298, its adoption of any limitation at all suggests an awareness that the desire to "make whole" must yield at some point to other considerations.

congressional debates leading to the introduction of § 703(h) indicate a concern that Title VII not be construed as requiring immediate and total restitution to the victims of discrimination regardless of cost in terms of other workers' legitimate expectations. Section 703(h) does not restrict the remedial powers of a district court once a discriminatory practice has been found, but neither are the concerns expressed therein irrelevant to a court's determination of "appropriate" equitable relief under § 706(g). Although the Court of Appeals read far too much into § 703(h), it properly recognized that the section does reflect congressional concern for existing rights under a "bona fide seniority or merit system."

Also relevant is § 703(j), which prohibits any interpretation of Title VII that would require an employer to grant "preferential treatment" to any individual because his race is underrepresented in the employer's work force in comparison with the community or the available work force.[10] A grant of competitive seniority to an identifiable victim of discrimination is not the kind of preferential treatment forbidden by § 703(j) but, as counsel for the Steelworkers admitted at oral argument, it certainly would be "preferential treatment." It constitutes a preference in the sense that the victim of discrimination henceforth will outrank, in the seniority system, the incumbents hired after the discrimination. Moreover, this is a preference based on a fiction, for the discrimination victim is placed ahead of others not because of time actually spent on the job but "as if" he had worked since he was denied employment. This also requires an assumption that nothing would have interrupted his employment, and that his performance would have justified a progression up the seniority ladder.[12] The incumbents, who in fact were on the job during the interim and performing satisfactorily, would be seriously disadvantaged. The congressional bar to one type of preferential treatment in § 703(j) should at least give the Court pause before it imposes upon district courts a duty to grant relief that creates another type of preference.

10. Section 703(j), 78 Stat. 257, 42 U.S.C. § 2000e–2(j), reads in full as follows:

"(j) Nothing contained in this subchapter shall be interpreted to require any employer, employment agency, labor organization, or joint labor-management committee subject to this subchapter to grant preferential treatment to any individual or to any group because of the race, color, religion, sex, or national origin of such individual or group on account of an imbalance which may exist with respect to the total number or percentage of persons of any race, color, religion, sex, or national origin employed by any employer, referred or classified for employment by any employment agency or labor organization, admitted to membership or classified by any labor organization, or admitted to, or employed in, any apprenticeship or other training program, in comparison with the total number or percentage of persons of such race, color, religion, sex, or national origin in any community, State, section, or other area, or in the available work force in any community, State, section, or other area."

12. It is true, of course, that backpay awards and retroactive grants of benefit-type seniority likewise are based on the same fiction and the same assumption. In the case of those remedies, however, no innocent persons are harmed by the use of the fiction, and any uncertainty about whether the victim of discrimination in fact would have retained the job and earned the benefits is properly borne by the wrongdoer.

IV

In expressing the foregoing views, I suggest neither that Congress intended to bar a retroactive grant of competitive-type seniority in all cases,[13] nor that district courts should indulge a presumption against such relief.[14] My point instead is that we are dealing with a congressional mandate to district courts to determine and apply equitable remedies. Traditionally this is a balancing process left, within appropriate constitutional or statutory limits, to the sound discretion of the trial court. At this time it is necessary only to avoid imposing, from the level of this Court, arbitrary limitations on the exercise of this traditional discretion specifically explicated in § 706(g). There will be cases where, under all of the circumstances, the economic penalties that would be imposed on innocent incumbent employees will outweigh the claims of discrimination victims to be made entirely whole even at the expense of others. Similarly, there will be cases where the balance properly is struck the other way.

The Court virtually ignores the only previous judicial discussion directly in point. The Court of Appeals for the Sixth Circuit, recently faced with the issue of retroactive seniority for victims of hiring discrimination, showed a fine appreciation of the distinction discussed above. Meadows v. Ford Motor Co., 510 F.2d 939 (1975), cert. pending, No. 74–1349.[15] That court began with the recognition that retroactive competitive-type seniority presents "greater problems" than a grant of

13. Nor is it suggested that incumbents have "indefeasibly vested rights" to their seniority status that invariably would foreclose retroactive seniority. But the cases cited by the Court for that proposition do not hold, or by analogy imply, that district courts operating under § 706(g) lack equitable discretion to take into account the rights of incumbents. In Tilton v. Missouri Pacific R. Co., 376 U.S. 169, 84 S.Ct. 595, 11 L.Ed.2d 590 (1964), and Fishgold v. Sullivan Corp., 328 U.S. 275, 66 S.Ct. 1105, 90 L.Ed. 1230 (1946), the Court only confirmed an express congressional determination, presumably made after weighing all relevant considerations, that for reasons of public policy veterans should receive seniority credit for their time in military service. See 376 U.S., at 174–175, 84 S.Ct., at 599–600, 11 L.Ed.2d, at 593–594. In Ford Motor Co. v. Huffman, 345 U.S. 330, 73 S.Ct. 681, 97 L.Ed. 1048 (1953), the Court affirmed the authority of a collective-bargaining agent, presumably after weighing the relative equities, see id., at 337–339, 73 S.Ct., at 685–687, 97 L.Ed., at 1057–1058, to advantage certain employees more than others. All I contend is that under § 706(g) a district court, like Congress in *Tilton* and *Fishgold*, and the bargaining agent in *Huffman*, also must be free to weigh the equities.

14. The Court, ante, at 764 n. 21, suggests I am arguing that retroactive competitive-type seniority should be "less available" as relief than backpay. This is not my position. All relief not specifically prohibited by the Act is equally "available" to the district courts. My point is that equitable considerations can make competitive-type seniority relief less "appropriate" in a particular situation than backpay or other relief. Again, the plain language of § 706(g) compels careful determination of the "appropriateness" of each "available" remedy in a specific case, and does not permit the inflexible approach taken by the Court.

15. From the briefs of the parties it appears that *Meadows* is one of only three reported appellate decisions dealing with the question of retroactive seniority relief to victims of discriminatory hiring practices. In the instant case, of course, the Court of Appeals for the Fifth Circuit held such relief barred by § 703(h). In Jurinko v. Edwin L. Wiegand Co., 477 F.2d 1038, vacated and remanded on other grounds, 414 U.S. 970, 94 S.Ct. 293, 38 L.Ed.2d 214 (1973), the Court of Appeals for the Third Circuit ordered the relief without any discussion of equitable considerations.

backpay because the burden falls upon innocent incumbents rather than the wrongdoing employer. Id., at 949.[16] The court further recognized that Title VII contains no prohibition against such relief. Then, noting that "the remedy for the wrong of discriminatory refusal to hire lies in the first instance *with the District Judge*," ibid. (emphasis added), the Court of Appeals for the Sixth Circuit stated:

> For his guidance on this issue we observe * * * that a grant of retroactive seniority would not depend solely upon the existence of a record sufficient to justify back pay * * *. The court would, in dealing with job [i.e., competitive-type] seniority, need also to consider the interests of the workers who might be displaced * * *. We do not assume * * * that such reconciliation is impossible, but as is obvious, we certainly do foresee genuine difficulties. * * * Ibid.

The Sixth Circuit suggested that the District Court seek enlightenment on the questions involved in the particular fact situation, and that it should allow intervention by representatives of the incumbents who stood to be disadvantaged.[17]

In attempted justification of its disregard of the explicit equitable mandate of § 706(g) the Court today relies almost exclusively on the practice of the National Labor Relations Board under § 10(c) of the National Labor Relations Act, 29 U.S.C. § 160(c).[18] It is true that in

16. The Sixth Circuit noted that no equitable considerations stand in the way of a district court's granting retroactive benefit-type seniority. 510 F.2d, at 949.

17. One of the commentators quoted by the Court today has endorsed the even-handed approach adopted by the Sixth Circuit: "In fashioning a remedy, * * * the courts should consciously assess the costs of relief to *all* the parties in the case, and then tailor the decree to minimize these costs while affording plaintiffs adequate relief. The best way to do this will no doubt vary from case to case depending on the facts: the number of plaintiffs, the number of [incumbents] affected and the alternatives available to them, the economic circumstances of the industry." Poplin, Fair Employment in a Depressed Economy: The Layoff Problem, 23 U.C.L.A.L.Rev. 177, 202 (1975) (emphasis in original); see id., at 224.

Another commentator has said that judges who fail to take account of equitable claims of incumbents are engaging in an "Alice in Wonderland" approach to the problem of Title VII remedies. See Rains, Title VII v. Seniority Based Layoffs: A Question of Who Goes First, 4 Hofstra L.Rev. 49, 53 (1975).

18. By gathering bits and pieces of the legislative history of the 1972 amendments, the Court attempts to patch together an argument that full retroactive seniority is a remedy equally "available" as backpay. Ante, at 1264–1265 n. 21. There are two short responses. First, as emphasized elsewhere, supra, at 1278 n. 14, no one contends that such relief is less *available*, but only that it may be less *equitable* in some situations. Second, insofar as the Court intends the legislative history to suggest some presumption in favor of this relief, it is irrefutably blocked by the plain language of § 706(g) calling for the exercise of *equitable* discretion in the fashioning of *appropriate* relief. There are other responses. As to the committee citations of lower court decisions and the Conference Report Analysis reference to "present case law," it need only be noted that as of the 1972 amendments no appellate court had considered a case involving retroactive seniority relief to victims of discriminatory hiring practices. Moreover, the cases were cited only in the context of a general discussion of the complexities of employment discrimination, never for their adoption of a "rightful place" theory of relief. And by the terms of the Conference Report Analysis itself, the existing case law could not take precedence over the explicit language of § 706(g), added by the amendments, that told courts to exercise *equitable* discretion in granting *appropriate* relief.

Moreover, I find no basis for the Court's statement that the Committee Reports indicated "rightful place" to be the objective

the two instances cited by the Court, and in the few others cited in the briefs of the parties,[19] the Board has ordered reinstatement of victims of discrimination "without prejudice to their seniority or other rights and privileges." But the alleged precedents are doubly unconvincing. First, in none of the cases is there a discussion of equities either by the Board or the enforcing court. That the Board has granted seniority relief in several cases may indicate nothing more than the fact that in the usual case no one speaks for the individual incumbents. This is the point recognized by the court in *Meadows,* and the impetus for its suggestion that a representative of their interests be entertained by the district court before it determines "appropriate" § 706(g) relief.

I also suggest, with all respect, that the Court's appeal to Board practice wholly misconceives the lesson to be drawn from it. In the seminal case recognizing the Board's power to order reinstatement for discriminatory refusals to hire, this Court in a reasoned opinion by Mr. Justice Frankfurter was careful to emphasize that the decision on the type and extent of relief rested in the Board's discretion, subject to limited review only by the courts.

> But in the nature of things Congress could not catalogue all the devices and strategems for circumventing the policies of the Act. Nor could it define the whole gamut of remedies to effectuate these policies in an infinite variety of specific situations. Congress met these difficulties by leaving the adaptation of means to end to the empiric process of administration. The exercise of the process was committed to the Board, subject to limited judicial review. * * *
>
> *   *   *   *   *   *   *   *
>
> * * * All these and other factors outside our domain of experience may come into play. Their relevance is for the Board, not for us. *In the exercise of its informed discretion the Board may find that effectuation of the Act's policies may or may not require reinstatement.* We have no warrant for speculating on matters of fact the determination of which Congress has entrusted to the Board. All we are entitled to ask is that the statute speak through the Board where the statute does not speak for itself. Phelps Dodge Corp. v. NLRB, 313 U.S. 177, 194–196, 61 S.Ct. 845, 852–853, 85 L.Ed. 1271, 1283–1284 (1941) (emphasis added).

The fallacy of the Court's reliance upon Board practice is apparent: the district courts under Title VII stand in the place of the Board under the NLRA. Congress entrusted to their discretion the appropriate remedies for violations of the Act, just as it previously had entrusted

of Title VII relief. In fact, in both instances cited by the Court the term was used in the context of a general comment that minorities were still "far from reaching their rightful place in society." S.Rep. No. 92–416, p. 6 (1971). There was no reference to the scope of relief under § 706(g), or indeed even to Title VII remedies at all.

19. The respondent Steelworkers cited seven Board decisions in addition to those mentioned in the Court's opinion. Brief for Respondent United Steelworkers of America AFL–CIO, and for American Federation of Labor and Congress of Industrial Organizations as *Amicus Curiae,* 27 n. 31.

discretion to the Board. The Court today denies that discretion to the district courts, when 35 years ago it was quite careful to leave discretion where Congress had entrusted it. It may be that the district courts, after weighing the competing equities, would order full retroactive seniority in most cases. But they should do so only after determining in each instance that it *is* appropriate, and not because this Court has taken from them the power—granted by Congress—to weigh the equities.

In summary, the decision today denying district courts the power to balance equities cannot be reconciled with the explicit mandate of § 706(g) to determine "appropriate" relief through the exercise of "equitable powers." Accordingly, I would remand this case to the District Court with instructions to investigate and weigh competing equities before deciding upon the appropriateness of retroactive competitive-type seniority with respect to individual claimants.[20]

Notes

1. *Reinstatement.* A finding of discrimination in Stage I of an employment discrimination case presumptively entitles a discriminatee to instatement (hiring), reinstatement in the discharge cases, or an immediate promotion in the failure to promote cases. Darnell v. City of Jasper, 730 F.2d 653, 655 (11th Cir.1984) (discharge); McCormick v. Attala County Board of Education, 541 F.2d 1094, 1095 (5th Cir.1976); Dickerson v. Deluxe Check Printers, Inc., 703 F.2d 276 (8th Cir.1983) (rejected applicant); Garza v. Brownsville Independent School Dist., 700 F.2d 253 (5th Cir.1983) (rejected applicant).

Instatement or reinstatement, which are forms of rightful place relief, has been denied where the plaintiff has found or could have found other work, Brito v. Zia Company, 478 F.2d 1200, 1204 (10th Cir.1973), where reinstatement would require the displacement or "bumping" of an incumbent or "innocent employee", see Smallwood v. United Air Lines, Inc., 661 F.2d 303 (4th Cir.1981), or where hostility would result, EEOC v. Kallir, Philips, Ross, Inc., 420 F.Supp. 919, 926–27 (S.D.N.Y.1976), affirmed 559 F.2d 1203 (2d Cir.1977), cert. denied 434 U.S. 920, 98 S.Ct. 395, 54 L.Ed.2d 277 (1977).

2. *Front Pay.* The back pay award is the remedy for economic loss which has occurred up to the date of the judgment. If a discriminatee

20. This is not to suggest that district courts should be left to exercise a standard-less, unreviewable discretion. But in the area of competitive-type seniority, unlike backpay and benefit-type seniority, the twin purposes of Title VII do not provide the standards. District courts must be guided in each instance by the mandate of § 706(g). They should, of course, record the considerations upon which they rely in granting or refusing relief, so that appellate review could be informed and precedents established in the area.

In this case, for example, factors that could be considered on remand and that could weigh in favor of full retroactive seniority, include Bowman's high employee turnover rate and the asserted fact that few victims of Bowman's discrimination have indicated a desire to be hired. Other factors, not fully developed in the record, also could require consideration in determining the balance of the equities. I would imply no opinion on the merits and would remand for full consideration in light of the views herein expressed.

cannot be awarded immediate rightful place relief in the form of immediate hiring or reinstatement at the date judgment is entered, front pay may be appropriate to effectuate the *Moody* "make whole" remedy. Front pay is a monetary award designed to compensate the discriminatee for future economic injury which occurs after the date of the judgment until he or she reaches rightful place. Awards of front pay are determined under the standards applied to all forms of relief: whether the award will aid in ending illegal discrimination and rectifying the harm it has caused. See Thompson v. Sawyer, 678 F.2d 257, 259 (D.C.Cir.1982); Note, "Front Pay— Prophylactic Relief under Title VII of the Civil Rights Act of 1964," 29 Vand.L.Rev. 211 (1976).

3. The scope of discretion under *Moody* and *Franks* is discussed in Belton, "Harnessing Discretionary Justice in Employment Discrimination Cases: The *Moody* and *Franks* Guidelines," 44 Ohio St.L.J. 571 (1983).

2. PROCEDURAL AND SUBSTANTIVE STANDARDS

INTERNATIONAL BROTHERHOOD OF TEAMSTERS v. UNITED STATES

Supreme Court of the United States, 1977.
431 U.S. 324, 97 S.Ct. 1843, 52 L.Ed.2d 396.

[Plaintiffs brought a class action consisting of three sub-classes: (1) pre-Act discriminatees which consisted of a group of black employees who were hired before the effective date of Title VII; (2) post-Act rejected black applicants which consisted of a group of blacks who were similarly situated to the class in Franks v. Bowman Transportation Co., i.e., had applied after the effective date of Title VII, had been initially rejected but later hired; and (3) post-Act non-applicants which consisted of a group of blacks who had not applied but arguably would have applied but for the reputation of the employer in discriminating against blacks. With respect to the third class, see Dothard v. Rawlinson, supra at 166. The basic facts are set out earlier at pp. 96, 220. After holding that the pre-Act discriminatees were entitled to no relief because the seniority system was bona fide within the meaning of Section 703(h), the Court discussed the standards for determining relief on remand for the other sub-classes of discriminatees].

The company contends that a grant of retroactive seniority to these nonapplicants is inconsistent with the make-whole purpose of a Title VII remedy and impermissibly will require the company to give preferential treatment to employees solely because of their race. The thrust of the company's contention is that unless a minority-group employee actually applied for a line-driver job, either for initial hire or for transfer, he has suffered no injury from whatever discrimination might have been involved in the refusal of such jobs to those who actually applied for them.

The Government argues in response that there should be no "immutable rule" that nonapplicants are nonvictims, and contends that a determination whether nonapplicants have suffered from unlawful discrimination will necessarily vary depending on the circumstances of each particular case. The Government further asserts that under the specific facts of this case, the Court of Appeals correctly determined that all qualified nonapplicants were likely victims and were therefore presumptively entitled to relief.

The question whether seniority relief may be awarded to nonapplicants was left open by our decision in *Franks,* since the class at issue in that case was limited to "identifiable applicants who were denied employment * * * after the effective date * * * of Title VII." 424 U.S., at 750, 96 S.Ct., at 1257. We now decide that an incumbent employee's failure to apply for a job is not an inexorable bar to an award of retroactive seniority. Individual nonapplicants must be given an opportunity to undertake their difficult task of proving that they should be treated as applicants and therefore are presumptively entitled to relief accordingly.

(1)

Analysis of this problem must begin with the premise that the scope of a district court's remedial powers under Title VII is determined by the purposes of the Act. Albemarle Paper Co. v. Moody, 422 U.S., at 417, 95 S.Ct., at 2371. In Griggs v. Duke Power Co., and again in *Albemarle,* the Court noted that a primary objective of Title VII is prophylactic: to achieve equal employment opportunity and to remove the barriers that have operated to favor white male employees over other employees. 401 U.S., at 429–430, 91 S.Ct., at 852–853; 422 U.S., at 417, 95 S.Ct., at 2371. The prospect of retroactive relief for victims of discrimination serves this purpose by providing the " 'spur or catalyst which causes employers and unions to self-examine and to self-evaluate their employment practices and to endeavor to eliminate, so far as possible, the last vestiges' " of their discriminatory practices. Id., at 417–418, 95 S.Ct., at 2371–2372. An equally important purpose of the Act is "to make persons whole for injuries suffered on account of unlawful employment discrimination." Id., at 418, 95 S.Ct., at 2372. In determining the specific remedies to be afforded, a district court is "to fashion such relief as the particular circumstances of a case may require to effect restitution." *Franks,* 424 U.S., at 764, 96 S.Ct., at 1264.

Thus, the Court has held that the purpose of Congress in vesting broad equitable powers in Title VII courts was "to make possible the 'fashion[ing] [of] the most complete relief possible,' " and that the district courts have " 'not merely the power but the duty to render a decree which will so far as possible eliminate the discriminatory effects of the past as well as bar like discrimination in the future.' " *Albemarle,* supra, 422 U.S., at 421, 418, 95 S.Ct., at 2373. More specifically, in *Franks* we decided that a court must ordinarily award a seniority remedy unless there exist reasons for denying relief " 'which, if applied generally, would not frustrate the central statutory purposes of eradicating discrimination * * * and making persons whole for injuries suffered.' " 424 U.S., at 771, 96 S.Ct., at 1267, quoting *Albemarle,* supra, 422 U.S., at 421, 95 S.Ct., at 2373.

Measured against these standards, the company's assertion that a person who has not actually applied for a job can *never* be awarded seniority relief cannot prevail. The effects of and the injuries suffered from discriminatory employment practices are not always confined to those who were expressly denied a requested employment opportunity. A consistently enforced discriminatory policy can surely deter job applications from those who are aware of it and are unwilling to subject themselves to the humiliation of explicit and certain rejection.

If an employer should announce his policy of discrimination by a sign reading "Whites Only" on the hiring-office door, his victims would not be limited to the few who ignored the sign and subjected themselves to personal rebuffs. The same message can be communicated to potential applicants more subtly but just as clearly by an employer's actual practices—by his consistent discriminatory treatment of actual applicants, by the manner in which he publicizes vacancies, his recruitment techniques, his responses to casual or tentative inquiries, and even by the racial or ethnic composition of that part of his work force from which he has discriminatorily excluded members of minority groups.[51] When a person's desire for a job is not translated into a formal application solely because of his unwillingness to engage in a futile gesture he is as much a victim of discrimination as is he who goes through the motions of submitting an application.

In cases decided under the National Labor Relations Act, the model for Title VII's remedial provisions, *Albemarle,* supra, 422 U.S., at 419, 95 S.Ct., at 2372; *Franks,* supra, 424 U.S., at 769, 96 S.Ct., at 1266, the National Labor Relations Board, and the courts in enforcing its orders, have recognized that the failure to submit a futile application does not bar an award of relief to a person claiming that he was denied employment because of union affiliation or activity. In NLRB v. Nevada Consolidated Copper Corp., 316 U.S. 105, 62 S.Ct. 960, 86 L.Ed. 1305, this Court enforced an order of the Board directing an employer to hire, with retroactive benefits, former employees who had not applied for newly available jobs because of the employer's well-known policy of refusing to hire union members. See In re Nevada Consolidated Copper Corp., 26 N.L.R.B. 1182, 1208, 1231. Similarly, when an application would have been no more than a vain gesture in light of

---

51. The far-ranging effects of subtle discriminatory practices have not escaped the scrutiny of the federal courts, which have provided relief from practices designed to discourage job applications from minority-group members. See, e.g., Franks v. Bowman Transportation Co., 495 F.2d 398, 418–419 (CA5) (public recruitment and advertising), rev'd on other grounds, 424 U.S. 747, 96 S.Ct. 1251, 47 L.Ed.2d 444; Carter v. Gallagher, 452 F.2d 315, 319 (CA8) (recruitment); United States v. Jacksonville Terminal Co., 451 F.2d, at 458 (posting of job vacancies and job qualification requirements); United States v. Local No. 86, Ironworkers, 315 F.Supp. 1202, 1238, 1245–1246 (WD Wash.) (dissemination of information), aff'd, 443 F.2d 544 (CA9). While these measures may be effective in preventing the deterrence of future applicants, they afford no relief to those persons who in the past desired jobs but were intimidated and discouraged by employment discrimination.

employer discrimination, the Courts of Appeals have enforced Board orders reinstating striking workers despite the failure of individual strikers to apply for reinstatement when the strike ended. E.g., NLRB v. Park Edge Sheridan Meats, Inc., 323 F.2d 956 (CA2); NLRB v. Valley Die Cast Corp., 303 F.2d 64 (CA6); Eagle-Picher Mining & Smelting Co. v. NLRB, 119 F.2d 903 (CA8). See also Piasecki Aircraft Corp. v. NLRB, 280 F.2d 575 (CA3); NLRB v. Anchor Rome Mills, 228 F.2d 775 (CA5); NLRB v. Lummus Co., 210 F.2d 377 (CA5). Consistent with the NLRA model, several Courts of Appeals have held in Title VII cases that a nonapplicant can be a victim of unlawful discrimination entitled to make-whole relief when an application would have been a useless act serving only to confirm a discriminatee's knowledge that the job he wanted was unavailable to him. Acha v. Beame, 531 F.2d 648, 656 (CA2); Hairston v. McLean Trucking Co., 520 F.2d 226, 231–233 (CA4); Bing v. Roadway Express, Inc., 485 F.2d 441, 451 (CA5); United States v. N.L. Industries, Inc., 479 F.2d 354, 369 (CA8).

The denial of Title VII relief on the ground that the claimant had not formally applied for the job could exclude from the Act's coverage the victims of the most entrenched forms of discrimination. Victims of gross and pervasive discrimination could be denied relief precisely because the unlawful practices had been so successful as totally to deter job applications from members of minority groups. A *per se* prohibition of relief to nonapplicants could thus put beyond the reach of equity the most invidious effects of employment discrimination—those that extend to the very hope of self-realization. Such a *per se* limitation on the equitable powers granted to courts by Title VII would be manifestly inconsistent with the "historic purpose of equity to 'secur[e] complete justice'" and with the duty of courts in Title VII cases "'to render a decree which will so far as possible eliminate the discriminatory effects of the past.'" Albemarle Paper Co. v. Moody, 422 U.S., at 418, 95 S.Ct., at 2372.

(2)

To conclude that a person's failure to submit an application for a job does not inevitably and forever foreclose his entitlement to seniority relief under Title VII is a far cry, however, from holding that nonapplicants are always entitled to such relief. A nonapplicant must show that he was a potential victim of unlawful discrimination. Because he is necessarily claiming that he was deterred from applying for the job by the employer's discriminatory practices, his is the not always easy burden of proving that he would have applied for the job had it not been for those practices. Cf. Mt. Healthy City Board of Education v. Doyle, 429 U.S. 274, 97 S.Ct. 568, 50 L.Ed.2d 471. When this burden is met, the nonapplicant is in a position analogous to that of an applicant and is entitled to the presumption discussed in Part III–A, supra.

The Government contends that the evidence it presented in this case at the liability stage of the trial identified all nonapplicants as victims of unlawful discrimination "with a fair degree of specificity," and that the Court of Appeals' determination that qualified nonapplicants are presumptively entitled to an award of seniority should accordingly be affirmed. In support of this contention the Government cites its proof of an extended pattern and practice of discrimination as evidence that an application from a minority employee for a line-driver job would have been a vain and useless act. It further argues that since the class of nonapplicant discriminatees is limited to incumbent employees, it is likely that every class member was aware of the futility of seeking a line-driver job and was therefore deterred from filing both an initial and a followup application.[52]

We cannot agree. While the scope and duration of the company's discriminatory policy can leave little doubt that the futility of seeking line-driver jobs was communicated to the company's minority employees, that in itself is insufficient. The known prospect of discriminatory rejection shows only that employees who wanted line-driving jobs may have been deterred from applying for them. It does not show which of the nonapplicants actually wanted such jobs, or which possessed the requisite qualifications.[53] There are differences between city- and line-driving jobs,[54] for example, but the desirability of the latter is not so self-evident as to warrant a conclusion that all employees would prefer to be line drivers if given a free choice.[55] Indeed, a substantial number

52. The limitation to incumbent employees is also said to serve the same function that actual job applications served in *Franks:* providing a means of distinguishing members of the excluded minority group from minority members of the public at large. While it is true that incumbency in this case and actual applications in *Franks* both serve to narrow what might otherwise be an impossible task, the statutes of nonincumbent applicant and nonapplicant incumbent differ substantially. The refused applicants in *Franks* had been denied an opportunity they clearly sought, and the only issue to be resolved was whether the denial was pursuant to a proved discriminatory practice. Resolution of the nonapplicant's claim, however, requires two distinct determinations: that he would have applied but for discrimination and that he would have been discriminatorily rejected had he applied. The mere fact of incumbency does not resolve the first issue, although it may tend to support a nonapplicant's claim to the extent that it shows he was willing and competent to work as a driver, that he was familiar with the tasks of line drivers, etc. An incumbent's claim that he would have applied for a line-driver job would certainly be more superficially plausible than a similar claim by a member of the general public who may never have worked in the trucking industry or heard of the company prior to suit.

53. Inasmuch as the purpose of the nonapplicant's burden of proof will be to establish that his status is similar to that of the applicant, he must bear the burden of coming forward with the basic information about his qualifications that he would have presented in an application. As in *Franks,* and in accord with Part III-A, supra, the burden then will be on the employer to show that the nonapplicant was nevertheless not a victim of discrimination. For example, the employer might show that there were other, more qualified persons who would have been chosen for a particular vacancy, or that the nonapplicant's stated qualifications were insufficient. See *Franks,* 424 U.S., at 773 n. 32, 96 S.Ct., at 1268.

54. Of the employees for whom the Government sought transfer to line-driving jobs, nearly one-third held city-driver positions.

55. The company's line drivers generally earned more annually than its city drivers, but the difference varied from under $1,000 to more than $5,000 depending on the terminal and the year. In 1971 city drivers at two California terminals, "LOS" and San Francisco, earned substantially more than the line drivers at those terminals. In addition to earnings, line drivers have the advantage of not being required to load and unload their trucks. City drivers, however, have regular working hours,

of white city drivers who were not subjected to the company's discriminatory practices were apparently content to retain their city jobs.[56]

In order to fill this evidentiary gap, the Government argues that a nonapplicant's current willingness to transfer into a line-driver position confirms his past desire for the job. An employee's response to the court-ordered notice of his entitlement to relief[57] demonstrates, according to this argument, that the employee would have sought a line-driver job when he first became qualified to fill one, but for his knowledge of the company's discriminatory policy.

This assumption falls short of satisfying the appropriate burden of proof. An employee who transfers into a line-driver unit is normally placed at the bottom of the seniority "board." He is thus in jeopardy of being laid off and must, at best, suffer through an initial period of bidding on only the least desirable runs. See supra, at 1858–1859, and n. 25. Non-applicants who chose to accept the appellate court's *post hoc* invitation, however, would enter the line-driving unit with retroactive seniority dating from the time they were first qualified. A willingness to accept the job security and bidding power afforded by retroactive seniority says little about what choice an employee would have made had he previously been given the opportunity freely to choose a starting line-driver job. While it may be true that many of the nonapplicant employees desired and would have applied for line-driver jobs but for their knowledge of the company's policy of discrimination, the Government must carry its burden of proof, with respect to each

are not required to spend extended periods away from home and family, and do not face the hazards of long-distance driving at high speeds. As the Government acknowledged at argument, the jobs are in some sense "parallel"—some may prefer one job and some may prefer another.

The District Court found generally that line-driver jobs "are considered the most desirable of the driving jobs." That finding is not challenged here, and we see no reason to disturb it. We observe only that the differences between city and line driving were not such that it can be said with confidence that all minority employees free from the threat of discriminatory treatment would have chosen to give up city for line driving.

56. In addition to the futility of application, the Court of Appeals seems to have relied on the minority employees' accumulated seniority in non-line-driver positions in concluding that nonapplicants had been unlawfully deterred from applying. See 517 F.2d, at 318, 320. The Government adopts that theory here, arguing that a nonapplicant who has accrued time at the company would be unlikely to have applied for transfer because he would have had to

forfeit all of his competitive seniority and the job security that went with it. In view of our conclusion in Part II–B, supra, this argument detracts from rather than supports a nonapplicant's entitlement to relief. To the extent that an incumbent was deterred from applying by his desire to retain his competitive seniority, he simply did not want a line-driver job requiring him to start at the bottom of the "board." Those nonapplicants who did not apply for transfer because they were unwilling to give up their previously acquired seniority suffered only from a lawful deterrent imposed on all employees regardless of race or ethnicity. The nonapplicant's remedy in such cases is limited solely to the relief, if any, to which he may be entitled because of the discrimination he encountered at a time when he wanted to take a starting line-driver job.

57. The District Court's final order required that the company notify each minority employee of the relief he was entitled to claim. The employee was then required to indicate, within 60 days, his willingness to accept the relief. Under the decision of the Court of Appeals, the relief would be qualification-date seniority.

specific individual, at the remedial hearings to be conducted by the District Court on remand.[58]

C

The task remaining for the District Court on remand will not be a simple one. Initially, the court will have to make a substantial number of individual determinations in deciding which of the minority employees were actual victims of the company's discriminatory practices. After the victims have been identified, the court must, as nearly as possible, " 'recreate the conditions and relationships that would have been had there been no' " unlawful discrimination. *Franks,* 424 U.S., at 769, 96 S.Ct., at 1266. This process of recreating the past will necessarily involve a degree of approximation and imprecision. Because the class of victims may include some who did not apply for line-driver jobs as well as those who did, and because more than one minority employee may have been denied each line-driver vacancy, the court will be required to balance the equities of each minority employee's situation in allocating the limited number of vacancies that were discriminatorily refused to class members.

Moreover, after the victims have been identified and their rightful place determined, the District Court will again be faced with the delicate task of adjusting the remedial interests of discriminatees and the legitimate expectations of other employees innocent of any wrongdoing. In the prejudgment consent decree, see n. 4, supra, the company and the Government agreed that minority employees would assume line-driver positions that had been discriminatorily denied to them by exercising a first-priority right to job vacancies at the company's terminals. The decree did not determine what constituted a vacancy, but in its final order the trial court defined "vacancy" to exclude any position that became available while there were laid-off employees awaiting an opportunity to return to work. Employees on layoff were given a preference to fill whatever openings might occur at their terminals during a three-year period after they were laid off. The Court of Appeals rejected the preference and held that all but "purely temporary" vacancies were to be filled according to an employee's seniority, whether as a member of the class discriminated against or as an incumbent line driver on layoff. 517 F.2d, at 322–323.

As their final contention concerning the remedy, the company and the union argue that the trial court correctly made the adjustment between the competing interests of discriminatees and other employees by granting a preference to laid-off employees, and that the Court of Appeals erred in disturbing it. The petitioners therefore urge the reinstatement of that part of the trial court's final order pertaining to

---

58. While the most convincing proof would be some overt act such as a pre-Act application for a line-driver job, the District Court may find evidence of an employee's informal inquiry, expression of interest, or even unexpressed desire credible and convincing. The question is a factual one for determination by the trial judge.

the rate at which victims will assume their rightful places in the line-driver hierarchy.

Although not directly controlled by the Act,[61] the extent to which the legitimate expectations of nonvictim employees should determine when victims are restored to their rightful place is limited by basic principles of equity. In devising and implementing remedies under Title VII, no less than in formulating any equitable decree, a court must draw on the "qualities of mercy and practicality [that] have made equity the instrument for nice adjustment and reconciliation between the public interest and private needs as well as between competing private claims." Hecht Co. v. Bowles, 321 U.S. 321, 329–330, 64 S.Ct. 587, 592, 88 L.Ed. 754. Cf. Phelps Dodge Corp. v. NLRB, 313 U.S., at 195–196, 61 S.Ct., at 852–853, modifying 113 F.2d 202 (CA2); 19 N.L. R.B. 547, 600; *Franks,* supra, 424 U.S., at 798–799, 96 S.Ct., at 1280–1281 (POWELL, J., concurring in part and dissenting in part). Especially when immediate implementation of an equitable remedy threatens to impinge upon the expectations of innocent parties, the courts must "look to the practical realities and necessities inescapably involved in reconciling competing interests," in order to determine the "special blend of what is necessary, what is fair, and what is workable." Lemon v. Kurtzman, 411 U.S. 192, 200–201, 93 S.Ct. 1463, 1469, 36 L.Ed.2d 151 (opinion of Burger, C.J.).

Because of the limited facts now in the record, we decline to strike the balance in this Court.

*   *   *

After the evidentiary hearings to be conducted on remand, both the size and the composition of the class of minority employees entitled to relief may be altered substantially. Until those hearings have been conducted and both the number of identifiable victims and the consequent extent of necessary relief have been determined, it is not possible to evaluate abstract claims concerning the equitable balance that should be struck between the statutory rights of victims and the contractual rights of nonvictim employees. That determination is best left, in the first instance, to the sound equitable discretion of the trial court.[62] See Franks v. Bowman Transportation Co., supra, 424 U.S., at

---

61. The petitioners argue that to permit a victim of discrimination to use his rightful-place seniority to bid on a line-driver job before the recall of all employees on layoff would amount to a racial or ethnic preference in violation of § 703(j) of the Act. Section 703(j) provides no support for this argument. It provides only that Title VII does not require an employer to grant preferential treatment to any group in order to rectify an imbalance between the composition of the employer's work force and the makeup of the population at large. See n. 20, supra. To allow identifiable victims of unlawful discrimination to participate in a layoff recall is not the kind of "preference" prohibited by § 703(j). If a discriminatee is ultimately allowed to secure a position before a laid-off line driver, a question we do not now decide, he will do so because of the bidding power inherent in his rightful-place seniority, and not because of a preference based on race. See *Franks,* 424 U.S., at 792, 96 S.Ct., at 1277 (Powell, J., concurring in part and dissenting in part).

62. Other factors, such as the number of victims, the number of nonvictim employees affected and the alternatives available to them, and the economic circumstances of the industry may also be

779, 96 S.Ct., at 1271; Albemarle Paper Co. v. Moody, 422 U.S., at 416, 95 S.Ct., at 2371. We observe only that when the court exercises its discretion in dealing with the problem of laid-off employees in light of the facts developed at the hearings on remand, it should clearly state its reasons so that meaningful review may be had on appeal. See *Franks,* supra, 424 U.S., at 774, 96 S.Ct., at 1269; Albemarle Paper Co. v. Moody, supra, 422 U.S., at 421 n. 14, 95 S.Ct., at 2373.

For all the reasons we have discussed, the judgment of the Court of Appeals is vacated, and the cases are remanded to the District Court for further proceedings consistent with this opinion.

It is so ordered.

MR. JUSTICE MARSHALL, with whom MR. JUSTICE BRENNAN joins, concurring in part and dissenting in part.

* * *

I also agree that incumbent minority-group employees who show that they applied for a line-driving job or that they would have applied but for the company's unlawful acts are presumptively entitled to the full measure of relief set forth in our decision last Term in Franks v. Bowman Transportation Co., 424 U.S. 747, 96 S.Ct. 1251, 47 L.Ed.2d 444 (1976).[1]

* * *

BIBBS v. BLOCK

United States Court of Appeals for the Eighth Circuit, 1985.
778 F.2d 1318.

ARNOLD, CIRCUIT JUDGE.

This is a Title VII case in which the plaintiff, an employee of the United States Department of Agriculture, claims that he was denied a promotion because of his race.[1] The District Court[2] found "that racial

relevant in the exercise of the District Court's discretion. See *Franks,* supra, at 796 n. 17, 96 S.Ct., at 1362 (Powell, J., concurring in part and dissenting in part).

1. In stating that the task nonapplicants face in proving that they should be treated like applicants is "difficult," ante, at 1869, I understand the Court simply to be addressing the facts of this case. There may well be cases in which the jobs that the nonapplicants seek are so clearly more desirable than their present jobs that proving that but for the employer's discrimination the nonapplicants previously would have applied will be anything but difficult.

Even in the present case, however, I believe the Court unnecessarily adds to the nonapplicants' burden. While I agree that proof of a nonapplicant's current willingness to accept a line-driver job is not dispositive of the question of whether the company's discrimination deterred the

nonapplicant from applying in the past, I do not agree that current willingness "says little," see ante, at 1873, about past willingness. In my view, we would do well to leave questions of this sort concerning the weight to be given particular pieces of evidence in the district courts rather than attempting to resolve them through overly broad and ultimately meaningless generalizations.

1. Plaintiff initially claimed age discrimination as well. The District Court found against this claim, and the panel to which this appeal was initially submitted affirmed that finding as not clearly erroneous. Bibbs v. Block, 749 F.2d 508, 509 (8th Cir.1984). This aspect of the case is not before the Court en banc.

2. The Hon. Howard F. Sachs, United States District Judge for the Western District of Missouri.

considerations probably did play a minor role in the selection process, * * * but that plaintiff would not have been selected for the position even if his race had been disregarded." Bibbs v. Block, No. 81–0227–CV–W–6, slip op. 7 (W.D.Mo. June 14, 1983). It added that "race was not a determining factor in the decision to promote [another employee] rather than plaintiff." Id. at 10. Judgment was entered in favor of defendant.

On appeal, a panel of this Court reversed. Bibbs v. Block, 749 F.2d 508 (8th Cir.1984). Pointing to the District Court's finding that "race was a discernible factor at the time of the decision," Bibbs v. Block, supra, slip op. 10, the panel took the view that the additional finding that "the same decision would have been made absent racial considerations" was "inherently inconsistent." 749 F.2d at 512. It vacated the judgment for defendant and remanded to the District Court "to enter a judgment in favor of plaintiff and to consider the necessary remedy to make plaintiff whole." Id. at 513.

The defendant petitioned for rehearing. He asked that the panel modify its opinion to make clear that any relief ordered 'on remand could not include retroactive promotion and back pay at the higher level plaintiff had unsuccessfully sought. Such relief, defendant argued, could not be appropriate where the trier of fact had found that plaintiff would not have been promoted in any event. In the alternative, defendant asked for rehearing en banc. We granted the petition for rehearing en banc, thus automatically vacating the panel opinion. After oral argument, we now hold that plaintiff, having shown that race was a discernible factor at the time of the decision not to promote him, has established a violation of Title VII. The cause will be remanded for a determination of appropriate relief. As to retroactive promotion and back pay, the District Court should make a new finding, this time placing the burden of persuasion on defendant. If the court finds that defendant has shown by a preponderance of the evidence that plaintiff would not have been promoted in any event, retroactive promotion and back pay may not be ordered.

I.

Bibbs, who is black, is employed by the Agricultural Stabilization and Conservation Service (ASCS), a division of the Department of Agriculture. In September 1976, Bibbs applied for, but was denied, a promotion to a supervisory position in the ASCS print shop. Bibbs was one of seven individuals who applied for the position; he was the only black applicant. All seven applications were forwarded to a selection committee comprised of three individuals, all of whom were white. The committee was dominated by one member, Joseph Tresnak, who was most familiar with the print shop and the print-shop employees. The District Court found that Tresnak was the "key figure" in making the selection. Tresnak's central role in the selection process is significant in light of the direct evidence of Tresnak's use of racial slurs. One witness testified Tresnak had characterized Bibbs as a "black militant," while another testified Tresnak referred to another print-shop employee who was black as "boy" and "nigger." After interviewing each of the seven candidates, the committee selected Dennis Laube, who was white, for the position. The three members of the committee, after conclusion of all the interviews and without having agreed on any criteria for selection, selected the same top three candidates and each chose them in the same order. They did not discuss their views of the relative merits of the candidates before, during, or after the interviews.

In determining that the decision not to promote Bibbs was not racially motivated, the trial court noted that the work force in the print shop was racially integrated.[3] The trial court also found that Bibbs had a history of disciplinary and interpersonal problems and was not selected in part because he was difficult to work with and caused irritation among fellow workers. Given the diverse factors each of the members of the selection committee used, and the alleged absence of any discussion among them during the deliberation process, the trial court judged the selection committee members "not particularly credible, either in demeanor or in the substance of their testimony. * * * The committee members were extremely guarded in their responses to questions and were quite defensive in their positions on matters that might reflect negatively on their decision. The Court is skeptical that it has heard the complete story concerning the committee's deliberations." Slip op. 5. The trial court was particularly concerned about the committee members' lack of credibility given the subjective criteria considered by the committee. The trial court observed that a subjective procedure may provide a "convenient screen for discriminatory decision making, and must be carefully scrutinized." Id. at 4.

After considering the evidence, the District Court made two factual findings. First, the court determined that race was a factor in the "selection process." Id. at 7. The court initially stated race played a "minor role in the selection process," ibid.; later, it stated race was a "discernible factor at the time of the decision." Id. at 10. Second, the court found that Bibbs "would not have been selected for the position even if his race had been disregarded," id. at 7. Thus, the court concluded race was not a "determining" factor or a "but for" factor, meaning a factor that ultimately made a difference in the decision, and that liability was therefore not established. It dismissed the complaint.

II.

In many Title VII cases, the proof proceeds on both sides on the premise that one motive only on the part of the employer—either an illegitimate one (e.g., race) or a legitimate one (e.g., ability to do the job)—has caused the adverse action of which the plaintiff complains. It is this type of case for which the familiar evidentiary framework of

---

3. Such "bottom line" statistics do not insulate an employer from liability for intentional discrimination against an individual employee. See Connecticut v. Teal, 457 U.S. 440, 454, 102 S.Ct. 2525, 2534, 73 L.Ed.2d 130 (1982). But they are relevant evidence, to be considered along with all other factors.

McDonnell Douglas Corp. v. Green, 411 U.S. 792, 93 S.Ct. 1817, 36 L.Ed. 2d 668 (1973), is designed. After the plaintiff establishes a *prima facie* case, and the defendant "articulates" (a verb that refers only to the burden of producing evidence) a legitimate, nondiscriminatory reason for the action complained of, the burden then shifts back to the plaintiff to persuade the trier of fact that the defendant's proffered reason was not the real one, but only a pretext hiding an impermissible racial motivation. Typically, the plaintiff will contend that one reason—race—was operative, the defendant will contend that another single reason—ability to do the job—motivated it, and the trier of fact will find one reason or the other (but not a combination) to be the true one. In such a case, the issues of motivation and causation are not distinctly separated, nor do they need to be. If the plaintiff shows the defendant's proffered reason to be a pretext for race, the case is over. Liability is established, and reinstatement is ordered (in a discharge case) absent extraordinary circumstances. The very showing that the defendant's asserted reason was a pretext for race is also a demonstration that but for his race plaintiff would have gotten the job. That is what pretext means: a reason *for the employment decision* that is not the true reason.

If the District Court in the case before us had found that defendant's reason or reasons for not promoting plaintiff were other than race, and that race played no part in the decisionmaking process, we should be required simply to affirm the dismissal of the complaint—assuming the finding was not clearly erroneous. But the court here conducted a more sensitive analysis of the various factors at work. It found that race was "a discernible factor," although not a but-for factor. It found, in other words, mixed motives.[4] In this situation, we believe analysis is aided best by separating the issues of liability and remedy. The District Court itself, citing Brodin, The Standard of Causation in the Mixed-Motive Title VII Action: A Social Policy Perspective, 82 Colum.L.Rev. 292 (1982), suggested such an approach, but decided, in view of its "novelty," to leave to us whether to pursue it. Slip op. 10 n. 5.

We accept the invitation. In doing so, we use as a factual predicate the District Court's findings of fact, which are not clearly erroneous. We look first to the statute. Section 703(a), 42 U.S.C. § 2000e–2(a) (1982), describes what conduct is unlawful:

Employer practices

It shall be an unlawful employment practice for an employer—

---

4. The District Court found that racial considerations were a discernible, though minor, factor in the selection process and in the decision of whom to promote, though not a determining factor in the "but for" sense. The court found that race was a motivating factor but that plaintiff had not shown that he would have received the job had race not been considered. In this situation, we think liability on the part of the defendant is established. The plaintiff, however, will actually be awarded the promotion (or comparable relief such as front pay or damages) only if defendant fails to show that it would have made the same decision absent consideration of the impermissible factor.

(1) to fail or refuse to hire or to discharge any individual, *or otherwise to discriminate against any individual with respect to his compensation, terms, conditions, or privileges of employment, because of such individual's race,* color, religion, sex, or national origin; or

(2) to limit, segregate, or classify his employees or applicants for employment in any way which would deprive *or tend to deprive* any individual of employment opportunities *or otherwise adversely affect his status as an employee, because of such individual's race,* color, religion, sex, or national origin.

(Emphasis added.)

As always, the words of the Congress are the best indications of its intention. It is not only failing to hire someone, or discharging him or her, because of race or sex, that is unlawful. The statute also forbids employers "otherwise to discriminate * * * with respect to compensation, terms, conditions, or privileges of employment, because of * * * race," § 703(a)(1), and makes it unlawful for employers "to limit * * * or classify * * * employees * * * in any way which would deprive *or tend to deprive* any individual of employment *opportunities or otherwise adversely affect* " him or her because of race. Section 703(a)(2). To put it in terms of the present case, it would be unlawful for defendant to put Bibbs at a disadvantage in the competition for promotion because of his race, as well as actually to deny him the promotion for this reason. (Indeed, if an employer requires black employees to meet a higher standard, the statute is violated even if they actually meet it and get the jobs in question.) Every kind of disadvantage resulting from racial prejudice in the employment setting is outlawed. Forcing Bibbs to be considered for promotion in a process in which race plays a discernible part is itself a violation of law, regardless of the outcome of the process. At the very least, such a process "tend[s] to deprive" him of an "employment opportunit[y]." Section 703(a)(2).

It does not follow, though, that retroactive promotion is an appropriate remedy. Unless the impermissible racial motivation was a but-for cause of Bibbs's losing the promotion, to place him in the job now would award him a windfall. He would be more than made whole. He would get a job that he would never have received whatever his race. At this point, we think, another provision of the statute, Section 706(g), 42 U.S.C. § 2000e–5(g) (1982), becomes important:

(g) If the court finds that the respondent has intentionally engaged in or is intentionally engaging in an unlawful employment practice charged in the complaint, the court may enjoin the respondent from engaging in such unlawful employment practice, and order such affirmative action as may be appropriate, which may include, but is not limited to, reinstatement or hiring of employees with or without back pay * * *, or any other equitable relief as the court deems appropriate. * * * No order of the court shall require the admission or reinstatement of an individual as a member of a union, or the hiring, reinstatement, or promotion of an individual as an employee, or the payment to him of any back pay, if such individual was refused admission, suspended, or expelled, or was refused employment or advancement, or was suspended or discharged *for any reason other than discrimination on account of race,* color, religion, sex, or national origin or in violation of section 2000e–3(a) of this title.

(Emphasis added.)

Thus, the language of Title VII supports the separation of liability and remedy and allows an award of reinstatement or promotion and back pay only after a finding that discrimination was the but-for cause of the employment decision. After defining unlawful employment practices of an employer in Subsection 703(a) of the statute, Congress set forth the conditions on which courts may grant injunctive and affirmative relief. By the terms of the statute, injunctive relief may be awarded after a finding of intentional discrimination; and affirmative relief such as reinstatement and back pay may not be awarded if the employment decision was "for any reason other than discrimination." The "but-for" determination required for an award of affirmative relief is consistent with Title VII's intended purpose of making persons whole for injuries suffered on account of unlawful employment discrimination. Albemarle Paper Co. v. Moody, 422 U.S. 405, 418, 95 S.Ct. 2362, 2372, 45 L.Ed.2d 280 (1975). Focusing on Subsection 706(g) of the statute, the Supreme Court recently reaffirmed the principle of make-whole relief, stating that competitive seniority can be awarded only to actual victims of discrimination. Firefighters Local Union No. 1784 v. Stotts, 467 U.S. 561, 104 S.Ct. 2576, 2589, 81 L.Ed.2d 483 (1984).

The Supreme Court has not expressly addressed the mixed-motives problem in a Title VII case, but it has focused on it in other contexts. For example, in the context of legislative and administrative decision making, the Court has considered whether a decision motivated by both lawful and unlawful considerations violated the Equal Protection Clause. See Village of Arlington Heights v. Metropolitan Housing Development Corp., 429 U.S. 252, 265–66, 97 S.Ct. 555, 563–64, 50 L.Ed. 2d 450 (1977) ("When there is proof that a discriminatory purpose has been a *motivating* factor in the decision, * * * judicial deference [to the legislative/administrative decision] is no longer justified.") (emphasis added). The Court established the so-called same-decision test to review such decisions:

> Proof that the decision by the Village was motivated in part by a racially discriminatory purpose would not necessarily have required invalidation of the challenged decision. Such proof would, however, have shifted to the Village the burden of establishing that the same decision would have resulted even had the impermissible purpose not been considered. If this were established, the complaining party in a case of this kind no longer fairly could attribute the injury complained of to improper consideration of a discriminatory purpose. In such circumstances, there would be no justification for judicial interference with the challenged decision.

Id. at 270 n. 21, 97 S.Ct. at 566 n. 21. The Court also adopted the same-decision test for First Amendment retaliatory-discharge cases in Mt. Healthy City School District Board of Education v. Doyle, 429 U.S. 274, 97 S.Ct. 568, 50 L.Ed.2d 471 (1977), decided the same day as *Arlington Heights*. See also Givhan v. Western Line Consolidated School District, 439 U.S. 410, 416–17, 99 S.Ct. 693, 697, 58 L.Ed.2d 619 (1979). The Court in *Mt. Healthy* articulated the proper standard of causation as follows:

> Initially, in this case, the burden was properly placed upon respondent to show that his conduct was constitutionally protected, and that this conduct was a "substantial factor"—or, to put it in other words, that it was a "motivating factor" in the Board's decision not to rehire him. Respondent having carried that burden, however, the District Court should have gone on to determine whether the Board had shown by a preponderance of the evidence that it would have reached the same decision as to respondent's reemployment even in the absence of the protected conduct.

429 U.S. at 287, 97 S.Ct. 568 at 576 (footnote omitted). See also NLRB v. Transportation Management Corp., 462 U.S. 393, 103 S.Ct. 2469, 76 L.Ed.2d 667 (1983) (similar mixed-motives analysis used in unfair-labor-practice cases).

In the *Mt. Healthy* group of cases, of course, the Supreme Court's mixed-motives analysis is used to establish the defendant's liability in the first place, not simply to determine the appropriate remedy. If the defendant establishes that it would have made the same decision in the absence of the illegitimate factor, it wins the case, and the complaint is dismissed. Our reading of Title VII is significantly different. In that statute, Congress has made unlawful any kind of racial discrimination, not just discrimination that actually deprives someone of a job. A defendant's showing that the plaintiff would not have gotten the job anyway does not extinguish liability. It simply excludes the remedy of retroactive promotion or reinstatement. In adopting this mode of analysis, we employ an approach similar to that used in King v. Trans-World Airlines, Inc., 738 F.2d 255, 259 (8th Cir.1984) (discrimination in interview process not cured by defendant's legitimate reasons for not hiring plaintiff), approved in Easley v. Anheuser-Busch, Inc., 758 F.2d 251, 262 (8th Cir.1985). See also, e.g., Caviale v. Wisconsin Department of Health and Social Services, 744 F.2d 1289, 1295–96 (7th Cir.1984); Fadhl v. San Francisco, 741 F.2d 1163, 1166–67 (9th Cir.1984); Pollard v. Grinstead, 741 F.2d 73, 75 (4th Cir.1984); Smallwood v. United Air Lines, Inc., 728 F.2d 614, 620 (4th Cir.), cert. denied, ___ U.S. ___, 105 S.Ct. 120, 83 L.Ed.2d 62 (1984); Toney v. Block, 705 F.2d 1364, 1370 (D.C.Cir.1983) (Tamm, J., concurring); Milton v. Weinberger, 696 F.2d 94, 98–99 (D.C.Cir.1982); Harbison v. Goldschmidt, 693 F.2d 115, 116–17 (10th Cir.1982); Nanty v. Barrows Co., 660 F.2d 1327, 1333 (9th Cir. 1981); League of United Latin American Citizens v. City of Salinas Fire Department, 654 F.2d 557, 558 (9th Cir.1981); Richerson v. Jones, 551 F.2d 918, 923–25 (3d Cir.1977); Day v. Mathews, 530 F.2d 1083, 1085

(D.C.Cir.1976) (per curiam); see generally Brodin, The Standard of Causation in the Mixed-Motive Title VII Action: A Social-Policy Perspective, 82 Colum.L.Rev. 292 (1982). Under this approach, once the plaintiff has established a violation of Title VII by proving that an unlawful motive played some part in the employment decision or decisional process, the plaintiff is entitled to some relief, including, as appropriate, a declaratory judgment, partial attorney's fees, and injunctive relief against future or continued discrimination. However, even after a finding of unlawful discrimination is made, the defendant is allowed a further defense in order to limit the relief. The defendant may avoid an award of reinstatement or promotion and back pay if it can prove by a preponderance of the evidence [5] that the plaintiff would not have been hired or promoted even in the absence of the proven discrimination.

This same-decision test will apply only to determine the appropriate remedy and only after plaintiff proves he or she was a victim of unlawful discrimination in some respect. *Toney,* 705 F.2d at 1370 (Tamm, J., concurring) (footnote omitted) ("It has no relevance to the liability phase of a Title VII suit."). For that reason, the burden of production *and* persuasion shifts from the plaintiff to the defendant. *King,* 738 F.2d at 259 ("The burden of showing that proven discrimination did not cause a plaintiff's rejection is properly placed on the defendant-employer because its unlawful acts have made it difficult to determine what would have transpired if all parties had acted properly.") (quoting League of United Latin American Citizens v. City of Salinas Fire Department, 654 F.2d 557, 559 (9th Cir.1981)).

In the instant case, Bibbs has proved race was a discernible factor in the decision not to promote him. We hold such proof is sufficient in a mixed-motive context to establish intentional discrimination and liability under Title VII. We therefore vacate the judgment dismissing the complaint and remand for the entry of a declaratory judgment in favor of Bibbs and an injunction prohibiting the ASCS from future or continued discrimination against Bibbs on the basis of race. In addition, the District Court should consider Bibbs a prevailing party for the purpose of an award of attorney's fees. See 42 U.S.C. § 2000e–5(k); *King,* 738 F.2d at 259; Nanty v. Barrows Co., 660 F.2d 1327, 1334 n. 10

5. Although several courts considering the weight of the employer's burden on the remedy question have imposed a "clear and convincing" proof requirement, see, e.g., *Toney,* 705 F.2d at 1373 (Tamm, J., concurring); Patterson v. Greenwood School District 50, 696 F.2d 293, 295; Ostroff v. Employment Exchange, Inc., 683 F.2d 302, 304 (9th Cir.1982), we recently rejected that higher standard of proof in Craik v. Minnesota State University Board, 731 F.2d 465, 470 n. 8 (8th Cir.1984) (Title VII class action alleging a pattern or practice of sex discrimination). But cf. *King,* 738 F.2d 255, 257 (8th Cir.1984). In *Craik* we stated: "The normal standard of proof in civil litigation is that of a preponderance of the evidence, and we do not believe that the public and private interests involved require altering that distribution of the risk of error between the litigants." 731 F.2d at 470 n. 8. We adhere to that view now. Cf. Herman & McLean v. Huddleston, 459 U.S. 375, 389–90, 103 S.Ct. 683, 685, 74 L.Ed.2d 548 (recovery under § 10(b) of the 1934 Securities Exchange Act, 15 U.S.C. § 78j(b), requires preponderance rather than clear and convincing evidence).

(9th Cir.1981). Of course, in determining a reasonable fee, an adjustment based on the extent to which Bibbs has succeeded will be appropriate. See Hensley v. Eckerhart, 461 U.S. 424, 435–36, 103 S.Ct. 1933, 1940–41, 76 L.Ed.2d 40 (1983) (applying 42 U.S.C. § 1988). Nevertheless, we emphasize that "by proving unlawful discrimination, appellant prevailed on a significant issue in the litigation," *King,* 738 F.2d at 259, and thereby vindicated a major purpose of Title VII, the rooting out and deterrence of job discrimination.

III.

On this rehearing en banc the government did not challenge the panel's holding that defendant is liable. Instead, it challenged the scope of relief available when there has been no finding that discrimination was the "but-for" cause of the denial of promotion. Because we agree that a but-for or same-decision finding must be made before affirmative relief such as retroactive promotion and back pay may be awarded, we remand the case for further analysis of the remedy issue. As stated above, the District Court must consider whether Bibbs would have received the promotion but for the discrimination in the selection process. While the trial court's statement that "[i]t cannot be concluded that plaintiff would have been selected by a committee free of racial considerations" would satisfy the same-decision standard, the trial court apparently placed the burden on Bibbs to show why he was denied the promotion. We reiterate that to avoid an award of retroactive promotion and back pay, the defendant must prove by a preponderance of evidence that Bibbs would not have received the promotion even if race had not been considered.

Vacated and remanded with instructions.

Lay, Chief Judge, with whom Heaney and McMillian, Circuit Judges, join, concurring.

I concur in Judge Arnold's well-written opinion.

I write separately for two reasons: (1) to voice my disagreement with the dissent and (2) to state specially, although I fully join Judge Arnold's opinion, that I seriously question the propriety of applying the "same decision" test to "mixed motive" cases in a Title VII context.[1]

In its petition for a rehearing en banc, the government *did not* dispute the finding of liability in the panel opinion and moved only to have this court adopt the "same decision" test for determining a remedy on remand. The liability issue was not argued by the respective parties nor was it considered by the court en banc. The dissent now, without discussion of the factual testimony, finds no liability at all and affirms the district court outright.

The original panel opinion, Bibbs v. Block, 749 F.2d 508 (8th Cir. 1984) (Lay, C.J., and Fairchild & McMillian, JJ.) reviewed the factual

---

1. Notwithstanding my disagreement with the same decision test, in order to provide a majority opinion and a clear test to follow in this circuit I join Judge Arnold's application of the same decision test.

findings of the district court and held that the district court's finding that race was not a "determining factor" in the employment decision was clearly erroneous and not supported by the record. The record reveals that Tresnak, who was shown to be racially biased, was the key figure in the promotion decision. The district court found that the selection committee lacked credibility in their testimony regarding the process of selection and that the selection process was suspect due to its subjective nature.

The dissent misreads Judge Arnold's opinion as establishing a new test, that of "discernible factor." The district court simply used the word "discernible" as an adjective to describe a racial factor which the court was able to "make out, * * * detect, * * * recognize, or identify as separate and distinct." [2] The majority opinion does not substitute the phrase "discernible factor" as a test to replace causation. Judge Arnold's analysis of the record, *ante* at 1323–1324, finds that:

> [O]nce the plaintiff has established a violation of Title VII by proving that an unlawful motive played some part in the employment decision or decisional process, the plaintiff is entitled to some relief, including, as appropriate, a declaratory judgment, partial attorney's fees, and injunctive relief against future or continued discrimination. However, even after a finding of unlawful discrimination is made, the defendant is allowed a further defense in order to limit the relief. The defendant may avoid an award of reinstatement or promotion and back pay if it can prove by a preponderance of the evidence that the plaintiff would not have been hired or promoted even in the absence of the proven discrimination.

This language does not establish a new test,[3] but simply restates the test in Texas Department of Community Affairs v. Burdine, 450 U.S. 248, 101 S.Ct. 1089, 67 L.Ed.2d 207 (1981), a different way.

In the dissent's focus on the word "discernible" it overlooks the fact that there are many ways to say the same thing. It also ignores the fact that the district court improperly quantified the employer's intent to discriminate when it found that although race was a discernible factor it was only a "minor" factor in the employment decision. The Supreme Court has expressly held that it is improper to quantify discriminatory intent. As the Supreme Court stated in Personnel Administrator of Massachusetts v. Feeney, 442 U.S. 256, 277, 99 S.Ct. 2282, 2295, 60 L.Ed.2d 870 (1979): "Discriminatory intent is simply not

---

2. Webster's Third New International Dictionary (Unabridged) 644 (1981).

3. Judge Arnold's reasoning is similar to the approach of the Eleventh Circuit in Title VII disparate treatment cases where there is direct evidence proving that the defendant-employer acted with a discriminatory motive. See e.g., Joshi v. Florida State University Health Center, 763 F.2d 1227, 1236 (11th Cir.1985), cert. denied, ___ U.S. ___, 106 S.Ct. 347, ___ L.Ed.2d ___ (1985) (defendants failed to meet burden to prove those ultimately employed were better qualified than plaintiff); Bell v. Birmingham Linen Service, 715 F.2d 1552, 1557 (11th Cir.1983), cert. denied, 467 U.S. 1204, 104 S.Ct. 2385, 81 L.Ed.2d 344 (1984) (absent finding that employer set aside own bias in hiring recommendations, court cannot conclude that employer met its burden to prove same decision would have been made absent discrimination).

amenable to calibration. It either is a factor that has influenced the legislative choice or it is not." [4]

The dissent's outright affirmance of the district court also fails to mention the fact that the district court, in using the same decision test, improperly placed the burden of proof onto the plaintiff to show that the same decision would not have been made absent race. Even under the principles articulated in Mt. Healthy City School District Board of Education v. Doyle, 429 U.S. 274, 97 S.Ct. 568, 50 L.Ed.2d 471 (1977), this is clear error. The plaintiff is asked to establish much more than "but for" causation—he is required improperly to prove that race was the sole cause.

THE SAME DECISION TEST

I now address my view that the same decision test should not apply to mixed motive cases, even when the burden of proof is properly placed on the employer.

Title VII is designed to protect victims against invidious discrimination which *in any way* influences or motivates an employment decision. That the employer has other nondiscriminatory reasons which enter into the decision is irrelevant. It is clear under the relevant case law that racial discrimination need not be the "sole" cause motivating the employer. Race is either a factor in the employment decision or it is not.

There is precedent for use of the same decision test in employment discrimination cases where liability is based upon a class action or disparate impact context.[5] But to extend such a test to cases of disparate treatment will provide hollow victories to most victims of racial discrimination and little real relief. Many litigants who successfully prove racial discrimination in the employment decision will now find that the spoils do not go to the victim but only to the victim's attorneys. Plaintiffs such as Bibbs will obtain attorneys' fees and perhaps injunctive or declaratory relief, but no award of back pay or reinstatement. After proving his or her case at the liability stage, to gain any other relief a plaintiff in an alleged mixed motive case will now face the additional uphill battle to rebut defendant's claim that the same decision would have been made absent race. Although Judge Arnold adopts the "but for" test for liability in McDonald v. Santa Fe

---

4. See also Village of Arlington Heights v. Metropolitan Housing Development Corp., 429 U.S. 252, 265, 97 S.Ct. 555, 563, 50 L.Ed.2d 450 (1977) ("Rarely can it be said that a legislature or administrative body operating under a broad mandate made a decision motivated solely by a single concern, or even that a particular purpose was the 'dominant' or 'primary' one.").

5. Cf. International Brotherhood of Teamsters v. United States, 431 U.S. 324, 359 n. 45, 97 S.Ct. 1843, 1867 n. 45, 52 L.Ed.2d 396 (1977). ("[T]he employer was in the best position to show why any individual employee was denied an employment opportunity. Insofar as the reasons related to available vacancies or the employer's evaluation of the applicant's qualifications, the company's records were the most relevant items of proof. If the refusal to hire was based on other factors, the employer and its agents knew best what those factors were and the extent to which they influenced the decision-making process.")

Trail Transportation Co., 427 U.S. 273, 282 n. 10, 96 S.Ct. 2574, 2580 n. 10, 49 L.Ed.2d 493 (1976), the practical effect will be that before a plaintiff can recover damages in a Title VII case, he or she will have to convince the court that race was the sole cause. Surely Congress did not intend such a result.

Certain well-established principles should govern our review of the district court's decision. First, under the teaching of *Burdine*, "the ultimate burden of persuading the trier of fact that the defendant intentionally discriminated against the plaintiff remains at all times with the plaintiff." *Burdine*, 450 U.S. at 253, 101 S.Ct. at 1093. Second, as the district court acknowledged and as stated above, in a Title VII disparate treatment action a plaintiff need not prove that the sole reason for the employment decision was the discrimination, but is required to show no more than that race was a "but for" cause. *McDonald*, 427 U.S. at 282 n. 10, 96 S.Ct. at 2580 n. 10. The district court, reciting the confusion of our own cases and those of other circuits,[6] resolved the apparent dilemma by finding that "racial considerations probably did play a minor role in the selection process, through the influence of Tresnak, but that plaintiff would not have been selected for the position even if his race had been disregarded." On the surface, the "same decision" reasoning is attractive and would simply relegate to appellate review the issue of whether the district court's factual findings are clearly erroneous. However, when race is shown to have been a discernible factor *in* the employment decision, as the district court found below, I conclude that the same decision test is inappropriate under the principles of *Burdine*. Here, plaintiff has done far more than put forth a prima facie case of discrimination. He has successfully proven that race was a discriminatory factor *in* his employer's refusal to promote him. Rather than requiring proof that race was a "substantial" as opposed to a "minor" factor in the decision, Title VII simply requires that a plaintiff prove his or her claim of unlawful discrimination by persuading the court that "a discriminatory reason more likely [than not] motivated the employer." *Burdine*, 450 U.S. at 256, 101 S.Ct. at 1095. Nothing more is required of a plaintiff to establish liability under Title VII.

Once the trier of fact has found that race was a factor "in any way" influencing the decision, it is error to attempt to quantify race as a minor factor. See 42 U.S.C. § 2000e–2(a)(2) (1970 ed. Supp. V). Under the factual record presented here, once race was found to be a discernible factor in or influencing the decision, the additional conclusion that it was a minor factor is irrelevant to the Title VII analysis.

---

6. See Tribble v. Westinghouse Electric Corp., 669 F.2d 1193, 1197 (8th Cir.1982), cert. denied, 460 U.S. 1080, 103 S.Ct. 1767, 76 L.Ed.2d 342 (1983) (determining factor); Nanty v. Barrows Co., 660 F.2d 1327, 1333 (9th Cir.1981) (same decision test at relief stage); Williams v. Boorstin, 663 F.2d 109, 117 (D.C.Cir.1980), cert. denied, 451 U.S. 985, 101 S.Ct. 2319, 68 L.Ed.2d 842 (1981) (same decision test at liability stage); Satz v. ITT Financial Corp., 619 F.2d 738, 746 (8th Cir.1980) (a factor); Marshall v. Kirkland, 602 F.2d 1282, 1289 (8th Cir.1979) (motivating factor); Cleverly v. Western Electric Co., 594 F.2d 638, 641 (8th Cir. 1979) (determining factor).

When race is shown at the liability stage to have been a factor in the employment decision, the employer should not be able to exculpate its proven invidious discriminatory practices by having a second chance to show that racial considerations did not affect the decision's outcome. This clearly contradicts Congress' purpose in enacting Title VII. I find that the record supports a finding that race clearly influenced the decision. Under these circumstances, I would reject as irrelevant and clearly erroneous the district court's unnecessary finding that "plaintiff would not have been selected for the position even if race had been disregarded."

The language of Title VII plainly recognizes the broad purpose of eliminating consideration of race from employment decisions. "Title VII prohibits *all* discrimination in employment based upon race, sex, and national origin. 'The broad, overriding interest, shared by employer, employee, and consumer, is efficient and trustworthy workmanship assured through fair and ∗ ∗ ∗ neutral employment and personnel decisions.'" *Burdine,* 450 U.S. at 259, 101 S.Ct. at 1096 (emphasis added) (quoting McDonnell Douglas Corp. v. Green, 411 U.S. 792, 801, 93 S.Ct. 1817, 1823, 36 L.Ed.2d 668 (1973)). As Justice Marshall has stated:

> [I]t is important to bear in mind that Title VII is a remedial statute designed to eradicate certain invidious employment practices. The evils against which it is aimed are defined broadly: "to fail ∗ ∗ ∗ to hire or to discharge ∗ ∗ ∗ or otherwise to discriminate ∗ ∗ ∗ with respect to ∗ ∗ ∗ compensation, terms, conditions, or privileges of employment [because of such individual's race ∗ ∗ ∗]" and "to limit, segregate, or classify ∗ ∗ ∗ in any way which would deprive or tend to deprive any individual of employment opportunities or otherwise adversely affect his status [∗ ∗ ∗ because of such individual's race ∗ ∗ ∗]." 42 U.S.C. § 2000e–2(a) (1970 ed., Supp. V) (emphasis deleted).

International Brotherhood of Teamsters, 431 U.S. at 381, 97 S.Ct. at 1878 (Marshall, J., concurring and dissenting).

Although proof of actual motivation would be within a defendant's knowledge, I find it highly inappropriate, under the *Burdine* principles governing Title VII cases, to adopt the *Mt. Healthy* rationale and shift the burden to the defendant to show that plaintiff would not have been promoted even if his race had not been considered. See also Givhan v. Western Line Consolidated School District, 439 U.S. 410, 99 S.Ct. 693, 58 L.Ed.2d 619 (1979); NLRB v. Wright Line, A Division of Wright Line, Inc., 251 N.L.R.B. 150 (1980), enforced, 662 F.2d 899 (1st Cir.1981), cert. denied, 455 U.S. 989, 102 S.Ct. 1612, 71 L.Ed.2d 848 (1982) (NLRB adopts the *Mt. Healthy* test to determine liability in § 8(a)(3) cases). *Mt. Healthy* exacts a distinctly different standard relating to recovery and burden of proof in constitutionally-protected conduct cases than does *Burdine* which applied Title VII. A mixed motive case should be tried under the same tests set forth in *McDonald* and *Burdine.* To hold otherwise is to inject total confusion into the already difficult process faced by litigants who pursue relief under Title VII.[7]

BRIGHT, SENIOR CIRCUIT JUDGE, separately concurring.

I concur in Judge Arnold's opinion. I write separately to indicate that I do not join the separate concurrences of Chief Judge Lay and Judge McMillian, and to emphasize my view that liability in this case rests upon the district court's finding of a causal relationship between race discrimination and the employment decision; that is, that race discrimination played a role, albeit a minor one, in selecting the person to be promoted.

In my opinion, the existence of some racial prejudice in the workplace that does not affect the employment decision will not support a determination of liability against an employer, where the discrimination and the decision are not shown to be causally connected.

Finally, I express disagreement with the suggestion in Chief Judge Lay's opinion that the "same decision test" should be rejected in mixed motive cases—"same decision" meaning that the employer would have made the same employment decision regardless of racial factors which might have entered into the hiring or promotion decision.

A simple hypothetical will illustrate the logic of applying the same decision test. Assume a college seeks a new president. Five candidates, four Caucasians and one black constitute the finalists. All are qualified but one Caucasian possesses clearly superior talents. That person is selected, but during the selection process an individual on the committee states that he or she would not vote for a black person for president under any circumstances, and that bias is shown to have a minor impact on the decisionmaking process of the entire committee.[1] The mixed motive analysis offered by Chief Judge Lay seems to suggest that the college would be forced to hire and give backpay to the black applicant who would not have been selected as college president under a completely racially neutral selection process.

Under Judge Arnold's opinion, which I join, the college could limit the remedy, avoiding backpay and having to hire the rejected applicant, by showing by a preponderance of the evidence that the black applicant would not have received the appointment in any event.

In his dissent, Judge Ross construes the majority's use of the term "discernible factor" as containing no causal requirement. I disagree. I

---

7. This discussion finds analogous aid in causation principles developed in tort law. In order to establish liability, a plaintiff does not have to show that the defendant's negligence (or here, racial discrimination) was *the* sole proximate cause of the accident. The burden is on the plaintiff only to show that the defendant's negligence was *a* proximate cause. In other words, the trier of fact must determine whether the defendant's negligence (dis-

crimination) was *a* factor which served as a proximate cause of the accident (employment decision).

1. To make my position clear, I would add that the presence of racial bias by one member of the selection committee which does not on a causal basis enter into the employment decision of the committee will not impose liability on the employer.

believe that term denotes the existence of a causal relationship in some degree in the present case, as shown by the district court's finding that "race played a minor role in the decision not to promote the plaintiff * * *." (Dist.Ct. Order at p. 8).

Thus, with the above explanation of my views, I agree with Judge Arnold's opinion for the court which imposes liability on the employer but permits the defendant to restrict the remedy by proving by a preponderance of the evidence that Bibbs would not have been promoted even if his race had not been considered in the employment decision.

McMILLIAN, CIRCUIT JUDGE, concurring.

I concur in the decision to remand this case to the district court to determine whether appellant would have received the promotion but for the employer's discrimination in the selection process.

I agree with most of the analysis set forth in the majority opinion. I agree that proof of unlawful discrimination requires only proof that race was "a discernible factor" in the employment decision, a finding which would ordinarily entitle the plaintiff to declaratory relief, partial attorney's fees and prospective injunctive relief, and that, following proof of unlawful discrimination, the burden of persuasion and the burden of producing evidence on the issue of the scope of available retroactive relief are properly shifted to the employer. "The burden of showing that proven discrimination did not cause a plaintiff's rejection is properly placed on the defendant-employer because its unlawful acts have made it difficult to determine what would have transpired if all parties had acted properly." League of United Latin American Citizens v. City of Salinas Fire Department, 654 F.2d 557, 559 (9th Cir.1981), citing Day v. Mathews, 530 F.2d 1083, 1086 (D.C.Cir.1976) (per curiam).

However, I do not agree with the preponderance of the evidence standard of proof and would instead require the employer to prove by clear and convincing evidence that appellant would not have been promoted in the absence of discrimination. See, e.g., King v. Trans World Airlines, Inc., 738 F.2d 255, 259 (8th Cir.1984).

> The requirement of clear and convincing proof * * * furthers Title VII's deterrent purpose. By making it more difficult for employers to defeat successful plaintiffs' claims to retroactive relief, the higher standard of proof may well discourage unlawful conduct by employers. In addition, the higher standard of proof is justified by the consideration that the employer is a wrongdoer whose unlawful conduct has made it difficult for the plaintiff to show what would have occurred in the absence of that conduct.

Toney v. Block, 705 F.2d 1364, 1373 (D.C.Cir.1983) (Tamm, J., concurring) (citations omitted).

I would remand the case to the district court to determine whether the employer has shown by clear and convincing evidence that appellant would not have been promoted even in the absence of unlawful discrimination.

Ross, Circuit Judge, with whom Fagg and Bowman, Circuit Judges, join, dissenting.

I dissent in part. I cannot agree with the majority's holding that proof that race was a "discernible factor" is sufficient in a mixed-motive context to establish intentional discrimination and liability under Title VII. I adhere to the position that when the evidence suggests mixed-motives the plaintiff must prove that race was a "motivating factor" before he or she can prevail at the liability stage. See Womack v. Munson, 619 F.2d 1292, 1297 n. 7 (8th Cir.1980), cert. denied, 450 U.S. 979, 101 S.Ct. 1513, 67 L.Ed.2d 814 (1981). Retention of this standard is warranted by the language of the statute, the case law and by practical considerations.

Notes

1. *"But For" Causation and Section 706(g).* Based in substantial part, on *Teamsters,* the courts of appeals are in agreement that, in class action cases when the liability and relief phases are generally bifurcated, an individual is not entitled to any form of relief under Section 706(g) unless the district court finds that "but for" the defendant's unlawful conduct the individual discriminatee would have received the employment opportunity at issue. The courts of appeals are split, however, on the applicability of the "but for" causation standard in the relief phase of an individual disparate treatment case. One of the leading and seminal cases holding that "but for" applies in the relief phase of an individual case is Day v. Mathews, 530 F.2d 1083 (D.C.Cir.1976). See also Milton v. Weinberger, 696 F.2d 94 (D.C.Cir.1982) (distinguishing between "but for" in liability and relief in individual cases). The Fourth, Seventh, Eighth, Ninth, Tenth, and Eleventh Circuits follow the Day v. Mathews rule. Smallwood v. United Air Lines, Inc., 728 F.2d 614 (4th Cir.1984); Caviale v. State of Wisconsin Dept. of Health and Social Services, 744 F.2d 1289 (7th Cir.1984); Bibbs v. Block, 778 F.2d 1318 (8th Cir.1985); Marotta v. Usery, 629 F.2d 615 (9th Cir.1980); Harbison v. Goldschmidt, 693 F.2d 115 (10th Cir.1982); Lewis v. Smith, 731 F.2d 1535 (11th Cir.1984). The Third Circuit has expressly held that the "but for" theory of causation is limited to the liability determination stage. Dillon v. Coles, 746 F.2d 998 (3d Cir.1984). And the District of Columbia Circuit expressly limited its Day v. Mathews rule to class action cases. Toney v. Block, 705 F.2d 1364 (D.C.Cir.1983). The role of causation in the mixed-motive cases is discussed in Brodin, "The Standard of Causation in the Mixed-Motive Title Action: A Social Policy Perspective," 82 Colum.L.Rev. 292 (1982).

2. Neither defendants nor plaintiffs are entitled, as a matter of right, to a *Teamsters*-type individualized hearing in the relief phase in class action cases. See Segar v. Smith, 738 F.2d 1249 (D.C.Cir.1984) (defendants); McKenzie v. Sawyer, 684 F.2d 62 (D.C.Cir.1982). Whether individualized hearings on relief will be allowed is determined under the discretionary authority a court has under Section 706(g) and the *Moody* and *Franks* guidelines.

3. RELIEF IN CLASS ACTIONS

DOMINGO v. NEW ENGLAND FISH COMPANY

United States Court of Appeals for the Ninth Circuit, 1984.
727 F.2d 1429.

PER CURIAM:

Nemesio Domingo, a Filipino, is a named plaintiff in a class action suit against his former employer, New England Fish Co. ("Nefco"). Domingo charged Nefco with employment discrimination on the basis of race in violation of Title VII of the Civil Rights Act of 1964, 42 U.S.C. § 2000e *et seq.*, and the Civil Rights Act of 1866, 42 U.S.C. § 1981. Following a bifurcated trial, the district court found for plaintiffs and awarded classwide and individual damages. We affirm in part and reverse in part.

I. BACKGROUND

As the facts of this case are reported more fully in the district court opinion, Domingo v. New England Fish Co., 445 F.Supp. 421 (W.D. Wash.1977), they only will be summarized here. Nefco operates salmon canneries located in remote, widely separated areas of Alaska. The facilities operate for only a limited period each year—typically less than 2 months—and lie vacant for the remainder of the year. Nefco hires employees from various area of Alaska and from Washington, Oregon, and northern California. It transports the employees to the canneries and houses and feeds them throughout the canning season. Employees are hired in a number of capacities, ranging from cannery workers and general maintenance personnel to administrators and engineers.

A. STATISTICS AND HIRING POLICIES

According to statistics compiled by Domingo and not challenged by Nefco, Nefco's work force was 47% nonwhite overall. However, nearly half of Nefco's hirings by job titles were racially segregated; in certain jobs 90% or more of the employees were white, while in others 90% or more were nonwhite. Many of the higher-paying job classifications were predominantly white, including jobs in the administrative department (100%), the tender department (96%), the quality control department (93%), and the machinist department (90%). The largest and lowest paying department, the cannery department, was 76% nonwhite.

The district court found that several company records labeled work crews by race. Time sheets contained job titles such as "Fil.[ipino] Crew—1st Foreman," "Fil. Crew—Inspector," "Native Cannery Foreman," or "White Bull Cook." Racial labels were also found in computer ledgers at Nefco's home office, on internal memoranda, and on budget forms prepared by cannery superintendents.

Nefco hired employees for each job department through separate channels. For the lower-paying cannery worker jobs, for example, Nefco recruited workers from native villages in Alaska and through a primarily Filipino ILWU local in Seattle. The resulting work force in the cannery department was almost entirely Alaska Native and Filipino. In contrast, the machinists and beach gangs were recruited by word of mouth. Friends and relatives of employees in those departments were thus the first to receive word about vacancies in the department. As the people in those departments were mostly white and the foremen who did the recruiting were white, most of the employees recruited were also white.

In addition, Nefco gave preference in hiring to relatives of company employees and business associates. This pervasive nepotism policy did help both whites and nonwhites obtain employment, but whites controlled the best jobs, and in those jobs the nepotism favored whites.

Finally, Nefco's criteria for employment were almost entirely subjective. The only criteria were: (1) job-related experience, (2) reputation for being a good worker, and (3) compatibility; even these criteria were not always adhered to. Each hiring decision was made by a cannery superintendent or a foreman on the basis of his personal judgment. Almost without exception, the hiring foremen and superintendents were white.

In order to justify its hiring decisions, Nefco introduced written job descriptions which purported to describe the necessary qualifications for many of its skilled jobs. However, the district court found that these job descriptions were largely pretextual since a number of Nefco's skilled employees could not meet the qualifications listed in the job descriptions as of the time they were hired.

B. Housing and Mess Halls

Although Nefco claimed that housing was assigned on the basis of crew and date of arrival at the cannery, employees found themselves in buildings that were either largely or entirely segregated. Even when integrated crews were assigned to the same bunkhouse, the floors of the bunkhouse were segregated by race. The best housing was assigned first and the worst assigned last, but the machinist, tender, carpenter, and other crews in which whites predominated were generally brought to the facilities first. The cannery crew (76% nonwhite) was generally the last to arrive.

Domingo also alleged that Nefco maintained segregated eating facilities at its canneries. However, Nefco did not assign seating in mess halls. In some of the mess halls, signs proclaimed that there were no seating restrictions. Generally, two types of food were served in the mess halls: American and Oriental. The Oriental food was provided at the request of Local 37, a Filipino union. At some of the canneries, the American and Oriental messes were in two different buildings. The Oriental mess was frequented mainly by Filipinos, and was known as the "Filipino mess." However, any employee could eat in either mess hall if he notified the cook in advance and if there was enough food and space to accommodate him. At other canneries, American and Oriental food was served in the same building. Employees usually sat at segregated tables because crews that worked and slept together generally ate together as well.

C. PROCEDURAL HISTORY

In this lawsuit, the district court certified Domingo's class as that of all nonwhites employed or deterred from employment at any one of five Nefco facilities at any time from January 30, 1971 to November 8, 1976. The court then bifurcated the trial, intending to determine liability on a classwide basis and damages individually. The liability phase of the trial occurred in November 1976, lasting 1½ days. Most of the evidence presented during this phase was in written form.

In the court's reported opinion on liability, the district court found that plaintiffs had established an unrebutted *prima facie* case of discriminatory employment practices in job allocation and in housing, and that plaintiffs had failed to establish a prima facie case of discrimination in messing.

Following the entry of the liability opinion,[1] individual notice and a claim form were mailed to 780 individuals. Notice was also published in a number of newspapers in Alaska, Washington, and California, and radio broadcasts in English and Yupik were made to native villages in Alaska. In the interim between the liability and the damages phases of the suit, however, the district court placed several restrictions on communications between class members and Domingo and his counsel. The notices did not include the name, address, or telephone number of Domingo's counsel. The court offered claimants the services of four magistrates to assist in filing claims, and it permitted Domingo and his counsel to assist class members in filing claims only when the class members initiated the contact. During some portion of the time before the damages hearings, the district court prohibited Domingo's counsel from interviewing claimants without giving Nefco's counsel the opportunity to attend and ask questions.

Claim forms were received from 205 individuals. Twelve were not members of the class. The district court dismissed the claims of 19 others before counsel had any contact with them. Thirty-one withdrew their claims.

1. The procedural history of the case in the interim between the time of the liability decision and the time of the damages hearings is quite extensive. After finding liability, the district court denied injunctive relief and appointed a monitor to gather information and review Nefco's employment practices. In January 1979, the court denied a preliminary injunction after reviewing the monitor's findings. Domingo took an interlocutory appeal. In May 1979, this court vacated the judgment and remanded for an immediate hearing on injunctive relief. A couple of weeks later, the court withdrew that order, set the appeal for an expedited hearing, and remanded for entry of findings and conclusions. The court delayed submission of the appeal, which was later dismissed as moot in June 1980, when Nefco petitioned for relief under the Bankruptcy Code. Domingo removed the case to bankruptcy court. At the request of Nefco's trustee in bankruptcy, the case was remanded and the automatic stay lifted.

Ultimately, 124 claims were heard by the district court. The court in November 1981 awarded individual damages to eight of the 124 claimants, and in addition made a lump-sum award of $55,000 in back pay to compensate for disparities in housing quality.

II. LIABILITY FOR DISCRIMINATION IN HIRING AND PROMOTION

* * *

Nefco challenges the district court's finding that Nefco discriminated on the basis of race, on the grounds that (1) the district court erred in analyzing Domingo's claims of discrimination under a disparate impact model; (2) it was inappropriate for the district court to base its finding of liability on general comparative statistics; and (3) Nefco successfully rebutted Domingo's prima facie case of discrimination. We hold that the plaintiffs established intentional discrimination; therefore, we need not decide the adequacy of the impact case. Nefco's other contentions are without merit.

* * *

IV. COMMUNICATION RESTRICTIONS

Plaintiffs contend the district court's imposition of restrictions on communications between potential class members and the plaintiffs and their counsel is error. They contend the restrictions violate Federal Rule of Civil Procedure 23, as interpreted by the Supreme Court in Gulf Oil Co. v. Bernard, 452 U.S. 89, 101 S.Ct. 2193, 68 L.Ed.2d 693 (1981).

The restrictions in this case were imposed under Local Rule 23(g), which prohibits parties and their counsel in a class action from communicating with actual or potential class members without prior approval of the court.[6] Plaintiffs contend the following restrictions, imposed

---

6. *Prevention of Potential Abuses of Class Actions*

In every potential and actual class action under Rule 23, F.R.Civ.P., all parties thereto and their counsel are hereby forbidden, directly or indirectly, orally or in writing, to communicate concerning such action with any potential or actual class member not a formal party to the action without the consent of and approval of the communication by order of the Court. Any such proposed communication shall be presented to the Court in writing with a designation of or description of all addresses and with a motion and proposed order for prior approval by the court of the proposed communications and proposed addressees. The communications forbidden by this rule, include, but are not limited to, (a) solicitation directly or indirectly of legal representation of potential and actual class members who are not formal parties to the class action; (b) solicitation of fees and expenses and agreements to pay

fees and expenses, from potential and actual class members who are not formal parties to the class action; (c) solicitation by formal parties to the class action of requests by class members to opt out in class actions under subparagraph (b)(3) of rule 23, F.R.Civ.P.; and (d) communications from counsel or a party which may tend to misrepresent the status, purposes and effects of the action, and of actual or potential Court orders therein, which may create impressions tending, without cause, to reflect adversely on any party, any counsel, the Court, or the administration of justice. The obligations and prohibitions of this rule are not exclusive. All other ethical, legal and equitable obligations are unaffected by this rule.

This rule does not forbid (1) communications between an attorney and his client or a prospective client, who has on the initiative of the client or prospective client consulted with, employed or proposed to employ the attorney, or (2) com-

before the damages phase of the trial, require reversal of the district court's denial of back-pay awards to the majority of claimants: (1) plaintiffs' counsel was denied the right to interview back-pay claimants outside the presence of Nefco's counsel; (2) counsel was prohibited from interviewing 19 claimants before their claims were dismissed; (3) the court limited the ability of plaintiffs and counsel to assist class members in filing back-pay claims; and (4) the court refused to identify plaintiffs' counsel in the notice, making it difficult for class members to direct inquiries to them. We hold the trial court erred in imposing these restrictions and remand for a new hearing on the claims of class members who wish to refile their claims or to file new ones.

In *Gulf Oil*, the Supreme Court held that a district court may not routinely restrict communications between class members and plaintiffs or their counsel. Before such restrictions may be imposed, the district court must carefully weigh the competing interests involved—the need for the restriction and the interference with the rights of the parties—and make specific findings that reflect that weighing. 452 U.S. at 101, 101 S.Ct. at 2200. The Court found the restrictions imposed in *Gulf Oil* were inconsistent with Rule 23 because they made it more difficult for the class representatives to obtain information about the merits of the case and interfered with efforts to inform potential class members of the existence of the law suit. Id.

It is undisputed that the district court did not make the specific findings required by *Gulf Oil*.[7] The record contains no specific findings

munications occurring in the regular course of business or in the performance of the duties of a public office or agency (such as the Attorney General) which do not have the effect of soliciting representation by counsel, or misrepresenting the status, purposes or effects of the action and orders therein.

Local Rule 23(g), Western District of Washington. This rule is based on the model provided in the Manual for Complex Litigation (rev. ed. 1973).

7. Nefco suggests that because *Gulf Oil* was decided after the restrictions in this case were imposed, it should not control our decision.

A reviewing court generally must apply the law as it exists at the time of its decision. United States v. Johnson, 457 U.S. 537, 548, 102 S.Ct. 2579, 2586-87, 73 L.Ed.2d 202 (1982). An exception to this rule may be made only after the court weighs three factors. First, the decision must establish a new principle of law. Second, the court must determine whether retrospective application would retard the policy behind the rule. Third, the court must consider whether retrospective application would be inequitable. Chevron Oil

Co. v. Huson, 404 U.S. 97, 106-07, 92 S.Ct. 349, 355-56, 30 L.Ed.2d 296 (1971).

Two other circuits have applied *Gulf Oil* retrospectively without discussion. See Williams v. United States District Court, 658 F.2d 430, 436 (6th Cir.) cert. denied, 454 U.S. 1128, 102 S.Ct. 980, 71 L.Ed.2d 116 (1981); Zinser v. Continental Grain Co., 660 F.2d 754, 762 (10th Cir.), cert. denied, 455 U.S. 941, 102 S.Ct. 1434, 71 L.Ed.2d 652 (1981).

We agree that the rule established in *Gulf Oil* should not be restricted to prospective application. A decision will be denied retrospective application only if it makes a "clear break" with past precedent. United States v. Johnson, 457 U.S. 537, 551 n. 12, 102 S.Ct. 2579, 2587 n. 12, 73 L.Ed.2d 202 (1982). Although *Gulf Oil* was a "new decision" in the sense that it decided an issue the Supreme Court had not previously addressed, the decision was not without precedent. In Rodgers v. United States Steel Corp., 508 F.2d 152 (3d Cir.1975), the Third Circuit invalidated a local rule prohibiting all communications with class members before certification unless approved by the court. The *Gulf Oil* opinion itself quotes from Coles v. Marsh, 560 F.2d

made before the restrictions were imposed that would justify them. "[T]he mere possibility of abuses does not justify routine adoption of a communications ban that interferes with the formation of a class or the prosecution of a class action in accordance with the Rules." *Gulf Oil*, 452 U.S. at 104, 101 S.Ct. at 2202. In its unpublished decision on damages, the district court suggested that plaintiffs' counsel may have overstepped ethical bounds in the zealousness of their handling of individual claims.[8] This after-the-fact pronouncement cannot substitute for a reasoned inquiry and findings supporting the restrictions prior to their imposition.[9]

186, 189 (3d Cir.) cert. denied, 484 U.S. 985, 98 S.Ct. 611, 54 L.Ed.2d 479 (1977), which held that a district court could not restrict communications in a class action absent a showing of the particular threatened abuses. 452 U.S. at 102, 101 S.Ct. at 2201. Analogous authority cited in *Gulf Oil* also imposed a duty in the context of issuance of protective orders. See In Re Halkin, 598 F.2d 176, 198 (D.C.Cir.1979) (Protective Order under Rule 26(c) "restrains plaintiff's expression yet the district court made no assessment of the strength of the continuing interest, the need for such a broad restriction, or the availability of alternate measures. In the absence of these findings, the petitioner's right to be free of the restriction is clear and undisputable"), cited at 452 U.S. at 102 n. 16, 101 S.Ct. at 2201 n. 16. The district court itself, in this case, acknowledged that the propriety and constitutionality of Local Rule 23(g) were in doubt.

8. The following comes from Judge Solomon's unpublished opinion in the damages phase of trial:

> In addition to the claim forms prepared by the claimants or by persons on behalf of the claimants, plaintiffs' counsel prepared written statements to supplement the claim forms, based upon their interviews with the claimants.
>
> * * *
>
>   * * *
>
> Many of the narrative statements prepared by plaintiffs' counsel went far beyond the contentions in the claim forms. The courtroom testimony and depositions revealed that these statements were inaccurate or exaggerated. Some of them contradicted statements in the claim forms, sometimes with the explanation that the claimant had not understood these simple forms.
>
> A more accurate explanation of these discrepancies is that certain named plaintiffs and others importuned many of these claimants to file claims or to testify contrary to the facts. For exam-

ple, one claimant testified at a court hearing that he was not qualified for the jobs he checked on the claim form, but had done so because of the urging of others. Another who apparently was making an equal pay claim testified that he was treated fairly. Many claimants knew nothing about the duties or qualifications of jobs which they had checked on the claim form.

> The questions asked claimants on their depositions, in the presence of defendant's counsel, were leading and suggestive. The claimants were asked to consider so-called facts and information, of which they had no knowledge when they worked for Nefco, as the basis for answering whether they sought particular jobs or whether they were deterred from asking for such jobs and whether they were qualified to hold those jobs.
>
> Their answers, often uncertain and equivocal, became positive assertions of interest, availability, and competence in the written narrative statements prepared for them by plaintiffs' counsel. These distortions may have been compounded in those interviews in which the claimants and plaintiffs' counsel refused to permit the questions and answers to be recorded.

Damages Op., supra note 5, at 5–6.

9. The first amendment interests involved here also would have required the district judge to make findings as to the necessity for the restrictions. Before a prior restraint on speech may be imposed, "the substantive evil must be extremely serious and the degree of imminence extremely high." Landmark Communications, Inc. v. Virginia, 435 U.S. 829, 845, 98 S.Ct. 1535, 1544, 56 L.Ed.2d 1 (1978). The Supreme Court has held that a "solidity of evidence" is necessary to make the requisite showing of imminence. Id. Moreover, "[t]he danger must not be remote or even probable; it must immediately imperil." Craig v. Harney, 331 U.S. 367, 376, 67 S.Ct.

Nefco contends *Gulf Oil* is inapplicable to this case because it involved a restriction on communications imposed before the certification of the class, while those at issue here were imposed after class certification. We reject this argument. If anything, the policies weighing in favor of communications restrictions after the class has been certified are much less compelling than before certification.

At the time the district court imposed restrictions in this case, the usual concerns weighing in favor of restrictions were not present. The Manual for Complex Litigation, and Local Rule 23(g), specifically identify the principal concerns: (1) solicitation of direct representation of class members who are not formal parties, (2) solicitation of funds and agreements to pay fees, (3) solicitation by defendants of requests to opt out, and (4) communications which may be confusing or misleading, or create an impression which reflects adversely on the court. Manual for Complex Litigation § 1.41 (1973). See also *Gulf Oil*, 452 U.S. at 100 & n. 12, 101 S.Ct. at 2200 & n. 12. The abuses at which communications restrictions are aimed arise from the fact that the class representative and his counsel may have interests that are in conflict with those of the class members. Thus, for example, counsel might want class members to participate in the litigation as named plaintiffs, when some class members might profit more from remaining inactive or opting out. It is hard to identify any conflict of interest that might have existed between plaintiffs' counsel and class members during the time at issue here. Nefco's liability had already been determined. Because the class had already been certified, class members who did not present their claims would be barred by *res judicata* from ever obtaining relief. Class members' only interest was in presenting their claims to the court in the best possible light. Plaintiffs' counsel, whatever their motives, had the same interest.

We must reverse if plaintiffs show that the restrictions on communications "created at least potential difficulties for them as they sought to vindicate the legal rights of a class of employees." *Gulf Oil*, 452 U.S. at 101, 101 S.Ct. at 2200. Plaintiffs contend that the restrictions interfered with their ability effectively to prosecute the individual claims for damages in the following ways: (1) the requirement that a Nefco attorney be present at the interviews discouraged confidentiality and hence hampered preparation of claim forms; (2) class members who were not willing to risk reprisals before even submitting a claim were discouraged from consulting with class counsel since a Nefco attorney would also be present; (3) the fact that English was a second

1249, 1255, 91 L.Ed. 1546 (1947). These standards apply to restrictions entered pursuant to Rule 23. See Gulf Oil Co. v. Bernard, 619 F.2d 459, 475–76 (5th Cir. 1980) (en banc), aff'd on other grounds, 452 U.S. 89, 101 S.Ct. 2193, 68 L.Ed.2d 693 (1981) ("Rule 23, as a specific aspect of the administration of justice, [does not] create an exception to the principles governing prior restraints. * * * The validity of a prior restraint entered under Rule 23 must be tested by the same standards utilized in other contexts."); accord Rodgers v. United States Steel Corp., 536 F.2d 1001, 1008 (3d Cir.1976).

language for many claimants gave rise to a special need for aid of counsel in preparing claims.

It is obvious that few, if any, of the claimants in this case could afford private counsel. The availability of a federal magistrate to help claimants is no substitute for an advocate who will help claimants to present their claims in the best possible light. The trial court seems unnecessarily concerned that counsel would be overzealous in the pursuit of claims. The advocacy system is designed to correct for excesses through response from opposing counsel, rather than through court-imposed restrictions which interfere with legal assistance to class members. The restrictions are particularly inappropriate where class members have no other effective means to secure counsel. Therefore, we reverse the trial court's findings on the individual claims and remand for a rehearing on the damage awards. The district court must allow all class members a reasonable time in which to submit claims prepared with the aid of counsel *ab initio* rather than supplementary to their original claims. The original claims should be disregarded unless no new claim is presented.

V. DEFINITION OF THE CLASS

In this case, the district court certified the plaintiff class as all nonwhites who either were employed by Nefco, applied for employment with Nefco, or were deterred from applying for employment with Nefco at any time between 300 days prior to November 26, 1971 (the date Domingo filed his charge with the EEOC) and the date of the damages phase of the trial. This definition covers the canning seasons 1971 through 1976, inclusive. Domingo challenges both the upper and lower limits of the time scope of the class. He contends that the continuing violation theory announced in cases such as Reed v. Lockheed Aircraft Corp., 613 F.2d 757, 759–61 (9th Cir.1980), permits victims of discrimination at an earlier time to recover. He also contends that the district court erred in failing to grant relief for discrimination after the 1976 season, citing United States v. Lee Way Motor Freight, Inc., 625 F.2d 918 (10th Cir.1979). We hold that the trial court was correct in establishing the starting date of the class action 300 days prior to the date Domingo filed his EEOC charge, but that it erred in refusing relief for discrimination after the date of trial.

As the district court correctly pointed out, a charge of employment discrimination under Title VII must be filed with the EEOC within 180 days of an alleged unlawful employment practice, or within 300 days of such a practice if the charging party has initially instituted proceedings with a state or local antidiscrimination agency. Title VII, § 706(e), 42 U.S.C. § 2000e–5(e) (1976).[10] It is now well settled that a named

---

10. At the time Domingo filed his charge, the relevant limitation periods under the Civil Rights Act of 1964 were 210 days if proceedings had been instituted with an appropriate state agency, and 90 days otherwise. Civil Rights Act of 1964, Pub.L. No. 88–352, § 706(d), 78 Stat. 241, 260. However, while Domingo's charge was pending before the EEOC Congress enacted the Equal Employment Opportunity Act of 1972, which lengthened the limitation periods. Equal Employment Oppor-

plaintiff who has filed a timely charge may bring a class action on behalf of class members who have not filed charges. Albemarle Paper Co. v. Moody, 422 U.S. 405, 414 n. 8, 95 S.Ct. 2362, 2370 n. 8, 45 L.Ed.2d 280 (1975); Oatis v. Crown Zellerbach Corp., 398 F.2d 496, 499 (5th Cir. 1968). In addition, the filing of a class action suspends the applicable statute of limitation for all class members. Crown, Cork, & Seal Co. v. Parker, 462 U.S. 345, 103 S.Ct. 2392, 2397, 76 L.Ed.2d 628 (1983); American Pipe & Construction Co. v. Utah, 414 U.S. 538, 554, 94 S.Ct. 756, 766, 38 L.Ed.2d 713 (1974). It follows, then, that Domingo may represent all class members whose claims were not already time-barred at the time he filed his charge, irrespective of whether the class members had filed charges of their own. Payne v. Travenol Laboratories, Inc., 673 F.2d 798, 813–14 (5th Cir.), cert. denied, 459 U.S. 1038, 103 S.Ct. 451, 74 L.Ed.2d 605 (1982); Laffey v. Northwest Airlines, Inc., 567 F.2d 429, 472 (D.C.Cir.1976), cert. denied, 434 U.S. 1086, 98 S.Ct. 1281, 55 L.Ed.2d 792 (1978); Wetzel v. Liberty Mutual Insurance Co., 508 F.2d 239, 246 (3d Cir.), cert. denied, 421 U.S. 1011, 95 S.Ct. 2415, 44 L.Ed.2d 679 (1975).

In this case, the district court allowed all class members to receive the benefit of the 300-day limitation period rather than the general 180-day period. Although Title VII seems to say that the longer period is to be used only for claimants who have instituted proceedings with an appropriate state agency, we have held the 300-day period applicable to the class. Williams v. Owens-Illinois, Inc., 665 F.2d 918, 923 n. 2 (9th Cir.), cert. denied, 459 U.S. 971, 103 S.Ct. 302, 74 L.Ed.2d 283 (1982); see Bartelt v. Berlitz School of Languages of America, Inc., 698 F.2d 1003, 1004 (9th Cir.), cert. denied, 464 U.S. 915, 104 S.Ct. 277, 78 L.Ed. 2d 257 (1983). The district court's class definition was therefore correct, although the definition would have to be modified if the action were brought today. *Williams*, 665 F.2d at 923–24 n. 2.

Domingo argues, nevertheless, that the continuing violation doctrine announced in this circuit operates to eliminate the limitation period. The continuing violation theory recognizes the principle that a plaintiff may be able to recover under Title VII if he or she can demonstrate a pattern or practice of discrimination that has continued into the present, notwithstanding his or her ability to prove specific instances of discrimination personally suffered at the hands of the defendant within the limitation period of Title VII. See O'Brien v. Sky Chefs, Inc., 670 F.2d 864, 868 (9th Cir.1982); Reed v. Lockheed Aircraft Corp., 613 F.2d 757, 761–62 (9th Cir.1980). Thus, Domingo reasons, if a continuing violation has been demonstrated a class member should be

tunity Act of 1972, Pub.L. No. 92–261, § 4(a), 86 Stat. 103, 104. The 1972 act stated that its provisions applied to all charges pending before the EEOC on the date of enactment or filed thereafter. Id. § 14, 86 Stat. at 113. We believe that the ends of efficiency and economy in class litigation, as well as the intent of Congress, are best effectuated by allowing the benefit of the lengthened limitation periods to inure to all members of the class. See American Pipe & Constr. Co. v. Utah, 414 U.S. 538, 553–54, 94 S.Ct. 756, 766, 38 L.Ed.2d 713 (1974).

able to recover regardless of when the class member was employed. That statement is not quite true.

We note, first, that the defendant's conduct, as found by the district court, did indeed constitute a continuing violation of Title VII. In order for a violation to be continuing, it must involve a practice, continued over a period of time, which operates to injure the plaintiff either individually or as a member of a class to which the plaintiff belongs. See Williams v. Owens-Illinois, Inc., 665 F.2d 918, 924–25 & n. 3 (9th Cir.), cert. denied, 459 U.S. 971, 103 S.Ct. 302, 74 L.Ed.2d 283 (1982); Reed v. Lockheed Aircraft Corp., 613 F.2d 757, 760 (9th Cir. 1980); Elliott v. Sperry Rand Corp., 79 F.R.D. 580, 585–86 (D.Minn. 1978). Here, plaintiffs have attacked Nefco's hiring and promotion systems and policies. There is no question that these policies remained intact from season to season. Moreover, the practices were not confined in application to any particular individual or group of individuals, but operated against the class generally. Indeed, the district court implicitly found, as a matter of fact, that Nefco's practices were classwide in application when it certified the class member under Fed. R.Civ.P. 23(b)(2).[11]

Domingo's argument, however, would effectively read the limitation period out of the statute, which we cannot do. As the Supreme Court has stated:

> A discriminatory act which is not made the basis for a timely charge is the legal equivalent of a discriminatory act which occurred before the statute was passed. It may constitute relevant background evidence in a proceeding in which the status of a current practice is at issue, but separately considered, it is merely an unfortunate event in history which has no present legal consequences.

United Air Lines, Inc. v. Evans, 431 U.S. 553, 558, 97 S.Ct. 1885, 1889, 52 L.Ed.2d 571 (1977). The continuing violation theory is a way of introducing this type of background evidence. In Reed v. Lockheed Aircraft Corp., 613 F.2d 757 (9th Cir.1980), the plaintiff launched a sweeping attack on Lockheed's systems of promotion, compensation, and training. She alleged three specific instances of discrimination, in 1963, 1969, and 1972, but filed her charge in 1976. The district court held her claim time-barred and we reversed, saying that the specific events of which plaintiff complained "are but evidence that a *policy* of discrimination pervaded Lockheed's personnel decisions. The violations of which she complains occurred each day of her employment, *including the days within the appropriate limitations period.*" Id. at 760 (latter emphasis added); accord Scott v. Pacific Maritime Association, 695 F.2d 1199, 1206 (9th Cir.1983). It follows that, as a prerequisite to obtaining relief, each class member must demonstrate, by fact of

---

11. We note that the drafters of Rule 23 specifically contemplated that suits against discriminatory hiring and promotion policies would be appropriately maintained under Rule 23(b)(2). Wetzel v. Liberty Mutu- al Ins. Co., 508 F.2d 239, 250 (3d Cir.), cert. denied, 421 U.S. 1011, 95 S.Ct. 2415, 44 L.Ed.2d 679 (1975). Such suits, then, may be particularly appropriate for continuing violation treatment.

employment or otherwise, that he or she had been discriminated against during the limitation period or was a member of a group exposed to discrimination during that time.

Domingo argues that the district court should have granted relief for discrimination after the 1976 season. We agree. In United States v. Lee Way Motor Freight, Inc., 625 F.2d 918, 945 (10th Cir.1979), the Tenth Circuit held it was error not to consider claims of discrimination which occurred after the complaint was filed, where there was no break in the pattern of discrimination. Here, the special master found that Nefco's employment practices had continued, unchanged, past the 1976 season. As in the *Lee Way* case, it would be inequitable to refuse to consider these claims, many of which might otherwise be time-barred.

Permitting post-1976 claims to be heard would also be consistent with two of the most important policies underlying Rule 23. One is the "vindication of the rights of individuals who otherwise might not consider it worth the candle to embark on litigation in which the optimum result might be more than consumed by the cost." Deposit Guaranty National Bank v. Roper, 445 U.S. 326, 338, 100 S.Ct. 1166, 1174, 63 L.Ed.2d 427 (1980). The other is the central purpose of Rule 23, that is, to have litigation in which common interests or common questions of law or fact prevail disposed of, where feasible in a single lawsuit. See Rodgers v. United States Steel Corp., 508 F.2d 152, 156, 163 (3d Cir.), cert. denied, 423 U.S. 832, 96 S.Ct. 54, 46 L.Ed.2d 50 (1975).

VI. DAMAGES

A. EMPLOYMENT DISCRIMINATION

Our decision on the communications issue requires reversal of the district court's denial of individual back-pay claims. Because the district court will have to redetermine these claims on remand, we address plaintiffs' contention that the district court should have awarded class-wide relief rather than attempting to determine the precise amount of back-pay owing to each individual claimant.

The facts of this case justify a departure from an individualized remedy for each claimant although we recognize that as a general rule that approach should be used. See Hameed v. International Association of Bridge Workers, 637 F.2d 506, 519 (8th Cir.1980); Stewart v. General Motors Corp., 542 F.2d 445, 452 (7th Cir.1976), cert. denied, 433 U.S. 919, 97 S.Ct. 2995, 53 L.Ed.2d 1105 (1977). Nefco's lack of objective hiring criteria and use of word-of-mouth recruitment directed at particular ethnic groups makes it difficult to determine precisely which of the claimants would have been given a better job absent discrimination, but it is clear that many should have. In such a situation, class-wide relief is appropriate.[12] "[W]hen the class size or

12. Because non-whites were not under-represented in Nefco's lower-paying cannery positions, class-wide relief is not appropriate for those class members denied those jobs. However, many claimants have alleged they were discharged from

the ambiguity of promotion or hiring practices or the illegal practices continued over an extended period of time calls forth [a] quagmire of hypothetical judgment * * * a class-wide approach to the measure of back-pay is necessitated." Pettway v. American Cast Iron Pipe Co., 494 F.2d 211, 261 (5th Cir.1974).

Determination of the award could proceed along any of several avenues, all of which are designed to estimate the difference between what non-whites actually earned and what they would have earned but for the discrimination. See, e.g., *Hameed*, 637 F.2d at 520–21; *Stewart*, 542 F.2d at 453–54; *Pettway*, 494 F.2d at 250. The court could determine a lump sum to be distributed among claimants in proportion to the number of seasons they worked or should have worked, or it could make individual awards based on the difference between what claimants actually earned and what they would have earned, on the average, had non-whites occupied their fair share of the better paying jobs. The district court should keep in mind that discrimination has already been proved; "proof of a discriminatory pattern and practice creates a rebuttable presumption in favor of relief." International Brotherhood of Teamsters v. United States, 431 U.S. 324, 359 n. 45, 97 S.Ct. 1843, 1867 n. 45, 52 L.Ed.2d 396 (1977).

In order to be eligible for back-pay, claimants need only prove they applied for a position or would have applied if not for Nefco's discriminatory practices. They may be required to show what their qualifications were, but do not have the burden of proving they were qualified for the position sought. Because class-wide discrimination has already been shown, the employer has the burden of proving that the applicant was unqualified or showing some other valid reason why the claimant was not, or would not have been, acceptable. See International Brotherhood of Teamsters, 431 U.S. at 362, 97 S.Ct. at 1868; Pettway v. American Cast Iron Pipe Co., 681 F.2d 1259, 1266 (11th Cir.1982), petition for cert. filed, 51 U.S.L.W. 3512 (U.S. Dec. 23, 1982) (No. 82–1074).

In determining whether claimants applied or were deterred from applying for a better position, the district court should not put an unrealistic burden on claimants. Given the extreme segregation in both living and working environments and Nefco's use of racial labels, it can be assumed that all Nefco employees were aware of its discriminatory hiring practices. Nefco's discriminatory hiring procedures, themselves, created the difficulty many claimants have experienced in attempting to prove application or deterrence. Application procedures were informal. Word-of-mouth recruitment, directed along racial lines, made it especially difficult for present or prospective employees to become aware of openings as they occurred. Such recruitment procedures also may have created confusion about what Nefco was looking

those positions, or refused a job, in retaliation for complaining about discrimination or for other discriminatory reasons. Such claimants may prove entitlement, on an individual basis, for back-pay relating to any of Nefco's job categories.

for by way of qualifications since non-whites were sought only for certain positions. Because Nefco lacked formal application procedures, any request for a better position made to a superior should suffice as an application. Denial of past applications, even in years prior to those at issue here, is more than enough proof of deterrence in later years. All uncertainties should be resolved against the employer. See *Stewart*, 542 F.2d at 452; *Pettway*, 494 F.2d at 261.

B. Housing Discrimination

Nefco argues that any award of damages for housing discrimination was inappropriate, while Domingo argues that the district court's damages award for housing discrimination was inadequate. Both contentions are without merit.

Nefco asserts that Title VII provides for only equitable relief and backpay and does not allow compensatory or punitive damages, Padway v. Palches, 665 F.2d 965, 968 (9th Cir.1982), and argues that the district court's award for housing discrimination cannot be characterized as backpay. If the class members had actually paid rent to Nefco for housing with a fair market rental value below the amount of rent paid, they could be awarded backpay in the amount of the difference between rent paid and the fair market rental value of the housing they received. Cf. Williams v. Yazoo Valley-Minter City Oil Mill, Inc., 469 F.Supp. 37, 54 (N.D.Miss.1978). However, since Nefco did not charge any rent to its employees, the company argues that any damage they suffered is not an identifiable economic loss, but is more closely analogous to the inferior working conditions for which the Sixth Circuit disallowed compensatory damages in Harrington v. Vandalia-Butler Board of Education, 585 F.2d 192, 194–97 (6th Cir.1978), cert. denied, 441 U.S. 932, 99 S.Ct. 2053, 60 L.Ed.2d 660 (1979).

In *Harrington,* a female physical education instructor sought damages based on the difference between her office facilities and those of her male counterparts. Male physical education instructors were given offices and private locker, toilet, and shower facilities. The female instructor had only a partitioned area for an office and was forced to share locker, toilet, and shower facilities with her students. The court found that a damage award on this basis would be an award of compensatory damages which would be inappropriate under Title VII.

We think, as the district court did, that Nefco supplied room and board as part of the compensation paid to its employees. The lodging provided by Nefco was for the personal use of its employees and was not part of the actual on-the-job work environment as were the office facilities in *Harrington.* On such facts, an award of backpay is proper under the Equal Pay Act, Laffey v. Northwest Airlines, Inc., 567 F.2d 429, 455 n. 175 (D.C.Cir.1976), cert. denied, 434 U.S. 1086, 98 S.Ct. 1281, 55 L.Ed.2d 792 (1978); 29 U.S.C. § 203(m) (1976), and there is no reason why a like award should be denied under Title VII. Thus, on these facts a measurable difference in the quality of housing provided to whites as opposed to nonwhites can be characterized as a wage differential for which relief is available under Title VII.

With respect to the amount of the district court's backpay award for the disparity in rental value between the white and nonwhite housing, Domingo argues that the $55,000 award was inadequate for several reasons.

Domingo claims that the district court erred in denying backpay for subjective disparities in housing, such as "squalor, stenches, peeling paint, unsanitary conditions, and defective plumbing." Domingo implies that the court failed to consider these subjective factors because their value was difficult to determine. Yet, the court spoke of the difficulty of determining the value of these factors as a rationale for not requiring individual proof of damages; it did not state that it was ignoring these factors in computing classwide damages. * * *. In fact, after discussing all the subjective factors that affected housing value, the district court stated that it was making its award "[t]aking all these adjustments into account, and recognizing the impossibility of precise calculations." Id. at 40.

Domingo also asserts that the district court erred in not awarding prejudgment interest on the amount of damages determined. Cases from other circuits have held that an award of prejudgment interest on a backpay award is appropriate. See, e.g., United States v. Lee Way Motor Freight, Inc., 625 F.2d 918, 940 (10th Cir.1979); Pettway v. American Cast Iron Pipe Co., 494 F.2d 211, 263 (5th Cir.1974). Such an award, however, is discretionary with the trial court. Taylor v. Phillips Industries, Inc., 593 F.2d 783, 787 (7th Cir.1979); see Twin City Sportservice, Inc. v. Charles O. Finley & Co., 676 F.2d 1291, 1310 (9th Cir.), cert. denied, 459 U.S. 1009, 103 S.Ct. 364, 74 L.Ed.2d 400 (1982). The fact that the amount of backpay is not readily determinable weighs against awarding prejudgment interest. See, e.g., Perkins v. Standard Oil Co., 487 F.2d 672, 675 (9th Cir.1973); Elte, Inc. v. S.S. Mullen, Inc., 469 F.2d 1127, 1133 (9th Cir.1972). In view of the many subjective factors the court valued in determining the amount of damages, we find no abuse of discretion.

* * *

4. ATTORNEY'S FEES

CHRISTIANBURG GARMENT CO. v. E.E.O.C.

Supreme Court of the United States, 1978.
434 U.S. 412, 98 S.Ct. 694, 54 L.Ed.2d 648.

MR. JUSTICE STEWART delivered the opinion of the Court.

Section 706(k) of Title VII of the Civil Rights Act of 1964 provides:

In any action or proceeding under this title the court in its discretion, may allow the prevailing party * * * a reasonable attorney's fee * * *.[1]

The question in this case is under what circumstances an attorney's fee should be allowed when the defendant is the prevailing party in a Title VII action—a question about which the federal courts have expressed divergent views.

I

Two years after Rosa Helm had filed a Title VII charge of racial discrimination against the petitioner Christiansburg Garment Co. (company), the Equal Employment Opportunity Commission notified her that its conciliation efforts had failed and that she had the right to sue the company in federal court. She did not do so. Almost two years later, in 1972, Congress enacted amendments to Title VII. Section 14 of these amendments authorized the Commission to sue in its own name to prosecute "charges pending with the Commission" on the effective date of the amendments. Proceeding under this section, the Commission sued the company, alleging that it had engaged in unlawful employment practices in violation of the amended Act. The company moved for summary judgment on the ground, *inter alia,* that the Rosa Helm charge had not been "pending" before the Commission when the 1972 amendments took effect. The District Court agreed and granted summary judgment in favor of the company. 376 F.Supp. 1067 (W.D.Va.).

The company then petitioned for the allowance of attorney's fees against the Commission pursuant to § 706(k) of Title VII. Finding that "the Commission's action in bringing the suit cannot be characterized as unreasonable or meritless," the District Court concluded that "an award of attorney's fees to petitioner is not justified in this case." A divided Court of Appeals affirmed, 550 F.2d 949 (CA4), and we granted certiorari to consider an important question of federal law, 432 U.S. 905, 97 S.Ct. 2948, 53 L.Ed.2d 1077.

II

It is the general rule in the United States that in the absence of legislation providing otherwise, litigants must pay their own attorney's fees. Alyeska Pipeline Co. v. Wilderness Society, 421 U.S. 240, 95 S.Ct. 1612, 44 L.Ed.2d 141. Congress has provided only limited exceptions to this rule "under selected statutes granting or protecting various federal rights." Id., at 260, 95 S.Ct. at 1623. Some of these statutes make fee awards mandatory for prevailing plaintiffs;[5] others make awards per-

---

1. Section 706(k) provides in full: "In any action or proceeding under this title the court, in its discretion, may allow the prevailing party, other than the Commission or the United States, a reasonable attorney's fee as part of the costs, and the Commission and the United States shall be liable for costs the same as a private person." 78 Stat. 261, 42 U.S.C. § 2000e–5(k).

5. See, e.g., Clayton Act, 38 Stat. 731, 15 U.S.C. § 15; Fair Labor Standards Act of 1938, 52 Stat. 1069, as amended, 29 U.S.C. § 216(b); Packers and Stockyards Act, 42 Stat. 165, 7 U.S.C. § 210(f); Truth

missive but limit them to certain parties, usually prevailing plaintiffs.[6] But many of the statutes are more flexible, authorizing the award of attorney's fees to either plaintiffs or defendants, and entrusting the effectuation of the statutory policy to the discretion of the district courts.[7] Section 706(k) of Title VII of the Civil Rights Act of 1964 falls into this last category, providing as it does that a district court may in its discretion allow an attorney's fee to the prevailing party.

In Newman v. Piggie Park Enterprises, 390 U.S. 400, 88 S.Ct. 964, 19 L.Ed.2d 1263, the Court considered a substantially identical statute authorizing the award of attorney's fees under Title II of the Civil Rights Act of 1964.[8] In that case the plaintiffs had prevailed, and the Court of Appeals had held that they should be awarded their attorney's fees "only to the extent that the respondents' defenses had been advanced 'for purposes of delay and not in good faith.' " Id., at 401, 88 S.Ct. at 966. We ruled that this "subjective standard" did not properly effectuate the purposes of the counsel-fee provision of Title II. Relying primarily on the intent of Congress to cast a Title II plaintiff in the role of "a 'private attorney general,' vindicating a policy that Congress considered of the highest priority," we held that a prevailing plaintiff under Title II "should ordinarily recover an attorney's fee unless special circumstances would render such an award unjust." Id., at 402, 88 S.Ct. at 966. We noted in passing that if the objective of Congress had been to permit the award of attorney's fees only against defendants who had acted in bad faith, "no new statutory provision would have been necessary," since even the American common-law rule allows the award of attorney's fees in those exceptional circumstances. Id., at 402, 88 S.Ct. at 966 n. 4.[9]

In Albemarle Paper Co. v. Moody, 422 U.S. 405, 95 S.Ct. 2362, 45 L.Ed.2d 280, the Court made clear that the *Piggie Park* standard of awarding attorney's fees to a successful plaintiff is equally applicable in an action under Title VII of the Civil Rights Act. 422 U.S., at 415, 95 S.Ct., at 2370. See also Northcross v. Memphis Board of Education, 412 U.S. 427, 428, 93 S.Ct. 2201, 37 L.Ed.2d 48. It can thus be taken as established, as the parties in this case both acknowledge, that under

in Lending Act, 82 Stat. 157, 15 U.S.C. § 1640(a); and Merchant Marine Act, 1936, 49 Stat. 2015, 46 U.S.C. § 1227.

6. See, e.g., Privacy Act of 1974, 88 Stat. 1897, 5 U.S.C. § 552a(g)(2)(B) (1976 ed.); Fair Housing Act of 1968, 82 Stat. 88, 42 U.S.C. § 3612(c).

7. See, e.g., Trust Indenture Act of 1939, 53 Stat. 1171, 15 U.S.C. § 77ooo(e); Securities Exchange Act of 1934, 48 Stat. 889, 897, 15 U.S.C. §§ 78i(e), 78r(a); Federal Water Pollution Control Act, 86 Stat. 889, 33 U.S.C. § 1365(d) (1970 ed., Supp. V); Clean Air Act, 84 Stat. 1706, 42 U.S.C. § 1857h–2(d); Noise Control Act of 1972, 86 Stat. 1244, 42 U.S.C. § 4911(d) (1970 ed., Supp. V).

8. "In any action commenced pursuant to this subchapter, the court, in its discretion, may allow the prevailing party, other than the United States, a reasonable attorney's fee as part of the costs, and the United States shall be liable for costs the same as a private person." 42 U.S.C. § 2000a–3(b).

9. The propriety under the American common-law rule of awarding attorney's fees against a losing party who has acted in bad faith was expressly reaffirmed in Alyeska Pipeline Co. v. Wilderness Society, 421 U.S. 240, 258–259, 95 S.Ct. 1612, 1622, 44 L.Ed.2d 141.

§ 706(k) of Title VII a prevailing *plaintiff* ordinarily is to be awarded attorney's fees in all but special circumstances.[10]

III

The question in the case before us is what standard should inform a district court's discretion in deciding whether to award attorney's fees to a successful *defendant* in a Title VII action. Not surprisingly, the parties in addressing the question in their briefs and oral arguments have taken almost diametrically opposite positions.

The company contends that the *Piggie Park* criterion for a successful plaintiff should apply equally as a guide to the award of attorney's fees to a successful defendant. Its submission, in short, is that every prevailing defendant in a Title VII action should receive an allowance of attorney's fees "unless special circumstances would render such an award unjust." The respondent Commission, by contrast, argues that the prevailing defendant should receive an award of attorney's fees only when it is found that the plaintiff's action was brought in bad faith. We have concluded that neither of these positions is correct.

A

Relying on what it terms "the plain meaning of the statute," the company argues that the language of § 706(k) admits of only one interpretation: "A prevailing defendant is entitled to an award of attorney's fees on the same basis as a prevailing plaintiff." But the permissive and discretionary language of the statute does not even invite, let alone require, such a mechanical construction. The terms of § 706(k) provide no indication whatever of the circumstances under which either a plaintiff *or* a defendant should be entitled to attorney's fees. And a moment's reflection reveals that there are at least two strong equitable considerations counseling an attorney's fee award to a prevailing Title VII plaintiff that are wholly absent in the case of a prevailing Title VII defendant.

First, as emphasized so forcefully in *Piggie Park*, the plaintiff is the chosen instrument of Congress to vindicate "a policy that Congress considered of the highest priority." 390 U.S., at 402, 88 S.Ct. at 966. Second, when a district court awards counsel fees to a prevailing plaintiff, it is awarding them against a violator of federal law. As the Court of Appeals clearly perceived, "these policy considerations which support the award of fees to a prevailing plaintiff are not present in the case of a prevailing defendant." 550 F.2d at 951. A successful defendant seeking counsel fees under § 706(k) must rely on quite different equitable considerations.

10. Chastang v. Flynn & Emrich Co., 541 F.2d 1040, 1045 (CA4) (finding "special circumstances" justifying no award to prevailing plaintiff); Carrion v. Yeshiva Univ., 535 F.2d 722, 727 (CA2); Johnson v. Georgia Highway Express, Inc., 488 F.2d 714, 716 (CA5); Parham v. Southwestern Bell Telephone Co., 433 F.2d 421, 429–430 (CA8).

But if the company's position is untenable, the Commission's argument also misses the mark. It seems clear, in short, that in enacting § 706(k) Congress did not intend to permit the award of attorney's fees to a prevailing defendant only in a situation where the plaintiff was motivated by bad faith in bringing the action. As pointed out in *Piggie Park*, if that had been the intent of Congress, no statutory provision would have been necessary, for it has long been established that even under the American common-law rule attorney's fees may be awarded against a party who has proceeded in bad faith.[13]

Furthermore, while it was certainly the policy of Congress that Title VII plaintiffs should vindicate "a policy that Congress considered of the highest priority," *Piggie Park*, 390 U.S., at 402, 88 S.Ct., at 966, it is equally certain that Congress entrusted the ultimate effectuation of that policy to the adversary judicial process, Occidental Life Ins. Co. v. EEOC, 432 U.S. 355, 97 S.Ct. 2447, 53 L.Ed.2d 402. A fair adversary process presupposes both a vigorous prosecution and a vigorous defense. It cannot be lightly assumed that in enacting § 706(k), Congress intended to distort that process by giving the private plaintiff substantial incentives to sue, while foreclosing to the defendant the possibility of recovering his expenses in resisting even a groundless action unless he can show that it was brought in bad faith.

B

The sparse legislative history of § 706(k) reveals little more than the barest outlines of a proper accommodation of the competing considerations we have discussed. The only specific reference to § 706(k) in the legislative debates indicates that the fee provision was included to "make it easier for a plaintiff of limited means to bring a meritorious suit." [14] During the Senate floor discussions of the almost identical attorney's fee provision of Title II, however, several Senators explained that its allowance of awards to defendants would serve "to deter the bringing of lawsuits without foundation," [15] "to discourage frivolous suits," [16] and "to diminish the likelihood of unjustified suits being brought." [17] If anything can be gleaned from these fragments of legislative history, it is that while Congress wanted to clear the way for suits to be brought under the Act, it also wanted to protect defendants from burdensome litigation having no legal or factual basis. The Court

---

13. See n. 9, supra. Had Congress provided for attorney's fee awards only to successful plaintiffs, an argument could have been made that the congressional action had pre-empted the common-law rule, and that, therefore, a successful defendant could not recover attorney's fees even against a plaintiff who had proceeded in bad faith. Cf. Byram Concretanks, Inc. v. Warren Concrete Products Company of New Jersey, 374 F.2d 649, 651 (CA3). But there is no indication whatever that the purpose of Congress in enacting § 706(k) in

the form that it did was simply to foreclose such an argument.

14. Remarks of Senator Humphrey, 110 Cong.Rec. 12724 (1964).

15. Remarks of Senator Lausche, id., at 13668.

16. Remarks of Senator Pastore, id., at 14214.

17. Remarks of Senator Humphrey, id., at 6534.

of Appeals for the District of Columbia Circuit seems to have drawn the maximum significance from the Senate debates when it concluded:

> [From these debates] two purposes for § 706(k) emerge. First, Congress desired to "make it easier for a plaintiff of limited means to bring a meritorious suit" * * *. But second, and equally important, Congress intended to "deter the bringing of lawsuits without foundation" by providing that the "prevailing party"—be it plaintiff or defendant—could obtain legal fees. Grubbs v. Butz, 179 U.S.App.D.C. 18, 20, 548 F.2d 973, 975.

The first federal appellate court to consider what criteria should govern the award of attorney's fees to a prevailing Title VII defendant was the Court of Appeals for the Third Circuit in United States Steel Corp. v. United States, 519 F.2d 359. There a District Court had denied a fee award to a defendant that had successfully resisted a Commission demand for documents, the court finding that the Commission's action had not been " 'unfounded, meritless, frivolous or vexatiously brought.' " Id., at 363. The Court of Appeals concluded that the District Court had not abused its discretion in denying the award. Id., at 365. A similar standard was adopted by the Court of Appeals for the Second Circuit in Carrion v. Yeshiva University, 535 F.2d 722. In upholding an attorney's fee award to a successful defendant, that court stated that such awards should be permitted "not routinely, not simply because he succeeds, but only where the action brought is found to be unreasonable, frivolous, meritless or vexatious." Id., at 727.[18]

To the extent that abstract words can deal with concrete cases, we think that the concept embodied in the language adopted by these two Courts of Appeals is correct. We would qualify their words only by pointing out that the term "meritless" is to be understood as meaning groundless or without foundation, rather than simply that the plaintiff has ultimately lost his case, and that the term "vexatious" in no way implies that the plaintiff's subjective bad faith is a necessary prerequisite to a fee award against him. In sum, a district court may in its discretion award attorney's fees to a prevailing defendant in a Title VII case upon a finding that the plaintiff's action was frivolous, unreasonable, or without foundation, even though not brought in subjective bad faith.

In applying these criteria, it is important that a district court resist the understandable temptation to engage in *post hoc* reasoning by concluding that, because a plaintiff did not ultimately prevail, his action must have been unreasonable or without foundation. This kind of hindsight logic could discourage all but the most airtight claims, for seldom can a prospective plaintiff be sure of ultimate success. No matter how honest one's belief that he has been the victim of discrimination, no matter how meritorious one's claim may appear at the

18. At least three other Circuits are in general agreement. See Bolton v. Murray Envelope Corp., 553 F.2d 881, 884 n. 2 (CA5); Grubbs v. Butz, 179 U.S.App.D.C. 18, 20–21, 548 F.2d 973, 975–976; Wright v. Stone Container Corp., 524 F.2d 1058, 1063–1064 (CA8).

outset, the course of litigation is rarely predictable. Decisive facts may not emerge until discovery or trial. The law may change or clarify in the midst of litigation. Even when the law or the facts appear questionable or unfavorable at the outset, a party may have an entirely reasonable ground for bringing suit.

That § 706(k) allows fee awards only to *prevailing* private plaintiffs should assure that this statutory provision will not in itself operate as an incentive to the bringing of claims that have little chance of success.[19] To take the further step of assessing attorney's fees against plaintiffs simply because they do not finally prevail would substantially add to the risks inhering in most litigation and would undercut the efforts of Congress to promote the vigorous enforcement of the provisions of Title VII. Hence, a plaintiff should not be assessed his opponent's attorney's fees unless a court finds that his claim was frivolous, unreasonable, or groundless, or that the plaintiff continued to litigate after it clearly became so. And, needless to say, if a plaintiff is found to have brought or continued such a claim in *bad faith,* there will be an even stronger basis for charging him with the attorney's fees incurred by the defense.[20]

19. See remarks of Senator Miller, 110 Cong.Rec. 14214 (1964), with reference to the parallel attorney's fee provision in Title II.

20. Initially, the Commission argued that the "costs" assessable against the Government under § 706(k) did not include attorney's fees. See, e.g., United States Steel Corp. v. United States, 519 F.2d 359, 362 (CA3); Van Hoomissen v. Xerox Corp., 503 F.2d 1131, 1132–1133 (CA9). But the Courts of Appeals rejected this position and, during the course of appealing this case, the Commission abandoned its contention that it was legally immune to adverse fee awards under § 706(k). 550 F.2d, at 951.

It has been urged that fee awards against the Commission should rest on a standard different from that governing fee awards against private plaintiffs. One *amicus* stresses that the Commission, unlike private litigants, needs no inducement to enforce Title VII since it is required by statute to do so. But this distinction between the Commission and private plaintiffs merely explains why Congress drafted § 706(k) to preclude the recovery of attorney's fees by the Commission; it does not support a difference in treatment among private and Government plaintiffs when a prevailing defendant seeks to recover his attorney's fees. Several courts and commentators have also deemed significant the Government's greater ability to pay adverse fee awards compared to a private litigant. See, e.g., United States Steel Corp. v. United States, supra, 519 F.2d, at 364 n. 24; Heinsz, Attorney's Fees for Prevailing Title VII Defendants: Toward a Workable Standard, 8 U.Toledo L.Rev. 259, 290 (1977); Comment, Title VII, Civil Rights Act of 1964: Standards for Award of Attorney's Fees to Prevailing Defendants, 1976 Wis.L.Rev. 207, 228. We are informed, however, that such awards must be paid from the Commission's litigation budget, so that every attorney's fee assessment against the Commission will inevitably divert resources from the agency's enforcement of Title VII. See 46 Comp.Gen. 98, 100 (1966); 38 Comp.Gen. 343, 344–345 (1958). The other side of this coin is the fact that many defendants in Title VII claims are small- and moderate-size employers for whom the expense of defending even a frivolous claim may become a strong disincentive to the exercise of their legal rights. In short, there are equitable considerations on both sides of this question. Yet § 706(k) explicitly provides that "the Commission and the United States shall be liable for costs the same as a private person." Hence, although a district court may consider distinctions between the Commission and private plaintiffs in determining the reasonableness of the Commission's litigation efforts, we find no grounds for applying a different general standard whenever the Commission is the losing plaintiff.

IV

In denying attorney's fees to the company in this case, the District Court focused on the standards we have discussed. The court found that "the Commission's action in bringing the suit could not be characterized as unreasonable or meritless" because "the basis upon which petitioner prevailed was an issue of first impression requiring judicial resolution" and because the "Commission's statutory interpretation of § 14 of the 1972 amendments was not frivolous." The court thus exercised its discretion squarely within the permissible bounds of § 706(k). Accordingly, the judgment of the Court of Appeals upholding the decision of the District Court is affirmed.

It is so ordered.

MR. JUSTICE BLACKMUN took no part in the consideration or decision of this case.

HENSLEY v. ECKERHART

Supreme Court of the United States, 1983.
461 U.S. 424, 103 S.Ct. 1933, 76 L.Ed.2d 40.

JUSTICE POWELL delivered the opinion of the Court.

Title 42 U.S.C. § 1988 provides that in federal civil rights actions "the court, in its discretion, may allow the prevailing party, other than the United States, a reasonable attorney's fee as part of the costs." The issue in this case is whether a partially prevailing plaintiff may recover an attorney's fee for legal services on unsuccessful claims.

I

A

Respondents brought this lawsuit on behalf of all persons involuntarily confined at the Forensic Unit of the Fulton State Hospital in Fulton, Missouri. The Forensic Unit consists of two residential buildings for housing patients who are dangerous to themselves or others. Maximum-security patients are housed in the Marion O. Biggs Building for the Criminally Insane. The rest of the patients reside in the less restrictive Rehabilitation Unit.

In 1972 respondents filed a three-count complaint in the District Court for the Western District of Missouri against petitioners, who are officials at the Forensic Unit and members of the Missouri Mental Health Commission. Count I challenged the constitutionality of treatment and conditions at the Forensic Unit. Count II challenged the placement of patients in the Biggs Building without procedural due process. Count III sought compensation for patients who performed institution-maintaining labor.

Count II was resolved by a consent decree in December 1973. Count III largely was mooted in August 1974 when petitioners began compensating patients for labor pursuant to the Fair Labor Standards Act, 29 U.S.C. § 201 et seq. In April 1975 respondents voluntarily dismissed the lawsuit and filed a new two-count complaint. Count I again related to the constitutionality of treatment and conditions at the Forensic Unit. Count II sought damages, based on the Thirteenth Amendment, for the value of past patient labor. In July 1976 respondents voluntarily dismissed this back-pay count. Finally, in August 1977 respondents filed an amended one-count complaint specifying the conditions that allegedly violated their constitutional right to treatment.

In August 1979, following a three-week trial, the District Court held that an involuntarily committed patient has a constitutional right to minimally adequate treatment. 475 F.Supp. 908, 915 (WD Mo.1979). The court then found constitutional violations in five of six general areas: physical environment; individual treatment plans; least restrictive environment; visitation, telephone, and mail privileges; and seclusion and restraint.[1] With respect to staffing, the sixth general area, the District Court found that the Forensic Unit's staffing levels, which had increased during the litigation, were minimally adequate. 475 F.Supp., at 919–920. Petitioners did not appeal the District Court's decision on the merits.

B

In February 1980 respondents filed a request for attorney's fees for the period from January 1975 through the end of the litigation. Their four attorneys claimed 2,985 hours worked and sought payment at rates varying from $40 to $65 per hour. This amounted to approximately $150,000. Respondents also requested that the fee be enhanced by thirty to fifty percent, for a total award of somewhere between $195,000 and $225,000. Petitioners opposed the request on numerous grounds, including inclusion of hours spent in pursuit of unsuccessful claims.

*   *   *

II

In Alyeska Pipeline Service Co. v. Wilderness Society, 421 U.S. 240, 95 S.Ct. 1612, 44 L.Ed.2d 141 (1975), this Court reaffirmed the "American Rule" that each party in a lawsuit ordinarily shall bear its own

---

1. Under "physical environment" the court found that certain physical aspects of the Biggs Building were not minimally adequate. 475 F.Supp., at 916–919.

Under "individual treatment plans" the court found that the existing plans were adequate, but that the long delay in preparation of initial plans after patients were admitted and the lack of regular review of the plans operated to deny patients minimally adequate plans. Id., at 921–922.

Under "least restrictive environment" the court found unconstitutional the delay in transfer of patients from the Biggs Building to the Rehabilitation Unit following a determination that they no longer

needed maximum-security confinement. Id., at 922–923.

Under "visitation, telephone and mail" the court found that the visitation and telephone policies at the Biggs Building were so restrictive that they constituted punishment and therefore violated patients' due-process rights. Id., at 923–925.

Under "seclusion and restraint" the court rejected respondents' claim that patients were given excessive medication as a form of behavior control. The court then found that petitioners' practices regarding seclusion and physical restraint were not minimally adequate. Id., at 925–928.

attorney's fees unless there is express statutory authorization to the contrary. In response Congress enacted the Civil Rights Attorney's Fees Awards Act of 1976, 42 U.S.C. § 1988, authorizing the district courts to award a reasonable attorney's fee to prevailing parties in civil rights litigation. The purpose of § 1988 is to ensure "effective access to the judicial process" for persons with civil rights grievances. H.R.Rep. No. 94–1558, p. 1 (1976). Accordingly, a prevailing plaintiff " 'should ordinarily recover an attorney's fee unless special circumstances would render such an award unjust.' " S.Rep. No. 94–1011, p. 4 (1976), U.S. Code Cong. & Admin.News 1976, p. 5912 (quoting Newman v. Piggie Park Enterprises, 390 U.S. 400, 402, 88 S.Ct. 964, 966, 19 L.Ed.2d 1263 (1968)).

The amount of the fee, of course, must be determined on the facts of each case. On this issue the House Report simply refers to twelve factors set forth in Johnson v. Georgia Highway Express, Inc., 488 F.2d 714 (CA5 1974).[3] The Senate Report cites to *Johnson* as well and also refers to three district court decisions that "correctly applied" the twelve factors.[4] One of the factors in *Johnson*, "the amount involved and the results obtained," indicates that the level of a plaintiff's success is relevant to the amount of fees to be awarded. The importance of this relationship is confirmed in varying degrees by the other cases cited approvingly in the Senate Report.

* * * The legislative history, therefore, does not provide a definitive answer as to the proper standard for setting a fee award where the plaintiff has achieved only limited success. Consistent with the legislative history, courts of appeals generally have recognized the relevance of the results obtained to the amount of a fee award. They have adopted varying standards, however, for applying this principle in cases where the plaintiff did not succeed on all claims asserted.[5]

3. The twelve factors are: (1) the time and labor required; (2) the novelty and difficulty of the questions; (3) the skill requisite to perform the legal service properly; (4) the preclusion of employment by the attorney due to acceptance of the case; (5) the customary fee; (6) whether the fee is fixed or contingent; (7) time limitations imposed by the client or the circumstances; (8) the amount involved and the results obtained; (9) the experience, reputation, and ability of the attorneys; (10) the "undesirability" of the case; (11) the nature and length of the professional relationship with the client; and (12) awards in similar cases. 488 F.2d, at 717–719. These factors derive directly from the American Bar Association Code of Professional Responsibility, Disciplinary Rule 2–106.

4. "It is intended that the amount of fees awarded * * * be governed by the same standards which prevail in other types of equally complex Federal litigation, such as antitrust cases[,] and not be re-

duced because the rights involved may be nonpecuniary in nature. The appropriate standards, see Johnson v. Georgia Highway Express, 488 F.2d 714 (5th Cir.1974), are correctly applied in such cases as Stanford Daily v. Zurcher, 64 F.R.D. 680 (ND Cal. 1974); Davis v. County of Los Angeles, 8 E.P.D. ¶ 9444 (CD Cal.1974); and Swann v. Charlotte-Mecklenburg Board of Education, 66 F.R.D. 483 (WDNC 1975). These cases have resulted in fees which are adequate to attract competent counsel, but which do not produce windfalls to attorneys. In computing the fee, counsel for a prevailing party should be paid, as is traditional with attorneys compensated by a fee-paying client, 'for all time reasonably expended on a matter.' *Davis,* supra; *Stanford Daily,* supra at 684." S.Rep. No. 94–1011, p. 6 (1976), U.S.Code Cong. & Admin.News 1976, pp. 5908, 5913.

5. Some courts of appeals have stated flatly that plaintiffs should not recover fees for any work on unsuccessful claims.

In this case petitioners contend that "an award of attorney's fees must be proportioned to be consistent with the extent to which a plaintiff has prevailed, and only time reasonably expended in support of successful claims should be compensated." Brief for Petitioners at 24. Respondents agree that a plaintiff's success is relevant, but propose a less stringent standard focusing on "whether the time spent prosecuting [an unsuccessful] claim in any way contributed to the results achieved." Brief for Respondents at 46. Both parties acknowledge the discretion of the district court in this area. We take this opportunity to clarify the proper relationship of the results obtained to an award of attorney's fees.[6]

III

A

A plaintiff must be a "prevailing party" to recover an attorney's fee under § 1988.[7] The standard for making this threshold determination has been framed in various ways. A typical formulation is that "plaintiffs may be considered 'prevailing parties' for attorney's fees purposes if they succeed on any significant issue in litigation which achieves some of the benefit the parties sought in bringing suit." Nadeau v. Helgemoe, 581 F.2d 275, 278–279 (CA1 1978).[8] This is a

---

See, e.g., Bartholomew v. Watson, 665 F.2d 910, 914 (CA9 1982); Muscare v. Quinn, 614 F.2d 577, 579–581 (CA7 1980); Hughes v. Repko, 578 F.2d 483, 486–487 (CA3 1978). Others have suggested that prevailing plaintiffs generally should receive a fee based on hours spent on all nonfrivolous claims. See, e.g., Sherkow v. Wisconsin, 630 F.2d 498, 504–505 (CA7 1980); Northcross v. Board of Educ. of Memphis City Schools, 611 F.2d 624, 636 (CA6 1979), cert. denied, 447 U.S. 911, 100 S.Ct. 2999, 64 L.Ed.2d 862 (1980); Brown v. Bathke, 588 F.2d 634, 636–637 (CA8 1978). Still other courts of appeals have held that recovery of a fee for hours spent on unsuccessful claims depends upon the relationship of those hours expended to the success achieved. See, e.g., Copeland v. Marshall, 205 U.S.App.D.C. 390, 401–402, n. 18, 641 F.2d 880, 891–892, n. 18 (1980) (en banc); Jones v. Diamond, 636 F.2d 1364, 1382 (CA5 1981) (en banc), cert. dism'd, 453 U.S. 950, 102 S.Ct. 27, 69 L.Ed.2d 1033 (1981); Gurule v. Wilson, 635 F.2d 782, 794 (CA10 1980) (opinion on rehearing); Lamphere v. Brown Univ., 610 F.2d 46, 47 (CA1 1979).

6. The parties disagree as to the results obtained in this case. Petitioners believe that respondents "prevailed only to an extremely limited degree." Brief for Petitioners at 22. Respondents contend that they "prevailed on practically every claim advanced." Brief for Respondents at 23. As discussed in Part IV, infra, we leave this dispute for the District Court on remand.

7. As we noted in Hanrahan v. Hampton, 446 U.S. 754, 758 n. 4, 100 S.Ct. 1987, 1989 n. 4, 64 L.Ed.2d 670 (1980) (per curiam), "[t]he provision for counsel fees in § 1988 was patterned upon the attorney's fees provisions contained in Title II and VII of the Civil Rights Act of 1964, 42 U.S.C. §§ 2000a–3(b) and 2000e–5(k), and § 402 of the Voting Rights Act Amendments of 1975, 42 U.S.C. § 1973l (e)." The legislative history of § 1988 indicates that Congress intended that "the standards for awarding fees be generally the same as under the fee provisions of the 1964 Civil Rights Act." S.Rep. No. 94–1011, p. 4 (1976), U.S.Code Cong. & Admin.News 1976, p. 5912. The standards set forth in this opinion are generally applicable in all cases in which Congress has authorized an award of fees to a "prevailing party."

8. See also Busche v. Burkee, 649 F.2d 509, 521 (CA7 1981), cert. denied, 454 U.S. 897, 102 S.Ct. 396, 70 L.Ed.2d 212 (1982); Sethy v. Alameda County Water Dist., 602 F.2d 894, 897–898 (CA9 1979) (per curiam). Cf. Taylor v. Sterrett, 640 F.2d 663, 669 (CA5 1981) ("[T]he proper focus is whether the plaintiff has been successful on the central issue as exhibited by the fact that he has acquired the primary relief sought").

generous formulation that brings the plaintiff only across the statutory threshold. It remains for the district court to determine what fee is "reasonable."

The most useful starting point for determining the amount of a reasonable fee is the number of hours reasonably expended on the litigation multiplied by a reasonable hourly rate. This calculation provides an objective basis on which to make an initial estimate of the value of a lawyer's services. The party seeking an award of fees should submit evidence supporting the hours worked and rates claimed. Where the documentation of hours is inadequate, the district court may reduce the award accordingly.

The district court also should exclude from this initial fee calculation hours that were not "reasonably expended." S.Rep. No. 94–1011, p. 6 (1976). Cases may be overstaffed, and the skill and experience of lawyers vary widely. Counsel for the prevailing party should make a good faith effort to exclude from a fee request hours that are excessive, redundant, or otherwise unnecessary, just as a lawyer in private practice ethically is obligated to exclude such hours from his fee submission. "In the private sector, 'billing judgment' is an important component in fee setting. It is no less important here. Hours that are not properly billed to one's *client* also are not properly billed to one's *adversary* pursuant to statutory authority." Copeland v. Marshall, 205 U.S.App. D.C. 390, 401, 641 F.2d 880, 891 (1980) (en banc) (emphasis in original).

B

The product of reasonable hours times a reasonable rate does not end the inquiry. There remain other considerations that may lead the district court to adjust the fee upward or downward, including the important factor of the "results obtained." [9] This factor is particularly crucial where a plaintiff is deemed "prevailing" even though he succeeded on only some of his claims for relief. In this situation two questions must be addressed. First, did the plaintiff fail to prevail on claims that were unrelated to the claims on which he succeeded? Second, did the plaintiff achieve a level of success that makes the hours reasonably expended a satisfactory basis for making a fee award?

In some cases a plaintiff may present in one lawsuit distinctly different claims for relief that are based on different facts and legal theories. In such a suit, even where the claims are brought against the same defendants—often an institution and its officers, as in this case— counsel's work on one claim will be unrelated to his work on another claim. Accordingly, work on an unsuccessful claim cannot be deemed to have been "expended in pursuit of the ultimate result achieved." Davis v. County of Los Angeles, 8 E.P.D. ¶ 9444, at 5049 (CD Cal.1974).

9. The district court also may consider other factors identified in Johnson v. Georgia Highway Express, Inc., 488 F.2d 714, 717–719 (CA5 1974), though it should note that many of these factors usually are subsumed within the initial calculation of hours reasonably expended at a reasonable hourly rate. See Copeland v. Marshall, 205 U.S.App.D.C. 390, 400, 641 F.2d 880, 890 (1980) (en banc).

The congressional intent to limit awards to prevailing parties requires that these unrelated claims be treated as if they had been raised in separate lawsuits, and therefore no fee may be awarded for services on the unsuccessful claim.[10]

It may well be that cases involving such unrelated claims are unlikely to arise with great frequency. Many civil rights cases will present only a single claim. In other cases the plaintiff's claims for relief will involve a common core of facts or will be based on related legal theories. Much of counsel's time will be devoted generally to the litigation as a whole, making it difficult to divide the hours expended on a claim-by-claim basis. Such a lawsuit cannot be viewed as a series of discrete claims. Instead the district court should focus on the significance of the overall relief obtained by the plaintiff in relation to the hours reasonably expended on the litigation.

Where a plaintiff has obtained excellent results, his attorney should recover a fully compensatory fee. Normally this will encompass all hours reasonably expended on the litigation, and indeed in some cases of exceptional success an enhanced award may be justified. In these circumstances the fee award should not be reduced simply because the plaintiff failed to prevail on every contention raised in the lawsuit. See Davis v. County of Los Angeles, 8 E.P.D. ¶ 9444, at 5049 (CD Cal.1974). Litigants in good faith may raise alternative legal grounds for a desired outcome, and the court's rejection of or failure to reach certain grounds is not a sufficient reason for reducing a fee. The result is what matters.[11]

If, on the other hand, a plaintiff has achieved only partial or limited success, the product of hours reasonably expended on the litigation as a whole times a reasonable hourly rate may be an excessive amount. This will be true even where the plaintiff's claims were interrelated, nonfrivolous, and raised in good faith. Congress has not authorized an award of fees whenever it was reasonable for a plaintiff to bring a lawsuit or whenever conscientious counsel tried the case with devotion and skill. Again, the most critical factor is the degree of success obtained.

Application of this principle is particularly important in complex civil rights litigation involving numerous challenges to institutional practices or conditions. This type of litigation is lengthy and demands many hours of lawyers' services. Although the plaintiff often may succeed in identifying some unlawful practices or conditions, the range

---

10. If the unsuccessful claim is frivolous, the defendant may recover attorney's fees incurred in responding to it.

11. We agree with the District Court's rejection of "a mathematical approach comparing the total number of issues in the case with those actually prevailed upon." Record 220. Such a ratio provides little aid in determining what is a reasonable fee in light of all the relevant factors. Nor is it necessarily significant that a prevailing plaintiff did not receive all the relief requested. For example, a plaintiff who failed to recover damages but obtained injunctive relief, or vice versa, may recover a fee award based on all hours reasonably expended if the relief obtained justified that expenditure of attorney time.

of possible success is vast. That the plaintiff is a "prevailing party" therefore may say little about whether the expenditure of counsel's time was reasonable in relation to the success achieved. In this case, for example, the District Court's award of fees based on 2,557 hours worked may have been reasonable in light of the substantial relief obtained. But had respondents prevailed on only one of their six general claims, for example the claim that petitioners' visitation, mail, and telephone policies were overly restrictive, see n. 1, supra, a fee award based on the claimed hours clearly would have been excessive.

There is no precise rule or formula for making these determinations. The district court may attempt to identify specific hours that should be eliminated, or it may simply reduce the award to account for the limited success. The court necessarily has discretion in making this equitable judgment. This discretion, however, must be exercised in light of the considerations we have identified.

C

A request for attorney's fees should not result in a second major litigation. Ideally, of course, litigants will settle the amount of a fee. Where settlement is not possible, the fee applicant bears the burden of establishing entitlement to an award and documenting the appropriate hours expended and hourly rates. The applicant should exercise "billing judgment" with respect to hours worked, see supra, at 1939–1940, and should maintain billing time records in a manner that will enable a reviewing court to identify distinct claims.[12]

We reemphasize that the district court has discretion in determining the amount of a fee award. This is appropriate in view of the district court's superior understanding of the litigation and the desirability of avoiding frequent appellate review of what essentially are factual matters. It remains important, however, for the district court to provide a concise but clear explanation of its reasons for the fee award. When an adjustment is requested on the basis of either the exceptional or limited nature of the relief obtained by the plaintiff, the district court should make clear that it has considered the relationship between the amount of the fee awarded and the results obtained.

IV

In this case the District Court began by finding that "[t]he relief [respondents] obtained at trial was substantial and certainly entitles them to be considered prevailing * * *, without the need of examining those issues disposed of prior to trial in order to determine which

---

12. We recognize that there is no certain method of determining when claims are "related" or "unrelated." Plaintiff's counsel, of course, is not required to record in great detail how each minute of his time was expended. But at least counsel should identify the general subject matter of his time expenditures. See Nadeau v. Helgemoe, 581 F.2d 275, 279 (CA1 1978)

("As for the future, we would not view with sympathy any claim that a district court abused its discretion in awarding unreasonably low attorney's fees in a suit in which plaintiffs were only partially successful if counsel's records do not provide a proper basis for determining how much time was spent on particular claims.").

went in [respondents'] favor." Record 219. It then declined to divide the hours worked between winning and losing claims, stating that this fails to consider "the relative importance of various issues, the interrelation of the issues, the difficulty in identifying issues, or the extent to which a party prevails on various issues." Record 220. Finally, the court assessed the "amount involved/results obtained" and declared: "Not only should [respondents] be considered prevailing parties, they are parties who have obtained relief of significant import. [Respondents'] relief affects not only them, but also numerous other institutionalized patients similarly situated. The extent of this relief clearly justifies the award of a reasonable attorney's fee." Record 231.

These findings represent a commendable effort to explain the fee award. Given the interrelated nature of the facts and legal theories in this case, the District Court did not err in refusing to apportion the fee award mechanically on the basis of respondents' success or failure on particular issues.[13] And given the findings with respect to the level of respondents' success, the District Court's award may be consistent with our holding today.

We are unable to affirm the decisions below, however, because the District Court's opinion did not properly consider the relationship between the extent of success and the amount of the fee award.[14] The court's finding that "the [significant] extent of the relief clearly justifies the award of a reasonable attorney's fee" does not answer the question of what is "reasonable" in light of that level of success. We emphasize that the inquiry does not end with a finding that the plaintiff obtained significant relief. A reduced fee award is appropriate if the relief,

13. In addition, the District Court properly considered the reasonableness of the hours expended, and reduced the hours of one attorney by thirty percent to account for his inexperience and failure to keep contemporaneous time records.

14. The District Court expressly relied on Brown v. Bathke, 588 F.2d 634 (CA8 1978), a case we believe understates the significance of the results obtained. In that case a fired school teacher had sought reinstatement, lost wages, $25,000 in damages, and expungement of derogatory material from her employment record. She obtained lost wages and the requested expungement, but not reinstatement or damages. The District Court awarded attorney's fees for the hours that it estimated the plaintiff's attorney had spent on the particular legal issue on which relief had been granted. The Eighth Circuit reversed. It stated that the results obtained may be considered, but that this factor should not "be given such weight that it reduces the fee awarded to a prevailing party below the 'reasonable attorney's fee'

authorized by the Act." 588 F.2d, at 637. The court determined that the unsuccessful issues that had been raised by the plaintiff were not frivolous, and then remanded the case to the District Court. Id., at 638.

Our holding today differs at least in emphasis from that of the Eighth Circuit in *Brown*. We hold that the extent of a plaintiff's success is a crucial factor that the district courts should consider carefully in determining the amount of fees to be awarded. In *Brown* the plaintiff had lost on the major issue of reinstatement. The District Court found that she had " 'obtained only a minor part of the relief she sought.' " Id., at 636. In remanding the Eighth Circuit implied that the District Court should not withhold fees for work on unsuccessful claims unless those claims were frivolous. Today we hold otherwise. It certainly was well within the *Brown* District Court's discretion to make a limited fee award in light of the "minor" relief obtained.

however significant, is limited in comparison to the scope of the litigation as a whole.

V

We hold that the extent of a plaintiff's success is a crucial factor in determining the proper amount of an award of attorney's fees under 42 U.S.C. § 1988. Where the plaintiff has failed to prevail on a claim that is distinct in all respects from his successful claims, the hours spent on the unsuccessful claim should be excluded in considering the amount of a reasonable fee. Where a lawsuit consists of related claims, a plaintiff who has won substantial relief should not have his attorney's fee reduced simply because the district court did not adopt each contention raised. But where the plaintiff achieved only limited success, the district court should award only that amount of fees that is reasonable in relation to the results obtained. On remand the District Court should determine the proper amount of the attorney's fee award in light of these standards.

The judgment of the Court of Appeals is vacated, and the case is remanded for further proceedings consistent with this opinion.

It is so ordered.

CHIEF JUSTICE BURGER, concurring.

I read the Court's opinion as requiring that when a lawyer seeks to have his adversary pay the fees of the prevailing party, the lawyer must provide detailed records of the time and services for which fees are sought. It would be inconceivable that the prevailing party should not be required to establish at least as much to support a claim under 42 U.S.C. § 1988 as a lawyer would be required to show if his own client challenged the fees. A District Judge may not, in my view, authorize the payment of attorney's fees unless the attorney involved has established by clear and convincing evidence the time and effort claimed and shown that the time expended was necessary to achieve the results obtained.

A claim for legal services presented by the prevailing party to the losing party pursuant to § 1988 presents quite a different situation from a bill that a lawyer presents to his own client. In the latter case, the attorney and client have presumably built up a relationship of mutual trust and respect; the client has confidence that his lawyer has exercised the appropriate "billing judgment," ante, at 1940, and unless challenged by the client, the billing does not need the kind of extensive documentation necessary for a payment under § 1988. That statute requires the losing party in a civil rights action to bear the cost of his adversary's attorney and there is, of course, no relationship of trust and confidence between the adverse parties. As a result, the party who seeks payment must keep records in sufficient detail that a neutral judge can make a fair evaluation of the time expended, the nature and need for the service, and the reasonable fees to be allowed.

JUSTICE BRENNAN, with whom JUSTICE MARSHALL, JUSTICE BLACKMUN, and JUSTICE STEVENS join, concurring in part and dissenting in part.

Notes

1.   In BLUM v. STENSON, 465 U.S. 886, 104 S.Ct. 1541, 79 L.Ed.2d 891 (1984), the Court held that non-profit legal services attorneys are entitled to be compensated at an hourly rate on the same basis, i.e., prevailing market rate theory, as are attorneys who work with for-profit law firms.

2.   A prevailing plaintiff is entitled to fees for services rendered on his or her behalf in state and local administrative proceedings initiated under Section 706 of Title VII. New York Gaslight Club, Inc. v. Carey, 447 U.S. 54, 100 S.Ct. 2024, 64 L.Ed.2d 723 (1980). Fees are not available for services rendered if a plaintiff pursues optional state administrative proceedings, unless those services were both useful and of the type ordinarily necessary to the action filed in federal court. Webb v. Board of Education of Dyer County, Tenn., ___ U.S. ___, 105 S.Ct. 1923, 85 L.Ed.2d 233 (1985).

3.   Under the offer of judgment rule, Rule 68 of the Federal Rules of Civil Procedure, a defendant can offer to allow judgment to be entered against him of a specified amount, provided the defendant offers to pay "costs" then accrued. In Marek v. Chesny, ___ U.S. ___, 105 S.Ct. 3012, 87 L.Ed.2d 1 (1985), the Court held that the term "costs" in Rule 68 includes attorney fees.

4.   In City of Riverside v. Rivera, ___ U.S. ___, 106 S.Ct. 2686, 91 L.Ed.2d 466 (1986), the plaintiffs recovered $33,350 in compensatory and punitive damages, and the district court awarded approximately $246,000 in fees. The Court rejected the argument that reasonable attorney's fees should be proportionate to the amount of the monetary award recovered in the underlying civil rights act. The Court also rejected the argument that a district court, in determining the amount of fees should consider prevailing contingent fee rates charged by counsel in personal injury cases.

5.   In Evans v. Jeff D., ___ U.S. ___, 106 S.Ct. 1531, 89 L.Ed.2d 747 (1986), the Court has held that in civil rights class actions, settlement terms on both the merits and attorney's fees not only may be negotiated simultaneously, but also may include a total waiver of fees award authorized by statute. In this case, an attorney employed by the Idaho Legal Aid Society was appointed by the federal district court to initiate and prosecute a class action challenging the educational programs and health care services provided by the State of Idaho for children suffering from emotional and mental handicaps. Before substantial work had been done on the case, the parties settled the educational claim in an agreement including a stipulation that each party bear its own fees and costs on the issue. Negotiations concerning the health care claim were unsuccessful, however, and the matter proceeded through cross-motions for summary judgment, class certification, and discovery. One week before trial the defendant proposed a new settlement offering the plaintiffs virtually all of the relief sought, on the condition that any claim to fees and costs be waived. Counsel for the plaintiff class decided that his ethical obligation to his clients mandated

acceptance of the proposed settlement, although he objected to the waiver of fees. The district court approved the entire settlement in effect. The Supreme Court reversed the Ninth Circuit, which had criticized both the simultaneous negotiation of settlement on substantive and fees issues and the conditioning of class action settlement on a waiver of attorney's fees and costs. The Court ruled that the lower courts had neither the power to compel an objecting party to accept a modified pretrial consent decree nor the duty to reject a proposed settlement because it included a waiver of statutory authorized attorney fees. ___ U.S. ___, 106 S.Ct. at 1537, 1545.

Justice Stevens, writing for the majority, saw no ethical bar to simultaneous negotiation of relief on the merits and a fees waiver, because counsel has an ethical duty only "to serve his clients loyally and competently, and not "to seek a statutory fee award." Id. at ___, 106 S.Ct. at 1537–1538. The majority of the Justices also agreed that nothing in the language or the legislative history of the Fees Act precluded a waiver of attorney's fees and costs as a condition of obtaining a settlement offering relief equal to or exceeding the probable outcome at trial. Id. at ___, 106 S.Ct. at 1538–1539. Eligibility for an attorney's fee award was viewed as a "bargaining chip," id. at ___ n. 20, 106 S.Ct. at 1539 n. 20, merely on the "arsenal of remedies" available for civil rights claimants to barter with; they might waive the right to fees and costs just as they might "conce[de] on damages to secure broader injunctive relief." Id. at ___, 106 S.Ct. at 1539–1540.

Chapter III

THE CIVIL RIGHTS ACT OF 1966—42 U.S.C. Section 1981

A. SCOPE OF COVERAGE

McDONALD v. SANTA FE TRAIL TRANSPORTATION COMPANY

Supreme Court of the United States, 1976.
427 U.S. 273, 96 S.Ct. 2574, 49 L.Ed.2d 493.

[The facts of the case are set out at pp. 81–82. In this portion of the opinion, the Court considered the question whether white persons are protected under 42 U.S.C. Section 1981.]

MR. JUSTICE MARSHALL delivered the opinion of the Court.

III

Title 42 U.S.C. § 1981 provides in pertinent part: "All persons within the jurisdiction of the United States shall have the same right in every State and Territory to make and enforce contracts * * * as is enjoyed by white citizens. * * *" We have previously held, where discrimination against Negroes was in question, that § 1981 affords a federal remedy against discrimination in private employment on the basis of race, and respondents do not contend otherwise. Johnson v. Railway Express Agency, 421 U.S. 454, 459–460, 95 S.Ct. 1716, 1719–1720, 44 L.Ed.2d 295 (1975). See also Runyon v. McCrary, 427 U.S. 160, 168, 96 S.Ct. 2586, 2593, 49 L.Ed.2d 415; Jones v. Alfred H. Mayer Co., 392 U.S. 409, 88 S.Ct. 2186, 20 L.Ed.2d 1189 (1968). The question here is whether § 1981 prohibits racial discrimination in private employment against whites as well as nonwhites.

While neither of the courts below elaborated its reasons for not applying § 1981 to racial discrimination against white persons, respondents suggest two lines of argument to support that judgment. First, they argue that by operation of the phrase "as is enjoyed by white citizens," § 1981 unambiguously limits itself to the protection of nonwhite persons against racial discrimination. Second, they contend that such a reading is consistent with the legislative history of the provision, which derives its operative language from § 1 of the Civil Rights Act of 1866, Act of Apr. 9, 1866, c. 31, § 1, 14 Stat. 27. See Runyon v. McCrary, supra, 427 U.S., at 168–170, n. 8, 96 S.Ct., at 2593; Tillman v. Wheaton-Haven Recreation Assn., 410 U.S. 431, 439, 93 S.Ct. 1090, 1094, 35 L.Ed.2d 403 (1973). The 1866 statute, they assert, was concerned predominantly with assuring specified civil rights to the former Negro slaves freed by virtue of the Thirteenth Amendment, and not at all with protecting the corresponding civil rights of white persons.

We find neither argument persuasive. Rather, our examination of the language and history of § 1981 convinces us that § 1981 is applicable to racial discrimination in private employment against white persons.

First, we cannot accept the view that the terms of § 1981 exclude its application to racial discrimination against white persons. On the contrary, the statute explicitly applies to "*all* persons" (emphasis added), including white persons. See, e.g., United States v. Wong Kim Ark, 169 U.S. 649, 675–676, 18 S.Ct. 456, 467–468, 42 L.Ed. 890 (1898). While a mechanical reading of the phrase "as is enjoyed by white citizens" would seem to lend support to respondents' reading of the statute, we have previously described this phrase simply as emphasizing "the racial character of the rights being protected," Georgia v. Rachel, 384 U.S. 780, 791, 86 S.Ct. 1783, 1789, 16 L.Ed.2d 925 (1966). In any event, whatever ambiguity there may be in the language of § 1981, * * * is clarified by an examination of the legislative history of § 1981's language as it was originally forged in the Civil Rights Act of 1866. Tidewater Oil Co. v. United States, 409 U.S. 151, 157, 93 S.Ct. 408, 412, 34 L.Ed.2d 375 (1972); Immigration Service v. Errico, 385 U.S. 214, 218, 87 S.Ct. 473, 476, 17 L.Ed.2d 318 (1966). It is to this subject that we now turn.

The bill ultimately enacted as the Civil Rights Act of 1866 was introduced by Senator Trumbull of Illinois as a "bill * * * to protect *all* persons in the United States in their civil rights * * *" (emphasis added), and was initially described by him as applying to "every race and color." Cong.Globe, 39th Cong., 1st Sess., 211 (1866) (hereinafter Cong.Globe). Consistent with the views of its draftsman,[17] and the prevailing view in the Congress as to the reach of its powers under the enforcement section of the Thirteenth Amendment,[18] the terms of the

---

17. Cf. Cong.Globe 474:

"I take it that any statute which is not equal to all, and which deprives any citizen of civil rights which are secured to other citizens, is an unjust encroachment upon his liberty; and is, in fact, a badge of servitude which, by the Constitution, is prohibited." (Emphasis added.)

18. See generally, e.g., Buchanan, The Quest for Freedom: A Legal History of the Thirteenth Amendment, 12 Hous.L.Rev. 1

(1974); Bickel, The Original Understanding and the Segregation Decision, 69 Harv. L.Rev. 1, 11–29 (1955). The Court has previously ratified the view that Congress is authorized under the Enforcement Clause of the Thirteenth Amendment to legislate in regard to "every race and individual." Hodges v. United States, 203 U.S. 1, 16–17, 27 S.Ct. 6, 8–9, 51 L.Ed. 65 (1906); see Jones v. Alfred H. Mayer Co., 392 U.S. 409,

bill prohibited any racial discrimination in the making and enforcement of contracts against whites as well as nonwhites. Its first section provided:

> [T]here shall be no discrimination in civil rights or immunities among the inhabitants of any State or Territory of the United States on account of race, color, or previous condition of slavery; but the inhabitants of every race and color, without regard to any previous condition of slavery or involuntary servitude, ＊ ＊ ＊ shall have the same right to make and enforce contracts, to sue, be parties, and give evidence, to inherit, purchase, lease, sell, hold, and convey real and personal property, and to full and equal benefit of all laws and proceedings for the security of person and property, and shall be subject to like punishment, pains, and penalties, and to none other, any law, statute, ordinance, regulation, or custom, to the contrary notwithstanding. Id., at 211.[19]

While it is, of course, true that the immediate impetus for the bill was the necessity for further relief of the constitutionally emancipated former Negro slaves, the general discussion of the scope of the bill did not circumscribe its broad language to that limited goal. On the contrary, the bill was routinely viewed, by its opponents and supporters alike, as applying to the civil rights of whites as well as nonwhites.[20] The point was most directly focused on in the closing debate in the Senate. During that debate, in response to the argument of Senator

441 n. 78, 88 S.Ct. 2186, 2204, 20 L.Ed.2d 1189 (1968).

19. The bill's concern with equal protection of civil rights for whites as well as nonwhites is also expressed in its § 4, which referred, as introduced, Cong.Globe 211, and enacted, 14 Stat. 28, to "protection to all persons in their constitutional rights of equality before the law, without distinction of race or color." The same concern is reflected in the evolution of an amendment offered by Senator Trumbull to provide, at the beginning of § 1: "That all persons of African descent born in the United States are hereby declared to be citizens of the United States ＊ ＊ ＊." Cong.Globe, 474. The amendment, accepted in principle, was itself amended to replace "all persons of African descent born in the United States" with "all persons born in the United States and not subject to any foreign power, excluding Indians not taxed," 14 Stat. 27. This provision was ultimately superseded by § 1 of the Fourteenth Amendment.

The congressional design to protect individuals of all races is further emphasized by re-enactment of the 1866 Act as part of the Enforcement Act of 1870, following ratification of the Fourteenth Amendment. See Jones v. Alfred H. Mayer Co., supra, at 436, 88 S.Ct., at 2201.

20. See, e.g., Cong.Globe 504 (remarks of Sen. Howard, a supporter: "[The bill] simply gives to persons who are of different races or colors the same civil rights"); id., at 505 (remarks of Sen. Johnson, an opponent: "[T]he white as well as the black is included in this first section ＊ ＊ ＊"); id., at 601 (remarks of Sen. Hendricks, an opponent: "[The bill] provides, in the first place, that the civil rights of *all* men, without regard to color, shall be equal). " (Emphasis added.)

Respondents reasonably assert that references to the bill's placing Negroes' and whites' civil rights "upon precisely the same footing," id., at 604 (remarks of Sen. Cowan, an opponent), and similar remarks might be read consistently either with the position that the measure was solely for relief of nonwhites, or with the position that it applies to protect whites as well. Respondents are unable, however, to summon any congressional debate from any stage in the bill's consideration to *contradict* the plain language of the bill as introduced and the explicit statements of Senator Trumbull, and others, that the bill, as introduced, did comprehend the prohibition of antiwhite discrimination.

Davis of Kentucky that by providing for the punishment of racial discrimination in its enforcement section, § 2, the bill extended to Negroes a protection never afforded whites, Senator Trumbull said:

> Sir, *this bill applies to white men as well as black men.* It declares that all persons in the United States shall be entitled to the same civil rights, the right to the fruit of their own labor, the right to make contracts, the right to buy and sell, and enjoy liberty and happiness; and that is abominable and iniquitous and unconstitutional! Could anything be more monstrous or more abominable than for a member of the Senate to rise in his place and denounce with such epithets as these a bill, the only object of which is to secure equal rights to all the citizens of the country, *a bill that protects a white man just as much as a black man?* With what consistency and with what face can a Senator in his place here say to the Senate and the country that this is a bill for the benefit of black men exclusively when there is no such distinction in it, and when *the very object of the bill is to break down all discrimination between black men and white men?* Id., at 599 (emphasis supplied).

So advised, the Senate passed the bill shortly thereafter. Id., at 606–607.

It is clear, thus, that the bill, as it passed the Senate, was not limited in scope to discrimination against nonwhites. Accordingly, respondents pitch their legislative history argument largely upon the House's amendment of the Senate bill to add the "as is enjoyed by white citizens" phrase. But the statutory history is equally clear that that phrase was not intended to have the effect of eliminating from the bill the prohibition of racial discrimination against whites.

Representative Wilson of Iowa, Chairman of the Judiciary Committee and the bill's floor manager in the House, proposed the addition of the quoted phrase immediately upon the introduction of the bill. The change was offered explicitly to technically "perfect" the bill, and was accepted as such without objection or debate. Id., at 1115.

That Wilson's amendment was viewed simply as a technical adjustment without substantive effect is corroborated by the structure of the bill as it then stood. Even as amended the bill still provided that "there shall be no discrimination in civil rights or immunities among citizens of the United States in any State or Territory of the United States on account of race, color, or previous condition of slavery." [21] To

---

21. After Representative Wilson's "perfecting" amendments, § 1 of the bill provided:

"[A]ll persons born in the United States and not subject to any foreign power, excluding Indians not taxed, are hereby declared to be citizens of the United States, without distinction of color, and there shall be no discrimination in civil rights or immunities among citizens of the United States in any State or Territory of the United States on account of race, color, or previous condition of slavery; and such citizens of every race and color, without regard to any previous condition of slavery or involuntary servitude, except as a punishment for crime whereof the party shall have been duly convicted, shall have the same right to make and enforce contracts, to sue, be parties and give evidence, to inherit, purchase, lease, sell, hold, and con-

read Wilson's amendment as excluding white persons from the particularly enumerated civil rights guarantees of the Act would contradict this more general language; and we would be unwilling to conclude, without further evidence, that in adopting the amendment without debate or discussion, the House so regarded it.[22]

Moreover, Representative Wilson's initial elaboration on the meaning of Senator Trumbull's bill, which immediately followed his securing passage of the foregoing amendment, fortifies our view that the amended bill was intended to protect whites as well as nonwhites. As Wilson described it, the purpose of the measure was to provide "for the equality of citizens * * * in the enjoyment of 'civil rights and immunities.'" Id., at 1117. Then, speaking in particular of "immunities" as "'freedom or exemption from obligation,'" he made clear that the bill "secures to citizens of the United States equality in the exemptions of the law. * * * Whatever exemptions there may be shall apply to all citizens alike. One race shall not be more favored in this respect than another," ibid.[23] Finally, in later dialogue Wilson made quite clear that the purpose of his amendment was not to affect the Act's protection of white persons. Rather, he stated, "the reason for offering [the amendment] was this: it was thought by some persons that unless these qualifying words were incorporated in the bill, those rights might be

vey real and personal property, and to full and equal benefit of all laws and proceedings for the security of person and property as is enjoyed by white citizens, and shall be subject to like punishment, pains, and penalties, and to none other, any law, statute, ordinance, regulation, or custom, to the contrary notwithstanding." S. 61, 39th Cong., 1st Sess., House Print, Mar. 2, 1866.

22. The provision generally forbidding "discrimination in civil rights or immunities * * * on account of race, color, or previous condition of slavery" was ultimately struck from the statute in the House. Cong.Globe 1366. This does not affect the analysis here, however, for two reasons. First, the debates make clear that the ground for objection to that provision, and the reason for its ultimate omission, was the breadth of the terms "civil rights and immunities," beyond those specifically enumerated in the second half of § 1, rather than an antagonism to the principle of protection for every race. See generally Georgia v. Rachel, 384 U.S. 780, 791–792, 86 S.Ct. 1783, 1789–1790, 16 L.Ed. 2d 925 (1966); Bickel, supra, n. 18, at 11–29. Second the point here is only that acceptance of respondents' interpretation of Congressman Wilson's amendment is inconsistent with the fact that the general provision against racial discrimination regarding civil rights remained in the bill *at*

the time of the amendment, and was not removed until debate had focused on its particular ambiguities more than a week later.

23. Wilson also urged that the bill should pass "to protect our citizens, from the highest to the lowest, from the whitest to the blackest, in the enjoyment of the great fundamental rights which belong to all men." Cong.Globe 1118.

Wilson's view that the Act applied equally to protect all races was echoed by other supporters of the bill in the House, as it had been in the Senate. See, e.g., the remarks of Representative Shallabarger:

"Its whole effect is to require that whatever rights as to each of those enumerated civil * * * matters the States may confer upon one race or color of the citizens shall be held by all races in equality. Your State may deprive women of the right to sue or contract or testify, and children from doing the same. But if you do so, or do not so as to one race, you shall treat the other likewise. * * * It secures—not to all citizens, but to all races as races who are citizens—equality of protection in those enumerated civil rights which the States may deem proper to confer upon any races." Id., at 1293. See also id., at 1159 (remarks of Rep. Windom); cf. id., at 1118 (remarks of Rep. Wilson).

extended to all citizens, whether male or female, majors or minors."
Cong.Globe, App. 157. Thus, the purpose of the amendment was simply
"to emphasize the racial character of the rights being protected,"
Georgia v. Rachel, 384 U.S., at 791, 86 S.Ct. at 1789, not to limit its
application to nonwhite persons.[24]

The senate debate on the House version of the bill [25] likewise
emphasizes that Representative Wilson's amendment was not viewed as
limiting the bill's prohibition of racial discrimination against white
persons. Senator Trumbull, still managing the bill on the floor of the
Senate, was asked whether there was not an inconsistency between the
application of the bill to all "citizens of every race and color" and the
statement that they shall have "the same right to make and enforce
contracts * * * *as is enjoyed by white persons,"* (emphasis supplied)
and it was suggested that the emphasized words were superfluous.
Cong.Globe 1413. Senator Trumbull responded in agreement with the
view that the words were merely "superfluous. I do not think they
alter the bill. * * * [A]nd as in the opinion of the [Senate Judiciary]
[C]ommittee which examined this matter they did not alter the meaning of the bill, the committee thought proper to recommend a concur-
rence * * *." Ibid.

Finally, after the Senate's acquiescence in the House version of the
bill, id., at 1413–1416, and the subsequent veto by President Johnson,[26]
the debate in both the Senate and the House again reflected the

24. Local 988 suggests that the pattern
for Wilson's "as enjoyed by white citizens"
amendment was similar language in § 2 of
the civil rights bill which, as introduced by
Senator Trumbull, Cong.Globe 211, and enacted, 14 Stat. 27, provided in pertinent
part:

"Any person who * * * shall subject
* * * any inhabitant of any State or
Territory * * * to different punishment, pains, or penalties * * * by reason of his color or race, than is prescribed for the punishment of white
persons, shall be deemed guilty of a misdemeanor, and, on conviction, shall be
punished by a fine * * * or imprisonment. * * *"

That this may have been the source of the
language of the amendment hardly explains its meaning. As recited above, the
prescriptive portion of the bill, § 1, provided, as introduced, see supra, at 2582, and
enacted see n. 25, infra, and provides as
currently codified, that punishments shall
be equal for members of all races. Section
2 of the bill is no different, as it criminal-
izes the application of "*different* punishment, pains, or penalties" (emphasis supplied) whether greater or lesser than what
white persons would be subject to. Even
were we to read § 2 of the Act as protect-

ing only nonwhites, however, the significance of such a conclusion to the interpretation of § 1 would be slight; for we have
previously explained that the 39th Congress apparently intended to apply criminal sanctions only to some, but not all,
violations of the Act. See Jones v. Alfred
H. Mayer Co., 392 U.S., at 424–425, 88
S.Ct. at 2195–2196.

25. Cong.Globe 1367. Section 1 of the
bill, as it then stood, and as it was ultimately enacted, provided in relevant part:

"[A]ll persons born in the United States,
and not subject to any foreign power,
excluding Indians not taxed, are hereby
declared to be citizens of the United
States; and such citizens, of every race
and color * * * shall have the same
right, in every State and Territory in the
United States, to make and enforce contracts * * * as is enjoyed by white
citizens, and shall be subject to like punishment, pains, and penalties, and to
none other, any law, statute, ordinance,
regulation, or custom, to the contrary
notwithstanding." 14 Stat. 27.

26. In his veto message, President
Johnson recognized that the bill attempted
to fix "a perfect equality of the white and
black races." Cong.Globe 1679.

proponents' views that the bill did not favor nonwhites. Senator Trumbull once more rejected the view that the bill "discriminates in favor of colored persons," id., at 1758, and in a similar vein, Representative Lawrence observed in the House that its "broad and comprehensive philanthropy which regards all men in their civil rights as equal before the law, is not made for any * * * race or color * * * but * * * will, if it become[s] a law, protect every citizen * * *." Id., at 1833. On these notes, both Houses passed the bill by the prescribed margins, and the veto was overridden. Id., at 1802, 1861.

This cumulative evidence of congressional intent makes clear, we think, that the 1866 statute, designed to protect the "same right * * * to make and enforce contracts" of "citizens of every race and color" was not understood or intended to be reduced by Representative Wilson's amendment, or any other provision, to the protection solely of nonwhites. Rather, the Act was meant, by its broad terms, to proscribe discrimination in the making or enforcement of contracts against, or in favor of, any race. Unlikely as it might have appeared in 1866 that white citizens would encounter substantial racial discrimination of the sort proscribed under the Act, the statutory structure and legislative history persuade us that the 39th Congress was intent upon establishing in the federal law a broader principle than would have been necessary simply to meet the particular and immediate plight of the newly freed Negro slaves. And while the statutory language has been somewhat streamlined in re-enactment and codification, there is no indication that § 1981 is intended to provide any less than the Congress enacted in 1866 regarding racial discrimination against white persons. Runyon v. McCrary, 427 U.S. 168, and n. 8, 96 S.Ct. 2586, 49 L.Ed.2d 415. Thus, we conclude that the District Court erred in dismissing petitioners' claims under § 1981 on the ground that the protections of that provision are unavailable to white persons.

The judgment of the Court of Appeals for the Fifth Circuit is reversed, and the case is remanded for further proceedings consistent with this opinion.

So ordered.

MR. JUSTICE WHITE and MR. JUSTICE REHNQUIST join Parts I and II of the Court's opinion, but for the reasons stated in MR. JUSTICE WHITE'S dissenting opinion in Runyon v. McCrary, 427 U.S. 160, 192, 96 S.Ct. 2586, 2604, 49 L.Ed.2d 415, cannot join Part III since they do not agree that § 1981 is applicable in this case. To that extent they dissent.

B. THEORY OF LIABILITY

GENERAL BUILDING CONTRACTORS ASSOCIATION, INC. v. PENNSYLVANIA

Supreme Court of the United States, 1982.
458 U.S. 375, 102 S.Ct. 3141, 73 L.Ed.2d 835.

JUSTICE REHNQUIST delivered the opinion of the Court.

Respondents, the Commonwealth of Pennsylvania and the representatives of a class of racial minorities who are skilled or seek work as operating engineers in the construction industry in Eastern Pennsylvania and Delaware, commenced this action under a variety of federal statutes protecting civil rights, including 42 U.S.C. § 1981. The complaint sought to redress racial discrimination in the operation of an exclusive hiring hall established in contracts between Local 542 of the International Union of Operating Engineers and construction industry employers doing business within the Union's jurisdiction. Respondents also alleged discrimination in the operation of an apprenticeship program established by Local 542 and several construction trade associations. Named as defendants were Local 542, the trade associations, the organization charged with administering the trade's apprenticeship program, and a class of approximately 1,400 construction industry employers. Petitioners, the defendant contractors and trade associations, seek review of a judgment granting an injunction against them. The questions we resolve are whether liability under 42 U.S.C. § 1981 requires proof of discriminatory intent and whether, absent such proof, liability can nevertheless be imposed vicariously on the employers and trade associations for the discriminatory conduct of the Union.

I

The hiring hall system that is the focus of this litigation originated in a collective-bargaining agreement negotiated in 1961 by Local 542 and four construction trade associations in the Philadelphia area, three of whom are petitioners in this Court. The agreement was concluded only after a 10-week strike prompted by the resistance of the trade associations to the Union's demand for an exclusive hiring hall. Under the terms of the agreement, the Union was to maintain lists of operating engineers, or would-be engineers, classified according to the extent of their recent construction experience. Signatory employers were contractually obligated to hire operating engineers only from among those referred by the Union from its current lists. Workers affiliated with the Union were barred from seeking work with those employers except through Union referrals. Thus, the collective-bargaining agreement effectively channeled all employment opportunities through the hiring hall. Since 1961 this requirement has been a constant feature of contracts negotiated with Local 542 by the trade associations, as well as of contracts signed with the Union by employers who were not represented by one of those associations in collective bargaining.

Among the means of gaining access to the Union's referral lists is an apprenticeship program established in 1965 by Local 542 and the trade associations. The program, which involves classroom and field training, is administered by the Joint Apprenticeship and Training Committee (JATC), a body of trustees half of whom are appointed by the Union and half by the trade associations. While enrolled in the program, apprentices are referred by the Union for unskilled construction work. Graduates of the program become journeymen operating engineers and are referred for heavy equipment jobs.

This action was filed in 1971 by the Commonwealth of Pennsylvania and 12 black plaintiffs representing a proposed class of minority group members residing within the jurisdiction of Local 542. The complaint charged that the Union and the JATC had violated numerous state and federal laws prohibiting employment discrimination, including Title VII of the Civil Rights Act of 1964, 78 Stat. 253, as amended, 42 U.S.C. § 2000e et seq. (1976 ed. and Supp. IV), and 42 U.S.C. § 1981. The complaint alleged that these defendants had engaged in a pattern and practice of racial discrimination, by systematically denying access to the Union's referral lists, and by arbitrarily skewing referrals in favor of white workers, limiting most minority workers who did gain access to the hiring hall to jobs of short hours and low pay. The contractor employers and trade associations were also named as defendants, although the complaint did not allege a Title VII cause of action against them.[4]

The District Court divided the trial into two stages. See Pennsylvania v. Local 542, Int'l Union of Operating Engineers, 469 F.Supp. 329, 348 (ED Pa.1978). The first stage, from which petitioners appeal, addressed issues of liability; assessment of damages was deferred to a second stage. For purposes of the first phase of the proceedings, the court certified a plaintiff class of minority operating engineers and would-be engineers, as well as a defendant class consisting of all trade associations and employers who had been parties to labor contracts with Local 542. A single employer, petitioner Glasgow, Inc., was certified to represent the defendant subclass of approximately 1,400 contractor employers.

The District Court's opinion in the liability phase of the trial is lengthy. For our purposes, however, the relevant findings and conclusions can be summarized briefly. First, the court found that the hiring hall system established by collective bargaining was neutral on its face.

4. The complaint did not assert a Title VII cause of action against petitioners because they were not named in the complaint filed by the plaintiffs with the Equal Employment Opportunity Commission, a precondition to suit in federal court. See Brief for Individual and Class Respondents 12, n. 18.

Id., at 342. Indeed, after May 1, 1971, the contracts contained a provision expressly prohibiting employment discrimination on the basis of race, religion, color, or national origin. Id., at 340, and n. 6. But the court found that Local 542, in administering the system, "practiced a pattern of intentional discrimination and that union practices in the over-all operation of a hiring hall for operating engineers created substantial racial disparities." Id., at 370. The court made similar findings regarding the JATC's administration of the job-training program. Id., at 384. On the basis of these findings, the District Court held that Local 542 and the JATC had violated Title VII, both because they intentionally discriminated and because they enforced practices that resulted in a disparate racial impact. Id., at 397–399. The court also interpreted 42 U.S.C. § 1981 to permit imposition of liability "on roughly the same basis as a Title VII claim," 469 F.Supp., at 401, and therefore concluded that the Union and the JATC had also violated § 1981. Id., at 399–401.

Turning to petitioners' liability under § 1981, the court found that the plaintiffs had failed to prove "that the associations or contractors viewed simply as a class were actually aware of the union discrimination," id., at 401, and had failed to show "intent to discriminate by the employers as a class," id., at 412. Nevertheless, the court held the employers and the associations liable under § 1981 for the purpose of imposing an injunctive remedy "as a result of their contractual relationship to and use of a hiring hall system which in practice effectuated intentional discrimination, whether or not the employers and associations knew or should have known [of the Union's conduct]." Id., at 401. The court reasoned that liability under § 1981 "requires no proof of purposeful conduct on the part of any of the defendants." Id., at 407. Instead, it was sufficient that "(1) the employers delegated an important aspect of their hiring procedure to the union; [and that] (2) the union, in effectuating the delegation, intentionally discriminated or, alternatively, produced a discriminatory impact." Id., at 412. "[P]laintiffs have shown that the requisite relationship exists among employers, associations, and union to render applicable the theory of *respondeat superior*, thus making employers and associations liable injunctively for the discriminatory acts of the union." Id., at 413.

Following an appeal authorized by 28 U.S.C. § 1292(b), the Court of Appeals for the Third Circuit, sitting en banc, affirmed the judgment of liability against petitioners by an equally divided vote. 648 F.2d 923 (1981). We granted certiorari, 454 U.S. 939, 102 S.Ct. 473, 70 L.Ed.2d 246 (1981), and we now reverse.

II

The District Court held that petitioners had violated 42 U.S.C. § 1981 notwithstanding its finding that, as a class, petitioners did not intentionally discriminate against minority workers and neither knew nor had reason to know of the Union's discriminatory practices. The first question we address, therefore, is whether liability may be imposed under § 1981 without proof of intentional discrimination.[8]

Title 42 U.S.C. § 1981 provides:

> All persons within the jurisdiction of the United States shall have the same right in every State and Territory to make and enforce contracts, to sue, be parties, give evidence, and to the full and equal benefit of all laws and proceedings for the security of persons and property as is enjoyed by white citizens, and shall be subject to like punishment, pains, penalties, taxes, licenses, and exactions of every kind, and to no other.

We have traced the evolution of this statute and its companion, 42 U.S.C. § 1982,[9] on more than one occasion, see, e.g., McDonald v. Santa Fe Trail Transp. Co., 427 U.S. 273, 287–296, 96 S.Ct. 2574, 2582–2586, 49 L.Ed.2d 493 (1976); Runyon v. McCrary, 427 U.S. 160, 168–170, 96 S.Ct. 2586, 2593–2594, 49 L.Ed.2d 415 (1976); Jones v. Alfred H. Mayer Co., 392 U.S. 409, 422–437, 88 S.Ct. 2186, 2194–2202, 20 L.Ed.2d 1189 (1968), and we will not repeat the narrative again except in broad outline.

The operative language of both laws apparently originated in § 1 of the Civil Rights Act of 1866, 14 Stat. 27, enacted by Congress shortly after ratification of the Thirteenth Amendment. "The legislative history of the 1866 Act clearly indicates that Congress intended to protect a limited category of rights, specifically defined in terms of racial equality." Georgia v. Rachel, 384 U.S. 780, 791, 86 S.Ct. 1783, 1789, 16 L.Ed. 2d 925 (1966). The same Congress also passed the Joint Resolution that was later adopted as the Fourteenth Amendment. See Cong.Globe, 39th Cong., 1st Sess., 3148–3149, 3042 (1866). As we explained in Hurd v. Hodge, 334 U.S. 24, 32–33, 68 S.Ct. 847, 851–852, 92 L.Ed. 1187 (1948) (footnotes omitted):

> Frequent references to the Civil Rights Act are to be found in the record of the legislative debates on the adoption of the Amendment. It is clear that in many significant respects the statute and the Amendment were expressions of the same general congressional policy. Indeed, as the legislative debates reveal, one of the primary purposes of many members of Congress in supporting the adoption of the Four-

---

8. The District Court concluded, by analogy to Title VII, that a violation of § 1981 could be made out by "proof of disparate impact alone." Id., at 401. The court referred to Griggs v. Duke Power Co., 401 U.S. 424, 91 S.Ct. 849, 28 L.Ed.2d 158 (1971), in which we held that Title VII forbids the use of employment tests that produce a disproportionate racial impact unless the employer shows "a manifest relationship to the employment in question," id., at 432, 91 S.Ct. at 854. See Teamsters v. United States, 431 U.S. 324, 335–336, 97 S.Ct. 1843, 1854, 52 L.Ed.2d 396 (1977).

The District Court's holding on this issue is contrary to the holding of every Court of Appeals that has addressed the matter, including that of the Third Circuit in a subsequent case.

* * *

9. Section 1982 provides:

"All citizens of the United States shall have the same right, in every State and Territory, as is enjoyed by white citizens thereof to inherit, purchase, lease, sell, hold, and convey real and personal property."

teenth Amendment was to incorporate the guaranties of the Civil Rights Act of 1866 in the organic law of the land. Others supported the adoption of the Amendment in order to eliminate doubt as to the constitutional validity of the Civil Rights Act as applied to the States.

Following ratification of the Fourteenth Amendment, Congress passed what has come to be known as the Enforcement Act of 1870, 16 Stat. 140, pursuant to the power conferred by § 5 of the Amendment. Section 16 of that Act contains essentially the language that now appears in § 1981. Indeed, the present codification is derived from § 1977 of the Revised Statutes of 1874, which in turn codified verbatim § 16 of the 1870 Act. Section 16 differed from § 1 of the 1866 Act in at least two respects. First, where § 1 of the 1866 Act extended its guarantees to "citizens, of every race and color," § 16 of the 1870 Act— and § 1981—protects "all persons." See United States v. Wong Kim Ark, 169 U.S. 649, 675, 18 S.Ct. 456, 467, 42 L.Ed. 890 (1898). Second, the 1870 Act omitted language contained in the 1866 Act, and eventually codified as § 1982, guaranteeing property rights equivalent to those enjoyed by white citizens. Thus, "[a]lthough the 1866 Act rested only on the Thirteenth Amendment * * * and, indeed, was enacted before the Fourteenth Amendment was formally proposed, * * * the 1870 Act was passed pursuant to the Fourteenth, and changes in wording may have reflected the language of the Fourteenth Amendment." Tillman v. Wheaton-Haven Recreation Assn., 410 U.S. 431, 439–440, n. 11, 93 S.Ct. 1090, 1095, n. 11, 35 L.Ed.2d 403 (1973). See Runyon v. McCrary, supra, 427 U.S. at 168–170, n. 8, 96 S.Ct. at 2593–2594, n. 8.

In determining whether § 1981 reaches practices that merely result in a disproportionate impact on a particular class, or instead is limited to conduct motivated by a discriminatory purpose, we must be mindful of the "events and passions of the time" in which the law was forged. United States v. Price, 383 U.S. 787, 803, 86 S.Ct. 1152, 1161, 16 L.Ed.2d 267 (1966). The Civil War had ended in April 1865. The First Session of the Thirty-ninth Congress met on December 4, 1865, some six months after the preceding Congress had sent to the States the Thirteenth Amendment and just two weeks before the Secretary of State certified the Amendment's ratification. On January 5, 1866, Senator Trumbull introduced the bill that would become the 1866 Act.

The principal object of the legislation was to eradicate the Black Codes, laws enacted by Southern legislatures imposing a range of civil disabilities on freedmen. Most of these laws embodied express racial classifications and although others, such as those penalizing vagrancy, were facially neutral, Congress plainly perceived all of them as consciously conceived methods of resurrecting the incidents of slavery. Senator Trumbull summarized the paramount aims of his bill:

> Since the abolition of slavery, the Legislatures which have assembled in the insurrectionary States have passed laws relating to the freedmen, and in nearly all the States they have discriminated against them. They deny them certain rights, subject them to severe penal-

ties, and still impose upon them the very restrictions which were imposed upon them in consequence of the existence of slavery, and before it was abolished. The purpose of the bill under consideration is to destroy all these discriminations, and "to carry into effect the [Thirteenth] amendment." Cong.Globe, 39th Cong., 1st Sess., 474 (1866).

Senator Trumbull emphasized: "This bill has nothing to do with the political rights or *status* of parties. It is confined exclusively to their civil rights, such rights as should appertain to every free man." Id., at 476 (emphasis in original).

Of course, this Court has found in the legislative history of the 1866 Act evidence that Congress sought to accomplish more than the destruction of state-imposed civil disabilities and discriminatory punishments. We have held that both § 1981 and § 1982 "prohibit all racial discrimination, whether or not under color of law, with respect to the rights enumerated therein." Jones v. Alfred H. Mayer Co., 392 U.S., at 436, 88 S.Ct., at 2201. See Johnson v. Railway Express Agency, Inc., 421 U.S. 454, 459–460, 95 S.Ct. 1716, 1719–1720, 44 L.Ed.2d 295 (1975); Runyon v. McCrary, 427 U.S., at 168, 96 S.Ct., at 2593. Nevertheless, the fact that the prohibitions of § 1981 encompass private as well as governmental action does not suggest that the statute reaches more than purposeful discrimination, whether public or private. Indeed, the relevant opinions are hostile to such an implication. Thus, although we held in *Jones,* supra, that § 1982 reaches private action, we explained that § 1 of the 1866 Act "was meant to prohibit *all racially motivated* deprivations of the rights enumerated in the statute." 392 U.S., at 426, 88 S.Ct., at 2196 (emphasis on "racially motivated" added). Similarly, in Runyon v. McCrary, supra, we stated that § 1981 would be violated "if a private offeror refuses to extend to a Negro, *solely because he is a Negro,* the same opportunity to enter into contracts as he extends to white offerees." 427 U.S., at 170–171, 96 S.Ct., at 2594.

The immediate evils with which the Thirty-ninth Congress was concerned simply did not include practices that were "neutral on their face, and even neutral in terms of intent," Griggs v. Duke Power Co., 401 U.S. 424, 430, 91 S.Ct. 849, 853, 28 L.Ed.2d 158 (1971), but that had the incidental effect of disadvantaging blacks to a greater degree than whites. Congress instead acted to protect the freedmen from intentional discrimination by those whose object was "to make their former slaves dependent serfs, victims of unjust laws, and debarred from all progress and elevation by organized social prejudices." Cong.Globe, 39th Cong., 1st Sess., 1839 (1866) (Rep. Clarke). See Memphis v. Greene, 451 U.S. 100, 131–135, 101 S.Ct. 1584, 1602–1604, 67 L.Ed.2d 769 (1981) (WHITE, J., concurring in judgment). The supporters of the bill repeatedly emphasized that the legislation was designed to eradicate blatant deprivations of civil rights, clearly fashioned with the purpose of oppressing the former slaves. To infer that Congress sought to accomplish more than this would require stronger evidence in the legislative record than we have been able to discern.[15]

Our conclusion that § 1981 reaches only purposeful discrimination is supported by one final observation about its legislative history. As noted earlier, the origins of the law can be traced to both the Civil Rights Act of 1866 and the Enforcement Act of 1870. Both of these laws, in turn, were legislative cousins of the Fourteenth Amendment. The 1866 Act represented Congress' first attempt to ensure equal rights for the freedmen following the formal abolition of slavery effected by the Thirteenth Amendment. As such, it constituted an initial blueprint of the Fourteenth Amendment, which Congress proposed in part as a means of "incorporat[ing] the guaranties of the Civil Rights Act of 1866 in the organic law of the land." Hurd v. Hodge, 334 U.S., at 32, 68 S.Ct., at 851. The 1870 Act, which contained the language that now appears in § 1981, was enacted as a means of enforcing the recently ratified Fourteenth Amendment. In light of the close connection between these Acts and the Amendment, it would be incongruous to construe the principal object of their successor, § 1981, in a manner markedly different from that of the Amendment itself.[17]

15. We attach significance to the fact that throughout much of the congressional debates, S.B. 61, which became the 1866 Act, contained an opening declaration that "there shall be no discrimination in civil rights or immunities among citizens of the United States in any State or Territory of the United States *on account of race, color, or previous condition of slavery.*" See Cong.Globe, 39th Cong., 1st Sess., 474 (1866). This passage had occasioned controversy in both the Senate and the House because of the breadth of the phrase "civil rights and immunities." After the Senate had passed the bill and as debates in the House were drawing to a close, the bill's floor manager, Representative Wilson, introduced an amendment proposed by the House Judiciary Committee, of which he was also the Chairman. That amendment deleted the language quoted above and left the bill as it would read when ultimately enacted. See n. 10, supra. Representative Wilson explained that the broad language of the original bill could have been interpreted to encompass the right of suffrage and other political rights. "To obviate that difficulty and the difficulty growing out of any other construction beyond the specific rights named in the section, our amendment strikes out all of those general terms and leaves the bill with the rights specified in the section." Cong.Globe, 39th Cong., 1st Sess., supra, at 1367. See McDonald v. Santa Fe Trail Transp. Co., 427 U.S. 273, 292, n. 22, 96 S.Ct. 2574, 2584, n. 22, 49 L.Ed.2d 493 (1976). The deleted language, emphasized above, strongly sug-

gests that Congress was primarily concerned with intentional discrimination. That the passage was removed in an effort to *narrow* the scope of the legislation sharply undercuts the view that the 1866 Act reflects broader concerns.

17. It is true that § 1981, because it is derived in part from the 1866 Act, has roots in the Thirteenth as well as the Fourteenth Amendment. Indeed, we relied on that heritage in holding that Congress could constitutionally enact § 1982, which is also traceable to the 1866 Act, without limiting its reach to "state action." See Jones v. Alfred H. Mayer Co., 392 U.S. 409, 438, 88 S.Ct. 2186, 2202, 20 L.Ed.2d 1189 (1968). As we have already intimated, however, the fact that Congress acted in the shadow of the Thirteenth Amendment does not demonstrate that Congress sought to eradicate more than purposeful discrimination when it passed the 1866 Act. For example, Congress also enacted 42 U.S.C. § 1985(3) (1976 ed., Supp. IV) in part to implement the commands of the Thirteenth Amendment. See Griffin v. Breckenridge, 403 U.S. 88, 104–105, 91 S.Ct. 1790, 1799, 29 L.Ed.2d 338 (1971). While holding that § 1985(3) does not require state action but also reaches private conspiracies, we have emphasized that a violation of the statute requires "some racial, or perhaps otherwise class-based, invidiously discriminatory animus behind the conspirators' action." Id., at 102, 91 S.Ct. at 1798.

We need not decide whether the Thirteenth Amendment itself reaches practices

With respect to the latter, "official action will not be held unconstitutional solely because it results in a racially disproportionate impact," Arlington Heights v. Metropolitan Housing Dev. Corp., 429 U.S. 252, 264–265, 97 S.Ct. 555, 562–563, 50 L.Ed.2d 450 (1977). "[E]ven if a neutral law has a disproportionately adverse impact upon a racial minority, it is unconstitutional under the Equal Protection Clause only if that impact can be traced to a discriminatory purpose." Personnel Administrator of Mass. v. Feeney, 442 U.S. 256, 272, 99 S.Ct. 2282, 2292, 60 L.Ed.2d 870 (1979). See Washington v. Davis, 426 U.S. 229, 96 S.Ct. 2040, 48 L.Ed.2d 597 (1976). The same Congress that proposed the Fourteenth Amendment also passed the Civil Rights Act of 1866, and the ratification of that Amendment paved the way for the Enforcement Act of 1870. These measures were all products of the same milieu and were directed against the same evils. Although Congress might have charted a different course in enacting the predecessors to § 1981 than it did in proposing the Fourteenth Amendment, we have found no convincing evidence that it did so.

We conclude, therefore, that § 1981, like the Equal Protection Clause, can be violated only by purposeful discrimination.

III

The District Court held petitioners liable under § 1981 notwithstanding its finding that the plaintiffs had failed to prove intent to discriminate on the part of the employers and associations as a class. In light of our holding that § 1981 can be violated only by intentional discrimination, the District Court's judgment can stand only if liability under § 1981 can properly rest on some ground other than the discriminatory motivation of the petitioners themselves. Both the District Court and respondents have relied on such grounds, but we find them unconvincing.

A

The District Court reasoned that liability could be vicariously imposed upon the employers and associations, based upon the intentional discrimination practiced by Local 542 in its operation of the hiring hall. The court's theory was that petitioners had delegated to the "union hiring hall" the authority to select workers as "the agent for two principals—the union and the contractors, with their respective associations." 469 F.Supp., at 411. Since the hiring hall came into existence only through the agreement of petitioners, and since the exclusive hiring hall was the means by which "the intentional discrimination of the union was able to work its way broadly into the common

with a disproportionate effect as well as those motivated by discriminatory purpose, or indeed whether it accomplished anything more than the abolition of slavery. See Memphis v. Greene, 451 U.S., at 125–126, 101 S.Ct., at 1598–1600. We conclude only that the existence of that Amend-ment, and the fact that it authorized Congress to enact legislation abolishing the "badges and incidents of slavery," Civil Rights Cases, 109 U.S. 3, 20, 3 S.Ct. 18, 27, 27 L.Ed. 835 (1883), do not evidence congressional intent to reach disparate effects in enacting § 1981.

workforce of operating engineers," id., at 412, the court concluded that "[t]he acts of the union therefore justify imposition of responsibility upon those employers participating in the original delegation," ibid. The effect of this holding, as the court recognized, was to impose a "duty to see that discrimination does not take place in the selection of one's workforce," regardless of where the discrimination originates. Ibid.

As applied to the petitioner associations, the District Court's theory is flawed on its own terms. The doctrine of *respondeat superior*, as traditionally conceived and as understood by the District Court, see id., at 411, enables the imposition of liability on a principal for the tortious acts of his agent and, in the more common case, on the master for the wrongful acts of his servant. See Restatement (Second) of Agency §§ 215–216, 219 (1958) (Restatement); W. Prosser, Law of Torts §§ 69–70 (4th ed. 1971) (Prosser); W. Seavey, Law of Agency § 83 (1964) (Seavey). "Agency is the fiduciary relation which results from the manifestation of consent by one person to another that the other shall act on his behalf and subject to his control, and consent by the other so to act." Restatement § 1. A master-servant relationship is a form of agency in which the master employs the servant as "an agent to perform service in his affairs" and "controls or has the right to control the physical conduct of the other in the performance of the service." Id., § 2. See 2 F. Harper & F. James, Law of Torts § 26.6 (1956) (Harper & James). Local 542, in its operation of the hiring hall, simply performed no function as the agent or servant of the associations. The record demonstrates that the associations themselves do not hire operating engineers, and never have. Their primary purpose is to represent certain employers in contract negotiations with the Union. Even if the doctrine of *respondeat superior* were broadly applicable to suits based on § 1981, therefore, it would not support the imposition of liability on a defendant based on the acts of a party with whom it had no agency or employment relationship.[18]

We have similar difficulty in accepting the application of traditional *respondeat superior* doctrine to the class of contractor employers. In the run of cases, the relationship between an employer and the union that represents its employees simply cannot be accurately characterized as one between principal and agent or master and servant. Indeed, such a conception is alien to the fundamental assumptions upon which the federal labor laws are structured.

---

18. In this case, the associations were held liable because they negotiated an agreement, fair on its face, which was later implemented by another party in a manner that was not only discriminatory but in violation of the agreement itself *and* in a manner of which the associations were neither aware nor had reason to be aware. Since the associations' only role was as agent for employers whose hiring would actually be governed by the agreement, the District Court's theory presumably would also permit the imposition of liability on the attorneys who actually conducted the contract negotiations. We are unaware of any authority supporting such an extended application of *respondeat superior*.

At the core of agency is a "fiduciary relation" arising from the "consent by one person to another that the other shall act on his behalf and subject to his control." Restatement § 1. Equally central to the master-servant relation is the master's control over or right to control the physical activities of the servant. See Restatement id., § 220; 2 Harper & James, § 26.3; Seavey, § 84, p. 142. See also Logue v. United States, 412 U.S. 521, 527, 93 S.Ct. 2215, 2219, 37 L.Ed.2d 121 (1973). The District Court found that the requirement of control was satisfied because "the employers retained power to oppose the union discrimination." 469 F.Supp., at 411, n. 61. However, the "power to oppose" the Union, even when the opposition is grounded in the terms of the collective-bargaining agreement, is not tantamount to a "right to control" the Union. See Lummus Co. v. NLRB, 119 U.S.App.D.C. 229, 236, 339 F.2d 728, 735 (1964).[19] Indeed, a rule equating the two would convert every contractual relationship into an agency relationship, a result clearly unsupported by the common-law doctrines on which the District Court relied.

The District Court's assumptions about the relation between the Union and the class of employers with whom it has contracted also runs counter to the premises on which the federal labor laws have been constructed. While authorizing collective bargaining and providing means of enforcing the resultant contracts, the National Labor Relations Act expressly prohibits employers from compromising the independence of labor unions. See 49 Stat. 452, as amended, 29 U.S.C. § 158(a); 61 Stat. 157, as amended, 29 U.S.C. § 186. The entire process of collective bargaining is structured and regulated on the assumption that "[t]he parties—even granting the modification of views that may come from a realization of economic interdependence—still proceed from contrary and to an extent antagonistic viewpoints and concepts of self-interest." NLRB v. Insurance Agents, 361 U.S. 477, 488, 80 S.Ct. 419, 426, 4 L.Ed.2d 454 (1960). See Vaca v. Sipes, 386 U.S. 171, 177, 87 S.Ct. 903, 909, 17 L.Ed.2d 842 (1967). We have no reason to doubt the validity of that assumption in the instant case.

Respondents also suggest that petitioners can be held vicariously liable for the discriminatory conduct of the JATC. They argue that the JATC is properly viewed as an agent of both Local 542 and the associations, emphasizing that half of the trustees charged with administering the JATC are appointed by the associations and that the JATC is wholly funded by mandatory contributions from the employers. We note initially that the District Court premised petitioners' liability not on the actions of the JATC, but on the discriminatory conduct of the Union. See 469 F.Supp., at 411–413. The record, therefore, con-

---

19. According to respondents, the District Court's conclusion that petitioners retained the power to control the hiring hall was a finding of fact that cannot be set aside unless clearly erroneous. We disagree. The District Court found that petitioners had the "power to oppose" the Union, a conclusion we do not question. Whether the power to oppose the Union is equivalent to a right of control sufficient to invoke the doctrine of *respondeat superior* is, however, a legal question to which we must devote our independent judgment.

tains no findings regarding the relationship between the JATC and petitioners, beyond those noted above, that might support application of *respondeat superior.*

The facts emphasized by respondents, standing alone, are inadequate. That the employers fund the activities of the JATC does not render the JATC the employers' servant or agent any more than an independent contractor is rendered an agent simply because he is compensated by the principal for his services. The employers must also enjoy a right to control the activities of the JATC, and there is no record basis for believing that to be the case. Neither is a right of control inferable merely from the power of the associations to appoint half of the JATC's trustees. It is entirely possible that the trustees, once appointed, owe a fiduciary duty to the JATC and the apprentices enrolled in its programs, rather than to the entities that appointed them. Cf. NLRB v. Amax Coal Co., 453 U.S. 322, 101 S.Ct. 2789, 69 L.Ed.2d 72 (1981). On the assumption that *respondeat superior* applies to suits based on § 1981, there is no basis for holding either the employers or the associations liable under that doctrine without evidence that an agency relationship existed at the time the JATC committed the acts on which its own liability was premised.

B

The District Court also justified its result by concluding that § 1981 imposes a "nondelegable duty" on petitioners "to see that discrimination does not take place in the selection of [their] workforce." 469 F.Supp., at 412. The concept of a nondelegable duty imposes upon the principal not merely an obligation to exercise care in his own activities, but to answer for the well-being of those persons to whom the duty runs. See Restatement § 214. The duty is not discharged by using care in delegating it to an independent contractor. Consequently, the doctrine creates an exception to the common-law rule that a principal normally will not be liable for the tortious conduct of an independent contractor. See 2 Harper & James, § 26.11, pp. 1405–1408; Prosser, § 70, p. 467, § 71, p. 470. So understood, a nondelegable duty is an affirmative obligation to ensure the protection of the person to whom the duty runs.

In a sense, to characterize such a duty as "nondelegable" is merely to restate the duty. Thus, in this litigation the question is not whether the employers and associations are free to delegate their duty to abide by § 1981, for whatever duty the statute imposes, they are bound to adhere to it. The question is *what* duty does § 1981 impose. More precisely, does § 1981 impose a duty to refrain from intentionally denying blacks the right to contract on the same basis as whites or does it impose an affirmative obligation to ensure that blacks enjoy such a right? The language of the statute does not speak in terms of duties. It merely declares specific rights held by "[a]ll persons within the jurisdiction of the United States." We are confident that the Thirty-ninth Congress meant to do no more than prohibit the employers and associations in these cases from intentionally depriving black workers of the rights enumerated in the statute, including the equal right to contract. It did not intend to make them the guarantors of the workers' rights as against third parties who would infringe them. Cf. Furnco Construction Corp. v. Waters, 438 U.S. 567, 577–578, 98 S.Ct. 2943, 2949–2950, 57 L.Ed.2d 957 (1978) (Title VII); Rizzo v. Goode, 423 U.S. 362, 376–377, 96 S.Ct. 598, 606–607, 46 L.Ed.2d 561 (1976) (42 U.S.C. § 1983).

Our earlier holding that § 1981 reaches only intentional discrimination virtually compels this conclusion. It would be anomalous to hold that § 1981 could be violated only by intentional discrimination and then to find this requirement satisfied by proof that the individual plaintiffs did not enjoy "the same right * * * to make and enforce contracts * * * as is enjoyed by white citizens" and that the defendants merely failed to ensure that the plaintiffs enjoyed employment opportunities equivalent to that of whites. Such a result would be particularly inappropriate in the case of the associations, who are not engaged in the construction business, do not employ operating engineers, and consequently did not delegate to the Union any hiring functions which they otherwise would have performed themselves. Neither the District Court nor respondents identify anything in the language or legislative history of the statute to support a contrary conclusion.[21]

* * *

The judgment of the Court of Appeals is reversed, and the case is remanded for proceedings consistent with this opinion.

It is so ordered.

JUSTICE O'CONNOR, with whom JUSTICE BLACKMUN joins, concurring.

* * *

JUSTICE STEVENS, concurring in part and concurring in the judgment.

As I noted in my separate opinion in Runyon v. McCrary, 427 U.S. 160, 189, 96 S.Ct. 2586, 2603, 49 L.Ed.2d 415, the Congress that enacted

---

21. Respondents also contend that petitioners can be held liable on the theory that the hiring hall was a "joint enterprise" involving petitioners as well as the Union. They point to language in the District Court's opinion holding that "the union hiring hall was the agent for two principals—the union and the contractors, with their respective associations." 469 F.Supp., at 411. Even this theory, however, requires, among other things, the existence of a mutual right of control as between the members of the enterprise. See Restatement § 491; 2 Harper & James, § 26.13, p. 1414. For reasons we have already stated, there is no record basis for finding that petitioners had a right to con-

trol Local 542 in its administration of the hiring hall. We also doubt the validity of the assumption that the hiring hall is a separate entity, except perhaps as a physical structure. The District Court did not find, and respondents do not assert, that the hiring hall has a separate judicial existence. Indeed, in discussing the operation of the hiring hall, the District Court made clear that it was imposing liability on the basis of *the Union's* conduct. As used in the court's opinion, the phrase "hiring hall" appears to be no more than a shorthand reference for the referral process administered on a day-to-day basis by the Union.

§ 1 of the Civil Rights Act of 1866 "intended only to guarantee all citizens the same legal capacity to make and enforce contracts, to obtain, own, and convey property, and to litigate and give evidence." Any violation of that guarantee—whether deliberate, negligent, or purely accidental—would, in my opinion, violate 42 U.S.C. § 1981. The statute itself contains no requirement that an intent to discriminate must be proved.

The Court has broadened the coverage of § 1981 far beyond the scope actually intended by its authors; in essence, the Court has converted a statutory guarantee of equal rights into a grant of equal opportunities. See Jones v. Alfred H. Mayer Co., 392 U.S. 409, 88 S.Ct. 2186, 20 L.Ed.2d 1189; Runyon v. McCrary, supra. Whether or not those decisions faithfully reflect the intent of Congress, the enlarged coverage of the statute "is now an important part of the fabric of our law." Runyon, supra, 427 U.S., at 190, 96 S.Ct., at 2604 (STEVENS, J., concurring).

Since I do not believe Congress intended § 1981 to have any application at all in the area of employment discrimination generally covered by Title VII of the Civil Rights Act of 1964, an analysis of the motives and intent of the Reconstruction Congress cannot be expected to tell us whether proof of intentional discrimination should be required in the judicially created portion of the statute's coverage. Since Congress required no such proof in the statute it actually enacted, a logician would be comfortable in concluding that no such proof should ever be required. Nevertheless, since that requirement tends to define the entire coverage of § 1981 in a way that better reflects the basic intent of Congress than would a contrary holding, I concur in the conclusion reached by the Court in Part II of its opinion insofar as it relates to the statutory protection of equal opportunity but, perhaps illogically, would reach a different conclusion in a case challenging a denial of a citizen's civil rights.

Accordingly, I join the Court's judgment and Parts III and IV of its opinion.

JUSTICE MARSHALL, with whom JUSTICE BRENNAN joins, dissenting.

Today the Court reaches out and decides that 42 U.S.C. § 1981 requires proof of an intent to discriminate—an issue that is not at all necessary to the disposition of these cases. Because I find no support for the majority's resolution of this issue, and because I disagree with its disposition of these cases even if proof of intent should ordinarily be required, I respectfully dissent.

I

The question whether intent generally should be required in § 1981 actions is at most tangentially related to these cases. There was unquestionably intentional discrimination on the part of both the union (Local 542) and the Joint Apprenticeship and Training Committee (JATC), a body composed of officials from the union and the petitioner contracting associations, which jointly administered the apprenticeship and training program. As a result, the only question that the Court need address today is whether limited injunctive liability may be vicariously imposed upon an employer when the person or entity to whom it delegates a large portion of its hiring decisions intentionally discriminates on the basis of race. However, because the majority has chosen to reach first the more general question whether proof of intent is a prerequisite to recovery in a § 1981 action, I likewise will address this issue first.

> All persons within the jurisdiction of the United States *shall have the same right* in every State and Territory to make and enforce contracts, to sue, be parties, give evidence, and to the full and equal benefit of all laws and proceedings for the security of persons and property as is enjoyed by white citizens. * * * 42 U.S.C. § 1981.

The plain language does not contain or suggest an intent requirement. A violation of § 1981 is not expressly conditioned on the motivation or intent of any person. The language focuses on the effects of discrimination on the protected class, and not on the intent of the person engaging in discriminatory conduct. Nothing in the statutory language implies that a right denied because of sheer insensitivity, or a pattern of conduct that disproportionately burdens the protected class of persons, is entitled to any less protection than one denied because of racial animus.

The Court attaches no significance to the broad and unqualified language of § 1981. Furthermore, the majority finds no support for its conclusion that intent should be required in the legislative history to § 1 of the 1866 Act, the precursor to § 1981. Instead, in the face of this unqualified language and the broad remedial purpose § 1981 was intended to serve, the majority assumes that Congress intended to restrict the scope of the statute to those situations in which racial animus can be proved on the ground that the legislative history contains no "convincing evidence" to the contrary. Ante, at 3150. In my view, this approach to statutory construction is not only unsound, it is also contrary to our prior decisions, which have consistently given § 1981 as broad an interpretation as its language permits. See, e.g., McDonald v. Santa Fe Trail Transp. Co., 427 U.S. 273, 96 S.Ct. 2574, 49 L.Ed.2d 493 (1976); Runyon v. McCrary, 427 U.S. 160, 96 S.Ct. 2586, 49 L.Ed.2d 415 (1976); Johnson v. Railway Express Agency, Inc., 421 U.S. 454, 95 S.Ct. 1716, 44 L.Ed.2d 295 (1975); Tillman v. Wheaton-Haven Recreation Assn., 410 U.S. 431, 93 S.Ct. 1090, 35 L.Ed.2d 403 (1973); Sullivan v. Little Hunting Park, Inc., 396 U.S. 229, 90 S.Ct. 400, 24 L.Ed.2d 386 (1969); Jones v. Alfred H. Mayer Co., 392 U.S. 409, 88 S.Ct. 2186, 20 L.Ed.2d 1189 (1968).

The fallacy in the Court's approach is that, in construing § 1981 and its legislative history, the Court virtually ignores Congress' broad remedial purposes and our paramount national policy of eradicating racial discrimination and its pernicious effects. When viewed in this light, it is clear that proof of intentional discrimination should not be required in order to find a violation of § 1981.

Although the Thirty-ninth Congress that passed the Civil Rights Act of 1866 did not specifically address the question whether intent should be required, the conclusion is inescapable that the congressional leadership intended to effectuate "the *result* of a change from a centuries old social system based on involuntary labor, with all the notions of racial unsuitability for the performance of anything but menial labor under close supervision, to the free labor system." Croker v. Boeing Co., 662 F.2d 975, 1006 (CA3 1981) (Gibbons, J., with whom Higginbotham and Sloviter, JJ., joined, dissenting in part) (emphasis in original). When this Congress convened, the Thirteenth Amendment had been ratified, abolishing slavery as a legal status. However it was clear that in reality, Negroes were hardly accorded the employment and other opportunities accorded white persons generally. Thus, this Congress undertook to provide *in fact* the rights and privileges that were available to Negroes in theory. See generally J. tenBroek, The Antislavery Origins of the Fourteenth Amendment 156–180 (1951) (discussing the intent of the Thirty-ninth Congress to ensure to Negroes the *practical* freedom and equality which was already present at law, to reach private, not merely governmental conduct, and to provide affirmative obligations on the government to protect Negroes from unequal treatment). Four separate but related measures were proposed in an effort to accomplish this purpose.[1]

In this general climate, the 1866 Civil Rights Act was not an isolated technical statute dealing with only a narrow subject. Instead, it was an integral part of a broad congressional scheme intended to work a major revolution in the prevailing social order.[2] It is inconceivable that the Congress which enacted this statute would permit this

1. These measures included the Civil Rights Act of 1866, passed over President Johnson's veto; the Freedman's Bureau bill, which would have created a federal agency to ensure that a free labor system in which Negroes had equal participation would *in fact* be accomplished, and which commanded a clear majority in Congress, but failed to pass over a Presidential veto; a constitutional amendment sponsored by Representative Bingham but not recommended; and the Fourteenth Amendment.

2. As the majority recognizes, ante, at 3148, one of the principal changes Congress hoped to achieve was the elimination of the infamous Black Codes. These included state laws regulating the terms and conditions of employment. In many States, these oppressive laws were facially neutral, literally applying to all laborers without regard to race. The laws prohibited such conduct as refusing to perform work and disobeying an employer, or inducing an employee away from his employ-

er, and many provided for forfeiture of wages if the employee did not fulfill the terms of his employment contract. Other Codes included vagrancy laws, which were vague and broad enough to encompass virtually all Negro adults, and many were facially neutral, applying to white persons as well as to Negroes. See Croker v. Boeing Co., 662 F.2d 975, 1004, n. 5 (CA3 1981) (Gibbons, J., dissenting in part) (citing E. McPherson, Political History of the United States of America During the Period of Reconstruction 30–44 (1871)). The Black Codes were constantly discussed during the debates over the Civil Rights Act of 1866, and Congress clearly intended that the Act would eliminate even those Codes which were facially neutral. See, e.g., Cong. Globe, 39th Cong., 1st Sess., 39–41, 118–125 (1865); id., at 1151–1160, 1838–1839 (1866). See also University of California Regents v. Bakke, 438 U.S. 265, 390–391, 98 S.Ct. 2733, 2799, 57 L.Ed.2d 750 (1978) (separate opinion of Marshall, J.).

purpose to be thwarted by excluding from the statute private action that concededly creates serious obstacles to the pursuit of job opportunities by Negroes solely because the aggrieved persons could not prove that the actors deliberately intended such a result. Even less conceivable is the notion, embraced by the Court's opinion today, that this Congress intended to absolve employers from even injunctive liability imposed as a result of intentional discrimination practiced by the persons to whom they had delegated their authority to hire employees. See infra, at 3162–3164.

The legislative history demonstrates that the Thirty-ninth Congress intended not merely to provide a remedy for preexisting rights, but to eradicate the "badges of slavery" that remained after the Civil War and the enactment of the Thirteenth Amendment. Congress was acutely aware of the difficulties that federal officials had encountered in effectuating the change from the system of slavery to a system of free labor even though the legal and constitutional groundwork for this change had already been laid. In the report that formed the working paper for the Joint Committee on Reconstruction and was of central importance to the deliberations of the Thirty-ninth Congress, General Schurz noted:

> That the result of the free labor experiment made under circumstances so extremely unfavorable should at once be a perfect success, no reasonable person would expect. Nevertheless, a large majority of the southern men with whom I came into contact announced their opinions with so positive an assurance as to produce the impression that their minds were fully made up. In at least nineteen cases of twenty the reply I received to my inquiry about their views on the new system was uniformly this: "You cannot make the negro work without physical compulsion." I heard this hundreds of times, heard it wherever I went, heard it in nearly the same words from so many different persons, that at last I came to the conclusion that this is the prevailing sentiment among the southern people. There are exceptions to the rule, but, as far as my information extends, far from enough to affect the rule. In the accompanying documents you will find an abundance of proof in support of this statement. There is hardly a paper relative to the negro question annexed to this report which does not, in some direct or indirect way, corroborate it. S.Exec.Doc. No. 2, 39th Cong., 1st Sess. (1865), reprinted in The Reconstruction Amendments' Debates 88 (Virginia Comm'n on Constitutional Government (1967).

Fully aware of this prevailing attitude, the leaders of Congress set about to enact legislation that would ensure to Negroes the opportunity to participate equally in the free labor system by providing an instrument by which they could strike down barriers to their participation, whether those barriers were erected with the conscious intent to exclude or with callous indifference to exclusionary effects. Congress knew that this attitude could manifest itself in a number of different ways and intended to protect Negro workers against not only flagrant, intentional discrimination, but also against more subtle forms of discrimination which might successfully camouflage the intent to oppress through facially neutral policies. Congressional awareness of the potential role that facially neutral measures might play in impeding the ability of Negroes to enjoy equal job opportunities is also reflected in the working paper which formed the basis for the 1866 Act. Addressing this problem, General Schurz stated:

> What particular shape the reactionary movement will assume it is at present unnecessary to inquire. There are a hundred ways of framing apprenticeship, vagrancy, or contract laws, which will serve the purpose. * * * Id., at 92.

Unfortunately, this awareness seems utterly lacking in the Court's opinion today. In order to hold that § 1981 requires a showing of intent, the majority must assume that the rights guaranteed under § 1981—to make and enforce contracts on the same basis as white persons—can be adequately protected by limiting the statute to cases where the aggrieved person can prove intentional discrimination. In taking this extraordinarily naive view, the Court shuts its eyes to reality, ignoring the manner in which racial discrimination most often infects our society. Today, although flagrant examples of intentional discrimination still exist, discrimination more often occurs "on a more sophisticated and subtle level," the effects of which are often as cruel and "devastating as the most crude form of discrimination." Pennsylvania v. Local 542, Int'l Union of Operating Engineers, 469 F.Supp. 329, 337 (ED Pa.1978) (Higginbotham, Circuit Judge, sitting by designation).[3] I think that Judge Higginbotham most accurately recognized this problem when he noted that "[t]he facts of the instant case * * * demonstrate the complexity and subtlety of the interrelationship of race, collective bargaining, craft unions, the employment process and that ultimate goal—real jobs." Ibid. He further noted that "[a]t the critical level of viable jobs and equal opportunities, there were intentional and persistent efforts to exclude and discourage most of the minorities who, but for their race, would have been considered for entry into the union and for the more lucrative jobs." Ibid.

Racial discrimination in all areas, and particularly in the areas of education and employment, is a devastating and reprehensible policy that must be vigilantly pursued and eliminated from our society:

> Racial discrimination can be the most virulent of strains that infect a society, and the illness in any society so infected can be quantified. Exposure to embarrassment, humiliation, and the denial of basic respect can and does cause psychological and physiological trauma to its victims. This disease must be recognized and vigorously eliminated wherever it occurs. But racial discrimination takes its

---

3. When discussing the scope of the Fifteenth Amendment in 1939, Justice Frankfurter was sensitive to the subtle forms that racial discrimination often takes. Writing for the Court in Lane v. Wilson, 307 U.S. 268, 275, 59 S.Ct. 872, 876, 83 L.Ed. 1281, he stated: "The Amendment nullifies sophisticated as well as simpleminded modes of discrimination." Unfortunately, the Court no longer seems sensitive to this reality.

most malevolent form when it occurs in employment, for prejudice here not only has an immediate economic effect, it has a fulminating integrant that perpetuates the pestilences of degraded housing, unsatisfactory neighborhood amenities, and unequal education. Croker v. Boeing Co., 662 F.2d, at 1002 (Aldisert, J., with whom Higginbotham, J., joined, dissenting in part).

The purposes behind § 1981, and the profound national policy of blotting out all vestiges of racial discrimination, are no less frustrated when equal opportunities are denied through cleverly masked or merely insensitive practices, where proof of actual intent is nearly impossible to obtain, than when instances of intentional discrimination escape unremedied. For this reason, I cannot accept the Court's glib and unrealistic view that requiring proof of intent in § 1981 actions does not frustrate that statute's purpose of protecting against the devastating effects of racial discrimination in employment.

II

Even if I agreed with the Court that intent must be proved in a § 1981 action, I could not agree with its conclusion that the petitioner contracting associations should be immunized, even from injunctive liability, for the intentional discrimination practiced by the union hall to which they delegated a major portion of their hiring decisions. Under § 1981, minorities have an unqualified right to enter into employment contracts on the same basis as white persons. It is undisputed that in these cases, the respondent class was denied this right through intentional discrimination. The fact that the associations chose to delegate a large part of the hiring process to the local union hiring hall, which then engaged in intentional discrimination, does not alter the fact that respondents were denied the right to enter into employment contracts with the associations on the same basis as white persons.

At the very least, § 1981 imposes on employers the obligation to make employment decisions free from racial considerations. The hiring decisions made by the contracting associations in these cases were fraught with racial discrimination. Solely because of their race, hundreds of minority operating engineers were totally excluded from the industry and could not enter into employment contracts with any employer. Those minorities allowed into the industry suffered discrimination in referrals, and thus they too were denied the same right as white persons to contract with the contracting associations. Not one of the petitioner contracting associations has ever claimed, nor could they, that minorities had the same right as white operating engineers to contract for employment.

Instead, the contracting associations attempt to hide behind the veil of ignorance, shifting their responsibility under § 1981 to the very entity which they chose to assist them in making hiring decisions. The suggestion that an employer's responsibility under § 1981 depends upon its own choice of a hiring agent finds no support in the statute, nor does any other source of law authorize the circumvention of § 1981 that the contracting associations seek here. Their obligation to make employment contracts free from racial discrimination is a nondelegable one—it does not disappear when, as is often the case, the actual employer designates a particular agent to assist in the hiring process. In my view, the fact that the discriminating entity here is a union hiring hall, and not a person or corporation which has a traditional agent-principal relationship with the employer, does not alter this analysis. Cf. Morrison-Knudsen Co. v. NLRB, 275 F.2d 914 (CA2 1960) (per Swan, J.) (employer cannot escape liability for discrimination against nonunion members by the union hiring hall to which it turns over the task of supplying men for employment), cert. denied, 366 U.S. 909, 81 S.Ct. 1082, 6 L.Ed.2d 234 (1961).

The majority does not really analyze the question whether petitioners should be held injunctively liable because § 1981 imposes upon them a nondelegable duty. Instead the majority argues that, because it has held that § 1981 is intended only to reach intentional discrimination, the statute cannot make employers "guarantors of the workers' rights as against third parties who would infringe them." Ante, at 3153. This argument does not withstand analysis. The majority does not assert that employers may escape liability under § 1981 by delegating their hiring decisions to a third-party agent. Indeed, in light of the importance attached to the rights § 1981 is intended to safeguard, the duty to abide by this statute must be nondelegable, as the majority apparently recognizes. Ante, at 3153. Instead, the majority argues that because § 1981 imposes only the duty to refrain from intentional discrimination in hiring, it somehow automatically follows that this duty could not have been violated in this case. However, it was precisely this duty that was violated here. The District Court found, and this Court does not disagree, that the entity to whom the petitioner associations effectively delegated their hiring decisions *intentionally discriminated* against the respondent class on the basis of race in making these decisions. Even under the Court's own narrow view of the scope of the duty imposed by § 1981, then, the duty was unquestionably violated in these cases.

The majority obfuscates the issue by suggesting that the District Court imposed upon the contracting associations an obligation to seek out and eliminate discrimination by unrelated third parties wherever it may occur. In reality, the District Court did nothing more than impose limited injunctive liability upon the associations for violating their nondelegable duty under § 1981 when the union hiring hall, which effectively made hiring decisions for the associations, engaged in intentional discrimination on the basis of race in making these decisions.

By immunizing the employer from the injunctive relief necessary to remedy the intentional discrimination practiced by those through whom the employer makes its hiring decisions, the Court removes the person most necessary to accord full relief—the entity with whom the aggrieved persons will ultimately make a contract. I believe that the District Court appropriately rejected the petitioners' argument when it explained: "With intensity some employers urge that they agreed to the exclusive hiring hall system solely as a matter of economic survival at the end of a destructive ten week strike when the union would not compromise for any other hiring alternative. Yet economic pressures, however strong and harmful they might be, do not create immunity for employers, at least not in [the injunctive] liability phase." 469 F.Supp., at 338.

Section 1981 provides Negroes "the same right" to make contracts as white persons enjoy. In the present cases, this unqualified right was violated, and the violation is made no more palatable because the persons who actually made the hiring decisions and referrals, and not the employer itself, engaged in intentional discrimination. The devastating violation of their rights under § 1981 remains the same and will go at least partially unremedied when the person with whom the ultimate employment contract must be made is immunized from even injunctive relief. I cannot impute to the Congress which enacted § 1981 the intention to reach such an inequitable and nonsensical result. Accordingly, I must dissent.

Notes

1. Johnson v. Railway Express Agency, Inc., 421 U.S. 454, 95 S.Ct. 1716, 44 L.Ed.2d 295 (1975), is the first Supreme Court case which held that Section 1981 reaches claims of racial discrimination in employment in the private sector. Unlike Title VII, Section 1981 is not limited to employers having fifteen or more employees.

2. Proof of discriminatory intent in the Section 1981 cases can be established through direct or circumstantial evidence. Carter v. Duncan-Huggins, Ltd., 727 F.2d 1225 (D.C.Cir.1984). The courts frequently rely on the Title VII disparate treatment analytical framework, i.e., prima facie case, legitimate nondiscriminatory reason, pretext, and order and allocation of the burdens of proof, to determine whether discriminatory intent has been shown in Section 1981 litigation. E.g., Murray v. Thistledown Racing Club, Inc., 770 F.2d 63 (6th Cir.1985); Gay v. Waiters' and Dairy Lunchmen's Union, 694 F.2d 531 (9th Cir.1982).

3. *Federal and State Employers.* Although federal employees may not sue under Section 1981, see Brown v. G.S.A., 425 U.S. 820, 96 S.Ct. 1961, 48 L.Ed.2d 402 (1976), state and local employees may sue under Section 1981. See, e.g., Bridgeport Guardians, Inc. v. Members of Bridgeport Civil Service Commission, 482 F.2d 1333 (2d Cir.1973), cert. denied 421 U.S. 991, 95 S.Ct. 1997, 44 L.Ed.2d 481 (1975). The Eleventh Amendment bars claims for money damages against state employers. Edelman v. Jordan, 415 U.S. 651, 94 S.Ct. 1347, 39 L.Ed.2d 662 (1974). Local municipalities are not covered under the Eleventh amendment and are thus subject to monetary awards in the Section 1981 employment discrimination cases. Monell v. Department of Social Services, 436 U.S. 658, 98 S.Ct. 2018, 56 L.Ed.2d 611 (1978).

4. *Alienage and National Origin:* Claims of discrimination on the basis of alienage have been allowed under Section 1981, see, e.g., Guerra v. Manchester Terminal Corp., 498 F.2d 641 (5th Cir.1974). As a general rule, however, the courts have allowed claims of discrimination based on national origin only to the extent that the plaintiff is a member of a group which is "of such an identifiable nature that the treatment afforded to its members may be measured against that afforded to Anglos." Manzanares v. Safeway Stores, Inc., 593 F.2d 968, 970 (10th Cir.1979). In discussing claims of national origin brought under Section 1981, the court, in Budinsky v. Corning Glass Works, 425 F.Supp. 786, 787–788 (W.D.Pa.1977), stated that:

> The terms "race" and "racial discrimination" may be of such doubtful sociological validity as to be scientifically meaningless, but these terms nonetheless are subject to a commonly-accepted, albeit sometimes vague understanding. Those courts which have extended coverage of Sec. 1981 have done so on a realistic basis, within the framework of this common meaning and understanding. On this admittedly unscientific basis, whites are plainly a "race" susceptible to "racial discrimination"; Hispanic persons and Indians, like blacks, have been traditional victims of group discrimination, and, however inaccurately or stupidly, are frequently and even commonly subject to a "racial" identification as "non-whites." There is accordingly both a practical need and a logical reason to extend Sec. 1981's proscription against exclusively "racial" employment discrimination to these groups of potential discriminatees.

5. *Sex Discrimination Claims:* The majority of the courts have held that sex discrimination claims cannot be brought under Section 1981. See Bobo v. ITT, Continental Baking Co., 662 F.2d 340 (5th Cir.1981). Cf. Runyon v. McCrary, 427 U.S. 160, 96 S.Ct. 2586, 49 L.Ed.2d 415 (1976) (Section 1981 does not apply to discrimination based on sex and religion).

6. *Right to Jury Trial:* The courts of appeals are split on the issue whether either party is entitled to a jury trial in a Section 1981 action. Compare Setser v. Novack Investment Co., 657 F.2d 962 (8th Cir.1981) (Section 1981 back pay suit gives rise to jury trial), cert. denied 454 U.S. 1064, 1066, 102 S.Ct. 615, 616, 70 L.Ed.2d 601 (1981) (White, J., dissenting from denial of certiorari because of conflict in the circuits) with Moore v. Sun Oil Co., 636 F.2d 154 (6th Cir.1980) (no right to jury trial); Lynch v. Pan American World Airways, Inc., 475 F.2d 764 (5th Cir.1973) (claim for reinstatement under Section 1981 equitable in nature and adding claim for monetary damages does not mandate jury trial).

7. *Procedural Requirements:* A claim brought under Section 1981 is not subject to an exhaustion of administrative remedies requirement. Johnson v. Railway Express Agency, Inc., supra, confirms this rule by noting specifically the independent nature of the Section 1981 remedy.

8. *Statute of Limitations:* The time within which to file a Section 1981 claim is controlled by the most appropriate state statute of limitations since Section 1981 does not have its own built-in statute of limitations. After the Supreme Court decided Wilson v. Garcia, ___ U.S. ___, 105 S.Ct. 1938, 85 L.Ed.2d 254 (1985), holding that the states' personal injury statute

of limitations is the most appropriate limitations period for claims brought under 42 U.S.C. Section 1983, lower courts have applied the same rule in the Section 1981 cases. See, e.g., Goodman v. Lukens Steel Co., 777 F.2d 113 (3d Cir.1985). A number of states have more than one statute of limitations for personal injury actions and the determination of which limitations period should apply has divided the lower courts. See Pruit & Mauldin v. Jones, 54 L.W. 3497 (U.S. Jan. 28, 1986) (White, J., dissenting from denial of certiorari to resolve the conflict in the lower courts on the question of which limitations to apply when a state has more than one personal injury statute of limitations).

9. The Civil Rights Attorney's Fees Awards Act of 1976, 42 U.S.C. Section 1988, provide for attorneys' fees in the Section 1981 cases. See Hensley v. Eckerhart, supra at p. 547.

Chapter IV

THE EXECUTIVE ORDER PROGRAM AND AFFIRMATIVE ACTION

A. THE EXECUTIVE POWER

1. HISTORICAL AND LEGISLATIVE BACKGROUND

EXCERPTS FROM EQUAL EMPLOYMENT OPPORTUNITY COMMISSION, LEGISLATIVE HISTORY OF TITLES VII AND XI OF THE CIVIL RIGHTS ACT OF 1964 (1968)

Adoption of the Civil Rights Act of 1964, with its Title VII equal employment opportunity provisions, culminated a drive begun many years before. It was a drive that gained fruition first in the area of government employment and much later in the area of government contract employment.

But efforts to enact federal legislation to deal with equal employment opportunity on a broad basis, some of which extended back into the 1940's, had been stymied in Congress. The only successes in legislating in this area had been achieved in the states.

GOVERNMENT EMPLOYMENT

Until the New Deal period of the 1930's, action by the federal government relating to employment discrimination was largely confined to government employees. The Civil Service Act of 1883, for example, sought to establish the principle of "merit employment." One of the first regulations issued under the law outlawed religious discrimination in federal employment. (The Pendleton Act [Civil Service Act], 22 Stat. 403, 1883, 5 U.S.C. ch. 12, 1958; U.S. Civil Service Commission, Rule VIII, 1883)

In 1940, a Civil Service rule forbade racial, as well as religious, discrimination in federal employment. (Executive Order 8587, 5 Fed. Reg. 445, 1940) Then, when Congress adopted the Ramspeck Act,

587

extending the coverage of the Civil Service Act and amending the Classification Act of 1923, the principle of "equal rights for all" in classified federal employment was established. The Act declared:

> In carrying out the provisions of this title, and the provisions of the Classification Act of 1923, as amended, there shall be no discrimination against any person, or with respect to the position held by any person, on account of race, creed, or color. (Ramspeck Act, 54 Stat. 1211, 1940, Title I, 5 U.S.C. sec. 631a, 1958)

NEW DEAL LEGISLATION

In the 1930's during the early New Deal period, a policy of equal opportunity in employment and training financed by federal funds was established by congressional and executive action. The policy extended not only to direct federal employment and employment by government contractors, but to employment and training opportunities provided by grant-in-aid programs as well.

The principle of equal job opportunity first was enunciated by Congress in the Unemployment Relief Act of 1933. It provided:

> "That in employing citizens for the purpose of this Act no discrimination shall be made on account of race, color, or creed." (Unemployment Relief Act of 1933, 48 Stat. 22)

Many of the laws passed under the New Deal contained similar provisions. If the laws themselves did not bar discrimination, the policy of nondiscrimination was enunciated by the executive branch. Regulations issued under the National Industrial Recovery Act and the laws providing for public low-rent housing and defense housing programs, for example, forbade discrimination based on race, color, or religion. (National Industrial Recovery Act of 1933, Title II, 48 Stat. 200; 44 C.F.R. sec. 265–33, 1938)

Although these pronouncements amounted to unequivocal declarations by the legislative and executive branches, they were of limited effect in most instances. In practice, they amounted to little more than expressions of policy. There were no standards by which discrimination could be determined, and machinery and sanctions for enforcement were rare.

Experience During World War II

The inclusion of nondiscrimination provisions in laws providing for federally financed training programs continued after the outbreak of World War II. Despite these provisions, leaders of the Negro community contended that Negroes still were being denied federally financed training for defense jobs. They threatened a Negro march on Washington.

THE FIRST FEPC

On June 25, 1941, President Roosevelt issued Executive Order 8802 establishing a five-man Fair Employment Practice Committee. The Committee was set up as an independent agency responsible solely to the President. The executive order declared the following to be the government's policy:

> To encourage full participation in the national defense program by all citizens of the United States, regardless of race, creed, color, or national origin, in the firm belief that the democratic way of life within the nation can be defended successfully only with the help and support of all groups within its borders. (Executive Order 8802, 6 Fed. Reg. 3109, 1941)

Broad in scope, the order applied to all defense contracts, to employment by the federal government, and to vocational and training programs administered by federal agencies. The FEPC was authorized to receive and investigate complaints of discrimination, to take "appropriate steps" to redress valid grievances, and to recommend to federal agencies and to the President whatever measures it deemed necessary and proper to carry out the purposes of the order.

The FEPC, nevertheless, had its weaknesses. It had a staff of only eight members, and it lacked direct enforcement powers. So it concentrated on drafting policies and conducting public hearings throughout the country.

The later transfer of the FEPC to the War Manpower Commission deprived it of its autonomy. A dispute with the Chairman of the Manpower Commission led to the resignation of several members of the FEPC, and the Committee, in effect, suspended operations early in 1943.

THE SECOND FEPC

Later in 1943, President Roosevelt issued Executive Order 9346 establishing a new Fair Employment Practices Committee and declaring it to be the policy of the government to promote the fullest utilization of manpower and to eliminate employment discrimination. (Executive Order 9346, 8 Fed.Reg. 7183, 1943)

A broader jurisdiction than that of its predecessor was given to the new FEPC. It extended to all employment by government contractors (not merely those in defense industries), recruitment and training for war production, and employment by the federal government. Moreover, its authority with regard to labor unions was extended to include discrimination in membership as well as in employment.

The second FEPC was much better staffed than its predecessor. Its budget permitted it to employ a staff of nearly 120 and to open 15 field offices. In its three years of existence, it processed approximately 8,000 complaints and conducted 30 public hearings. It still lacked power, however, to enforce its decisions except by negotiation, moral suasion, and the pressure of public opinion. Its authority expired at the end of June 1946.

Government Contracts

From 1946 until 1964, the principal government efforts to eliminate racial and religious discrimination in employment were in the area of government contracts. A major step was taken by President Truman in 1951 when he issued a series of executive orders directing certain government agencies to include nondiscrimination clauses in their contracts.

THE TRUMAN COMMITTEE

On December 3, 1951, Truman issued Executive Order 10308 creating the Committee on Government Contract Compliance. It was an 11-member group composed of representatives of industry, the public, and the five principal government contracting agencies. (16 Fed.Reg. 12303, 1951)

After studying the effectiveness of the existing program, the Committee made more than 20 recommendations for improving the program. Many were aimed at the establishment of effective enforcement procedures for the nondiscrimination clause.

THE EISENHOWER COMMITTEE

On August 13, 1953, President Eisenhower issued an order replacing the Truman Committee with the President's Committee on Government Contracts—a 15-member group composed of representatives of industry, labor, government, and the public. (Executive Order 10479, 18 Fed.Reg. 4899, 1953)

The Eisenhower Committee was given the following duties:

1. To make recommendations to contracting agencies for improving nondiscrimination provisions in government contracts.

2. To serve as a clearing house for complaints alleging violation of the nondiscrimination clauses.

3. To encourage and assist with educational programs by nongovernmental groups.

Once again, however, the Committee had no power to enforce its recommendations. It had to rely on the procurement agencies to adjust complaints, although a report on the disposition of each complaint had to be made to the Committee.

THE KENNEDY COMMITTEE

The policy of nondiscrimination by government contractors was given teeth under the Kennedy Administration. In Executive Order 10925 issued on March 6, 1961, President Kennedy created a new President's Committee on Equal Employment Opportunity charged with the responsibility of effectuating equal employment opportunity both in government employment and in employment on government contracts. (26 Fed.Reg. 1977, 1961)

There was a dramatic break with the past under the new order. While earlier orders had imposed an obligation on contractors not to discriminate on the basis of race, creed, color, or national origin, the Kennedy order also required the contractors to take affirmative action to make the policy effective.

Government contractors were required to do the following:

1. Not to discriminate against any employee or job applicant because of race, creed, color, or national origin.

2. To take affirmative action to ensure that applicants are employed and employees are treated during their employment without regard to race, creed, color, or national origin.

3. To state in all solicitations or advertisements for employees that all qualified applicants will receive consideration without regard to race, creed, color, or national origin.

4. To advise each labor union with which they deal of their commitments under the order.

5. To include the obligations under the order in every subcontract or purchase order, unless specifically exempted.

6. To comply with all provisions of the order and the rules and regulations issued by the Committee; to furnish all information and reports required by the Committee; to permit access to books, records, and accounts for the purpose of investigation to ascertain compliance.

7. To file regular compliance reports describing hiring and employment practices.

ENFORCEMENT

The new order had teeth in it. In addition to requiring contractors to file compliance reports, it gave the Committee specific enforcement powers. To assure compliance, the Committee was authorized to do the following:

1. Publish the names of noncomplying contractors and unions.

2. Recommend suits by the Justice Department to compel compliance.

3. Recommend criminal actions by the Justice Department against contractors who furnish false information.

4. Terminate the contract of a noncomplying employer.

5. Forbid the contracting agencies to enter into new contracts with contractors who have discriminated unless they can demonstrate that they have changed their policies.

The most effective method of achieving compliance, however, was the "plan for progress"—described by the Committee as a procedure for effecting compliance through cooperation. At the time the Civil Rights Act was passed, there were more than 200 large companies operating under such plans. They required the contractor to set up effective recruitment programs to give members of minority groups equal opportunity of employment.

PROGRAM BROADENED

Under Executive Order 11114 issued by President Kennedy on June 22, 1963, the no-discrimination requirement was extended to all construction contracts paid for in whole or in part with funds obtained from the federal government or borrowed on the credit of the government pursuant to a grant, contract, loan, insurance, or guarantee. It also was extended to contracts undertaken pursuant to any federal program involving such a grant, contract, loan, insurance, or guarantee.

On February 13, 1964, President Johnson issued Executive Order 11141 declaring a federal policy under which federal supply contractors and subcontractors are forbidden (1) to discriminate because of age in hiring, promoting, or discharging employees, or in connection with working conditions or privileges, and (2) to specify an age limit in help-wanted ads. Both prohibitions are subject to a qualification permitting discrimination based upon a bona fide occupational qualification, retirement plan, or statutory requirement.

DISCRIMINATION BY UNIONS

The Committee set up by President Kennedy was directed to use its best efforts to get unions to cooperate with and comply in the implementation of the executive orders, but the Committee had no direct means of compelling compliance by unions. The obligation not to discriminate runs from the contractor to the government.

The standards and compliance procedures for apprenticeship under federal programs were issued in December 1963. * * *

2. OFCCP 1965–1978: THE AGE OF ADMINISTRATIVE EVOLUTION

A great many changes took place, primarily through administrative evolution, between 1965 and 1978 when President Carter's reorganization went into effect. The following overview was taken from an OFCCP Basic Compliance Training Course which was in use for the training of compliance personnel immediately prior to the 1978 reorganization.

A BRIEF HISTORY OF CONTRACT COMPLIANCE *

* * *

On September 24, 1965, President Johnson issued Executive Order 11246. The new Executive Order established a new administrative arrangement with the Secretary of Labor, rather than a Presidential Committee, charged with supervising and coordinating the activities of

---

* This excerpt was taken from a very elaborate set of materials prepared by Pacifica Consultants for OFCCP and the contents thereof are the property of OFCCP. Originally designated Office of Federal Contract Compliance, the agency was renamed Office of Federal Contract Compliance Programs on June 17, 1975. Both acronyms—OFCC and OFCCP—are used herein.

the contracting agencies. The contracting agencies maintained primary responsibility for obtaining compliance. The Secretary of Labor was empowered to issue regulations implementing the Order, investigate complaints, conduct compliance reviews, hold hearings and impose sanctions. The Secretary was also given authority to direct contracting agencies to conduct such complaint investigations, compliance reviews, hold hearings and impose sanctions as he deemed necessary for implementation of the Order. The Office of Federal Contract Compliance was established in the Office of the Secretary of Labor on October 5, 1965, to administer the new Executive Order. The Secretary of Labor has delegated the authority for carrying out the responsibilities under such order to the Director of the Office of Federal Contract Compliance. The Director of OFCC has delegated some authority to contracting Federal agencies to enforce contract compliance regulation; but this authority is to be exercised only under the Director's general guidance and control.

Under Executive Order 11246, a Federal contractor is now required to include in each contract a seven-point equal opportunity clause in which the employer agrees not to discriminate against anyone in the hiring process or during employment on the basis of race, color, creed, or national origin. In 1967, Executive Order 11246 was amended by Executive Order 11375 to "prohibit discrimination in employment because of race, color, religion, sex or national origin." (The effect of the amendment was to eliminate "creed" as prohibited criteria, but add "religion" and "sex.") In addition, the contractor also agrees to take "affirmative action" to ensure that applicants are employed, and that employees are treated during their employment, without regard to their race, color, religion, sex, or national origin. Some contracts are not required to contain the equal opportunity clause. For exemptions from the requirement, refer to 41 CFR 60–1.5.

Affirmative Action Requirements

OFCC regulations issued May 1, 1968, explained for the first time the meaning of the affirmative action requirement and also required each Federal contractor with 50 or more employees, and a Federal contract of $50,000 or more to develop for each of its establishments a written plan of affirmative action. These regulations were supplemented on February 5, 1970, by adding an entirely new part amending and clarifying the sections of the regulation on affirmative action.

This addition to the regulations, referred to as Order 4, stated that any contractor required to develop affirmative action compliance programs had not complied fully with the Executive Order until a program was developed and found acceptable by using standards and guidelines of Order 4. Order 4 set forth three basic requirements and eight additional guidelines for affirmative action compliance programs. The three basic obligations imposed on the contractors were (1) to perform an analysis of minority utilization in all job categories, (2) establish goals and a timetable to correct deficiencies, and (3) develop data collection systems and reporting plans documenting progress in achieving affirmative action goals. These general affirmative requirements were clarified and expanded by a second set of regulations, issued in 1970 and significantly revised in 1971. The second set of regulations, Revised Order 4, required contractors for the first time to include women in affirmative action programs. In addition, Revised Order 4 introduced the requirements that contractors remedy the effects of past discrimination experienced by incumbent employees. Finally, the regulation established a procedure to be followed by Federal agencies prior to imposing sanctions for failure to comply with affirmative action requirements (41 CFR 60–2.2 (1974)).

In October of 1971, OFCC issued the Testing and Selection Order (41 CFR 60–3). This Order required that if tests and other selection procedures used by contractors caused an adverse impact on minorities or women, then such tests and other procedures must be shown to be job related (valid).

The Testing Order was amended in January of 1974 to add specific documentation requirements for elements to be included in studies of job relatedness (validity) of selection procedures. In December of 1976 the Testing Order was replaced by the Federal Executive Agency Guidelines on Employee Selection Procedures (41 CFR 60–3), a joint document of the Departments of Labor and Justice and the Civil Service Commission. The new Guidelines lay out more specific requirements for validity studies done by contractors, while taking into account changes in the field of personnel psychology since the Testing Order was issued in 1971.

In March 1972, OFCC instructed the compliance agencies to implement a review procedure called Order 14. The compliance agencies objected to certain aspects of the order and formed an Interagency Committee on Order 14 to make recommendations to OFCC.

Revised Order 14 was issued to the compliance agencies by the Secretary of Labor in January 1973. Compliance agencies were critical of Revised Order 14 and they felt that the confidentiality provisions of the order would seriously inhibit the review process. By July 1974, OFCC had issued a substantially improved version of Revised Order 14. The order instructed the compliance agencies routinely to select contractors for review and delineated the various aspects and steps of the review process.

In September 1974, OFCC and EEOC signed a Memorandum of Understanding which provided that all Executive Order complaints would be referred to EEOC. This Memorandum superseded a similar agreement signed on May 20, 1970, which was never fully implemented. The 1970 Memorandum provided that OFCC and EEOC would routinely exchange information concerning pending investigations, employers under investigation, as well as outstanding and resolved complaints or charges. The only provision even partially carried out was that which stipulated that complaints filed with OFCC would be deemed EEOC charges and would be promptly transmitted to EEOC. In practice, OFCC directed the compliance agencies to refer to EEOC individual complaints, but not those alleging systemic or class-wide discrimination.

The 1974 agreement, like the one in 1970, provided that the agencies would exchange data on outstanding Title VII charges and Executive Order compliance reviews, as well as information concerning specific respondents. Each agency also agreed to notify the other before conducting an investigation or compliance review. In addition the 1974 agreement provided for each agency (1) to notify the other before issuing a debarment notice or instituting a Title VII lawsuit, and (2) to coordinate their efforts with regard to industry-wide projects. The 1974 memorandum did not alter the practice of handling complaints between the two agencies. The complaints received by OFCCP that allege class or systemic discrimination are usually investigated under the auspices of OFCCP, while complaints alleging individual discrimination are generally referred to EEOC.

3. OFCCP—THE EARLY 80's

THE OFFICE OF FEDERAL CONTRACT COMPLIANCE PROGRAMS *

Perhaps the most direct effect that the Federal Government has in eliminating private sector employment discrimination rests in its relationships with those firms that enter into contracts with Federal agencies. These agencies can and do establish various requirements for contractors, including equal employment opportunity and affirmative action requirements. According to one estimate, approximately 40 percent of the civilian work force is employed by companies that receive Federal contracts.[1] The Federal agency that is responsible for ensuring equal employment opportunity by Federal contractors is the Office of Federal Contract Compliance Programs (OFCCP) of the U.S. Department of Labor.

LAW AND OFFICIAL POLICY

Generally, firms that contract with the Federal Government to provide goods, services, or real property, and construction contractors whose work is paid in whole or in part by Federal funds, must make a written contractual commitment not to discriminate against applicants or employees because of their race, color, religion, sex, or national origin and to take affirmative action to eliminate such discrimination and to ensure equal employment opportunity for all applicants and employees.[2] In addition, contractors must take affirmative action to

---

* Excerpted from "Promises and Perceptions—Federal Efforts to Eliminate Discrimination Through Affirmative Action", U.S. Commission on Civil Rights, Oct. 1981, chapter 2 pp. 5–6.

1. Victor Perlo, Economics of Racism, USA (New York: International Publishers, 1976), p. 225.

2. Exec.Order No. 11246, 3 C.F.R. 339 (1964–1965 Comp.), and 30 Fed.Reg. 12319 (1965), as amended by Exec.Order No. 11375, 3 C.F.R. 684 (1966–70 Comp.), 32

employ and promote qualified handicapped persons,[3] as well as qualified disabled veterans and Vietnam veterans.[4] These provisions mean that the right to receive Federal monies for doing business with the Federal Government is contingent upon compliance with explicit equal employment opportunity and affirmative action requirements.

The basic equal employment opportunity requirements for government contractors and federally assisted construction contractors are set forth in Executive Order 11246, as amended,[5] in the Rehabilitation Act of 1973, as amended,[6] and in the Vietnam Era Veterans Readjustment Assistance Act of 1974, as amended.[7] An Executive order such as 11246 has the same legal force and effect as a statute enacted by Congress.[8]

Under its authority, the Department of Labor has established the OFCCP. The enforcement responsibilities for Executive Order 11246 were consolidated in OFCCP by Executive Order 12086.[9] The OFCCP has issued and enforces a series of regulations and orders, discussed below, to implement the provisions of Executive Order 11246, as amended,[10] section 503 of the Rehabilitation Act of 1973, as amended,[11] and section 402 of the Vietnam Era Veterans Readjustment Assistance Act of 1974, as amended.[12]

Certain contractors are exempt by statute, by regulation, and by order from the provisions of the foregoing equal opportunity requirements. Most contractors and subcontractors whose individual con-

Fed.Reg. 14303 (1967), and as amended by Exec.Order 12086, 3 C.F.R. 230 (1978 Comp.), 43 Fed.Reg. 46501 (1978), hereafter cited as Exec.Order No. 11246, as amended. For exceptions see 41 C.F.R. § 60–1.4 (1980).

3. Section 503 of the Rehabilitation Act of 1973, Pub.L. 93–1112, 29 U.S.C. § 793 (1976), as amended by Pub.L. 93–516, 29 U.S.C. § 706 and Exec.Order No. 11758. See also 41 C.F.R. § 60–741 et seq. (1980).

4. Section 402 of the Vietnam Era Veterans Readjustment Act of 1974, 38 U.S.C. § 2012 (1976). See also 41 C.F.R. § 60–250 et seq. (1980).

5. Exec.Order No. 11246, as amended.

6. 29 U.S.C. § 793 (1976).

7. 38 U.S.C. § 2012 (1976). Regulations amending a limited number of provisions under Executive Order 11246, as amended, section 402 of the Vietnam Era Veterans Readjustment Act of 1973, as amended, and section 503 of the Rehabilitation Act of 1973 were published as a final rule at 45 Fed.Reg. 86216 (1980). These regulations were to take effect on Jan. 29, 1981. On Jan. 28, 1981, the effective date of the regulations was deferred until Apr. 29, 1981, to allow the Department of Labor to review fully the regulations, 46 Fed.Reg.

9084 (1981). On Apr. 28, 1981, the effective date of OFCCP's Dec. 30, 1980, regulations was further deferred until June 29, 1981. These proposed regulations may, therefore, undergo further revisions.

8. Farkas v. Texas Instruments Inc., 375 F.2d 629 (5th Cir.1967), cert. denied, 389 U.S. 977 (1967); See also, Letter Carriers v. Austin, 418 U.S. 264, 273 (1973); Contractors Assn. of Eastern Pennsylvania v. Secretary of Labor, 442 F.2d 159 (3rd Cir.1971), cert. granted, 404 U.S. 854; United States v. New Orleans Public Service, Inc., 553 F.2d 459 (5th Cir.1977), cert. denied, vacated and remanded for reconsideration on other grounds, 436 U.S. 942 (1978), decision reaffirmed after reconsideration but remanded on other grounds, 638 F.2d 899 (5th Cir.1981); Legal Aid Society of Alameda County v. Brennan, 608 F.2d 1319 (9th Cir.1979), cert. denied, 447 U.S. 921 (1980).

9. Exec.Order No. 12086, 3 C.F.R. 230 (1978 Comp.).

10. E.g., 41 C.F.R. §§ 60–1, 60–2, 60–3, 60–4, 60–20, 60–50 (1979).

11. 41 C.F.R. §§ 60–741.1–60–741.54 (1980).

12. 41 C.F.R. §§ 60–250.1–60–250.23 (1980).

tracts with the Federal Government or contracts aggregated over a 12-month period total $10,000 or less, or whose federally assisted construction contracts are below that amount, are exempt from the requirements of Executive Order 11246 and its implementing regulations and orders.[13]   However, depositories of Federal funds, financial institutions issuing United States savings bonds and notes, and holders of government bills of lading for freight shipments are not exempt, regardless of the size of their financial dealings with the Federal Government.[14] Other exemptions include contracts and subcontracts to be performed outside the United States by employees recruited from outside the country.[15]   A contractor whose contract with the Federal Government is $2,500 or less is not covered by the affirmative action requirements for qualified handicapped applicants and employees.[16]   A Federal contractor whose contract is less than $10,000 is not covered by the affirmative action obligation with respect to veterans.[17]

Certain other nonconstruction contractors must develop written affirmative action programs to attempt to eliminate the underutilization of members of minority groups and women protected by Executive Order 11246 and to correct problems in their work forces regarding treatment of minorities and women.[18]   Under current regulations, all nonconstruction contractors and subcontractors with the Federal Government who employ more than 50 workers and who have a nonconstruction contract or subcontract for at least $50,000, or who hold $50,000 or more in bills of lading for freight shipments in a 12-month period, or who are a depository of Federal funds in any amount, or who are issuing or paying agents for United States savings bonds or notes in any amount are required to develop and implement written affirmative action programs for each establishment.[19]   State and local government agencies other than schools and hospitals are specifically exempted from that requirement,[20] although other regulations require written plans of them, as indicated in chapter 4.

The written affirmative action program must be developed by a nonconstruction contractor for each of its establishments within 120 days from the beginning of the contract.[21]   The aim of the program is to eliminate discriminatory practices and to promote equal employment opportunity by determining the extent to which minorities and women are underutilized by the contractor and by then developing and implementing affirmative steps to eliminate the problem.[22]   To accomplish this goal, a contractor must analyze its existing work force by job title based upon such factors as duties and rates of pay.[23]   Utilization of

13. 41 C.F.R. § 60–1.5(a)(1) (1980).

14. Id.

15. 41 C.F.R. § 60–1.5(a)(3) (1980).

16. 29 U.S.C. § 793(a) (1976).

17. 38 U.S.C. § 2012(a) (1976). See also 41 C.F.R. § 60–250.1 (1980).

18. 41 C.F.R. § 60–1.2(a) (1980).

19. 41 C.F.R. § 60–1.40(a) (1980).

20. 41 C.F.R. § 60–1.5(a)(4) (1980).

21. 41 C.F.R. § 60–1.40(a) (1980), and 41 C.F.R. § 60–2 (1980).

22. Id.

23. Id.

minority groups and women within the total work force of the contractor must be analyzed for each major job group.[24] In addition, hiring practices, including recruitment and testing, as well as upgrading, transfer, and promotion of existing employees must be reviewed on an annual basis.[25]

These general requirements for affirmative action programs are developed more fully for nonexempt nonconstruction contractors in OFCCP Revised Order No. 4.[26] Affirmative action requirements for construction contractors are described in other regulations.[27] According to Revised Order No. 4, "an affirmative action program is a set of specific and result-oriented procedures" that includes an analysis of areas where the contractor is underutilizing minorities and women, as well as goals and timetables to correct any deficiencies revealed by the self-analysis.[28] Underutilization is defined as "having fewer minorities or women in a particular job group than would reasonably be expected by their availability."[29] To perform an availability analysis, an employer must separately determine the percentage of minorities and women in each job group and compare it to the percentage of minority and female representation in the relevant labor area from which the contractor hires its employees.[30]

* * *

When a contractor determines that women or minorities are being underutilized in its work force, the contractor must develop goals and timetables for ending the underutilization.[33] In addition, the contractor is required to remedy deficiencies.[34] The goals and timetables must be specific and reasonably capable of attainment.[35] By regulation, the affirmative action program must be signed by an executive-level official of the contractor.[36] In addition, it is recommended that an executive of the contractor be appointed as director or manager of the company's equal employment opportunity programs.[37] His or her specific duties as set forth in the regulations are intended to ensure that problems are identified, effective solutions are proposed and implemented, information is disseminated up and down the line of command, regular liaison with community groups is maintained, and that any other steps necessary to assure success of the program are taken.[38]

24. 41 C.F.R. § 60–1.40(b) (1980), and 41 C.F.R. §§ 60–2.10–2.15 (1980).

25. Id. See also Uniform Guidelines on Employee Selection Procedures, which were adopted in 1978 by the EEOC, 29 C.F.R. § 1607 (1979), the Civil Service Commission, 5 C.F.R. § 300.103(c) 1979, the Department of Justice, 28 C.F.R. § 50.14 (1979), and OFCCP, 41 C.F.R. § 60–3 (1980).

26. 41 C.F.R. §§ 60–2.1–60–2.32 (1980).

27. See e.g., 41 C.F.R. §§ 60–4.1–60–4.9 (1980).

28. 41 C.F.R. § 60–2.10 (1980).

29. 41 C.F.R. § 60–2.11(b) (1980).

30. Id. See also U.S., Department of Labor, Office of Federal Contract Compliance Programs, Federal Contract Compliance Manual (1979), ch. 2, sec. 160, hereafter cited as OFCCP, Federal Contract Compliance Manual.

33. 41 C.F.R. § 1.40(a) (1980) and 41 C.F.R. § 60–2.12 (1980).

34. 41 C.F.R. § 60–2.10 (1980).

35. 41 C.F.R. § 60–2.12(a) (1980).

36. 41 C.F.R. § 60–1.40 (1980).

37. 41 C.F.R. § 60–2.22 (1980).

38. Id.

Construction contractors, both those contracting directly with the Federal Government and those receiving Federal monies for the performance of contracts with State and local public and private agencies, are also subject to affirmative action standards.[39] Such contractors are required to take affirmative measures such as steps to provide a working environment free of harassment, maintain a current file of minority and female job applicants as well as action taken by the contractor on those applications, notify the Director of OFCCP whenever a union with which the contractor has an agreement impedes the ability of the contractor to comply with equal employment opportunity requirements, develop on-the-job training and apprenticeship programs to upgrade women and minorities, review and disseminate equal employment information in advertisements and within the contractor's establishments, and validate selection criteria.[40]

To implement Executive Order 11246, OFCCP has approved several cooperative plans such as the "Hometown Plan." [41] (Hometown Plans are agreements among local contractors, unions, and minority groups to increase minority and female employment in the construction industry.) In addition, OFCCP issues goals and timetables for minority employment by geographical areas and for female employment on a nationwide basis as often as is deemed necessary.[42] Thus, unlike nonconstruction contractors who develop their own goals and timetables, goals and timetables for construction contractors to end the underutilization of minorities and women are determined by OFCCP unless the contractor is working under an approved Hometown Plan.[43]

Each nonconstruction contractor who is required to develop a written affirmative action program is also required to maintain data necessary to support its affirmative action program.[44] These data include progression line charts, applicant flow, seniority rosters, and applicant rejection ratios indicating minority and sex status.[45]

OFCCP evaluates these data through the compliance review process.[46] With nonconstruction contracts in excess of $1 million, where a review has not been conducted within 12 months, a preaward compliance review is mandatory.[47] With all other contracts subject to OFCCP regulations, however, review is not a precondition to the award of a contract, but may occur during the life of a contract. The compliance review process as set forth in regulations, orders, and the comprehensive OFCCP *Contract Compliance Manual* consists of three phases: desk

---

39. 41 C.F.R. § 60–4.1–60–4.9 (1980).

40. 41 C.F.R. § 60–4.3 (1980). Equal Employment Opportunity Construction Contract Specifications, §§ 7(a)–(p) (1980).

41. 41 C.F.R. §§ 60–4.4, 60–4.5 (1980); OFCCP, Federal Contract Compliance Manual, ch. 4, sec. 40.3.

42. 41 C.F.R. § 60–4.6 (1980).

43. Compare 41 C.F.R. § 60–2.12 (1980) with 41 C.F.R. § 60–4.6 (1980).

44. 41 C.F.R. § 60–2.12(m) (1980).

45. Id.

46. Revised Order No. 14, 41 C.F.R. §§ 60–60.1–60.8 (1980).

47. 41 C.F.R. § 60–1.20(d) (1979).

audit, onsite review, and offsite analysis.[48] Although not every nonconstruction contractor reviewed is subjected to all three phases, all nonexempt contractors must maintain the data essential to permit such a comprehensive review.[49]

Construction contractors are also subject to compliance reviews. They are required to document their affirmative actions to achieve equal employment opportunity and to keep comprehensive, identifiable, and easily retrievable records of personnel actions and of their work force for evaluation by OFCCP.[50]

Individual complaints of employment discrimination against contractors are normally referred by OFCCP to the Equal Employment Opportunity Commission (EEOC) for processing under Title VII rather than under Executive Order 11246, the authority under which OFCCP functions.[51] If OFCCP does elect to proceed under its authority, it will thoroughly investigate the complaint and develop a complete case record.[52] OFCCP generally retains and investigates class type complaints of employment discrimination.

If OFCCP determines in a compliance review or complaint investigation that a contractor is in violation of Executive Order 11246, it can move in several directions to secure compliance. In all cases, however, informal means of resolving violations of equal employment opportunity requirements are preferred over formal enforcement proceedings.[53] That is, OFCCP is expressly encouraged to rely on conciliation and persuasion to secure compliance as opposed to instituting formal enforcement procedures.[54] If, however, OFCCP has reason to believe a contractor is violating its responsibilities and if the agency is unable to resolve the matter informally, it will issue a show cause notice that offers the contractor the opportunity to demonstrate why it should not be subject to enforcement proceedings.[55] If conciliation does not result in compliance or if a contractor continues to violate a conciliation agreement after being notified of its conduct, OFCCP may request the Office of the Solicitor, Department of Labor, to institute administrative enforcement proceedings.[56] OFCCP may also elect to refer the matter to the Department of Justice for judicial proceedings.[57] There are no procedural prerequisites (e.g., completion of a compliance review or issuance of a show cause notice) to a referral to the Department of Justice.[58] In addition, the Department of Justice may, subject to approval by the Director of OFCCP, independently initiate its own

---

48. Revised Order No. 14, 41 C.F.R. § 60–60.3(a), (b), (c), (d) (1980), OFCCP, Federal Contract Compliance Manual.

49. See e.g., 41 C.F.R. § 60–1.43, § 60–1.7, and § 60–2.12(m) (1980).

50. 41 C.F.R. § 60–4.3 Standard Federal Equal Employment Opportunity Construction Contract Specifications, § 7, (1980).

51. Exec.Order No. 11246 § 209(a)(3); 41 C.F.R. § 60–1.24(a) (1980).

52. 41 C.F.R. § 60–1.24(b) (1980).

53. 41 C.F.R. § 60–1.24(c)(2) (1980).

54. Exec.Order No. 11246 § 209(b); 41 C.F.R. § 60–1.20(b) (1980).

55. 41 C.F.R. § 60–1.28 (1980).

56. 41 C.F.R. § 60–1.26(a)(2) (1980).

57. Id.

58. Id.

investigation of contractors it believes to be violating equal employment opportunity requirements.[59]

Where administrative or judicial proceedings against a contractor result in a determination that Executive Order 11246 has been violated, sanctions may be imposed and remedies required. Sanctions include both injunction of the conduct that constitutes the violation and cancellation of, or debarment from, future government contracts.[60] Remedies include assistance to victims of violations such as the award of back pay and retroactive seniority.[61] If debarred, which is the ultimate sanction, a contractor must request reinstatement and demonstrate its compliance with the requirements of equal employment opportunity as established by Executive Order 11246.[62] A list of debarred or otherwise ineligible contractors and subcontractors is periodically updated and circulated to all Federal agencies and departments.[63]

IMPLEMENTATION PROCEDURES

The principal steps OFCCP takes to fulfill its responsibility of assuring equal employment opportunity among Federal contractors are: (1) selection of contractors for review; (2) preaward reviews; (3) normal compliance reviews involving desk audits, onsite reviews, and where necessary conciliation and use of sanctions; (4) followup; and (5) processing of complaints.

The initial step, of course, is to select those contractors to be reviewed. OFCCP's national office establishes certain guidelines for selecting contractors to be reviewed, and the regional offices exercise some discretion to allow for industrial and other variations from region to region.

Discretion in selection of contractors is limited to some extent by the requirement to conduct preaward reviews of bidders being awarded contracts in excess of $1 million and by conciliation agreements or court decrees that must be monitored. * * *

Generally, however, the criteria utilized to select contractors include: (1) size of establishments, with larger contractors more likely to be reviewed; (2) availability of employment and career opportunities, with more attention paid to those establishments that afford greater likelihood of significant hiring and advancement to higher paid positions; (3) availability of minorities and women in the labor force, with those establishments located in areas containing large concentrations of these workers given higher priority; (4) contractors' previous record, with greater attention paid to those who have exhibited poor performance in the past in the area of equal employment opportunity; and (5) complaints, including allegations of discrimination against large classes

59.   41 C.F.R. § 60–1.26(f) (1980).

60.   Exec.Order No. 11246 § 209; 41 C.F.R. § 60–1.26(f); 41 C.F.R. § 60–30.30; 41 C.F.R. § 60–1.26(a)(2)(e) (1980).

61.   41 C.F.R. § 60–1.26(d) (1980).

62.   41 C.F.R. § 60–1.31 (1980).

63.   41 C.F.R. § 60–1.30 (1980).

of employees or applicants, with priority given to those contractors which are the source of a relatively high number of complaints.[65]

* * *

Once contractors have been identified for review, the initial step in the actual review process is a desk audit. At this stage the compliance officer reviews documents submitted by the contractors to make an initial evaluation of the affirmative action program and to identify the existence of any deficiencies for indepth examination during the onsite review. The reviewer checks such things as the work force analysis, availability analysis, whether jobs are properly grouped, whether or not deficiencies are properly identified, goals and timetables, evidence of adverse impact or disparate treatment caused by selection practices, evidence of good faith to meet all requirements, and other information.[70] During the desk audit, the compliance officer is instructed not to focus on those job groups where acceptable goals are being met or are within 5 percent of being met.[71] The compliance officer cannot normally conclude from the desk audit alone whether or not there are compliance problems, but a desk audit can be useful in helping to determine problem areas to focus on during the onsite review.[72]

If the desk audit suggests a need for additional information to demonstrate conclusively a contractor's compliance or noncompliance, an onsite review is conducted.[73] Among the items examined at this stage are the following:

1. EEO policies and procedures;

2. Contractor records to determine sufficiency and whether those records support what was stated in the affirmative action report;

3. Personnel practices to determine if there is evidence of possible adverse impact or disparate treatment;

4. Recruitment, hiring, promotion, transfer, layoff, and recall procedures;

5. Grievance, disciplinary, and termination procedures;

6. Compliance with guidelines on discrimination because of religion or national origin;

7. Compliance with guidelines on handicapped persons and veterans;

8. Compliance with technical requirements (such as posting EEO employer poster); and

9. Whether on the basis of the above analysis there are systemic discrimination or affected class problems.

65. Kansas City Transcript, p. 209; Boston Transcript, pp. 419–20 and 433. Also see Weldon J. Rougeau, "Enforcing a National Mandate"; Janet Regan and John M. Heneghan, "The Compliance Review and Beyond"; and Edward E. Mitchell, "A Year of Accomplishment," in Journal of Intergroup Relations, November 1979.

70. OFCCP, Federal Contract Compliance Manual, ch. 2, sec. 50.

71. Ibid., ch. 2, sec. 30.4.

72. Ibid., ch. 2, sec. 50.

73. Ibid., ch. 2, sec. 300.2–2g.

*   *   *

Entrance and exit interviews are conducted with the contractor as part of the review.[77] If no deficiencies are found, OFCCP issues a letter indicating the contractor's affirmative action program is accepted.[78] Where minor violations are found, a letter of commitment from the contractor to remedy the violations is sufficient for OFCCP to make a similar finding that the contractor's affirmative action plan is acceptable.[79]

If the deficiencies are major, however, a conciliation agreement must be negotiated to find the affirmative action program acceptable. This agreement spells out the problem areas and the corrective action to be taken.

B. ENFORCING THE CONTRACTUAL OBLIGATION

FARMER v. PHILADELPHIA ELECTRIC COMPANY, 215 F.Supp. 729 (E.D.Pa.1963).

It should come as no surprise that the early efforts to enforce the contractual obligations under the executive order looked to concepts from contract law as the basis of the legal action. In Farmer v. The Philadelphia Electric Co., the first case of record under the 1961 Executive Order, the court dismissed the plaintiff's action against the government contractor which alleged racial discrimination in violation of Executive Order 10925. That court looked at the plaintiff's case from the point of view of a contract action and concluded that it had no jurisdiction because there was a lack of diversity. Looking at the matter as an action arising under the executive order, assuming the order had the force and effect of law, the court concluded that there was no private right of action granted under the order. Only administrative remedies were intended to be available to the plaintiff. 215 F.Supp. at 733–34.

On appeal to the Third Circuit, the court affirmed the decision below. 329 F.2d 3 (3d Cir.1964.) That court assumed the executive order and its regulations had the force and effect of law, but held that they did not provide a remedy to the plaintiff under the Third Party Beneficiary Theory. The court noted that the plaintiffs had not complied with the rules and procedures for filing complaints which were provided under the executive order and therefore the case was a proper one for the application of the doctrine of "exhaustion of administrative remedies." 329 F.2d at 10.

---

77. OFCCP, Federal Contract Compliance Manual, ch. 3, secs. 60 and 180.

78. Ibid., ch. 3, sec. 43.

79. 41 C.F.R. § 60–1.20(b)(1980).

TODD v. JOINT APPRENTICESHIP COMMITTEE, 223 F.Supp. 12 (N.D.Ill.1963), vacated 332 F.2d 243 (7th Cir.1964), cert. denied 380 U.S. 914, 85 S.Ct. 880, 13 L.Ed.2d 800 (1965). In October of 1963, lawyers went to court on a combination of constitutional, federal statutory, and executive order grounds and sought direct action against the contractor under a third party beneficiary theory in Todd v. Joint Apprenticeship Committee. This suit involved state, federal and private entities subject to Executive Order 10925. The court rejected the third party beneficiary theory (223 F.Supp. at 16) but sustained the right of the plaintiffs to sue and granted relief under other provisions of law without specific attention to whether there was a right of action for the plaintiff under the executive order. On appeal the case was vacated and remanded for dismissal as moot by the Seventh Circuit.

FARKAS v. TEXAS INSTRUMENT, INC., 375 F.2d 629 (5th Cir. 1967), cert. denied 389 U.S. 977, 88 S.Ct. 480, 19 L.Ed.2d 471 (1967). In Farkas v. Texas Instrument, Inc., the Fifth Circuit reviewed the dismissal for want of jurisdiction of a complaint against a government contractor by an individual. The court below had considered it lacked jurisdiction and dismissed the complaint accordingly. The Court of Appeals disagreed with the court below regarding the lack of jurisdiction but sustained the dismissal of the complaint. Citing Farmer v. The Philadelphia Electric, supra, it concluded that a private civil action was not a permissible method of enforcing the executive order. The court noted that the plaintiff could have taken his case to the President's Committee, referring to the complaint procedures of the then applicable rules and regulations. In response to the plaintiff's allegation that he sought a remedy before the Committee and that relief was refused, the court said that in the light of the executive orders emphasis upon administrative method that refusal was final, citing Switchmen's Union of North America v. N.M.B., 320 U.S. 297, 64 S.Ct. 5, 88 L.Ed. 61 (1943).

The majority of cases have held, virtually uniformly, that there is no third party right of action under the executive order against a contractor. See e.g. Cohen v. I.I.T., 524 F.2d 818 (7th Cir.1975), cert. denied 425 U.S. 943, 96 S.Ct. 1683, 48 L.Ed.2d 187 (1976); Cap v. Lehigh University, 433 F.Supp. 1275 (E.D.Pa.1977); Gorman v. University of Miami, 414 F.Supp. 1022 (S.D.Fla.1976); Jackson v. University of Pittsburgh, 405 F.Supp. 607 (W.D.Pa.1975). See also, United States v. East Texas Motor Freight Systems, Inc., 564 F.2d 179 (5th Cir.1977), for the proposition that a union, not being a contractor with the government, cannot be subject to an independent cause of action under the executive order. But, cf. Eatmon v. Bristol Steel & Iron Works, Inc., 769 F.2d 1503 (11th Cir.1985) upholding plaintiff's rights to enforce a conciliation agreement arrived at under Executive Order 11246 in an action in federal district court. See also, Jones v. Local 520 International Union of Operating Engineers, 603 F.2d 664 (7th Cir.1979), cert. denied 444

U.S. 1071, 100 S.Ct. 669, 62 L.Ed.2d 647 (1980). In *Jones* the Seventh Circuit held that an employee could sue under 42 U.S.C. § 1981 to enforce a 11246 contract establishing a preferential minority hiring.

That third party beneficiary claims are not available for individual affected classes under the executive order does not establish that no relief might be forthcoming through attempts to utilize the courts.

HADNOTT v. LAIRD, 463 F.2d 304 (D.C.Cir.1972). In Hadnott v. Laird, plaintiff sued the Secretary of Defense to enjoin the award of future contracts to eleven textile companies who allegedly were guilty of discrimination and to require the federal government to terminate the existing contracts until the discriminatory practices were eliminated. The District Court dismissed the complaint on the grounds of sovereign immunity and failure of the plaintiffs to exhaust administrative remedies. 317 F.Supp. 379 (D.D.C.1970). The D.C. Circuit Court of Appeals sustained the dismissal on the failure to exhaust theory and declined to address the sovereign immunity issue. The Court of Appeals noted that nowhere in the record was there an assertion that any of the plaintiffs had filed the complaint seeking to invoke the administrative process. It refused to accept the plaintiffs allegations that attempting to exhaust the administrative remedies would be futile.

The court chose to read the plaintiff's effort as an original court action demanding the remedy of government contract termination with all companies found racially discriminating in employment practice, with the remedy derived directly from the Due Process Clause of the Fifth Amendment of the U.S. Constitution. It felt that to read the Due Process Clause as containing the remedy of government contract cancellation, available to be invoked by an aggrieved party, was a bit unprecedented and, likewise, fraught with the possibility of complete disruption of the usual procedures for statutory enforcement. It noted that the availability of alternate judicial and administrative remedies made it particularly inappropriate for the court to involve itself with constitutional claims at a point prior to the plaintiffs' efforts to avail themselves of those other remedies.

This case is the strongest authority for the availability of judicial review of the administrative process provided under the executive order and its rules and regulations, although the Fifth Circuit had suggested in Farkas v. Farmer that the actions under the executive order were committed to agency discretion and unreviewable.

The D.C. Circuit emphasized its view as follows: "We cannot say with exactitude what will occur if plaintiffs go to the Office of Federal Contract Compliance and file a complaint in each of the eleven instances which they cite to the District Court and now cite to this small court. But we are assured that one of several things will happen: (1) the Office of Federal Contract Compliance may actually reject the complaint on the ground that the matter has already been investigated, compliance assured, and the matter closed; (2) the OFCC may accept the complaint, reopen the investigation, but deny plaintiffs any role in such investigation by offering testimony or otherwise; or (3) the OFCC may reopen the investigation, conduct an open hearing, in which plaintiffs are allowed to participate. In either eventuality, the plaintiffs will have definite administrative action to which to point when they then come into the United States District Court for review under the provisions of the Administrative Procedure Act. (469 F.2d at 308–309, footnotes omitted.)

Notes

For discussions of right of action by implication see e.g. "Implied Rights of Action to Enforce Civil Rights: The Case for a Sympathetic View," 87 Yale L.J. 1378 (1978), and "Implied Private Actions Under Federal Statutes—The Emergence of a Conservative Doctrine," 18 William & Mary L. Rev. 429 (1976).

See also Cannon v. The University of Chicago, 441 U.S. 677, 99 S.Ct. 1946, 60 L.Ed.2d 560 (1979), in which the Supreme Court concluded that a cause of action existed by implication under the provisions of Title IX. In North Haven Board of Education v. Bell, 456 U.S. 612, 102 S.Ct. 1912, 72 L.Ed.2d 299 (1982) the Court concluded that employment discrimination comes within the scope of Title IX of the Education Act of 1972. The argument had been made that because Title IX was modeled on Title VI of the Civil Rights Act of 1964 it excluded employment unless the purpose of the grant was related to employment. While Title VI has a specific provision to that effect, Title IX contains no such language. The Supreme Court concluded that employment discrimination is covered by Title IX and that the agency's regulations were valid in light of the fact that its authority was subject to program specific limitations and the regulations were not inconsistent with that restriction.

LEGAL AID SOC. OF ALAMEDA CTY. v. BRENNAN
United States Court of Appeals for the Ninth Circuit, 1979.
608 F.2d 1319, cert. denied 447 U.S. 921, 100 S.Ct. 3010,
65 L.Ed.2d 1112 (1980.)

BROWNING, CHIEF JUDGE:

As a condition of doing business with the federal government, larger federal contractors are required to develop "written affirmative action compliance programs" designed to further equal employment opportunity. The contents of these programs are specified by regulation. 41 C.F.R. §§ 60–1.40, 60–2.10 to 13.

Several Black residents of Alameda County, California and organizations representing them, brought this suit against responsible federal officials, alleging they had failed to discharge their duty to ensure the maintenance by food processing contractors of adequate affirmative action programs. The district court granted partial summary judgment and injunctive relief.   Legal Aid Society v. Brennan, 381 F.Supp. 125 (N.D.Cal.1974).

I.

A.

Executive Order 11246 requires government contracting agencies to include in most federal and federally-assisted contracts dual covenants (1) that the contractor "will not discriminate against any employee or applicant for employment because of race, color, religion, sex, or national origin," and (2) that the contractor will "take affirmative action to ensure that applicants are employed, and that employees are treated during employment without regard to their race, color, religion, sex, or national origin."   This suit concerns the second covenant—the "affirmative action" obligation—which was added to the "nondiscrimination" obligation in 1961 in response to "an urgent need for expansion and strengthening of efforts to promote full equality of employment opportunity * * * " 26 Fed.Reg. 1977 (March 8, 1961).

B.

Appellees' complaint contained two central allegations.   First appellees charged that responsible USDA officials failed to review the affirmative action programs of a majority of federal contractors within USDA's compliance jurisdiction.[6]   This portion of the case is still pending below.   Second, appellees alleged that where compliance reviews were undertaken, USDA officials regularly approved programs that did not comply with Revised Order No. 4.   In discovery proceedings in support of the second claim, appellees obtained the affirmative action programs of 29 contractors in Alameda County, California, that had been reviewed and approved by USDA from August 1972 through January 1973.   These included the programs of all Alameda County contractors within USDA's compliance jurisdiction.   Based upon these programs and letters from the officials approving them, appellees moved for partial summary judgment on the complaint that USDA officials had regularly approved noncomplying programs.   Appellees asked that the officials be restrained from approving noncomplying programs, and that they be required to rescind approval of deficient plans and initiate enforcement proceedings against companies submitting these plans.

The district court granted appellees' motion.   It concluded that components of affirmative action programs that were mandated by Revised Order No. 4 were nonetheless absent from the programs approved by the officials.   It declared ten specific programs to be violative of the regulations, and therefore illegally approved.   The court enjoined USDA officials from approving programs that did not comply with Revised Order No. 4.   They were ordered to rescind

---

6.   Named as defendants were the Secretary of Labor, the Director of OFCCP, the Secretary of Agriculture, and the Chief of the Contract Compliance Division of USDA's Office of Equal Opportunity.

approval of the ten noncomplying programs, to issue show cause notices to the contractors submitting them, and to seek sanctions against any contractor that did not develop and implement a complying program.[7]

The federal officials filed, then withdrew, a notice of appeal, and have appeared in this court in support of the judgment.

The appellants are contractors whose affirmative action plans formed the basis for the court's order. The plans of four appellants were among the ten specifically declared unacceptable.[8]

Appellants were not parties to the proceedings below. After partial summary judgment was granted, appellants sought to intervene generally for the purpose of reopening the proceedings. The district court denied their motion, but permitted intervention for the purpose of appeal.

Appellants present five issues. First, they contend that approval of affirmative action plans by a compliance agency is not subject to judicial review or remedies, at least not at the behest of these appellees. Second, they contend that judicial review, if available, was premature because appellees had not exhausted administrative remedies. Third, they argue that they were entitled to participate in the proceedings below, and that entry of summary judgment without their presence deprived them of due process. Fourth, they contend that in finding the affirmative action programs inadequate and in formulating the decree, the district court relied upon standards that were erroneous in substance and not lawfully promulgated. Finally, they argue that the decree imposes hiring and promotion quotas in violation of the Constitution and of Title VII of the Civil Rights Act of 1964.

The federal appellees argue that appellants lack the requisite interest to maintain this appeal. Appellants counter that their interests were sufficient not only to permit intervention to appeal but also to require that the judgment be set aside because they were not parties to the proceedings in the court below.

* * *

III.

A.

The provisions of Revised Order No. 4, issued under Executive Order 11246, have the force of law.[14] Appellants do not disagree. They

---

7. The court's order also established a reporting and monitoring system requiring USDA officials to submit newly approved affirmative action programs to the court and to appellees' counsel for inspection. This part of the decree is not contested.

8. Appellant Chamber of Commerce appears as a representative of various contractors.

14. See United States v. New Orleans Pub. Serv., Inc., 553 F.2d 459, 465–68 (5th Cir.1977), vacated and remanded on other grounds, 436 U.S. 942, 98 S.Ct. 2841, 56 L.Ed.2d 783 (1978). Provisions of the regulations governing disclosure of information secured from contractors may not be sufficiently rooted in a grant of authority from Congress to have the force of law, see Chrysler Corp. v. Brown, 441 U.S. 281, 99 S.Ct. 1705, 1718–1721, 60 L.Ed.2d 208 (1979), but there can be no doubt that the essential features of the affirmative action program reflected in the regulations promulgated in Revised Order No. 4 were

contend, however, that the terms of the Executive Order and Revised Order No. 4 are not enforceable in the courts.

Administrative action is subject to judicial review unless it is clear that such review was not to be available. Morris v. Gressette, 432 U.S. 491, 500–01, 97 S.Ct. 2411, 53 L.Ed.2d 506 (1977); Barlow v. Collins, 397 U.S. 159, 166–67, 90 S.Ct. 832, 25 L.Ed.2d 192 (1970); Arizona Power Pooling Ass'n v. Morton, 527 F.2d 721, 727 (9th Cir.1975).[15] Nothing in Executive Order 11246 precludes judicial review. Indeed, the Order appears to anticipate such review by preserving, in addition to sanctions expressly authorized by the Order, remedies "as otherwise provided by law." E.O. 11246, § 202(6).

Although the Executive Order and implementing regulations place heavy reliance upon administrative expertise and discretion, not all compliance review action is committed to discretion of the agency. In these circumstances, judicial review limited to the non-discretionary aspects of agency action is appropriate. Ness Investment Corp. v. USDA Forest Service, 512 F.2d 706, 714–15 (9th Cir.1975); East Oakland-Fruitville Planning Council v. Rumsfeld, 471 F.2d 524, 533–34 (9th Cir.1972).[16] The regulations sought to be enforced here identify in clear

effectively ratified by Congress in adopting the Equal Employment Opportunity Enforcement Act of 1972. Several frontal attacks on the OFCC goal-and-timetable enforcement system were defeated during congressional consideration of the 1972 Act. Court decisions upholding the validity of the affirmative action program under the Executive Order were before the legislators and figured prominently in the debates. See 118 Cong.Rec. 1664–72, 4918 (1972) (remarks of Sen. Javits, reprinting decision in Contractors Ass'n of Eastern Pa. v. Secretary of Labor, 442 F.2d 159 (3d Cir.1971)); id. 1386 (Sen. Saxbe); id. 1663–64 (Sen. Ervin); 117 Cong.Rec. 32089 (Rep. Dent); id. 31965 (Rep. Green), H.R.Rep. No. 92–238, 92nd Cong., 2d Sess. (1971) (separate views of Rep. Green); reprinted at [1972] U.S.Code Cong. & Admin.News, pp. 2137, 2176–77. In rejecting the assault on the OFCC affirmative action approach, Congress approved the exercise of executive authority to issue binding regulations regarding minority utilization. See Comment, The Philadelphia Plan: A Study in the Dynamics of Executive Power, 39 U.Chi.L.Rev. 723, 757 (1972).

Independent Meat Packers Ass'n v. Butz, 526 F.2d 228 (8th Cir.1975), which appellants cite, is not to the contrary. That court held that Executive Order 11821 was not judicially enforceable. Executive Order 11821 requires executive agencies to evaluate the inflationary impact of major legislative proposals, rules, and regulations emanating from the executive branch.

The court's conclusion that the Executive Order lacked legal force rested on the premise that the Order "was intended primarily as a managerial tool for implementing the President's personal economic policies," and had been issued as a housekeeping measure rather than pursuant to constitutional or statutory authority. 526 F.2d at 235–36. See also Manhattan-Bronx Postal Union v. Gronouski, 121 U.S.App. D.C. 321, 350 F.2d 451 (D.C.Cir.1965). Executive Order 11246 rests upon statutory and other congressional authorization. See United States v. New Orleans Pub. Serv., Inc., supra.

15. It is questionable whether an Executive Order could of its own force preclude judicial review of action taken pursuant to it. Congress may create regulatory bodies with lawmaking powers and insulate those bodies from judicial oversight. It does not follow that the President may do so solely by Executive Order, without congressional ratification. In any event, Executive Order 11246 rests upon statute and other congressional authorization (see note 14), and neither the President nor Congress has indicated an intent to preclude judicial review of action taken by compliance authorities under the Executive Order.

16. Compare Peters v. Hobby, 349 U.S. 331, 345, 75 S.Ct. 790, 797, 99 L.Ed. 1129 (1954) ("Agencies, whether created by statute or [by] Executive Order, must of course be free to give reasonable scope to the terms conferring their authority. But they

mandatory terms elements that must be included in affirmative action programs before they may be deemed acceptable by compliance officials. Programs "*must* include an analysis of the areas within which the contractor is deficient in the utilization of minorities and women," 41 C.F.R. § 60–2.10. This analysis "*must* contain" the work force breakdown spelled out in 41 C.F.R. § 60.211, plus a utilization-availability study in which the contractor "will consider" at least eight enumerated factors. 41 C.F.R. § 60–2.11(a)(1) (1973).[17] Programs also "*must* include * * * goals and timetables," 41 C.F.R. § 60–2.10, which "*must* be designed to correct any identifiable deficiencies." 41 C.F.R. § 60–2.12(g).[18] Affirmative action programs "*shall* contain" the additional ingredients listed in 41 C.F.R. § 60–2.13.

There is no discretion as to the presence of these components in an acceptable affirmative action plan. Programs that lack them do not comply with Revised Order No. 4. Judicial review is available to insure that compliance officials perform their non-discretionary duty to refrain from approving plans that do not contain the elements mandated by the regulations. The remedies available under the Administrative Procedure Act—setting aside unlawful program approvals, 5 U.S.C. § 706(2), and compelling unlawfully withheld agency rejection of non-complying programs, 5 U.S.C. § 706(1)—may be invoked against compliance officials who violate this duty.[19]

Relief in the nature of mandamus is also appropriate. 28 U.S.C. § 1361. In arguing to the contrary, appellants stress the informality and flexibility of the enforcement scheme under the Executive Order, pointing to its emphasis on mediation and conciliation, 41 C.F.R. §§ 60–2.2(c)(2),[20] 60–1.24(c)(2) (1973), and to the express reservation that "[n]o contractor's compliance status shall be judged alone by whether he meets his goals and timetables * * * [but] shall be reviewed and determined by * * * his good faith efforts to make his program work * * *." 41 C.F.R. § 60–2.14. As appellants correctly argue, areas of the administrative process so laced with discretion are traditionally shielded from direct judicial intervention. Smith v. Grimm, 534 F.2d

---

are not free to ignore plain limitations on that authority.").

17. In the most recent version of Revised Order No. 4, this provision appears in 41 C.F.R. § 60–2.11(b)(1) (1977). See 43 Fed.Reg. 49240, 49250–51 (October 20, 1978).

18. Similarly, "program[s] *shall* provide * * * when there are deficiencies, [for] the development of specific goals and timetables for the prompt achievement of full and equal employment opportunity." 41 C.F.R. § 60–1.40(a).

19. Adams v. Richardson, 156 U.S.App. D.C. 267, 480 F.2d 1159 (D.C.Cir.1973) (en banc), supports this conclusion. *Adams* held reviewable the alleged consistent failure of the Department of Health, Educa-

tion and Welfare to enforce Title VI of the Civil Rights Act of 1964 against public school districts receiving federal funds. Appellants distinguish *Adams* on the ground that Title VI specifically permits a judicial role in its enforcement. Nothing in the *Adams* opinion suggests that HEW enforcement orders were made reviewable expressly. 480 F.2d at 1161–63. In any event, judicial review need not be expressly authorized; availability of judicial review is presumed unless clear evidence precludes it.

20. In the current regulations this provision appears as 41 C.F.R. § 60–2.2(c)(3) (1977). See 43 Fed.Reg. 49240, 49250 (October 20, 1978).

1346, 1352 (9th Cir.1976); Jarrett v. Resor, 426 F.2d 213, 216 (9th Cir. 1970); Wilmot v. Doyle, 403 F.2d 811, 816 (9th Cir.1968). But these are not the areas as to which appellees sought and obtained relief. Appellees' claim went to a threshold matter—the required content of acceptable affirmative action plans. This issue is distinct from such subsequent questions as to whether a contractor is in compliance with a valid affirmative action program (to which the good faith standard is relevant), or what should be done to secure compliance once it is determined that a contractor has violated his affirmative action obligations (to which the conciliation provisions are directed).[21] Appellees seek only to "require * * * [compliance] officers * * * to perform the ministerial duty of complying with their own regulations" by disapproving programs that do not contain the elements required by the regulations. Workman v. Mitchell, 502 F.2d 1201, 1205 (9th Cir.1974). See also Elliott v. Weinberger, 564 F.2d 1219, 1226 (9th Cir.1977), aff'd in part, rev'd in part sub nom. Califano v. Yamasaki, ___ U.S. ___, 99 S.Ct. 2545, 61 L.Ed.2d 176 (1979). For this an order in the nature of mandamus will lie. It is no bar to such relief that the court may be required to interpret Revised Order No. 4 to determine the precise scope of the agency's duties. "[O]nce the court interprets the law, the defendant's duty will become clear; the court is not telling the defendant how to exercise his discretion." Knuckles v. Weinberger, 511 F.2d 1221, 1222 (9th Cir.1975).

Appellants rely on three Court of Appeals' holdings that Executive Order 11246 does not afford a basis for a private right of action by an employee against an employer for alleged discrimination. These cases are inapposite. Two involved suits for damages for alleged violation of nondiscrimination covenants in private employers' contracts with the government.[22] The courts held that a private right to initiate judicial enforcement of such a covenant independently of the government would be inconsistent with the enforcement scheme created by the Executive Order. The third case involved a suit by a government employee against the government as an employer, and was based primarily upon sovereign immunity.[23]

Appellees do not seek recognition of a supplemental private enforcement mechanism. They do not seek damages for specific acts of discrimination against themselves. They ask only that the court review the government's own enforcement effort against the standards established by the Executive Order and regulations. Review of this sort is an ordinary element of administrative enforcement schemes,

---

21. As Revised Order No. 4 recognizes, the complex task of "transform[ing] * * * paper commitments into equal employment opportunity" requires leeway for the operation of discretion and good faith. But "developing and judging" the initial adequacy of the paper commitments can be carried out according to clearly stated criteria. 41 C.F.R. § 60–2.1.

22. Farmer v. Philadelphia Electric Co., 329 F.2d 3 (3d Cir.1964); Farkas v. Texas Instrument, Inc., 375 F.2d 629 (5th Cir. 1967).

23. Gnotta v. United States, 415 F.2d 1271, 1275 (8th Cir.1969).

absent clear indication to the contrary. Since the only relief sought in such a suit is that government officials be required to perform the non-discretionary duties imposed upon them by the Executive Order and regulations, the action is by definition compatible with the scheme established by the Order and regulations. The reluctance of courts to imply separate private enforcement rights from statutes or regulations which provide explicitly only for government enforcement procedures and penalties, see, e.g., Cort v. Ash, 422 U.S. 66, 78–80, 95 S.Ct. 2080, 45 L.Ed.2d 26 (1975); National R.R. Passenger Corp. v. National Ass'n of R.R. Passengers, 414 U.S. 453, 458, 94 S.Ct. 690, 38 L.Ed.2d 646 (1974), is not applicable to such a private proceeding as this.

If the cases on which appellants rely correctly deny the right to initiate a private suit against a discriminating employer under Executive Order 11246, judicial oversight of enforcement efforts of government officials through such a suit as this becomes doubly important; without it, no remedy would be available against compliance agencies that ignore the specific requirements of the Executive Order and regulations.

The argument that sovereign immunity bars this suit is no longer available. After briefs were filed, Congress amended the Administrative Procedure Act to remove the sovereign immunity defense to judicial review of administrative action where nonmonetary relief is sought. See Pub.L. 94–574, § 1, Oct. 21, 1976, 90 Stat. 2721, amending 5 U.S.C. § 702. The amendment is applicable on this appeal. Hill v. United States, 571 F.2d 1098 (9th Cir.1978).

B.

Appellant Chamber of Commerce contends that even if a private judicial remedy is available, appellees have no standing to pursue it.[24]

* * *

The argument advanced by the Chamber of Commerce—the only objection to standing actually raised by any party—is all but frivolous. The Chamber does not suggest that appellees were not injured nor that the decree, if complied with, would not have alleviated this injury. The Chamber's argument is that the contractors might elect to forego their contracts with the government rather than comply with affirmative action programs of the kind appellees assert to be required, and if they did so the injury to appellees would persist. The record reflects no substantial additional cost or other factor that might have led the contractors to abandon existing and presumably profitable contracts with the government, and accept debarment from future contracts, rather than correct deficiencies in their affirmative action programs. On the contrary, the record suggests both that the increase in the

---

24. The Legal Aid Society of Alameda County and the Western Regional Job Council appear as representatives of the individual appellees. Their standing turns on that of the individuals they represent,

Hunt v. Washington Apple Advertising Commission, 432 U.S. 333, 342–43, 97 S.Ct. 2434, 53 L.Ed.2d 383 (1977), and is not challenged separately by appellants.

available labor supply that would have resulted from elimination of discrimination against women and minorities would have reduced the contractors' costs, and that the opportunity to contract with the government was of great value to the contractors.[30]   Compare Simon v. Eastern Kentucky Welfare Rights Organization, 426 U.S. 26, 43–44, 96 S.Ct. 1917, 48 L.Ed.2d 450 (1976).

Castillo and the other appellees also satisfy the prudential limitations on standing.   Like the individual plaintiff in *Arlington Heights*, appellees assert more than a generalized grievance shared in equal measure by many others.   Appellees' injury as minority job seekers among the Alameda County contractors is "peculiar to [themselves] or to a distinct group of which [they are] a part."   Gladstone, Realtors v. Bellwood, 441 U.S. at 100, 99 S.Ct. at 1608.   They assert their own rights, not those of third parties.   Id.[31]   As set forth in part IIIA of this opinion, plaintiffs have a right to seek judicial relief under Executive Order 11246 and Revised Order No. 4.   Warth v. Seldin, supra, 422 U.S. at 500, 95 S.Ct. 2197.

IV.

Appellants argue the district court acted prematurely by granting relief without requiring appellees to exhaust the administrative remedy available under 41 C.F.R. § 60–1.21 et seq. (1973).   These provisions apply to complaints by employers, or applicants for employment, against individual employers for alleged acts of discrimination violating the employer's contractual obligations to the government.[32]   Although the complaint in this case alleges such acts as the immediate source of the "distinct and palpable injury" to individual appellees essential to standing, these acts are not the primary target of the litigation.   The complaint is directed instead at the ultimate cause of appellees' injury—the systematic approval by government officials of affirmative action programs that did not contain the provisions mandated by the

30. The Chamber does not suggest the record could have been supplemented with concrete evidence to support the Chamber's speculation about contractor withdrawal, had the Chamber had an opportunity to participate below.   At any rate, the Chamber must accept the record as it stands, since the Chamber has appealed only the summary judgment and not the denial of intervention.   See note 13.

31. If the "zone of interests" limitation on standing survives, at least as to matters of review under the Administrative Procedure Act, see Gladstone, Realtors v. Bellwood, 441 U.S. 91, 99 S.Ct. at 1608 n. 6 (1979); compare Simon v. Eastern Kentucky Welfare Rights Org., 426 U.S. 26, 38–39 n. 19, 96 S.Ct. 1917 (1976); K. Davis, Administrative Law in the Seventies § 22.02–11 at 509–15 (1976); 13 Wright, Miller & Cooper, Federal Practice & Proce-

dure: Civil § 3531 at 87 (Supp.1978), as a member of a minority group seeking a job with federal contractors, Castillo falls easily within the zone of interests protected by Executive Order 11246 and Revised Order No. 4.

32. The complaint procedure in force when appellees began this action permitted any employee or applicant of a federal contractor to file "a complaint of alleged discrimination in violation of the equal opportunity clause."   41 C.F.R. §§ 60–1.21, 1.22 (1973).   The procedure was apparently designed to handle complaints that specific employment decisions violated the nondiscrimination covenant of the employer's federal contract.   Thus, the complaint must identify the contractor "committing the alleged discrimination" and must describe "the acts considered to be discriminatory."   41 C.F.R. § 60–1.23.

regulations to expose and eliminate discriminatory employment practices. Appellees seek a declaration of the standards by which the
adequacy of affirmative action plans must be judged and a declaration
of the duties of compliance officials in implementing those standards.
The administrative procedures to which appellants point are not designed for processing claims of this sort or to provide relief of this scope.
With respect to this major aspect of appellees' claim, there was no
administrative remedy to be exhausted. Rosado v. Wyman, 397 U.S.
397, 406 & n. 8, 90 S.Ct. 1207, 25 L.Ed.2d 442 (1970).[33]

Moreover, even if the complaint procedures were applicable to
appellees' primary claim, we would not reverse because appellees failed
formally to exhaust them. This is not a case in which exhaustion of
administrative remedies is required by statute as a prerequisite to
judicial intervention. As applied here, the requirement that administrative remedies be exhausted is a judicially created doctrine to be
employed in the manner that best serves the competing interests of the
court, the agency, and the aggrieved individual in the circumstances of
the particular case. Montgomery v. Rumsfeld, 572 F.2d 250, 253–54
(9th Cir.1978). None of the interests served by the exhaustion requirement would be advanced by a reversal in this case.

The private appellees did not deliberately flout the administrative
process. It is questionable whether the formal remedy provided by the
regulations was applicable to any part of appellees' claims. Appellees
submitted their grievance to the agency by informal means before filing
suit, and the agency ruled against them on the merits, finding the
affirmative action programs acceptable. After litigation was commenced, the district court, following the procedures approved in State
of Washington v. Udall, 417 F.2d 1310, 1319 n. 14 (9th Cir.1969),
required the private appellees to present their claims to compliance
officials a second time, but to no avail.[34] Thus agency officials were
afforded an opportunity to correct their errors, to make their expertise

33. Freeman v. Schultz, 153 U.S.App.
D.C. 152, 468 F.2d 120 (D.C.Cir.1972), and
Hadnott v. Laird, 149 U.S.App.D.C. 358,
463 F.2d 304 (D.C.Cir.1972), on which appellants rely, are distinguishable. In both
cases, the complaint was directed at discriminatory acts of a particular contractor
or contractors. The relief sought (cancellation of existing contracts and debarment
from future contracts) was that authorized
in such cases by the Executive Order and
regulations. Executive Order 11246,
§ 209(a) (1965); 41 C.F.R. § 60–1.24(c)(3)
(1973). Hadnott did seek relief against the
responsible enforcement officials, and the
dissenting judge would have read the complaint as directed to the failure of these
officials to perform their duty, but the majority treated the complaint as seeking relief against specific offending companies
and relegated the plaintiffs to the adminis-

trative remedy available for processing
such complaints. See also note 35 infra.

34. Before filing this lawsuit, private
appellees requested federal officials to in-
tensify enforcement of the Executive Order
and regulations. In response, the agency
conducted reviews of all Alameda County
contractors within its compliance jurisdiction. The agency concluded all had acceptable affirmative action programs. After
appellees filed suit, the court ordered proceedings stayed "to permit disposition of
all issues herein involved at the administrative level of each of the offices affected
by the complaint." Appellees submitted a
detailed memorandum to the agency discussing the various areas in which appellees believed administrative enforcement
of the regulations to be deficient. The
agency took no action.

available, and to develop an administrative record for review, see Weinberger v. Salfi, 422 U.S. 749, 765, 95 S.Ct. 2457, 45 L.Ed.2d 522 (1975), and declined to do so. Moreover, as defendants in this litigation, responsible officials provided the court with the counsel of their experience and expertise to the extent expertise was relevant. They participated actively in the proceedings below and made their views as to the correct construction of the regulations known to the court. Finally, no factual determinations were involved for which agency procedures or creation of an administrative record could have been especially useful. See McGee v. United States, 402 U.S. 479, 485, 91 S.Ct. 1565, 29 L.Ed.2d 47 (1971). The allegation was that the responsible agency officials approved affirmative action programs that were facially inadequate in light of the Executive Order and regulations. Only the documents themselves were relevant. Thus, while resolution of some charges of affirmative action clause violations might require detailed fact-finding and record-building—for example, a charge that the contractor had not sought in good faith to implement his affirmative action program—the court in this case was not disadvantaged by the lack of formal agency complaint proceedings below.[35]

V.

The legitimacy of the standards applied by the district court in evaluating affirmative action programs and in formulating the decree is challenged on procedural grounds.

The district court concluded that compliance officials approved affirmative action programs that were in violation of Revised Order No. 4 in one or more of the following respects: (1) they contained inadequate utilization analyses, 41 C.F.R. § 60–2.11; (2) they failed to establish adequate goals and timetables designed to correct underutilization of minorities and women within the minimum period necessary, 41 C.F.R. §§ 60–2.12, 60–1.20(b); and (3) they failed to include the required additional ingredients listed in 41 C.F.R. § 60–2.13.

---

35. These factors further distinguish *Freeman* and *Hadnott.* See note 33. Those cases involved alleged violations of the nondiscrimination clause in particular contracts. Such violations usually raise factual issues as to the relationship between the employer and the alleged discriminatee. Compare Furnco Construction Corp. v. Waters, 438 U.S. 567, 575, 98 S.Ct. 2943, 57 L.Ed.2d 957 (1978). Agency investigatory procedures may be especially valuable in ferreting out these facts, and the administrative record compiled by the agency may be essential to judicial review. This fact-finding and record-building were absent in *Freeman* and *Hadnott,* see, 153 U.S.App.D.C. at 155 & n. 6, 468 F.2d at 123 & n. 6; 149 U.S.App.D.C. at 362, 463 F.2d at 308. As a consequence, the reviewing court had no basis, short of hearing the testimony itself, upon which to judge

whether the agency determination of nondiscrimination was justified.

Further, in this case appellees' letters and subsequent communications with the agency and their detailed informal complaint to the agency cataloging the asserted flaws in the approved affirmative action plans, together with the court's decision to stay its hand for further administrative-level negotiations, gave the agency a significantly greater opportunity to correct the asserted errors than did the single, unpursued oral complaint in *Freeman,* 153 U.S.App.D.C. at 153–54, 468 F.2d at 121–22, or the apparent lack of any resort to the agency at all in *Hadnott.* Indeed, in *Hadnott* there was every indication that the agency was correcting *sua sponte* the errors of which plaintiffs complained. 149 U.S.App.D.C. at 360, 463 F.2d at 306.

In the course of its analysis, the court referred to Technical Guidance Memo No. 1, issued to compliance agencies "to give specific guidance on the proper interpretation of certain selected issues that have been or continue to be raised regarding Revised Order 4." [36] Appellants contend that as used by the district court Technical Guidance Memo No. 1 was a legislative rule having a substantial impact upon the rights and obligations of federal contractors, and was invalid because not issued pursuant to the rule-making procedures of 5 U.S.C. § 553, citing Texaco, Inc. v. FPC, 412 F.2d 740, 745 (3d Cir.1969), and related cases. Appellees respond that Technical Guidance Memo No. 1 is an interpretive rule exempt from notice-and-comment requirements under subsection (b)(A) of 5 U.S.C. § 553. See, e.g., Energy Reserves Group, Inc. v. Department of Energy, 589 F.2d 1082 (Em.App.1978).

We need not decide whether the Technical Guidance Memo is to be classified as a legislative rule and, if so, whether it was lawfully issued. Although the district court found support for its holding in the Technical Guidance Memo (381 F.Supp. at 135–39), the court also concluded that reference to the Memo was not necessary to the decision of this case (381 F.Supp. at 135–36 n. 16). We agree. It is clear without reference to the Memo that appellee officials repeatedly approved affirmative action programs that failed to satisfy the fundamental requirements of Revised Order No. 4.

Although approved by compliance officials, none of the affirmative action programs contained an analysis of all eight factors specified in Revised Order No. 4, 41 C.F.R. § 60–2.11, for determining underutilization in any job category.[37] Most of the programs failed to establish goals and timetables designed to correct the underutilization of minorities and women, 41 C.F.R. § 60–2.12(g), in a manner that would assure the "prompt achievement of full and equal employment opportunity."

---

36. The Memo was issued by the Office of Federal Contract Compliance of the Department of Labor on February 22, 1974, a few months before partial summary judgment was granted. Although the Memo has not been published, its provisions are virtually identical to those of OFCCP's Standard Contractor Review Report, Part B, § XII.B(a)–(c), published in the Federal Register three weeks after entry of the district court's order. See 39 Fed.Reg. 25655 (1974), codified at 41 C.F.R. § 60–60.9 (1977); 43 Fed.Reg. 49240 (1978).

37. 41 C.F.R. § 60–2.11(b)(1) reads:

In determining whether minorities are being underutilized in any job classification the contractors will consider at least the following factors:

(i) The minority population of the labor area surrounding the facility;

(ii) The size of the minority unemployment force in the labor area surrounding the facility;

(iii) The percentage of the minority work force as compared with the total work force in the immediate labor area;

(iv) The general availability of minorities having requisite skills in the immediate labor area;

(v) The availability of minorities having requisite skills in an area in which the contractor can reasonably recruit;

(vi) The availability of promotable and transferable minorities within the contractor's organization;

(vii) The existence of training institutions capable of training persons in the requisite skills; and

(viii) The degree of training which the contractor is reasonably able to undertake as a means of making all job classes available to minorities.

A similar analysis is required for utilization of women by section 60–2.11(b)(2).

41 C.F.R. § 60–1.40(a). The goals set forth in the programs neither established long-range targets to complete the correction of underutilizations, 41 C.F.R. § 60–2.12(e), nor committed the contractor to eradicating underutilizations within any period of time, 41 C.F.R. §§ 60–2.12(d), 60–1.20(b). The annual numerical goals of a number of the programs rested on unexplained underprojection of job openings anticipated by the contractor for the forthcoming year.[38] All the programs failed to contain one or more of the "additional ingredients" required by 41 C.F.R. § 60–2.13, including development and implementation of affirmative action recruiting programs for minorities and women, 41 C.F.R. § 60–2.13(f)(j), plans for support of community-based programs designed to improve employment opportunities for minorities and women, 41 C.F.R. § 60–2.13(i), and development of internal audit and reporting systems for measuring the effectiveness of the program, 41 C.F.R. § 60–2.13(g).

VI.

Appellants object that certain provisions of the decree are at variance with the Executive Order and implementing regulations.

The court ordered compliance officials to approve only affirmative action programs containing the utilization analyses, goals and timetables, and additional ingredients called for by Revised Order No. 4. The decree imposes specific requirements with respect to each of these components. The utilization analysis in each affirmative action program must compare, separately for each set of similar jobs, the percentage of women and of each of specified minority groups in the contractor's existing work force with the percentage of available women and members of each minority group in the applicable labor area. The applicable labor area must be defined as either the city, county or Standard Metropolitan Statistical Area, depending upon which of the three has the highest minority population, unless the contractor justifies use of an area with fewer minority residents.[39] The decree requires

---

38. See 351 F.Supp. at 137 & n. 19.

39. The portion of the decree dealing with utilization analyses provides:

(a) Each program must contain a utilization analysis that satisfies each of the following requirements:

(i) The analysis must include a list of all major job categories (hereinafter referred to as "job groups") in the contractor's work force and, for each such job group, a statement of the total number of male and female incumbents for each of the following ethnic groups: Blacks, Spanish-Surnamed Americans, American Indians and Orientals.

(ii) Minority and female "availability" must be separately analyzed for each job group. The availability analysis must include a statement of the specific per-

centages of minority persons (stated separately for Blacks, Spanish-Surnamed Americans, American Indians and Orientals) and minority and non-minority women determined to be available in the applicable labor area for each job group.

(iii) Whenever the percentage of total minorities or of any ethnic group exceeding 2% of the surrounding population or of women in a job group is lower than the percentage of such persons available in that job group within the applicable labor area, the affirmative action program must specifically state that underutilization exists in that job group.

(iv) For purposes of determining availability, the labor area must not be defined in such a way as to minimize the

that an ultimate goal be set for each job group at least equal to the percentage of women and minority workers in the job group available in the applicable labor market; that a minimum feasible period be established for achieving this goal; and that interim percentage hiring rates be fixed and remain in effect until that underutilization is completely corrected.[40] Each program must contain specific and detailed action-oriented recruitment and training programs.[41]

Appellants object that the decree requires compliance officials to apply rigid standards and criteria in testing the adequacy of the utilization analysis, goals and timetables, and compliance programs in affirmative action plans, and that this is inconsistent with Revised Order No. 4 which imposes flexible standards and leaves determinations of compliance largely to the discretion of compliance officials. Appellants misread the regulations and the decree.

Appellants argue, for example, that the regulations do not require affirmative action programs to contain "ultimate goals" for female and

availability of minorities or women. In defining the relevant labor area, the contractor must set forth statistics showing the ethnic and sexual composition (including specific data for the four minority ethnic groups) of the population of the Standard Metropolitan Statistical Area, county and city in which the establishment is located and other appropriate adjacent areas. Any program which adopts a labor area which has a minority population lower than the highest of the SMSA, county or city must be rejected unless the program provides an appropriate written justification for the use of such area.

40. The goals-and-timetables portion of the decree provides:

(b) Each program must contain goals and timetables which satisfy each of the following requirements:

(i) An ultimate goal must be established for each job group in which underutilization exists and must be designed to completely correct the underutilization. The ultimate goal must be stated as a percentage of the total employees in the job group and must be at least equal to the percentage of minorities or women available for work in the job group in the labor market.

(ii) For each job group in which underutilization exists, a specific timetable must be established for reaching the ultimate goal in the minimum feasible time period.

(iii) For each job group in which underutilization exists, the contractor must

establish rates for hiring or promoting the minorities and women. The rates must be stated as a percentage of new placements in the job group, and they must remain in effect (unless specifically modified on the basis of subsequent data) until the underutilization is completely corrected. The percentage rates must be the maximum rates that can be achieved through the contractor's putting forth every good faith effort, including the use of available recruitment and training facilities, and must not be lower than the percentages set in the ultimate goals. Numerical goals based on projected openings are permissible but cannot be used in place of percentage rates.

41. The action-oriented-program requirement of the decree provides:

(c) Each program must contain specific and detailed action oriented programs, including recruitment and training programs, which comply with the requirements of Revised Order No. 4. These programs must, at a minimum, commit the contractor to undertake every good faith effort to contact and use in some concrete and specific manner relevant recruitment and training resources for recruitment and training minorities and women to fill positions in job groups where underutilization exists. Data regarding promotable employees, community training facilities and company training facilities must be prepared by the contractor itself and related to the locality.

minority utilization as distinguished from annual or interim goals, or indeed, no goals at all; and that the regulations do not require goals tied to the percentage of available women and minorities in the job groups or in the labor pool, as distinguished from flexible goals or goals keyed to a lower level that is more practical in the particular circumstances.

The regulations do not explicitly require that ultimate goals be fixed, but they do so by inescapable implication. Goals are to be directed toward achieving *"full* and equal employment opportunity." 41 C.F.R. § 60–1.40(a) by correcting *"any* identifiable deficiencies" in female or minority utilization. 41 C.F.R. § 60–2.12(g). Affirmative action programs must be "result-oriented," and the result to which they are to be directed under the current regulations is not merely "to increase materially the utilization of minorities and women"—as it once was, 41 C.F.R. § 60–2.10 (1973)—but "to achieve prompt and *full* utilization of minorities and women" in deficient segments of the contractor's work force. 41 C.F.R. § 60–2.10 (1978). Goals that must be stated in terms of "full utilization" and correction of "any deficiencies" can hardly be less than ultimate goals.[42]

Similarly, although the regulations do not state in so many words that acceptable ultimate goals must reflect a level of female and minority employment in the contractor's establishment at least equal to the percentage of women and minorities available in the job group in the contractor's labor area, no other inference is consistent with what the regulations do state. Under the regulations, goals in affirmative action programs are designed to correct underutilizations. 41 C.F.R. § 60–2.12(g). Underutilizations are "fewer minorities or women in a particular job group than would reasonably be expected by their availability." 41 C.F.R. § 60–2.11(b). Availability figures are to reflect only qualified workers reasonably available in the relevant labor pool. Id. It follows that, absent discrimination utilization will not be less than availability, and that to correct underutilization goals must be set to achieve parity with the level of available women and minority workers in the relevant labor pool. To say that compliance officials may accept employment goals lower than the level of qualified women or minority workers in the relevant labor area, as appellants do, is inconsistent with the simple central canon of the regulations that underutilization must be corrected.[43]

42. As appellants note, the regulations anticipate that goals will not be established in some circumstances. For example, 41 C.F.R. § 60–2.12(k) provides that when no goal is provided the affirmative action program must detail reasons for the omission. Appellants argue that the decree conflicts with the regulations in this respect because the decree provides without qualification that "Each program must contain goals and timetables." However, it is clear from the decree as a whole, and

federal appellees concede that if goals are inappropriate under the regulations in any circumstances, the exception would be equally applicable under the decree.

43. In this and other respects the district court's interpretation of the regulations reflected in the decree is consistent with that found in Technical Guidance Memo No. 1. See note 36. Although we have refrained from deciding whether the Memo is a lawfully published rule having

This analysis of the decree and the regulations also suggests the error in appellants' argument that by determining underutilization and setting goals and hiring rates on the basis of a comparison of percentages of women and minorities in job categories in a contractor's work force and in the relevant labor area, the decree substitutes a rigid mathematical formula for the flexible determination encompassing all relevant factors contemplated by the regulations. The percentage of women and minorities available in a contractor's work force is to be determined by a consideration of the eight variables specified in the regulations, including, as noted above, possession of the necessary skills for the particular job category. The same is true of the determination of the percentage of such persons available in the work force in the relevant labor area. The comparison of percentages is mechanical, but the percentages to be compared are computed on the basis of the full range of variables specified in the regulations.

Appellants also argue that the decree substitutes a rigid definition of the relevant labor area for flexible guidelines in Revised Order No. 4. The regulations require that the contractor's availability analysis account for potential minority employees in the area "surrounding [his] facility," "in the immediate labor area," and "in an area in which [he] can reasonably recruit." 41 C.F.R. § 60–2.11(b)(1)(i)–(v), (2)(i)–(v). The decree provides that a program which adopts a labor area having a lower minority population than the highest in three standard geographical statistical units (Standard Metropolitan Statistical Area, County, and City) "must be rejected unless the program provides an appropriate written justification for the use of such areas." [44] This provision of the decree does not displace the regulatory standard. It simply provides a triggering mechanism for requiring a more explicit demonstration on the written record that the standard has been met when it appears that the boundaries of the labor market may have been skewed to exclude minority workers.

The district court found that compliance officials repeatedly approved affirmative action programs containing over or under-inclusive labor area definitions which minimized minority availability. 381 F.Supp. at 135. Requiring a full written exposition in the affirmative action program of the justification for the boundaries drawn, when the circumstances suggest manipulation, will make it more difficult for compliance officials to approve noncomplying programs in the future, and easier to detect abuses if they occur. At the same time, the power of the agency to determine the appropriate labor market by careful analysis of the commuting distances, communications channels, and related factors, remains unimpaired. If the written justification satis-

---

the force of law, unquestionably it reflects a construction of Revised Order No. 4 by the agency responsible for its promulgation and enforcement. As such it is entitled to weight (Udall v. Tallman, 380 U.S. 1, 16, 85 S.Ct. 792, 13 L.Ed.2d 616 (1965)), even though it may not be binding authority

because of formal deficiencies. Skidmore v. Swift & Co., 323 U.S. 134, 140, 65 S.Ct. 161, 89 L.Ed. 124 (1944).

44. See Para. (1)(a)(iv) of the decree, note 39.

fies compliance officials that the portions of the municipal unit with the highest minority population are beyond reasonable commuting or recruiting range, for example, a more limited labor area may be approved though its minority population is lower.

This provision of the decree reflects an appropriate exercise of the court's power, in fashioning a remedy on administrative review, to "adjust its relief to the exigencies of the case in accordance with the equitable principles governing judicial action." Ford Motor Co. v. NLRB, 305 U.S. 364, 373, 59 S.Ct. 301, 307, 83 L.Ed. 221 (1939). The court's power is broad, so long as the court acts "within the bounds of the [regulation] and without intruding upon the administrative province." Id. The decree violates neither the language of Revised Order No. 4 nor the "administrative province" of compliance authorities. Cf. Mitchell v. DeMario Jewelry, 361 U.S. 288, 290–92, 80 S.Ct. 332, 4 L.Ed. 2d 323 (1960); Indiana & Michigan Electric Co. v. FPC, 163 U.S.App. D.C. 334, 344, 502 F.2d 336, 346 (D.C.Cir.1974).

Finally, basing goals on availability levels does not restrict administrative flexibility "in deciding when compliance has been achieved," as appellants argue. However the goals are stated, they remain only "targets reasonably attainable by means of applying every good faith effort" by the contractor. 41 C.F.R. § 2.12(e). Compliance is measured by good faith efforts to attain them, not by whether they are realized. 41 C.F.R. § 2.14. The decree does not alter this key tenet. It affects only how the goals must be set, not how they are to be met.

VII.

Appellants argue that the provision in the decree restraining compliance officials from approving affirmative action plans unless they include hiring and promotion rates equalling the percentage of minorities and women available in the relevant labor market, requires preferential hiring and promotion on the basis of race and sex and is incompatible with section 703(a)(1), (2), (d) and (j) of Title VII of the Civil Rights Act of 1964, 42 U.S.C. § 2000e–2(a)(1), (2), (d) & (j), and with the equal protection component of the Due Process Clause of the Fifth Amendment.

Appellants' argument rests on the premise that this provision of the decree requires preferential hiring and promotion of underutilized minorities and women, and consequent "reverse discrimination" against individuals not in these groups. Appellants' premise is false. Nothing in the decree or inherent in the circumstances of this case requires preferential treatment or discrimination on the basis of race or sex. We therefore need not consider when if ever racial and sexual preferences and discrimination undertaken to comply with Executive Order 11246 can be lawful under either Title VII or the Constitution. Cf. United Steelworkers of America v. Weber, ___ U.S. ___, ___, 99 S.Ct. 2721, 2726, 2730, 61 L.Ed.2d 480 (1979); id. at ___, 99 S.Ct. at 2726 (Rehnquist, J., dissenting).

The source of hiring and promotion goals and rates required by the decree to be included in acceptable affirmative action programs is significant. As noted earlier (see text at note 43), these goals and rates reflect the contractor's own determination of the percentage of minority and female workers qualified for the particular job group who are reasonably available for employment by that contractor. The goals and rates thus represent the contractor's own judgment as to the percentage of females and minority members that would be found in his work force if all available qualified persons applied for employment and if all selection processes operated in a completely nondiscriminatory manner. Given this premise, it is entirely reasonable to assume that a contractor who finds a lower percentage of women or minority members in a particular job category in his work force may well be able to correct the deficiency simply by removing obstacles to fair and equal employment, without reliance upon racial preference or discrimination.

Underutilization may be traced to failure of available women and minority workers to apply, for a variety of reasons, in the expected numbers. They may not be aware of job openings. If this is the problem, contacts may be established with local organizations, institutions, or individuals who are in a position to refer women and minority applicants; advantage may be taken of media and events through which potential women and minority applicants can be reached; and word-of-mouth recruiting by women and minority employees and applicants may be encouraged.[45] Perhaps the contractor will discover that potential applicants are discouraged by the contractor's negative image among women workers or in the minority community. If so, the problem may be solved by designating minority liaison officers, 41 C.F.R. § 60–2.22(a)(b), or by widening dissemination of the contractor's fair employment policy and practices, id. § 60–2.21(a)(b). Or deficiency in the flow of applications from women and minority workers may be attributable to persons other than the contractor—to labor unions or subcontractors, for example—whom the contractor can persuade to abandon exclusionary practices. Id. § 60–2.23(b)(17).

If the contractor is attracting a balanced flow of applicants, underutilization may be the product of improper screening or selection processes. Facially objective job criteria that screen out women and minority workers disproportionately may prove to be irrelevant or only marginally related to job performance, and new and validated criteria can be substituted. Id. § 60–2.24(b); [1976] Empl.Prac.Guide (CCH) ¶¶ 1416, 1418. Or the contractor may discover that hiring personnel entertain subjective biases (conscious or not) that can be corrected by instruction or training, or by removing biased officials from the hiring process. 41 C.F.R. § 60–2.24(d).

Under most conditions these and similar steps to correct flaws in the contractor's hiring system will involve neither preference nor

---

45. See 41 C.F.R. § 60–2.24(e). See also [1976] Empl.Prac. Guide (CCH) ¶ 1414; Fiss, A Theory of Fair Employment Laws, 38 U.Chi.L.Rev. 235, 282–85 (1971).

discrimination, yet they may be adequate to enable the contractor to comply fully with hiring and promotion goals and rates required under the decree. Of course, it may prove otherwise. Employers may find it expedient to adopt, indeed compliance officials may require, affirmative action programs that involve preference and discrimination.[46] Both administrative and judicial remedies will be available to test the lawfulness of such provisions on the basis of a specific record. But because the hiring and promotion requirements of the Revised Order and decree may lead in some circumstances to the adoption of questionable programs is not a sufficient ground for condemning the requirement on its face: "A hypothetical threat is not enough," United Public Workers v. Mitchell, 330 U.S. 75, 90, 67 S.Ct. 556, 564, 91 L.Ed. 754 (1947).

Paragraph (2) of the decree is stricken as moot. The remainder of the decree is affirmed.

C. GOVERNMENT ENFORCEMENT OF THE CONTRACTUAL OBLIGATIONS

1. PROHIBITING INTERFERENCE WITH THE CONTRACT

The federal government was rather slow to seek the aid of the courts to prohibit outside interference with the contractual requirements against employment discrimination. The earliest effort of the government to prevent interference with these contractual obligations occurred in United States v. Building & Construction Trades Council of St. Louis, 271 F.Supp. 447 (E.D.Mo.1966) and United States v. Sheet Metal Workers International Association, Local 36, 280 F.Supp. 719 (E.D.Mo.1968), judgment reversed, 416 F.2d 123 (8th Cir.1969). In those cases, however, the government's theory that the federal courts had jurisdiction to restrain tortious interference with its contractual relationship with the employer subject to the executive order was rejected. It was not until United States by Clark v. Local 189, United Papermakers & Paperworkers & the Crown Zellerbach Corp., 282 F.Supp. 39 (E.D. La.1968) that the government was successful in this regard.

The case is most known for its disposition of contested seniority issues at the Court of Appeals level, 416 F.2d 980 (5th Cir.1969), cert. denied 397 U.S. 919, 90 S.Ct. 926, 25 L.Ed.2d 100 (1970). However, in the lower court action the district court held as a matter of law that it had jurisdiction and that the discrimination with respect to employment opportunities was properly subject to attack by the government pursuant not only to Title VII of the Civil Rights Act of 1964, but also under § 209 of Executive Order 11246. It concluded that that order was to be accorded the force and effect of statutory law. Additionally,

---

46. See Associated General Contractors of Mass., Inc. v. Altshuler, 490 F.2d 9, 19 (1st Cir.1973); Note, A Proposal for Reconciling Affirmative Action and Nondiscrimination Under the Contractor Antidiscrimination Program, 30 Stan.L.Rev. 803, 817–18 & n. 68 (1978); Venick & Lane, Doubling the Price of Past Discrimination: The Employer's Burden After McDonald v. Santa Fe Trail Transportation Co., 8 Loy.Uni.L.J. 789.

the court granted a permanent injunction against the company and the union and all persons and organizations in active concert or participation with them from discriminating in violation of Title VII and in violation of the obligations imposed pursuant to Executive Order 11246. (United States v. Papermakers & Paperworkers, Local 189, 301 F.Supp. 906 (E.D.La.1969), affirmed 416 F.2d 980 (5th Cir.1969), cert. denied 397 U.S. 919, 90 S.Ct. 926, 25 L.Ed.2d 100 (1970).)

It took the federal government somewhat longer to venture into federal court seeking the assistance of the court under other traditional contract remedies at common law.

2. SPECIFIC ENFORCEMENT OF THE CONTRACTUAL OBLIGATIONS OF THE EXECUTIVE ORDER

UNITED STATES v. NEW ORLEANS PUBLIC SERVICE, INC.,

United States Court of Appeals for the Fifth Circuit, 1977.
553 F.2d 459, vacated and remanded 436 U.S. 942, 98 S.Ct. 2841,
56 L.Ed.2d 783 (1978).

Before AINSWORTH and CLARK, CIRCUIT JUDGES, and HUGHES,* DISTRICT JUDGE.

AINSWORTH, CIRCUIT JUDGE:

Appellant, New Orleans Public Service, Inc. (hereinafter NOPSI), appeals from an adverse decision of the district court holding that NOPSI is a government contractor subject to Executive Order 11246,[1] and permanently enjoining NOPSI from failing and refusing to comply with the Order, as amended, and the implementing rules and regulations. Questions as to the force, coverage and enforcement of the Executive Order are involved. The principal issue today before us is whether a public utility which, under a city permit, enjoys a local monopoly in the sale of electricity and a near-monopoly in the sale of natural gas and which sells such energy to the Government in substantial amount can be required by the Government to comply with the equal opportunity obligations of Executive Order 11246, even though the utility has not agreed to be so bound. We hold that the Government can compel such a utility to follow the Order; however, we disagree with the district court as to the appropriate remedy.

Executive Order 11246 prohibits employment discrimination by government contractors. The Order was issued by President Johnson in 1965, and requires that all covered government contracts contain a nondiscrimination clause, including an agreement to take affirmative

---

* Senior District Judge of the Northern District of Texas sitting by designation.

1. 30 Fed.Reg. 12319 (1965), 3 C.F.R. 339 (1964–1965 Compilation), as amended by Exec.Order No. 11375, 32 Fed.Reg. 14303 (1967), 3 C.F.R. 406 (1969), 42 U.S. C.A. § 2000e note (1974), superseded in part (irrelevant for purposes herein) by Exec.Order No. 11478, 34 Fed.Reg. 12985 (1969), 3 C.F.R. 133 (1969 Compilation), 42 U.S.C.A. § 2000e note (1974).

action to achieve the equal opportunity goals of the Executive Order's mandate. Id. § 202.

NOPSI is a public utility which produces, distributes and sells electric power to consumers located in that part of New Orleans, Louisiana, on the east bank of the Mississippi River, and sells and distributes natural gas to consumers throughout the city. The company sells its gas and electricity pursuant to indeterminate permits,[2] like franchises, issued by the City Council of New Orleans. NOPSI is the only company with indeterminate permits to supply New Orleans with gas, and the east bank of the city with electricity. If any New Orleans consumer (including the Federal Government) on the east bank wishes to buy electric service, the consumer must purchase from NOPSI. NOPSI also provides most of the natural gas service to consumers (including the Federal Government) throughout the city, and in those cases where companies receive their gas from other sources, NOPSI has agreed to the arrangement and has built and maintained the transmission line connecting the company with the parish boundary. The federal agencies which buy electricity from NOPSI are on the east bank, and have no alternative source of electric power. NOPSI is regulated by the City Council, which in 1973 granted the company rate increases for its electric and natural gas services to customers.

A number of federal agencies and installations in New Orleans are major purchasers of electricity and natural gas from NOPSI. In 1973 NOPSI supplied such federal users with nearly $2 million worth of electric utility service, and with more than $2,680,000 worth of electric and natural gas utility services combined. There are nine federal agencies which at the present time and during the period 1965–1973 each have received over $10,000 annually in combined gas and electric services from NOPSI; some of those each have received more than $50,000 in such utility services annually. The biggest user, the Michoud Assembly Facility (hereinafter Michoud) of the National Aeronautics and Space Administration (hereinafter NASA), alone received approximately $1.4 million worth of electricity and natural gas in 1973. The agencies are billed monthly and pay for the services on a regular basis.

According to the district court opinion, NOPSI supplies the Government with utility services pursuant to various contractual arrangements. The court found that NOPSI is supplying 22 federal agencies under written agreements. Some of those contracts predated the Executive Order, but the court found that they were modified by, *inter alia*, the 1973 revised rate schedules which were approved by the City Council; were applied to the particular contract by NOPSI; and were accepted, through payment, by the agency. A few of those contracts contained nondiscrimination clauses required by earlier Executive Or-

2. Under an indeterminate permit, the company is granted the right to supply such services indefinitely, but the grantor City Council retains the right to buy the utility operation from the company, thus terminating the permit.

ders. In the case of two agencies in the group, the Government had sent NOPSI a proposed new contract, containing the nondiscrimination clause required by Executive Order 11246, but NOPSI rejected the proposed contract on the ground that the clause was unsatisfactory. Other contracts were signed in 1972 or on dates not specified by the district court opinion and were modified by the revised rate schedules in 1973.

In addition, the district court found that NOPSI is supplying six other federal agencies pursuant to contracts which were not formal, written agreements. Some of those contracts, for example, were based on letter requests from the federal agencies; another was based on an oral agreement.

Somewhat more complicated is the relationship between NOPSI and NASA's Michoud facility. Disagreement in that relationship precipitated the instant litigation. NOPSI supplied Michoud with electricity and natural gas under a written contract between the utility and the space agency which was signed in 1965 and terminated according to its own terms in June 1970. That contract contained an equal opportunity clause which was required by Executive Order 10925, the predecessor of Executive Order 11246. The contract also contained a limitation clause restricting the scope of the contract to the Michoud operations. Because of the NASA–NOPSI relationship involving utilities service at Michoud, the Government has tried in the past to review NOPSI's compliance with Executive Order 11246, but NOPSI has resisted on the ground that it was not covered by the Order. Attempts between the Government and NOPSI to negotiate a new utilities contract for Michoud broke down, with the Government unwilling to agree to a scope limitation like that in the 1965 contract, and NOPSI unwilling to agree to an equal opportunity clause without such a limitation. Nevertheless, NASA asked NOPSI to continue supplying Michoud, and NOPSI has continued to do so even though the formal contract has expired, subject to the rate schedules set out by NOPSI at the time of the termination of the written contract. The district court, after surveying the preceding facts, held that a contract existed between NASA and NOPSI.[3]

The Government's efforts to conduct a compliance review of NOPSI began in 1969, and further unsuccessful attempts were made through 1972. This action was initiated by the Government through the Justice Department in 1973 to compel NOPSI's compliance with the Executive Order. After holding that NOPSI was covered by the Order, the district court permanently enjoined the utility from failing or refusing to comply with the Order and implementing regulations. The injunc-

___

3. The facts indicating the circumstances under which NOPSI supplied energy to the various government agencies are laid out fully in the district court's opinion, and are incorporated herein except insofar as they indicate specific contractual arrangements between NOPSI and the Government. The long-standing seller-purchaser relationship indisputedly makes NOPSI a government contractor, and further contractual underpinning is unnecessary for our holding.

tion reached NOPSI's refusal to allow the Government to conduct compliance reviews of NOPSI, and authorized the parties to begin discovery. In addition, the court retained continuing jurisdiction to effectuate NOPSI's full compliance with the Executive Order.

I. THE VALIDITY AND APPLICABILITY OF THE EXECUTIVE ORDER

A. THE EXECUTIVE ORDER PROGRAM

* * *

For purposes of the instant case, the critical—and disputed—provision of the federal contract compliance program is found in the Secretary of Labor's regulations, 41 C.F.R. § 60–1, as amended by 42 Fed.Reg. 3454, et seq. (1977), and states:

> (e) *Incorporation by operation of the Order.*—By operation of the Order, the equal opportunity clause shall be considered to be a part of every contract and subcontract required by the Order and the regulations in this part to include such a clause whether or not it is physically incorporated in such contracts and whether or not the contract between the agency and the contractor is written.

§ 60–1.4(e).[5] Cf. id. § 60–1.4(d) (incorporation by reference). The "equal opportunity clause" referred to in the regulation is the nondiscrimination clause set forth in the Executive Order. "Contract" means any "government contract," and "government contract" is defined to include "any agreement or modification thereof between any contracting agency and any person for the furnishing of supplies or services." Id. § 60–1.3. The term "services," as used in the regulation, includes utility services. Id. Executive Order 11246 states in section 202 that the Order applies to every government contract entered into after the effective date unless the contract is specifically exempted under section 204. No such exemption is applicable in the instant case.[6] Therefore, assuming no problems concerning the Order's basic

5. We note that, although certain changes in the regulations have occurred as a result of the 1977 amendments, the result we reach today would be the same whether or not the new regulations were in effect. Furthermore, we would apply the current version of the regulations in any event, since this appeal involves both a program requiring present compliance by NOPSI and a continuing injunctive order of the district court.

The language of the provision cited in the accompanying text reflects a minor change. The Labor Department's comments state:

> The effect of the change in § 60–1.4(e) is to make it clear that, consistent with the intent of the Secretary and with existing case law, the equal opportunity clause is considered a part of all nonexempt contracts, including unwritten contracts. * * *

42 Fed.Reg. 3454 (1977).

6. Section 204 of the Order provides that the Secretary of Labor may grant an exemption to a specific contract because of "special circumstances," or may exempt

> facilities of a contractor which are in all respects separate and distinct from activities of the contractor related to the performance of the contract: Provided, That such an exemption will not interfere with or impede the effectuation of the purposes of this Order. * * *

No such exemption has been granted to NOPSI. Section 204(3) also provides for a class exemption, by rule or regulation, for contracts involving less than specified amounts of money. A contract which exceeds $10,000 (or a contract of a government contractor having an aggregate total of government contracts within a twelve-month period in excess of $10,000) is not

validity or its application herein, NOPSI is clearly subject to the requirements of the program.

B. NOPSI's Argument

NOPSI argues that the Executive Order and the regulations do not give the Labor Department's Office of Federal Contract Compliance—the agency which administers the Executive Order—authority to compel the company to fulfill the affirmative action obligations of the program. In support of its position, NOPSI offers three arguments which speak to the validity of the regulations as herein applied, from the point of view of both executive power and general contract law.

First, NOPSI points out that it did not seek the Government's business or any government contracts. NOPSI contends that the relevant judicial decisions on the Executive Order all involved employers that sought the Government's business, e.g., by bidding for government contracts, or were unquestionably government contractors, and that each case therefore presented an element of consent which is here lacking. Second, the company argues that it has consistently refused to accept the Order's affirmative action obligation. This argument, related to the first, assumes the necessity of NOPSI's consent in order for the company to be bound by the nondiscrimination clause. Third, NOPSI contends that it is not furnishing energy to the Government pursuant to any contract, but instead is supplying such energy pursuant to its franchises, granted by the City, which require NOPSI to provide power to all consumers who request it. Under that argument, NOPSI's status as a City franchisee precludes its having the status of a Federal Government contractor, given the fact that NOPSI has refused to accede to the contract terms required by the Government. Accordingly, NOPSI and amicus Mississippi Power & Light Company, appellant in No. 75–2590, 5 Cir., 1977, 553 F.2d 480, the companion case which we also decide today, challenge the application of the Executive Order both on the ground that it conflicts with the contractual principle of consent, and that it is action taken without authority from Congress.

C. The Program's Force and Effect

The starting point of our analysis is the well-established proposition that the Order has the force and effect of law. (Citations omitted). From that proposition flows our ultimate conclusion as to the validity of applying the Order to NOPSI in the instant case.

* * *

D. Executive and Legislative Action

* * *

Congress not only has refused to circumscribe the role of the Office of Federal Contract Compliance in combating employment discrimina-

exempt under section 204(3) from the requirements of the nondiscrimination clause. 41 C.F.R. 60–1.5, 42 Fed.Reg. 3454, 3459 (1977). Therefore, NOPSI is a nonexempt contractor. The effective date of the Order causes no problem since the case involves a contractual relationship which, in particular instances, has been renewed or modified by the parties since such effective date. See discussion infra.

tion, but has indicated a concern for the efficacy of such efforts and an intent that they would continue. The regulation in controversy is an integral part of a long-standing program which Congress has recognized and approved. We have no difficulty, therefore, in finding congressional authorization for the provision.[8] It follows that the application of the Order to NOPSI is also authorized, for such action requires no extension of the regulation's coverage. The regulation incorporating by operation of the Order the nondiscrimination clause into every govern-

---

8. NOPSI argues that application of the Executive Order herein contravenes the principle in Youngstown Sheet & Tube Co. v. Sawyer, 343 U.S. 579, 72 S.Ct. 863, 96 L.Ed. 1153 (1952), in which the Supreme Court held that President Truman's seizure of the steel mills was unlawful. In *Youngstown*, however, Congress had refused to authorize governmental seizure of property as was therein attempted. Therefore, the President had acted in the face of that congressional decision and in the absence of any other power authorizing his action. See 343 U.S. at 585–89, 72 S.Ct. at 866–67. The instant case is thus distinguishable, since the Executive acted here pursuant to congressional authorization. The application of the Order today before us falls within the first category of executive power—that of maximum power—which Justice Jackson identified in his concurring opinion in *Youngstown*, 343 U.S. at 635–37, 72 S.Ct. at 870–71; see Contractors Ass'n, supra, 442 F.2d at 168–71. Furthermore, the analogy to a seizure is manifestly imprecise.

At oral argument, NOPSI also cited NAACP v. FPC, 425 U.S. 662, 96 S.Ct. 1806, 48 L.Ed.2d 284 (1976), in which the Supreme Court held that the Federal Power Commission did not have authority under the Federal Power Act and the Natural Gas Act to issue a rule prohibiting discriminatory employment practices by the agency's regulatees. However, *FPC* does not aid appellant's position. The opinion does not hold that an agency cannot issue regulations concerning affirmative action, assuming the agency has a statutory basis for doing so, nor does it suggest that issuance of such regulations is prohibited unless Congress has authorized the agency to promulgate them. Furthermore, the Court did hold that the FPC indirectly could regulate discriminatory employment practices by its regulatees, to the extent that such practices demonstrably affected a regulatee company's labor costs. Id., 425 U.S. at 666–670, 96 S.Ct. at 1810–11. Therefore, under *FPC*, a government agency can regulate discriminatory employment practices to the extent that such discrimination

is related directly to the agency's functions. That principle should be read in light of *Rosetti Contracting* and *Northeast Constr.*, which involve the Executive Order herein and require only a loose relationship between the noneconomic objective, *i.e.*, regulating employment discrimination, and the procurement function. *Rosetti Contracting*, supra, 508 F.2d at 1045 n. 18; *Northeast Constr.*, supra, 485 F.2d at 760–61. We also note Mississippi Power & Light's citation of Hampton v. Mow Sun Wong, 426 U.S. 88, 96 S.Ct. 1895, 48 L.Ed. 2d 495 (1976), apparently to rebut the proposition that Congress ratifies executive orders by subsequently recognizing their existence and making reference to them. However, to the extent that the Supreme Court addressed this issue in *Mow Sun Wong*, the opinion turned on the particular facts in controversy. That case involved, *inter alia*, the question whether acquiescence by the Executive and Congress in a Civil Service Commission policy imposing a citizenship requirement on federal employees was sufficient to give the Commission rule the same support as an express statutory or presidential command. The Court held that neither appropriations acts nor executive orders in which Congress and the President, respectively, had considered the policy and spoken to it in some fashion could fairly be read as evidencing either approval or disapproval of the policy by either branch. Id. 426 U.S. at 104–114, 96 S.Ct. at 1906–10. The opinion makes clear, though, that the legislative history and executive orders there in dispute could arguably be taken either way, i.e., they might be read as evidencing either disapproval or approval, and it was that ambiguity which gave rise to the Court's statement. Thus, *Mow Sun Wong* is clearly distinguishable from the case at bar. The legislative history behind the program today before us lacks such ambiguity as dictated the *Mow Sun Wong* result. Furthermore, the cited case lacked the clear directive from the Executive—by Executive Order—which is the very source of the program we confront and uphold herein.

ment contract would be a dead letter if the Government could not apply it to a government contractor like NOPSI, merely because the company refused to consent.

Although no circuit has confronted the precise legal issue today before us, we find the *Contractors Ass'n* case to be a very persuasive precedent. There the Third Circuit specifically considered the validity of the Philadelphia Plan, relating to minority hiring in federally-assisted construction projects, which was promulgated pursuant to Executive Order 11246. The court upheld the Plan, on the ground that it was within the implied authority of the President. Insofar as the Philadelphia Plan was instituted to implement the mandate of the Executive Order in a particular geographic area and industry, the court's holding clearly flowed from a view that the Executive Order program itself was valid, at least with respect to federally-assisted construction contracts. Moreover, in language on all fours, the Third Circuit specifically stated that Executive imposition of nondiscrimination contract provisions (including an affirmative action clause) in the Government procurement area is action pursuant to the express or implied authorization of Congress. 442 F.2d at 170.

In response to the argument that a decision for the Government in this case would go beyond the Third Circuit's holding in *Contractors Ass'n*, we believe that our decision today fits within that precedent and, in fact, approves a more confined power than did the *Contractors Ass'n* court. We here impose the nondiscrimination obligation on a company which, as a public utility, holds City-granted franchises and, pursuant thereto, (1) enjoys special economic advantages, including a monopoly, and (2) sells directly to the Government. To so apply the provision is far easier, in our judgment, than to apply it, as in *Contractors Ass'n*, to a mere bidder for federally-assisted construction project contracts. The ease of application is a function of both the Government's legal power and the utility's economic power in their direct contractual relationship.

E. CONTRACT LAW

The second aspect of NOPSI's attack on the Executive Order as herein applied focuses on contract law. The company contends that its lack of consent to be bound by the nondiscrimination clause distinguishes the prior cases involving the validity of the Order. Whatever, if any, authorization exists for the program is vitiated when, as here, it is imposed on a nonconsenting public utility, the company argues, because the contractual consent principle is violated. We disagree.

We find that the absence of NOPSI's consent to the Executive Order is not determinative, and does not render the prior caselaw distinguishable. Furthermore, we reject the company's contention that NOPSI is not a government contractor.

Government contracts are different from contracts between ordinary parties. See M. Steinthal & Co. v. Seamans, 1971, 147 U.S.App.D.C. 221, 455 F.2d 1289, 1304. See also Vacketta & Wheeler, A Government Contractor's Right to Abandon Performance, 65 Geo.L.J. 27 (1976). The Government has the unrestricted power to determine those with whom it will deal, and to fix the terms and conditions upon which it will make needed purchases. Perkins v. Lukens Steel Co., 310 U.S. 113, 127, 60 S.Ct. 869, 876, 84 L.Ed. 1108 (1940); Southern Ill. Bldrs. Ass'n v. Ogilvie, S.D.Ill., 1971, 327 F.Supp. 1154, aff'd, 471 F.2d 680 (7 Cir., 1972); cf. King v. Smith, 392 U.S. 309, 88 S.Ct. 2128, 20 L.Ed.2d 1118 (1968); *Vacketta & Wheeler,* supra. Agreement to such conditions is unnecessary: where regulations apply and require the inclusion of a contract clause in every contract, the clause is incorporated into the contract, even if it has not been expressly included in a written contract or agreed to by the parties. *M. Steinthal,* supra, at 1304; J.W. Bateson Co. v. United States, 1963, 162 Ct.Cl. 566, 569; *G.L. Christian,* supra, 312 F.2d at 424; see Russell Motor Car Co. v. United States, 261 U.S. 514, 43 S.Ct. 428, 67 L.Ed. 778 (1923). See also De Laval Steam Turbine Co. v. United States, 284 U.S. 61, 52 S.Ct. 78, 76 L.Ed. 168 (1931); College Point Boat Corp. v. United States, 267 U.S. 12, 45 S.Ct. 199, 69 L.Ed. 490 (1925).[9]

A contractual relationship obviously exists between NOPSI and the Government, notwithstanding the company's attempt to disclaim government-contractor status. This contractual relationship exists by virtue of the fact that the company sells millions of dollars worth of utility services to various agencies of the Federal Government, and has done so for many years. The district court's extensive factual findings as to particular contracts aids us in this determination; however, we would reach it even in the absence of any oral or written agreements to particular terms, because the relationship so clearly reflects a contract.

Furthermore, we cannot understand how NOPSI seriously can deny status as a government contractor for the reason that it is supplying utility services to the Government pursuant to local franchises which require the company to furnish such energy to all consumers who request it. That the company services customers under local franchises does not negate the obvious fact that NOPSI renders such services to individual customers pursuant to contracts, whether written or parol, and whether explicit or implicit in the parties' course of dealing.

NOPSI's status as a public utility, operating under local franchises granted by the City of New Orleans, and providing services to the

---

9. A contract between the Government and one of its contractors need not be in writing in order to be enforceable. See, e.g., Patten, Government Contracts—Are They Enforceable If Not in Writing?, 7 Pub. Contract L.J. 232 (1975). Similarly, the applicability of the Executive Order to NOPSI does not depend upon the existence of a formal written contract. We do not say today that no such contract exists between NOPSI and the Government, since resolution of that question is unnecessary to our holding.

United States, renders the utility's express consent unnecessary in light of the Executive Order. Acceptance of the benefits of the local franchises subjected NOPSI to the obligations attached thereto. Cf. Almeida-Sanchez v. United States, 413 U.S. 266, 271, 93 S.Ct. 2535, 2538, 37 L.Ed.2d 596 (1973). When NOPSI undertook to satisfy those obligations by selling energy to the Government, the company did so according to the terms imposed by the Government.[10]

NOPSI implies, in addition, that because of its public-utility status, imposition of the Executive Order's requirements would be unfair. The unfairness, the company suggests, stems from NOPSI's lack of choice as to whether to accept the Government's business. However, the fact that NOPSI is a public utility militates strongly in *favor* of allowing the Government to impose the obligations of the Executive Order on the company. NOPSI's franchises give it a local monopoly in the sale of electricity and a near-monopoly in the sale of natural gas. A monopolistic government supplier, unlike a seller in an ordinary market, has the economic power to resist the Executive Order. In the situation under consideration, the Government needs to buy electric energy in the New Orleans area. If NOPSI were allowed to prevail in its contentions, the Government would have to either acquiesce or else go without necessary services. Obviously, a local utility cannot force such a dilemma upon the Government. Otherwise, a valid and important nationwide federal program, set in place by the President over a third of a century ago, continued by every one of his successors, approved by Congress and applicable to all government contractors, could be nullified by any seller with a monopoly in a service, supply or property needed by the Government, just by virtue of the seller's economic position. Here, NOPSI's monopoly exists only because of local legislative action. The supremacy clause of the Constitution obviously cannot countenance such a result. We hold, therefore, that the Government can compel NOPSI to comply with the equal opportunity obligations of Executive Order 11246, even though the company has not expressly consented to be bound by that Order.

II. NOPSI'S FOURTH AMENDMENT CONTENTIONS

NOPSI next contends that the Executive Order and implementing regulations violate the fourth amendment when applied to a public utility which does not seek to do business with the Government and has not consented to the provisions of the Order. This argument parallels the company's central contention in the case, and is similarly without merit.

* * *

10. We are not inferring here any implied or constructive agreement by NOPSI to the terms of the Executive Order. Our holding is dictated by (1) the sale by the company of energy to the Government, *and* (2) the fact that such sale of services was made by a company which, under City franchises, enjoyed a local monopoly in such services needed by the Government. The presence of both those elements triggered the regulation, 41 C.F.R. § 60–1.4(e), and thus, the application of the program's obligations by operation of the Order.

We note finally that, under the inspection procedure contemplated by the Executive Order program, "the possibilities of abuse and the threat to privacy are not of impressive dimensions," see *Biswell*, supra, 406 U.S. at 317, 92 S.Ct. at 1597, and accordingly, we sustain the program against attack on fourth amendment grounds.[12]

III. The District Court's Injunctive Order

We turn finally to NOPSI's disagreement with the district court's injunctive order. The company argues that the court lacked jurisdiction to issue that order, under which the court retained jurisdiction over this action for the purpose of enforcing the substantive provisions of the Executive Order.

We hold that, the district court having found NOPSI to be covered by the Executive Order, the task of obtaining NOPSI's compliance with the program should be left to the Government's own administrative compliance processes. Accordingly, we modify that part of the district court's opinion which retained jurisdiction over this suit and which dictated a mandate of injunction clearly contemplating substantive enforcement of the Executive Order. Our decision is based on equitable considerations, and should not be read as holding that the district court lacked jurisdiction in any respect for its ruling. Resolution of NOPSI's objections to the court's injunctive order is therefore unnecessary to our holding; however, we proceed to dismiss all of the company's present objections in order that they may not be interposed again as obstacles to enforcement of the program herein.

NOPSI makes two major arguments in this regard. The first is that the Government has failed to follow the procedural requirements of the Executive Order and implementing regulations. NOPSI alleges

12. Mississippi Power & Light argues that the Executive Order's provision for Government access to a contractor's books and records is unconstitutional because: (1) the provision is without statutory authorization, and (2) it does not contain a procedure for judicial review. The argument about lack of statutory authorization is without merit in light of the pattern of congressional approval for the Executive Order program which we found in section I of this opinion. The argument about lack of judicial review is also without merit since, in the setting of the instant controversy, it is purely hypothetical. Here there has been no attempt to obtain access by force to the company's records without judicial approval; in fact, there has been ample judicial review in these proceedings of the Government's attempt to conduct a compliance review of NOPSI.

Since oral argument, Mississippi Power & Light has called our attention to Brennan v. Gibson's Products, Inc., E.D.Tex., 1976, 407 F.Supp. 154, appeal docketed, No. 76–

1526 (5 Cir. Feb. 27, 1976), a case in which a three-judge court held that an attempt by Department of Labor officials to conduct a warrantless inspection of a business, pursuant to the Occupational Safety and Health Act of 1970, violated the fourth amendment. However, *Gibson's Products* does not deter us from the conclusion we have reached. As the three-judge court pointed out, the company involved there was not licensed and had no history of close regulation, and the statutory provisions which appeared to authorize the search were not limited to such businesses, but instead embraced "the whole spectrum of unrelated and disparate activities which compose private enterprise in the United States." Id., 407 F.Supp. at 161–62. Furthermore, there was no reason to believe that the thing sought to be controlled by the regulatory system before the court existed in the area to be searched. Id. at 162. Therefore, *Gibson's Products* is manifestly distinguishable from both the instant case and those cases upon which we have relied.

that the Government was required to proceed by conciliation and persuasion, but instead chose to pursue litigation in its compliance strategy. In addition, NOPSI contends that the Government has failed to afford the company a hearing mandated under the program. In support of these assertions, NOPSI relies on a number of regulatory provisions. We need not respond to each assertion specifically, in view of the fact that the Government's attempts to conduct a voluntary compliance review of NOPSI date back to 1969.

The regulations now in effect [13] provide for the institution of administrative *or* judicial enforcement proceedings in response to violations of the Executive Order. Violations may be found, based upon, *inter alia,*

> (iv) a contractor's refusal to submit an affirmative action program; (v) a contractor's refusal to allow an on-site compliance review to be conducted; (vi) a contractor's refusal to supply records or other information as required by these regulations * * * or (vii) any substantial or material violation or the threat of [such] a * * * violation of the contractual provisions of the Order, or of the rules or regulations issued pursuant thereto.

41 C.F.R. § 60–1.26(a)(1). The district court found such a violation. The regulations further provide that whenever the Director of the Office of Federal Contract Compliance has reason to believe that there exists the threat or fact of violation of the Order or regulations, the Director

> may institute administrative enforcement proceedings * * * *or* refer the matter to the Department of Justice to enforce the contractual provisions of the Order, to seek injunctive relief * * * and to seek such additional relief, including back pay, as may be appropriate. *There are no procedural prerequisites to a referral to the Department of Justice* by the Director, and *such referrals may be accomplished without proceeding through the conciliation procedures* in this chapter, *and a referral may be made at any stage in the procedures* under this chapter.

Id. § 60–1.26(a)(2) (emphasis added).

The preceding regulation plainly rebuts NOPSI's first contention.[14] And the regulation also refutes NOPSI's second major assertion, which is that the Justice Department cannot bring judicial proceedings to enforce the provisions of the Executive Order until the OFCC or the compliance agency (here the General Services Administration) has first

---

13. See note 5 supra.

14. As to NOPSI's argument that the Government was required to proceed by conciliation and persuasion, we think that the facts described at the outset of our opinion indicate that such efforts took place. In addition, we find no conflict between 41 C.F.R. § 60–1.26(a)(2) and section 209(b) of the Executive Order. While section 209(b) directs the contracting agency to make reasonable efforts to achieve compliance by conciliation and persuasion, those efforts are to be made pursuant to the regulations issued by the Secretary of Labor. Id. Thus, section 60–1.26(a)(2) qualifies the Government's responsibilities under section 209(b) of the Order, rather than vice versa, and the two provisions can be read consistently.

exhausted the administrative procedures of the program. Two more observations are in order as to the exhaustion argument. First, the cases cited by NOPSI in support of that contention involve private actions and are, therefore, inapposite to the situation where the Government itself has decided to pursue judicial litigation in enforcing Executive Order 11246.[15] Second, while we recognize that, as NOPSI argues, substantial arguments can be mustered for application of the exhaustion doctrine, we nevertheless have no reason to read an exhaustion requirement into a program which clearly and deliberately provides judicial enforcement as an alternative to administrative enforcement, and which explicitly rejects procedural prerequisites to judicial enforcement.

Despite our conclusion that the district court had both the jurisdiction and the power to direct by injunctive order NOPSI's compliance, we conclude that the enforcement function in this case would be better carried out administratively by the compliance agencies. This decision is reached in the exercise of our equitable discretion, for "the manner, means and method for resolving" this dispute must be devised under "inherent equitable principles." R.L. Johnson v. Goodyear Tire & Rubber Co., 5 Cir., 1974, 491 F.2d 1364, 1367.[16] In light of our holding that NOPSI is covered by the Executive Order and has violated it, our primary mission at this point, of course, is to render such relief as is necessary and appropriate to effectuate the mandate of the Executive Order as fully and expeditiously as possible. However, the relief imposed should not "run against the grain of fundamental fairness which should hopefully be the outcome of any equitable decree." Id. at 1379. In the particular setting of this case, where NOPSI has never agreed to be bound by the Order, we believe that fundamental fairness requires that the Government, armed this time with this court's opinion, now obtain the company's voluntary compliance before calling for the support of our injunctive powers.

Other equitable factors support this result. The basic approach of the Executive Order program, as implemented, is enforcement by Executive agencies, in particular the Department of Labor, even though the Order itself provides the judicial enforcement alternative in section 209(a)(2). The Executive has expertise, which this court lacks, in the administration of the program, and that expertise can profitably be brought to bear on the problem at bar. Further, we see no reason to burden our scarce judicial resources with the task of supervising the

15. For example, to the extent that the exhaustion argument is rooted in notions of deference to the administrative process and the administrative agency, the argument has no bearing in the instant context.

16. *Johnson* is one of the cases cited by the Government for the proposition that the district court's retention of jurisdiction and injunctive order were justified. While those cases indicate that the district court had the authority to take the action which it took—a conclusion we do not dispute—they in no way suggest that the district court's injunctive order was required in the circumstances before us. Since we have concluded that our remedial tack will best effectuate the Executive Order, discussion of those cases is unnecessary.

enforcement of the federal contract compliance program, unless such judicial enforcement becomes necessary.

Our decision today is not an invitation to further delay by NOPSI in complying with the Executive Order. Such delay would be intolerable. In its brief, NOPSI states:

> If a court of final appellant (sic) resort upholds the District Court determination that NOPSI is a government contractor notwithstanding its refusal to consent to the contractual equal opportunity provisions of Executive Order 11246, the General Services Administration and OFCC should then be afforded the opportunity to work with NOPSI in developing an appropriate affirmative action program, if indeed one is found necessary . . . .

Brief for Appellant at 46–47.[17] That statement underlies the remedial approach which we today require. We assume, based on the quoted passage, NOPSI's good faith in complying with the Order, given our holding that the company is covered by it.

To restate our decision, then, the appropriate government compliance agency—whether OFCC or GSA—may proceed by administrative action to obtain NOPSI's compliance with the Executive Order. Though we are removing the injunctive mandate of the district court, our decision contemplates good faith negotiations between the parties, and certain issues decided herein are precluded from further negotiation. The company cannot any longer dispute its coverage under the Executive Order, nor can the company attempt to nullify the effect of the Order's application by demanding limitation-of-scope language in any contract or proposed affirmative action program that would restrict the impact of the Order. Moreover, NOPSI has no valid fourth amendment objections to the Government's demands for access either to the company's facilities or to the company's books and records, nor can NOPSI further delay or resist compliance by insisting on merely technical or unnecessary procedural niceties.

The Government may proceed at once in enforcing the Executive Order by administrative action. The parties are advised that, having fashioned our relief on the assumption of NOPSI's good faith in complying with our decision herein, this court will look with disfavor on any future attempts to delay compliance.

Modified and Affirmed.

CLARK, CIRCUIT JUDGE, DISSENTING:

The decisive question in both this case and United States v. Mississippi Power & Light Co., 553 F.2d 480 (5th Cir.1977), which we also decide today, is whether the federal government may impose a substantial contract obligation on a public utility simply because that utility supplies energy to federal installations as required by state law

---

17. NOPSI's statement suggests the possibility that an affirmative action program might not be found necessary. We read the regulations, however, to require a written affirmative action program. See 41 C.F.R. § 60–1.40(a).

and the terms of its state or municipal franchise. The majority answers in the affirmative. I respectfully disagree.

I.

In order to determine whether New Orleans Public Service, Inc. [NOPSI], or Mississippi Power & Light Co. [MP & L] must comply with a comprehensive equal opportunity clause despite their explicit refusals to subject themselves to it, three issues must be resolved. First, was the issuance of the Executive Order which requires the clause be included in every federal contract a valid exercise of Presidential power? Second, what relation must exist between a person and the federal government before that person is subject to the dictates of the equal opportunity clause by operation of the Executive Order? And third, does the requisite relation exist between the federal government and either NOPSI or MP & L? Since the resolution of the second and third issues furnishes a sufficient ground for the decision of this case, I do not reach the constitutional puzzles presented by the first.[1]

* * *

Although the Executive Order does not explicitly define the term "government contract," there is nothing in its language which suggests that anything less than a contractual relation—as those words are commonly understood in the law—between a person and the federal government was intended to suffice for coverage. The word "contract" is an unambiguous legal term of art connoting an enforceable promise or set of promises between mutually consenting parties. Turning to the "executive history" of the Order or to the Secretary's implementing regulations to vary this unambiguous meaning would be unjustifiable. "[W]here the words are plain there is no room for construction." Osaka Shoshen Kaisha Line v. United States, 300 U.S. 98, 101, 57 S.Ct. 356, 357, 81 L.Ed. 532 (1937), quoted in, Hodgson v. Mauldin, 344 F.Supp. 302, 307 (N.D.Ala.1972), aff'd, 478 F.2d 702 (5th Cir.1973); Souder v. Brennan, 367 F.Supp. 808, 812 (D.D.C.1973). Although these cases involved the interpretation of a statute rather than an executive order, there is no reason why the cannons of construction should not be the same.

The regulations promulgated by the Secretary pursuant to his authority to issue such rules as he deems necessary to accomplish the purposes of the Executive Order,[6] however, might be read as taking a broader view of the meaning of the word "contract" as it is used in the Executive Order. 41 C.F.R. § 60–1.3 (1976), as amended, 42 Fed.Reg. 3454, 3458 (1977), provides:

1. For the purposes of this dissent, I make two assumptions. The first is that the Executive Order is valid and possesses the force and effect of law. The second is that the Secretary of Labor did not exceed the rulemaking authority granted him by the Executive Order when he issued 41 C.F.R. § 60–1.4(e) (1976), as amended, 42 Fed.Reg. 3454, 3459 (1977), which incorporates the equal opportunity clause into all non-exempt government contracts by operation of the Executive Order.

6. 3 C.F.R. 169, § 201 (1974).

"Government Contract" means any agreement or modification thereof between any contracting agency and any person for the furnishing of supplies or services or for the use of real or personal property, including lease arrangements. The term "services," as used in this section includes, but is not limited to the following services:

Utility * * *

"Modification" means any alteration in the terms and conditions of a contract, including supplemental agreements, amendments, and extensions.

Since regulations issued pursuant to a valid executive order stand on no better footing than regulations issued pursuant to a statute, it follows that the Secretary's regulations possess the force and effect of law only if they are "(a) within the granted power, (b) issued pursuant to proper procedure, and (c) reasonable." 1 K. Davis, Administrative Law Treatise § 5.03, p. 299 (1958) & § 29.01–1, p. 654 (Supp.1976). The Executive Order requires the presence of the equal opportunity clause only in contracts. If the term "agreement" used in Section 60–1.3 was intended to be more inclusive it would be void since it would exceed the scope of the Secretary's rulemaking authority. As the Supreme Court recently stated:

> The rulemaking power granted to an administrative agency charged with the administration of a federal statute is not the power to make law. Rather, it is 'the power to adopt regulations to carry into effect the will of Congress as expressed by the statute."

Ernst & Ernst v. Hochfelder, 425 U.S. 185, 213, 96 S.Ct. 1375, 1391, 47 L.Ed.2d 668, 688 (1976), quoting Manhattan General Equipment Co. v. Commissioner of Internal Revenue, 297 U.S. 129, 134, 56 S.Ct. 397, 399, 80 L.Ed. 528, 531 (1936). The same principle is applicable here.

Moreover, even if the Executive Order could be read to cover parties to unenforceable agreements or non-contracts, the federal government's position would not be measurably advanced. The Executive Order merely requires contracting agencies to include the equal opportunity clause in their bid lettings and contracts. The supplementary regulation, Section 60–1.4(e), provides only that the clause is in the contract whether or not the agency remembered to put it there. Therefore, it is necessary that an enforceable contract exist between a person and the government if there is to be a basis for the enforcement of the clause. If the clause were placed in a void agreement, it would fail with the rest.

NOPSI and MP & L are public utility companies. Although their arrangements with their respective regulatory authorities are not identical in form,[7] the effect is the same. Because they hold franchises granted by a state or a city, are engaged in an enterprise affected with

---

7. NOPSI supplies electricity and natural gas to residents of New Orleans pursuant to an indeterminate permit issued by the New Orleans City Council in 1922. MP & L operates under a franchise granted to it by the Mississippi Public Service Commission in 1956.

the public interest, and hold themselves out as being willing to serve all members of the public, both NOPSI and MP & L have a duty to provide the types of energy they distribute to anyone within their certificated area who requests it and complies with reasonable conditions of service. Morehouse Natural Gas Co. v. Louisiana Public Service Commission, 242 La. 985, 999–1000, 140 So.2d 646, 651 (1962); Capital Electric Power Association v. Mississippi Power & Light Co., 218 So.2d 707, 713 (Miss. 1968). In exchange, they receive the right, to some extent exclusively, to supply utility service to customers within their certificated area at a price set by their regulatory authority, and they are guaranteed a reasonable rate of return on their investment.

Since the majority has described the history of NOPSI's interaction with the federal government, only brief recap is necessary here. NOPSI has furnished federal installations with utility service for more than 50 years. In United States v. New Orleans Public Service, Inc., 8 Fair Empl.Prac.Cas. 1089, 8 Empl.Prac.Dec. 9795 (E.D.La.1974), the court found that NOPSI currently supplied 22 federal facilities with electricity, natural gas, or both. In some instances there is a written agreement between NOPSI and the federal government concerning essential terms, such as the applicable rate and volume of service demanded, while in others the understanding is unwritten. Although most of these arrangements pre-date the Executive Order, a few were entered into after it became effective. The price term of every agreement was changed as recently as 1973, when the New Orleans City Council revised NOPSI's rate schedule, and on at least one occasion since the issuance of the Order the government requested and received additional service at one of its locations. Recently, when NASA insisted that its proposed written agreement with NOPSI contain the equal opportunity clause NOPSI refused to capitulate. Instead, NOPSI informed NASA it would continue to supply NASA's energy requirements at the regulated price as both its franchise and Louisiana law require, but expressly refused to subject itself to the equal opportunity clause.[8]

Government contracts do differ from contracts between private parties in some respects, see J. Paul, United States Government-Contracts and Subcontracts 69–75 (1964), but no such difference affects the result here. Although contracts of the United States are governed by federal law, United States v. Seckinger, 397 U.S. 203, 210, 90 S.Ct. 880, 884, 25 L.Ed.2d 224, 232 (1970), "[i]t is customary, where Congress has not adopted a different standard, to apply to the construction of government contracts the principles of general contract law." Priebe & Sons, Inc. v. United States, 332 U.S. 407, 410–412, 68 S.Ct. 123, 125–26, 92 L.Ed. 32, 37–38 (1947), quoted in, Security Life & Accident Insurance

8. Since MP & L's interaction with the federal government contains the same essential elements—written and unwritten arrangements for service consummated before and after the issuance of the Order, changes in the rate applicable to the government since 1965, and an express refusal to be bound by the equal opportunity clause—MP & L stands in the same posture as NOPSI, and I shall not needlessly prolong this dissent by recounting its course of dealing in detail.

Co. v. United States, 357 F.2d 145, 148 (5th Cir.1966). One of the most fundamental of those principles is that to be enforceable, a contract must be supported by valid consideration. Estate of Bogley v. United States, 514 F.2d 1027, 1033, Ct.Cl. (1976); 1 S. Williston, Contracts § 99, p. 367 (3d ed. 1957); 1A A. Corbin, Contracts § 114, p. 498 (1963). There is no reason why this rule should not apply to contracts with the federal government; at least one court has assumed that it does. See United States v. Marchetti, 466 F.2d 1309, 1317 n. 6 (4th Cir.), cert. denied, 409 U.S. 1063, 93 S.Ct. 553, 34 L.Ed.2d 516 (1972).

A promise to perform a service which one is under a pre-existing legal obligation to perform is not valid consideration for a return promise. United States v. Bridgeman, 173 U.S.App.D.C. 150, 523 F.2d 1099, 1110 (1975), cert. denied, 425 U.S. 961, 96 S.Ct. 1744, 48 L.Ed.2d 206 (1976); 1 S. Williston, supra, § 132, p. 557; 1A A. Corbin, supra, § 171, p. 105. Nor is it merely the return promise that is unenforceable. Because the return promise is unenforceable, there is no mutuality of obligation and therefore no contract is ever formed. Of course, in the event that the party subject to the pre-existing obligation does more than his duty requires, he creates consideration sufficient to support the return promise. 1 S. Williston, supra, § 132, pp. 558–59; 1A A. Corbin, supra, § 192, p. 180.

The application of these principles to the facts of this case is straightforward. Since both NOPSI and MP & L have a pre-existing legal obligation to supply utility service to the federal installations within their certificated area at the applicable rate irrespective of their agreement to do so, their arrangements with the federal government were instances of performance of their duty to serve customers, not contracts with the federal government. Moreover, an examination of the record reveals that none of the agreements between the utilities and the federal government purported to bind either utility to treat the government any differently from the way state law obliged it to treat other customers of equal size. Therefore, neither utility is a government contractor within the meaning of the Executive Order, and neither has an enforceable obligation to comply with the equal opportunity clause.

The majority takes the position that by accepting their franchises, NOPSI and MP & L assumed an obligation to furnish the federal government with energy on whatever terms it might wish to impose, including a requirement that they comply with the provisions of the equal opportunity clause. But there is nothing in the record which supports the notion that either the utilities or their respective regulatory authorities were aware that NOPSI and MP & L were undertaking such an obligation at the time the franchise agreements were executed. And since the franchises were agreements with a state or city rather than the federal government, no such obligation can be implied as a matter of law under Section 60–1.4(e) of the regulations. In addition, both utilities accepted their franchises long before Executive Order

11246 was issued. To impose the burden of complying with the equal opportunity clause on them because of actions pre-dating the Order would be inconsistent with Sections 202 & 405 which indicate that the order is triggered only by actions taken after October 24, 1965.

The majority also suggests that because NOPSI and MP & L are public utilities it is justifiable to saddle them with the recordkeeping, expense, and other burdens that compliance with the equal opportunity clause entails. It contends that to permit them to use their position as the sole sources of energy within their certificated areas to force the federal government to choose between bargaining over the inclusion of the clause and doing without energy, would be inconsistent with the Supremacy Clause.[9] The premise of this argument is that the utilities' economic leverage is the result of state action, because purely private action cannot violate the Supremacy Clause. This premise is not supported by the record.

* * *

II.

Had the court adopted the position of this dissent, the effectiveness of the Executive Order as a tool for eliminating discrimination in employment would not have been destroyed. The vast majority of those supplying goods and services to the federal government are not under a pre-existing legal obligation to do so but rather are contractors within the meaning of the Order. Nothing said here would affect the applicability of the provisions of the equal opportunity clause to them. Nor would such a decision leave public utilities at liberty to treat their employees as they pleased. They are subject to a plethora of state and federal measures designed to eliminate discriminatory employment practices.

I do not dissent to defend discriminatory employment practices. But when the government has chosen to attack them through the mechanism of inserting a nondiscrimination clause in its contracts rather than by enacting a statute, there are limits to what it can accomplish. Those limits have been exceeded here. The majority makes a mistake when it allows the government to forge ahead to a desirable end by means that stand the law of contracts on its head.

Notes

1. *NOPSI*, along with its companion case United States v. Mississippi Power & Light, 553 F.2d 480 (5th Cir.1977) were both vacated and remanded for reconsideration in light of Marshall v. Barlow's Inc., 436 U.S. 307, 98 S.Ct. 1816, 56 L.Ed.2d 305 (1978), an occupational health and safety case in which the Court concluded that warrantless searches violate the Fifth Amendment. The district court at 480 F.Supp. 705 (E.D.La.1979) concluded that *Barlows* did not render the Executive Order 11246 as amended or the rules and regulations issued thereunder invalid and reaffirmed its earlier

9. U.S. Const., Art. VI, cl. 2.

decision. On review the Fifth Circuit sustained the lower court, United States v. Mississippi Power & Light Co., 638 F.2d 899 (5th Cir.1981), but remanded the case yet again to determine whether the searches were based on specific evidence of existing violations and to determine whether there was a showing that reasonable or legislative standards were satisfied for conducting the investigations with respect to a particular establishment, or on assuring that the search was pursuant to an administrative plan containing specific neutral criteria. If the court found the standards set forth by the Fifth Circuit satisfied reasonableness standards under the Fourth Amendment, the injunctions against the utilities should issue. The Supreme Court declined to review this determination of the court of appeals. 454 U.S. 892, 102 S.Ct. 387, 70 L.Ed.2d 206 (1981).

For a discussion of problems raised by these cases see "Imposition of Affirmative Action Obligations on Non-Consenting Government Contractors," 91 Harv.L.Rev. 506 (1977).

The final chapter in the saga of United States v. NOPSI ended with a determination that existing neutral criteria for selecting the utilities for compliance reviews could not be established to have existed at the time the original investigation had been undertaken.

In United States v. New Orleans Public Service Inc., 723 F.2d 422 (5th Cir.1984) the court of appeals determined that the selection of the government contractor in 1971 for review of its compliance with Executive Order 11246 violated the standards which it had set forth where there was no evidence that the selection was based on neutral criteria. This was so despite the contention that the regulation required compliance review before government contracts of more than $1,000,000 could be awarded. On June 14, 1984, in United States v. NOPSI, 34 FEP Cases 1801, the Fifth Circuit denied a rehearing on the case concluding that Donovan v. Lone Steer Inc., 464 U.S. 408, 104 S.Ct. 769, 78 L.Ed.2d 567 (1984), involving an administrative subpoena duces tecum, did not alter the application of the *Barlows* standard which the Fifth Circuit had used.

2. In United States v. Duquesne Light Co., 423 F.Supp. 507 (W.D.Pa. 1976), the court sustained the government's claim that under the executive order it was entitled to seek back pay for victims of racial or sexual discrimination practiced by government contractors. The court reasoned that the government has the discretion to invoke equitable judicial powers and that absent a congressional limitation on those powers, it may seek any remedy to effectuate the purposes of the executive order, including back pay. Cited with approval in United States v. Lee Way Motor Freight Inc., 625 F.2d 918 (10th Cir.1979).

D.   CHALLENGES TO GOVERNMENTAL ACTION

Unlike the difficulties that affected class members have had in obtaining judicial oversight of the government's executive order program, contractors have usually been able to obtain the assistance of the court, at times in pre-enforcement challenges to agency action. Crown Zellerbach Corp. v. Wirtz, 281 F.Supp. 337 (D.D.C.1968); see also e.g.

Copper Plumbing & Heating Co. v. Campbell, 290 F.2d 368 (D.C.Cir. 1961); Gonzalez v. Freeman, 334 F.2d 570 (D.C.Cir.1964); Gantt & Panzer, "The Government Blacklist: Debarment and Suspension of Bidders on Government Contracts," 25 George Washington L.Rev. 175 (1976); Note, "The Blacklisted Contractor and the Question of Standing to Sue," 56 N.W.Univ.L.Rev. 811 (1962).

The theory underlying the plaintiffs' case in Crown Zellerbach v. Wirtz was that the government was about to engage in conduct which was unauthorized under the executive order. Challenges to *ultra vires* acts of administrative agencies are generally appropriate in the pre-enforcement stage. However, frequently in early phases of a program parties attempt to use the courts to challenge the constitutionality or legality of the program itself without first going through the administrative process. Court challenges to the executive order program did not start until the late 1960's and there is a sufficient body of law in place now supporting the general validity of the executive order so that broadscale, pre-enforcement challenges are infrequent.

UNIROYAL INC. v. MARSHALL, 579 F.2d 1060 (7th Cir.1978). In Uniroyal Inc. v. Marshall, the company sought to challenge the validity of the OFCC's pre-hearing discovery rules and administrative subpoenas on the ground that the rules were not specifically authorized by the Administrative Procedure Act, the executive order or the Federal Property and Administrative Services Act. In 41 C.F.R. § 60–30 the agency provides rules of practice for the trial of a contested case under the executive order. The company essentially claimed that the government acted *ultra vires* in promulgating rules which were not authorized under the legal instruments under which it purported to act.

Under the then existing rules, contracting agencies had the compliance responsibility. The agency had conducted an on site review of one of the company's plants and found a number of deficiencies, including a failure to supply complete and accurate data to investigators. The company also failed to identify areas where women and minorities were under-utilized and to set goals and timetables for an affirmative action program.

When negotiations for a settlement failed during the show-cause period, a formal complaint was issued against the company and the case set for hearing before an administrative law judge. Uniroyal refused to cooperate during the pre-hearing discovery phase and refused to comply with orders of the administrative law judge. The government moved to terminate its contracts and debar the company from future contracts for its failures with regard to discovery. Uniroyal sued in the federal district court seeking to bar enforcement of the rules, to enjoin any administrative hearing, and to bar the company from imposing any sanctions for its non-compliance with the rules. It sought a declaratory judgment that the rules were an unconstitutional exercise of governmental authority. The district court granted the government's motion for summary judgment on the basis that the case met none of the requirements for pre-enforcement review of agency action and was not ripe for judicial review. It held the rules were valid contract terms not in excess of the authority under the executive order.

The Seventh Circuit Court of Appeals denied the company's motion for an injunction against proceeding with the administrative hearing. (579 F.2d 1060, at 1064 (7th Cir.1978).) It affirmed the decision below on the basis of the company's failure to exhaust the administrative procedures but did not decide the question of validity of the rules. The court found that the case did not come within any exceptions to the exhaustion requirement.

The administrative hearing on the merits in *Uniroyal* was concluded and a final order was issued on June 28, 1979. (In the Matter of Department of Labor and Uniroyal, Number OFCCP 1977–1). The company got a temporary restraining order in the district court of the District of Columbia on July 2, 1979 barring any action by the government until approved by the court. On July 20, the court sustained the Department of Labor and upheld the validity of the regulations under challenge. It also concluded that the company was properly debarred from present and future contracts for violation of the discovery regulations. (482 F.Supp. 364 (D.D.C.1979).) The Court of Appeals for the District of Columbia denied the company's request for an injunction pending appeal to the district court's decision, but before the case could be appealed the parties reached an agreement on the matters in dispute and the appeal was dismissed.

St. Regis Paper Co. v. Marshall, 591 F.2d 612 (10th Cir.1979).

In this case the government had found that the Saint Regis Co. had deviated from its affirmative action plan in the employment of women. It issued a notice to the company to show cause why sanctions shouldn't be applied and the parties proceeded to negotiate on corrective measures. When negotiations broke down the company brought an action in the district court which was dismissed for failure to exhaust administrative procedures. On appeal the company argued that its action was excepted from the exhaustion requirement on one or more of the following grounds:

1. The complaint raises important questions of law involving statutory interpretation and the constitutionality of regulations, which are within the expertise of courts rather than agencies.

2. Review by the agency would be expensive and fruitless, since the agency is not likely to void its own regulations.

3. Agency rules constitute "final agency action" subject to pre-enforcement court review under the Administrative Procedure Act.

4. Plaintiff is prejudiced by the administrative delay in that it is subject to further show cause notices at its other facilities and

is subject to *de facto* debarment nationally by virtue of the show cause notice.

5. If plaintiff loses at the administrative level it will likely be permanently debarred with no assurance of being granted a stay pending court review. (591 F.2d at 614.)

The court of appeals rejected the plaintiff's argument and noted that agency action must not only be final to be properly reviewable, but also the controversy must be ripe for review. It ruled that agency review of challenged regulations is desirable, even where pure questions of law are concerned, in order to provide the court with the agency's views and to preserve the opportunity for the agency to correct an ill-conceived regulation and moot the issue. This is particularly desirable where the challenge is to the regulation as applied to a specific set of facts, as well as on its face so that ultimate judicial review if necessary would be facilitated by a complete administrative record. The Supreme Court refused to hear the case.

ILLINOIS TOOL WORKS, INC. v. MARSHALL, 601 F.2d 943 (7th Cir.1979). In this case the contractor successfully challenged an OFCCP rule which, in effect, permitted debarment until disputed matters were resolved. Under the rule, which the Labor Department subsequently abandoned, a contractor could be determined to be a non-responsible bidder or designated in a non-awardable category without there being any administrative process to determine or to enable the contractor to challenge the status. With such a cloud upon their status, another regulation prohibited them from bidding on future contracts. The Seventh Circuit held that the government may not take any action which debars, or has the effect of debarring, a contractor without first having a hearing on the merits at which the contractor may be found guilty of non-compliance. Any rule permitting such an action violated the executive order. No issue of exhaustion of administrative remedies was raised in this case.

LIBERTY MUT. INS. CO. v. FRIEDMAN

United States Court of Appeals for the Fourth Circuit, 1981.
639 F.2d 164.

JAMES DICKSON PHILLIPS, CIRCUIT JUDGE:

Liberty Mutual Insurance Company and two related insurance companies (Liberty) challenge the district court's conclusion that defendant Rougeau [1] validly issued a determination by letter that the companies are government subcontractors and thus subject to the recordkeeping and affirmative action requirements of Executive Order 11,246.[2]

1. Defendant Rougeau, director of the Office of Federal Contract Compliance Programs, and the other defendants-appellees are federal government officials assigned responsibility in the Executive Order program.

2. Exec.Order No. 11,246, 3 C.F.R. 339 (1964–1965 Compilation), as amended by Exec.Order No. 11,375, 3 C.F.R. 684 (1966–1970 Compilation).

We conclude that defendants' action was outside any statutory authorization and reverse.

I

Under § 202 of Executive Order 11,246, as amended, contractors and subcontractors [3] with the government are prohibited from discriminating in employment on the basis of "race, color, religion, sex, or national origin" and are required to take affirmative action to ensure equal employment opportunity. Section 201 of the Executive Order provides that the Secretary of Labor shall administer and enforce the order and grants rulemaking power to the Secretary. The Department of Labor's Office of Federal Contract Compliance Programs (OFCCP) has promulgated regulations that require government contractors and subcontractors to furnish reports and other information about their affirmative action programs.[4]

Liberty underwrites workers' compensation insurance for many companies that contract with the government. Ordinarily, this type of insurance provides blanket coverage for all employees of the insured company whether or not the employees are performing work under a government contract or subcontract. During the time period involved in this case, Liberty has not written any insurance policies for any federal governmental agency and has not signed any contracts or subcontracts that include the antidiscrimination or affirmative action clauses required to be included in covered contracts by Executive Order 11,246.

In October 1977, defendant Friedman notified Liberty that Liberty was a government subcontractor under the definition found in 41 C.F.R. § 60–1.3 and therefore subject to the requirements of Executive Order 11,246. Section 60–1.3 defines subcontract as:

> any agreement or arrangement between a contractor and any person (in which the parties do not stand in the relationship of an employer and an employee):
>
> (1) For the furnishing of supplies or services or for the use of real or personal property, including lease arrangements, which, in whole or in part, is necessary to the performance of any one or more contracts; or
>
> (2) Under which any portion of the contractor's obligation under any one or more contracts is performed, undertaken, or assumed.

Because all states in the United States have enacted workers' compensation laws, and employers, including government contractors, are obligated by statute to provide workers' compensation insurance, defendant determined that Liberty was providing a service necessary to the

---

3. Section 202(7) requires the contractor to include the antidiscrimination and affirmative action clauses in all nonexempt subcontracts.

4. 41 C.F.R. § 60–1.7.

performance of the federal contract and was, therefore, covered under subsection 1 of the definition above.

Liberty contested the Government's determination that providers of workers' compensation insurance to government contractors are government subcontractors and brought this declaratory judgment action under 28 U.S.C. §§ 2201, 2202. The district court rejected the challenge to defendants' authority to classify Liberty as a subcontractor and entered judgment for defendants.

On this appeal Liberty argues that it is outside the definition of subcontractor found in the regulations; that, if Liberty is found to be within the subcontractor definition, the regulation is either outside the scope of Executive Order 11,246 or beyond the legislative grant of authority of Congress; that, if Executive Order 11,246 covers the insurance policies issued by Liberty, Executive Order 11,246 is an unlawful delegation of legislative authority; and that the Government may not bind Liberty to a contractual obligation to which it did not consent. Because we conclude that, although the regulatory definition of subcontract includes workers' compensation insurance contracts, application of the Executive Order to Liberty is outside the scope of any grant of legislative authority, we need not address Liberty's other contentions.

II

* * *

We conclude, as did the district court, that Liberty's workers' compensation policies issued to government contractors are subcontracts under the regulations.

III

Liberty's second argument, that the broad definition of subcontractor, with its attendant consequences for meeting the recordkeeping and affirmative action requirements of Executive Order 11,246, is outside the scope of the Order or beyond any legislative grant of authority presents a more difficult question.

The history of Executive Order 11,246 is discussed in detail in Contractors Association v. Secretary of Labor, 442 F.2d 159, 168–71 (3d Cir.1971), and need not be recounted here. Executive Order 11,246, as amended, "charge[s] the Secretary of Labor with ensuring that corporations that benefit from government contracts provide equal employment opportunity regardless of race or sex." Chrysler Corp. v. Brown, 441 U.S. 281, 286, 99 S.Ct. 1705, 1709, 60 L.Ed.2d 208 (1979) (footnote omitted). Although the Executive Order is written in broad terms, the prohibition against discrimination in employment is clearly intended to cover both government contractors and their subcontractors. Section 202(7) of the Order specifically requires contractors to include in all subcontracts the antidiscrimination, affirmative action, and recordkeeping provisions required by Executive Order 11,246. Subcontract is not defined within the Executive Order, but § 201 provides that the Secretary of Labor "shall adopt such rules and regulations * * * as are deemed necessary and appropriate to achieve the purposes" of the Order. Those purposes, as declared by the Supreme Court in *Chrysler,* "are an end to discrimination in employment by the Federal Government and those who deal with the Federal Government." 441 U.S. at 307, 99 S.Ct. at 1720. Because Executive Order 11,246 is clearly intended to cover subcontractors and because the term "subcontractor" has no "single exact meaning," [5] the Secretary had the power to define, by regulation, which subcontracts are covered so long as the definition is within the purposes of the Executive Order and the statutory grant of authority. See Chrysler Corp. v. Brown, 441 U.S. at 306–07, 99 S.Ct. at 1720. Although the regulation's broad-ranging definition of subcontract is arguably consistent with the purposes of the Executive Order, we conclude that application of the Executive Order to plaintiffs is not reasonably within the contemplation of any statutory grant of authority.

The question before us is not whether Congress could require insurance companies providing workers' compensation insurance to federal contractors to comply with the affirmative action requirements of Executive Order 11,246, the question is "whether or to what extent Congress did grant * * * such authority" to the executive branch of the government. See NAACP v. Federal Power Commission, 425 U.S. 662, 665, 96 S.Ct. 1806, 1809, 48 L.Ed.2d 284 (1976). Determining whether defendants have the statutory authorization to require Liberty to comply with Executive Order 11,246 is rendered difficult because "[t]he origins of the congressional authority for Executive Order 11,246 are somewhat obscure and have been roundly debated by commentators and courts." Chrysler Corp. v. Brown, 441 U.S. at 304, 99 S.Ct. at 1719.

The *Chrysler* Court acknowledged that several sources of congressional authorization have been suggested by lower courts,[6] including the Federal Property and Administrative Services Act of 1949,[7] Titles

---

5. MacEvoy Co. v. United States, 322 U.S. 102, 108, 64 S.Ct. 890, 894, 88 L.Ed. 1163 (1944). In *MacEvoy*, the Supreme Court judicially defined "subcontractor" under the Miller Act, 40 U.S.C. § 270a et seq. The Act itself did not define the term, and the Court noted,

In a broad, generic sense a subcontractor includes anyone who has a contract to furnish labor or material to a prime contractor. * * * But under the more technical meaning, as established by usage in the building trades, a subcontractor is one who performs for and takes from the prime contractor a specific part of the labor or material requirements of the original contract, thus excluding ordinary laborers and materialmen.

Id. at 108–09, 64 S.Ct. at 894–5. Because the term is not susceptible to a uniform definition, we do not attempt to state the precise boundaries within which the Secretary may validly require compliance with the Executive Order, but we do note that the Secretary's definition of subcontractor is beyond the scope even of the "broad, generic" sense of the term.

6. The Executive Order states that it is promulgated "[u]nder and by virtue of the authority vested in [the] President of the United States by the Constitution and statutes of the United States. * * *" 3 C.F.R. 339 (1964–1965 Compilation). There is no reference to a specific statutory source.

7. 40 U.S.C. § 471 et seq.

VI and VII of the Civil Rights Act of 1964,[8] the Equal Employment Opportunity Act of 1972,[9] and "some more general notion that the Executive can impose reasonable contractual requirements in the exercise of its procurement authority." Id. at 305–06, 99 S.Ct. at 1720. For the purposes of decision in *Chrysler* the Court was not required to determine the precise source of authority for Executive Order 11,246 because it held that the regulation there being challenged was not authorized by any of the arguable statutory grants of authority. Id. at 304–06, 99 S.Ct. at 1719–20.

The challenge in *Chrysler* was to OFCCP rules that provided for disclosure of reports submitted by an employer pursuant to Executive Order 11,246. The Court refused to accord the challenged rule the "force and effect of law" in part because none of the arguable statutory grants of authority contemplated the disclosure rule being challenged. Id. at 304–08, 99 S.Ct. at 1719–1721. Although *Chrysler* involved a challenge to a particular aspect of the OFCCP's administration of Executive Order 11,246 instead of a threshold challenge, as here, to the legitimacy of the order's attempted application for any purpose to the challenging employer, we think the method of analysis used in *Chrysler* is equally applicable here, and to that we now turn.[10]

IV

A congressional grant of legislative authority need not be specific in order to sustain the validity of regulations promulgated pursuant to the grant, but a court must "reasonably be able to conclude that the grant of authority contemplates the regulations issued." Id. at 308, 99 S.Ct. at 1721. Our examination of the possible statutory sources of congressional authorization for Executive Order 11,246 convinces us that none of the statutes reasonably contemplates that Liberty, as a provider of workers' compensation insurance to government contractors, may be required to comply with Executive Order 11,246. We conclude therefore that none of the cited statutes authorize the action taken by defendants.

A.

First, we consider as a possible source the general procurement power of Congress as delegated to the Executive by the Federal Proper-

---

8. 42 U.S.C. §§ 2000d to 2000d–4, 2000e to 2000e–17.

9. 42 U.S.C. §§ 2000e, 2000e–1 to –6, –8, –9, –13 to –17.

10. In response to Liberty's contention that authorization for the challenged application of Executive Order 11,246 must be found in a particular legislative grant, defendants take the position that "there is no * * * burden on the government" to identify the legislative grant. Brief for Appellee at 17. Consistent with this position, defendants have declined to stake their claim of authority on any particular statutory or constitutional sources, relying instead on a general contention that "Congress has generally approved of, and given its sanction to, the executive order program. * * *" Id. Because we believe that the particular source must be found, our analysis must proceed, as in *Chrysler*, to consider all reasonably arguable sources. These are generally deducible from the authorities relied upon by defendants in their argument addressed to the lack of authorization. Generally, we run the gamut of the possible sources identified in *Chrysler*.

ty and Administrative Services Act. 40 U.S.C. § 471 et seq. (The Procurement Act). Congress has said of this Act that its purpose is to provide "an economical and efficient system" for, among other objectives, the procurement of personal property and services. Id. § 471. The Act authorizes Executive Orders "necessary to effectuate [its] provisions," id. § 486(a), but does not mention employment discrimination. See also Chrysler Corp. v. Brown, 441 U.S. at 304 n. 34, 99 S.Ct. at 1719 n. 34.

Several cases, some specifically relied upon by defendants, arguably support the view that this Act provides the necessary authorization for application of the Order to Liberty. We think that, rightly analyzed, they do not. In Farmer v. Philadelphia Electric Co., 329 F.2d 3 (3d Cir. 1964), the court stated that the delegation to the President in § 486(a) was the statutory authorization for a predecessor of Executive Order 11,246, id. at 7–8, but that conclusion was not necessary to the decision in *Farmer*. The court in Farkas v. Texas Instrument, Inc., 375 F.2d 629 (5th Cir.1967), reached the same conclusion, id. at 632 n. 1, but that conclusion was also dictum. See Chrysler Corp. v. Brown, 441 U.S. at 304 n. 34, 99 S.Ct. at 1719 n. 34, citing Contractors Association v. Secretary of Labor, 442 F.2d at 167.

More apposite, and to be reckoned with, is *Contractors Association* in which the court squarely faced the question whether the Executive may impose the contract terms required by Executive Order 11,246 upon federally assisted state construction contracts. The court noted that neither *Farkas* nor *Farmer* had analyzed the relation between the statutory grant of authority in § 486(a) and the nondiscrimination objectives of the Executive Orders, 442 F.2d at 167; see Chrysler Corp. v. Brown, 441 U.S. at 304 n. 34, 99 S.Ct. at 1719 n. 34, but went on to find that relationship sufficiently established in respect of federally assisted construction projects because of the strong federal interest in ensuring that the cost and progress of these projects were not adversely affected by an artificial restriction of the labor pool caused by discriminatory employment practices. As the court noted, the Executive Order applies to all direct federal procurement contracts but, with respect to federally assisted contracts, extends its coverage to construction contracts only. This choice was significant to the court because it involved the one type of federally assisted contract in which discrimination would be most likely adversely to affect cost and progress of projects. Id. at 170. The Government's interest in keeping costs low and ensuring completion of state construction projects that receive federal assistance was considered identical to the Government's interest with respect to direct procurement contracts. Id.

Contractors Association thus found in the Procurement Act both a general source of congressional authority for Executive Order 11,246 and a specific source of authority for the particular application there being challenged. Reserving judgment on the first of these, cf. Cramer v. Virginia Commonwealth Univ., 415 F.Supp. 673, 680 (E.D.Va.1976) (questioning *Contractors Association's* analysis); Note, Doing Good the Wrong Way: The Case for Delimiting Presidential Power Under Executive Order No. 11,246, 33 Vand.L.Rev. 921, 931 (1980) (questionable as general source), we conclude that under the test applied in *Contractors Association* there can be found in the Procurement Act no authorization for the specific application being challenged in the instant case.

The key point in *Contractors Association* is its recognition that any application of the Order must be reasonably related to the Procurement Act's purpose of ensuring efficiency and economy in government procurement (whether direct or assisted) in order to lie within the statutory grant. This requirement of a reasonably close nexus between the efficiency and economy criteria of the Procurement Act and any exactions imposed upon federal contractors by Executive Orders promulgated under its authority has recently been highlighted by the District of Columbia Circuit in a closely related context. In AFL–CIO v. Kahn, 618 F.2d 784 (1979) (en banc), the court upheld as having the force and effect of law the requirement of Executive Order 12,092 that federal contractors certify compliance with voluntary wage and price guidelines established by the Council on Wage and Price Stability. Though, as in *Contractors Association,* the *Kahn* court found the Executive Order's requirements to fall within the statutory authority of the Procurement Act, the several opinions of the court took great pains to emphasize that the court's holding was rested narrowly upon the manifestly close nexus between the Procurement Act's criteria of efficiency and economy and the Executive Order's predominant objective of containing procurement costs. Id. at 792–93 (majority opinion); id. at 796–97 (Bazelon, J. concurring); id. at 797 (Tamm, J. concurring); cf. id. at 797 (MacKinnon, J. dissenting) (no statutory authority for order).

Assuming, without deciding, that the Procurement Act does provide constitutional authorization for some applications of Executive Order 11,246, we conclude that, in any event, the authorization could validly extend no further than to those applications satisfying the nexus test used in *Contractors Association* and *Kahn.* Applying that test here, we are satisfied that it is not met.

In applying the test, it is important first to note a respect in which the record before the *Contractors Association* court differed materially from that developed in this case to show the relationship between Procurement Act criteria and Executive Order application. In *Contractors Association,* but not in the instant case, there were factual findings in the record which tended to show a demonstrable relationship between the two which was not apparent from a consideration alone of the Act and the Order.

Before the plan challenged in *Contractors Association* was implemented, a series of public hearings was held in the targeted area that resulted in administrative findings which reflected serious underrepresentation of minority employees in six trades. The mathematical disparity was found to be caused by exclusionary practices of trade unions rather than any lack of qualified minority applicants in the labor pool. 442 F.2d at 164, 173. These findings buttressed the *Contractors Association* court's conclusion that the Executive was acting to protect the federal government's financial interest in the state projects thereby establishing the sufficiently close nexus sought by both the *Contractors Association* and *Kahn* courts. Cf. Fullilove v. Klutznick, ___ U.S. ___, ___, 100 S.Ct. 2758, 2785–90, 65 L.Ed.2d 902 (1980) (Powell, J., concurring: importance of legislative findings of discrimination to sustain Act of Congress mandating affirmative action in federal grants for local public works projects).

By contrast, no such findings were made in the case before us. Liberty is not itself a federal contractor and there is, therefore, no direct connection to federal procurement. Instead, Liberty provides blanket workers' compensation insurance to employers that hold federal contracts. There are no findings that suggest what percentage of the total price of federal contracts may be attributed to the cost of this insurance. Further, there is no suggestion that insurers have practiced the deliberate exclusion of minority employees found to have occurred in *Contractors Association.* The connection between the cost of workers' compensation policies, for which employers purchase a single policy to cover employees working on both federal and nonfederal contracts without distinction between the two, and any increase in the cost of federal contracts that could be attributed to discrimination by these insurers is simply too attenuated to allow a reviewing court to find the requisite connection between procurement costs and social objectives.

Defendants rely upon, and we of course recognize that there are decisions from other courts that can be read to reject the need for any such nexus between Procurement Act economy/efficiency criteria and Executive Order social objectives in order to uphold challenged applications of the Order. See United States v. New Orleans Public Service, Inc., 553 F.2d 459 (5th Cir.1977), vacated and remanded on other grounds, 436 U.S. 942, 98 S.Ct. 2841, 56 L.Ed.2d 783 (1978); Rossetti Contracting Co. v. Brennan, 508 F.2d 1039, 1045 n. 18 (7th Cir.1975); Northeast Construction Co. v. Romney, 485 F.2d 752, 760–61 (D.C.Cir. 1973). In what could be taken as the most extreme view expressed in these decisions, one characterizes the other two as standing for "the proposition that equal employment goals themselves, reflecting important national policies, validate the use of the procurement power in the context of the [Executive] Order." *New Orleans Public Service,* 553 F.2d at 467. To the extent this quotation rightly characterizes these holdings, and to the extent it reflects a considered rejection of the requirement of nexus between Procurement Act purposes and Executive Order objectives that we read in *Contractors Association* and *Kahn* and that we apply here,[11] we simply disagree. The plain implication of

---

11. On careful analysis, this might be questioned. The discussion of this general proposition in *Northeast,* for example, is technically dicta, since the court there simply assumed the validity of the Executive Order, and the nexus-issue was not directly in contention. See id. at 760–61. Furthermore, in all three cases, whatever the

such a rejection would be that regulations promulgated under an Executive Order that traces its lawmaking authority to a particular statute need bear no relation to the purposes of that authorizing statute so long as the regulations bear relation to national policies reflected in other sources—common law, statutory, or constitutional. This would render meaningless the simple, fundamental separation of powers requirement, recently reasserted by the Supreme Court in *Chrysler*, that such an "exercise of quasi-legislative authority by governmental departments and agencies must be rooted in a grant of [legislative] power by the Congress ＊ ＊ ＊," 441 U.S. at 302, 99 S.Ct. at 1718, and lie "reasonably within the contemplation of that grant of authority." Id. at 306, 99 S.Ct. at 1720.

As indicated, we think that this fundamental requirement dictates application of the sort of nexus test we apply here, and that when applied to the regulations here in question and the Procurement Act it is plain that the former do not lie "reasonably within the contemplation of" the latter.

B.

We next consider as possible sources of statutory authorization for the Executive Order Titles VI and VII of the Civil Rights Act of 1964. The short answer to this possibility is that neither Title contains any express delegation of substantive lawmaking authority to the President. *Chrysler*, 441 U.S. at 305 n. 35, 99 S.Ct. at 1719 n. 35.

Indeed, as the Supreme Court pointed out in *Chrysler*, the question of the relationship of these Titles to Executive Order 11,246 has "usually been put in terms of whether Executive Order 11,246 is inconsistent with these titles ＊ ＊ ＊," 441 U.S. at 305 n. 35, 99 S.Ct. at 1719 n. 35, rather than in terms of whether the latter provide authorization for the former.

C.

The final possible source of congressional authorization to be considered is that contended by defendants to have occurred by "ratification" or "negative authorization" of the Executive Order flowing from the rejection in 1972 of several amendments intended to circumscribe the role of the Executive Order program. The argument depends essentially upon the congressional debates surrounding adoption of the Equal Employment Opportunity Act of 1972. 42 U.S.C. §§ 2000e to 2000e–17 (1976). See *Chrysler*, 441 U.S. at 306 n. 36, 99 S.Ct. at 1720 n. 36; Legal Aid Society v. Brennan, 608 F.2d 1319, 1329 n. 14 (9th Cir.

course of general discussion in the opinions, there is great likelihood that upon a *Contractors Association*-type analysis, a sufficient efficiency/economy nexus might well have been demonstrable. All three involved construction contractors as to whom the restricted labor pool analysis might well have applied. Certainly in all three such a nexus is more readily surmised from the mere nature of the contracts than could possibly be shown in relation to the insurance "sub-contracts" involved in the instant case.

1979); United States v. New Orleans Public Service, Inc., 553 F.2d at 467.

Even if "ratification" by such a process might in some circumstances be properly found—a matter of some general dubiety when its potential effect upon the dynamics of the legislative process is carefully considered [12]—we do not think it can properly be found here. The rejection in 1972 of a series of amendments which would have cut back the Executive Order program in existence at that time, cannot fairly be considered to contemplate a grant of authority to the Executive to extend the program to Liberty in 1977.

V

Defendants acted outside any grant of legislative authority when they sought to impose the requirements of Executive Order 11,246 upon plaintiffs. Without this critical connection to legislative authorization, defendants' action cannot be given effect.[13] The decision of the district court is reversed.

Reversed.

BUTZNER, CIRCUIT JUDGE, concurring in part and dissenting in part:

I concur in Parts I and III of the court's opinion to the extent that they set forth the factual and legal background of this case. I also concur in Part II which holds that workmen's compensation policies issued to government contractors are subcontracts within the meaning of the regulations that implement Executive Order 11,246.

I dissent from the conclusion reached in Parts IV and V of the court's opinion holding that there is no congressional authority for imposing the requirements of Executive Order 11,246 on Liberty Mutual Insurance Company.

* * *

Indeed, among the courts of appeals, this court alone impugns the authority of the Secretary, as the President's delegate, to enforce Executive Order 11,246 against a subcontractor. Dissenting, I would affirm the judgment of the district court.

12. See Note, Doing Good the Wrong Way: The Case for Delimiting Presidential Power Under Executive Order No. 11,246, 33 Vand.L.Rev. 921, 946–47 (1980).

13. The possibility that authorization for the Executive Order might be found independently of statutory sources in the "inherent powers" of the President inferable from the general powers conferred directly upon him by article II of the Constitution is completely foreclosed by Youngstown Sheet & Tube Co. v. Sawyer, 343 U.S. 579, 72 S.Ct. 863, 96 L.Ed. 1153 (1952). There the Supreme Court held that the "inherent powers" of the President under his constitutional authority as Commander-in-Chief did not support his executive order directing seizure of the steel mills during the Korean conflict. This was legislative action and in the absence of any delegation of lawmaking power by the Congress, none could be inferred from the President's constitutional powers to see that the laws are faithfully executed. Id. at 587, 72 S.Ct. at 866. The same reasoning must apply to the lawmaking power clearly assumed in Executive Order 11,246.

E. AFFIRMATIVE ACTION CONCEPTS

Executive Order 10925, the Kennedy order, contained two elements of great significance which distinguished it from its predecessors: (1) the affirmative action requirement, and (2) the specification, in the order, of sanctions for violations, which in prior executive orders were there only by implication.

By far the most significant conceptual innovation in the civil rights field is the use of affirmative action. In the Kennedy order this remedial concept, ordinarily utilized as a remedy after determination of fault, is imposed as a condition of doing government business. The assurance of affirmative action to facilitate equal employment opportunity is an undertaking *in addition* to the undertaking not to discriminate on the basis of race, creed, color, or national origin.

Specific inclusion of the sanctions to be imposed for violation of the contractual commitment clearly signaled a governmental intention, or pretention as history has revealed it, to enforce the obligations.

The affirmative action concept was conceived as a response during the Eisenhower Administration to a criticism of the President's committee programs in the final report of the committee chaired by then Vice President Nixon. That report advised as follows: "Overt discrimination . . . is not as prevalent as is generally believed. To a greater degree, *the indifference of employers to establishing a positive policy* of nondiscrimination hinders qualified applicants and employees from being hired and promoted on the basis of equality." (Emphasis in original.) This sound advice regarding the nature of discrimination was not duplicated with recommendations regarding the nature of administrative organizations which could most effectively pursue the goals of affirmative action.

Before the potential of the affirmative action concept of the executive order could be effectively implemented, it was necessary for the government to come to grips with the use of numbers. Numbers raised the spectre of quotas and the fear that any use of goals or timetables would be declared illegal. The principal case in which these issues are joined follows.

CONTRACTORS ASSOCIATION OF EASTERN PENNSYLVANIA v. SECRETARY OF LABOR

United States Court of Appeals for the Third Circuit, 1971.
442 F.2d 159.

OPINION OF THE COURT

GIBBONS, CIRCUIT JUDGE.

The original plaintiff, the Contractors Association of Eastern Pennsylvania (the Association) and the intervening plaintiffs,[1] construction

1. James D. Morrissey, Inc.; The Conduit & Foundation Corp.; Glasgow, Inc.; Buckley & Company; The Nyleve Company; Erb Engineering & Constr. Co.; Per-

contractors doing business in the Philadelphia area (the Contractors), appeal from an order of the district court which denied their motion for summary judgment, granted the motion of the federal defendants [2] to dismiss the Association complaint for lack of standing, and granted the cross-motion of the federal defendants for summary judgment.[3] When deciding these motions, the district court had before it the Association's verified complaint, a substantially identical complaint of the Contractors, the affidavits of Vincent G. Macaluso and Ward McCreedy on behalf of the federal defendants which identified certain relevant documents, a stipulation by the parties as to certain facts, and two affidavits of Howard G. Minckler on behalf of the plaintiffs.

The complaint challenges the validity of the Philadelphia Plan, promulgated by the federal defendants under the authority of Executive Order No. 11246.[4] That Plan is embodied in two orders issued by officials of the United States Department of Labor, dated June 27, 1969 and September 23, 1969, respectively. Copies of these orders were annexed to the verified complaint as exhibits 1 and 2, respectively, and to the Macaluso affidavit as appendices B and C respectively. In summary, they require that bidders on any federal or federally assisted construction contracts for projects in a five-county area around Philadelphia,[5] the estimated total cost of which exceeds $500,000, shall submit an acceptable affirmative action program which includes specific goals for the utilization of minority manpower in six skilled crafts: ironworkers, plumbers and pipefitters, steamfitters, sheetmetal workers, electrical workers, and elevator construction workers.

Executive Order No. 11246 requires all applicants for federal assistance to include in their construction contracts specific provisions respecting fair employment practices, including the provision:

> The contractor will take affirmative action to ensure that applicants are employed, and that employees are treated during employment, without regard to their race, color, religion, sex or national origin.[6]

The Executive Order empowers the Secretary of Labor to issue rules and regulations necessary and appropriate to achieve its purpose. On June 27, 1969 Assistant Secretary of Labor Fletcher issued an order

---

kins, Kanak, Foster, Inc.; and Lansdowne Constructors, Inc.

2. The Secretary of Labor, George P. Shultz; The Assistant Secretary of Labor, Arthur A. Fletcher; The Director, Office of Federal Contract Compliance, John L. Wilks; The Secretary of Agriculture, Clifford M. Hardin.

3. An additional defendant, the General State Authority of the Commonwealth of Pennsylvania, has not participated in this appeal.

4. 30 Fed.Reg. 12319 (Sept. 24, 1965), as amended by Exec.Order No. 11375, 32 Fed. Reg. 14303 (Oct. 13, 1967), 3 C.F.R. 406

(1969), 42 U.S.C.A. § 2000e note (1970), superseded in part by Exec.Order No. 11478, 34 Fed.Reg. 12985 (Aug. 8, 1969), 3 C.F.R., 1969 Comp. 133, 42 U.S.C. § 2000e note (1970).

5. Encompassing Bucks, Chester, Delaware, Montgomery and Philadelphia Counties in Pennsylvania.

6. § 202(1). This wording comes from Exec.Order No. 11375, see note 4 supra, and represents a minor change from the original designed to parallel the classes of discrimination prohibited by Title VII of the Civil Rights Act of 1964, 42 U.S.C. § 2000e et seq.

implementing the Executive Order in the five-county Philadelphia area. The order required bidders, prior to the award of contracts, to submit "acceptable affirmative action" programs "which shall include specific goals of minority manpower utilization." The order contained a finding that enforcement of the "affirmative action" requirement of Executive Order No. 11246 had posed special problems in the construction trades.[7] Contractors and subcontractors must hire a new employee complement for each job, and they rely on craft unions as their prime or sole source for labor. The craft unions operate hiring halls. "Because of the exclusionary practices of labor organizations," the order finds "there traditionally has been only a small number of Negroes employed in these seven trades."[8] The June 27, 1969 order provided that the Area Coordinator of the Office of Federal Contract Compliance, in conjunction with the federal contracting and administering agencies in the Philadelphia area, would determine definite standards for specific goals in a contractor's affirmative action program. After such standards were determined, each bidder would be required to commit itself to specific goals for minority manpower utilization. The order set forth factors to be considered in determining definite standards, including:

"1) The current extent of minority group participation in the trade.

2) The availability of minority group persons for employment in such trade.

3) The need for training programs in the area and/or the need to assure demand for those in or from existing training programs.

4) The impact of the program upon the existing labor force."

Acting pursuant to the June 29, 1969 order, representatives of the Department of Labor held public hearings in Philadelphia on August 26, 27 and 28, 1969. On September 23, 1969, Assistant Secretary Fletcher made findings with respect to each of the listed factors.

* * *

The order of September 23, 1969 specified that on each invitation to bid each bidder would be required to submit an affirmative action program. The order further provided:

"4. No bidder will be awarded a contract unless his affirmative action program contains goals falling within the range set forth * * * above. * * *

---

7. Recognition of this problem antedated the present Plan. Under the Philadelphia Pre-Award Plan, which was put into effect on November 30, 1967 by the Philadelphia Federal Executive Board, each apparent low bidder was required to submit a written affirmative action program assuring minority group representation in eight specified trades as a precondition to qualifying for a construction contract or subcontract. This predecessor Plan was suspended due to an Opinion letter by the Comptroller General stating that it violated the principles of competitive bidding. 48 Comp.Gen. 326 (1968).

8. The order of June 27, 1969 listed "roofers and water proofers" among the trades underrepresented by minority craftsmen. The order of September 23, 1969 dropped this category from the list, leaving the six trades previously named.

*   *   *   *   *   *   *   *   *

6. The purpose of the contractor's commitment to specific goals as to minority manpower utilization is to meet his affirmative action obligations under the equal opportunity clause of the contract. This commitment is not intended and shall not be used to discriminate against any qualified applicant or employee. Whenever it comes to the bidder's attention that the goals are being used in a discriminatory manner, he must report it to the Area Coordinator of the Office of Federal Contract Compliance of the U.S. Department of Labor in order that appropriate sanction proceedings may be instituted.

*   *   *   *   *   *   *   *   *

8. The bidder agrees to keep such records and file such reports relating to the provisions of this order as shall be required by the contracting or administering agency."

In November, 1969, the General State Authority of the Commonwealth of Pennsylvania issued invitations to bid for the construction of an earth dam on Marsh Creek in Chester County, Pennsylvania. Although this dam is a Commonwealth project, part of the construction cost, estimated at over $3,000,000 is to be funded by federal monies under a program administered by the Department of Agriculture.[9] The Secretary of Agriculture, one of the federal defendants, as a condition for payment of federal financial assistance for the project, required the inclusion in each bid of a Philadelphia Plan Commitment in compliance with the order of September 23, 1969. On November 14, 1969, the General State Authority issued an addendum to the original invitation for bids requiring all bidders to include such a commitment in their bids. It is alleged and not denied that except for the requirement by the Secretary of Agriculture that the Philadelphia Plan Commitment be included, the General State Authority would not have imposed such a requirement on bidders.

The Association consists of more than eighty contractors in the five-county Philadelphia area who regularly employ workers in the six specified crafts, and who collectively perform more than $150,000,000 of federal and federally assisted construction in that area annually. Each of the contractor plaintiffs is a regular bidder on federal and federally assisted construction projects. The complaint was filed prior to the opening of bids on the Marsh Creek dam. It sought injunctive relief against the inclusion of a Philadelphia Plan Commitment requirement in the invitation for bids. By virtue of a stipulation that the General State Authority would issue a new and superseding invitation for bids if the district court held the Plan to be unlawful, the parties agreed that bids could be received without affecting the justiciability of the controversy. Bids were received on January 7, 1970. One of the intervening

9. Federal assistance was authorized under the Watershed Protection and Flood Prevention Act, 16 U.S.C. § 1001 et seq.

contractor plaintiffs submitted a low bid and appeared at the time of the district court decision to be entitled to an award of the contract.

The complaints of the Association and the Contractors refer to the fact that the Comptroller General of the United States has opined that the Philadelphia Plan Commitment is illegal and that disbursement of federal funds for the performance of a contract containing such a promise will be treated as unlawful.[10] The plaintiffs point out that the withholding of funds after a contractor has commenced performance would have catastrophic consequences, since contractors depend upon progress payments, and are in no position to complete their contracts without such payments. They allege that the Philadelphia Plan is illegal and void for the following reasons:

1. It is action by the Executive branch not authorized by the constitution or any statute and beyond Executive power.

2. It is inconsistent with Title VII of the Civil Rights Act of 1964.[11]

3. It is inconsistent with Title VI of the Civil Rights Act of 1964.[12]

4. It is inconsistent with the National Labor Relations Act.[13]

5. It is substantively inconsistent with and was not adopted in procedural accordance with Executive Order No. 11246.

6. It violates due process because

   a) it requires contradictory conduct impossible of consistent attainment;

   b) it unreasonably requires contractors to undertake to remedy an evil for which the craft unions, not they, are responsible;

   c) it arbitrarily and without basis in fact singles out the five-county Philadelphia area for discriminatory treatment without adequate basis in fact or law; and

   d) it requires quota hiring in violation of the Fifth Amendment.

The federal defendants moved both to dismiss the complaint under Rule 12(b)(1), Fed.R.Civ.P. and for summary judgment under Rule 56(b), Fed. R.Civ.P. They asserted that the plaintiffs lacked standing and that they were entitled to judgment as a matter of law. The plaintiffs moved for summary judgment. The district court held that the Association lacked standing to maintain the suit, that the Contractors had

---

10. Comp.Gen.Op., Letter to Sec. of Labor George P. Shultz, August 5, 1969, 115 Cong.Rec. 17.201–04 (daily ed. Dec. 18, 1969). The Comptroller General had objected to earlier efforts at implementing the "affirmative action" aspect of Exec. Order No. 11246 on the ground that these plans failed to inform prospective bidders of definite minimum standards for acceptable programs. In his negative opinion letter in response to the original Philadel-phia Pre-Award Plan, he had also adverted to the possibility of conflict with Title VII of the Civil Rights Act of 1964. See note 7 supra. The Title VII objections became the heart of the opinion of August 5, 1969 which challenged the validity of the Revised Philadelphia Plan.

11. 42 U.S.C. § 2000e et seq.

12. 42 U.S.C. § 2000d et seq.

13. 29 U.S.C. § 151 et seq.

such standing, and that the Plan was valid, 311 F.Supp. 1002. It granted summary judgment for the federal defendants, and the plaintiffs appeal.

* * *

EXECUTIVE POWER

The plaintiffs contend that the Philadelphia Plan is social legislation of local application enacted by the Executive without the benefit of statutory or constitutional authority. They point out, probably correctly, that the Plan imposes on the successful bidder on a project of the Commonwealth of Pennsylvania record keeping and hiring practices which violate Pennsylvania law.[14] If the Plan was adopted pursuant to a valid exercise of presidential power its provisions would, of course, control over local law. See United States v. City of Chester, 144 F.2d 415, 420 (3d Cir.1944); cf. United States v. Allegheny County, 322 U.S. 174, 183, 64 S.Ct. 908, 88 L.Ed. 1209 (1944); Panhandle Oil Co. v. State of Mississippi ex rel. Knox, 277 U.S. 218, 221, 48 S.Ct. 451, 72 L.Ed. 857 (1928). But, say the plaintiffs, where there is neither statutory authorization nor constitutional authority for the Executive action, no substantive federal requirements may be imposed upon a contract between the Commonwealth and its contractor.

The district court's answer is that the federal government "has the unrestricted power to fix the terms, conditions and those with whom it will deal."[15] For this proposition it cites Perkins v. Lukens Steel Co., 310 U.S. 113, 60 S.Ct. 869, 84 L.Ed. 1108 (1940) and King v. Smith, 392 U.S. 309, 333, 88 S.Ct. 2128, 20 L.Ed.2d 1118 (1968). Neither case is in point, however on the issue of Executive as distinguished from federal power. King v. Smith held that the Alabama substitute father regulation was inconsistent with the Social Security Act, 42 U.S.C. § 606(a), and points out that the federal government may impose the terms and conditions upon which its money allotments may be disbursed. The conditions referred to were imposed by Congress, not by the Executive branch. Perkins v. Lukens Steel Co. interprets the Public Contracts Act of June 30, 1936[16] which requires that sellers to the federal government pay prevailing minimum wages. It holds that an administrative determination of prevailing wages in a given industry made by the Secretary of Labor is not subject to judicial review on behalf of a potential seller.[17] The opinion contains the language:

14. The Pennsylvania Human Relations Act, 43 P.S. § 951 et seq. (Supp.1970), specifically prohibits an employer from keeping any record of or using any form of application with respect to the race, color, religion, ancestry, sex or national origin of an applicant for employment. 43 P.S. § 955(b)(1). The Act also prohibits the use of a quota system for employment based on the same criteria. 43 P.S. § 955(b)(3). The record keeping prohibition may be of limited force due to certain requirements of Title VII of the Civil Rights Act of 1964.

42 U.S.C. § 2000e–8(e). Moreover, we do not know how the Pennsylvania courts or the Pennsylvania Human Relations Commission would react to a scheme of "benign" quota hiring.

15. 311 F.Supp. 1002, 1011 (E.D.Pa. 1970).

16. 49 Stat. 2036–2039, 41 U.S.C. §§ 35–45.

17. The actual holding of *Perkins* was subsequently nullified by Congress. 66

Like private individuals and businesses, the Government enjoys the unrestricted power to produce its own supplies, to determine those with whom it will deal, and to fix the terms and conditions upon which it will make needed purchases.[18]

The quoted language refers to federal power exercised pursuant to a statutory mandate. The case is not in point on the issue of Executive power absent such a mandate.

The federal defendants and several amici [19] contend that Executive power to impose fair employment conditions incident to the power to contract has been upheld in this circuit and in the Fifth Circuit. They cite Farmer v. Philadelphia Electric Company, 329 F.2d 3 (3d Cir.1964) and Farkas v. Texas Instrument, Inc., 375 F.2d 629 (5th Cir.), cert. denied, 389 U.S. 977, 88 S.Ct. 480, 19 L.Ed.2d 471 (1967). Both cases discussed the Executive Order program for achieving fair employment in the context of Government contracts rather than federally assisted state contracts, and both assumed the validity of the Executive Order then applicable.[20] Both cases held that even assuming the validity of the Executive Order, it did not give rise to a private cause of action for damages by a party subjected to discrimination. Discussion of the validity of the Executive Order was in each case dictum. Moreover, both *Farmer* and *Farkas* refer to 40 U.S.C. § 486(a) as the source of the Executive power to issue the order. That subsection authorizes the President to prescribe such policies and directives as he deems necessary to effectuate the provisions of Chapter 10 of Title 40 [21] and Chapter 4 of Title 41.[22] These chapters deal with procurement of Government property and services, not with federal assistance programs. Thus even if *Farmer* and *Farkas* were holdings rather than dicta as to Executive power, the holdings would not reach the instant case. The validity of the Executive Order program as applied to the construction industry in state government contracts by virtue of federal assistance has not been litigated, so far as we have been able to determine, in any case reaching the courts of appeals.[23] Certainly no case has arisen which considers Executive power to impose, by virtue of federal assistance, contract terms in a state construction contract which are at variance with state law.

Stat. 308 (1952), 41 U.S.C. § 43a. See 4 K. Davis, Administrative Law § 28.06 (1958).

18. 310 U.S. at 127, 60 S.Ct. at 876.

19. Amici favoring the Plan include the City of Philadelphia, the Urban League of Philadelphia, Wives for Equal Employment Opportunity, the Lawyers' Committee for Civil Rights Under Law, and the N.A. A.C.P. Appearing as amici in opposition to the Plan are the Building and Construction Trades Dep't, AFL–CIO, the Building and Construction Trades Council of Philadelphia and Vicinity, AFL–CIO, the General Building Contractors Ass'n, Inc., the National Electrical Contractors Ass'n, and the Associated General Contractors of America.

20. Exec.Order No. 10925, 26 Fed.Reg. 1977 (March 6, 1961), 3 C.F.R., 1961 Comp. 86.

21. Management and Disposal of Government Property.

22. Procurement Procedures.

23. But cf. Weiner v. Cuyahoga Community College, 19 Ohio St.2d 35, 249 N.E.2d 907 (1969), cert. denied, 396 U.S. 1004, 90 S.Ct. 554, 24 L.Ed.2d 495 (1970); Ethridge v. Rhodes, 268 F.Supp. 83 (S.D. Ohio 1967).

The limitations of Executive power have rarely been considered by the courts. One of those rare instances is Youngstown Sheet & Tube Co. v. Sawyer, 343 U.S. 579, 72 S.Ct. 863, 96 L.Ed. 1153 (1952). From the six concurring opinions and one dissenting opinion in that case, the most significant guidance for present purposes may be found in that of Justice Jackson:

> We may well begin by a somewhat oversimplified grouping of practical situations in which a President may doubt, or others may challenge, his powers, and by distinguishing roughly the legal consequences of this factor of relativity.

> 1. When the President acts pursuant to an express or implied authorization of Congress, his authority is at its maximum, for it includes all that he possesses in his own right plus all that Congress can delegate. In these circumstances, and in these only, may he be said (for what it may be worth) to personify the federal sovereignty. If his act is held unconstitutional under these circumstances, it usually means that the Federal Government as an undivided whole lacks power. A seizure executed by the President pursuant to an Act of Congress would be supported by the strongest of presumptions and the widest latitude of judicial interpretation, and the burden of persuasion would rest heavily on any who might attack it.

> 2. When the President acts in absence of either a congressional grant or denial of authority, he can only rely upon his own independent powers, but there is a zone of twilight in which he and Congress may have concurrent authority, or in which its distribution is uncertain. Therefore, congressional inertia, indifference or quiescence may sometimes, at least as a practical matter, enable, if not invite, measures on independent presidential responsibility. In this area, any actual test of power is likely to depend on the imperatives of events and contemporary imponderables rather than on abstract theories of law.

> 3. When the President takes measures incompatible with the expressed or implied will of Congress, his power is at its lowest ebb, for then he can rely only upon his own constitutional powers minus any constitutional powers of Congress over the matter. Courts can sustain exclusive presidential control in such a case only by disabling the Congress from acting upon the subject. Presidential claim to a power at once so conclusive and preclusive must be scrutinized with caution, for what is at stake is the equilibrium established by our constitutional system.[24]

Plaintiffs contend that the Philadelphia Plan is inconsistent with the will of Congress expressed in several statutes. We deal with these statutory contentions hereinafter. Thus for the moment we may set to one side consideration of Justice Jackson's third category, and turn to category (1), action expressly or impliedly authorized, and category (2), action in which the President has implied power to act in the absence of

24. 343 U.S. at 635–638, 72 S.Ct. at 870–871 (footnotes omitted).

congressional preemption. To determine into which category the Philadelphia Plan falls a review of Executive Orders in the field of fair employment practices is helpful.

* * *

In the area of Government procurement Executive authority to impose non-discrimination contract provisions falls in Justice Jackson's first category: action pursuant to the express or implied authorization of Congress.

Executive Order No. 10925 [41] signed by President Kennedy on March 6, 1961, among other things enlarged the notice requirements and specified that the President's Committee on Equal Employment Opportunity could by rule, regulation or order impose sanctions for violation. Coverage still extended only to federal government contracts. Significantly for purposes of this case, however, the required contract language was amended to add the provision:

> The Contractor will take affirmative action to ensure that applicants are employed, and that employees are treated during employment, without regard to their race, creed, color, or national origin.[42]

The Philadelphia Plan is simply a refined approach to this "affirmative action" mandate. Applied to federal procurement the affirmative action clause is supported by the same Presidential procurement authority that supports the non-discrimination clause generally.

The most significant change in the Executive Order program for present purposes occurred on June 22, 1963 when the President signed Executive Order No. 11114,[43] which amended Executive Order No. 10925 by providing that the same non-discrimination contract provisions heretofore required in all federal procurement contracts must also be included in all federally assisted construction contracts. By way of Executive Order No. 11246 [44] issued in 1965, President Johnson transferred to the Secretary of Labor the functions formerly specified in Executive Order Nos. 10925 and 11114, and he continued both the affirmative action requirement and the coverage of federally assisted construction contracts.

While all federal procurement contracts must include an affirmative action covenant,[45] the coverage on federally assisted contracts has been extended to construction contracts only. This choice is significant, for it demonstrates that the Presidents were not attempting by the Executive Order program merely to impose their notions of desira-

---

41. 26 Fed.Reg. 1977, 3 C.F.R., 1959–63 Comp. 448.

42. Id., pt. III, § 301(1).

43. 28 Fed.Reg. 6485, 3 C.F.R., 1959–63 Comp. 774.

44. See note 4 supra.

45. Section 204 of Exec.Order No. 11246 provides that the Secretary of Labor may exempt certain contracts and purchase orders from the requirements of the order because of special circumstances in the national interest and that he may by rule or regulation exempt certain classes of contracts (1) to be performed outside the United States, (2) for standard commercial supplies or raw materials, (3) involving insubstantial amounts of money or workers, or (4) involving subcontracts below a specified tier.

ble social legislation on the states wholesale. Rather, they acted in the one area in which discrimination in employment was most likely to affect the cost and the progress of projects in which the federal government had both financial and completion interests. In direct procurement the federal government has a vital interest in assuring that the largest possible pool of qualified manpower be available for the accomplishment of its projects. It has the identical interest with respect to federally assisted construction projects. When the Congress authorizes an appropriation for a program of federal assistance, and authorizes the Executive branch to implement the program by arranging for assistance to specific projects, in the absence of specific statutory regulations it must be deemed to have granted to the President a general authority to act for the protection of federal interests. In the case of Executive Order Nos. 11246 and 11114 three Presidents have acted by analogizing federally assisted construction to direct federal procurement. If such action has not been authorized by Congress (Justice Jackson's first category), at the least it falls within the second category. If no congressional enactments prohibit what has been done, the Executive action is valid. Particularly is this so when Congress, aware of Presidential action with respect to federally assisted construction projects since June of 1963, has continued to make appropriations for such projects. We conclude, therefore, that unless the Philadelphia Plan is prohibited by some other congressional enactment, its inclusion as a pre-condition for federal assistance was within the implied authority of the President and his designees. We turn, then to a consideration of the statutes on which plaintiffs rely.

THE CIVIL RIGHTS ACT OF 1964

Plaintiffs suggest that by enacting Title VII of the Civil Rights Act of 1964, 42 U.S.C. § 2000e et seq., which deals comprehensively with discrimination in employment, Congress occupied the field. The express reference in that statute to Executive Order No. 10925 or any other Executive Order prescribing fair employment practices for Government contractors, 42 U.S.C. § 2000e–8(d), indicates, however, that Congress contemplated continuance of the Executive Order program. Moreover we have held that the remedies established by Title VII are not exclusive. Young v. International Telephone & Telegraph Co., 438 F.2d 757 (3d Cir.1971).

But while Congress has not prohibited Presidential action in the area of fair employment on federal or federally assisted contracts, the Executive is bound by the express prohibitions of Title VII. The argument most strenuously advanced against the Philadelphia Plan is that it requires action by employers which violates the Act. Plaintiffs point to § 703(j), 42 U.S.C. § 2000e–2(j):

> Nothing contained in this subchapter shall be interpreted to require any employer * * * [or] labor organization * * * to grant preferential treatment to any individual or to any group because of the race * * * of such individual or groups on account of an imbalance which

may exist with respect to the total number or percentage of persons of any race * * * employed * * * in comparison with the total number or percentage of persons of such race * * * in the available work force in any community * * * or other area.

The Plan requires that the contractor establish specific goals for utilization of available minority manpower in six trades in the five-county area. Possibly an employer could not be compelled, under the authority of Title VII, to embrace such a program, although § 703(j) refers to percentages of minorities in an area work force rather than percentages of minority tradesmen in an available trade work force. We do not meet that issue here, however, for the source of the required contract provision is Executive Order No. 11246. Section 703(j) is a limitation only upon Title VII not upon any other remedies, state or federal.

Plaintiffs, and more particularly the union amici, contend that the Plan violates Title VII because it interferes with a bona fide seniority system. Section 703(h), 42 U.S.C. § 2000e–2(h), provides:

Notwithstanding any other provision of this subchapter, it shall not be an unlawful employment practice for an employer to employ different standards of compensation, or different terms, conditions, or privileges of employment pursuant to a bona fide seniority or merit system * * *.

The unions, it is said, refer men from the hiring halls on the basis of seniority, and the Philadelphia Plan interferes with this arrangement since few minority tradesmen have high seniority. Just as with § 703(j), however, § 703(h) is a limitation only upon Title VII, not upon any other remedies.[46]

Plaintiffs contend that the Plan, by imposing remedial quotas, requires them to violate the basic prohibitions of Section 703(a), 42 U.S.C. § 2000e–2(a):

It shall be an unlawful employment practice for an employer—

(1) to fail or refuse to hire * * * any individual * * * because of such individual's race * * * or

(2) to * * * classify his employees in any way which would deprive * * * any individual of employment opportunities * * * because of such individual's race * * *.

Because the Plan requires that the contractor agree to specific goals for minority employment in each of the six trades and requires a good faith effort to achieve those goals, they argue, it requires (1) that they refuse

---

46. This same subsection refers to ability tests. The Supreme Court recently in Griggs v. Duke Power Co., 401 U.S. 424, 91 S.Ct. 849, 28 L.Ed.2d 158 (1971) considered the extent to which such tests are permissible. The Court said:

"But Congress directed the thrust of the Act to the *consequences* of employment practices, not simply the motivation." 91 S.Ct. at 854.

It held that the tests must be job related. Nor can seniority make permanent the effects of past discrimination. Local 189, United Papermakers & Paperworkers v. United States, 416 F.2d 980 (5th Cir.1969), cert. denied, 397 U.S. 919, 90 S.Ct. 926, 25 L.Ed.2d 108 (1970); Quarles v. Philip Morris, Inc., 279 F.Supp. 505 (E.D.Va.1968).

to hire some white tradesmen, and (2) that they classify their employees by race, in violation of § 703(a). This argument rests on an overly simple reading both of the Plan and of the findings which led to its adoption.

The order of September 23, 1969 contained findings that although overall minority group representation in the construction industry in the five-county Philadelphia area was thirty per cent, in the six trades representation was approximately one per cent. It found, moreover, that this obvious underrepresentation was due to the exclusionary practices of the unions representing the six trades. It is the practice of building contractors to rely on union hiring halls as the prime source for employees. The order made further findings as to the availability of qualified minority tradesmen for employment in each trade, and as to the impact of an affirmative action program with specific goals upon the existing labor force. The Department of Labor found that contractors could commit to the specific employment goals "without adverse impact on the existing labor force." Some minority tradesmen could be recruited, in other words, without eliminating job opportunities for white tradesmen.

To read § 703(a) in the manner suggested by the plaintiffs we would have to attribute to Congress the intention to freeze the status quo and to foreclose remedial action under other authority designed to overcome existing evils. We discern no such intention either from the language of the statute or from its legislative history. Clearly the Philadelphia Plan is color-conscious. Indeed the only meaning which can be attributed to the "affirmative action" language which since March of 1961 has been included in successive Executive Orders is that Government contractors must be color-conscious. Since 1941 the Executive Order program has recognized that discriminatory practices exclude available minority manpower from the labor pool. In other contexts color-consciousness has been deemed to be an appropriate remedial posture. Porcelli v. Titus, 302 F.Supp. 726 (D.N.J.1969), aff'd, 431 F.2d 1254 (3d Cir.1970); Norwalk CORE v. Norwalk Redevelopment Agency, 395 F.2d 920, 931 (2d Cir.1968); Offermann v. Nitkowski, 378 F.2d 22, 24 (2d Cir.1967). It has been said respecting Title VII that "Congress did not intend to freeze an entire generation of Negro employees into discriminatory patterns that existed before the Act." Quarles v. Philip Morris, Inc., supra, 279 F.Supp. at 514. The *Quarles* case rejected the contention that existing, nondiscriminatory seniority arrangements were so sanctified by Title VII that the effects of past discrimination in job assignments could not be overcome.[47] We reject the contention that Title VII prevents the President acting through the Executive Order program from attempting to remedy the absence from

47. The federal courts in overcoming the effects of past discrimination are expressly authorized in Title VII to take affirmative action. 42 U.S.C. § 2000e–5(g). See Vogler v. McCarty, 294 F.Supp. 368 (E.D.La.1968), aff'd sub nom. International Ass'n Heat & Frost Insulation & Asbestos Workers v. Vogler, 407 F.2d 1047 (5th Cir. 1969).

the Philadelphia construction labor of minority tradesmen in key trades.

What we have said about Title VII applies with equal force to Title VI of the Civil Rights Act of 1964, 42 U.S.C. § 2000d et seq. That Title prohibits racial and other discrimination in any program or activity receiving federal financial assistance.[48] This general prohibition against discrimination cannot be construed as limiting Executive authority in defining appropriate affirmative action on the part of a contractor.

We hold that the Philadelphia Plan does not violate the Civil Rights Act of 1964.

THE NATIONAL LABOR RELATIONS ACT

The June 27, 1969 order, par. 8(b) provides:

> It is no excuse that the union with which the contractor has a collective bargaining agreement failed to refer minority employees. Discrimination in referral for employment, even if pursuant to provisions of a collective bargaining agreement, is prohibited by the National Labor Relations Act and the Civil Rights Act of 1964. It is the longstanding uniform policy of OFCC that contractors and subcontractors have a responsibility to provide equal employment opportunity if they want to participate in federally involved contracts. To the extent they have delegated the responsibility for some of their employment practices to some other organization or agency which prevents them from meeting their obligations pursuant to Executive Order 11246, as amended, such contractors cannot be considered to be in compliance with Executive Order 11246, as amended, or the implementing rules, regulations and orders.

The union amici vigorously contend that the Plan violates the National Labor Relations Act by interfering with the exclusive union referral systems to which the contractors have in collective bargaining agreements bound themselves. Exclusive hiring hall contracts in the building and construction industry are validated by Section 8(f) of the National Labor Relations Act, 29 U.S.C. § 158(f). In Teamsters Local 357 v. NLRB, 365 U.S. 667, 81 S.Ct. 835, 6 L.Ed.2d 11 (1961), the Supreme Court held that the National Labor Relations Board could not proscribe exclusive hiring hall agreements as illegal per se since Congress had not chosen to prohibit hiring halls. It is argued that the President is attempting to do what the Supreme Court said the National Labor Relations Board could not do—prohibit a valid hiring hall agreement. Of course collective bargaining agreements which perpetuate the effects of past discrimination are unlawful under Title VII. Local 189, United Papermakers & Paperworkers v. United States,

---

48. Section 604 of Title VI, 42 U.S.C. § 2000d–3, states that nothing in the Title authorizes agency action under the Title with respect to employment practices of any employer, except where federal assistance is primarily aimed at providing employment. However, since the Philadelphia Plan does not purport to derive its authorization from Title VI, this section does not affect its validity.

supra; United States v. Sheet Metal Workers, Local 36, 416 F.2d 123, 132 (8th Cir.1969). The findings of past discrimination which justified remedial action in these cases were made in judicial proceedings, however. See 42 U.S.C. § 2000e–5(g). The amici contend that the Assistant Secretary's nonjudicial finding of prior exclusionary practices is insufficient to support the Plan's implied requirement that the contractor look to other sources for employees if the unions fail to refer sufficient minority group members.

It is clear that while hiring hall arrangements are permitted by federal law they are not required. Nothing in the National Labor Relations Act purports to place any limitation upon the contracting power of the federal government. We have said hereinabove that in imposing the affirmative action requirement on federally assisted construction contracts the President acted within his implied contracting authority. The assisted agency may either agree to do business with contractors who will comply with the affirmative action covenant, or forego assistance. The prospective contractors may either agree to undertake the affirmative action covenant, or forego bidding on federally assisted work. If the Plan violates neither the Constitution nor federal law, the fact that its contractual provisions may be at variance with other contractual undertakings of the contractor is legally irrelevant. Factually, of course, that variance is quite relevant. Factually it is entirely likely that the economics of the marketplace will produce an accommodation between the contract provisions desired by the unions and those desired by the source of the funds. Such an accommodation will be no violation of the National Labor Relations Act.

The absence of a judicial finding of past discrimination is also legally irrelevant. The Assistant Secretary acted not pursuant to Title VII but pursuant to the Executive Order. Regardless of the cause, exclusion from the available labor pool of minority tradesmen is likely to have an adverse effect upon the cost and completion of construction projects in which the federal government is interested. Even absent a finding that the situation found to exist in the five-county area was the result of deliberate past discrimination, the federal interest in improving the availability of key tradesmen in the labor pool would be the same. While a court must find intentional past discrimination before it can require affirmative action under 42 U.S.C. § 2000e–5(g), that section imposes no restraint upon the measures which the President may require of the beneficiaries of federal assistance. The decision of his designees as to the specific affirmative action which would satisfy the local situation did not violate the National Labor Relations Act and was not prohibited by 42 U.S.C. § 2000e–5(g).

CONSISTENCY WITH EXECUTIVE ORDER NO. 11246

The plaintiffs argue that the affirmative action mandate of § 202 of Executive Order No. 11246 is limited by the more general requirement in the same section, "The contractor will not discriminate against any employee or applicant for employment because of race, creed, color, or national origin." They contend that properly construed the affirmative action referred to means only policing against actual present discrimination, not action looking toward the employment of specific numbers of minority tradesmen.

Section 201 of the Executive Order provides:

> The Secretary of Labor shall be responsible for the administration of Parts II [Government contracts] and III [federal assistance] of this Order and shall adopt such rules and regulations and issue such orders as he deems necessary and appropriate to achieve the purposes thereof.

Acting under this broad delegation of authority the Labor Department in a series of orders of local application made it clear that it interpreted "affirmative action" to require more than mere policing against actual present discrimination.[49] Administrative action pursuant to an Executive Order is invalid and subject to judicial review if beyond the scope of the Executive Order. Peters v. Hobby, 349 U.S. 331, 75 S.Ct. 790, 99 L.Ed. 1129 (1955). But the courts should give more than ordinary deference to an administrative agency's interpretation of an Executive Order or regulation which it is charged to administer. Udall v. Tallman, 380 U.S. 1, 85 S.Ct. 792, 13 L.Ed.2d 616 (1965); Bowles v. Seminole Rock & Sand Co., 325 U.S. 410, 413, 65 S.Ct. 1215, 89 L.Ed. 1700 (1945). The Attorney General has issued an opinion that the Philadelphia Plan is valid,[50] and the President has continued to acquiesce in the interpretation of the Executive Order made by his designee. The Labor Department interpretation of the affirmative action clause must, therefore, be deferred to by the courts.

Plaintiffs also contend that the signing of the June 27, 1969 and September 23, 1969 orders by an assistant secretary rather than by the Secretary of Labor makes those orders procedurally invalid. Here they rely on § 401 which provides:

> The Secretary of Labor may delegate to any officer, agency, or employee in the Executive branch of the Government, any function or duty of the Secretary under Parts II and III of this Order, except authority to promulgate rules and regulations of a general nature.

The Plan, they say, is a rule or regulation of a general nature, and could have been issued only by the Secretary. In the first place the Plan is not general. It is based upon findings as to the available construction manpower in a specific labor market. Moreover, the interpretation of § 401 made by the administrator requires the same deference from the courts as is required toward his other interpretations of the order. We will not second guess his delegation to the Assistant Secretary of the duty of enforcing the affirmative action covenant.

49. See United States Commission on Civil Rights, The Federal Civil Rights Enforcement Effort at 167–72 (1970).

50. Att'y Gen. Op., Letter to Sec. of Labor Shultz, Sept. 22, 1969, 115 Cong.Rec. 17.204–06 (daily ed. Dec. 18, 1969).

THE DUE PROCESS CONTENTIONS

Plaintiffs urge that the Plan violates the Due Process Clause of the Fifth Amendment in several ways.

First, they allege that it imposes on the contractors contradictory duties impossible of attainment. This impossibility arises, they say, because the Plan requires both an undertaking to seek achievement of specific goals of minority employment and an undertaking not to discriminate against any qualified applicant or employee, and because a decision to hire any black employee necessarily involves a decision not to hire a qualified white employee. This is pure sophistry. The findings in the September 23, 1969 order disclose that the specific goals may be met, considering normal employee attrition and anticipated growth in the industry, without adverse effects on the existing labor force. According to the order the construction industry has an essentially transitory labor force and is often in short supply in key trades. The complaint does not allege that these findings misstate the underlying facts.

Next the plaintiffs urge that the Plan is arbitrary and capricious administrative action, in that it singles out the contractors and makes them take action to remedy the situation created by acts of past discrimination by the craft unions. They point to the absence of any proceedings under Title VII against the offending unions, and urge that they are being discriminated against. This argument misconceives the source of the authority for the affirmative action program. Plaintiffs are not being discriminated against. They are merely being invited to bid on a contract with terms imposed by the source of the funds. The affirmative action covenant is no different in kind than other covenants specified in the invitation to bid. The Plan does not impose a punishment for past misconduct. It exacts a covenant for present performance.

Some amici urge that selection of the five-county Philadelphia area was arbitrary and capricious and without basis in fact. The complaint contains a conclusive allegation to this effect. No supporting facts are alleged. It is not alleged, for example, that the specific goals for minority manpower utilization would be different if more or fewer counties were to be included in the September 23, 1969 order. The union amici do question the findings made by the Assistant Secretary of Labor, but the complaint, fairly read, does not put these findings in issue. We read the allegation with respect to the five-county area as putting in issue the legal authority of the Secretary to impose a specific affirmative action requirement in any separate geographic area. The simple answer to this contention is that federally assisted construction contracts are performed at specific times and in specific places. What is appropriate affirmative action will very according to the local manpower conditions prevailing at the time.

Finally, the plaintiffs urge that the specific goals specified by the Plan are racial quotas prohibited by the equal protection aspect of the

Fifth Amendment. See Shapiro v. Thompson, 394 U.S. 618, 641–642, 89 S.Ct. 1322, 22 L.Ed. 600 (1969); Schneider v. Rusk, 377 U.S. 163, 84 S.Ct. 1187, 12 L.Ed.2d 218 (1964); Bolling v. Sharpe, 347 U.S. 497, 74 S.Ct. 693, 98 L.Ed. 884 (1954). The Philadelphia Plan is valid Executive action designed to remedy the perceived evil that minority tradesmen have not been included in the labor pool available for the performance of construction projects in which the federal government has a cost and performance interest. The Fifth Amendment does not prohibit such action.

* * *

The federal interest is in maximum availability of construction tradesmen for the projects in which the federal government has a cost and completion interest. A finding as to the historical reason for the exclusion of available tradesmen from the labor pool is not essential for federal contractual remedial action.

The judgment of the district court will be affirmed.

ASSOCIATED GENERAL CONTRACTORS OF MASSACHUSETTS, INC. v. ALTSHULER

United States Court of Appeals for the First Circuit, 1973.
490 F.2d 9.
Certiorari denied April 22, 1974.
See 94 S.Ct. 1971.

COFFIN, CHIEF JUDGE.

This is an appeal from a judgment sustaining, as constitutional and in accord with state law, certain contract requirements imposed by the Commonwealth of Massachusetts upon contractors engaged in publicly funded construction work at Boston State College. Appellants are thirteen individual construction companies, now engaged in construction of public buildings for the Commonwealth, and a membership corporation comprised of one hundred forty-five general contracting firms which together perform approximately eighty per cent of all construction in the Commonwealth. Each of the appellants was a prospective bidder for the Boston State College contract.

In relevant part, § 1B of the contract requires that the contractor

* * * maintain on his project, which is located in an area in which there are high concentrations of minority group persons, a not less than twenty percent ratio of minority employee man hours to total employee man hours in each job category * * *.

Section V, ¶ 3, of the contract provides, however, that the contractor must hire only "competent" workers. The Secretary of Transportation and Construction for the Commonwealth, who is charged with enforcing the contract provisions, interprets this to mean that § 1B requires the hiring of only "qualified" workers. The district court has interpreted the contract in the same way.

The contract also requires that the contractor engage in special referral procedures as well as traditional referral methods, cooperate with a Liaison Committee composed of various representatives from community groups, make weekly compliance reports to the Liaison Committee and the Massachusetts Commission Against Discrimination (M.C.A.D.), and permit the M.C.A.D. access to books, records, and accounts containing employment information.

The contract further stipulates that the M.C.A.D. will investigate any alleged non-compliance with the contract terms and notify the contractor of both its findings and recommendations as to how he might comply with the terms. If the contractor fails to accept the recommendations and in addition the M.C.A.D. determines that the contractor has not taken "every possible measure to achieve compliance", the M.C.A.D. will report its findings to the Bureau of Construction and recommend that specific sanctions be imposed. Before imposing any sanctions, however, pursuant to the Commonwealth's Administrative Procedures Act, M.G.L.A. c. 30A §§ 10, 11, and according to the Secretary of Transportation and Construction, the Bureau will provide the contractor with notice of the findings and a hearing in which he may challenge them.

Because the federal government pays a portion of the construction costs of the Boston State project, contractors are also required to accept federal bid conditions, promulgated by the United States Secretary of Labor pursuant to § 201 of Executive Order No. 11246 (30 F.R. 12319, as amended, 32 F.R. 14303; 34 F.R. 12985) and 41 C.F.R. 60. The specific contractual elements of the federal bid conditions are derived from the Boston Area Construction Program (the Boston Plan), a "hometown" equal employment opportunity plan prepared by the local construction industry in cooperation with the Department of Labor. Unlike the Commonwealth's § 1B, the federal Boston Plan sets area-wide percentage objectives for minority hiring within each trade, rather than percentage goals for each project. Under the Boston Plan the responsibility for fulfilling the objectives does not lie with the individual contractor; he merely agrees to hire whatever minority workers are referred to him by the trades unions in the course of the plan's operation. Moreover, while § 1B requires that contractors take "every possible measure" to comply with the contract terms, the Boston Plan necessitates merely a "good faith" effort by the contractor. A fourth point of difference between the two plans is that the Boston Plan places the burden of proving non-compliance upon the government agency, while § 1B places the burden of proving compliance, once non-compliance has been alleged, upon the contractor himself.

Appellants challenge the constitutionality of § 1B of the contract requirements imposed by the Commonwealth on three grounds: They contend, first, that § 1B varies so significantly from the federal bid conditions of the Boston Plan that it violates the Supremacy Clause of Article VI; second, that § 1B imposes a fixed racial hiring quota which violates the Equal Protection Clause of the Fourteenth Amendment; and finally, that § 1B permits the imposition of sanctions without proper notice or an opportunity to be heard, in violation of the Due Process Clause of the Fourteenth Amendment. Appellants also contend, pursuant to the pendent jurisdiction of this court, that § 1B involves the M.C.A.D. in activities which go beyond the scope of its enabling legislation.

I

In order to deal with appellants' first contention, that § 1B violates the Supremacy Clause because the federal Boston Plan must necessarily preempt § 1B, it is necessary to set out the context in which this case arises.

We note at the outset that the construction industry has been particularly slow, throughout the nation, to open itself to racial minorities.[1] For this reason, in 1967 the federal government launched pilot plans in several cities designed to increase minority employment on federally funded construction projects by way of "affirmative action" programs. Executive Order 11246,[2] under which the Secretary of Labor was authorized to promulgate such programs,[3] required that contractors "take affirmative action to ensure that applicants are employed * * * without regard to race * * *." Affirmative action itself was defined as "specific steps to guarantee equal employment opportunity keyed to the problems and needs of members of minority groups, including, when there are deficiencies, the development of specific goals and time tables * * *."[4]

After several different affirmative action programs had been implemented, with varying degrees of success,[5] in 1970 the government permitted particular communities to develop their own "hometown" affirmative action programs.[6] If the Secretary of Labor approved the

1. See Marshall, The Negro and Organized Labor, 118–28 (1965); Hill, The Racial Practices of Organized Labor: The Contemporary Record, in The Negro and the American Labor Movement 313–314 (J. Jacobson, ed., 1968).

As of May 19, 1970, only 11.8% of the 1.1 million members of the construction unions in America were members of racial minorities. The higher the skilled union, the smaller the percentage of minority workers becomes: 38.3% of construction laborers are members of racial minorities, while 5.1% of electrical workers, and 2.1% of plumbers. Equal Employment Opportunity Commission Release No. 70–15 (May 19, 1970).

2. 30 Fed.Reg. 12319, as amended 32 Fed.Reg. 14303.

3. Under the Secretary of Labor's regulations, the Director of the Office of Contract Compliance (O.F.C.C.) has full authority to implement the policies of the Secretary. Thus, the position of the O.F. C.C. is analogous to that of the Commonwealth's Bureau of Construction.

4. 41 C.F.R. § 60.–1.40(a) (Supp.1970).

5. Plans have been promulgated for Philadelphia, Washington, D.C., St. Louis, Atlanta, and Camden, N.J. See 41 C.F.R. 60.5, 60.6, 60.8, and 38 F.R. 21533 (Aug. 10, 1973). Such "imposed" plans operate only on the contractors; they do not require, and typically do not have, the cooperation of the unions involved.

6. There are now approximately forty-seven hometown plans finally approved by the O.F.C.C., including approximately twenty-nine federally funded training programs.

plans,[7] the plans would receive federal funding, and local contractors who complied with them would thereby comply with the mandate of Executive Order 11246.[8]

The Boston Plan emerged from negotiations between representatives of buildings trades unions, contractors, and minority communities in the Boston area, and was approved by the Secretary of Labor in the fall of 1970. Although it fulfilled its first year goal of training and placing three hundred sixty minority workers, relationships with the minority community representatives deteriorated to the extent that the Department of Labor withheld second year funding until a revised plan could be negotiated. The new plan, beginning operations in January, 1972, did not have the participation of representatives of Boston's minority communities.[9] In addition, although put into effect two years after the original Boston Plan had commenced, the revised plan retained the same minority employment goal as that of the original plan.

At about the same time as the revised Boston Plan was put into effect, the Commonwealth began an inquiry of its own into the need for a separate state affirmative action program. The inquiry revealed that despite the existence of the federal Boston Plan, minority membership in all of the nineteen participating unions amounted to less than four per cent of union membership, while minorities comprised approximately twenty-three per cent of the population of Boston. Since virtually all of the contractors who engage in state funded projects rely upon these predominantly white unions for workers, minority employment in the construction trades continued to be extremely low. The Commonwealth also determined that the Boston Plan had no provision for the collection of reliable data on the actual number of hours worked by minority workers placed on construction jobs. Finally, in the opinion of the Commonwealth's Office of Transportation and Construction, the Boston Plan lacked adequate enforcement machinery.[10] On

7. The O.F.C.C. determines the adequacy of the hometown plan by considering such factors as (1) the minority population of the area to be covered by the plan; (2) the minority manpower utilization in the industry (on a trade by trade basis); (3) the availability of minorities for employment; (4) the need and availability of training programs; and (5) the projected growth and attrition factors of the area industry in the near future.

8. For any trades or contractors not participating in the hometown plan, Part II of the federal bid conditions sets forth mandatory affirmative action requirements for each individual contractor, generally paralleling those of the hometown plan. The principal distinction with respect to Parts I and II of the bid conditions is that the obligations under Part II are individual obligations that run to a contractor's own work forces, with each con-

tractor responsible for its own training program. Under Part I (the hometown plan), the minority hiring goals are obligations of the trade, and it is the administrative committee of the hometown plan that assigns fair share goals to the individual contractors.

9. The United States Department of Labor is now funding a subcontract with the Recruiting and Training Program (formerly the Workers Defense League), a minority organization which is providing recruiting, training, and referrals for the Boston Plan.

10. The Commonwealth was also of the view that it is desirable to concentrate minority employment in the trade in projects in or near minority neighborhoods. Thus, the Commonwealth contends that its plan is not designed simply for the purpose of increasing minority employment but al-

the basis of these findings the Commonwealth concluded that the federal Boston Plan had not gone far enough, and that a separate, state affirmative action program was required for construction projects in which state funds were committed.

The contract for the construction of Boston State College is the first to incorporate both the Commonwealth's own § 1B bid conditions, promulgated under authority of the Governor's Executive Order No. 74, and the federal Boston Plan bid conditions. The Assistant Secretary of Transportation and Construction for the Commonwealth has determined that there exist adequate journeymen, apprentices, and trainees within Boston's minority community to provide at least twenty per cent of the work force for the project, as well as for other projects anticipated in the area.[11] It is estimated that the total work force required for the Boston State Project will vary between forty-seven and one hundred fifty persons; contractors on the project must therefore take "every possible measure" to employ between ten and thirty qualified minority workers.

Appellants contend that because the Commonwealth's § 1B affirmative action program places different requirements upon contractors than those of the Boston Plan, the two are in conflict, and that the state plan must therefore be declared invalid. Appellants point out, most particularly, that under § 1B, contractors must bear the burden of showing that they have taken "every possible measure" to comply, whereas under the Boston Plan, they must have made merely a "good faith effort" and the burden of showing non-compliance rests with the government agency. They also stress that the record keeping and referral requirements of § 1B are more onerous than those of the Boston Plan.

In deciding whether state regulations should be invalidated because they conflict with federal law, courts have tended to examine both the possibility of broad conflict in "purposes and objectives" between the two schemes, Hines v. Davidowitz, 312 U.S. 52, 67, 61 S.Ct. 399, 85 L.Ed. 581 (1940), and the likelihood of specific conflict in the implementation of the two programs.

Clearly, the broad purposes which lay behind the federal Boston Plan and the Commonwealth's § 1B are congruent. Affirmative action, defined in the President's Executive Order as " * * * steps to guarantee equal employment * * * including * * * the development of specific goals and time tables * * * " has the same meaning as affirmative action as defined in the Governor's Executive Order: " * * * positive and aggressive measures to insure equal opportunity." Both plans envisage minority hiring goals as a means of achieving equal opportunity.

so for altering the geographic distribution of placements.

11. The district court found that the minority populations of neighborhoods in

which the Commonwealth's plan is to be applied is approximately 40%.

Nothing in the President's Executive Order requires that affirmative action taken under the Order be uniform throughout the country, nor does it necessitate that the federal government be the source for every program. An important aspect of federal implementation is the development of "hometown" plans, conceived and developed by local contractors, unions, and minority representatives. And in at least one instance the federal government has relied upon a plan originally conceived by state officials for their own state funded contracts. See Illinois Builders Ass'n v. Ogilvie, 327 F.Supp. 1154 (S.D.Ill.1971), aff'd. 471 F.2d 680 (7th Cir.1972).

Nor is there any indication that the federal government has intended to preempt this field. Federal preemption should not be presumed, absent "a clear manifestation of intention" to preempt the field. Schwartz v. Texas, 344 U.S. 199, 202–203, 73 S.Ct. 232, 97 L.Ed. 231 (1952); see also New York State Department of Social Service v. Dublino, 405 U.S. 413, 93 S.Ct. 2507, 37 L.Ed.2d 688 (1973). The President's Executive Order merely requires that contractors take some "affirmative action" and directs the Secretary of Labor to "use his best efforts" through "state and local agencies" as well as federal agencies. The Secretary of Labor has stated, as amicus curiae, that the federal program is not meant to preempt state programs such as the Commonwealth's § 1B. And congressional policy in this area, as expressed in Title VII of the Civil Rights Act of 1964, the statute most closely analogous to the President's Executive Order, is clearly one of encouraging state cooperation and initiative in remedying racial discrimination. Title VII, 42 U.S.C. § 2000h–4 expressly disclaims any intent to preempt state action. See also Voutsis v. Union Carbide, 452 F.2d 889 (2d Cir.1971), cert. denied, 406 U.S. 918, 92 S.Ct. 1768, 32 L.Ed.2d 117 (1971).

Even if there is no conflict between the purposes and objectives of the two schemes, the state plan might still be invalid if there is a showing of "such actual conflict between the two schemes of regulation that both cannot stand in the same area * * *." Florida Lime and Avocado Growers, Inc. v. Paul, 373 U.S. 132, 141, 83 S.Ct. 1210, 1217, 10 L.Ed.2d 248 (1963); see also Perez v. Campbell, 402 U.S. 637, 649–653, 91 S.Ct. 1704, 29 L.Ed.2d 233 (1971). While we acknowledge that § 1B may be more demanding than the Boston Plan, and may well involve higher administrative costs, there is no reason to suppose that contractors could not comply with both at the same time. By complying with § 1B's minority hiring goals on projects funded by both the state and the federal government, contractors would also comply with the Boston Plan's goals. The reporting requirements are different for the two plans, but this merely necessitates the filing of two different sets of reports.

* * *

II

Appellant's second contention, that the Commonwealth's § 1B imposes a fixed racial hiring quota which violates the Equal Protection Clause of the Fourteenth Amendment, presents a more difficult issue, the implications of which stretch far beyond this particular dispute.

The first Justice Harlan's much quoted observation that "the Constitution [is colorblind] * * * [and] does not * * * permit any public authority to know the race of those entitled to be protected in the enjoyment of such rights", Plessy v. Ferguson, 163 U.S. 537, 554, 16 S.Ct. 1138, 1145, 41 L.Ed. 256 (1896) (dissenting opinion) has come to represent a long-term goal. It is by now well understood, however, that our society cannot be completely colorblind in the short term if we are to have a colorblind society in the long term. After centuries of viewing through colored lenses, eyes do not quickly adjust when the lenses are removed. Discrimination has a way of perpetuating itself, albeit unintentionally, because the resulting inequalities make new opportunities less accessible. Preferential treatment is one partial prescription to remedy our society's most intransigent and deeply rooted inequalities.

Intentional, official recognition of race has been found necessary to achieve fair and equal opportunity in the selection of grand juries, Brooks v. Beto, 366 F.2d 1 (5th Cir.1966); tenants for public housing, Otero v. New York City Housing Authority, 484 F.2d 1122 (2d Cir.1973); Norwalk CORE v. Norwalk Redevelopment Agency, 395 F.2d 920 (2d Cir.1968); Gautreaux v. Chicago Housing Authority, 304 F.Supp. 736 (N.D.Ill.1969); school administrators, Porcelli v. Titus, 431 F.2d 1254 (3d Cir.1970); and children who are to attend a specific public school, Swann v. Charlotte-Mecklenburg Board of Education, 402 U.S. 1, 91 S.Ct. 1267, 28 L.Ed.2d 554 (1971).

The intentional, official recognition of race in the selection of union members or construction workers has been constitutionally tested and upheld in two contexts. The first is where courts have ordered, pursuant to Title VII of the Civil Rights Act of 1964, 42 U.S.C. § 2000e–5(g), remedial action for past discrimination. In fulfilling their "duty to render a decree which will so far as possible eliminate the discriminatory effects of the past * * *", Louisiana v. United States, 380 U.S. 145, 154, 85 S.Ct. 817, 822, 13 L.Ed.2d 709 (1965), courts have ordered unions to grant immediate membership to a number of minority applicants, United States v. Wood, Wire, and Metal Lathers International Union, Local No. 46, 471 F.2d 408 (2d Cir.1973), cert. denied, 412 U.S. 939, 93 S.Ct. 2773, 37 L.Ed.2d 398 (1973); to begin an affirmative minority recruitment program, United States v. Sheet Metal Workers International Ass'n, Local No. 36, 416 F.2d 123 (8th Cir.1969); to match normal referrals with minority referrals until a specific objective has been obtained, Heat and Frost Workers, Local 53 v. Vogler, 407 F.2d 1047 (5th Cir.1969); or to take on a certain number of minority apprentices for each class of workers, United States v. Ironworkers

Local 86, 443 F.2d 544 (9th Cir.1971), cert. denied, 404 U.S. 984, 92 S.Ct. 447, 30 L.Ed.2d 367 (1971). Courts have also ordered employers to hire minority employees up to thirty per cent of the total work force, Stamps v. Detroit Edison, 365 F.Supp. 87 (E.D.Mich.1973); to hire one minority worker every time two white workers were hired, up to a certain number, Carter v. Gallagher, 452 F.2d 315 (8th Cir.1971), cert. denied, 406 U.S. 950, 92 S.Ct. 2045, 32 L.Ed.2d 338 (1972); and in our own Castro v. Beecher, 459 F.2d 725 (1972), we order that black and Spanish-speaking applicants for police positions, who had failed to measure up to a constitutionally impermissible set of hiring standards, be given priority in future hiring.

The second context in which race has been recognized as a permissible criterion for employment is where courts have upheld federal affirmative action programs against challenges under the Equal Protection clause or under the anti-preference provisions of Title VII of the Civil Rights Act of 1964, 42 U.S.C. § 2000e–2(j). Recognizing that the discretionary power of public authorities to remedy past discrimination is even broader than that of the judicial branch, see Swann v. Charlotte-Mecklenburg, supra at 16 of 402 U.S., 91 S.Ct. 1267; cf. Katzenbach v. Morgan, 384 U.S. 641, 653, 86 S.Ct. 1717, 16 L.Ed.2d 828 (1966), courts have upheld the specific percentage goals and time tables for minority hiring found in the Philadelphia Plan, Contractors Ass'n of Eastern Pennsylvania v. Secretary of Labor, 311 F.Supp. 1002 (E.D.Pa. 1970), aff'd, 442 F.2d 159 (3d Cir.1971), cert. denied, 404 U.S. 854, 92 S.Ct. 98, 30 L.Ed.2d 95 (1971), the Cleveland Plan, Weiner v. Cuyahoga Community College District, 19 Ohio St.2d 35, 249 N.E.2d 907, 908 (1969), cert. denied, 396 U.S. 1004 (1970), the Newark Plan, Joyce v. McCrane, 320 F.Supp. 1284 (D.N.J.1970), and the Illinois Ogilvie Plan, Southern Illinois Builders Ass'n v. Ogilvie, 327 F.Supp. 1154 (S.D.Ill. 1971), aff'd, 471 F.2d 680 (7th Cir.1972).

Despite ample precedent for using race as a criterion of selection where the goal is equal opportunity, we approach its use in the present case with care. This marks the first time, to our knowledge, that a court has been asked to sanction a plan for hiring a specific percentage of minority workers that requires an employer to take "every possible measure" to reach the goal on each job site, and places upon him the burden of proving compliance, under threat of serious penalties if that burden is not sustained. It is but a short step from these requirements to a demand that an employer give an absolute percentage preference to members of a racial minority, regardless of their qualifications and without consideration for their availability within the general population. The Commonwealth's affirmative action plan forces us to address a fundamental question: are there constitutional limits to the means by which racial criteria may be used to remedy the present effects of past discrimination and achieve equal opportunity in the future?

There are good reasons why the use of racial criteria should be strictly scrutinized and given legal sanction only where a compelling need for remedial action can be shown. Norwalk CORE v. Norwalk Redevelopment Agency, 395 F.2d 920, 931–932 (2d Cir.1969). Government recognition and sanction of racial classifications may be inherently divisive, reinforcing prejudices, confirming perceived differences between the races, and weakening the government's educative role on behalf of equality and neutrality.[13] It may also have unexpected results, such as the development of indicia for placing individuals into different racial categories. Once racial classifications are imbedded in the law, their purpose may become perverted: a benign preference under certain conditions may shade into a malignant preference at other times.[14] Moreover, a racial preference for members of one minority might result in discrimination against another minority, a higher proportion of whose members had previously enjoyed access to a certain opportunity.

In the present instance, there is no question that a compelling need exists to remedy serious racial imbalance [15] in the construction trades, particularly in Roxbury, Dorchester, and South End, where minorities constitute approximately forty per cent of the population, and yet only about four per cent of the membership of buildings trades unions, and where there has been a long history of racial discrimination in those unions. Such an imbalance within the relatively lucrative, highly visible, and expanding construction trades undermines efforts at achieving equal opportunity elsewhere in the economy, and contributes to racial tensions.[16]

Even where a long history of discrimination and continuing racial imbalance compels the remedial use of racial criteria, however, the means chosen to implement the compelling interest should be reasonably related to the desired end. See Contractors Ass'n of Eastern Pennsylvania v. Secretary of Labor, supra, 311 F.Supp. at 1011; cf. McLaughlin v. Florida, 379 U.S. 184, 193, 85 S.Ct. 283, 13 L.Ed.2d 222 (1964). A program which included unrealistic minority hiring goals might impose an unreasonable burden on the employer and upon qualified workers who were denied jobs because they were not members of the racial minority. Unrealistically high goals are likely, in addi-

---

13. See Kaplan, Equal Justice in an Unequal World: Equality for the Negro— The Problem of Special Treatment, 61 Nw. U.L.Rev. 363 (1966).

14. For example, a preference for induction into the armed services might appear to some to be a positive opportunity for training and steady work, yet might also appear at other times or to other people to be a somewhat negative opportunity.

15. Based upon information revealed in the depositions of several union officials, and other statistical information such as the "Equal Employment Opportunity Local Union Reports", the district court concluded that racial imbalance does exist in the Boston construction trades and such imbal-

ance is the result of past discriminatory practices on the part of many "entities" in that industry. Such inferences from statistical showings of racial imbalance are permitted. See, e.g., Carter v. Gallagher, 452 F.2d 315, 323 (8th Cir.1971); Parkham v. Southwestern Bell Telephone, 433 F.2d 421, 426 (8th Cir.1970); Jones v. Lee Way Motor Freight, 431 F.2d 245, 247 (10th Cir. 1970).

16. If, at some future time, racial balance were to be achieved in Boston's construction trades, we assume that there would no longer exist a compelling need for remedial action, and the use of such racial criteria would no longer be warranted.

tion, to foment racial tensions and to prompt employers to circumvent the rules.

A program of affirmative action might be considered to impose unrealistic and unreasonable hiring goals if it included a racial preference that could not be fulfilled, or could be fulfilled only by taking on workers who were unqualified for the trainee, apprentice, or journeyman status for which they were hired. Equal opportunity is an elusive concept, but at its core it carries the simple mandate that opportunities should be open to all on the basis of competence alone. Thus, it would be consistent with the goal of equal opportunity to give first priority to members of a minority that had previously been denied equal opportunity, if those members were otherwise as qualified as were qualified members of the majority population. In order that this special treatment be meaningful, of course, there should be equal opportunity to gain the training necessary to qualify.[17]

While § 1B says nothing about hiring "qualified" minority workers, § V, ¶ 3 of the same contract requires that the contractor hire only "competent" workers. The district court has interpreted § 1B in light of § V, ¶ 3, to require that the twenty per cent minority employees of § 1B be "qualified" for the status to which they were assigned. The Commonwealth's Secretary of Transportation and Construction, who is charged with implementing these provisions, has interpreted § 1B in the same way.

Appellants maintain, however, that the goal of twenty per cent minority workers on each construction site, combined with the contractor's burden of proving that he has taken "every possible measure to achieve compliance" with the goal, will necessarily move the contractor to hire unqualified minority workers, rather than run the risk of incurring sanctions. While we think that this is an unwarranted concern, given that the Boston State College project will require approximately thirty minority workers, we concede that, in principle, a high percentage goal for minority hiring combined with a high burden of proving compliance might create the likelihood that unqualified workers would be hired.

Despite the fact that the Secretary of Transportation and Construction alleges that the twenty per cent goal was based upon an assessment of current availability of minority journeymen, apprentices, and trainees, courts are ill equipped to judge the accuracy of such assessments. It becomes important, therefore, that affirmative action plans, such as the Commonwealth's § 1B, contain fair procedures for contractors to make a showing that insufficient qualified minority workers are available. Thus, any reasonable program designed to remedy racial imbalance must incorporate the necessary elements of due process. So long as contractors receive notice and a meaningful opportunity to challenge any allegations of non-compliance and prove that they have

17. Thus, presumably, to be "qualified" for a training program would require less competence than to be "qualified" for apprenticeship or journeyman status.

taken whatever efforts are required of them to comply, it is less important that a particular percentge goal might be slightly optimistic or unrealistic, given current availability of qualified minority workers.

Appellants' contention that § 1B violates the Equal Protection clause is therefore intimately tied to their contention that § 1B, in violation of the Due Process clause, permits the imposition of sanctions without proper notice or an opportunity to be heard, an issue to which we now turn.

III

Appellants' due process claim concerns § 1B.2 of the contract provisions, which sanctions listed below * * *. [T]he Commission (M.C.A.D.) shall make a final report of non-compliance, and recommend to the Bureau [of Construction] the imposition of one or more of the sanctions listed below * * *. [T]he Bureau shall impose one or more of the following sanctions, as it may deem appropriate * * *.

The M.C.A.D.'s determination of noncompliance is made ex parte. Contractors are notified of the findings and given an opportunity to take specific steps which would, in the opinion of the M.C.A.D., bring them into compliance, but contractors are not permitted to challenge the findings of non-compliance at this juncture.

The Bureau of Construction is required, pursuant to the Commonwealth's Administrative Procedure Act, M.G.L.A. c. 30A §§ 10, 11, to hold a hearing before any penalties may be imposed on the contractors for non-compliance. What is in dispute is the scope of this hearing. Appellants maintain that § 1B.2 allows, at most, a challenge to the particular sanction which the M.C.A.D. has recommended, in favor of what might be contended to be a more appropriate sanction, but not a challenge to the truth of the M.C.A.D.'s basic findings of non-compliance. If appellants' interpretation of § 1B.2 were correct, their due process claim would have some merit because contractors would be subject to serious penalties, such as debarment from participation in state contracts for three years, without having had an opportunity to contest the findings on which the imposition of the penalty was based. See Boddie v. Connecticut, 401 U.S. 371, 377–379, 91 S.Ct. 780, 28 L.Ed. 2d 113 (1971); cf. Fuentes v. Shevin, 407 U.S. 67, 92 S.Ct. 1983, 32 L.Ed. 2d 556 (1972); Sniadach v. Family Finance Corp., 395 U.S. 337, 89 S.Ct. 1820, 23 L.Ed.2d 349 (1969).

We do not think, however, that § 1B.2 must necessarily be interpreted to require such a narrowing of the scope of the administrative hearing. The contract states that the Bureau "shall impose" one of the sanctions only "as it may deem appropriate to attain full and effective enforcement." It would seem perfectly consistent with this mandate for the Bureau to determine for itself that the contractor had in fact taken "every possible measure" to achieve compliance, despite the findings of the M.C.A.D. to the contrary, and that any sanction would be inappropriate. The presumption of constitutionality customarily accorded state statutes, e.g., United States v. Carolene Products, 304 U.S. 144, 152, 58 S.Ct. 778, 82 L.Ed. 1234 (1938), would dictate that we apply this interpretation. The Supreme Judicial Court of Massachusetts has, moreover, construed certain other Commonwealth statutes, facially lacking express provisions for notice and hearing, as impliedly calling for such due process requirements. See Rohrer, Petitioner, 353 Mass. 282, 230 N.E.2d 915 (1967); O'Leary, Petitioner, 325 Mass. 179, 89 N.E.2d 769 (1950).

The Commonwealth's Secretary of Transportation and Construction has given the foregoing interpretation to § 1B.2, and has stipulated that no sanctions may be imposed against a contractor until he has had a full hearing before officials of the Bureau of Construction in which he may challenge any findings of non-compliance by the M.C.A.D. Since the Secretary is entrusted with interpretation and implementation of the contract provisions, his view is at least entitled to "respectful consideration", Fox v. Standard Oil Co., 294 U.S. 87, 96, 55 S.Ct. 333, 79 L.Ed. 780 (1935). We see no reason not to accept his interpretation in this case, Law Students Research Council v. Wadmond, 401 U.S. 154, 162, 91 S.Ct. 720, 27 L.Ed.2d 749 (1971), and indeed condition our holding on the consistent application of this interpretation. We conclude, therefore, that § 1B so construed does not violate the Due Process clause of the Fourteenth Amendment.

Since contractors are provided with notice and a full opportunity to contest allegations of non-compliance, they may thereby show that insufficient qualified minority workers were available. Therefore, in light of our preceding analysis, we find that § 1B does not violate the Equal Protection clause of the Fourteenth Amendment.

IV

Appellants' final contention, which comes within the compass of our pendent jurisdiction, is that the Commonwealth's § 1B program involves the M.C.A.D. in activities that are prohibited by the anti-preference clause of M.G.L.A. c. 151B, § 4. This clause provides, in relevant part that " * * * nothing contained in this chapter or in any rule or regulation issued by the Commission [M.C.A.D.] shall be interpreted as requiring any employer, employment agency or labor organization to grant preferential treatment to any individual or to any group because of the race * * * of such individual or group * * *."

The anti-preference clause has not been interpreted by Massachusetts courts. The district court determined, however, that the statute is inapplicable to activities of the M.C.A.D. carried on pursuant to § 1B for two reasons. The first is that the anti-preference clause applies only to regulations issued by the M.C.A.D., while under § 1B the M.C.A.D. merely investigates and makes recommendations under regulations promulgated by the Secretary of Transportation and Construction. The second reason is that, contrary to the assertions of appellants, the clause applies only to authority vested in the statute itself, while the authority for § 1B stems from the Governor's Executive Order No. 74

and from M.G.L.A. c. 6A § 24 and c. 149 § 44A, both of which provide for the acceptance or the rejection of bids. We agree with this analysis.

In addition, we would point to the way in which federal courts have dealt with the anti-preference provision of Title VII of the Civil Rights Act of 1964, 42 U.S.C. § 2000e–2(j), which is analogous to the Commonwealth's anti-preference clause. In United States v. I.B.E.W. Local 38, 428 F.2d 144 (6th Cir.1970), cert. denied, 400 U.S. 943, 91 S.Ct. 245, 27 L.Ed.2d 248 (1970), the court construed that provision to mean that an employer was not required to grant preferential treatment to minorities merely because of racial imbalance on his work force, but that some preference might be required to remedy the present effects of past discrimination. "Any other interpretation would allow complete nullification of the stated purpose of the Civil Rights Act of 1964". Id. at 149–150. See also Carter v. Gallagher, supra.

It is undisputed that past racial discrimination in Boston's construction trades is in large part responsible for the present racial imbalance. Given this fact, we find it difficult to conceive that Massachusetts would interpret its own anti-preference provision in such a way as to prohibit programs designed to remedy that imbalance.

We conclude, therefore, that the Commonwealth's § 1B is violative of neither state law nor the federal Constitution.

Affirmed.

Notes

The Supreme Court has so far declined to review any of the cases directly involving the legality of the executive order programs prohibiting discrimination and requiring affirmative action. The following case, involving a federal minority contract set-aside program, raises many similar issues. The contract set-aside program originated pursuant to an executive order. The requirements were included in a statute in 1977 which is the subject of the court challenge.

FULLILOVE v. KLUTZNICK, SECRETARY OF COMMERCE OF THE UNITED STATES

Supreme Court of the United States, 1980.
448 U.S. 448, 100 S.Ct. 2758, 65 L.Ed.2d 902.

MR. CHIEF JUSTICE BURGER announced the judgment of the Court and delivered an opinion, in which MR. JUSTICE WHITE and MR. JUSTICE POWELL joined.

We granted certiorari to consider a facial constitutional challenge to a requirement in a congressional spending program that, absent an administrative waiver, 10% of the federal funds granted for local public works projects must be used by the state or local grantee to procure services or supplies from businesses owned and controlled by members of statutorily identified minority groups. 441 U.S. 960, 99 S.Ct. 2403, 60 L.Ed.2d 1064 (1979).

I

In May 1977, Congress enacted the Public Works Employment Act of 1977, Pub.L. 95–28, 91 Stat. 116, which amended the Local Public Works Capital Development and Investment Act of 1976, Pub.L. 94–369, 90 Stat. 999, 42 U.S.C. § 6701 et seq. The 1977 amendments authorized an additional $4 billion appropriation for federal grants to be made by the Secretary of Commerce, acting through the Economic Development Administration (EDA), to state and local governmental entities for use in local public works projects. Among the changes made was the addition of the provision that has become the focus of this litigation. Section 103(f)(2) of the 1977 Act, referred to as the "minority business enterprise" or "MBE" provision, requires that:[1]

> Except to the extent that the Secretary determines otherwise, no grant shall be made under this Act for any local public works project unless the applicant gives satisfactory assurance to the Secretary that at least 10 per centum of the amount of each grant shall be expended for minority business enterprises. For purposes of this paragraph, the term "minority business enterprise" means a business at least 50 per centum of which is owned by minority group members or, in case of a publicly owned business, at least 51 per centum of the stock of which is owned by minority group members. For the purposes of the preceding sentence minority group members are citizens of the United States who are Negroes, Spanish-speaking, Orientals, Indians, Eskimos, and Aleuts.

In late May 1977, the Secretary promulgated regulations governing administration of the grant program which were amended two months later.[2] In August 1977, the EDA issued guidelines supplementing the statute and regulations with respect to minority business participation in local public works grants,[3] and in October 1977, the EDA issued a technical bulletin promulgating detailed instructions and information to assist grantees and their contractors in meeting the 10% MBE requirement.[4]

On November 30, 1977, petitioners filed a complaint in the United States District Court for the Southern District of New York seeking declaratory and injunctive relief to enjoin enforcement of the MBE provision. Named as defendants were the Secretary of Commerce, as the program administrator, and the State and City of New York, as actual and potential project grantees. Petitioners are several associa-

---

1. 91 Stat. 116, 42 U.S.C. § 6705(f)(2) (1976 ed., Supp. II).

2. 42 Fed.Reg. 27432 (1977), as amended by 42 Fed.Reg. 35822 (1977); 13 CFR Part 317 (1978).

3. U.S. Dept. of Commerce, Economic Development Administration, Local Public Works Program, Round II, Guidelines For 10% Minority Business Participation In LPW Grants (1977) (hereinafter Guidelines); App. 156a–167a.

4. U.S. Dept. of Commerce, Economic Development Administration, EDA Minority Business Enterprise (MBE) Technical Bulletin (Additional Assistance and Information Available to Grantees and Their Contractors In Meeting The 10% MBE Requirement) (1977) (hereinafter Technical Bulletin); App. 129a–155a.

tions of construction contractors and subcontractors, and a firm engaged in heating, ventilation, and air conditioning work. Their complaint alleged that they had sustained economic injury due to enforcement of the 10% MBE requirement and that the MBE provision on its face violated the Equal Protection Clause of the Fourteenth Amendment, the equal protection component of the Due Process Clause of the Fifth Amendment, and various statutory antidiscrimination provisions.[5]

After a hearing held the day the complaint was filed, the District Court denied a requested temporary restraining order and scheduled the matter for an expedited hearing on the merits. On December 19, 1977, the District Court issued a memorandum opinion upholding the validity of the MBE program and denying the injunctive relief sought. Fullilove v. Kreps, 443 F.Supp. 253 (1977).

The United States Court of Appeals for the Second Circuit affirmed, 584 F.2d 600 (1978), holding that "even under the most exacting standard of review the MBE provision passes constitutional muster." Id., at 603. Considered in the context of many years of governmental efforts to remedy past racial and ethnic discrimination, the court found it "difficult to imagine" any purpose for the program other than to remedy such discrimination. Id., at 605. In its view, a number of factors contributed to the legitimacy of the MBE provision, most significant of which was the narrowed focus and limited extent of the statutory and administrative program, in size, impact, and duration, id., at 607–608; the court looked also to the holdings of other Courts of Appeals and District Courts that the MBE program was constitutional, id., at 608–609.[6] It expressly rejected petitioners' contention that the 10% MBE requirement violated the equal protection guarantees of the Constitution.[7] Id., at 609.

5. 42 U.S.C. §§ 1981, 1983, 1985; Title VI, § 601 of the Civil Rights Act of 1964, 78 Stat. 252, 42 U.S.C. § 2000d; Title VII, § 701 et seq. of the Civil Rights Act of 1964, 78 Stat. 253, as amended, 42 U.S.C. § 2000e et seq.

6. Ohio Contractors Assn. v. Economic Development Administration, 580 F.2d 213 (CA6 1978); Constructors Assn. v. Kreps, 573 F.2d 811 (CA3 1978); Rhode Island Chapter, Associated General Contractors v. Kreps, 450 F.Supp. 338 (R.I.1978); Associated General Contractors v. Secretary of Commerce, No. 77–4218 (Kan. Feb. 9, 1978); Carolinas Branch, Associated General Contractors v. Kreps, 442 F.Supp. 392 (S.C.1977); Ohio Contractors Assn. v. Economic Development Administration, 452 F.Supp. 1013 (SD Ohio 1977); Montana Contractors' Assn. v. Secretary of Commerce, 439 F.Supp. 1331 (Mont.1977); Florida East Coast Chapter v. Secretary of Commerce, No. 77–8351 (SD Fla. Nov. 3, 1977); but see Associated General Contractors v. Secretary of Commerce, 441 F.Supp. 955 (CD Cal.1977), vacated and remanded for consideration of mootness, 438 U.S. 909, 98 S.Ct. 3132, 57 L.Ed.2d 1153 (1978), on remand, 459 F.Supp. 766 (CD Cal.), vacated and remanded sub nom. Armistead v. Associated General Contractors of California, 448 U.S. 908, 100 S.Ct. 3052, 65 L.Ed.2d 1138.

7. Both the Court of Appeals and the District Court rejected petitioners' various statutory arguments without extended discussion. 584 F.2d, at 608, n. 15; 443 F.Supp., at 262.

II

A

The MBE provision was enacted as part of the Public Works Employment Act of 1977, which made various amendments to Title I of the Local Public Works Capital Development and Investment Act of 1976. The 1976 Act was intended as a short-term measure to alleviate the problem of national unemployment and to stimulate the national economy by assisting state and local governments to build needed public facilities.[8] To accomplish these objectives, the Congress authorized the Secretary of Commerce, acting through the EDA, to make grants to state and local governments for construction, renovation, repair, or other improvement of local public works projects.[9] The 1976 Act placed a number of restrictions on project eligibility designed to assure that federal moneys were targeted to accomplish the legislative purposes.[10] It established criteria to determine grant priorities and to apportion federal funds among political jurisdictions.[11] Those criteria directed grant funds toward areas of high unemployment.[12] The statute authorized the appropriation of up to $2 billion for a period ending in September 1977;[13] this appropriation was soon consumed by grants made under the program.

Early in 1977, Congress began consideration of expanded appropriations and amendments to the grant program. Under administration of the 1976 appropriation, referred to as "Round I" of the local public works program, applicants seeking some $25 billion in grants had competed for the $2 billion in available funds; of nearly 25,000 applications, only some 2,000 were granted.[14] The results provoked widespread concern for the fairness of the allocation process.[15] Because the 1977 Act would authorize the appropriation of an additional $4 billion to fund "Round II" of the grant program,[16] the congressional hearings and debates concerning the amendments focused primarily on the politically sensitive problems of priority and geographic distribution of grants under the supplemental appropriation.[17] The result of this attention was inclusion in the 1977 Act of provisions revising the

8. H.R.Rep.No.94–1077, p. 2 (1976), U.S. Code Cong. & Admin.News 1976, p. 1746. The bill discussed in this Report was accepted by the Conference Committee in preference to the Senate version. S.Conf. Rep.No.94–939, p. 1 (1976); H.R.Conf.Rep. No.94–1260, p. 1 (1976), U.S.Code Cong. & Admin.News 1976, p. 1746.

9. 90 Stat. 999, 42 U.S.C. § 6702.

10. 90 Stat. 1000, 42 U.S.C. § 6705.

11. 90 Stat. 1000, 42 U.S.C. § 6707.

12. 90 Stat. 1001, 42 U.S.C. § 6707(c).

13. 90 Stat. 1002, 42 U.S.C. § 6710. The actual appropriation of the full amount authorized was made several weeks later. Pub.L. 94–447, 90 Stat. 1497.

14. 123 Cong.Rec. 2136 (1977) (remarks of Sen. Randolph).

15. See, e.g., Hearings on H.R. 11 and Related Bills before the Subcommittee on Economic Development of the House Committee on Public Works and Transportation, 95th Cong., 1st Sess. (1977); H.R.Rep. No. 95–20 (1977); S.Rep.No. 95–38 (1977), U.S.Code Cong. & Admin.News 1977, p. 150.

16. 91 Stat. 119, 42 U.S.C. § 6710 (1976 ed., Supp. II). The actual appropriation of the full authorized amount was made the same day. Pub.L. 95–29, 91 Stat. 123.

17. E.g., Hearings, supra, n. 15; 123 Cong.Rec. 5290–5353 (1977); id., at 7097–7176.

allocation criteria of the 1976 legislation. Those provisions, however, retained the underlying objective to direct funds into areas of high unemployment.[18] The 1977 Act also added new restrictions on applicants seeking to qualify for federal grants;[19] among these was the MBE provision.

The origin of the provision was an amendment to the House version of the 1977 Act, H.R. 11, offered on the floor of the House on February 23, 1977, by Representative Mitchell of Maryland.[20] As offered, the amendment provided:[21]

> Notwithstanding any other provision of law, no grant shall be made under this Act for any local public works project unless at least 10 per centum of the articles, materials, and supplies which will be used in such project are procured from minority business enterprises. For purposes of this paragraph, the term "minority business enterprise" means a business at least 50 percent of which is owned by minority group members or, in case of publicly owned businesses, at least 51 percent of the stock of which is owned by minority group members. For the purposes of the preceding sentence, minority group members are citizens of the United States who are Negroes, Spanish-speaking, Orientals, Indians, Eskimos, and Aleuts.

The sponsor stated that the objective of the amendment was to direct funds into the minority business community, a sector of the economy sorely in need of economic stimulus but which, on the basis of past experience with Government procurement programs, could not be expected to benefit significantly from the public works program as then formulated.[22] He cited the marked statistical disparity that in fiscal year 1976 less than 1% of all federal procurement was concluded with minority business enterprises, although minorities comprised 15–18% of the population.[23] When the amendment was put forward during debate on H.R. 11,[24] Representative Mitchell reiterated the need to ensure that minority firms would obtain a fair opportunity to share in the benefits of this Government program.[25]

The amendment was put forward not as a new concept, but rather one building upon prior administrative practice. In his introductory remarks, the sponsor rested his proposal squarely on the ongoing program under § 8(a) of the Small Business Act, Pub.L. 85–536, § 2, 72

---

18. 91 Stat. 117, 42 U.S.C. § 6707 (1976 ed., Supp. II).

19. 91 Stat. 116, 42 U.S.C. § 6705 (1976 ed., Supp. II).

20. 123 Cong.Rec. 5097 (1977) (remarks of Rep. Mitchell).

21. Id., at 5098.

22. Id., at 5097–5098.

23. Id., at 5098.

24. Id., at 5327. As reintroduced, the first sentence of the amendment was modified to provide:

"Notwithstanding any other provision of law, no grant shall be made under this Act for any local public works project unless at least 10 per centum of the dollar volume of each contract shall be set aside for minority business enterprise and, or, unless at least 10 per centum of the articles, materials, and supplies which will be used in such project are procured from minority business enterprises."

25. Id., at 5327–5328.

Stat. 389, which, as will become evident, served as a model for the administrative program developed to enforce the MBE provision: [26]

> The first point in opposition will be that you cannot have a set-aside. Well, Madam Chairman, we have been doing this for the last 10 years in Government. The 8–A set aside under SBA has been tested in the courts more than 30 times and has been found to be legitimate and bona fide. We are doing it in this bill.

> * * *

The Senate adopted the amendment without debate.[36] The Conference Committee, called to resolve differences between the House and Senate versions of the Public Works Employment Act of 1977, adopted the language approved by the House for the MBE provision.[37] The Conference Reports added only the comment: "This provision shall be dependent on the availability of minority business enterprises located in the project area." [38]

The device of a 10% MBE participation requirement, subject to administrative waiver, was thought to be required to assure minority business participation; otherwise it was thought that repetition of the prior experience could be expected, with participation by minority business accounting for an inordinately small percentage of government contracting. The causes of this disparity were perceived as involving the longstanding existence and maintenance of barriers impairing access by minority enterprises to public contracting opportunities, or sometimes as involving more direct discrimination, but not as relating to lack—as Senator Brooke put it—"of capable and qualified minority enterprises who are ready and willing to work." [39] In the words of its sponsor, the MBE provision was "designed to begin to redress this grievance that has been extant for so long." [40]

B

The legislative objectives of the MBE provision must be considered against the background of ongoing efforts directed toward deliverance of the century-old promise of equality of economic opportunity. The sponsors of the MBE provision in the House and the Senate expressly linked the provision to the existing administrative programs promoting minority opportunity in government procurement, particularly those related to § 8(a) of the Small Business Act of 1953.[41] Section 8(a) delegates to the Small Business Administration (SBA) an authority and an obligation "whenever it determines such action is necessary" to enter into contracts with any procurement agency of the Federal

---

26. Id., at 5327.

36. Ibid.

37. S.Conf.Rep. No. 95–110, p. 11 (1977); H.R.Conf.Rep.No.95–230, p. 11 (1977).

38. Ibid. The Conference Committee bill was agreed to by the Senate, 123 Cong. Rec. 12941–12942 (1977), and by the House, id., at 13242–13257, and was signed into law on May 13, 1977.

39. Id., at 7156 (remarks of Sen. Brooke).

40. Id., at 5330 (remarks of Rep. Mitchell).

41. Id., at 5327; id., at 7156 (remarks of Sen. Brooke).

Government to furnish required goods or services, and, in turn, to enter into subcontracts with small businesses for the performance of such contracts. This authority lay dormant for a decade. Commencing in 1968, however, the SBA was directed by the President [42] to develop a program pursuant to its § 8(a) authority to assist small business concerns owned and controlled by "socially or economically disadvantaged" persons to achieve a competitive position in the economy.

* * *

III

When we are required to pass on the constitutionality of an Act of Congress, we assume "the gravest and most delicate duty that this Court is called on to perform." Blodgett v. Holden, 275 U.S. 142, 148, 48 S.Ct. 105, 107, 72 L.Ed. 206 (1927) (opinion of Holmes, J.). A program that employs racial or ethnic criteria, even in a remedial context, calls for close examination; yet we are bound to approach our task with appropriate deference to the Congress, a co-equal branch charged by the Constitution with the power to "provide for the * * * general Welfare of the United States" and "to enforce, by appropriate legislation," the equal protection guarantees of the Fourteenth Amendment. Art. I, § 8, cl. 1; Amdt. 14, § 5. In Columbia Broadcasting System, Inc. v. Democratic National Committee, 412 U.S. 94, 102, 93 S.Ct. 2080, 2086, 36 L.Ed.2d 772 (1973), we accorded "great weight to the decisions of Congress" even though the legislation implicated fundamental constitutional rights guaranteed by the First Amendment. The rule is not different when a congressional program raises equal protection concerns. See, e.g., Cleland v. National College of Business, 435 U.S. 213, 98 S.Ct. 1024, 55 L.Ed.2d 225 (1978); Mathews v. De Castro, 429 U.S. 181, 97 S.Ct. 431, 50 L.Ed.2d 389 (1976).

Here we pass, not on a choice made by a single judge or a school board, but on a considered decision of the Congress and the President. However, in no sense does that render it immune from judicial scrutiny, and it "is not to say we 'defer' to the judgment of the Congress * * * on a constitutional question," or that we would hesitate to invoke the Constitution should we determine that Congress has overstepped the bounds of its constitutional power. *Columbia Broadcasting,* supra, at 103, 93 S.Ct., at 2087.

The clear objective of the MBE provision is disclosed by our necessarily extended review of its legislative and administrative background. The program was designed to ensure that, to the extent federal funds were granted under the Public Works Employment Act of 1977, grantees who elect to participate would not employ procurement practices that Congress had decided might result in perpetuation of the effects of prior discrimination which had impaired or foreclosed access by minority businesses to public contracting opportunities. The MBE

42. Exec.Order No. 11375, 3 CFR 684 (1966–1970 Comp.); Exec.Order No. 11518, 3 CFR 907 (1966–1970 Comp.).

program does not mandate the allocation of federal funds according to inflexible percentages solely based on race or ethnicity.

Our analysis proceeds in two steps. At the outset, we must inquire whether the *objectives* of this legislation are within the power of Congress. If so, we must go on to decide whether the limited use of racial and ethnic criteria, in the context presented, is a constitutionally permissible *means* for achieving the congressional objectives and does not violate the equal protection component of the Due Process Clause of the Fifth Amendment.

A

(1)

In enacting the MBE provision, it is clear that Congress employed an amalgam of its specifically delegated powers. The Public Works Employment Act of 1977, by its very nature, is primarily an exercise of the Spending Power. U.S.Const., Art. I, § 8, cl. 1. This Court has recognized that the power to "provide for the * * * general Welfare" is an independent grant of legislative authority, distinct from other broad congressional powers. Buckley v. Valeo, 424 U.S. 1, 90–91, 96 S.Ct. 612, 668–669, 46 L.Ed.2d 659 (1976); United States v. Butler, 297 U.S. 1, 65–66, 56 S.Ct. 312, 319, 80 L.Ed. 477 (1936). Congress has frequently employed the Spending Power to further broad policy objectives by conditioning receipt of federal moneys upon compliance by the recipient with federal statutory and administrative directives. This Court has repeatedly upheld against constitutional challenge the use of this technique to induce governments and private parties to cooperate voluntarily with federal policy. E.g., California Bankers Assn. v. Shultz, 416 U.S. 21, 94 S.Ct. 1494, 39 L.Ed.2d 812 (1974); Lau v. Nichols, 414 U.S. 563, 94 S.Ct. 786, 39 L.Ed.2d 1 (1974); Oklahoma v. CSC, 330 U.S. 127, 67 S.Ct. 544, 91 L.Ed. 794 (1947); Helvering v. Davis, 301 U.S. 619, 57 S.Ct. 904, 81 L.Ed. 1307 (1937); Steward Machine Co. v. Davis, 301 U.S. 548, 57 S.Ct. 883, 81 L.Ed. 1279 (1937).

The MBE program is structured within this familiar legislative pattern.

Here we need not explore the outermost limitations on the objectives attainable through such an application of the Spending Power. The reach of the Spending Power, within its sphere, is at least as broad as the regulatory powers of Congress. If, pursuant to its regulatory powers, Congress could have achieved the objectives of the MBE program, then it may do so under the Spending Power. And we have no difficulty perceiving a basis for accomplishing the objectives of the MBE program through the Commerce Power insofar as the program objectives pertain to the action of private contracting parties, and through the power to enforce the equal protection guarantees of the Fourteenth Amendment insofar as the program objectives pertain to the action of state and local grantees.

(2)

We turn first to the Commerce Power. U.S.Const., Art. I, § 8, cl. 3. Had Congress chosen to do so, it could have drawn on the Commerce Clause to regulate the practices of prime contractors on federally funded public works projects. Katzenbach v. McClung, 379 U.S. 294, 85 S.Ct. 377, 18 L.Ed.2d 290 (1964); Heart of Atlanta Motel, Inc. v. United States, 379 U.S. 241, 85 S.Ct. 348, 13 L.Ed.2d 258 (1964). The legislative history of the MBE provision shows that there was a rational basis for Congress to conclude that the subcontracting practices of prime contractors could perpetuate the prevailing impaired access by minority businesses to public contracting opportunities, and that this inequity has an effect on interstate commerce. Thus Congress could take necessary and proper action to remedy the situation. Ibid.

It is not necessary that these prime contractors be shown responsible for any violation of antidiscrimination laws. Our cases dealing with application of Title VII of the Civil Rights Act of 1964, 78 Stat. 253, as amended, express no doubt of the congressional authority to prohibit practices "challenged as perpetuating the effects of [not unlawful] discrimination occurring prior to the effective date of the Act." Franks v. Bowman Transportation Co., 424 U.S. 747, 761, 96 S.Ct. 1251, 1263, 47 L.Ed.2d 444 (1976); see California Brewers Assn. v. Bryant, 444 U.S. 598, 100 S.Ct. 814, 63 L.Ed.2d 55 (1980); Teamsters v. United States, 431 U.S. 324, 97 S.Ct. 1843, 52 L.Ed.2d 396 (1977); Albermarle Paper Co. v. Moody, 422 U.S. 405, 95 S.Ct. 2362, 45 L.Ed.2d 280 (1975); Griggs v. Duke Power Co., 401 U.S. 424, 91 S.Ct. 849, 28 L.Ed.2d 158 (1971). Insofar as the MBE program pertains to the actions of private prime contractors, the Congress could have achieved its objectives under the Commerce Clause. We conclude that in this respect the objectives of the MBE provision are within the scope of the Spending Power.

(3)

In certain contexts, there are limitations on the reach of the Commerce Power to regulate the actions of state and local governments. National League of Cities v. Usery, 426 U.S. 833, 96 S.Ct. 2465, 49 L.Ed.2d 245 (1976). To avoid such complications, we look to § 5 of the Fourteenth Amendment for the power to regulate the procurement practices of state and local grantees of federal funds. Fitzpatrick v. Bitzer, 427 U.S. 445, 96 S.Ct. 2666, 49 L.Ed.2d 614 (1976). A review of our cases persuades us that the objectives of the MBE program are within the power of Congress under § 5 "to enforce, by appropriate legislation," the equal protection guarantees of the Fourteenth Amendment.

* * *

With respect to the MBE provision, Congress had abundant evidence from which it could conclude that minority businesses have been denied effective participation in public contracting opportunities by procurement practices that perpetuated the effects of prior discrimination.

*   *   *

B

We now turn to the question whether, as a *means* to accomplish these plainly constitutional objectives, Congress may use racial and ethnic criteria, in this limited way, as a condition attached to a federal grant. We are mindful that "[i]n no matter should we pay more deference to the opinion of Congress than in its choice of instrumentalities to perform a function that is within its power," National Mutual Insurance Co. v. Tidewater Transfer Co., 337 U.S. 582, 603, 69 S.Ct. 1173, 1183, 93 L.Ed. 1556 (1949) (opinion of Jackson, J.). However, Congress may employ racial or ethnic classifications in exercising its Spending or other legislative powers only if those classifications do not violate the equal protection component of the Due Process Clause of the Fifth Amendment. We recognize the need for careful judicial evaluation to assure that any congressional program that employs racial or ethnic criteria to accomplish the objective of remedying the present effects of past discrimination is narrowly tailored to the achievement of that goal.

Again, we stress the limited scope of our inquiry. Here we are not dealing with a remedial decree of a court but with the legislative authority of Congress. Furthermore, petitioners have challenged the constitutionality of the MBE provision on its face; they have not sought damages or other specific relief for injury allegedly flowing from specific applications of the program; nor have they attempted to show that as applied in identified situations the MBE provision violated the constitutional or statutory rights of any party to this case.[71] In these circumstances, given a reasonable construction and in light of its projected administration, if we find the MBE program on its face to be free of constitutional defects, it must be upheld as within congressional power. Parker v. Levy, 417 U.S. 733, 760, 94 S.Ct. 2547, 2563, 41 L.Ed. 2d 439 (1974); Fortson v. Dorsey, 379 U.S. 433, 438–439, 85 S.Ct. 498, 501, 13 L.Ed.2d 401 (1965); Aptheker v. Secretary of State, 378 U.S. 500, 515, 84 S.Ct. 1659, 1668, 12 L.Ed.2d 992 (1964); see United States v. Raines, 362 U.S. 17, 20–24, 80 S.Ct. 519, 522–524, 4 L.Ed.2d 524 (1960).

Our review of the regulations and guidelines governing administration of the MBE provision reveals that Congress enacted the program as a strictly remedial measure; moreover, it is a remedy that functions prospectively, in the manner of an injunctive decree.

*   *   *

71. In their complaint, in order to establish standing to challenge the validity of the program, petitioners alleged as "[s]pecific examples" of economic injury three instances where one of their number assertedly would have been awarded a public works contract but for enforcement of the MBE provision. Petitioners requested only declaratory and injunctive relief against continued enforcement of the MBE provision; they did not seek any remedy for these specific instances of assertedly unlawful discrimination. App. 12a–13a, 17a–19a.

(1)

As a threshold matter, we reject the contention that in the remedial context the Congress must act in a wholly "color-blind" fashion. In Swann v. Charlotte-Mecklenburg Board of Education, 402 U.S. 1, 18–21, 91 S.Ct. 1267, 1277–1278, 28 L.Ed.2d 554 (1971), we rejected this argument in considering a court-formulated school desegregation remedy on the basis that examination of the racial composition of student bodies was an unavoidable starting point and that racially based attendance assignments were permissible so long as no absolute racial balance of each school was required. In McDaniel v. Barresi, 402 U.S. 39, 41, 91 S.Ct. 1287, 1289, 28 L.Ed.2d 582 (1971), citing Swann, we observed: "In this remedial process, steps will almost invariably require that students be assigned 'differently because of their race.' Any other approach would freeze the status quo that is the very target of all desegregation processes." (Citations omitted.) And in North Carolina Board of Education v. Swann, 402 U.S. 43, 91 S.Ct. 1284, 28 L.Ed.2d 586 (1971), we invalidated a state law that absolutely forbade assignment of any student on account of race because it foreclosed implementation of desegregation plans that were designed to remedy constitutional violations. We held that "[j]ust as the race of students must be considered in determining whether a constitutional violation has occurred, so also must race be considered in formulating a remedy." Id., at 46, 91 S.Ct., at 1286.

In these school desegregation cases we dealt with the authority of a federal court to formulate a remedy for unconstitutional racial discrimination. However, the authority of a court to incorporate racial criteria into a remedial decree also extends to statutory violations. Where federal antidiscrimination laws have been violated, an equitable remedy may in the appropriate case include a racial or ethnic factor. Franks v. Bowman Transportation Co., 424 U.S. 747, 96 S.Ct. 1251, 47 L.Ed.2d 444 (1976); see Teamsters v. United States, 431 U.S. 324, 97 S.Ct. 1843, 52 L.Ed.2d 396 (1977); Albemarle Paper Co. v. Moody, 422 U.S. 405, 95 S.Ct. 2362, 45 L.Ed.2d 280 (1975). In another setting, we have held that a state may employ racial criteria that are reasonably necessary to assure compliance with federal voting rights legislation, even though the state action does not entail the remedy of a constitutional violation. United Jewish Organizations of Williamsburgh, Inc. v. Carey, 430 U.S. 144, 147–165, 97 S.Ct. 996, 1000–1009, 51 L.Ed.2d 229 (1977) (opinion of WHITE, J., joined by BRENNAN, BLACKMUN, and STEVENS, JJ.); id., at 180–187, 97 S.Ct., at 1017–1020 (BURGER, C.J., dissenting on other grounds).

When we have discussed the remedial powers of a federal court, we have been alert to the limitation that "[t]he power of the federal courts to restructure the operation of local and state governmental entities 'is not plenary. * * *' [A] federal court is required to tailor 'the scope of the remedy' to fit the nature and extent of the * * * violation." Dayton Board of Education v. Brinkman, 433 U.S. 406, 419–420, 97 S.Ct.

2766, 2775, 53 L.Ed.2d 851 (1977) (quoting Milliken v. Bradley, 418 U.S. 717, 738, 94 S.Ct. 3112, 3124, 41 L.Ed.2d 1069 (1974), and Swann v. Charlotte-Mecklenburg Board of Education, supra, at 16, 91 S.Ct., at 1276).

Here we deal, as we noted earlier, not with the limited remedial powers of a federal court, for example, but with the broad remedial powers of Congress. It is fundamental that in no organ of government, state or federal, does there repose a more comprehensive remedial power than in the Congress, expressly charged by the Constitution with competence and authority to enforce equal protection guarantees. Congress not only may induce voluntary action to assure compliance with existing federal statutory or constitutional antidiscrimination provisions, but also, where Congress has authority to declare certain conduct unlawful, it may, as here, authorize and induce state action to avoid such conduct. Supra, at 2772–2775.

(2)

A more specific challenge to the MBE program is the charge that it impermissibly deprives nonminority businesses of access to at least some portion of the government contracting opportunities generated by the Act. It must be conceded that by its objective of remedying the historical impairment of access, the MBE provision can have the effect of awarding some contracts to MBE's which otherwise might be awarded to other businesses, who may themselves be innocent of any prior discriminatory actions. Failure of nonminority firms to receive certain contracts is, of course, an incidental consequence of the program, not part of its objective; similarly, past impairment of minority-firm access to public contracting opportunities may have been an incidental consequence of "business as usual" by public contracting agencies and among prime contractors.

It is not a constitutional defect in this program that it may disappoint the expectations of nonminority firms. When effectuating a limited and properly tailored remedy to cure the effects of prior discrimination, such "a sharing of the burden" by innocent parties is not impermissible. *Franks,* supra, 424 U.S., at 777, 96 S.Ct., at 1270; see *Albermarle Paper Co.,* supra; *United Jewish Organizations,* supra. The actual "burden" shouldered by nonminority firms is relatively light in this connection when we consider the scope of this public works program as compared with overall construction contracting opportunities.[72] Moreover, although we may assume that the complaining parties are innocent of any discriminatory conduct, it was within congressional power to act on the assumption that in the past some

---

72. The Court of Appeals relied upon Department of Commerce statistics to calculate that the $4.2 billion in federal grants conditioned upon compliance with the MBE provision amounted to about 2.5% of the total of nearly $170 billion spent on construction in the United States during 1977. Thus, the 10% minimum minority business participation contemplated by this program would account for only 0.25% of the annual expenditure for construction work in the United States. Fullilove v. Kreps, 584 F.2d, at 607.

nonminority businesses may have reaped competitive benefit over the years from the virtual exclusion of minority firms from these contracting opportunities.

(3)

Another challenge to the validity of the MBE program is the assertion that it is underinclusive—that it limits its benefit to specified minority groups rather than extending its remedial objectives to all businesses whose access to government contracting is impaired by the effects of disadvantage or discrimination. Such an extension would, of course, be appropriate for Congress to provide; it is not a function for the courts.

Even in this context, the well-established concept that a legislature may take one step at a time to remedy only part of a broader problem is not without relevance. See Dandridge v. Williams, 397 U.S. 471, 90 S.Ct. 1153, 25 L.Ed.2d 491 (1970); Williamson v. Lee Optical Co., 348 U.S. 483, 75 S.Ct. 461, 99 L.Ed. 563 (1955). We are not reviewing a federal program that seeks to confer a preferred status upon a nondisadvantaged minority or to give special assistance to only one of several groups established to be similarly disadvantaged minorities. Even in such a setting, the Congress is not without a certain authority. See, e.g., Personnel Administrator of Massachusetts v. Feeney, 442 U.S. 256, 99 S.Ct. 2282, 60 L.Ed.2d 870 (1979); Califano v. Webster, 430 U.S. 313, 97 S.Ct. 1192, 51 L.Ed.2d 360 (1977); Morton v. Mancari, 417 U.S. 535, 94 S.Ct. 2474, 41 L.Ed.2d 290 (1974).

The Congress has not sought to give select minority groups a preferred standing in the construction industry, but has embarked on a remedial program to place them on a more equitable footing with respect to public contracting opportunities. There has been no showing in this case that Congress has inadvertently effected an invidious discrimination by excluding from coverage an identifiable minority group that has been the victim of a degree of disadvantage and discrimination equal to or greater than that suffered by the groups encompassed by the MBE program. It is not inconceivable that on very special facts a case might be made to challenge the congressional decision to limit MBE eligibility to the particular minority groups identified in the Act. See Vance v. Bradley, 440 U.S. 93, 109–112, 99 S.Ct. 939, 949–950, 59 L.Ed.2d 171 (1979); Oregon v. Mitchell, 400 U.S., at 240, 91 S.Ct., at 322 (opinion of BRENNAN, WHITE, and MARSHALL, JJ.). But on this record we find no basis to hold that Congress is without authority to undertake the kind of limited remedial effort represented by the MBE program. Congress, not the courts, has the heavy burden of dealing with a host of intractable economic and social problems.

(4)

It is also contended that the MBE program is overinclusive—that it bestows a benefit on businesses identified by racial or ethnic criteria which cannot be justified on the basis of competitive criteria or as a remedy for the present effects of identified prior discrimination. It is conceivable that a particular application of the program may have this effect; however, the peculiarities of specific applications are not before us in this case. We are not presented here with a challenge involving a specific award of a construction contract or the denial of a waiver request; such questions of specific application must await future cases.

This does not mean that the claim of overinclusiveness is entitled to no consideration in the present case. The history of governmental tolerance of practices using racial or ethnic criteria for the purpose or with the effect of imposing an invidious discrimination must alert us to the deleterious effects of even benign racial or ethnic classifications when they stray from narrow remedial justifications. Even in the context of a facial challenge such as is presented in this case, the MBE provision cannot pass muster unless, with due account for its administrative program, it provides a reasonable assurance that application of racial or ethnic criteria will be limited to accomplishing the remedial objectives of Congress and that misapplications of the program will be promptly and adequately remedied administratively.

It is significant that the administrative scheme provides for waiver and exemption. Two fundamental congressional assumptions underlie the MBE program: (1) that the present effects of past discrimination have impaired the competitive position of businesses owned and controlled by members of minority groups; and (2) that affirmative efforts to eliminate barriers to minority-firm access, and to evaluate bids with adjustment for the present effects of past discrimination, would assure that at least 10% of the federal funds granted under the Public Works Employment Act of 1977 would be accounted for by contracts with available, qualified, bona fide minority business enterprises. Each of these assumptions may be rebutted in the administrative process.

The administrative program contains measures to effectuate the congressional objective of assuring legitimate participation by disadvantaged MBE's. Administrative definition has tightened some less definite aspects of the statutory identification of the minority groups encompassed by the program.[73] There is administrative scrutiny to

---

73. The MBE provision, 42 U.S.C. § 6705(f)(2) (1976 ed., Supp. II), classifies as a minority business enterprise any "business at least 50 per centum of which is owned by minority group members or, in the case of a publicly owned business, at least 51 per centum of the stock of which is owned by minority group numbers." Minority group members are defined as "citizens of the United States who are Negroes, Spanish-speaking, Orientals, Indians, Eskimos and Aleuts." The administrative definitions are set out in the Appendix to this opinion, ¶ 3. These categories also are classified as minorities in the regulations implementing the nondiscrimination requirements of the Railroad Revitalization

and Regulatory Reform Act of 1976, 45 U.S.C. § 803, see 49 CFR § 265.5(i) (1978), on which Congress relied as precedent for the MBE provision. See 123 Cong.Rec. 7156 (1977) (remarks of Sen. Brooke). The House Subcommittee on SBA Oversight and Minority Enterprise, whose activities played a significant part in the legislative history of the MBE provision, also recognized that these categories were included within the Federal Government's definition of "minority business enterprise." H.R.Rep. No. 94–468, pp. 20–21 (1975). The specific inclusion of these groups in the MBE provision demonstrates that Congress concluded they were victims of discrimination. Petitioners did not press any

identify and eliminate from participation in the program MBE's who are not "bona fide" within the regulations and guidelines; for example, spurious minority-front entities can be exposed. A significant aspect of this surveillance is the complaint procedure available for reporting "unjust participation by an enterprise or individuals in the MBE program." Supra, at 2771. And even as to specific contract awards, waiver is available to avoid dealing with an MBE who is attempting to exploit the remedial aspects of the program by charging an unreasonable price, i.e., a price not attributable to the present effects of past discrimination. Supra, at 2770–2771. We must assume that Congress intended close scrutiny of false claims and prompt action on them.

Grantees are given the opportunity to demonstrate that their best efforts will not succeed or have not succeeded in achieving the statutory 10% target for minority firm participation within the limitations of the program's remedial objectives. In these circumstances a waiver or partial waiver is available once compliance has been demonstrated. A waiver may be sought and granted at any time during the contracting process, or even prior to letting contracts if the facts warrant.

Nor is the program defective because a waiver may be sought only by the grantee and not by prime contractors who may experience difficulty in fulfilling contract obligations to assure minority participation. It may be administratively cumbersome, but the wisdom of concentrating responsibility at the grantee level is not for us to evaluate; the purpose is to allow the EDA to maintain close supervision of the operation of the MBE provision. The administrative complaint mechanism allows for grievances of prime contractors who assert that a grantee has failed to seek a waiver in an appropriate case. Finally, we note that where private parties, as opposed to governmental entities, transgress the limitations inherent in the MBE program, the possibility of constitutional violation is more removed. See Steelworkers v. Weber, 443 U.S. 193, 200, 99 S.Ct. 2721, 2726, 61 L.Ed.2d 480 (1979).

That the use of racial and ethnic criteria is premised on assumptions rebuttable in the administrative process gives reasonable assurance that application of the MBE program will be limited to accomplishing the remedial objectives contemplated by Congress and that misapplications of the racial and ethnic criteria can be remedied. In dealing with this facial challenge to the statute, doubts must be resolved in support of the congressional judgment that this limited program is a necessary step to effectuate the constitutional mandate for equality of economic opportunity. The MBE provision may be viewed as a pilot project, appropriately limited in extent and duration, and subject to reassessment and reevaluation by the Congress prior to any extension or re-enactment.[74] Miscarriages of administration could have

challenge to Congress' classification categories in the Court of Appeals; there is no reason for this Court to pass upon the issue at this time.

74. Cf. GAO, Report to the Congress, Minority Firms on Local Public Works Projects—Mixed Results, CED–79–9 (Jan. 16, 1979); U.S. Dept. of Commerce, Eco-

only a transitory economic impact on businesses not encompassed by the program, and would not be irremediable.

IV

Congress, after due consideration, perceived a pressing need to move forward with new approaches in the continuing effort to achieve the goal of equality of economic opportunity. In this effort, Congress has necessary latitude to try new techniques such as the limited use of racial and ethnic criteria to accomplish remedial objectives; this is especially so in programs where voluntary cooperation with remedial measures is induced by placing conditions on federal expenditures. That the program may press the outer limits of congressional authority affords no basis for striking it down.

* * *

Any preference based on racial or ethnic criteria must necessarily receive a most searching examination to make sure that it does not conflict with constitutional guarantees. This case is one which requires, and which has received, that kind of examination. This opinion does not adopt, either expressly or implicitly, the formulas of analysis articulated in such cases as University of California Regents v. Bakke, 438 U.S. 265, 98 S.Ct. 2733, 57 L.Ed.2d 750 (1978). However, our analysis demonstrates that the MBE provision would survive judicial review under either "test" articulated in the several *Bakke* opinions. The MBE provision of the Public Works Employment Act of 1977 does not violate the Constitution.[77]

Affirmed.

MR. JUSTICE POWELL, concurring.

Although I would place greater emphasis than THE CHIEF JUSTICE on the need to articulate judicial standards of review in conventional terms, I view his opinion announcing the judgment as substantially in accord with my own views. Accordingly, I join that opinion and write separately to apply the analysis set forth by my opinion in University of California v. Bakke, 438 U.S. 265, 98 S.Ct. 2733, 57 L.Ed.2d 750 (1978) (hereinafter *Bakke*).

* * *

MR. JUSTICE MARSHALL, with whom MR. JUSTICE BRENNAN and MR. JUSTICE BLACKMUN join, concurring in the judgment.

My resolution of the constitutional issue in this case is governed by the separate opinion I coauthored in University of California Regents v. Bakke, 438 U.S. 265, 324–379, 98 S.Ct. 2733, 2766–2794, 57 L.Ed.2d 750 (1978). In my view, the 10% minority set-aside provision of the Public

---

nomic Development Administration, Local Public Works Program Interim Report on 10 Percent Minority Business Enterprise Requirement (Sept. 1978).

77. Although the complaint alleged that the MBE program violated several

federal statutes, n. 5, supra, the only statutory argument urged upon us is that the MBE provision is inconsistent with Title VI of the Civil Rights Act of 1964.

Works Employment Act of 1977 passes constitutional muster under the standard announced in that opinion.

* * *

MR. JUSTICE STEWART, with whom MR. JUSTICE REHNQUIST joins, dissenting.

"Our Constitution is color-blind, and neither knows nor tolerates classes among citizens. * * * The law regards man as man, and takes no account of his surroundings or of his color * * *." Those words were written by a Member of this Court 84 years ago. Plessy v. Ferguson, 163 U.S. 537, 559, 16 S.Ct. 1138, 1146, 41 L.Ed. 256 (Harlan, J., dissenting). His colleagues disagreed with him, and held that a statute that required the separation of people on the basis of their race was constitutionally valid because it was a "reasonable" exercise of legislative power and had been "enacted in good faith for the promotion [of] the public good * * *." Id., at 550, 16 S.Ct., at 1143. Today, the Court upholds a statute that accords a preference to citizens who are "Negroes, Spanish-speaking, Orientals, Indians, Eskimos, and Aleuts," for much the same reasons. I think today's decision is wrong for the same reason that Plessy v. Ferguson was wrong, and I respectfully dissent.

* * *

MR. JUSTICE STEVENS, dissenting.

* * *

F. AFFIRMATIVE ACTION OR IMPERMISSIBLE PREFERENCES— THE CONTINUING CONFLICTS

1. **In the preceding cases we have considered challenges to affirmative action programs which were *imposed* upon nonconsenting contractors. The following cases illustrate problems with voluntary or "quasi-voluntary" implementation of affirmative action plans.**

UNITED STEELWORKERS OF AMERICA, AFL–CIO–CLC v. WEBER

Supreme Court of the United States, 1979.
443 U.S. 193, 99 S.Ct. 2721, 61 L.Ed.2d 480.

MR. JUSTICE BRENNAN delivered the opinion of the Court.

Challenged here is the legality of an affirmative action plan— collectively bargained by an employer and a union—that reserves for black employees 50% of the openings in an in-plant craft-training program until the percentage of black craftworkers in the plant is commensurate with the percentage of blacks in the local labor force. The question for decision is whether Congress, in Title VII of the Civil Rights Act of 1964, 78 Stat., 253, as amended, 42 U.S.C. § 2000e et seq., left employers and unions in the private sector free to take such race-conscious steps to eliminate manifest racial imbalances in traditionally segregated job categories. We hold that Title VII does not prohibit such race-conscious affirmative action plans.

I

In 1974, petitioner United Steelworkers of America (USWA) and petitioner Kaiser Aluminum & Chemical Corp. (Kaiser) entered into a master collective-bargaining agreement covering terms and conditions of employment at 15 Kaiser plants. The agreement contained, *inter alia,* an affirmative action plan designed to eliminate conspicuous racial imbalances in Kaiser's then almost exclusively white craft-work forces. Black craft-hiring goals were set for each Kaiser plant equal to the percentage of blacks in the respective local labor forces. To enable plants to meet these goals, on-the-job training programs were established to teach unskilled production workers—black and white—the skills necessary to become craftworkers. The plan reserved for black employees 50% of the openings in these newly created in-plant training programs.

This case arose from the operation of the plan at Kaiser's plant in Gramercy, La. Until 1974, Kaiser hired as craftworkers for that plant only persons who had had prior craft experience. Because blacks had long been excluded from craft unions,[1] few were able to present such credentials. As a consequence, prior to 1974 only 1.83% (5 out of 273) of the skilled craftworkers at the Gramercy plant were black, even though the work force in the Gramercy area was approximately 39% black.

Pursuant to the national agreement Kaiser altered its craft-hiring practice in the Gramercy plant. Rather than hiring already trained outsiders, Kaiser established a training program to train its production workers to fill craft openings. Selection of craft trainees was made on the basis of seniority, with the proviso that at least 50% of the new trainees were to be black until the percentage of black skilled craftworkers—in the Gramercy plant approximated the percentage of blacks in the local labor force. See 415 F.Supp. 761, 764.

1. Judicial findings of exclusion from crafts on racial grounds are so numerous as to make such exclusion a proper subject for judicial notice. See, e.g., United States v. Elevator Constructors, 538 F.2d 1012 (CA3 1976); Associated General Contractors of Massachusetts v. Altshuler, 490 F.2d 9 (CA1 1973); Southern Illinois Builders Assn. v. Ogilvie, 471 F.2d 680 (CA7 1972); Contractors Assn. of Eastern Pennsylvania v. Secretary of Labor, 442 F.2d 159 (CA3 1971); Insulators & Asbestos Workers v. Vogler, 407 F.2d 1047 (CA5 1969); Buckner v. Goodyear Tire & Rubber Co., 339 F.Supp. 1108 (ND Ala.1972), aff'd without opinion, 476 F.2d 1287 (CA5 1973).

See also U.S. Commission on Civil Rights, The Challenge Ahead: Equal Opportunity in Referral Unions 58–94 (1976) (summarizing judicial findings of discrimination by craft unions); G. Myrdal, An American Dilemma 1079–1124 (1944); F. Marshall & V. Briggs, The Negro and Apprenticeship (1967); S. Spero & A. Harris, The Black Worker (1931); U.S. Commission on Civil Rights, Employment 97 (1961); State Advisory Committees, U.S. Commission on Civil Rights, 50 States Report 209 (1961); Marshall, The Negro in Southern Unions, in The Negro and the American Labor Movement 145 (J. Jacobson, ed. 1968); App. 63, 104.

During 1974, the first year of the operation of the Kaiser-USWA affirmative action plan, 13 craft trainees were selected from Gramercy's production work force. Of these, seven were black and six white. The most senior black selected into the program had less seniority than several white production workers whose bids for admission were rejected. Thereafter one of those white production workers, respondent Brian Weber (hereafter respondent), instituted this class action in the United States District Court for the Eastern District of Louisiana.

The complaint alleged that the filling of craft trainee positions at the Gramercy plant pursuant to the affirmative action program had resulted in junior black employees receiving training in preference to senior white employees, thus discriminating against respondent and other similarly situated white employees in violation of §§ 703(a)[2] and (d)[3] of Title VII. The District Court held that the plan violated Title VII, entered a judgment in favor of the plaintiff class, and granted a permanent injunction prohibiting Kaiser and the USWA "from denying plaintiffs, Brian F. Weber and all other members of the class, access to on-the-job training programs on the basis of race." App. 171. A divided panel of the Court of Appeals for the Fifth Circuit affirmed, holding that all employment preferences based upon race, including those preferences incidental to bona fide affirmative action plans, violated Title VII's prohibition against racial discrimination in employment. 563 F.2d 216 (1977). We granted certiorari. 439 U.S. 1045, 99 S.Ct. 720, 58 L.Ed.2d 704 (1978). We reverse.

II

We emphasize at the outset the narrowness of our inquiry. Since the Kaiser-USWA plan does not involve state action, this case does not present an alleged violation of the Equal Protection Clause of the Fourteenth Amendment. Further, since the Kaiser-USWA plan was adopted voluntarily, we are not concerned with what Title VII requires or with what a court might order to remedy a past proved violation of the Act. The only question before us is the narrow statutory issue of whether Title VII *forbids* private employers and unions from voluntari-

---

2. Section 703(a), 78 Stat. 255, as amended, 86 Stat. 109, 42 U.S.C. § 2000e–2(a), provides:

"(a) * * * It shall be an unlawful employment practice for an employer—

"(1) to fail or refuse to hire or to discharge any individual, or otherwise to discriminate against any individual with respect to his compensation, terms, conditions, or privileges of employment, because of such individual's race, color, religion, sex, or national origin; or

"(2) to limit, segregate, or classify his employees or applicants for employment in any way which would deprive or tend to deprive any individual of employment opportunities or otherwise adversely af-

fect his status as an employee, because of such individual's race, color, religion, sex, or national origin."

3. Section 703(d), 78 Stat. 256, 42 U.S.C. § 2000e–2(d), provides:

"It shall be an unlawful employment practice for any employer, labor organization, or joint labor-management committee controlling apprenticeship or other training or retraining, including on-the-job training programs to discriminate against any individual because of his race, color, religion, sex, or national origin in admission to, or employment in, any program established to provide apprenticeship or other training."

ly agreeing upon bona fide affirmative action plans that accord racial preferences in the manner and for the purpose provided in the Kaiser-USWA plan. That question was expressly left open in McDonald v. Santa Fe Trail Transp. Co., 427 U.S. 273, 281 n. 8, 96 S.Ct. 2574, 2579, 49 L.Ed.2d 493 (1976), which held, in a case not involving affirmative action, that Title VII protects whites as well as blacks from certain forms of racial discrimination.

Respondent argues that Congress intended in Title VII to prohibit all race-conscious affirmative action plans. Respondent's argument rests upon a literal interpretation of §§ 703(a) and (d) of the Act. Those sections make it unlawful to "discriminate * * * because of * * * race" in hiring and in the selection of apprentices for training programs. Since, the argument runs, McDonald v. Sante Fe Trail Transp. Co., supra, settled that Title VII forbids discrimination against whites as well as blacks, and since the Kaiser-USWA affirmative action plan operates to discriminate against white employees solely because they are white, it follows that the Kaiser-USWA plan violates Title VII.

Respondent's argument is not without force. But it overlooks the significance of the fact that the Kaiser-USWA plan is an affirmative action plan voluntarily adopted by private parties to eliminate traditional patterns of racial segregation. In this context respondent's reliance upon a literal construction of §§ 703(a) and (d) and upon McDonald is misplaced. See McDonald v. Sante Fe Trail Transp. Co., supra, at 281 n. 8, 96 S.Ct., at 2579. It is a "familiar rule that a thing may be within the letter of the statute and yet not within the letter of the statute and yet not within the statute, because not within its spirit nor within the intention of its makers." Holy Trinity Church v. United States, 143 U.S. 457, 459, 12 S.Ct. 511, 512, 36 L.Ed. 226 (1892). The prohibition against racial discrimination in §§ 703(a) and (d) of Title VII must therefore be read against the background of the legislative history of Title VII and the historical context from which the Act arose. See Train v. Colorado Public Interest Research Group, 426 U.S. 1, 10, 96 S.Ct. 1938, 1942, 48 L.Ed.2d 434 (1976); National Woodwork Mfrs. Assn. v. NLRB, 386 U.S. 612, 620, 87 S.Ct. 1250, 1255, 18 L.Ed.2d 357 (1967); United States v. American Trucking Assns., 310 U.S. 534, 543–544, 60 S.Ct. 1059, 1063–1064, 84 L.Ed. 1345 (1940). Examination of those sources makes clear that an interpretation of the sections that forbade all race-conscious affirmative action would "bring about an end completely at variance with the purpose of the statute" and must be rejected. United States v. Public Utilities Comm'n, 345 U.S. 295, 315, 73 S.Ct. 706, 718, 97 L.Ed. 1020 (1953). See Johansen v. United States, 343 U.S. 427, 431, 72 S.Ct. 849, 852, 96 L.Ed. 1051 (1952); Longshoremen v. Juneau Spruce Corp., 342 U.S. 237, 243, 72 S.Ct. 235, 239, 96 L.Ed. 275 (1952); Texas & Pacific R. Co. v. Abilene Cotton Oil Co., 204 U.S. 426, 27 S.Ct. 350, 51 L.Ed. 553 (1907).

Congress' primary concern in enacting the prohibition against racial discrimination in Title VII of the Civil Rights Act of 1964 was with "the plight of the Negro in our economy." 110 Cong.Rec. 6548 (1964) (remarks of Sen. Humphrey). . . .

As Senator Clark told the Senate:

The rate of Negro unemployment has gone up consistently as compared with white unemployment for the past 15 years. This is a social malaise and a social situation which we should not tolerate. That is one of the principal reasons why the bill should pass. Id., at 7220.

Congress feared that the goals of the Civil Rights Act—the integration of blacks into the mainstream of American society—could not be achieved unless this trend were reversed. As Senator Humphrey explained to the Senate:

What good does it do a Negro to be able to eat in a fine restaurant if he cannot afford to pay the bill? What good does it do him to be accepted in a hotel that is too expensive for his modest income? How can a Negro child be motivated to take full advantage of integrated educational facilities if he has no hope of getting a job where he can use that education? Id., at 6547.

It plainly appears from the House Report accompanying the Civil Rights Act that Congress did not intend wholly to prohibit private and voluntary affirmative action efforts as one method of solving this problem. The Report provides:

No bill can or should lay claim to eliminating all of the causes and consequences of racial and other types of discrimination against minorities. There is reason to believe, however, that national leadership provided by the enactment of Federal legislation dealing with the most troublesome problems *will create an atmosphere conducive to voluntary or local resolution of other forms of discrimination.* H.R.Rep. No. 914, 88th Cong., 1st Sess., pt. 1, p. 18 (1963); U.S.Code Cong. & Admin.News 1964, pp. 2355, 2393. (Emphasis supplied.)

Given this legislative history, we cannot agree with respondent that Congress intended to prohibit the private sector from taking effective steps to accomplish the goal that Congress designed Title VII to achieve. The very statutory words intended as a spur or catalyst to cause "employers and unions to self-examine and to self-evaluate their employment practices and to endeavor to eliminate, so far as possible, the last vestiges of an unfortunate and ignominious page in this country's history," Albemarle Paper Co. v. Moody, 422 U.S. 405, 418, 95 S.Ct. 2362, 2372, 45 L.Ed.2d 280 (1975), cannot be interpreted as an absolute prohibition against all private, voluntary, race-conscious affirmative action efforts to hasten the elimination of such vestiges.[4] It would be ironic indeed if a law triggered by a Nation's concern over centuries of racial injustice and intended to improve the lot of those

4. The problem that Congress addressed in 1964 remains with us. In 1962, the nonwhite unemployment rate was 124% higher than the white rate. See 110 Cong.Rec. 6547 (1964) (remarks of Sen. Humphrey). In 1978, the black unemployment rate was 129% higher. See Monthly Labor Review, U.S. Department of Labor, Bureau of Labor Statistics 78 (Mar. 1979).

who had "been excluded from the American dream for so long," 110 Cong.Rec. 6552 (1964) (remarks of Sen. Humphrey), constituted the first legislative prohibition of all voluntary, private, race-conscious efforts to abolish traditional patterns of racial segregation and hierarchy.

Our conclusion is further reinforced by examination of the language and legislative history of § 703(j) of Title VII.[5] Opponents of Title VII raised two related arguments against the bill. First, they argued that the Act would be interpreted to *require* employers with racially imbalanced work forces to grant preferential treatment to racial minorities in order to integrate. Second, they argued that employers with racially imbalanced work forces would grant preferential treatment to racial minorities, even if not required to do so by the Act. See 110 Cong.Rec. 8618–8619 (1964) (remarks of Sen. Sparkman). Had Congress meant to prohibit all race-conscious affirmative action, as respondent urges, it easily could have answered both objections by providing that Title VII would not require or *permit* racially preferential integration efforts. But Congress did not choose such a course. Rather, Congress added § 703(j) which addresses only the first objection. The section provides that nothing contained in Title VII "shall be interpreted to *require* any employer ＊ ＊ ＊ to grant preferential treatment ＊ ＊ ＊ to any group because of the race ＊ ＊ ＊ of such ＊ ＊ ＊ group on account of" a *de facto* racial imbalance in the employer's work force. The section does *not* state that "nothing in Title VII shall be interpreted to *permit*" voluntary affirmative efforts to correct racial imbalances. The natural inference is that Congress chose not to forbid all voluntary race-conscious affirmative action.

The reasons for this choice are evident from the legislative record. Title VII could not have been enacted into law without substantial support from legislators in both Houses who traditionally resisted federal regulation of private business. Those legislators demanded as a price for their support that "management prerogatives, and union freedoms ＊ ＊ ＊ be left undisturbed to the greatest extent possible."

---

5. Section 703(j) of Title VII, 78 Stat. 257, 42 U.S.C. § 2000e–2(j), provides:

"Nothing contained in this title shall be interpreted to require any employer, employment agency, labor organization, or joint labor-management committee subject to this title to grant preferential treatment to any individual or to any group because of the race, color, religion, sex, or national origin of such individual or group on account of an imbalance which may exist with respect to the total number or percentage of persons of any race, color, religion, sex, or national origin employed by any employer, referred or classified for employment by any employment agency or labor organization, admitted to membership or classified by any labor organization, admitted to membership or classified by any labor organization, or admitted to, or employed in, any apprenticeship or other training program, in comparison with the total number or percentage of persons of such race, color, religion, sex, or national origin in any community, State, section, or other area, or in the available work force in any community, State, section, or other area."

Section 703(j) speaks to substantive liability under Title VII, but it does not preclude courts from considering racial imbalance as evidence of a Title VII violation. See Teamsters v. United States, 431 U.S. 324, 339–340, n. 20, 97 S.Ct. 1843, 1856, 52 L.Ed.2d 396 (1977). Remedies for substantive violations are governed by § 706(g), 42 U.S.C. § 2000e–5(g).

H.R.Rep. No. 914, 88th Cong., 1st Sess., pt. 2, p. 29 (1963), U.S.Code Cong. & Admin.News 1964, p. 2391. Section 703(j) was proposed by Senator Dirksen to allay any fears that the Act might be interpreted in such a way as to upset this compromise. The section was designed to prevent § 703 of Title VII from being interpreted in such a way as to lead to undue "Federal Government interference with private businesses because of some Federal employee's ideas about racial balance or racial imbalance." 110 Cong.Rec. 14314 (1964) (remarks of Sen. Miller).[6] See also id., at 9881 (remarks of Sen. Allott); id., at 10520 (remarks of Sen. Carlson); id., at 11471 (remarks of Sen. Javits); id., at 12817 (remarks of Sen. Dirksen). Clearly, a prohibition against all voluntary, race-conscious, affirmative action efforts would disserve these ends. Such a prohibition would augment the powers of the Federal Government and diminish traditional management prerogatives while at the same time impeding attainment of the ultimate statutory goals. In view of this legislative history and in view of Congress' desire to avoid undue federal regulation of private businesses, use of the word "require" rather than the phrase "require or permit" in § 703(j) fortifies the conclusion that Congress did not intend to limit traditional business freedom to such a degree as to prohibit all voluntary, race-conscious affirmative action.[7]

---

6. Title VI of the Civil Rights Act of 1964, considered in University of California Regents v. Bakke, 438 U.S. 265, 98 S.Ct. 2733, 57 L.Ed.2d 750 (1978), contains no provision comparable to § 703(j). This is because Title VI was an exercise of federal power over a matter in which the Federal Government was already directly involved: the prohibitions against race-based conduct contained in Title VI governed "program[s] or activit[ies] receiving Federal financial assistance." 42 U.S.C. § 2000d. Congress was legislating to assure federal funds would not be used in an improper manner. Title VII, by contrast, was enacted pursuant to the commerce power to regulate purely private decision-making and was not intended to incorporate and particularize the commands of the Fifth and Fourteenth Amendments. Title VII and Title VI, therefore, cannot be read *in pari materia.* See 110 Cong.Rec. 8315 (1964) (remarks of Sen. Cooper). See also id., at 11615 (remarks of Sen. Cooper).

7. Respondent argues that our construction of § 703 conflicts with various remarks in the legislative record. See, e.g., 110 Cong.Rec. 7213 (1964) (Sens. Clark and Case); id., at 7218 (Sens. Clark and Case); id., at 6549 (Sen. Humphrey); id., at 8921 (Sen. Williams). We do not agree. In Senator Humphrey's words, these comments were intended as assurances that Title VII would not allow establishment of systems "to *maintain* racial balance in em-

ployment." Id., at 11848 (emphasis added). They were not addressed to temporary, voluntary, affirmative action measures undertaken to eliminate manifest racial imbalance in traditionally segregated job categories. Moreover, the comments referred to by respondent all preceded the adoption of § 703(j), 42 U.S.C. § 2000e–2(j). After § 73(j) was adopted, congressional comments were all to the effect that employers would not be *required* to institute preferential quotas to avoid Title VII liability, see, e.g., 110 Cong.Rec. 12819 (1964) (remarks of Sen. Dirksen); id., at 13079–13080 (remarks of Sen. Clark); id., at 15876 (remarks of Rep. Lindsay). There was no suggestion after the adoption of § 703(j) that wholly voluntary, race-conscious, affirmative action efforts would in themselves constitute a violation of Title VII. On the contrary, as Representative MacGregor told the House shortly before the final vote on Title VII:

"Important as the scope and extent of this bill is, it is also vitally important that all Americans understand what this bill does not cover.

"Your mail and mine, your contacts and mine with our constituents, indicates a great degree of misunderstanding about this bill. People complain about * * * preferential treatment or quotas in employment. There is a mistaken belief that Congress is legislating in

We therefore hold that Title VII's prohibition in §§ 703(a) and (d) against racial discrimination does not condemn all private, voluntary, race-conscious affirmative action plans.

III

We need not today define in detail the line of demarcation between permissible and impermissible affirmative action plans. It suffices to hold that the challenged Kaiser-USWA affirmative action plan falls on the permissible side of the line. The purposes of the plan mirror those of the statute. Both were designed to break down old patterns of racial segregation and hierarchy. Both were structured to "open employment opportunities for Negroes in occupations which have been traditionally closed to them." 110 Cong.Rec. 6548 (1964) (remarks of Sen. Humphrey).[8]

At the same time, the plan does not unnecessarily trammel the interests of the white employees. The plan does not require the discharge of white workers and their replacement with new black hirees. Cf. McDonald v. Santa Fe Trail Transp. Co., 427 U.S. 273, 96 S.Ct. 2574, 49 L.Ed.2d 493 (1976). Nor does the plan create an absolute bar to the advancement of white employees; half of those trained in the program will be white. Moreover, the plan is a temporary measure; it is not intended to maintain racial balance, but simply to eliminate a manifest racial imbalance. Preferential selection of craft trainees at the Gramercy plant will end as soon as the percentage of black skilled craftworkers in the Gramercy plant approximates the percentage of blacks in the local labor force. See 415 F.Supp., at 763.

We conclude, therefore, that the adoption of the Kaiser-USWA plan for the Gramercy plant falls within the area of discretion left by Title VII to the private sector voluntarily to adopt affirmative action plans designed to eliminate conspicuous racial imbalance in traditionally segregated job categories.[9] Accordingly, the judgment of the Court of Appeals for the Fifth Circuit is

Reversed.

MR. JUSTICE POWELL and MR. JUSTICE STEVENS took no part in the consideration or decision of these cases.

MR. JUSTICE BLACKMUN, concurring.

these areas in this bill. When we drafted this bill we excluded these issues largely because the problems raised by these controversial questions are more properly handled at a governmental level closer to the American people and by communities and individuals themselves." 110 Cong.Rec. 15893 (1964).

8. See n. 1, supra. This is not to suggest that the freedom of an employer to undertake race-conscious affirmative action efforts depends on whether or not his effort is motivated by fear of liability under Title VII.

9. Our disposition makes unnecessary consideration of petitioners' argument that their plan was justified because they feared that black employees would bring suit under Title VII if they did not adopt an affirmative action plan. Nor need we consider petitioners' contention that their affirmative action plan represented an attempt to comply with Exec. Order No. 11246, 3 CFR 339 (1964–1965 Comp.).

While I share some of the misgivings expressed in MR. JUSTICE REHNQUIST'S dissent, post, p. 2736, concerning the extent to which the legislative history of Title VII clearly supports the result the Court reaches today, I believe that additional considerations, practical and equitable, only partially perceived, if perceived at all, by the 88th Congress, support the conclusion reached by the Court today, and I therefore join its opinion as well as its judgment.

I

In his dissent from the decision of the United States Court of Appeals for the Fifth Circuit, Judge Wisdom pointed out that this litigation arises from a practical problem in the administration of Title VII. The broad prohibition against discrimination places the employer and the union on what he accurately described as a "high tightrope without a net beneath them." 563 F.2d 216, 230. If Title VII is read literally, on the one hand they face liability for past discrimination against blacks, and on the other they face liability to whites for any voluntary preferences adopted to mitigate the effects of prior discrimination against blacks.

In this litigation, Kaiser denies prior discrimination but concedes that its past hiring practices may be subject to question. Although the labor force in the Gramercy area was proximately 39% black, Kaiser's work force was less than 15% black, and its craftwork force was less than 2% black. Kaiser had made some effort to recruit black painters, carpenters, insulators, and other craftsmen, but it continued to insist that those hired have five years' prior industrial experience, a requirement that arguably was not sufficiently job related to justify under Title VII any discriminatory impact it may have had. See Parson v. Kaiser Aluminum & Chemical Corp., 575 F.2d 1374, 1389 (CA5 1978), cert. denied, sub nom. Steelworkers v. Parson, 441 U.S. 968, 99 S.Ct. 2417, 60 L.Ed.2d 1073 (1979). The parties dispute the extent to which black craftsmen were available in the local labor market. They agree, however, that after critical reviews from the Office of Federal Contract Compliance, Kaiser and the Steelworkers established the training program in question here and modeled it along the lines of a Title VII consent decree later entered for the steel industry. See United States v. Allegheny-Ludlum Industries, Inc., 517 F.2d 826 (CA5 1975). Yet when they did this, respondent Weber sued, alleging that Title VII prohibited the program because it discriminated against him as a white person and it was not supported by a prior judicial finding of discrimination against blacks.

Respondent Weber's reading of Title VII endorsed by the Court of Appeals, places voluntary compliance with Title VII in profound jeopardy. The only way for the employer and the union to keep their footing on the "tightrope" it creates would be to eschew all forms of voluntary affirmative action. Even a whisper of emphasis on minority recruiting would be forbidden. Because Congress intended to encourage private efforts to come into compliance with Title VII, see

Alexander v. Gardner-Denver Co., 415 U.S. 36, 44, 94 S.Ct. 1011, 1017, 39 L.Ed.2d 147 (1974), Judge Wisdom concluded that employers and unions who had committed "arguable violations" of Title VII should be free to make reasonable responses without fear of liability to whites. 563 F.2d, at 230. Preferential hiring along the lines of the Kaiser program is a reasonable response for the employer, whether or not a court, on these facts, could order the same step as a remedy. The company is able to avoid identifying victims of past discrimination, and so avoids claims for backpay that would inevitably follow a response limited to such victims. If past victims should be benefited by the program, however, the company mitigates its liability to those persons. Also, to the extent that Title VII liability is predicated on the "disparate effect" of an employer's past hiring practices, the program makes it less likely that such an effect could be demonstrated. Cf. County of Los Angeles v. Davis, 440 U.S. 625, 633–634, 99 S.Ct. 1379, 1384, 59 L.Ed.2d 642 (1979) (hiring could moot a past Title VII claim). And the Court has recently held that work-force statistics resulting from private affirmative action were probative of benign intent in a "disparate treatment" case. Furnco Construction Corp. v. Waters, 438 U.S. 567, 579–580, 98 S.Ct. 2943, 2950–951, 57 L.Ed.2d 957 (1978).

The "arguable violation" theory has a number of advantages. It responds to a practical problem in the administration of Title VII not anticipated by Congress. It draws periodically from the outline of present law and closely effectuates the purpose of the Act. Both Kaiser and the United States urge its adoption here. Because I agree that it is the soundest way to approach this case, my preference would be to resolve this litigation by applying it and holding that Kaiser's craft training program meets the requirement that voluntary affirmative action be a reasonable response to an "arguable violation" of Title VII.

* * *

III

I also think it significant that, while the Court's opinion does not foreclose other forms of affirmative action, the Kaiser program it approves is a moderate one. The opinion notes that the program does not afford an absolute preference for blacks, and that it ends when the racial composition of Kaiser's craftwork force matches the racial composition of the local population. It thus operates as a temporary tool for remedying past discrimination without attempting to "maintain" a previously achieved balance. See University of California Regents v. Bakke, 438 U.S. 265, 342 n. 17, 98 S.Ct. 2733, 2775, 57 L.Ed.2d 750 (1978) (opinion of BRENNAN, WHITE, MARSHALL, and BLACKMUN, JJ.). Because the duration of the program is finite, it perhaps will end even before the "stage of maturity when action along this line is no longer necessary." Id., at 403, 98 S.Ct., at 2806 (opinion of BLACKMUN, J.). And if the Court has misperceived the political will, it has the assurance that because the question is statutory Congress may set a different course if it so chooses.

MR. CHIEF JUSTICE BURGER, dissenting.

The Court reaches a result I would be inclined to vote for were I a Member of Congress considering a proposed amendment of Title VII. I cannot join the Court's judgment, however, because it is contrary to the explicit language of the statute and arrived at by means wholly incompatible with long-established principles of separation of powers. Under the guise of statutory "construction," the Court effectively rewrites Title VII to achieve what it regards as a desirable result. It "amends" the statute to do precisely what both its sponsors and its opponents agreed the statute was not intended to do.

* * *

MR. JUSTICE REHNQUIST, with whom THE CHIEF JUSTICE joins, dissenting.

In a very real sense, the Court's opinion is ahead of its time: it could more appropriately have been handed down five years from now, in 1984, a year coinciding with the title of a book from which the Court's opinion borrows, perhaps subconsciously, at least one idea. Orwell describes in his book a governmental official of Oceania, one of the three great world powers, denouncing the current enemy, Eurasia, to an assembled crowd:

> It was almost impossible to listen to him without being first convinced and then maddened. * * * The speech had been proceeding for perhaps twenty minutes when a messenger hurried onto the platform and a scrap of paper was slipped into the speaker's hand. He unrolled and read it without pausing in his speech. Nothing altered in his voice or manner, or in the content of what he was saying, but suddenly the names were different. Without words said, a waive of understanding rippled through the crowd. Oceania was at war with Eastasia! * * * The banners and posters with which the square was decorated were all wrong! * * *

> [T]he speaker had switched from one line to the other actually in mid-sentence, not only without a pause, but without even breaking the syntax. G. Orwell, Nineteen Eighty-Four 181–182 (1949).

Today's decision represents an equally dramatic and equally unremarked switch in this Court's interpretation of Title VII.

The operative sections of Title VII prohibit racial discrimination in employment *simpliciter*. Taken in its normal meaning and as understood by all Members of Congress who spoke to the issue during the legislative debates, see infra, at 2741–2751, this language prohibits a covered employer from considering race when making an employment decision, whether the race be black or white. Several years ago, however, a United States District Court held that "the dismissal of white employees charged with misappropriating company property while not dismissing a similarly charged Negro employee does not raise a claim upon which Title VII relief may be granted." McDonald v. Santa Fe Trail Transp. Co., 427 U.S. 273, 278, 96 S.Ct. 2574, 2578, 49 L.Ed.2d 493 (1976). This Court unanimously reversed, concluding from the "uncontradicted legislative history" that "[T]itle VII prohibits racial discrimination against the white petitioners in this case upon the same standards as would be applicable were they Negroes * * *." Id., at 280, 96 S.Ct., at 2579.

We have never wavered in our understanding that Title VII "prohibits *all* racial discrimination in employment, without exception for any group of particular employees." Id., at 283, 96 S.Ct., at 2580 (emphasis in original). In Griggs v. Duke Power Co., 401 U.S. 424, 431, 91 S.Ct. 849, 853, 28 L.Ed.2d 158 (1971), our first occasion to interpret Title VII, a unanimous Court observed that "[d]iscriminatory preference, for any group, minority or majority, is precisely and only what Congress has proscribed." And in our most recent discussion of the issue, we uttered words seemingly dispositive of this case: "It is clear beyond cavil that the obligation imposed by Title VII is to provide an equal opportunity for *each* applicant regardless of race, without regard to whether members of the applicant's race are already proportionately represented in the work force." Furnco Construction Corp. v. Waters, 438 U.S. 567, 579, 98 S.Ct. 2943, 2951, 57 L.Ed.2d 957 (1978) (emphasis in original).[1]

Today, however, the Court behaves much like the Orwellian speaker earlier described, as if it had been handed a note indicating that Title VII would lead to a result unacceptable to the Court if interpreted here as it was in our prior decisions. Accordingly, without even a break in syntax, the Court rejects "a literal construction of § 703(a)" in favor of newly discovered "legislative history," which leads it to a conclusion directly contrary to that compelled by the "uncontradicted legislative history" unearthed in *McDonald* and our other prior decisions. Now we are told that the legislative history of Title VII shows that employers are free to discriminate on the basis of race: an employer may, in the Court's words, "trammel the interests of the white employees" in favor of black employees in order to eliminate "racial imbalance." Ante, at 2730. Our earlier interpretations of Title VII, like the banners and posters decorating the square in Oceania, were all wrong.

* * *

II

Were Congress to act today specifically to prohibit the type of racial discrimination suffered by Weber, it would be hard pressed to draft language better tailored to the task than that found in § 703(d) of Title VII:

> It shall be an unlawful employment practice for any employer, labor organization, or joint labor-management committee controlling apprenticeship or other training or retraining, including on-the-job training programs to discriminate against any individual because of his race, color, religion, sex, or national origin in admission to, or

---

1. Our statements in *Griggs* and *Furnco Construction* patently inconsistent with today's holding, are not even mentioned, much less distinguished, by the Court.

employment in, any program established to provide apprenticeship or other training. 78 Stat. 256, 42 U.S.C. § 2000e–2(d).

Equally suited to the task would be § 703(a)(2), which makes it unlawful for an employer to classify his employees "in any way which would deprive or tend to deprive any individual of employment opportunities or otherwise adversely affect his status as an employee, because of such individual's race, color, religion, sex, or national origin." 78 Stat. 255, 42 U.S.C. § 2000e–2(a)(2).[7]

Entirely consistent with these two express prohibitions is the language of § 703(j) of Title VII, which provides that the Act is not to be interpreted "to require any employer ＊ ＊ ＊ to grant preferential treatment to any individual or to any group because of the race ＊ ＊ ＊ of such individual or group" to correct a racial imbalance in the employer's work force. 42 U.S.C. § 2000e–2(j).[8] Seizing on the word "require," the Court infers that Congress must have intended to "permit" this type of racial discrimination. Not only is this reading of § 703(j) outlandish in the light of the flat prohibitions of §§ 703(a) and (d), but also, as explained in Part III, it is totally belied by the Act's legislative history.

Quite simply, Kaiser's racially discriminatory admission quota is flatly prohibited by the plain language of Title VII. This normally dispositive fact,[9] however, gives the Court only momentary pause. An "interpretation" of the statute upholding Weber's claim would, according to the Court, " 'bring about an end completely at variance with the purpose of the statute.' " Ante, at 2727, quoting United States v. Public Utilities Comm'n, 345 U.S. 295, 315, 73 S.Ct. 706, 718, 97 L.Ed. 1020 (1953). To support this conclusion, the Court calls upon the "spirit" of the Act, which it divines from passages in Title VII's legislative history indicating that enactment of the statute was prompted by Congress' desire " 'to open employment opportunities for Negroes in occupations which [had] been traditionally closed to them.' " Ante, at 2728, quoting 110 Cong.Rec. 6548 (1964) (remarks of Sen. Humphrey).[10] But the legislative history invoked by the Court to avoid

7. (omitted).

8. (omitted).

9. "If the words are plain, they give meaning to the act, and it is neither the duty nor the privilege of the courts to enter speculative fields in search of a different meaning.

" ＊ ＊ ＊ [W]hen words are free from doubt they must be taken as the final expression of the legislative intent, and are not to be added to or subtracted from by considerations drawn ＊ ＊ ＊ from any extraneous source." Caminetti v. United States, 242 U.S. 470, 490, 37 S.Ct. 192, 196, 61 L.Ed. 442 (1917).

10. In holding that Title VII cannot be interpreted to prohibit use of Kaiser's ra-

cially discriminatory admission quota, the Court reasons that it would be "ironic" if a law inspired by the history of racial discrimination in employment against blacks forbade employers from voluntarily discriminating against whites in favor of blacks. I see no irony in a law that prohibits *all* voluntary racial discrimination, even discrimination directed at whites in favor of blacks. The evil inherent in discrimination against Negroes is that it is based on an immutable characteristic, utterly irrelevant to employment decisions. The characteristic becomes no less immutable and irrelevant, and discrimination based thereon becomes no less evil, simply because the person excluded is a member of one race rather than another. Far from

the plain language of §§ 703(a) and (d) simply misses the point. To be sure, the reality of employment discrimination against Negroes provided the primary impetus for passage of Title VII. But this fact by no means supports the proposition that Congress intended to leave employers free to discriminate against white persons.[11] In most cases, "[l]egislative history * * * is more vague than the statute we are called upon to interpret." supra, at 320, 73 S.Ct., at 720 (Jackson, J., concurring). Here, however, the legislative history of Title VII is as clear as the language of §§ 703(a) and (d), and it irrefutably demonstrates that Congress meant precisely what it said in §§ 703(a) and (d)— that *no* racial discrimination in employment is permissible under Title

ironic, I find a prohibition on all preferential treatment based on race as elementary and fundamental as the principle that "two wrongs do not make a right."

11. The only shred of legislative history cited by the Court in support of the proposition that "Congress did not intend wholly to prohibit private and voluntary affirmative action efforts," ante, at 2728, is the following excerpt from the Judiciary Committee Report accompanying the civil rights bill reported to the House:

"No bill can or should lay claim to eliminating all of the causes and consequences of racial and other types of discrimination against minorities. There is reason to believe, however, that national leadership provided by the enactment of Federal legislation dealing with the most troublesome problems *will create an atmosphere conducive to voluntary or local resolution of other forms of discrimination.*" H.R.Rep. No. 914, 88th Cong., 1st Sess., pt. 1, p. 18 (1963), U.S.Code Cong. & Admin.News 1964, p. 2393 (hereinafter H.R.Rep.), quoted ante, at 2728.

The Court seizes on the italicized language to support its conclusion that Congress did not intend to prohibit voluntary imposition of racially discriminatory employment quotas. The Court, however, stops too short in its reading of the House Report. The words immediately following the material excerpted by the Court are as follows:

"It is, however, possible and necessary for the Congress to enact legislation which prohibits and provides the means of terminating *the most serious types of discrimination.* This H.R. 7152, as amended, would achieve in a number of related areas. It would reduce discriminatory obstacles to the exercise of the right to vote and provide means of expediting the vindication of that right. It would make it possible to remove the daily affront and humiliation involved in

discriminatory denials of access to facilities ostensibly open to the general public. It would guarantee that there will be no discrimination upon recipients of Federal financial assistance. It would prohibit discrimination in employment, and provide means to expedite termination of discrimination in public education. It would open additional avenues to deal with redress of denials of equal protection of the laws on account of race, color, religion, or national origin by State or local authorities." H.R.Rep., pt. 1 p. 18 (emphasis added).

When thus read in context, the meaning of the italicized language in the Court's excerpt of the House Report becomes clear. By dealing with "the most serious types of discrimination," such as discrimination in voting, public accommodations, employment, etc., H.R. 7152 would hopefully inspire "voluntary or local resolution of other forms of discrimination," that is, forms other than discrimination in voting, public accommodations, employment, etc.

One can also infer from the House Report that the Judiciary Committee hoped that federal legislation would inspire voluntary elimination of discrimination against minority groups other than those protected under the bill, perhaps the aged and handicapped to name just two. In any event, the House Report does not support the Court's proposition that Congress, by banning racial discrimination in employment, intended to permit racial discrimination in employment.

Thus, examination of the House Judiciary Committee's report reveals that the Court's interpretation of Title VII, far from being compelled by the Act's legislative history, is utterly without support in that legislative history. Indeed, as demonstrated in Part III, infra, the Court's interpretation of Title VII is totally refuted by the Act's legislative history.

VII, not even preferential treatment of minorities to correct racial imbalance.

* * *

WYGANT v. JACKSON BOARD OF EDUCATION, etc. et al.

Supreme Court of the United States, 1986.
__ U.S. __, 106 S.Ct. 1842, 90 L.Ed.2d 260.

JUSTICE POWELL announced the judgment of the Court and delivered an opinion in which THE CHIEF JUSTICE and JUSTICE REHNQUIST joined, and which JUSTICE O'CONNOR joined in parts I, II, III–A, III–B, and V.

This case presents the question whether a school board, consistent with the Equal Protection Clause, may extend preferential protection against layoffs to some of its employees because of their race or national origin.

I

In 1972 the Jackson Board of Education, because of racial tension in the community that extended to its schools, considered adding a layoff provision to the Collective Bargaining Agreement (CBA) between the Board and the Jackson Education Association (the Union) that would protect employees who were members of certain minority groups against layoffs.[1] The Board and the Union eventually approved a new provision, Article XII of the CBA, covering layoffs. It stated:

"In the event that it becomes necessary to reduce the number of teachers through layoff from employment by the Board, teachers with the most seniority in the district shall be retained, except that at no time will there be a greater percentage of minority personnel laid off than the current percentage of minority personnel employed at the time of the layoff. In no event will the number given notice of possible layoff be greater than the number of positions to be eliminated. Each teacher so affected will be called back in reverse order for positions for which he is certificated maintaining the above minority balance." App. 13.[2]

When layoffs became necessary in 1974, it was evident that adherence to the CBA would result in the layoff of tenured nonminority teachers while minority teachers on probationary status were retained. Rather than complying with Article XII, the Board retained the tenured teachers and laid off probationary minority teachers, thus failing

1. Prior to bargaining on this subject, the Minority Affairs Office of the Jackson Public Schools sent a questionnaire to all teachers, soliciting their views as to a layoff policy. The questionnaire proposed two alternatives: continuation of the existing straight seniority system, or a freeze of minority layoffs to ensure retention of minority teachers in exact proportion to the minority student population. Ninety-six percent of the teachers who responded to the questionnaire expressed a preference for the straight seniority system.

2. Article VII of the CBA defined "minority group personnel" as "those employees who are Black, American Indian, Oriental, or of Spanish descendancy." App. 15.

to maintain the percentage of minority personnel that existed at the time of the layoff. The Union, together with two minority teachers who had been laid off, brought suit in federal court, id., at 30, (*Jackson Education Assn. v. Board of Education, (Jackson I)* (mem. op.)), claiming that the Board's failure to adhere to the layoff provision violated the Equal Protection Clause of the Fourteenth Amendment and Title VII of the Civil Rights Act of 1964. They also urged the District Court to take pendent jurisdiction over state law contract claims. * * * After dismissing the federal claims, the District Court declined to exercise pendent jurisdiction over the state law contract claims.

Rather than taking an appeal, the plaintiffs instituted a suit in state court, *Jackson Education Assn. v. Board of Education*, No. 77–011484CZ (Jackson County Circuit Court, 1979) *(Jackson II)*, raising in essence the same claims that had been raised in *Jackson I*. In rejecting the Board's argument that the layoff provision violated the Civil Rights Act of 1964, the state court found that it "ha[d] not been established that the board had discriminated against minorities in its hiring practices. The minority representation on the faculty was the result of societal racial discrimination." App. 43. The state court also found that "[t]here is no history of overt past discrimination by the parties to this contract." Id., at 49. Nevertheless, the court held that Article XII was permissible, despite its discriminatory effect on nonminority teachers, as an attempt to remedy the effects of societal discrimination.

After *Jackson II,* the Board adhered to Article XII. As a result, during the 1976–1977 and 1981–1982 school years, nonminority teachers were laid off, while minority teachers with less seniority were retained. The displaced nonminority teachers, petitioners here, brought suit in Federal District Court, alleging violations of the Equal Protection Clause, Title VII, 42 U.S.C. § 1983, and other federal and state statutes. On cross motions for summary judgment, the District Court dismissed all of petitioners' claims. * * *

The Court of Appeals for the Sixth Circuit affirmed, largely adopting the reasoning and language of the District Court. 746 F.2d 1152 (1984). We granted certiorari, 471 U.S. ___, 105 S.Ct. 2015, 85 L.Ed.2d 298 (1985), to resolve the important issue of the constitutionality of race-based layoffs by public employers. We now reverse.

II

Petitioners' central claim is that they were laid off because of their race in violation of the Equal Protection Clause of the Fourteenth Amendment. Decisions by faculties and administrators of public schools based on race or ethnic origin are reviewable under the Fourteenth Amendment.[4] This Court has "consistently repudiated '[d]istinctions between citizens solely because of their ancestry' as being 'odious to a free people whose institutions are founded upon the

---

4. School district collective bargaining agreements constitute state action for purposes of the Fourteenth Amendment. Abood v. Detroit Board of Ed., 431 U.S. 209, 218, and n. 12, 97 S.Ct. 1782, 1790, and n. 12, 52 L.Ed.2d 261 (1977).

doctrine of equality,' " Loving v. Virginia, 388 U.S. 1, 11, 87 S.Ct. 1817, 1823, 18 L.Ed.2d 1010 (1967) quoting Hirabayashi v. United States, 320 U.S. 81, 100, 63 S.Ct. 1375, 1385, 87 L.Ed. 1774 (1943). "Racial and ethnic distinctions of any sort are inherently suspect and thus call for the most exacting judicial examination." Regents of University of California v. Bakke, 438 U.S. 265, 291, 98 S.Ct. 2733, 2748, 57 L.Ed.2d 750 (1978) (opinion of POWELL, J., joined by WHITE, J.)

The Court has recognized that the level of scrutiny does not change merely because the challenged classification operates against a group that historically has not been subject to governmental discrimination. Mississippi University for Women v. Hogan, 458 U.S. 718, 724 n. 9, 102 S.Ct. 3331, 3336 n. 9, 73 L.Ed.2d 1090 (1982); Bakke, 438 U.S., at 291–299, 98 S.Ct., at 2748–2752; see Shelley v. Kraemer, 334 U.S. 1, 22, 68 S.Ct. 836, 846, 92 L.Ed. 1161 (1948); see also A. Bickel, The Morality of Consent 133 (1975). In this case, Article XII of the CBA operates against whites and in favor of certain minorities, and therefore constitutes a classification based on race. "Any preference based on racial or ethnic criteria must necessarily receive a most searching examination to make sure that it does not conflict with constitutional guarantees." Fullilove v. Klutznick, 448 U.S. 448, 491, 100 S.Ct. 2758, 2781, 65 L.Ed.2d 902 (1980) (opinion of BURGER, C.J.). There are two prongs to this examination. First, any racial classification "must be justified by a compelling governmental interest." Palmore v. Sidoti, 466 U.S. 429, 432, 104 S.Ct. 1879, 1882, 80 L.Ed.2d 421 (1984); see Loving v. Virginia, 388 U.S. 1, 11, 87 S.Ct. 1817, 1823, 18 L.Ed.2d 1010 (1967); cf. Graham v. Richardson, 403 U.S. 365, 375, 91 S.Ct. 1848, 1853, 29 L.Ed.2d 534 (1971) (alienage). Second, the means chosen by the State to effectuate its purpose must be "narrowly tailored to the achievement of that goal." Fullilove, 448 U.S., at 480, 100 S.Ct., at 2776. We must decide whether the layoff provision is supported by a compelling state purpose and whether the means chosen to accomplish that purpose are narrowly tailored.

III

A

The Court of Appeals, relying on the reasoning and language of the District Court's opinion, held that the Board's interest in providing minority role models for its minority students, as an attempt to alleviate the effects of societal discrimination, was sufficiently important to justify the racial classification embodied in the layoff provision. 746 F.2d, at 1156–1157. The court discerned a need for more minority faculty role models by finding that the percentage of minority teachers was less than the percentage of minority students. Id., at 1156.

This Court never has held that societal discrimination alone is sufficient to justify a racial classification. Rather, the Court has insisted upon some showing of prior discrimination by the governmental unit involved before allowing limited use of racial classifications in order to remedy such discrimination. This Court's reasoning in Hazel-wood School District v. United States, 433 U.S. 299, 97 S.Ct. 2736, 53 L.Ed.2d 768 (1977), illustrates that the relevant analysis in cases involving proof of discrimination by statistical disparity focuses on those disparities that demonstrate such prior governmental discrimination. In *Hazelwood* the Court concluded that, absent employment discrimination by the school board, " 'nondiscriminatory hiring practices will in time result in a work force more or less representative of the racial and ethnic composition of the population in the community from which the employees are hired.' " Id., at 307, 97 S.Ct., at 2741, quoting Teamsters v. United States, 431 U.S. 324, 340, n. 20, 97 S.Ct. 1843, 1856, n. 20, 52 L.Ed.2d 396 (1977). * * * *Hazelwood* demonstrates this Court's focus on prior discrimination as the justification for, and the limitation on, a State's adoption of race-based remedies. See also Swann v. Charlotte-Mecklenburg Board of Education, 402 U.S. 1, 91 S.Ct. 1267, 28 L.Ed.2d 554 (1971).

Unlike the analysis in *Hazelwood,* the role model theory employed by the District Court has no logical stopping point. The role model theory allows the Board to engage in discriminatory hiring and layoff practices long past the point required by any legitimate remedial purpose. Indeed, by tying the required percentage of minority teachers to the percentage of minority students, it requires just the sort of year-to-year calibration the Court stated was unnecessary in Swann, 402 U.S., at 31–32, 91 S.Ct., at 1283–1284:

* * *

Societal discrimination, without more, is too amorphous a basis for imposing a racially classified remedy. The role model theory announced by the District Court and the resultant holding typify this indefiniteness. There are numerous explanations for a disparity between the percentage of minority students and the percentage of minority faculty, many of them completely unrelated to discrimination of any kind. In fact, there is no apparent connection between the two groups. Nevertheless, the District Court combined irrelevant comparisons between these two groups with an indisputable statement that there has been societal discrimination, and upheld state action predicated upon racial classifications. No one doubts that there has been serious racial discrimination in this country. But as the basis for imposing discriminatory *legal* remedies that work against innocent people, societal discrimination is insufficient and over expansive. In the absence of particularized findings, a court could uphold remedies that are ageless in their reach into the past, and timeless in their ability to affect the future.

B

Respondents also now argue that their purpose in adopting the layoff provision was to remedy prior discrimination against minorities by the Jackson School District in hiring teachers. Public schools, like other public employers, operate under two interrelated constitutional duties. They are under a clear command from this Court, starting with Brown v. Board of Education, 349 U.S. 294, 75 S.Ct. 753, 99 L.Ed. 1083 (1955), to eliminate every vestige of racial segregation and discrimination in the schools. Pursuant to that goal, race-conscious remedial action may be necessary. North Carolina State Board of Education v. Swann, 402 U.S. 43, 46, 91 S.Ct. 1284, 1286, 28 L.Ed.2d 586 (1971). On the other hand, public employers, including public schools, also must act in accordance with a "core purpose of the Fourteenth Amendment" which is to "do away with all governmentally imposed distinctions based on race." Palmore v. Sidoti, 466 U.S., at 432, 104 S.Ct., at 1881–1882. These related constitutional duties are not always harmonious; reconciling them requires public employers to act with extraordinary care. In particular, a public employer like the Board must ensure that, before it embarks on an affirmative action program, it has convincing evidence that remedial action is warranted. That is, it must have sufficient evidence to justify the conclusion that there has been prior discrimination.

* * *

Despite the fact that Article XII has spawned years of litigation and three separate lawsuits, no such determination ever has been made. Although its litigation position was different, the Board in *Jackson I* and *Jackson II* denied the existence of prior discriminatory hiring practices. App. 33. This precise issue was litigated in both those suits. Both courts concluded that any statistical disparities were the result of general societal discrimination, not of prior discrimination by the Board. The Board now contends that, given another opportunity, it could establish the existence of prior discrimination. Although this argument seems belated at this point in the proceedings, we need not consider the question since we conclude below that the layoff provision was not a legally appropriate means of achieving even a compelling purpose.

IV

The Court of Appeals examined the means chosen to accomplish the Board's race-conscious purposes under a test of "reasonableness." That standard has no support in the decisions of this Court. As demonstrated in Part II above, our decisions always have employed a more stringent standard—however articulated—to test the validity of the means chosen by a state to accomplish its race-conscious purposes. See, e.g., Palmore, 466 U.S., at 432, 104 S.Ct., at 1882 ("to pass constitutional muster, [racial classifications] must be necessary * * * to the accomplishment of their legitimate purpose") (quoting McLaughlin v. Florida, 379 U.S. 184, 196, 85 S.Ct. 283, 290, 13 L.Ed.2d 222 (1964); Fullilove, 448 U.S., at 480, 100 S.Ct., at 2775 (opinion of Burger, C.J.) ("We recognize the need for careful judicial evaluation to assure that any * * * program that employs racial or ethnic criteria to accomplish the objective of remedying the present effects of past discrimination is narrowly tailored to the achievement of that goal").[6] Under strict scrutiny the means chosen to accomplish the State's asserted purpose must be specifically and narrowly framed to accomplish that purpose. Fullilove, 448 U.S., at 480, 100 S.Ct., at 2775 (opinion of BURGER, C.J.). "Racial classifications are simply too pernicious to permit any but the most exact connection between justification and classification." Id., at 537, 100 S.Ct., at 2805 (STEVENS, J., dissenting).

We have recognized, however, that in order to remedy the effects of prior discrimination, it may be necessary to take race into account. As part of this Nation's dedication to eradicating racial discrimination, innocent persons may be called upon to bear some of the burden of the remedy. "When effectuating a limited and properly tailored remedy to cure the effects of prior discrimination, such a 'sharing of the burden' by innocent parties is not impermissible." Id., at 484, 100 S.Ct., at 2778, quoting Franks v. Bowman Transportation Co., 424 U.S. 747, 96 S.Ct. 1251, 47 L.Ed.2d 444 (1976).[8] In *Fullilove*, the challenged statute

---

6. The term "narrowly tailored," so frequently used in our cases, has acquired a secondary meaning. More specifically, as commentators have indicated, the term may be used to require consideration whether lawful alternative and less restrictive means could have been used. Or, as Professor Ely has noted, the classification at issue must "fit" with greater precision than any alternative means. Ely, The Constitutionality of Reverse Racial Discrimination, 41 U.Chi.L.Rev. 723, 727, n. 26 (1974) (hereinafter Ely). "[Courts] should give particularly intense scrutiny to whether a nonracial approach or a more narrowly tailored racial classification could promote the substantial interest about as well and at tolerable administrative expense." Greenawalt, Judicial Scrutiny of "Benign" Racial Preference in Law School Admissions, 75 Colum.L.Rev. 559, 578–579 (1975) (hereinafter Greenawalt).

8. Of course, when a state implements a race-based plan that requires such a sharing of the burden, it cannot justify the discriminatory effect on some individuals because other individuals had approved the plan. Any "waiver" of the right not to be dealt with by the government on the basis of one's race must be made by those affected. Yet JUSTICE MARSHALL repeatedly contends that the fact that Article XII was approved by a majority vote of the Union somehow validates this plan. He sees this case not in terms of individual constitutional rights, but as an allocation of burdens "between two racial groups." Post, at 1864. Thus, Article XII becomes a political compromise that "avoided placing the entire burden of layoffs on either the white teachers as a group or the minority teach-

ers as a group." Post, at 1859. But the petitioners before us today are not "the white teachers as a group." They are Wendy Wygant and other individuals who claim that they were fired from their jobs because of their race. That claim cannot be waived by petitioners' more senior colleagues. In view of the way union seniority works, it is not surprising that while a straight freeze on minority layoffs was overwhelmingly rejected, a "compromise" eventually was reached that placed the entire burden of the compromise on the most junior union members. The more senior union members simply had nothing to lose from such a compromise. See Post, at 1860 ("To petitioners, at the bottom of the seniority scale among white teachers, fell the lot of bearing the white group's proportionate share of layoffs that became necessary in 1982.") The fact that such a painless accommodation was approved by the more senior union members six times since 1972 is irrelevant. The Constitution does not allocate constitutional rights to be distributed like bloc grants within discrete racial groups; and until it does, petitioners' more senior union colleagues cannot vote away petitioners' rights.

JUSTICE MARSHALL also attempts to portray the layoff plan as one that has no real invidious effect, stating that "within the confines of constant minority proportions, it preserves the hierarchy of seniority in the selection of individuals for layoff." Post, at 1865. That phrase merely expresses the tautology that layoffs are based on seniority except as to those nonminority teachers who are displaced by minority teachers with less seniority. This is really nothing more than group-based analysis:

required at least 10 percent of federal public works funds to be used in contracts with minority-owned business enterprises. This requirement was found to be within the remedial powers of Congress in part because the "actual burden shouldered by nonminority firms is relatively light." 448 U.S., at 484, 100 S.Ct., at 2778.[9]

Significantly, none of the cases discussed above involved layoffs.[10] Here, by contrast, the means chosen to achieve the Board's asserted purposes is that of laying off nonminority teachers with greater seniority in order to retain minority teachers with less seniority. We have previously expressed concern over the burden that a preferential layoffs scheme imposes on innocent parties. See Firefighters v. Stotts, 467 U.S. 561, 574–576, 578–579, 104 S.Ct. 2576, ___–___, ___–___, 81 L.Ed.2d 483 (1984); see also Weber, n. 9, supra this page, 443 U.S., at 208, 99 S.Ct., at 2730 ("The plan does not require the discharge of white workers and their replacement with new black hirees"). In cases involving valid *hiring* goals, the burden to be borne by innocent individuals is diffused to a considerable extent among society generally. Though hiring goals may burden some innocent individuals, they simply do not impose the same kind of injury that layoffs impose. Denial of a future employment opportunity is not as intrusive as loss of an existing job.

Many of our cases involve union seniority plans with employees who are typically heavily dependent on wages for their day-to-day living. Even a temporary layoff may have adverse financial as well as psychological effects. A worker may invest many productive years in one job and one city with the expectation of earning the stability and security of seniority. "At that point, the rights and expectations surrounding seniority make up what is probably the most valuable capital asset that the worker 'owns,' worth even more than the current equity in his home." Fallon & Weiler, Conflicting Models of Racial Justice, 1984 S.Ct.Rev. 1, 58. Layoffs disrupt these settled expectations in a way that general hiring goals do not.

While hiring goals impose a diffuse burden, often foreclosing only one of several opportunities,[11] layoffs impose the entire burden of

"each group would shoulder a portion of [the layoff] burden equal to its portion of the faculty." Post, at 1859. The constitutional problem remains: the decision that petitioners would be laid off was based on their race.

9. Similarly, the Court approved the hiring program in Steelworkers v. Weber, 443 U.S. 193, 208, 99 S.Ct. 2721, 2729, 61 L.Ed.2d 480 (1979), in part because the plan did not "unnecessarily trammel the interests of the white employees." Since *Weber* involved a private company, its reasoning concerning the validity of the hiring plan at issue there is not directly relevant to this case, which involves a state-imposed plan. No equal protection claim was presented in *Weber.*

10. There are cases involving alteration of strict seniority layoffs, see, e.g., Ford Motor Co. v. Huffman, 345 U.S. 330, 73 S.Ct. 681, 97 L.Ed. 1048 (1953); Aeronautical Industrial District Lodge 727 v. Campbell, 337 U.S. 521, 69 S.Ct. 1287, 93 L.Ed. 1513 (1949), but they do not involve the critical element here—layoffs based on race. The Constitution does not require layoffs to be based on strict seniority. But it does require the state to meet a heavy burden of justification when it implements a layoff plan based on race.

11. The "school admission" cases, which involve the same basic concepts as cases involving hiring goals, illustrate this principle. For example, in DeFunis v. Odegaard, 416 U.S. 312, 94 S.Ct. 1704, 40

achieving racial equality on particular individuals, often resulting in serious disruption of their lives. That burden is too intrusive. We therefore hold that, as a means of accomplishing purposes that otherwise may be legitimate, the Board's layoff plan is not sufficiently narrowly tailored.[12] Other, less intrusive means of accomplishing similar purposes—such as the adoption of hiring goals—are available. For these reasons, the Board's selection of layoffs as the means to accomplish even a valid purpose cannot satisfy the demands of the Equal Protection Clause.[13]

V

We accordingly reverse the judgment of the Court of Appeals for the Sixth Circuit.

It is so ordered.

JUSTICE O'CONNOR, concurring in part and concurring in the judgment.

This case requires us to define and apply the standard required by the Equal Protection Clause when a governmental agency agrees to give preferences on the basis of race or national origin in making layoffs of employees. The specific question posed is, as JUSTICE MARSHALL puts it, "whether the Constitution prohibits a union and a local school board from developing a collective-bargaining agreement that apportions layoffs between two racially determined groups as a means of preserving the effects of an affirmative hiring policy." Post, at 1860 (MARSHALL, J., dissenting). There is no issue here of the interpretation and application of Title VII of the Civil Rights Act; accordingly, we have only the constitutional issue to resolve.

The Equal Protection Clause standard applicable to racial classifications that work to the disadvantage of "nonminorities" has been articulated in various ways. See, e.g., Post, at ___–___ (MARSHALL, J., dissenting). JUSTICE POWELL now would require that: (1) the racial classification be justified by a " 'compelling governmental interest,' " and (2) the means chosen by the State to effectuate its purpose be

L.Ed.2d 164 (1974), while petitioner's complaint alleged that he had been denied admission to the University of Washington Law School because of his race, he also had been accepted at the Oregon, Idaho, Gonzaga, and Willamette Law Schools. DeFunis v. Odegaard, 82 Wash.2d 11, 30, n. 11, 507 P.2d 1169, 1181, n. 11 (1973). The injury to DeFunis was not of the same kind or degree as the injury that he would have suffered had he been removed from law school in his third year. Even this analogy may not rise to the level of harm suffered by a union member who is laid off.

12. We have recognized, however, that in order to provide make-whole relief to the actual, identified victims of individual discrimination, a court may in an appropri-

ate case award competitive seniority. See Franks v. Bowman Transportation Co., 424 U.S. 747, 96 S.Ct. 1251, 47 L.Ed.2d 444 (1976).

13. The Board's definition of minority to include Blacks, Orientals, American Indians, and persons of Spanish descent, n. 2, supra, further illustrates the undifferentiated nature of the plan. There is no explanation of why the Board chose to favor these particular minorities or how in fact members of some of the categories can be identified. Moreover, respondents have never suggested—much less formally found—that they have engaged in prior, purposeful discrimination against members of each of these minority groups.

"narrowly tailored." Ante, at 1867. This standard reflects the belief, apparently held by all members of this Court, that racial classifications of any sort must be subjected to "strict scrutiny," however defined. See, e.g., Fullilove v. Klutznick, 448 U.S. 448, 491, 100 S.Ct. 2758, 2781, 65 L.Ed.2d 902 (1980), (opinion of BURGER, C.J., joined by WHITE, J.) ("Any preference based on racial or ethnic criteria must necessarily receive a most searching examination to make sure that it does not conflict with constitutional guarantees"); id., at 537, 100 S.Ct., at 2805 (STEVENS, J., dissenting) ("Racial classifications are simply too pernicious to permit any but the most exact connection between justification and classification"); Regents of University of California v. Bakke, 438 U.S. 265, 291, 98 S.Ct. 2733, 2748, 57 L.Ed.2d 750 (1978) (opinion of POWELL, J., joined by WHITE, J.) ("Racial and ethnic distinctions of any sort are inherently suspect and thus call for the most exacting judicial examination"); id., at 361–362, 98 S.Ct., at 2784 ("[O]ur review under the Fourteenth Amendment should be strict—not ' "strict" in theory and fatal in fact,' because it is stigma that causes fatality—but strict and searching nonetheless") (opinion of BRENNAN, WHITE, MARSHALL, and BLACKMUN, JJ.). JUSTICES MARSHALL, BRENNAN, and BLACKMUN, however, seem to adhere to the formulation of the "strict" standard that they authored, with JUSTICE WHITE, in *Bakke*: "remedial use of race is permissible if it serves 'important governmental objectives' and is 'substantially related to achievement of those objectives.' " Post, at 1861 (MARSHALL, J., dissenting), quoting Bakke, supra, at 359, 98 S.Ct. at 2783 (opinion of BRENNAN, WHITE, MARSHALL, and BLACKMUN, JJ.).

I subscribe to JUSTICE POWELL's formulation because it mirrors the standard we have consistently applied in examining racial classifications in other contexts. In my view,

> "the analysis and level of scrutiny applied to determine the validity of [a racial] classification do not vary simply because the objective appears acceptable to individual Members of the Court. While the validity and importance of the objective may affect the outcome of the analysis, the analysis itself does not change." Mississippi University for Women v. Hogan, 458 U.S. 718, 724, n. 9, 102 S.Ct. 3331, 3336, n. 9, 73 L.Ed.2d 1090 (1982).

Although JUSTICE POWELL's formulation may be viewed as more stringent than that suggested by JUSTICES BRENNAN, WHITE, MARSHALL, and BLACKMUN, the disparities between the two tests do not preclude a fair measure of consensus. In particular, as regards certain state interests commonly relied upon in formulating affirmative action programs, the distinction between a "compelling" and an "important" governmental purpose may be a negligible one. The Court is in agreement that, whatever the formulation employed, remedying past or present racial discrimination by a state actor is a sufficiently weighty state interest to warrant the remedial use of a carefully constructed affirmative action program. This remedial purpose need not be accompanied by contemporaneous findings of actual discrimination to be accepted as legitimate as long as the public actor has a firm basis for believing that remedial action is required. See infra, at ___; ante, at ___. See also post, at ___ (MARSHALL, J., dissenting). Additionally, although its precise contours are uncertain, a state interest in the promotion of racial diversity has been found sufficiently "compelling," at least in the context of higher education, to support the use of racial considerations in furthering that interest. See, e.g., Bakke, 438 U.S., at 311–315, 98 S.Ct., at 2759–2761 (opinion of POWELL, J.). See also post, at ___ (MARSHALL, J., dissenting); id., at ___ – ___ (STEVENS, J., dissenting). And certainly nothing the Court has said today necessarily forecloses the possibility that the Court will find other governmental interests which have been relied upon in the lower courts but which have not been passed on here to be sufficiently "important" or "compelling" to sustain the use of affirmative action policies.

It appears, then, that the true source of disagreement on the Court lies not so much in defining the state interests which may support affirmative action efforts as in defining the degree to which the means employed must "fit" the ends pursued to meet constitutional standards. See, e.g., ante, at 1863, nn. 6–7. Yet even here the Court has forged a degree of unanimity; it is agreed that a plan need not be limited to the remedying of specific instances of identified discrimination for it to be deemed sufficiently "narrowly tailored," or "substantially related," to the correction of prior discrimination by the state actor. See infra, at ___; ante, at ___; post, at ___ (MARSHALL, J., dissenting).

In the final analysis, the diverse formulations and the number of separate writings put forth by various members of the Court in these difficult cases do not necessarily reflect an intractable fragmentation in opinion with respect to certain core principles. Ultimately, the Court is at least in accord in believing that a public employer, consistent with the Constitution, may undertake an affirmative action program which is designed to further a legitimate remedial purpose and which implements that purpose by means that do not impose disproportionate harm on the interests, or unnecessarily trammel the rights, of innocent individuals directly and adversely affected by a plan's racial preference.

* * *

* * * The courts below ruled that a particularized, contemporaneous finding of discrimination was not necessary and upheld the plan as a remedy for "societal" discrimination, apparently on the assumption that in the absence of a specific, contemporaneous finding, any discrimination addressed by an affirmative action plan could only be termed "societal." See, e.g., 546 F.Supp., at 1199. I believe that this assumption is false and therefore agree with the Court that a contemporaneous or antecedent finding of past discrimination by a court or other competent body is not a constitutional prerequisite to a public employer's voluntary agreement to an affirmative action plan. See ante, at ___.

A violation of federal statutory or constitutional requirements does not arise with the making of a finding; it arises when the wrong is committed. Contemporaneous findings serve solely as a means by which it can be made absolutely certain that the governmental actor truly is attempting to remedy its own unlawful conduct when it adopts an affirmative action plan, rather than attempting to alleviate the wrongs suffered through general societal discrimination. See, e.g., Fullilove v. Klutznick, 448 U.S., at 498, 100 S.Ct., at 2784 (POWELL, J., concurring). Such findings, when voluntarily made by a public employer, obviously are desirable in that they provide evidentiary safeguards of value both to nonminority employees and to the public employer itself, should its affirmative action program be challenged in court. If contemporaneous findings were *required* of public employers in every case as a precondition to the constitutional validity of their affirmative action efforts, however, the relative value of these evidentiary advantages would diminish, for they could be secured only by the sacrifice of other vitally important values.

The imposition of a requirement that public employers make findings that they have engaged in illegal discrimination before they engage in affirmative action programs would severely undermine public employers' incentive to meet voluntarily their civil rights obligations. See e.g. Bakke, supra, 438 U.S. at 364, 98 S.Ct., at 2785 (opinion of BRENNAN, WHITE, MARSHALL, and BLACKMUN, JJ.) Cf. Steelworkers v. Weber, 443 U.S. 193, 210–211, 99 S.Ct. 2721, 2730–2731, 61 L.Ed.2d 480 (1979) (BLACKMUN, J., concurring). This result would clearly be at odds with this Court's and Congress' consistent emphasis on "the value of voluntary efforts to further the objectives of the law." Bakke supra, 438 U.S., at 364, 98 S.Ct. at 2785 (opinion of BRENNAN, WHITE, MARSHALL, and BLACKMUN, JJ.); see also Albemarle Paper Co. v. Moody, 422 U.S. 405, 417–418, 95 S.Ct. 2362, 2371–2372, 45 L.Ed.2d 280 (1975); Alexander v. Gardner-Denver Co., 415 U.S. 36, 44, 94 S.Ct. 1011, 1017, 39 L.Ed.2d 147 (1974). The value of voluntary compliance is doubly important when it is a public employer that acts, both because of the example its voluntary assumption of responsibility sets and because the remediation of governmental discrimination is of unique importance. See S. Rep. No. 92–415, p. 10 (1971) (accompanying the amendments extending coverage of Title VII to the States) ("Discrimination by government * * * serves a doubly destructive purpose. The exclusion of minorities from effective participation in the bureaucracy not only promotes ignorance of minority problems in that particular community, but also creates mistrust, alienation, and all too often hostility toward the entire process of government"). Imposing a contemporaneous findings requirement would produce the anomalous result that what private employers may voluntarily do to correct apparent violations of Title VII, Steelworkers v. Weber, supra, public employers are constitutionally forbidden to do to correct their statutory and constitutional transgressions.

Such results cannot, in my view, be justified by reference to the incremental value a contemporaneous findings requirement would have as an evidentiary safeguard. As is illustrated by this case, public employers are trapped between the competing hazards of liability to minorities if affirmative action *is not* taken to remedy apparent employment discrimination and liability to nonminorities if affirmative action *is* taken. Where these employers, who are presumably fully aware both of their duty under federal law to respect the rights of *all* their employees and of their potential liability for failing to do so, act on the basis of information which gives them a sufficient basis for concluding that remedial action is necessary, a contemporaneous findings requirement should not be necessary.

This conclusion is consistent with our previous decisions recognizing the States' ability to take voluntary race-conscious action to achieve compliance with the law even in the absence of a specific finding of past discrimination. See, e.g. United Jewish Organizations of Williamsburgh, Inc. v. Carey, 430 U.S. 144, 165–166, 97 S.Ct. 996, 1009–1010, 51 L.Ed.2d 229 (1977) (reapportionment); McDaniel v. Barresi, 402 U.S. 39, 91 S.Ct. 1287, 28 L.Ed.2d 582 (1971) (school desegregation). Indeed, our recognition of the responsible state actor's competency to take these steps is assumed in our recognition of the States' constitutional *duty* to take affirmative steps to eliminate the continuing effects of past unconstitutional discrimination. See e.g., Swann v. Charlotte-Mecklenburg Board of Education, 402 U.S. 1, 15, 91 S.Ct. 1267, 1275, 28 L.Ed.2d 554 (1971); Green v. New Kent County School Board, 391 U.S. 430, 437–438, 88 S.Ct. 1689, 1693–1694, 20 L.Ed.2d 716 (1968).

Of course, as the Court notes, the public employer must discharge this sensitive duty with great care; in order to provide some measure of protection to the interests of its nonminority employees and the employer itself in the event that its affirmative action plan is challenged, the public employer must have a firm basis for determining that affirmative action is warranted. Public employers are not without reliable benchmarks in making this determination. For example, demonstrable evidence of a disparity between the percentage of qualified blacks on a school's teaching staff and the percentage of qualified minorities in the relevant labor pool sufficient to support a prima facie Title VII pattern or practice claim by minority teachers would lend a compelling basis for a competent authority such as the School Board to conclude that implementation of a voluntary affirmative action plan is appropriate to remedy apparent prior employment discrimination.

To be sure, such a conclusion is not unassailable. If a voluntary affirmative action plan is subsequently challenged in court by nonminority employees, those employees must be given the opportunity to prove that the plan does not meet the constitutional standard this Court has articulated. However, as the Court suggests, the institution of such a challenge does not automatically impose upon the public employer the burden of convincing the court of its liability for prior unlawful discrimination; nor does it mean that the court must make an actual finding of prior discrimination based on the employer's proof before the employer's affirmative action plan will be upheld. See ante, at ___. In "reverse discrimination" suits, as in any other suit, it is the plaintiffs who must bear the burden of demonstrating that their rights have been violated. The findings a court must make before upholding an affirmative action plan reflect this allocation of proof and the nature of the challenge asserted. For instance, in the example posed above, the nonminority teachers could easily demonstrate that the purpose and effect of the plan is to impose a race-based classification. But when the Board introduces its statistical proof as evidence of its remedial purpose, thereby supplying the court with the means for determining that the Board had a firm basis for concluding that remedial action was appropriate, it is incumbent upon the nonminority teachers to prove their case; they continue to bear the ultimate burden of persuading the court that the Board's evidence did not support an inference of prior discrimination and thus a remedial purpose, or that the plan instituted on the basis of this evidence was not sufficiently "narrowly tailored." Only by meeting this burden could the plaintiffs establish a violation of their constitutional rights, and thereby defeat the presumption that the Board's assertedly remedial action based on the statistical evidence was justified.

In sum, I do not think that the layoff provision was constitutionally infirm simply because the School Board, the Commission or a court had not made particularized findings of discrimination at the time the provision was agreed upon. But when the plan was challenged, the District Court and the Court of Appeals did not make the proper inquiry into the legitimacy of the Board's asserted remedial purpose; instead, they relied upon governmental purposes that we have deemed insufficient to withstand strict scrutiny, and therefore failed to isolate a sufficiently important governmental purpose that could support the challenged provision.

There is, however, no need to inquire whether the provision actually had a legitimate remedial purpose based on the record, such as it is, because the judgment is vulnerable on yet another ground: the courts below applied a "reasonableness" test in evaluating the relationship between the ends pursued and the means employed to achieve them that is plainly incorrect under any of the standards articulated by this Court. Nor is it necessary, in my view, to resolve the troubling questions of whether any layoff provision could survive strict scrutiny or whether this particular layoff provision could, when considered without reference to the hiring goal it was intended to further, pass the onerous "narrowly tailored" requirement. Petitioners have met their burden of establishing that this layoff provision is not "narrowly tailored" to achieve its asserted remedial purpose by demonstrating that the provision is keyed to a hiring goal that itself has no relation to the remedying of employment discrimination.

Although the constitutionality of the hiring goal as such is not before us, it is impossible to evaluate the necessity of the layoff provision as a remedy for the apparent prior employment discrimination absent reference to that goal. See, e.g., post, at 1858, (MARSHALL, J., dissenting). In this case, the hiring goal that the layoff provision was designed to safeguard was tied to the percentage of minority students in the school district, not to the percentage of qualified minority teachers within the relevant labor pool. The disparity between the percentage of minorities on the teaching staff and the percentage of minorities in the student body is not probative of employment discrimination; it is only when it is established that the availability of minorities in the relevant labor pool substantially exceeded those hired that one may draw an inference of deliberate discrimination in employment. See Hazelwood School District v. United States, 433 U.S. 299, 308, 97 S.Ct. 2736, 2741, 53 L.Ed.2d 768 (1977) (Title VII context). Because the layoff provision here acts to maintain levels of minority hiring that have no relation to remedying employment discrimination, it cannot be adjudged "narrowly tailored" to effectuate its asserted remedial purpose.

I therefore join in parts I, II, III–A, III–B, and V of the Court's opinion, and concur in the judgment.

JUSTICE WHITE, concurring in the judgment.

* * *

JUSTICE MARSHALL, with whom JUSTICE BRENNAN and JUSTICE BLACKMUN join, dissenting.

When this Court seeks to resolve farranging constitutional issues, it must be especially careful to ground its analysis firmly in the facts of the particular controversy before it. Yet in this significant case, we are hindered by a record that is informal and incomplete. Both parties now appear to realize that the record is inadequate to inform the Court's decision. Both have lodged with the Court voluminous "submissions" containing factual material that was not considered by the District Court or the Court of Appeals. Petitioners have submitted 21 separate items, predominantly statistical charts, which they assert are relevant to their claim of discrimination. Respondents have submitted public documents that tend to substantiate the facts alleged in the brief accompanying their motion for summary judgment in the District Court. These include transcripts and exhibits from two prior proceedings, in which certain questions of discrimination in the Jackson schools were litigated, Jackson Education Association v. Board of Education, No. 4–72340 (ED Mich.1976) (Jackson I), and Jackson Education Association v. Board of Education, No. 77–011484CZ (Jackson Cty. Cir. Ct.1979) (Jackson II).

We should not acquiesce in the parties' attempt to try their case before this Court. Yet it would be just as serious a mistake simply to ignore altogether, as the plurality has done, the compelling factual setting in which this case evidently has arisen. No race-conscious provision that purports to serve a remedial purpose can be fairly assessed in a vacuum.

The haste with which the District Court granted summary judgment to respondents, without seeking to develop the factual allegations contained in respondents' brief, prevented the full exploration of the facts that are now critical to resolution of the important issue before us. Respondents' acquiescence in a premature victory in the District Court should not now be used as an instrument of their defeat. Rather, the District Court should have the opportunity to develop a factual record adequate to resolve the serious issue raised by the case. I believe, therefore, that it is improper for this Court to resolve the constitutional issue in its current posture. But, because I feel that the plurality has also erred seriously in its legal analysis of the merits of this case, I write further to express my disagreement with the conclusions that it has reached.

I, too, believe that layoffs are unfair. But unfairness ought not be confused with constitutional injury. Paying no heed to the true circumstances of petitioners' plight, the plurality would nullify years of negotiation and compromise designed to solve serious educational problems in the public schools of Jackson, Michigan. Because I believe that a public employer, with the full agreement of its employees, should be permitted to preserve the benefits of a legitimate and constitutional affirmative-action hiring plan even while reducing its work force, I dissent.

I

*   *   *

II

From the outset, it is useful to bear in mind what this case is not. There has been no court order to achieve racial balance, which might require us to reflect upon the existence of judicial power to impose obligations on parties not proven to have committed a wrong. See Swann v. Charlotte-Mecklenburg Board of Education, 402 U.S. 1, 16, 91 S.Ct. 1267, 1276, 28 L.Ed.2d 554 (1971). There is also no occasion here to resolve whether a white worker may be required to give up his or her job in order to be replaced by a black worker. See Steelworkers v. Weber, 443 U.S. 193, 208, 99 S.Ct. 2721, 2729, 61 L.Ed.2d 480 (1979). Nor are we asked to order parties to suffer the consequences of an agreement that they had no role in adopting. See Firefighters v. Stotts, 467 U.S. 561, 575, 104 S.Ct. 2576, ___, 81 L.Ed.2d 483 (1984). Moreover, this is not a case in which a party to a collective-bargaining agreement has attempted unilaterally to achieve racial balance by refusing to comply with a contractual, seniority-based layoff provision. Cf. Teamsters v. United States, 431 U.S. 324, 350, 352, 97 S.Ct. 1843, 1862, 1863, 52 L.Ed.2d 396 (1977).

The sole question posed by this case is whether the Constitution prohibits a union and a local school board from developing a collective-bargaining agreement that apportions layoffs between two racially determined groups as a means of preserving the effects of an affirmative hiring policy, the constitutionality of which is unchallenged.[3]

III

Agreement upon a means for applying the Equal Protection Clause to an affirmative-action program has eluded this Court every time the issue has come before us. * * *

* * *

Despite the Court's inability to agree on a route, we have reached a common destination in sustaining affirmative action against constitutional attack. * * *

In this case, it should not matter which test the Court applies. What is most important, under any approach to the constitutional analysis, is that a reviewing court genuinely consider the circumstances of the provision at issue. The history and application of Article XII, assuming verification upon a proper record, demonstate that this provision would pass constitutional muster, no matter which standard the Court should adopt.

IV

The principal state purpose supporting Article XII is the need to preserve the levels of faculty integration achieved through the affirmative hiring policy adopted in the early 1970's. Brief for Respondents 41–43. Justification for the hiring policy itself is found in the turbulent history of the effort to integrate the Jackson Public Schools—not even mentioned in the majority opinion—which attests to the bona fides of the Board's current employment practices.

3. JUSTICE O'CONNOR rests her disposition of this case on the propriety of the hiring plan, even though petitioners have not challenged it. She appears to rely on language in the preamble to the collective-bargaining agreement, which suggests that the "goal of such [affirmative-action] policy shall be to have at least the same percentage of minority racial representation on each individual staff as is represented by the student population of the Jackson Public Schools." Article VII.D.1, App. to Pet. for Cert. 1a. Believing that the school system's hiring "goal" ought instead to be the percentage of qualified minorities in the labor pool, JUSTICE O'CONNOR concludes that the challenged layoff provision itself is overly broad. Ante, at ___. Among the materials considered by the District Court and Court of Appeals, however, there is no evidence to show the actual proportion of minority teachers in the Jackson schools, either in relation to the qualified minority labor force or in relation to the number of minority students. If the distinction between the two goals is to be considered critical to the constitutionality of the affirmative-action plan, it is incumbent on petitioners—plaintiffs below—to demonstrate that, at the time they were laid off, the proportion of minority teachers had equaled or exceeded the appropriate percentage of the minority labor force, and that continued adherence to affirmative-action goals, therefore, unjustifiably caused their injuries. This petitioners have failed to do. Outside of the First Amendment context, I know of no justification for invalidating a provision because it might, in a hypothetical case, apply improperly to other potential plaintiffs. Petitioners have attempted to fill the gap in their case by supplying statistical charts to this Court. See, e.g., Petitioners' Lodging, pp. 56–62. Clearly, however, we are not equipped for such factfinding, and if the hortatory ceiling of the affirmative-action plan is indeed to be considered a significant aspect of the case, then that would be an appropriate subject of inquiry on remand.

The record and lodgings indicate that the Commission, endowed by the State Constitution with the power to investigate complaints of discrimination and the duty to secure the equal protection of the laws, Mich.Const., Art. V, § 29, prompted and oversaw the remedial steps now under attack.[4] When the Board agreed to take specified remedial action, including the hiring and promotion of minority teachers, the Commission did not pursue its investigation of the apparent violations to the point of rendering formal findings of discrimination.

* * *

An explicit Board admission or judicial determination of culpability, which the petitioners and even the Solicitor General urge us to hold was required before the Board could undertake a race-conscious remedial plan, see Brief for Petitioners 27–29; Brief for United States as *Amicus Curiae* 29, would only have exposed the Board in this case to further litigation and liability, including individual liability under 42 U.S.C. § 1983, for past acts. It would have contributed nothing to the advancement of the community's urgent objective of integrating its schools.

* * * The Court is correct to recognize, as it does today, that formal findings of past discrimination are not a necessary predicate to the adoption of affirmative-action policies, and that the scope of such policies need not be limited to remedying specific instances of identifiable discrimination. See ante, at 1844 (opinion of POWELL, J.); ante, at 1852 (opinion of O'CONNOR, J.).

Moreover, under the apparent circumstances of this case, we need not rely on any general awareness of "societal discrimination" to conclude that the Board's purpose is of sufficient importance to justify its limited remedial efforts. * * *

Were I satisfied with the record before us, I would hold that the state purpose of preserving the integrity of a valid hiring policy—which in turn sought to achieve diversity and stability for the benefit of *all* students—was sufficient, in this case, to satisfy the demands of the Constitution.

V

The second part of any constitutional assessment of the disputed plan requires us to examine the means chosen to achieve the state purpose. Again, the history of Article XII, insofar as we can determine it, is the best source of assistance.

---

4. The Commission currently describes its participation in the Jackson matter as follows: "[T]he Commission investigated the allegations and sought *to remedy the apparent violations* by negotiating an order of adjustment with the Jackson Board * * *. [T]he out-of-line seniority layoff provisions in the Jackson Board of Educa-tion's employment contracts with its teachers since 1972 are consistent with overall desegregation efforts undertaken *in compliance with* the Commission's order of adjustment." Brief for Michigan Civil Rights Commission, Michigan Dept. of Civil Rights as *Amicus Curiae* 14 (emphasis added).

A

Testimony of both Union and school officials illustrates that the Board's obligation to integrate its faculty could not have been fulfilled meaningfully as long as layoffs continued to eliminate the last hired. See App. 41; Respondents' Lodging No. 3, p. 69 (deposition of Superintendent of Schools); Respondents' Lodging No. 2, pp. 16–20 (testimony of Union Executive Director, *Jackson I*). In addition, qualified minority teachers from other States were reluctant to uproot their lives and move to Michigan without any promise of protection from imminent layoff. The testimony suggests that the lack of some layoff protection would have crippled the efforts to recruit minority applicants. Id., at 20, 55, 56. Adjustment of the layoff hierarchy under these circumstances was a necessary corollary of an affirmative hiring policy.

B

Under JUSTICE POWELL's approach, the community of Jackson, having painfully watched the hard-won benefits of its integration efforts vanish as a result of massive layoffs, would be informed today, simply, that preferential layoff protection is never permissible because hiring policies serve the same purpose at a lesser cost. See ante, at 1851–1852. As a matter of logic as well as fact, a hiring policy achieves no purpose at all if it is eviscerated by layoffs. JUSTICE POWELL's position is untenable.

JUSTICE POWELL has concluded, by focusing exclusively on the undisputed hardship of losing a job, that the Equal Protection Clause always bars race-conscious layoff plans. This analysis overlooks, however, the important fact that Article XII does not cause the loss of jobs; someone will lose a job under any layoff plan and, whoever it is, that person will not deserve it. Any *per se* prohibition against layoff protection, therefore, must rest upon a premise that the tradition of basing layoff decisions on seniority is so fundamental that its modification can never be permitted. Our cases belie that premise.

* * *

C

Article XII is a narrow provision because it allocates the impact of an unavoidable burden proportionately between two racial groups. It places no absolute burden or benefit on one race, and, within the confines of constant minority proportions, it preserves the hierarchy of seniority in the selection of individuals for layoff. Race is a factor, along with seniority, in determining which individuals the school system will lose; it is not alone dispositive of any individual's fate. Cf. Bakke, 438 U.S., at 318, 98 S.Ct., at 2762 (opinion of POWELL, J.). Moreover, Article XII does not use layoff protection as a tool for *increasing* minority representation; achievement of that goal is entrusted to the less severe hiring policies.[5] And Article XII is narrow in the

---

5. JUSTICE WHITE assumes that respondents' plan is equivalent to one that deliberately erately seeks to change the racial composition of a staff by firing and hiring

temporal sense as well. The very bilateral process that gave rise to Article XII when its adoption was necessary will also occasion its demise when remedial measures are no longer required. Finally, Article XII modifies contractual expectations that do not themselves carry any connotation of merit or achievement; it does not interfere with the "cherished American ethic" of "[f]airness in individual competition," Bakke, supra, at 319, n. 53, 98 S.Ct., at 2763, n. 53, depriving individuals of an opportunity that they could be said to deserve. In all of these important ways, Article XII metes out the hardship of layoffs in a manner that achieves its purpose with the smallest possible deviation from established norms.

The Board's goal of preserving minority porportions could have been achieved, perhaps, in a different way. For example, if layoffs had been determined by lottery, the ultimate effect would have been retention of current racial percentages. A random system, however, would place every teacher in equal jeopardy, working a much greater upheaval of the seniority hierarchy than that occasioned by Article XII; it is not at all a less restrictive means of achieving the Board's goal. Another possible approach would have been a freeze on layoffs of minority teachers. This measure, too, would have been substantially more burdensome than Article XII, not only by necessitating the layoff of a greater number of white teachers, but also by erecting an absolute distinction between the races, one to be benefited and one to be burdened, in a way that Article XII avoids. Indeed, neither petitioners nor any Justice of this Court has suggested an alternative to Article XII that would have attained the stated goal in any narrower or more equitable a fashion. Nor can I conceive of one.

VI

It is no accident that this least burdensome of all conceivable options is the very provision that the parties adopted. For Article XII was forged in the crucible of clashing interests. All of the economic powers of the predominantly white teachers' union were brought to bear against those of the elected Board, and the process yielded consensus.

The concerns that have prompted some Members of this Court to call for narrowly tailored, perhaps court-ordered, means of achieving racial balance spring from a legitimate fear that racial distinctions will again be used as a means to persecute individuals, while couched in benign phraseology. That fear has given rise to mistrust of those who profess to take remedial action, and concern that any such action "work the least harm possible to other innocent persons competing for the benefit." * * *

members of predetermined races. Ante, at 1857. That assumption utterly ignores the fact that the Jackson plan involves only the means for selecting the employees who will be chosen for layoffs already necessi- tated by external economic conditions. This plan does not seek to supplant whites with blacks, nor does it contribute in any way to the number of job losses.

The collective-bargaining process is a legitimate and powerful vehicle for the resolution of thorny problems, and we have favored "minimal supervision by courts and other governmental agencies over the substantive terms of collective-bargaining agreements." American Tobacco Co. v. Patterson, 456 U.S. 63, 76–77, 102 S.Ct. 1534, 1541, 71 L.Ed.2d 748 (1982). We have also noted that "[s]ignificant freedom must be afforded employers and unions to create differing seniority systems," California Brewers Assn. v. Bryant, 444 U.S. 598, 608, 100 S.Ct. 814, 820, 63 L.Ed.2d 55 (1980).[6] The perceived dangers of affirmative action misused, therefore, are naturally averted by the bilateral process of negotiation, agreement, and ratification. The best evidence that Article XII is a narrow means to serve important interests is that representatives of all affected persons, starting from diametrically opposed perspectives, have agreed to it—not once, but six times since 1972.

VII

The narrow question presented by this case, if indeed we proceed to the merits, offers no occasion for the Court to issue broad proclamations of public policy concerning the controversial issue of affirmative action. Rather, this case calls for calm, dispassionate reflection upon exactly what has been done, to whom, and why. If one honestly confronts each of those questions against the factual background suggested by the materials submitted to us, I believe the conclusion is inescapable that Article XII meets, and indeed surpasses, any standard for ensuring that race-conscious programs are necessary to achieve remedial purposes. * * * To attempt to resolve the constitutional issue either with no historical context whatever, as the plurality has done, or on the basis of a record devoid of established facts, is to do a grave injustice not only to the Board and teachers of Jackson and to the State of Michigan, but also to individuals and governments committed to the goal of eliminating all traces of segregation throughout the country. Most of all, it does an injustice to the aspirations embodied in the Fourteenth Amendment itself. I would vacate the judgment of the Court of Appeals and remand with instructions that the case be remanded to the District Court for further proceedings consistent with the views I have expressed.[7]

JUSTICE STEVENS, dissenting.

6. This deference is warranted only if the union represents the interests of the workers fairly; a union's breach of that duty in the form of racial discrimination gives rise to an action by the worker against the union. See Steele v. Louisville & Nashville R. Co., 323 U.S. 192, 207, 65 S.Ct. 226, 234, 89 L.Ed. 173 (1944).

7. I do not envy the District Court its task of sorting out what this Court has and has not held today. It is clear, at any rate, that from among the many views expressed today, two noteworthy results emerge: a majority of the Court has explicitly rejected the argument that an affirmative-action plan must be preceded by a formal finding that the entity seeking to institute the plan has committed discriminatory acts in the past; and the Court has left open whether layoffs may be used as an instrument of remedial action.

In my opinion, it is not necessary to find that the Board of Education has been guilty of racial discrimination in the past to support the conclusion that it has a legitimate interest in employing more black teachers in the future. Rather than analyzing a case of this kind by asking whether minority teachers have some sort of special entitlement to jobs as a remedy for sins that were committed in the past, I believe that we should first ask whether the Board's action advances the public interest in educating children for the future. If so, I believe we should consider whether that public interest, and the manner in which it is pursued, justifies any adverse effects on the disadvantaged group.[1]

I

The Equal Protection Clause absolutely prohibits the use of race in many governmental contexts. To cite only a few: the government may not use race to decide who may serve on juries,[2] who may use public services,[3] who may marry,[4] and who may be fit parents.[5] The use of race in these situations is "utterly irrational" because it is completely unrelated to any valid public purpose;[6] moreover, it is particularly pernicious because it constitutes a badge of oppression that is unfaithful to the central promise of the Fourteenth Amendment.

Nevertheless, in our present society, race is not always irrelevant to sound governmental decisionmaking.[7] To take the most obvious example, in law enforcement, if an undercover agent is needed to

---

1. In every equal protection case, we have to ask certain basic questions.

"What class is harmed by the legislation, and has it been subjected to a 'tradition of disfavor' by our laws? What is the public purpose that is being served by the law? What is the characteristic of the disadvantaged class that justifies the disparate treatment?"

Cleburne v. Cleburne Living Center, 473 U.S. ___, ___, 105 S.Ct. 3249, 3261–3262, 87 L.Ed.2d 313 (1985) (STEVENS, J., concurring).

2. Batson v. Kentucky, 476 U.S. ___, 106 S.Ct. 1712, 89 L.Ed.2d ___ (1986); Vasquez v. Hillery, 474 U.S. ___, 106 S.Ct. 617, 88 L.Ed.2d 598 (1985); Rose v. Mitchell, 443 U.S. 545, 99 S.Ct. 2993, 61 L.Ed.2d 739 (1979); Strauder v. West Virginia, 10 Otto 303, 100 U.S. 303, 25 L.Ed. 664 (1880).

3. Turner v. City of Memphis, 369 U.S. 350, 82 S.Ct. 805, 7 L.Ed.2d 762 (1962) (per curiam); Burton v. Wilmington Parking Authority, 365 U.S. 715, 81 S.Ct. 856, 6 L.Ed.2d 45 (1961).

4. Loving v. Virginia, 388 U.S. 1, 87 S.Ct. 1817, 18 L.Ed.2d 1010 (1967).

5. Palmore v. Sidoti, 466 U.S. 429, 104 S.Ct. 1879, 80 L.Ed.2d 421 (1984).

6. Cleburne, supra, 473 U.S., at ___, 105 S.Ct., at ___ (STEVENS, J., concurring in judgment) ("It would be utterly irrational to limit the franchise on the basis of height or weight; it is equally invalid to limit it on the basis of skin color"). See also Palmore v. Sidoti, 466 U.S., at 432, 104 S.Ct., at 1882 (1984) ("Classifying persons according to their race is more likely to reflect racial prejudice than legitimate public concerns; the race, not the person, dictates the category").

7. As JUSTICE MARSHALL explains, although the Court's path in University of California Regents v. Bakke, 438 U.S. 265, 98 S.Ct. 2733, 57 L.Ed.2d 750 (1978) and Fullilove v. Klutznick, 448 U.S. 448, 100 S.Ct. 2758, 65 L.Ed.2d 902 (1980) is tortuous, the path at least reveals that race consciousness does not automatically violate the Equal Protection Clause. In those opinions, only two Justices of the Court suggested that race conscious governmental efforts were inherently unconstitutional. See id., at 522, 100 S.Ct., at 2797 (STEWART, J., dissenting, joined by REHNQUIST, J.). Cf. id., at 548, 100 S.Ct., at 2810 (STEVENS, J., dissenting) ("Unlike Mr. JUSTICE STEWART and Mr. JUSTICE REHNQUIST, * * * I am not convinced that the Clause contains an absolute prohibition against any statu-

infiltrate a group suspected of ongoing criminal behavior—and if the members of the group are all of the same race—it would seem perfectly rational to employ an agent of that race rather than a member of a different racial class. Similarly, in a city with a recent history of racial unrest, the superintendent of police might reasonably conclude that an integrated police force could develop a better relationship with the community and thereby do a more effective job of maintaining law and order than a force composed only of white officers.

In the context of public education,[8] it is quite obvious that a school board may reasonably conclude that an integrated faculty will be able to provide benefits to the student body that could not be provided by an all white, or nearly all white, faculty. One of the most important lessons that the American public schools teach is that the diverse ethnic, cultural, and national backgrounds that have been brought together in our famous "melting pot" do not identify essential differences among the human beings that inhabit our land. It is one thing for a white child to be taught by a white teacher that color, like beauty, is only "skin deep"; it is far more convincing to experience that truth on a day to day basis during the routine, ongoing learning process.

In this case, the collective-bargaining agreement between the Union and the Board of Education succinctly stated a valid public purpose—"recognition of the desirability of multi-ethnic representation on the teaching faculty," and thus "a policy of actively seeking minority group personnel." App. to Pet. for Cert. 22a. Nothing in the record—not a shred of evidence—contradicts the view that the Board's attempt to employ, and to retain, more minority teachers in the Jackson public school system served this completely sound educational purpose. Thus, there was a rational and unquestionably legitimate basis for the Board's decision to enter into the collective-bargaining agreement that petitioners have challenged, even though the agreement required special efforts to recruit and retain minority teachers.

tory classification based on race"). Notably, in this Court, petitioners have presented solely a constitutional theory, and have not pursued any statutory claims. Cf. Bakke, 438 U.S. at 408, 98 S.Ct., at 2808 (STEVENS, J., concurring in judgment in part and dissenting in part) (suggesting that constitutional issue need not be reached because statutory issue was dispositive).

8. The Court has frequently emphasized the role of public schools in our national life. See Board of Education v. Pico, 457 U.S. 853, 864, 102 S.Ct. 2799, 2806, 73 L.Ed.2d 435 (1982) (plurality opinion) ("[P]ublic schools are vitally important * * * as vehicles for 'inculcating fundamental values necessary to the maintenance of a democratic political system'"); Ambach v. Norwick, 441 U.S. 68, 76, 99 S.Ct. 1589, 1594, 60 L.Ed.2d 49 (1979) ("The

importance of public schools in the preparation of individuals for participation as citizens, and in the preservation of the values on which our society rests, long has been recognized by our decisions"); San Antonio Independent School District v. Rodriguez, 411 U.S. 1, 30, 93 S.Ct. 1278, 1295, 36 L.Ed.2d 16 (1973) (" 'the grave significance of education both to the individual and to our society' cannot be doubted"); Brown v. Board of Education, 347 U.S. 483, 493, 74 S.Ct. 686, 691, 98 L.Ed. 873 (1954) ("[E]ducation * * * is the very foundation of good citizenship. Today it is a principal instrument in awakening the child to cultural values, in preparing him for later professional training, and in helping him to adjust normally to his environment").

II

* * *

III

Even if there is a valid purpose to the race consciousness, however, the question that remains is whether that public purpose transcends the harm to the white teachers who are disadvantaged by the special preference the Board has given to its most recently hired minority teachers. In my view, there are two important inquiries in assessing the harm to the disadvantaged teacher. The first is an assessment of the procedures that were used to adopt, and implement, the race-conscious action.[10] The second is an evaluation of the nature of the harm itself.

* * *

IV

We should not lightly approve the government's use of a race-based distinction. History teaches the obvious dangers of such classifications.[15] Our ultimate goal must, of course, be "to eliminate entirely from governmental decisionmaking such irrelevant factors as a human being's race." [16] In this case, however, I am persuaded that the decision to include more minority teachers in the Jackson, Michigan, school system served a valid public purpose, that it was adopted with fair procedures and given a narrow breadth, that it transcends the harm to petitioners, and that it is a step toward that ultimate goal of eliminating entirely from governmental decisionmaking such irrelevant factors as a human being's race. I would therefore affirm the judgment of the Court of Appeals.

---

2. "The cases that follow illustrate the contested issues which arise when affirmative action is used as 'remedy' after trial or as part of a consent decree."

10. Cf. Fullilove, 448 U.S., at 548–549, 100 S.Ct., at 2810–2811 (STEVENS, J., dissenting) (a race-based classification "does impose a special obligation to scrutinize any governmental decisionmaking process that draws nationwide distinctions between citizens on the basis of their race and incidentally also discriminates against noncitizens in the preferred racial classes. For just as procedural safeguards are necessary to guarantee impartial decisionmaking in the judicial process, so can they play a vital part in preserving the impartial character of the legislative process"). That observation is, of course, equally applicable to a context in which the governmental decision is reached through a nonlegislative process. Significantly, a reason given for what this Court frequently calls "strict scrutiny" of certain classifications is the notion that the disadvantaged class is one that has been unable to enjoy full procedural participation. See United States v. Carolene Products, Co., 304 U.S. 144, 152–153, n. 4, 58 S.Ct. 778, 783–784, n. 4, 82 L.Ed. 1234 (1938) ("[P]rejudice against discrete and insular minorities may be a special condition, which tends seriously to curtail the operation of those political processes ordinarily to be relied upon to protect minorities, and which may call for a correspondingly more searching judicial inquiry"); J. Ely, Democracy and Distrust 75–77 (1980).

15. See, e.g., Fullilove, 448 U.S., at 534, n. 5, 100 S.Ct., at 2804, n. 5 (STEVENS, J., dissenting).

16. Id., at 547, 100 S.Ct., at 2810.

FIREFIGHTERS LOCAL UNION
NO. 1784 v. STOTTS

The Supreme Court of the United States, 1984.
467 U.S. 561, 104 S.Ct. 2576, 81 L.Ed.2d 483.

JUSTICE WHITE delivered the opinion of the Court.

Petitioners challenge the Court of Appeals' approval of an order enjoining the City of Memphis from following its seniority system in determining who must be laid off as a result of a budgetary shortfall. Respondents contend that the injunction was necessary to effectuate the terms of a Title VII consent decree in which the City agreed to undertake certain obligations in order to remedy past hiring and promotional practices. Because we conclude that the order cannot be justified, either as an effort to enforce the consent decree or as a valid modification, we reverse.

I

In 1977 respondent Carl Stotts, a black holding the position of fire-fighting captain in the Memphis, Tennessee, Fire Department, filed a class action complaint in the United States District Court for the Western District of Tennessee. The complaint charged that the Memphis Fire Department and other city officials were engaged in a pattern or practice of making hiring and promotion decisions on the basis of race in violation of Title VII of the Civil Rights Act of 1964, 42 U.S.C. § 2000e et seq., as well as 42 U.S.C. §§ 1981 and 1983. The District Court certified the case as a class action and consolidated it with an individual action subsequently filed by respondent Fred Jones, a black fire-fighting private in the Department, who claimed that he had been denied a promotion because of his race. Discovery proceeded, settlement negotiations ensued, and in due course, a consent decree was approved and entered by the District Court on April 25, 1980.

The stated purpose of the decree was to remedy the hiring and promotion practices "of the Department with respect to blacks." 679 F.2d 541, 575–576 (CA6 1982) (Appendix). Accordingly, the City agreed to promote 13 named individuals and to provide backpay to 81 employees of the Fire Department. It also adopted the long-term goal of increasing the proportion of minority representation in each job classification in the Fire Department to approximately the proportion of blacks in the labor force in Shelby County, Tennessee. However, the City did not, by agreeing to the decree, admit "any violations of law, rule or regulation with respect to the allegations" in the complaint. Id., at 574. The plaintiffs waived any further relief save to enforce the decree, ibid., and the District Court retained jurisdiction "for such further orders as may be necessary or appropriate to effectuate the purposes of this decree." Id., at 578.

The long-term hiring goal outlined in the decree paralleled the provisions of a 1974 consent decree, which settled a case brought against the City by the United States and which applied citywide. Like the 1974 decree, the 1980 decree also established an interim hiring goal of filling on an annual basis 50 percent of the job vacancies in the Department with qualified black applicants. The 1980 decree contained an additional goal with respect to promotions: the Department was to attempt to ensure that 20 percent of the promotions in each job classification be given to blacks. Neither decree contained provisions for layoffs or reductions in rank, and neither awarded any competitive seniority. The 1974 decree did require that for purposes of promotion, transfer, and assignment, seniority was to be computed "as the total seniority of that person with the City." Id., at 572.

In early May, 1981, the City announced that projected budget deficits required a reduction of non-essential personnel throughout the City Government. Layoffs were to be based on the "last hired, first fired" rule under which city-wide seniority, determined by each employee's length of continuous service from the latest date of permanent employment, was the basis for deciding who would be laid off. If a senior employee's position were abolished or eliminated, the employee could "bump down" to a lower ranking position rather than be laid off. As the Court of Appeals later noted, this layoff policy was adopted pursuant to the seniority system "mentioned in the 1974 decree and * * * incorporated in the City's memorandum with the Union." 679 F.2d, at 549.

On May 4, at respondents' request, the District Court entered a temporary restraining order forbidding the layoff of any black employee. The Union, which previously had not been a party to either of these cases, was permitted to intervene. At the preliminary injunction hearing, it appeared that 55 then-filled positions in the Department were to be eliminated and that 39 of these positions were filled with employees having "bumping" rights. It was estimated that 40 least-senior employees in the fire-fighting bureau of the Department [1] would be laid off and that of these 25 were white and 15 black. It also appeared that 56 percent of the employees hired in the Department since 1974 had been black and that the percentage of black employees had increased from approximately 3 or 4 percent in 1974 to 11½ percent in 1980.

On May 18, the District Court entered an order granting an injunction. The Court found that the consent decree "did not contemplate the method to be used for reduction in rank or lay-off," and that the layoff policy was in accordance with the City's seniority system and was not adopted with any intent to discriminate. Nonetheless, concluding that the proposed layoffs would have a racially discriminatory effect and that the seniority system was not a bona fide one, the District Court ordered that the City "not apply the seniority policy insofar as it

1. The Memphis Fire Department is divided into several bureaus, including fire-fighting, alarm office, administration, apparatus, maintenance, and fire prevention. Of the positions covered by the original injunction, all but one were in the fire-fighting bureau.

will decrease the percentage of black lieutenants, drivers, inspectors and privates that are presently employed. * * *" On June 23, the District Court broadened its order to include three additional classifications. A modified layoff plan, aimed at protecting black employees in the seven classifications so as to comply with the court's order, was presented and approved. Layoffs pursuant to the modified plan were then carried out. In certain instances, to comply with the injunction, non-minority employees with more seniority than minority employees were laid off or demoted in rank.[2]

On appeal, the Court of Appeals for the Sixth Circuit affirmed despite its conclusion that the District Court was wrong in holding that the City's seniority system was not bona fide. 679 F.2d, at 551, n. 6. Characterizing the principal issue as "whether the district court erred in modifying the 1980 Decree to prevent minority employment from being affected disproportionately by unanticipated layoffs," id., at 551, the Court of Appeals concluded that the District Court had acted properly. After determining that the decree was properly approved in the first instance, the court held that the modification was permissible under general contract principles because the City "contracted" to provide "a substantial increase in the number of minorities in supervisory positions" and the layoffs would breach that contract. Id., at 561. Alternatively, the court held that the District Court was authorized to modify the decree because new and unforeseen circumstances had created a hardship for one of the parties to the decree. Id., at 562–563. Finally, articulating three alternative rationales, the court rejected petitioners' argument that the modification was improper because it conflicted with the City's seniority system, which was immunized from Title VII attack under § 703(h) of that Act, 42 U.S.C. § 2000e–2(h).

II

We deal first with the claim that these cases are moot. Respondents submit that the injunction entered in this case was a preliminary injunction dealing only with the 1981 layoffs, that all white employees laid off as a result of the injunction were restored to duty only one month after their layoff, and that those who were demoted have now been offered back their old positions. Assertedly, the injunction no longer has force or effect, and the cases are therefore moot. For several reasons, we find the submission untenable.

Accordingly, the inquiry is not merely whether the injunction is still in effect, but whether the mandated modification of the consent decree continues to have an impact on the parties such that the case remains alive.[3] We are quite unconvinced—and it is the respondents'

---

2. The City ultimately laid off 24 privates, three of whom were black. Had the seniority system been followed, six blacks would have been among the 24 privates laid off. Thus, three white employees were laid off as a direct result of the District Court's order. The number of whites de-

moted as a result of the order is not clear from the record before us.

3. The Court of Appeals, recognizing that the District Court had done more than temporarily preclude the City from applying its seniority system, stated that the "principal issue" before it was "whether

burden to convince us, County of Los Angeles v. Davis, 440 U.S. 625, 631, 99 S.Ct. 1379, 1383, 59 L.Ed.2d 642 (1979)—that the modification of the decree and the *pro tanto* invalidation of the seniority system is of no real concern to the City because it will never again contemplate layoffs that if carried out in accordance with the seniority system would violate the modified decree.[4] For this reason alone, the case is not moot.

* * *

III

The issue at the heart of this case is whether the District Court exceeded its powers in entering an injunction requiring white employees to be laid off, when the otherwise applicable seniority system [7] would have called for the layoff of black employees with less seniority.[8]

the district court erred in modifying the 1980 Decree to prevent minority employment from being affected disproportionately by unanticipated layoffs." 679 F.2d, at 551.

4. Of course if layoffs become necessary, both the City and respondents will be affected by the modified decree, the City because it will be unable to apply its seniority system, respondents because they will be given greater protection than they would otherwise receive under that system. Moreover, the City will be immediately affected by the modification even though no layoff is currently pending. If the lower courts' ruling is left intact, the City will no longer be able to promise current or future employees that layoffs will be conducted solely on the basis of seniority. Against its will, the City has been deprived of the power to offer its employees one of the benefits that make employment with the City attractive to many workers. Seniority has traditionally been, and continues to be, a matter of great concern to American workers. "[M]ore than any other provision of the collective [bargaining] agreement * * * seniority affects the economic security of the individual employee covered by its terms." Franks v. Bowman Transportation Co., 424 U.S. 747, 766, 96 S.Ct. 1251, 1265, 47 L.Ed.2d 444 (1976) (quoting Aaron, Reflections on the Legal Nature and Enforceability of Seniority Rights, 75 Harv.L.Rev. 1532, 1535 (1962)). It is not idle speculation to suppose that the City will be required to offer greater monetary compensation or fringe benefits in order to attract and retain the same caliber and number of workers as it could without offering such benefits were it completely free to implement its seniority system. The extent to which the City's employment efforts will be harmed by the loss of this "bargaining chip" may be difficult

to measure, but in view of the importance that American workers have traditionally placed on such benefits, the harm cannot be said to be insignificant. Certainly, an employer's bargaining position is as substantially affected by a decree precluding it from offering its employees the benefits of a seniority system as it is by a state statute that provides economic benefits to striking employees. Super Tire Engineering Co. v. McCorkle, 416 U.S. 115, 122–125, 94 S.Ct. 1694, 1698–1699, 40 L.Ed.2d 1 (1974).

7. Respondents contend that the memorandum of understanding between the Union and the City is unenforceable under state law, citing Fulenwider v. Firefighters Association Local Union 1784, 649 S.W.2d 268 (Tenn.1982). However, the validity of that memorandum under state law is unimportant for purposes of the issues presented in this case. First, the Court of Appeals assumed that the memorandum was valid in reaching its decision. 679 F.2d, at 564, n. 20. Since we are reviewing that decision, we are free to assume the same. Moreover, even if the memorandum is unenforceable, the City's seniority system is still in place. The City unilaterally adopted the seniority system citywide in 1973. That policy was incorporated into the memorandum of understanding with the Firefighters Union in 1975, but its citywide effect, including its application to the Fire Department, continues irrespective of the status of the memorandum.

8. The dissent's contention that the only issue before us is whether the District Court so misapplied the standards for issuing a preliminary injunction that it abused its discretion, post, at 2600, overlooks what the District Court did in this case. The District Court did not purport to apply the standards for determining whether to issue a preliminary injunction. It did not even

We are convinced that the Court of Appeals erred in resolving this issue and in affirming the District Court.

* * *

A

The Court of Appeals first held that the injunction did no more than enforce the terms of the agreed-upon consent decree. This specific-performance approach rests on the notion that because the City was under a general obligation to use its best efforts to increase the proportion of blacks on the force, it breached the decree by attempting to effectuate a layoff policy reducing the percentage of black employees in the Department even though such a policy was mandated by the seniority system adopted by the City and the Union. A variation of this argument is that since the decree permitted the District Court to enter any later orders that "may be necessary or appropriate to effectuate the purposes of this decree," 679 F.2d, at 578 (Appendix), the City had agreed in advance to an injunction against layoffs that would reduce the proportion of black employees. We are convinced, however, that both of these are improvident constructions of the consent decree.

It is to be recalled that the "scope of a consent decree must be discerned within its four corners, and not by reference to what might satisfy the purposes of one of the parties to it" or by what "might have been written had the plaintiff established his factual claims and legal theories in litigation." United States v. Armour & Co., 402 U.S. 673, 681–682, 91 S.Ct. 1752, 1757, 29 L.Ed.2d 256 (1971). Here, as the District Court recognized, there is no mention of layoffs or demotions within the four corners of the decree; nor is there any suggestion of an intention to depart from the existing seniority system or from the City's arrangements with the Union. We cannot believe that the parties to the decree thought that the City would simply disregard its arrangements with the Union and the seniority system it was then following. Had there been any intention to depart from the seniority plan in the event of layoffs or demotions, it is much more reasonable to believe that there would have been an express provision to that effect. This is particularly true since the decree stated that it was not "intended to conflict with any provisions" of the 1974 decree, 679 F.2d, at 574 (Appendix), and since the latter decree expressly anticipated that the City would recognize seniority, id., at 572. It is thus not surprising that when the City anticipated layoffs and demotions, it in the first instance

mention them. Instead, having found that the consent decree did "not contemplate what method would be used for a reduction in rank or layoff," the court considered "whether or not * * * it should exercise its authority to modify the consent decree. * * *" Petition for Certiorari, at A73. As noted above, the Court of Appeals correctly recognized that more was at stake than a mere preliminary injunction, stating that the "principal issue" was "wheth-er the district court erred in modifying the 1980 Decree to prevent minority employment from being affected disproportionately by unanticipated layoffs." 679 F.2d, at 551. By deciding whether the District Court erred in interpreting or modifying the consent decree so as to preclude the City from applying its seniority system, we do not, as the dissent shrills, attempt to answer a question never faced by the lower courts.

faithfully followed its preexisting seniority system, plainly having no thought that it had already agreed to depart from it. It therefore cannot be said that the express terms of the decree contemplated that such an injunction would be entered.

The argument that the injunction was proper because it carried out the purposes of the decree is equally unconvincing. The decree announced that its purpose was "to remedy past hiring and promotion practices" of the Department, id., at 575–576, and to settle the dispute as to the "appropriate and valid procedures for hiring and promotion," id., at 574. The decree went on to provide the agreed-upon remedy, but as we have indicated, that remedy did not include the displacement of white employees with seniority over blacks. Furthermore, it is reasonable to believe that the "remedy", which it was the purpose of the decree to provide, would not exceed the bounds of the remedies that are appropriate under Title VII, at least absent some express provision to that effect. As our cases have made clear, however, and as will be reemphasized below, Title VII protects bona fide seniority systems, and it is inappropriate to deny an innocent employee the benefits of his seniority in order to provide a remedy in a pattern or practice suit such as this. We thus have no doubt that the City considered its system to be valid and that it had no intention of departing from it when it agreed to the 1980 decree.

Finally, it must be remembered that neither the Union nor the non-minority employees were parties to the suit when the 1980 decree was entered. Hence the entry of that decree cannot be said to indicate any agreement by them to any of its terms. Absent the presence of the Union or the non-minority employees and an opportunity for them to agree or disagree with any provisions of the decree that might encroach on their rights, it seems highly unlikely that the City would purport to bargain away non-minority rights under the then-existing seniority system. We therefore conclude that the injunction does not merely enforce the agreement of the parties as reflected in the consent decree. If the injunction is to stand, it must be justified on some other basis.

B

The Court of Appeals held that even if the injunction is not viewed as compelling compliance with the terms of the decree, it was still properly entered because the District Court had inherent authority to modify the decree when an economic crisis unexpectedly required layoffs which, if carried out as the City proposed, would undermine the affirmative action outlined in the decree and impose an undue hardship on respondents. This was true, the court held, even though the modification conflicted with a bona fide seniority system adopted by the City. The Court of Appeals erred in reaching this conclusion.[9]

9. The dissent seems to suggest, post, at 2604–2605, and n. 9, and Justice Stevens expressly states, post, at 2594, that Title VII is irrelevant in determining whether the District Court acted properly in modifying the consent decree. However, this was Title VII litigation, and in affirming modifications of the decree, the Court of

Section 703(h) of Title VII provides that it is not an unlawful employment practice to apply different standards of compensation, or different terms, conditions, or privileges of employment pursuant to a bona fide seniority system, provided that such differences are not the result of an intention to discriminate because of race.[10] It is clear that the City had a seniority system, that its proposed layoff plan conformed to that system, and that in making the settlement the City had not agreed to award competitive seniority to any minority employee whom the City proposed to lay off. The District Court held that the City could not follow its seniority system in making its proposed layoffs because its proposal was discriminatory in effect and hence not a bona fide plan. Section 703(h), however, permits the routine application of a seniority system absent proof of an intention to discriminate. Teamsters v. United States, 431 U.S. 324, 352, 97 S.Ct. 1843, 1863, 52 L.Ed.2d 396 (1977). Here, the District Court itself found that the layoff proposal was not adopted with the purpose or intent to discriminate on the basis of race. Nor had the City in agreeing to the decree admitted in any way that it had engaged in intentional discrimination. The Court of Appeals was therefore correct in disagreeing with the District Court's holding that the layoff plan was not a bona fide application of the seniority system, and it would appear that the City could not be faulted for following the seniority plan expressed in its agreement with the Union. The Court of Appeals nevertheless held that the injunction was proper even though it conflicted with the seniority system. This was error.

To support its position, the Court of Appeals first proposed a "settlement" theory, i.e., that the strong policy favoring voluntary

Appeals relied extensively on what it considered to be its authority under Title VII. That is the posture in which the case comes to us. Furthermore, the District Court's authority to impose a modification of a decree is not wholly dependent on the decree. "[T]he District's Court's authority to adopt a consent decree comes only from the statute which the decree is intended to enforce," not from the parties' consent to the decree. System Federation No. 91 v. Wright, 364 U.S. 642, 651, 81 S.Ct. 368, 373, 5 L.Ed.2d 349 (1961). In recognition of this principle, this Court in *Wright* held that when a change in the law brought the terms of a decree into conflict with the statute pursuant to which the decree was entered, the decree should be modified over the objections of one of the parties bound by the decree. By the same token, and for the same reason, a district court cannot enter a disputed modification of a consent decree in Title VII litigation if the resulting order is inconsistent with that statute.

Thus, Title VII necessarily acted as a limit on the District Court's authority to

modify the decree over the objections of the City; the issue cannot be resolved solely by reference to the terms of the decree and notions of equity. Since, as we note, infra, at ——, Title VII precludes a district court from displacing a non-minority employee with seniority under the contractually established seniority system absent either a finding that the seniority system was adopted with discriminatory intent or a determination that such a remedy was necessary to make whole a proven victim of discrimination, the District Court was precluded from granting such relief over the City's objection in this case.

10. Section 703(h) provides that "it shall not be an unlawful employment practice for an employer to apply different standards of compensation, or different terms, conditions, or privileges of employment pursuant to a bona fide seniority or merit system * * * provided that such differences are not the result of an intention to discriminate because of race, color, religion, sex, or national origin. * * *" 42 U.S.C. § 2000e-2(h).

settlement of Title VII actions permitted consent decrees that encroached on seniority systems. But at this stage in its opinion, the Court of Appeals was supporting the proposition that even if the injunction was not merely enforcing the agreed-upon terms of the decree, the District Court had the authority to modify the decree over the objection of one of the parties. The settlement theory, whatever its merits might otherwise be, has no application when there is no "settlement" with respect to the disputed issue. Here, the agreed-upon decree neither awarded competitive seniority to the minority employees nor purported in any way to depart from the seniority system.

A second ground advanced by the Court of Appeals in support of the conclusion that the injunction could be entered notwithstanding its conflict with the seniority system was the assertion that "[i]t would be incongruous to hold that the use of the preferred means of resolving an employment discrimination action decreases the power of a court to order relief which vindicates the policies embodied within Title VII, and 42 U.S.C. §§ 1981 and 1983." 679 F.2d, at 566. The court concluded that if the allegations in the complaint had been proved, the District Court could have entered an order overriding the seniority provisions. Therefore, the court reasoned, "[t]he trial court had the authority to override the Firefighter's Union seniority provisions to effectuate the purpose of the 1980 Decree." 679 F.2d, at 566.

The difficulty with this approach is that it overstates the authority of the trial court to disregard a seniority system in fashioning a remedy after a plaintiff has successfully proved that an employer has followed a pattern or practice having a discriminatory effect on black applicants or employees. If individual members of a plaintiff class demonstrate that they have been actual victims of the discriminatory practice, they may be awarded competitive seniority and given their rightful place on the seniority roster. This much is clear from Franks v. Bowman Transportation Co., 424 U.S. 747, 96 S.Ct. 1251, 47 L.Ed.2d 444 (1976) and Teamsters v. United States, 431 U.S. 324, 97 S.Ct. 1843, 52 L.Ed.2d 396 (1977). *Teamsters*, however, also made clear that mere membership in the disadvantaged class is insufficient to warrant a seniority award; each individual must prove that the discriminatory practice had an impact on him. 431 U.S., at 367–371, 97 S.Ct., at 1870–1872. Even when an individual shows that the discriminatory practice has had an impact on him, he is not automatically entitled to have a non-minority employee laid off to make room for him. He may have to wait until a vacancy occurs,[11] and if there are non-minority employees on layoff, the Court must balance the equities in determining who is entitled to the job. *Teamsters,* supra, 431 U.S., at 371–376, 97 S.Ct., at 1872–1875.

---

11. Lower courts have uniformly held that relief for actual victims does not extend to bumping employees previously occupying jobs. See e.g., Patterson v. American Tobacco Co., 535 F.2d 257, 267 (CA4), cert. denied, 429 U.S. 920, 97 S.Ct. 314, 50 L.Ed.2d 286 (1976); Local 189, United Papermakers and Paperworkers v. United States, 416 F.2d 980, 988 (CA5 1969), cert. denied, 397 U.S. 919, 90 S.Ct. 926, 25 L.Ed. 2d 100 (1970).

See also Ford Motor Co. v. EEOC, 458 U.S. 219, 236–240, 102 S.Ct. 3057, 3068–3070, 73 L.Ed.2d 721 (1982). Here, there was no finding that any of the blacks protected from layoff had been a victim of discrimination and no award of competitive seniority to any of them. Nor had the parties in formulating the consent decree purported to identify any specific employee entitled to particular relief other than those listed in the exhibits attached to the decree. It therefore seems to us that in light of *Teamsters,* the Court of Appeals imposed on the parties as an adjunct of settlement something that could not have been ordered had the case gone to trial and the plaintiffs proved that a pattern or practice of discrimination existed.

Our ruling in *Teamsters* that a court can award competitive seniority only when the beneficiary of the award has actually been a victim of illegal discrimination is consistent with the policy behind § 706(g) of Title VII, which affects the remedies available in Title VII litigation. That policy, which is to provide make-whole relief only to those who have been actual victims of illegal discrimination, was repeatedly expressed by the sponsors of the Act during the congressional debates.

*   *   *

Similar assurances concerning the limits on a court's authority to award make-whole relief were provided by supporters of the bill throughout the legislative process.

*   *   *

For example, following passage of the bill in the House, its Republican House sponsors published a memorandum describing the bill. Referring to the remedial powers given the courts by the bill, the memorandum stated: "Upon conclusion of the trial, the federal court may enjoin an employer or labor organization from practicing further discrimination and may order the hiring or reinstatement of an employee or the acceptance or reinstatement of a union member. *But Title VII does not permit the ordering of racial quotas in business or unions.* *   *   ** " Id., at 6566 (emphasis added). In like manner, the principal Senate sponsors, in a bi-partisan news letter delivered during an attempted filibuster to each senator supporting the bill, explained that "[u]nder title VII, not even a Court, much less the Commission, could order racial quotas or the hiring, reinstatement, admission to membership or payment of back pay for anyone who is not discriminated against in violation of this title." Id., at 14465.[15]

---

15. The dissent suggests that Congress abandoned this policy in 1972 when it amended § 706(g) to make clear that a court may award "any other equitable relief" that the court deems appropriate. Post, at 2609–2610. As support for this proposition the dissent notes that prior to 1972, some federal courts had provided remedies to those who had not proven that they were victims. It then observes that in a section-by-section analysis of the bill, its sponsors stated that "in any areas where a specific contrary intention is not indicated, it was assumed that the present case law as developed by the courts would continue to govern the applicability and construction of Title VII." 118 Cong.Rec. 7167 (1972).

We have already rejected, however, the contention that Congress intended to codify all existing Title VII decisions when it made this brief statement. See *Teamsters,* supra, 431 U.S., at 354, n. 39, 97 S.Ct., at

The Court of Appeals holding that the District Court's order was permissible as a valid Title VII remedial order ignores not only our ruling in *Teamsters* but the policy behind § 706(g) as well. Accordingly, that holding cannot serve as a basis for sustaining the District Court's order.[16]

Finally, the Court of Appeals was of the view that the District Court ordered no more than that which the City unilaterally could have done by way of adopting an affirmative action program. Whether the City, a public employer, could have taken this course without violating the law is an issue we need not decide. The fact is that in this case the City took no such action and that the modification of the decree was imposed over its objection.[17]

We thus are unable to agree either that the order entered by the District Court was a justifiable effort to enforce the terms of the decree to which the City had agreed or that it was a legitimate modification of the decree that could be imposed on the City without its consent. Accordingly, the judgment of the Court of Appeals is reversed.

It is so ordered.

JUSTICE O'CONNOR, concurring.

The various views presented in the opinions in this case reflect the unusual procedural posture of the case and the difficulties inherent in allocating the burdens of recession and fiscal austerity. I concur in the

1864, n. 39. Moreover, the statement on its face refers only to those sections not changed by the 1972 amendments. It cannot serve as a basis for discerning the effect of the changes that were made by the amendment. Finally, and of most importance, in a later portion of the same section-by-section analysis, the sponsors explained their view of existing law and the effect that the amendment would have on that law.

"The provisions of this subsection are intended to give the courts wide discretion exercising their equitable powers to fashion the most complete relief possible. In dealing with the present § 706(g) *the courts have stressed that the scope of relief under that section of the Act is intended to make victims of unlawful discrimination whole,* and that the attainment of this objective rests not only upon the elimination of the particular unlawful employment practice complained of, but also requires that *persons aggrieved by the consequences and effects of the unlawful employment practice* be, so far as possible, restored to a position where they would have been were it not for the unlawful discrimination." Id., at 7168 (emphasis added).

As we noted in *Franks*, the 1972 amendments evidence "emphatic confirmation

that federal courts are empowered to fashion such relief as the particular circumstances of a case may require to effect restitution, making whole insofar as possible *the victims of racial discrimination.*" 424 U.S., at 764, 96 S.Ct., at 1264 (emphasis added).

16. Neither does it suffice to rely on the District Court's remedial authority under §§ 1981 and 1983. Under those sections relief is authorized only when there is proof or admission of intentional discrimination. Washington v. Davis, 426 U.S. 229, 96 S.Ct. 2040, 48 L.Ed.2d 597 (1976); General Building Contractors Association v. Pennsylvania, 458 U.S. 375, 102 S.Ct. 3141, 73 L.Ed.2d 835 (1982). Neither precondition was satisfied here.

17. The Court of Appeals also suggested that under United States v. Swift & Co., 286 U.S. 106, 114–115, 52 S.Ct. 460, 462, 76 L.Ed. 999 (1932), the decree properly was modified pursuant to the District Court's equity jurisdiction. But *Swift* cannot be read as authorizing a court to impose a modification of a decree that runs counter to statutory policy, see n. 9, supra, here §§ 703(h) and 706(g) of Title VII.

Court's treatment of these difficult issues, and write separately to reflect my understanding of what the Court holds today.

II

My understanding of the Court's holding on the merits also is aided by a review of the place this case takes in the history of the parties' litigation. The city entered into a consent decree with respondents, agreeing to certain hiring and promotional goals, backpay awards, and individual promotions. The city was party both to another consent decree and to an agreement with the union concerning application of the seniority system at the time it made these concessions. Respondents did not seek the union's participation in the negotiation of their consent decree with the city, did not include the seniority system as a subject of negotiation, and waived all rights to seek further relief. When the current dispute arose, the District Court rejected respondents' allegation that the seniority system had been adopted or applied with any discriminatory animus. It held, however, that "modification" was appropriate because of the seniority system's discriminatory effects. Under these circumstances, the Court's conclusion that the District Court had no authority to order maintenance of racial percentages in the Department is, in my view, inescapable.

Had respondents presented a plausible case of discriminatory animus in the adoption or application of the seniority system, then the Court would be hard pressed to consider entry of the preliminary injunction an abuse of discretion. But that is not what happened here. To the contrary, the District Court rejected the claim of discriminatory animus, and the Court of Appeals did not disagree. Furthermore, the District Court's erroneous conclusion to the contrary, maintenance of racial balance in the Department could not be justified as a correction of an employment policy with an unlawful disproportionate impact. Title VII affirmatively protects bona fide seniority systems, including those with discriminatory effects on minorities. See American Tobacco Co. v. Patterson, 456 U.S. 63, 65, 102 S.Ct. 1534, 71 L.Ed.2d 748 (1982); Teamsters v. United States, 431 U.S. 324, 352, 97 S.Ct. 1843, 1863, 52 L.Ed.2d 396 (1977).

Therefore, the preliminary injunction could only be justified as a reasonable interpretation of the consent decree or as a permissible exercise of the District Court's authority to modify that consent decree. Neither justification was present here. For the reasons stated by the Court, ante, at 2586–2587, and JUSTICE STEVENS, post, at 2595, the consent decree itself cannot fairly be interpreted to bar use of the seniority policy or to require maintenance of racial balances previously achieved in the event layoffs became necessary. Nor can a district court unilaterally modify a consent decree to adjust racial imbalances or to provide retroactive relief that abrogates legitimate expectations of other employees and applicants. See Steelworkers v. Weber, 443 U.S. 193, 205–207, 99 S.Ct. 2721, 2728–2729, 61 L.Ed.2d 480 (1979); Pasadena City Bd. of Education v. Spangler, supra, 427 U.S., at 436–438, 96 S.Ct., at 2704–2705. A court may not grant preferential treatment to any individual or group simply because the group to which they belong is adversely affected by a bona fide seniority system. Rather, a court may use its remedial powers, including its power to modify a consent decree, only to prevent future violations and to compensate identified victims of unlawful discrimination. See Teamsters v. United States, supra, 431 U.S., at 367–371, 97 S.Ct., at 1870–1872; Milliken v. Bradley, 433 U.S. 267, 280–281, 97 S.Ct. 2749, 2757, 53 L.Ed.2d 745 (1977); see also University of California Regents v. Bakke, 438 U.S. 265, 307–309, and n. 44, 98 S.Ct. 2733, 2757–2758, and n. 44, 57 L.Ed.2d 750 (1978) (POWELL, J., announcing the judgment of the Court). Even when its remedial powers are properly invoked, a district court may award preferential treatment only after carefully balancing the competing interests of discriminatees, innocent employees, and the employer. See Ford Motor Co. v. EEOC, 458 U.S., at 239–240, 102 S.Ct., at 3070; Teamsters v. United States, supra, 431 U.S., at 371–376, 97 S.Ct., at 1872–1875. In short, no matter how significant the change in circumstance, a district court cannot unilaterally modify a consent decree to adjust racial balances in the way the District Court did here.[2]

To be sure, in 1980, respondents could have gone to trial and established illegal discrimination in the Department's past hiring practices, identified its specific victims, and possibly obtained retroactive seniority for those individuals. Alternatively, in 1980, in negotiating the consent decree, respondents could have sought the participation of the union,[3] negotiated the identities of the specific victims with the union and employer, and possibly obtained limited forms of retroactive relief. But respondents did none of these things. They chose to avoid the costs and hazards of litigating their claims. They negotiated with the employer without inviting the union's participation. They entered into a consent decree without establishing any specific victim's identity. And, most importantly, they waived their right to seek further relief. To allow respondents to obtain relief properly reserved for only identified victims or to prove their victim status now would undermine the certainty of obligation that is condition precedent to employers' acceptance of, and unions' consent to, employment discrimination settlements. See Steelworkers v. Weber, supra, 443 U.S., at 211, 99 S.Ct., at 2731 (BLACKMUN, J., concurring) (employers enter into settlements to avoid back pay responsibilities and to reduce disparate impact claims). Modifications requiring maintenance of racial balance would not en-

---

2. Unlike the dissenters and Justice Stevens, I find persuasive the Court's reasons for holding Title VII relevant to analysis of the modification issue, see ante, at 2587, and n. 12, and the Court's application of Title VII's provisions to the facts of the present controversy.

3. "Absent a judicial determination, * * * the Company * * * cannot alter

the collective-bargaining agreement without the Union's consent." W. R. Grace & Co. v. Local 759, 461 U.S. ___, ___, 103 S.Ct. 2177, 2179, 76 L.Ed.2d 298 (1983). Thus, if innocent employees are to be required to make any sacrifices in the final consent decree, they must be represented and have had full participation rights in the negotiation process.

courage valid settlements [4] of employment discrimination cases. They would impede them. Thus, when the Court states that this preferential relief could not have been awarded even had *this case* gone to trial, see *ante,* at 2589, it is holding respondents to the bargain they struck during the consent decree negotiations in 1980 and thereby furthering the statutory policy of voluntary settlement. See Carson v. American Brands, Inc., 450 U.S. 79, 88, and n. 14, 101 S.Ct. 993, 998, and n. 14, 67 L.Ed.2d 59 (1981).

In short, the Court effectively applies the criteria traditionally applicable to the review of preliminary injunctions. See Doran v. Salem Inn, Inc., 422 U.S. 922, 931, 95 S.Ct. 2561, 2567, 45 L.Ed.2d 648 (1975). When the Court disapproves the preliminary injunction issued in this case, it does so because respondents had no chance of succeeding on the merits of their claim. The District Court had no authority to order the Department to maintain its current racial balance or to provide preferential treatment to blacks. It therefore abused its discretion. On this understanding, I join the opinion and judgment rendered by the Court today.

JUSTICE STEVENS, concurring in the judgment.

In my judgment, the Court's discussion of Title VII is wholly advisory. This case involves no issue under Title VII; it only involves the administration of a consent decree. ＊ ＊ ＊

Accordingly, because I conclude that the District Court abused its discretion in entering the preliminary injunction at issue here, I concur in the judgment.

JUSTICE BLACKMUN, with whom JUSTICE BRENNAN and JUSTICE MARSHALL join, dissenting.

Today's opinion is troubling less for the law it creates than for the law it ignores. The issues in these cases arose out of a preliminary injunction that prevented the city of Memphis from conducting a particular layoff in a particular manner. Because that layoff has ended, the preliminary injunction no longer restrains any action that the city wishes to take. The Court nevertheless rejects respondents' claim that these cases are moot because the Court concludes that there are continuing effects from the preliminary injunction and that these create a continuing controversy. The Court appears oblivious, however, to the fact that any continuing legal consequences of the preliminary

---

4. The policy favoring voluntary settlement does not, of course, countenance unlawful discrimination against existing employees or applicants. See McDonald v. Santa Fe Trail Transportation Co., 427 U.S. 273, 278–296, 96 S.Ct. 2574, 2577–2586, 49 L.Ed.2d 493 (1976) (Title VII and 42 U.S.C. § 1981 prohibit discrimination against whites as well as blacks); Steelworkers v. Weber, 443 U.S. 193, 208–209, 99 S.Ct. 2721, 2729–2730, 61 L.Ed.2d 480 (1979) (listing attributes that would make affirmative action plan impermissible); cf. id., at 215, 99 S.Ct., at 2733 (Blackmun, J., concurring) ("seniority is not in issue because the craft training program is new and does not involve an abrogation of pre-existing seniority rights").

injunction would be erased by simply vacating the Court of Appeals' judgment, which is this Court's longstanding practice with cases that become moot.

Having improperly asserted jurisdiction, the Court then ignores the proper standard of review. The District Court's action was a preliminary injunction reviewable only on an abuse of discretion standard; the Court treats the action as a permanent injunction and decides the merits, even though the District Court has not yet had an opportunity to do so. On the merits, the Court ignores the specific facts of these cases that make inapplicable the decisions on which it relies. Because, in my view, the Court's decision is demonstrably in error, I respectfully dissent.

*   *   *

B

After ignoring the appropriate standard of review, the Court then focuses on an issue that is not in these cases. It begins its analysis by stating that the "issue at the heart of this case" is the District Court's power to "ente[r] an injunction requiring white employees to be laid off." Ante, at 2585. That statement, with all respect, is simply incorrect. On its face, the preliminary injunction prohibited the city from conducting layoffs in accordance with its seniority system "insofar as it will decrease the percentage of black[s] *   *   * presently employed" in certain job categories. App. to Pet. for Cert. in No. 82–229, p. A80. The preliminary injunction did not require the city to lay off any white employees at all. In fact, several parties interested in the suit, including the union, attempted to persuade the city to avoid layoffs entirely by reducing the working hours of all fire department employees. See Brief for Respondents 73. Thus, although the District Court ordered reduced the city's options in meeting its fiscal crisis, it did not require the dismissal of white employees. The choice of a modified layoff plan remained that of the city.

This factual detail is important because it makes clear that the preliminary injunction did not abrogate the contractual rights of white employees. If the modified layoff plan proposed by the city to comply with the District Court's order abrogated contractual rights of the union, those rights remained enforceable. This Court recognized this principle just last Term in W. R. Grace & Co. v. Local Union 759, ___ U.S. ___, 103 S.Ct. 2177, 76 L.Ed.2d 298 (1983), which presented a situation remarkably similar to the one here. In that case, an employer sought to conduct layoffs and faced a conflict between a Title VII conciliation agreement protecting its female employees and the seniority rights of its male employees. The employer chose to lay off male employees, who filed grievances and obtained awards for the violation of their contractual rights. In upholding the awards, this Court explained that the dilemma faced by the employer did not render the male employees' contractual rights unenforceable:

> Given the Company's desire to reduce its workforce, it is undeniable that the Company was faced with a dilemma: it could follow the conciliation agreement as mandated by the District Court and risk liability under the collective bargaining agreement, or it could follow the bargaining agreement and risk both a contempt citation and Title VII liability. The dilemma, however, was of the Company's own making. The Company committed itself voluntarily to two conflicting contractual obligations. Id., at ___, 103 S.Ct., at 2184.

It is clear, therefore, that the correctness of the District Court's interpretation of the decree is irrelevant with respect to the enforceability of the union's contractual rights; those rights remained enforceable regardless of whether the city had an obligation not to lay off blacks.[8] The question in these cases remains whether the District Court's authority pursuant to the consent decree enabled it to enjoin a layoff of more than a certain number of blacks. The issue is not whether the District Court could require the city to layoff whites, or whether the District Court could abrogate contractual rights of white firefighters.

III

Assuming, as the Court erroneously does, that the District Court entered a permanent injunction, the question on review then would be whether the District Court had authority to enter it. In affirming the District Court, the Court of Appeals suggested at least two grounds on which respondents might have prevailed on the merits.

The first of these derives from the contractual characteristics of a consent decree. Because a consent decree "is to be construed for enforcement purposes essentially as a contract," United States v. ITT Continental Baking Co., 420 U.S. 223, 238, 95 S.Ct. 926, 935, 43 L.Ed.2d 148 (1975), respondents had the right to specific performance of the terms of the decree. If the proposed layoffs violated those terms, the District Court could issue an injunction requiring compliance with them. Alternatively, the Court of Appeals noted that a court of equity has inherent power to modify a consent decree in light of changed circumstances. 679 F.2d 541, 560–561 (CA6 1982). Thus, if respondents could show that changed circumstances justified modification of the decree, the District Court would have authority to make such a change.

*   *   *

The Court of Appeals also suggested that respondents could have prevailed on the merits because the 1981 layoffs may have justified a modification of the consent decree. This Court frequently has recognized the inherent "power of a court of equity to modify an injunction

---

8. Judge Martin's opinion concurring in part and dissenting in part from the Sixth Circuit's decision is based on precisely this point. See 679 F.2d, at 569.

in adaptation to changed conditions though it was entered by consent." United States v. Swift & Co., 286 U.S. 106, 114, 52 S.Ct. 460, 462, 76 L.Ed. 999 (1932); accord, Pasadena City Board of Education v. Spangler, 427 U.S. 424, 437, 96 S.Ct. 2697, 2705, 49 L.Ed.2d 599 (1976); United States v. United Shoe Machinery Corp., 391 U.S. 244, 251, 88 S.Ct. 1496, 1500, 20 L.Ed.2d 562 (1968). "The source of the power to modify is of course the fact that an injunction often requires a continuing willingness to apply its powers and processes on behalf of the party who obtained that equitable relief." System Federation v. Wright, 364 U.S. 642, 647, 81 S.Ct. 368, 371, 5 L.Ed.2d 349 (1961). The test for ruling on a plaintiff's request for a modification of a consent decree is "whether the change serve[s] to effectuate * * * the basic purpose of the original consent decree." Chrysler Corp. v. United States, 316 U.S., at 562, 62 S.Ct., at 1149.

The Court rejects this ground for affirming the preliminary injunction, not by examining the purposes of the *consent decree* and whether the proposed layoffs justified a modification of the decree, but rather by reference to Title VII. The Court concludes that the preliminary injunction was improper because it "imposed on the parties as an adjunct of settlement something that could not have been ordered had the case gone to trial and the plaintiffs proved that a pattern or practice of discrimination existed." Ante, at 2588. Thus, the Court has chosen to evaluate the propriety of the preliminary injunction by asking what type of relief the District Court could have awarded had respondents litigated their Title VII claim and prevailed on the merits. Although it is far from clear whether that is the right question,[9] it is clear that the Court has given the wrong answer.

Had respondents prevailed on their Title VII claims at trial, the remedies available would have been those provided by § 706(g), 42 U.S.C. § 2000e–5(g). Under that section, a court that determines that an employer has violated Title VII may "enjoin the respondent from engaging in such unlawful employment practice, and order such affirm-

---

9. The Court's analysis seems to be premised on the view that a consent decree cannot provide relief that could not be obtained at trial. In addressing the Court's analysis, I do not mean to imply that I accept its premise as correct. In Steelworkers v. Weber, 443 U.S. 193, 99 S.Ct. 2721, 61 L.Ed.2d 480 (1979), this Court considered whether an affirmative action plan adopted voluntarily by an employer violated Title VII because it discriminated against whites. In holding that the plan was lawful, the Court stressed that the voluntariness of the plan informed the nature of its inquiry. Id., at 200, 99 S.Ct., at 2725; see also id., at 211, 99 S.Ct., at 2731 (concurring opinion). Because a consent decree is an agreement that is enforceable in court, it has qualities of both voluntariness and compulsion. The Court has explained that Congress intended to encourage voluntary settlement of Title VII suits, Carson v. American Brands, Inc., 450 U.S. 79, 88, n. 14, 101 S.Ct. 993, 998, n. 14, 67 L.Ed.2d 59 (1981), and cooperative private efforts to eliminate the lingering effects of past discrimination. *Weber*, 443 U.S., at 201–207, 99 S.Ct., at 2726–2729. It is by no means clear, therefore, that the permissible scope of relief available under a consent decree is the same as could be ordered by a court after a finding of liability at trial.

ative action as may be appropriate, which may include, *but is not limited to,* reinstatement or hiring of employees, with or without back pay * * *, *or any other equitable relief as the court deems appropriate*" (emphasis added). The scope of the relief that could have been entered on behalf of respondents had they prevailed at trial therefore depends on the nature of relief that is "appropriate" in remedying Title VII violations.

In determining the nature of "appropriate" relief under § 706(g), courts have distinguished between individual relief and race-conscious class relief. Although overlooked by the Court, this distinction is highly relevant here. In a Title VII class-action suit of the type brought by respondents, an individual plaintiff is entitled to an award of individual relief only if he can establish that he was the victim of discrimination. That requirement grows out of the general equitable principles of "make whole" relief; an individual who has suffered no injury is not entitled to an individual award. See Teamsters v. United States, 431 U.S. 324, 347–348, 364–371, 97 S.Ct. 1843, 1860–1861, 1869–1872, 52 L.Ed.2d 396 (1977). If victimization is shown, however, an individual is entitled to whatever retroactive seniority, backpay, and promotions are consistent with the statute's goal of making the victim whole. Franks v. Bowman Transportation Co., 424 U.S. 747, 762–770, 96 S.Ct. 1251, 1263–1266, 47 L.Ed.2d 444 (1976).

In Title VII class-action suits, the Courts of Appeals are unanimously of the view that race-conscious affirmative relief can also be "appropriate" under § 706(g).[10] See University of California Regents v. Bakke, 438 U.S. 265, 301–302, 98 S.Ct. 2733, 2753–2754, 57 L.Ed.2d 750 (opinion of POWELL, J.); id., at 353, n. 28, 98 S.Ct., at 2780, n. 28 (1978) (opinion of BRENNAN, WHITE, MARSHALL and BLACKMUN, JJ.). The purpose of such relief is not to make whole any particular individual, but rather to remedy the present class-wide effects of past discrimination or to prevent similar discrimination in the future. Because the discrimination sought to be alleviated by race-conscious relief is the class-wide effects of past discrimination, rather than discrimination against identified members of the class, such relief is provided to the class as a whole

10. See e.g., Boston Chapter, NAACP, Inc. v. Beecher, 504 F.2d 1017, 1027–1028 (CA1 1974), cert. denied, 421 U.S. 910, 95 S.Ct. 1561, 43 L.Ed.2d 775 (1975); Rios v. Enterprise Ass'n Steamfitters Local 638, 501 F.2d 622, 629 (CA2 1974); E.E.O.C. v. American Tel. & Tel. Co., 556 F.2d 167, 174–177 (CA3 1977), cert. denied, 438 U.S. 915, 98 S.Ct. 3145, 57 L.Ed.2d 1161 (1978); Chisholm v. United States Postal Service, 665 F.2d 482, 499 (CA4 1981); United States v. City of Alexandria, 614 F.2d 1358, 1363–1366 (CA5 1980); United States v. I.B.E.W., Local No. 38, 428 F.2d 144 (CA6), cert. denied, 400 U.S. 943, 91 S.Ct. 245, 27 L.Ed.2d 248 (1970); United States v. City of Chicago, 663 F.2d 1354 (CA7 1981) (en banc); Firefighters Institute v. City of St. Louis, 616 F.2d 350, 364 (CA8 1980), cert. denied, 452 U.S. 938, 101 S.Ct. 3079, 69 L.Ed.2d 951 (1981); United States v. Ironworkers Local 86, 443 F.2d 544, 553–554 (CA9), cert. denied, 404 U.S. 984, 92 S.Ct. 447, 30 L.Ed.2d 367 (1971); United States v. Lee Way Motor Freight, Inc., 625 F.2d 918, 944 (CA10 1979); Thompson v. Sawyer, 219 U.S.App.D.C. 393, 430, 678 F.2d 257, 294 (1982).

rather than to its individual members. The relief may take many forms, but in class actions it frequently involves percentages—such as those contained in the 1980 consent decree between the city and respondents—that require race to be taken into account when an employer hires or promotes employees. The distinguishing feature of race-conscious relief is that no individual member of the disadvantaged class has a claim to it, and individual beneficiaries of the relief need not show that they were themselves victims of the discrimination for which the relief was granted.

In the instant case, respondents' request for a preliminary injunction did not include a request for individual awards of retroactive seniority—and, contrary to the implication of the Court's opinion, the District Court did not make any such awards. Rather, the District Court order required the city to conduct its layoffs in a race-conscious manner; specifically, the preliminary injunction prohibited the city from conducting layoffs that would "decrease the percentage of black[s]" in certain job categories. The city remained free to lay off any individual black so long as the percentage of black representation was maintained.

Because these cases arise out of a consent decree, and a trial on the merits has never taken place, it is of course impossible for the Court to know the extent and nature of any past discrimination by the city. For this reason, to the extent that the scope of appropriate relief would depend upon the facts found at trial, it is impossible to determine whether the relief provided by the preliminary injunction would have been appropriate following a trial on the merits. Nevertheless, the Court says that the preliminary injunction was inappropriate because, it concludes, respondents could not have obtained similar relief had their cases been litigated instead of settled by a consent decree.

The Court's conclusion does not follow logically from its own analysis.

* * *

The Court's reliance on *Teamsters* is mistaken at a more general level as well, because *Teamsters* was concerned with individual relief, whereas these cases are concerned exclusively with classwide, race-conscious relief. *Teamsters* arose out of two pattern-or-practice suits filed by the Government alleging that a union and an employer had discriminated against minorities in hiring truck drivers. Prior to a finding of liability, the Government entered into a consent decree in partial resolution of the suit. In that decree, the defendants agreed to a variety of race-conscious remedial actions, including a requirement that the company hire "one Negro or Spanish-surnamed person for every white person" until a certain percentage of minority representation was achieved. 431 U.S., at 330–331, n. 4, 97 S.Ct., at 1852, n. 4. The decree did not settle the claims of individual class members, however, and allowed the individuals whom the court found to be victims of discrimination to seek whatever retroactive seniority was appropriate under Title VII. Ibid.

In *Teamsters*, therefore, all class-wide claims had been settled before the case reached this Court. The case concerned only the problems of determining victims and the nature of appropriate individual relief. *Teamsters* did not consider the nature of appropriate affirmative class relief that would have been available had such relief not been provided in the consent decree between the parties. The issue in the present cases, as posed by the Court, is just the reverse. Respondents have not requested individual awards of seniority, and the preliminary injunction made none. Thus, the issue in these cases is the appropriate scope of classwide relief—an issue not present in *Teamsters* when that case came here. *Teamsters* therefore has little relevance for these cases.

The Court seeks to buttress its reliance on *Teamsters* by stressing on the last sentence of § 706(g). That sentence states that a court cannot order the "hiring, reinstatement, or promotion of an individual as an employee ∗ ∗ ∗ if such individual ∗ ∗ ∗ was refused employment or advancement or was suspended or discharged for any reason other than discrimination" in violation of Title VII. The nature of the Court's reliance on that sentence is unclear, however, because the Court states merely that the District Court "ignores" the "policy behind § 706(g)." Ante, at 2588, 2590. For several reasons, however, it appears that the Court relies on the policy of § 706(g) only in making a particularized conclusion concerning the relief granted in these cases, rather than a conclusion about the general availability of race-conscious remedies.

In discussing § 706(g), the Court relies on several passages from the legislative history of the Civil Rights Act of 1964 in which individual legislators stated their views that Title VII would not authorize the imposition of remedies based upon race. And while there are indications that many in Congress at the time opposed the use of race-conscious remedies, there is authority that supports a narrower interpretation of § 706(g). Under that interpretation, the last sentence of § 706(g) addresses only the situation in which a plaintiff demonstrates that an employer has engaged in unlawful discrimination, but the employer can show that a particular individual would not have received the job, promotion or reinstatement even in the absence of discrimination because there was also a lawful justification for the action. See Patterson v. Greenwood School District 50, 696 F.2d 293, 295 (CA4 1982); E.E.O.C. v. American Tel. & Tel. Co., 556 F.2d 167, 174–177 (CA3 1977), cert. denied, 438 U.S. 915, 98 S.Ct. 3145, 51 L.Ed.2d 1161 (1978); Day v. Mathews, 174 U.S.App.D.C. 231, 233, 530 F.2d 1083, 1085 (1976); King v. Laborers Int'l Union, Local No. 818, 443 F.2d 273, 278–279 (CA6

1971). See also Brodin, The Standard of Causation in the Mixed-Motive Title VII Action: A Social Policy Perspective, 82 Colum.L.Rev. 292 (1982). The provision, for example, prevents a court from granting relief where an employment decision is based in part upon race, but where the applicant is unqualified for the job for nondiscriminatory reasons. In that sense, the section merely prevents a court from ordering an employer to hire someone unqualified for the job, and has nothing to do with prospective class-wide relief.

Much of the legislative history supports this view. What is now § 706(g) had its origin in § 707(e) of H.R. 7152, 88th Cong.,

* * *

In any event, § 706(g) was amended by the Equal Employment Opportunity Act of 1972, 86 Stat. 107. The legislative history of that amendment strongly supports the view that Congress endorsed the remedial use of race under Title VII. The amendment added language to the first sentence of § 706(g) to make clear the breadth of the remedial authority of the courts. As amended, the first sentence authorizes a court to order "such affirmative action as may be appropriate, which may include, *but is not limited to,* reinstatement or hiring of employees, with or without backpay * * * *or any other equitable relief as the court deems appropriate."* 42 U.S.C. § 2000e–5(g) (emphasized language added in 1972).

In addition, during consideration of the amendment, Congress specifically rejected an attempt to amend Title VII to *prohibit* the use of prospective race-conscious employment goals to remedy discrimination. Senator Ervin proposed an amendment to Title VII intended to prohibit government agencies from requiring employers to adopt goals or quotas for the hiring of minorities. 118 Cong.Rec. 1663–1664 (1972). Senator Javits led the debate against the amendment. Id., at 1664–1676. Significantly, Senator Javits stressed that the amendment would affect not only the activities of federal agencies, but also the scope of judicial remedies available under Title VII. He referred repeatedly to court decisions ordering race-conscious remedies, and asked that two such decisions be printed in the Congressional Record. Id., at 1665–1675.[12] He stated explicitly his view that "[w]hat this amendment seeks to do is to undo * * * those court decisions." Id., at 1665. The amendment was rejected by a 2 to 1 margin. Id., at 1676.

---

12. The two cases placed in the Congressional Record were United States v. Ironworkers Local 86, 443 F.2d 544 (CA9), cert. denied, 404 U.S. 984, 92 S.Ct. 447, 30 L.Ed.2d 367 (1971) (a percentage goal for black participation in apprenticeship program as part of remedy for Title VII violation), and Contractors Association of Eastern Pennsylvania v. Secretary of Labor, 442 F.2d 159 (CA3), cert. denied, 404 U.S. 854, 92 S.Ct. 98, 30 L.Ed.2d 95 (1971) (upheld lawfulness of a plan requiring contractors on federally assisted projects to adopt goals for minority employment). Senator Javits also noted the Justice Department's practice of seeking consent decrees in Title VII cases containing percentage hiring goals. 118 Cong.Rec. 1675 (1972).

With clear knowledge, therefore, of courts' use of race-conscious remedies to correct patterns of discrimination, the 1972 Congress rejected an attempt to amend Title VII to prohibit such remedies. In fact, the Conference Committee stated: "In any area where the new law does not address itself, or in any areas where a specific contrary intention is not indicated, it was assumed that the present case law as developed by the courts would continue to govern the applicability and construction of Title VII." 118 Cong.Rec. 7166 (1972). Relying on this legislative history of the 1972 amendment and other actions by the Executive and the courts, four members of this Court, including the author of today's opinion, stated in University of California Regents v. Bakke, 438 U.S. 265, 353, n. 28, 98 S.Ct. 2733, 2780, n. 28, 57 L.Ed.2d 750. "Executive, judicial, and congressional action subsequent to the passage of Title VII conclusively established that the Title did not bar the remedial use of race" (opinion of BRENNAN, WHITE, MARSHALL, and BLACKMUN, JJ.). As has been observed, supra, n. 10, moreover, the Courts of Appeals are unanimously of the view that race-conscious remedies are not prohibited by Title VII. Because the Court's opinion does not even acknowledge this consensus, it seems clear that the Court's conclusion that the District Court "ignored the policy" of § 706(g) is a statement that the race-conscious relief ordered in these cases was broader than necessary, not that race-conscious relief is never appropriate under Title VII.

* * *

LOCAL 28 OF THE SHEET METAL WORKERS' INTERNATIONAL ASSOCIATION AND LOCAL 28 JOINT APPRENTICESHIP COMMITTEE, PETITIONERS, v. EQUAL EMPLOYMENT OPPORTUNITY COMMISSION ET AL.

Supreme Court of the United States, 1986.
__ U.S. __, 106 S.Ct. 3019, 92 L.Ed. 344.

JUSTICE BRENNAN announced the judgment of the Court and delivered the opinion of the Court with respect to Parts I, II, III, and VI, and an opinion with respect to Parts IV, V, and VII in which JUSTICE MARSHALL, JUSTICE BLACKMUN, and JUSTICE STEVENS join.

In 1975, petitioners were found guilty of engaging in a pattern and practice of discrimination against black and Hispanic individuals (nonwhites) in violation of Title VII of the Civil Rights Act of 1964, 42 U.S.C. § 2000e et seq., and ordered to end their discriminatory practices, and to admit a certain percentage of nonwhites to union membership by July 1982. In 1982 and again in 1983, petitioners were found guilty of civil contempt for disobeying the District Court's earlier orders. They now challenge the District Court's contempt finding, and also the remedies the court ordered both for the Title VII violation and for contempt. Principally, the issue presented is whether the remedial provision of Title VII, see 42 U.S.C. § 2000e–5(g), empowers a district court to order race-conscious relief that may benefit individuals who are not identified victims of unlawful discrimination.

I

Petitioner Local 28 of the Sheet Metal Workers' International Association (Local 28) represents sheet metal workers employed by contractors in the New York City metropolitan area. Petitioner Local 28 Joint Apprenticeship Committee (JAC) is a management-labor committee which operates a 4-year apprenticeship training program designed to teach sheet metal skills. Apprentices enrolled in the program receive training both from classes and from on the job work experience. Upon completing the program, apprentices become journeyman members of Local 28. Successful completion of the program is the principal means of attaining union membership.[1]

In 1964, the New York State Commission for Human Rights determined that petitioners had excluded blacks from the union and the apprenticeship program in violation of state law. The State Commission found, among other things, that Local 28 had never had any black members or apprentices, and that "admission to apprenticeship is conducted largely on a nepot[is]tic basis involving sponsorship by incumbent union members," App. JA–407, creating an impenetrable barrier for nonwhite applicants.[2] Petitioners were ordered to "cease and desist" their racially discriminatory practices. The New York State Supreme Court affirmed the State Commission's findings, and directed petitioners to implement objective standards for selecting apprentices. State Comm'n for Human Rights v. Farrell, 43 Misc.2d 958, 252 N.Y.S.2d 649 (1964).

When the court's orders proved ineffective, the State Commission commenced other state-court proceedings in an effort to end petitioners' discriminatory practices. Petitioners had originally agreed to indenture two successive classes of apprentices using nondiscriminatory selection procedures, but stopped processing applications for the second apprentice class, thus requiring that the State Commission seek a court order requiring petitioners to indenture the apprentices. State

---

1. In addition to completing the apprenticeship program, an individual can gain membership in Local 28 by (1) transferring directly from a "sister" union; (2) passing a battery of journeyman level tests administered by the union; and (3) gaining admission at the time a nonunion sheet metal shop is organized by Local 28. In addition, during periods of full employment, Local 28 issues temporary work permits which allow nonmembers to work within its jurisdiction.

2. The Sheet Metal Workers' International Union was formed in 1888, under a Constitution which provided for the establishment of "white local unions" and relegated blacks to membership in subordinate locals. Local 28 was established in 1913 as a "white local union." Although racial restrictions were formally deleted from the International Constitution in 1946, Local 28 refused to admit blacks until 1969.

Comm'n for Human Rights v. Farrell, 47 Misc.2d 244, 262 N.Y.S.2d 526, aff'd, 24 App.Div.2d 128, 264 N.Y.S.2d 489 (1st Dept.1965). The court subsequently denied the union's request to reduce the size of the second apprentice class, and chastized the union for refusing "except for token gestures, to further the integration process." State Comm'n for Human Rights v. Farrell, 47 Misc.2d 799, 800, 263 N.Y.S.2d 250, 252 (1965). Petitioners proceeded to disregard the results of the selection test for a third apprentice class on the ground that nonwhites had received "unfair tutoring" and had passed in unreasonably high numbers. The state court ordered petitioners to indenture the apprentices based on the examination results. State Comm'n for Human Rights v. Farrell, 52 Misc.2d 936, 277 N.Y.S.2d 287, aff'd, 27 App.Div.2d 327, 278 N.Y.S.2d 982 (1st Dept.), aff'd 19 N.Y.2d 974, 281 N.Y.S.2d 521, 228 N.E.2d 691 (1967).

In 1971, the United States initiated this action under Title VII and Executive Order 11246, 3 CFR 339 (1964–1965 Comp.) to enjoin petitioners from engaging in a pattern and practice of discrimination against black and Hispanic individuals (nonwhites).[3] The New York City Commission on Human Rights (City) intervened as plaintiff to press claims that petitioners had violated municipal fair employment laws, and had frustrated the City's efforts to increase job opportunities for minorities in the construction industry. 347 F.Supp. 164 (1972). In 1970, the City had adopted a plan requiring contractors on its projects to employ one minority trainee for every four journeyman union members. Local 28 was the only construction local which refused to comply voluntarily with the plan. In early 1974, the City attempted to assign six minority trainees to sheet metal contractors working on municipal construction projects. After Local 28 members stopped work on the projects, the District Court directed the JAC to admit the six trainees into the apprenticeship program, and enjoined Local 28 from causing any work stoppage at the affected job sites. The parties subsequently agreed to a consent order that required the JAC to admit up to 40 minorities into the apprenticeship program by September 1974. The JAC stalled compliance with the consent order, and only completed the indenture process under threat of contempt.

* * *

[In 1975, the District Court found petitioner union and petitioner apprenticeship committee of the union guilty of violating Title VII of the Civil Rights Act of 1964 by discriminating against nonwhite workers in recruitment, selection, training, and admission to the union. The court ordered petitioners to end their discriminatory practices, established a 29% nonwhite membership goal, based on the percentage of nonwhites in the relevant labor pool in New York City, to be achieved

---

3. The Equal Employment Opportunity Commission was substituted as named plaintiff in this case. The Sheet Metal and Air Conditioning Contractors' Association of New York City (Contractor's Associa- tion) was also named as a defendant. The New York State Division of Human Rights (State), although joined as a third and fourth-party defendant in this action, re- aligned itself as a plaintiff.

by July 1981, and also ordered petitioners to implement procedures designed to achieve this goal under the supervision of a court-appointed administrator. Thereafter, the administrator proposed and the court adopted an affirmative-action program. The Court of Appeals affirmed, with modifications. On remand, the District Court adopted a revised affirmative-action program, and extended the time to meet the 29% membership goal. The Court of Appeals again affirmed. In 1982 and again in 1983, the District Court found petitioners guilty of civil contempt for disobeying the court's earlier orders. The court imposed a fine to be placed in a special Employment, Training, Education, and Recruitment Fund (Fund), to be used to increase nonwhite membership in the union and its apprenticeship program. The District Court ultimately entered an amended affirmative-action program establishing a 29.23% nonwhite membership goal to be met by August 1987. The Court of Appeals affirmed the District Court's contempt findings (with one exception), the contempt remedies, including the Fund order, and the affirmative-action program with modifications, holding that the 29.23% nonwhite membership goal was proper and did not violate Title VII or the Constitution. * * *

Local 28 and the JAC filed a petition for a writ of certiorari. They present several claims for review: (1) that the District Court relied on incorrect statistical data; (2) that the contempt remedies ordered by the District Court were criminal in nature and were imposed without due process; (3) that the appointment of an administrator to supervise membership practices interferes with their right to self-governance; and (4) that the membership goal and Fund are unconstitutional. Principally, however, petitioners, supported by the Solicitor General, maintain that the membership goal and Fund exceed the scope of remedies available under Title VII because they extend race-conscious preferences to individuals who are not the identified victims of petitioners' unlawful discrimination. We granted the petition, 474 U.S. ___, 106 S.Ct. 58, 88 L.Ed.2d 47 (1985), and now affirm the Court of Appeals.

II

Petitioners argue that the District Court relied on incorrect statistical evidence in violation of Title VII and of petitioners' right to due process.

A

Under the O & J and RAAPO, petitioners were directed to attain a 29% nonwhite membership goal by July of 1981. This goal was based on the percentage of minorities in the relevant labor pool within New York City. Petitioners argue that because members and applicants for Local 28 membership have always been drawn from areas outside of New York City, the nonwhite membership goal should have accounted for the percentage of minorities in the relevant labor pool in these

* (Excerpted from the syllabus prepared by the Reporter of Decisions—Ed.)

areas. Although they concede that there is no evidence in the record from which the correct percentage could be derived, they insist that the District Court's figure is erroneous, and that this error was "significant." [20]

The 29% nonwhite membership goal was established more than a decade ago and was twice affirmed by the Court of Appeals. Petitioners did not seek certiorari from this Court to review either of the Court of Appeals' judgments. Consequently, we do not have before us any issue as to the correctness of the 29% figure. See Pasadena City Board of Education v. Spangler, 427 U.S. 424, 432, 96 S.Ct. 2697, 2703, 49 L.Ed.2d 599 (1976). Under AAAPO, petitioners are now obligated to attain a 29.23% nonwhite-membership goal by August 1987. AAAPO adjusted the original 29% membership goal to account for the fact that Local 28's members were now drawn from areas outside of New York City. Thus, even assuming that the original 29% membership goal was erroneous, it would not affect petitioners' existing obligations under AAAPO, or any other issue now before us.[21]

B

Petitioners argue that the District Court also relied on incorrect data in finding that they had underutilized the apprenticeship program. The Court of Appeals recognized this error, see n. 20, supra, but affirmed the finding based on other evidence presented to the District Court.[22] Petitioners do not explain whether, and if so, why, the Court

20. In their brief, petitioners also suggest that the District Court's 29% membership goal was used to confirm its original finding of discrimination, and was therefore invalid under Hazelwood School District v. United States, 433 U.S. 299, 97 S.Ct. 2736, 53 L.Ed.2d 768 (1977) (proof of a pattern of discrimination by statistical evidence must be drawn from relevant geographical locations). However, the Court of Appeals recognized that the District Court's finding of liability "did not rely on inferences from racial ratios of population and employment in the area," but rather "was based on direct and overwhelming evidence of purposeful racial discrimination over a period of many years." 565 F.2d 31, n. 8, (1977). In any event, petitioners conceded at oral argument that they do not "challeng[e] any finding that there was deliberate discrimination." Tr. of Oral Arg. 7.

21. Petitioners   contend   that "[i]nasmuch as [they] have now been held in contempt for not achieving the [29% membership] quota, the propriety of the evidence upon which it was derived is relevant." Brief for Petitioners 35–36. In the first place, the District Court expressly stated that petitioners were not held in contempt for failing to attain the 29%

membership goal. In any event, a "contempt proceeding does not open to reconsideration the legal or factual basis of the order alleged to have been disobeyed and thus become a retrial of the original controversy." Maggio v. Zeitz, 333 U.S. 56, 69, 68 S.Ct. 401, 408, 92 L.Ed. 476 (1948); see also Walker v. City of Birmingham, 388 U.S. 307, 313–314, 87 S.Ct. 1824, 1828, 18 L.Ed.2d 1210 (1967); United States v. Rylander, 460 U.S. 752, 756–757, 103 S.Ct. 1548, 1552–1553, 75 L.Ed.2d 521 (1983); C. Wright & A. Miller, Federal Practice and Procedure § 2960, pp. 597–598.

22. The court pointed to evidence before the District Court showing that after the O & J was entered: (1) there was a "sharp increase" in the ratio of journeymen to apprentices employed by contractors; (2) the average number of hours worked annually by journeymen "increased dramatically"; (3) the percentage of unemployed apprentices decreased; and (4) the union issued hundreds of temporary work permits, mostly to white journeymen. Based on this evidence, the Court of Appeals concluded that despite the need for more apprentices, Local 28 had deliberately shifted employment opportunities from apprentices to predominately white journeymen, and had refused to conduct the

of Appeals' evaluation of the evidence was incorrect. Based on our own review of the record, we cannot say that the District Court's resolution of the evidence presented on this issue was clearly erroneous. Cf. National Collegiate Athletic Assn. v. Board of Regents of Univ. of Okla., 468 U.S. 85, 98, n. 15, 104 S.Ct. 2948, 2959, n. 15, 82 L.Ed.2d 70 (1984); Rogers v. Lodge, 458 U.S. 613, 623, 102 S.Ct. 3272, 3278–3279, 73 L.Ed.2d 1012 (1982). Moreover, because petitioners do not challenge three of the findings on which the first contempt order was based, any alleged use of incorrect statistical evidence by the District Court provides no basis for disturbing the contempt citation. As the Court of Appeals observed, petitioners' "failure to have the apprentices employed is both an independent ground for contempt and a symptom of the effects of defendants' other kinds of contemptuous conduct." 753 F.2d, at 1183.

III

The District Court imposed a variety of contempt sanctions in this case, including fines to finance the Fund, a computerized recordkeeping requirement, and attorney's fees and expenses. Petitioners claim that these sanctions, while ostensibly imposed for civil contempt, are in fact punitive, and were issued without the procedures required for criminal contempt proceedings, see Fed.Rule Crim.Proc. 42(b); 42 U.S.C. § 2000h. We reject this contention.

Criminal contempt sanctions are punitive in nature and are imposed to vindicate the authority of the court. United States v. Mine Workers, 330 U.S. 258, 302, 67 S.Ct. 677, 700, 91 L.Ed. 884 (1947). On the other hand, sanctions in civil-contempt proceedings may be employed "for either or both of two purposes: to coerce the defendant into compliance with the court's order, and to compensate the complainant for losses sustained." Id., at 303–304, 67 S.Ct., at 701; see also McComb v. Jacksonville Paper Co., 336 U.S. 187, 191, 69 S.Ct. 497, 499, 93 L.Ed. 599 (1949); Penfield Co. of California v. S.E.C., 330 U.S. 585, 590, 67 S.Ct. 918, 921, 91 L.Ed. 1117 (1947); Nye v. United States, 313 U.S. 33, 42, 61 S.Ct. 810, 813, 85 L.Ed. 1172 (1941); McCrone v. United States, 307 U.S. 61, 64, 59 S.Ct. 685, 686–687, 83 L.Ed. 1108 (1939); 42 U.S.C. § 2000h. Under this standard, the sanctions issued by the District Court were clearly civil in nature.

* * * [T]he sanctions levied by the District Court were clearly designed to coerce compliance with the court's orders, rather than to punish petitioners for their contemptuous conduct.[23]

general publicity campaign required by RAAPO to attract nonwhites to the apprenticeship program.

23. The District Court had also determined that petitioners had failed to comply with the detailed recordkeeping requirements of the O & J and RAAPO. The

computerized recordkeeping system was clearly designed to foster petitioners' compliance with these provisions. Finally, the assessment of attorney fees and expenses compensated respondents for costs occasioned by petitioners' contemptuous conduct.

IV

Petitioners, joined by the Solicitor General, argue that the membership goal, the Fund order, and other orders which require petitioners to grant membership preferences to nonwhites are expressly prohibited by § 706(g), 42 U.S.C. § 2000e–5(g), which defines the remedies available under Title VII. Petitioners and the Solicitor General maintain that § 706(g) authorizes a district court to award preferential relief only to the actual victims of unlawful discrimination.[24] They maintain that the membership goal and the Fund violate this provision, since they require petitioners to admit to membership, and otherwise to extend benefits to black and Hispanic individuals who are not the identified victims of unlawful discrimination.[25] We reject this argument, and hold that § 706(g) does not prohibit a court from ordering, in appropriate circumstances, affirmative race-conscious relief as a remedy for past discrimination. Specifically, we hold that such relief may be appropriate where an employer or a labor union has engaged in persistent or egregious discrimination, or where necessary to dissipate the lingering effects of pervasive discrimination.

24. Both petitioners and the Solicitor General present this challenge from a rather curious position. Petitioners did not seek review in this Court of the 29% membership goal twice approved by the Court of Appeals, even though that goal was similar to the 29.23% goal they now challenge. However, we reject the State's contention that either res judicata or the law of the case prohibits us from now addressing the legality of the membership goal. See United States v. A.S. Kreider Co., 313 U.S. 443, 445–446, 61 S.Ct. 1007, 1009, 85 L.Ed. 1447 (1941); Southern R. Co. v. Clift, 260 U.S. 316, 319, 43 S.Ct. 126, 127, 67 L.Ed. 283 (1922); Messenger v. Anderson, 225 U.S. 436, 444, 32 S.Ct. 739, 740, 56 L.Ed. 1152 (1912); 1B J. Moore, J. Lucas, & T. Currier, Moore's Federal Practice ¶ 0.404 [4.6], p. 141 (2d ed. 1984).

The Solicitor General challenges the membership goal and Fund order even though the EEOC has, throughout this litigation, joined the other plaintiffs in asking the courts to order numerical goals, implementing ratios, and timetables. In the complaint, the Government sought the "selection of sufficient apprentices from among qualified non-white applicants to overcome the effects of past discrimination." App. JA–374. In its post-trial memorandum, the Government urged the court to "establish a goal of no less than 30 per cent non white membership in Local 28." Id., at JA–277. To achieve this goal, the Government asked the court to order petitioners to select apprentices based on a one-to-one white to nonwhite ratio, and argued that "a reasonable preference in favor of minority persons to remedy past discriminatory injustices is permissable [sic]." Ibid.

25. The last sentence of § 706(g) addresses only court orders requiring the "admission or reinstatement of an individual as a member of a union." 42 U.S.C. § 2000e–5(g). Thus, even under petitioners' reading of § 706(g), that provision would not apply to several of the benefits conferred by the Fund, to wit the tutorial, liaison, counseling, stipend, and loan programs extended to nonwhites. Moreover, the District Court established the Fund in the exercise of its contempt powers. Thus, even assuming that petitioners correctly read § 706(g) to limit the remedies a court may impose for a violation of Title VII, that provision would not necessarily limit the District Court's authority to order petitioners to implement the Fund. The Solicitor General, without citing any authority, maintains that "contempt sanctions imposed to enforce Title VII must not themselves violate the statute's policy of providing relief only to the actual victims of discrimination." Brief for EEOC 11. We need not decide whether § 706(g) restricts a court's contempt powers, since we reject the proposition that § 706(g) always prohibits a court from ordering affirmative race-conscious relief which might incidentally benefit individuals who were not the actual victims of discrimination.

A

* * *

The language of § 706(g) plainly expresses Congress's intent to vest district courts with broad discretion to award "appropriate" equitable relief to remedy unlawful discrimination. Teamsters v. United States, 431 U.S. 324, 364, 97 S.Ct. 1843, 1869, 52 L.Ed.2d 396 (1977); Franks v. Bowman Transportation Co., 424 U.S. 747, 771, 96 S.Ct. 1251, 1267, 47 L.Ed.2d 444 (1976); Albemarle Paper Co. v. Moody, 422 U.S. 405, 421, 95 S.Ct. 2362, 2373, 45 L.Ed.2d 280 (1975).[26] Nevertheless, petitioners and the Solicitor General argue that the last sentence of § 706(g) prohibits a court from ordering an employer or labor union to take affirmative steps to eliminate discrimination which might incidentally benefit individuals who are not the actual victims of discrimination. This reading twists the plain language of the statute.

The last sentence of § 706(g) prohibits a court from ordering a union to admit an individual who was "refused admission * * * for any reason other than discrimination." It does not, as petitioners and the Solicitor General suggest, say that a court may order relief only for the actual victims of past discrimination. The sentence on its face addresses only the situation where a plaintiff demonstrates that a union (or an employer) has engaged in unlawful discrimination, but the union can show that a particular individual would have been refused admission even in the absence of discrimination, for example because that individual was unqualified. In these circumstances, § 706(g) confirms that a court could not order the union to admit the unqualified individual. Patterson v. Greenwood School District 50, 696 F.2d 293, 295 (CA4 1982); EEOC v. American Tel. & Tel. Co., 556 F.2d 167, 174–177 (CA3 1977), cert. denied, 438 U.S. 915, 98 S.Ct. 3145, 57 L.Ed.2d 1161 (1978); Day v. Mathews, 174 U.S.App.D.C. 231, 233, 530 F.2d 1083, 1085 (1976); King v. Laborers' International Union, Local No. 818, 443 F.2d 273, 278–279 (CA6 1971). In this case, neither the membership goal nor the Fund order required petitioners to admit to membership individuals who had been refused admission for reasons unrelated to

---

26. Section 706(g) was modeled after § 10(c) of the National Labor Relations Act, 29 U.S.C. § 160(c). See Franks v. Bowman Transportation Co., 424 U.S., at 769, 96 S.Ct., at 1266; Albemarle Paper Co. v. Moody, 422 U.S., at 419, 95 S.Ct., at 2372. Principles developed under the National Labor Relations Act "guide, but do not bind, courts tailoring remedies under Title VII." Ford Motor Co. v. EEOC, 458 U.S. 219, 226, n. 8, 102 S.Ct. 3057, 3062–3063, n. 8, 73 L.Ed.2d 721 (1982). Section 10(c) as we have noted, was intended to give the National Labor Relations Board broad authority to formulate appropriate remedies:

"[I]n the nature of things Congress could not catalogue all the devices and strategems for circumventing the policies of the Act. Nor could it define the whole gamut of remedies to effectuate these policies in an infinite variety of specific situations. Congress met these difficulties by leaving the adaption of means to end to the empiric process of administration." Phelps Dodge Corp. v. NLRB, 313 U.S. 177, 194, 61 S.Ct. 845, 852, 85 L.Ed. 1271 (1941).

See also Franks, supra, 424 U.S., at 769, n. 29, 96 S.Ct., at 1266 ("§ 706(g) grants * * * broader discretionary powers than those granted the [NLRB under section 10(c)].")

discrimination. Thus, we do not read § 706(g) to prohibit a court from ordering the kind of affirmative relief the District Court awarded in this case.

B

The availability of race-conscious affirmative relief under § 706(g) as a remedy for a violation of Title VII also furthers the broad purposes underlying the statute. Congress enacted Title VII based on its determination that racial minorities were subject to pervasive and systematic discrimination in employment. "[I]t was clear to Congress that '[t]he crux of the problem [was] to open employment opportunities for Negroes in occupations which have been traditionally closed to them,' * * * and it was to this problem that Title VII's prohibition against racial discrimination in employment was primarily addressed." Steelworkers v. Weber, 443 U.S. 193, 203, 99 S.Ct. 2721, 2727, 61 L.Ed.2d 480 (1979) (quoting 110 Cong.Rec. 6548 (1964) (remarks of Sen. Humphrey)). Title VII was designed "to achieve equality of employment opportunities and remove barriers that have operated in the past to favor an identifiable group of white employees over other employees." Griggs v. Duke Power Co., 401 U.S. 424, 429–430, 91 S.Ct. 849, 853, 28 L.Ed.2d 158 (1971); see Teamsters, supra, 431 U.S., at 364–365, 97 S.Ct., at 1869–1870; Franks, supra, 424 U.S., at 763, 771, 96 S.Ct., at 1263–1264, 1267; Albemarle Paper, 422 U.S., at 417–18, 95 S.Ct., at 2371–2372. In order to foster equal employment opportunities, Congress gave the lower courts broad power under § 706(g) to fashion "the most complete relief possible" to remedy past discrimination. Franks, supra, 424 U.S., at 770, 96 S.Ct., at 1267; Albemarle Paper, supra, 422 U.S., at 418, 95 S.Ct., at 2372.

In most cases, the court need only order the employer or union to cease engaging in discriminatory practices, and award make-whole relief to the individuals victimized by those practices. In some instances, however, it may be necessary to require the employer or union to take affirmative steps to end discrimination effectively to enforce Title VII. Where an employer or union has engaged in particularly longstanding or egregious discrimination, an injunction simply reiterating Title VII's prohibition against discrimination will often prove useless and will only result in endless enforcement litigation. In such cases, requiring recalcitrant employers or unions to hire and to admit qualified minorities roughly in proportion to the number of qualified minorities in the work force may be the only effective way to ensure the full enjoyment of the rights protected by Title VII. See e.g., Thompson v. Sawyer, 219 U.S.App.D.C. 393, 430, 678 F.2d 257, 294 (1982); Chisholm v. United States Postal Service, 665 F.2d 482, 499 (CA4 1981); United States v. Lee Way Motor Freight, Inc., 625 F.2d 918, 943–945 (CA10 1979); United States v. City of Chicago, 549 F.2d 415, 437 (CA7 1977), cert. denied, 434 U.S. 875, 98 S.Ct. 225, 54 L.Ed.2d 155 (1977), modified 663 F.2d 1354, 1362 (1981) (en banc); Rios v. Enterprise

Assn. Steamfitters Local 638, 501 F.2d 622, 631–32 (CA2 1974); NAACP v. Allen, 340 F.Supp. 703 (1972), sub nom. United States v. Dothard, 373 F.Supp. 504, 506–507 (MD Ala.1974) (Johnson, J.); see also Edwards & Zaretsky, Preferential Remedies for Employment Discrimination, 74 Mich.L.Rev. 1, 9 (1976) ("a number of courts have held that some form of preferential remedy is the most effective means of enforcing equal employment opportunity when the facts show a long history of discrimination against a protected class").

Further, even where the employer or union formally ceases to engage in discrimination, informal mechanisms may obstruct equal employment opportunities. An employer's reputation for discrimination may discourage minorities from seeking available employment. See Morrow v. Crisler, 491 F.2d 1053, 1056 (CA5) (en banc), cert. denied, 419 U.S. 895, 95 S.Ct. 173, 42 L.Ed.2d 139 (1974); Carter v. Gallagher, 452 F.2d 315, 331 (CA8 1971), cert. denied, 406 U.S. 950, 92 S.Ct. 2045, 32 L.Ed.2d 338 (1972); Spiegelman, Court-Ordered Hiring Quotas after Stotts: A Narrative on the Role of the Moralities of the Web and the Ladder in Employment Discrimination Doctrine, 20 Harv.Civ.Rights-Civ.Lib.L.Rev. 339, 388 (1985); see also Taylor v. Jones, 653 F.2d 1193, 1203 (CA8 1981) ("in cases where a discriminatory atmosphere has been shown, the more common forms of relief, * * * may not be appropriate or adequate"); Edwards & Zaretsky, supra, at 6. In these circumstances, affirmative race-conscious relief may be the only means available "to assure equality of employment opportunities and to eliminate those discriminatory practices and devices which have fostered racially stratified job environments to the disadvantage of minority citizens." McDonnell Douglas Corp. v. Green, 411 U.S. 792, 800, 93 S.Ct. 1817, 1823, 36 L.Ed.2d 668 (1973); see Teamsters, 431 U.S., at 348, 97 S.Ct., at 1861.[27] Affirmative action "promptly operates to change the outward and visible signs of yesterday's racial distinctions and thus, to provide an impetus to the process of dismantling the barriers, psychological or

27. We have steadfastly recognized that affirmative race-conscious relief may provide an effective means of remedying the effects of past discrimination. See Wygant v. Jackson Board of Education, 476 U.S. ___, 106 S.Ct. 1842, 90 L.Ed.2d 260 (1986) (opinion of POWELL, J.) ("to eliminate every vestige of racial segregation and discrimination * * * race-conscious remedial action may be necessary"); id., at ___, 106 S.Ct., at 1861 (MARSHALL, J., dissenting) ("racial distinctions * * * are highly relevant to the one legitimate state objective of eliminating the pernicious vestiges of past discrimination"); Fullilove v. Klutznick, 448 U.S. 448, 100 S.Ct. 2758, 65 L.Ed.2d 902 (1980) (upholding 10% set aside of federal contract funds for minority businesses); University of California Regents v. Bakke, 438 U.S. 265, 98 S.Ct. 2733, 57 L.Ed.2d 750 (1978) (state university may consider race as a factor in admissions process); United Jewish Organizations of Williamsburgh Inc. v. Carey, 430 U.S. 144, 97 S.Ct. 996, 51 L.Ed.2d 229 (1977) (reapportionment of voting districts in accordance with specific numerical racial goals permissible under Voting Rights Act of 1965); McDaniel v. Barresi, 402 U.S. 39, 91 S.Ct. 1287, 28 L.Ed.2d 582 (1971) (School Board properly took race into account in redrawing school districts); Swann v. Charlotte-Mecklenburg Board of Education, 402 U.S. 1, 91 S.Ct. 1267, 28 L.Ed.2d 554 (1971) (court may use mathematical racial ratios as starting point for remedying school segregation); United States v. Montgomery County Board of Education, 395 U.S. 225, 89 S.Ct. 1670, 23 L.Ed.2d 263 (1969) (court may properly impose flexible racial ratios for faculty and staff).

otherwise, erected by past practices." NAACP v. Allen, 493 F.2d 614, 621 (CA5 1974).

Finally, a district court may find it necessary to order interim hiring or promotional goals pending the development of nondiscriminatory hiring or promotion procedures. In these cases, the use of numerical goals provides a compromise between two unacceptable alternatives: an outright ban on hiring or promotions, or continued use of a discriminatory selection procedure.

We have previously suggested that courts may utilize certain kinds of racial preferences to remedy past discrimination under Title VII. See Fullilove v. Klutznick, 448 U.S. 448, 483, 100 S.Ct. 2758, 2777, 65 L.Ed.2d 902 (1980) (opinion of BURGER, C.J.) University of California Regents v. Bakke, 438 U.S. 265, 353, 98 S.Ct. 2733, 2780, 57 L.Ed.2d 750 (1978) (opinion of BRENNAN, WHITE, MARSHALL, and BLACKMUN, JJ.) The Courts of Appeals have unanimously agreed that racial preferences may be used, in appropriate cases, to remedy past discrimination under Title VII.[28]

C

Despite the fact that the plain language of § 706(g) and the purposes of Title VII suggest the opposite, petitioners and the Solicitor General maintain that the legislative history indicates that Congress intended that affirmative relief under § 706(g) benefit only the identified victims of past discrimination. To support this contention, petitioners and the Solicitor General rely principally on statements made throughout the House and Senate debates to the effect that Title VII would not require employers or labor unions to adopt quotas or preferences that would benefit racial minorities.

Our examination of the legislative history of Title VII convinces us that, when examined in context, the statements relied upon by petitioners and the Solicitor General do not indicate that Congress intended to limit relief under § 706(g) to that which benefits only the actual victims of unlawful discrimination. * * *

* * *

* * * Our task then, is to determine whether Congress intended to preclude a district court from ordering affirmative action in appropriate circumstances as a remedy for past discrimination. See Brooklyn Savings Bank v. O'Neil, 324 U.S. 697, 706, 65 S.Ct. 895, 902, 89 L.Ed. 1296 (1945); Burnet v. Guggenheim, 288 U.S. 280, 285, 53 S.Ct. 369, 370–371, 77 L.Ed. 748 (1933). Our examination of the legislative

---

28. [Citations omitted]

Given the consistent record in the Courts of Appeals, some commentators have concluded that the legality of court-ordered race-conscious affirmative action under Title VII was "settled." See B. Schlei & P. Grossman, Employment Discrimination Law, ch. 37, p. 1200, and n. 20 (1976); C. Sullivan, M. Zimmer & R. Richards, Federal Statutory Law of Employment Discrimination § 13.2, p. 815, and n. 11 (1980); Blumrosen, Affirmative Action in Employment After Weber, 34 Rutgers L.Rev. 1, 39–41 (1981).

policy behind Title VII leads us to conclude that Congress did not intend to prohibit a court from exercising its remedial authority in that way.[37] Congress deliberately gave the district courts broad authority under Title VII to fashion the most complete relief possible to eliminate "the last vestiges of an unfortunate and ignominious page in this country's history," Albemarle Paper, 422 U.S., at 418, 95 S.Ct., at 2372. As we noted above, affirmative race-conscious relief may in some instances be necessary to accomplish this task. In the absence of any indication that Congress intended to limit a district court's remedial authority in a way which would frustrate the court's ability to enforce Title VII's mandate, we decline to fashion such a limitation ourselves.

4

Our reading of the scope of the district court's remedial powers under § 706(g) is confirmed by the contemporaneous interpretations of the EEOC and the Justice Department.[38] * * *

37. We also reject petitioners' argument that the District Court's remedies contravened § 703(j), since they require petitioners to grant preferential treatment to blacks and Hispanics based on race. Our examination of the legislative history convinces us that § 703(j) was added to Title VII to make clear that an employer or labor union does not engage in "discrimination" simply because of a racial imbalance in its workforce or membership, and would not be required to institute preferential quotas to avoid Title VII liability. See Weber, 443 U.S., at 205, n. 5, 99 S.Ct., at 2728, n. 5 ("§ 703(j) speaks to substantive liability under Title VII"); Teamsters, 431 U.S., at 339–340, n. 20, 97 S.Ct., at 1856–1857, n. 20 ("§ 703(j) makes clear that Title VII imposes no requirement that a work force mirror the general population"); Franks, 424 U.S., at 758, 96 S.Ct., at 1261 ("the * * * provisions of § 703 * * * delineat[e] which employment practices are illegal and thereby prohibited and which are not"). We reject the notion that § 703(j) somehow qualifies or proscribes a court's authority to order relief otherwise appropriate under § 706(g) in circumstances where an illegal discriminatory act or practice is established. See EEOC v. American Tel. & Tel. Co., 556 F.2d at 174; United States v. International Union of Elevator Constructors, 538 F.2d, at 1019; Patterson v. American Tobacco Co., 535 F.2d, at 273; Boston Chapter, NAACP, Inc., 504 F.2d 1028; cert. denied, 421 U.S. 910, 95 S.Ct. 1561, 43 L.Ed.2d 775 (1975); Rios v. Enterprise Assn. Steamfitters, Local 638, 501 F.2d 622, 631 (CA2 1974); Blumrosen, Affirmative Action in Employ-

ment After Weber, 34 Rutgers L.Rev. 1, 39 (1981).

38. Although the Solicitor General now makes a contrary argument, we note that the brief for the EEOC submitted by the Solicitor General in Weber, supra, described the 1964 legislative history as follows:

"To be sure, there was considerable concern that the Act would be construed to require the use of quota systems to establish and maintain racial balance in employers' work forces. [citations omitted]. The sponsors of the bill repeatedly assured its opponents that this was not the intent and would not be the effect of the statute. [citations omitted]. But these assurances did not suggest restrictions on remedies that could be ordered after a finding of discrimination. Instead, they made it clear that the statute would not impose a duty on employers to establish racially balanced work forces and that it would not require or even permit employers to establish racial quotas for employment in the absence of discrimination of the kind prohibited by the Act. [citations omitted]." Brief for the United States and the Equal Employment Opportunity Commission in United Steelworkers of America v. Weber, O.T. 1978. Nos. 432, 435 and 436, pp. 29–30.

The brief concludes that "the last sentence of Section 706(g) simply state[s] that a court could not order relief under the authority of the Act if employers took action against employees or applicants on grounds other than those prohibited by the Act." Id., at 30–31.

5

Finally, our interpretation of § 706(g) is confirmed by the legislative history of the Equal Employment Opportunity Act of 1972, 86 Stat. 103, which amended Title VII in several respects. One such change modified the language of § 706(g) to empower a court to order "such affirmative action as may be appropriate, which may include, but is not limited to reinstatement or hiring of employees * * * *or any other equitable relief as the court deems appropriate.*" 42 U.S.C. § 2000e–5(g) (emphasized language added in 1972). This language was intended "to give the courts wide discretion exercising their equitable powers to fashion the most complete relief possible." 118 Cong.Rec. 7168 (1972). While the section-by-section analysis undertaken in the Conference Committee Report stressed the need for "make-whole" relief for the "victims of unlawful discrimination," id., at 7168, 7565, nowhere did Congress suggest that a court lacked the power to award preferential remedies that might benefit nonvictims. Indeed, the Senate's rejection of two other amendments supports a contrary conclusion.

During the 1972 debates, Senator Ervin introduced an amendment to counteract the effects of the Department of Labor's so-called Philadelphia Plan. The Philadelphia Plan was established pursuant to Executive Order No. 11246, 3 CFR 339 (1964–1965 comp.), and required prospective federal contractors to submit affirmative-action programs including "specific goals of minority manpower utilization." Contractors Assn. of Eastern Pa. v. Secretary of Labor, 442 F.2d 159, 163 (CA3), cert. denied, 404 U.S. 854, 92 S.Ct. 98, 30 L.Ed.2d 95 (1971). Attacking the Plan as "[t]he most notorious example of discrimination in reverse," 118 Cong.Rec., at 1663, Senator Ervin proposed an amendment to Title VII that read, in relevant part: "No department, agency, or officer of the United States shall require an employer to practice discrimination in reverse by employing persons of a particular race * * * in either fixed or variable numbers, proportions, percentages, quotas, goals, or ranges." Id., at 1662. Senator Ervin complained that the amendment was needed because both the Department of Labor and the EEOC were ignoring § 703(j)'s prohibition against requiring employers to engage in preferential hiring for racial minorities. Id., at 1663–1664.

Senator Javits vigorously opposed Senator Ervin's proposal. First, he recognized that the amendment, while targeted at the Philadelphia Plan, would also jettison "the whole concept of 'affirmative action' as it has been developed under Executive Order 11246 *and as a remedial concept under Title VII.*" Id., at 1664 (emphasis added). He explained that the amendment would "deprive the courts of the opportunity to order affirmative action under Title VII of the type which they have sustained in order to correct a history of unjust and illegal discrimination in employment." Id., at 1665. To emphasize this point, Senator Javits had printed in the Congressional Record both the decision of the Court of Appeals for the Third Circuit sustaining the Philadelphia Plan, and a decision by the Court of Appeals for the Ninth Circuit affirming a District Court's Title VII remedial order requiring a union to indenture a certain percentage of black apprentices and to offer special programs for certain black applicants. Id., at 1665–1675 (reprinting Contractors Assn., and Ironworkers Local 86, supra).[39] Senator Javits summarized his attack on the Ervin amendment as follows:

> "[I]t would torpedo orders of courts seeking to correct a history of unjust discrimination in employment on racial or color grounds, because it would prevent the court from ordering specific measures which could assign specific percentages of minorities that had to be hired, and that could apply to government as well as private employers." Id., at 1675.

Senator Williams, referring to Senator Javits' examples of "the kind of situation that could be affected adversely" by Senator Ervin's amendment, argued that the "amendment would strip Title VII * * * of all its basic fiber. It can be read to deprive even the courts of any power to remedy clearly proven cases of discrimination." Id., at 1676. The Ervin amendment was defeated by a margin of 2 to 1. Ibid.

Senator Ervin proposed a second amendment that would have extended § 703(j)'s prohibition against racial preferences to "Executive Order Numbered 11246, or any other law or Executive Order," id., at 4917–4918; this amendment was also defeated resoundingly. Id., at 4918.[40] Thus, the legislative history of the 1972 amendments to Title VII confirms the availability of race-conscious affirmative action as a remedy under the statute. Congress was aware that both the Executive and Judicial Branches had used such measures to remedy past discrimination,[41] and rejected amendments that would have barred such reme-

---

39. Senator Javits also referred to the decision in United States v. Enterprise Assn. Steamfitters Local 638, 337 F.Supp. 217 (SDNY 1972): "I am told, and I believe the information to be reliable, that under the decision made last week by Judge Bonsal in New York, in the Steamfitters case, an affirmative order was actually entered requiring a union local to take in a given number of minority-group apprentices." 118 Cong.Rec. 1665 (1972).

40. The House considered a bill that would have transferred administration of Executive Order 11246 from the Department of Labor's Office of Federal Contract Compliance (OFCC) to the EEOC. See H.R. 1746, 92d Cong., 1st Sess. § 717(f) (1971); H.R.Rep. No. 238, 92d Cong. 1st Sess. 14–16, 57 (1971). Because OFCC had required contractors to adopt hiring goals in order to bid on federal projects, opponents feared that the bill would give the EEOC the authority to order racial quotas. Representative Dent proposed an amendment that read: "The Commission shall be prohibited from imposing or requiring a quota or preferential treatment with re-

spect to numbers of employees, or percentage of employees of any race, color, religion, sex, or national origin." 117 Cong.Rec. 31784 (1971). Supporters of this amendment repeated what the 1964 Congress had adamantly insisted upon: that "[s]uch a prohibition against the imposition of quotas or preferential treatment already applies to actions brought under Title VII." Ibid. (remarks of Rep. Dent); see id., at 32091 (remarks of Rep. Erlenborn). The bill ultimately passed by the House left the OFCC intact, and the Dent amendment never came to a vote.

41. In addition to the decisions cited by Senator Javits, other federal courts had, prior to the passage of the 1972 amendments, approved of the use of racial preferences to remedy the effects of illegal employment discrimination. See e.g., Carter v. Gallagher, 452 F.2d 315, 330 (CA8 1971) (en banc), cert. denied, 406 U.S. 950, 92 S.Ct. 2045, 32 L.Ed.2d 338 (1972); Local 53, Heat & Frost Insulators v. Volger, 407 F.2d 1047, 1055 (CA5 1969); United States v. Central Motor Lines, Inc., 338 F.Supp. 532, 560–562 (WDNC 1971); United States v.

dies. Instead, Congress reaffirmed the breadth of the court's remedial powers under § 706(g) by adding language authorizing courts to order "any other equitable relief as the court deems appropriate." 42 U.S.C. § 2000e–5(g). The section-by-section analysis undertaken by the Conference Committee Report confirms Congress' resolve to accept prevailing judicial interpretations regarding the scope of Title VII: "[I]n any area where the new law does not address itself, or in any area where a specific contrary intention is not indicated, it was assumed that the present case law as developed by the courts would continue to govern the applicability and construction of Title VII." 118 Cong.Rec., at 7166, 7564. Thus, "[e]xecutive, judicial, and congressional action subsequent to the passage of Title VII conclusively established that the Title did not bar the remedial use of race." Bakke, 438 U.S., at 353, n. 28, 98 S.Ct., at 2780 (opinion of BRENNAN, WHITE, MARSHALL, and BLACKMUN, JJ.); see also Boston Chapter, NAACP, Inc. v. Beecher, 504 F.2d 1017, 1027–1028 (CA1 1974), cert. denied, 421 U.S. 910, 95 S.Ct. 1561, 43 L.Ed.2d 775 (1975); United States v. Local 212, *IBEW,* 472 F.2d 634, 636 (CA6 1973); United States v. International Union of Elevator Constructors, Local 5, 538 F.2d 1012, 1017–1020 (CA3 1976); cf. North Haven Board of Education v. Bell, 456 U.S. 512, 534–535, 102 S.Ct. 1912, 1924–1925, 72 L.Ed.2d 299 (1982); Lorillard v. Pons, 434 U.S. 575, 580–581, 98 S.Ct. 866, 870, 55 L.Ed.2d 40 (1978).[42]

D

Finally, petitioners and the Solicitor General find support for their reading of § 706(g) in several of our decisions applying that provision. Petitioners refer to several cases for the proposition that court-ordered remedies under § 706(g) are limited to make-whole relief benefiting actual victims of past discrimination. See Ford Motor Co. v. EEOC, 458 U.S. 219, 102 S.Ct. 3057, 73 L.Ed.2d 721 (1982); Connecticut v. Teal, 457 U.S. 440, 102 S.Ct. 2525, 73 L.Ed.2d 130 (1982); Teamsters v. United States, 431 U.S. 324, 97 S.Ct. 1843, 52 L.Ed.2d 396 (1977); Franks v. Bowman Transportation Co., 424 U.S. 747, 96 S.Ct. 1251, 47 L.Ed.2d 444 (1976); Albemarle Paper Co. v. Moody, 422 U.S. 405, 95 S.Ct. 2362, 45 L.Ed.2d 280 (1975). This reliance is misguided. The cases cited hold only that a court may order relief designed to make individual victims of racial discrimination whole. See Teamsters, supra (competitive seniority); Franks, supra, 424 U.S., at 779, 96 S.Ct., at 1271 (competi-

Sheet Metal Workers International Association, Local 10, 3 Empl.Prac.Dec. ¶ 8068 (D NJ 1970).

42. Again, we note that the brief submitted by the Solicitor General in Weber urged this reading of the 1972 legislative history. The Solicitor General argued that "[a]ny doubts that Title VII authorized the use of race-conscious remedies were put to rest with the enactment of the Equal Employment Opportunity Act of 1972." Brief for the United States and the EEOC 31. Referring specifically to the amendment to the language of § 706(g), the Government argued:

"In light of Congress's keen awareness of the kinds of remedies courts had been granting in Title VII cases, and in light of the protests from Senator Ervin and others over the use of race-conscious remedies, this amendment to Section 706(g) provides substantial support for the proposition that Congress intended that numerical, race-conscious relief is available under Title VII to remedy employment discrimination." Id., at 35.

tive seniority); Albemarle Paper, supra, 422 U.S., at 422, 95 S.Ct., at 2373–2374 (backpay). None of these decisions suggested that individual "make-whole" relief was the *only* kind of remedy available under the statute, on the contrary, several cases emphasized that the district court's remedial powers should be exercised both to eradicate the effects of unlawful discrimination as well as to make the victims of past discrimination whole. Teamsters, supra, 431 U.S., at 364, 97 S.Ct., at 1869; Franks, supra, 424 U.S., at 771, 96 S.Ct., at 1267; Albemarle Paper, supra, 422 U.S., at 421, 95 S.Ct., at 2373. Neither do these cases suggest that § 706(g) prohibits a court from ordering relief which might benefit nonvictims; indeed several cases acknowledged that the district court has broad authority to "devise prospective relief designed to assure that employers found to be in violation of [Title VII] eliminate their discriminatory practices and the effects therefrom." Teamsters, supra, 431 U.S., at 361, n. 47, 97 S.Ct., at 1868, n. 47; see also Franks, supra, 424 U.S., at 770, 96 S.Ct., at 1267; Albemarle Paper, supra, 422 U.S., at 418, 95 S.Ct., at 2372.

Petitioners claim to find their strongest support in Firefighters v. Stotts, 467 U.S. 561, 104 S.Ct. 2576, 81 L.Ed.2d 483 (1984). * * *

* * *

* * * Relying on Teamsters, supra, we observed that a court may abridge a bona fide seniority system in fashioning a Title VII remedy only to make victims of intentional discrimination whole, that is, a court may award competitive seniority to individuals who show that they had been discriminated against. However, because none of the firefighters protected by the court's order was a proven victim of illegal discrimination, we reasoned that at trial the District Court would have been without authority to override the city's seniority system, and therefore the court could not enter such an order merely to effectuate the purposes of the consent decree.

While not strictly necessary to the result, we went on to comment that "[o]ur ruling in Teamsters that a court can award competitive seniority only when the beneficiary of the award has actually been a victim of illegal discrimination is consistent with the policy behind § 706(g)" which, we noted, "is to provide 'make-whole' relief only to those who have been actual victims of illegal discrimination." Id., at 579–580. Relying on this language, petitioners, joined by the Solicitor General, argue that both the membership goal and the Fund order contravene the policy behind § 706(g) since they extend preferential relief to individuals who were not the actual victims of illegal discrimination. We think this argument both reads Stotts too broadly and ignores the important differences between Stotts and this case.

* * * The purpose of affirmative action is not to make identified victims whole, but rather to dismantle prior patterns of employment discrimination and to prevent discrimination in the future. Such relief is provided to the class as a whole rather than to individual members; no individual is entitled to relief, and beneficiaries need not show that

they were themselves victims of discrimination.[45] * * * We decline petitioners' invitation to read Stotts to prohibit a court from ordering any kind of race-conscious affirmative relief that might benefit nonvictims.[46] This reading would distort the language of § 706(g), and would deprive the courts of an important means of enforcing Title VII's guarantee of equal employment opportunity.[47]

E

Although we conclude that § 706(g) does not foreclose a district court from instituting some sorts of racial preferences where necessary to remedy past discrimination, we do not mean to suggest that such relief is always proper. While the fashioning of "appropriate" remedies for a particular Title VII violation invokes the "equitable discretion of the district courts," Franks, 424 U.S., at 770, 96 S.Ct., at 1267, we emphasize that a court's judgment should be guided by sound legal principles. In particular, the court should exercise its discretion with an eye towards Congress' concern that race-conscious affirmative measures not be invoked simply to create a racially balanced work force. In the majority of Title VII cases, the court will not have to impose

45. Even where the district court orders such relief, we note that § 706(g) protects the right of the employer or the union to exclude a particular individual from its workforce or membership for reasons unrelated to discrimination.

46. The Government urged a different interpretation of Stotts earlier in this lawsuit. In July 1984, petitioners' counsel, in a letter to the Court of Appeals, argued that Stotts "affects the propriety [of the remedies ordered] by the district court." App. 5. In response, counsel for the EEOC submitted that "the decision in Stotts does not affect the disposition of the issues in this appeal." Ibid. Counsel explained that "the court's discussion [in Stotts] of § 706(g) is not relevant to the relief challenged by the appellants since it relates only to the award of retroactive or 'make-whole' relief and not to the use of prospective remedies," like those ordered by the District Court. Id., at 6. With respect to the last sentence of § 706(g), counsel stated:

"The last sentence of § 706(g) * * * deals with 'make-whole' relief and does not even address prospective relief, let alone state that all prospective remedial orders must be limited so that they only benefit the specific victims of the employer's or union's past discriminatory acts. Moreover, the language and the legislative history of § 706(g) support the Commissions's position that carefully tailored prospective race-conscious measures are permissible Title VII remedies

* * *. [T]he fact that this interpretation was consistently followed by the Commission and the Department of Justice, during the years immediately following enactment of Title VII entitles the interpretation to great deference." App., at 7–8.

47. The federal courts have declined to read Stotts broadly, and have instead limited the decision to its facts. See Pennsylvania v. International Union of Operating Engineers, 770 F.2d 1068 (CA3 1985), cert. denied 474 U.S. ___, 106 S.Ct. 803, 88 L.Ed.2d 779 (1986); Paradise v. Prescott, 767 F.2d, at 1527–1530; Turner v. Orr, 759 F.2d 817, 823–826 (CA11 1985); Vanguards of Cleveland v. City of Cleveland, 753 F.2d, at 485–489, aff'd ___ U.S. ___, 106 S.Ct. ___, 90 L.Ed.2d ___ (1986); Diaz v. American Telephone & Telegraph, 752 F.2d 1356, 1360 n. 5 (CA9 1985); Van Aken v. Young, 750 F.2d 43, 44–45 (CA6 1984); Wygant v. Jackson Bd. of Educ., 746 F.2d 1152, 1157–1159 (CA6 1984), rev'd on other grounds, 476 U.S. ___, 106 S.Ct. 1842, 90 L.Ed.2d 260 (1986); Kromnick v. School Dist. of Philadelphia, 739 F.2d 894, 911 (CA3 1984), cert. denied, 469 U.S. 1107, 105 S.Ct. 782, 83 L.Ed.2d 777 (1985); Grann v. City of Madison, 738 F.2d 786, 795, n. 5 (CA7), cert. denied, 469 U.S. 918, 105 S.Ct. 296, 83 L.Ed.2d 231 (1984); Deveraux v. Geary, 596 F.Supp. 1481, 1485–1487 (Mass.1984), aff'd, 765 F.2d 268 (CA1 1985); NAACP v. Detroit Police Officers Assn., 591 F.Supp. 1194, 1202–1203 (ED Mich.1984).

affirmative action as a remedy for past discrimination, but need only order the employer or union to cease engaging in discriminatory practices and award make-whole relief to the individuals victimized by those practices. However, in some cases, affirmative action may be necessary in order effectively to enforce Title VII. As we noted before, a court may have to resort to race-conscious affirmative action when confronted with an employer or labor union that has engaged in persistent or egregious discrimination. Or, such relief may be necessary to dissipate the lingering effects of pervasive discrimination. Whether there might be other circumstances that justify the use of court-ordered affirmative action is a matter that we need not decide here. We note only that a court should consider whether affirmative action is necessary to remedy past discrimination in a particular case before imposing such measures, and that the court should also take care to tailor its orders to fit the nature of the violation it seeks to correct.[48]

* * *

V

Petitioners also allege that the membership goal and Fund order contravene the equal protection component of the Due Process Clause of the Fifth Amendment because they deny benefits to white individuals based on race. We have consistently recognized that government bodies constitutionally may adopt racial classifications as a remedy for past discrimination. See Wygant v. Jackson Board of Education, 476 U.S. ___, 106 S.Ct. 1842, 90 L.Ed.2d 260 (1986); Fullilove v. Klutznick, 448 U.S. 448, 100 S.Ct. 2758, 65 L.Ed.2d 902 (1980); University of California Regents v. Bakke, 438 U.S. 265, 98 S.Ct. 2733, 57 L.Ed.2d 750 (1978); Swann v. Charlotte-Mecklenburg Board of Education, 402 U.S. 1, 91 S.Ct. 1267, 28 L.Ed.2d 554 (1971). We have not agreed, however, on the proper test to be applied in analyzing the constitutionality of race-conscious remedial measures. * * * We need not resolve this dispute here, since we conclude that the relief ordered in this case passes even the most rigorous test—it is narrowly tailored to further the Government's compelling interest in remedying past discrimination.

In this case, there is no problem, as there was in Wygant, with a proper showing of prior discrimination that would justify the use of remedial racial classifications. Both the District Court and Court of Appeals have repeatedly found petitioners guilty of egregious violations of Title VII, and have determined that affirmative measures were

---

48. This cautious approach to the use of racial preferences has been followed by the Courts of Appeals. As one commentator has noted:

"While the circuit courts of appeals have indicated that they possess [the] power [to award race-conscious affirmative relief], they have been reluctant to exercise it. The federal appellate courts have

preferred to issue less harsh orders such as recruiting and posting of notices of vacancies. They have tended to impose hiring orders only after employer recalcitrance has been demonstrated." Blumrosen, 34 Rutgers L.Rev., at 41.

See also Edwards & Zaretsky, Preferential Remedies for Employment Discrimination, 74 Mich.L.Rev. 1, 6–7 (1975).

necessary to remedy their racially discriminatory practices. More importantly, the District Court's orders were properly tailored to accomplish this objective.

VII

To summarize our holding today, six members of the Court agree that a district court may, in appropriate circumstances, order preferential relief benefitting individuals who are not the actual victims of discrimination as a remedy for violations of Title VII, see supra, Parts IV–A—IV–D (opinion of BRENNAN J., joined by MARSHALL, J., BLACKMUN, J., and STEVENS, J.); post, at ___ (POWELL J., concurring in part and concurring in the judgment); post, at ___ (WHITE, J., dissenting), that the District Court did not use incorrect statistical evidence in establishing petitioners' nonwhite membership goal, see supra, Part II–A, that the contempt fines and Fund order were proper remedies for civil contempt, see supra, Part III, and that the District Court properly appointed an administrator to supervise petitioners' compliance with the court's orders, see supra, Part VI. Five members of the Court agree that in this case, the District Court did not err in evaluating petitioners' utilization of the apprenticeship program, see supra, Part II–B, and that the membership goal and the Fund order are not violative of either Title VII or the Constitution, see supra, Parts IV–E, V (opinion of BRENNAN, J., joined by MARSHALL, J., BLACKMUN, J., AND STEVENS, J.); post, at ___ (POWELL, J., concurring in part and concurring in the judgment). The judgment of the Court of Appeals is hereby

Affirmed.

Justice POWELL, concurring in part and concurring in the judgment.

I join Parts I, II, III, and VI of JUSTICE BRENNAN's opinion. I further agree that § 706(g) does not limit a court in all cases to granting relief only to actual victims of discrimination. I write separately with respect to the issues raised in Parts IV and V to explain why I think the remedy ordered under the circumstances of this case violated neither Title VII nor the Constitution.

I

Petitioners contend that the Fund order and the membership goal imposed by the District Court and upheld by the Court of Appeals are forbidden by § 706(g) because that provision authorizes an award of preferential relief only to the actual victims of unlawful discrimination. The plain language of Title VII does not clearly support a view that all remedies must be limited to benefiting victims. And although the matter is not entirely free from doubt, I am unpersuaded by petitioners' reliance on the legislative history of Title VII. Rather, in cases involving particularly egregious conduct a District Court may fairly conclude that an injunction alone is insufficient to remedy a proven violation of Title VII. This is such a case.

* * *

The flexible application of the goal requirement in this case demonstrates that it is not a means to achieve racial balance. The contempt order was not imposed for the Union's failure to achieve the goal, but for its failure to take the prescribed steps that would facilitate achieving the goal. Additional flexibility is evidenced by the fact that this goal, originally set to be achieved by 1981, has been twice delayed and is now set for 1987.

It is also important to emphasize that on the record before us, it does not appear that nonminorities will be burdened directly, if at all.

* * *

* * *

JUSTICE O'CONNOR, concurring in part and dissenting in part.

I join Parts II–A, III, and VI of the Court's opinion. I would reverse the judgment of the Court of Appeals on statutory grounds insofar as the membership "goal" and the Fund order are concerned, and I would not reach petitioners' constitutional claims. I agree with JUSTICE WHITE, however, that the membership "goal" in this case operates as a rigid racial quota that cannot feasibly be met through good-faith efforts by Local 28. In my view, § 703(j), 42 U.S.C. § 2000e–2(j), and § 706(g), 42 U.S.C. § 2000e–5(g), read together, preclude courts from ordering racial quotas such as this. I therefore dissent from the Court's judgment insofar as it affirms the use of these mandatory quotas.

In Firefighters v. Stotts, 467 U.S. 561, 104 S.Ct. 2576, 81 L.Ed.2d 483 (1984), the Court interpreted § 706(g) as embodying a policy against court-ordered remedies under Title VII that award racial preferences in employment to individuals who have not been subjected to unlawful discrimination. See id., at 579–583, 104 S.Ct., at 2588–2590. The dissenting opinion in *Stotts* urged precisely the position advanced by JUSTICE BRENNAN's plurality opinion today—that any such policy extends only to awarding make-whole relief to particular non-victims of discrimination, and does not bar class-wide racial preferences in certain cases. Id., at 612–614, 104 S.Ct., at 2605–2607 (BLACKMUN, J., dissenting). The Court unquestionably rejected that view in Stotts. Although technically dicta, the discussion of § 706(g) in *Stotts* was an important part of the Court's rationale for the result it reached, and accordingly is entitled to greater weight than the Court gives it today. See id., at 582–583, 104 S.Ct., at 2590.

It is now clear, however, that a majority of the Court believes that the last sentence of § 706(g) does not in all circumstances prohibit a court in a Title VII employment discrimination case from ordering relief that may confer some racial preferences with regard to employment in favor of nonvictims of discrimination. Even assuming that some forms of race-conscious affirmative relief, such as racial hiring goals, are permissible as remedies for egregious and pervasive violations of Title VII, in my view the membership "goal" and Fund order in this case were impermissible because they operate not as goals but as racial quotas. Such quotas run counter to § 703(j) of Title VII, and are thus impermissible under § 706(g) when that section is read in light of § 703(j), as I believe it should be.

*   *   *

The plurality correctly indicates that, as to any racial goal ordered by a court as a remedy for past discrimination, the employer *always* has a potential defense by virtue of § 706(g) against a claim that it was required to hire a particular employee, to wit, that the employee was not hired for "reasons unrelated to discrimination." Ante, at 3049, n. 45. Although the plurality gives no clues as to the scope of this defense, it is clear that an employer would remain free to refuse to hire unqualified minority applicants, even if as a result the employer failed to meet a racial hiring goal. Thus, an employer's undoubted freedom to refuse to hire unqualified minority applicants, even in the face of a court-ordered racial hiring goal, operates as one important limitation on the extent of any racially preferential treatment that can result from such a goal.

The plurality offers little guidance as to what separates an impermissible quota from a permissible goal. *   *   *

To be consistent with § 703(j), a racial hiring or membership goal must be intended to serve merely as a benchmark for measuring compliance with Title VII and eliminating the lingering effects of past discrimination, rather than as a rigid numerical requirement that must unconditionally be met on pain of sanctions. To hold an employer or union to achievement of a particular percentage of minority employment or membership, and to do so regardless of circumstances such as economic conditions or the number of available qualified minority applicants, is to impose an impermissible quota. By contrast, a permissible goal should require only a good faith effort on the employer's or union's part to come within a range demarcated by the goal itself.

This understanding of the difference between goals and quotas essentially comports with the definitions jointly adopted by the EEOC and the Departments of Justice and Labor in a 1973 memorandum, and reaffirmed on several occasions since then by the EEOC and the Department of Labor. Memorandum—Permissible Goals and Timetables in State and Local Government Employment Practices (Mar. 23, 1973), reprinted in 2 CCH Employment Practices ¶3776 (1985) (hereinafter Memorandum); see 41 Fed.Reg. 38815 (1976) (EEOC Policy Statement on Affirmative Action Programs for State and Local Government Agencies); Office of Federal Contract Compliance Programs v. Priester Construction Co., No. 78–OFCCP–11 (Feb. 22, 1983), summarized in OFCCP Order No. 970a3, reprinted in 2 BNA AACM D:9121 (1983). In the view of these federal agencies, which are charged with responsibility for enforcing equal employment opportunity laws, a quota "would impose a fixed number or percentage which must be attained, or which cannot be exceeded," and would do so "regardless of the number of potential applicants who meet necessary qualifications." Memorandum, 2 CCH Employment Practices, at 3856. By contrast, a goal is "a numerical objective, fixed realistically in terms of the number of vacancies expected, and the number of qualified applicants available in the relevant job market." Ibid. An employer's failure to meet a goal despite good faith efforts "is not subject to sanction, because [the employer] is not expected to displace existing employees or to hire unneeded employees to meet [the] goal." Ibid. This understanding of the difference between goals and quotas seems to me workable and far more consistent with the policy underlying § 703(j) and § 706(g) than the plurality's forced distinction between make-whole relief and class-wide relief. If, then, some racial preferences may be ordered by a court as a remedy for past discrimination even though the beneficiaries may be nonvictims, I would employ a distinction such as this between quotas and goals in setting standards to inform use by district courts of their remedial powers under § 706(g) to fashion such relief.

* * *

I do not question that petitioners' past violations of Title VII were egregious, or that in some respects they exhibited inexcusable recalcitrance in the face of the District Court's earlier remedial orders. But the timetable with which petitioners were ordered to comply was quite unrealistic and clearly could not be met by good-faith efforts on petitioners' part. In sum, the membership goal operates as a rigid membership quota, which will in turn spawn a sharp curtailment in the opportunities of nonminorities to be admitted to the apprenticeship program. Indeed, in order for the District Court's timetable to be met, this fixed quota would appear to require "the replacement of journeymen by apprentices on a strictly racial basis." 753 F.2d, at 1195 (WINTER, J., dissenting).

Whether the unequivocal rejection of racial quotas by the Congress that enacted Title VII is said to be expressed in § 706(g), in § 703(j), or in both, a "remedy" such as this membership quota cannot stand. For similar reasons, I believe that the Fund order, which created benefits for minority apprentices that nonminority apprentices were precluded from enjoying, operated as a form of racial quota. Accordingly, I would reverse the judgment of the Court of Appeals on statutory grounds insofar as the membership "goal" and Fund order are concerned, without reaching petitioners' constitutional claims.

JUSTICE WHITE, dissenting.

As the Court observes, the general policy under Title VII is to limit relief for racial discrimination in employment practices to actual victims of the discrimination. But I agree that § 706(g) does not bar relief for nonvictims in all circumstances. * * * The remedy is inequitable in my view, and for this reason I dissent from the judgment affirming the Court of Appeals.

JUSTICE REHNQUIST, with whom THE CHIEF JUSTICE joins, dissenting.

Today, in Local Number 93 v. City of Cleveland, ___ U.S. ___, 106 S.Ct. 3063, 90 L.Ed.2d ___ (REHNQUIST, J., dissenting), I express my belief that § 706(g) forbids a court from ordering racial preferences that effectively displace non-minorities except to minority individuals who have been the actual victims of a particular employer's racial discrimination. Although the pervasiveness of the racial discrimination practiced by a particular union or employer is likely to increase the number of victims who are entitled to a remedy under the Act, § 706(g) does not allow us to go further than that and sanction the granting of relief to those who were not victims at the expense of innocent non-minority workers injured by racial preferences. I explain that both the language and the legislative history of § 706(g) clearly support this reading of § 706(g), and that this Court stated as much just two Terms ago in Firefighters v. Stotts, 467 U.S. 561, 104 S.Ct. 2576, 81 L.Ed.2d 483 (1984). Because of this, I would not reach the equal protection question. * * *

LOCAL NO. 93, INTERNATIONAL ASSOCIATION OF FIREFIGHTERS, AFL–CIO C.L.C. v. CLEVELAND ET AL.

The Supreme Court of the United States, 1986.
—— U.S. ——, 106 S.Ct. 3063, 92 L.Ed.2d 405.

JUSTICE BRENNAN delivered the Opinion of the Court.

The question presented in this case is whether § 706(g) of Title VII of the Civil Rights Act of 1964, as amended, 42 U.S.C. § 2000e–5(g), precludes the entry of a consent decree which provides relief that may benefit individuals who were not the actual victims of defendant's discriminatory practice.

[On October 23, 1980, the Vanguard of Cleveland an organization of Black and Hispanic Firefighters employed by the City of Cleveland (hereinafter the City), filed a complaint charging the City and various municipal employees with discrimination on the basis of race and national origin in the hiring, assignment and promotion of firefighters within the City Fire Department.

The Vanguards claimed the City had violated the rights of the Plaintiff class under the Thirteenth and Fourteenth Amendments to the United States Constitution, Title VII of the Civil Rights Act of 1964, and 42 U.S.C. §§ 1981 and 1983.

The complaint alleged that discrimination was effectuated by intentional practices of the City, use of discriminatory written examinations in making promotions, that the discriminatory test was reenforced by the use of seniority points and manipulation of retirement dates, and that the City limited minority advancement by refusing to administer a new promotional examination thereby cancelling the effects of increased minority hiring that had resulted from earlier litigation.

Previously, the City had lost a suit charging race discrimination and hiring and promotion (the Police Department) see Shield Club v. Cleveland, 370 F.Supp. 251 (N.D. Ohio 1972). That law suit resulted in an injunction against certain hiring and promotion practices and established minority hiring goals. Subsequently, the hiring goals were adjusted and promotion goals were established pursuant to a consent decree. Thereafter, litigation raising similar claims was commenced against the Fire Department and resulted in a judicial finding of unlawful discrimination and an entry of a consent decree imposing hiring goals similar to the *Shield Club* litigation. See Headon v. City of Cleveland, C73–330 (N.D. Ohio 1975).

When the Vanguards filed their complaint the City had unsuccessfully contested many of the basic factual issues in other law suits.

In 1981, Local 93 of the International Association of Firefighters was permitted to intervene as a party plaintiff in the Vanguard suit. A proposed consent decree was submitted to the District Court in 1981 pursuant to negotiations between the Vanguards and the City. A two day fairness hearing on the proposed consent decree was held at which time Local 93 objected to the use of minority promotional goals and the nine year life of the decree. Additionally, the Union protested the fact that it had not been included in the negotiations. The Court deferred the proceedings and mandated that the Firefighters be included in discussions.

At a second hearing the Union continued to oppose any form of affirmative action. Pursuant to testimony at that hearing, the Judge persuaded the parties to consider revamping the consent decree along the lines of the Atlanta Plan and referred the matter to a United States Magistrate. After 40 hours of intensive negotiations under the Magistrate's supervision, the parties agreed to a revised consent decree that incorporated a modified version of the Atlanta Plan but submission of the proposed decree to the Court was conditioned upon approval by the membership of the local union. The membership rejected the proposal.

In 1983 the Vanguards and the City lodged a second consent decree with the Court and moved for its approval. Local 93 submitted its objections to the decree in writing but apart from expressing its opinion as to the wisdom and the necessity of the proposed decree, the Union failed to assert any legal claims against either the Vanguards or the City.

The District Court approved the consent decree finding that the statistics and testimony at the hearings revealed an historical pattern of racial discrimination in the promotions in the City Fire Department. It concluded that the decree was neither unreasonable nor unfair and that the amended proposal was more reasonable and less burdensome than the nine year plan that had been originally proposed. The Judge overruled the Union's objections and adopted the consent decree as fair, reasonable and adequate resolution of the claims raised in the action.

On appeal, the Sixth Circuit Court of Appeals affirmed, one judge consenting. (Vanguards of Cleveland v. Cleveland, 753 F.2d 749 (6th Cir. 1985)). The Court of Appeals found the consent decree to be fair and reasonable to nonminority firefighters and emphasized that the goals set forth in the plan were relatively modest and that the plan did not require the hiring of unqualified minority firefighters or the discharge of any nonminority firefighters. Moreover, the plan did not create an absolute bar to advancement of nonminority employees and was of short duration.

After oral argument before the Court of Appeals, the Supreme Court decided Firefighters v. Stotts, 467 U.S. 561, 104 S.Ct. 2576, 81 L.Ed.2d 483 (1984). Concern with the potential impact of *Stotts*, the Court of Appeals ordered the parties to submit supplemental briefs but ultimately concluded that *Stotts* did not affect the outcome of the case. It noted that in *Stotts* an injunction modifying the consent decree had been issued over the objection of the City, while in the instant case the City of Cleveland had agreed to the plan. Moreover, it distinguished *Stotts* on the grounds that the injunction imposed by the District Court had the direct effect of abrogating a valid seniority system to the detriment of nonminority workers while in the *Cleveland* case the consent decree assured the integrity of the existing seniority system.] *(Editor's Summary)

Local 93 petitioned this Court for a writ of certiorari. The sole issue raised by the petition is whether the consent decree is an impermissible remedy under § 706(g) of Title VII.[5] Local 93 argues that the consent decree disregards the express prohibition of the last sentence of § 706(g) that

> "*[n]o order of the court shall require* the admission or reinstatement of an individual as a member of a union, or *the hiring, reinstatement, or promotion of an individual as an employee,* or the payment to him of any back pay, *if such individual* was refused admission, suspended, or expelled, or *was refused employment or advancement* or was suspended or discharged *for any reason other than discrimination on account of race,* color, religion, sex, or national origin or

---

5. The petition for certiorari sets forth two questions:

"1. May a District Court adopt provisions in a consent decree purporting to remedy a Title VII violation that it would have had no authority to order as a remedy if the matter had gone to trial?

"2. May a municipal employer voluntarily adopt an affirmative action promotional scheme over the objections of an intervenor union duly elected to represent all employees when said promotional scheme adversely affects the rights and interests of the employees and awards relief to minority employees regardless of whether they were actual victims of past racial discrimination?"

The first of these questions plainly asks only whether Title VII precludes the entry of this consent decree. Although the sec-

ond question can conceivably be read to embody a more general challenge respecting the effect of the consent decree on petitioner's legal rights, neither the petition for certiorari nor the brief on the merits discusses any issue other than whether this consent decree was prohibited by § 706(g) of Title VII. Moreover, petitioner limited its challenge below to whether the consent decree was "reasonable," and then, after *Stotts* was decided, to whether the consent decree was permissible under § 706(g). Finally, the District Court's retention of jurisdiction leaves it open for petitioner to press whatever other claims it might have before that court, see infra, at ___. Therefore, we deem it necessary to decide only the question whether § 706(g) precluded the District Court from entering this consent degree.

in violation of section 2000e–3(a) of this title." 42 U.S.C. § 2000e–5(g) (emphasis added).

According to Local 93, this sentence precludes a court from awarding relief under Title VII that may benefit individuals who were not the actual victims of the employer's discrimination. The Union argues further that the plain language of the provision that "[n]o order of the court" shall provide such relief extends this limitation to orders entered by consent in addition to orders issued after litigation. Consequently, the Union concludes that a consent decree entered in Title VII litigation is invalid if—like the consent decree approved in this case—it utilizes racial preferences that may benefit individuals who are not themselves actual victims of an employer's discrimination. The Union is supported by the United States as *amicus curiae*.[6]

We granted the petition in order to answer this important question of federal law. 474 U.S. ___, 106 S.Ct. 59, 88 L.Ed.2d 48 (1985). The Court holds today in Sheet Metal Workers v. EEOC, ___ U.S. ___, 106 S.Ct. 3019, 90 L.Ed.2d ___ (1986), that courts may, in appropriate cases, provide relief under Title VII that benefits individuals who were not the actual victims of a defendant's discriminatory practices. We need not decide whether this is one of those cases, however. For we hold that whether or not § 706(g) precludes a court from imposing certain forms of race-conscious relief after trial, that provision does not apply to relief awarded in a consent decree.[7] We therefore affirm the judgment of the Court of Appeals.

II

We have on numerous occasions recognized that Congress intended for voluntary compliance to be the preferred means of achieving the objectives of Title VII. Alexander v. Gardner-Denver Co., 415 U.S. 36, 44, 94 S.Ct. 1011, 1017, 39 L.Ed.2d 147 (1974); Albemarle Paper Co. v. Moody, 422 U.S. 405, 417–418, 95 S.Ct. 2362, 2371–72, 45 L.Ed.2d 280 (1975) (quoting United States v. N.L. Industries, Inc., 479 F.2d 354, 379 (CA8 1973)) (Title VII sanctions intended to cause employers " 'to self-examine and self-evaluate their employment practices and to endeavor to eliminate, so far as possible, the last vestiges of an unfortunate and ignominious page in this country's history' "). See also Teamsters v. United States, 431 U.S. 324, 364, 97 S.Ct. 1843, 1869, 52 L.Ed.2d 396 (1977); Ford Motor Co. v. EEOC, 458 U.S. 219, 228, 102 S.Ct. 3057, 3063, 73 L.Ed.2d 721 (1982); W.R. Grace & Co. v. Rubber Workers, 461 U.S. 757, 770–771, 103 S.Ct. 2177, 2185–86, 76 L.Ed.2d 298 (1983). This view is shared by the Equal Employment Opportunity Commission (EEOC),

---

6. The United States took exactly the opposite position in Steelworkers v. Weber, 443 U.S. 193, 99 S.Ct. 2721, 61 L.Ed.2d 480 (1979). See Brief for United States and EEOC in Steelworkers v. Weber, O.T. 1978, Nos. 432, 435, and 436, pp. 26–38.

7. We emphasize that, in light of this holding, nothing we say here is intended to express a view as to the extent of a court's remedial power under § 706(g) in cases where that provision does apply. That question is addressed in Sheet Metal Workers v. EEOC, ___ U.S., at ___, 106 S.Ct., at ___.

which has promulgated guidelines setting forth its understanding that "Congress strongly encouraged employers * * * to act on a voluntary basis to modify employment practices and systems which constituted barriers to equal employment opportunity * * *." 29 CFR § 1608.1(b) (1985). * * *

It is equally clear that the voluntary action available to employers and unions seeking to eradicate race discrimination may include reasonable race-conscious relief that benefits individuals who were not actual victims of discrimination. This was the holding of Steelworkers v. Weber, 443 U.S. 193, 99 S.Ct. 2721, 61 L.Ed.2d 480 (1979). * * *

Of course, *Weber* involved a purely private contractual agreement rather than a consent decree. But, at least at first blush, there does not seem to be any reason to distinguish between voluntary action taken in a consent degree and voluntary action taken entirely outside the context of litigation.[8] Indeed, in Carson v. American Brands, Inc., 450 U.S. 79, 88, n. 14, 101 S.Ct. 993, 998, n. 14, 67 L.Ed.2d 59 (1981), we held that a District Court's order denying entry of a consent decree is appealable under 28 U.S.C. § 1292(a)(1) because such an order undermines Congress' "strong preference for encouraging voluntary settlement of employment discrimination claims" under Title VII. Moreover, the EEOC's guidelines concerning "Affirmative Action Appropriate Under Title VII of the Civil Rights Act of 1964," 29 CFR pt. 1608 (1985), plainly contemplate the use of consent decrees as an appropriate form of voluntary affirmative action. See, e.g., § 1608.8.[9] True, these guidelines do not have the force of law, General Electric Co. v. Gilbert, 429 U.S. 125, 141, 97 S.Ct. 401, 410, 50 L.Ed.2d 343 (1976), but still they " 'constitute a body of experience and informed judgment to which courts and litigants may properly resort for guidance.' " *Id.,*

---

8. Unlike *Weber*, which involved a private employer, this case involves a public employer whose voluntary actions are subject to the strictures of the Fourteenth Amendment as well as to the limitations of § 703 of Title VII. In the posture in which this case comes to us, we have no occasion to address the circumstances, if any, in which voluntary action by a public employer that is permissible under § 703 would nonetheless be barred by the Fourteenth Amendment. Rather, as is explained below, *infra*, at ___–___, we leave questions regarding the application of the Fourteenth Amendment to the underlying agreement to further proceedings before the District Court. Nor need we decide what limits § 703 places on an employer's ablity to agree to race-conscious relief in a voluntary settlement that is not embodied in a consent degree, or what showing the employer would be required to make concerning possible prior discrimination on its part against minorities in order to defeat a challenge by nonminority employees based

on § 703. Cf. Wygant v. Jackson Board of Education, 476 U.S. ___, 106 S.Ct. 1842, 90 L.Ed.2d 260 (1986). In any event, there may be instances in which a public employer, consistent with both the Fourteenth Amendment as interpreted in *Wygant* and § 703 as interpreted in *Weber*, could voluntarily agree to take race-conscious measures in pursuance of a legitimate remedial purpose. The only issue before us is whether, assuming *arguendo* that § 706(g) would bar a court from ordering such race-conscious relief after trial in some of these instances, § 706(g) also bars a court from approving a consent decree entered into by the employer and providing for such relief.

9. The EEOC has not joined the Brief for United States in this case. The Solicitor General's brief has been filed only on behalf of the Attorney General, who has some limited enforcement responsibility under Title VII, see 42 U.S.C. § 2000e-5(f) (1), and the Federal Government in its capacity as an employer, § 2000e-16.

at 142, 97 S.Ct., at 411 (quoting Skidmore v. Swift & Co., 323 U.S. 134, 140, 65 S.Ct. 161, 164, 89 L.Ed. 124 (1944)). Therefore, absent some contrary indication, there is no reason to think that voluntary, race-conscious affirmative action such as was held permissible in *Weber* is rendered impermissible by Title VII simply because it is incorporated into a consent decree.

* * *

To be sure, consent decrees bear some of the earmarks of judgments entered after litigation. At the same time, because their terms are arrived at through mutual agreement of the parties, consent decrees also closely resemble contracts. See United States v. ITT Continental Baking Co., 420 U.S. 223, 235–237, 95 S.Ct. 926, 933–35, 43 L.Ed.2d 148 (1975); United States v. Armour & Co., 402 U.S. 673, 91 S.Ct. 1752, 29 L.Ed.2d 256 (1971). More accurately, then, as we have previously recognized, consent decrees "have attributes both of contracts and of judicial decrees," a dual character that has resulted in different treatment for different purposes. United States v. ITT Continental Baking Co., supra, 420 U.S., at 235–237, and n. 10, 95 S.Ct., at 934, and n. 10. The question is not whether we can label a consent decree as a "contract" or a "judgment," for we can do both. The question is whether, given their hybrid nature, consent decrees implicate the concerns embodied in § 706(g) in such a way as to require treating them as "orders" within the meaning of that provision.

Because this Court's cases do not treat consent decrees as judicial decrees in all respects and for all purposes, we think that the language of § 706(g) does not so clearly include consent decrees as to preclude resort to the voluminous legislative history of Title VII. The issue is whether, when Congress used the phrase "[n]o order of the court shall require" in § 706(g), it unmistakably intended to refer to *consent* decrees. In addition to the fact that consent decrees have contractual as well as judicial features, the use of the verb "require" in § 706(g) suggests that it was the coercive aspect of a judicial decree that Congress had in mind. * * *

* * *

* * * [W]hatever the extent of the limits § 706(g) places on the power of the federal courts to compel employers and unions to take certain actions that the employers or unions oppose and would not otherwise take, § 706(g) by itself does not restrict the ability of employers or unions to enter into voluntary agreements providing for race-conscious remedial action. The limits on such agreements must be found outside § 706(g).[11]

11. Thus, we do not suggest that voluntary action by employers or unions is outside the ambit of Title VII regardless of its effect on non-minorities. We already rejected such arguments in McDonald v. Santa Fe Trail Transp. Co., 427 U.S. 273, 96 S.Ct. 2574, 49 L.Ed.2d 493 (1976), and Steelworkers v. Weber, 443 U.S. 193, 99 S.Ct. 2721, 61 L.Ed.2d 480 (1979). Section 706(g) by its own terms, limits courts, not employers or unions, and focuses on preserving certain management prerogatives from interference by the federal courts. The rights of non-minorities with respect to action by their employers are delineated in § 703 of Title VII, 42 U.S.C. § 2000e–2,

From this, it is readily apparent that consent decrees are not included among the "orders" referred to in § 706(g), for the voluntary nature of a consent decree is its most fundamental characteristic. As we observed in *United States v. Armour & Co.*:

> "Consent decrees are entered into by parties to a case after careful negotiation has produced agreement on their precise terms. The parties waive their right to litigate the issues involved in the case and thus save themselves the time, expense, and inevitable risk of litigation. Naturally, the agreement reached normally embodies a compromise; in exchange for the saving of cost and elimination of risk, the parties each give up something they might have won had they proceeded with the litigation. Thus, the *decree* itself cannot be said to have a purpose; rather the *parties* have purposes, generally opposed to each other, and the resultant decree embodies as much of those opposing purposes as the respective parties have the bargaining power and skill to achieve." 402 U.S., at 681–682, 91 S.Ct., at 1757 (emphasis in original) (footnote omitted).

Indeed, it is the parties' agreement that serves as the source of the court's authority to enter any judgment at all. See United States v. Ward Baking Co., 376 U.S. 327, 84 S.Ct. 763, 11 L.Ed.2d 743 (1964) (cannot enter consent decree to which one party has not consented); Ashley v. City of Jackson, supra, 464 U.S., at 902, 104 S.Ct., at 257 (REHNQUIST, J., dissenting from denial of certiorari). More importantly, it is the agreement of the parties, rather than the force of the law upon which the complaint was originally based, that creates the obligations embodied in a consent decree. Consequently, whatever the limitations Congress placed in § 706(g) on the power of federal courts to impose obligations on employers or unions to remedy violations of Title VII, these simply do not apply when the obligations are created by a consent decree.

* * *

III

Relying upon Firefighters v. Stotts, 467 U.S. 561, 104 S.Ct. 2576, 81 L.Ed.2d 483 (1984), and Railway Employees v. Wright, 364 U.S. 642, 81 S.Ct. 368, 5 L.Ed.2d 349 (1961), Local 93—again joined by the Solicitor General—contends that we have recognized as a general principle that a consent decree cannot provide greater relief than a court could have decreed after a trial. They urge that even if § 706(g) does not directly invalidate the consent decree, that decree is nonetheless void because the District Court "would have been powerless to order [such an injunction] under Title VII, had the matter actually gone to trial." Brief for Petitioner 17.

We concluded above that voluntary adoption in a consent decree of race-conscious relief that may benefit nonvictims does not violate the

and, in cases involving governmental employees, by the Fourteenth Amendment. See Weber, supra; Wygant v. Jackson

Board of Education, 476 U.S. ___, 106 S.Ct. 1842, 90 L.Ed.2d 260 (1986).

congressional objectives of § 706(g). It is therefore hard to understand the basis for an independent judicial canon or "common law" of consent decrees that would give § 706(g) the effect of prohibiting such decrees anyway. To be sure, a federal court is more than "a recorder of contracts" from whom parties can purchase injunctions; it is "an organ of government constituted to make judicial decisions * * *." * * *

This is not to say that the parties may agree to take action that conflicts with or violates the statute upon which the complaint was based. As noted above, the fact that the parties have consented to the relief contained in a decree does not render their action immune from attack on the ground that it violates § 703 of Title VII or the Fourteenth Amendment. However, inasmuch as the limits placed by § 706(g) on the remedial authority of a federal court—whatever these may be—are not implicated by voluntary agreements, there is no conflict with or violation of § 706(g) when a federal court enters a consent decree that provides such relief. Accordingly, to the extent that the consent decree is not otherwise shown to be unlawful, the court is not barred from entering a consent decree merely because it might lack authority under § 706(g) to do so after a trial.

This simply was not the case in either Railway Employees v. Wright or Firefighters v. Stotts, in both of which the Court found conflicts between a judicial decree and the underlying statute. * * *

Because § 706(g) is not concerned with voluntary agreements by employers or unions to provide race-conscious relief, there is no inconsistency between it and a consent decree providing such relief, although the court might be barred from ordering the same relief after a trial or, as in *Stotts*, in disputed proceedings to modify a decree entered upon consent.

IV

Local 93 and the Solicitor General also challenge the validity of the consent decree on the ground that it was entered without the consent of the Union. They take the position that because the Union was permitted to intervene as of right, its consent was required before the court could approve a consent decree. This argument misconceives the Union's rights in the litigation.

A consent decree is primarily a means by which parties settle their disputes without having to bear the financial and other costs of litigating. It has never been supposed that one party—whether an original party, a party that was joined later, or an intervenor—could preclude other parties from settling their own disputes and thereby withdrawing from litigation. Thus, while an intervenor is entitled to present evidence and have its objections heard at the hearings on whether to approve a consent decree, it does not have power to block the decree merely by withholding its consent. See Zipes v. Trans World Airlines, Inc., 455 U.S. 385, 392, 400, 102 S.Ct. 1127, 1131, 1136, 71 L.Ed.2d 234 (1982); Kirkland v. New York State Dept. of Correctional Services, 711 F.2d 1117, 1126 (CA2 1983), cert. denied, 465 U.S. 1005, 104 S.Ct. 997,

79 L.Ed.2d 230 (1984). Here, Local 93 took full advantage of its opportunity to participate in the District Court's hearings on the consent decree. It was permitted to air its objections to the reasonableness of the decree and to introduce relevant evidence; the District Court carefully considered these objections and explained why it was rejecting them. Accordingly, "the District Court gave the union all the process that [it] was due * * *." Zipes, supra, 455 U.S., at 400, 102 S.Ct., at 1136.

Of course, parties who choose to resolve litigation through settlement may not dispose of the claims of a third party, and *a fortiori* may not impose duties or obligations on a third party, without that party's agreement. A court's approval of a consent decree between some of the parties therefore cannot dispose of the valid claims of nonconsenting intervenors; if properly raised, these claims remain and may be litigated by the intervenor. 3B Moore ¶ 24.16[6], p. 181; see also, United States Steel Corp. v. EPA, 614 F.2d 843, 845–846 (CA3 1979); Wheeler v. American Home Products Corp., 563 F.2d 1233, 1237–1238 (CA5 1977). And, of course, a court may not enter a consent decree that imposes obligations on a party that did not consent to the decree. See, e.g., United States v. Ward Baking Co., 376 U.S. 327, 84 S.Ct. 763, 11 L.Ed.2d 743 (1964); Hughes v. United States, 342 U.S. 353, 72 S.Ct. 306, 96 L.Ed. 394 (1952); Ashley v. City of Jackson, 464 U.S., at 902, 104 S.Ct., at 257 (REHNQUIST, J., dissenting from denial of certiorari); 1B Moore ¶ 0.409[5], p. 326, n. 2. However, the consent decree entered here does not bind Local 93 to do or not to do anything. It imposes no legal duties or obligations on the Union at all; only the parties to the decree can be held in contempt of court for failure to comply with its terms. See United States v. Armour & Co., 402 U.S., at 676–677, 91 S.Ct., at 1754–55. Moreover, the consent decree does not purport to resolve any claims the Union might have under the Fourteenth Amendment, see Wygant v. Jackson Board of Education, 476 U.S. ___, 106 S.Ct. 1842, 90 L.Ed.2d 260 (1986), § 703 of Title VII, see McDonald v. Santa Fe Trail Transp. Co., 427 U.S. 273, 96 S.Ct. 2574, 49 L.Ed.2d 493 (1976); Steelworkers v. Weber, 443 U.S. 193, 99 S.Ct. 2721, 61 L.Ed.2d 480 (1979), or as a matter of contract, see W.R. Grace & Co. v. Rubber Workers, 461 U.S. 757, 103 S.Ct. 2177, 76 L.Ed.2d 298 (1983). Indeed, despite the efforts of the District Judge to persuade it to do so, the Union failed to raise any substantive claims. Whether it is now too late to raise such claims, or—if not—whether the Union's claims have merit are questions that must be presented in the first instance to the District Court, which has retained jurisdiction to hear such challenges. The only issue before us is whether § 706(g) barred the District Court from approving this consent decree. We hold that it did not. Therefore, the judgment of the Court of Appeals is

Affirmed.

JUSTICE O'CONNOR, concurring.

* * *

JUSTICE WHITE, dissenting.

For several reasons, I am unable to join either the Court's opinion or judgment.

Title VII forbids racially discriminatory employment practices. The general proscription of § 703 is that an employer may not discriminate against either blacks or whites in either hiring or promotion. An employer may not, without violating Title VII, simply decide for itself or in agreement with its employees to have a racially balanced work force and displace employees of any race to make room for employees of another race. Even without displacing any present employees, Title VII would forbid quota hiring or promotion such as reserving every third vacancy or promotion for a black, or for a white for that matter. And if this is the case, it must be wholly untenable to permit a court to enter a consent decree requiring conduct that would violate Title VII.

Under the present law, an employer may adopt or be ordered to adopt racially discriminatory hiring or promotion practices favoring actual or putative employees of a particular race only as a remedy for its own prior discriminatory practices disfavoring members of that race. The Court's opinion pays scant attention to this necessary predicate for race-conscious practices, whether judicially imposed or voluntarily adopted, favoring one race over another. Instead, the Court seeks to avoid the issue whether the consent decree at issue violates the Title VII rights of nonminority employees by limiting itself to holding that § 706(g), which deals with remedies for violations of Title VII, has no application whatsoever to agreements and consent decrees such as are involved in this case. In so doing, the Court not only ignores the fact that the intervenors in this case have never restricted their claims to those based on § 706(g), see Pet. for Cert., at 7, but also adopts an unduly restricted view of the place of § 706(g) in the statute.

The Court purports to find support for its position in *Weber*, but this is not my understanding of that case. There, it was clear that the company had been hiring only those craft workers with prior experience and that the craft unions had excluded blacks. Hence, the company's craft workers were almost totally white. The company and the union negotiated a contract to break this discriminatory pattern, and we held that there was no violation of Title VII. But the company's prior discriminatory conduct provided the predicate for a temporary remedy favoring black employees. The *Weber* opinion stated that the agreement was a voluntary, private, race-conscious effort to abolish traditional patterns of segregation and hierarchy, 443 U.S., at 204, 99 S.Ct., at ___, and held that the agreement was not an undue attempt to overcome these racial barriers. The case did not hold that without such a predicate, an employer, alone or in agreement with the union, may adopt race-conscious hiring practices without violating Title VII.

Under current law, an employer who litigates a Title VII case to judgment cannot lose unless it is proved that it has discriminated within the meaning of § 703. It is therefore, untenable to conclude, as the Court does, that a district court may nevertheless enter a consent decree ordering an employer to hire or promote on a racial basis in a way that could not be ordered after a contested trial. Title VII was not enacted to protect employers against themselves, but to protect applicants and employees from racially discriminatory practices. There is no statutory authority for concluding that if an employer desires to discriminate against a white applicant or employee on racial grounds he may do so without violating Title VII but may not be ordered to do so if he objects. In either case, the harm to the discriminatee is the same, and there is no justification for such conduct other than as a permissible remedy for prior racial discrimination practiced by the employer involved. The Court should not deprecate that requirement and in effect make Title VII's proscription a one-way racial street, thus disserving the goal of ending racial discrimination in this country.

I agree with JUSTICE REHNQUIST that the consent decree in this case was not immune from examination under § 706(g). I also agree with JUSTICE BRENNAN's opinion in *Local 28* that in Title VII cases enjoining discriminatory practices and granting relief only to victims of past discrimination is the general rule, with relief for non-victims being reserved for particularly egregious conduct that a District Court concludes cannot be cured by injunctive relief alone. I disagree, however, with the Court in this case that we need not decide whether the remedy conforms to the limitations of § 706(g). * * *

* * *

JUSTICE REHNQUIST, with whom THE CHIEF JUSTICE joins, dissenting.

Petitioners challenge a District Court decree that ordered preferential treatment in promotions for minority firefighters at the expense of nonminority firefighters who would have been promoted under the City's existing seniority system. There was no requirement in the decree that the minority beneficiaries have been victims of the City's allegedly discriminatory policies. One would have thought that this question was governed by our opinion only two Terms ago in Firefighters v. Stotts, 467 U.S. 561, 578–579, 104 S.Ct. 2576, 2588, 81 L.Ed.2d 483 (1984), in which we said:

"If individual members of a plaintiff class demonstrate that they have been actual victims of the discriminatory practice, they may be awarded competitive seniority and given their rightful place on the seniority roster. This much is clear from Franks v. Bowman Transportation Co., 424 U.S. 747 [96 S.Ct. 1251, 47 L.Ed.2d 444] (1976), and Teamsters v. United States, [431 U.S. 324 [97 S.Ct. 1843, 52 L.Ed.2d 396] (1977)]. *Teamsters*, however, also made clear that mere membership in the disadvantaged class is insufficient to warrant a seniority award; each individual must prove that the discriminatory practice had an impact on him * * *. Here, there was no finding that any of the blacks protected from layoff had been a victim of discrimination and no award of competitive seniority to any of them. Nor had the parties in formulating the consent decree purported to identify any specific employee entitled to particular relief other than those listed in the exhibits attached to the decree. It therefore seems to us that in light of *Teamsters*, the Court of Appeals imposed on the parties as an adjunct of settlement something that could not have been ordered had the case gone to trial and the plaintiffs proved that a pattern or practice of discrimination existed."

But a majority of the Court todays holds that the District Court properly entered the decree in this case because it was a consent decree, whereas *Stotts* involved the *modification* of a consent decree. The Court apparently views a consent decree as one which may be structured almost entirely by the parties, even though the statute which the decree enforces may not authorize any such relief, and, indeed, may actually prohibit such relief.

*　*　*

The Court today repeats arguments made by the dissenters in *Stotts*, which did not command a majority two years ago, and also suggests that a restriction such as § 706(g) should apparently be narrowly construed because, if it were to limit the authority of the Court to enter a consent decree, it might hinder settlement of some cases. It would be just as sensible to say that the Norris-LaGuardia Act should be narrowly construed so as not to prevent a consent decree which would violate the Norris-LaGuardia Act since more consent decrees might be entered under that construction of the statute. Congress undoubtedly expressed a preference for conciliation in cases arising under Title VII, but not conciliation reached by violation of its express statutory commands.

Legislative history can obviously be mustered in support of the Court's interpretation of § 706(g), just as *Stotts* referred to the legislative history supporting the construction adopted in that case. But while the legislative history may be fairly apportioned among both sides, the language of the statutes is clear. *No order of the Court* shall require promotion of an individual whose failure to receive promotion was for a reason other than discrimination prohibited by the statute. Here the failure of the District Court to make any finding that the minority firemen who will receive preferential promotions were the victims of racial discrimination requires us to conclude on this record that the City's failure to advance them was *not* "on account of race, color, religion, sex, or national origin."

Chapter V

EEO AND LABOR RELATIONS LAWS

A. DUTY OF FAIR REPRESENTATION

STEELE v. LOUISVILLE & N.R. CO.

Supreme Court of the United States, 1944.
323 U.S. 192, 65 S.Ct. 226, 89 L.Ed. 173.

MR. CHIEF JUSTICE STONE delivered the opinion of the Court.

The question is whether the Railway Labor Act, 48 Stat. 1185, 45 U.S.C. § 151 et seq., 45 U.S.C.A. § 151 et seq., imposes on a labor organization, acting by authority of the statute as the exclusive bargaining representative of a craft or class of railway employees, the duty to represent all the employees in the craft without discrimination because of their race, and, if so, whether the courts have jurisdiction to protect the minority of the craft or class from the violation of such obligation.

* * *

The allegations of the bill of complaint, so far as now material, are as follows: Petitioner, a Negro, is a locomotive fireman in the employ of respondent railroad, suing on his own behalf and that of his fellow employees who, like petitioner, are Negro firemen employed by the Railroad. Respondent Brotherhood, a labor organization, is, as provided under § 2, Fourth of the Railway Labor Act, the exclusive bargaining representative of the craft of firemen employed by the Railroad and is recognized as such by it and the members of the craft. The majority of the firemen employed by the Railroad are white and are members of the Brotherhood, but a substantial minority are Negroes who, by the constitution and ritual of the Brotherhood, are excluded from its membership. As the membership of the Brotherhood constitutes a majority of all firemen employed on respondent Railroad, and as under § 2, Fourth, the members because they are the majority have the right to choose and have chosen the Brotherhood to represent the craft, petitioner and other Negro firemen on the road have been required to accept the Brotherhood as their representative for the purposes of the Act.

On March 28, 1940, the Brotherhood, purporting to act as representative of the entire craft of firemen, without informing the Negro firemen or giving them opportunity to be heard, served a notice on respondent Railroad and on twenty other railroads operating principally in the southeastern part of the United States. The notice announced the Brotherhood's desire to amend the existing collective bargaining agreement in such manner as ultimately to exclude all Negro firemen from the service. By established practice on the several railroads so notified only white firemen can be promoted to serve as engineers, and the notice proposed that only "promotable", i.e., white, men should be employed as firemen or assigned to new runs or jobs or permanent vacancies in established runs or jobs.

On February 18, 1941, the railroads and the Brotherhood, as representative of the craft, entered into a new agreement which provided that not more than 50% of the firemen in each class of service in each seniority district of a carrier should be Negroes; that until such percentage should be reached all new runs and all vacancies should be filled by white men; and that the agreement did not sanction the employment of Negroes in any seniority district in which they were not working. The agreement reserved the right of the Brotherhood to negotiate for further restrictions on the employment of Negro firemen on the individual railroads. On May 12, 1941, the Brotherhood entered into a supplemental agreement with respondent Railroad further controlling the seniority rights of Negro firemen and restricting their employment. The Negro firemen were not given notice or opportunity to be heard with respect to either of these agreements, which were put into effect before their existence was disclosed to the Negro firemen.

Until April 8, 1941, petitioner was in a "passenger pool", to which one white and five Negro firemen were assigned. These jobs were highly desirable in point of wages, hours and other considerations. Petitioner had performed and was performing his work satisfactorily. Following a reduction in the mileage covered by the pool, all jobs in the pool were, about April 1, 1941, declared vacant. The Brotherhood and the Railroad, acting under the agreement, disqualified all the Negro firemen and replaced them with four white men, members of the Brotherhood, all junior in seniority to petitioner and no more competent or worthy. As a consequence petitioner was deprived of employment for sixteen days and then was assigned to more arduous, longer, and less remunerative work in local freight service. In conformity to the agreement, he was later replaced by a Brotherhood member junior to him, and assigned work on a switch engine, which was still harder and less remunerative, until January 3, 1942. On that date, after the bill of complaint in the present suit had been filed, he was reassigned to passenger service.

Protests and appeals of petitioner and his fellow Negro firemen, addressed to the Railroad and the Brotherhood, in an effort to secure relief and redress, have been ignored. Respondents have expressed their intention to enforce the agreement of February 18, 1941, and its subsequent modifications. The Brotherhood has acted and asserts the right to act as exclusive bargaining representative of the firemen's craft. It is alleged that in that capacity it is under an obligation and duty imposed by the Act to represent the Negro firemen impartially and in good faith; but instead, in its notice to and contracts with the railroads, it has been hostile and disloyal to the Negro firemen, has deliberately discriminated against them, and has sought to deprive them of their seniority rights and to drive them out of employment in their craft, all in order to create a monopoly of employment for Brotherhood members.

The Supreme Court of Alabama took jurisdiction of the cause but held on the merits that petitioner's complaint stated no cause of action.

It thought that the Brotherhood was empowered by the statute to enter into the agreement of February 18, 1941, and that by virtue of the statute the Brotherhood has power by agreement with the Railroad both to create the seniority rights of petitioner and his fellow Negro employees and to destroy them. It construed the statute, not as creating the relationship of principal and agent between the members of the craft and the Brotherhood, but as conferring on the Brotherhood plenary authority to treat with the Railroad and enter into contracts fixing rates of pay and working conditions for the craft as a whole without any legal obligation or duty to protect the rights of minorities from discrimination or unfair treatment, however gross. Consequently it held that neither the Brotherhood nor the Railroad violated any rights of petitioner or his fellow Negro employees by negotiating the contracts discriminating against them.

If, as the state court has held, the Act confers this power on the bargaining representative of a craft or class of employees without any commensurate statutory duty toward its members, constitutional questions arise. For the representative is clothed with power not unlike that of a legislature which is subject to constitutional limitations on its power to deny, restrict, destroy or discriminate against the rights of those for whom it legislates and which is also under an affirmative constitutional duty equally to protect those rights. If the Railway Labor Act purports to impose on petitioner and the other Negro members of the craft the legal duty to comply with the terms of a contract whereby the representative has discriminatorily restricted their employment for the benefit and advantage of the Brotherhood's own members, we must decide the constitutional questions which petitioner raises in his pleading.

But we think that Congress, in enacting the Railway Labor Act and authorizing a labor union, chosen by a majority of a craft, to represent the craft, did not intend to confer plenary power upon the union to sacrifice, for the benefit of its members, rights of the minority of the craft, without imposing on it any duty to protect the minority. Since petitioner and the other Negro members of the craft are not members of the Brotherhood or eligible for membership, the authority to act for them is derived not from their action or consent but wholly from the command of the Act.

Unless the labor union representing a craft owes some duty to represent non-union members of the craft, at least to the extent of not discriminating against them as such in the contracts which it makes as their representative, the minority would be left with no means of protecting their interests, or indeed, their right to earn a livelihood by pursuing the occupation in which they are employed. While the majority of the craft chooses the bargaining representative, when chosen it represents, as the Act by its terms makes plain, the craft or class, and not the majority. The fair interpretation of the statutory language is that the organization chosen to represent a craft is to represent all its members, the majority as well as the minority, and it is to act for and not against those whom it represents.[3] It is a principle of general application that the exercise of a granted power to act in behalf of others involves the assumption toward them of a duty to exercise the power in their interest and behalf, and that such a grant of power will not be deemed to dispense with all duty toward those for whom it is exercised unless so expressed.

We think that the Railway Labor Act imposes upon the statutory representative of a craft at least as exacting a duty to protect equally the interests of the members of the craft as the Constitution imposes upon a legislature to give equal protection to the interests of those for whom it legislates. Congress has seen fit to clothe the bargaining representative with powers comparable to those possessed by a legislative body both to create and restrict the rights of those whom it represents, cf. J.I. Case Co. v. National Labor Relations Board, supra, 321 U.S. 335, 64 S.Ct. 579, but it has also imposed on the representative a corresponding duty. We hold that the language of the Act to which we have referred, read in the light of the purposes of the Act, expresses the aim of Congress to impose on the bargaining representative of a craft or class of employees the duty to exercise fairly the power conferred upon it in behalf of all those for whom it acts, without hostile discrimination against them.

This does not mean that the statutory representative of a craft is barred from making contracts which may have unfavorable effects on some of the members of the craft represented. Variations in the terms

3. Compare the House Committee Report on the N.L.R.A. (H.Rep. No. 1147, 74th Cong., 1st Sess., pp. 20–22) indicating that although the principle of majority rule "written into the statute books by Congress in the Railway Labor Act of 1934" was to be applicable to the bargaining unit under the N.L.R.A., the employer was required to give "equally advantageous terms to nonmembers of the labor organization negotiating the agreement." See also the Senate Committee Report on the N.L.R.A. to the same effect. S.Rep. No. 573, 74th Cong., 1st Sess., p. 13.

of the contract based on differences relevant to the authorized purposes of the contract in conditions to which they are to be applied, such as differences in seniority, the type of work performed, the competence and skill with which it is performed, are within the scope of the bargaining representation of a craft, all of whose members are not identical in their interest or merit. * * * Without attempting to mark the allowable limits of differences in the terms of contracts based on differences of conditions to which they apply, it is enough for present purposes to say that the statutory power to represent a craft and to make contracts as to wages, hours and working conditions does not include the authority to make among members of the craft discriminations not based on such relevant differences. Here the discriminations based on race alone are obviously irrelevant and invidious. Congress plainly did not undertake to authorize the bargaining representative to make such discriminations. Cf. Yick Wo v. Hopkins, 118 U.S. 356, 6 S.Ct. 1064, 30 L.Ed. 220; Yu Cong Eng v. Trinidad, 271 U.S. 500, 46 S.Ct. 619, 70 L.Ed. 1059; State of Missouri ex rel. Gaines v. Canada, 305 U.S. 337, 59 S.Ct. 232, 83 L.Ed. 208; Hill v. Texas, 316 U.S. 400, 62 S.Ct. 1159, 86 L.Ed. 1559.

The representative which thus discriminates may be enjoined from so doing, and its members may be enjoined from taking the benefit of such discriminatory action. No more is the Railroad bound by or entitled to take the benefit of a contract which the bargaining representative is prohibited by the statute from making. In both cases the right asserted, which is derived from the duty imposed by the statute on the bargaining representative, is a federal right implied from the statute and the policy which it has adopted. It is the federal statute which condemns as unlawful the Brotherhood's conduct. "The extent and nature of the legal consequences of this condemnation, though left by the statute to judicial determination, are nevertheless to be derived from it and the federal policy which it has adopted."

* * *

We conclude that the duty which the statute imposes on a union representative of a craft to represent the interests of all its members stands on no different footing and that the statute contemplates resort to the usual judicial remedies of injunction and award of damages when appropriate for breach of that duty.

The judgment is accordingly reversed and remanded for further proceedings not inconsistent with this opinion.

Reversed.

MR. JUSTICE BLACK concurs in the result.

MR. JUSTICE MURPHY, concurring.

Notes

In Wallace Corporation v. The National Labor Relations Board, 323 U.S. 248, 65 S.Ct. 238, 89 L.Ed. 216 (1944), which was decided on the same day as Steele v. The Louisville & Nashville Railroad, supra, the Supreme Court determined that the duty of fair representation applied to labor organizations operating under the Wagner Act as well. The case involved an unfair labor practice committed by the employer in setting up and maintaining a union in order to frustrate unionization of its plant by an outside union, an unfair labor practice under the law in 1944. The Wagner Act did not include any union unfair labor practices. However, the court declared that: "The duties of a bargaining agent selected under the terms of the Act extend beyond the mere representation of the interests of its own group members. By its selection as bargaining representative, it has become the agent of all employees, charged with the responsibility of representing their interests fairly and impartially. Otherwise, employees who are not members of a selected union at the time it is chosen by the majority would be left without adequate representation." This case is oft overlooked as the first case in which the Court concluded that the duty of fair representation was applicable to unions operating under the National Labor Relations Act. Ford Motor Company v. Huffman, 345 U.S. 330, 73 S.Ct. 681, 97 L.Ed. 1048 (1953) is frequently cited as the authority for the applicability of the duty of fair representation to National Labor Relations Act matters. That case, which also involved a challenge to fictional seniority, does indeed invoke the union's duty of fair representation. It also makes clear that labor organizations have a wide range of reasonableness in choice of positions in representing the diverse membership. Neither the *Wallace Corporation* case nor Ford Motor Company v. Huffman involved racial discrimination. Thus, from the inception of the duty of fair representation it was not restricted to race. The Supreme Court made clear, however, in Syres v. Oil Workers International Union, 223 F.2d 739 (5th Cir.1955), reversed and remanded per curiam 350 U.S. 892, 76 S.Ct. 152, 100 L.Ed. 785 (1955) that the duty of fair representation under the National Labor Relations Act was applicable to racial discrimination. The Court has also made clear that the duty is applicable to the administration and enforcement of collective bargaining agreements as well as to the negotiation process. Conley v. Gibson, 355 U.S. 41, 78 S.Ct. 99, 2 L.Ed.2d 80 (1957); Humphrey v. Moore, 375 U.S. 335, 84 S.Ct. 363, 11 L.Ed.2d 370 (1964).

Although the duty from its inception was more comprehensive than just racial discrimination, during the first twenty years of its existence it was used primarily in race cases. It was also not a very effective mechanism for dealing with employment discrimination. See Herring, "The Fair Representation Doctrine: An Effective Weapon Against Union Racial Discrimination?" 24 Md.L.Rev. 113 (1964).

The National Labor Relations Board and the DFR

In 1962, the National Labor Relations Board, badly divided, concluded that if a union breached its duty of fair representation, it committed an unfair labor practice under the National Labor Relations Act. Miranda Fuel Co., 140 N.L.R.B. 181 (1972), enforcement denied 326 F.2d 172 (2d Cir.1973). The genesis of the Board's applicability of the unfair labor practice provisions of the National Labor Relations Act to the union's breach of the duty of fair representation was an article by Cox entitled "The Duty of Fair Representation," 2 Villanova L.Rev. 151 (1957).

Undaunted by the mixed reception of its first venture into the DFR as ULP arena, the Board on July 1, 1964, one day before Congress passed the Civil Rights Act of 1964, issued its decision in the Hughes Tool Co., 147 N.L.R.B. 1573 (1964), finding racial discrimination by a labor organization a breach of the duty of fair representation. The Court of Appeals, in Local Union No. 12, United Rubber Workers v. N.L.R.B., 368 F.2d 12 (5th Cir.1966); and N.L.R.B. v. Local 1367, International Longshoremen's Association, 368 F.2d 1010 (5th Cir.1966) sustained the Board's interpretation of its statute.

Although the Supreme Court of the United States has not yet directly addressed the issue, in Vaca v. Sipes, 386 U.S. 171, 87 S.Ct. 903, 17 L.Ed.2d 842 (1967) the Supreme Court assumed, without deciding, that the union's alleged breach of its duty of fair representation would have constituted an unfair labor practice. In declining in that case to conclude that the NLRB's tardy assumption of jurisdiction of duty of fair representation breach cases preempted the field, the Supreme Court seems, at least implicitly, to have accepted the Board's interpretation of the statute.

The Board has held, and the Court of Appeals has sustained the interpretation, that a union commits an unfair labor practice by maintaining two different locals segregated on the basis of sex and by sex segregated processing of grievances. N.L.R.B. v. Glass Bottle Blowers Association, Local 106, 520 F.2d 693 (6th Cir.1975); Farmer v. ARA Services, Inc., 660 F.2d 1096 (6th Cir.1981).

In United Packing House, Food & Allied Workers International Union v. The National Labor Relations Board, 416 F.2d 1126 (D.C.Cir. 1969), cert. denied 396 U.S. 903, 90 S.Ct. 216, 24 L.Ed.2d 179 (1969) the United States Court of Appeals for the District of Columbia concluded that an employer's policy and practice of invidious discrimination against its employees on account of race or national origin inhibited its victims from asserting themselves against their employer to improve their lot. The court concluded that employer racial discrimination set up an unjustified clash of interests between groups of workers which tends to reduce the likelihood and effectiveness of their working in concert to achieve their legitimate goals under the Act; and racial discrimination creates in its victims an apathy or docility which inhibits them from asserting their rights against the perpetrator of the discrimination. The court found confluence of those two factors sufficiently deterred the exercise of Section 7 rights as to violate Section 8(a) (1). The court remanded the case to the Board for its consideration. On remand the Board found insufficient evidence to justify findings of racial discrimination. 194 N.L.R.B. No. 3 (1972). Subsequently, in Jubilee Manufacturing Co., 202 N.L.R.B. No. 2 (1973) the Board declined to accept the D.C. Court of Appeals' interpretation of the law in its *Packinghouse* decision.

The Supreme Court seems to be close to explicit acceptance of the Board's exercise of jurisdiction in DFR cases. In Del Costello v. Teamsters, the Court said "Even if not all breaches of the duty are unfair labor practices, however, the family resemblance is undeniable, and indeed there is substantial overlap. Many fair representation claims * * * include allegations of discrimination based on membership status or dissident views, which would be unfair labor practices under 8(a)(1) or (2). Aside from these clear cases, duty of fair representation claims are allegations of unfair, arbitrary, or discriminatory treatment of workers by unions—as are virtually all unfair labor practice charges made by workers against unions. * * * Similarly, it may be the case that alleged violations by an employer of a collective bargaining agreement will also amount to unfair labor practices." 462 U.S. 151 at 170, 103 S.Ct. 2281 at 2293.

It should be noted, however, as the membership and the philosophy of the National Labor Relations Board changes so too may its approach to the breach of the duty of fair representation.

The Board has had a longer history of policing its election and certification process for invidious and hostile discrimination. The following Board decision in *Handy Andy* traces the Board's past and enunciates a new policy.

B. DISCRIMINATION AND THE NLRB ELECTION AND CERTIFICATION PROCESS

HANDY ANDY, INC. v. TEAMSTERS, LOCAL 657

National Labor Relations Board, 1977.
228 NLRB No. 59, 94 LRRM 1354.

Before NLRB: MURPHY, CHAIRMAN; FANNING, JENKINS, PENELLO, and WALTHER, Members. * * *

The employer's sole objection to the issuance of a certification to the Union is that

[t]he Union * * * practices invidious discrimination by engaging in practices such as excluding persons from membership on the basis of race, alienage or national origin and/or is shown to have a propensity to fail to represent employees fairly.

The Employer contends that the Union's alleged discriminatory practices preclude it from being certified as an exclusive bargaining representative, citing Bekins Moving & Storage Co. of Florida, Inc., supra. As evidence in support of its objection, the Employer relies primarily upon several decisions by the United States Court of Appeals for the Fifth Circuit. In these cases, the court held, inter alia, that certain seniority provisions of the National Master Freight Agreement, to which the Union is a party together with various employers (but not the Employer herein), were unlawful because they perpetuated the effects of the employers' past discrimination. Consequently, the court found that the Union, by being party to such an agreement, had violated Title VII of the Civil Rights Act of 1964.

The Employer's reliance on *Bekins* is based on the majority's holding in that case that the Board is constitutionally required to consider issues raised by an objection grounded on alleged invidious discrimination prior to issuance of a Board certification of representative. As the majority noted in *Bekins*, however, the question of whether a labor organization's invidious discrimination constitutes objectionable conduct warranting withholding certification was a novel issue and one on which the Supreme Court has not ruled. We now conclude that the policies of the Act are better effectuated by considering allegations that a labor organization practices invidious discrimination in appropriate unfair labor practice rather than representation proceedings. Accordingly, for the reasons set forth hereafter, the *Bekins* decision is overruled.

In our view neither the Fifth Amendment to the Constitution nor the National Labor Relations Act, as amended, requires the Board to resolve questions of alleged invidious discrimination by a labor organization before it may lawfully certify the union as the exclusive bargaining representative of employees in an appropriate unit. Indeed, it appears to us that the contrary is true; namely, that the Board is not authorized to withhold certification of a labor organization duly selected by a majority of the unit employees. In so holding, we are fully cognizant of our continuing obligation under the statute to police the conduct of certified unions as it relates to their duty of fair representation. Issues relating to whether a union engages in unlawful race, sex, or other invidious forms of discrimination have historically been considered by the Board in the context of unfair labor practice proceedings. Such a proceeding, for the reasons discussed below, continues to be the appropriate vehicle for resolving such issues and for devising the appropriate remedies for unlawful discrimination including revocation of certification. This route recognizes the substantive and procedural differences between representation and unfair labor practice proceedings and affords the charged party the full panoply of due process of law without at the same time denying or delaying the employees' right to the services of their designated bargaining agent.

The majority in *Bekins* concluded that precertification consideration of alleged invidious discrimination by labor organizations is required by the Fifth Amendment to the Constitution because the Board may not lawfully bestow its certification upon a union which in fact discriminates on the basis of such considerations. The majority stated that, under the principle enunciated by the Supreme Court in Shelley v. Kraemer and subsequent cases, were the Board, as a Federal agency, to confer the benefits of certification on a labor organization which practices unlawful discrimination "the power of the Federal Government would surely appear to be sanctioning, and indeed furthering, the continued practice of such discrimination, thereby running afoul of the due process clause of the fifth amendment."

The foregoing statement misconstrues the "state action" doctrine as defined in Shelley v. Kraemer, supra, and its progeny. In *Shelley,* petitioners were blacks seeking to buy property covered by private restrictive covenants which prohibited occupancy of the covered premises by persons "not of the Caucasian race." The state courts had enforced the covenants and, consequently, had found that petitioner could not obtain valid title. The Supreme Court held that the agreement, standing alone, did not violate any constitutional right of petitioners, emphasizing that:

> [T]he principle has become firmly embedded in our constitutional law that the action inhibited by the [equal protection clause] of the Fourteenth Amendment is only such action as may fairly be said to be that of the States. That Amendment erects no shield against merely private conduct, however discriminatory or wrongful. [Footnote omitted].

The Court concluded, however, that enforcement of the covenants by state courts was state action subject to the equal protection clause. In so concluding, the Court commented:

> It is clear that but for the *active intervention* of the state courts, supported by the full panoply of state power, petitioners would have been free to occupy the properties in question without restraint.

> These are not cases * * * in which the States have merely abstained from action, leaving private individuals free to impose such discriminations as they see fit. Rather, these are *cases in which the States have made available to such individuals the full coercive power of government to deny to petitioners, on the grounds of race or color, the enjoyment of property rights* in premises which petitioners are willing and financially able to acquire and which the grantors are willing to sell. [Emphasis supplied.]

Thus, the prohibited state action in Shelley v. Kraemer was the *affirmative enforcement* by the State of a private agreement to discriminate.

Similarly, in Peterson et al. v. City of Greenville, 10 blacks were arrested for trespassing after refusing to leave a segregated lunch counter. In reversing their convictions, the Supreme Court noted that a local ordinance requiring segregation at lunch counters had removed the decision to segregate from the sphere of private choice, and thus sufficiently involved the State in the counter manager's discrimination to violate the equal protection clause. Thus, the case stands for the principle that a governmental body which *requires* a private party to discriminate runs afoul of the Fifth or Fourteenth Amendments.

The governmental action doctrine, as applied to statutes and regulations, was further expanded in Reitman v. Mulkey to extend to mere "authorization" of private discrimination. In that case, an amendment to the California state constitution, which prohibited any governmental agency within the State from abridging the absolute discretion of any property owner to sell or lease, or to refuse to sell or lease, his property to anyone for any reason, was declared unconstitutional. Although purporting to remain neutral on the question of private racial discrimination in housing, the amendment repealed two open housing statutes, and erected a barrier to attaining any such legislation in the future. The Court held that, taken in the context of the conditions and attitudes of its passage, the amendment "was intended to authorize, and does authorize, racial discrimination in the housing market." Thus, the prohibited state action in *Reitman* was *authorization* by the State of private discrimination.

Finally, in Moose Lodge No. 107 v. Irvis, a state liquor control agency, in granting liquor licenses, promulgated numerous regulations with which licensees had to comply. One of these required that "[e]very club licensee shall adhere to all of the provisions of its Constitution and By-laws." *Moose Lodge* had a provision in its constitution which denied membership to blacks. The trial court had relied on the pervasive regulation of the club's activity by the liquor control board in ruling that the agency was sufficiently implicated with the discriminating club to violate the fourteenth amendment. But the Court, in analyzing the amount of government involvement necessary to raise constitutional issues, rejected the trial court's reasoning, noting that "[h]owever detailed this type of regulation may be in some particulars, it cannot be said to in any way *foster* or *encourage* racial discrimination." (Emphasis supplied.) The Court held that only one regulation which had the effect of specifically requiring the club to discriminate was sufficiently involved with the private club's racially discriminatory policy to run afoul of the Constitution. None of the other regulations governing the operation of *Moose Lodge* were so entwined with the racial policies as to trigger the equal protection clause, because they did not specifically support the racial discrimination. * * *

* * *

We recognize, of course, that certification of a labor organization confers substantial benefits. The Board does not, however, by certifying a labor organization, place its imprimatur on all the organization's activity, lawful or otherwise. On the contrary, a certification is neither more nor less than an acknowledgment that a majority of the employees in an appropriate bargaining unit have selected the union as their exclusive bargaining representative. The choice of representative is made by the employees, and may not be exercised by this Board. * * *

Clearly, certification does not constitute enforcement or even approval of a labor organization's activities, and should not be construed as "state action" restricted by the Fifth Amendment.

* * *

* * * The Act and the Board's implementation of it can hardly be said to be "significantly involved" in the union's discrimination, since the duty of fair representation in its various forms *specifically prohibits* a union from practicing unlawful discrimination under the authority of the Act. Therefore, the Board, while it may extend the Act's protection to the union, is not involved in the union's discriminatory activities, a requirement of the governmental action doctrine.

* * *

A logical consequence of the *Bekins* constitutional determination is the conclusion that in their respective areas of authority the Federal agencies have overlapping responsibility for remedying any invidious discrimination by private parties. For example, one might argue that the Interstate Commerce Commission may not constitutionally approve a route of a common carrier which engages in discriminatory hiring practices or that the Securities and Exchange Commission is prohibited from approving a prospectus of a corporation which engages in such practices. This argument was recently rejected by the Supreme Court in National Association for the Advancement of Colored People v. Federal Power Commission, in which the Court held that the FPC does not have the authority to promulgate rules prohibiting its regulatees from engaging in discriminatory employment practices, but that the Commission does have authority to consider the consequences of employment discrimination in performing its mandated regulatory functions. * * *

* * *

Not only does the *Bekins* approach impair the national labor policy favoring collective bargaining, but it is ineffective in implementing an antidiscrimination policy. Denying certification and bargaining orders to discriminating unions may seem to be an effective sanction as the status of bargaining representative is the source of a union's power. However, many unions have no need of Board aid to gain or keep the position of bargaining representative. Most unions do not resort to certification elections to establish their majority status, and many unions which are certified would not be harmed by losing their certifications. Entrenched unions, which already have well-established bargaining relationships with employers, need no aid from the Board in maintaining their positions. Powerful unions, which can make effective use of such traditional self-help remedies as striking and picketing to force employers to bargain, have no need for bargaining orders. These powerful and entrenched unions are the ones with the least natural incentive to lower racial barriers, because they do not have to worry about attracting votes at representation elections as the weaker unions must. Thus the *Bekins* remedies fail to reach those unions likely to be the worst offenders. In addition, *Bekins*, by increasing the duration of representation cases, would create problems in applying Section 8(b)(7)(C) to picketing by unions whose representational eligibility is being litigated or has been denied by the Board. To prevent a union found ineligible for certification from engaging in recognitional picketing and thereby to secure the representative status unavailable through the Board's usual representation case processes, and to prevent the prospect of a series of election petitions followed by recognitional picketing, the Board would be under pressure to disregard the literal language of Section 8(b)(7)(C) by making any recognitional picketing by an ineligible union a violation of that section.

Also, under the majority *Bekins* holding, a labor organization could be denied certification upon the mere presumption that it will fail to discharge its responsibility to represent employees in *this* unit fairly solely because it has failed to represent employees fairly in some *other* bargaining unit, rather than on proof of such dereliction as to unit employees in a revocation proceeding. In fact, the Employer herein, in seeking to prevent the issuance of certification, relies upon discriminatory provisions in the Union's contracts in other bargaining units with other employers, contracts to which this Employer has never been a party and which were found to be unlawful solely because they perpetuated the other employers' past discrimination. For the Board to conclude that there will be further unlawful conduct solely on the basis of such evidence is directly contrary to our longstanding policy. Traditionally, as is true of virtually all court and administrative determinations, the Board's findings and remedies apply only to the particular parties before us.

The *Bekins* holding further would lead to anomalous situations such as that where an employer exercises exclusive control over hiring, resulting in the total absence of female and black employees in the unit, yet it is argued that this situation constitutes evidence of the union's propensity to practice discrimination and certification of the union would perpetuate this condition. In these circumstances it would be ludicrous to excuse the employer from its bargaining obligation.

* * *

We conclude that our statutory function of eliminating invidious discrimination of labor organizations is best served by scrutinizing their activities when they are subject to our adversary procedures and remedial orders. Indeed, the Board has long utilized unfair labor practice procedures to consider allegations of invidious discrimination by labor organizations and employers which interferes with Section 7 rights. We have done so with respect to unions by policing their conduct *vis-a-vis* the employees in units they represent through our power to remedy a labor organization's breach of its duty of fair representation. This doctrine was first enunciated by the Board in *Miranda Fuel Company, Inc.*:

> Section 7 thus gives employees the right to be free from unfair or irrelevant or invidious treatment by their exclusive bargaining agent in matters affecting their employment. This right of employees is a statutory limitation on statutory bargaining representatives, and we conclude that Section 8(b)(1)(A) of the Act accordingly prohibits labor organizations, when acting in a statutory representative capacity, from

taking action against any employee upon considerations or classifications which are irrelevant, invidious, or unfair. [Footnote omitted.]

This doctrine of the duty of fair representation was derived from the Supreme Court's decision in three companion cases: Steele v. Louisville & Nashville Railroad Co.; Tunstall v. Brotherhood of Locomotive Firemen & Enginemen; and Wallace Corporation v. N.L.R.B. In *Steele* and *Tunstall*, both of which involved racial discrimination by a union which was statutory representative under the Railway Labor Act, the Court concluded that such a representative "cannot rightly refuse to perform the duty, which is inseparable from the power of representation conferred upon it, to represent the entire membership of the craft." In *Wallace*, which did not involve race discrimination, the Court held that the same duty of fair representation was required of bargaining representatives selected under the National Labor Relations Act.

The duty of fair representation has become the touchstone of the Board's concern with invidious discrimination by unions. For example, it is well established that a labor organization's rejection of an employee's grievance solely because of his or her race breaches the duty of fair representation and violates Section 8(b)(1)(A), 8(b)(2), and 8(b)(3) of the Act. Similarly, we have held that a union's refusal to process grievances filed to protest an employer's segregated plant facilities constitutes a violation of Section 8(b)(1)(A).

In *Galveston Maritime Association, Inc.,* the Board held, again relying on the duty of fair representation, that a union's maintenance of a collective-bargaining agreement which allocated work on the basis of race violated Section 8(b)(1)(A), 8(b)(2), and 8(b)(3) of the Act. The Board premised the 8(b)(2) violation on its conclusion that the establishment, maintenance, and enforcement of discriminatory work quotas based on irrelevant, invidious, and unfair considerations of race and union membership discriminated against employees in violation of Section 8(a)(3) of the Act and that, by causing an employer to so discriminate, a union violates Section 8(b)(2). In holding that the work allocation violated Section 8(b)(3), the Board concluded that "a labor organization's duty to bargain collectively includes the duty to represent fairly," on grounds that collective-bargaining agreements which discriminate invidiously are not lawful under the Act and therefore do not meet the good faith requirements of Section 8(d).

The duty of fair representation is not limited to present discrimination, but is also breached by union policies which perpetuate past discrimination. Thus, in *Houston Maritime Association*, the union had a policy prior to September 1963 of refusing to accept black applicants for membership. In the latter part of that month, the union adopted a policy of closing its register of applicants and refusing to accept any further applications regardless of the applicant's race. In addition to finding that the union's new policy violated Section 8(b)(1)(A) and Section 8(b)(2) of the Act as an attempt to perpetuate past discrimination, the Board found that the employers who had participated in the pattern of unlawful conduct had thereby violated Section 8(a)(1) and (3).

While these cases clearly illustrate that we provide a remedy for breach of the duty of fair representation, thereby protecting employees from invidious discrimination by their bargaining representative, other remedies for a union's unlawful discrimination are also available. For example, we have held that a union commits unfair labor practices by attempting to force an employer to continue discriminatory practices even though no breach of the duty of fair representative is involved. Additionally, the Board has, in appropriate cases, revoked the certification of unions which engage in unlawful invidious discrimination.

As the foregoing discussion indicates, the Board has long recognized its obligation to consider issues concerning discrimination on the basis of race, sex, national origin, or other unlawful, invidious, or irrelevant reasons when they are raised in an appropriate context, and we shall continue to do so.

However, on the basis of all the foregoing, although we neither approve nor condone discriminatory practices on the part of unions, we hereby overrule *Bekins* as we conclude that the holding of that case is neither mandated by the Constitution nor by the Act and is destructive of the policies embodied in Section 9(c) of the Act. We further conclude that issues such as those raised by the Employer herein are best considered in the context of appropriate unfair labor practice proceedings. We do so on the basis of the paramount importance of avoidance of delay in representation cases, the procedural safeguards afforded in unfair labor practice proceedings which are not available in representation proceedings, the somewhat different purposes served by Section 8 and Section 9 of the Act, and the fact that effective procedures already exist for litigation of the type of discrimination alleged by the Employer herein.

We therefore overrule the Employer's objection and shall certify the Union as the representative of the employees in the unit found appropriate above.

* * *

JENKINS, Member, dissenting. * * *

In an attempt to rationalize their conclusion that the due process clause of the fifth amendment does not prohibit the Board's certification of a discriminating union, my colleagues assert that the view of the majority in *Bekins* that certification of a discriminating union violates constitutional restrictions misconstrued the Supreme Court delineation of the scope of prohibited state action. After reviewing a number of cases in which the Supreme Court held state action involved with invidious discrimination exceeded constitutional bounds, my colleagues state that such an involvement is found in circumstances, among others, where the government authorized private discrimination or fostered and encouraged private discrimination. They conclude, however, that certification of a discriminating union does not sufficiently involve the Board in the union's invidiously discriminatory practices to render its action unconstitutional because "a certification is neither more nor less than an acknowledgement that a majority of the employees in an appropriate bargaining unit have selected the union as their exclusive bargaining representative" and does not authorize the union to engage in discrimination.

This evaluation of the Board's involvement in the union's discriminatory practices is a patent understatement of the significant effects of certification. By certification the union becomes the statutory bargaining agent with statutory rights. Improper interference with the selection of the bargaining representative is the violation of "public, not private, rights."

* * *

"[W]hen a governmental agency recognizes such a union to be the bargaining representative it significantly becomes a willing participant in the union's discriminatory practices." *Mansion House, supra,* 473 F.2d at 473. The Board's conferring the status of statutory bargaining agent upon a union which engages in invidious discrimination clearly fosters and supports the union's discriminatory practices and this constitutes the Board's involvement in them under the standards which my colleagues acknowledge but contend are not applicable here. As the Supreme Court stated in Burton v. Wilmington Parking Authority, supra, where the state authority merely leased space in a public building to a private restaurant which denied service to blacks, there existed "that degree of state participation and involvement in discriminatory action which it was the design of the Fourteenth Amendment to condemn."

The Board's decisions holding breach of the duty of fair representation to be an unfair labor practice, with which I of course fully agree, are no substitute for the disqualification of a discriminating union in a representation proceeding. The Fifth Amendment does not permit a Government agency to provide the instrument for practicing discrimination merely because at some uncertain future date the Board may have an opportunity to terminate this discrimination in unfair labor practice proceedings set in motion by the charges of private parties if the General Counsel decides to file a complaint. The Board cannot initiate unfair labor practice proceedings. Moreover, for a variety of reasons, such proceedings may never be instituted notwithstanding the discriminatory exclusion of minorities from the union or from employment in the certified unit.

Notes

Bell & Howell Co. v. N.L.R.B., 598 F.2d 136 (D.C.Cir.1979), cert. denied, 442 U.S. 942, 99 S.Ct. 2885, 61 L.Ed.2d 312 (1979) the Court of Appeals concluded that nothing in the National Labor Relations Act required the National Labor Relations Board to consider allegations of discrimination prior to certifying a victorious union at least where the proffered evidence of discrimination related to past union misconduct outside the bargaining unit that the union sought to represent. This is a court acceptance of the Board's approach in Handy Andy and there seems little indication that reversal of that approach is likely to be successful in the near term.

NATIONAL LABOR RELATIONS BOARD v. EURODRIVE, INC.

United States Court of Appeals for the Sixth Circuit, 1984.
724 F.2d 556.

CELEBREZZE, SENIOR CIRCUIT JUDGE.

National Labor Relations Board (Board) applies for enforcement of its order, issued to Respondent Eurodrive, Inc. (Company), directing the Company to bargain collectively with Teamsters Local No. 957, International Brotherhood of Teamsters, Chauffeurs, Warehousemen and Helpers (Union). On February 20, 1981, the Union filed a representation petition with the Board, seeking to represent the Company's production and maintenance employees. The Company and Union thereafter entered into a Stipulation for Certification Upon Consent Election. On April 30, 1981, twenty-eight ballots were cast in the election; fifteen employees voted for and twelve voted against union representation. The Company challenged the conduct of Richard Loy, the Union's representative and requested that either the election be set aside or a hearing be held to resolve issues raised.[1] The Regional Director investigated the Company's allegations of pre-election misconduct and recommended that the Company's objections be dismissed. Following the Board's adoption of the Regional Director's recommendation, the Company filed a motion for reconsideration with the Board. This motion was denied and, after the Company refused to bargain collectively, the Union filed an unfair labor practice charge with the Board. By Decision and Order, dated March 31, 1982, the Board granted general counsel's motion for summary judgment on the unfair labor practice charge and subsequently filed this application for enforcement. We deny enforcement of the Board's order.

The dispute in this instance concerns the conduct of Teamster organizer, Richard Loy. According to the Company, Loy held two meetings for employees prior to the election. At the first meeting, held eight days prior to the election, Loy indicated that, unlike the Company's sole black employee, Robert Howard, white employees needed the Union to protect their jobs because white employees were not protected by the equal opportunity laws. In an attempt to illustrate the "white's

---

1. The Company initially raised four objections to the conduct of the election. In its Exceptions to the Regional Director's Report on Objections, the Company sought review of the Regional Director's recommendations with respect to only three of the objections. However, in its brief to this court, the Company contends that only Objection No. 3, concerning the conduct of the Union's representative, should not have been overruled. Accordingly, only the Board's decision regarding Objection No. 3 is before this Court. See 29 U.S.C. 160(e); NLRB v. Tennessee Packers, Inc., Frosty Morn Division, 344 F.2d 948, 949 (6th Cir.1965).

need for protection", Loy discussed the discharge of a white employee named Kim Morse. Morse had been dismissed approximately four weeks prior to the election because, despite repeated warnings, he directed racial harassment toward Howard. The harassment of Howard by Morse, which included racial slurs, jokes, insults and other comments, was tolerated by Howard for a considerable period of time before a complaint was made to management. Loy told those present at the meeting that Morse's discharge exemplified the "white's need for protection" and, further, promised that the Union could and would obtain his reinstatement with backpay. The Company also alleges that Loy pointed to Howard and stated that Howard would soon receive a paper to sign and, should he sign it, that Morse's reinstatement would be assured.[2] On the evening before the election, another meeting was held at which time Loy repeated his promise to have Morse reinstated. Based on these allegations, the Company claims that union organizer Loy made an effective appeal to racial prejudice which interfered with the employee's ability to make a reasoned choice in the election.

When the party objecting to pre-election conduct can establish that an evidentiary hearing is required to resolve substantial and material factual issues, the Board may order the Regional Director to hold such a hearing. NLRB v. Tennessee Packers, Inc., Frosty Morn Division, 379 F.2d 172 (6th Cir.1967). In order to obtain a hearing, the party objecting to the pre-election conduct must proffer specific evidence which demonstrates that the election was unfair, NLRB v. Basic Wire Products, 516 F.2d 261, 263 (6th Cir.1975); Harlan No. 4 Coal Co. v. NLRB, 490 F.2d 117, 120 (6th Cir.), cert. denied, 416 U.S. 986, 94 S.Ct. 2390, 40 L.Ed.2d 763 (1974), and this evidence must "prima facie warrant setting aside the election." NLRB v. Silverman's Men's Wear, Inc., 656 F.2d 53, 55 (3rd Cir.1981). In reviewing whether the Board properly denied a hearing to the objecting party, the court must determine whether the Board acted arbitrarily in exercising its discretion. E.g., NLRB v. A.J. Tower Co., 329 U.S. 324, 67 S.Ct. 324, 91 L.Ed. 322 (1946); Harlan No. 4 Coal Co. v. NLRB, 490 F.2d 117 (6th Cir.), cert. denied, 416 U.S. 986, 94 S.Ct. 2390, 40 L.Ed.2d 763 (1974).

An election will be set aside when the objecting party demonstrates that pre-election conduct "seeks to overstress and exacerbate racial feelings" through a deliberate appeal to racial prejudice.[3] Sewell

2. The affidavit of Andrew Nuss, who had been employed at Eurodrive for approximately four years, indicates:

"During this meeting [on August 22, 1981] Mr. Loy also singled out our only black employee, Bobby Howard. He said that Bobby did not need the Union because he had the protection of the Equal Opportunity laws, while the rest of us had no protection without the Union."

Furthermore, Nuss' affidavit indicates that Loy used phrases such as "it was no sweat", "he had it in the bag", and "there was no way he could lose" in referring to the Union's ability to effect Morse's reinstatement.

3. We are mindful that the Board has retreated from its earlier requirement that elections be conducted under "laboratory conditions." General Shoe Corporation, 77 NLRB 124 (1948). However, the Board still seeks to create "ideal (election) conditions insofar as possible", The Liberal Market, Inc., 108 NLRB 1481, 1482 (1954), and has repeatedly emphasized the importance of employees' free choice. See, e.g., TRW-

Manufacturing Company, Inc., 138 NLRB 66, 71 (1962). See Silverman's Men's Wear, Inc., 656 F.2d 53 (3rd Cir.1981). The Board itself enunciated the test used to determine whether pre-election appeals or arguments have no purpose except to exacerbate racial feelings:

> So long *   *   * as a party limits itself to *truthfully* setting forth another party's position on matters of racial interest *   *   * we shall not set aside an election on this ground. However, the burden will be on the party making use of a racial message to establish that it was truthful and germane, and where there is doubt as to whether the *total conduct* of such party is within the described bounds, the doubt will be resolved against him.

Sewell Manufacturing Company, 138 NLRB 66, 71–72 (1962) (emphasis added). The principle to be applied from *Sewell* is that "an effective appeal to racial *   *   * prejudice prima facie warrants setting aside an election." [4] NLRB v. Silverman's Men's Wear, Inc., 656 F.2d 53, 58 (3rd Cir.1981). See NLRB v. Katz, 701 F.2d 703 (7th Cir.1983) (The company's allegation that pre-election racial and religious slurs were made at a union organizational meeting established a prima facie case for setting aside the election.).

The Board acknowledges that Loy made the challenged comments, but asserts that the comments were merely "intemperate, abusive and inaccurate statements made by a union during an attempt to organize employees which statements are to be tolerated under the Act." Baker Canning Company v. NLRB, 505 F.2d 574, 576 (7th Cir.1974). Loy's comments concerning the equal employment opportunity laws, according to the Board, simply expressed his opinion that the sole black employee, as a member of a protected class, had more job security than the other employees. The Board further contends that Loy's statements indicating that the Company would have to reinstate Morse with backpay were no more than an expression of confidence that the Board would find that Morse had been unlawfully discharged. Accordingly, the Board does not believe that Loy's statements constituted an appeal to racial prejudice of sufficient seriousness to warrant a hearing. We disagree.

Pre-election statements which indicate that a union has made a deliberate appeal to racial prejudice prior to an election are material.

United Greenfield Division, 245 NLRB 1135 (1979); EDM of Texas, Div. of Chromalloy American Corp., 245 NLRB 934 (1979); El Fenix Corporation, 234 NLRB 1212 (1978).

4. The Board's decision in Sewell, which applies when the only purpose for challenged conduct is to arouse the racial feelings of voters in an election, Bancroft Manufacturing Company, Inc., 210 NLRB 1007, 1008 (1974), requires that an election be set aside if "the uninhibited desires of the employees cannot be determined". The Gummed Products Company, 112 NLRB 1092, 1093 (1955). The principle underlying this policy is that members of one race should "not be persuaded to vote for or against a union on the basis of invidious prejudices they might have against individuals of another race." NLRB v. Sumter Plywood Corp., 535 F.2d 917, 924–25 (5th Cir.1976), cert. denied, 429 U.S. 1092, 97 S.Ct. 1105, 51 L.Ed.2d 538 (1977).

E.g., Sewell Manufacturing Company, 138 NLRB 66, 71 (1962). In determining whether pre-election statements were intended to appeal to racial prejudice, both the Board and the reviewing court must consider the context in which these statements were made, see, e.g., NLRB v. General Telephone Directory Company, 602 F.2d 912, 915 (9th Cir.1979) (prior to determining whether an employer's pre-election statements are protected, court will consider the context in which the statements were made), and the "total conduct" of the person who made the statements. E.g. Sewell Manufacturing Company, 138 NLRB 66, 71 (1962). Prior to the election, racial tension existed between Howard and the Company's other employees; [5] this tension was due, in part, to the Company's decision to discharge Morse for racially harassing Howard. Accordingly, Loy's pre-election statements must be viewed in light of the pre-existing racial tension that existed at the time the alleged statements were made.

Loy's statement concerning the white employees' need for protection is, in itself, insufficient to establish any particular intent to exacerbate racial feelings among the employees prior to the election. Loy, however, did not simply inform the employees of the legal benefits available to minorities under the law or of the benefits available to all employees as a consequence of unionization. Instead, Loy decided to illustrate the "white's need for protection" by discussing the Company's recent decision to discharge Morse. Knowing that the Company discharged Morse for racially harassing Howard, the Company's sole black employee, and knowing that Morse's discharge aroused racial tension between Howard and the Company's other employees, Loy promised the other employees that the union could reinstate Morse with backpay if only Howard would cooperate. Loy then singled out Howard and informed the other employees that Howard's signature would assure Morse's reinstatement. Although some of Loy's statements were tangentially related to legitimate campaign issues, viewed in the context in which they were made, Loy's statements and total conduct placed undue emphasis on a racial issue which Loy must have known would exacerbate pre-existing racial tension among the employees prior to the election. Clearly, the Company's allegations raised a substantial and material issue; whether Loy made a deliberate appeal to racial prejudice which interfered with the employee's freedom of choice.

5. The Board concedes that "bigoted conduct" and racial tension existed among the employees prior to the election. It asserts, however, that the racial tension which existed between the Company's sole black employee and the other employees prior to the election was not a result of the Union's pre-election conduct. We accept the Board's conclusion in this regard. Clearly, the racial tension that existed in this case was not initially brought about as a result of the Union's actions. The crucial determination whether pre-election conduct is likely to affect the employee's ability to make a well reasoned and independent decision, however, does not depend necessarily upon the fault of the party *initially* responsible for the racial tension. In our view, a union that makes a deliberate attempt to exacerbate *existing* racial tensions prior to an election is as culpable as a union who *creates* racial tension to enhance its political strength.

Accordingly, we believe that the Board abused its discretion by refusing to grant the Company's request for a hearing.

Generally, when a reviewing court determines that a substantial and material question was presented to the Board, it remands the case for a hearing. E.g., Kitchen Fresh, Inc. v. NLRB, 716 F.2d 351 (6th Cir. 1983). In this instance, however, we can discern no useful purpose to be served by a remand. The Board has conceded that union organizer Loy's pre-election statements were made,[6] and that his statements were made in an atmosphere of racial tension.[7] In our view, the undisputed evidence is alone sufficient to establish that Loy engaged in a subtle, but deliberate attempt to exacerbate racial feelings among the employees prior to the election.

The sole question which remains is whether Loy's attempt to exacerbate racial feelings among the employees was "likely to have an appreciable effect" on the employees' selection. NLRB v. Gorbea, Perez & Morrell, S. en. C., 328 F.2d 679, 680 (1st Cir.1964). See e.g., NLRB v. Katz, 701 F.2d 703, 707 (7th Cir.1983) (Board's petition for enforcement of its bargaining order denied when court found that pre-election inflammatory comments "could have impaired" employees' freedom of choice); Advertisers Manufacturing Company v. NLRB, 677 F.2d 544 (7th Cir.1982) (Party challenging pre-election conduct must establish that such conduct impaired employees' freedom of choice); NLRB v. Basic Wire Products, 516 F.2d 261 (6th Cir.1975) (When pre-election conduct is challenged on the basis that it interfered with the election, the critical inquiry is whether employees were able to exercise free choice.).

In our view, Loy's statements were likely to have an appreciable effect on the employees' free choice. The proposed bargaining unit was small; that any employee would have been unaware of the racial harassment directed toward Howard is unlikely. Thus, the effectiveness of Loy's statements was multiplied by the already existing racial tension brought about by Morse's conduct and subsequent discharge. Moreover, Loy's racial appeal was made twice during the eight day period before the election. Loy's second appeal occurred on the eve of the election. The Company was therefore powerless to respond to the remarks: Indeed, even if the Company had the opportunity to respond, to have done so may have further inflamed racial feelings. In light of these circumstances, we believe that Loy's attempt to exacerbate the

6. In its brief, the Board states:

"With respect to job security, Loy stated that the Company's black employee, Howard, did not need the protection of the Union because he was protected by the equal opportunity laws, but that the white employees needed the Union to protect their jobs. At the same time, Loy indicated that Morse would be reinstated with backpay and that Howard would be receiving a paper that he should sign so that Morse could be reinstated. (Citation to affidavits omitted). On April 29, the day before the election, the Union held another meeting, and Loy repeated that Morse would be reinstated with backpay (Citation to affidavit omitted).

7. See note 5, supra.

racial tension that existed prior to the election was likely to have had an appreciable effect upon the employees' freedom of choice.

In summary, the undisputed facts are sufficient to establish that union organizer Loy engaged in a subtle, but deliberate attempt to exacerbate existing feelings of racial tension, and that this attempt was likely to have affected appreciably the employees' decision to vote for or against union representation. Accordingly, the Board's petition for enforcement of its order requiring the Company to bargain with the Union is Denied.

C. SELF–HELP AGAINST RACIAL DISCRIMINATION—PROTECTED CONCERTED ACTIVITY UNDER THE NLRA * * *

EMPORIUM CAPWELL CO. v. WESTERN ADDITION COMMUNITY ORGANIZATION

Supreme Court of the United States, 1975.
420 U.S. 50, 95 S.Ct. 977, 43 L.Ed.2d 12.

Opinion of the Court by MR. JUSTICE MARSHALL, announced by MR. CHIEF JUSTICE BURGER.

This litigation presents the question whether, in light of the national policy against racial discrimination in employment, the National Labor Relations Act protects concerted activity by a group of minority employees to bargain with their employer over issues of employment discrimination. The National Labor Relations Board held that the employees could not circumvent their elected representative to engage in such bargaining. The Court of Appeals for the District of Columbia Circuit reversed and remanded, holding that in certain circumstances the activity would be protected. 158 U.S.App.D.C. 138, 485 F.2d 917. Because of the importance of the issue to the administration of the Act, we granted certiorari. 415 U.S. 913, 94 S.Ct. 1407, 39 L.Ed.2d 466. We now reverse.

I

The Emporium Capwell Co. (Company) operates a department store in San Francisco. At all times relevant to this litigation it was a party to the collective-bargaining agreement negotiated by the San Francisco Retailer's Council, of which it was a member, and the Department Store Employees Union (Union) which represented all stock and marking area employees of the Company. The agreement, in which the Union was recognized as the sole collective-bargaining agency for all covered employees, prohibited employment discrimination by reason of race, color, creed, national origin, age, or sex, as well as union activity. It had a no-strike or lockout clause, and it established grievance and arbitration machinery for processing any claimed violation of the contract, including a violation of the anti-discrimination clause.[1]

On April 3, 1968, a group of Company employees covered by the agreement met with the secretary-treasurer of the Union, Walter Johnson, to present a list of grievances including a claim that the Company was discriminating on the basis of race in making assignments and promotions. The Union official agreed to take certain of the grievances and to investigate the charge of racial discrimination. He appointed an investigating committee and prepared a report on the employees' grievances, which he submitted to the Retailer's Council and which the Council in turn referred to the Company. The report described "the possibility of racial discrimination" as perhaps the most important issue raised by the employees and termed the situation at the Company as potentially explosive if corrective action were not taken. It offered as an example of the problem the Company's failure to promote a Negro stock employee regarded by other employees as an outstanding candidate but a victim of racial discrimination.

Shortly after receiving the report, the Company's labor relations director met with Union representatives and agreed to "look into the matter" of discrimination and see what needed to be done. Apparently unsatisfied with these representations, the Union held a meeting in September attended by Union officials, Company employees, and representatives of the California Fair Employment Practices Committee (FEPC) and the local anti-poverty agency. The secretary-treasurer of the Union announced that the Union had concluded that the Company was discriminating, and that it would process every such grievance through to arbitration if necessary. Testimony about the Company's practices was taken and transcribed by a court reporter, and the next day the Union notified the Company of its formal charge and demanded that the joint union-management Adjustment Board be convened "to hear the entire case."

At the September meeting some of the Company's employees had expressed their view that the contract procedures were inadequate to handle a systemic grievance of this sort; they suggested that the Union instead begin picketing the store in protest. Johnson explained that the collective agreement bound the Union to its processes and expressed his view that successful grievants would be helping not only themselves but all others who might be the victims of invidious discrim-

---

1. Section 5B provided:

"Any act of any employer, representative of the Union, or any employe that is interfering with the faithful performance of this agreement, or a harmonious relationship between the employers and the UNION, may be referred to the Adjustment Board for such action as the Adjustment Board deems proper, and is permissive within this agreement." App. 100–101.

Section 36B established an Adjustment Board consisting of three Union and three management members. Section 36C provided that if any matter referred to the Adjustment Board remained unsettled after seven days, either party could insist that the dispute be submitted to final and binding arbitration. App. 100–101.

ination as well. The FEPC and antipoverty agency representatives offered the same advice. Nonetheless, when the Adjustment Board meeting convened on October 16, James Joseph Hollins, Tom Hawkins, and two other employees whose testimony the Union had intended to elicit refused to participate in the grievance procedure. Instead, Hollins read a statement objecting to reliance on correction of individual inequities as an approach to the problem of discrimination at the store and demanding that the president of the Company meet with the four protestants to work out a broader agreement for dealing with the issue as they saw it. The four employees then walked out of the hearing.

Hollins attempted to discuss the question of racial discrimination with the Company president shortly after the incidents of October 16. The president refused to be drawn into such a discussion but suggested to Hollins that he see the personnel director about the matter. Hollins, who had spoken to the personnel director before, made no effort to do so again. Rather, he and Hawkins and several other dissident employees held a press conference on October 22 at which they denounced the store's employment policy as racist, reiterated their desire to deal directly with "the top management" of the Company over minority employment conditions, and announced their intention to picket and institute a boycott of the store. On Saturday, November 2, Hollins, Hawkins, and at least two other employees picketed the store throughout the day and distributed at the entrance handbills urging consumers not to patronize the store.[2] Johnson encountered the picketing employees, again urged them to rely on the grievance process, and warned that they might be fired for their activities. The pickets, however, were not dissuaded, and they continued to press their demand to deal directly with the Company president.[3]

2. The full text of the handbill read:

"* * * BEWARE * * * BEWARE
* * * BEWARE * * *
"EMPORIUM SHOPPERS
"'Boycott Is On' 'Boycott Is On' 'Boycott
Is On'

"For years at The Emporium black, brown, yellow and red people have worked at the lowest jobs, at the lowest levels. Time and time again we have seen intelligent, hard working brothers and sisters denied promotions and respect.

"The Emporium is a 20th Century colonial plantation. The brothers and sisters are being treated the same way as our brothers are being treated in the slave mines of Africa.

"Whenever the racist pig at The Emporium injures or harms a black sister or brother, they injure and insult all black people. THE EMPORIUM MUST PAY

FOR THESE INSULTS. Therefore, we encourage all of our people to take their money out of this racist store, until black people have full employment and are promoted justly through out The Emporium.

"We welcome the support of our brothers and sisters from the churches, unions, sororities, fraternities, social clubs, Afro-American Institute, Black Panther Party, W. A. C. O. and the Poor Peoples Institute." App. 107.

3. Johnson testified that Hollins "informed me that the only one they wanted to talk to was Mr. Batchelder [the Company president] and I informed him that we had concluded negotiations in 1967 and I was a spokesman for the union and represented a few thousand clerks and I have never met Mr. Batchelder * * *." App. 76.

On November 7, Hollins and Hawkins were given written warnings that a repetition of the picketing or public statements about the Company could lead to their discharge.[4] When the conduct was repeated the following Saturday, the two employees were fired.

Western Addition Community Organization (hereinafter respondent), a local civil rights association of which Hollins and Hawkins were members, filed a charge against the Company with the National Labor Relations Board. The Board's General Counsel subsequently issued a complaint alleging that in discharging the two the Company had violated § 8(a)(1) of the National Labor Relations Act, as amended, 61 Stat. 140, 29 U.S.C. § 158(a)(1). After a hearing, the NLRB Trial Examiner found that the discharged employees had believed in good faith that the Company was discriminating against minority employees, and that they had resorted to concerted activity on the basis of that belief. He concluded, however, that their activity was not protected by § 7 of the Act and that their discharges did not, therefore, violate § 8(a) (1).

The Board, after oral argument, adopted the findings and conclusions of its Trial Examiner and dismissed the complaint. 192 N.L.R.B. 173. Among the findings adopted by the Board was that the discharged employees' course of conduct

> was no mere presentation of a grievance but nothing short of a demand that the [Company] bargain with the picketing employees for the entire group of minority employees.[5]

The Board concluded that protection of such an attempt to bargain would undermine the statutory system of bargaining through an exclusive, elected representative, impede elected union's efforts at bettering the working conditions of minority employees, "and place on the

---

4. The warning given to Hollins read:

"On October 22, 1968, you issued a public statement at a press conference to which all newspapers, radio, and TV stations were invited. The contents of this statement were substantially the same as those set forth in the sheet attached. This statement was broadcast on Channel 2 on October 22, 1968 and Station KDIA.

"On November 2nd you distributed copies of the attached statement to Negro customers and prospective customers, and to other persons passing by in front of The Emporium.

"These statements are untrue and are intended to and will, if continued injure the reputation of The Emporium.

"These are ample legal remedies to correct any discrimination you may claim to exist. Therefore, we view your activities as a deliberate and unjustified attempt to injure your employer.

"This is to inform you that you may be discharged if you repeat any of the above acts or make any similar public statement."

That given to Hawkins was the same except that the first paragraph was not included. Id., at 106.

5. 192 N.L.R.B., at 185. The evidence marshaled in support of this finding consisted of Hollins' meeting with the Company president in which he said that he wanted to discuss the problem perceived by minority employees; his statement that the pickets would not desist until the president treated with them; Hawkins' testimony that their purpose in picketing was to "talk to the top management to get better conditions"; and his statement that they wanted to achieve their purpose through "group talk and through the president if we could talk to him," as opposed to use of the grievance-arbitration machinery.

Employer an unreasonable burden of attempting to placate self-designated representatives of minority groups while abiding by the terms of a valid bargaining agreement and attempting in good faith to meet whatever demands the bargaining representative put forth under that agreement." [6]

On respondent's petition for review the Court of Appeals reversed and remanded. The court was of the view that concerted activity directed against racial discrimination enjoys a "unique status" by virtue of the national labor policy against discrimination, as expressed in both the NLRA, see United Packinghouse Workers v. NLRB, 135 U.S.App.D.C. 111, 416 F.2d 1126, cert. denied, 396 U.S. 903, 90 S.Ct. 216, 24 L.Ed.2d 179 (1969), and in Title VII of the Civil Rights Act of 1964, 78 Stat. 253, as amended, 42 U.S.C. § 2000e et seq., and that the Board had not adequately taken account of the necessity to accommodate the exclusive bargaining principle of the NLRA to the national policy of protecting action taken in opposition to discrimination from employer retaliation.[7] The court recognized that protection of the minority-group concerted activity involved in this case would interfere to some extent with the orderly collective-bargaining process, but it considered the disruptive effect on that process to be outweighed where protection of minority activity is necessary to full and immediate realization of the policy against discrimination. In formulating a standard for distinguishing between protected and unprotected activity, the majority held that the "Board should inquire, in cases such as this, whether the union was actually remedying the discrimination to the

6. The Board considered but stopped short of resolving the question of whether the employees' incentive and call for a boycott of the Company bespoke so malicious an attempt to harm their employer as to deprive them of the protection of the Act. The Board decision is therefore grounded squarely on the view that a minority group member may not bypass the Union and bargain directly over matters affecting minority employees, and not at all on the tactics used in this particular attempt to obtain such bargaining.

Member Jenkins dissented on the ground that the employees' activity was protected by § 7 because it concerned the terms and conditions of their employment. Member Brown agreed but expressly relied upon his view that the facts revealed no attempt to bargain "but simply to urge [the Company] to take action to correct conditions of racial discrimination which the employees reasonably believed existed at the Emporium." 192 N.L.R.B., at 179.

7. Section 9(a) of the NLRA, 29 U.S.C. § 159(a), provides in part:

"Representatives designated or selected for the purposes of collective bargain-

ing by the majority of the employees in a unit appropriate for such purposes, shall be the exclusive representatives of all the employees in such unit for the purposes of collective bargaining in respect to rates of pay, wages, hours of employment, or other conditions of employment * * *."

Section 704(a) of Title VII, 42 U.S.C. § 2000e–3(a) (1970 ed., Supp. III), provides:

"It shall be an unlawful employment practice for an employer to discriminate against any of his employees or applicants for employment, for an employment agency or joint labor-management committee controlling apprenticeship or other training or retraining, including on-the-job training programs, to discriminate against any individual; or for a labor organization to discriminate against any member thereof or applicant for membership, because he has opposed any practice made an unlawful employment practice by this subchapter, or because he has made a charge, testified, assisted, or participated in any manner in an investigation, proceeding, or hearing under this subchapter."

fullest extent possible, by the most expedient and efficacious means. Where the union's efforts fall short of this high standard, the minority group's concerted activities cannot lose [their] section 7 protection." [8] Accordingly, the court remanded the case for the Board to make this determination and, if it found in favor of the employees, to consider whether their particular tactics were so disloyal to their employer as to deprive them of § 7 protection under our decision in NLRB v. Electrical Workers, 346 U.S. 464, 74 S.Ct. 172, 98 L.Ed. 195 (1953).[9]

II

Before turning to the central questions of labor policy raised by these cases, it is important to have firmly in mind the character of the underlying conduct to which we apply them. As stated, the Trial Examiner and the Board found that the employees were discharged for attempting to bargain with the Company over the terms and conditions of employment as they affected racial minorities. Although the Court of Appeals expressly declined to set aside this finding,[10] respondent has devoted considerable effort to attacking it in this Court,[11] on the theory that the employees were attempting only to present a grievance to their employer within the meaning of the first provision to 9(a).[12] We see no

8. 158 U.S.App.D.C., at 152, 485 F.2d at 931 (emphasis in original). We hasten to point out that it had never been determined in any forum, at least as of the time that Hollins and Hawkins engaged in the activity for which they were discharged, that the Company had engaged in any discriminatory conduct. The Board found that the employees believed that the Company had done so, but that no evidence introduced in defense of their resort to self-help supported this belief.

9. Judge Wyzanski dissented insofar as the Board was directed on remand to evaluate the adequacy of the Union's efforts in opposing discrimination. He was of the view that minority concerted activity against discrimination would be protected regardless of the Union's efforts.

10. Id., at 150 n. 34, 485 F.2d at 929 n. 34 (majority opinion); id., at 158, 485 F.2d at 937 (dissenting opinion) ("There could not be a plainer instance of an attempt to bargain respecting working conditions, as distinguished from an adjustment of grievances").

11. Brief for Respondent 27–34; Tr. of Oral Arg. 34, 37–40, 44, 49.

12. That proviso states:

"That any individual employee or a group of employees shall have the right at any time to present grievances to their employer and to have such grievances adjusted, without the intervention of the bargaining representative, as long as the adjustment is not inconsistent with the terms of a collective-bargaining contract or agreement then in effect * * *."

Respondent clearly misapprehends the nature of the "right" conferred by this section. The intendment of the proviso is to permit employees to present grievances and to authorize the employer to entertain them without opening itself to liability for dealing directly with employees in derogation of the duty to bargain only with the exclusive bargaining representative, a violation of § 8(a)(5). H.R.Rep.No.245, 80th Cong., 1st Sess., 7 (1947); H.R.Conf.Rep.No. 510, 80th Cong., 1st Sess. (House manager's statement), 46 (1947); U.S.Code Cong.Serv. 1947, p. 1135. The Act nowhere protects this "right" by making it an unfair labor practice for an employer to refuse to entertain such a presentation, nor can it be read to authorize resort to economic coercion. This matter is fully explicated in Black-Clawson Co. v. Machinists, 313 F.2d 179 (CA2 1962). See also Republic Steel v. Maddox, 379 U.S. 650, 85 S.Ct. 614, 13 L.Ed.2d 580 (1965). If the employees' activity in the present litigation is to be deemed protected, therefore, it must be so by reason of the reading given to the main part of § 9(a), in light of Title VII and the national policy against employment discrimination, and not by burdening the proviso to that section with a load it was not meant to carry.

occasion to disturb the finding of the Board. Universal Camera Corp. v. NLRB, 340 U.S. 474, 491, 71 S.Ct. 456,466, 95 L.Ed. 456 (1951). The issue, then, is whether such attempts to engage in separate bargaining are protected by 7 of the Act or proscribed by 9(a).

A

Section 7 affirmatively guarantees employees the most basic rights of industrial self-determination, "the right to self-organization, to form, join, or assist labor organizations, to bargain collectively through representatives of their own choosing, and to engage in other concerted activities for the purpose of collective bargaining or other mutual aid or protection," as well as the right to refrain from these activities. These are, for the most part, collective rights, rights to act in concert with one's fellow employees; they are protected not for their own sake but as an instrument of the national labor policy of minimizing industrial strife "by encouraging the practice and procedure of collective bargaining." 29 U.S.C. § 151.

Central to the policy of fostering collective bargaining, where the employees elect that course, is the principle of majority rule. See NLRB v. Jones & Laughlin Steel Corp., 301 U.S. 1, 57 S.Ct. 615, 81 L.Ed. 893 (1937). If the majority of a unit chooses union representation, the NLRA permits it to bargain with its employer to make union membership a condition of employment, thereby imposing its choice upon the minority. 29 U.S.C. §§ 157, 158(a)(3). In establishing a regime of majority rule, Congress sought to secure to all members of the unit the benefits of their collective strength and bargaining power, in full awareness that the superior strength of some individuals or groups might be subordinated to the interest of the majority. Vaca v. Sipes, 386 U.S. 171, 182, 87 S.Ct. 903, 912, 17 L.Ed.2d 842 (1967); J. I. Case Co. v. NLRB, 321 U.S. 332, 338–339, 64 S.Ct. 576, 580, 88 L.Ed. 762 (1944); H.R.Rep. No. 972, 74th Cong., 1st Sess., 18 (1935). As a result, "[t]he complete satisfaction of all who are represented is hardly to be expected." Ford Motor Co. v. Huffman, 345 U.S. 330, 338, 73 S.Ct. 681, 686, 97 L.Ed. 1048 (1953).

In vesting the representatives of the majority with this broad power Congress did not, of course, authorize a tyranny of the majority over minority interests. First, it confined the exercise of these powers to the context of a " 'unit appropriate' for the purposes of collective bargaining," i.e., a group of employees with a sufficient commonality of circumstances to ensure against the submergence of a minority with distinctively different interests in the terms and conditions of their employment. See Chemical Workers v. Pittsburgh Glass, 404 U.S. 157, 171, 92 S.Ct. 383, 393, 30 L.Ed.2d 341 (1971). Second, it undertook in the 1959 Landrum-Griffin amendments, 73 Stat. 519, to assure that minority voices are heard as they are in the functioning of a democratic institution. Third, we have held, by the very nature of the exclusive bargaining representative's status as representative of *all* unit employees, Congress implicitly imposed upon it a duty fairly and in good faith to represent the interests of minorities within the unit. Vaca v. Sipes, supra; Wallace Corp. v. NLRB, 323 U.S. 248, 65 S.Ct. 238, 89 L.Ed. 216 (1944); cf. Steele v. Louisville & N. R. Co., 323 U.S. 192, 65 S.Ct. 226, 89 L.Ed. 173 (1944). And the Board has taken the position that a union's refusal to process grievances against racial discrimination, in violation of that duty, is an unfair labor practice. Hughes Tool Co., 147 N.L.R.B. 1573 (1964); see Miranda Fuel Co., 140 N.L.R.B. 181 (1962), enforcement denied, 326 F.2d 172 (CA2 1963). Indeed, the Board has ordered a union implicated by a collective-bargaining agreement in discrimination with an employer to propose specific contractual provisions to prohibit racial discrimination. See Local Union No. 12, United Rubber Workers of America v. NLRB, 368 F.2d 12 (CA5 1966) (enforcement granted).

B

Against this background of long and consistent adherence to the principle of exclusive representation tempered by safeguards for the protection of minority interests, respondent urges this Court to fashion a limited exception to that principle: employees who seek to bargain separately with their employer as to the elimination of racially discriminatory employment practices peculiarly affecting them,[15] should be free from the constraints of the exclusivity principle of § 9(a). Essentially because established procedures under Title VII or, as in this case, a grievance machinery, are too time consuming, the national labor policy against discrimination requires this exception, respondent argues, and its adoption would not unduly compromise the legitimate interests of either unions or employers.[16]

Plainly, national labor policy embodies the principles of nondiscrimination as a matter of highest priority, Alexander v. Gardner-Denver Co., 415 U.S. 36, 47, 94 S.Ct. 1011, 39 L.Ed.2d 147 (1974), and it is a commonplace that we must construe the NLRA in light of the broad national labor policy of which it is a part. See Textile Workers v.

---

15. As respondent conceded at oral argument, the rule it espouses here would necessarily have equal application to any identifiable group of employees—racial or religious groups, women, etc.—that reasonably believed themselves to be the object of invidious discrimination by their employer. Tr. of Oral Arg. 30–31. As seemingly limited by the Court of Appeals, however, such a group would have to give their elected representative an opportunity to adjust the matter in some way before resorting to self-help.

16. Our analysis of respondent's argument in favor of the exception makes it unnecessary either to accept or reject its factual predicate, *viz.*, that the procedures now established for the elimination of discrimination in employment are too cumbersome to be effective. We note, however, that the present record provides no support for the proposition. Thus, while respondent stresses the fact that Hollins and Hawkins had brought their evidence of discrimination to the Union in April 1968 but did not resort to self-help until the following October, it overlooks the fact that although they had been in contact with the state FEPC they did not file a charge with that agency or the Equal Employment Opportunity Commission (EEOC). Further, when they abandoned the procedures to which the union was bound because they thought "the Union was sort of putting us off and on and was going into a lot of delay that we felt was unnecessary," App. 26, it was at the very moment that the Adjustment Board had been convened to hear their testimony.

Lincoln Mills, 353 U.S. 448, 456–458, 77 S.Ct. 923, 1 L.Ed.2d 972 (1957). These general principles do not aid respondent, however, as it is far from clear that separate bargaining is necessary to help eliminate discrimination. Indeed, as the facts of this litigation demonstrate, the proposed remedy might have just the opposite effect. The collective-bargaining agreement involved here prohibited without qualification all manner of invidious discrimination and made any claimed violation a grievable issue. The grievance procedure is directed precisely at determining whether discrimination has occurred.[17] That orderly determination, if affirmative, could lead to an arbitral award enforceable in court.[18] Nor is there any reason to believe that the processing of grievances is inherently limited to the correction of individual cases of discrimination. Quite apart from the essentially contractual question of whether the Union could grieve against a "pattern or practice" it deems inconsistent with the nondiscrimination clause of the contract, one would hardly expect an employer to continue in effect an employment practice that routinely results in adverse arbitral decisions.[19]

* * *

What has been said here in evaluating respondent's claim that the policy against discrimination requires § 7 protection for concerted efforts at minority bargaining has obvious implications for the related claim that legitimate employer and union interests would not be unduly compromised thereby. The court below minimized the impact on the Union in this case by noting that it was not working at cross-purposes with the dissidents, and that indeed it could not do so consistent with its duty of fair representation and perhaps its obligations under Title VII. As to the Company, its obligations under Title VII are cited for the proposition that it could have no legitimate objection to bargaining with the dissidents in order to achieve full compliance with that law.

This argument confuses the employees' substantive right to be free of racial discrimination with the procedures available under the NLRA for securing these rights. Whether they are thought to depend upon Title VII or have an independent source in the NLRA,[23] they cannot be pursued at the expense of the orderly collective-bargaining process contemplated by the NLRA.

17. The Union in this case had been "prepared to go into arbitration" to enforce its position, but was advised by its attorney that it would be difficult to do so without the dissident members' testimony. Testimony of Walter Johnson, App. 76.

18. Even if the arbitral decision denies the putative discriminatee's complaint his access to the processes of Title VII and thereby to the federal courts is not foreclosed. Alexander v. Gardner-Denver Co., 415 U.S. 36, 94 S.Ct. 1011, 39 L.Ed.2d 147.

19. "The processing of disputes through the grievance machinery is actually a vehi-cle by which meaning and content are given to the collective bargaining agreement," Steelworkers v. Warrior & Gulf Co., 363 U.S. 574, 581, 80 S.Ct. 1347, 1352, 4 L.Ed. 2d 1409 (1960): hence the " 'common law of the shop.' " Id., at 580, 80 S.Ct. at 1351, quoting Cox, Reflections Upon Labor Arbitration, 72 Harv.L.Rev. 1492, 1499 (1959).

23. See United Packinghouse Workers v. NLRB, 135 U.S.App.D.C. 111, 416 F.2d 1126, cert. denied, 396 U.S. 903 (1969); Local Union No. 12, United Rubber Workers of America v. NLRB, 368 F.2d 12 (CA 5 1966).

Accordingly, we think neither aspect of respondent's contention in support of a right to short-circuit orderly, established processes for eliminating discrimination in employment is well-founded. The policy of industrial self-determination as expressed in § 7 does not require fragmentation of the bargaining unit along racial or other lines in order to consist with the national labor policy against discrimination. And in the face of such fragmentation, whatever its effect on discriminatory practices, the bargaining process that the principle of exclusive representation is meant to lubricate could not endure unhampered.

III

Even if the NLRA, when read in the context of the general policy against discrimination, does not sanction these employees' attempt to bargain with the Company, it is contended that it must do so if a specific element of that policy is to be preserved. The element in question is the congressional policy of protecting from employer reprisal employee efforts to oppose unlawful discrimination, as expressed in § 704(a) of Title VII. See n. 7, supra. Since the discharged employees here had, by their own lights, "opposed" discrimination, it is argued that their activities "fell plainly within the scope of," and their discharges therefore violated, § 704(a).[24] The notion here is that if the discharges did not also violate § 8(a)(1) of the NLRA, then the integrity of § 704(a) will be seriously undermined. We cannot agree.

Even assuming that § 704(a) protects employees' picketing and instituting a consumer boycott of their employer,[25] the same conduct is

24. This argument as advanced by respondent is somewhat weakened by its context of insistence that the discharged employees were not seeking to bargain with the Company. The same argument is made in the *amicus curiae* brief of the National Association for the Advancement of Colored People, pp. 9–14, on the assumption, however, that bargaining—over the issue of racial discrimination alone—was their objective. In light of our declination to upset the finding to that effect, we take the argument as the *amicus* makes it.

25. The question of whether § 704(a) is applicable to the facts of this case is not as free from doubt as the respondent and *amicus* would have it. In its brief the NLRB argues that § 704(a) is directed at protecting access to the EEOC and federal courts. Pettway v. American Cast Iron Pipe Co., 411 F.2d 998 (CA5 1969). We have previously had occasion to note that "[n]othing in Title VII compels an employer to absolve and rehire one who has engaged in * * * deliberate, unlawful activity against it." McDonnell Douglas Corp. v. Green, 411 U.S. 792, 803, 93 S.Ct. 1817, 1825, 36 L.Ed.2d 668 (1973). Whether the protection afforded by § 704(a) extends only to the right of access or well beyond it,

however, is not a question properly presented by these cases. Nor is it an appropriate question to be answered in the first instance by the NLRB. Questions arising under Title VII must be resolved by the means that Congress provided for that purpose.

In the course of arguing for affirmance of the decision below, under which the NLRB would be called upon to evaluate the effectiveness of a union's efforts to oppose employer discrimination in the bargaining unit, respondent takes the position that the Board is well equipped by reason of experience and perspective to play a major role in the process of eliminating discrimination in employment. The Board-enforced duty of fair representation, it is noted, has already exposed it to the problems that inhere in detecting and deterring racial discrimination within unions. What is said above does not call into question either the capacity or the propriety of the Board's sensitivity to questions of discrimination. It pertains, rather, to the proper allocation of a particular function—adjudication of claimed violations of Title VII—that Congress has assigned elsewhere.

not necessarily entitled to affirmative protection from the NLRA. Under the scheme of that Act, conduct which is not protected concerted activity may lawfully form the basis for the participants' discharge. That does not mean that the discharge is immune from attack on other statutory grounds in an appropriate case. If the discharges in these cases are violative of § 704(a) of Title VII, the remedial provisions of that Title provide the means by which Hollins and Hawkins may recover their jobs with backpay. 42 U.S.C. § 2000e–5(g) (1970 ed., Supp. III).

Respondent objects that reliance on the remedies provided by Title VII is inadequate effectively to secure the rights conferred by Title VII. There are indeed significant differences between proceedings initiated under Title VII and an unfair labor practice proceeding. Congress chose to encourage voluntary compliance with Title VII by emphasizing conciliatory procedures before federal coercive powers could be invoked. Even then it did not provide the EEOC with the power of direct enforcement, but made the federal courts available to the agency or individual to secure compliance with Title VII. See Alexander v. Gardner-Denver Co., 415 U.S., at 44–45, 94 S.Ct. 1011. By contrast, once the General Counsel of the NLRB decides to issue a complaint, vindication of the charging party's statutory rights becomes a public function discharged at public expense, and a favorable decision by the Board brings forth an administrative order. As a result of these and other differences, we are told that relief is typically available to the party filing a charge with the NLRB in a significantly shorter time, and with less risk, than obtains for one filing a charge with the EEOC.

Whatever its factual merit, this argument is properly addressed to the Congress and not to this Court or the NLRB. In order to hold that employer conduct violates § 8(a)(1) of the NLRA *because* it violates § 704(a) of Title VII, we would have to override a host of consciously made decisions well within the exclusive competence of the Legislature.[26] This obviously, we cannot do.

Reversed.

Mr. Justice Douglas, dissenting.

The Court's opinion makes these Union members—and others similarly situated—prisoners of the Union. The law, I think, was designed to prevent that tragic consequence. Hence, I dissent.

* * *

26. In Alexander v. Gardner-Denver Co., 415 U.S., at 48 n. 9, 94 S.Ct. at 1019, n. 9, we had occasion to refer to Senator Clark's interpretive memorandum stating that "[n]othing in Title VII or anywhere else in this bill affects rights and obligations under the NLRA * * *." Since the Senator's remarks were directed to the suggestion that enactment of Title VII would somehow constrict an employee's access to redress under other statutory regimes, we do not take them as foreclosing the possibility that in some circumstances rights created by the NLRA and related laws affecting the employment relationship must be broadened to accommodate the policies of Title VII.

The law should facilitate the involvement of unions in the quest for racial equality in employment, but it should not make the individual a prisoner of the union. While employees may reasonably be required to approach the union first, as a kind of "exhaustion" requirement before resorting to economic protest, cf. NLRB v. Tanner Motor Livery, 419 F.2d 216 (CA9), they should not be under continued inhibition when it becomes apparent that the union response is inadequate. The Court of Appeals held that the employees should be protected from discharge unless the Board found on remand that the Union had been prosecuting their complaints "to the *fullest extent possible, by the most expedient and efficacious means.*" 158 U.S.App.D.C. 138, 152, 485 F.2d 917, 931. I would not disturb this standard.

* * *

FRANK BRISCOE INCORPORATED v. NATIONAL LABOR RELATIONS BOARD

United States Court of Appeals for the Third Circuit, 1981.
637 F.2d 946.

OPINION OF THE COURT

SEITZ, CHIEF JUDGE.

Frank Briscoe, Inc. (Briscoe) petitions for review, and the National Labor Relations Board (Board) cross-petitions for enforcement, of an order of the Board. The order of the Board is based on the finding that Briscoe violated section 8(a)(1) of the National Labor Relations Act (NLRA) when it refused to recall certain employees because some of them had engaged in protected, concerted activity by filing charges against Briscoe with the Equal Employment Opportunity Commission (EEOC). See 247 NLRB No. 6 (1980). We have jurisdiction under 29 U.S.C. § 160(e) & (f) (1976).

I.

Briscoe, a New Jersey corporation engaged in general contracting in the construction industry, was the general contractor for the construction of the multi-million dollar convention center in Pittsburgh, Pennsylvania. Briscoe employed between twenty and fifty ironworkers to work on the convention-center project, the number varying according to the working conditions at a given time. Pursuant to Briscoe's national collective bargaining agreement with the International Association of Bridge, Structural and Ornamental Workers (Union), the vast majority of these ironworkers were hired through the Union's hiring hall.[1]

During January and February of 1979, production problems plagued the convention-center project. The entire project was shut

---

1. Under the national agreement with the Union. Briscoe is not required to hire all its workers directly through the hiring hall, it also may accept on-the-job applica-   tions. However, since early March 1979, Briscoe has hired primarily through the hiring hall.

down during the second week of February because of poor weather conditions. On February 13, 1979, Ironworker Superintendent Jack Godwin informed Union Steward George Cook that certain workers would have to be laid off.

Cook, accompanied by the general foreman, then went to a "shanty" where the ironworkers gathered before work. There, he read the names of twelve ironworkers, including Jeffrey, a trainee, who were to be laid off. According to Cook, he was instructed to tell the men that this was a general layoff, and that they would be recalled.

On February 14 and 16, four of the laid-off ironworkers, including Jeffrey, and a fifth ironworker who had been demoted but not laid off, filed charges of racial discrimination with the EEOC. Each of the five complainants is black. Two of these ironworkers filed charges on February 14, and the other three filed charges on February 16. Briscoe received notice of these charges on February 22 and 23.

After the layoff, each of the eight ironworkers involved in this unfair labor practice suit requested, either at the jobsite or at the Union hiring hall, that he be recalled when Briscoe began rehiring. Mr. Hanna, whose testimony the administrative law judge credited, is the Union's business representative in charge of referring workers to jobs from the hiring hall. He testified that temporarily laid-off ironworkers requesting to be recalled normally would be preferentially referred back to the job. However, Mr. Hanna testified that none of the ironworkers laid off on February 13 were referred back to the convention-center jobsite because he had been told by Briscoe's Job Superintendent that Briscoe "didn't intend to hire the men back and * * * as long as [the] discrimination charges [were] filed with the EEOC, if [Briscoe] did take some of the people back, then there would be definite grounds for discrimination." Mr. Hanna informed those ironworkers who requested to be recalled that he would not refer them back to the jobsite, because Briscoe would not recall any of the workers who had been laid off on February 13 as long as the EEOC charges were pending. According to Mr. Hanna, had it not been for Briscoe's refusal to recall these workers, he would have referred these workers back to the job.

Briscoe began hiring ironworkers again on March 5, hiring twenty-nine workers between that date and April 2. With the sole exception of Jeffrey,[2] none of the ironworkers laid off on February 13 was, or has since been, recalled.

Eight of the workers, including three of the black ironworkers who had filed discrimination charges, brought an unfair labor practice charge against Briscoe for refusing to recall them because some of the

----

2. Briscoe explains that Jeffrey was laid off on February 13 because of its mistaken impression that the collective bargaining agreement required that all train- ees be laid off before any journeyman could be laid off. When Briscoe realized this mistake, it recalled Jeffrey on February 27.

workers had filed charges with the EEOC.[3] After conducting the hearing, the administrative law judge found that the black workers who had filed the EEOC charges had engaged in concerted activity protected under section 7 of the NLRA. Further, he found that Briscoe had refused to recall any of the ironworkers laid off on February 13 because some of them had filed EEOC charges. He concluded that this failure to recall the workers violated section 8(a)(1) of the NLRA. The Board affirmed the rulings, findings, and conclusions of the administrative law judge, and adopted his order with one minor modification. Briscoe petitions for review, and the Board cross-petitions for enforcement, of this order.

II.

First, Briscoe argues that the record does not support the Board's holding that the ironworkers engaged in protected, concerted activity when they filed discrimination charges with the EEOC. Briscoe also argues that the Board erroneously relied on the "constructive concerted activity" doctrine enunciated in Interboro Contractors, Inc., 157 N.L. R.B. 1295 (1966), *enforced* 388 F.2d 495 (2d Cir.1967), which was rejected by this court in NLRB v. Northern Metal Co., 440 F.2d 881 (3d Cir. 1971).

We have consistently held that to qualify as concerted activity, "it must appear at the very least that [the conduct] was engaged in with the object of initiating or inducing or preparing for group action or that it had *some relation to group action in the interest of the employees.*" Mushroom Transportation Co. v. NLRB, 330 F.2d 683, 685 (3d Cir.1964) (emphasis added). Determining whether particular conduct constitutes "concerted activity" is basically a factual inquiry. See Edward Blankstein, Inc. v. NLRB, 623 F.2d 320, 321 (3d Cir.1980). We are bound to uphold the Board's determination if it is supported by substantial evidence on the record as a whole. See Universal Camera Corp. v. NLRB, 340 U.S. 474, 71 S.Ct. 456, 95 L.Ed. 456 (1951); 29 U.S.C. § 160(e) & (f) (1976).

The witnesses who testified before the administrative law judge concentrated on the reasons for Briscoe's refusal to recall the workers laid off on February 13, and thus their testimony is not directed to whether filing the EEOC charges was concerted activity. We believe, however, that the following evidence supports the Board's finding: (1) All five of the EEOC complainants filed charges within three days of the layoff (two of them filed on February 14, and the other three filed on February 16); (2) these complaints are similar in nature; (3) the complaints filed by the two trainees who had been laid off referred to discrimination against other trainees, and a third complaint alleged that the complainant had previously complained that Briscoe discrimi-

---

3. Seven of these workers, including two EEOC complainants, filed the unfair labor practice charge on April 20. An eighth worker, who also had filed an EEOC charge, was added to the unfair labor practice complaint at the beginning of the hearing before the administrative law judge.

nated against blacks by not hiring enough trainees, thus indicating that the individual complainants intended to benefit workers other than themselves. Compare Wheeling-Pittsburgh Steel Corp. v. NLRB, 618 F.2d 1009 (3d Cir.1980) (employee refusing to work because unsafe conditions endangered not only himself but also other employees engaging in concerted activity) *with Northern Metal Co.*, 440 F.2d 881 (employee attempting to secure holiday pay only for himself not engaging in concerted activity).

Further, the testimony before the administrative law judge contains ample evidence that Briscoe lumped the charges together and viewed "the blacks" as a group with respect to those charges. The evidence that Briscoe clearly knew of the EEOC charges and viewed the complainants as a group distinguishes this case from Tri-State Truck Service v. NLRB, 616 F.2d 65, 71 (3d Cir.1980) (employer "must have knowledge, or reason to know, that employee activities have coalesced into group action for mutual aid or protection"). After reviewing the record, we are satisfied that there is substantial evidence on the record as a whole to support the Board's determination that the ironworkers engaged in concerted activity by filing the EEOC charges.

Having found that substantial evidence supports the Board's conclusion that filing the EEOC charges constituted concerted activity, we must examine the Board's conclusion that this activity was protected under section 7. In order to be protected under section 7, the concerted activity must be "for the purpose of collective bargaining or other mutual aid or protection." 29 U.S.C. § 157 (1976). Activities relating to conditions of employment are for "mutual aid or protection." We conclude that concerted activity directed toward ending alleged discriminatory employment practices falls within this standard, and thus deserves protection under section 7, at least as long as it does not violate another important principle of labor law, such as the principle of exclusive representation. See, e.g., Emporium Capwell Co. v. Western Addition Community Organization, 420 U.S. 50, 70, 95 S.Ct. 977, 988, 43 L.Ed.2d 12 (1975) (national labor policy embodying principles of nondiscrimination does not require an exception to the exclusivity principles of section 9(a)); United Packinghouse Workers v. NLRB, 416 F.2d 1126, 1135 (D.C.Cir.) ("racially integrated working conditions are valid objects for employee action"), cert. denied sub nom., Farmers' Cooperative Compress v. United Packinghouse Workers, 396 U.S. 903, 90 S.Ct. 216, 24 L.Ed.2d 179 (1969). The record amply supports the conclusion that the EEOC complainants, by seeking to end Briscoe's alleged discriminatory practices against other workers as well as against themselves, were acting for "mutual aid or protection," and thus were protected under section 7.[5]

---

5. Briscoe also argues that, by relying on the "presumption" of concerted activity derived from the *Interboro* line of cases, the Board erroneously shifted the burden of proof and required Briscoe to demonstrate the reason for its initial decision to lay off the workers, which will be the issue in each of the EEOC charges. Briscoe thus appears to be arguing that the Board forced it to try the EEOC charges in an

III.

Next, Briscoe argues that the evidence on the record does not support the Board's finding that Briscoe refused to recall the ironworkers because some of them had filed EEOC charges. After reviewing the testimony presented to the administrative law judge, we are satisfied that substantial evidence supports the finding that Briscoe intended the February 13th layoff to be a temporary cutback because of poor weather, and that it later refused to recall the workers because of the pending EEOC charges.

IV.

Finally, Briscoe argues that the only remedy available to the workers for Briscoe's refusal to rehire them is section 704(a) of title VII, 42 U.S.C. § 2000e–3(a) (1976) (prohibiting retaliation by an employer when an employee has opposed the employer's discriminatory practices or has participated in any title VII proceeding). We cannot determine whether Briscoe is arguing that the Board erred in finding that filing the EEOC charges was concerted activity protected under section 7, and thus that section 8(a)(1) of the NLRA was not implicated, or that section 704(a) of title VII is the exclusive remedy for retaliation against employees who oppose employer discrimination regardless of whether such opposition may also constitute concerted activity protected under section 7. We have already addressed and rejected the contentions that filing the EEOC charges was not concerted, protected activity, and that the Board erroneously relied on the "constructive concerted activity" doctrine enunciated in Interboro Contractors, Inc., 157 N.L.R.B. 1295, enforced 388 F.2d 495 (2d Cir.1967). Thus, we will enforce the order of the Board unless section 704(a) of title VII provides the exclusive remedy for the ironworkers here involved.

Nothing in the text of title VII itself addresses the relation between section 704(a) and section 8(a)(1). However, the legislative history of title VII demonstrates that Congress intended to allow an individual to pursue rights independently under both title VII and other applicable statutes, including the NLRA.

*   *   *

We do not believe that the holding of the Supreme Court in Great American Federal Savings & Loan Association v. Novotny, 442 U.S. 366, 99 S.Ct. 2345, 60 L.Ed.2d 957 (1979), is inconsistent with our conclusion. In *Novotny*, the Court did not consider whether title VII provides the exclusive remedy when the same factual occurrence gives rise to violations of "two 'independent' rights," id. at 378, 99 S.Ct. at

unfair labor practice proceeding. We disagree. Any shifting of the burden was not the result of this alleged presumption, but was the result of the Board's demonstrating that Briscoe had retaliated against the protected, concerted activity engaged in by these workers. Any duplication in what Briscoe will try to prove in the EEOC and the Board proceedings derives not from any attempt on the Board's part to try an EEOC charge, but from the fact that Briscoe's alleged nonretaliatory reason for not rehiring the workers, i.e. that they were poor performers, necessarily implicates the reason for the original layoff.

2352, which is the issue we address in this case. Instead, the Court held "that § 1985(c) may not be invoked to redress violations of Title VII." Id. Nor do we believe that the Court's holding in Emporium Capwell Co. v. Western Addition Community Organization, 420 U.S. 50, 70, 95 S.Ct. 977, 988, 43 L.Ed.2d 12 (1975), supports Briscoe's suggestion that section 704(a) should be the exclusive remedy even when the employees' conduct is also protected by section 7 of the NLRA. On the contrary, we believe that *Emporium Capwell* supports our conclusion that section 8(a)(1) protects employees from employer retaliation for engaging in protected, concerted activity even when section 704(a) also provides protection.

* * *

We conclude that, when the Board finds that the conduct of employees constitutes concerted activity protected under section 7, and that the employer has refused to recall a group of employees because some of them were exercising these section 7 rights, the fact that some of the employees [6] also have a remedy under section 704(a) does not deprive the Board of jurisdiction.

* * *

MURRAY M. SCHWARTZ, DISTRICT JUDGE, dissenting. * * *

D. LABOR ARBITRATION AND TITLE VII

ALEXANDER v. GARDNER–DENVER CO.

415 U.S. 36, 94 S.Ct. 1011, 39 L.Ed.2d 147 (1974).

MR. JUSTICE POWELL delivered the opinion of the Court.

This case concerns the proper relationship between federal courts and the grievance-arbitration machinery of collective-bargaining agreements in the resolution and enforcement of an individual's rights to equal employment opportunities under Title VII of the Civil Rights Act of 1964, 78 Stat. 253, 42 U.S.C. § 2000e et seq. Specifically, we must decide under what circumstances, if any, an employee's statutory right to a trial *de novo* under Title VII may be foreclosed by prior submission of his claim to final arbitration under the nondiscrimination clause of a collective-bargaining agreement.

I.

In May 1966, petitioner Harrell Alexander, Sr., a black, was hired by respondent Gardner-Denver Co. (the company) to perform maintenance work at the company's plant in Denver, Colorado. In June 1968, petitioner was awarded a trainee position as a drill operator. He remained at that job until his discharge from employment on Septem-

---

6. Although Briscoe argues that § 704(a) is the exclusive remedy for all the ironworkers laid off on February 13, it never addresses whether those ironworkers who did not file EEOC charges would have a remedy under title VII. The record does not disclose whether they also "opposed" Briscoe's alleged racial discrimination and thus would be protected from retaliation by § 704(a). Because we reject Briscoe's contention that § 704(a) provides the exclusive remedy for an employer's retaliatory conduct that also violates § 8(a)(1), we need not address this issue.

ber 29, 1969. The company informed petitioner that he was being discharged for producing too many defective or unusable parts that had to be scrapped. 415 U.S. at 38, 94 S.Ct. at 1015.

(Summary) Following his discharge by the Gardner-Denver Company, the petitioner Harrell Alexander, Sr., a black, filed a grievance under the collective bargaining agreement between the company and Local No. 3029 of the United Steel Workers of America protesting his discharge.

> The grievant stated: "I feel I have been unjustly discharged and ask that I be reinstated with full seniority and pay." No explicit claim of racial discrimination was made.

The collective bargaining agreement provided for the company's right to discharge for cause and included both a prohibition against discrimination on account of race, color and other relevant classes, as well as a broad arbitration clause. The grievance procedure contained four steps prior to the requirement that unresolved matters be remitted to compulsory arbitration. It also provided that the arbitrator's decision must be based solely on an interpretation of provisions of the contract.

The union processed his grievance through the contractual machinery and, apparently for the first time, at the final pre-arbitration step the grievant raised the claim that his discharge resulted from racial discrimination. Prior to arbitration hearing Alexander filed a complaint with the Colorado Civil Rights Commission of racial discrimination which complaint was referred to the EEOC on November 5, 1969.

The arbitration hearing was held on November 20, 1969 and on December 30th the arbitrator ruled that the grievant had been discharged for just cause. He made no reference to the claim of racial discrimination. On July 25, 1970, the EEOC determined that there was not reasonable cause to believe that a violation of Title VII had occurred but later notified the grievant of his right to institute a civil action in federal court within thirty days.

The grievant filed his claim in the federal court alleging that his discharge resulted from a racially discriminatory employment practice in violation of Section 703(a)(1) of Title VII. The district court granted the company's motion for summary judgment and dismissed the case. 346 F.Supp. 1012 (D.Colo.1971). The court found that the claim for racial discrimination had been submitted to the arbitrator and resolved adversely to the grievant. It then held that having voluntarily elected to pursue his grievance to final arbitration under the non-discriminatory clause of the collective bargaining agreement, the plaintiff was bound by the arbitral decision and thereby precluded from suing his employer under Title VII. The Court of Appeals for the 10th Circuit affirmed per curiam on the basis of the district court's opinion. 466 F.2d 1209 (10th Cir.1972).

The Supreme Court granted the petitioner's application for certiorari and reversed.

The Supreme Court held that Title VII was designed to supplement, rather than supplant existing laws prohibiting employment discrimination and that the legislative history of the act manifests a congressional intent to allow an individual to pursue independently his rights under both Title VII and other applicable state and federal statutes. In filing a lawsuit under Title VII, the court held an employee asserts independent statutory rights accorded by Congress and there was no inconsistency in permitting both rights to be enforced in their respectively appropriate forms.

The Court rejected the proposition that plaintiff waives his cause of action under Title VII by proceeding in arbitration concluding that there was no prospective waiver under Title VII. It declared "Title VII strictures are absolute and represent a congressional command that each employee be free from discriminatory practices. Of necessity, the rights conferred can form no part of the collective bargaining process since waiver of these rights would defeat the paramount congressional purpose behind Title VII. In these circumstances, an employee's rights under Title VII are not susceptible to prospective waiver. * * *" (415 U.S. at 51, 94 S.Ct. at 1021.)

The Court noted that an arbitrator has authority to resolve only questions of contractual rights, and this authority remains regardless of whether certain contractual rights are similar to, or duplicative of, the substantive rights secured by Title VII. It noted that as proctor of the bargain, the arbitrator's task is to effectuate the intent of the parties and he has no general authority to invoke public laws that conflict with the bargain between the parties. (415 U.S. at 53, 94 S.Ct. at 1022.) The Court felt the arbitration procedures were inappropriate for the final resolution of rights created by Title VII. It noted that where the collective bargaining agreement conflicts with Title VII, the arbitrator must follow the agreement. The fact finding process in arbitration is usually not equivalent to judicial fact finding; the usual rules of evidence do not apply; and rights and procedures common to civil trials, such as discovery, compulsory process, cross-examination and testimony under oath are often severely limited or unavailable.

With regard to the doctrine of election of remedies, the Court noted that the doctrine refers to a situation where an individual pursues remedies that are legally or factually inconsistent but that it had no application in the instant case. By going to arbitration an employee seeks to vindicate his contractual right under a collective bargaining agreement. In filing a lawsuit under Title VII an employee asserts independent statutory rights accorded by Congress. It noted that the resulting scheme was somewhat analogous to procedures under the National Labor Relations Act which permit pursuit of an issue under a collective bargaining agreement or before the Board. Citing Carey v. Westinghouse Electric Corp., 375 U.S. 261, 84 S.Ct. 401, 11 L.Ed.2d 320 (1964); cf. Smith v. Evening News Assoc., 371 U.S. 195, 83 S.Ct. 267, 9 L.Ed.2d 246 (1962).

In addition to rejecting the company's request for a preclusion rule, the Court also declined to defer to arbitral decisions. (See Spielberg Manufacturing Co., 112 N.L.R.B. 1080 (1955). Under this proposal a court would grant summary judgment and dismiss an employee's action if the claim was before the arbitrator; the collective bargaining agreement prohibited the form of discrimination charged in the suit under Title VII; and the arbitrator had authority to rule on the claim and to fashion a remedy. The Court rejected deferral even under a more demanding standard than that proposed such as was adopted by the Fifth Circuit in Rios v. Reynolds Metals Co., 467 F.2d 54 (5th Cir.1972). It held that the federal court should consider the employee's claim *de novo*. The arbitral decision may be admitted as evidence and accorded such weight as the court deems appropriate. The judgment of the Court of Appeals was reversed. The weight to be accorded an arbitration decision was not determined by the court but it set forth the relevant standards in footnote [21] reproduced below:

W.R. GRACE AND CO. v. LOCAL UNION 759

The Supreme Court of the United States, 1983.
461 U.S. 757, 103 S.Ct. 2177, 76 L.Ed.2d 298.

JUSTICE BLACKMUN delivered the opinion of the Court.

Faced with the prospect of liability for violations of Title VII of the Civil Rights Act of 1964, as amended, petitioner signed with the Equal Employment Opportunity Commission (Commission or EEOC) a conciliation agreement that was in conflict with its collective bargaining agreement with respondent. Petitioner then obtained a court order, later reversed on appeal, that the conciliation agreement should prevail. The issue presented is whether the Court of Appeals was correct in enforcing an arbitral award of backpay damages against petitioner under the collective bargaining agreement for layoffs pursuant to the conciliation agreement.

I

A

In October 1973, after a lengthy investigation, the EEOC's District Director determined that there was reasonable cause to believe that petitioner W.R. Grace and Company (Company) had violated Title VII

21. We adopt no standards as to the weight to be accorded an arbitral decision, since this must be determined in the court's discretion with regard to the facts and circumstances of each case. Relevant factors include the existence of provisions in the collective-bargaining agreement that conform substantially with Title VII, the degree of procedural fairness in the arbitral forum, adequacy of the record with respect to the issue of discrimination, and the special competence of particular arbitrators. Where an arbitral determination gives full consideration to an employee's Title VII rights, a court may properly accord it great weight. This is especially true where the issue is solely one of fact, specifically addressed by the parties and decided by the arbitrator on the basis of an adequate record. But courts should ever be mindful that Congress, in enacting Title VII, thought it necessary to provide a judicial forum for the ultimate resolution of discriminatory employment claims. It is the duty of courts to assure the full availability of this forum.

of the Civil Rights Act of 1964, 78 Stat. 253, as amended, 42 U.S.C. §§ 2000e to 2000e–17 (1976 ed. and Supp. IV), by discriminating in the hiring of Negroes and women at its Corinth, Miss., plastics manufacturing facility. App. 2. In addition, the Director found that the departmental and plant-wide seniority systems, mandated by the Company's collective bargaining agreement with respondent Local Union No. 759 (Union), were unlawful because they perpetuated the effects of the Company's past discrimination. The Company was invited, pursuant to § 706(b) of the Act, 42 U.S.C. § 2000e–5(b), to conciliate the dispute. Although the Commission also invited the Union to participate, the Union declined to do so.

B

A collective bargaining agreement between petitioner and respondent expired in March 1974, and failed negotiations led to a strike. The Company hired strike replacements, some of whom were women who took Company jobs never before held by women. The strike was settled in May with the signing of a new agreement that continued the plant seniority system specified by the expired agreement. The strikers returned to work, but the Company also retained the strike replacements. The women replacements were assigned to positions in the Corinth plant ahead of men with greater seniority. Specifically, the Company prevented men from exercising the shift preference seniority (to which they were entitled under the collective bargaining agreement) to obtain positions held by the women strike replacements. The men affected by this action filed grievances under the procedures established by the collective bargaining agreement.

The Company refused to join the ultimate arbitration. Instead, it filed an action under § 301 of the Labor Management Relations Act of 1947, 61 Stat. 156, 29 U.S.C. § 185, in the United States District Court for the Northern District of Mississippi. The Company sought an injunction prohibiting arbitration of the grievances while the Company negotiated a conciliation agreement with the Commission. The Union counterclaimed to compel arbitration.

Before the District Court took any action, the Company and the Commission signed a conciliation agreement dated December 11, 1974. App. 10. In addition to ratifying the Company's position with respect to the shift preference dispute, the conciliation agreement provided that in the event of layoffs, the Company would maintain the existing proportion of women in the plant's bargaining unit. App. 15–16. The Company then amended its § 301 complaint to add the Commission as a defendant and to request an injunction barring the arbitration of grievances seeking relief that conflicted with the terms of the conciliation agreement. The Commission cross-claimed against the Union and counterclaimed against the Company for a declaratory judgment that the conciliation agreement prevailed, or, in the alternative, for a declaratory judgment that the seniority provisions were not a bona fide seniority system protected by § 703(h) of the Civil Rights Act, 78 Stat. 259, 42 U.S.C. § 2000e–2(h).[1]

While cross-motions for summary judgment were under consideration, the Company laid off employees pursuant to the conciliation agreement. Several men affected by the layoff, who would have been protected under the seniority provisions of the collective bargaining agreement, filed grievances. In November 1975, with the Company still refusing to arbitrate, the District Court granted summary judgment for the Commission and the Company. It held that under Title VII the seniority provisions could be modified to alleviate the effects of past discrimination. Southbridge Plastics Division, W.R. Grace & Co. v. Local 759, 403 F.Supp. 1183, 1188 (1975). The court declared that the terms of the conciliation agreement were binding on all parties and that "all parties * * * shall abide thereby." App. 44.[2] The Union appealed, and no party sought a stay.

With the Union's appeal pending before the United States Court of Appeals for the Fifth Circuit, the Company, following the terms of the conciliation agreement, laid off more employees. Again, adversely affected male employees filed grievances. In January 1978, over two years after the District Court's decision, the Court of Appeals reversed. Southbridge Plastics Division, W.R. Grace & Co. v. Local 759, 565 F.2d 913. Applying Teamsters v. United States, 431 U.S. 324, 97 S.Ct. 1843, 52 L.Ed.2d 396 (1977), which was decided after the District Court's decision, the Court of Appeals held that because the seniority system was not animated by a discriminatory purpose, it was lawful and could not be modified without the Union's consent. 565 F.2d, at 916. The court granted the Union's counterclaim, compelling the Company to arbitrate the grievances.

In response to this decision, the Company reinstated the male employees to the positions to which they were entitled under the collective bargaining agreement. The pending grievances, seeking backpay, then proceeded to arbitration. The first to reach arbitration was that of a male employee who had been demoted while the District Court order was in effect. Arbitrator Anthony J. Sabella, in August 1978, concluded that although the grievant was entitled to an award under the collective bargaining agreement, it would be inequitable to

---

1. The Company's amended complaint, unlike the Commission's pleadings, did not expressly request a declaratory judgment under 28 U.S.C. §§ 2201 and 2202. See App. in Southbridge Plastics Division, W.R. Grace & Co. v. Local 759, No. 75–4416 (CA5), pp. 98, 123–124, 129–130. The United States Court of Appeals for the Fifth Circuit, however, viewed the Company's complaint as seeking a declaration of its obligations under the respective contracts. See 565 F.2d 913, 915 (1978).

2. The relevant text of the order is as follows:

"(1) The terms of the conciliation agreement executed on December 11, 1974, by the plaintiff and the defendant, EEOC, are binding upon all the parties to this action; and

"(2) Where the provisions of the collective bargaining agreement executed by the plaintiff and defendant, Local 759, conflict with the provisions of the conciliation agreement executed by the plaintiff and defendant, EEOC, the provisions of the conciliation agreement are controlling and all parties to this action shall abide thereby." App. 44.

penalize the Company for conduct that complied with an outstanding court order. App. 45. He thus denied the grievance. Id., at 47. Instead of filing an action to set aside that award, the Union chose to contest Sabella's reasoning in later arbitrations.

C

The next grievance to be arbitrated resulted in the award in dispute here. App. 48. Arbitrator Gerald A. Barrett was presented with the complaints of two men who had been laid off before, and one man who had been laid off after, the entry of the District Court order.[3] Acknowledging that the Sabella arbitration resolved the same contractual issue, id., at 51, Barrett first considered whether the collective bargaining agreement required him to follow the Sabella arbitration award. He concluded that it did not. The collective bargaining agreement limited the arbitrator's authority, Barrett found, to considering whether the express terms of the contract had been violated.[4] Because Sabella had considered the fairness of enforcing the terms of the contract, he had acted outside his contractually defined jurisdiction. Id., at 55–56. Barrett determined that the finality clause of the collective bargaining agreement [5] therefore did not require him to follow Sabella's award. Ibid.

Arbitrator Barrett then turned to the grievances before him. The Company did not dispute that it had violated the seniority provisions of the collective bargaining agreement,[6] id., at 56, and Barrett also accepted the Company's contention that it had acted in good faith in following the conciliation agreement. He found, however, that the collective bargaining agreement made no exception for good faith violations of the seniority provisions, and that the Company had acted at its own risk in breaching the agreement. The Company, he held, could not complain that the law ultimately had made this out to be an unfortunate decision. Ibid. In essence, Barrett interpreted the collective

3. Neither the parties nor the District Court nor the Court of Appeals attached significance to this distinction between the grievants. See Brief for EEOC as *Amicus Curiae* 6, n. 6. Our resolution of the case eliminates any need to consider it.

4. The 1974 collective bargaining agreement and the succeeding 1977 agreement each defined the arbitrator's jurisdiction as follows:

"The jurisdiction and authority of the Arbitrator of the grievance and his opinion and award shall be confined exclusively to the interpretation and application of the express provision or provisions of this Agreement at issue between the Union and the Company. He shall have no authority to add to, adjust, change, or modify any provision of this Agreement." Art. IV, § 3; App. 19, 31.

5. The finality clause in each of the 1974 and 1977 collective bargaining agreements provided in relevant part: "The decision of the Arbitrator on the merits of any grievance adjudicated within his jurisdiction and authority as specified in this Agreement shall be final and binding on the aggrieved employee or employees, the Union and the Company." Art. IV, § 4; App. 20, 32.

6. The 1974 and 1977 collective bargaining agreements each provided: "If it is determined in the grievance procedure that an employee has been unjustly discharged or suspended the employee shall be reinstated to his former job and shall be compensated at his regular hourly earnings for the time lost less any penalty time decided upon." Art. IV, § 7(a); App. 21, 32–33.

bargaining agreement as providing that the District Court's order did not extinguish the Company's liability for its breach.

D

The Company then instituted another action under § 301 of the Labor Management Relations Act to overturn the award. The United States District Court for the Northern District of Mississippi entered summary judgment for the Company, finding that public policy prevented enforcement of the collective bargaining agreement during the period prior to the Court of Appeals' reversal. App. 58–69. The United States Court of Appeals for the Fifth Circuit reversed. 652 F.2d 1248 (1981). We granted certiorari to decide the important issue of federal labor law that the case presents. 458 U.S. ___, 102 S.Ct. 3481, 73 L.Ed. 2d 1365 (1982).

II

The sole issue before the Court is whether the Barrett award should be enforced. Under well established standards for the review of labor arbitration awards, a federal court may not overrule an arbitrator's decision simply because the court believes its own interpretation of the contract would be the better one. Steelworkers v. Enterprise Wheel & Car Corp., 363 U.S. 593, 596, 80 S.Ct. 1358, 1360, 4 L.Ed.2d 1424 (1960). When the parties include an arbitration clause in their collective bargaining agreement, they choose to have disputes concerning constructions of the contract resolved by an arbitrator. Unless the arbitral decision does not "dra[w] its essence from the collective bargaining agreement," id., at 597, 80 S.Ct., at 1361, a court is bound to enforce the award and is not entitled to review the merits of the contract dispute. This remains so even when the basis for the arbitrator's decision may be ambiguous. Id., at 598, 80 S.Ct., at 1361.

Under this standard, the Court of Appeals was correct in enforcing the Barrett award, although it seems to us to have taken a somewhat circuitous route to this result.[7] Barrett's initial conclusion that he was not bound by the Sabella decision was based on his interpretation of the bargaining agreement's provisions defining the arbitrator's jurisdiction and his perceived obligation to give a prior award a preclusive effect. See nn. 4 and 5, supra. Because the authority of arbitrators is a subject of collective bargaining, just as is any other contractual provision, the scope of the arbitrator's authority is itself a question of contract interpretation that the parties have delegated to the arbitrator. Barrett's conclusions that Sabella acted outside his jurisdiction and that this deprived the Sabella award of precedential force under the contract draw their "essence" from the provisions of the collective bargaining

---

7. Although the court believed that the validity of the Sabella award was the dispositive issue, 652 F.2d, at 1252, the Union raised and argued the question whether the Barrett award itself was enforceable. Brief for Appellant in No. 80–3661 (CA5), pp. 18–30. We disagree with the court's initial premise that the validity of the Sabella award is relevant. Only the enforceability of the Barrett award is at issue.

agreement. Regardless of what our view might be of the correctness of Barrett's contractual interpretation, the Company and the Union bargained for that interpretation. A federal court may not second-guess it. Steelworkers v. Enterprise Wheel & Car Corp., 363 U.S., at 599, 80 S.Ct., at 1362.

Barrett's analysis of the merits of the grievances is entitled to the same deference. He found that the collective bargaining agreement provided no good faith defense to claims of violations of the seniority provisions, and gave him no authority to weigh in some other fashion the Company's good faith. Again, although conceivably we could reach a different result were we to interpret the contract ourselves,[8] we cannot say that the award does not draw its essence from the collective bargaining agreement.

III

As with any contract, however, a court may not enforce a collective bargaining agreement that is contrary to public policy. See Hurd v. Hodge, 334 U.S. 24, 34–35, 68 S.Ct. 847, 852–53, 92 L.Ed. 1187 (1948). Barrett's view of his own jurisdiction precluded his consideration of this question, and, in any event, the question of public policy is ultimately one for resolution by the courts. See International Brotherhood of Teamsters v. Washington Employers, Inc., 557 F.2d 1345, 1350 (CA9 1977); Local 453 v. Otis Elevator Co., 314 F.2d 25, 29 (CA2 1963), cert. denied, 373 U.S. 949, 83 S.Ct. 1680, 10 L.Ed.2d 705 (1963); Kaden, Judges and Arbitrators: Observations on the Scope of Judicial Review, 80 Colum.L.Rev. 267, 287 (1980). If the contract as interpreted by Barrett violates some explicit public policy, we are obliged to refrain from enforcing it. Hurd v. Hodge, 334 U.S., at 35, 68 S.Ct., at 853. Such a public policy, however, must be well defined and dominant, and is to be ascertained "by reference to the laws and legal precedents and not from general considerations of supposed public interests." Muschany v. United States, 324 U.S. 49, 66, 65 S.Ct. 442, 451, 89 L.Ed. 744 (1945).

A

It is beyond question that obedience to judicial orders is an important public policy. An injunction issued by a court acting within its jurisdiction must be obeyed until the injunction is vacated or withdrawn. Walker v. City of Birmingham, 388 U.S. 307, 313–314, 87 S.Ct.

---

8. The 1974 and 1977 collective bargaining agreements each contained a clause that provided: "In the event that any provision of this Agreement is found to be in conflict with any State or Federal Laws now existing or hereinafter enacted, it is agreed that such laws shall supersede the conflicting provisions without affecting the remainder of these provisions." Art. XIV, § 7; App. 29, 42. Before the Court of Appeals, the Company argued that under this "legality" clause the seniority provi-sion was superceded by the District Court's determination that the provision was illegal. The Court of Appeals responded that its decision reversing the District Court had retroactive effect because it declared the law as it always had existed. 652 F.2d, at 1255. It seems to us, however, that the Company's argument was that the court should interpret the legality clause itself, a privilege not permitted to federal courts in reviewing an arbitral award.

1824, 1828, 18 L.Ed.2d 1210 (1967); United States v. United Mine Workers, 330 U.S. 258, 293–294, 67 S.Ct. 677, 695–96, 91 L.Ed. 884 (1947); Howat v. Kansas, 258 U.S. 181, 189–190, 42 S.Ct. 277, 280–81, 66 L.Ed. 550 (1922). A contract provision the performance of which has been enjoined is unenforceable. See Restatement (Second) of Contracts §§ 261, 264 (1981). Here, however, enforcement of the collective bargaining agreement as interpreted by Barrett does not compromise this public policy.

Given the Company's desire to reduce its workforce, it is undeniable that the Company was faced with a dilemma: it could follow the conciliation agreement as mandated by the District Court and risk liability under the collective bargaining agreement, or it could follow the bargaining agreement and risk both a contempt citation and Title VII liability. The dilemma, however, was of the Company's own making. The Company committed itself voluntarily to two conflicting contractual obligations. When the Union attempted to enforce its contractual rights, the Company sought a judicial declaration of its respective obligations under the contracts. During the course of this litigation, before the legal rights were finally determined,[9] the Company again laid off employees and dishonored its contract with the Union. For these acts, the Company incurred liability for breach of contract. In effect, Barrett interpreted the collective bargaining agreement to allocate to the Company the losses caused by the Company's decision to follow the District Court order that proved to be erroneous.[10]

Even assuming that the District Court's order was a mandatory injunction,[11] nothing in the collective bargaining agreement as inter-

---

9. We do not decide whether some public policy would be violated by an arbitral award for a breach of seniority provisions ultimately found to be illegal under Teamsters v. United States, 431 U.S. 324, 355–356, 97 S.Ct. 1843, 1864–65, 52 L.Ed.2d 396 (1977). Neither do we decide whether such an award could be enforced in the face of a valid judicial alteration of seniority provisions, pursuant to Franks v. Bowman Transportation Co., 424 U.S. 747, 778–779, 96 S.Ct. 1251, 1270–71, 47 L.Ed.2d 444 (1976), to provide relief to discriminatees under Title VII or other law. See Dennison v. City of Los Angeles Department of Water and Power, 658 F.2d 694, 695–696 (CA9 1981); EEOC v. McCall Printing Corp., 633 F.2d 1232, 1237 (CA6 1980).

10. Although Barrett could have considered the District Court order to cause impossibility of performance and thus to be a defense to the Company's breach, he did not do so. Impossibility is a doctrine of contract interpretation. See 18 W. Jaeger, Williston on Contracts §§ 1931–1979 (3d ed. 1978). For the reasons stated in the text, we cannot revise Barrett's implicit rejection of the impossibility defense.

Even if we were to review the issue de novo, moreover, it is far from clear that the defense is available to the Company, whose own actions created the condition of impossibility. See id., § 1939, p. 50; Uniform Commercial Code § 2–615(a) and comment 10, 1A U.L.A. 335, 338 (1976); Lowenschuss v. Kane, 520 F.2d 255, 265 (CA2 1975).

11. As a threshold matter, we doubt that the District Court in this case ordered specific performance of the conciliation agreement or granted any other type of injunctive relief. That court, in "considering the declaratory relief sought," 403 F.Supp., at 1187, stated that the issue was "whether the terms of the conciliation agreement override the terms of the bargaining agreement." Ibid. Both the Company's amended complaint and the Union's counterclaim invoked only the cause of action provided by § 301 of the Labor Management Relations Act. Although the Commission filed a counterclaim against the Company alleging that the Company had violated Title VII, the Court of Appeals treated the case as a § 301 action. See 565 F.2d, at 917. See generally Airline

preted by Barrett required the Company to violate that order. Barrett's award neither mandated layoffs [12] nor required that layoffs be conducted according to the collective bargaining agreement. The award simply held, retrospectively, that the employees were entitled to damages for the prior breach of the seniority provisions.[13]

In this case, the Company actually complied with the District Court's order, and nothing we say here causes us to believe that it would disobey the order if presented with the same dilemma in the future. Enforcement of Barrett's award will not create intolerable incentives to disobey court orders. Courts have sufficient contempt powers to protect their injunctions, even if the injunctions are issued erroneously. See Walker v. City of Birmingham, 388 U.S., at 315, 87 S.Ct., at 1829. In addition to contempt sanctions, the Company here was faced with possible Title VII liability if it departed from the conciliation agreement in conducting its layoffs. The Company was cornered by its own actions, and it cannot argue now that liability under the collective bargaining agreement violates public policy.

Stewards & Stewardesses Assn. v. American Airlines, Inc., 573 F.2d 960, 963 (CA7), cert. denied, 439 U.S. 876, 99 S.Ct. 214, 58 L.Ed.2d 190 (1978) (judicial review of Title VII settlement agreement is not review of judgment of Title VII liability after trial). Consistent with this view, the court expressly stated that the action was not brought under Title VII, 565 F.2d, at 917, and refused to remand to permit individual women employees to meet the standards set forth in Teamsters v. United States, 431 U.S. 324, 97 S.Ct. 1843, 52 L.Ed.2d 396 (1977). See 565 F.2d, at 917. Thus, the courts had no occasion to order injunctive relief under Title VII. The decision of the District Court instead seems to be a declaration of the rights and obligations of the parties under the conflicting agreements, and not a mandatory injunction. Given the ambiguity, however, we assume for purposes of decision that the District Court's order constituted an injunction.

12. Economic necessity is not recognized as a commercial impracticability defense to a breach of contract claim. Uniform Commercial Code § 2–615, comment 4, 1A U.L.A. 336 (1976) (increased cost of performance does not constitute impossibility); 18 W. Jaeger, Williston on Contracts § 1931, pp. 7–8 (3d ed. 1978) (same). Thus, while it may have been economic misfortune for the Company to postpone or forgo its layoff plans, its extant, conflicting, and voluntarily assumed contractual obligations exposed it to liability regardless of the layoff procedure it followed. In order to avoid liability under either contract, the Company, of course, could have accepted the economic losses of foregoing its reduction-in-force plans.

This is not to say that in the face of the economic necessity of the layoffs, the Company had no way whatsoever to avoid the injury. Prior to conducting the layoffs, the Company could have requested a stay from the District Court to permit it to follow the collective bargaining agreement pending review by the Court of Appeals. It was the Company, which had sought the declaration of rights and obligations, and which chose to act before the determination of its respective contractual obligations was final; the Union most likely would have preferred that no lay-offs occur at all. Although the Union could have requested a stay, there is no rule requiring a party to ask for prospective relief from a possible contractual breach. The Union justifiably relied on its right to backpay damages. Moreover, the Company, in future contract negotiations, may seek to bargain for a contract provision expressly allocating the loss to its employees in a case such as this one.

13. Compensatory damages may be available to a plaintiff injured by a breach of contract even when specific performance of the contract would violate public policy. Restatement (Second) of Contracts § 365, comment a (1981). This principle is particularly applicable here; since the employees' Union had no responsibility for the events giving rise to the injunction, and entered into the collective bargaining agreement ignorant of any illegality, the employees are not precluded from recovery for the breach. Id., at § 180, comment a.

Nor is placing the Company in this position with respect to the court order so unfair as to violate public policy. Obeying injunctions often is a costly affair.[14] Because of the Company's alleged prior discrimination against women, some readjustments and consequent losses were bound to occur. The issue is whether the Company or the Union members should bear the burden of those losses. As interpreted by Barrett, the collective bargaining agreement placed this unavoidable burden on the Company. By entering into the conflicting conciliation agreement, by seeking a court order to excuse it from performing the collective bargaining agreement, and by subsequently acting on its mistaken interpretation of its contractual obligations, the Company attempted to shift the loss to its male employees, who shared no responsibility for the sex discrimination. The Company voluntarily assumed its obligations under the collective bargaining agreement and the arbitrators' interpretations of it. No public policy is violated by holding the Company to those obligations, which bar the Company's attempted reallocation of the burden.

IV

For the foregoing reasons, the Barrett award is properly to be enforced. The judgment of the Court of Appeals is therefore affirmed.

It is so ordered.

---

14. A party injured by the issuance of an injunction later determined to be erroneous has no action for damages in the absence of a bond. Russell v. Farley, 105 U.S. 433, 437, 26 L.Ed. 1060 (1882); Buddy Systems, Inc. v. Exer-Genie, Inc., 545 F.2d 1164, 1167–1168 (CA9 1976), cert. denied, 431 U.S. 903, 97 S.Ct. 1694, 52 L.Ed.2d 387 (1977). Enforcing the Barrett award to compensate the injuries suffered by the male employees does not violate this principle. The only party injured by the injunction itself has been the Company; the proof of this is that if the Company had done nothing at all, see n. 12, supra, the economic loss from failing to reduce the workforce would have fallen on the Company. By an independent and voluntary act, the Company shifted this loss to its male employees and thereby caused the injury remedied by the Barrett award.

Chapter VI

AGE DISCRIMINATION

A. DISPARATE TREATMENT

TRANS WORLD AIRLINES, INC. v. THURSTON

Supreme Court of the United States, 1985.
469 U.S. 111, 105 S.Ct. 613, 83 L.Ed.2d 523.

JUSTICE POWELL delivered the opinion of the Court.

Trans World Airlines, Inc. (TWA), a commercial airline, permits captains disqualified from serving in that capacity for reasons other than age to transfer automatically to the position of flight engineer. In this case, we must decide whether the Age Discrimination in Employment Act of 1967 (ADEA), 29 U.S.C. § 621 et seq., requires the airline to afford this same "privilege of employment" to those captains disqualified by their age. We also must decide what constitutes a "willful" violation of the ADEA, entitling a plaintiff to "liquidated" or double damages.

I

A

TWA has approximately 3,000 employees who fill the three cockpit positions on most of its flights.[1] The "captain" is the pilot and controls the aircraft. He is responsible for all phases of its operation. The "first officer" is the copilot and assists the captain. The "flight engineer" usually monitors a side-facing instrument panel. He does not operate the flight controls unless the captain and the first officer become incapacitated.

In 1977, TWA and the Air Line Pilots Association (ALPA) entered into a collective-bargaining agreement, under which every employee in a cockpit position was required to retire when he reached the age of 60. This provision for mandatory retirement was lawful under the ADEA,

---

1. On certain long-distance flights, a fourth crew member, the "international relief officer," is in the cockpit. On some types of aircraft, there are only two cockpit positions.

as part of a "bona fide seniority system." See United Air Lines, Inc. v. McMann, 434 U.S. 192, 98 S.Ct. 444, 54 L.Ed.2d 402 (1977). On April 6, 1978, however, the Act was amended to prohibit the mandatory retirement of a protected individual because of his age.[2] TWA officials became concerned that the company's retirement policy, at least as it applied to flight engineers, violated the amended ADEA.[3]

On July 19, 1978, TWA announced that the amended ADEA prohibited the forced retirement of flight engineers at age 60. The company thus proposed a new policy, under which employees in all three cockpit positions, upon reaching age 60, would be allowed to continue working as flight engineers. TWA stated that it would not implement its new policy until it "had the benefit of [ALPA's] views." ALPA's views were not long in coming. The Union contended that the collective-bargaining agreement prohibited the employment of a flight engineer after his 60th birthday and that the proposed change was not required by the recently amended ADEA.

Despite opposition from the Union, TWA adopted a modified version of its proposal. Under this plan, any employee in "flight engineer status" at age 60 is entitled to continue working in that capacity. The new plan, unlike the initial proposal, does not give 60-year-old captains [6] the right automatically to begin training as flight engineers. Instead, a captain may remain with the airline only if he has been able to obtain "flight engineer status" through the bidding procedures outlined in the collective-bargaining agreement. These procedures require a captain, prior to his 60th birthday, to submit a "standing bid" for the position of flight engineer. When a vacancy occurs, it is assigned to the most senior captain with a standing bid. If no vacancy occurs prior to his 60th birthday, or if he lacks sufficient seniority to bid successfully for those vacancies that do occur, the captain is retired.[7]

Under the collective-bargaining agreement, a captain displaced for any reason besides age need not resort to the bidding procedures. For example, a captain unable to maintain the requisite first-class medical certificate, see 14 CFR § 67.13 (1984), may displace automatically, or

---

2. Section 2(a) of the Age Discrimination in Employment Act Amendments of 1978, Pub.L. 95–256, 92 Stat. 189, 29 U.S.C. § 623(f)(2).

3. A regulation promulgated by the Federal Aviation Administration prohibits anyone from serving after age 60 as a pilot on a commercial carrier. 14 CFR § 121.383(c) (1984). Captains and first officers are considered "pilots" subject to this regulation; flight engineers are not. Therefore, TWA officials were concerned primarily with the effect that the 1978 amendments had on the company's policy of mandatory retirement of flight engineers.

6. The term "captain" will hereinafter be used to refer to both the positions of captain and first officer.

7. In 1980, TWA imposed an additional restriction on captains bidding for flight engineer positions. Successful bidders were required to "fulfill their bids in a timely manner." Under this amended practice, captains who bid successfully for positions as flight engineers were required to "activate" their bids immediately. As a result, many captains under age 60 were trained for and assumed flight engineer positions, with resulting lower pay and responsibility.

"bump," a less senior flight engineer.[8]   The medically disabled captain's ability to bump does not depend upon the availability of a
vacancy.[9]   Similarly, a captain whose position is eliminated due to
reduced manpower needs can "bump" a less senior flight engineer.[10]
Even if a captain is found to be incompetent to serve in that capacity,
he is not discharged,[11] but is allowed to transfer to a position as flight
engineer without resort to the bidding procedures.[12]

Respondents Harold Thurston, Christopher J. Clark, and Clifton A.
Parkhill, former captains for TWA, were retired upon reaching the age
of 60.   Each was denied an opportunity to "bump" a less senior flight
engineer.   Thurston was forced to retire on May 26, 1978, before the
company adopted its new policy.   Clark did not attempt to bid because
TWA had advised him that bidding would not affect his chances of
obtaining a transfer.   These two captains thus effectively were denied
an opportunity to become flight engineers through the bidding procedures.   The third captain, Parkhill, did file a standing bid for the
position of flight engineer.   No vacancies occurred prior to Parkhill's
60th birthday, however, and he too was forced to retire.

B

Thurston, Clark, and Parkhill filed this action against TWA and
ALPA in the United States District Court for the Southern District of
New York.   They argued that the company's transfer policy violated
ADEA § 4(a)(1), 29 U.S.C. § 623(a)(1).   The airline allowed captains
displaced for reasons other than age to "bump" less senior flight
engineers.   Captains compelled to vacate their positions upon reaching
age 60, they claimed, should be afforded this same "privilege of employment."   The Equal Employment Opportunity Commission intervened
on behalf of 10 other age-disqualified captains who had been discharged
as a result of their inability to displace less senior flight engineers.

The District Court entered a summary judgment in favor of defendants TWA and ALPA.   Air Line Pilots Assn. v. Trans World Air Lines,
547 F.Supp. 1221 (SDNY 1982).   The court held that the plaintiffs had
failed to establish a prima facie case of age discrimination under the
test set forth in McDonnell Douglas Corp. v. Green, 411 U.S. 792, 93

---

8. The pilot must be able to obtain the
second-class medical certificate that is required for the position of flight engineer.
See 14 CFR § 67.15 (1984).

9. If the disabled captain lacks sufficient seniority to displace, he is not discharged.   Rather, he is entitled to go on
unpaid medical leave for up to five years,
during which time he retains and continues to accrue seniority.

10. Only those flight engineers in the
current and last former domiciles of the
displaced captain may be "bumped."   If a
captain has insufficient seniority to displace a flight engineer at either of these
domiciles, he is not discharged.   Instead,

he is placed in furlough status for a period
of up to 10 years, during which time he
continues to accrue seniority for purposes
of a recall.

11. Although the collective-bargaining
agreement does not address disciplinary
downgrades, TWA's Vice President of
Flight Operations, J.E. Frankum, stated
that such downgrades had occurred "many
times over many years."

12. Captains disqualified for other reasons also are allowed to "bump" less senior
flight engineers.   For example, the collective-bargaining agreement provides that a
captain who fails to "requalify" in that
position will not be discharged.

S.Ct. 1817, 36 L.Ed.2d 668 (1973). None could show that at the time of his transfer request a vacancy existed for the position of flight engineer. See id., at 802, 93 S.Ct., at 1824. Furthermore, the court found that two affirmative defenses justified the company's transfer policy. 29 U.S.C. § 623(f)(1) and (f)(2). The United States Court of Appeals for the Second Circuit reversed the District Court's judgment. 713 F.2d 940 (1983). It found the *McDonnell Douglas* formula inapposite because the plaintiffs had adduced *direct* proof of age discrimination. Captains disqualified for reasons other than age were allowed to "bump" less senior flight engineers. Therefore, the company was required by ADEA § 4(a)(1), 29 U.S.C. § 623(a)(1), to afford 60-year-old captains this same "privilege of employment." The Court of Appeals also held that the affirmative defenses of the ADEA did not justify the company's discriminatory transfer policy.[14] 713 F.2d, at 949–951. TWA was held liable for "liquidated" or double damages because its violation of the ADEA was found to be "willful." According to the court, an employer's conduct is "willful" if it "knows or shows reckless disregard for the matter of whether its conduct is prohibited by the ADEA." Because "TWA was clearly aware of the 1978 ADEA amendments," the Court of Appeals found the respondents entitled to double damages. Id., at 956–957.

TWA filed a petition for a writ of certiorari in which it challenged the Court of Appeals' holding that the transfer policy violated the ADEA and that TWA's violation was "willful." The Union filed a cross-petition raising only the liability issue. We granted certiorari in both cases, and consolidated them for argument. We now affirm as to the violation of the ADEA, and reverse as to the claim for double damages.

II

A

The ADEA "broadly prohibits arbitrary discrimination in the workplace based on age." Lorillard v. Pons, 434 U.S. 575, 577, 98 S.Ct. 866, 868, 55 L.Ed.2d 40 (1978). Section 4(a)(1) of the Act proscribes differential treatment of older workers "with respect to * * * [a] privileg[e] of employment." 29 U.S.C. § 623(a). Under TWA's transfer policy, 60-year-old captains are denied a "privilege of employment" on the basis of age. Captains who become disqualified from serving in that position

---

14. The Court of Appeals also found that ALPA had violated ADEA § 4(c), 29 U.S.C. § 623(c), which prohibits unions from causing or attempting to cause an employer to engage in unlawful discrimination. The court found, however, that ALPA was not liable for damages. It held that the ADEA does not permit the recovery of monetary damages, including back pay, against a labor organization. It noted that the ADEA incorporates the remedial scheme of the FLSA, which does not allow actions against unions to recover damages. 713 F.2d, at 957.

In its petition for a writ of certiorari, TWA raised the issue of a union's liability for damages under the ADEA. Although we granted the petition in full, we now conclude that the Court is without jurisdiction to consider this question. TWA was not the proper party to present this question. The airline cannot assert the right of others to recover damages against the Union.

for reasons other than age automatically are able to displace less senior flight engineers. Captains disqualified because of age are not afforded this same "bumping" privilege. Instead, they are forced to resort to the bidding procedures set forth in the collective-bargaining agreement. If there is no vacancy prior to a bidding captain's 60th birthday, he must retire.[15]

The Act does not require TWA to grant transfer privileges to disqualified captains. Nevertheless, if TWA does grant some disqualified captains the "privilege" of "bumping" less senior flight engineers, it may not deny this opportunity to others because of their age. In Hishon v. King & Spalding, 457 U.S. ___, 104 S.Ct. 2229, 81 L.Ed.2d 59 (1984), we held that "[a] benefit that is part and parcel of the employment relationship may not be doled out in a discriminatory fashion, even if the employer would be free * * * not to provide the benefit at all." Id., at ___, 104 S.Ct., at 2234. This interpretation of Title VII of the Civil Rights Act of 1964, 42 U.S.C. § 2000e et seq., applies with equal force in the context of age discrimination, for the substantive provisions of the ADEA "were derived in *haec verba* from Title VII." Lorillard v. Pons, supra, 434 U.S., at 584, 98 S.Ct., at 872.

TWA contends that the respondents failed to make out a prima facie case of age discrimination under McDonnell Douglas v. Green, 411 U.S. 792, 93 S.Ct. 1817, 36 L.Ed.2d 668 (1973), because at the time they were retired, no flight engineer vacancies existed. This argument fails, for the *McDonnell Douglas* test is inapplicable where the plaintiff presents direct evidence of discrimination. See Teamsters v. United States, 431 U.S. 324, 358 n. 44, 97 S.Ct. 1843, 1866 n. 44, 52 L.Ed.2d 396 (1977). The shifting burdens of proof set forth in *McDonnell Douglas* are designed to assure that the "plaintiff [has] his day in court despite the unavailability of direct evidence." Loeb v. Textron, Inc., 600 F.2d 1003, 1014 (CA1 1979). In this case there is direct evidence that the method of transfer available to a disqualified captain depends upon his age. Since it allows captains who become disqualified for any reason other than age to "bump" less senior flight engineers, TWA's transfer policy is discriminatory on its face. Cf. Los Angeles Dept. of Water & Power v. Manhart, 435 U.S. 702, 98 S.Ct. 1370, 55 L.Ed.2d 657 (1978) (employer's policy requiring female employees to make larger contribution to pension fund than male employees is discriminatory on its face).

B

Although we find that TWA's transfer policy discriminates against disqualified captains on the basis of age, our inquiry cannot end here.

---

15. The discriminatory transfer policy may violate the Act even though 83% of the 60-year-old captains were able to obtain positions as flight engineers through the bidding procedures. See Phillips v. Martin Marietta Corp., 400 U.S. 542, 91 S.Ct. 496, 27 L.Ed.2d 613 (1971) (*per curiam*).

It also should be noted that many of the captains who obtained positions as flight engineers were forced to assume that position prior to reaching age 60. See n. 7, supra. They were adversely affected by the discriminatory transfer policy despite the fact that they obtained positions as flight engineers.

Petitioners contend that the age-based transfer policy is justified by two of the ADEA's five affirmative defenses. Petitioners first argue that the discharge of respondents was lawful because age is a "bona fide occupational qualification" (BFOQ) for the position of captain. 29 U.S.C. § 623(f)(1). Furthermore, TWA claims that its retirement policy is part of a "bona fide seniority system," and thus exempt from the Act's coverage. 29 U.S.C. § 623(f)(2).

Section 4(f)(1) of the ADEA provides that an employer may take "any action otherwise prohibited" where age is a "bona fide occupational qualification." 29 U.S.C. § 623(f)(1). In order to be permissible under § 4(f)(1), however, the age-based discrimination must relate to a "particular business." Ibid. Every court to consider the issue has assumed that the "particular business" to which the statute refers is the job from which the protected individual is excluded. In Weeks v. Southern Bell Tel. & Tel. Co., 408 F.2d 228 (CA5 1969), for example, the court considered the Title VII claim of a female employee who, because of her sex, had not been allowed to transfer to the position of switchman. In deciding that the BFOQ defense was not available to the defendant, the court considered only the job of switchman.

TWA's discriminatory transfer policy is not permissible under § 4(f)(1) because age is not a BFOQ for the "particular" position of flight engineer. It is necessary to recognize that the airline has two age-based policies: (i) captains are not allowed to serve in that capacity after reaching the age of 60; and (ii) age-disqualified captains are not given the transfer privileges afforded captains disqualified for other reasons. The first policy, which precludes individuals from serving as captains, is not challenged by respondents.[17] The second practice does not operate to exclude protected individuals from the position of captain; rather it prevents qualified 60-year-olds from working as flight engineers. Thus, it is the "particular" job of flight engineer from which the respondents were excluded by the discriminatory transfer policy. Because age under 60 is not a BFOQ for the position of flight engineer,[18] the age-based discrimination at issue in this case cannot be justified by § 4(f)(1).

TWA nevertheless contends that its BFOQ argument is supported by the legislative history of the amendments to the ADEA. In 1978, Congress amended ADEA § 4(f)(2), 29 U.S.C. § 623(f)(2), to prohibit the involuntary retirement of protected individuals on the basis of age. Some Members of Congress were concerned that this amendment might be construed as limiting the employer's ability to terminate workers subject to a valid BFOQ. The Senate proposed an amendment to § 4(f)

17. In this litigation, the respondents have not challenged TWA's claim that the FAA regulation establishes a BFOQ for the position of captain. The EEOC guidelines, however, do not list the FAA's age-60 rule as an example of a BFOQ because the EEOC wishes to avoid any appearance that it endorses the rule. 46 Fed.Reg. 47724, 47725 (1981).

18. The petitioners do not contend that age is a BFOQ for the position of flight engineer. Indeed, the airline has employed at least 148 flight engineers who are over 60 years old.

(1) providing that an employer could establish a mandatory retirement age where age is a BFOQ. S.Rep.No. 95–493, pp. 11, 24 (1977), U.S.Code Cong. & Admin.News 1978, p. 504. In the Conference Committee, however, the proposed amendment was withdrawn because "the [Senate] conferees agreed that * * * [it] neither added to nor worked any change upon present law." H.R.Conf.Rep. No. 95–950, p. 7 (1978), U.S. Code Cong. & Admin.News 1978, p. 529. The House Committee Report also indicated that an individual could be compelled to retire from a position for which age was a BFOQ. H.R.Rep. No. 95–527 pt. 1, p. 12 (1977).

The legislative history of the 1978 Amendments does not support petitioners' position. The history shows only that the ADEA does not prohibit TWA from retiring all disqualified captains, including those who are incapacitated because of age. This does not mean, however, that TWA can make dependent upon the age of the individual the availability of a transfer to a position for which age is not a BFOQ. Nothing in the legislative history cited by petitioners indicates a congressional intention to allow an employer to discriminate against an older worker seeking to transfer to another position, on the ground that age was a BFOQ for his *former* job.

TWA also contends that its discriminatory transfer policy is lawful under the Act because it is part of a "bona fide seniority system." 29 U.S.C. § 623(f)(2). The Court of Appeals held that the airline's retirement policy is not mandated by the negotiated seniority plan. We need not address this finding; any seniority system that includes the challenged practice is not "bona fide" under the statute. The Act provides that a seniority system may not "require or permit" the involuntary retirement of a protected individual because of his age. Ibid. Although the FAA "age 60 rule" may have caused respondents' retirement, TWA's seniority plan certainly "permitted" it within the meaning of the ADEA. Ibid. Moreover, because captains disqualified for reasons other than age are allowed to "bump" less senior flight engineers, the mandatory retirement was age-based. Therefore, the "bona fide seniority system" defense is unavailable to the petitioners.

In summary, TWA's transfer policy discriminates against protected individuals on the basis of age, and thereby violates the Act. The two statutory defenses raised by petitioners do not support the argument that this discrimination is justified. The BFOQ defense is meritless because age is not a bona fide occupational qualification for the position of flight engineer, the job from which the respondents were excluded. Nor can TWA's policy be viewed as part of a bona fide seniority system. A system that includes this discriminatory transfer policy permits the forced retirement of captains on the basis of age.

III

A

Section 7(b) of the ADEA, 29 U.S.C. § 626(b), provides that the rights created by the Act are to be "enforced in accordance with the powers, remedies, and procedures" of the Fair Labor Standards Act. See Lorillard v. Pons, 434 U.S., at 579, 98 S.Ct., at 869 (1978). But the remedial provisions of the two statutes are not identical. Congress declined to incorporate into the ADEA several FLSA sections. Moreover, § 16(b) of the FLSA, which makes the award of liquidated damages mandatory, is significantly qualified in ADEA § 7(b) by a proviso that a prevailing plaintiff is entitled to double damages "only in cases of willful violations." 29 U.S.C. § 626(b). In this case, the Court of Appeals held that TWA's violation of the ADEA was "willful," and that the respondents therefore were entitled to double damages. 713 F.2d, at 957. We granted certiorari to review this holding.

The legislative history of the ADEA indicates that Congress intended for liquidated damages to be punitive in nature. The original bill proposed by the administration incorporated § 16(a) of the FLSA, which imposes criminal liability for a willful violation. See 113 Cong.Rec. 2199 (1967). Senator Javits found "certain serious defects" in the administration bill. He stated that "difficult problems of proof * * * would arise under a criminal provision," and that the employer's invocation of the Fifth Amendment might impede investigation, conciliation, and enforcement. 113 Cong.Rec. 7076 (1967). Therefore, he proposed that "the [FLSA's] criminal penalty in cases of willful violation * * * [be] eliminated and a double damage liability substituted." Ibid. Senator Javits argued that his proposed amendment would "furnish an effective deterrent to willful violations [of the ADEA]," ibid., and it was incorporated into the ADEA with only minor modification, S. 788, 90th Cong., 1st Sess. (1967).

This Court has recognized that in enacting the ADEA, "Congress exhibited * * * a detailed knowledge of the FLSA provisions and their judicial interpretation * * *." Lorillard v. Pons, 434 U.S. 575, 581, 98 S.Ct. 866, 870, 55 L.Ed.2d 40 (1978). The manner in which FLSA § 16(a) has been interpreted therefore is relevant. In general, courts have found that an employer is subject to criminal penalties under the FLSA when he "wholly disregards the law * * * without making any reasonable effort to determine whether the plan he is following would constitute a violation of the law." Nabob Oil Co. v. United States, 190 F.2d 478, 479 (CA10), cert. denied, 342 U.S. 876, 72 S.Ct. 167, 96 L.Ed. 659 (1951); see also Darby v. United States, 132 F.2d 928 (CA5 1943).[19] This standard is substantially in accord with the

19. Courts below have held that an employer's action may be "willful," within the meaning of § 16(a) of the FLSA, even though he did not have an evil motive or bad purpose. See Nabob Oil Co. v. United States, 190 F.2d 478 (CA10), cert. denied, 342 U.S. 876, 72 S.Ct. 167, 96 L.Ed. 659 (1951). We do not agree with TWA's argument that unless it intended to violate the Act, double damages are inappropriate un-

interpretation of "willful" adopted by the Court of Appeals in interpreting the liquidated damages provision of the ADEA. The court below stated that a violation of the Act was "willful" if "the employer * * * knew or showed reckless disregard for the matter of whether its conduct was prohibited by the ADEA." 713 F.2d, at 956. Given the legislative history of the liquidated damages provision, we think the "reckless disregard" standard is reasonable.

The definition of "willful" adopted by the above cited courts is consistent with the manner in which this Court has interpreted the term in other criminal and civil statutes. In United States v. Murdock, 290 U.S. 389, 54 S.Ct. 223, 78 L.Ed. 381 (1933), the defendant was prosecuted under the Revenue Acts of 1926 and 1928, which made it a misdemeanor for a person "willfully" to fail to pay the required tax. The *Murdock* Court stated that conduct was "willful" within the meaning of this criminal statute if it was "marked by careless disregard [for] whether or not one has the right so to act." Id., at 395, 54 S.Ct., at 225. In United States v. Illinois Central R., 303 U.S. 239, 58 S.Ct. 533, 82 L.Ed. 773 (1938), the Court applied the *Murdock* definition of "willful" in a civil case. There, the defendant's failure to unload a cattle car was "willful," because it showed a disregard for the governing statute and an indifference to its requirements. Id., at 242–243, 58 S.Ct., at 534–535.[20]

The respondents argue that an employer's conduct is willful if he is "cognizant of an appreciable possibility that the employees involved were covered by the [ADEA]." In support of their position, the respondents cite § 6 of the Portal-to-Portal Act of 1947 (PPA), 29 U.S.C. § 255(a), which is incorporated in both the ADEA and the FLSA. Section 6 of the PPA provides for a 2-year statute of limitations period unless the violation is willful, in which case the limitations period is extended to three years. 29 U.S.C. § 255(a). Several courts have held that a violation is willful within the meaning of § 6 if the employer knew that the ADEA was "in the picture." See, e.g., Coleman v. Jiffy June Farms, Inc., 458 F.2d 1139, 1142 (CA5 1971), cert. denied, 409 U.S. 948, 93 S.Ct. 292, 34 L.Ed.2d 219 (1972); EEOC v. Central Kansas Medical Center, 705 F.2d 1270, 1274 (CA10 1983). Respondents contend that the term "willful" should be interpreted in a similar manner in applying the liquidated damages provision of the ADEA.

We are unpersuaded by respondents' argument that a violation of the Act is "willful" if the employer simply knew of the potential applicability of the ADEA. Even if the "in the picture" standard were appropriate for the statute of limitations, the same standard should not

der § 7(b) of the ADEA. Only one court of appeals has expressed approval of this position. See Loeb v. Textron, Inc., 600 F.2d 1003, 1020 n. 27 (CA1 1979).

20. The definition of "willful" set forth in *Murdock* and *Illinois Central* has been applied by courts interpreting numerous other criminal and civil statutes. See, e.g., Alabama Power Co. v. Federal Energy Regulatory Comm'n, 584 F.2d 750 (CA5 1978); F.X. Messina Construction Corp. v. Occupational Safety & Health Review Comm'n, 505 F.2d 701 (CA1 1974).

govern a provision dealing with liquidated damages.[21]   More importantly, the broad standard proposed by the respondents would result in an award of double damages in almost every case.   As employers are required to post ADEA notices, it would be virtually impossible for an employer to show that he was unaware of the Act and its potential applicability.   Both the legislative history and the structure of the statute show that Congress intended a two-tiered liability scheme.   We decline to interpret the liquidated damages provision of ADEA § 7(b) in a manner that frustrates this intent.[22]

B

As noted above, the Court of Appeals stated that a violation is "willful" if "the employer either knew or showed reckless disregard for the matter of whether its conduct was prohibited by the ADEA." 713 F.2d, at 956.   Although we hold that this is an acceptable way to articulate a definition of "willful," the court below misapplied this standard.   TWA certainly did not "know" that its conduct violated the Act.   Nor can it fairly be said that TWA adopted its transfer policy in "reckless disregard" of the Act's requirements.   The record makes clear that TWA officials acted reasonably and in good faith in attempting to determine whether their plan would violate the ADEA.   See Nabob Oil Co. v. United States, supra.

Shortly after the ADEA was amended, TWA officials met with their lawyers to determine whether the mandatory retirement policy violated the Act.   Concluding that the company's existing plan was inconsistent with the ADEA, David Crombie, the airline's Vice President for Administration, proposed a new policy.   Despite opposition from the Union, the company adopted a modified version of this initial proposal.   Under the plan adopted on August 10, 1978, any pilot in "flight engineer status" on his 60th birthday could continue to work for the airline.   On the day the plan was adopted, the union filed suit against the airline claiming that the new retirement policy constituted

---

21. The Courts of Appeals are divided over whether Congress intended the "willfulness" standard to be identical for determining liquidated damages and for purposes of the limitations period.   Compare Spagnuolo v. Whirlpool Corp., 641 F.2d 1109, 1113 (CA4), cert. denied, 454 U.S. 860, 102 S.Ct. 316, 70 L.Ed.2d 158 (1981) (standards are identical), with Kelly v. American Standard, Inc., 640 F.2d 974, 979 (CA9 1981) (standards are different).

22. The "in the picture" standard proposed by the respondents would allow the recovery of liquidated damages even if the employer acted reasonably and in complete "good faith."   Congress hardly intended such a result.

The Court interpreted the FLSA, as originally enacted, as allowing the recovery of liquidated damages any time that there

was a violation of the Act.   See Overnight Motor Transportation Co. v. Missel, 316 U.S. 572, 62 S.Ct. 1216, 86 L.Ed. 1682 (1942).   In response to its dissatisfaction with that harsh interpretation of the provision, Congress enacted the Portal-to-Portal Act of 1947.   See Lorillard v. Pons, 434 U.S. 575, 581–582 n. 8, 98 S.Ct. 866, 870 n. 8, 55 L.Ed.2d 40 (1978).   Section 11 of the PPA, 29 U.S.C. § 260, provides the employer with a defense to a mandatory award of liquidated damages when it can show good faith and reasonable grounds for believing it was not in violation of the FLSA.   Section 7(b) of the ADEA does not incorporate § 11 of the PPA, contra Hays v. Republic Steel Corp., 531 F.2d 1307 (CA5 1976). Nevertheless, we think that the same concerns are reflected in the proviso to § 7(b) of the ADEA.

a "major" change in the collective-bargaining agreement, and thus was barred by the § 6 of the Railway Labor Act, 45 U.S.C. § 156. Nevertheless, TWA adhered to its new policy.

As evidence of "willfulness," respondents point to comments made by J.E. Frankum, the Vice President of Flight Operations. After Crombie was hospitalized in August 1978, Frankum assumed responsibility for bringing TWA's retirement policy into conformance with the ADEA. Despite legal advice to the contrary, Frankum initially believed that the company was not required to allow any pilot over 60 to work. Frankum later abandoned this position in favor of the plan approved on August 10, 1978. Frankum apparently had been concerned only about whether flight engineers could work after reaching the age of 60. There is no indication that TWA was ever advised by counsel that its new transfer policy discriminated against captains on the basis of age.

There simply is no evidence that TWA acted in "reckless disregard" of the requirements of the ADEA. The airline had obligations under the collective-bargaining agreement with the Air Line Pilots Association. In an attempt to bring its retirement policy into compliance with the ADEA, while at the same time observing the terms of the collective-bargaining agreement, TWA sought legal advice and consulted with the Union. Despite opposition from the Union, a plan was adopted that permitted cockpit employees to work as "flight engineers" after reaching age 60. Apparently TWA officials and the airline's attorneys failed to focus specifically on the effect of each aspect of the new retirement policy for cockpit personnel. It is reasonable to believe that the parties involved, in focusing on the larger overall problem, simply overlooked the challenged aspect of the new plan. We conclude that TWA's violation of the Act was not willful within the meaning of § 7(b), and that respondents therefore are not entitled to liquidated damages.

IV

The ADEA requires TWA to afford 60-year-old captains the same transfer privileges that it gives to captains disqualified for reasons other than age. Therefore, we affirm the Court of Appeals on this issue. We do not agree with its holding that TWA's violation of the Act was willful. We accordingly reverse its judgment that respondents are entitled to liquidated or double damages.

It is so ordered.

WILHELM v. BLUE BELL, INC.

United States Court of Appeals for the Fourth Circuit, 1985.
773 F.2d 1429.

CHAPMAN, CIRCUIT JUDGE:

Plaintiffs Frank Wilhelm, Karl Gatlin, and Harold Kogut brought this age discrimination suit against their former employer, Blue Bell,

Inc., under the Age Discrimination in Employment Act of 1967 (ADEA), 29 U.S.C. § 621 et seq. Plaintiffs Wilhelm and Gatlin alleged that Blue Bell had discharged them because of their ages and that their respective discharges were without just cause and in violation of an implied covenant of good faith and fair dealing. Plaintiff Kogut later intervened and alleged that Blue Bell had discharged him because of his age. The plaintiffs' state law claims were dismissed prior to trial.

The jury found that Blue Bell had discharged plaintiffs Wilhelm and Kogut because of their ages in violation of the ADEA, awarded them damages, and concluded that Blue Bell's discrimination was "willful" within the meaning of § 7(b) of the ADEA, 29 U.S.C. § 626(b). The jury also found that plaintiff Gatlin had not filed his age claim with the Equal Employment Opportunity Commission within the applicable time period and accordingly awarded him no damages. In conformity with the jury's verdict the district court awarded Wilhelm and Kogut back pay, liquidated damages equal to the back pay amounts, reinstatement, attorneys' fees and costs. These orders were stayed pending appeal.

Blue Bell appeals claiming that the district court erred in denying its motions for judgment notwithstanding the verdict or a new trial and in instructing the jury on the issue of willfulness. We affirm the district court's denial of Blue Bell's motion for judgment notwithstanding the verdict but remand the case for a new trial on the issue of damages under a proper willfulness instruction.

I

Blue Bell manufactures and markets outer wearing apparel. Its most common product lines are blue jeans and related sportswear bearing the "Wrangler" brand name. Plaintiffs Wilhelm and Kogut were both Field Sales Representatives in the Southeastern Region of Blue Bell's Wrangler Boyswear Division. Wilhelm was responsible for the western half of North Carolina and Kogut was responsible for the southern half of Florida.

Wilhelm was fired on February 2, 1982. Wilhelm was forty-nine years old and had been employed by Blue Bell for eight and one-half years when he was fired. At trial Blue Bell claimed that it fired Wilhelm because he refused to make "line presentations" as instructed by his supervisor, William Wise, and because he essentially ceased working in January 1982 after finishing a one year probationary period. Specifically, the evidence reveals that Wilhelm had worked only thirty accounts since January 1, the lowest of any salesman in the region. Blue Bell also notes that Wilhelm's relative salesman efficiency was the lowest in the region and his total number of accounts developed was the lowest in the region. In addition, Wilhelm's own contact reports indicate that he had made only one line presentation the first week in January, only two the second week, and only four the third week instead of the twenty per week required. As a result, Wilhelm had the lowest bookings in the region.

Wilhelm presents an entirely different picture of his performance. According to Wilhelm, as of January 29, 1982, he had secured four new accounts, was twenty-four percent ahead of his prior year's sales, was number one in the Southeastern Region in sales, and was number eleven out of eighty-five sales persons in the nation. Furthermore, Wilhelm notes that these figures do not even take into account sales for the last week in January. Wilhelm states that had he received credit for all of the sales he made, his actual percentage ahead of sales for the year before would have been thirty-four percent and his position nationally would have been number nine out of eighty-five.

Kogut was fired on May 16, 1983. Kogut was fifty-two years old and had been employed by Blue Bell for twelve years when he was fired. At trial, Blue Bell claimed that it fired Kogut and an under forty salesman named Randy Cloud because they both failed, after specific counseling and warning, to fulfill the evaluation criteria imposed on all the Boyswear salesmen in the Southeastern Region as part of an intensive eight-week period of evaluation. Blue Bell replaced Kogut with a twenty-eight year old salesman.

Kogut also presents a different picture of his performance. According to Kogut, at the time he was fired he was number one in the six-man district in accomplishing percent of sales quota and was number two in the entire Southeastern Region in acquiring new accounts. Kogut's immediate supervisor during the evaluation period, District Manager Joe C. Glover, testified that as of May 19, 1983, Kogut was at seventy-eight percent of quota with approximately four and one half months left in the fiscal year. In addition, Kogut notes that Blue Bell fired him approximately one month after he gave deposition testimony unfavorable to Blue Bell as part of the discovery proceedings in the Gatlin and Wilhelm lawsuit.

II

To establish discrimination in an age discrimination case, the plaintiff must prove by a preponderance of the evidence that "but for" the defendant's motive to discriminate against an older employee, he would not have been terminated. E.E.O.C. v. Western Electric Co., Inc., 713 F.2d 1011, 1014 (4th Cir.1983); Lovelace v. Sherwin-Williams Co., 681 F.2d 230, 239 (4th Cir.1982); Loeb v. Textron, Inc., 600 F.2d 1003, 1019 (1st Cir.1979). The plaintiff may meet this burden "under ordinary principles of proof by any direct or indirect evidence relevant to and sufficiently probative of the issue. * * * " Lovelace, 681 F.2d at 239. Alternatively, the plaintiff may rely on the judicially created proof scheme for Title VII cases, see McDonnell Douglas Corp. v. Green, 411 U.S. 792, 93 S.Ct. 1817, 36 L.Ed.2d 668 (1973); Texas Department of Community Affairs v. Burdine, 450 U.S. 248, 101 S.Ct. 1089, 67 L.Ed.2d 207 (1981), which has been adopted for application in ADEA litigation.

In this case it is undisputed that plaintiffs Wilhelm and Kogut were in the protected age bracket when Blue Bell fired them. Accordingly, the sole issue for trial was whether age was a determining factor

in the discharge of each plaintiff. In *Lovelace* this court established
that the dispositive motivational issue of whether the plaintiff was
discharged because of his age can be proven without resort to the
McDonnell Douglas format:

> Where—as here, and ordinarily—coverage and unfavorable action
> are not disputed, the dispositive and only issue is a difficult, but
> narrow, motivational one: whether the employee "was [discharged]
> because of his age." This may of course be proved under ordinary
> principles of proof by any direct or indirect evidence relevant to and
> sufficiently probative of the issue, * * * *without resort to any special
> judicially created presumption or inferences related to the evidence.*

In *Lovelace* this court held that direct evidence of age discrimination is sufficient to overcome a motion for a directed verdict or judgment notwithstanding the verdict. There, this court stated that in
ruling upon a sufficiency motion in an ADEA case:

> The first question is whether plaintiff's evidence may have carried the
> original production burden without need to invoke the *McDonnell-
> Douglas* presumption. This may have occurred, for example, through
> direct evidence of a stated purpose to disfavor because of age. . . .
> If this is the judicial assessment, inquiry of course ceases, no further
> production burdens are put in play, and the motion can be denied.

681 F.2d at 240 (emphasis added) (citation omitted). Furthermore, in
Spagnuolo v. Whirlpool Corp., 641 F.2d 1109 (4th Cir.1981), this court
ruled that where the plaintiff in an ADEA case relies primarily upon
direct evidence of a discriminatory motive by the employer, the case
" 'simply does not fit the mold of the *McDonnell Douglas* formula,' "
and the plaintiff has no need to prove independently that the defendant's articulated reasons for a discharge were "pretextual."

In considering the motion for judgment notwithstanding the verdict, the district court was required to view the evidence in the light
most favorable to Wilhelm and Kogut and to draw all reasonable
inferences in their favor. The district court could not weigh evidence
or assess the credibility of witnesses. The test for determining whether
judgment notwithstanding the verdict should be entered is whether,
viewing the evidence in the light most favorable to the appellee-
plaintiff, there is substantial evidence in the record to support the
jury's findings.

Unlike the motion for judgment notwithstanding the verdict, the
district court may weigh evidence and assess credibility in ruling on a
motion for a new trial. Indeed, the district court had a duty to order a
new trial if "this action [was] required in order to prevent injustice."
However, the grant or denial of a motion for a new trial is within the
sound discretion of the district court and will not be disturbed absent a
clear showing of abuse of discretion.

III

A

The first issue on appeal is whether the district court erred in denying Blue Bell's motions for judgment notwithstanding the verdict or a new trial. Blue Bell argues that the plaintiffs have failed to establish a prima facie case of age discrimination because the record conclusively shows that neither Wilhelm nor Kogut was subjected to any disparate treatment because of his age. Blue Bell emphasizes that between 1977 and 1983 only two over-forty Boyswear salesmen in the Southeastern Region (plaintiffs Wilhelm and Kogut) were discharged. During the same period, however, four other under-forty salesmen were also discharged. Furthermore, Blue Bell maintains that it fired both Wilhelm and Kogut because they failed adequately to discharge their duties as measured by objective-criteria. Blue Bell also argues that there is no substantial evidence to support the jury's findings that both Wilhelm and Kogut had successfully rebutted Blue Bell's legitimate, nondiscriminatory reasons for its employment decisions.

The plaintiffs introduced ample direct evidence suggesting that Blue Bell fired them because of their ages. This direct evidence of age discrimination consisted of testimony relating how various Blue Bell officials had indicated an intent to replace older salesmen with younger salesmen. For example, plaintiffs introduced evidence of a conversation between Wilhelm and his immediate supervisor, William Wise, in February 1981, less than one year before Wilhelm's discharge, relating to various personnel changes in the company. Wilhelm testified that Wise told him that "eventually Blue Bell is going to have $15,000 a year college boys for salesmen. * * * Blue Bell cannot stand these five and six percent commission rates; so, in time they will have all young college guys on a salary, being paid expenses and going around taking inventory in Blue Bell accounts." App. at 406.

The plaintiffs also introduced evidence of a conversation between Wilhelm and Wise in September 1981 when Wise placed Wilhelm on probation. At that time Wilhelm protested that his performance was better than the other salesmen in the Region and accused Blue Bell of being "on a youth campaign" and wanting "to get rid of the older guys and replace them with younger people." App. at 423. Instead of denying that accusation, Wise confirmed that he believed that "older people tend to become complacent whereas younger people generally have more drive and ambition." Id. Wilhelm testified that Wise told him that "He was going to take care of him first and then there were going to be some others." Id.

Kogut testified that in September or October 1981 Wise conceded that he believed that "younger salesmen do a much better job than older salesmen." App. at 580. According to Kogut, Wise further stated that "in the not too distant future, all Wrangler salesmen would be young, college boys driving leased Chevrolets, taking inventory on big

Wrangler accounts." Id. Kogut testified to these statements by Wise while he was a Blue Bell employee and prior to becoming a plaintiff in this case.

Wilhelm and Kogut testified that they informed Jerry Poole, the president of the Boyswear Division of Blue Bell, about the statements made by Wise that younger salesmen do a much better job than older salesmen and that the future Blue Bell salesman would be a young college boy. According to Wilhelm and Kogut, in each instance Poole responded, "That really doesn't bother me too much." App. at 440, 776. At trial Poole admitted that Wilhelm and Kogut had informed him of Wise's age related remarks prior to their termination and that he had, in fact, responded to each that the statements did not bother him. App. at 776. Poole explained that these threats to terminate older salesmen and replace them with "college boys" did not bother him because he was not "going to let it happen." Id. Furthermore, the uncontradicted evidence at trial established that when Poole was first informed that Wise had placed Wilhelm on probation in September 1981, five months prior to his firing, Poole responded, "you have to understand that Bill Wise is of the opinion that the younger salesmen do a much better job than you older fellows. You older fellows have a tendency to become complacent after you have been around a while and run out of steam." App. at 579.

Wise ceased to be Kogut's manager and was replaced by Joe Glover. The plaintiffs offered evidence that in December 1981 Glover told Kogut, Wilhelm and another Blue Bell salesmen that "Blue Bell doesn't want salesmen with good records anymore. * * * They want young men who can do the work for a lot less money." App. at 445–46, 597–98. The plaintiffs further offered evidence that in December 1981, one month prior to Wilhelm's firing, the National Sales Manager of Blue Bell, Ed Weymeth, approached Wilhelm, Kogut, and one other older salesman and said, "My God, [are] you old guys still around. I thought we got rid of you at the last sales meeting." App. at 596, 445.

We conclude that there is substantial evidence in the record to support the jury's findings that Blue Bell discharged Wilhelm and Kogut because of their ages. The plaintiffs introduced ample direct evidence of age discrimination from which the jury could have concluded that Blue Bell fired Wilhelm and Kogut because of their ages. This direct evidence of age discrimination, if believed by the jury, was sufficient by itself to support a verdict for the plaintiffs and, concomitantly, to survive a motion for a directed verdict or a judgment notwithstanding the verdict. Lovelace v. Sherwin-Williams Co., 681 F.2d at 240. In addition, this direct evidence of age discrimination obviated the need for an independent showing by plaintiffs that Blue Bell's articulated reasons for their discharges were "pretextual." Spagnuolo v. Whirlpool Corp., 641 F.2d at 1113. Thus, the district court did not err in denying Blue Bell's motion for judgment notwithstanding the verdict. For the same reasons, the district court did not abuse its discretion in denying Blue Bell's motion for a new trial.

THORNBROUGH v. COLUMBUS AND GREENVILLE RAILROAD COMPANY

United States Court of Appeals for the Fifth Circuit, 1985.
760 F.2d 633.

GOLDBERG, CIRCUIT JUDGE:

Grow old along with me!

The best is yet to be,

The last of life, for which the first was made.

—Robert Browning, *Rabbi Ben Ezra* st. 1 (1864)

For many elder Americans, Browning's verse is a cruel jest rather than a reassuring vision. Not only must they face the inexorable advance of nature—they must face the biases of their fellow man. In 1967, recognizing that one of the tests of a civilized society is its treatment of the elderly, Congress enacted the Age Discrimination in Employment Act ("ADEA"). The Act has as its purpose the "elimination of discrimination from the workplace," Lorillard v. Pons, 434 U.S. 575, 584, 98 S.Ct. 866, 872, 55 L.Ed.2d 40 (1978), by making it unlawful for employers to discriminate against persons between the ages of forty and seventy based on their age.

In February 1983, Maud Lee Thornbrough brought suit against the Columbus & Greenville Railroad, alleging that he had been dismissed because of his age, in violation of the ADEA. The district court held that Thornbrough had failed to present a prima facie case of age discrimination and granted summary judgment for the Railroad. Because we conclude that Thornbrough raised a genuine issue of material fact, we hold that summary judgment was improperly granted. Accordingly, we reverse the judgment below and remand for further proceedings.

I. FACTS

At the time of his discharge from the C & G Railroad, Thornbrough was fifty-six years old and held the position of Vice President of Federal Projects. He had worked in the railroad business for approximately thirty-one years—the last five with the C & G Railroad, from 1977 to 1982. During this time, he held a variety of positions, including Assistant Chief Engineer, Vice President-Chief Engineer, Vice President of Transportation, and Vice President of Operations.

The C & G Railroad was established in 1975. From its inception, it was plagued with financial problems. Indeed, between the years 1975 and 1982, the Railroad made a net profit in only one year and accumulated net losses of $1.6 million. Its losses exclusive of real property gains totaled $3.58 million.

In 1982, the Railroad determined that in order to cut these losses, it had to reduce its work force. Between February and November 1982, the Railroad "furloughed" (that is, fired) forty-three employees. Including retirements, the Railroad's work force was reduced by forty-six employees, from 106 to 60. In addition, the Railroad went on a four-day work week, and management deferred payment of approximately ten percent of its own salary.

On June 30, 1982, the Railroad furloughed Thornbrough. Apparently, no one replaced Thornbrough in his position as Vice President of Federal Projects. Instead, his position was eliminated and its duties divided up among the Railroad's Chief Engineer, Accountant, and General Supervisor of Maintenance of Ways and Structures. These individuals were approximately forty-seven, thirty, and fifty-four years old, respectively. The Railroad also retained several other younger employees in positions similar to Thornbrough's and hired two new employees with little railroad experience. The precise ages of these retained and new employees are somewhat unclear. At least one was clearly outside of the protected ADEA class at the time of Thornbrough's furlough, and several others may also have been outside of the protected class.

Thornbrough brought suit against the Railroad on February 11, 1983, alleging both a violation of the ADEA and breach of contract. In support of the ADEA claim, Thornbrough alleged that he was better qualified than the younger employees whom the Railroad retained and hired, including the three persons who assumed his former duties. According to Thornbrough, the fact that younger, less well-qualified employees were retained and hired in preference to him was evidence that the Railroad had discriminated based on age.

Following limited discovery, the district court granted the Railroad's motion for summary judgment on the ADEA claim on the ground that Thornbrough had failed to establish a prima facie case, and dismissed without prejudice Thornbrough's pendent state claim for breach of contract. Thornbrough now appeals.

II. Elements of a Prima Facie Employment Discrimination Case

In a disparate treatment suit, the ultimate issue is whether the employer intentionally discriminated against the plaintiff. Thus, if a plaintiff is able to offer sufficient direct evidence of intentional discrimination, he obviously should prevail. Usually, however, this is not the case. Unless the employer is a latter-day George Washington, employment discrimination is as difficult to prove as who chopped down the cherry tree. See Mendez, Presumptions of Discriminatory Motive in Title VII Disparate Treatment Cases, 32 Stan.L.Rev. 1129 (1980). Employers are rarely so cooperative as to include a notation in the personnel file, "fired due to age," or to inform a dismissed employee candidly that he is too old for the job.

To ease the evidentiary burdens on employment discrimination plaintiffs, courts have fashioned special rules of proof, in order "progressively to sharpen the inquiry into the elusive factual question of intentional discrimination." [4] Initially, a plaintiff can create a rebuttable presumption of intentional discrimination by establishing a "prima facie case." Generally, to establish a prima facie case, a plaintiff need only make a very minimal showing. He can meet his initial burden by showing merely that he was within the protected class, that he was qualified for the job in question, and that employees outside of the protected class were more favorably treated—for example, by being hired to a job for which the plaintiff was turned down or by replacing the plaintiff in the job from which the plaintiff was discharged.

Once an employee has established a prima facie case, the burden of production shifts to the employer. In order to rebut the presumption of intentional discrimination, the employer must articulate "some legitimate, nondiscriminatory reason" why the plaintiff was rejected or someone else was preferred; otherwise, the factfinder is required to find for the plaintiff.

By articulating legitimate reasons for his decision, the employer rebuts the initial presumption of intentional discrimination created by the plaintiff's prima facie case. The burden of production therefore shifts back to the plaintiff, albeit at "a new level of specificity," to prove that the reasons articulated by the employer are not true reasons but

4. These special rules governing the order of proof were first set forth in McDonnell Douglas Corp. v. Green, 411 U.S. 792, 93 S.Ct. 1817, 36 L.Ed.2d 668 (1973), and were later explicated and refined in Furnco Const. Corp. v. Waters, 438 U.S. 567, 98 S.Ct. 2943, 57 L.Ed.2d 957 (1978), Board of Trustees v. Sweeney, 439 U.S. 24, 99 S.Ct. 295, 58 L.Ed.2d 216 (1978), *Burdine,* 450 U.S. 248, 101 S.Ct. 1089, and *Aikens,* 460 U.S. 711, 103 S.Ct. 1478. Although *McDonnell Douglas* itself was technically a failure to rehire case, not a discharge case, both the Supreme Court and this court have applied the *McDonnell Douglas* rules of proof in discharge cases, see, e.g., *Burdine,* 450 U.S. 248, 101 S.Ct. 1089; Williams v. General Motors Corp., 656 F.2d 120 (5th Cir.1981), cert. denied, 455 U.S. 943, 102 S.Ct. 1439, 71 L.Ed.2d 655 (1982); Price v. Maryland Casualty Co., 561 F.2d 609 (5th Cir.1977), as well as in other types of disparate treatment cases, see generally B. Schlei & P. Grossman, Employment Discrimination Law 1153 & nn. 5–12 (1976).

Moreover, although the special rules of proof developed in *McDonnell Douglas* and its progeny arose in the context of Title VII of the Civil Rights Act of 1964, 42 U.S.C. §§ 2000e to 2000e–17 (1982), ever since our maiden ADEA case, Hodgson v. First Federal Savings & Loan Ass'n, 455 F.2d 818 (5th Cir.1972), we have looked to Title VII decisions to interpret the ADEA. Recently, we adopted in the ADEA context both the *McDonnell Douglas* test of a prima facie case, *Price,* 561 F.2d at 612; Marshall v. Goodyear Tire & Rubber Co., 554 F.2d 730, 735 (5th Cir.1977), and the accompanying rules regarding the order and burdens of proof, Reeves v. General Foods Corp., 682 F.2d 515, 520–23 (5th Cir. 1982) (establishing a prima facie case may not always satisfy plaintiff's burden of production); Smith v. Farah Mfg. Co., 650 F.2d 64, 67 (5th Cir.1981) (burden of persuasion remains at all times on plaintiff). In this respect, we agree with most other circuits that have considered the question. See Loeb v. Textron, Inc., 600 F.2d 1003, 1014–16 (1st Cir.1979); Duffy v. Wheeling Pittsburgh Steel Corp., 738 F.2d 1393, 1396 (3rd Cir.), cert. denied, __ U.S. __, 105 S.Ct. 592, 83 L.Ed.2d 702 (1984); Douglas v. Anderson, 656 F.2d 528, 531–32 (9th Cir. 1981); Schwager v. Sun Oil Co., 591 F.2d 58, 60–61 (10th Cir.1979). But see Laugesen v. Anaconda Co., 510 F.2d 307, 312 (6th Cir.1975). Thus, even though the present case is an ADEA rather than a Title VII case, the rules of proof developed in *McDonnell Douglas* and its progeny are controlling.

only pretexts. The plaintiff can do this in two ways, "either [1] directly by persuading the court that a discriminatory reason more likely motivated the employer or [2] indirectly by showing that the employer's proffered explanation is unworthy of credence." The first of these alternatives is the alternative that is always open to the plaintiff in an employment discrimination case: producing "evidence from which a trier of fact might reasonably conclude that the employer intended to discriminate in reaching the decision at issue." The second, however, depends upon the resurrection of the presumption initially created by the plaintiff's prima facie case. By disproving the reasons offered by the employer to rebut the plaintiff's prima facie case, the plaintiff recreates the situation that obtained when the prima facie case was initially established: in the absence of any known reasons for the employer's decision, we presume that the employer was motivated by discriminatory reasons. As the Court explained in *Furnco*,

> [W]e are willing to presume this largely because we know from our experience that more often than not people do not act in a totally arbitrary manner, without any underlying reasons, especially in a business setting. Thus, when all legitimate reasons for rejecting an applicant have been eliminated as possible reasons for the employer's actions, it is more likely than not the employer, who we generally assume acts only with *some* reason, based his decision on an impermissible consideration such as race.

438 U.S. at 577, 98 S.Ct. at 2950. Thus, in our view, unlike Humpty-Dumpty, the employee's prima facie case can be put back together again, through proof that the employer's proffered reasons are pretextual.

III. STANDARD OF REVIEW

Under Fed.R.Civ.P. 56(c), summary judgment is proper only if "there is no genuine issue as to any material fact and * * * the moving party is entitled to a judgment as a matter of law." In reviewing a motion for summary judgment, "the court must indulge every reasonable inference from [the underlying] facts in favor of the party opposing the motion." The party who defended against the motion for summary judgment must have his allegations taken as true and must receive the benefit of the doubt when his assertions conflict with those of the movant.

In general, summary judgment is an inappropriate tool for resolving claims of employment discrimination, which involve nebulous questions of motivation and intent. Often, motivation and intent can only be proved through circumstantial evidence; determinations regarding motivation and intent depend on complicated inferences from the evidence and are therefore peculiarly within the province of the factfinder. In reviewing a case on appeal, it is difficult to determine what evidence might legitimately sway the factfinder and hence be material. Thus, if any facts are in dispute, summary judgment is generally inappropriate.

IV. VALIDITY OF SUMMARY JUDGMENT

The district court granted summary judgment on the ground that Thornbrough failed to present a prima facie case of employment discrimination. In reviewing this holding, we must consider two questions: (1) Did Thornbrough present a genuine issue of fact as to the existence of a prima facie case, and (2) if so, did he present a genuine issue of fact as to whether the reasons articulated by the Railroad for discharging him were pretextual? We hold that Thornbrough presented genuine issues of fact regarding both issues.

A. PRIMA FACIE CASE

The necessary elements of a prima facie employment discrimination case are not Platonic forms, pure and unchanging; rather, they vary depending on the facts of a particular case. In *McDonnell Douglas*, when the Supreme Court first articulated the elements of a prima facie case, it recognized that "specification * * * of the prima facie proof required from respondent is not necessarily applicable in every respect to differing factual situations." As we later stated, since discrimination exists "in forms as myriad as the creative perverseness of human beings can provide," McCorstin v. United States Steel Corp., 621 F.2d 749, 753–54 (5th Cir.1980), certain specific elements do not constitute "the alpha and omega" of a prima facie ADEA case, id. at 753.

In Williams v. General Motors Corp., 656 F.2d 120 (5th Cir.1981), cert. denied, 455 U.S. 943, 102 S.Ct. 1439, 71 L.Ed.2d 655 (1982), we modified the McDonnell Douglas test in the context of cases that, like the present one, involve a general reduction in an employer's workforce. As we noted, "Reduction-in-force cases are obviously outside the embrace of [*McDonnell Douglas*] since reduction-case plaintiffs are simply laid off and thus incapable of proving the third [*McDonnell Douglas*] element, i.e., actual replacement by a younger employee." Id. at 128. We therefore elaborated a different standard for reduction-in-force cases, under which a plaintiff must (1) satisfy the standing requirements of the statute by showing that he is within the protected group and that he has been adversely affected—e.g., discharged or demoted—by the employer's decisions; (2) show that he was qualified to assume another position at the time of the discharge or demotion; and (3) produce "evidence, circumstantial or direct, from which a fact-finder might reasonably conclude that the employer intended to discriminate in reaching the decision at issue." Id. at 129.

The principal novelty of the *Williams* test is its third requirement. At first glance, this requirement may seem to represent a considerable heightening of the proof required for a prima facie case. In a non-reduction-in-force suit, the plaintiff must make only a very minimal showing to establish this aspect of his prima facie case: He must simply show that he was discharged from a position for which he was qualified, and that he was replaced by someone outside of the protected class. He need not introduce any evidence, either direct or circumstantial, that the employer in fact engaged in intentional discrimination; instead, discrimination is presumed from his replacement. By contrast, under the *Williams* version of a prima facie case, the plaintiff must "produce some evidence that an employer has not treated age neutrally, but has instead discriminated based upon it. Specifically, the evidence must lead the factfinder reasonably to conclude either (1) that defendant consciously refused to consider retaining or relocating a plaintiff because of his age, or (2) that defendant regarded age as a negative factor in such consideration." 656 F.2d at 129–30.

Williams, however, does not answer the crucial question: What quantum of evidence might lead the factfinder reasonably to conclude that the defendant has not treated age neutrally? Or, put differently, what quantum of evidence is sufficient to create a presumption of intentional discrimination? By failing to specify what evidence is and is not sufficient, it is ambiguous whether *Williams* represents a stricter or merely a more flexible standard for a prima facie case. An argument could be made that *Williams* eased rather than heightened the burden on employment discrimination plaintiffs by eliminating the necessity of showing actual replacement by a younger worker; instead, *Williams* allows employees to establish a prima facie case through any type of circumstantial evidence that younger employees were more favorably treated than older employees.

In examining whether Thornbrough alleged a prima facie case, we note at the outset what Thornbrough did not attempt to prove. He did not attempt to prove that the Railroad's officers made any remarks indicating that age was a factor in their employment decisions. In his deposition, he admitted that no one ever told him that he was too old for the job. Thornbrough Deposition at 50. He did not introduce any statistical evidence that the Railroad tended to disfavor older employees. Indeed, what little statistical evidence there was indicated the reverse: The overall effect of the Railroad's lay-offs was to increase the average age of its work-force from thirty-six to thirty-nine. Record at 22. Finally, Thornbrough did not present much, if any, evidence that the Railroad's general employment practices tended to discriminate against older employees.

Instead, the only evidence offered by Thornbrough in support of his claim of age discrimination was that several younger, allegedly less well-qualified employees were retained during the Railroad's reduction-in-force, and that, at the time of his discharge, two younger, allegedly less well-qualified employees were hired. Record at 4, 31–33; Thornbrough Deposition at 48–49.[14] In our view, these allegations, limited

14. Although Thornbrough compared his treatment not merely to employees outside of the protected ADEA class, but also to employees within the protected class, this is not decisive. We have never demanded rigid adherence to the requirement that the plaintiff establish that he was treated unfavorably as compared with people outside of the protected class—i.e., under age forty. For example, in Wilson v. Sealtest Foods Div. of Kraftco Corp., 501 F.2d 84 (5th Cir.1974), we reversed a direct-

though they are, are sufficient to support a prima facie case. They exude that faint aroma of impropriety that is sufficient to justify requiring the Railroad to give reasons for its decision.

A prima facie case "raises an inference of discrimination only because we presume [the employer's] acts, if otherwise unexplained, are more likely than not based on the consideration of impermissible factors." *Furnco*, 438 U.S. at 577, 98 S.Ct. at 2949–50. In a reduction-in-force case, what creates the presumption of discrimination is not the discharge itself, but rather the discharge coupled with the retention of younger employees. Unlike in an ordinary discharge case, where the mere discharge creates a presumption of discrimination because we assume that an employer does not fire a qualified employee, in a reduction-in-force case, discharges are readily explicable in terms of the employer's economic problems. Consequently, the fact that qualified, older employees are laid off is not inherently suspicious and does not in itself warrant shifting the burden of production to the employer to justify his actions.

Instead, what is suspicious in reduction-in-force cases is that the employer fired a qualified, older employee but retained younger ones. If we focus not on why employees, in general, were discharged, as the district court did, but instead on why the plaintiff rather than another employee was discharged, the discharge of an older employee rather than a younger one is initially unexplained. Under these circumstances, requiring the employer to articulate reasons for his decision to fire the plaintiff is appropriate. It serves the primary function of the prima facie case doctrine: "to sharpen the inquiry into the elusive factual question of intentional discrimination." *Burdine*, 450 U.S. at 255 n. 8, 101 S.Ct. at 1094 n. 8.

We note that this conclusion is consistent with the approach taken by several other circuit courts. In Coburn v. Pan American World Airways, 711 F.2d 339 (D.C.Cir.), cert. denied, ___ U.S. ___, 104 S.Ct. 488, 78 L.Ed.2d 683 (1983), for example, the District of Columbia Circuit held that in a reduction-in-force suit, an employee can establish a prima facie case merely by proving that, while he was fired from a job for

ed verdict in favor of the employer, even though the plaintiff was replaced simply by someone younger, not by someone outside of the protected ADEA class. Id. at 86. As we noted in McCorstin v. United States Steel Corp., 621 F.2d 749 (5th Cir.1980).

[B]ecause the discrimination involves age, rather than sex or race, a requirement that the replacement be from a nonprotected group fails to take the reality of the working place into account. Because of the value of experience rarely are sixty-year-olds replaced by those under forty. The replacement process is more subtle but just as injurious to the worker who has been discharged. That the person is replaced by a person ten

years younger rather than twenty years does not diminish the discrimination; the subtlety only tends to disguise it.

Id. at 754; see also McCuen v. Home Ins. Co., 633 F.2d 1150, 1151–52 (5th Cir.1981) (summary judgment reversed even though the younger employees who were retained were over forty years of age). Moreover, in the present case, although several of the retained or new employees with whom Thornbrough compares his treatment may have been within the protected class, at least two clearly were not: the Railroad's Accountant, who was approximately thirty years old in 1982, and the newly-promoted Vice President of Transportation, who was in his early thirties.

which he was qualified, "younger persons were retained and others later promoted." Id. at 343. In support of this conclusion, the court stated, "We believe the exigencies of a reduction-in-force can best be analyzed at the stage where the employer puts on evidence of a nondiscriminatory reason for the firing." Id. Similarly, in Massarsky v. General Motors Corp., 706 F.2d 111 (3d Cir.), cert. denied, ___ U.S. ___, 104 S.Ct. 348, 78 L.Ed.2d 314 (1983), the Third Circuit stated that "a plaintiff alleging a discriminatory layoff need show only that he is a member of the protected class and that he was laid off from a job for which he was qualified while others not in the protected class were treated more favorably." Id. at 118. The court held that the plaintiff had established a prima facie case by proving that while he was laid off, a younger person outside of the protected class was retained.

The conclusion that we reach is also supported by our approach in non-reduction-in-force cases. Although we require more than a conclusory allegation of age discrimination to establish a prima facie case we do not require much more. Generally, we demand only that a plaintiff present some evidence of differential treatment between older and younger employees. If a younger employee was promoted, but an older employee in a similar position was not, or if a younger employee was hired in preference to an older one, this creates a presumption of discrimination. We do not require the plaintiff initially to provide any additional evidence of discrimination. Nor is the fact that the employer cannot promote every employee, or that he cannot hire every applicant, decisive. Instead, we are concerned with why the younger employee was promoted, or the younger applicant hired, rather than the older one. Similarly, in reduction-in-force cases, the fact that the employer cannot retain every employee is not conclusive. The question is why, given the employer's need to reduce his workforce, he chose to discharge the older rather than the younger employee. By shifting the burden of production to the employer, this is the question that we hope to answer.[19]

19. In holding that the plaintiff has met his burden of establishing a prima facie case, and that therefore summary judgment was improperly granted, we do not mean to belittle the salutary function of summary judgment in the employment discrimination arena: summary judgment allows patently meritless cases to be nipped in the bud, before valuable judicial resources are expended. Where there is only an "attenuated possibility that a jury would infer a discriminatory motive," Pace v. Southern Ry. Sys., 701 F.2d 1383, 1391 (11th Cir.), cert. denied, ___ U.S. ___, 104 S.Ct. 549, 78 L.Ed.2d 724 (1983), proceeding with a case serves no useful function. The problem, however, is that there is no bright line demarcating when a "genuine issue of fact" degenerates into an "attenuated possibility." Consequently, our cases display no clear pattern. Compare McCuen v. Home Ins. Co., 633 F.2d 1150 (5th Cir. 1981) (summary judgment reversed, where plaintiff alleged only that while he was laid off, several younger employees were retained, and where employer had articulated legitimate, nondiscriminatory reasons for its actions) and Wilson v. Sealtest Foods Div. of Kraftco Corp., 501 F.2d 84 (5th Cir.1974) (directed verdict in favor of employer reversed where plaintiff alleged simply that he was forced to retire from job for which he was qualified, and that younger employee who was retained replaced him) with Stendebach v. CPC Int'l, Inc., 691 F.2d 735, 738 (5th Cir.1982) (directed verdict affirmed on ground that employee's evidence was, "at best, a mere scintilla which is insufficient to present a jury question"), cert. denied, 461 U.S. 944, 103 S.Ct. 2122, 77 L.Ed.2d 1302 (1983) and Baldwin v. Sears, Roebuck & Co., 667 F.2d 458 (5th Cir.1982) (summary judgment affirmed in reduction-in-force case on ground

B. Pretext

Although we reject the district court's holding that the plaintiff failed to allege sufficient facts to establish a prima facie case, the Railroad urges that summary judgment is nevertheless warranted. A prima facie case raises only a *rebuttable* presumption of discrimination. If the employer articulates legitimate, nondiscriminatory reasons for his actions, the presumption created by the plaintiff's prima facie case dissolves and the burden reverts to the plaintiff to prove that the employer's reasons are pretextual. *Burdine,* 450 U.S. at 253–55, 101 S.Ct. at 1093–94. According to the Railroad, Thornbrough failed to meet this burden because he was unable to rebut the Railroad's articulated reasons for furloughing Thornbrough rather than another employee. The Railroad claims, therefore, that summary judgment was justified.[20]

We disagree. In the context of a summary judgment proceeding, the question is not whether the plaintiff proves pretext, but rather whether the plaintiff raises a genuine issue of fact regarding pretext. Here, Thornbrough did so. Although the Railroad offered a number of reasons for its decision to fire Thornbrough, Thornbrough questioned the objective truth of each of them. The Railroad claimed that Thornbrough was a less effective worker than the other employees in question—that he was not a "self-starter"; in response, Thornbrough argued that he was an experienced and effective worker, and that several of the employees retained or hired by the Railroad were extremely

that employee presented no statistical or direct evidence of intentional discrimination) and *Williams,* 656 F.2d at 130 (finding of intentional discrimination reversed on ground that plaintiff failed to establish a prima facie case). In the present case, although the plaintiff's odds of prevailing may not be high, we are not prepared to say that they are so minute that proceeding with the case would be pointless.

20. The Railroad also cites undisputed statistical evidence indicating that it did not engage in age discrimination. This evidence shows that, as a result of the Railroad's reduction in force, the average age of its employees increased. While this evidence is probative of the age discrimination issue, it is not dispositive. The issue in this case is whether the Railroad discriminated against Thornbrough, not whether it discriminated against other older employees. "It is clear that Congress never intended to give an employer license to discriminate against some employees * * * merely because he favorably treats other members of the employees' group. * * * [I]rrespective of the form taken by the discriminatory practice, an employer's treatment of other members of the plaintiffs' group can be 'of little comfort to the victims of * * * discrimination.' " Connecticut v. Teal, 457 U.S. 440, 455, 102 S.Ct. 2525, 2535, 73 L.Ed.2d 130 (1982) (quoting International Bhd. of Teamsters v. United States, 431 U.S. 324, 342, 97 S.Ct. 1843, 1858, 52 L.Ed.2d 396 (1977); cf. Cooper v. Federal Reserve Bank, ___ U.S. ___, 104 S.Ct. 2794, 81 L.Ed.2d 718 (1984) (adverse judgment in class action suit not res judicata in subsequent suit by individuals, since employer may have committed individual acts of discrimination without engaging in general pattern of discrimination). As the Court put it in *Cooper,* "a piece of fruit may well be bruised without being rotten to the core." ___ U.S. at ___, 104 S.Ct. at 2802. Moreover, the fact that the Railroad retained many older employees does not prove that the Railroad did not regard age as a negative factor; perhaps these older employees were so far superior to their younger colleagues that, even though their age was regarded as a disadvantage, the Railroad did not want to discharge them. Thus, the Railroad's statistical evidence does not warrant summary judgment. Instead, it should be weighed by the factfinder along with the other evidence presented by the parties.

inexperienced.   Record at 31–33;   Thornbrough Deposition at 47–49. The Railroad claimed that Thornbrough was unqualified for several of the positions held by the employees who were retained (for example, the accountant's position and the position of securing industrial development prospects and business); Thornbrough claimed that, with his experience in the railroad industry, he could have filled virtually any position in the Railroad.   Record at 33;   Thornbrough Deposition at 47. The Railroad claimed that Thornbrough's position was not full-time and was more easily divisible than those of the other employees;   Thornbrough responded that his job was full-time.   Record at 31.[22]

These disputed factual issues are clearly material.   Although the Railroad makes much of Thornbrough's lack of affirmative proof of discrimination, Thornbrough is not required to prove that the Railroad was motivated by bad reasons;   he need only persuade the factfinder that the Railroad's purported good reasons were untrue.   While Thornbrough's case would be considerably stronger if he could point to a smoking personnel file, if he can undermine the Railroad's articulated reasons, the factfinder would be entitled to conclude that the Railroad engaged in intentional discrimination.[23]

Of course, the issue in this case is not whether Thornbrough or the retained employees were better qualified.   The Railroad is entitled to make that decision for itself.   The ADEA was not intended to be a vehicle for judicial second-guessing of business decisions, nor was it intended to transform the courts into personnel managers.   See *Elliott,* 714 F.2d at 567.   However, if the factfinder determines that Thornbrough was clearly better qualified than the employees who were retained, it is entitled to conclude that the Railroad's articulated reasons are pretexts.   Everyone can make a mistake—but if the mistake is large enough, we may begin to wonder whether it was a mistake at all.

22.   Despite the sparseness of proof in favor of Thornbrough, we are unwilling to say that the disputes raised by Thornbrough are not genuine.   Here we are not faced merely with the conclusory allegation of Thornbrough that he was well qualified for his job.   Cf. EEOC v. Exxon Shipping Co., 745 F.2d 967, 976 (5th Cir.1984) ("[P]retext cannot be established by mere 'conclusory statements' of a plaintiff who feels he has been discriminated against."). Instead, according to Thornbrough's counsel, if Thornbrough's presentation of proof had not been abruptly terminated by the summary judgment, Thornbrough was prepared to present witnesses who would have testified as to his qualifications and abilities.   Moreover, if the case had continued, Thornbrough could have cross-examined the retained and new employees about their qualifications.   Through this comparison of his qualifications with those of his "competitors," Thornbrough may have

been able to persuade the factfinder that he was the clearly superior employee.   Cf. Causey v. Ford Motor Co., 516 F.2d 416, 423 (5th Cir.1975) (where employer alleges that he hired one employee rather than another because, in his subjective view, the chosen employee was better qualified, court should scrutinize this explanation very carefully);   Pond v. Braniff Airways, Inc., 500 F.2d 161, 166 (5th Cir.1974) (same).

23.   See, e.g., Exxon Shipping, 745 F.2d at 974–77 (affirmed finding of pretext where plaintiff was denied promotion even though clearly less-qualified person was promoted);   Martinez v. El Paso County, 710 F.2d 1102, 1104–05 (5th Cir.1983) (affirmed finding of pretext based on testimonial evidence that discharged employee was clearly better qualified than retained employee).

V. Conclusion

In Williams v. General Motors, we enunciated the general principle that the ADEA "does not place an affirmative duty upon an employer to accord special treatment to members of the protected age group;" it only "mandates that an employer reach employment decisions without regard to age." 656 F.2d at 129. We recognize that this decision stretches this principle to its limit. By allowing an employee to bring suit merely because an employer fires him rather than a younger, allegedly less well-qualified employee, we may, to some degree, induce employers to lay off younger employees instead of older ones.

However, we are unwilling to embrace the alternative. We are unwilling to hold that even if an older employee can prove that he was clearly better qualified than younger employees who were kept on, he is precluded as a matter of law from bringing an age discrimination suit. Such a ruling would go far toward shielding a clever employer from the reach of the ADEA. Given the difficulties of demonstrating age discrimination, we believe that the better course is to allow the factfinder to determine whether the plaintiff's evidence justifies an inference of age discrimination.

In Simmons v. McGuffey Nursing Home, 619 F.2d 369 (5th Cir. 1980), we upheld a grant of summary judgment, noting, "The possibility of a jury drawing a contrary inference sufficient to create a dispute as to a material fact does not reify to the point even of a thin vapor capable of being seen or realized by a reasonable jury." Id. at 371. Here, through the dim mists, we perceive a thin vapor. Whether it will precipitate into a victorious shower is a question for the jury. It should not have been dispersed by means of summary judgment.

Reversed and Remanded.

Notes

1. Former EEOC Commissioner Cathy Shattuck conducted surveys of persons seeking relief under the ADEA during the period 1978–83. Copies of the surveys, summaries of which were made public at the time, were made available to one of the editors in private correspondence. The surveys produced the following profile of the typical ADEA plaintiff: A white male, aged 55, with 20 years service, employed in a white collar position earning $32,000 a year, who was terminated by his employer.

2. Almost all the Courts of Appeals have ruled that neither compensatory damages for pain and suffering nor punitive damages are allowable under the ADEA. See the discussion in an early leading case, *Rogers v. Exxon Research and Engineering*, 550 F.2d 834 (3d Cir. 1977) cert. denied 434 U.S. 1022, 98 S.Ct. 749, 54 L.Ed.2d 770 (1978). Such damages may be recoverable, however, under a pendent state claim. See e.g., *Cancellier v. Federated Department Shares*, 672 F.2d 1312 (9th Cir. 1981) cert. denied 459 U.S. 859, 103 S.Ct. 131, 74 L.Ed.2d 113 (1982). On the other hand, almost all circuits have authorized the award of "front pay" in lieu of reinstatement where circumstances render the latter remedy inappropriate. See, the discussion in *Wildman v. Lerner Stores*, 771 F.2d 605 (1st Cir. 1985).

B. DISPARATE IMPACT

GELLER v. MARKHAM

United States Court of Appeals for the Second Circuit, 1980.
635 F.2d 1027.

MANSFIELD, CIRCUIT JUDGE:

Miriam Geller, a 55-year-old teacher, brought a class action in the District Court for the District of Connecticut under the Age Discrimination in Employment Act of 1967 (ADEA), 29 U.S.C. §§ 621, et seq., claiming that defendants-appellants violated her rights by denying her employment as a teacher because of her age. She sought damages, equitable relief (including reinstatement, pension rights, benefits and seniority) and attorney's fees. A jury trial before Judge M. Joseph Blumenfeld resulted in an award of $15,190 damages. Following the trial, Judge Blumenfeld denied her application for equitable relief but awarded attorney's fees. From this denial she appeals. Defendants cross-appeal from the judgment against them, asserting that the court erred in its conclusions as to governing legal principles and in its instructions to the jury regarding causation.

We affirm the finding of defendants' liability, since the record reveals that defendants subjected Ms. Geller to a hiring practice with both discriminatory impact, see Griggs v. Duke Power Co., 401 U.S. 424, 91 S.Ct. 849, 28 L.Ed.2d 158 (1971), and illegally disparate treatment, see McDonnell Douglas Co. v. Green, 411 U.S. 792, 93 S.Ct. 1817, 36 L.Ed.2d 668 (1973), the principles of which may be applied in ADEA cases. See Lorillard v. Pons, 434 U.S. 575, 584, 98 S.Ct. 866, 872, 55 L.Ed.2d 40 (1978). We also affirm the district court's refusal to award reinstatement, but reverse its decision not to award pension benefits.

Ms. Geller applied for a position as a teacher at Bugbee School in West Hartford in late August, 1976. She was then 55 years old. She had gained considerable experience as a tenured teacher in New Jersey, where she had lived until shortly before applying for the Bugbee job, and she had done some work as a substitute teacher in the Connecticut schools. She was interviewed for a permanent position to fill a "sudden opening" in the Bugbee School on September 3, 1976, and was told to be ready to begin teaching art on September 7. Meanwhile, school officials continued to interview other candidates for the job.

Ms. Geller prepared the art room over Labor Day weekend, and taught school until September 17, when she was replaced by a 25-year-old woman who had not applied for the job until September 10. Shortly thereafter, Ms. Geller brought the present suit, alleging violations of ADEA, and pointing in particular to the "Sixth Step Policy" adopted by the West Hartford Board of Education ("Board"). This cost-cutting policy, which was derived from a statement included by the previous Bugbee School Superintendent in his budget report to the Board, read:

> Except in special situations and to the extent possible, teachers needed in West Hartford next year will be recruited at levels below the sixth step of the salary schedule.

The sixth step is the salary grade reached by teachers with more than five years' experience.

At trial plaintiff introduced expert statistical testimony establishing that 92.6% of Connecticut teachers between 40 and 65 years old (the protected age group under ADEA) have more than 5 years experience, while only 62% of teachers under 40 have taught more than five years. She also presented considerable evidence in the form of witnesses' testimony that individual defendants had discussed the "sixth step" policy with her, and had taken the policy into account when deciding to replace her. Defendants countered that the ratio of hirees over 40 years of age to under-40 hirees had not changed substantially since the announcement of the "sixth step" policy. From these latter statistics, which were offered not by an expert statistician but by Mr. Hedrick, a named defendant, defendants argued that the "sixth step" policy had never been applied to discriminate on the basis of age. They claimed that Ms. Geller had been replaced by a younger woman because hiring officials considered the younger woman more qualified, not because the school board was unwilling to pay a woman with her experience. Defendants also argue that even if the "sixth step" was applied, they were justified in applying it because an "experience-cost criterion" for hiring was necessary in view of declining enrollments and rising school costs.

Largely on the strength of plaintiff's expert statistical evidence, Judge Blumenfeld found that defendants' "sixth step" policy was discriminatory as a matter of law. He found the case to be governed by the line of cases regulating facially neutral employment policies which have a discriminatory impact, see Griggs v. Duke Power Co., supra; Dothard v. Rawlinson, 433 U.S. 321, 97 S.Ct. 2720, 53 L.Ed.2d 786 (1977); Washington v. Davis, 426 U.S. 229, 247, 96 S.Ct. 2040, 2051, 48 L.Ed.2d 597 (1976). He declined to accept defendants' contention that proof of a violation of ADEA required establishment of discriminatory motive. With respect to plaintiff's claim of disparate treatment, see McDonnell Douglas Co. v. Green, supra, however, he took the view that to sustain this claim plaintiff must ultimately prove a discriminatory motive on the defendants' part and that proof that they discharged her because of the application of the "sixth step" policy was insufficient, rendering McDonnell Douglas "inapplicable."

After instructing the jury that the "sixth step" policy was discriminatory on the basis of age as a matter of law, Judge Blumenfeld submitted to it the question of whether this policy had been applied to Ms. Geller. First, in his oral instructions to the jury, he asked it to determine "if the decision about Mrs. Geller was made in whole or in part, because she was above the fifth step," and if the "sixth step" policy "made a difference" in the decision to replace her with the younger woman, stating:

> There could have been more than one reason for defendants' decision about [Mrs. Geller's] employment but she is nevertheless entitled to

recover if one factor was her [age] and if it made a difference in determining whether she would be employed. If it did not make any difference, if it was not a reason that entered into the decision, then of course she has not proved her case. But if it did, then she has.

If defendants' decision about Mrs. Geller was made in whole or in part because she was above the fifth step on the salary scale, * * * Mrs. Geller is entitled to recover. * * *

He then submitted special interrogatories to the jury, as follows:

THE COURT: I propose to submit some Special Interrogatories.

1. Was the sixth step guideline one reason for Mrs. Geller not being hired for the permanent art teacher's position at the Bugbee Elementary School? Answer: Yes or No.

MR. POST: Sir, could I ask that that interrogatory track with your charge to the Jury and say, "One reason that made a difference"?

THE COURT: No. If it was one reason, that is sufficient.

MR. POST: That made a difference in their decision.

THE COURT: No. If it was one reason.

The jury found for Ms. Geller, answering the first Special Interrogatory in the affirmative. It then responded to Judge Blumenfeld's charge to award "damages equal to the amount of losses plaintiff suffered due to defendants' discriminatory actions, less amounts earned through reasonable efforts at mitigation," by awarding $15,190 in back pay, which equalled the salary Ms. Geller would have earned at the Bugbee School in 1976. In answer to another interrogatory, the jury did not find that the defendants' discrimination was "willful."

In post-trial motions plaintiffs applied for equitable relief based upon the jury's verdict, specifically requesting reinstatement, pension benefits, and attorney's fees. All of these requests except for the request for attorney's fees were denied. Plaintiff has assigned as error the denial of these requests for relief, while defendants attack Judge Blumenfeld's instructions to the jury and his ruling that the "sixth step" policy was discriminatory as a matter of law.

DISCUSSION

As the Supreme Court pointed out in International Brotherhood of Teamsters v. United States, 431 U.S. 324, 335–36 n. 15, 97 S.Ct. 1843, 1854 n. 15, 52 L.Ed.2d 396 (1977), discriminatory or disparate treatment in violation of Title VII occurs where "[t]he employer simply treats some people less favorably than others because of their race, color, religion, sex or national origin. Proof of discriminatory motive is critical, although it can in some situations be inferred from the mere fact of differences in treatment." "Disparate impact," on the other hand, results from the use of "employment practices that are facially neutral in their treatment of different groups but that in fact fall more harshly on one group than another and cannot be justified by business necessity." Id., 431 U.S. at 336 n. 15, 97 S.Ct. at 1854. Proof of motive is not required to sustain a claim of disparate impact.

Defendants argue that principles with respect to discriminatory racist impact in violation of Title VII should not govern age discrimination cases instituted under 29 U.S.C. § 626(c)(1). We disagree. In Lorillard v. Pons, 434 U.S. 575, 584, 98 S.Ct. 866, 872, 55 L.Ed.2d 40 (1978), the Court noted that "the [substantive] prohibitions of the ADEA were derived *in haec verba* from Title VII." Although the ADEA did not adopt Title VII's procedural rules entirely, the rule permitting a case to be established by a showing of discriminatory impact or treatment cannot reasonably be viewed as merely procedural. See Oscar Mayer Co. v. Evans, 441 U.S. 750, 755–56, 99 S.Ct. 2066, 2071, 60 L.Ed.2d 609 (1979).

DISPARATE IMPACT

A prima facie case of discriminatory impact may be established by showing that an employer's facially neutral practice has a disparate impact upon members of plaintiff's class, in this case teachers over 40 years of age. Griggs v. Duke Power Co., 401 U.S. 424, 429–30, 91 S.Ct. 849, 852–53, 28 L.Ed.2d 158 (1970). Such a discriminatory impact is frequently evidenced by statistics from which it may be inferred that an employer's selection methods or employment criteria result in employment of a larger share of one group (here, teachers under 40 years of age) than of another (teachers over 40). Intl. Brotherhood of Teamsters v. United States, 431 U.S. 324, 335 n. 15, 339, 97 S.Ct. 1843, 1854 n. 15, 1856, 52 L.Ed.2d 396 (1977); Hazelwood School Dist. v. United States, 433 U.S. 299, 97 S.Ct. 2736, 53 L.Ed.2d 768 (1977). The employer may defend by showing that the employment practice is justified by business necessity or need and is related to successful performance of the job for which the practice is used, Griggs v. Duke Power Co., supra, 401 U.S. at 424, 432, 91 S.Ct. 849, 854, 28 L.Ed.2d 168. In that event the plaintiff must be given an opportunity to show that other selection methods having less discriminatory effects would serve the employer's legitimate interest in competent performance of the job. Albemarle Paper Co. v. Moody, 422 U.S. 405, 425, 95 S.Ct. 2362, 2375, 45 L.Ed.2d 280 (1975); Dothard v. Rawlinson, 433 U.S. 321, 329, 97 S.Ct. 2720, 2726, 53 L.Ed.2d 786 (1977); United States v. Bethlehem Steel Corp., 446 F.2d 652, 662 (2d Cir.1971).

A prima facie case of discriminatory treatment may be made out by the plaintiff's showing:

(i) that he belongs to a racial minority;

(ii) that he applied and was qualified for a job for which the employer was seeking applicants; (iii) that, despite his qualifications, he was rejected; and (iv) that, after his rejection, the position remained open and the employer continued to seek applicants from persons of complainant's qualifications.

McDonnell Douglas Corp. v. Green, 411 U.S. 792, 802, 93 S.Ct. 1817, 1824, 36 L.Ed.2d 668 (1973); Furnco Construction Corp. v. Waters, 438 U.S. 567, 582, 98 S.Ct. 2943, 2952, 57 L.Ed.2d 957 (1978). The burden then shifts to the employer to go forward with evidence of "some legitimate, nondiscriminatory reason for the employee's rejection," *Mc-*

Donnell Douglas Corp., supra, 411 U.S. at 802, 93 S.Ct. at 1824, in which event the plaintiff, who has the ultimate burden, must be afforded the opportunity to demonstrate by competent evidence that the employer's presumptively valid reasons are a cover-up or pretext. Id. at 805, 93 S.Ct. at 1825. If the plaintiff succeeds in this showing the employer's articulated reason will not stand. Board of Trustees of Keene State College v. Sweeney, 439 U.S. 24, 99 S.Ct. 295, 58 L.Ed.2d 216 (1978).

Turning to the present case, the plaintiff showed through an accredited expert (Dr. Alan Hunt), based on his statistical analysis of the relationship between age and years of experience for teachers in Connecticut, that 92.6% of all teachers over 40 years of age have five or more years of teaching experience, which he characterized as "very significant" statistically or about "600 times the level generally required for statistical significance." Although the significance of the 92.6% figure is somewhat weakened by evidence that over 60% of teachers under 40 also have had more than five years experience, we agree with Judge Blumenfeld's finding that the high correlation between experience and membership in the protected age group (40 to 65 years of age) would render application of the "sixth step" policy discriminatory as a matter of law, see Coates v. National Cash Register Co., 433 F.Supp. 655, 661 (W.D.Va.1977), since, absent countervailing statistics, the likelihood of a person over 40 being selected under the policy would be substantially less than that of a person under 40. The purpose of the "sixth step" policy was to economize by employing less experienced teachers, which would inevitably open more teaching opportunities to younger less experienced applicants than to the older, who were more experienced.

Defendants have offered two lines of defense, both of which are unpersuasive. First they contend that, although the "sixth step" policy appears to be correlated strongly to membership in the group over 40, the policy did not in fact result in discrimination against this group since the percentage of over-40 teachers hired to fill job openings before and after the application of the policy was about the same. The uncorroborated statistics offered in support of this contention, however, were so defective as to justify the district court's refusal to give them any weight. They were prepared by a named defendant in the case, a former Personnel Director for the West Hartford schools who had no expertise as a statistician and had a direct interest in the outcome of the case.[1] He not only failed to produce any competent evidence of the applicant pool for the periods, which is essential to a statistical determination of hiring patterns, but he employed such dubious analytical techniques as obtaining an overall percentage figure by averaging

---

1. In Albemarle Paper Co. v. Moody, 422 U.S. 405, 433 n. 32, 95 S.Ct. 2362, 2379 n. 32, 45 L.Ed.2d 280 (1974), the Supreme Court recognized the problematic validity of statistics produced by such a source:

"It cannot escape notice that Albemarle's study was conducted by plant officials, without neutral, on-the-scene oversight, at a time when this litigation was about to come to trial. Studies so closely controlled by an interested party in litigation must be examined with great care."

annual percentages for several different years, thus contravening the basic, well-recognized principle that such averaging by percentages produces meaningless and misleading results. Moreover it appears that there were dramatic changes in the size of the applicant pool and in the number of teachers hired in the West Hartford School District during the mid-1970's, which cast serious doubt upon the statistical significance of the defendants' evidence of allegedly unchanging hiring patterns. In 1968 and 1969, according to defendants' own figures, West Hartford hired 129 and 136 teachers, of whom 28 and 33, respectively, were above the fifth step, and 17 (13%) and 15 (8%), respectively, were over 40. In 1975 and 1976, by contrast, the District hired only 35 and 53 teachers, a substantially smaller group, of whom 7 and 10 were above the fifth step and 2 (6%) and 4 (8%), respectively, were over 40.[2]

Cases involving statistics can pose a formidable challenge to a court. As the Supreme Court has observed, " 'Statistics * * * come in infinite variety. * * * [T]heir usefulness depends on all the surrounding facts and circumstances' * * *. Only the trial court is in a position to make the appropriate determination." Hazelwood v. United States, 433 U.S. 299, 312, 97 S.Ct. 2736, 2744, 53 L.Ed.2d 768 (1977), quoting International Brotherhood of Teamsters v. United States, 431 U.S. 324, 340, 97 S.Ct. 1843, 1856, 52 L.Ed.2d 396 (1977). A trial court is best able to evaluate the credibility and professionality of the witnesses who provide statistical evidence, to consider all the statistical evidence advanced, to draw inferences from different parties' failure to include relevant statistics that are available to them, and to assess the validity of assertedly objective numerical evidence by considering the influence of unaccounted-for factors upon the numbers presented. Where, as here, the statistical evidence, or its absence, leads to an indisputable result, the judge is justified in taking the evaluation of the statistics away from the jury.

Here Judge Blumenfeld rightly found that the "sixth step" policy was discriminatory on its face. From there, he apparently declined to rely on statistics either to establish as a matter of law plaintiff's position that the policy was applied or to support defendants' position that it was not applied. Absent statistics regarding any changes in the applicant pool for teaching jobs as overall hiring decreased, comparative evidence of overall hiring percentages carries little weight, since these percentages may have remained constant despite an increase or fall-off in over-40 applicants. In the face of these deficiencies in the statistical proof and the existence of testimony that the "sixth step" policy was applied in Ms. Geller's individual case, which was disputed, Judge Blumenfeld properly submitted the issue of whether it was applied to the jury, which resolved the question in her favor by finding that the "sixth step" policy was one reason for the hiring of a younger replacement.

Defendants' second line of defense, somewhat inconsistent with their contention that the "sixth step" policy was never followed, is that

2. Ms. Geller has conceded that the "sixth step" policy was never applied as an absolute exclusionary barrier to applicants over 40.

the policy, if applied, was supportable as a necessary cost-cutting gesture in the face of tight budgetary constraints. This cost justification must fail, however, because of the clear rule that

> a general assertion that the average cost of employing older workers as a group is higher than the average cost of employing younger workers as a group will not be recognized as a differentiation under the terms and provisions of the Act, unless one of the other statutory exceptions applies. To classify or group employees solely on the basis of age for the purpose of comparing costs, or for any other purpose, necessarily rests on the assumption that the age factor alone may be used to justify a differentiation—an assumption plainly contrary to the terms of the Act and the purpose of Congress in enacting it. Differentials so based would serve only to perpetuate and promote the very discrimination at which the Act is directed. 29 C.F.R. § 860.103(h) (1979).

Accord, Marshall v. Arlene Knitwear, Inc., 454 F.Supp. 715, 728 (E.D. N.Y.1978) ("Where economic savings and expectation of longer future service are directly related to an employee's age, it is a violation of the ADEA to discharge the employee for those reasons" (citations omitted)); Laugeson v. Anaconda Co., 510 F.2d 307, 316 (6th Cir.1975) ("Since it was obvious that economic conditions had to play an important part in the decision, it was vital for the jury to know that this alone would not dispose of the case if Laugeson's age induced Anaconda to discharge him instead of someone else"). Accordingly, we conclude, that Ms. Geller established disparate impact by proving that she was subjected to a facially neutral policy disproportionately disadvantaging her as a member of a protected class. Griggs v. Duke Power Co., supra; Dothard v. Rawlinson, supra.

DISPARATE TREATMENT

The record also reveals that, in addition to making out a case of disparate impact, Ms. Geller established a prima facie case of discriminatory treatment under McDonnell Douglas, supra, satisfying the oft-repeated four conditions prescribed by the Court in that case. At age 55 she was clearly within the protected group under ADEA. She applied for the teaching job, was concededly qualified for it, and was even hired temporarily to perform it. She was then released, and saw a younger person placed in the job for which she was concededly qualified. These undisputed facts are sufficient to place upon the defendants the burden of rebutting her prima facie case.[3] For reasons already stated, the defenses that the "sixth step" policy was not applied to Ms. Geller and that, if applied, it was cost-justified, must be rejected. The only other defense, that the discharge of Ms. Geller in favor of a

---

3. Discriminatory treatment analysis is no less applicable to this case because the trial court failed to instruct the jury on the specific elements of a McDonnell Douglas prima facie case. See Furnco Construction Co. v. Waters, 438 U.S. 567, 577, 98 S.Ct. 2943, 2949, 57 L.Ed.2d 957 (1978) ("The method suggested in *McDonnell Douglas* is merely a sensible, orderly way to evaluate the evidence in light of common experience as it bears on the critical question of discrimination"); Loeb v. Textron, Inc., 600 F.2d 1003, 1014 (1st Cir.1979).

younger teacher, was not motivated by the policy but by the superior competence of the latter candidate, was rejected by the jury's findings.

CAUSATION

This leads us to defendants' final contention, that the court erred in instructing the jury as to the part age must play in determining whether they violated ADEA in discharging Ms. Geller. In order to make out a case under ADEA, Ms. Geller was not required to show that age discrimination was the sole cause of her discharge. Where an employer acts out of mixed motives in discharging or refusing to hire an employee, the plaintiff must show that age was a causative or determinative factor, one that made a difference in deciding whether the plaintiff should be employed. See Loeb v. Textron, Inc., 600 F.2d 1003, 1019 (1st Cir.1979) (plaintiff must prove that age was the " 'determining factor' in his discharge in the sense that 'but for' his employer's motive to discriminate against him because of age, he would not have been discharged"; Laugeson v. Anaconda Co., supra, 510 F.2d at 317 ("We believe it was essential for the jury to understand from the instructions that there could be more than one factor in the decision to discharge him and that he was nevertheless entitled to recover if one such factor was his age and if in fact it made a difference in determining whether he was to be retained or discharged. This is so even though the need to reduce the employee force generally was also a strong, and perhaps even more compelling reason"). Accord, Cova v. Coca Cola Bottling Co., 574 F.2d 958 (8th Cir.1978).

Both parties here suggest that the *Laugeson* and *Cova* standard is in conflict with the *Loeb* rule. We disagree. If age discrimination was a "factor * * * [which] made a difference," then the employee's fortunes would have been "different" without the discriminatory action and age discrimination was therefore a "but for" cause of the result that did take place.

In the present case Judge Blumenfeld submitted to the jury a special interrogatory which asked whether the "sixth step" guideline was "one reason" for Ms. Geller's not being hired for the permanent art teacher's position. He refused to amend the interrogatory to read "one reason that made a difference." Standing alone, this refusal to amend might entitle defendants to a retrial since the jury, absent further instructions, could have found that the "sixth step" guideline, although considered by the Board as a factor, may not have been a determinative one. However, the interrogatory followed hard on the heels of an instruction in which the jury was told that it could find liability only if Ms. Geller's age "made a difference in determining whether she would be employed" and that "[i]f it did not make any difference—then of course she has not proved her case. But if it did, then she has." We conclude that, while it would have been advisable to repeat the gist of the latter language in the interrogatory, the instructions and the interrogatory, read together, were adequate. In this context the words "a reason," as used in the interrogatory, meant a reason which made a difference and hence were sufficient. Our view is fortified by undisputed evidence, including testimony of Dr. Johnson and Messrs. Metzger and Hedrick, as well as tape recordings of conversations between Ms. Geller and the various defendants, that the "key factor" was the "sixth step" policy. The principal of the school, Dr. Johnson, testified that she "rendered an excellent service. I have nothing but praise for her."

EQUITABLE RELIEF

We next turn to Ms. Geller's contention that the district court erred in denying her equitable relief beyond the damages awarded by the jury. Title 29 U.S.C. § 626(c)(1) provides, "Any person aggrieved [by an alleged violation of the ADEA] may bring a civil action in any court of competent jurisdiction for such legal or equitable relief as will effectuate the purposes of this chapter." Section 626(b) defines the available legal and equitable relief as "including without limitation judgments compelling employment, reinstatement or promotion, or enforcing the liability of amounts deemed to be unpaid minimum wages or unpaid overtime compensation under this section." The Supreme Court, defining which forms of relief were legal and which equitable so that it could determine which should be submitted to a jury, has noted that § 626

> does not specify which of the listed categories of relief are legal and which are equitable. However, since it is clear that judgments compelling "employment, reinstatement of promotion" are equitable, see 5 J. Moore, Federal Practice Par. 38.21 (1977), Congress must have meant the phrase "legal relief" to refer to judgments "enforcing * * * liability for amounts deemed to be unpaid minimum wages or unpaid overtime compensation." Lorillard v. Pons, supra, 434 U.S. at 583 n. 11, 98 S.Ct. at 871 n. 11.

Judge Blumenfeld viewed reinstatement as inappropriate because he interpreted the jury's decision granting damages equal to one year's salary at Bugbee School as a factual conclusion that Ms. Geller was deprived of only one year's employment by the defendants' discriminatory action. We agree with this conclusion. Ms. Geller had never formally been hired as a permanent teacher during the time she was working but had merely been told to get started. Permanent reinstatement therefore is unwarranted.

On the other hand, we disagree with the trial judge's refusal to consider Ms. Geller's request for lost pension benefits on the ground that "[d]amages for lost pension benefits are one component of the overall damages suffered by a plaintiff, which a jury may assess in ADEA actions." Despite some case law that supports viewing lost pension rights as an aspect of damages, see Fellows v. Medford Corp., 431 F.Supp. 199, 201 (D.Or.1977), the better view is that these rights fall within the category of equitable relief, see Cleverly v. Western Electric Co., 450 F.Supp. 507, 510 (W.D.Mo.1978), affd., 594 F.2d 638, 640 (8th Cir.1979). As distinguished from damage awards, which are payable to the plaintiff, pension benefits are paid into pension annuity funds. They merely replace the benefits that would have accrued during the year of employment wrongfully denied to Ms. Geller. Because a judge exercising his equitable power over a discrimination action should afford "make-whole" relief to wronged plaintiffs, Rodriguez v. Taylor, 569 F.2d 1231, 1238 (3d Cir.1977), we remand to the district court with directions to award pension rights to plaintiff for the 1976–77 year, to be paid into the Connecticut Teachers' Pension Fund. Plaintiffs' application for reasonable attorney's fees in prosecuting this appeal is granted in the sum of $500 plus her costs in prosecuting the appeal and defending against defendants' cross-appeal.

The judgment appealed from by the defendants is affirmed. The district court's order denying equitable relief to the plaintiff is affirmed except as to the denial of pension benefits which is reversed to the extent indicated.

LUMBARD, CIRCUIT JUDGE (dissenting):

I dissent.

We all agree that the crucial question for the jury's determination was whether age discrimination was a factor which made a difference in determining whether plaintiff was to be retained or discharged. Although the trial judge so told the jury in his oral instructions, he refused to word the written interrogatory submitted to the jury in accordance with his oral instructions. Thus, what the jury took into the juryroom read as follows:

> 1. Was the sixth step guideline one reason for Mrs. Geller not being hired for the permanent art teacher's position at the Bugbee Elementary School?

The trial judge had previously advised counsel of his proposed wording of the interrogatory. Counsel for the defendants specifically objected in the following colloquy:

> Mr. Post: Sir, could I ask that that interrogatory track with your charge to the Jury and say, "One reason that made a difference"?
>
> The Court: No. If it was one reason, that is sufficient.
>
> Mr. Post: That made a difference in their decision.
>
> The Court: No. If it was one reason.

I cannot escape the conclusion that the special interrogatory must have been uppermost in the jury's mind during its deliberation. Even if any juror had remembered the oral instructions, the written interrogatory would surely settle conclusively any question in the mind of any juror. And it was the question in the interrogatory which the jury answered and not anything else.

It follows that the restriction of the written interrogatory was error and that it was an error which could have resulted in a different verdict. It is not so overwhelmingly clear to me as it seems to be to my brothers that the jury would have decided the same way if the trial judge had conformed the wording of the interrogatory to his oral instructions, as he certainly should have done. In this case the jury should have made their decision on a proper instruction; it is not enough for my brothers to do it for them. So that a jury may decide the case on a proper instruction, and on an interrogatory in accordance with the instruction, I would reverse and remand for a new trial.

MARKHAM v. GELLER

The Supreme Court of the United States, 1981.
451 U.S. 945, 101 S.Ct. 2028, 68 L.Ed.2d 332.

JUSTICE REHNQUIST, dissenting from the denial of certiorari.

This case presents the question whether a school board may enact a policy which, for budgetary reasons, favors the hiring of less experienced teachers. Because I think the Court of Appeals for the Second Circuit erred in holding that such a policy violates the Age Discrimination in Employment Act of 1967 (ADEA), 29 U.S.C. § 621 et seq., I dissent from the denial of the petition for a writ of certiorari.

In my opinion, the decision of the Court of Appeals is inconsistent with the express provisions of the ADEA and is not supported by any prior decision of this Court. The ADEA makes it unlawful for any employer "to fail or refuse to hire or to discharge any individual or otherwise discriminate against any individual with respect to his compensation, terms, conditions, or privileges of employment, because of such individual's age." 29 U.S.C. § 623(a)(1). The policy under attack in this case, however, makes no reference to age. For budgetary reasons, a school board simply adopted a policy to hire teachers with fewer years of experience. No one contends that the Board discriminated against teachers over the age of 40 who had fewer than five years of prior teaching experience and who sought employment. In spite of this, the courts below found the Board's policy unlawful because it has a greater "impact" on teachers between the ages of 40 and 65 than it has on teachers under the age of 40. They reached this conclusion even though over 60% of all teachers under the age of 40 also have more than five years of experience and are detrimentally affected by the Board's policy. This Court has never held that proof of discriminatory impact can establish a violation of the ADEA, and it certainly has never sanctioned a finding of a violation where the statistical evidence revealed that a policy, neutral on its face, has such a significant impact on all candidates concerned, not simply the protected age group.

Of greater importance, however, is the rationale employed by the Court of Appeals in rejecting the Board's "cost" justification for its policy. The court held that such justification conflicted with 29 CFR § 860.103(h) (1979), which is one of the many guidelines that has been issued by the Secretary of Labor in this area. By its express terms, however, this regulation is inapplicable to the present situation. The Board has not made a general assertion that "the average cost of employing older workers as a group is higher than the average cost of employing younger workers," nor does this involve an attempt "[t]o classify or group employees solely on the basis of age for the purpose of comparing costs. * * * " Rather, this is a policy which by its express terms makes no reference to age and which in practice has had a significant impact on teachers under the age of 40 as well as those over that age. The Court of Appeals' opinion manages to tie the hands of local school boards in dealing with ever-increasing costs without the sanction of the Act which Congress passed to protect older workers. Presumably, the Court of Appeals' rationale would similarly prohibit the Board from deciding no longer to give full credit for teaching experience received at other school districts. Such a policy, although neutral on its face with regard to age and affecting all teachers, would no doubt have a statistically different impact on teachers over the age of 40 than on those under that age.

In my view, Congress did not intend the ADEA to have the restraining influence on local governments which will result from the decision below. Congress revealed this intention in 29 U.S.C. § 623(f)(1), which provides that it shall not be unlawful for an employer to take any action otherwise prohibited "where the differentiation is based on reasonable factors other than age." Because the differential based on experience in petitioners' sixth-step policy has nothing to do with age, I would grant the petition for a writ of certiorari and give plenary consideration to the decision of the Court of Appeals.

C. RETIREMENT

EQUAL EMPLOYMENT OPPORTUNITY COMMISSION v. CHRYSLER CORPORATION

United States Court of Appeals for the Sixth Circuit, 1984.
733 F.2d 1183.

MERRITT, CIRCUIT JUDGE.

In this age discrimination case, we conclude that the District Court did not err in issuing an injunction requiring the Chrysler Corporation to offer certain forced retirees "layoff status," a status which allows an employee the possibility of recall to active duty. We, therefore, affirm.

I.

In 1979 Chrysler's management determined that a drastic reduction in its work force was necessary for the company's survival. When its policies failed to reduce the work force sufficiently, Chrysler identified about fifty employees age fifty-five and over for a special early retirement "at corporate option." These employees would otherwise simply have been laid off under a company policy entitling them to return by seniority to active duty if the company's prospects for survival improved. The employees forced to retire were provided the same special benefits provided those employees who had voluntarily accepted early retirement, including a temporary pension supplement and pension benefits not actuarily reduced. These forced retirees were not, however, provided the option of taking "layoff status" which had been provided to employees under age fifty-five, whose age did not qualify them for special early retirement "at corporate option."

The Equal Employment Opportunity Commission (EEOC) filed suit against Chrysler alleging that Chrysler's forced retirement policy violates section 4 of the Age Discrimination in Employment Act, (ADEA), which provides that "no * * * [bona fide] employee benefit plan shall require or permit the involuntary retirement of any individual [between the ages of 40 and 70] because of the age of such individual." The EEOC requested that the District Court award preliminary injunctive relief.

United States District Judge Philip Pratt of the Eastern District of Michigan ordered Chrysler to provide the group of forced retirees the opportunity to be placed on "layoff status." The District Court determined that the EEOC had established a "strong" likelihood of success on the merits of the claims of the forced retirees and those who accepted "mutually satisfactory" retirement under protest. The District Court held that Chrysler's decision to identify certain employees for involuntary retirement was clearly based on age because "those over 55 with requisite corporate service were involuntarily retired with no chance of recall" while "those under 55 * * * were laid off with the possibility of recall in the order of seniority." Although Chrysler offered the so-called "failing company doctrine" as a justification for its employment decisions, the District Court concluded that "no reason for retirement vis-a-vis layoff was implicated 'other than age.' "

The District Court reasoned that the legislative history of the 1978 amendment to section 4(f)(2) of the ADEA establishes that the qualifying statutory terms were meant to legitimate only forced retirements based on an individual's personal inability to continue to perform his or her job duties adequately. The District Court held that there is no case law to support the "proposition that job elimination or a reduction in [work] force is a factor which renders an otherwise illegal involuntary retirement lawful."

II.

On this appeal Chrysler argues primarily that the District Court abused its discretion in determining that the EEOC had established a substantial likelihood of success on the merits of its claims against Chrysler. In particular, as its rebuttal to the EEOC's claim that Chrysler's forced retirement policy was based on age, Chrysler attempts here to justify the forced retirements on the basis of an economic necessity to reduce costs in the face of possible insolvency. Such economic necessity, it argues, is a "reasonable factor other than age" within the meaning of 29 U.S.C. § 623(f)(1).

Chrysler's argument regarding its economic justifications for the forced retirements requires close scrutiny in light of the 1978 amendments to the ADEA forbidding forced early retirement before age 70, amendments which overruled the Supreme Court's decision to the contrary in United Air Lines v. McMann, 434 U.S. 192, 98 S.Ct. 444, 54 L.Ed.2d 402 (1977). Chrysler argues that the legislative history of the 1978 amendments indicates that the plaintiff's ultimate burden under section 4(f)(2) of the ADEA is to establish that age is the sole and arbitrary basis for Chrysler's forced retirement policy. Under Chrysler's interpretation of the 1978 amendments, Chrysler's poor financial condition in 1979 was an additional factor other than age and, thus, was a legitimate basis for Chrysler's forced retirements.

We read the plain language and legislative history of the 1978 amendments, however, as indicating that the plaintiff in the instant case had to establish that age was a "determining" factor in Chrysler's formulation of its forced retirement policy in order for that policy to violate the ADEA. Thus, the critical question on this appeal is whether the prospect of imminent bankruptcy legitimates the use of age as a factor in determining those employees who shall receive a pension and those who shall be laid off subject to recall.

Forced early retirements based on economic necessity are unacceptable under the ADEA unless they meet two tests. First, the necessity for drastic cost reduction obviously must be real. A similar showing has been required in antitrust cases involving the "failing company" defense. Second, the forced early retirements must be the least-detrimental-alternative means available to reduce costs. This standard has been developed in Title VII cases. See, e.g., United States v. Bethlehem Steel Corp., 446 F.2d 652 (2d Cir.1971); Robinson v. Lorillard Corp., 444 F.2d 791 (4th Cir.), cert. dismissed, 404 U.S. 1006, 92 S.Ct. 573, 30 L.Ed.2d 655 (1971). See generally Note, The Cost of Growing Old: Business Necessity and the Age Discrimination in Employment Act, 88 Yale L.J. 565 (1979).

In the instant case, there is no dispute that Chrysler's financial difficulties were real in 1979. As the District Court indicated, Congressional findings establish that at the time of these forced retirement decisions Chrysler was on the verge of insolvency.

Chrysler's program to force certain employees to retire early, however, does not meet the least-detrimental-alternative standard. In order to meet this standard, Chrysler would have had to give the employees subject to forced early retirements the same right of recall as the younger employees were given. As the District Court noted, Chrysler has presented no reason why the need to implement a reduction in work force precluded a certain class of employees—employees age 55 or over with at least 10 years of service—from choosing layoff. Thus, we agree with the District Court's conclusion that there is a substantial likelihood of success on the merits of the EEOC's claims against Chrysler.

Chrysler also argues on this appeal that the District Court abused its discretion in finding that the forced retirees suffered irreparable harm as a result of Chrysler's discriminatory policy. The District Court found that Chrysler's decision to force certain individuals to retire early caused loss of work and loss of future prospects for work as well as causing individuals to suffer from such problems as emotional distress, depression, increased drug use, decrease in feelings of a useful life, a contracted social life, increased cigarette consumption, lassitude, sexual problems, and a reduced sense of well-being. We conclude that the District Court's findings are not clearly erroneous and that, as the District Court noted, the forced retirees' problems are "the very type of injur[ies] Congress sought to avert when it banned involuntary retirement." Such findings support irreparable injury in other kinds of discrimination cases, and we believe the same factors support such a finding in this age discrimination case.

For the reasons stated herein, we affirm the District Court's judgment entering the preliminary injunction against Chrysler.

D. BONA FIDE OCCUPATIONAL QUALIFICATION

WESTERN AIR LINES, INC. v. CRISWELL

The Supreme Court of the United States, 1985.
__ U.S. __, 105 S.Ct. 2743, 86 L.Ed.2d 321.

JUSTICE STEVENS delivered the opinion of the Court.

The petitioner, Western Air Lines, Inc., requires that its flight engineers retire at age 60. Although the Age Discrimination in Employment Act of 1967 (ADEA), 29 U.S.C. §§ 621–634, generally prohibits mandatory retirement before age 70, the Act provides an exception "where age is a bona fide occupational qualification [BFOQ] reasonably necessary to the normal operation of the particular business." [1] A jury concluded that Western's mandatory retirement rule did not qualify as a BFOQ even though it purportedly was adopted for safety reasons. The question here is whether the jury was properly instructed on the elements of the BFOQ defense.

I

In its commercial airline operations, Western operates a variety of aircraft, including the Boeing 727 and the McDonnell-Douglas DC–10. These aircraft require three crew members in the cockpit: a captain, a first officer, and a flight engineer. "The 'captain' is the pilot and controls the aircraft. He is responsible for all phases of its operation. The 'first officer' is the copilot and assists the captain. The 'flight engineer' usually monitors a side-facing instrument panel. He does not operate the flight controls unless the captain and the first officer become incapacitated." Trans World Airlines, Inc. v. Thurston, __ U.S. __, __, 105 S.Ct. 613, 618, 83 L.Ed.2d 523 (1985).

---

1. Section 4(f)(1) of the ADEA provides:

"It shall not be unlawful for an employer * * *

"(1) to take any action otherwise prohibited * * * where age is a bona fide occupational qualification reasonably necessary to the normal operation of the particular business. * * *" 81 Stat. 603, 29 U.S.C. § 623(f)(1)

A regulation of the Federal Aviation Administration prohibits any person from serving as a pilot or first officer on a commercial flight "if that person has reached his 60th birthday." 14 CFR § 121.383(c) (1985). The FAA has justified the retention of mandatory retirement for pilots on the theory that "incapacitating medical events" and "adverse psychological, emotional, and physical changes" occur as a consequence of aging. "The inability to detect or predict with precision an individual's risk of sudden or subtle incapacitation, in the face of known age-related risks, counsels against relaxation of the rule." 49 Fed.Reg. 14695 (1984). See also 24 Fed.Reg. 9776 (1959).

At the same time, the FAA has refused to establish a mandatory retirement age for flight engineers. "While a flight engineer has important duties which contribute to the safe operation of the airplane, he or she may not assume the responsibilities of the pilot in command." 49 Fed.Reg., at 14694. Moreover, available statistics establish that flight engineers have rarely been a contributing cause or factor in commercial aircraft "accidents" or "incidents." Ibid.

In 1978, respondents Criswell and Starley were Captains operating DC–10s for Western. Both men celebrated their 60th birthdays in July 1978. Under the collective-bargaining agreement in effect between Western and the union, cockpit crew members could obtain open positions by bidding in order of seniority. In order to avoid mandatory retirement under the FAA's under-age-60 rule for pilots, Criswell and Starley applied for reassignment as flight engineers. Western denied both requests, ostensibly on the ground that both employees were members of the company's retirement plan which required all crew members to retire at age 60.[4] For the same reason, respondent Ron, a career flight engineer, was also retired in 1978 after his 60th birthday.

Mandatory retirement provisions similar to those contained in Western's pension plan had previously been upheld under the ADEA. United Air Lines, Inc. v. McMann, 434 U.S. 192, 98 S.Ct. 444, 54 L.Ed. 2d 402 (1977). As originally enacted in 1967, the Act provided an exception to its general proscription of age discrimination for any actions undertaken "to observe the terms of a * * * bona fide employee benefit plan such as a retirement, pension, or insurance plan, which is not a subterfuge to evade the purposes of this Act." In April 1978, however, Congress amended the statute to prohibit employee

---

4. The Western official who was responsible for the decision to retire the plaintiffs conceded that "the sole basis" for the denial of the applications of Criswell, Starley and Ron was the same: "the provision in the pension plan regarding retirement at age 60." Tr. 1163. In addition, he admitted that he had "no personal knowledge" of any safety rationale for the under-age-60 rule for flight engineers, id., at 2059, nor had it played any significant role in his decision to retire them. See id., at 61, 2027–2033, 2056–2057. The airline sent Starley and Ron form letters informing them of its "considered judgment after examining all of the applicable statutory law that since you have been a member of our Pilot retirement plan, that we cannot continue your employment beyond the normal retirement date of age 60." See App. 89, 91.

benefit plans from requiring the involuntary retirement of any employee because of age.

Criswell, Starley, and Ron brought this action against Western
contending that the under-age-60 qualification for the position of flight
engineer violated the ADEA. In the District Court, Western defended,
in part, on the theory that the age-60 rule is a BFOQ "reasonably
necessary" to the safe operation of the airline.[7] All parties submitted
evidence concerning the nature of the flight engineer's tasks, the
physiological and psychological traits required to perform them, and
the availability of those traits among persons over age 60.

As the District Court summarized, the evidence at trial established
that the flight engineer's "normal duties are less critical to the safety of
flight than those of a pilot." 514 F.Supp. 384, 390 (CD Cal.1981). The
flight engineer, however, does have critical functions in emergency
situations and, of course, might cause considerable disruption in the
event of his own medical emergency.

The actual capabilities of persons over age 60, and the ability to
detect disease or a precipitous decline in their faculties, were the
subject of conflicting medical testimony. Western's expert witness, a
former FAA Deputy Federal Air Surgeon,[8] was especially concerned
about the possibility of a "cardiovascular event" such as a heart attack.
He testified that "with advancing age the likelihood of onset of disease
increases and that in persons over age 60 it could not be predicted
whether and when such diseases would occur." Id., at 389.

The plaintiffs' experts, on the other hand, testified that physiological deterioration is caused by disease, not aging, and that "it was
feasible to determine on the basis of individual medical examinations
whether flight deck crew members, including those over age 60, were
physically qualified to continue to fly." Ibid. These conclusions were
corroborated by the nonmedical evidence:

> The record also reveals that both the FAA and the airlines have
> been able to deal with the health problems of pilots on an individual-
> ized basis. Pilots who have been grounded because of alcoholism or
> cardiovascular disease have been recertified by the FAA and allowed
> to resume flying. Pilots who were unable to pass the necessary
> examination to maintain their FAA first class medical certificates, but
> who continued to qualify for second class medical certificates were
> allowed to "down-grade" from pilot to [flight engineer]. There is
> nothing in the record to indicate that these flight deck crew members
> are physically better able to perform their duties than flight engineers

7. Western also contended that its denials of the downbids by pilots Starley and
Criswell were based on "reasonable factors
other than age [RFOA]." 29 U.S.C.
§ 623(f)(1); see n. 10, infra.

8. Although the witness had served
with FAA for 7 years ending in 1979, he
conceded that throughout his tenure at the
FAA, he never had advocated that the
Agency extend the age-60 rule to flight
engineers. Tr. 1521.

over age 60 who have not experienced such events or that they are less likely to become incapacitated. Id., at 390.

Moreover, several large commercial airlines have flight engineers over age 60 "flying the line" without any reduction in their safety record. Ibid.

The jury was instructed that the "BFOQ defense is available only if it is reasonably necessary to the normal operation or essence of defendant's business." Tr. 2626. The jury was informed that "the essence of Western's business is the safe transportation of their passengers." Ibid. The jury was also instructed:

One method by which defendant Western may establish a BFOQ in this case is to prove:

(1) That in 1978, when these plaintiffs were retired, it was highly impractical for Western to deal with each second officer over age 60 on an individualized basis to determine his particular ability to perform his job safely; and

(2) That some second officers over age 60 possess traits of a physiological, psychological or other nature which preclude safe and efficient job performance that cannot be ascertained by means other than knowing their age.

In evaluating the practicability to defendant Western of dealing with second officers over age 60 on an individualized basis, with respect to the medical testimony, you should consider the state of the medical art as it existed in July 1978. Id., at 2627.

The jury rendered a verdict for the plaintiffs, and awarded damages. After trial, the District Court granted equitable relief, explaining in a written opinion why he found no merit in Western's BFOQ defense to the mandatory retirement rule. 514 F.Supp. at 389–391.

On appeal, Western made various arguments attacking the verdict and judgment below, but the Court of Appeals affirmed in all respects. 709 F.2d 544 (CA9 1983). In particular, the Court of Appeals rejected Western's contention that the instruction on the BFOQ defense was insufficiently deferential to the airline's legitimate concern for the safety of its passengers. Id., at 549–551. We granted certiorari to consider the merits of this question. 469 U.S. ___, 105 S.Ct. 80, 83 L.Ed. 2d 28 (1984).[10]

---

10. One of Western's claims in the trial court was that its refusal to allow pilots to serve as flight engineers after they reached age 60 was based on "reasonable factors other than age," namely a facially neutral policy embodied in its collective bargaining agreement which prohibited downbidding. See nn. 3 and 7, supra. The jury rejected this defense in its verdict. On appeal, Western claimed that the instructions had improperly required it to bear the burden of proof on the RFOA issue inasmuch as the burden of persuasion on the issue of age discrimination is at all times on the plaintiff. Cf. Texas Department of Community Affairs v. Burdine, 450 U.S. 248, 101 S.Ct. 1089, 67 L.Ed.2d 207 (1981); Furnco Construction Co. v. Waters, 438 U.S. 567, 98 S.Ct. 2943, 57 L.Ed.2d 957 (1978). The Court of Appeals rejected this claim on the merits. 709 F.2d, at 552–553. We granted certiorari to consider the merits of this question, 469 U.S. ___, 105 S.Ct. 80, 83 L.Ed.2d 28 (1984), but as we read the instructions the burden was placed on the plaintiffs on the RFOA issue. The general instruction on the question of discrimination provided that the "burden of proof is

II

Throughout the legislative history of the ADEA, one empirical fact is repeatedly emphasized: the process of psychological and physiological degeneration caused by aging varies with each individual. "The basic research in the field of aging has established that there is a wide range of individual physical ability regardless of age." [11] As a result, many older American workers perform at levels equal or superior to their younger colleagues.

In 1965, the Secretary of Labor reported to Congress that despite these well-established medical facts there "is persistent and widespread use of age limits in hiring that in a great many cases can be attributed only to arbitrary discrimination against older workers on the basis of age and regardless of ability." Two years later, the President recommended that Congress enact legislation to abolish arbitrary age limits on hiring. Such limits, the President declared, have a devastating effect on the dignity of the individual and result in a staggering loss of human resources vital to the national economy. [13]

After further study, Congress responded with the enactment of the ADEA. The preamble declares that the purpose of the ADEA is "to promote employment of older persons based on their ability rather than age [and] to prohibit arbitrary age discrimination in employment." 81 Stat. 602, 29 U.S.C. § 621(b). Section 4(a)(1) makes it "unlawful for an employer * * * to fail or refuse to hire or to discharge any individual or otherwise discriminate against any individual with respect to his compensation, terms, conditions, or privileges of employment, because of such individual's age." 81 Stat. 603, 29 U.S.C. § 623(a)(1). This proscription presently applies to all persons between the ages of 40 and 70. 29 U.S.C. § 631(a).

The legislative history of the 1978 Amendments to the ADEA makes quite clear that the policies and substantive provisions of the

on the plaintiffs to show discriminatory treatment on the basis of age." App. 58. The instructions expressly informed the jury when the burden shifted to the defendant to prove various issues, e.g., id., at 60 (business necessity); id., at 61 (BFOQ), but did not so inform the jury in the RFOA instruction, id., at 62–63. Because the plaintiffs were assigned the burden of proof, we need not consider whether it would have been error to assign it to the defendant.

11. Report of the Secretary of Labor, The Older American Worker: Age Discrimination in Employment 9 (1965) (hereinafter Report), EEOC, Legislative History of the Age Discrimination in Employment Act 26 (1981) (hereinafter Legislative History). See also S.Rep. No. 95–493, p. 2 (1977), U.S.Code Cong. & Admin.News 1978, pp. 504, 505, Legislative History 435

("Scientific research . . . indicates that chronological age alone is a poor indicator of ability to perform a job").

13. "Hundreds of thousands not yet old, not yet voluntarily retired, find themselves jobless because of arbitrary age discrimination. Despite our present low rate of unemployment, there has been a persistent average of 850,000 people age 45 and over who are unemployed.

*   *   *   *   *

"In economic terms, this is a serious—and senseless—loss to a nation on the move. But the greater loss is the cruel sacrifice in happiness and well-being which joblessness imposes on these citizens and their families." H.R.Doc. No. 40, 90th Cong., 1st Sess., 7 (1967), Legislative History 61.

Act apply with especial force in the case of mandatory retirement provisions. The House Committee on Education and Labor reported:

> Increasingly, it is being recognized that mandatory retirement based solely upon age is arbitrary and that chronological age alone is a poor indicator of ability to perform a job. Mandatory retirement does not take into consideration actual differing abilities and capacities. Such forced retirement can cause hardships for older persons through loss of roles and loss of income. Those older persons who wish to be re-employed have a much more difficult time finding a new job than younger persons.
>
> Society, as a whole, suffers from mandatory retirement as well. As a result of mandatory retirement, skills and experience are lost from the work force resulting in reduced GNP. Such practices also add a burden to Government income maintenance programs such as social security.[15]

In the 1978 Amendments, Congress narrowed an exception to the ADEA which had previously authorized involuntary retirement under limited circumstances.

In both 1967 and 1978, however, Congress recognized that classifications based on age, like classifications based on religion, sex, or national origin, may sometimes serve as a necessary proxy for neutral employment qualifications essential to the employer's business. The diverse employment situations in various industries, however, forced Congress to adopt a "case-by-case basis * * * as the underlying rule in the administration of the legislation." H.R.Rep. No. 805, 90th Cong., 1st Sess., 7 (1967), U.S.Code Cong. & Admin.News 1967, pp. 2213, 2220, Legislative History 80.[16] Congress offered only general guidance on when an age classification might be permissible by borrowing a concept and statutory language from Title VII of the Civil Rights Act of 1964 and providing that such a classification is lawful "where age is a bona fide occupational qualification reasonably necessary to the normal operation of the particular business." 29 U.S.C. § 623(f)(1).

Shortly after the passage of the Act, the Secretary of Labor, who was at that time charged with its enforcement, adopted regulations declaring that the BFOQ exception to ADEA has only "limited scope and application" and "must be construed narrowly." 33 Fed.Reg. 9172 (1968), 29 CFR § 860.102(b) (1984). The EEOC adopted the same narrow construction of the BFOQ exception after it was assigned authority for enforcing the statute. 46 Fed.Reg. 47727 (1981), 29 CFR

---

15. H.R.Rep. No. 95–527, pt. 1, p. 2 (1977), Legislative History 362. Cf. S.Rep. 95–493, p. 4, Legislative History 437 ("The committee believes that the arguments for retaining existing mandatory retirement policies are largely based on misconceptions rather than upon a careful analysis of the facts").

16. "Many different types of employment situations prevail. Administration of

this law must place emphasis on case-by-case basis, with unusual working conditions weighed on their own merits. The purpose of this legislation, simply stated, is to insure that age, within the limits prescribed herein, is not a determining factor in a refusal to hire." S.Rep. 723, 90th Cong., 1st Sess., 7 (1967), Legislative History 111.

§ 1625.6 (1984). The restrictive language of the statute, and the consistent interpretation of the administrative agencies charged with enforcing the statute convince us that, like its Title VII counterpart, the BFOQ exception "was in fact meant to be an extremely narrow exception to the general prohibition" of age discrimination contained in the ADEA. Dothard v. Rawlinson, 433 U.S. 321, 334, 97 S.Ct. 2720, 2729, 53 L.Ed.2d 786 (1977).

III

In Usery v. Tamiami Trail Tours, Inc., 531 F.2d 224 (1976), the Court of Appeals for the Fifth Circuit was called upon to evaluate the merits of a BFOQ defense to a claim of age discrimination. Tamiami Trail Tours, Inc., had a policy of refusing to hire persons over-age-40 as intercity bus drivers. At trial, the bus company introduced testimony supporting its theory that the hiring policy was a BFOQ based upon safety considerations—the need to employ persons who have a low risk of accidents. In evaluating this contention, the Court of Appeals drew on its Title VII precedents, and concluded that two inquiries were relevant.

First, the court recognized that some job qualifications may be so peripheral to the central mission of the employer's business that *no* age discrimination can be "reasonably *necessary* to the normal operation of the particular business." [18] 29 U.S.C. § 623(f)(1). The bus company justified the age qualification for hiring its drivers on safety considerations, but the court concluded that this claim was to be evaluated under an objective standard:

> [T]he job qualifications which the employer invokes to justify his discrimination must be *reasonably necessary* to the essence of his business—here, the *safe* transportation of bus passengers from one point to another. The greater the safety factor, measured by the likelihood of harm in case of an accident, the more stringent may be the job qualifications designed to insure safe driving. 531 F.2d, at 236.

This inquiry "adjusts to the safety factor" by ensuring that the employer's restrictive job qualifications are "reasonably necessary" to further the overriding interest in public safety. Ibid. In *Tamiami,* the court noted that no one had seriously challenged the bus company's safety justification for hiring drivers with a low risk of having accidents.

Second, the court recognized that the ADEA requires that age qualifications be something more than "convenient" or "reasonable";

---

18. Diaz v. Pan American World Airways, Inc., 442 F.2d 385 (CA5), cert. denied, 404 U.S. 950, 92 S.Ct. 275, 30 L.Ed.2d 267 (1971), provided authority for this proposition. In Diaz the court had rejected Pan Am's claim that a female-only qualification for the position of in-flight cabin attendant was a BFOQ under Title VII. The District Court had upheld the qualification as a BFOQ finding that the airline's passengers preferred the "pleasant environment" and the "cosmetic effect" provided by female attendants, and that most men were unable to perform effectively the "non-mechanical functions" of the job. The Court of Appeals rejected the BFOQ defense concluding that these considerations "are tangential to the essence of the business involved." Id., at 388.

they must be "reasonably necessary * * * to the particular business," and this is only so when the employer is compelled to rely on age as a proxy for the safety-related job qualifications validated in the first inquiry.[19] This showing could be made in two ways. The employer could establish that it " 'had reasonable cause to believe, that is, a factual basis for believing, that all or substantially all [persons over the age qualifications] would be unable to perform safely and efficiently the duties of the job involved.' " [20] In *Tamiami*, the employer did not seek to justify its hiring qualification under this standard.

Alternatively, the employer could establish that age was a legitimate proxy for the safety-related job qualifications by proving that it is " 'impossible or highly impractical' " to deal with the older employees on an individualized basis.[21] "One method by which the employer can carry this burden is to establish that some members of the discriminated-against class possess a trait precluding safe and efficient job performance that cannot be ascertained by means other than knowledge of the applicant's membership in the class." Id., at 235. In *Tamiami*, the medical evidence on this point was conflicting, but the District Court had found that individual examinations could not determine which individuals over the age of 40 would be unable to operate the buses safely. The Court of Appeals found that this finding of fact was not "clearly erroneous," and affirmed the District Court's judgment for the bus company on the BFOQ defense. Id., at 238.

Congress, in considering the 1978 Amendments, implicitly endorsed the two-part inquiry identified by the Fifth Circuit in the *Tamiami* case. The Senate Committee Report expressed concern that the amendment prohibiting mandatory retirement in accordance with pension plans might imply that mandatory retirement could not be a BFOQ:

> For example, in certain types of particularly arduous law enforcement activity, there may be a factual basis for believing that substantially all employees above a specified age would be unable to continue to perform safely and efficiently the duties of their particular jobs, and it may be impossible or impractical to determine through medical examinations, periodic reviews of current job performance and other objective tests the employees' capacity or ability to continue to perform the jobs safely and efficiently.

19. Weeks v. Southern Bell Telephone & Telegraph Co., 408 F.2d 228 (CA5 1969), provided authority for this proposition. In *Weeks* the court rejected Southern Bell's claim that a male-only qualification for the position of switchman was a BFOQ under Title VII. Southern Bell argued, and the District Court had found, that the job was "strenuous," but the court observed that "finding is extremely vague." Id., at 234. The court rejected the BFOQ defense concluding that "using these class stereotypes denies desirable positions to a great many women perfectly capable of performing the duties involved." Id., at 236. Moreover, the employer had made no showing that it was "impossible or highly impractical to deal with women on an individualized basis." Id., at 235, n. 5.

20. Usery v. Tamiami Trail Tours, Inc., 531 F.2d, at 235 (quoting Weeks v. Southern Bell Telephone & Telegraph Co., 408 F.2d, at 235).

21. Usery v. Tamiami Trail Tours, Inc., 531 F.2d, at 235 (quoting Weeks v. Southern Bell Telephone & Telegraph Co., 408 F.2d, at 235, n. 5).

Accordingly, the committee adopted an amendment to make it clear that where these two conditions are satisfied and where such a bona fide occupational qualification has therefore been established, an employer may lawfully require mandatory retirement at that specified age. S.Rep. No. 95–493, p. 10–11 (1977), U.S.Code Cong. & Admin. News 1978, pp. 513, 514, Legislative History 443–444.

The amendment was adopted by the Senate, but deleted by the Conference Committee because it "neither added to nor worked any change upon present law." [22] H.R.Conf.Rep. No. 95–950, p. 7 (1978), U.S.Code Cong. & Admin.News 1978, p. 528, Legislative History 518.

Every Court of Appeals that has confronted a BFOQ defense based on safety considerations has analyzed the problem consistently with the *Tamiami* standard.[23] An EEOC regulation embraces the same criteria.[24] Considering the narrow language of the BFOQ exception, the parallel treatment of such questions under Title VII, and the uniform application of the standard by the federal courts, the EEOC and Congress, we conclude that this two-part inquiry properly identifies the relevant considerations for resolving a BFOQ defense to an age-based qualification purportedly justified by considerations of safety.

IV

In the trial court, Western preserved an objection to any instruction in the *Tamiami* mold, claiming that "any instruction pertaining to the statutory phrase 'reasonably necessary to the normal operation of [defendant's] business' * * * is irrelevant to and confusing for the deliberations of the jury." Western proposed an instruction that would have allowed it to succeed on the BFOQ defense by proving "that in

22. Senator Javits, an active proponent of the legislation, obviously viewed the BFOQ defense as a narrow one when he explained that it could be proved when "the employer can demonstrate that there is an objective, factual basis for believing that virtually all employees above a certain age are unable to safely perform the duties of their jobs and where, in addition, there is no practical medical or performance test to determine capacity." 123 Cong.Rec. 34319 (1977), Legislative History 506. See also H.R.Rep. No. 95–527, pt. 1, p. 12, Legislative History 372.

23. See, e.g., Monroe v. United Air Lines, Inc., 736 F.2d 394 (CA7 1984), cert. denied, 469 U.S. ___, 105 S.Ct. 983, 83 L.Ed.2d 984 (1985); Johnson v. American Airlines, Inc., 745 F.2d 988, 993–994 (CA5 1984), cert. pending, No. 84–1271; 709 F.2d, at 550 (case below); Orzel v. City of Wauwatosa Fire Department, 697 F.2d 743, 752–753 (CA7), cert. denied, 464 U.S. 992, 104 S.Ct. 484, 78 L.Ed.2d 680 (1983); Tuohy v. Ford Motor Co., 675 F.2d 842, 844–845 (CA6 1982); Smallwood v. United Air Lines, Inc., 661 F.2d 303, 307 (CA4 1981),

cert. denied, 456 U.S. 1007, 102 S.Ct. 2299, 73 L.Ed.2d 1302 (1982); Arritt v. Grisell, 567 F.2d 1267, 1271 (CA4 1977). Cf. Harriss v. Pan American World Airways, Inc., 649 F.2d 670, 676–677 (CA9 1980) (Title VII).

24. 46 Fed.Reg. 47727 (1981), 29 CFR § 1625.6(b) (1984):

"An employer asserting a BFOQ defense has the burden of proving that (1) the age limit is reasonably necessary to the essence of the business, and either (2) that all or substantially all individuals excluded from the job involved are in fact disqualified, or (3) that some of the individuals so excluded possess a disqualifying trait that cannot be ascertained except by reference to age. If the employer's objective in asserting a BFOQ is the goal of public safety, the employer must prove that the challenged practice does indeed effectuate that goal and that there is no acceptable alternative which would better advance it or equally advance it with less discriminatory impact."

1978, when these plaintiffs were retired, there existed a *rational basis in fact* for defendant to believe that use of [flight engineers] over age 60 on its DC–10 airliners would increase the likelihood of risk to its passengers." [26] The proposed instruction went on to note that the jury might rely on the FAA's age-60 rule for pilots to establish a BFOQ under this standard "without considering any other evidence." It also noted that the medical evidence submitted by the parties might provide a "rational basis in fact."

On appeal, Western defended its proposed instruction, and the Court of Appeals' soundly rejected it. 709 F.2d, at 549–551. In this Court, Western slightly changes its course. The airline now acknowledges that the *Tamiami* standard identifies the relevant general inquiries that must be made in evaluating the BFOQ defense. However, Western claims that in several respects the instructions given below were insufficiently protective of public safety. Western urges that we interpret or modify the *Tamiami* standard to weigh these concerns in the balance.

Reasonably Necessary Job Qualifications

Western relied on two different kinds of job qualifications to justify its mandatory retirement policy. First, it argued that flight engineers should have a low risk of incapacitation or psychological and physiological deterioration. At this vague level of analysis the plaintiffs have not seriously disputed—nor could they—that the qualification of good health for a vital crew member is reasonably necessary to the essence of the airline's operations. Instead, they have argued that age is not a necessary proxy for that qualification.

On a more specific level, Western argues that flight engineers must meet the same stringent qualifications as pilots, and that it was therefore quite logical to extend to flight engineers the FAA's age-60 retirement rule for pilots. Although the FAA's rule for pilots, adopted for safety reasons, is relevant evidence in the airline's BFOQ defense, it is not to be accorded conclusive weight. Johnson v. Mayor and City Council of Baltimore, ___ U.S. ___, ___, 105 S.Ct. 2717, ___, 85 L.Ed.2d ___. The extent to which the rule is probative varies with the weight of the evidence supporting its safety rationale and "the congruity between the * * * occupations at issue." Ibid. In this case, the evidence clearly established that the FAA, Western, and other airlines all recognized that the qualifications for a flight engineer were less rigorous than those required for a pilot.[28]

---

26. Ibid. (Defendant's Proposed Instruction No. 19) (emphasis added). In support of the "rational basis in fact" language in the proposed instruction Western cited language in the Seventh Circuit's opinion in Hodgson v. Greyhound Lines, Inc., 499 F.2d 859 (CA7 1974), cert. denied, 419 U.S. 1122, 95 S.Ct. 805, 42 L.Ed.2d 822 (1975) which had been criticized by the Fifth Circuit panel in *Tamiami* and which the Seventh Circuit later repudiated. Orzel v. City of Wauwatosa Fire Department, 697 F.2d, at 752–753. Western also relied on the District Court's opinion in Tuohy v. Ford Motor Co., 490 F.Supp. 258 (ED Mich.1980), which was reversed on appeal, 675 F.2d 842 (CA6 1982).

28. As the Court of Appeals noted, the "jury heard testimony that Western itself

In the absence of persuasive evidence supporting its position, Western nevertheless argues that the jury should have been instructed to defer to "Western's selection of job qualifications for the position of [flight engineer] that are reasonable in light of the safety risks." Brief for Petitioner 30. This proposal is plainly at odds with Congress' decision, in adopting the ADEA, to subject such management decisions to a test of objective justification in a court of law. The BFOQ standard adopted in the statute is one of "reasonable necessity," not reasonableness.

In adopting that standard, Congress did not ignore the public interest in safety. That interest is adequately reflected in instructions that track the language of the statute. When an employer establishes that a job qualification has been carefully formulated to respond to documented concerns for public safety, it will not be overly burdensome to persuade a trier of fact that the qualification is "reasonably necessary" to safe operation of the business. The uncertainty implicit in the concept of managing safety risks always makes it "reasonably necessary" to err on the side of caution in a close case.[29] The employer cannot be expected to establish the risk of an airline accident "to a certainty, for certainty would require running the risk until a tragic accident would prove that the judgment was sound." Usery v. Tamiami Trail Tours, Inc., 531 F.2d, at 238. When the employer's argument has a credible basis in the record, it is difficult to believe that a jury of lay persons—many of whom no doubt have flown or could expect to fly on commercial air carriers—would not defer in a close case to the airline's judgment. Since the instructions in this case would not have prevented the airline from raising this contention to the jury in closing argument, we are satisfied that the verdict is a consequence of a defect in Western's proof rather than a defect in the trial court's instructions.

WESTERN'S STATUTORY SAFETY OBLIGATION

The instructions defined the essence of Western's business as "the safe transportation of their passengers." Tr. 2626. Western complains that this instruction was defective because it failed to inform the jury

allows a captain under the age of sixty who cannot, for health reasons, continue to fly as a captain or co-pilot to downbid to a position as second officer. [In addition,] half the pilots flying in the United States are flying for major airlines which do not require second officers to retire at the age of sixty, and * * * there are over 200 such second officers currently flying on wide-bodied aircraft." 709 F.2d, at 552. See also supra, at 2748.

29. Several Courts of Appeals have recognized that safety considerations are relevant in making or reviewing findings of fact. See, e.g., Levin v. Delta Air Lines, Inc., 730 F.2d 994, 998 (CA5 1984); Orzel v. City of Wauwatosa Fire Department, 697 F.2d, at 755; Tuohy v. Ford Motor Co., 675 F.2d, at 845; Murnane v. American Airlines, Inc., 215 U.S.App.D.C. 55, 58, 667 F.2d 98, 101 (1981), cert. denied, 456 U.S. 915, 102 S.Ct. 1770, 72 L.Ed.2d 174 (1982); Hodgson v. Greyhound Lines, Inc., 499 F.2d, at 863. Such considerations, of course, are only relevant at the margin of a close case, and do not relieve the employer from its burden of establishing the BFOQ by the preponderance of credible evidence.

that an airline must conduct its operations "with the highest possible degree of safety." [31]

Jury instructions, of course, "may not be judged in artificial isolation," but must be judged in the "context of the overall charge" and the circumstances of the case. See Cupp v. Naughten, 414 U.S. 141, 147, 94 S.Ct. 396, 400, 38 L.Ed.2d 368 (1973). In this case, the instructions characterized safe transportation as the "essence" of Western's business and specifically referred to the importance of "safe and efficient job performance" by flight engineers. Tr. 2627. Moreover, in closing argument counsel pointed out that because "safety is the essence of Western's business," the airline strives for "the highest degree possible of safety." [32] Viewing the record as a whole, we are satisfied that the jury's attention was adequately focused on the importance of safety to the operation of Western's business. Cf. United States v. Park, 421 U.S. 658, 674, 95 S.Ct. 1903, 1912, 44 L.Ed.2d 489 (1975).

AGE AS A PROXY FOR JOB QUALIFICATIONS

Western contended below that the ADEA only requires that the employer establish "a rational basis in fact" for believing that identification of those persons lacking suitable qualifications cannot occur on an individualized basis. This "rational basis in fact" standard would have been tantamount to an instruction to return a verdict in the defendant's favor. Because that standard conveys a meaning that is significantly different from that conveyed by the statutory phrase "reasonably necessary," it was correctly rejected by the trial court.[34]

Western argues that a "rational basis" standard should be adopted because medical disputes can never be proved "to a certainty" and because juries should not be permitted "to resolve bona fide conflicts among medical experts respecting the adequacy of individualized testing." Reply Brief for Petitioner 9, n. 10. The jury, however, need not be convinced beyond all doubt that medical testing is impossible, but only that the proposition is true "on a preponderance of the evidence." Moreover, Western's attack on the wisdom of assigning the resolution

---

31. This standard is set forth in the Federal Aviation Act, which provides, in part:

"In prescribing standards, rules, and regulations, and in issuing certificates under this subchapter, the Secretary of Transportation shall give full consideration to the duty resting upon air carriers to perform their services with *the highest possible degree of safety* in the public interest. * * * " 49 U.S.C.App. § 1421(b) (emphasis added).

32. "We have tried to present, throughout the case, our view that safety is the essence of Western's business. It is the core, it is what the air passenger service business is all about. We have a duty to our passengers, which we consider to be the most important duty of all the business operations that we engage in, including making money. Our first duty is that the passengers and the crews on all our aircraft are safe. And we attempt to render to them the highest degree possible of safety." Tr. 2514.

34. This standard has been rejected by nearly every court to consider it. 709 F.2d, at 550–551 (case below); Orzel v. City of Wauwatosa Fire Department, 697 F.2d, at 755–756; Tuohy v. Ford Motor Co., 675 F.2d, at 845; Harriss v. Pan American World Airways, Inc., 649 F.2d, at 677; Arritt v. Grisell, 567 F.2d, at 1271; Usery v. Tamiami Trail Tours, Inc., 531 F.2d, at 235–236.

of complex questions to 12 lay persons is inconsistent with the structure of the ADEA. Congress expressly decided that problems involving age discrimination in employment should be resolved on a "case-by-case basis" by proof to a jury.[35]

The "rational basis" standard is also inconsistent with the preference for individual evaluation expressed in the language and legislative history of the ADEA. Under the Act, employers are to evaluate employees between the ages of 40 and 70 on their merits and not their age. In the BFOQ defense, Congress provided a limited exception to this general principle, but required that employers validate any discrimination as "reasonably necessary to the normal operation of the particular business." It might well be "rational" to require mandatory retirement at *any* age less than 70, but that result would not comply with Congress' direction that employers must justify the rationale for the age chosen. Unless an employer can establish a substantial basis for believing that all or nearly all employees above an age lack the qualifications required for the position, the age selected for mandatory retirement less than 70 must be an age at which it is highly impractical for the employer to insure by individual testing that its employees will have the necessary qualifications for the job.

Western argues that its lenient standard is necessary because "where qualified experts disagree as to whether persons over a certain age can be dealt with on an individual basis, an employer must be allowed to resolve that controversy in a conservative manner." Reply Brief for Petitioner 8–9. This argument incorrectly assumes that all expert opinion is entitled to equal weight, and virtually ignores the function of the trier of fact in evaluating conflicting testimony. In this case, the jury may well have attached little weight to the testimony of Western's expert witness. See supra, at 2747–2748, and n. 8. A rule that would require the jury to defer to the judgment of any expert witness testifying for the employer, no matter how unpersuasive, would allow some employers to give free reign to the stereotype of older workers that Congress decried in the legislative history of the ADEA.

When an employee covered by the Act is able to point to reputable businesses in the same industry that choose to eschew reliance on mandatory retirement earlier than age 70, when the employer itself relies on individualized testing in similar circumstances, and when the administrative agency with primary responsibility for maintaining airline safety has determined that individualized testing is not impractical for the relevant position, the employer's attempt to justify its decision on the basis of the contrary opinion of experts—solicited for the purposes of litigation—is hardly convincing on any objective standard short of complete deference. Even in cases involving public safety, the

---

35. Supra, at 2750 and n. 16; 29 U.S.C. § 626(c)(2); Lorillard v. Pons, 434 U.S. 575, 98 S.Ct. 866, 55 L.Ed.2d 40 (1978).

ADEA plainly does not permit the trier of fact to give complete deference to the employer's decision.

The judgment of the Court of Appeals is

Affirmed.

JUSTICE POWELL took no part in the decision of this case.

JOHNSON v. MAYOR AND CITY COUNCIL OF BALTIMORE

Supreme Court of the United States, 1985.
___ U.S. ___, 105 S.Ct. 2717, 86 L.Ed.2d 286.

JUSTICE MARSHALL delivered the opinion of the Court.

The issue is whether a federal statute generally requiring federal firefighters to retire at age 55 establishes, as a matter of law, that age 55 is a bona fide occupational qualification (BFOQ) for nonfederal firefighters within the meaning of the Age Discrimination in Employment Act of 1967, 81 Stat. 602, as amended, 29 U.S.C. § 621 et seq. (ADEA or Act).

I

Congress enacted the ADEA "to promote employment of older persons based on their ability rather than age; to prohibit arbitrary age discrimination in employment; [and] to help employers and workers find ways of meeting problems arising from the impact of age on employment." 29 U.S.C. § 621(b). To this end, the Act today prohibits virtually all employers from discriminating on the basis of age against employees or applicants for employment who are between the ages of 40 and 70, for example, by discharging them or requiring them to retire involuntarily. §§ 623(a), 631(a). The Act contains one general exception to this prohibition: when age is shown to be "a bona fide occupational qualification [BFOQ] reasonably necessary to the normal operation of the particular business," § 623(f)(1), an employee may be terminated on the basis of his age before reaching age 70.[1]

Since enacting the ADEA in 1967, Congress has amended its provisions several times. The ADEA originally did not apply to the Federal Government, to the States or their political subdivisions, or to employers with fewer than 25 employees, but in 1974 Congress extended coverage to Federal, State and local Governments, and to employers with at least 20 workers. §§ 630(b), 633a.[2] Also, while the Act initially

---

1. Federal employees are covered in a separate section of the Act and are treated differently from nonfederal employees in various ways not relevant to this case. See 29 U.S.C. § 633a (extending antidiscrimination provisions to federal employees, but providing such employees a different remedy for violations); § 631 (establishing 70 as a permissible retirement age for all but federal employees, for whom there is no permissible cap). Cf.

Vance v. Bradley, 440 U.S. 93, 99 S.Ct. 939, 59 L.Ed.2d 171 (1979) (lower retirement age for federal employees covered by Foreign Service retirement system does not violate equal protection).

2. See Senate Special Committee on Aging, Improving the Age Discrimination Law, 93d Cong., 1st Sess. 14, 17–18 (Comm. Print 1973); EEOC, Legislative History of the Age Discrimination in Employment

covered employees only up to age 65, in 1978 Congress raised the maximum age to 70 for state, local and private employees and eliminated the cap entirely for federal workers. Age Discrimination in Employment Act Amendments of 1978, § 3(a), 92 Stat. 189, 29 U.S.C. § 631(b) (hereinafter 1978 Amendments).

The 1978 Amendments eliminated substantially all federal age limits on employment, but they left untouched several mandatory retirement provisions of the federal civil-service statute applicable to specific federal occupations, including firefighters, air traffic controllers, and law enforcement officers, as well as mandatory retirement provisions applicable to the Foreign Service and the Central Intelligence Agency. Among the provisions that were left unaffected by the 1978 Amendments is 5 U.S.C. § 8335(b), which requires certain federal law enforcement officers and firefighters to retire at age 55 if they have sufficient years of service to qualify for a pension and their agency does not find that it is in the public interest to continue their employment.[3] As a result, most federal firefighters must retire at age 55, despite the provisions of the ADEA. At issue here is the effect of this age limit for federal firefighters on the ADEA's application to state and local firefighters.

A

Six firefighters brought this action in the District Court for the District of Maryland challenging the City of Baltimore's municipal code provisions that establish for firefighters and police personnel a mandatory retirement age lower than 70. They claimed that these provisions violate the ADEA. The Equal Employment Opportunity Commission (EEOC) subsequently intervened to support the six plaintiffs.

Until 1962, all Baltimore employees, including firefighters, were covered by the Employees Retirement System (ERS), which provided for mandatory retirement at age 70. App. 4. In 1962, the City established

Act 215, 231, 234–235 (1981) (hereinafter Legislative History).

The Act contains several minor exemptions not at issue here. See, e.g., 29 U.S.C. §§ 630(f), 631(c)(1). It additionally empowers the EEOC to determine BFOQs for federal employees, 29 U.S.C. § 633a(b), and also to establish general exemptions from the ADEA if it finds them to be reasonable and "necessary and proper in the public interest." 29 U.S.C. § 628. In 1980, the EEOC examined the desirability of fixing a retirement age for local firefighters and concluded that such an exemption from the ADEA was not warranted. The Commission found that individual assessments of fitness would be feasible and that age alone would be a poor indicator of ability in this occupation. See App. 5–23.

3. Title 5 U.S.C. § 8335(b) provides:

"A law enforcement officer or a firefighter who is otherwise eligible for immediate retirement under section 8336(c) of this title shall be separated from the service on the last day of the month in which he becomes 55 years of age or completes 20 years of service if then over that age. The head of the agency, when in his judgment the public interest so requires, may exempt such an employee from automatic separation under this subsection until that employee becomes 60 years of age. The employing office shall notify the employee in writing of the date of separation at least 60 days in advance thereof. Action to separate the employee is not effective, without the consent of the employee, until the last day of the month in which the 60-day notice expires."

the Fire and Police Employee Retirement System (FPERS), which generally requires that all firefighting personnel below the rank of lieutenant retire at age 55. See FPERS, Baltimore City Code, Art. 22, § 34(a)1–4 (1983); App. 3. Lieutenants and other higher-ranking officers may work until age 65. Ibid. When the FPERS was implemented in 1962, special provision was made for personnel hired before 1962, who were given the option of remaining in the ERS or transferring to the FPERS under a special grandfather provision. Firefighters hired before 1962 who chose to remain in the ERS may continue to work until age 70 even today. See 515 F.Supp. 1287, 1297, n. 10 (Md.1981). Firefighters hired before 1962 who are covered by the newer FPERS may work until age 60 or, in some limited circumstances, until age 65. Ibid. The plaintiffs here include five firefighters covered by this grandfather clause who are subject to retirement at age 60, and one firefighter hired after 1962, who is subject to retirement at age 55.

The City asserted as an affirmative defense that age is a BFOQ for the position of firefighter and that the mandatory retirement provision therefore was permissible under the ADEA. After a 6-day bench trial, at which each side presented expert and nonexpert testimony on the validity of the BFOQ defense, the District Court held that the City had failed to produce sufficient evidence to make out its BFOQ defense. The court considered both the particular condition of the plaintiff firefighters and the general operation of the Baltimore Fire Department, noting that "historically Baltimore firemen have always worked past [age 60] and even up to age seventy," 515 F.Supp., at 1297. It then applied the two-pronged test developed by the Court of Appeals for the Fifth Circuit in Usery v. Tamiami Trail Tours, Inc., 531 F.2d 224 (1976), and adopted by the Fourth Circuit.[6] The trial court concluded that the City had shown neither "that there is a factual basis for [it] to believe that all or substantially all Baltimore City firefighters between the ages of sixty and sixty-five, other than officers, would be unable to perform their job safely and efficiently," id., at 1296, nor that "it is impossible or impractical to deal with firefighters between sixty and sixty-five on an individualized basis." Ibid. The court therefore struck down the City's mandatory retirement plan for firefighters.

A divided panel of the Court of Appeals for the Fourth Circuit reversed. 731 F.2d 209 (1984). The majority did not take issue with the District Court's findings that the City had failed to prove that age was a BFOQ for firefighters. Instead, the court held that the City was entitled to the BFOQ defense as a matter of law. To reach that conclusion, the appellate court relied on language from this Court's

6. The District Court required the City to show (1) that the BFOQ it invokes " 'is reasonably necessary to the essence of its business' of operating an efficient fire department within the City of Baltimore, and (2) that defendants have 'reasonable cause, i.e., a factual basis for believing that all or substantially all persons within the class * * * would be unable to perform safely and efficiently the duties of the job involved, or that it is impossible or impractical to deal with persons over the age limit on an individualized basis.' " 515 F.Supp., at 1295 (quoting Arritt v. Grisell, 567 F.2d 1267, 1271 (CA4 1977)).

decision in EEOC v. Wyoming, 460 U.S. 226, 103 S.Ct. 1054, 75 L.Ed.2d 18 (1983), in which we upheld the constitutionality of Congress' extension of the ADEA to state and local governments. In that decision we observed that the ADEA tests a State's discretion to impose a mandatory retirement age "against a reasonable federal standard." Id., at 240, 103 S.Ct., at 1062. The Court of Appeals undertook a "search for a 'reasonable federal standard'" by which to test the asserted BFOQ; it found that standard in the federal civil service statute, 5 U.S.C. § 8335(b), which generally requires federal firefighters to retire at age 55. See n. 3, supra. The court held that, because Congress has selected age 55 as the retirement age for most federal firefighters, as a matter of law the same age constitutes a BFOQ for all state and local firefighters as well. Therefore, the court concluded, the City was not required to make any factual showing at trial as to its need for the mandatory retirement age.[7]

Because this case presents serious questions about the administration of the ADEA, we granted certiorari to review the decision of the Court of Appeals.

B

EEOC v. Wyoming arose out of a lawsuit filed by a Wyoming state game warden who was required under state law to retire at age 55. He brought an action against the State and various of its officials claiming that its mandatory requirement violated the ADEA. The District Court held that the ADEA violated the Tenth Amendment insofar as it regulated Wyoming's employment relationship with its game wardens and other law enforcement officers and dismissed the suit. In rejecting that argument, we explained that the ADEA did not unduly intrude into the exercise of governmental functions because it did not require employers to retain unfit employees, but only at most to make more individualized determinations about fitness. Moreover, we noted that, in light of the BFOQ defense, States might in fact remain free from the obligation even to make more individualized showings:

> Perhaps more important, appellees remain free under the ADEA to continue to do *precisely what they are doing now,* if they can demonstrate that age is a "bona fide occupational qualification" for the job of game warden. ＊ ＊ ＊ Thus, ＊ ＊ ＊ even the State's discretion to achieve its goals *in the way it thinks best* is not being overridden entirely, but is merely being tested against a reasonable federal standard. 460 U.S., at 240, 103 S.Ct., at 1062 (emphasis in original).

We remanded to give Wyoming an opportunity to prove at trial that age 55 was in fact a BFOQ for Wyoming game wardens.

---

7. Chief Judge Winter dissented. He rejected the panel's conclusion that the civil service provision necessarily constituted a congressional determination that age 55 is a BFOQ for federal firefighters but asserted that even if it were a BFOQ for federal firefighters, that fact would not ex- cuse the City from proving facts necessary to establish a BFOQ under 29 U.S.C. § 623(f)(1) of the ADEA. Concluding that the District Court's factual findings on the City's proof were not clearly erroneous, he would have affirmed the District Court.

In this case, the Court of Appeals interpreted our use of the term "reasonable federal standard" in the quoted passage to mean that the question whether an age limit for nonfederal employees is permissible under the ADEA may be resolved simply by reference to a federal statute establishing a retirement age for a class of federal employees. It seized on the retirement provisions of the federal civil service statute, which require that federal firefighters retire at age 55. Then, without considering the intent underlying that provision, it held that, as a matter of law, age must therefore be a BFOQ for local firefighters.

The "reasonable federal standard" to which we referred in EEOC v. Wyoming, however, is the standard supplied by the ADEA itself—that is, whether the age limit is a bona fide occupational qualification. By use of that phrase, we intended only to reaffirm that the BFOQ standard permits an employer to maintain a mandatory retirement age as long as the employer makes the requisite showing that age is a BFOQ. Nothing in the ADEA or our decision in *Wyoming* warrants the conclusion that a federal rule, not found in the ADEA, and by its terms applicable only to federal employees, *necessarily* authorizes a state or local government employer to maintain a mandatory retirement age as a matter of law. To make the fact that the Federal Government has imposed a mandatory age limit on its own firefighters automatically dispositive of the question whether the same age limit is appropriate for state and local officers, without in any way examining the provision, would extend the federal rule far beyond its scope. It would apply to state and local employees a statute applicable by its terms only to federal officers. The mere fact that some federal firefighters are required to cease work at age 55 does not provide an absolute defense to an ADEA action challenging state and local age limits for firefighters.

The Court of Appeals in this case failed to focus on the City's factual showing and instead centered its attention on the federal retirement provisions of the United States Code. We would be remiss, in light of Congress' indisputable intent to permit deviations from the mandate of the ADEA only in light of a particularized, factual showing, see H.R.Rep. No. 805, 90th Cong., 1st Sess., 7 (1967); Legislative History 80; S.Rep. No. 723, 90th Cong., 1st Sess., 7 (1967); Legislative History 111, U.S.Code Cong. & Admin.News 1967, p. 2213,[8] to permit nonfederal employers to circumvent this plan by mere citation to an unrelated statutory provision that is not even mentioned in the ADEA.

II

The City, supported by several *amici*, argues for affirmance nonetheless. It asserts first that the federal civil service statute is not just a federal retirement provision unrelated to the ADEA but *in fact* estab-

---

8. To this end, the lower courts have fashioned tests for finding a BFOQ that focus first, on the individual employer's need for an age limit and second, on the factual basis for his belief that all workers above a certain age are not qualified and on his proof that individual testing is highly impractical. We recently have elaborated on the precise standard to be applied. Western Air Lines, Inc. v. Criswell, ___ U.S. ___, ___, 105 S.Ct. 2743, ___, 85 L.Ed. 2d ___ (1985).

lishes age as a BFOQ for federal firefighters based on factors that properly go into that determination under the ADEA, see Western Air Lines, Inc. v. Criswell, ___ U.S. ___, 105 S.Ct. 2743, 85 L.Ed.2d ___ (1985). Second, the City asserts, a congressional finding that age is a BFOQ for a certain occupation is dispositive of that determination with respect to nonfederal employees in that occupation. We consider each of these contentions in turn.

A

We must first resolve whether the age-55 retirement for federal firefighters reflects a congressional determination that age 55 is a BFOQ within the meaning of the ADEA, as the City urges, or whether Congress established the mandatory retirement age based on an analysis different from that mandated by the BFOQ standard. On this question, the statute is silent. Section 8335(b), the federal civil service provision, does not by its terms or history evince an intent to cover nonfederal employees, or to limit the scope of the ADEA. Nor does the ADEA, which was passed later, cross-reference the civil service statute or in any way express a congressional desire to exempt any firefighters from the full effect of the Act's reach.[9] In other words, in the language of neither statute has Congress indicated that the civil service provision reflects anything more than a congressional decision that federal firefighters must retire, as a general matter, at the age of 55.

The history of the civil service provision, however, makes clear that the decision to retire certain federal employees at an early age was not based on bona fide occupational qualifications for the covered employment. This history demonstrates instead that Congress has acted to deal with the idiosyncratic problems of federal employees in the federal civil service. The Federal Government first introduced early retirement for certain employees in 1947 with passage of legislation *permitting* investigatory personnel of the Federal Bureau of Investigation to retire at age 50 at an enhanced annuity. Act of July 11, 1947, ch. 219, 61 Stat. 307. Congress in 1948 extended this program to anyone whose duties for at least 20 years were primarily the investigation, apprehension, or detention of persons suspected or convicted of federal criminal law violations, see Act of July 2, 1948, ch. 807, 62 Stat. 1221. In 1972, this voluntary retirement provision was further extended to federal firefighters. See Act of Aug. 14, 1972, Pub.L. No. 92–382, 86 Stat. 539.

The provision as initially passed was intended only to give certain employees the option to retire early. It was designed in part as "an added stimulus to morale in the Federal Bureau of Investigation.
* * *

*   *   *   *   *   *   *   *   *

9. Recently, legislation to exempt state and local firefighters and law enforcement officers from the ADEA has been introduced in both the Senate and the House of Representatives. See S. 698, 99th Cong., 1st Sess. (introduced March 20, 1985); H.R. 1435, 99th Cong., 1st Sess. (introduced March 6, 1985).

"[To] stabilize the service of the Federal Bureau of Investigation into a career service * * * [and to] act as an incentive to investigative personnel of the [FBI] to remain in the Federal service until a reasonable retirement age is reached." S.Rep. No. 76, 80th Cong., 1st Sess., 1–2 (1947). In addition, as then-Attorney General Tom C. Clark explained, the Department of Justice sought to maintain the FBI "as a 'young man's service.'" He added that "men in their 60's and 70's, forced to remain in the service, faced with the rigors of arduous service demanded of special agents and others, be not forced to carry on for lack of an adequate retirement plan to fit the needs of the FBI service." Id., at 2.

In 1974, Congress amended the statute to provide that these same federal employees *must* retire at age 55 if they had completed 20 years of service, and it provided an enhanced annuity. As with the voluntary retirement scheme, one goal of the 1974 amendment was to maintain "relatively young, vigorous, and effective law enforcement and firefighting workforces." H.R.Rep. No. 93–463, p. 2 (1973). The amendment also was designed to replace the existing provision, which was having an adverse impact on the quality of older federal employees, because "most of those who retire in their early fifties are the more alert and aggressive employees who have found desirable jobs outside of Government," id., at 3; in contrast, the newer mandatory scheme would enable management to "retire, without stigma, one who suffers a loss of proficiency." Retirement for Certain Hazardous Duty Personnel: Hearing on H.R. 6078 and H.R. 9281 before the Subcommittee on Compensation and Employment Benefits of the Senate Committee on Post Office and Civil Service, 93d Cong., 2d Sess., 134 (1974) (testimony of Rep. Brasco, sponsor of House bill).

Congress undoubtedly sought in significant part to maintain a youthful workforce and took steps through the civil service retirement provisions to make early retirement both attractive and financially rewarding. However, neither the language of the 1974 amendment nor its legislative history offers any indication why Congress wanted to maintain the image of a "young man's service," or why Congress thought that 55 was the proper cut-off age, or whether Congress believed that older employees in fact could not meet the demands of these occupations. Indeed, Congressmen who opposed the bill voiced their concern for the singling out of one group of employees for preferential treatment through enhanced annuities and early retirement, and did not even acknowledge that the exigencies of the job might have anything to do with Congress' willingness to accord special treatment to a group of employees. H.R.Rep. No. 93–463, supra, at 20. Moreover, the allowance that firefighters who had not yet served for 20 years could remain in their jobs, see id., at 6, along with other exceptions to the general rule of retirement, casts serious doubt on any argument that Congress in fact believed that either the employee or the public would be jeopardized by the employment of older firefighters.

The absence of any indication that Congress established the age limit based on the demands of the occupation raises the possibility that the federal rule is merely "an example of the sort of age stereotyping without factual basis that was one of the primary targets of the reforms of the ADEA," Brief for Petitioner in No. 84–710, p. 38, and surely belies any contention that the age limit is based on actual occupational qualifications. Without knowing whether Congress passed the statute based on factual support, legislative balancing of competing policy concerns, or stereotypical assumptions, we simply have no way to decipher whether it is consistent with the policies underlying the ADEA.[10]

Congress' treatment of the civil service provision when it extended the ADEA to federal employees in 1978 conclusively demonstrates that the retirement statute does not represent a congressional determination that age is an occupational qualification for federal firefighters. The decision to retain mandatory retirement provisions for certain federal employees resulted not from a finding that the provisions met the standards of the ADEA, but rather from an agreement to provide to the congressional Committees with jurisdiction over the retirement programs at issue the opportunity to review those provisions. Instead of delaying passage of the ADEA while those Committees studied the mandatory retirement provisions in light of the proposed ADEA, Congress decided to preserve the status quo, with respect to the retirement program, pending further study. This express purpose definitively rules out any conclusion that Congress approved the retirement programs in light of the ADEA.

In sum, almost four decades of legislative history establish that Congress at no time has indicated that the federal retirement age for federal firefighters is based on a determination that age 55 is a bona fide occupational qualification within the meaning of the ADEA. Congress adopted what might well have been an arbitrarily designated retirement age in an era not concerned with the pervasive discrimination against the elderly that eventually gave rise to the ADEA. There-

10. Congress, of course, may exempt federal employees from application of the ADEA and otherwise treat federal employees, whose employment relations it may directly supervise, differently from those of other employers, see, e.g., 26 U.S.C. § 3306(c)(6) (unemployment compensation not applicable to federal employees); 29 U.S.C. § 152(2) (exempting federal employees from labor relations legislation); indeed it has done so elsewhere in the ADEA. While Congress at first exempted federal employees from the reach of the Act, it now applies even more protective rules to older federal employees than it imposes on other employers. See 29 U.S.C. §§ 631(a), 631(b) (federal employees generally cannot be forced to retire at any age, while similarly situated nonfederal em-

ployees may be forced to retire at age 70). It might be that congressional findings leading to the conclusion that age is a BFOQ for a certain federal occupation would be of relevance to a judicial inquiry into age as a BFOQ for other employers, even absent express congressional direction on this point. See infra. But this relevance derives from a recognition that Congress might already have engaged in the same inquiry that a district court must make, and a district court might find congressionally gathered evidence useful and congressional factfinding persuasive. Contrary to the suggestion of the Court of Appeals, 731 F.2d, at 212–213, Congress is not always required to treat federal and nonfederal employees in the same way.

after, although Congress retained mandatory limitations in 1978, while questioning whether they continued to make good policy sense, it did so for the sake of expediency alone. On considering the language and history of the civil service provision, we find it quite possible that factors other than conclusive determinations of occupational qualifications might originally have led to passage of this federal rule, and that the reason for its retention after 1978 further undercuts any argument that Congress has determined that age is a BFOQ for federal firefighters.

In the absence of an indication that Congress in fact grounded the age limit on occupational qualifications, we will not presume that it did so intend. The myriad political purposes for which Congress might properly make decisions affecting federal employees, and that body's uncontested authority to exempt federal employees from the requirements of federal regulatory statutes, simply do not permit the conclusion that Congress passed or retained this retirement provision because it reflects bona fide occupational qualifications.[12] We therefore conclude that this civil service provision does not articulate a BFOQ for firefighters, that its presence in the United States Code is not relevant to the question of a BFOQ for firefighters, and that it would be error for a court, faced with a challenge under the ADEA to an age limit for firefighters, to give any weight, much less conclusive weight, to the federal retirement provision.

B

Were there evidence that Congress in fact determined that a class of federal employees must retire early based on the same considerations that support a finding of a BFOQ under the Act, the situation might differ. Of course, if Congress expressly extended the BFOQ to nonfederal occupations, that determination would be dispositive. But if it did not, the federal exemption nevertheless might be relevant to an appropriate employer when deciding whether to impose a mandatory retirement age, and to a district court engaged in reviewing an employer's BFOQ defense. The evidence Congress has considered, and the conclusions it has drawn therefrom, might be admissible as evidence in judicial proceedings to determine the existence of a BFOQ for nonfederal employees. The extent to which these factors are probative would, of course, vary depending at least on the congruity between the federal and nonfederal occupations at issue. Indeed, the need to consider the actual tasks of the nonfederal employees and the circumstances of

---

12. Nor do we have any reason to believe that, when the City imposed its mandatory retirement scheme in 1962, it was relying on a congressional determination of any kind. The history of the civil service provision up to that time reveals no congressional finding of an occupational qualification, and in fact in 1962 the congressional scheme remained completely voluntary. It was not until 1974 that Congress even rendered early retirement mandatory. Indeed, the City pointed out to the Court of Appeals that it instituted its mandatory retirement plan "more than a decade before the federal government did likewise." Answer of Appellant City to Petition for Rehearing with Suggestion for Rehearing en Banc in No. 81–1965 (CA4), pp. 9–10.

employment, in order to determine the extent to which congressional conclusions about federal employees in fact are relevant, would preclude the kind of wholesale reliance on the federal rule that the City suggests. See supra, at 2722. Because in this case the evidence supports no such finding of congressional intent to establish a BFOQ, however, we decline to speculate on the manner in which a different federal rule might affect nonfederal employment.

III

We accordingly reverse the Court of Appeals' holding that the federal retirement provision at issue in this case provides an absolute defense in an ADEA action. We remand to the Court of Appeals for further proceedings consistent with this opinion.

It is so ordered.

Chapter VII

HANDICAP

A. COVERAGE

CONSOLIDATED RAIL CORPORATION v. DARRONE

Supreme Court of the United States, 1984.
465 U.S. 624, 104 S.Ct. 1248, 79 L.Ed.2d 568.

JUSTICE POWELL delivered the opinion of the Court.

This case requires us to clarify the scope of the private right of action to enforce § 504 of the Rehabilitation Act of 1973, 29 U.S.C. (Supp. V) § 794, that prohibits discrimination against the handicapped by federal grant recipients. There is a conflict among the circuits.

I

The Rehabilitation Act of 1973 establishes a comprehensive federal program aimed at improving the lot of the handicapped. Among its purposes are to "promote and expand employment opportunities in the public and private sectors for handicapped individuals and place such individuals in employment." 29 U.S.C. § 701(8). To further these purposes, Congress enacted § 504 of the Act. That section provides that:

> No otherwise qualified handicapped individual *   *   * shall, solely by reason of his handicap, be excluded from the participation in, be denied the benefits of, or be subjected to discrimination under any program or activity receiving Federal financial assistance.

The language of the section is virtually identical to that of § 601 of Title VI of the Civil Rights Act of 1964, 42 U.S.C. § 2000d, that similarly bars discrimination (on the ground of race, color, or national origin) in federally-assisted programs.

In 1978, Congress amended the Rehabilitation Act to specify the means of enforcing its ban on discrimination. In particular, § 505(a)(2), 29 U.S.C. §§ 794a, made available the "remedies, procedure, and rights set forth in Title VI of the Civil Rights Acts of 1964" to victims of discrimination in violation of § 504 of the Act.[1]

Petitioner, Consolidated Rail Corporation ("Conrail"), was formed pursuant to subchapter III of the Regional Rail Reorganization Act, 45 U.S.C. §§ 701 et seq. The Act, passed in response to the insolvency of a number of railroads in the Northeast and Midwest, established Conrail to acquire and operate the rail properties of the insolvent railroads and to integrate these properties into an efficient national rail transportation system. Under § 216 of the Act, 45 U.S.C. § 726, the United States, acting through the United States Railway Association, purchases debentures and series A preferred stock of the corporation "at such times and in such amounts as may be required and requested by the corporation," but "in accordance with the terms and conditions * * * prescribed by the Association * * *." Id. § 726(b)(1). The statute permits the proceeds from these sales to be devoted to maintenance of rail properties, capital needs, refinancing of indebtedness, or working capital. Ibid. Under this statutory authorization, Conrail has sold the United States $3.28 billion in securities. See App. A–15.

Conrail also received federal funds under subchapter V of the Act, now repealed, to provide for reassignment and retraining of railroad workers whose jobs were affected by the reorganization. And Conrail now receives federal funds under § 1143(a) of the Northeast Rail Service Act, 45 U.S.C. § 797a, that provides termination allowances of up to $25,000 to workers who lose their jobs as a result of reorganization.

II

In 1979, Thomas LeStrange filed suit against petitioner for violation of rights conferred by § 504 of the Rehabilitation Act. The complaint alleged that the Erie Lackawanna Railroad, to which Conrail is the successor in interest, had employed the plaintiff as a locomotive engineer; that an accident had required amputation of plaintiff's left hand and forearm in 1971; and that, after LeStrange was disabled, the Erie Lackawanna Railroad, and then Conrail, had refused to employ him although it had no justification for finding him unfit to work.

The District Court, following the decision of Trageser v. Libbie Rehabilitation Center, Inc., 590 F.2d 87 (CA4 1978), cert. denied, 442 U.S. 947, 99 S.Ct. 2895, 61 L.Ed.2d 318 (1979), granted petitioner's motion for summary judgment on the ground that the plaintiff did not have "standing" to bring a private action under § 504. In *Trageser*, the Fourth Circuit had held that § 505(a)(2) of the Rehabilitation Act

---

1. Section 505(a)(2) provides in full: "The remedies, procedures, and rights set forth in title VI of the Civil Rights Act of 1964 shall be available to any person aggrieved by any act or failure to act by any recipient of Federal assistance or Federal provider of such assistance under § 794 of this title."

Section 505(a)(1) generally makes available the remedies of Title VII of the Civil Rights Act to persons aggrieved by violation of § 791 of the Rehabilitation Act, which governs the federal government's employment of the handicapped.

incorporated into that act the limitation found in § 604 of Title VI, which provides that employment discrimination is actionable only when the employer receives federal financial assistance the "primary objective" of which is "to provide employment." The District Court concluded that the aid provided to petitioner did not satisfy the "primary objective" test.

The Court of Appeals reversed and remanded to the District Court. 687 F.2d 767 (CA3 1982). There was no opinion for the court, but all three judges of the panel agreed that the cause of action for employment discrimination under § 504 was not properly limited to situations "where a primary objective of the federal financial assistance is to provide employment."

We granted certiorari to resolve the conflict among the circuits and to consider other questions under the Rehabilitation Act. We affirm.

III

We are met initially by petitioner's contention that the death of the plaintiff LeStrange has mooted the case and deprives the Court of jurisdiction for that reason. Petitioner concedes, however, that there remains a case or controversy if LeStrange's estate may recover money that would have been owed to LeStrange. Without determining the extent to which money damages are available under § 504, we think it clear that § 504 authorizes a plaintiff who alleges intentional discrimination to bring an equitable action for backpay. The case therefore is not moot.

In Guardians Ass'n v. Civil Service Comm'n, 463 U.S. 582, 103 S.Ct. 3221, 77 L.Ed.2d 866 (1983), a majority of the Court expressed the view that a private plaintiff under Title VI could recover backpay; and no member of the Court contended that backpay was unavailable, at least as a remedy for intentional discrimination.[9] It is unnecessary to review here the grounds for this interpretation of Title VI. It suffices to state that we now apply this interpretation to § 505(a)(2), that, as we have noted, provides to plaintiffs under § 504 the remedies set forth in

---

9. A majority of the Court agreed that retroactive relief is available to private plaintiffs for all discrimination, whether intentional or unintentional, that is actionable under Title VI. Justice Marshall, and Justice Stevens, joined by Justices Brennan and Blackmun, argued that both prospective and retroactive relief were fully available to Title VI plaintiffs. ___ U.S., at ___, ___, 103 S.Ct., at 3245–3249. Justice O'Connor agreed that both prospective and retroactive equitable relief were available, while reserving judgment on the question whether there is a private cause of action for damages relief under Title VI. Id., at ___, n. 1, 103 S.Ct., at 3237, n. 1.

Justice White, joined by Justice Rehnquist, while contending that only relief ordering future compliance with legal obligations was available in other private actions under Title VI, put aside the situation of the private plaintiff who alleged intentional discrimination. Id., at ___, 103 S.Ct., at 3237. The Chief Justice and Justice Powell did not reach the question, as they would have held that petitioners in that case had no private right of action and had not made the showing of intentional discrimination required to establish a violation of Title VI. Id., at ___, 103 S.Ct., at 3236.

Title VI. Therefore, respondent, having alleged intentional discrimination, may recover backpay in the present § 504 suit.[10]

IV

A

The Court of Appeals rejected the argument that petitioner may be sued under § 504 only if the primary objective of the federal aid that it receives is to promote employment. Conrail relies particularly on § 604 of Title VI. This section limits the applicability of Title VI to "employment practice[s] * * * where a *primary objective* of the federal financial assistance is to provide employment" (emphasis added).[11] As noted above, § 505(a)(2) of the Rehabilitation Act, as amended in 1978, adopted the remedies and rights provided in Title VI. Accordingly, Conrail's basic position in this case is that § 604's limitation was incorporated expressly into the Rehabilitation Act. The decision of the Court of Appeals therefore should be reversed, Conrail contends, as the primary objective of the federal assistance received by Conrail was not to promote employment.

It is clear that § 504 itself contains no such limitation. Section 504 neither refers explicitly to § 604 nor contains analogous limiting language; rather, that section prohibits discrimination against the handicapped under "*any* program or activity receiving Federal financial assistance." And it is unquestionable that the section was intended to reach employment discrimination.[12] Indeed, enhancing employment of the handicapped was so much the focus of the 1973 legislation that Congress the next year felt it necessary to amend the statute to clarify whether § 504 was intended to prohibit other types of discrimination as well. See § 111(a), Pub.L. 93–516, 88 Stat. 1617, 1619 (1974), amending 29 U.S.C. § 706(6); S.Rep. No. 93–1297, p. 37 (1974), U.S.Code Cong. &

---

10. Although the legislative history of the 1978 amendments does not explicitly indicate that Congress intended to preserve the full measure of courts' equitable power to award backpay, the few references to the question are consistent with our holding. Congress clearly intended to make backpay available to victims of discrimination by the federal government, see S.Rep. No. 95–890, p. 19 (1978); and statements made in relation to subsequent legislation by the Senate Committee on Labor and Human Resources, the committee responsible for the 1978 amendments, endorse the availability of backpay. S.Rep. No. 96–316, pp. 12–13 (1979).

11. Section 604 provides in full: "Nothing contained in this subchapter shall be construed to authorize action under this subchapter by any department or agency with respect to any employment practice of any employer, employment agency, or la-

bor organization except where a primary objective of the Federal financial assistance is to provide employment." 42 U.S.C. § 2000d–3.

12. Congress recognized that vocational rehabilitation of the handicapped would be futile if those who were rehabilitated could not obtain jobs because of discrimination. Employment discrimination thus would have "a profound effect on the provision of relevant and effective [rehabilitation] services." 119 Cong.Rec. 5862 (1973) (remarks of Sen. Williams). See, e.g., S.Rep. No. 93–318, p. 4 (1973); 119 Cong.Rec. 24587 (1973) (remarks of Sen. Taft), 24588 (remarks of Sen. Williams). Several other sections of Title V of the Rehabilitation Act also were aimed at discrimination in employment: § 501 and § 503 require all federal employers and federal contractors to adopt affirmative action programs for the handicapped.

Admin.News 1974, 6373.[13]   Thus, the language of § 504 suggests that its bar on employment discrimination should not be limited to programs that receive federal aid the primary purpose of which is to promote employment.

The legislative history, executive interpretation, and purpose of the 1973 enactment all are consistent with this construction.   The legislative history contains no mention of a "primary objective" limitation, although the legislators on numerous occasions adverted to § 504's prohibition against discrimination in employment by programs assisted with federal funds.   See, e.g., S.Rep. No. 93–318, at 4, 18, 50, 70 (1973), U.S.Code Cong. & Admin.News 1973, 2076;   119 Cong.Rec. 5862 (remarks of Sen. Cranston), 24587–24588 (1973) (remarks of Sen. Williams, chairman of the Committee on Labor and Public Welfare).   Moreover, the Department of Health, Education and Welfare, the agency designated by the President to be responsible for coordinating enforcement of § 504, see Exec. Order No. 11914, from the outset has interpreted that section to prohibit employment discrimination by all recipients of

---

13. We note further that the Court in an analogous statutory context rejected the contention that the terms used in § 504 implicitly contain a "primary objective" limitation.   § 901 of Title IX, like § 504, borrowed the language of § 601 of Title VI. North Haven Board of Education v. Bell, 456 U.S. 512, 102 S.Ct. 1912, 72 L.Ed.2d 299 (1982), found, however, that Title IX's prohibition of employment discrimination did not incorporate § 604's "primary objective" requirement.   The Court stated that, had Congress wished so to limit Title IX, it would have enacted in that Title counterparts to both § 601 and § 604.   Id., at 530, 102 S.Ct., at 1922–1923.

Petitioner suggests that *North Haven* is inapplicable to the construction of § 504 because the Congress considered but rejected a provision explicitly incorporating the language of § 604 of Title VI into Title IX.   And other aspects of the legislative history also supported the Court's interpretation of § 901, see id., at 523–529, 102 S.Ct., at 1919–1922.   In contrast, Congress did not advert to a "primary objective" limitation when drafting § 504.

Clearly, petitioner's observations do not touch on that aspect of *North Haven*—its analysis of the language of § 601—that is relevant to the present case.   But even without the analysis of *North Haven*, petitioner's interpretation of § 504's language is unfounded.   For language as broad as that of § 504 cannot be read in isolation from its history and purposes.   See, e.g., Chapman v. Houston Welfare Rights Org., 441 U.S. 600, 608, 99 S.Ct. 1905, 1911, 60 L.Ed.2d 508 (1979);   Philbrook v. Glodgett, 421 U.S. 707, 713, 95 S.Ct. 1893, 1898, 44

L.Ed.2d 525 (1975).   In these respects, § 504 differs from Title VI in ways that suggest that § 504 cannot sensibly be interpreted to ban employment discrimination only in programs that receive federal aid the "primary objective" of which is to promote employment.   The "primary objective" limitation of Title VI gave the antidiscrimination provision of that Title a scope that well fits its underlying purposes—to ensure "that funds of the United States are not used to support racial discrimination" but "are spent in accordance with the Constitution and the moral sense of the Nation."   110 Cong.Rec. 6544 (1964) (remarks of Sen. Humphrey).   As the Court of Appeals observed, it was unnecessary to extend Title VI more generally to ban employment discrimination, as Title VII comprehensively regulates such discrimination.

In contrast, the primary goal of the Act is to increase employment of the handicapped, see supra, at 1253 and n. 13.   However, Congress chose to ban employment discrimination against the handicapped, not by all employers, but only by the federal government and recipients of federal contracts and grants.   As to the latter, Congress apparently determined that it would require contractors and grantees to bear the costs of providing employment for the handicapped as a *quid pro quo* for the receipt of federal funds.   Cf. 118 Cong.Rec. 32305 (1972) (remarks of Sen. Javits).   But this decision to limit § 504 to the recipients of federal aid does not require us to limit that section still further, as petitioner urges.

federal financial aid, regardless of the primary objective of that aid.[14] This Court generally has deferred to contemporaneous regulations issued by the agency responsible for implementing a congressional enactment. See, e.g., NLRB v. Bell Aerospace Co., 416 U.S. 267, 274–275, 94 S.Ct. 1757, 1761–1762, 40 L.Ed.2d 134 (1974). The regulations particularly merit deference in the present case: the responsible congressional committees participated in their formulation, and both these committees and Congress itself endorsed the regulations in their final form.[15] Finally, application of § 504 to all programs receiving federal financial assistance fits the remedial purpose of the Rehabilitation Act "to promote and expand employment opportunities" for the handicapped. 29 U.S.C. § 701(8).

B

Nor did Congress intend to enact the "primary objective" requirement of § 604 into the Rehabilitation Act when it amended that Act in 1978. The amendments, as we have noted, make "available" the remedies, procedures and rights of Title VI for suits under § 504 against "*any* recipient of federal assistance." § 505(a)(2), 29 U.S.C. § 794a(a)(2). These terms do not incorporate § 604's "primary objective" limitation. Rather, the legislative history reveals that this section was intended to codify the regulations of the Department of Health, Education and Welfare governing enforcement of § 504, see S.Rep. No. 95–890, at 19, that prohibited employment discrimination regardless of the purpose of federal financial assistance.[16] And it would be anomalous to conclude that the section, "designed to enhance the ability of handicapped individuals to assure compliance with [§ 504]," id., at 18, silently adopted a drastic limitation on the handicapped individual's right to sue federal grant recipients for employment discrimination.

---

14. See 39 Fed.Reg. 18562, 18582 (1974) (revising pre-existing provisions to implement § 504); 41 Fed.Reg. 29548, 29552, 29563 (1976) (proposed department regulations), *promulgated,* 42 Fed.Reg. 22678 (§ 84.2), 22680 (§ 84.11), 22688 ("Employment Practices") (1977); 43 Fed.Reg. 2132, 2138 (1978) (final coordinating regulations).

The Department of Justice, now responsible for coordinating agency implementation of § 504, see Executive Order No. 12250, 45 Fed.Reg. 72995 (1980), adopted the HEW guidelines, 46 Fed.Reg. 440686 (1981). The Department of Transportation, from which Conrail receives federal aid, also has construed § 504 to prohibit employment discrimination in all programs receiving federal financial assistance. 44 Fed.Reg. 31442, 31468 (1979), codified at 49 CFR Pt. 27. See id. § 27.31.

15. See S.Rep. No. 93–1297, p. 25 (1974). In adopting § 505(a)(2) in the amendments of 1978, Congress incorporated the substance of the Department's regulations into the statute. See infra, at n. 17.

16. The Committee noted that "the regulations promulgated by the Department of Health, Education and Welfare with respect to procedures, remedies, and rights under § 504 conform with those promulgated under title VI. Thus, this amendment codifies existing practice as a specific statutory requirement." S.Rep. No. 95–890, at 19. Although these Department regulations incorporated Title VI regulations governing "complaint and enforcement procedures," see 42 Fed.Reg., at 22685, 22694–22701, the regulations implementing § 504 did not incorporate § 80.3 of the Title VI regulations, which limit Title VI's application to employment discrimination in federal programs to increase employment. The § 504 regulations banned employment discrimination in programs receiving any form of federal financial assistance. See n. 15, supra.

V

Section 504, by its terms, prohibits discrimination only by a "program or activity receiving Federal financial assistance." This Court on two occasions has considered the meaning of the terms "program or activity" as used in Title IX. Grove City College v. Bell, ___ U.S. ___, 104 S.Ct. 1211, 78 L.Ed.2d ___ (1984); North Haven Board of Education v. Bell, 456 U.S., at 535–540, 102 S.Ct., at 1925–1928. Clearly, this language limits the ban on discrimination to the specific program that receives federal funds. Neither opinion, however, provides particular guidance as to the appropriate treatment of the programs before us. *Grove City College* considered grants of financial aid to students. The Court specifically declined to analogize these grants to nonearmarked direct grants and, indeed, characterized them as *"sui generis."* ___ U.S., at ___, 104 S.Ct., at 1221. *North Haven Board of Education* did not undertake to define the term "program" at all, finding that, in the procedural posture of that case, that task should be left to the District Court in the first instance. 456 U.S., at 540, 102 S.Ct., at 1928.

The procedural posture of the case before us is the same as that of *North Haven Board of Education.* The District Court granted a motion for summary judgment on grounds unrelated to the issue of "program specificity." That judgment was reversed by the Court of Appeals and the case remanded for further proceedings. Thus, neither the District Court nor the Court of Appeals below considered the question whether respondent's decedent had sought and been denied employment in a "program * * * receiving federal financial assistance." Nor did the District Court develop the record or make the factual findings that would be required to define the relevant "program." We therefore do not consider whether federal financial assistance was received by the "program or activity" that discriminated against LeStrange.

VI

We conclude that respondent may recover backpay due to her decedent under § 504 and that this suit for employment discrimination may be maintained even if petitioner receives no federal aid the primary purpose of which is to promote employment. The judgment of the Court of Appeals is therefore affirmed.

It is so ordered.

Note

The United States provides financial assistance to airport operators through grants from a Trust Fund created by the Airport and Airway Development Act of 1970. The Government also operates a nationwide air traffic control system. In *United States Department of Transportation v. Paralyzed Veterans of America,* ___ U.S. ___, 106 S.Ct. 2705, 91 L.Ed.2d 494 (1986) the Supreme Court, in an opinion by Justice Powell, held that the above facts did not make commercial airlines which used the airports recipients of federal financial assistance under § 504. The court drew a sharp distinction between direct recipients and indirect recipients or beneficiaries. Justices Marshall, Brennan and Blackmun dissented.

SOUTHEASTERN COMMUNITY COLLEGE v. DAVIS

The Supreme Court of the United States, 1979.
442 U.S. 397, 99 S.Ct. 2361, 60 L.Ed.2d 980.

MR. JUSTICE POWELL delivered the opinion of the Court.

This case presents a matter of first impression for this Court: Whether § 504 of the Rehabilitation Act of 1973, which prohibits discrimination against an "otherwise qualified handicapped individual" in federally funded programs "solely by reason of his handicap," forbids professional schools from imposing physical qualifications for admission to their clinical training programs.

I

Respondent, who suffers from a serious hearing disability, seeks to be trained as a registered nurse. During the 1973–1974 academic year she was enrolled in the College Parallel program of Southeastern Community College, a state institution that receives federal funds. Respondent hoped to progress to Southeastern's Associate Degree Nursing program, completion of which would make her eligible for state certification as a registered nurse. In the course of her application to the nursing program, she was interviewed by a member of the nursing faculty. It became apparent that respondent had difficulty understanding questions asked, and on inquiry she acknowledged a history of hearing problems and dependence on a hearing aid. She was advised to consult an audiologist.

On the basis of an examination at Duke University Medical Center, respondent was diagnosed as having a "bilateral, sensorineural hearing loss." A change in her hearing aid was recommended, as a result of which it was expected that she would be able to detect sounds "almost as well as a person would who has normal hearing." But this improvement would not mean that she could discriminate among sounds sufficiently to understand normal spoken speech. Her lip-reading skills would remain necessary for effective communication: "While wearing the hearing aid, she is well aware of gross sounds occurring in the listening environment. However, she can only be responsible for speech spoken to her, when the talker gets her attention and allows her to look directly at the talker."

Southeastern next consulted Mary McRee, Executive Director of the North Carolina Board of Nursing. On the basis of the audiologist's report, McRee recommended that respondent not be admitted to the nursing program. In McRee's view, respondent's hearing disability made it unsafe for her to practice as a nurse. In addition, it would be impossible for respondent to participate safely in the normal clinical training program, and those modifications that would be necessary to enable safe participation would prevent her from realizing the benefits of the program: "To adjust patient learning experiences in keeping with [respondent's] hearing limitations could, in fact, be the same as denying her full learning to meet the objectives of your nursing programs."

After respondent was notified that she was not qualified for nursing study because of her hearing disability, she requested reconsideration of the decision. The entire nursing staff of Southeastern was assembled, and McRee again was consulted. McRee repeated her conclusion that on the basis of the available evidence, respondent "has hearing limitations which could interfere with her safely caring for patients." Upon further deliberation, the staff voted to deny respondent admission.

Respondent then filed suit in the United States District Court for the Eastern District of North Carolina, alleging both a violation of § 504 of the Rehabilitation Act of 1973, and a denial of equal protection and due process. After a bench trial, the District Court entered judgment in favor of Southeastern. It confirmed the findings of the audiologist that even with a hearing aid respondent cannot understand speech directed to her except through lip-reading, and further found:

> [I]n many situations such as an operation room intensive care unit, or post-natal care unit, all doctors and nurses wear surgical masks which would make lip reading impossible. Additionally, in many situations a Registered Nurse would be required to instantly follow the physician's instructions concerning procurement of various types of instruments and drugs where the physician would be unable to get the nurse's attention by other than vocal means.

Accordingly, the court concluded:

> [Respondent's] handicap actually prevents her from safely performing in both her training program and her proposed profession. The trial testimony indicated numerous situations where [respondent's] particular disability would render her unable to function properly. Of particular concern to the court in this case is the potential of danger to future patients in such situations.

Based on these findings, the District Court concluded that respondent was not an "otherwise qualified handicapped individual" protected against discrimination by § 504. In its view, "[o]therwise qualified, can only be read to mean otherwise able to function sufficiently in the position sought in spite of the handicap, if proper training and facilities are suitable and available." 424 F.Supp., at 1345. Because respondent's disability would prevent her from functioning "sufficiently" in Southeastern's nursing program, the court held that the decision to exclude her was not discriminatory within the meaning of § 504.[3]

On appeal, the Court of Appeals for the Fourth Circuit reversed. It did not dispute the District Court's findings of fact, but held that the

---

3. The District Court also dismissed respondent's constitutional claims. The Court of Appeals affirmed that portion of the order, and respondent has not sought review of this ruling.

court had misconstrued § 504. In light of administrative regulations
that had been promulgated while the appeal was pending, see 42 Fed.
Reg. 22676 (1977),[4] the appellate court believed that § 504 required
Southeastern to "reconsider plaintiff's application for admission to the
nursing program without regard to her hearing ability." It concluded
that the District Court had erred in taking respondent's handicap into
account in determining whether she was "otherwise qualified" for the
program, rather than confining its inquiry to her "academic and
technical qualifications." The Court of Appeals also suggested that
§ 504 required "affirmative conduct" on the part of Southeastern to
modify its program to accommodate the disabilities of applicants, "even
when such modifications become expensive."

Because of the importance of this issue to the many institutions
covered by § 504, we granted certiorari. We now reverse.[5]

II

As previously noted, this is the first case in which this Court has
been called upon to interpret § 504. It is elementary that "[t]he
starting point in every case involving construction of a statute is the
language itself." Section 504 by its terms does not compel educational
institutions to disregard the disabilities of handicapped individuals or
to make substantial modifications in their programs to allow disabled
persons to participate. Instead, it requires only that an "otherwise
qualified handicapped individual" not be excluded from participation in
a federally funded program "solely by reason of his handicap," indicating only that mere possession of a handicap is not a permissible ground
for assuming an inability to function in a particular context.[6]

---

4. Relying on the plain language of the
Act, the Department of Health, Education,
and Welfare (HEW) at first did not promulgate any regulations to implement § 504.
In a subsequent suit against HEW, however, the United States District Court for the
District of Columbia held that Congress
had intended regulations to be issued and
ordered HEW to do so. Cherry v. Mathews, 419 F.Supp. 922 (1976). The ensu-
ing regulations currently are embodied in
45 CFR pt. 84 (1978).

5. In addition to challenging the construction of § 504 by the Court of Appeals,
Southeastern also contends that respondent cannot seek judicial relief for violations of that statute in view of the absence
of any express private right of action. Respondent asserts that whether or not § 504
provides a private action, she may maintain her suit under 42 U.S.C. § 1983. In
light of our disposition of this case on the
merits, it is unnecessary to address these
issues and we express no views on them.

6. The Act defines "handicapped individual" as follows:

"The term 'handicapped individual'
means any individual who (A) has a
physical or mental disability which for
such individual constitutes or results in
a substantial handicap to employment
and (B) can reasonably be expected to
benefit in terms of employability from
vocational rehabilitation services provided pursuant to subchapters I and III of
this chapter. For the purposes of subchapters IV and V of this chapter, such
term means any person who (A) has a
physical or mental impairment which
substantially limits one or more of such
person's major life activities, (B) has a
record of such an impairment, or (C) is
regarded as having such an impairment." § 7(6) of the Rehabilitation Act
of 1973, 87 Stat. 361, as amended, 88
Stat. 1619, 89 Stat. 2–5, 29 U.S.C.
§ 706(6).

This definition comports with our understanding of § 504. A person who has a
record of, or is regarded as having, an
impairment may at present have no actual
incapacity at all. Such a person would be
exactly the kind of individual who could be

The court below, however, believed that the "otherwise qualified" persons protected by § 504 include those who would be able to meet the requirements of a particular program in every respect except as to limitations imposed by their handicap. Taken literally, this holding would prevent an institution from taking into account any limitation resulting from the handicap, however disabling. It assumes, in effect, that a person need not meet legitimate physical requirements in order to be "otherwise qualified." We think the understanding of the District Court is closer to the plain meaning of the statutory language. An otherwise qualified person is one who is able to meet all of a program's requirements in spite of his handicap.

The regulations promulgated by the Department of HEW to interpret § 504 reinforce, rather than contradict, this conclusion. According to these regulations, a "[q]ualified handicapped person" is, "[w]ith respect to postsecondary and vocational education services, a handicapped person who meets the academic and technical standards requisite to admission or participation in the [school's] education program or activity * * *." 45 CFR § 84.3(k)(3) (1978). An explanatory note states:

> The term "technical standards" refers to *all* nonacademic admissions criteria that are essential to participation in the program in question. 45 CFR pt. 84, App. A, p. 405 (1978) (emphasis supplied).

A further note emphasizes that legitimate physical qualifications may be essential to participation in particular programs.[7] We think it clear, therefore, that HEW interprets the "other" qualifications which a handicapped person may be required to meet as including necessary physical qualifications.

III

The remaining question is whether the physical qualifications Southeastern demanded of respondent might not be necessary for participation in its nursing program. It is not open to dispute that, as Southeastern's Associate Degree Nursing program currently is consti-

---

"otherwise qualified" to participate in covered programs. And a person who suffers from a limiting physical or mental impairment still may possess other abilities that permit him to meet the requirements of various programs. Thus, it is clear that Congress included among the class of "handicapped" persons covered by § 504 a range of individuals who could be "otherwise qualified." See S.Rep. No. 93–1297, pp. 38–39 (1974), U.S.Code Cong. & Admin. News, p. 6373.

7. The note states:

"Paragraph (k) of § 84.3 defines the term 'qualified handicapped person.' Throughout the regulation, this term is used instead of the statutory term 'otherwise qualified handicapped person.' The

Department believes that the omission of the word 'otherwise' is necessary in order to comport with the intent of the statute because, read literally, 'otherwise' qualified handicapped persons include persons who are qualified except for their handicap, rather than in spite of their handicap. Under such a literal reading, a blind person possessing all the qualifications for driving a bus except sight could be said to be 'otherwise qualified' for the job of driving. Clearly, such a result was not intended by Congress. In all other respects, the terms 'qualified' and 'otherwise qualified' are intended to be interchangeable." 45 CFR pt. 84, App. A, p. 405 (1978).

tuted, the ability to understand speech without reliance on lipreading is necessary for patient safety during the clinical phase of the program. As the District Court found, this ability also is indispensable for many of the functions that a registered nurse performs.

Respondent contends nevertheless that § 504, properly interpreted, compels Southeastern to undertake affirmative action that would dispense with the need for effective oral communication. First, it is suggested that respondent can be given individual supervision by faculty members whenever she attends patients directly. Moreover, certain required courses might be dispensed with altogether for respondent. It is not necessary, she argues, that Southeastern train her to undertake all the tasks a registered nurse is licensed to perform. Rather, it is sufficient to make § 504 applicable if respondent might be able to perform satisfactorily some of the duties of a registered nurse or to hold some of the positions available to a registered nurse.[8]

Respondent finds support for this argument in portions of the HEW regulations discussed above. In particular, a provision applicable to postsecondary educational programs requires covered institutions to make "modifications" in their programs to accommodate handicapped persons, and to provide "auxiliary aids" such as sign-language interpreters. Respondent argues that this regulation imposes an obligation to ensure full participation in covered programs by handicapped individuals and, in particular, requires Southeastern to make the kind of adjustments that would be necessary to permit her safe participation in the nursing program.

We note first that on the present record it appears unlikely respondent could benefit from any affirmative action that the regulation reasonably could be interpreted as requiring. Section 84.44(d)(2), for example, explicitly excludes "devices or services of a personal nature" from the kinds of auxiliary aids a school must provide a handicapped individual. Yet the only evidence in the record indicates that nothing less than close, individual attention by a nursing instructor would be sufficient to ensure patient safety if respondent took part in the clinical phase of the nursing program. Furthermore, it also is reasonably clear that § 84.44(a) does not encompass the kind of curricu-

---

8. The court below adopted a portion of this argument:

"[Respondent's] ability to read lips aids her in overcoming her hearing disability; however, it was argued that in certain situations such as in an operating room environment where surgical masks are used, this ability would be unavailing to her.

"Be that as it may, in the medical community, there does appear to be a number of settings in which the plaintiff could perform satisfactorily as an RN, such as in industry or perhaps a physician's office. Certainly [respondent]

could be viewed as possessing extraordinary insight into the medical and emotional needs of those with hearing disabilities.

"If [respondent] meets all the other criteria for admission in the pursuit of her RN career, under the relevant North Carolina statutes, N.C.Gen.Stat. §§ 90–158, *et seq.*, it should not be foreclosed to her simply because she may not be able to function effectively in all the roles which registered nurses may choose for their careers." 574 F.2d 1158, 1161 n. 6 (1978).

lar changes that would be necessary to accommodate respondent in the nursing program. In light of respondent's inability to function in clinical courses without close supervision, Southeastern, with prudence, could allow her to take only academic classes. Whatever benefits respondent might realize from such a course of study, she would not receive even a rough equivalent of the training a nursing program normally gives. Such a fundamental alteration in the nature of a program is far more than the "modification" the regulation requires.

Moreover, an interpretation of the regulations that required the extensive modifications necessary to include respondent in the nursing program would raise grave doubts about their validity. If these regulations were to require substantial adjustments in existing programs beyond those necessary to eliminate discrimination against otherwise qualified individuals, they would do more than clarify the meaning of § 504. Instead, they would constitute an unauthorized extension of the obligations imposed by that statute.

The language and structure of the Rehabilitation Act of 1973 reflect a recognition by Congress of the distinction between the even-handed treatment of qualified handicapped persons and affirmative efforts to overcome the disabilities caused by handicaps. Section 501(b), governing the employment of handicapped individuals by the Federal Government, requires each federal agency to submit "an affirmative action program plan for the hiring, placement, and advancement of handicapped individuals * * *." These plans "shall include a description of the extent to which and methods whereby the special needs of handicapped employees are being met." Similarly, § 503(a), governing hiring by federal contractors, requires employers to "take affirmative action to employ and advance in employment qualified handicapped individuals * * *." The President is required to promulgate regulations to enforce this section.

Under § 501(c) of the Act, by contrast, state agencies such as Southeastern are only "encourage[d] * * * to adopt and implement such policies and procedures." Section 504 does not refer at all to affirmative action, and except as it applies to federal employers it does not provide for implementation by administrative action. A comparison of these provisions demonstrates that Congress understood accommodation of the needs of handicapped individuals may require affirmative action and knew how to provide for it in those instances where it wished to do so.

Although an agency's interpretation of the statute under which it operates is entitled to some deference, "this deference is constrained by our obligation to honor the clear meaning of a statute, as revealed by its language, purpose, and history." Here, neither the language, purpose, nor history of § 504 reveals an intent to impose an affirmative-action obligation on all recipients of federal funds. Accordingly, we hold that even if HEW has attempted to create such an obligation itself, it lacks the authority to do so.

IV

We do not suggest that the line between a lawful refusal to extend affirmative action and illegal discrimination against handicapped persons always will be clear. It is possible to envision situations where an insistence on continuing past requirements and practices might arbitrarily deprive genuinely qualified handicapped persons of the opportunity to participate in a covered program. Technological advances can be expected to enhance opportunities to rehabilitate the handicapped or otherwise to qualify them for some useful employment. Such advances also may enable attainment of these goals without imposing undue financial and administrative burdens upon a State. Thus, situations may arise where a refusal to modify an existing program might become unreasonable and discriminatory. Identification of those instances where a refusal to accommodate the needs of a disabled person amounts to discrimination against the handicapped continues to be an important responsibility of HEW.

In this case, however, it is clear that Southeastern's unwillingness to make major adjustments in its nursing program does not constitute such discrimination. The uncontroverted testimony of several members of Southeastern's staff and faculty established that the purpose of its program was to train persons who could serve the nursing profession in all customary ways. This type of purpose, far from reflecting any animus against handicapped individuals is shared by many if not most of the institutions that train persons to render professional service. It is undisputed that respondent could not participate in Southeastern's nursing program unless the standards were substantially lowered. Section 504 imposes no requirement upon an educational institution to lower or to effect substantial modifications of standards to accommodate a handicapped person.

One may admire respondent's desire and determination to overcome her handicap, and there well may be various other types of service for which she can qualify. In this case, however, we hold that there was no violation of § 504 when Southeastern concluded that respondent did not qualify for admission to its program. Nothing in the language or history of § 504 reflects an intention to limit the freedom of an educational institution to require reasonable physical qualifications for admission to a clinical training program. Nor has there been any showing in this case that any action short of a substantial change in Southeastern's program would render unreasonable the qualifications it imposed.

V

Accordingly, we reverse the judgment of the court below, and remand for proceedings consistent with this opinion.

So ordered.

McCLEOD v. CITY OF DETROIT

U.S. District Court for the Eastern District of Michigan, 1985.
39 FEP Cases 225

COHN, DISTRICT JUDGE:

I.

A.

This case involves a challenge to the City of Detroit's use of particular drug screening tests for the presence of marihuana in the urine and the rejection of plaintiffs as candidates for firefighting positions in 1982 on the basis of positive test results. On May 21, 1985, a partial judgment was entered in favor of defendants on a jury verdict dismissing plaintiffs' 42 U.S.C. § 1983 claims against the City of Detroit and James Duncan (Duncan), Senior Examining Physician in the Medical Division of the Detroit Fire Department. Now before me for decision are plaintiffs' claims under the Rehabilitation Act of 1973.

B.

As part of the examination process for the position of firefighter, the City of Detroit requires applicants to submit to drug screening tests for the presence of marihuana. Each plaintiff tested positive on two different tests, each of which tests was administered a week apart. As a consequence of the positive test results, plaintiffs were rejected. Plaintiffs say that under the Act they are considered handicapped and have been discriminated against as a consequence of their handicap. Plaintiffs also say that the Charter requires that employment be based on merit and, because the tests utilized have no scientific validity, denial of employment based on the positive test results was arbitrary and capricious.

The City of Detroit says that plaintiffs are not handicapped individuals as defined by the Act and that there is a rational relationship between testing positive for the presence of marihuana, as did plaintiffs, and disqualification for the job of firefighter.

C.

For the reasons that follow, which constitute the findings of fact and conclusions of law required by Fed.R.Civ.P. 52(a), I find that the City's position is correct and, therefore, plaintiffs' claims will be dismissed.

II.

A.

At trial, plaintiffs' case was put through plaintiffs' cross-examination of Duncan and the testimony of Thomas Regent and Arthur McVey, expert toxologists, as well as a number of exhibits. Plaintiffs established that they were fully qualified for the firefighter position except for the positive test results. Their proof established that the

City began drug screening tests generally in 1973, and in 1981 included a test for the presence of marihuana when Sylva Corporation (Sylva) began marketing the EMIT (Enzyme Multiple Immunoassay Technique) test for the presence of marihuana. When the use of this test was challenged as unreliable because of the possibility of false positives, the City directed the laboratory administering the tests to confirm a positive test result by the EMIT method with an RIA (Radio Immunoassay) test as recommended by Sylva. According to the plaintiffs' experts' testimony, each of these tests has too high a probability of false positives and therefore the only reliable confirmatory test is a GC–MS (gas chromatography-mass spectrometry) test. The experts opined that the positive test results of plaintiffs demonstrated at most the presumptive use of marihuana and that a decision to reject them for employment as firefighters on the basis that they were marihuana users was inappropriate. Important to plaintiffs' proofs at trial was a study (Px21) describing the problems of detecting marihuana use and the limitations of each of the tests, i.e., EMIT, RIA, and GC/MS. While the study tended to support the experts' opinion on the lack of reliability in the EMIT/RIA combination, it stated that the cost of the EMIT/RIA combination was less than $5.00 while the cost of a GC/MS test was $50–$100.

B.

The City's proofs were put through the testimony of staff members of its Personnel Department, Frank L. Smith and Arnold Bauer; the Chief of Fire Operations, Walter Chapman; and Robert DePont, former Director of the National Institute for Drug Abuse, currently in private practice as a treating physician for drug abusers and a consultant on problems of drug abuse and treatment. Plaintiffs' (sic) proofs established that within minutes of ingestion marihuana can cause physical reactions such as short-term memory loss, problems with coordination and thinking, and diminishment of the ability to take risks. This evidence proved that the use of marihuana by a firefighter constituted a direct threat to the property and safety of the community.

The Personnel Department witnesses expressed the opinion, which I find credible, that positive test results demonstrated that plaintiffs, after being expressly warned against use of marihuana, did use it and were thus users of an illegal substance,[2] conduct incompatible with public employment.

2. In the Fall of 1982, as part of the application process each plaintiff signed a form that reads:

I declare that I am not currently taking any controlled narcotic substance on a regular basis; and do not use illegal drugs *including marihuana.*

I understand that I am subject to screening for drug use, and that positive find-ings with subsequent confirmations will disqualify me for employment as a firefighter.

Plaintiffs were tested for marihuana use in December 1982, some three months after signing the forms.

As to the appropriateness of the use of the EMIT/RIA combination for the presence of marihuana, and hence proof of the fact that plaintiffs were marihuana users, the City's proofs established the relatively modest cost of this form of testing, the general reliability of these tests as opined by Dr. DuPont, the acceptance of the EMIT test as a useful drug screen, and the express recommendation of Sylva that the RIA test be used to confirm a positive test result by the EMIT method.

The City acknowledged, as explained by Sylva in its instruction booklet (Px24), that the usefulness of the tests was limited to indicating the recent use of marihuana and not as a measure of the level of use or the effect of use on the person tested.[3]

III.

Plaintiffs' case under the Act fails because they are not handicapped as defined in the Act, and even if they are defined as handicapped under the Act the City legitimately disqualified them from the job of firefighter.

A.

To make out a claim of discrimination because of a physical handicap, plaintiffs have to satisfy the threshold requirement of being a handicapped individual.

29 U.S.C. § 794 provides that:

No otherwise qualified *handicapped individual* in the United States, as defined in section 706(7) of this title, shall, solely by reason of his handicap, be excluded from the participation in, be denied the benefits of, or be subject to discrimination under any program or activity receiving Federal financial assistance * * *. [Emphasis added.]

A handicapped individual is defined under 29 U.S.C. § 706 as:

any person who (i) has a physical or mental impairment which substantially limits one or more of such person's major life activities, (ii) has a record of such impairment, or (iii) is regarded as having any impairment.

The Act also affords a cause of action not only to a person excluded because he or she is actually handicapped, 29 U.S.C. § 794, but also to those excluded from participation in a federally funded program because they have been incorrectly classified and treated as being handi-

---

3. My description of the proofs at trial is obviously simplified. The experts went into some detail as to the composition of marihuana, its principle psychoactive ingredient, the difficulties of detecting its presence in the human body, the manner of detecting it, the way the tests work, their technical limitations, and the literature relating to marihuana use and detection. The burden was on plaintiffs to make out a case for lack of scientific validity of the test methods used by the City and the arbitrary relationship between positive test results indicating the use of marihuana and firefighter qualifications. As was explained on the record on June 17, 1985, the jury heard the proofs and was fairly instructed. It was satisfied that plaintiffs did not make a case. As will be seen from my discussion, I agree with the jury's conclusion.

There is no dispute over the fact that the Detroit Fire Department receives federal funds and therefore is subject to the Act.

capped when in fact they are not. Carter v. Orleans Parish Public Schools, 725 F.2d 261 (5th Cir.1984).

Importantly, therefore, plaintiffs must establish an impairment that substantially limits one or more of their major life activities. "Major life activities" are defined in the regulations as such actions as caring for one's self, performing manual tasks, walking, seeing, hearing, speaking, breathing, learning, and working. 29 C.F.R. § 1613.702(c).

B.

Jasany v. United States Postal Service, 755 F.2d 1244, 37 FEP Cases 210 (6th Cir.1985), involved a postal worker with a mild case of strobismus, i.e., crossed eyes. The affliction did not have any effect on any of plaintiff's activities, including his work history, apart from the operation of a mail sorting machine at his post office job. The district court found that work on the sorting machine qualified as a major life activity and that plaintiff was handicapped within the meaning of § 706. The Court of Appeals reversed the district court decision, holding that an impairment that affects only a narrow range of jobs can be regarded either as or as not reaching a major life activity or as or as not substantially limiting, that the burden is on the plaintiff to establish the existence of an impairment that substantially limits a major life activity as an element of a *prima facie* case, and that plaintiff had failed to do so.

In E.E. Black, Ltd. v. Marshall, 497 F.Supp. 1088, 23 FEP Cases 1253 (D.C.1980), the court had under consideration the definition of a handicapped individual under § 706 and held that an impairment that interfered with an individual's ability to do a particular job, but did not significantly decrease the ability to obtain satisfactory employment otherwise, was not substantially limiting within the meaning of the Act.

Here, the question is whether the plaintiffs suffer from an impairment that significantly altered a major life activity. Even if the use of marihuana qualifies as an impairment, there was no evidence at trial that being a firefighter was a major life activity. "One particular job for one particular employer cannot be a major life activity." Salt Lake City Corp. v. Confer, 674 P.2d 632, 636, 37 FEP Cases 283 (Utah 1983).

C.

Assuming that drug use is a handicap and that plaintiffs are drug users, the Act excludes them from its benefits. 29 U.S.C. § 706 reads:

> For purposes of sections 793 and 794 of this title as such sections relate to employment, such term (handicapped individuals) does not include any individual who is an alcoholic or drug abuser whose current *use of alcohol or drugs prevents such individual from performing the duties of the job in question or whose employment, by reason of such current alcohol or drug abuse, would constitute a direct threat to property or the safety of others.* [Emphasis added.]

Plaintiffs' contention, that because the City takes the position that their memory, coordination and risk-taking ability are impaired it also must view them as handicapped even though its view of these qualities is erroneous, confuses the distinction between a handicap and a job qualification.

Certainly the Act makes clear that "no otherwise qualified individual is to be denied employment based on his or her handicap," 29 U.S.C. § 794. And certainly Congress intended to include an individual with a history of drug abuse as "handicapped," 28 C.F.R. § 540; Davis v. Bucher, 451 F.Supp. 791, 17 FEP Cases 918 (E.D.Pa.1978). This circumstance obtains, however, only where the drug addiction substantially affects the addict's ability to perform a major life activity, id., and here plaintiffs failed to show that their ability to perform a major life activity had been impaired.

If plaintiffs had established the existence of an impairment that substantially limited a major life activity, the burden would have shifted to the City to demonstrate that the challenged criteria were job related and required by job necessity. Prewitt v. United States Postal Service, 662 F.2d 292, 27 FEP Cases 1043 (5th Cir.1981). Assuming that plaintiffs established they were handicapped, they were not "qualified handicapped", i.e., those "who, with or without reasonable accommodations can perform essential functions of the position in question." 29 C.F.R. § 1613.702(f); Jasany, supra, 755 F.2d at 1250. As already described, use of marihuana can adversely affect a firefighter's ability to do his or her job. The challenged criteria were, therefore, job related and required by business necessity. Prewitt, id., because they implicated the possibility of endangering the property and safety of others. The plaintiffs therefore had no coverage under 29 U.S.C. § 706(7)(B).

B.

To find that the standard used by the City to deny employment to plaintiffs was not job related I would have to find that plaintiffs proved that the use of marihuana was job disqualifying and that the use of the EMIT/RIA combination was arbitrary and capricious. As already described, I am satisfied it was reasonable for the City to disqualify a marihuana user from being considered for the position of firefighter; but plaintiffs certainly did not prove that use of marihuana has no rational relationship to the job of firefighter. Likewise, I am also satisfied that use of the EMIT/RIA combination, given its relative cost and relative reliability, was a reasonable method of testing for the use of marihuana and an appropriate method of screening candidates for the job of firefighter. Certainly plaintiffs did not prove that the test methods used by the City were arbitrary and capricious.

Notes

Unlike Title VII and the Age Discrimination in Employment Act, whose coverage is based on interstate commerce and is very broad, the

Vocational Rehabilitation Act of 1973 applies only to the federal government itself (§ 501), contractors with the federal government (§ 503) and recipients of federal financial assistance (§ 504).

By 1986 forty-eight states had laws prohibiting discrimination against the handicapped. Because of the limited coverage of the federal law, state laws are especially important in the handicap area. Thus, there is considerable litigation under the state laws. The reported decisions deal with a wide range of handicaps. E.g., on the question whether obesity is a handicap, compare S.D.H.R. v. Xerox Corp., 65 N.Y.2d 213, 491 N.Y.S.2d 106, 480 N.E.2d 695 (1985) with Philadelphia Electric Co. v. Pennsylvania Human Relations Commission, 68 Pa.Cmwlth. 212, 448 A.2d 701 (1982). Numerous state court decisions examine the safety defense, which is sometimes accepted, e.g., Boynton Cab Co. v. D.I.L.H.R., 96 Wis.2d 396, 291 N.W.2d 850 (1980) and Lewis v. Metropolitan Transit Commission, 320 N.W.2d 426 (Minn.1982) and sometimes rejected, e.g., M.H.R.C. v. Canadian Pacific, 458 A.2d 1225 (Me.1983) and Chicago & North Western R.R. v. L.I. R.C., 98 Wis.2d 592, 297 N.W.2d 819 (1980).

B. DISPARATE TREATMENT

PREWITT v. UNITED STATES POSTAL SERVICE

United States Court of Appeals for the Fifth Circuit, 1981.
662 F.2d 292.

TATE, CIRCUIT JUDGE:

Claiming that the United States Postal Service unlawfully denied him employment due to his physical handicap, the plaintiff, George Dunbar Prewitt, Jr., brought this action against the postal service. Prewitt contended that he was physically able to perform the job for which he applied despite his handicap, even though the postal service's physical requirements indicate that only persons in "good physical condition" can perform the job because it involves "arduous" work. Prewitt alleged, inter alia, that the postal service thus violated his rights under the Rehabilitation Act of 1973, as amended, 29 U.S.C. § 701 et seq. Prewitt filed this suit as a class action, after he was denied employment as a clerk/carrier at the Greenville, Mississippi post office. The district court granted the postal service's motion for summary judgment. On Prewitt's appeal, we find that the plaintiff has raised genuine issues of material fact as to 1) whether the postal service's physical requirements for postal employment are sufficiently "job related" to provide lawful grounds for the refusal to hire Prewitt, and 2) whether the postal service has breached its duty to make "reasonable accommodation" for handicapped persons such as Prewitt. Accordingly, we reverse the summary judgment of the district court, and remand the case for further proceedings in accordance with this opinion.

THE FACTUAL BACKGROUND

The plaintiff Prewitt is a disabled Vietnam war veteran. Due to gunshot wounds, he must endure limited mobility of his left arm and shoulder. Nevertheless, in May *1970* (prior to his rejection for re-employment in 1978 that gave rise to this lawsuit), Prewitt applied for a position as a distribution clerk in the Jackson, Mississippi post office, a position which, according to the job description, "require[s] arduous physical exertion involving prolonged standing, throwing, reaching, and may involve lifting sacks of mail up to 80 pounds." [1] Prewitt was hired after passing the requisite written and medical examinations, and it is undisputed that, despite his handicap, he performed his duties in a competent, entirely satisfactory manner.

Prewitt resigned his position at the Jackson post office in September 1970 to return to school. He testified in his affidavit, which we must regard as true for summary judgment purposes, that his physical condition did not diminish in any significant way between May 1970 and September 1978, when he applied for the position at the Greenville post office that gave rise to this lawsuit. Prewitt questions the failure of the postal service to re-employ him in 1978, due to a physical handicap, for a position as clerk/carrier, a position with similar physical requirements to those of the job that he had satisfactorily performed in 1970.

After applying for the clerk/carrier position at Greenville in 1978, Prewitt took and passed a standard written examination. He received a final rating of 92.8 (basic rating of 82.8 plus a 10 point compensable veteran's preference), which placed him second on the roster of eligible applicants. Physical suitability for the position, however, remained to be determined.

According to the postal services qualification standards, the duties of a carrier "are arduous and require that the incumbent be in good physical condition." Thus, a medical form which was given to Prewitt indicates that applicants for this position must meet a wide range of physical criteria, including, inter alia, the ability to see, hear, lift heavy weights, carry moderate weights, reach above shoulder, and use fingers and both hands. According to the affidavit of Postmaster Charles Hughes, the duties of a clerk/carrier require stooping, bending, squatting, lifting up to seventy pounds, standing for long periods, stretching arms in all directions, reaching above and below the shoulder, and some twisting of the back.

To determine whether Prewitt could meet these physical standards, the Greenville postal authorities asked Prewitt to authorize the Veteran's Administration (VA) to release his medical records to the postal service for examination, and Prewitt complied with this request. The VA records, which apparently were made in 1970 before Prewitt was

---

1. These physical requirements of Prewitt's 1970 position as distribution clerk are similar to those for the position of clerk/carrier for which he applied in 1978.

awarded disability benefits, indicated that Prewitt had a 30% service-related disability that caused "limitation of motion of left shoulder and atrophy of trapezius," as well as that he had a kidney disease, hypertension, and an eye condition not related to his armed forces service. The VA report was analyzed by Dr. Cenon Baltazar, a postal medical officer, who reported: "Limited records pertaining to [Prewitt] showed limitation of left shoulder and atrophy of trapezius muscle. This is not suitable for full performance as required of postal service positions unless it is a desk job." Prewitt subsequently received from Hughes a terse, two sentence letter informing him that Dr. Baltazar had determined that he was "medically unsuitable for postal employment." The letter did not state any reasons for this finding of unsuitability.

After receiving word of this adverse determination, Prewitt contacted Hughes to dispute the conclusion of the medical officer. Hughes told Prewitt that there was no appeal from the decision, but that the decision would be reconsidered at the local level if Prewitt would undergo an examination, at his own expense, by a private physician. In fact, Prewitt did have the right to appeal to the postal service's regional medical director. After belatedly learning of this right, Prewitt exercised his right to appeal, but he chose not to undergo a new physical examination. The regional medical officer, Dr. Gedney, examined the VA report and concluded that Prewitt was medically unsuitable. Unlike Dr. Baltazar, who relied solely on Prewitt's shoulder injury as the basis for his adverse determination, Dr. Gedney also mentioned the kidney disease (which Dr. Gedney stated is an unpredictably progressive disease that could possibly be aggravated by arduous duty) and hypertension. Based on Dr. Gedney's report, the regional office sustained the adverse determination and told Prewitt that there were no further medical appeal rights. Again, the letter did not inform Prewitt of the medical reasons upon which this conclusion was based.

Although the regional office correctly stated that there were no further *medical* appeal rights, in fact Prewitt had available to him an entirely independent chain of administrative review of the adverse determination through the postal service's equal employment opportunity (EEO) office. Prewitt filed an EEO complaint, alleging that the postal service had discriminated against him on the basis of his handicap by finding him unsuitable for postal employment. The EEO office conducted an investigation and found that the same medical officer who had disqualified Prewitt had ruled three other disabled or physically handicapped applicants suitable for postal employment. The investigation also revealed that the Greenville post office had hired fourteen persons classified as disabled and/or physically handicapped. Relying on these findings, the EEO office found no discrimination and advised Prewitt that he could appeal its decision to the Office of Appeals and Review of the Equal Employment Opportunity Commission (EEOC).[8]

8. The proposed disposition of Prewitt's complaint which was adopted as the final agency decision, states in pertinent part: You allege that you were discriminated against because of your physical handicap in that you were ruled unsuitable for

As permitted by statute, 42 U.S.C. § 2000e–16(c), made applicable to the handicapped by 29 U.S.C. § 794a(a)(1), instead of appealing to the EEOC, Prewitt filed this suit in the district court. No contention is made by the postal service that Prewitt did not exhaust administrative remedies. The postal service responded to Prewitt's complaint with a motion for summary judgment, contending that it had rejected Prewitt for valid medical reasons, and that Prewitt's refusal to take a physical examination had precluded it from making a re-evaluation. The plaintiff responded that postal service regulations required that applicants be given a current physical examination before a medical determination is made, and therefore, even though Prewitt was afforded an opportunity to take a physical after his determination was made, the determination of medical unfitness was invalid. Prewitt further argued that the regulations entitled him to a free physical examination, so that he was not required to bear the expense of an examination by a private physician. Finally, Prewitt noted that in view of the undisputed fact that he had been able to perform competently a similar job in 1970, the postal service had failed to articulate any legitimate reason for its finding of medical unsuitability.

1. THE APPLICABILITY OF THE REHABILITATION ACT TO FEDERAL GOVERNMENT HIRING

Only since 1978 have handicapped individuals been entitled to bring private actions against federal agencies for violations of the Rehabilitation Act. This is apparently the first case in which a federal appellate court has been called upon to determine the nature and extent of this newly-created private right. We shall therefore examine the history of this legislation in some detail.

Congress passed the Rehabilitation Act of 1973 for the express purpose, inter alia, of "promot[ing] and expand[ing] employment opportunities in the public and private sectors for handicapped individuals." 29 U.S.C. § 701(8). In addition to creating a number of wide-ranging federally-funded programs designed to aid handicapped persons in assuming a full role in society, the Act, in its Title V, established the principle that (a) the federal government, (b) federal contractors, and (c) recipients of federal funds cannot discriminate against the handicapped.

The duties of each of these three classes of entities were set forth in separate sections. Section 503 of the Act, 29 U.S.C. § 793, required federal contractors to include in their contracts with the United States

postal employment on February 2, 1979, at the Greenville, MS, Post Office. The facts developed during the investigation of August 23, 1979, revealed that you were considered for employment along with several other "non-handicapped" and "physically-handicapped" applicants. Appropriate medical authorities ruled that you were medically unsuitable for the postal clerk-carrier position.

Three disabled or physically handicapped applicants were ruled suitable for employment by the same medical officer. The records further reveal that the Greenville, MS, Post Office has hired fourteen employees who are classified as disabled and/or physically handicapped. There is no indication that you were treated differently because of your physical handicap.

a provision mandating that, in employing persons to carry out the contract, "the party contracting with the United States shall take affirmative action to employ and advance in employment qualified handicapped individuals. * * * " Section 504, 29 U.S.C. § 794, which imposed duties on recipients of federal funds, provided: "No otherwise qualified handicapped individual * * * shall, solely by reason of his handicap, be excluded from participation in, be denied the benefits of, or be subjected to discrimination under any program or activity receiving federal financial assistance."

The duties of the federal government itself were set forth in section 501(b), 29 U.S.C. § 791(b) which stated:

> Each department, agency, and instrumentality (including the United States Postal Service and the Postal Rate Commission) in the executive branch shall * * * submit to the Civil Service Commission and to the [Interagency Committee on Handicapped Employees] an affirmative action program plan for the hiring, placement, and advancement of handicapped individuals in such department, agency, or instrumentality. Such plan shall include a description of the extent to which and methods whereby the special needs of handicapped employees are being met. * * *

A Senate committee report commenting on section 501 emphasized that "the Federal Government must be an equal opportunity employer, and that this equal opportunity must apply fully to handicapped individuals." [9] As Senator Cranston subsequently commented in connection with 1978 amendments strengthening the federal employment rights of the handicapped, "[t]he legislative history of the section 501 illustrates that with respect to the employment of handicapped individuals, Congress expected the Federal Government should be a leader." In the words of Senator Williams, Congress enacted section 501 "to require that the Federal Government itself act as the model employer of the handicapped and take affirmative action to hire and promote the disabled." [11]

Under the original 1973 Rehabilitation Act, a private cause of action founded on handicap discrimination was not recognized upon section 501 as against a federal government employer; the literal statutory wording merely required federal agencies to *submit* affirmative actions plans. However, due to differences in statutory wording, all courts that considered the issue found that section 504 established a private cause of action for handicapped persons subjected to discrimination by recipients of federal funds, while the federal courts split on the

---

9. S.Rep. No. 93–318, 93d Cong., 1st Sess., at 49 (1973), U.S.Code Cong. & Admin.News 1973, pp. 2076, 2122.

11. Rehabilitation of the Handicapped Programs 1976: Hearings Before the Subcommittee on the Handicapped of the Committee on Labor and Public Welfare, 94th

Cong., 2d Sess., at 1502 (1976), quoted in Linn, Uncle Sam Doesn't Want You: Entering the Federal Stronghold of Employment Discrimination Against Handicapped Individuals, 27 DePaul L.Rev. 1047, 1060 (1978).

question whether the same was true under section 503 for individuals subjected to handicap discrimination by federal contractors.

In 1978, the Rehabilitation Act was amended to provide a private cause of action in favor of persons subjected to handicap discrimination by the federal government employing agencies. In the House, an amendment was adopted and ultimately enacted by the Congress that extended section 504's proscription against handicap discrimination to "any program or activity conducted by an Executive agency or by the United States Postal Service;" the legislative history, as well as the judicial interpretations (see note 13), fully recognized that a private right of action had been created by section 504.

The Senate, at the same time, added a new section 505(a)(1) to the Rehabilitation Act, which created a private right of action under section 501. The provision states:

> The remedies, procedures, and rights set forth in section 717 of the Civil Rights Act of 1964 [42 U.S.C. § 2000e–16], including the application of sections 706(f) through 706(k), [42 U.S.C. § 2000e–5], shall be available, with respect to any complaint under section 501 of this Act, to any employee or applicant for employment aggrieved by the final deposition of such complaint, or by the failure to take final action on such complaint.

Section 717 of Title VII of the Civil Rights Act, 42 U.S.C. § 2000e–16, to which section 501 is explicitly tied by the new section 505, mandates that all federal personnel actions be made "free from any discrimination based on race, color, religion, sex, or national origin." The provision further provides for a private right of action in favor of those whose claims of discrimination have not been satisfactorily resolved by administrative procedures. However, before an individual can bring a section 717 action in court, strict procedural requirements with respect to exhaustion of administrative remedies must be fulfilled. See 42 U.S.C. § 2000e–16(c). Once administrative remedies have been exhausted, however, an individual is entitled to de novo consideration of his discrimination claims in the district court; however, prior administrative findings made with respect to an employment discrimination claim may be admitted into evidence at the trial de novo.

The scope of the federal government's obligations under section 501 received Senate attention during debate on a proposed amendment to the proposed new section 505(a)(1). An amendment offered by Senator McClure would have added the following clause at the end of section 505(a)(1): "provided, however, that no equitable relief or affirmative action remedy disproportionately exceeding actual damages in the case shall be available under this section." Cong.Rec. S15664 (Daily ed. Sept. 21, 1978). Senator McClure explained that his amendment "would provide that the federally financed affirmative action remedy * * * could not be used to initiate massive construction projects for relatively minor temporal damages." Id.

Senators Cranston and Stafford spoke in opposition to the McClure amendment. Senator Cranston remarked:

> I believe that the requirement with respect to Federal Contractors and grantees should be no less stringent than the requirements attached to the Federal Government. The amendment offered by the Senator from Idaho would create an unwise and unrealistic distinction with respect of employment between the obligations of the Federal Government and the obligations of Federal contractors and grantees. Ironically, the Senator's amendment would limit—with a financial test—the Federal Government's obligation of being an equal opportunity employer. Federal contractors and grantees would—appropriately—continue to be required to be equal opportunity employers. Rather than a leader in this field, the Federal Government would become a distant also-ran requiring more of its grantees and contractors than it would be willing to require of itself.

Id. at S15665–66.

The dispute was resolved when Senator McClure and the managers of the bill agreed upon the following compromise language: "In fashioning an equitable or affirmative action remedy under such section [section 501], a court may take into account the reasonableness of the cost of any necessary workplace accommodation, and the availability of alternative therefor or other appropriate relief." Id. at S15667. As thus amended, the new section 505(a)(1) was enacted into law, and is now codified as 29 U.S.C. § 794a(a)(1).[17]

In summary, the 1978 amendments to the Rehabilitation Act 1) established a private right of action, subject to the same procedural constraints (administrative exhaustion, etc.) set forth in Title VII of the Civil Rights Act, in favor of section 501 claimants, and 2) extended section 504's proscription against handicap employment discrimination to cover the activities of the federal government itself.

Thus, by its 1978 amendments to the Rehabilitation Act, Congress clearly recognized both in section 501 and in section 504 that individuals now have a private cause of action to obtain relief for handicap discrimination on the part of the federal government and its agencies. The amendments to section 504 were simply the House's answer to the same problem that the Senate saw fit to resolve by strengthening section 501. The joint House-Senate conference committee could have chosen to eliminate the partial overlap between the two provisions, but

---

17. The new section 505(a)(1), 29 U.S.C. § 794a(a)(1), added by the Senate amendment to the Rehabilitation Act provides:

The remedies, procedures, and rights set forth in section 717 of the Civil Rights Act of 1964, including the application of sections 706(f) through 706(k), shall be available, with respect to any complaint under section 791 of this title, to any employee or applicant for employment aggrieved by the final disposition of such complaint, or by the failure to take final action on such complaint. In fashioning an equitable or affirmative action remedy under such section, a court may take into account the reasonableness of the cost of any necessary work place accommodation, and the availability of alternatives therefor or other appropriate relief in order to achieve an equitable and appropriate remedy.

instead the conference committee, and subsequently Congress as a whole, chose to pass both provisions, despite the overlap. "When there are two acts upon the same subject, the rule is to give effect to both if possible." United States v. Borden Co., 308 U.S. 188, 198, 60 S.Ct. 182, 188, 84 L.Ed. 181 (1939). By this same principle, in order to give effect to *both* the House and the Senate 1978 amendments finally enacted, we must read the exhaustion of administrative remedies requirement of section 501 into the private remedy recognized by both section 501 and section 504 for federal government handicap discrimination.

2. Prewitt's Present Claim(s) of Handicap Discrimination

In the present suit, Prewitt claims that, despite his handicap, he is physically able to perform the job for which he applied, but that the postal service's physical requirements, neutral on their face, had *disparate impact* upon a person with his particular handicap and that they excluded him from employment that in fact he was physically able to perform. The present case was dismissed on summary judgment, through a failure to take into account the principles applicable to the federal government by the Rehabilitation Act of 1973, as amended in 1978; due to disputed issues of material fact, as will be stated, summary judgment was improvidently granted.

One of the chief physical factors upon which the postal service bases its refusal to hire Prewitt is that, due to Prewitt's inability to lift his left arm above shoulder level, the employing authority feels that he cannot "case" (sort) the mail that he would be required to deliver on his route. Because a carrier is required to lift above shoulder level with both hands to remove stacks of mail from a six-foot-high top ledge, the postal service contends that Prewitt would not be able to do this part of the job without some workplace modification—however, the postal service witness admitted, for instance, that Prewitt could be accommodated simply by lowering the legs to which the shelves are attached.[18] Only if Prewitt, despite his handicap, can perform the essential duties of the position in question, without the need for any workplace accommodation, can it be said that he was a victim of "disparate impact" discrimination. However, even if Prewitt cannot so perform, he might still be entitled to relief if he was a victim of "surmountable barrier" discrimination, i.e., if he was rejected even though he could have performed the essentials of the job if afforded reasonable accommodation.[19]

18. The second principal factor upon which the postal service relies is the severe pain that a VA report indicates that Prewitt suffers after lifting. Prewitt denies the pain or at least its severity. This type of handicap may be either a surmountable or insurmountable employment barrier. See text and note 25 infra.

19. Commentators have identified four distinct types of discriminatory barriers that handicapped persons must confront when seeking employment: 1. Intentional discrimination for reasons of social bias (racial, sexual, religion, handicap, etc.); 2. neutral standards with disparate impact; 3. surmountable impairment barriers; and 4. insurmountable impairment barriers. See Note, Accommodating the Handicapped: The Meaning of Discrimination Under Section 504 of the Rehabilitation Act, 55 N.Y.U.L.Rev. 881, 883–84 (1980). See also Gittler, Fair Employment and the

Since both issues will arise on the remand, we will therefore note the principles applicable to judicial determination of both cases involving claims of "disparate impact" and also of "surmountable barrier" ("the duty to make reasonable accommodation") discrimination against a handicapped person.

Preliminarily, however, we should observe that section 501 requires affirmative action on the part of federal agencies; unlike section 504 of the Rehabilitation Act and Title VII of the Civil Rights Act which usually require only nondiscrimination. In Ryan v. Federal Deposit Insurance Corp., 565 F.2d 762, 763 (D.C.Cir.1977), the court held, and we agree, especially in light of the 1978 amendments, that section 501 requires that federal agencies do more than just *submit* affirmative plans—section 501 "impose[s] a duty upon federal agencies to structure their procedures and programs so as to ensure that handicapped individuals are afforded equal opportunity in both job assignment and promotion." Although *Ryan,* which was decided prior to the 1978 amendments, did not recognize a private right of action under section 501, the court held that the defendant federal agency should amend its procedures to provide an administrative forum through which handicapped individuals could enforce their section 501 rights. Id. at 764. Subsequent to *Ryan,* the Civil Service Commission, and its successor enforcement agency, the EEOC, promulgated administrative regulations that define the section 501 duties of federal agencies, see 29 C.F.R. §§ 1613.701 et seq., which for instance (see below) include the duty to make reasonable accommodation to employ a handicapped person, see 29 C.F.R. § 1613.704. These regulations are the administrative interpretation of the Act by the enforcing agency and are therefore entitled to some deference in our attempt to determine the applications of this statute. See Southeastern Community College v. Davis, 442 U.S. 397, 99 S.Ct. 2361, 2369, 60 L.Ed.2d 980 (1979); Albemarle Paper Co. v. Moody, 422 U.S. 405, 431, 95 S.Ct. 2362, 2378, 45 L.Ed.2d 280 (1975); Griggs v. Duke Power Co., 401 U.S. 424, 433–34, 91 S.Ct. 849, 854–55, 28 L.Ed.2d 158 (1971).

The EEOC regulations adopt a *Griggs*-type approach in the disparate impact handicap discrimination context. They require federal agencies not to use any selection criterion that "screens out or tends to screen out qualified handicapped persons or any class of handicapped persons" unless the criterion, as used by the agency, is shown to be

Handicapped: A Legal Perspective, 27 DePaul L.Rev. 953, 958–66 (1978).

The present complaints by Prewitt involve alleged "disparate impact" and a "surmountable barrier" handicap-discrimination.

The Title VII jurisprudence is, we believe, for the most part applicable to intentional social-bias discrimination against handicapped persons. See Texas Department of Corrections v. Burdine, 450 U.S.

248, 101 S.Ct. 1089, 67 L.Ed.2d 207 (1981) and McDonnell Douglas Corp. v. Green, 411 U.S. 792, 93 S.Ct. 1817, 36 L.Ed.2d 668 (1973). Likewise, as will be noted in the text, the Title VII disparate impact decisions are relevant in the determination of disparate impact handicap discrimination. Surmountable and insurmountable barriers raise issues that for the most part are peculiar to handicap discrimination.

"job-related for the position in question." 29 C.F.R. § 1613.705. The test is whether a handicapped individual who meets all employment criteria except for the challenged discriminatory criterion "can perform the essential functions of the position in question without endangering the health and safety of the individuals or others." If the individual can so perform, he must not be subjected to discrimination. 28 C.F.R. §§ 1613.702(f) & 703. Cf. New York State Association for Retarded Children v. Carey, 612 F.2d 644, 649–50 (2d Cir.1979) (discriminatory exclusion of handicapped children from regular public school classes unlawful in the absence of "at least some substantial showing" by the school authorities that the exclusion is necessary).

In our opinion, in the disparate impact context, there should be only minor differences in the application of the *Griggs* principles to handicap discrimination claims. One difference, however, is that, when assessing the disparate impact of a facially-neutral criterion, courts must be careful not to group all handicapped persons into one class, or even into broad subclasses. This is because "the fact that an employer employs fifteen epileptics is not necessarily probative of whether he or she has discriminated against a blind person." [20]

In a section 504 handicap discrimination case, the Supreme Court held that the Rehabilitation Act does not require redress of "insurmountable barrier" handicap discrimination—that the statutory language prohibiting discrimination against an "otherwise qualified handicapped individual" means qualified *"in spite"* of his handicap, not qualified in all respects except for being handicapped. Southeastern Community College v. Davis, 442 U.S. 397, 406, 99 S.Ct. 2361, 2367, 60 L.Ed.2d 980 (1979) (emphasis added).

The *Davis* rationale is equally controlling in the employment discrimination context. Accordingly, employers subject to the Rehabilitation Act need not hire handicapped individuals who cannot fully perform the required work, even with accommodation. However, while Davis demonstrates that only individuals who are qualified "in spite of" their handicaps need be hired, *Griggs* and its progeny dictate that the employer must bear the burden of proving that the physical criteria are job related. If the employer does this, then the burden of persuasion to show that he can satisfy these criteria rests on the handicapped applicant.

4. "SURMOUNTABLE BARRIER" DISCRIMINATION, OR THE DUTY TO MAKE REASONABLE ACCOMMODATION

Federal employers, including the postal service, are obliged by section 501(b) to provide reasonable accommodation for the handicapped.[21] As the Davis Court pointed out, 442 U.S. at 410, 99 S.Ct. at

---

20. Gittler, supra note 19, at 972. Thus, the postal service's reliance on the fact that the Greenville office has hired numerous handicapped persons is misplaced.

21. This court has consistently held that section 504 also mandates reasonable accommodation, thus prohibiting surmountable barrier discrimination by federal grantees against the handicapped. See

2369, section 501(b), unlike section 504, explicitly requires federal government employers to undertake "affirmative action" on behalf of the handicapped. And the new section 505, added by Congress in 1978, explicitly permits courts to fashion "an equitable or affirmative action remedy" for violations of section 501, with the caveat that "the reasonableness of the cost of any necessary workplace accommodation" should be taken into account. The legislative intent reflected in the creation of a handicap discrimination private action clearly shows that federal government employers must make reasonable accommodation for handicapped job applicants.

There is a dearth of decisional law on this issue.[22] However, the EEOC administrative regulations, which, as noted above, are entitled to deference, provide some basis for outlining the contours of the surmountable barrier accommodation duty.

The relevant EEOC regulation, 29 C.F.R. § 1613.704, provides:

(a) An agency shall make reasonable accommodation to the known physical or mental limitations of a qualified handicapped applicant or employee unless the agency can demonstrate that the accommodation would impose an undue hardship on the operation of its program.

(b) Reasonable accommodation may include, but shall not be limited to: (1) Making facilities readily accessible to and usable by handicapped persons, and (2) job restructuring, part-time or modified work schedules, acquisition or modification of equipment or devices, appropriate adjustment or modification of examinations, the provision of readers and interpreters, and other similar actions.

(c) In determining pursuant to paragraph (a) of this section whether an accommodation would impose an undue hardship on the operation of the agency in question, factors to be considered include: (1) The overall size of the agency's program with respect to the number of employees, number and type of facilities and size of budget; (2) the type of agency operation, including the composition and structure of

Majors v. Housing Authority of the County of DeKalb Georgia, 652 F.2d 454, 457–58 (5th Cir.1981); Tatro v. State of Texas, 625 F.2d 557, 564 (5th Cir.1980); Camenisch v. University of Texas, 616 F.2d 127, 132–33 (5th Cir.1980), vacated on other grounds, 451 U.S. 390, 101 S.Ct. 1830, 68 L.Ed.2d 175 (1981).

22. Outside the handicap discrimination context, the "reasonable accommodation" issue has arisen in cases involving persons who claim a right to accommodation of their religious duty to refrain from working on certain days. In Trans World Airlines v. Hardison, 432 U.S. 63, 84, 97 S.Ct. 2264, 2277, 53 L.Ed.2d 113 (1977), the Supreme Court interpreted § 701(j) of the Civil Rights Act of 1964, 42 U.S.C. § 2000e(j), which requires employers to accommodate such religious practices, unless

to do so would impose "undue hardship." The Court held that an employer need not accommodate such persons if the accommodation would require "more than a *de minimis* cost."

The *Hardison* principles are not applicable in the federal-employer handicap discrimination context. Congress clearly intended the federal government to take measures that would involve more than a *de minimis* cost. As the debate over the McClure amendment shows, Congress was even unwilling to approve language that would have limited the government's duty to make reasonable accommodation to instances in which the cost of accommodation does not "disproportionately exceed[ ] actual damages." See text at note 17 supra.

the agency's work force; and (3) the nature and the cost of the accommodation.

Thus, under subsection (a) of this provision, the burden of proving inability to accommodate is upon the employer. The administrative reasons for so placing the burden likewise justify a similar burden of proof in a private action based upon the Rehabilitation Act. The employer has greater knowledge of the essentials of the job than does the handicapped applicant. The employer can look to its own experience, or, if that is not helpful, to that of other employers who have provided jobs to individuals with handicaps similar to those of the applicant in question. Furthermore, the employer may be able to obtain advice concerning possible accommodations from private and government sources. See Note, Accommodating the Handicapped: Rehabilitating Section 504 After Southeastern, 80 Colum.L.Rev. 171, 187–88 (1980).

Although the burden of persuasion in proving inability to accommodate always remains on the employer, we must add one caveat. Once the employer presents credible evidence that indicates accommodation of the plaintiff would not reasonably be possible, the plaintiff may not remain silent. Once the employer presents such evidence, the plaintiff has the burden of coming forward with evidence concerning his individual capabilities and suggestions for possible accommodations to rebut the employer's evidence. See Note, supra, 80 Colum.L.Rev. at 189.

In addition, subsections (a) and (c) of 29 C.F.R. § 1613.704, which limit the employer's duty to accommodate to instances where accommodation would not impose "undue hardship" and define the factors to be used in determining whether a particular accommodation would impose "undue hardship," accurately express congressional intent. The second sentence of section 505, which admonishes the courts to "take into account the reasonableness of the cost of any necessary workplace accommodation," was added as compromise language in response to Senator McClure's concern that federal employers might be obliged "to initiate massive construction projects." The EEOC regulations adequately respond to this concern.

GENUINE DISPUTED ISSUES OF MATERIAL FACT PRECLUDE
SUMMARY JUDGMENT

The factual showing before the district court was that the postal service rejected Prewitt's application for employment because it felt, on the basis of the medical records supplied to it, that Prewitt could not perform the "arduous" duties of the position. In view of the undisputed fact that Prewitt had satisfactorily performed a similar postal job in 1970 despite his physical handicap, as well as of his *uncontradicted* affidavit that his physical condition was substantially unchanged since then, Prewitt raised a genuine issue of material fact as to whether the postal service's physical standards for employment are sufficiently "job related" to justify the employer's refusal to hire him. Under the applicable legal principles earlier set forth, therefore, the postal service is not shown under the facts thus far educed to have been justified as a matter of law in denying Prewitt's application. The summary judgment must therefore be reversed.

We should note that the postal service contends that the postal service rejected him because he refused its request that he take a current physical examination to establish his medical suitability for employment. This contention is based upon the showing that, *after* Prewitt was found medically unsuitable for employment, he was informally advised by the local postmaster that he would be reconsidered if he secured a new medical examination.

However, the record reveals that Prewitt's application was rejected because he was found to be medically unsuitable (without notifying Prewitt of the specific medical reasons), not because he refused to furnish any further or more current medical information. Indeed, Prewitt's essential position was that his physical condition and the effect of his disability was unchanged since 1970 and that, even accepting the disability reflected by the VA medical reports upon which the postal service relied, he was physically qualified to perform the duties of the position for which he applied, as instanced by his earlier satisfactory performance of the duties of a similar postal position.

On the Remand

On the basis of the factual showing thus far made, we reverse the summary judgment dismissing Prewitt's handicap-discrimination claim. We remand for further proceedings in accordance with the views set forth in this opinion. To summarize:

(1) Prewitt, the disabled claimant, may establish a prima facie case of unlawful discrimination by proving that: (a) except for his physical handicap, he is qualified to fill the position; (b) he has a handicap that prevents him from meeting the physical criteria for employment; and (c) the challenged physical standards have a disproportionate impact on persons having the same handicap from which he suffers. To sustain this prima facie case, there should also be a facial showing or at least plausible reasons to believe that the handicap can be accommodated or that the physical criteria are not "job related."

(2) Once the prima facie case of handicap discrimination is established, the burden of persuasion shifts to the federal employer to show that the physical criteria offered as justification for refusal to hire the plaintiff are "job related," i.e., that persons who suffer from the handicap plaintiff suffers and who are, therefore, unable to meet the challenged standards, cannot safely and efficiently perform the essentials of the position in question. If the issue of reasonable accommodation is raised, the agency must then be prepared to make a further showing that accommodation cannot reasonably be made that would enable the handicapped applicant to perform the essentials of the job adequately and safely; in this regard, the postal service must "demon-

strate that the accommodation would impose an undue hardship on the operation of its program," 29 C.F.R. § 1613.704(a), taking into consideration the factors set forth by 704(c) of the cited regulation.

(3) If the employer proves that the challenged requirements are job related, the plaintiff may then show that other selection criteria without a similar discriminatory effect would also serve the employer's legitimate interest in efficient and trustworthy workmanship. Dothard v. Rawlinson, 433 U.S. 321, 329, 97 S.Ct. 2720, 2726, 53 L.Ed.2d 786 (1977); Johnson v. Uncle Ben's, Inc., 657 F.2d 750, 752 (5th Cir.1981). When the issue of reasonable accommodation is raised, the burden of persuasion in proving inability to accommodate always remains on the employer; however, once the employer presents credible evidence that reasonable accommodation is not possible or practicable, the plaintiff must bear the burden of coming forward with evidence that suggests that accommodation may in fact be reasonably made.

CONCLUSION

We of course express no opinion as to the merits of Prewitt's claim. If he is unable to perform the essentials of the position for which he has applied, with or without reasonable accommodation, the postal service need not hire him. The ultimate test is whether, with or without reasonable accommodation, a handicapped individual who meets all employment criteria except for the challenged discriminatory criterion "can perform the essential functions of the position in question without endangering the health and safety of the individuals or others." 28 C.F.R. § 1613.702(f). Since a disputed issue of material fact is shown as to this issue, the summary judgment granted by the district court must be Reversed.

C. DISPARATE IMPACT

ALEXANDER v. CHOATE

The Supreme Court of the United States, 1985.
469 U.S. 287, 105 S.Ct. 712, 83 L.Ed.2d 661.

JUSTICE MARSHALL delivered the opinion of the Court.

In 1980, Tennessee proposed reducing the number of annual days of inpatient hospital care covered by its state Medicaid program. The question presented is whether the effect upon the handicapped that this reduction will have is cognizable under § 504 of the Rehabilitation Act of 1973 or its implementing regulations. We hold that it is not.

I

Faced in 1980–1981 with projected state Medicaid [1] costs of $42 million more than the State's Medicaid budget of $388 million, the

1. Medicaid was established by Title XIX of the Social Security Act of 1965, 79 Stat. 343 and amended, 42 U.S.C. § 1396 et seq. (1982). Medicaid is a joint state-federal funding program for medical assistance in which the Federal Government approves

directors of the Tennessee Medicaid program decided to institute a variety of cost-saving measures. Among these changes was a reduction from 20 to 14 in the number of inpatient hospital days per fiscal year that Tennessee Medicaid would pay hospitals on behalf of a Medicaid recipient. Before the new measures took effect, respondents, Tennessee Medicaid recipients, brought a class action for declaratory and injunctive relief in which they alleged, *inter alia,* that the proposed 14-day limitation on inpatient coverage would have a discriminatory effect on the handicapped. Statistical evidence, which petitioners do not dispute, indicated that in the 1979–1980 fiscal year, 27.4% of all handicapped users of hospital services who received Medicaid required more than 14 days of care, while only 7.8% of nonhandicapped users required more than 14 days of inpatient care.

Based on this evidence, respondents asserted that the reduction would violate § 504 of the Rehabilitation Act of 1973, 29 U.S.C. § 794, and its implementing regulations. Section 504 provides that:

> No otherwise qualified handicapped individual * * * shall, solely by reason of his handicap, be excluded from the participation in, be denied the benefits of, or be subjected to discrimination under any program or activity receiving Federal financial assistance * * *. 29 U.S.C. § 794.

Respondents' position was twofold. First, they argued that the change from 20 to 14 days of coverage would have a disproportionate effect on the handicapped and hence was discriminatory.[3] The second, and major, thrust of respondents' attack was directed at the use of *any* annual limitation on the number of inpatient days covered, for respondents acknowledged that, given the special needs of the handicapped for medical care, any such limitation was likely to disadvantage the handicapped disproportionately. Respondents noted, however, that federal law does not require States to impose any annual durational limitation on inpatient coverage, and that the Medicaid programs of only 10 States impose such restrictions. Respondents therefore suggested that Tennessee follow these other States and do away with any limitation on the number of annual inpatient days covered. Instead, argued respondents, the State could limit the number of days of hospital coverage on a perstay basis, with the number of covered days to vary depending on the recipient's illness (for example, fixing the number of days covered for an appendectomy); the period to be covered for each illness could then be set at a level that would keep Tennessee's Medicaid program as a whole within its budget. The State's refusal to adopt this plan was

a State plan for the funding of medical services for the needy and then subsidizes a significant portion of the financial obligations the state has agreed to assume. Once a State voluntarily chooses to participate in Medicaid, the State must comply with the requirements of Title XIX and applicable regulations. Harris v. McRae,

448 U.S. 297, 301, 100 S.Ct. 2671, 2680, 65 L.Ed.2d 784 (1980).

3. The evidence indicated that, if 19 days of coverage were provided, 16.9% of the handicapped, as compared to 4.2% of the nonhandicapped, would not have their needs for inpatient care met.

said to result in the imposition of gratuitous costs on the handicapped and thus to constitute discrimination under § 504.

A divided panel of the Court of Appeals for the Sixth Circuit held that respondents had indeed established a prima facie case of a § 504 violation. The majority apparently concluded that any action by a federal grantee that disparately affects the handicapped states a cause of action under § 504 and its implementing regulations. Because both the 14-day rule and any annual limitation on inpatient coverage disparately affected the handicapped, the panel found that a prima facie case had been made out, and the case was remanded to give Tennessee an opportunity for rebuttal. According to the panel majority, the State on remand could either demonstrate the unavailability of alternative plans that would achieve the State's legitimate cost-saving goals with a less disproportionate impact on the handicapped, or the State could offer "a substantial justification for the adoption of the plan with the greater discriminatory impact." Jennings v. Alexander, 715 F.2d 1036, 1045 (CA6 1983). We granted certiorari to consider whether the type of impact at issue in this case is cognizable under § 504 or its implementing regulations, 465 U.S. ___, 104 S.Ct. 1271, 79 L.Ed.2d 677 (1984) and we now reverse.

II

The first question the parties urge on the Court is whether proof of discriminatory animus is always required to establish a violation of § 504 and its implementing regulations, or whether federal law also reaches action by a recipient of federal funding that discriminates against the handicapped by effect rather than by design. The State of Tennessee argues that § 504 reaches only purposeful discrimination against the handicapped. As support for this position, the State relies heavily on our recent decision in Guardians Assn. v. Civil Service Comm'n of New York City, 463 U.S. 582, 103 S.Ct. 3221, 77 L.Ed.2d 866 (1983).

In *Guardians*, we confronted the question whether Title VI of the Civil Rights Act of 1964, 42 U.S.C. § 2000d et seq., which prohibits discrimination against racial and ethnic minorities in programs receiving federal aid, reaches both intentional and disparate-impact discrimination.[7] No opinion commanded a majority in *Guardians*, and mem-

---

7. Section 601 of the Civil Rights Act of 1964, 42 U.S.C. § 2000d, provides:

"No person in the United States shall, on the ground of race, color, or national origin, be excluded from participation in, be denied the benefits of, or be subjected to discrimination under any program or activity receiving Federal financial assistance."

The premise of the State's reliance on *Guardians* is that § 504 was modelled in part on Title VI, and that the evolution of Title VI regulatory and judicial law is therefore relevant to ascertaining the intended scope of § 504. We agree with this basic premise. See S.Rep. No. 93–1297, pp. 6390–91 (1974) U.S.Code Cong. & Admin. News 1974, pp. 6373, 6390–91 ("Section 504 was patterned after and is almost identical to, the antidiscrimination language of section 601 of the Civil Rights Act of 1964, 42 U.S.C. 2000d–1 (relating to race, color, or national origin) and section 901 of the Education Amendments of 1972, 42 U.S.C. 1683 (relating to sex)"). Nonetheless, as we point out infra, at 719–721 and n. 13,

bers of the Court offered widely varying interpretations of Title VI. Nonetheless, a two-pronged holding on the nature of the discrimination proscribed by Title VI emerged in that case. First, the Court held that Title VI itself directly reached only instances of intentional discrimination. Second, the Court held that actions having an unjustifiable disparate impact on minorities could be redressed through agency regulations designed to implement the purposes of Title VI. In essence, then, we held that Title VI had delegated to the agencies in the first instance the complex determination of what sorts of disparate impacts upon minorities constituted sufficiently significant social problems, and were readily enough remediable, to warrant altering the practices of the federal grantees that had produced those impacts.

Guardians, therefore, does not support petitioners' blanket proposition that federal law proscribes only intentional discrimination against the handicapped. Indeed, to the extent our holding in *Guardians* is relevant to the interpretation of § 504, *Guardians* suggests that the regulations implementing § 504, upon which respondents in part rely, could make actionable the disparate impact challenged in this case. Moreover, there are reasons to pause before too quickly extending even the first prong of *Guardians* to § 504. Cf. Consolidated Rail Corp. v. Darrone, 465 U.S. ___, n. 13, 104 S.Ct. 1248, n. 13, 79 L.Ed.2d 568 (1984) (recognizing distinctions between Title VI and § 504).

Discrimination against the handicapped was perceived by Congress to be most often the product, not of invidious animus, but rather of thoughtlessness and indifference—of benign neglect.[12] Thus, Representative Vanik, introducing the predecessor to § 504 in the House, described the treatment of the handicapped as one of the country's "shameful oversights," which caused the handicapped to live among society "shunted aside, hidden, and ignored." 117 Cong.Rec. 45974 (1971). Similarly, Senator Humphrey, who introduced a companion measure in the Senate, asserted that "we can no longer tolerate the invisibility of the handicapped in America * * *." 118 Cong.Rec. 525–526 (1972). And Senator Cranston, the Acting Chairman of the Subcommittee that drafted § 504, described the Act as a response to "previous societal neglect." 119 Cong.Rec. 5880, 5883 (1973). See also 118 Cong.Rec. 526 (1972) (statement of cosponsor Sen. Percy) (describing the legislation leading to the 1973 Act as a national commitment to eliminate the "glaring neglect" of the handicapped). Federal agencies and commentators on the plight of the handicapped similarly have found that discrimination against the handicapped is primarily the result of apathetic attitudes rather than affirmative animus.[16]

too facile an assimilation of Title VI law to § 504 must be resisted.

12. To be sure, well-catalogued instances of invidious discrimination against the handicapped do exist. See, e.g., United States Commission on Civil Rights, Accommodating The Spectrum of Individual Abilities, Ch. 2 (1983); Wegner, The Antidis-

crimination Model Reconsidered: Ensuring Equal Opportunity Without Respect to Handicap Under Section 504 of the Rehabilitation Act of 1973, 69 Cornell L.Rev. 401, 403, n. 2 (1984).

16. See, e.g., United States Commission on Civil Rights, Accommodating the Spectrum of Individual Abilities 17 (1983);

In addition, much of the conduct that Congress sought to alter in passing the Rehabilitation Act would be difficult if not impossible to reach were the Act construed to proscribe only conduct fueled by a discriminatory intent. For example, elimination of architectural barriers was one of the central aims of the Act, see, e.g., S.Rep. No. 93–318, p. 4 (1973), U.S.Code Cong. & Admin.News 1973, pp. 2076, 2080, yet such barriers were clearly not erected with the aim or intent of excluding the handicapped. Similarly, Senator Williams, the chairman of the Labor and Public Welfare Committee that reported out § 504, asserted that the handicapped were the victims of "[d]iscrimination in access to public transportation" and "[d]iscrimination because they do not have the simplest forms of special educational and rehabilitation services they need * * *." 118 Cong.Rec. 3320 (1972). And Senator Humphrey, again in introducing the proposal that later became § 504, listed, among the instances of discrimination that the section would prohibit, the use of "transportation and architectural barriers," the "discriminatory effect of job qualification * * * procedures," and the denial of "special educational assistance" for handicapped children. 118 Cong.Rec. 525–526 (1972). These statements would ring hollow if the resulting legislation could not rectify the harms resulting from action that discriminated by effect as well as by design.[17]

At the same time, the position urged by respondents—that we interpret § 504 to reach all action disparately affecting the handicapped—is also troubling. Because the handicapped typically are not similarly situated to the nonhandicapped, respondents' position would in essence require each recipient of federal funds first to evaluate the effect on the handicapped of every proposed action that might touch the interests of the handicapped, and then to consider alternatives for achieving the same objectives with less severe disadvantage to the handicapped. The formalization and policing of this process could lead to a wholly unwieldy administrative and adjudicative burden. See Note, Employment Discrimination Against the Handicapped and Section 504 of the Rehabilitation Act: An Essay on Legal Evasiveness, 97 Harv.L.Rev. 997, 1008 (1984) (describing problems with pure disparate impact model in context of employment discrimination against the handicapped). Had Congress intended § 504 to be a National Environ-

---

Note, Accommodating the Handicapped: The Meaning of Discrimination Under Section 504 of the Rehabilitation Act, 55 N.Y. U.L.R. 881, 883 (1980).

17. All the Courts of Appeals that have addressed the issue have agreed that, at least under some circumstances, § 504 reaches disparate-impact discrimination. See, e.g., New Mexico Assn. for Retarded Citizens v. New Mexico, 678 F.2d 847, 854 (CA10 1982); Pushkin v. Regents of University of Colorado, 658 F.2d 1372, 1384–1385 (CA10 1981); Dopico v. Goldschmidt, 687 F.2d 644, 652–653 (CA2 1982); NAACP v. Wilmington Medical Center, 657 F.2d

1322, 1331 (CA3 1981) (en banc); Majors v. Housing Authority of the County of DeKalb, Georgia, 652 F.2d 454, 457–458 (CA5 1981); Jones v. Illinois Dept. of Rehabilitation Services, 689 F.2d 724 (CA7 1982); Stutts v. Freeman, 694 F.2d 666 (CA11 1983); Georgia Assn. of Retarded Citizens v. McDaniel, 716 F.2d 1565, 1578–1580 (CA11 1983), vacated for further consideration in light of Smith v. Robinson, 468 U.S. ___, 104 S.Ct. 3457, 82 L.Ed.2d 746 (1984); 468 U.S. 104 S.Ct. 3581, 82 L.Ed.2d 880 (1984).

At least 24 federal agencies have reached the same conclusion.

mental Policy Act [18] for the handicapped, requiring the preparation of "Handicapped Impact Statements" before any action was taken by a grantee that affected the handicapped, we would expect some indication of that purpose in the statute or its legislative history. Yet there is nothing to suggest that such was Congress' purpose. Thus, just as there is reason to question whether Congress intended § 504 to reach only intentional discrimination, there is similarly reason to question whether Congress intended § 504 to embrace all claims of disparate-impact discrimination.

Any interpretation of § 504 must therefore be responsive to two powerful but countervailing considerations—the need to give effect to the statutory objectives and the desire to keep § 504 within manageable bounds. Given the legitimacy of both of these goals and the tension between them, we decline the parties' invitation to decide today that one of these goals so overshadows the other as to eclipse it. While we reject the boundless notion that all disparate-impact showings constitute prima facie cases under § 504, we assume without deciding that § 504 reaches at least some conduct that has an unjustifiable disparate impact upon the handicapped. On that assumption, we must then determine whether the disparate effect of which respondents complain is the sort of disparate impact that federal law might recognize.

III

To determine which disparate impacts § 504 might make actionable, the proper starting point is Southeastern Community College v. Davis, 442 U.S. 397, 99 S.Ct. 2361, 60 L.Ed.2d 980 (1979), our major previous attempt to define the scope of § 504.[19] *Davis* involved a plaintiff with a major hearing disability who sought admission to a college to be trained as a registered nurse, but who would not be capable of safely performing as a registered nurse even with fulltime personal supervision. We stated that, under some circumstances, a "refusal to modify an existing program might become unreasonable and discriminatory. Identification of those instances where a refusal to accommodate the needs of a disabled person amounts to discrimination against the handicapped [is] an important responsibility of HEW." 442 U.S., at 413, 99 S.Ct., at 2370. We held that the college was not required to admit Davis because it appeared unlikely that she could benefit from any modifications that the relevant HEW regulations required, id., at 409, 99 S.Ct., at 2368, and because the further modifications Davis sought—fulltime, personal supervision whenever she attended patients and elimination of all clinical courses—would have compromised the essential nature of the college's nursing program, id.,

---

18. 42 U.S.C. §§ 4321 et seq.

19. *Davis* addressed that portion of § 504 which requires that a handicapped individual be "otherwise qualified" before the nondiscrimination principle of § 504 becomes relevant. However, the question of who is "otherwise qualified" and what actions constitute "discrimination" under the Section would seem to be two sides of a single coin; the ultimate question is the extent to which a grantee is required to make reasonable modifications in its programs for the needs of the handicapped.

at 413–414, 99 S.Ct., at 2370–2371. Such a "fundamental alteration in the nature of a program" was far more than the reasonable modifications the statute or regulations required. Id., at 410, 99 S.Ct., at 2369. *Davis* thus struck a balance between the statutory rights of the handicapped to be integrated into society and the legitimate interests of federal grantees in preserving the integrity of their programs: while a grantee need not be required to make "fundamental" or "substantial" modifications to accommodate the handicapped, it may be required to make "reasonable" ones. Compare 442 U.S., at 410, 99 S.Ct., at 2369 with id., at 412–413, 99 S.Ct., at 2370.[20]

The balance struck in *Davis* requires that an otherwise qualified handicapped individual must be provided with meaningful access to the benefit that the grantee offers. The benefit itself, of course, cannot be defined in a way that effectively denies otherwise qualified handicapped individuals the meaningful access to which they are entitled; to assure meaningful access, reasonable accommodations in the grantee's program or benefit may have to be made.[21] In this case, respondents argue that the 14-day rule, or any annual durational limitation, denies

20. In *Davis*, we stated that § 504 does not impose an "affirmative-action obligation on all recipients of federal funds." 442 U.S., at 411, 99 S.Ct., at 2369–2370. Our use of the term affirmative action in this context has been severely criticized for failing to appreciate the difference between affirmative action and reasonable accommodation; the former is said to refer to a remedial policy for the victims of past discrimination, while the latter relates to the elimination of existing obstacles against the handicapped. See Note, Accommodating the Handicapped: The Meaning of Discrimination Under Section 504 of the Rehabilitation Act, 55 N.Y.U.L.R. 881, 885–86 (1980); Note, Accommodating the Handicapped: Rehabilitating Section 504 After *Southeastern*, 80 Colum.L.Rev. 171, 185–86 (1980); see also Dopico v. Goldschmidt, 687 F.2d 644, 652 (CA2 1982) ("Use of the phrase 'affirmative action' in this context is unfortunate, making it difficult to talk about any kind of affirmative efforts without importing the special legal and social connotations of that term."). Regardless of the aptness of our choice of words in *Davis*, it is clear from the context of *Davis* that the term affirmative action referred to those "changes," "adjustments," or "modifications" to existing programs that would be "substantial," 442 U.S., at 410, 411, n. 10, 413, 99 S.Ct., at 2369, 2369–2370, n. 10, 2370, or that would constitute "fundamental alteration[s] in the nature of a program * * *," id., at 410, 99 S.Ct., at 2369, rather than to those changes that would be reasonable accommodations.

21. As the Solicitor General states, "Antidiscrimination legislation can obviously be emptied of meaning if every discriminatory policy is 'collapsed' into one's definition of what is the relevant benefit." Brief for the United States As *Amicus Curiae* at 29, n. 36. At oral argument, the government also acknowledged that "special measures for the handicapped, as the *Lau* case shows, may sometimes be necessary * * *." Tr. of Oral Arg. 14–15 (referring to Lau v. Nichols, 414 U.S. 563, 94 S.Ct. 786, 39 L.Ed.2d 1 (1974)).

The regulations implementing § 504 are consistent with the view that reasonable adjustments in the nature of the benefit offered must at times be made to assure meaningful access. See, e.g., 45 CFR § 84.12(a) (1983) (requiring an employer to make "reasonable accommodations to the known physical or mental limitations" of a handicapped individual); 45 CFR § 84.22 and § 84.23 (1983) (requiring that new buildings be readily accessible, building alterations be accessible "to the maximum extent feasible," and existing facilities eventually be operated so that a program or activity inside is, "when viewed in its entirety," readily accessible); 45 CFR § 84.44(a) (1983) (requiring certain modifications to the regular academic programs of secondary education institutions, such as changes in the length of time permitted for the completion of degree requirements, substitution of specific courses required for the completion of degree requirements, and adaptation of the manner in which specific courses are conducted).

meaningful access to Medicaid services in Tennessee. We examine each of these arguments in turn.

A

The 14-day limitation will not deny respondents meaningful access to Tennessee Medicaid services or exclude them from those services. The new limitation does not invoke criteria that have a particular exclusionary effect on the handicapped; the reduction, neutral on its face, does not distinguish between those whose coverage will be reduced and those whose coverage will not on the basis of any test, judgment, or trait that the handicapped as a class are less capable of meeting or less likely of having. Moreover, it cannot be argued that "meaningful access" to state Medicaid services will be denied by the 14-day limitation on inpatient coverage; nothing in the record suggests that the handicapped in Tennessee will be unable to benefit meaningfully from the coverage they will receive under the 14-day rule. The reduction in inpatient coverage will leave both handicapped and nonhandicapped Medicaid users with identical and effective hospital services fully available for their use, with both classes of users subject to the same durational limitation. The 14-day limitation, therefore, does not exclude the handicapped from or deny them the benefits of the 14 days of care the State has chosen to provide. Cf. Jefferson v. Hackney, 406 U.S. 535, 92 S.Ct. 1724, 32 L.Ed.2d 285 (1972).

To the extent respondents further suggest that their greater need for prolonged inpatient care means that, to provide meaningful access to Medicaid services, Tennessee must single out the handicapped for *more* than 14 days of coverage, the suggestion is simply unsound. At base, such a suggestion must rest on the notion that the benefit provided through state Medicaid programs is the amorphous objective of "adequate health care." But Medicaid programs do not guarantee that each recipient will receive that level of health care precisely tailored to his or her particular needs. Instead, the benefit provided through Medicaid is a particular package of health care services, such as 14 days of inpatient coverage. That package of services has the general aim of assuring that individuals will receive necessary medical care, but the benefit provided remains the individual services offered— not "adequate health care."

The federal Medicaid Act makes this point clear. The Act gives the States substantial discretion to choose the proper mix of amount, scope, and duration limitations on coverage, as long as care and services are provided in "the best interests of the recipients." 42 U.S.C. § 1396a(a)(19). The District Court found that the 14-day limitation would fully serve 95% of even handicapped individuals eligible for Tennessee Medicaid, and both lower courts concluded that Tennessee's proposed Medicaid plan would meet the "best interests" standard. That unchallenged conclusion indicates that Tennessee is free, as a matter of the Medicaid Act, to choose to define the benefit it will be providing as 14 days of inpatient coverage.

Section 504 does not require the State to alter this definition of the benefit being offered simply to meet the reality that the handicapped have greater medical needs. To conclude otherwise would be to find that the Rehabilitation Act requires States to view certain illnesses, i.e., those particularly affecting the handicapped, as more important than others and more worthy of cure through government subsidization. Nothing in the legislative history of the Act supports such a conclusion. Cf. Doe v. Colautti, 592 F.2d 704 (CA3 1979) (State may limit covered-private-inpatient-psychiatric care to 60 days even though State sets no limit on duration of coverage for physical illnesses). Section 504 seeks to assure evenhanded treatment and the opportunity for handicapped individuals to participate in and benefit from programs receiving federal assistance. Southeastern Community College v. Davis, 442 U.S. 397, 99 S.Ct. 2361, 60 L.Ed.2d 980 (1979). The Act does not, however, guarantee the handicapped equal results from the provision of state Medicaid, even assuming some measure of equality of health could be constructed. Ibid.

Regulations promulgated by the Department of Health and Human Services (HHS) pursuant to the Act further support this conclusion.[24] These regulations state that recipients of federal funds who provide health services cannot "provide a qualified handicapped person with benefits or services that are not as effective (as defined in § 84.4(b)) as the benefits or services provided to others." 45 CFR § 84.52(a)(3) (1984). The regulations also prohibit a recipient of federal funding from adopting "criteria or methods of administration that have the purpose or effect of defeating or substantially impairing accomplishment of the objectives of the recipient's program with respect to the handicapped." 45 CFR § 84.4(b)(4)(ii) (1984).

While these regulations, read in isolation, could be taken to suggest that a State medicaid program must make the handicapped as healthy as the nonhandicapped, other regulations reveal that HHS does not contemplate imposing such a requirement. Title 45 CFR § 84.4(b)(2) (1984), referred to in the regulations quoted above, makes clear that:

> For purposes of this part, aids, benefits, and services, to be equally effective, are not required to produce the identical result or level of achievement for handicapped and nonhandicapped persons, but must

---

24. We have previously recognized these regulations as an important source of guidance on the meaning of § 504. See Consolidated Rail Corp. v. Darrone, 465 U.S. __, 104 S.Ct. 1248, 79 L.Ed.2d 568 (1984) (holding that 1978 Amendments to the Act were intended to codify the regulations enforcing § 504); Southeastern Community College v. Davis, 442 U.S., at 413, 99 S.Ct., at 2370 ("Identification of those instances where a refusal to accommodate the needs of a disabled person amounts to discrimination against the handicapped person continues to be an important re-

sponsibility of HEW"); see generally Guardians Association v. Civil Service Commission of New York, 463 U.S. 582, 103 S.Ct. 3221, 77 L.Ed.2d 866 (1983). 1974 Amendments to the Act clarified the scope of § 504 by making clear that those charged with administering the Act had substantial leeway to explore areas in which discrimination against the handicapped posed particularly significant problems and to devise regulations to prohibit such discrimination. See, e.g., S.Rep. No. 93–1297, at 40–41, 56 (1974).

afford handicapped persons equal opportunity to obtain the same result, to gain the same benefit, or to reach the same level of achievement * * *. 45 CFR 84.4(b)(2) (1984).

This regulation, while indicating that adjustments to existing programs are contemplated, also makes clear that Tennessee is not required to assure that its handicapped Medicaid users will be as healthy as its nonhandicapped users. Thus, to the extent respondents are seeking a distinct durational limitation for the handicapped, Tennessee is entitled to respond by asserting that the relevant benefit is 14 days of coverage. Because the handicapped have meaningful and equal access to that benefit, Tennessee is not obligated to reinstate its 20-day rule or to provide the handicapped with more than 14 days of inpatient coverage.

B

We turn next to respondents' alternative contention, a contention directed not at the 14-day rule itself but rather at Tennessee's Medicaid *plan* as a whole. Respondents argue that the inclusion of any annual durational limitation on inpatient coverage in a state Medicaid plan violates § 504. The thrust of this challenge is that all annual durational limitations discriminate against the handicapped because (1) the effect of such limitations falls most heavily on the handicapped and because (2) this harm could be avoided by the choice of other Medicaid plans that would meet the State's budgetary constraints without disproportionately disadvantaging the handicapped. Viewed in this light, Tennessee's current plan is said to inflict a gratuitous harm on the handicapped that denies them meaningful access to Medicaid services.

Whatever the merits of this conception of meaningful access, it is clear that § 504 does not require the changes respondents seek. In enacting the Rehabilitation Act and in subsequent amendments, Congress did focus on several substantive areas—employment,[28] education, and the elimination of physical barriers to access—in which it considered the societal and personal costs of refusals to provide meaningful access to the handicapped to be particularly high. But nothing in the pre- or post-1973 legislative discussion of § 504 suggests that Congress desired to make major inroads on the States' longstanding discretion to choose the proper mix of amount, scope, and duration limitations on services covered by state Medicaid, see Beal v. Doe, 432 U.S. 438, 444, 97 S.Ct. 2366, 2370, 53 L.Ed.2d 464 (1977). And, more generally, we have already stated, supra, at 719–720, that § 504 does not impose a general NEPA-like requirement on federal grantees.

The costs of such a requirement would be far from minimal, and thus Tennessee's refusal to pursue this course does not, as respondents suggest, inflict a "gratuitous" harm on the handicapped. On the contrary, to require that the sort of broad-based distributive decision at

28. "The primary goal of the Act is to increase employment." Consolidated Rail Corp. v. Darrone, 465 U.S., at ___, n. 13, 104 S.Ct., at 1254, n. 13. See also 29 U.S.C. § 701(11) (1976 ed.).

issue in this case always be made in the way most favorable, or least disadvantageous, to the handicapped, even when the same benefit is meaningfully and equally offered to them, would be to impose a virtually unworkable requirement on state Medicaid administrators. Before taking any across-the-board action affecting Medicaid recipients, an analysis of the effect of the proposed change on the handicapped would have to be prepared. Presumably, that analysis would have to be further broken down by class of handicap—the change at issue here, for example, might be significantly less harmful to the blind, who use inpatient services only minimally, than to other subclasses of handicapped Medicaid recipients; the State would then have to balance the harms and benefits to various groups to determine, on balance, the extent to which the action disparately impacts the handicapped. In addition, respondents offer no reason that similar treatment would not have to be accorded other groups protected by statute or regulation from disparate-impact discrimination.

It should be obvious that administrative costs of implementing such a regime would be well beyond the accommodations that are required under *Davis*. As a result, Tennessee need not redefine its Medicaid program to eliminate durational limitations on inpatient coverage, even if in doing so the State could achieve its immediate fiscal objectives in a way less harmful to the handicapped.

IV

The 14-day rule challenged in this case is neutral on its face, is not alleged to rest on a discriminatory motive, and does not deny the handicapped access to or exclude them from the particular package of Medicaid services Tennessee has chosen to provide. The State has made the same benefit—14 days of coverage—equally accessible to both handicapped and nonhandicapped persons, and the State is not required to assure the handicapped "adequate health care" by providing them with more coverage than the nonhandicapped. In addition, the State is not obligated to modify its Medicaid program by abandoning reliance on annual durational limitations on inpatient coverage. Assuming, then, that § 504 or its implementing regulations reach some claims of disparate-impact discrimination, the effect of Tennessee's reduction in annual inpatient coverage is not among them. For that reason, the Court of Appeals erred in holding that respondents had established a prima facie violation of § 504. The judgment below is accordingly reversed.

It is so ordered.

D. REASONABLE ACCOMMODATION

STRATHIE v. DEPARTMENT OF TRANSPORTATION

United States Court of Appeals for the Third Circuit, 1983.
716 F.2d 227.

SEITZ, CHIEF JUDGE.

James Strathie appeals an order of the district court granting judgment in favor of appellees in his civil rights suit after a final hearing.

I.

The district court found the following facts, which are undisputed on appeal. Appellant Strathie was hired and trained as a school bus driver by Van Trans, Inc., a private bus company which provides transportation for students in certain Pennsylvania public school districts. After completing his training, Strathie took and passed the school bus driver's license test required by the Pennsylvania Department of Transportation. Strathie was issued a Class 4 license, which authorized him to drive a school bus.

After working for Van Trans as a school bus driver for one day, Strathie was notified by the Department of Transportation that his Class 4 license was suspended indefinitely and until his competency was established. The reason for the suspension was that Strathie wore a hearing aid, in violation of one of the Department's regulations, 67 Pa. Code § 71.3(b)(5). This regulation provides that in order to obtain a school bus driver's license, an applicant must have "[n]o hearing loss greater than 25 decibels at frequencies of 500, 1,000, and 2,000 in the better ear, without a hearing aid." The regulation was formulated by the Medical Advisory Board of the Department of Transportation, and adopted by the Department effective July 1, 1970.

At the time his school bus driver's license was suspended, Strathie was in every respect other than his hearing, qualified under Department of Transportation regulations to continue to be licensed to drive a school bus. With the use of his hearing aid, Strathie's hearing is corrected within the decibel requirements of 67 Pa.Code § 71.3(b)(5).

II.

In enacting and amending section 504 of the Rehabilitation Act, Congress "made a commitment to the handicapped, that, to the maximum extent possible they shall be fully integrated into the mainstream of life in America." S.Rep. No. 890, 95th Cong., 2d Sess. 39 (1978). Section 504 provides, in pertinent part, that:

No otherwise qualified handicapped individual * * * shall, solely by reason of his handicap, be excluded from the participation in, be denied the benefits of, or be subjected to discrimination under any program or activity receiving Federal financial assistance. * * *

29 U.S.C. § 794. Section 504 creates a private right of action in favor of persons who allege to have been subjected to illegal discrimination based on handicap.

In order to make out a case under section 504 of the Rehabilitation Act, a plaintiff must prove (1) that he is a "handicapped individual" under the Act, (2) that he is "otherwise qualified" for the position sought, (3) that he was excluded from the position sought solely by reason of his handicap, and (4) that the program or activity in question receives federal financial assistance.

It is undisputed that Strathie is a handicapped person, and that his license was suspended solely by reason of his handicap. With regard to federal funding, the parties have stipulated that both the Pennsylvania Department of Transportation and the Department of Education receive federal financial assistance. Thus, the school bus driver licensing program qualifies as a recipient of federal funds for purposes of section 504, regardless of whether any of the federal funding in question is earmarked for that program.

Thus, the principal issue presented in this appeal is whether Strathie is "otherwise qualified" to be a school bus driver. Strathie bears the ultimate burden of proof as to this issue.

A.

In Southwestern Community College v. Davis, 442 U.S. 397, 99 S.Ct. 2361, 60 L.Ed.2d 980 (1979), the United States Supreme Court held that an "otherwise qualified" handicapped individual is one who can meet all of a program's requirements in spite of his handicap. In dictum, however, the Court indicated that an individual may be "otherwise qualified" in some instances even though he cannot meet all of a program's requirements. This is the case when the refusal to modify an existing program to accommodate the handicapped individual would be unreasonable, and thereby discriminatory. Id. at 412–13, 99 S.Ct. at 2370.

In Davis, the Supreme Court indicated that two factors pertain to the reasonableness of a refusal to accommodate a handicapped individual. First, requiring accommodation is unreasonable if it would necessitate modification of the essential nature of the program. Second, requiring accommodation is unreasonable if it would place undue burdens, such as extensive costs, on the recipient of federal funds.

Notably absent from the Supreme Court's opinion in Davis, however, is any discussion of the scope of judicial review with regard to the reasonableness of a refusal to accommodate a handicapped individual. Program administrators surely are entitled to some measure of judicial deference in this matter, by reason of their experience with and knowledge of the program in question. On the other hand, broad judicial deference resembling that associated with the "rational basis" test would substantially undermine Congress' intent in enacting section 504 that stereotypes or generalizations not deny handicapped individuals equal access to federally-funded programs.

We believe the following standard effectively reconciles these competing considerations: A handicapped individual who cannot meet all of a program's requirements is not otherwise qualified if there is a factual basis in the record reasonably demonstrating that accommodating that individual would require either a modification of the essential nature of the program, or impose an undue burden on the recipient of federal funds.

In the present case, it is undisputed that Strathie cannot meet all the requirements necessary to obtain a school bus driver's license because he wears a hearing aid. Strathie contends that he is otherwise qualified to obtain this type of license because the Department of Transportation's refusal to accommodate him is unreasonable. The Department's response is that, for several reasons, no hearing aid wearer can be issued a school bus driver's license without jeopardizing the essential purpose of the school bus driver licensing program.[7]

B.

The first step in resolving this dispute must be to ascertain the essential nature of the school bus driver licensing program. The district court held that the essence of the licensing program is to ensure that school bus drivers are able to provide control over and safety to school bus passengers. The Department contends, however, that the purpose of the licensing program is not only to provide for the safety of school bus passengers, but to ensure the highest level of safety. The Department views its responsibility under the program as requiring it to eliminate as many potential safety risks as it can.

Although we fully appreciate the Department's concern for the safety and discipline of school bus passengers, we believe the Department's characterization of the essential nature of its licensing program is overbroad. In our view, the essential nature of the program is to prevent any and all *appreciable* risks that a school bus driver will be unable to provide for the control over and safety of his passengers. For example, we note that the Department allows the granting of school bus driver's licenses to individuals who must wear eyeglasses in order to meet Department vision standards. If such a person's eyeglasses were to be removed, either voluntarily or involuntarily, while he was driving a school bus, he would certainly present a danger to the safety of his passengers. That such an individual is allowed to obtain a school

---

7. Implicit in the modifications proposed by Strathie in rebuttal to the Department's safety concerns is that the Department will have to conduct, at least in some cases, individualized examinations of hearing aid wearers who apply for a school bus driver's license. The Department does not argue in this appeal that such individualized examinations, or any of the program modifications suggested by Strathie, would place an undue burden on the Department. See Southeastern Community College v. Davis, 442 U.S. at 412, 99 S.Ct. at 2370.

bus driver's license indicates that the Department views some safety risks as too remote to justify the denial of a school bus driver's license.

Department of Transportation Regulations concerning other physical disabilities confirm our description of the essential purpose of the school bus driver licensing program. For example, several physical ailments will prevent an individual from obtaining such a license only if the ailment is "*likely* to interfere with the ability to drive a school bus with safety." 67 Pa.Code § 71.3(b). These ailments include (1) color blindness, (2) respiratory disfunctions, (3) rheumatic, arthritic, orthopedic, muscular or neuromuscular disease, and (4) mental, nervous, organic or functional diseases. Id. Similarly, the Department's regulations authorize the Medical Advisory Board to waive the requirement that a school bus driver applicant have no loss or impairment of the use of any foot, leg, arm, hand, fingers or thumb "upon determining that the impairment will not interfere with the ability of the driver to drive a school bus with safety." 67 Pa.Code § 71.3(b)(2).

Having thus identified the essential nature of the Department's licensing program, we are prepared to address the Department's several reasons why an accommodation of hearing aid wearers would be inconsistent with this purpose. First, the Department points out that hearing aids can become dislodged. Therefore, the Department argues that even if an individual could meet the minimum hearing level standards prescribed in 67 Pa.Code § 71.3(b)(5) with the use of a hearing aid, there is an appreciable danger that he may lose the hearing aid and thus be unable to provide for the safety and control of his passengers.

Strathie responds by suggesting that the Department could require hearing-impaired school bus drivers to wear an eyeglass type of hearing aid, such as he wears. This type of hearing aid is built into the temples of a person's eyeglasses, and is fitted tightly against the bone over the ear. There is record evidence, in the form of depositions from experts Leidy and Jewell, that this type of hearing aid is less likely to become dislodged than are regular eyeglasses. App. 163, 213. Based on this evidence, and the fact that the Department allows eyeglass wearers to obtain school bus driver's licenses, Strathie argues that a school bus driver who wears this type of hearing aid is not so likely to have it dislodged that he poses an appreciable risk to the safety of his passengers.

The district court accepted the Department's reliance on the risk of hearing aid dislodgement without addressing Strathie's proposed modification. Given the considerations noted above, we cannot say at this stage that a reasonable fact finder would have no alternative but to find a factual basis in the record reasonably demonstrating that Strathie's proposal would require a modification of the essential purpose of the licensing program. Thus, we cannot affirm the district court on the basis of risk of dislodgement.

Second, the Department of Transportation points out that a hearing aid, like any other active mechanical device, is subject to sudden mechanical failure. This might occur, for example, if a hearing aid battery were to wear out. The Department argues that there is an appreciable risk that the mechanical failure of a hearing aid may endanger the wearer's ability to provide for the control and safety of school bus passengers.

Strathie rejoins that the Department could eliminate all appreciable risk of mechanical failure by requiring a periodic inspection of hearing aids. Similarly, Strathie says the Department could require each user to purchase an inexpensive battery tester, app. 157–58 (Jewell deposition), and to check the power and operability of his hearing aid before each school bus trip.

Strathie also contends that the Department could adopt regulations which would eliminate any appreciable risk that, even were a hearing aid to fail suddenly, the user would lose control over his passengers or endanger their safety. For example, Strathie says the Department could require hearing aid wearers to carry a spare aid and extra batteries. If a hearing aid were to fail suddenly, Strathie argues, neither the process of replacing the aid or its batteries, nor the time spent in so doing would jeopardize the driver's ability to provide for the control over and safety of his passengers to an appreciable extent.

The district court accepted the Department's reliance on the mechanical failure argument without addressing any of the possible modifications suggested by Strathie. We cannot at this stage say that a reasonable fact finder would have no choice but to find these modifications unreasonable, under the standard we have set forth. Therefore, we cannot affirm the district court on this ground.

Third, the Department argues that hearing aid wearers cannot be accommodated into the school bus driver licensing program because those individuals may turn the volume of their hearing aids down or off. The Department relies on the depositions of experts who say that in noisy situations, such as on a school bus, hearing aid wearers have an incentive to reduce the volume of their aids. Strathie responds that the Department could require hearing aid wearers to purchase and use a hearing aid with a pre-set volume that cannot be routinely altered. See App. 160 (Jewell deposition); App. 207 (Leidy deposition).

The district court accepted the Department's hearing aid turn-off argument, based on expert testimony that there is no way to test whether a school bus driver will turn off his hearing aid. Obviously, this argument does not pertain to Strathie's proposal that hearing aid wearers be required to use aids the volume of which can be pre-set. The district court did not comment on this proposed modification. Given the existence of the Jewell and Leidy depositions in the record, we cannot say at this stage that a reasonable fact finder would have to conclude that Strathie's proposed modification would not alleviate any and all appreciable risks that hearing impaired school bus drivers would turn off their hearing aids. Therefore, we cannot affirm the district court on this ground.

Finally, the Department contends that the inability of hearing aid wearers to localize sound may render them unable to provide for the safety and control of their passengers in certain situations. In response, Strathie proposes that the Department could require hearing aid wearers to purchase and use a stereo hearing aid, similar to the type that he uses. There is expert testimony in the record that, at least for some hearing impaired individuals, a stereo hearing aid totally cures the problem of sound localization. App. 120–21 (Cole deposition); App. 203 (Leidy deposition). Moreover, there is expert testimony that audiological testing can identify which hearing-impaired individuals can localize sound with the use of stereo hearing aids, and which cannot. App. 115 (Cole deposition); App. 188 (Leidy deposition).

The district court held that accommodating wearers of stereo hearing aids within the school bus driver licensing program would require a modification of the essential purpose of the program, for two reasons. First, the court said that stereo hearing aid wearers would not be able to localize sound if the volume control for one side were set higher than for the other. In our view, this objection is no different than the Department's "turn-off" argument. Therefore, we cannot rely on this aspect of the court's holding as grounds for affirmance.

Second, the district court said that "[a]lthough [a stereo] type of hearing aid undoubtedly enables the wearer to localize sound better than other types, the wearer still may not be able to distinguish the direction from which sound comes as well as a person with normal hearing." This statement is ambiguous. On the one hand, the statement may mean that although some wearers could localize sound with the use of stereo hearing aids as well as a person with normal hearing, others could not. We are not free to affirm on this ground, because the district court failed to address Strathie's contention that mandatory audiological testing would reveal which stereo hearing aid wearers would be able to localize sound sufficiently well, and which would not.

On the other hand, the district court could have meant to say that no wearer of stereo hearing aids can localize sound as well as a normal person. We have three difficulties with this conclusion. First, we are not convinced that the deposition of Dr. Cole supports the district court's conclusion. Although Dr. Cole's deposition says that stereo hearing aids do not "always compensate" with regard to sound localization, Dr. Cole does not state whether a stereo hearing aid compensates fully for some hearing-impaired individuals but not for others, or whether that type of hearing aid does not fully compensate any hearing-impaired individual's sound localization difficulties. App. 117–18.

Second, even if Dr. Cole's deposition could be read to say that a stereo hearing aid does not fully cure the sound localization difficulties of any hearing aid wearer, there is testimony from expert Leidy which is clearly to the contrary. App. 203. Because the district court's opinion does not refer to the Leidy deposition, we cannot be certain that the court took this evidence into account in evaluating the sound localization question.

Finally, we are not at all satisfied that the proper question with regard to sound localization is whether an individual wearer of stereo hearing aids can localize sound as well as a normal person. Instead, we believe the correct statement of the issue is whether there is a factual basis in the record reasonably demonstrating that accommodating a wearer of a stereo hearing aid would present an appreciable risk to the safety and control of school bus passengers if permitted to drive school buses. Therefore, for all of the above reasons, we cannot accept the Department's sound localization argument as grounds for affirmance.

III.

We will vacate the district court's judgment and remand for further proceedings.

VICKERS v. VETERANS ADMINISTRATION

United States District Court for the W.D. Washington, 1982.
549 F.Supp. 85.

VOORHEES, DISTRICT JUDGE.

From the credible evidence presented at the trial of this cause, the Court now renders the following decision:

1. The issues before this Court are these: * * *

5. The question then remains as to whether plaintiff is entitled to any kind of relief against the Veterans Administration as a handicapped person under the Rehabilitation Act of 1973, as amended, 29 U.S.C. § 794. The Court ruled prior to trial that § 794 does permit a private right of action for damages or for equitable relief.

6. The Court finds that plaintiff is a handicapped person within the meaning of the term "handicapped person" as defined in 29 U.S.C. § 706(7)(B). That subsection provides that any person is a "handicapped" person within the contemplation of 29 U.S.C. § 794 if that person has a physical impairment which substantially limits one or more of his or her major life activities. It appears from the evidence in this cause that plaintiff is unusually sensitive to tobacco smoke and that this hypersensitivity does in fact limit at least one of his major life activities, that is, his capacity to work in an environment which is not completely smoke free.

7. The finding by the Court that plaintiff is a handicapped person within the meaning of the Act does not, however, dispose of this matter. In order for the Court to find that plaintiff is entitled to recover money damages from the Veterans Administration or that plaintiff is entitled to some kind of equitable relief, the Court must find that the Veterans Administration discriminated against plaintiff by reason of his handicap. * * *

12. Plaintiff asserts, however, that he has been discriminated against because of the failure of the Veterans Administration "to make reasonable accommodations to his physical handicap by providing a work environment that is free of tobacco smoke."

13. Plaintiff has failed to cite any authority from the decided cases to the effect that the Veterans Administration was under a duty to make "reasonable accommodations" to plaintiff's sensitivity to tobacco smoke. Assuming, but not deciding, that the Veterans Administration was under such a duty, the Court finds from the evidence that the Veterans Administration did make reasonable efforts to accommodate to plaintiff's handicap.

14. Plaintiff is employed in the Purchasing and Contracts Section of the Supply Service Department at the Veterans Administration Medical Center. The employees in that section have their desks in Room 105–C in Building 15. This building is a temporary one. It is contemplated that within two years all of the Supply Service employees will be moved out of that building and into new quarters in a building now under construction. Ten employees have their desks in Room 105–C. Some of them smoke; some do not. Room 105–C is relatively quite crowded as there are more desks and more employees in that room than the available space can comfortably accommodate. In that room are seven windows, which can be opened and closed, and one double door. This double door may be opened or "cracked" to admit fresh air. Two rather large circulating fans are located in this room.

15. Immediately adjacent to Room 105–C is Room 105–D in which are located those employees who are in the Personal Property Management Section of the Supply Service Department. There are eight employees in this section. Some of these employees smoke; some do not.

16. In February, 1979 the Deputy Administrator of the Veterans Administration at the direction of the Administrator promulgated a nationwide policy relative to smoking at the facilities of the Veterans Administration. One of the provisions of that policy was as follows:

> In establishing and continuing a smoking policy in work areas under their jurisdiction, supervisors should strive to maintain an equitable balance between the rights of smokers and nonsmokers.

17. In February, 1980 the Director of the Veterans Administration Medical Center in Seattle promulgated a policy relative to smoking in the facility. That policy provided that smoking was to be permitted in office areas. By virtue of that promulgated policy employees were permitted to smoke in Rooms 105–C and 105–D.

18. From time to time plaintiff has made known to his superiors his sensitivity to tobacco smoke and has urged that action be taken by them to make it possible for him to work in a smoke-free environment.

19. In an effort to accommodate to plaintiff's handicap the following has been done by the Veterans Administration:

(a) After plaintiff's initial complaint the desks of smokers were physically separated in the office from the desks of the non-smokers.

(b) Thereafter Mr. Radke sought and was able to secure a voluntary agreement by those who work in the same office as plaintiff (Room 105–C) not to smoke at any time in that room.

(c) Later, Mr. Radke sought and was able to secure a voluntary agreement by those who work in Room 105–D, the office adjacent to Room 105–C, that they would not smoke at any time in that room.

(d) Mr. Radke submitted a requisition for an exhaust system to be installed in Room 105–C in the hope that this system would remove whatever tobacco smoke might drift into Room 105–C from rooms where smoking was still permitted. This request was, however, turned down by the Engineering Department because its cost was considered to be excessive in light of the fact that Building 15 was only a temporary building and the employees in Supply Service were to be transferred from that building to a new building.

(e) Mr. Radke was able to have two vents installed in the ceiling of Room 105–C in an effort to withdraw from that room any tobacco smoke that might drift into it from other areas.

(f) Mr. Radke purchased at his own expense an air purifier in an effort to alleviate the effects of his smoking in his own private office, Room 105–B.

(g) Mr. Radke offered to have a partition constructed around plaintiff's desk. This partition would have extended from floor to ceiling and have a door.

(h) Plaintiff was given the opportunity to move his desk farther away from the door leading from Room 105–C to 105–D and closer to a window.

(i) Plaintiff has been offered an outside maintenance job by defendant Veterans Administration.

20. The voluntary action by the smokers in Rooms 105–C and 105–D has significantly reduced the presence of tobacco smoke in plaintiff's work space in Room 105–C.

21. At the time plaintiff complained to his supervisor about the adverse effects of tobacco smoke upon his health, Mr. Radke was faced with the problem of trying to accommodate the desires of plaintiff with the desires of the smokers whose desks were in Rooms 105–C and 105–D. It appears from the testimony of plaintiff that some of those individuals were "heavy" or "very heavy" smokers. Under the national policy of the Veterans Administration he was under a duty to "strive to maintain an equitable balance between the rights of smokers and nonsmokers." In light of the policy promulgated by the Director of the Veterans Administration Medical Center in Seattle that smoking was

to be permitted in offices, Mr. Radke could not have ordered that there be no smoking in Rooms 105–C and 105–D without running into the objection by the smokers in those rooms that they were permitted by the Director's policy to smoke at their desks and that Mr. Radke did not have the authority to override that policy. He was faced, too, with the problem that some of the employees in Room 105–C wanted to have the windows open; some insisted that they be closed. Some wanted the temperature of the room relatively high; some wanted it relatively low. These opposing attitudes made it, of course, difficult to arrive at a mutually satisfactory arrangement with respect to whether the windows would be open or closed.

22. The only tobacco smoke to which plaintiff is now exposed is that which may at times drift into Room 105–C from Room 105–A or 105–B. This drifting in of smoke is not a constant phenomenon and, when it does occur, the smoke is normally not heavy in concentration. At the time of the voluntary commitments by the smokers in Rooms 105–C or 105–D, and as an accommodation to them in exchange for their agreeing not to smoke at their desks, Mr. Radke gave them permission to smoke in Room 105–A, the office of the Assistant Chief of Supply Service, or, when on business, to smoke in his own office, Room 105–B.

23. In light of all of the foregoing the Court finds that the Veterans Administration did make a reasonable effort to accommodate to plaintiff's handicap while at the same time attempting to accommodate to those who felt the need to smoke during working hours.

24. Plaintiff would like to have everyone in Supply Service be forbidden to smoke in order that he would not be exposed at any time to tobacco smoke. The Director of the Medical Center has not, however, banned smoking in any of the office spaces of the Center. The Veterans Administration has not adopted a policy against smoking in any of its offices. Congress has not enacted any legislation which forbids smoking in office working spaces in any of the office buildings owned by the United States.

25. Had Congress enacted legislation or the Veterans Administration adopted a policy or the Director of the Medical Center promulgated a directive forbidding the smoking of tobacco in any office space, this Court would readily enforce that ban. In the absence, however, of a statute or regulation forbidding the smoking of tobacco in government office spaces those Supply Service employees who smoke have certain rights which must be balanced against the desire of plaintiff that his working environment be completely free of tobacco smoke. Until and unless Congress enacts a statute banning the smoking of tobacco in government offices or the Veterans Administration promulgates a policy against smoking in its offices, the desires of those employees who wish to smoke cannot be disregarded.

26. In order to minimize the effect of tobacco smoke upon himself, plaintiff must himself take action to avoid his exposure to tobacco

smoke. It appears that plaintiff can at any time close the door which separates Room 105–C from 105–D and that this would have the effect of preventing the entrance into Room 105–C of any smoke which might drift out of Room 105–A or 105–B. Although it is somewhat of an inconvenience and perhaps a nuisance to close that door, it appears to the Court that plaintiff would choose to do that rather than to have himself exposed to the tobacco smoke to which he is sensitive. There is no prohibition against the closing of that door, and the Chief of the Purchasing and Contracts Section testified that it was immaterial to him whether that door was kept in a closed or an open position.

27. In addition the desk of plaintiff is located but one desk away from the door which separates Rooms 105–C and 105–D. Plaintiff was advised that he could move his desk farther away from that door and closer to a window if he desired to do so, but he has chosen to have his desk remain in its present position. The Court is of the opinion that moving his desk would undoubtedly reduce his exposure to smoke.

28. By reason of the foregoing the Court finds that plaintiff is not entitled to injunctive relief nor to damages as against defendant Veterans Administration.

29. This Memorandum Decision will be in lieu of formal findings of fact and conclusions of law.

E. REMEDY AGAINST THE STATE

ATASCADERO STATE HOSPITAL v. SCANLON

Supreme Court of the United States, 1985.
___ U.S. ___, 105 S.Ct. 3142, 87 L.Ed.2d 171.

JUSTICE POWELL delivered the opinion of the Court.

This case presents the question whether States and state agencies are subject to suit in federal court by litigants seeking retroactive monetary relief under § 504 of the Rehabilitation Act of 1973, 29 U.S.C. § 794, or whether such suits are proscribed by the Eleventh Amendment.

II

The Eleventh Amendment provides: "The Judicial power of the United States shall not be construed to extend to any suit in law or equity, commenced or prosecuted against one of the United States by Citizens of another State, or by Citizens or Subjects of any Foreign State." As we have recognized, the significance of this Amendment "lies in its affirmation that the fundamental principle of sovereign immunity limits the grant of judicial authority in Article III" of the Constitution. Pennhurst State School & Hospital v. Halderman, 465 U.S. 89, ___, 104 S.Ct. 900, 906, 79 L.Ed.2d 67 (1984) (Pennhurst II). Thus, in Hans v. Louisiana, 134 U.S. 1, 10 S.Ct. 504, 33 L.Ed. 842 (1890), the Court held that the Amendment barred a citizen from bringing a suit against his own State in federal court, even though the express terms of the Amendment do not so provide.

There are, however, certain well-established exceptions to the reach of the Eleventh Amendment. For example, if a State waives its immunity and consents to suit in federal court, the Eleventh Amendment does not bar the action. See, e.g., Clark v. Barnard, 108 U.S. 436, 447, 2 S.Ct. 878, 883, 27 L.Ed. 780 (1883). Moreover, the Eleventh Amendment is "necessarily limited by the enforcement provisions of § 5 of the Fourteenth Amendment," that is, by Congress' power "to enforce, by appropriate legislation, the substantive provisions of the Fourteenth Amendment." Fitzpatrick v. Bitzer, 427 U.S. 445, 456, 96 S.Ct. 2666, 2671, 49 L.Ed.2d 614 (1976). As a result, when acting pursuant to § 5 of the Fourteenth Amendment, Congress can abrogate the Eleventh Amendment without the States' consent. Ibid.

But because the Eleventh Amendment implicates the fundamental constitutional balance between the Federal Government and the States, this Court consistently has held that these exceptions apply only when certain specific conditions are met. Thus, we have held that a State will be deemed to have waived its immunity "only where stated 'by the most express language or by such overwhelming implication from the text as [will] leave no room for any other reasonable construction.' " Edelman v. Jordan, supra, 415 U.S., at 673, 94 S.Ct., at 1361, quoting Murray v. Wilson Distilling Co., 213 U.S. 151, 171, 29 S.Ct. 458, 464, 53 L.Ed. 742 (1909). Likewise, in determining whether Congress in exercising its Fourteenth Amendment powers has abrogated the States' Eleventh Amendment immunity, we have required "an unequivocal expression of congressional intent to 'overturn the constitutionally guaranteed immunity of the several States.' " *Pennhurst II*, supra, 465 U.S., at ___, 104 S.Ct., at 907, quoting Quern v. Jordan, 440 U.S. 332, 342, 99 S.Ct. 1139, 1146, 59 L.Ed.2d 358 (1979).

IV

Respondents also contend that in enacting the Rehabilitation Act, Congress abrogated the States' constitutional immunity. In making this argument, respondent relies on the pre- and post-enactment legislative history of the Act and inferences from general statutory language. To reach respondent's conclusion, we would have to temper the requirement, well established in our cases, that Congress unequivocally express its intention to abrogate the Eleventh Amendment bar to suits against the States in federal court. *Pennhurst II*, 465 U.S., at ___, 104 S.Ct., at ___; Quern v. Jordan, supra, 440 U.S., at 342–345, 99 S.Ct., at 1145–1147. We decline to do so, and affirm that Congress may abrogate the States' constitutionally secured immunity from suit in federal court only by making its intention unmistakably clear in the language of the statute. The fundamental nature of the interests implicated by the Eleventh Amendment dictates this conclusion.

Only recently the Court reiterated that "the States occupy a special and specific position in our constitutional system. * * *" Garcia v.

San Antonio Metropolitan Transit Authority, 469 U.S. ___, ___, 105 S.Ct. 1005, 1020, 83 L.Ed.2d 1016 (1985). The "constitutionally mandated balance of power" between the States and the Federal Government was adopted by the Framers to ensure the protection of "our fundamental liberties." Id., at ___, 105 S.Ct., at 1029 (POWELL, J., dissenting). By guaranteeing the sovereign immunity of the States against suit in federal court, the Eleventh Amendment serves to maintain this balance. "Our reluctance to infer that a State's immunity from suit in the federal courts has been negated stems from recognition of the vital role of the doctrine of sovereign immunity in our federal system." *Pennhurst II,* supra, 465 U.S., at ___, 104 S.Ct., at 907.

Congress' power to abrogate a State's immunity means that in certain circumstances the usual constitutional balance between the States and Federal Government does not obtain. "Congress may, in determining what is 'appropriate legislation' for the purpose of enforcing the provisions of the Fourteenth Amendment, provide for private suits against States or state officials which are constitutionally impermissible in other contexts." *Fitzpatrick,* 427 U.S., at 456, 96 S.Ct., at 2671. In view of this fact, it is incumbent upon the federal courts to be certain of Congress' intent before finding that federal law overrides the guarantees of the Eleventh Amendment. The requirement that Congress unequivocally express this intention in the statutory language ensures such certainty.

It is also significant that in determining whether Congress has abrogated the States' Eleventh Amendment immunity, the courts themselves must decide whether their own jurisdiction has been expanded. Although it is of course the duty of this Court "to say what the law is," Marbury v. Madison, 1 Cranch 137, 177, 2 L.Ed. 60 (1803), it is appropriate that we rely only on the clearest indications in holding that Congress has enhanced our power. See American Fire & Cas. Co. v. Finn, 341 U.S. 6, 17, 71 S.Ct. 534, 542, 95 L.Ed. 702 (1951) ("The jurisdiction of the federal courts is carefully guarded against expansion by judicial interpretation * * *").

For these reasons, we hold consistent with *Quern, Edelman,* and *Pennhurst II,*—that Congress must express its intention to abrogate the Eleventh Amendment in unmistakable language in the statute itself.

In light of this principle, we must determine whether Congress, in adopting the Rehabilitation Act, has chosen to override the Eleventh Amendment.[4] Section 504 of the Rehabilitation Act provides in pertinent part:

4. Petitioners assert that the Rehabilitation Act of 1973 does not represent an exercise of Congress' Fourteenth Amendment authority, but was enacted pursuant to the Spending Clause, Art. I, § 8, cl. 1. Petitioners conceded below, however, that the Rehabilitation Act was passed pursuant to § 5 of the Fourteenth Amendment. Thus, we first analyze § 504 in light of Congress' power under the Fourteenth Amendment to subject unconsenting States to federal court jurisdiction. See Fitzpatrick v. Bitzer, 427 U.S. 445, 96 S.Ct. 2666, 49 L.Ed.2d 614 (1976). In Part V, infra, at 3150, we address the reasoning of the Court of Appeals and conclude that by accepting funds under the Act, the State

No otherwise qualified handicapped individual in the United States, as defined in section 706(7) of this title, shall, solely by reason of his handicap, be excluded from the participation in, be denied the benefits of, or be subjected to discrimination under any program or activity receiving Federal financial assistance or under any program or activity conducted by any Executive agency or by the United States Postal Service. 87 Stat. 394, as amended, 29 U.S.C. § 794.

Section 505, which was added to the Act in 1978, describes, as set forth in 29 U.S.C. § 794a, the available remedies under the Act, including the provisions pertinent to this case:

(a)(2) The remedies, procedures, and rights set forth in title VI of the Civil Rights Act of 1964 [42 U.S.C. 2000d et seq.] shall be available to any person aggrieved by any act or failure to act by any recipient of Federal assistance or Federal provider of such assistance under section 794 of this title.

(b) In any action or proceeding to enforce or charge a violation of a provision of this subchapter, the court, in its discretion, may allow the prevailing party, other than the United States, a reasonable attorney's fee as part of the costs.

The statute thus provides remedies for violations of § 504 by "*any* recipient of Federal assistance." There is no claim here that the State of California is not a recipient of federal aid under the statute. But given their constitutional role, the States are not like any other class of recipients of federal aid. A general authorization for suit in federal court is not the kind of unequivocal statutory language sufficient to abrogate the Eleventh Amendment. When Congress chooses to subject the States to federal jurisdiction, it must do so specifically. *Pennhurst II*, 465 U.S., at ___, 104 S.Ct., at ___, citing Quern v. Jordan, 440 U.S. 332, 99 S.Ct. 1139, 59 L.Ed.2d 358 (1979). Accordingly, we hold that the Rehabilitation Act does not abrogate the Eleventh Amendment bar to suits against the States.

V

Finally, we consider the position adopted by the Court of Appeals that the State consented to suit in federal court by accepting funds under the Rehabilitation Act.[5] 735 F.2d, at 361–362. In reaching this conclusion, the Court of Appeals relied on "the extensive provisions [of the Act] under which the states are the express intended recipients of federal assistance." Id., at 360. It reasoned that "this is a case in which a 'congressional enactment * * * by its terms authorized suit by designated plaintiffs against a general class of defendants which literally included States or state instrumentalities,' and 'the State by its participation in the program authorized by Congress had in effect

did not "implicitly consent[ ] to be sued * * *." 735 F.2d, at 362.

5. Although the Court of Appeals seemed to state that the Rehabilitation Act was adopted pursuant to § 5 of the Four-

teenth Amendment, by focusing on whether the State consented to federal jurisdiction it engaged in analysis relevant to Spending Clause enactments.

consented to the abrogation of that immunity,' " id., at 361; citing Edelman v. Jordan, 415 U.S., at 672, 94 S.Ct., at 1360. The Court of Appeals thus concluded that if the State "has participated in and received funds from programs under the Rehabilitation Act, [it] has implicitly consented to be sued as a recipient under 29 U.S.C. § 794." 735 F.2d, at 362.

The court properly recognized that the mere receipt of federal funds cannot establish that a State has consented to suit in federal court. Ibid., citing Florida Dept. of Health v. Florida Nursing Home Assn., 450 U.S., at 150, 101 S.Ct., at 1034; Edelman v. Jordan, supra, 415 U.S., at 673, 94 S.Ct., at 1360. The court erred, however, in concluding that because various provisions of the Rehabilitation Act are addressed to the States, a State necessarily consents to suit in federal court by participating in programs funded under the statute. We have decided today that the Rehabilitation Act does not evince an unmistakable congressional purpose, pursuant to § 5 of the Fourteenth Amendment, to subject unconsenting States to the jurisdiction of the federal courts. The Act likewise falls far short of manifesting a clear intent to condition participation in the programs funded under the Act on a State's consent to waive its constitutional immunity. Thus, were we to view this statute as an enactment pursuant to the Spending Clause, Art. I, § 8, see n. 2, supra, we would hold that there was no indication that the State of California consented to federal jurisdiction.

VI

The provisions of the Rehabilitation Act fall far short of expressing an unequivocal congressional intent to abrogate the States' Eleventh Amendment immunity. Nor has the State of California specifically waived its immunity to suit in federal court. In view of these determinations, the judgment of the Court of Appeals must be reversed.

JUSTICE BRENNAN, with whom JUSTICE MARSHALL, JUSTICE BLACKMUN and JUSTICE STEVENS join, dissenting.

I

I first address the Court's holding that Congress did not succeed in abrogating the States' sovereign immunity when it enacted § 504 of the Rehabilitation Act, 29 U.S.C. § 794. If this holding resulted from the Court's examination of the statute and its legislative history to determine whether Congress intended in § 504 to impose an obligation on the states enforceable in federal court, I would confine my dissent to the indisputable evidence to the contrary in the language and history of § 504.

Section 504 imposes an obligation not to discriminate against the handicapped in "any program or activity receiving Federal financial assistance." This language is general and unqualified, and contains no indication whatsoever that an exemption for the States was intended. Moreover, state governmental programs and activities are undoubtedly the recipients of a large percentage of federal funds.[2]   Given this widespread state dependence on federal funds, it is quite incredible to assume that Congress did not intend that the states should be fully subject to the strictures of § 504.

The legislative history confirms that the States were among the primary targets of § 504.   In introducing the predecessor of § 504 as an amendment to Title VI of the Civil Rights Act of 1964, 42 U.S.C. § 2000d, Rep. Vanik clearly indicated that governments would be among the primary targets of the legislation: "Our Governments tax [handicapped] people, their parents and relatives, but fail to provide services for them.   *   *   *   The opportunities provided by the Government almost always exclude the handicapped."   117 Cong.Rec. 45,974 (1971).   He further referred approvingly to a federal court suit against the State of Pennsylvania raising the issue of educational opportunities for the handicapped.   See 117 Cong.Rec. 45,974–45,975 (citing Pennsylvania Assoc. for Retarded Children v. Pennsylvania, 343 F.Supp. 279 (ED Pa. 1972), and characterizing it as a "suit against the State").   Two months later, Rep. Vanik noted the range of state actions that could disadvantage the handicapped.   He said that state governments "lack funds and facilities" for medical care for handicapped children and "favor the higher income families" in tuition funding.   118 Cong.Rec. 4341 (1972).   He pointed out that "the States are unable to define and deal with" the illnesses of the handicapped child, and that "[e]xclusion of handicapped children [from public schools] is illegal in some States, but the States plead lack of funds."   Id.   Similarly, Senator Humphrey, the bill's sponsor in the Senate, focused particularly on a suit against a state-operated institution for the mentally retarded as demonstrating the need for the bill.   See 118 Cong.Rec. 9495, 9501 (1972).

The language used in the statute ("any program or activity receiving Federal financial assistance") has long been used to impose obligations on the States under other statutory schemes.   For example, Title VI, enacted in 1964, bans discrimination on the basis of race, color or national origin by "any program or activity receiving Federal financial assistance."   42 U.S.C. § 2000d.   Soon after its enactment, seven agencies promulgated regulations that defined a recipient of federal financial assistance to include "any State, political subdivision of any State or instrumentality of any State or political subdivision."   See, e.g., 29 Fed.Reg. 16274, § 15.2(e) (1964).   See generally Guardians Assn. v. Civil Service Comm'n, 463 U.S. 582, 618, 103 S.Ct. 3221, 3240, 77 L.Ed.2d 866 (1983) (MARSHALL, J., dissenting).   Over forty federal agencies and every Cabinet department adopted similar regulations.   Id., at 619, 103 S.Ct., at 3241.   As Senator Javits remarked in the debate on Title VI, "[w]e are primarily trying to reach units of government, not individuals." 110 Cong.Rec. 13700 (1964).

2. For instance, in 1972–1973, the year in which Congress was considering § 504, state governments received over $31 billion in revenue from the federal government.   By 1981–1982, this had grown to $66 billion.   Bureau of the Census, Historical Statistics on Governmental Finances and Employment, at 34 (1982).

Similarly Title IX of the Education Amendments of 1972, 20 U.S.C. § 1681(a), prohibits discrimination on the basis of sex by "any education program or activity receiving Federal financial assistance." The regulations governing Title IX use the same definition of "recipient"—which explicitly includes the States—as do the Title VI regulations. See 34 CFR § 106.2(h). The Congress that enacted § 504 had the examples of Titles VI and IX before it, and plainly knew that the language of the statute would include the States.[3]

Implementing regulations promulgated for § 504 included the same definition of "recipient" that had previously been used to implement Title VI and Title IX. See 45 CFR § 84.3(f). In 1977, Congress held hearings on the implementation of § 504, and subsequently produced amendments to the statute enacted in 1978. Pub.L. 95–602, § 505(a)(2), 29 U.S.C. § 794a. The Senate Report accompanying the amendments explicitly approved the implementing regulations. S.Rep. No. 95–890, at 19. No member of Congress questioned the reach of the regulations. In describing another section of the 1978 amendments which brought the Federal Government within the reach of § 504, Rep. Jeffords noted that the section "applies 504 to the Federal Government as well as State and local recipients of Federal dollars." 124 Cong.Rec. 13,901 (1978). Rep. Sarasin emphasized that "[n]o one should discriminate against an individual because he or she suffers from a handicap—not private employers, not State and local governments, and most certainly, not the Federal Government." 124 Cong.Rec. 38,552 (1978).

The 1978 amendments also addressed the remedies for violations of § 504:

> The remedies, procedures, and rights set forth in title VI of the Civil Rights Act of 1964[, 42 U.S.C. § 2000d et seq.] shall be available to any person aggrieved by any act or failure to act by any recipient of Federal assistance or Federal provider of such assistance under section 794 of this title. 29 U.S.C. § 794a.

Again, the amendment referred in general and unqualified terms to "any recipient of Federal assistance." An additional provision of the 1978 amendments made available attorney's fees to prevailing parties in actions brought to enforce § 504. Discussing these two provisions, Senator Cranston presupposed that States would be subject to suit under this section:

> [W]ith respect to State and local bodies or State and local officials, attorney's fees, similar to other items of cost, would be collected from the official, in his official capacity from funds of his or her agency or

---

3. The Rehabilitation Act was amended in 1974, a year after its original enactment. Pub.L. 93–516, 88 Stat. 1617 (1974). The Senate Report that accompanied the amendment acknowledged that "Section 504 was patterned after, and is almost identical to, the antidiscrimination language of section 601 of the Civil Rights Act of 1964, * * * and section 901 of the Education Amendments of 1974 [sic]." S.Rep. No. 93–1297, at 39–40, U.S.Code Cong. & Admin.News 1974, pp. 6373, 6390. These amendments and their history "clarified the scope of § 504" and "shed significant light on the intent with which § 504 was enacted." Alexander v. Choate, ___ U.S. ___, ___, n. 27, 105 S.Ct. 712, 724, n. 27, 83 L.Ed.2d 661 (1985).

under his or her control; or from the State or local government—regardless of whether such agency or Government is a named party. 124 Cong.Rec. 30,347 (1978)

Given the unequivocal legislative history, the Court's conclusion that Congress did not abrogate the States' sovereign immunity when it enacted § 504 obviously cannot rest on an analysis of what Congress intended to do or on what Congress thought it was doing. Congress intended to impose a legal obligation on the States not to discriminate against the handicapped. In addition, Congress fully intended that whatever remedies were available against *other* entities—including the Federal Government itself after the 1978 amendments—be equally available against the States. There is simply not a shred of evidence to the contrary.

Appendix A

STATUTORY MATERIAL

CONSTITUTION OF THE UNITED STATES OF AMERICA

Fifth Amendment (1791)

No person shall be held to answer for a capital, or otherwise infamous crime, unless on a presentment or indictment of a Grand Jury, except in cases arising in the land or naval forces, or in the militia, when in actual service in time of war or public danger; nor shall any person be subject for the same offence to be twice put in jeopardy of life or limb; nor shall be compelled in any criminal case to be a witness against himself, nor be deprived of life, liberty, or property, without due process of law; nor shall private property be taken for public use, without just compensation.

Thirteenth Amendment (1865)

Section 1. Neither slavery nor involuntary servitude, except as a punishment for crime whereof the party shall have been duly convicted, shall exist within the United States, or any place subject to their jurisdiction.

Section 2. Congress shall have power to enforce this article by appropriate legislation.

Fourteenth Amendment (1868)

Section 1. All persons born or naturalized in the United States, and subject to the jurisdiction thereof, are citizens of the United States and of the State wherein they reside. No State shall make or enforce any law which shall abridge the privileges or immunities of citizens of the United States; nor shall any State deprive any person of life, liberty, or property, without due process of law; nor deny to any person within its jurisdiction the equal protection of the laws.

* * *

Section 5. The Congress shall have power to enforce, by appropriate legislation, the provisions of this article.

———

CIVIL RIGHTS ACT OF 1866 (42 U.S.C. SEC. 1981)

Equal rights under the law

All persons within the jurisdiction of the United States shall have the same right in every State and Territory to make and enforce contracts, to sue, be parties, give evidence, and to the full and equal benefit of all laws and proceedings for the security of persons and property as is enjoyed by white citizens, and shall be subject to like punishment, pains, penalties, taxes, licenses, and exactions of every kind, and to no other.

———

CIVIL RIGHTS ACT OF 1870 (42 U.S.C. SEC. 1982)

Property rights of citizens

All citizens of the United States shall have the same right, in every State and Territory, as is enjoyed by white citizens thereof to inherit, purchase, lease, sell, hold, and convey real and personal property.

———

CIVIL RIGHTS ACT OF 1871 (42 U.S.C. SEC. 1983)

Civil action for deprivation of rights

Every person who, under color of any statute, ordinance, regulation, custom, or usage, of any State or Territory, subjects, or causes to be subjected, any citizen of the United States or other person within the jurisdiction thereof to the deprivation of any rights, privileges, or immunities secured by the Constitution and laws, shall be liable to the party injured in an action at law, suit in equity, or other proper proceeding for redress.

———

CIVIL RIGHTS ACT OF 1964

Title VI.   Nondiscrimination in Federally Assisted
Programs

(42 U.S.C. Sec. 2000d)

§ 2000d.

No person in the United States shall, on the ground of race, color, or national origin, be excluded from participation in, be denied the benefits of, or be subjected to discrimination under any program or activity receiving Federal financial assistance.

(Pub.L. 88–352, title VI, § 601, July 2, 1964, 78 Stat. 252.)

§ 2000d–1.

Each Federal department and agency which is empowered to extend Federal financial assistance to any program or activity, by way of grant, loan, or contract other than a contract of insurance or guaranty, is authorized and directed to effectuate the provisions of section 2000d of this title with respect to such program or activity by issuing rules, regulations, or orders of general applicability which shall be consistent with achievement of the objectives of the statute authorizing the financial assistance in connection with which the action is taken.   No such rule, regulation, or order shall become effective unless and until approved by the President.   Compliance with any requirement adopted pursuant to this section may be effected (1) by the termination of or refusal to grant or to continue assistance under such program or activity to any recipient as to whom there has been an express finding on the record, after opportunity for hearing, of a failure to comply with such requirement, but such termination or refusal shall be limited to the particular political entity, or part thereof, or other recipient as to whom such a finding has been made and, shall be limited in its effect to the particular program, or part thereof, in which such noncompliance has been so found, or (2) by any other means authorized by law: Provided, however, That no such action shall be taken until the department or agency concerned has advised the appropriate person or persons of the failure to comply with the requirement and has determined that compliance cannot be secured by voluntary means.   In the case of any action terminating, or refusing to grant or continue, assistance because of failure to comply with a requirement imposed pursuant to this section, the head of the Federal department or agency shall file with the committees of the House and Senate having legislative jurisdiction over the program or activity involved a full written report of the circumstances and the grounds for such action.   No such action shall become effective until thirty days have elapsed after the filing of such report.

(Pub.L. 88–352, title VI, § 602, July 2, 1964, 78 Stat. 252.)

§ 2000d–2.

Any department or agency action taken pursuant to section 2000d–1 of this title shall be subject to such judicial review as may otherwise be provided by law for similar action taken by such department or agency on other grounds. In the case of action, not otherwise subject to judicial review, terminating or refusing to grant or to continue financial assistance upon a finding of failure to comply with any requirement imposed pursuant to section 2000d–1 of this title, any person aggrieved (including any State or political subdivision thereof and any agency of either) may obtain judicial review of such action in accordance with chapter 7 of title 5, and such action shall not be deemed committed to unreviewable agency discretion within the meaning of that chapter.

(Pub.L. 88–352, title VI, § 603, July 2, 1964, 78 Stat. 253.)

§ 2000d–3.

Nothing contained in this subchapter shall be construed to authorize action under this subchapter by any department or agency with respect to any employment practice of any employer, employment agency, or labor organization except where a primary objective of the Federal financial assistance is to provide employment.

(Pub.L. 88–352, title VI, § 604, July 2, 1964, 78 Stat. 253.)

§ 2000d–4.

Nothing in this subchapter shall add to or detract from any existing authority with respect to any program or activity under which Federal financial assistance is extended by way of a contract of insurance or guaranty.

(Pub.L. 88–352, title VI, § 605, July 2, 1964, 78 Stat. 253.)

CIVIL RIGHTS ACT OF 1964 AS AMENDED

Title VII. Equal Employment Opportunity [1]

(42 U.S.C. Sections 2000e–2000e–17)

DEFINITIONS

Sec. 701. For the purposes of this title—

(a) The term "person" includes one or more individuals, *governments, governmental agencies, political subdivisions,* labor unions, partnerships, associations, corporations, legal representatives, mutual companies, joint-stock companies, trusts, unincorporated organizations, trustees, trustees in bankruptcy, or receivers.

---

1. Includes 1972 amendments made by P.L. 92–261 printed in italic.

(b) The term "employer" means a person engaged in an industry affecting commerce who has *fifteen* or more employees for each working day in each of twenty or more calendar weeks in the current or preceding calendar year, and any agent of such a person, but such term does not include (1) the United States, a corporation wholly owned by the Government of the United States, an Indian tribe, or *any department or agency of the District of Columbia subject by statute to procedures of the competitive service (as defined in section 2102 of title 5 of the United States Code), or* (2) a bona fide private membership club (other than a labor organization) which is exempt from taxation under section 501(c) of the Internal Revenue Code of 1954, *except that during the first year after the date of enactment of the Equal Employment Opportunity Act of 1972,* persons having fewer than *twenty-five* employees (and their agents) shall not be considered *employers.*

(c) The term "employment agency" means any person regularly undertaking with or without compensation to procure employees for an employer or to procure for employees opportunities to work for an employer and includes an agent of such a person.

(d) The term "labor organization" means a labor organization engaged in an industry affecting commerce, and any agent of such an organization, and includes any organization of any kind, any agency, or employee representation committee, group, association, or plan so engaged in which employees participate and which exists for the purpose, in whole or in part, of dealing with employers concerning grievances, labor disputes, wages, rates of pay, hours, or other terms or conditions of employment, and any conference, general committee, joint or system board, or joint council so engaged which is subordinate to a national or international labor organization.

(e) A labor organization shall be deemed to be engaged in an industry affecting commerce if (1) it maintains or operates a hiring hall or hiring office which procures employees for an employer or procures for employees opportunities to work for an employer, or (2) the number of its members (or, where it is a labor organization composed of other labor organizations or their representatives, if the aggregate number of the members of such other labor organization) is (A) *twenty-five* or more during the first year after the *date of enactment of the Equal Employment Opportunity Act of 1972, or (B) fifteen* or more thereafter, and such labor organization—

(1) is the certified representative of employees under the provisions of the National Labor Relations Act, as amended, or the Railway Labor Act, as amended;

(2) although not certified, is a national or international labor organization or a local labor organization recognized or acting as the representative of employees of an employer or employers engaged in an industry affecting commerce; or

(3) has chartered a local labor organization or subsidiary body which is representing or actively seeking to represent employees of employers within the meaning of paragraph (1) or (2); or

(4) has been chartered by a labor organization representing or actively seeking to represent employees within the meaning of paragraph (1) or (2) as the local or subordinate body through which such employees may enjoy membership or become affiliated with such labor organization; or

(5) is a conference, general committee, joint or system board, or joint council subordinate to a national or international labor organization, which includes a labor organization engaged in an industry affecting commerce within the meaning of any of the preceding paragraphs of this subsection.

(f) The term "employee" means an individual employed by an employer, *except that the term 'employee' shall not include any person elected to public office in any State or political subdivision of any State by the qualified voters thereof, or any person chosen by such officer to be on such officer's personal staff, or an appointee on the policymaking level or an immediate adviser with respect to the excercise of the constitutional or legal powers of the office. The exemption set forth in the preceding sentence shall not include employees subject to the civil service laws of a State government, governmental agency or political subdivision.*

(g) The term "commerce" means trade, traffic, commerce, transportation, transmission, or communication among the several States; or between a State and any place outside thereof; or within the District of Columbia, or a possession of the United States; or between points in the same State but through a point outside thereof.

(h) The term "industry affecting commerce" means any activity, business, or industry in commerce or in which a labor dispute would hinder or obstruct commerce or the free flow of commerce and includes any activity or industry "affecting commerce" within the meaning of the Labor-Management Reporting and Disclosure Act of 1959, *and further includes any governmental industry, business, or activity.*

(i) The term "State" includes a State of the United States, the District of Columbia, Puerto Rico, the Virgin Islands, American Samoa, Guam, Wake Island, the Canal Zone, and Outer Continental Shelf lands defined in the Outer Continental Shelf Lands Act.

(j) The term "religion" includes all aspects of religious observance and practice, as well as belief, unless an employer demonstrates that he is unable to reasonably accommodate to an employee's or prospective employee's, religious observance or practice without undue hardship on the conduct of the employer's business.

(k) The terms "because of sex" or "on the basis of sex" include, but are not limited to, because of or on the basis of pregnancy, childbirth, or related medical conditions; and women affected by pregnancy, childbirth, or related medical conditions shall be treated the same for all employment-related purposes, including receipt of benefits under fringe benefit programs, as other persons not so affected but similar in their ability or inability to work, and nothing in section 2000e–2(h) of this title shall be interpreted to permit otherwise. This subsection shall not require an employer to pay for health insurance benefits for abortion, except where the life of the mother would be endangered if the fetus were carried to term, or except where medical complications have arisen from an abortion: *Provided,* That nothing herein shall preclude an employer from providing abortion benefits or otherwise affect bargaining agreements in regard to abortion.[2]

EXEMPTION

Sec. 702. This title shall not apply to an employer with respect to the employment of aliens outside any State, or to a religious corporation, association, *educational institution,* or society with respect to the employment of individuals of a particular religion to perform work connected with the carrying on by such corporation, association, *educational institution,* or society of its *activities.*

DISCRIMINATION BECAUSE OF RACE, COLOR, RELIGION, SEX, OR NATIONAL ORIGIN

Sec. 703. (a) It shall be an unlawful employment practice for an employer—

(1) to fail or refuse to hire or to discharge any individual, or otherwise to discriminate against any individual with respect to his compensation, terms, conditions, or privileges of employment, be-

2. 1978 amendment made by P.L. 95–555

Effective Date of 1978 Amendment; Exceptions to Application

Section 2 of Pub.L. 95–555 provided that:

"(a) Except as provided in subsection (b), the amendment made by this Act [amending this section] shall be effective on the date of enactment [Oct. 31, 1978].

"(b) The provisions of the amendment made by the first section of this Act [amending this section] shall not apply to any fringe benefit program or fund, or insurance program which is in effect on the date of enactment of this Act [Oct. 31, 1978] until 180 days after enactment of this Act."

Readjustment of Benefits

Section 3 of Pub.L. 95–555 provided that: "Until the expiration of a period of one year from the date of enactment of this Act [Oct. 31, 1978] or, if there is an applicable collective-bargaining agreement in effect on the date of enactment of this Act, until

the termination of that agreement, no person who, on the date of enactment of this Act is providing either by direct payment or by making contributions to a fringe benefit fund or insurance program, benefits in violation with this Act [amending this section, and enacting provisions set out as a note above] shall, in order to come into compliance with this Act, reduce the benefits or the compensation provided any employee on the date of enactment of this Act, either directly or by failing to provide sufficient contributions to a fringe benefit fund or insurance program: Provided, That where the costs of such benefits on the date of enactment of this Act are apportioned between employers and employees, the payments or contributions required to comply with this Act may be made by employers and employees in the same proportion: And provided further, That nothing in this section shall prevent the readjustment of benefits or compensation for reasons unrelated to compliance with this Act."

cause of such individual's race, color, religion, sex, or national origin; or

(2) to limit, segregate, or classify his employees *or applicants for employment* in any way which would deprive or tend to deprive any individual of employment opportunities or otherwise adversely affect his status as an employee, because of such individual's race, color, religion, sex, or national origin.

(b) It shall be an unlawful employment practice for an employment agency to fail or refuse to refer for employment, or otherwise to discriminate against, any individual because of his race, color, religion, sex, or national origin, or to classify or refer for employment any individual on the basis of his race, color, religion, sex, or national origin.

(c) It shall be an unlawful employment practice for a labor organization—

(1) to exclude or to expel from its membership, or otherwise to discriminate against, any individual because of his race, color, religion, sex, or national origin;

(2) to limit, segregate, or classify its membership, *or applicants for membership* or to classify or fail or refuse to refer for employment any individual, in any way which would deprive or tend to deprive any individual of employment opportunities, or would limit such employment opportunities or otherwise adversely affect his status as an employee or as an applicant for employment, because of such individual's race, color, religion, sex, or national origin; or

(3) to cause or attempt to cause an employer to discriminate against an individual in violation of this section.

(d) It shall be an unlawful employment practice for any employer, labor organization, or joint labor-management committee controlling apprenticeship or other training or retraining, including on-the-job training programs to discriminate against any individual because of his race, color, religion, sex, or national origin in admission to, or employment in, any program established to provide apprenticeship or other training.

(e) Notwithstanding any other provision of this title, (1) it shall not be an unlawful employment practice for an employer to hire and employ employees, for an employment agency to classify, or refer for employment any individual, for a labor organization to classify its membership or to classify or refer for employment any individual, or for an employer, labor organization, or joint labor-management committee controlling apprenticeship or other training or retraining programs to admit or employ any individual in any such program, on the basis of his religion, sex, or national origin in those certain instances where religion, sex, or national origin is a bona fide occupational qualification reasonably necessary to the normal operation of that particular business or enterprise, and (2) it shall not be an unlawful employment practice for a school, college, university, or other educational institution or institution of learning to hire and employ employees of a particular religion if such school, college, university, or other educational institution or institution of learning is, in whole or in substantial part, owned, supported, controlled, or managed by a particular religion or by a particular religious corporation, association, or society, or if the curriculum of such school, college, university, or other educational institution or institution of learning is directed toward the propagation of a particular religion.

(f) As used in this title, the phrase "unlawful employment practice" shall not be deemed to include any action or measure taken by an employer, labor organization, joint labor-management committee, or employment agency with respect to an individual who is a member of the Communist Party of the United States or of any other organization required to register as a Communist-action or Communist-front organization by final order of the Subversive Activities Control Board pursuant to the Subversive Activities Control Act of 1950.

(g) Notwithstanding any other provision of this title, it shall not be an unlawful employment practice for an employer to fail or refuse to hire and employ any individual for any position, for an employer to discharge any individual from any position, or for an employment agency to fail or refuse to refer any individual for employment in any position, or for a labor organization to fail or refuse to refer any individual for employment in any position, if—

    (1) the occupancy of such position, or access to the premises in or upon which any part of the duties of such position is performed or is to be performed, is subject to any requirement imposed in the interest of the national security of the United States under any security program in effect pursuant to or administered under any statute of the United States or any Executive order of the President; and

    (2) such individual has not fulfilled or has ceased to fulfill that requirement.

(h) Notwithstanding any other provision of this title, it shall not be an unlawful employment practice for an employer to apply different standards of compensation, or different terms, conditions, or privileges of employment pursuant to a bona fide seniority or merit system, or a system which measures earnings by quantity or quality of production or to employees who work in different locations, provided that such differences are not the result of an intention to discriminate because of race, color, religion, sex, or national origin, nor shall it be an unlawful employment practice for an employer to give and to act upon the results of any professionally developed ability test provided that such test, its administration or action upon the results is not designed, intended or used to discriminate because of race, color, religion, sex or national origin. It shall not be an unlawful employment practice under this title for an employer to differentiate upon the basis of sex in determining the amount of the wages or compensation paid or to be paid to employees of such employer if such differentiation is authorized by the provisions of section 6(d) of the Fair Labor Standards Act of 1938, as amended (29 U.S.C. 206(d)).

(i) Nothing contained in this title shall apply to any business or enterprise on or near an Indian reservation with respect to any publicly announced employment practice of such business or enterprise under which a preferential treatment is given to any individual because he is an Indian living on or near a reservation.

(j) Nothing contained in this title shall be interpreted to require any employer, employment agency, labor organization, or joint labor-management committee subject to this title to grant preferential treatment to any individual or to any group because of the race, color, religion, sex, or national origin of such individual or group on account of an imbalance which may exist with respect to the total number or percentage of persons of any race, color, religion, sex, or national origin employed by any employer, referred or classified for employment by any employment agency or labor organization, admitted to membership or classified by any labor organization, or admitted to, or employed in, any apprenticeship or other training program, in comparison with the total number or percentage of persons of such race, color, religion, sex, or national origin in any community, State, section, or other area, or in the available work force in any community, State, section, or other area.

OTHER UNLAWFUL EMPLOYMENT PRACTICES

Sec. 704. (a) It shall be an unlawful employment practice for an employer to discriminate against any of his employees or applicants for employment, for an employment agency, *or joint labor-management committee controlling apprenticeship or other training or retraining, including on-the-job training programs,* to discriminate against any individual, or for a labor organization to discriminate against any member thereof or applicant for membership, because he has opposed any practice made an unlawful employment practice by this title, or because he has made a charge, testified, assisted, or participated in any manner in an investigation, proceeding, or hearing under this title.

(b) It shall be an unlawful employment practice for an employer, labor organization, employment *agency, or joint labor-management committee controlling apprenticeship or other training or retraining, including on-the-job training programs,* to print or publish or cause to be printed or published any notice or advertisement relating to employment by such an employer or membership in or any classification or referral for employment by such a labor organization, or relating to any classification or referral for employment by such an employment *agency, or relating to admission to, or employment in, any program established to provide apprenticeship or other training by such a joint labor-management committee* indicating any preference, limitation, specification, or discrimination, based on race, color, religion, sex, or national origin, except that such a notice or advertisement may indicate a preference, limitation, specification, or discrimination based on religion, sex, or national origin when religion, sex, or national origin is a bona fide occupational qualification for employment.

EQUAL EMPLOYMENT OPPORTUNITY COMMISSION

Sec. 705. (a) There is hereby created a Commission to be known as the Equal Employment Opportunity Commission, which shall be composed of five members, not more than three of whom shall be members of the same political party. *Members of the Commission* shall be appointed by the President by and with the advice and consent of the *Senate* for a term of five *years. Any individual chosen to fill a vacancy shall be appointed only for the unexpired term of the member whom he shall succeed, and all members of the Commission shall continue to serve until their successors are appointed and qualified, except that no such member of the Commission shall continue to serve (1) for more than sixty days when the Congress is in session unless a nomination to fill such vacancy shall have been submitted to the Senate, or (2) after the adjournment sine die of the session of the Senate in which such nomination was submitted.* The President shall designate one member to serve as Chairman of the Commission, and one member to serve as Vice Chairman. The Chairman shall be responsible on behalf of the Commission for the administrative operations of the Commission, and *except as provided in subsection (b),* shall appoint, in accordance with the *provisions of title 5, United States Code, governing appointments in the competitive service, such officers, agents, attorneys, hearing examiners, and employees as he deems necessary to assist it in the performance of its functions and to fix their compensation in accordance with the provisions of chapter 51 and subchapter III of chapter 53 of title 5, United States Code, relating to classification and General Schedule pay rates: Provided, That assignment, removal, and compensation of hearing examiners shall be in accordance with sections 3105, 3344, 5362, and 7521 of title 5, United States Code.*

(b)(1) There shall be a General Counsel of the Commission appointed by the President, by and with the advice and consent of the Senate, for a term of four years. The General Counsel shall have responsibility for the conduct of litigation as provided in sections 706 and 707 of this title. The General Counsel shall have such other duties as the Commission may prescribe or as may be provided by law and shall concur with the Chairman of the Commission on the appointment and supervision of regional attorneys. The General Counsel of the Commission on the effective date of this Act shall continue in such position and perform the functions specified in this subsection until a successor is appointed and qualified.

(2) Attorneys appointed under this section may, at the direction of the Commission, appear for and represent the Commission in any case in court, provided that the Attorney General shall conduct all litigation to

which the Commission is a party in the Supreme Court pursuant to this title.

(c) A vacancy in the Commission shall not impair the right of the remaining members to exercise all the powers of the Commission and three members thereof shall constitute a quorum.

(d) The Commission shall have an official seal which shall be judicially noticed.

(e) The Commission shall at the close of each fiscal year report to the Congress and to the President concerning the action it has taken; the names, salaries, and duties of all individuals in its employ and the moneys it has disbursed; and shall make such further reports on the cause of and means of eliminating discrimination and such recommendations for further legislation as may appear desirable.

(f) The principal office of the Commission shall be in or near the District of Columbia, but it may meet or exercise any or all its powers at any other place. The Commission may establish such regional or State offices as it deems necessary to accomplish the purpose of this title.

(g) The Commission shall have power—

(1) to cooperate with and, with their consent, utilize regional, State, local, and other agencies, both public and private, and individuals;

(2) to pay to witnesses whose depositions are taken or who are summoned before the Commission or any of its agents the same witness and mileage fees as are paid to witnesses in the courts of the United States;

(3) to furnish to persons subject to this title such technical assistance as they may request to further their compliance with this title or an order issued thereunder;

(4) upon the request of (i) any employer, whose employees or some of them, or (ii) any labor organization, whose members or some of them, refuse or threaten to refuse to cooperate in effectuating the provisions of this title, to assist in such effectuation by conciliation or such other remedial action as is provided by this title;

(5) to make such technical studies as are appropriate to effectuate the purposes and policies of this title and to make the results of such studies available to the public;

(6) to *intervene* in a civil action brought *under section 706* by an aggrieved party *against a respondent other than a government, governmental agency, or political subdivision.*

(h) The Commission shall, in any of its educational or promotional activities, cooperate with other departments and agencies in the performance of such educational and promotional activities.

(*i*) All officers, agents, attorneys, and employees of the Commission shall be subject to the provisions of section 9 of the Act of August 2, 1939, as amended (the Hatch Act), notwithstanding any exemption contained in such section.

PREVENTION OF UNLAWFUL EMPLOYMENT PRACTICES

Sec. 706. (*a*) *The Commission is empowered, as hereinafter provided, to prevent any person from engaging in any unlawful employment practice as set forth in section 703 or 704 of this title.*

(*b*) Whenever *a charge is filed by or on behalf of a* person claiming to be aggrieved, or by a member of the Commission, *alleging* that an employer, employment agency, labor *organization, or joint labor-management committee controlling apprenticeship or other training or retraining, including on-the-job training programs,* has engaged in an unlawful employment practice, the Commission shall *serve a notice of the charge (including the date, place and circumstances of the alleged unlawful employment practice) on* such employer, employment agency, labor *organization, or joint labor-management committee* (hereinafter referred to as the "respondent") *within ten days, and shall make an investigation thereof. Charges shall be in writing under oath or affirmation and shall contain such information and be in such form as the Commission requires. Charges* shall not be made public by the Commission. If the Commission *determines* after such investigation that there is *not* reasonable cause to believe that the charge is true, *it shall dismiss the charge and promptly notify the person claiming to be aggrieved and the respondent of its action. In determining whether reasonable cause exists, the Commission shall accord substantial weight to final findings and orders made by State or local authorities in proceedings commenced under State or local law pursuant to the requirements of subsections (c) and (d). If the Commission determines after such investigation that there is reasonable cause to believe that the charge is true,* the Commission shall endeavor to eliminate any such alleged unlawful employment practice by informal methods of conference, conciliation, and persuasion. Nothing said or done during and as a part of such *informal* endeavors may be made public by the *Commission, its officers or employees, or used as evidence in a subsequent proceeding* without the written consent of the *persons concerned.* Any *person* who *makes* public information in violation of this subsection shall be fined not more than $1,000 or imprisoned *for* not more than one *year, or both. The Commission shall make its determination on reasonable cause as promptly as possible and, so far as practicable, not later than one hundred and twenty days from the filing of the charge or, where applicable under subsection (c) or (d) from the date upon which the Commission is authorized to take action with respect to the charge.*

(*c*) In the case of an alleged unlawful employment practice occurring in a State, or political subdivision of a State, which has a State or local law prohibiting the unlawful employment practice alleged and establishing or authorizing a State or local authority to grant or seek relief from such practice or to institute criminal proceedings with respect thereto upon receiving notice thereof, no charge may be filed under subsection (a) by the person aggrieved before the expiration of sixty days after proceedings have been commenced under the State or local law, unless such proceedings have been earlier terminated, provided that such sixty-day period shall be extended to one hundred and twenty days during the first year after the effective date of such State or local law. If any requirement for the commencement of such proceedings is imposed by a State or local authority other than a requirement of the filing of a written and signed statement of the facts upon which the proceeding is based, the proceeding shall be deemed to have been commenced for the purposes of this subsection at the time such statement is sent by registered mail to the appropriate State or local authority.

(*d*) In the case of any charge filed by a member of the Commission alleging an unlawful employment practice occurring in a State or political subdivision of a State which has a State or local law prohibiting the practice alleged and establishing or authorizing a State or local authority to grant or seek relief from such practice or to institute criminal proceedings with respect thereto upon receiving notice thereof, the Commission shall, before taking any action with respect to such charge, notify the appropriate State or local officials and, upon request, afford them a reasonable time, but not less than sixty days (provided that such sixty-day period shall be extended to one hundred and twenty days during the first year after the effective *date* of such State or local law), unless a shorter period is requested, to act under such State or local law to remedy the practice alleged.

(*e*) A charge under *this section* shall be filed within *one hundred and eighty* days after the alleged unlawful employment practice *occurred and notice of the charge (including the date, place and circumstances of the alleged unlawful employment practice) shall be served upon the person against whom such charge is made within ten days thereafter,* except that in *a* case of an unlawful employment practice with respect to which the person aggrieved has *initially instituted proceedings with a State or local agency with authority to grant or seek relief from such practice or to institute criminal proceedings with respect thereto upon receiving notice thereof,* such charge shall be filed by *or on behalf of* the person aggrieved within *three hundred* days after the alleged unlawful employment practice occurred, or within thirty days after receiving notice that the State or local agency has terminated the proceedings under the State or local law, whichever is earlier, and a copy of such charge shall be filed by the Commission with the State or local agency.

(*f*)(*1*) If within thirty days after a charge is filed with the Commission or within thirty days after expiration of any period of reference under subsection (*c*) *or* (*d*), the Commission has been unable to *secure from the respondent a conciliation agreement acceptable to the Commis-*

sion, the Commission *may bring a civil action against any respondent not a government, governmental agency, or political subdivision named in the charge. In the case of a respondent which is a government, governmental agency, or political subdivision, if the Commission has been unable to secure from the respondent a conciliation agreement acceptable to the Commission, the Commission shall take no further action and shall refer the case to the Attorney General who may bring a civil action against such respondent in the appropriate United States district court. The person or persons aggrieved shall have the right to intervene in a civil action brought by the Commission or the Attorney General in a case involving a government, governmental agency, or political subdivision. If a charge filed with the Commission pursuant to subsection (b) is dismissed by the Commission, or if within one hundred and eighty days from the filing of such charge or the expiration of any period of reference under subsection (c) or (d), whichever is later, the Commission has not filed a civil action under this section or the Attorney General has notified a civil action in a case involving a government, governmental agency, or political subdivision, or the Commission has not entered into a conciliation agreement to which the person aggrieved is a party, the Commission, or the Attorney General in a case involving a government, governmental agency, or political subdivision, shall so notify the person aggrieved and within ninety days after the giving of such notice a civil action may* be brought against the respondent named in the charge (A) by the person claiming to be aggrieved, or (B) if such charge was filed by a member of the Commission, by any person whom the charge alleges was aggrieved by the alleged unlawful employment practice. Upon application by the complainant and in such circumstances as the court may deem just, the court may appoint an attorney for such complainant and may authorize the commencement of the action without the payment of fees, costs, or security. Upon timely application, the court may, in its discretion, permit the *Commission,* or the Attorney General in a case involving a government, governmental agency, or political subdivision, to intervene in such civil action *upon certification* that the case is of general public importance. Upon request, the court may, in its discretion, stay further proceedings for not more than sixty days pending the termination of State or local proceedings described in subsections *(c) or (d) of this section or further* efforts of the Commission to obtain voluntary compliance.

(2) Whenever a charge is filed with the Commission and the Commission concludes on the basis of a preliminary investigation that prompt judicial action is necessary to carry out the purposes of this Act, the Commission, or the Attorney General in a case involving a government, governmental agency, or political subdivision, may bring an action for appropriate temporary or preliminary relief pending final disposition of such charge. Any temporary restraining order or other order granting preliminary or temporary relief shall be issued in accordance with rule 65 of the Federal Rules of Civil Procedure. It shall be the duty of a

court having jurisdiction over proceedings under this section to assign cases for hearing at the earliest practicable date and to cause such cases to be in every way expedited.

(3) Each United States district court and each United States court of a place subject to the jurisdiction of the United States shall have jurisdiction of actions brought under this title. Such an action may be brought in any judicial district in the State in which the unlawful employment practice is alleged to have been committed, in the judicial district in which the employment records relevant to such practice are maintained and administered, or in the judicial district in which the aggrieved person would have worked but for the alleged unlawful employment practice, but if the respondent is not found within any such district, such an action may be brought within the judicial district in which the respondent has his principal office. For purposes of sections 1404 and 1406 of title 28 of the United States Code, the judicial district in which the respondent has his principal office shall in all cases be considered a district in which the action might have been brought.

(4) It shall be the duty of the chief judge of the district (or in his absence, the acting chief judge) in which the case is pending immediately to designate a judge in such district to hear and determine the case. In the event that no judge in the district is available to hear and determine the case, the chief judge of the district, or the acting chief judge, as the case may be, shall certify this fact to the chief judge of the circuit (or in his absence, the acting chief judge) who shall then designate a district or circuit judge of the circuit to hear and determine the case.

(5) It shall be the duty of the judge designated pursuant to this subsection to assign the case for hearing at the earliest practicable date and to cause the case to be in every way expedited. If such judge has not scheduled the case for trial within one hundred and twenty days after issue has been joined, that judge may appoint a master pursuant to rule 53 of the Federal Rules of Civil Procedure.

(g) If the court finds that the respondent has intentionally engaged in or is intentionally engaging in an unlawful employment practice charged in the complaint, the court may enjoin the respondent from engaging in such unlawful employment practice, and order such affirmative action as may be appropriate, which may include, but is not limited to, reinstatement or hiring of employees, with or without back pay (payable by the employer, employment agency, or labor organization, as the case may be, responsible for the unlawful employment practice), or any other equitable relief as the court deems appropriate. Back pay liability shall not accrue from a date more than two years prior to the filing of a charge with the Commission. Interim earnings or amounts earnable with reasonable diligence by the person or persons discriminated against shall operate to reduce the back pay otherwise allowable. No order of the court shall require the admission or reinstatement of an individual as a member of a union, or the hiring, reinstatement, or

promotion of an individual as an employee, or the payment to him of any back pay, if such individual was refused admission, suspended, or expelled, or was refused employment or advancement or was suspended or discharged for any reason other than discrimination on account of race, color, religion, sex, or national origin or in violation of section 704(a).

(h) The provisions of the Act entitled "An Act to amend the Judicial Code and to define and limit the jurisdiction of courts sitting in equity, and for other purposes," approved March 23, 1932 (29 U.S.C. 101–115), shall not apply with respect to civil actions brought under this section.

(i) In any case in which an employer, employment agency, or labor organization fails to comply with an order of a court issued in a civil action brought under *this section*, the Commission may commence proceedings to compel compliance with such order.

(j) Any civil action brought under *this section* and any proceedings brought under subsection (i) shall be subject to appeal as provided in sections 1291 and 1292, title 28, United States Code.

(k) In any action or proceeding under this title the court, in its discretion, may allow the prevailing party, other than the Commission or the United States, a reasonable attorney's fee as part of the costs, and the Commission and the United States shall be liable for costs the same as a private person.

Sec. 707. (a) Whenever the Attorney General has reasonable cause to believe that any person or group of persons is engaged in a pattern or practice of resistance to the full enjoyment of any of the rights secured by this title, and that the pattern or practice is of such a nature and is intended to deny the full exercise of the rights herein described, the Attorney General may bring a civil action in the appropriate district court of the United States by filing with it a complaint (1) signed by him (or in his absence the Acting Attorney General), (2) setting forth facts pertaining to such pattern or practice, and (3) requesting such relief, including an application for a permanent or temporary injunction, restraining order or other order against the person or persons responsible for such pattern or practice, as he deems necessary to insure the full enjoyment of the rights herein described.

(b) The district courts of the United States shall have and shall exercise jurisdiction of proceedings instituted pursuant to this section, and in any such proceeding the Attorney General may file with the clerk of such court a request that a court of three judges be convened to hear and determine the case. Such request by the Attorney General shall be accompanied by a certificate that, in his opinion, the case is of general public importance. A copy of the certificate and request for a three-judge court shall be immediately furnished by such clerk to the chief judge of the circuit (or in his absence, the presiding circuit judge of the circuit) in which the case is pending. Upon receipt of such request it shall be the duty of the chief judge of the circuit or the presiding circuit judge, as the case may be, to designate immediately three judges in such circuit, of whom at least one shall be a circuit judge and another of whom shall be a district judge of the court in which the proceeding was instituted, to hear and determine such case, and it shall be the duty of the judges so designated to assign the case for hearing at the earliest practicable date, to participate in the hearing and determination thereof, and to cause the case to be in every way expedited. An appeal from the final judgment of such court will lie to the Supreme Court.

In the event the Attorney General fails to file such a request in any such proceeding, it shall be the duty of the chief judge of the district (or in his absence, the acting chief judge) in which the case is pending immediately to designate a judge in such district to hear and determine the case. In the event that no judge in the district is available to hear and determine the case, the chief judge of the district, or the acting chief judge, as the case may be, shall certify this fact to the chief judge of the circuit (or in his absence, the acting chief judge) who shall then designate a district or circuit judge of the circuit to hear and determine the case.

It shall be the duty of the judge designated pursuant to this section to assign the case for hearing at the earliest practicable date and to cause the case to be in every way expedited.

(c) Effective two years after the date of enactment of the Equal Employment Opportunity Act of 1972, the functions of the Attorney General under this section shall be transferred to the Commission, together with such personnel, property, records, and unexpended balances of appropriations, allocations, and other funds employed, used, held, available, or to be made available in connection with such functions unless the President submits, and neither House of Congress vetoes, a reorganization plan pursuant to chapter 9, of title 5, United States Code, inconsistent with the provisions of this subsection. The Commission shall carry out such functions in accordance with subsections (d) and (e) of this section.

(d) Upon the transfer of functions provided for in subsection (c) of this section, in all suits commenced pursuant to this section prior to the date of such transfer, proceedings shall continue without abatement, all court orders and decrees shall remain in effect, and the Commission shall be substituted as a party for the United States of America, the Attorney General, or the Acting Attorney General, as appropriate.

(e) Subsequent to the date of enactment of the Equal Employment Opportunity Act of 1972, the Commission shall have authority to investigate and act on a charge of a pattern or practice of discrimination, whether filed by or on behalf of a person claiming to be aggrieved or by a member of the Commission. All such actions shall be conducted in accordance with the procedures set forth in section 706 of this Act.

Effect on State Laws

Sec. 708. Nothing in this title shall be deemed to exempt or relieve any person from any liability, duty, penalty, or punishment provided by any present or future law of any State or political subdivision of a State, other than any such law which purports to require or permit the doing of any act which would be an unlawful employment practice under this title.

Investigations, Inspections, Records, State Agencies

Sec. 709. (a) In connection with any investigation of a charge filed under section 706, the Commission or its designated representative shall at all reasonable times have access to, for the purposes of examination, and the right to copy any evidence of any person being investigated or proceeded against that relates to unlawful employment practices covered by this title and is relevant to the charge under investigation.

(b) The Commission may cooperate with State and local agencies charged with the administration of State fair employment practices laws and, with the consent of such agencies, may, for the purpose of carrying out its functions and duties under this title and within the limitation of funds appropriated specifically for such purpose, *engage in and contribute to the cost of research and other projects of mutual interest undertaken by such agencies, and* utilize the services of such agencies and their employees, and, notwithstanding any other provision of law, *pay by advance or reimbursement* such agencies and their employees for services rendered to assist the Commission in carrying out this title. In furtherance of such cooperative efforts, the Commission may enter into written agreements with such State or local agencies and such agreements may include provisions under which the Commission shall refrain from processing a charge in any cases or class of cases specified in such agreements or under which the Commission shall relieve any person or class of persons in such State or locality from requirements imposed under this section. The Commission shall rescind any such agreement whenever it determines that the agreement no longer serves the interest of effective enforcement of this title.

(c) *Every* employer, employment agency, and labor organization subject to this title shall (1) make and keep such records relevant to the determinations of whether unlawful employment practices have been or are being committed, (2) preserve such records for such periods, and (3) make such reports therefrom, as the Commission shall prescribe by regulation or order, after public hearing, as reasonable, necessary, or appropriate for the enforcement of this title or the regulations or orders thereunder. The Commission shall, by regulation, require each employer, labor organization, and joint labor-management committee subject to this title which controls an apprenticeship or other training program to maintain such records as are reasonably necessary to carry out the purpose of this title, including, but not limited to, a list of applicants who wish to participate in such program, including the chronological order in which applications were received, and *to* furnish to the Commission upon request, a detailed description of the manner in which persons are selected to participate in the apprenticeship or other training program. Any employer, employment agency, labor organization, or joint labor-management committee which believes that the application to it of any regulation or order issued under this section would result in undue hardship may apply to the Commission for an exemption from the application of such regulation or order, *and, if such application for an exemption is denied,* bring a civil action in the United States district court for the district where such records are kept. If the Commission or the court, as the case may be, finds that the application of the regulation or order to the employer, employment agency, or labor organization in question would impose an undue hardship, the Commission or the court, as the case may be, may grant appropriate relief. *If any person required to comply with the provisions of this subsection fails or refuses to do so, the United States district court for the district in which such person is found, resides, or transacts business, shall, upon application of the Commission, or the Attorney General in a case involving a government, governmental agency or political subdivision, have jurisdiction to issue to such person an order requiring him to comply.*

(d) In prescribing requirements pursuant to subsection (c) of this section, the Commission shall consult with other interested State and Federal agencies and shall endeavor to coordinate its requirements with those adopted by such agencies. The Commission shall furnish upon request and without cost to any State or local agency, charged with the administration of a fair employment practice law information obtained pursuant to subsection (c) of this section from any employer, employment agency, labor organization, or joint labor-management committee subject to the jurisdiction of such agency. Such information shall be furnished on condition that it not be made public by the recipient agency prior to the institution of a proceeding under State or local law involving such information. If this condition is violated by a recipient agency, the Commission may decline to honor subsequent requests pursuant to this subsection.

(e) It shall be unlawful for any officer or employee of the Commission to make public in any manner whatever any information obtained by the Commission pursuant to its authority under this section prior to the institution of any proceeding under this title involving such information. Any officer or employee of the Commission who shall make public in any manner whatever any information in violation of this subsection shall be guilty of a misdemeanor and upon conviction thereof, shall be fined not more than $1,000, or imprisoned not more than one year.

INVESTIGATORY POWERS

Sec. 710. *For the purpose of all hearings and investigations conducted by the Commission or its duly authorized agents or agencies, section 11 of the National Labor Relations Act (49 Stat. 455; 29 U.S.C. 161) shall apply.*

NOTICES TO BE POSTED

Sec. 711. (a) Every employer, employment agency, and labor organization, as the case may be, shall post and keep posted in conspicuous places upon its premises where notices to employees, applicants for employment, and members are customarily posted a notice to be prepared or approved by the Commission setting forth excerpts from, or summaries of, the pertinent provisions of this title and information pertinent to the filing of a complaint.

(b) A willful violation of this section shall be punishable by a fine of not more than $100 for each separate offense.

VETERANS' PREFERENCE

Sec. 712. Nothing contained in this title shall be construed to repeal or modify any Federal, State, territorial, or local law creating special rights or preference for veterans.

RULES AND REGULATIONS

Sec. 713. (a) The Commission shall have authority from time to time to issue, amend, or rescind suitable procedural regulations to carry out the provisions of this title. Regulations issued under the section shall be in conformity with the standards and limitations of the Administrative Procedure Act.

(b) In any action or proceeding based on any alleged unlawful employment practice, no person shall be subject to any liability or punishment for or on account of (1) the commission by such person of an unlawful employment practice if he pleads and proves that the act or omission complained of was in good faith, in conformity with, and in reliance on any written interpretation or opinion of the Commission, or (2) the failure of such person to publish and file any information required by any provision of this title if he pleads and proves that he failed to publish and file such information in good faith, in conformity with the instructions of the Commission issued under this title regarding the filing of such information. Such a defense, if established, shall be a bar to the action or proceeding, notwithstanding that (A) after such act or omission, such interpretation or opinion is modified or rescinded or is determined by judicial authority to be invalid or of no legal effect, or (B) after publishing or filing the description and annual reports, such publication or filing is determined by judicial authority not to be in conformity with the requirements of this title.

FORCIBLY RESISTING THE COMMISSION OR ITS REPRESENTATIVES

Sec. 714. The provisions of *sections 111 and 1114* title 18, United States Code, shall apply to officers, agents, and employees of the Commission in the performance of their official duties. *Notwithstanding the provisions of sections 111 and 1114 of title 18, United States Code, whoever in violation of the provisions of section 1114 of such title kills a person while engaged in or on account of the performance of his official functions under this Act shall be punished by imprisonment for any term of years or for life.*

EQUAL EMPLOYMENT OPPORTUNITY COORDINATING COUNCIL

Sec. 715. *There shall be established an Equal Employment Opportunity Coordinating Council (hereinafter referred to in this section as the Council) composed of the Secretary of Labor, the Chairman of the Equal Employment Opportunity Commission, the Attorney General, the Chairman of the United States Civil Service Commission, and the Chairman of the United States Civil Rights Commission, or their respective delegates. The Council shall have the responsibility for developing and implementing agreements, policies and practices designed to maximize effort, promote efficiency, and eliminate conflict, competition, duplication and inconsistency among the operations, functions and jurisdictions of the various departments, agencies and branches of the Federal government responsible for the implementation and enforcement of equal employment opportunity legislation, orders, and policies. On or before July 1 of each year, the Council shall transmit to the President and to the Congress a report of its activities, together with such recommendations for legislative or administrative changes as it concludes are desirable to further promote the purposes of this section.*

EFFECTIVE DATE

Sec. 716. (a) This title shall become effective one year after the date of its enactment.

(b) Notwithstanding subsection (a), sections of this title other than sections 703, 704, 706, and 707 shall become effective immediately.

(c) The President shall, as soon as feasible after the enactment of this title, convene one or more conferences for the purpose of enabling the leaders of groups whose members will be affected by this title to become familiar with the rights afforded and obligations imposed by its provisions, and for the purpose of making plans which will result in the fair and effective administration of this title when all of its provisions become effective. The President shall invite the participation in such conference or conferences of (1) the members of the President's Committee on Equal Employment Opportunity, (2) the members of the Commission on Civil Rights, (3) representatives of State and local agencies engaged in furthering equal employment opportunity, (4) representatives of private agencies engaged in furthering equal employment opportunity, and (5) representatives of employers, labor organizations, and employment agencies who will be subject to this title.

NONDISCRIMINATION IN FEDERAL GOVERNMENT EMPLOYMENT

Sec. 717. *(a) All personnel actions affecting employees or applicants for employment (except with regard to aliens employed outside the limits of the United States) in military departments as defined in section 102 of title 5, United States Code, in executive agencies (other than the General Accounting Office) as defined in section 105 of title 5, United States Code (including employees and applicants for employment who are paid from nonappropriated funds), in the United States Postal Service and the Postal Rate Commission, in those units of the Government of the District of Columbia having positions in the competitive service, and in those units of the legislative and judicial branches of the Federal Government having positions in the competitive service, and in the Library of Congress shall be made free from any discrimination based on race, color, religion, sex, or national origin.*

(b) Except as otherwise provided in this subsection, the Civil Service Commission shall have authority to enforce the provisions of subsection (a) through appropriate remedies, including reinstatement or hiring of employees with or without back pay, as will effectuate the policies of this section, and shall issue such rules, regulations, orders, and instructions as it deems necessary and appropriate to carry out its responsibilities under this section. The Civil Service Commission shall—

(1) be responsible for the annual review and approval of a national and regional equal employment opportunity plan which each department and agency and each appropriate unit referred to in subsection (a) of this section shall submit in order to maintain an affirmative program of equal employment opportunity for all such employees and applicants for employment;

(2) be responsible for the review and evaluation of the operation of all agency equal employment opportunity programs, periodically obtaining and publishing (on at least a semiannual basis) progress reports from each such department, agency, or unit; and

(3) consult with and solicit the recommendations of interested individuals, groups, and organizations relating to equal employment opportunity.

The head of each such department, agency, or unit shall comply with such rules, regulations, orders, and instructions which shall include a provision that an employee or applicant for employment shall be notified of any final action taken on any complaint of discrimination filed by him thereunder. The plan submitted by each department, agency, and unit shall include, but not be limited to—

(1) provision for the establishment of training and education programs designed to provide a maximum opportunity for employees to advance so as to perform at their highest potential; and

(2) a description of the qualifications in terms of training and experience relating to equal employment opportunity for the principal and operating officials of each such department, agency, or unit

responsible for carrying out the equal employment opportunity program and of the allocation of personnel and resources proposed by such department, agency, or unit to carry out its equal employment opportunity program.

With respect to employment in the Library of Congress, authorities granted in this subsection to the Civil Service Commission shall be exercised by the Librarian of Congress.

(c) Within thirty days of receipt of notice of final action taken by a department, agency, or unit referred to in subsection 717(a), or by the Civil Service Commission upon an appeal from a decision or order of such department, agency, or unit on a complaint of discrimination based on race, color, religion, sex, or national origin, brought pursuant to subsection (a) of this section, Executive Order 11478 or any succeeding Executive orders, or after one hundred and eighty days from the filing of the initial charge with the department, agency, or unit or with the Civil Service Commission on appeal from a decision or order of such department, agency, or unit until such time as final action may be taken by a department, agency, or unit, an employee or applicant for employment, if aggrieved by the final disposition of his complaint, or by the failure to take final action on his complaint, may file a civil action as provided in section 706, in which civil action the head of the department, agency, or unit, as appropriate, shall be the defendant.

(d) The provisions of section 706(f) through (k), as applicable, shall govern civil actions brought hereunder.

(e) Nothing contained in this Act shall relieve any Government agency or official of its or his primary responsibility to assure nondiscrimination in employment as required by the Constitution and statutes or of its or his responsibilities under Executive Order 11478 relating to equal employment opportunity in the Federal Government.

SPECIAL PROVISIONS WITH RESPECT TO DENIAL, TERMINATION, AND SUSPENSION OF GOVERNMENT CONTRACTS

Sec. 718. *No Government contract, or portion thereof, with any employer, shall be denied, withheld, terminated, or suspended, by any agency or officer of the United States under any equal employment opportunity law or order, where such employer has an affirmative action plan which has previously been accepted by the Government for the same facility within the past twelve months without first according such employer full hearing and adjudication under the provisions of title 5, United States Code, section 554, and the following pertinent sections: Provided, That if such employer has deviated substantially from such previously agreed to affirmative action plan, this section shall not apply: Provided further, That for the purposes of this section an affirmative action plan shall be deemed to have been accepted by the Government at the time the appropriate compliance agency has accepted such plan* *unless within forty-five days thereafter the Office of Federal Contract Compliance has disapproved such plan.*

CIVIL RIGHTS ACT OF 1964

Subchapter IX. Miscellaneous Provisions

(42 U.S.C. Section 2000h)

§ 2000h–2. Intervention by Attorney General; denial of equal protection on account of race, color, religion, sex or national origin

Whenever an action has been commenced in any court of the United States seeking relief from the denial of equal protection of the laws under the fourteenth amendment to the Constitution on account of race, color, religion, sex or national origin, the Attorney General for or in the name of the United States may intervene in such action upon timely application if the Attorney General certifies that the case is of general public importance. In such action the United States shall be entitled to the same relief as if it had instituted the action.

(Pub.L. 88–352, title IX, § 902, July 2, 1964, 78 Stat. 266; Pub.L. 92–318, title IX, § 906(a), June 23, 1972, 86 Stat. 375.)

AMENDMENTS

1972—Pub.L. 92–318 included the term "sex" after the word "religion".

CIVIL RIGHTS ACT OF 1964

Title XI. Miscellaneous

(42 U.S.C. Section 2000h–6)

Sec. 1101. In any proceeding for criminal contempt arising under title II, III, IV, V, VI, or VII of this Act, the accused, upon demand therefor, shall be entitled to a trial by jury, which shall conform as near as may be to the practice in criminal cases. Upon conviction, the accused shall not be fined more than $1,000 or imprisoned for more than six months.

This section shall not apply to contempts committed in the presence of the court, or so near thereto as to obstruct the administration of justice, nor to the misbehavior, misconduct, or disobedience of any officer of the court in respect to writs, orders, or process of the court. No person shall be convicted of criminal contempt hereunder unless the act or omission constituting such contempt shall have been intentional, as required in other cases of criminal contempt.

Nor shall anything herein be construed to deprive courts of their power, by civil contempt proceedings, without a jury, to secure compliance with or to prevent obstruction of, as distinguished from punishment for violations of, any lawful writ, process, order, rule, decree, or command of the court in accordance with the prevailing usages of law and equity, including the power of detention.

Sec. 1102. No person should be put twice in jeopardy under the laws of the United States for the same act or omission. For this reason, an acquittal or conviction in a prosecution for a specific crime under the laws of the United States shall bar a proceeding for criminal contempt, which is based upon the same act or omission and which arises under the provisions of this Act; and an acquittal or conviction in a proceeding for criminal contempt, which arises under the provisions of this Act, shall bar a prosecution for a specific crime under the laws of the United States based upon the same act or omission.

Sec. 1103. Nothing in this Act shall be construed to deny, impair, or otherwise affect any right or authority of the Attorney General or of the United States or any agency or officer thereof under existing law to institute or intervene in any action or proceeding.

Sec. 1104. Nothing contained in any title of this Act shall be construed as indicating an intent on the part of Congress to occupy the field in which any such title operates to the exclusion of State laws on the same subject matter, nor shall any provision of this Act be construed as invalidating any provision of State law unless such provision is inconsistent with any of the purposes of this Act, or any provision thereof.

Sec. 1105. There are hereby authorized to be appropriated such sums as are necessary to carry out the provisions of this Act.

Sec. 1106. If any provision of this Act or the application thereof to any person or circumstances is held invalid, the remainder of the Act and the application of the provision to other persons not similarly situated or to other circumstances shall not be affected thereby.

Approved July 2, 1964.

EXECUTIVE ORDER 11246—EQUAL EMPLOYMENT OPPORTUNITY

Source: The provisions of Executive Order 11246 of Sept. 24, 1965, appear at 30 FR 12319, 12935, 3 CFR, 1964–1965 Comp., p. 339, unless otherwise noted.

Under and by virtue of the authority vested in me as President of the United States by the Constitution and statutes of the United States, it is ordered as follows:

Part I. Nondiscrimination in Government Employment

[Part I superseded by EO 11478 of Aug. 8, 1969, 34 FR 12985, 3 CFR, 1966–1970 Comp., p. 803]

Part II. Nondiscrimination in Employment by Government Contractors and Subcontractors

SUBPART A. DUTIES OF THE SECRETARY OF LABOR

Sec. 201. The Secretary of Labor shall be responsible for the administration and enforcement of Parts II and III of this Order. The Secretary shall adopt such rules and regulations and issue such orders as are deemed necessary and appropriate to achieve the purposes of Parts II and III of this Order.

[Sec. 201 amended by EO 12086 of Oct. 5, 1978, 43 FR 46501, 3 CFR, 1978 Comp., p. 230]

SUBPART B. CONTRACTORS' AGREEMENTS

Sec. 202. Except in contracts exempted in accordance with Section 204 of this Order, all Government contracting agencies shall include in every Government contract hereafter entered into the following provisions:

During the performance of this contract, the contractor agrees as follows:

(1) The contractor will not discriminate against any employee or applicant for employment because of race, color, religion, sex, or national origin. The contractor will take affirmative action to ensure that applicants are employed, and that employees are treated during employment, without regard to their race, color, religion, sex or national origin. Such action shall include, but not be limited to the following: employment, upgrading, demotion, or transfer; recruitment or recruitment advertising; layoff or termination; rates of pay or other forms of compensation; and selection for training, including apprenticeship. The contractor agrees to post in conspicuous places, available to employees and applicants for employment, notices to be provided by the contracting officer setting forth the provisions of this nondiscrimination clause.

(2) The contractor will, in all solicitations or advertisements for employees placed by or on behalf of the contractor, state that all qualified applicants will receive consideration for employment without regard to race, color, religion, sex or national origin.

(3) The contractor will send to each labor union or representative of workers with which he has a collective bargaining agreement or other contract or understanding, a notice, to be provided by the agency contracting officer, advising the labor union or workers' representative of the contractor's commitments under Section 202 of Executive Order No. 11246 of September 24, 1965, and shall post copies of the notice in

conspicuous places available to employees and applicants for employment.

(4) The contractor will comply with all provisions of Executive Order No. 11246 of Sept. 24, 1965, and of the rules, regulations, and relevant orders of the Secretary of Labor.

(5) The contractor will furnish all information and reports required by Executive Order No. 11246 of September 24, 1965, and by the rules, regulations, and orders of the Secretary of Labor, or pursuant thereto, and will permit access to his books, records, and accounts by the contracting agency and the Secretary of Labor for purposes of investigation to ascertain compliance with such rules, regulations, and orders.

(6) In the event of the contractor's noncompliance with the nondiscrimination clauses of this contract or with any of such rules, regulations, or orders, this contract may be cancelled, terminated or suspended in whole or in part and the contractor may be declared ineligible for further Government contracts in accordance with procedures authorized in Executive Order No. 11246 of Sept. 24, 1965, and such other sanctions may be imposed and remedies invoked as provided in Executive Order No. 11246 of September 24, 1965, or by rule, regulation, or order of the Secretary of Labor, or as otherwise provided by law.

(7) The contractor will include the provisions of paragraphs (1) through (7) in every subcontract or purchase order unless exempted by rules, regulations, or orders of the Secretary of Labor issued pursuant to Section 204 of Executive Order No. 11246 of September 24, 1965, so that such provisions will be binding upon each subcontractor or vendor. The contractor will take such action with respect to any subcontract or purchase order as may be directed by the Secretary of Labor as a means of enforcing such provisions including sanctions for noncompliance: Provided, however, that in the event the contractor becomes involved in, or is threatened with, litigation with a subcontractor or vendor as a result of such direction, the contractor may request the United States to enter into such litigation to protect the interests of the United States.

[Sec. 202 amended by EO 11375 of Oct. 13, 1967, 32 FR 14303, 3 CFR, 1966–1970 Comp., p. 684; EO 12086 of Oct. 5, 1978, 43 FR 46501, 3 CFR, 1978 Comp., p. 230]

Sec. 203. (a) Each contractor having a contract containing the provisions prescribed in Section 202 shall file, and shall cause each of his subcontractors to file, Compliance Reports with the contracting agency or the Secretary of Labor as may be directed. Compliance Reports shall be filed within such times and shall contain such information as to the practices, policies, programs, and employment policies, programs, and employment statistics of the contractor and each subcontractor, and shall be in such form, as the Secretary of Labor may prescribe.

(b) Bidders or prospective contractors or subcontractors may be required to state whether they have participated in any previous contract subject to the provisions of this Order, or any preceding similar Executive order, and in that event to submit, on behalf of themselves and their proposed subcontractors, Compliance Reports prior to or as an initial part of their bid or negotiation of a contract.

(c) Whenever the contractor or subcontractor has a collective bargaining agreement or other contract or understanding with a labor union or an agency referring workers or providing or supervising apprenticeship or training for such workers, the Compliance Report shall include such information as to such labor union's or agency's practices and policies affecting compliance as the Secretary of Labor may prescribe: Provided, That to the extent such information is within the exclusive possession of a labor union or an agency referring workers or providing or supervising apprenticeship or training and such labor union or agency shall refuse to furnish such information to the contractor, the contractor shall so certify to the Secretary of Labor as part of its Compliance Report and shall set forth what efforts he has made to obtain such information.

(d) The Secretary of Labor may direct that any bidder or prospective contractor or subcontractor shall submit, as part of his Compliance Report, a statement in writing, signed by an authorized officer or agent on behalf of any labor union or any agency referring workers or providing or supervising apprenticeship or other training, with which the bidder or prospective contractor deals, with supporting information, to the effect that the signer's practices and policies do not discriminate on the grounds of race, color, religion, sex or national origin, and that the signer either will affirmatively cooperate in the implementation of the policy and provisions of this order or that it consents and agrees that recruitment, employment, and the terms and conditions of employment under the proposed contract shall be in accordance with the purposes and provisions of the order. In the event that the union, or the agency shall refuse to execute such a statement, the Compliance Report shall so certify and set forth what efforts have been made to secure such a statement and such additional factual material as the Secretary of Labor may require.

[Sec. 203 amended by EO 11375 of Oct. 13, 1967, 32 FR 14303, 3 CFR, 1966–1970 Comp., p. 684.; EO 12086 of Oct. 5, 1978, 43 FR 46501, 3 CFR, 1978 Comp., p. 230]

Sec. 204. The Secretary of Labor may, when he deems that special circumstances in the national interest so require, exempt a contracting agency from the requirement of including any or all of the provisions of Section 202 of this Order in any specific contract, subcontract, or purchase order. The Secretary of Labor may, by rule or regulation, also exempt certain classes of contracts, subcontracts, or purchase orders (1) whenever work is to be or has been performed outside the United States and no recruitment of workers within the limits of the United States is involved; (2) for standard commercial supplies or raw materials; (3) involving less than specified amounts of money or specified numbers of workers; or (4) to the extent that they involve subcontracts below a specified tier. The Secretary of Labor may also provide, by rule, regulation, or order, for the exemption of facilities of a contractor which are in all respects separate and distinct from activities of the contractor related to the performance of the contract: Provided, That such an exemption will not interfere with or impede the effectuation of the purposes of this Order: And provided further, That in the absence of such an exemption all facilities shall be covered by the provisions of this Order.

SUBPART C. POWERS AND DUTIES OF THE SECRETARY OF LABOR
AND THE CONTRACTING AGENCIES

Sec. 205. The Secretary of Labor shall be responsible for securing compliance by all Government contractors and subcontractors with this Order and any implementing rules or regulations. All contracting agencies shall comply with the terms of this Order and any implementing rules, regulations, or orders of the Secretary of Labor. Contracting agencies shall cooperate with the Secretary of Labor and shall furnish such information and assistance as the Secretary may require.

[Sec. 205 amended by EO 12086 of Oct. 5, 1978, 43 FR 46501, 3 CFR, 1978 Comp., p. 230]

Sec. 206. (a) The Secretary of Labor may investigate the employment practices of any Government contractor or subcontractor to determine whether or not the contractual provisions specified in Section 202 of this Order have been violated. Such investigation shall be conducted in accordance with the procedures established by the Secretary of Labor.

(b) The Secretary of Labor may receive and investigate complaints by employees or prospective employees of a Government contractor or subcontractor which allege discrimination contrary to the contractual provisions specified in Section 202 of this Order.

[Sec. 206 amended by EO 12086 of Oct. 5, 1978, 43 FR 46501, 3 CFR, 1978 Comp., p. 230]

Sec. 207. The Secretary of Labor shall use his best efforts, directly and through interested Federal, State, and local agencies, contractors, and all other available instrumentalities to cause any labor union engaged in work under Government contracts or any agency referring workers or providing or supervising apprenticeship or training for or in the course of such work to cooperate in the implementation of the purposes of this Order. The Secretary of Labor shall, in appropriate cases, notify the Equal Employment Opportunity Commission, the Department of Justice, or other appropriate Federal agencies whenever it has reason to believe that the practices of any such labor organization or agency violate Title VI or Title VII of the Civil Rights Act of 1964 or other provision of Federal law.

[Sec. 207 amended by EO 12086 of Oct. 5, 1978, 43 FR 46501, 3 CFR, 1978 Comp., p. 230]

Sec. 208. (a) The Secretary of Labor, or any agency, officer, or employee in the executive branch of the Government designated by rule, regulation, or order of the Secretary, may hold such hearings, public or private, as the Secretary may deem advisable for compliance, enforcement, or educational purposes.

(b) The Secretary of Labor may hold, or cause to be held, hearings in accordance with Subsection (a) of this Section prior to imposing, ordering, or recommending the imposition of penalties and sanctions under this Order. No order for debarment of any contractor from further Government contracts under Section 209(a)(6) shall be made without affording the contractor an opportunity for a hearing.

SUBPART D. SANCTIONS AND PENALTIES

Sec. 209. (a) In accordance with such rules, regulations, or orders as the Secretary of Labor may issue or adopt, the Secretary may:

(1) Publish, or cause to be published, the names of contractors or unions which it has concluded have complied or have failed to comply with the provisions of this Order or of the rules, regulations, and orders of the Secretary of Labor.

(2) Recommend to the Department of Justice that, in cases in which there is substantial or material violation or the threat of substantial or material violation of the contractual provisions set forth in Section 202 of this Order, appropriate proceedings be brought to enforce those provisions, including the enjoining, within the limitations of applicable law, of organizations, individuals, or groups who prevent directly or indirectly, or seek to prevent directly or indirectly, compliance with the provisions of this Order.

(3) Recommend to the Equal Employment Opportunity Commission or the Department of Justice that appropriate proceedings be instituted under Title VII of the Civil Rights Act of 1964.

(4) Recommend to the Department of Justice that criminal proceedings be brought for the furnishing of false information to any contracting agency or to the Secretary of Labor as the case may be.

(5) After consulting with the contracting agency, direct the contracting agency to cancel, terminate, suspend, or cause to be cancelled, terminated, or suspended, any contract, or any portion or portions thereof, for failure of the contractor or subcontractor to comply with equal employment opportunity provisions of the contract. Contracts may be cancelled, terminated, or suspended absolutely or continuance of contracts may be conditioned upon a program for future compliance approved by the Secretary of Labor.

(6) Provide that any contracting agency shall refrain from entering into further contracts, or extensions or other modifications of existing contracts, with any noncomplying contractor, until such contractor has satisfied the Secretary of Labor that such contractor has established and will carry out personnel and employment policies in compliance with the provisions of this Order.

(b) Pursuant to rules and regulations prescribed by the Secretary of Labor, the Secretary shall make reasonable efforts, within a reasonable time limitation, to secure compliance with the contract provisions of this Order by methods of conference, conciliation, mediation, and persuasion before proceedings shall be instituted under subsection (a)(2) of this Section, or before a contract shall be cancelled or terminated in whole or in part under subsection (a)(5) of this Section.

[Sec. 209 amended by EO 12086 of Oct. 5, 1978, 43 FR 46501, 3 CFR, 1978 Comp., p. 230]

Sec. 210. Whenever the Secretary of Labor makes a determination under Section 209, the Secretary shall promptly notify the appropriate agency. The agency shall take the action directed by the Secretary and shall report the results of the action it has taken to the Secretary of Labor within such time as the Secretary shall specify. If the contracting agency fails to take the action directed within thirty days, the Secretary may take the action directly.

[Sec. 210 amended by EO 12086 of Oct. 5, 1978, 43 FR 46501, 3 CFR, 1978 Comp., p. 230]

Sec. 211. If the Secretary shall so direct, contracting agencies shall not enter into contracts with any bidder or prospective contractor unless the bidder or prospective contractor has satisfactorily complied with the provisions of this Order or submits a program for compliance acceptable to the Secretary of Labor.

[Sec. 211 amended by EO 12086 of Oct. 5, 1978, 43 FR 46501, 3 CFR, 1978 Comp., p. 230]

Sec. 212. When a contract has been cancelled or terminated under Section 209(a)(5) or a contractor has been debarred from further Government contracts under Section 209(a)(6) of this Order, because of noncompliance with the contract provisions specified in Section 202 of this Order, the Secretary of Labor shall promptly notify the Comptroller General of the United States.

[Sec. 212 amended by EO 12086 of Oct. 5, 1978, 43 FR 46501, 3 CFR, 1978 Comp., p. 230]

SUBPART E. CERTIFICATES OF MERIT

Sec. 213. The Secretary of Labor may provide for issuance of a United States Government Certificate of Merit to employers or labor unions, or other agencies which are or may hereafter be engaged in work under Government contracts, if the Secretary is satisfied that the personnel and employment practices of the employer, or that the personnel, training, apprenticeship, membership, grievance and representation, upgrading, and other practices and policies of the labor union or other agency conform to the purposes and provisions of this Order.

Sec. 214. Any Certificate of Merit may at any time be suspended or revoked by the Secretary of Labor if the holder thereof, in the judgment of the Secretary, has failed to comply with the provisions of this Order.

Sec. 215. The Secretary of Labor may provide for the exemption of any employer, labor union, or other agency from any reporting requirements imposed under or pursuant to this Order if such employer, labor union, or other agency has been awarded a Certificate of Merit which has not been suspended or revoked.

Part III. Nondiscrimination Provisions in Federally Assisted Construction Contracts

Sec. 301. Each executive department and agency which administers a program involving Federal financial assistance shall require as a condition for the approval of any grant, contract, loan, insurance, or guarantee thereunder, which may involve a construction contract, that the applicant for Federal assistance undertake and agree to incorporate, or cause to be incorporated, into all construction contracts paid for in whole or in part with funds obtained from the Federal Government or borrowed on the credit of the Federal Government pursuant to such grant, contract, loan, insurance, or guarantee, or undertaken pursuant to any Federal program involving such grant, contract, loan, insurance, or guarantee, the provisions prescribed for Government contracts by Section 202 of this Order or such modification thereof, preserving in substance the contractor's obligations thereunder, as may be approved by the Secretary of Labor, together with such additional provisions as the Secretary deems appropriate to establish and protect the interest of the United States in the enforcement of those obligations. Each such applicant shall also undertake and agree (1) to assist and cooperate actively with the Secretary of Labor in obtaining the compliance of contractors and subcontractors with those contract provisions and with the rules, regulations and relevant orders of the Secretary, (2) to obtain and to furnish to the Secretary of Labor such information as the Secretary may require for the supervision of such compliance, (3) to carry out sanctions and penalties for violation of such obligations imposed upon contractors and subcontractors by the Secretary of Labor pursuant to Part II, Subpart D, of this Order, and (4) to refrain from entering into any contract subject to this Order, or extension or other modification of such a contract with a contractor debarred from Government contracts under Part II, Subpart D, of this Order.

[Sec. 301 amended by EO 12086 of Oct. 5, 1978, 43 FR 46501, 3 CFR, 1978 Comp., p. 230]

Sec. 302. (a) "Construction contract" as used in this Order means any contract for the construction, rehabilitation, alteration, conversion, extension, or repair of buildings, highways, or other improvements to real property.

(b) The provisions of Part II of this Order shall apply to such construction contracts, and for purposes of such application the administering department or agency shall be considered the contracting agency referred to therein.

(c) The term "applicant" as used in this Order means an applicant for Federal assistance or, as determined by agency regulation, other program participant, with respect to whom an application for any grant, contract, loan, insurance, or guarantee is not finally acted upon prior to the effective date of this Part, and it includes such an applicant after he becomes a recipient of such Federal assistance.

Sec. 303. (a) The Secretary of Labor shall be responsible for obtaining the compliance of such applicants with their undertakings under this Order. Each administering department and agency is directed to cooperate with the Secretary of Labor and to furnish the Secretary such information and assistance as the Secretary may require in the performance of the Secretary's functions under this Order.

(b) In the event an applicant fails and refuses to comply with the applicant's undertakings pursuant to this Order, the Secretary of Labor may, after consulting with the administering department or agency, take any or all of the following actions: (1) direct any administering department or agency to cancel, terminate, or suspend in whole or in part the agreement, contract or other arrangement with such applicant with respect to which the failure or refusal occurred; (2) direct any administering department or agency to refrain from extending any further assistance to the applicant under the program with respect to which the failure or refusal occurred until satisfactory assurance of future compliance has been received by the Secretary of Labor from such applicant; and (3) refer the case to the Department of Justice or the Equal Employment Opportunity Commission for appropriate law enforcement or other proceedings.

(c) In no case shall action be taken with respect to an applicant pursuant to clause (1) or (2) of subsection (b) without notice and opportunity for hearing.

[Sec. 303 amended by EO 12086 of Oct. 5, 1978, 43 FR 46501, 3 CFR, 1978 Comp., p. 230]

Sec. 304. Any executive department or agency which imposes by rule, regulation, or order requirements of nondiscrimination in employment, other than requirements imposed pursuant to this Order, may delegate to the Secretary of Labor by agreement such responsibilities with respect to compliance standards, reports, and procedures as would tend to bring the administration of such requirements into conformity with the administration of requirements imposed under this Order: *Provided,* That actions to effect compliance by recipients of Federal financial assistance with requirements imposed pursuant to Title VI of the Civil Rights Act of 1964 shall be taken in conformity with the procedures and limitations prescribed in Section 602 thereof and the regulations of the administering department or agency issued thereunder.

Part IV. Miscellaneous

Sec. 401. The Secretary of Labor may delegate to any officer, agency, or employee in the Executive branch of the Government, any function or duty of the Secretary under Parts II and III of this Order.

[Sec. 401 amended by EO 12086 of Oct. 5, 1978, 43 FR 46501, 3 CFR, 1978 Comp., p. 230]

Sec. 402. The Secretary of Labor shall provide administrative support for the execution of the program known as the "Plans for Progress."

Sec. 403. (a) Executive Orders Nos. 10590 (January 19, 1955), 10722 (August 5, 1957), 10925 (March 6, 1961), 11114 (June 22, 1963), and 11162 (July 28, 1964), are hereby superseded and the President's Committee on Equal Employment Opportunity established by Executive Order No. 10925 is hereby abolished. All records and property in the custody of the Committee shall be transferred to the Office of Personnel Management and the Secretary of Labor, as appropriate.

(b) Nothing in this Order shall be deemed to relieve any person of any obligation assumed or imposed under or pursuant to any Executive Order superseded by this Order. All rules, regulations, orders, instructions, designations, and other directives issued by the President's Committee on Equal Employment Opportunity and those issued by the heads of various departments or agencies under or pursuant to any of the Executive orders superseded by this Order, shall, to the extent that they are not inconsistent with this Order, remain in full force and effect unless and until revoked or superseded by appropriate authority. References in such directives to provisions of the superseded orders shall be deemed to be references to the comparable provisions of this Order.

[Sec. 403 amended by EO 12107 of Dec. 28, 1978, 44 FR 1055, 3 CFR, 1978 Comp., p. 264]

Sec. 404. The General Services Administration shall take appropriate action to revise the standard Government contract forms to accord with the provisions of this Order and of the rules and regulations of the Secretary of Labor.

Sec. 405. This Order shall become effective thirty days after the date of this Order.

CIVIL RIGHTS ATTORNEY'S FEES AWARD OF 1976 (42 U.S.C. SEC. 1988)

§ 1988. Proceedings in vindication of civil rights; attorney's fees

The jurisdiction in civil and criminal matters conferred on the district courts by the provisions of this Title, and of Title "CIVIL RIGHTS," and of Title "CRIMES," for the protection of all persons in the United States in their civil rights, and for their vindication, shall be exercised and enforced in conformity with the laws of the United States, so far as such laws are suitable to carry the same into effect; but in all cases where they are not adapted to the object, or are deficient in the provisions necessary to furnish suitable remedies and punish offenses against law, the common law, as modified and changed by the constitution and statutes of the State wherein the court having jurisdiction of such civil or criminal cause is held, so far as the same is not inconsistent with the Constitution and laws of the United States, shall be extended to and govern the said courts in the trial and disposition of the cause, and, if it is of a criminal nature, in the infliction of punishment on the party found guilty. In any action or proceeding to enforce a provision of sections 1981, 1982, 1983, 1985, and 1986 of this title, title IX of Public Law 92–318 [20 U.S.C. 1681 et seq.], or title VI of the Civil Rights Act of 1964 [42 U.S.C. 2000d et seq.], the court, in its discretion, may allow the prevailing party, other than the United States, a reasonable attorney's fee as part of the costs.

(R.S. § 722; Pub.L. 94–559, § 2, Oct. 19, 1976, 90 Stat. 2641; Pub.L. 96–481, title II, § 205(c), Oct. 21, 1980, 94 Stat. 2330.)

AN OVERVIEW OF THE 1978 UNIFORM GUIDELINES ON EMPLOYEE SELECTION PROCEDURES *

I. Background

One problem that confronted the Congress which adopted the Civil Rights Act of 1964 involved the effect of written preemployment tests on equal employment opportunity. The use of these test scores frequently denied employment to minorities in many cases without evidence that the tests were related to success on the job. Yet employers wished to continue to use such tests as practical tools to assist in the selection of qualified employees. Congress sought to strike a balance which would proscribe discrimination, but otherwise permit the use of tests in the selection of employees. Thus, in title VII, Congress authorized the use of "any professionally developed ability test provided that

---

* Federal Register, August 25, 1978, Part IV.

such test, its administration or action upon the results is not designed, intended or used to discriminate * * * ".[1]

At first, some employers contended that, under this section, they could use any test which had been developed by a professional so long as they did not intend to exclude minorities, even if such exclusion was the consequence of the use of the test. In 1966, the Equal Employment Opportunity Commission (EEOC) adopted guidelines to advise employers and other users what the law and good industrial psychology practice required.[2] The Department of Labor adopted the same approach in 1968 with respect to tests used by Federal contractors under Executive Order 11246 in a more detailed regulation. The Government's view was that the employer's intent was irrelevant. If tests or other practices had an adverse impact on protected groups, they were unlawful unless they could be justified. To justify a test which screened out a higher proportion of minorities, the employer would have to show that it fairly measured or predicted performance on the job. Otherwise, it would not be considered to be "professionally developed."

In succeeding years, the EEOC and the Department of Labor provided more extensive guidance which elaborated upon these principles and expanded the guidelines to emphasize all selection procedures. In 1971 in Griggs v. Duke Power Co.,[3] the Supreme Court announced the principle that employer practices which had an adverse impact on minorities and were not justified by business necessity constituted illegal discrimination under title VII. Congress confirmed this interpretation in the 1972 amendments to title VII. The elaboration of these principles by courts and agencies continued into the mid-1970's,[4] but differences between the EEOC and the other agencies (Justice, Labor, and Civil Service Commission) produced two different sets of guidelines by the end of 1976.

With the advent of the Carter administration in 1977, efforts were intensified to produce a unified government position. The following document represents the result of that effort. This introduction is intended to assist those not familiar with these matters to understand the basic approach of the uniform guidelines. While the guidelines are complex and technical, they are based upon the principles which have been consistently upheld by the courts, the Congress, and the agencies.

The following discussion will cite the sections of the Guidelines which embody these principles.

II. ADVERSE IMPACT

The fundamental principle underlying the guidelines is that employer policies or practices which have an adverse impact on employment opportunities of any race, sex, or ethnic group are illegal under

1. Section 703(h), 42 U.S.C. 2000e(2)(h).

2. See 35 U.S.L.W. 2137 (1966).

3. 401 U.S. 424 (1971).

4. See, e.g., Albemarle Paper Co. v. Moody, 422 U.S. 405 (1975).

title VII and the Executive order unless justified by business necessity.[5] A selection procedure which has no adverse impact generally does not violate title VII or the Executive order.[6] This means that an employer may usually avoid the application of the guidelines by use of procedures which have no adverse impact.[7] If adverse impact exists, it must be justified on grounds of business necessity. Normally, this means by validation which demonstrates the relation between the selection procedure and performance on the job.

The guidelines adopt a "rule of thumb" as a practical means of determining adverse impact for use in enforcement proceedings. This rule is known as the "⅘ths" or "80 percent" rule.[8] It is not a legal definition of discrimination, rather it is a practical device to keep the attention of enforcement agencies on serious discrepancies in hire or promotion rates or other employment decisions. To determine whether a selection procedure violates the "⅘ths rule", an employer compares its hiring rates for different groups.[9] But this rule of thumb cannot be applied automatically. An employer who has conducted an extensive recruiting campaign may have a larger than normal pool of applicants, and the "⅘ths rule" might unfairly expose it to enforcement proceedings.[10] On the other hand, an employer's reputation may have discouraged or "chilled" applicants of particular groups from applying because they believed application would be futile. The application of the "⅘ths" rule in that situation would allow an employer to evade scrutiny because of its own discrimination.[11]

III. Is Adverse Impact to Be Measured by the Overall Process?

In recent years some employers have eliminated the overall adverse impact of a selection procedure and employed sufficient numbers of minorities or women to meet this "⅘th's rule of thumb". However, they might continue use of a component which does have an adverse impact. For example, an employer might insist on a minimum passing score on a written test which is not job related and which has an adverse impact on minorities.[12] However, the employer might compensate for this adverse impact by hiring a sufficient proportion of minorities who do meet its standards, so that its overall hiring is on a par with or higher than the applicant flow. Employers have argued that as long as their "bottom line" shows no overall adverse impact, there is no violation at all, regardless of the operation of a particular component of the process.

---

5. *Griggs,* note 3, supra; uniform guidelines on employee selection procedures (1978), section 3A, (hereinafter cited by section number only).

6. Furnco v. Waters, 98 S.Ct. 2943 (1978).

7. Section 6.

8. Section 4D.

9. Section 16R (definition of selection rate).

10. Section 4D (special recruiting programs).

11. Ibid (user's actions have discouraged applicants).

12. See, e.g., Griggs v. Duke Power Co., 401 U.S. 424 (1971).

Employee representatives have argued that rights under equal employment opportunity laws are individual, and the fact that an employer has hired some minorities does not justify discrimination against other minorities. Therefore, they argue that adverse impact is to be determined by examination of each component of the selection procedure, regardless of the "bottom line." This question has not been answered definitively by the courts. There are decisions pointing in both directions.

These guidelines do not address the underlying question of law. They discuss only the exercise of prosecutorial discretion by the Government agencies themselves.[13] The agencies have decided that, generally, their resources to combat discrimination should be used against those respondents whose practices have restricted or excluded the opportunities of minorities and women. If an employer is appropriately including all groups in the workforce, it is not sensible to spend Government time and effort on such a case, when there are so many employers whose practices do have adverse effects which should be challenged. For this reason, the guidelines provide that, in considering whether to take enforcement action, the Government will take into account the general posture of the employer concerning equal employment opportunity, including its affirmative action plan and results achieved under the plan.[14] There are some circumstances where the government may intervene even though the "bottom line" has been satisfied. They include the case where a component of a selection procedure restricts promotional opportunities of minorities or women who were discriminatorily assigned to jobs, and where a component, such as a height requirement, has been declared unlawful in other situations.[15]

What of the individual who is denied the job because of a particular component in a procedure which otherwise meets the "bottom line" standard? The individual retains the right to proceed through the appropriate agencies, and into Federal court.[16]

IV. WHERE ADVERSE IMPACT EXISTS: THE BASIC OPTIONS

Once an employer has established that there is adverse impact, what steps are required by the guidelines? As previously noted, the employer can modify or eliminate the procedure which produces the adverse impact, thus taking the selection procedure from the coverage of these guidelines. If the employer does not do that, then it must justify the use of the procedure on grounds of "business necessity."[17]

---

13. Section 4C.

14. Section 4E.

15. Section 4C.

16. The processing of individual cases is excluded from the operation of the bottom line concept by the definition of "enforcement action," section 16I. Under section 4C, where adverse impact has existed, the

employer must keep records of the effect of each component for 2 years after the adverse effect has dissipated.

17. A few practices may be used without validation even if they have adverse impact. See, e.g., McDonnell Douglas v. Green, 411 U.S. 792 (1973) and section 6B.

This normally means that it must show a clear relation between performance on the selection procedure and performance on the job. In the language of industrial psychology, the employer must validate the selection procedure. Thus the bulk of the guidelines consist of the Government's interpretation of standards for validation.

V. VALIDATION: CONSIDERATION OF ALTERNATIVES

The concept of validation as used in personnel psychology involves the establishment of the relationship between a test instrument or other selection procedure and performance on the job. Federal equal employment opportunity law has added a requirement to the process of validation. In conducting a validation study, the employer should consider available alternatives which will achieve its legitimate business purpose with lesser adverse impact.[18] The employer cannot concentrate solely on establishing the validity of the instrument or procedure which it has been using in the past.

This same principle of using the alternative with lesser adverse impact is applicable to the manner in which an employer uses a valid selection procedure.[19] The guidelines assume that there are at least three ways in which an employer can use scores on a selection procedure: (1) To screen out of consideration those who are not likely to be able to perform the job successfully; (2) to group applicants in accordance with the likelihood of their successful performance on the job, and (3) to rank applicants, selecting those with the highest scores for employment.[20]

The setting of a "cutoff score" to determine who will be screened out may have an adverse impact. If so, an employer is required to justify the initial cutoff score by reference to its need for a trustworthy and efficient work force.[21] Similarly, use of results for grouping or for rank ordering is likely to have a greater adverse effect than use of scores solely to screen out unqualified candidates. If the employer chooses to use a rank order method, the evidence of validity must be sufficient to justify that method of use.[22]

VI. TESTING FOR HIGHER LEVEL JOBS

Normally, employers test for the job for which people are hired. However, there are situations where the first job is temporary or transient, and the workers who remain are promoted to work which involves more complex activities. The guidelines restrict testing for higher level jobs to users who promote a majority of the employees who

---

18. Albemarle Paper Co. v. Moody, 422 U.S. 405 (1975); Robinson v. Lorillard Corp., 444 F.2d 791 (4th Cir.1971).

19. Sections 3B; 5G.

20. Ibid.

21. See sections 3B; 5H. See also sections 14B(6) (criterion-related validity); 14C(9) (content validity); 14D(1) (construct validity).

22. Sections 5G, 14B(6); 14C(9); 14D(1).

remain with them to the higher level job within a reasonable period of time.[23]

VII. How is Validation to Be Conducted

Validation has become highly technical and complex, and yet is constantly changing as a set of concepts in industrial psychology. What follows here is a simple introduction to a highly complex field. There are three concepts which can be used to validate a selection procedure. These concepts reflect different approaches to investigating the job relatedness of selection procedures and may be interrelated in practice. They are (1) criterion-related validity,[24] (2) content validity,[25] and (3) construct validity.[26] In criterion-related validity, a selection procedure is justified by a statistical relationship between scores on the test or other selection procedure and measures of job performance. In content validity, a selection procedure is justified by showing that it representatively samples significant parts of the job, such as a typing test for a typist. Construct validity involves identifying the psychological trait (the construct) which underlies successful performance on the job and then devising a selection procedure to measure the presence and degree of the construct. An example would be a test of "leadership ability."

The guidelines contain technical standards and documentation requirements for the application of each of the three approaches.[27] One of the problems which the guidelines attempt to meet is the "border-line" between "content validity" and "construct validity." The extreme cases are easy to understand. A secretary, for example, may have to type. Many jobs require the separation of important matters which must be handled immediately from those which can be handled routinely. For the typing function, a typing test is appropriate. It is justifiable on the basis of content validity because it is a sample of an important or critical part of the job. The second function can be viewed as involving a capability to exercise selective judgment in light of the surrounding circumstances, a mental process which is difficult to sample.

In addressing this situation, the guidelines attempt to make it practical to validate the typing test by a content strategy,[28] but do not allow the validation of a test measuring a construct such as "judgment" by a content validity strategy.

The bulk of the guidelines deals with questions such as those discussed in the above paragraphs. Not all such questions can be answered simply, nor can all problems be addressed in the single

---

23. Section 5I.

24. Sections 5B, (General Standards); 14B (Technical Standards); 15B (Documentation); 16F (Definition).

25. Sections 5B (General Standards); 14C (Technical Standards); 15C (Documentation); 16D (Definition).

26. Sections 5B (General Standards); 14D (Technical Standards); 15D (Documentation); 16E (Definition).

27. Technical standards are in section 14; documentation requirements are in section 15.

28. Section 14C.

document. Once the guidelines are issued, they will have to be inter-preted in light of changing factual, legal, and professional circum-stances.

VIII. SIMPLIFICATION OF REPORTING AND RECORDKEEPING REQUIREMENTS

The reporting and recordkeeping provisions which appeared in the December 30 draft which was published for comment have been careful-ly reviewed in light of comments received and President Carter's direction to limit paperwork burdens on those regulated by Govern-ment to the minimum necessary for effective regulation. As a result of this review, two major changes have been made in the documentation requirements of the guidelines:

(1) A new section 15A(1) provides a simplified recordkeeping option for employers with fewer than 100 employees;

(2) Determinations of the adverse impact of selection procedures need not be made for groups which constitute less than 2 percent of the relevant labor force.

Also, the draft has been changed to make clear that users can assess adverse impact on an annual basis rather than on a continuing basis.

Analysis of comments. The uniform guidelines published today are based upon the proposition that the Federal Government should speak to the public and to those whom it regulates with one voice on this important subject; and that the Federal Government ought to impose upon itself obligations for equal employment opportunity which are at least as demanding as those it seeks to impose on others. These guidelines state a uniform Federal position on this subject, and are intended to protect the rights created by title VII of the Civil Rights Act of 1964, as amended, Executive Order 11246, as amended, and other provisions of Federal law. The uniform guidelines are also intended to represent "professionally acceptable methods" of the psychological pro-fession for demonstrating whether a selection procedure validly predicts or measures performance for a particular job. Albemarle Paper Co. v. Moody, 442 U.S. 405, 425. They are also intended to be consistent with the decisions of the Supreme Court and authoritative decisions of other appellate courts.

Although the development of these guidelines preceded the issu-ance by President Jimmy Carter of Executive Order 12044 designed to improve the regulatory process, the spirit of his Executive order was followed in their development. Initial agreement among the Federal agencies was reached early in the fall of 1977, and the months from October 1977 until today have been spent in extensive consultation with civil rights groups whose clientele are protected by these guide-lines; employers, labor unions, and State and local governments whose employment practices are affected by these guidelines; State and local government antidiscrimination agencies who share with the Federal

Government enforcement responsibility for discriminatory practices; and appropriate members of the general public. For example, an earlier draft of these guidelines was circulated informally for comment on October 28, 1977, pursuant to OMB Circular A–85. Many comments were received from representatives of State and local governments, psychologists, private employers, and civil rights groups. Those comments were taken into account in the draft of these guidelines which was published for comment December 30, 1977, 42 FR 66542.

More than 200 organizations and individuals submitted written comments on the December 30, 1977, draft. These comments were from representatives of private industry, public employers, labor organizations, civil rights groups, the American Psychological Association and components thereof, and many individual employers, psychologists, and personnel specialists. On March 3, 1978, notice was given of a public hearing and meeting to be held on April 10, 1978, 43 FR 9131. After preliminary review of the comments, the agencies identified four issues of particular interest, and invited testimony particularly on those issues, 43 FR 11812 (March 21, 1978). In the same notice the agencies published questions and answers on four issues of concern to the commenters. The questions and answers were designed to clarify the intent of the December 30, 1977, draft, so as to provide a sharper focus for the testimony at the hearing.

At a full day of testimony on April 10, 1978, representatives of private industry, State and local governments, labor organizations, and civil rights groups, as well as psychologists, personnel specialists, and others testified at the public hearing and meeting. The written comments, testimony, and views expressed in subsequent informal consultations have been carefully considered by the four agencies. We set forth below a summary of the comments, and the major issues raised in the comments and testimony, and attempt to explain how we have resolved those issues.

The statement submitted by the American Psychological Association (A.P.A.) stated that "these guidelines represent a major step forward and with careful interpretation can provide a sound basis for concerned professional work." Most of the A.P.A. comments were directed to clarification and interpretation of the present language of the proposal. However, the A.P.A. recommended substantive change in the construct validity section and in the definition of work behavior.

Similarly, the Division of Industrial and Organizational Psychology (division 14) of the A.P.A. described the technical standards of the guidelines as "superior" in terms of congruence with professional standards to "most previous orders and guidelines but numerous troublesome aspects remain." Division 14 had substantial concerns with a number of the provisions of the general principles of the draft.

Civil rights groups generally found the uniform guidelines far superior to the FEA guidelines, and many urged their adoption, with modifications concerning ranking and documentation. Others raised concerns about the "bottom line" concept and other provisions of the guidelines.

The Ad Hoc Group on Employee Selection Procedures representing many employers in private industry supported the concept of uniform guidelines, but had a number of problems with particular provisions, some of which are described below. The American Society for Personnel Administration (ASPA) and the International Personnel Management Association, which represents State and local governments, generally took the same position as the ad hoc group. Major industrial unions found that the draft guidelines were superior to the FEA guidelines, but they perceived them to be inferior to the EEOC guidelines. They challenged particularly the bottom line concept and the construct validity section.

The building trade unions urged an exclusion of apprenticeship programs from coverage of the guidelines. The American Council on Education found them inappropriate for employment decisions concerning faculty at institutions of higher education. Other particular concerns were articulated by organizations representing the handicapped, licensing and certifying agencies, and college placement offices.

General Principles

1. *Relationship between validation and elimination of adverse impact, and affirmative action.* Federal equal employment opportunity law generally does not require evidence of validity for a selection procedure if there is no adverse impact; e.g., Griggs v. Duke Power Co., 401 U.S. 424. Therefore, a user has the choice of complying either by providing evidence of validity (or otherwise justifying use in accord with Federal law), or by eliminating the adverse impact. These options have always been present under Federal law, 29 CFR 1607.3; 41 CFR 60–3.3(a); and the Federal Executive Agency Guidelines, 41 FR 51734 (November 23, 1976). The December 30 draft guidelines, however, clarified the nature of the two options open to users.

Psychologists expressed concern that the December 30 draft of section 6A encouraged the use of invalid procedures as long as there is no adverse impact. Employers added the concern that the section might encourage the use of illegal procedures not having an adverse impact against the groups who have historically suffered discrimination (minorities, women), even if they have an adverse impact on a different group (whites, males).

Section 6A was not so intended, and we have revised it to clarify the fact that illegal acts purporting to be affirmative action are not the goal of the agencies or of the guidelines; and that any employee selection procedure must be lawful and should be as job related as possible. The delineation of examples of alternative procedures was eliminated to avoid the implication that particular procedures are either prescribed or are necessarily appropriate. The basic thrust of section 6A, that elimination of adverse impact is an alternative to validation, is retained.

The inclusion of excerpts from the 1976 Equal Employment Opportunity Coordinating Council Policy Statement on Affirmative Action in section 13B of the December 30 draft was criticized as not belonging in a set of guidelines for the validation of selection procedures. Section 13 has been revised. The general statement of policy in support of voluntary affirmative action, and the reaffirmation of the policy statement have been retained, but this statement itself is now found in the appendix to the guidelines.

2. *The "bottom line" (section 4C)*. The guidelines provide that when the overall selection process does not have an adverse impact the Government will usually not examine the individual components of that process for adverse impact or evidence of validity. The concept is based upon the view that the Federal Government should not generally concern itself with individual components of a selection process, if the overall effect of that process is nonexclusionary. Many commenters criticized the ambiguity caused by the word "generally" in the December 30 draft of section 4C which provided, "the Federal enforcement agencies * * * generally will not take enforcement action based upon adverse impact of any component" of a process that does not have an overall adverse impact. Employer groups stated the position that the "bottom line" should be a rule prohibiting enforcement action by Federal agencies with respect to all or any part of a selection process where the bottom line does not show adverse impact. Civil rights and some labor union representatives expressed the opposing concerns that the concept may be too restrictive, that it may be interpreted as a matter of law, and that it might allow certain discriminatory conditions to go unremedied.

The guidelines have been revised to clarify the intent that the bottom line concept is based upon administrative and prosecutorial discretion. The Federal agencies cannot accept the recommendation that they never inquire into or take enforcement action with respect to any component procedure unless the whole process of which it is a part has an adverse impact. The Federal enforcement agencies believe that enforcement action may be warranted in unusual circumstances, such as those involving other discriminatory practices, or particular selection procedures which have no validity and have a clear adverse impact on a national basis. Other unusual circumstances may warrant a high level agency decision to proceed with enforcement actions although the "bottom line" has been satisfied. At the same time the agencies adhere to the bottom line concept of allocating resources primarily to those users whose overall selection processes have an adverse impact. See overview, above, part III.

3. *Investigation of alternative selection procedures and alternative methods of use (section 3B)*. The December 30 draft included an obligation on the user, when conducting a validity study, to investigate

alternative procedures and uses, in order to determine whether there are other procedures which are substantially equally valid, but which have less adverse impact. The American Psychological Association stated:

> We would concur with the drafters of the guidelines that it is appropriate in the determination of a selection strategy to consider carefully a variety of possible procedures and to think carefully about the question of adverse impact with respect to each of these procedures. Nevertheless, we feel it appropriate to note that a rigid enforcement of these sections, particularly for smaller employers, would impose a substantial and expensive burden on these employers.

Since a reasonable consideration of alternatives is consistent with the underlying principle of minimizing adverse impact consistent with business needs, the provision is retained.

Private employer representatives challenged earlier drafts of these guidelines as being inconsistent with the decision of the Supreme Court in Albemarle Paper Co. v. Moody, 422 U.S. 405. No such inconsistency was intended. Accordingly, the first sentence of section 3B was revised to paraphrase the opinion in the *Albemarle* decision, so as to make it clear that section 3B is in accord with the principles of the *Albemarle* decision.

Section 3B was further revised to clarify the intent of the guidelines that the obligation to investigate alternative procedures is a part of conducting a validity study, so that alternative procedures should be evaluated in light of validity studies meeting professional standards, and that section 3B does not impose an obligation to search for alternatives if the user is not required to conduct a validity study.

Just as, under section 3B of the guidelines, a user should investigate alternative selection procedures as a part of choosing and validating a procedure, so should the user investigate alternative uses of the selection device chosen to find the use most appropriate to his needs. The validity study should address the question of what method of use (screening, grouping, or rank ordering) is appropriate for a procedure based on the kind and strength of the validity evidence shown, and the degree of adverse impact of the different uses.

4. *Establishment of cutoff scores and rank ordering.* Some commenters from civil rights groups believed that the December 30 draft guidelines did not provide sufficient guidance as to when it was permissible to use a selection procedure on a ranking basis rather than on a pass-fail basis. They also objected to section 5G in terms of setting cutoff scores. Other comments noted a lack of clarity as to how the determination of a cutoff score or the use of a procedure for ranking candidates relates to adverse impact.

As we have noted, users are not required to validate procedures which do not have an adverse impact. However, if one way of using a procedure (e.g., for ranking) results in greater adverse impact than another way (e.g., pass/fail), the procedure must be validated for that use. Similarly, cutoff scores which result in adverse impact should be justified. If the use of a validated procedure for ranking results in greater adverse impact than its use as a screening device, the evidence of validity and utility must be sufficient to warrant use of the procedures as a ranking device.

A new section 5G has been added to clarify these concepts. Section 5H (formerly section 5G) addresses the choice of a cutoff score when a procedure is to be used for ranking.

5. *Scope: Requests for exemptions for certain classes of users.* Some employer groups and labor organizations (e.g., academic institutions, large public employers, apprenticeship councils) argued that they should be exempted from all or some of the provisions of these guidelines because of their special needs. The intent of Congress as expressed in Federal equal employment opportunity law is to apply the same standards to all users, public and private.

These guidelines apply the same principles and standards to all employers. On the other hand, the nature of the procedures which will actually meet those principles and standards may be different for different employers, and the guidelines recognize that fact. Accordingly, the guidelines are applicable to all employers and other users who are covered by Federal equal employment opportunity law.

Organizations of handicapped persons objected to excluding from the scope of these guidelines the enforcement of laws prohibiting discrimination on the basis of handicap, in particular the Rehabilitation Act of 1973, sections 501, 503, and 504. While this issue has not been addressed in the guidelines, nothing precludes the adoption of the principles set forth in these guidelines for other appropriate situations.

Licensing and certification boards raised the question of the applicability of the guidelines to their licensing and certification functions. The guidelines make it clear that licensing and certification are covered "to the extent" that licensing and certification may be covered by Federal equal employment opportunity law.

Voluntary certification boards, where certification is not required by law, are not users as defined in section 16 with respect to their certifying functions and therefore are not subject to these guidelines. If an employer relies upon such certification in making employment decisions, the employer is the user and must be prepared to justify, under Federal law, that reliance as it would any other selection procedure.

6. *The "Four-Fifths Rule of Thumb" (section 4D).* Some representatives of employers and some professionals suggest that the basic test for adverse impact should be a test of statistical significance, rather than the four-fifths rule. Some civil rights groups, on the other hand, still regard the four-fifths rule as permitting some unlawful discrimination.

The Federal agencies believe that neither of these positions is correct. The great majority of employers do not hire, promote, or assign enough employees for most jobs to warrant primary reliance upon statistical significance. Many decisions in day-to-day life are made on the basis of information which does not have the justification of a test of statistical significance. Courts have found adverse impact without a showing of statistical significance. Griggs v. Duke Power Co., supra; Vulcan Society of New York v. CSC of N.Y., 490 F.2d 387, 393 (2d Cir.1973); Kirkland v. New York St. Dept. of Corr. Serv., 520 F.2d 420, 425 (2d Cir.1975).

Accordingly, the undersigned believe that while the four-fifths rule does not define discrimination and does not apply in all cases, it is appropriate as a rule of thumb in identifying adverse impact.

Technical Standards

7. *Criterion-related validity (section 14B)*. This section of the guidelines found general support among the commenters from the psychological profession and, except for the provisions concerning test fairness (sometimes mistakenly equated with differential prediction or differential validity), generated relatively little comment.

The provisions of the guidelines concerning criterion-related validity studies call for studies of fairness of selection procedures where technically feasible.

Section 14B(8). Some psychologists and employer groups objected that the concept of test fairness or unfairness has been discredited by professionals and pointed out that the term is commonly misused. We recognize that there is serious debate on the question of test fairness; however, it is accepted professionally that fairness should be examined where feasible. The A.P.A. standards for educational and psychological tests, for example, direct users to explore the question of fairness on finding a difference in group performances (section E9, pp. 43–44). Similarly the concept of test fairness is one which is closely related to the basic thrust of Federal equal employment opportunity law; and that concept was endorsed by the Supreme Court in Albemarle Paper Co. v. Moody, 422 U.S. 405.

Accordingly, we have retained in the guidelines the obligation upon users to investigate test fairness where it is technically feasible to do so.

8. *Content validity*. The Division of Industrial and Organizational Psychology of A.P.A. correctly perceived that the provisions of the draft guidelines concerning content validity, with their emphasis on observable work behaviors or work products, were "greatly concerned with minimizing the inferential leap between test and performance." That division expressed the view that the draft guidelines neglected situations where a knowledge, skill or ability is necessary to an outcome but where the work behavior cannot be replicated in a test. They recommended that the section be revised.

We believe that the emphasis on observable work behaviors or observable work products is appropriate; and that in order to show content validity, the gap between the test and performance on the job should be a small one. We recognize, however, that content validity may be appropriate to support a test which measures a knowledge, skill, or ability which is a necessary prerequisite to the performance of the job, even though the test might not be close enough to the work behavior to be considered a work sample, and the guidelines have been revised appropriately. On the other hand, tests of mental processes which are not directly observable and which may be difficult to determine on the basis of observable work behaviors or work products should not be supported by content validity.

Thus, the Principles for the Validation and Use of Personnel Selection Procedures (Division of Industrial and Organizational Psychology, American Psychological Association, 1975, p. 10), discuss the use of content validity to support tests of "specific items of knowledge, or specific job skills," but call attention to the inappropriateness of attempting to justify tests for traits or constructs on a content validity basis.

9. *Construct validity (section 14D).* Business groups and professionals expressed concern that the construct validity requirements in the December 30 draft were confusing and technically inaccurate. As section 14D indicates, construct validity is a relatively new procedure in the field of personnel selection and there is not yet substantial guidance in the professional literature as to its use in the area of employment practices. The provisions on construct validity have been revised to meet the concerns expressed by the A.P.A. The construct validity section as revised clarifies what is required by the Federal enforcement agencies at this stage in the development of construct validity. The guidelines leave open the possibility that different evidence of construct validity may be accepted in the future, as new methodologies develop and become incorporated in professional standards and other professional literature.

10. *Documentation (section 15).* Commenters stated that the documentation section did not conform to the technical requirements of the guidelines or was otherwise inadequate. Section 15 has been clarified and two significant changes have been made to minimize the record-keeping burden. (See overview, part VIII.)

11. *Definitions (section 16).* The definition of work behavior in the December 30, 1977 draft was criticized by the A.P.A. and others as being too vague to provide adequate guidance to those using the guidelines who must identify work behavior as a part of any validation technique. Other comments criticized the absence or inadequacies of other definitions, especially "adverse impact." Substantial revisions of and additions to this section were therefore made.

PART 1604—GUIDELINES ON DISCRIMINATION BECAUSE OF SEX

Authority: Sec. 713(b), 78 Stat. 265, 42 U.S.C. 2000e–12.
Source: 37 FR 6836, April 5, 1972, unless otherwise noted.

§ 1604.1   General principles

(a) References to "employer" or "employers" in this Part 1604 state principles that are applicable not only to employers but also to labor organizations and to employment agencies insofar as their action or inaction may adversely affect employment opportunities.

(b) To the extent that the views expressed in prior Commission pronouncements are inconsistent with the views expressed herein, such prior views are hereby overruled.

(c) The Commission will continue to consider particular problems relating to sex discrimination on a case-by-case basis.

§ 1604.2   Sex as a bona fide occupational qualification

(a) The commission believes that the bona fide occupational qualification exception as to sex should be interpreted narrowly. Label—"Men's jobs" and "Women's jobs"—tend to deny employment opportunities unnecessarily to one sex or the other.

(1) The Commission will find that the following situations do not warrant the application of the bona fide occupational qualification exception:

(i) The refusal to hire a woman because of her sex based on assumptions of the comparative employment characteristics of women in general. For example, the assumption that the turnover rate among women is higher than among men.

(ii) The refusal to hire an individual based on stereotyped characterizations of the sexes. Such stereotypes include, for example, that men are less capable of assembling intricate equipment: that women are less capable of aggressive salesmanship. The principle of nondiscrimination requires that individuals be considered on the basis of individual capacities and not on the basis of any characteristics generally attributed to the group.

(iii) The refusal to hire an individual because of the preferences of coworkers, the employer, clients or customers except as covered specifically in paragraph (a)(2) of this section.

(2) Where it is necessary for the purpose of authenticity or genuineness, the Commission will consider sex to be a bona fide occupational qualification, e.g., an actor or actress.

(b) Effect of sex-oriented State employment legislation.

(1) Many States have enacted laws or promulgated administrative regulations with respect to the employment of females. Among these laws are those which prohibit or limit the employment of females, e.g., the employment of females in certain occupations, in jobs requiring the lifting or carrying of weights exceeding certain prescribed limits, during certain hours of the night, for more than a specified number of hours per day or per week, and for certain periods of time before and after childbirth. The Commission has found that such laws and regulations do not take into account the capacities, preferences, and abilities of individual females and, therefore, discriminate on the basis of sex. The Commission has concluded that such laws and regulations conflict with and are superseded by title VII of the Civil Rights Act of 1964. Accordingly, such laws will not be considered a defense to an otherwise established unlawful employment practice or as a basis for the application of the bona fide occupational qualification exception.

(2) The Commission has concluded that State laws and regulations which discriminate on the basis of sex with regard to the employment of minors are in conflict with and are superseded by title VII to the extent that such laws are more restrictive for one sex. Accordingly, restrictions on the employment of minors of one sex over and above those imposed on minors of the other sex will not be considered a defense to an otherwise established unlawful employment practice or as a basis for the application of the bona fide occupational qualification exception.

(3) A number of States require that minimum wage and premium pay for overtime be provided for female employees. An employer will be deemed to have engaged in an unlawful employment practice if:

(i) It refuses to hire or otherwise adversely affects the employment opportunities of female applicants or employees in order to avoid the payment of minimum wages or overtime pay required by State law; or

(ii) It does not provide the same benefits for male employees.

(4) As to other kinds of sex-oriented State employment laws, such as those requiring special rest and meal periods or physical facilities for women, provision of these benefits to one sex only will be a violation of title VII. An employer will be deemed to have engaged in an unlawful employment practice if:

(i) It refuses to hire or otherwise adversely affects the employment opportunities of female applicants or employees in order to avoid the provision of such benefits; or

(ii) It does not provide the same benefits for male employees. If the employer can prove that business necessity precludes providing these benefits to both men and women, then the State law is in conflict with and superseded by title VII as to this employer. In this situation, the employer shall not provide such benefits to members of either sex.

(5) Some States require that separate restrooms be provided for employees of each sex. An employer will be deemed to have engaged in an unlawful employment practice if it refuses to hire or otherwise adversely affects the employment opportunities of applicants or employees in order to avoid the provision of such restrooms for persons of that sex.

§ 1604.3 Separate lines of progression and seniority systems

(a) It is an unlawful employment practice to classify a job as "male" or "female" or to maintain separate lines of progression or separate seniority lists based on sex where this would adversely affect any employee unless sex is a bona fide occupational qualification for that job. Accordingly, employment practices are unlawful which arbitrarily classify jobs so that:

(1) A female is prohibited from applying for a job labeled "male," or for a job in a "male" line of progression; and vice versa.

(2) A male scheduled for layoff is prohibited from displacing a less senior female on a "female" seniority list; and vice versa.

(b) A Seniority system or line of progression which distinguishes between "light" and "heavy" jobs constitutes an unlawful employment practice if it operates as a disguised form of classification by sex, or creates unreasonable obstacles to the advancement by members of either sex into jobs which members of that sex would reasonably be expected to perform.

§ 1604.4 Discrimination against married women

(a) The Commission has determined that an employer's rule which forbids or restricts the employment of married women and which is not applicable to married men is a discrimination based on sex prohibited by title VII of the Civil Rights Act. It does not seem to us relevant that the rule is not directed against all females, but only against married females, for so long as sex is a factor in the application of the rule, such application involves a discrimination based on sex.

(b) It may be that under certain circumstances, such a rule could be justified within the meaning of section 703(e)(1) of title VII. We express no opinion on this question at this time except to point out that sex as a bona fide occupational qualification must be justified in terms of the peculiar requirements of the particular job and not on the basis of a general principle such as the desirability of spreading work.

§ 1604.5   Job opportunities advertising

It is a violation of title VII for a help-wanted advertisement to indicate a preference, limitation, specification, or discrimination based on sex unless sex is a bona fide occupational qualification for the particular job involved. The placement of an advertisement in columns classified by publishers on the basis of sex, such as columns headed "Male" or "Female," will be considered an expression of a preference, limitation, specification, or discrimination based on sex.

§ 1604.6   Employment agencies

(a) Section 703(b) of the Civil Rights Act specifically states that it shall be unlawful for an employment agency to discriminate against any individual because of sex. The Commission has determined that private employment agencies which deal exclusively with one sex are engaged in an unlawful employment practice, except to the extent that such agencies limit their services to furnishing employees for particular jobs for which sex is a bona fide occupational qualification.

(b) An employment agency that receives a job order containing an unlawful sex specification will share responsibility with the employer placing the job order if the agency fills the order knowing that the sex specification is not based upon a bona fide occupational qualification. However, an employment agency will not be deemed to be in violation of the law, regardless of the determination as to the employer, if the agency does not have reason to believe that the employer's claim of bona fide occupations qualification is without substance and the agency makes and maintains a written record available to the Commission of each such job order. Such record shall include the name of the employer, the description of the job and the basis for the employer's claim of bona fide occupational qualification.

(c) It is the responsibility of employment agencies to keep informed of opinions and decisions of the Commission on sex discrimination.

§ 1604.7   Pre-employment inquiries as to sex

A pre-employment inquiry may ask "Male ___, Female ___"; or "Mr. Mrs. Miss," provided that the inquiry is made in good faith for a nondiscriminatory purpose. Any pre-employment inquiry in connection with prospective employment which expresses directly or indirectly any limitation, specification, or discrimination as to sex shall be unlawful unless based upon a bona fide occupational qualification.

§ 1604.8   Relationship of title VII to the Equal Pay Act

(a) The employee coverage of the prohibitions against discrimination based on sex contained in title VII is coextensive with that of the other prohibitions contained in title VII and is not limited by section 703(h) to those employees covered by the Fair Labor Standards Act.

(b) By virtue of section 703(h), a defense based on the Equal Pay Act may be raised in a proceeding under title VII.

(c) Where such a defense is raised the Commission will give appropriate consideration to the interpretations of the Administrator, Wage and Hour Division, Department of Labor, but will not be bound thereby.

§ 1604.9 Fringe benefits

(a) "Fringe benefits," as used herein, includes medical, hospital, accident, life insurance and retirement benefits; profit-sharing and bonus plans; leave; and other terms, conditions, and privileges of employment.

(b) It shall be an unlawful employment practice for an employer to discriminate between men and women with regard to fringe benefits.

(c) Where an employer conditions benefits available to employees and their spouses and families on whether the employee is the "head of the household" or "principal wage earner" in the family unit, the benefits tend to be available only to male employees and their families. Due to the fact that such conditioning discriminatorily affects the rights of women employees, and that "head of household" or "principal wage earner" status bears no relationship to job performance, benefits which are so conditioned will be found a prima facie violation of the prohibitions against sex discrimination contained in the act.

(d) It shall be an unlawful employment practice for an employer to make available benefits for the wives and families of male employees where the same benefits are not made available for the husbands and families of female employees; or to make available benefits for the wives of male employees which are not made available for female employees; or to make available benefits to the husbands of female employees which are not made available for male employees. An example of such an unlawful employment practice is a situation in which wives of male employees receive maternity benefits while female employees receive no such benefits.

(e) It shall not be a defense under title VIII to a charge of sex discrimination in benefits that the cost of such benefits is greater with respect to one sex than the other.

(f) It shall be an unlawful employment practice for an employer to have a pension or retirement plan which establishes different optional or compulsory retirement ages based on sex, or which differentiates in benefits on the basis of sex. A statement of the General Counsel of September 13, 1968, providing for a phasing out of differentials with regard to optional retirement age for certain incumbent employees is hereby withdrawn.

§ 1604.10 Employment policies relating to pregnancy and childbirth

(a) A written or unwritten employment policy or practice which excludes from employment applicants or employees because of pregnancy, childbirth or related medical conditions is in prima facie violation of Title VII.

(b) Disabilities caused or contributed to by pregnancy, childbirth, or related medical conditions, for all job-related purposes, shall be treated the same as disabilities caused or contributed to by other medical conditions, under any health or disability insurance or sick leave plan available in connection with employment. Written or unwritten employment policies and practices involving matters such as the commencement and duration of leave, the availability of extensions, the accrual of seniority and other benefits and privileges, reinstatement, and payment under any health or disability insurance or sick leave plan, formal or informal, shall be applied to disability due to pregnancy, childbirth or related medical conditions on the same terms and conditions as they are applied to other disabilities. Health insurance benefits for abortion, except where the life of the mother would be endangered if the fetus were carried to term or where medical complications have arisen from an abortion, are not required to be paid by an employer; nothing herein, however, precludes an employer from providing abortion benefits or otherwise affects bargaining agreements in regard to abortion.

(c) Where the termination of an employee who is temporarily disabled is caused by an employment policy under which insufficient or no leave is available, such a termination violates the Act if it has a disparate impact on employees of one sex and is not justified by business necessity.

(d)(1) Any fringe benefit program, or fund, or insurance program which is in effect on October 31, 1978, which does not treat women affected by pregnancy, childbirth, or related medical conditions the same as other persons not so affected but similar in their ability or inability to work, must be in compliance with the provisions of § 1604.10(b) by April 29, 1979. In order to come into compliance with the provisions of 1604.10(b), there can be no reduction of benefits or compensation which were in effect on October 31, 1978, before October 31, 1979 or the expiration of a collective bargaining agreement in effect on October 31, 1978, whichever is later.

(2) Any fringe benefit program implemented after October 31, 1978, must comply with the provisions of § 1604.10(b) upon implementation.

[44 FR 23805, Apr. 20, 1979]

§ 1604.11 Sexual harassment

(a) Harassment on the basis of sex is a violation of Sec. 703 of Title VII.[1] Unwelcome sexual advances, requests for sexual favors, and other verbal or physical conduct of a sexual nature constitute sexual harassment when (1) submission to such conduct is made either explicitly or implicitly a term or condition of an individual's employment, (2) submission to or rejection of such conduct by an individual is used as the basis for employment decisions affecting such individual, or (3) such conduct has the purpose or effect of unreasonably interfering with an individual's work performance or creating an intimidating, hostile, or offensive working environment.

(b) In determining whether alleged conduct constitutes sexual harassment, the Commission will look at the record as a whole and at the totality of the circumstances, such as the nature of the sexual advances and the context in which the alleged incidents occurred. The determination of the legality of a particular action will be made from the facts, on a case by case basis.

(c) Applying general Title VII principles, an employer, employment agency, joint apprenticeship committee or labor organization (hereinafter collectively referred to as "employer") is responsible for its acts and those of its agents and supervisory employees with respect to sexual harassment regardless of whether the specific acts complained of were authorized or even forbidden by the employer and regardless of whether the employer knew or should have known of their occurrence. The Commission will examine the circumstances of the particular employment relationship and the job junctions performed by the individual in determining whether an individual acts in either a supervisory or agency capacity.

(d) With respect to conduct between fellow employees, an employer is responsible for acts of sexual harassment in the workplace where the employer (or its agents or supervisory employees) knows or should have known of the conduct, unless it can show that it took immediate and appropriate corrective action.

(e) An employer may also be responsible for the acts of non-employees, with respect to sexual harassment of employees in the workplace, where the employer (or its agents or supervisory employees) knows or should have known of the conduct and fails to take immediate and appropriate corrective action. In reviewing these cases the Commission will consider the extent of the employer's control and any other legal responsibility which the employer may have with respect to the conduct of such non-employees.

(f) Prevention is the best tool for the elimination of sexual harassment. An employer should take all steps necessary to prevent sexual harassment from occurring, such as affirmatively raising the subject,

---

1. The principles involved here continue to apply to race, color, religion or national origin.

expressing strong disapproval, developing appropriate sanctions, informing employees of their right to raise and how to raise the issue of harassment under Title VII, and developing methods to sensitize all concerned.

(g) Other related practices: Where employment opportunities or benefits are granted because of an individual's submission to the employer's sexual advances or requests for sexual favors, the employer may be held liable for unlawful sex discrimination against other persons who were qualified for but denied that employment opportunity or benefit.

(Title VII, Pub.L. 88–352, 78 Stat. 253 (42 U.S.C. 2000e et seq.))

[45 FR 74677, Nov. 10, 1980]

PART 1605—GUIDELINES ON DISCRIMINATION BECAUSE OF RELIGION

Sec.

1605.1   "Religious" nature of a practice or belief.
1605.2   Reasonable accommodation without undue hardship as required by Section 701(j) of Title VII of the Civil Rights Act of 1964.
1605.3   Selection practices.
Appendix A to §§ 1605.2 and 1605.3—Background Information
Authority: Title VII of the Civil Rights Act of 1964, as amended, 42 U.S.C. 2000e et seq.
Source: 45 FR 72612, Oct. 31, 1980, unless otherwise noted.

§ 1605.1 "Religious" nature of a practice or belief

In most cases whether or not a practice or belief is religious is not at issue. However, in those cases in which the issue does exist, the Commission will define religious practices to include moral or ethical beliefs as to what is right and wrong which are sincerely held with the strength of traditional religious views. This standard was developed in United States v. Seeger, 380 U.S. 163 (1965) and Welsh v. United States, 398 U.S. 333 (1970). The Commission has consistently applied this standard in its decisions.[1] The fact that no religious group espouses such beliefs or the fact that the religious group to which the individual professes to belong may not accept such belief will not determine whether the belief is a religious belief of the employee or prospective employee. The phrase "religious practice" as used in these Guidelines includes both religious observances and practices, as stated in Section 701(j), 42 U.S.C. 2000e(j).

----

1. See CD 76–104 (1976), CCH ¶ 6500; CD 71–2620 (1971), CCH ¶ 6283; CD 71–779 (1970), CCH ¶ 6180.

§ 1605.2 Reasonable accommodation without undue hardship as required by Section 701(j) of Title VII of the Civil Rights Act of 1964

(a) *Purpose of this section.* This section clarifies the obligation imposed by Title VII of the Civil Rights Act of 1964, as amended, (sections 701(j), 703 and 717) to accommodate the religious practices of employees and prospective employees. This section does not address other obligations under Title VII not to discriminate on grounds of religion, nor other provisions of Title VII. This section is not intended to limit any additional obligations to accommodate religious practices which may exist pursuant to constitutional, or other statutory provisions; neither is it intended to provide guidance for statutes which require accommodation on bases other than religion such as section 503 of the Rehabilitation Act of 1973. The legal principles which have been developed with respect to discrimination prohibited by Title VII on the basis of race, color, sex, and national origin also apply to religious discrimination in all circumstances other than where an accommodation is required.

(b) *Duty to accommodate.* (1) Section 701(j) makes it an unlawful employment practice under section 703(a)(1) for an employer to fail to reasonably accommodate the religious practices of an employee or prospective employee, unless the employer demonstrates that accommodation would result in undue hardship on the conduct of its business.[2]

(2) Section 701(j) in conjunction with section 703(c), imposes an obligation on a labor organization to reasonably accommodate the religious practices of an employee or prospective employee, unless the labor organization demonstrates that accommodation would result in undue hardship.

(3) Section 1605.2 is primarily directed to obligations of employers or labor organizations, which are the entities covered by Title VII that will most often be required to make an accommodation. However, the principles of § 1605.2 also apply when an accommodation can be required of other entities covered by Title VII, such as employment agencies (Section 703(b)) or joint labor-management committees controlling apprenticeship or other training or retraining (Section 703(d)). (See, for example, § 1605.3(a) "Scheduling of Tests or Other Selection Procedures.")

(c) *Reasonable accommodation.* (1) After an employee or prospective employee notifies the employer or labor organization of his or her need for a religious accommodation, the employer or labor organization has an obligation to reasonably accommodate the individual's religious practices. A refusal to accommodate is justified only when an employer or labor organization can demonstrate that an undue hardship would in fact result from each available alternative method of accommodation. A mere assumption that many more people, with the same

2. See Trans World Airlines, Inc. v. Hardison, 432 U.S. 63, 74 (1977).

religious practices as the person being accommodated, may also need accommodation is not evidence of undue hardship.

(2) When there is more than one method of accommodation available which would not cause undue hardship, the Commission will determine whether the accommodation offered is reasonable by examining:

(i) The alternatives for accommodation considered by the employer or labor organization; and

(ii) The alternatives for accommodation, if any, actually offered to the individual requiring accommodation. Some alternatives for accommodating religious practices might disadvantage the individual with respect to his or her employment opportunities, such as compensation, terms, conditions, or privileges of employment. Therefore, when there is more than one means of accommodation which would not cause undue hardship, the employer or labor organization must offer the alternative which least disadvantages the individual with respect to his or her employment opportunities.

(d) *Alternatives for accommodating religious practices.* (1) Employees and prospective employees most frequently request an accommodation because their religious practices conflict with their work schedules. The following subsections are some means of accommodating the conflict between work schedules and religious practices which the Commission believes that employers and labor organizations should consider as part of the obligation to accommodate and which the Commission will consider in investigating a charge. These are not intended to be all-inclusive. There are often other alternatives which would reasonably accommodate an individual's religious practices when they conflict with a work schedule. There are also employment practices besides work scheduling which may conflict with religious practices and cause an individual to request an accommodation. See, for example, the Commission's finding number (3) from its Hearings on Religious Discrimination, in Appendix A to §§ 1605.2 and 1605.3. The principles expressed in these Guidelines apply as well to such requests for accommodation.

(i) Voluntary Substitutes and "Swaps".

Reasonable accommodation without undue hardship is generally possible where a voluntary substitute with substantially similar qualifications is available. One means of substitution is the voluntary swap. In a number of cases, the securing of a substitute has been left entirely up to the individual seeking the accommodation. The Commission believes that the obligation to accommodate requires that employers and labor organizations facilitate the securing of a voluntary substitute with substantially similar qualifications. Some means of doing this which employers and labor organizations should consider are: to publicize policies regarding accommodation and voluntary substitution; to promote an atmosphere in which such substitutions are favorably regarded; to provide a central file, bulletin board or other means for matching voluntary substitutes with positions for which substitutes are needed.

(ii) Flexible Scheduling.

One means of providing reasonable accommodation for the religious practices of employees or prospective employees which employers and labor organizations should consider is the creation of a flexible work schedule for individuals requesting accommodation.

The following list is an example of areas in which flexibility might be introduced: flexible arrival and departure times; floating or optional holidays; flexible work breaks; use of lunch time in exchange for early departure; staggered work hours; and permitting an employee to make up time lost due to the observance of religious practices.[3]

(iii) Lateral Transfer and Change of Job Assignments.

When an employee cannot be accommodated either as to his or her entire job or an assignment within the job, employers and labor organizations should consider whether or not it is possible to change the job assignment or give the employee a lateral transfer.

(2) Payment of Dues to a Labor Organization.

Some collective bargaining agreements include a provision that each employee must join the labor organization or pay the labor organization a sum equivalent to dues. When an employee's religious practices do not permit compliance with such a provision, the labor organization should accommodate the employee by not requiring the employee to join the organization and by permitting him or her to donate a sum equivalent to dues to a charitable organization.

(e) *Undue hardship.* (1) Cost. An employer may assert undue hardship to justify a refusal to accommodate an employee's need to be absent from his or her scheduled duty hours if the employer can demonstrate that the accommodation would require "more than a *de minimis* cost".[4] The Commission will determine what constitutes "more than a *de minimis* cost" with due regard given to the identifiable cost in relation to the size and operating cost of the employer, and the number of individuals who will in fact need a particular accommodation. In general, the Commission interprets this phrase as it was used in the *Hardison* decision to mean that costs similar to the regular payment of premium wages of substitutes, which was at issue in *Hardison,* would constitute undue hardship. However, the Commission will presume that the infrequent payment of premium wages for a substitute or the payment of premium wages while a more permanent accommodation is being sought are costs which an employer can be required to bear as a means of providing a reasonable accommodation. Further, the Commission will presume that generally, the payment of administrative costs necessary for providing the accommodation will not constitute more than a *de minimis* cost. Administrative costs, for

---

3. On September 29, 1978, Congress enacted such a provision for the accommodation of Federal employees' religious practices. See Pub.L 95–390, 5 U.S.C. 5550a

"Compensatory Time Off for Religious Observances."

4. *Hardison,* supra, 432 U.S. at 84.

example, include those costs involved in rearranging schedules and recording substitutions for payroll purposes.

(2) Seniority Rights. Undue hardship would also be shown where a variance from a bona fide seniority system is necessary in order to accommodate an employee's religious practices when doing so would deny another employee his or her job or shift preference guaranteed by that system. *Hardison, supra,* 432 U.S. at 80. Arrangements for voluntary substitutes and swaps (see paragraph (d)(1)(i) of this section) do not constitute an undue hardship to the extent the arrangements do not violate a bona fide seniority system. Nothing in the Statute or these Guidelines precludes an employer and a union from including arrangements for voluntary substitutes and swaps as part of a collective bargaining agreement.

§ 1605.3 Selection practices

(a) Scheduling of Tests or Other Selection Procedures. When a test or other selection procedure is scheduled at a time when an employee or prospective employee cannot attend because of his or her religious practices, the user of the test should be aware that the principles enunciated in these guidelines apply and that it has an obligation to accommodate such employee or prospective employee unless undue hardship would result.

(b) Inquiries Which Determine An Applicant's Availability to Work During An Employer's Scheduled Working Hours.

(1) The duty to accommodate pertains to prospective employees as well as current employees. Consequently, an employer may not permit an applicant's need for a religious accommodation to affect in any way its decision whether to hire the applicant unless it can demonstrate that it cannot reasonably accommodate the applicant's religious practices without undue hardship.

(2) As a result of the oral and written testimony submitted at the Commission's Hearings on Religious Discrimination, discussions with representatives of organizations interested in the issue of religious discrimination, and the comments received from the public on these Guidelines as proposed, the Commission has concluded that the use of pre-selection inquiries which determine an applicant's availability has an exclusionary effect on the employment opportunities of persons with certain religious practices. The use of such inquiries will, therefore, be considered to violate Title VII unless the employer can show that it:

(i) Did not have an exclusionary effect on its employees or prospective employees needing an accommodation for the same religious practices; or

(ii) Was otherwise justified by business necessity.

Employers who believe they have a legitimate interest in knowing the availability of their applicants prior to selection must consider procedures which would serve this interest and which would have a lesser exclusionary effect on persons whose religious practices need accommodation. An example of such a procedure is for the employer to state the normal work hours for the job and, after making it clear to the applicant that he or she is not required to indicate the need for any absences for religious practices during the scheduled work hours, ask the applicant whether he or she is otherwise available to work those hours. Then, after a position is offered, but before the applicant is hired, the employer can inquire into the need for a religious accommodation and determine, according to the principles of these Guidelines, whether an accommodation is possible. This type of inquiry would provide an employer with information concerning the availability of most of its applicants, while deferring until after a position is offered the identification of the usually small number of applicants who require an accommodation.

(3) The Commission will infer that the need for an accommodation discriminatorily influenced a decision to reject an applicant when: (i) prior to an offer of employment the employer makes an inquiry into an applicant's availability without having a business necessity justification; and (ii) after the employer has determined the applicant's need for an accommodation, the employer rejects a qualified applicant. The burden is then on the employer to demonstrate that factors other than the need for an accommodation were the reason for rejecting the qualified applicant, or that a reasonable accommodation without undue hardship was not possible.

APPENDIX A TO §§ 1605.2 AND 1605.3—BACKGROUND INFORMATION

In 1966, the Commission adopted guidelines on religious discrimination which stated that an employer had an obligation to accommodate the religious practices of its employees or prospective employees unless to do so would create a "serious inconvenience to the conduct of the business". 29 CFR 1605.1(a)(2), 31 FR 3870 (1966).

In 1967, the Commission revised these guidelines to state that an employer had an obligation to reasonably accommodate the religious practices of its employees or prospective employees, unless the employer could prove that to do so would create an "undue hardship". 29 CFR 1605.1(b)(c), 32 FR 10298.

In 1972, Congress amended Title VII to incorporate the obligation to accommodate expressed in the Commission's 1967 Guidelines by adding section 701(j).

In 1977, the United States Supreme Court issued its decision in the case of Trans World Airlines, Inc. v. Hardison, 432 U.S. 63 (1977). *Hardison* was brought under section 703(a)(1) because it involved facts occurring before the enactment of Section 701(j). The Court applied the Commission's 1967 Guidelines, but indicated that the result would be the same under Section 701(j). It stated that Trans World Airlines had made reasonable efforts to accommodate the religious needs of its employee, Hardison. The Court held that to require Trans World

Airlines to make further attempts at accommodations—by unilaterally violating a seniority provision of the collective bargaining agreement, paying premium wages on a regular basis to another employee to replace Hardison, or creating a serious shortage of necessary employees in another department in order to replace Hardison—would create an undue hardship on the conduct of Trans World Airlines' business, and would therefore, exceed the duty to accommodate Hardison.

In 1978, the Commission conducted public hearings on religious discrimination in New York City, Milwaukee, and Los Angeles in order to respond to the concerns raised by *Hardison*. Approximately 150 witnesses testified or submitted written statements.[5] The witnesses included employers, employees, representatives of religious and labor organizations and representatives of Federal, State and local governments.

The Commission found from the hearings that:

(1) There is widespread confusion concerning the extent of accommodation under the *Hardison* decision.

(2) The religious practices of some individuals and some groups of individuals are not being accommodated.

(3) Some of those practices which are not being accommodated are:

—Observance of a Sabbath or religious holidays;

—Need for prayer break during working hours;

—Practice of following certain dietary requirements;

—Practice of not working during a mourning period for a deceased relative;

—Prohibition against medical examinations;

—Prohibition against membership in labor and other organizations; and

—Practices concerning dress and other personal grooming habits.

(4) Many of the employers who testified had developed alternative employment practices which accommodate the religious practices of employees and prospective employees and which meet the employer's business needs.

(5) Little evidence was submitted by employers which showed actual attempts to accommodate religious practices with resultant unfavorable consequences to the employer's business. Employers appeared to have substantial anticipatory concerns but no, or very little, actual experience with the problems they theorized would emerge by providing reasonable accommodation for religious practices.

5. The transcript of the Commission's Hearings on Religious Discrimination can be examined by the public at: The Equal Employment Opportunity Commission, 2401 E Street NW., Washington, D.C. 20506.

Based on these findings, the Commission is revising its Guidelines to clarify the obligation imposed by Section 701(j) to accommodate the religious practices of employees and prospective employees.

EXECUTIVE ORDER 12068

Providing for Transfer to the Attorney General of Certain Functions Under Section 707 of Title VII of the Civil Rights Act of 1964, as Amended

By virtue of the authority vested in me as President of the United States by the Constitution and laws of the United States, including Section 9 of Reorganization Plan Number 1 of 1978 (43 FR 19807), in order to clarify the Attorney General's authority to initiate public sector litigation under Section 707 of Title VII of the Civil Rights Act of 1964, as amended (42 U.S.C. 2000e–6), it is ordered as follows:

1–1. *Section 707 Functions of the Attorney General*

1–101. Section 5 of Reorganization Plan Number 1 of 1978 (43 FR 19807) shall become effective on July 1, 1978.

1–102. The functions transferred to the Attorney General by Section 5 of Reorganization Plan Number 1 of 1978 shall, consistent with Section 707 of Title VII of the Civil Rights Act of 1964, as amended, be performed in accordance with Department of Justice procedures heretofore followed under Section 707.

JIMMY CARTER

THE WHITE HOUSE,
June 30, 1978.

OFCCP—RULES AND REGULATIONS
(41 CFR 60–1)
Obligations of Contractors and Subcontractors

SUBPART A. PRELIMINARY MATTERS; EQUAL OPPORTUNITY CLAUSE; COMPLIANCE REPORTS

§ 60–1.1 Purpose and application

The purpose of the regulations in this part is to achieve the aims of parts II, III, and IV of Executive Order 11246 for the promotion and insuring of equal opportunity for all persons, without regard to race, color, religion, sex, or national origin, employed or seeking employment with Government contractors or with contractors performing under federally assisted construction contracts. The regulations in this part apply to all contracting agencies of the Government and to contractors and subcontractors who perform under Government contracts, to the extent set forth in this part. The regulations in this part apply to all agencies of the Government administering programs involving Federal financial assistance which may include a construction contract, and to all contractors and subcontractors performing under construction contracts which are related to any such programs. The procedures set forth in the regulations in this part govern all disputes relative to a contractor's compliance with his obligations under the equal opportunity clause regardless of whether or not his contract contains a "Disputes" clause. Failure of a contractor or applicant to comply with any provision of the regulations in this part shall be grounds for the imposition of any or all of the sanctions authorized by the order. The regulations in this part do not apply to any action taken to effect compliance with respect to employment practices subject to title VI of the Civil Rights Act of 1964. The rights and remedies of the Government hereunder are not exclusive and do not affect rights and remedies provided elsewhere by law, regulation, or contract; neither do the regulations limit the exercise by the Secretary or Government agencies of powers not herein specifically set forth, but granted to them by the order.

§ 60–1.2 Administrative responsibility

The Director has been delegated authority and assigned responsibility for carrying out the responsibilities assigned to the Secretary under the Executive order. All correspondence regarding the order should be directed to the Director, Office of Federal Contract Compliance Programs, Employment Standards Administration, U.S. Department of Labor, 200 Constitution Avenue NW., Washington, D.C. 20210.

§ 60–1.3 Definitions

"Administering agency" means any department, agency and establishment in the executive branch of the Government, including any wholly owned Government corporation, which administers a program involving federally assisted construction contracts.

"Administrative law judge" means an administrative law judge appointed as provided in 5 U.S.C. 3105 and Subpart B of Part 930 of Title 5 of the *Code of Federal Regulations* (see 37 FR 16787) and qualified to preside at hearings under 5 U.S.C. 557.

"Agency" means any contracting or any administering agency of the Government.

"Applicant" means an applicant for Federal assistance involving a construction contract, or other participant in a program involving a construction contract as determined by regulation of an administering agency. The term also includes such persons after they become recipients of such Federal assistance.

"Construction work" means the construction, rehabilitation, alteration, conversion, extension, demolition or repair of buildings, highways, or other changes or improvements to real property, including facilities providing utility services. The term also includes the supervision, inspection, and other onsite functions incidental to the actual construction.

"Contract" means any Government contract or any federally assisted construction contract.

"Contracting agency" means any department, agency, establishment, or instrumentality in the executive branch of the Government, including any wholly owned Government corporation, which enters into contracts.

"Contractor" means, unless otherwise indicated, a prime contractor or subcontractor.

"Director" means the Director, Office of Federal Contract Compliance Programs (OFCCP), U.S. Department of Labor or any person to whom he delegates authority under the regulations in this chapter.

"Equal opportunity clause" means the contract provisions set forth in § 60–1.4(a) or (b), as appropriate.

"Federally assisted construction contract" means any agreement or modification thereof between any applicant and a person for construction work which is paid for in whole or in part with funds obtained from the Government or borrowed on the credit of the Government pursuant to any Federal program involving a grant, contract, loan, insurance, or guarantee, or undertaken pursuant to any Federal program involving such grant, contract, loan, insurance, or guarantee, or any application or modification thereof approved by the Government for a grant, contract, loan, insurance, or guarantee under which the applicant itself participates in the construction work.

"Government" means the government of the United States of America.

"Government contract" means any agreement or modification thereof between any contracting agency and any person for the furnishing of supplies or services or for the use of real or personal property, including lease arrangements. The term "services", as used in this section includes, but is not limited to the following services: Utility, construction, transportation, research, insurance, and fund depository. The term "Government contract" does not include (1) agreements in which the parties stand in the relationship of employer and employee, and (2) federally assisted construction contracts.

"Minority group" as used herein shall include, where appropriate, female employees and perspective female employees.

"Modification" means any alteration in the terms and conditions of a contract, including supplemental agreements, amendments, and extensions.

"Order," "Executive order," or "Executive Order 11246" means parts II, III, and IV of the Executive Order 11246 dated September 24,

1965 (30 FR 12319), any Executive order amending such order, and any other Executive order superseding such order.

"Person" means any natural person, corporation, partnership, unincorporated association, State or local government, and any agency, instrumentality, or subdivision of such a government.

"Prime contractor" means any person holding a contract and, for the purposes of Subpart B of this part, any person who has held a contract subject to the order.

"Recruiting and training agency" means any person who refers workers to any contractor or subcontractor or who provides for employment by any contractor or subcontractor.

"Rules, regulations, and relevant orders of the Secretary of Labor" used in paragraph (4) of the equal opportunity clause means rules, regulations, and relevant orders of the Secretary of Labor or his designee issued pursuant to the order.

"Secretary" means the Secretary of Labor, U.S. Department of Labor.

"Site of construction" means the general physical location of any building, highway, or other change or improvement to real property which is undergoing construction, rehabilitation, alteration, conversion, extension, demolition, or repair and any temporary location or facility at which a contractor, subcontractor, or other participating party meets a demand or performs a function relating to the contract or subcontract.

"Subcontract" means any agreement or arrangement between a contractor and any person (in which the parties do not stand in the relationship of an employer and an employee):

(1) For the furnishing of supplies or services or for the use of real or personal property, including lease arrangements, which, in whole or in part, is necessary to the performance of any one or more contracts; or

(2) Under which any portion of the contractor's obligation under any one or more contracts is performed, undertaken, or assumed.

"Subcontractor" means any person holding a subcontract and, for the purposes of Subpart B of this part, any person who has held a subcontract subject to the order. The term "First-tier subcontractor" refers to a subcontractor holding a subcontract with a prime contractor.

"United States" as used herein shall include the several States, the District of Columbia, the Commonwealth of Puerto Rico, the Panama Canal Zone, and the possessions of the United States.

§ 60-1.4 Equal opportunity clause

(a) *Government contracts.* Except as otherwise provided, each contracting agency shall include the following equal opportunity clause contained in section 202 of the order in each of its Government contracts (and modifications thereof if not included in the original contract):

During the performance of this contract, the contractor agrees as follows:

(1) The contractor will not discriminate against any employee or applicant for employment because of race, color, religion, sex, or national origin. The contractor will take affirmative action to ensure that applicants are employed, and that employees are treated during employment, without regard to their race, color, religion, sex, or national origin. Such action shall include, but not be limited to the following: Employment, upgrading, demotion, or transfer, recruitment or recruitment advertising; layoff or termination; rates of pay or other forms of compensation; and selection for training, including apprenticeship. The contractor agrees to post in conspicuous places, available to employees and applicants for employment, notices to be provided by the contracting officer setting forth the provisions of this non-discrimination clause.

(2) The contractor will, in all solicitations or advertisements for employees placed by or on behalf of the contractor, state that all qualified applicants will receive consideration for employment without regard to race, color, religion, sex, or national origin.

(3) The contractor will send to each labor union or representative of workers with which he has a collective bargaining agreement or other contract or understanding, a notice to be provided by the agency contracting officer, advising the labor union or workers' representative of the contractor's commitments under section 202 of Executive Order 11246 of September 24, 1965, and shall post copies of the notice in conspicuous places available to employees and applicants for employment.

(4) The contractor will comply with all provisions of Executive Order 11246 of September 24, 1965, and of the rules, regulations, and relevant orders of the Secretary of Labor.

(5) The contractor will furnish all information and reports required by Executive Order 11246 of September 24, 1965, and by the rules, regulations, and orders of the Secretary of Labor, or pursuant thereto, and will permit access to his books, records, and accounts by the contracting agency and the Secretary of Labor for purposes of investigation to ascertain compliance with such rules, regulations, and orders.

(6) In the event of the contractor's noncompliance with the non-discrimination clauses of this contract or with any of such rules, regulations, or orders, this contract may be canceled, terminated or suspended in whole or in part and the contractor may be declared ineligible for further Government contracts in accordance with procedures authorized in Executive Order 11246 of September 24, 1965, and such other sanctions may be imposed and remedies invoked as provided in Executive Order 11246 of September 24, 1965, or by rule,

regulation, or order of the Secretary of Labor, or as otherwise provided by law.

(7) The contractor will include the provisions of paragraphs (1) through (7) in every subcontract or purchase order unless exempted by rules, regulations, or orders of the Secretary of Labor issued pursuant to section 204 of Executive Order 11246 of September 24, 1965, so that such provisions will be binding upon each subcontractor or vendor. The contractor will take such action with respect to any subcontract or purchase order as may be directed by the Secretary of Labor as a means of enforcing such provisions including sanctions for noncompliance: *Provided, however,* that in the event the contractor becomes involved in, or is threatened with, litigation with a subcontractor or vendor as a result of such direction, the contractor may request the United States to enter into such litigation to protect the interests of the United States.

(b) *Federally assisted construction contracts.* (1) Except as otherwise provided, each administering agency shall require the inclusion of the following language as a condition of any grant, contract, loan, insurance, or guarantee involving federally assisted construction which is not exempt from the requirements of the equal opportunity clause:

The applicant hereby agrees that it will incorporate or cause to be incorporated into any contract for construction work, or modification thereof, as defined in the regulations of the Secretary of Labor at 41 CFR Chapter 60, which is paid for in whole or in part with funds obtained from the Federal Government or borrowed on the credit of the Federal Government pursuant to a grant, contract, loan insurance, or guarantee, or undertaken pursuant to any Federal program involving such grant, contract, loan, insurance, or guarantee, the following equal opportunity clause:

During the performance of this contract, the contractor agrees as follows:

(1) The contractor will not discriminate against any employee or applicant for employment because of race, color, religion, sex, or national origin. The contractor will take affirmative action to ensure that applicants are employed, and that employees are treated during employment without regard to their race, color, religion, sex, or national origin, such action shall include, but not be limited to the following: Employment, upgrading, demotion, or transfer; recruitment or recruitment advertising; layoff or termination; rates of pay or other forms of compensation; and selection for training, including apprenticeship. The contractor agrees to post in conspicuous places, available to employees and applicants for employment, notices to be provided setting forth the provisions of this nondiscrimination clause.

(2) The contractor will, in all solicitations or advertisements for employees placed by or on behalf of the contractor, state that all qualified applicants will receive considerations for employment without regard to race, color, religion, sex, or national origin.

(3) The contractor will send to each labor union or representative of workers with which he has a collective bargaining agreement or other contract or understanding, a notice to be provided advising the said labor union or workers' representatives of the contractor's commitments under this section, and shall post copies of the notice in conspicuous places available to employees and applicants for employment.

(4) The contractor will comply with all provisions of Executive Order 11246 of September 24, 1965, and of the rules, regulations, and relevant orders of the Secretary of Labor.

(5) The contractor will furnish all information and reports required by Executive Order 11246 of September 24, 1965, and by rules, regulations, and orders of the Secretary of Labor, or pursuant thereto, and will permit access to his books, records, and accounts by the administering agency and the Secretary of Labor for purposes of investigation to ascertain compliance with such rules, regulations, and orders.

(6) In the event of the contractor's noncompliance with the non-discrimination clauses of this contract or with any of the said rules, regulations, or orders, this contract may be canceled, terminated, or suspended in whole or in part and the contractor may be declared ineligible for further Government contracts or federally assisted construction contracts in accordance with procedures authorized in Executive Order 11246 of September 24, 1965, and such other sanctions may be imposed and remedies invoked as provided in Executive Order 11246 of September 24, 1965, or by rule, regulation, or order of the Secretary of Labor, or as otherwise provided by law.

(7) The contractor will include the portion of the sentence immediately preceding paragraph (1) and the provisions of paragraphs (1) through (7) in every subcontract or purchase order unless exempted by rules, regulations, or orders of the Secretary of Labor issued pursuant to section 204 of Executive Order 11246 of September 24, 1965, so that such provisions will be binding upon each subcontractor or vendor. The contractor will take such action with respect to any subcontract or purchase order as the administering agency may direct as a means of enforcing such provisions, including sanctions for noncompliance: *Provided, however,* That in the event a contractor becomes involved in, or is threatened with, litigation with a subcontractor or vendor as a result of such direction by the administering agency the contractor may request the United States to enter into such litigation to protect the interests of the United States.

The applicant further agrees that it will be bound by the above equal opportunity clause with respect to its own employment practices when it participates in federally assisted construction work: *Provided,* That if the applicant so participating is a State or local government, the above equal opportunity clause is not applicable to any agency, instrumentality or subdivision of such government which does not participate in work on or under the contract.

The applicant agrees that it will assist and cooperate actively with the administering agency and the Secretary of Labor in obtaining the compliance of contractors and subcontractors with the equal opportunity clause and the rules, regulations, and relevant orders of the Secretary of Labor, that it will furnish the administering agency and the Secretary of Labor such information as they may require for the supervision of such compliance, and that it will otherwise assist the administering agency in the discharge of the agency's primary responsibility for securing compliance.

The applicant further agrees that it will refrain from entering into any contract or contract modification subject to Executive Order 11246 of September 24, 1965, with a contractor debarred from, or who has not demonstrated eligibility for, Government contracts and federally assisted construction contracts pursuant to the Executive order and will carry out such sanctions and penalties for violation of the equal opportunity clause as may be imposed upon contractors and subcontractors by the administering agency or the Secretary of Labor pursuant to Part II, Subpart D of the Executive order. In addition, the applicant agrees that if it fails or refuses to comply with these undertakings, the administering agency may take any or all of the following actions: Cancel, terminate, or suspend in whole or in part this grant (contract, loan, insurance, guarantee); refrain from extending any further assistance to the applicant under the program with respect to which the failure or refund occurred until satisfactory assurance of future compliance has been received from such applicant; and refer the case to the Department of Justice for appropriate legal proceedings.

(c) *Subcontracts.* Each nonexempt prime contractor or subcontractor shall include the equal opportunity clause in each of its nonexempt subcontracts.

(d) *Incorporation by reference.* The equal opportunity clause may be incorporated by reference in all Government contracts and subcontracts, including Government bills of lading, transportation requests, contracts for deposit of Government funds, and contracts for issuing and paying U.S. savings bonds and notes, and such other contracts and subcontracts as the Director may designate.

(e) *Incorporation by operation of the order.* By operation of the order, the equal opportunity clause shall be considered to be a part of every contract and subcontract required by the order and the regulations in this part to include such a clause whether or not it is physically incorporated in such contracts and whether or not the contract between the agency and the contractor is written.

(f) *Adaptation of language.* Such necessary changes in language may be made in the equal opportunity clause as shall be appropriate to identify properly the parties and their undertakings.

§ 60–1.5 Exemptions

(a) *General*—(1) *Transactions of $10,000 or under.* Contracts and subcontracts not exceeding $10,000, other than Government bills of lading, and other than contracts and subcontracts with depositories of Federal funds in any amount and with financial institutions which are issuing and paying agents for U.S. savings bonds and savings notes, are exempt from the requirements of the equal opportunity clause. In determining the applicability of this exemption to any federally assisted construction contract, or subcontract thereunder, the amount of such contract or subcontract rather than the amount of the Federal financial assistance shall govern. No agency, contractor, or subcontractor shall procure supplies or services in a manner so as to avoid applicability of the equal opportunity clause: *Provided,* that where a contractor has contracts or subcontracts with the Government in any 12-month period which have an aggregate total value (or can reasonably be expected to have an aggregate total value) exceeding $10,000, the $10,000 or under exemption does not apply, and the contracts are subject to the order and the regulations issued pursuant thereto regardless of whether any single contract exceeds $10,000.

(2) *Contracts and subcontracts for indefinite quantities.* With respect to contracts and subcontracts for indefinite quantities (including, but not limited to, open end contracts, requirement-type contracts, Federal Supply Schedule contracts, "call-type" contracts, and purchase notice agreements), the equal opportunity clause shall be included unless the purchaser has reason to believe that the amount to be ordered in any year under such contract will not exceed $10,000. The applicability of the equal opportunity clause shall be determined by the purchaser at the time of award for the first year, and annually thereafter for succeeding years, if any. Notwithstanding the above, the equal opportunity clause shall be applied to such contract whenever the amount of a single order exceeds $10,000. Once the equal opportunity clause is determined to be applicable, the contract shall continue to be subject to such clause for its duration, regardless of the amounts ordered, or reasonably expected to be ordered in any year.

(3) *Work outside the United States.* Contracts and subcontracts are exempt from the requirements of the equal opportunity clause with regard to work performed outside the United States by employees who were not recruited within the United States.

(4) *Contracts with State or local governments.* The requirements of the equal opportunity clause in any contract or subcontract with a State or local government (or any agency, instrumentality or subdivision thereof) shall not be applicable to any agency, instrumentality or subdivision of such government which does not participate in work on or under the contract or subcontract. In addition, any agency, instrumentality or subdivision of such government, except for educational institutions and medical facilities, are exempt from the requirements of filing the annual compliance report provided for by § 60–1.7(a)(1) and maintaining a written affirmative action compliance program prescribed by § 60–1.40 and Part 60–2 of this chapter.

(5) *Contracts with certain educational institutions.* It shall not be a violation of the equal opportunity clause for a school, college, univer-

sity, or other educational institution or institution of learning to hire and employ employees of a particular religion if such school, college, university, or other educational institution or institution of learning is, in whole or in substantial part, owned, supported, controlled, or managed by a particular religion or by a particular religious corporation, association, or society, or if the curriculum of such school, college, university, or other educational institution or institution of learning is directed toward the propagation of a particular religion. The primary thrust of this provision is directed at religiously oriented church-related colleges and universities and should be so interpreted.

(6) *Work on or near Indian reservations.* It shall not be a violation of the equal opportunity clause for a construction or nonconstruction contractor to extend a publicly announced preference in employment to Indians living on or near an Indian reservation in connection with employment opportunities on or near an Indian reservation. The use of the word "near" would include all that area where a person seeking employment could reasonably be expected to commute to and from in the course of a work day. Contractors or subcontractors extending such a preference shall not, however, discriminate among Indians on the basis of religion, sex, or tribal affiliation, and the use of such a preference shall not excuse a contractor from complying with the other requirements contained in this chapter.

(b) *Specific contracts and facilities—*(1) *Specific contracts.* The Director may exempt an agency or any person from requiring the inclusion of any or all of the equal opportunity clause in any specific contract or subcontract when he deems that special circumstances in the national interest so require. The Director may also exempt groups or categories of contracts or subcontracts of the same type where he finds it impracticable to act upon each request individually or where group exemptions will contribute to convenience in the administration of the order.

(2) *Facilities not connected with contracts.* The Director may exempt from the requirements of the equal opportunity clause any of a prime contractor's or subcontractor's facilities which he finds to be in all respects separate and distinct from activities of the prime contractor or subcontractor related to the performance of the contract or subcontract, provided that he also finds that such an exemption will not interfere with or impede the effectuation of the order.

(c) *National security.* Any requirement set forth in these regulations in this part shall not apply to any contract or subcontract whenever the head of an agency determines that such contract or subcontract is essential to the national security and that its award without complying with such requirement is necessary to the national security. Upon making such a determination, the head of the agency will notify the Director in writing within 30 days.

(d) *Withdrawal of exemption.* When any contract or subcontract is of a class exempted under this section, the Director may withdraw the exemption for a specific contract or subcontract or group of contracts or subcontracts when in his judgment such action is necessary or appropriate to achieve the purposes of the order. Such withdrawal shall not apply to contracts or subcontracts awarded prior to the withdrawal, except that in procurements entered into by formal advertising, or the various forms of restricted formal advertising, such withdrawal shall not apply unless the withdrawal is made more than 10 calendar days before the date set for the opening of the bids.

[43 FR 49240, Oct. 20, 1978; 43 FR 51400, Nov. 3, 1978]

§ 60–1.6 [Reserved]

§ 60–1.7 Reports and other required information

(a) *Requirements for prime contractors and subcontractors.* (1) Each prime contractor and subcontractor shall file annually, on or before the 31st day of March, complete and accurate reports on Standard Form 100 (EEO–1) promulgated jointly by the Office of Federal Contract Compliance Programs, the Equal Employment Opportunity Commission and Plans for Progress or such form as may hereafter be promulgated in its place if such prime contractor or subcontractor (i) is not exempt from the provisions of these regulations in accordance with § 60–1.5; (ii) has 50 or more employees; (iii) is a prime contractor or first tier subcontractor; and (iv) has a contract, subcontract or purchase order amounting to $50,000 or more or serves as a depository of Government funds in any amount, or is a financial institution which is an issuing and paying agent for U.S. savings bonds and savings notes: Provided, That any subcontractor below the first tier which performs construction work at the site of construction shall be required to file such a report if it meets requirements of paragraphs (a)(1)(i), (ii), and (iv) of this section.

(2) Each person required by § 60–1.7(a)(1) to submit reports shall file such a report with the contracting or administering agency within 30 days after the award to him of a contract or subcontract, unless such person has submitted such a report within 12 months preceding the date of the award. Subsequent reports shall be submitted annually in accordance with § 60–1.7(a)(1), or at such other intervals as the Director may require. The Director may extend the time for filing any report.

(3) The Director or the applicant, on their own motions, may require a contractor to keep employment or other records and to furnish, in the form requested, within reasonable limits, such information as the Director or the applicant deems necessary for the administration of the order.

(4) Failure to file timely, complete and accurate reports as required constitutes noncompliance with the prime contractor's or subcontractor's obligations under the equal opportunity clause and is ground for the imposition by the Director, an applicant, prime contractor or

subcontractor, of any sanctions as authorized by the order and the regulations in this part.

(b) *Requirements for bidders or prospective contractors—*(1) *Certification of compliance with Part 60–2: Affirmative Action Programs.* Each agency shall require each bidder or prospective prime contractor and proposed subcontractor, where appropriate, to state in the bid or in writing at the outset of negotiations for the contract: (i) Whether it has developed and has on file at each establishment affirmative action programs pursuant to Part 60–2 of this chapter; (ii) whether it has participated in any previous contract or subcontract subject to the equal opportunity clause; (iii) whether it has filed with the Joint Reporting Committee, the Director or the Equal Employment Opportunity Commission all reports due under the applicable filing requirements.

(2) *Additional information.* A bidder or prospective prime contractor or proposed subcontractor shall be required to submit such information as the Director requests prior to the award of the contract or subcontract. When a determination has been made to award the contract or subcontract to a specific contractor, such contractor shall be required, prior to award, or after the award, or both, to furnish such other information as the applicant or the Director requests.

(c) *Use of reports.* Reports filed pursuant to this section shall be used only in connection with the administration of the order, the Civil Rights Act of 1964, or in furtherance of the purposes of the order and said Act.

§ 60–1.8 Segregated facilities

(a) *General.* In order to comply with his obligations under the equal opportunity clause, a prime contractor or subcontractor must insure that facilities provided for employees are provided in such a manner that segregation on the basis of race, color, religion, or national origin cannot result. He may neither require such segregated use by written or oral policies nor tolerate such use by employee custom. His obligation extends further to insuring that his employees are not assigned to perform their services at any location, under his control, where the facilities are segregated. This obligation extends to all contracts containing the equal opportunity clause regardless of the amount of the contract. The term "facilities" as used in this section means waiting rooms, work areas, restaurants and other eating areas, time clocks, restrooms, washrooms, locker rooms, and other storage or dressing areas, parking lots, drinking fountains, recreation or entertainment areas, transportation, and housing facilities provided for employees.

(b) *Certification by prime contractors and subcontractors.* Prior to the award or any nonexempt Government contract of subcontract or federally assisted construction contract or subcontract, each agency or applicant shall require the prospective prime contractor and each prime contractor and subcontractor shall require each subcontractor to submit a certification, in the form approved by the Director, that the prospective prime contractor or subcontractor does not and will not maintain any facilities he provides for his employees in a segregated manner, or permit his employees to perform their services at any location, under his control, where segregated facilities are maintained; and that he will obtain a similar certification in the form approved by the Director, prior to the award of any nonexempt subcontract.

[43 FR 49240, Oct. 20, 1978; 43 FR 51400, Nov. 3, 1978]

§ 60–1.9 Compliance by labor unions and by recruiting and training agencies

(a) Whenever compliance with the equal opportunity clause may necessitate a revision of a collective bargaining agreement the labor union or unions which are parties to such an agreement shall be given an adequate opportunity to present their views to the director.

(b) The Director shall use his best efforts, directly and through agencies, contractors, subcontractors, applicants, State and local officials, public and private agencies, and all other available instrumentalities, to cause any labor union, recruiting and training agency or other representative of workers who are or may be engaged in work under contracts and subcontracts to cooperate with, and to comply in the implementation of, the purposes of the order.

(c) In order to effectuate the purposes of paragraph (a) of this section, the Director may hold hearings, public or private, with respect to the practices and policies of any such labor union or recruiting and training agency.

(d) The Director may notify any Federal, State, or local agency of his conclusions and recommendations with respect to any such labor organization or recruiting and training agency which in his judgment has failed to cooperate with himself, agencies, prime contractors, subcontractors, or applicants in carrying out the purposes of the order. The Director also may notify the Equal Employment Opportunity Commission, the Department of Justice, or other appropriate Federal agencies whenever he has reason to believe that the practices of any such labor organization or agency violates title VII of the Civil Rights Act of 1964 or other provisions of Federal law.

§ 60–1.10 Foreign government practices

Contractors shall not discriminate on the basis of race, color, religion, sex, or national origin when hiring or making employee assignments for work to be performed in the United States or abroad. Contractors are exempted from this obligation only when hiring persons outside the United States for work to be performed outside the United States (see 41 CFR 60–1.5(a)(3)). Therefore, a contractor hiring workers in the United States for either Federal or nonfederally connected work shall be in violation of Executive Order 11246, as amended, by refusing to employ or assign any person because of race, color, religion, sex, or national origin regardless of the policies of the country where the work is to be performed or for whom the work will be performed. Should any contractor be unable to acquire a visa of entry for any employee or potential employee to a country in which or with which it is doing business, and which refusal it believes is due to the race, color, religion, sex, or national origin of the employee or potential employee, the contractor must immediately notify the Department of State and the Director of such refusal.

§ 60–1.11 Payment or reimbursement of membership fees and other expenses to private clubs

(a)(1) A contractor which maintains a policy or practice of paying membership fees or other expenses for employee participation in private clubs or organizations shall ensure that the policy or practice is administered without regard to the race, color, religion, sex, or national origin of employees.

(2) Payment or reimbursement by contractors of membership fees and other expenses for participation by their employees in a private club or organization which bars, restricts or limits its membership on the basis of race, color, sex, religion, or national origin constitutes a violation of Executive Order 11246 except where the contractor can provide evidence that such restrictions or limitations do not abridge the promotional opportunities, status, compensation or other terms and conditions of employment of those of its employees barred from membership because of their race, color, religion, sex, or national origin. OFCCP shall provide the contractor with the opportunity to present evidence in defense of its actions.

(b) The contractor has the responsibility of determining whether the club or organization restricts membership on the basis of race, color, religion, sex, or national origin. The contractor may make separate determinations for different chapters of an organization, and where it does so, may limit any necessary corrective action to the particular chapters which observe discriminatory membership policies and practices.

[46 FR 3896, Jan. 16, 1981]

Effective Date Note: at 46 FR 3896, Jan. 16, 1981, § 60–1.11 was added. At 46 FR 18951, Mar. 27, 1981, the effective date was deferred until further notice.

SUBPART B. GENERAL ENFORCEMENT; COMPLIANCE REVIEW AND COMPLAINT PROCEDURE

§ 60–1.20 Compliance reviews

(a) The purpose of a compliance review is to determine if the prime contractor or subcontractor maintains nondiscriminatory hiring and employment practices and is taking affirmative action to insure that applicants are employed and that employees are placed, trained, upgraded, promoted, and otherwise treated during employment without regard to race, color, religion, sex, or national origin. It shall consist of a comprehensive analysis and evaluation of each aspect of the afore-mentioned practices, policies, and conditions resulting therefrom. Where necessary, recommendations for appropriate sanctions shall be made.

(b) Where deficiencies are found to exist, reasonable efforts shall be made to secure compliance through conciliation and persuasion. Be-fore the contractor can be found to be in compliance with the order, it must make a specific commitment, in writing, to correct any such deficiencies. The commitment must include the precise action to be taken and dates for completion. The time period allotted shall be no longer than the minimum period necessary to effect such changes. Upon approval of the commitment, the contractor may be considered in compliance, on condition that the commitments are faithfully kept. The contractor shall be notified that making such commitments does not preclude future determinations of noncompliance based on a find-ing that the commitments are not sufficient to achieve compliance.

(c) [Reserved]

(d) Each agency shall include in the invitation for bids for each formally advertised nonconstruction contract or state at the outset of negotiations for each negotiated contract, that if the award, when let, should exceed the amount of $1 million or more, the prospective contractor and his known first-tier subcontractors with subcontracts of $1 million or more will be subject to a compliance review before the award of the contract. No such contract shall be awarded unless a preaward compliance review of the prospective contractor and his known first-tier $1 million subcontractors has been conducted within 12 months prior to the award. The awarding agency will notify OFCCP and request appropriate action and findings in accordance with this subsection. OFCCP will provide awarding agencies with written re-ports of compliance within 30 days following the request. In order to qualify for the award of a contract, a contractor and such first-tier subcontractors must be found to be in compliance pursuant to para-graph (b) of this section, and with Part 60–2 of these regulations.

[43 FR 49240, Oct. 20, 1978; 43 FR 51400, Nov. 3, 1978]

§ 60–1.21 Filing complaints

Complaints shall be filed within 180 days of the alleged violation unless the time for filing is extended by the Director for good cause shown.

[43 FR 49240, Oct. 20, 1978; 43 FR 51400, Nov. 3, 1978]

§ 60–1.22 Where to file

Complaints may be filed with the OFCCP, 200 Constitution Ave-nue, NW., Washington, D.C. 20210, or with any OFCCP regional or area office.

§ 60–1.23 Contents of complaint

(a) The complaint shall include the name, address, and telephone number of the complainant, the name and address of the contractor or subcontractor committing the alleged discrimination, a description of the acts considered to be discriminatory, and any other pertinent information which will assist in the investigation and resolution of the complaint. The complaint shall be signed by the complainant or his/her authorized representative. Complaints alleging class-type violations which do not identify the alleged discriminatee or discriminatees will be accepted, provided the other requirements of this paragraph are met.

(b) If a complaint contains incomplete information, OFCCP shall seek the needed information from the complainant. In the event such information is not furnished to the Director within 60 days of the date of such request, the case may be closed.

§ 60–1.24 Processing of matters

(a) *Complaints.* OFCCP may refer appropriate complaints to the Equal Employment Opportunity Commission (EEOC) for processing under Title VII of the Civil Rights Act of 1964, as amended, rather than processing under E.O. 11246 and the regulations in this chapter. Upon referring complaints to the EEOC, OFCCP shall promptly notify complainant(s) and the contractor of such referral.

(b) *Complaint investigations.* In conducting complaint investigations, OFCCP shall, as a minimum, conduct a thorough evaluation of the allegations of the complaint and shall be responsible for developing a complete case record. The case record should contain the name, address, and telephone number of each person interviewed, the interview statements, copies, transcripts, or summaries (where appropriate) of pertinent documents, a reference to at least one covered contract, and a narrative report of the investigation with references to exhibits and other evidence which relate to the alleged violations.

(c)(1) [Reserved]

(2) If any complaint investigation or compliance review indicates a violation of the equal opportunity clause, the matter should be resolved by informal means whenever possible. Such informal means may include the holding of a compliance conference.

(3) Where any complaint investigation or compliance review indicates a violation of the equal opportunity clause and the matter has not been resolved by informal means, the Director shall proceed in accordance with § 60–1.26.

(4) When a prime contractor or subcontractor, without a hearing, shall have complied with the recommendations or orders of the Director and believes such recommendations or orders to be erroneous, he shall, upon filing a request therefor within ten days of such compliance, be

afforded an opportunity for a hearing and review of the alleged errone-ous action.

(5) For reasonable cause shown, the Director may reconsider or cause to be reconsidered any matter on his/her own motion or pursuant to a request.

(d) *Reports to the Director.* (1) With the exception of complaints which have been referred to EEOC, within 60 days from receipt of a complaint or within such additional time as may be allowed by the Director for good cause shown, the complaint shall be processed and the case record developed containing the following information:

(i) Name and address of the complainant;

(ii) Brief summary of findings, including a statement regarding the contractor's compliance or noncompliance with the requirements of the equal opportunity clause;

(iii) A statement of the disposition of the case, including any corrective action taken and any sanctions or penalties imposed or, whenever appropriate, the recommended corrective action and sanc-tions or penalties.

(2) A written report of every preaward compliance review required by this regulation or otherwise required by the Director, shall be developed and maintained.

(3) A written report of every other compliance review or any other matter processed involving an apparent violation of the equal opportu-nity clause shall be made. Such report shall contain a brief summary of the findings, including a statement of conclusions regarding the contractor's compliance or noncompliance with the requirements of the order, and a statement of the disposition of the case, including any corrective action taken or recommended and any sanctions or penalties imposed or recommended.

§ 60–1.25 Assumption of jurisdiction by or referrals to the Direc-tor

The Director may inquire into the status of any matter pending before an agency. Where he considers it necessary or appropriate to the achievement of the purposes of the order, he may assume jurisdic-tion over the matter and proceed as provided herein. Whenever the Director assumes jurisdiction over any matter, or an agency refers any matter he may conduct, or have conducted, such investigations, hold such hearings, make such findings, issue such recommendations and directives, order such sanctions and penalties, and take such other action as may be necessary or appropriate to achieve the purposes of the order. The Director shall promptly notify the agency of any corrective action to be taken or any sanctions to be taken or any sanction to be imposed by the agency. The agency shall take such action, and report the results thereof to the Director within the time specified.

§ 60–1.26   Enforcement proceedings

(a) *General.* (1) Violations of the order, equal opportunity clause, the regulations in this chapter, or of applicable construction industry equal employment opportunity requirements, may result in the institution of administrative or judicial enforcement proceedings to enforce the order and to seek appropriate relief. Violations may be found based upon, inter alia, any of the following: (i) The results of a complaint investigation; (ii) analysis of an affirmative action program; (iii) the results of an on-site review of the contractor's compliance with the order and its implementing regulations; (iv) a contractor's refusal to submit an affirmative action program; (v) a contractor's refusal to allow an on-site compliance review to be conducted; (vi) a contractor's refusal to supply records or other information as required by these regulations or applicable construction industry requirements; or (vii) any substantial or material violation or the threat of a substantial or material violation of the contractual provisions of the order, or of the rules or regulations issued pursuant thereto.

(2) If the investigation of a complaint, or a compliance review, results in a determination that the order, equal opportunity clause or regulations issued pursuant thereto, have been violated, and the violations have not been corrected in accordance with the conciliation procedures in this chapter, OFCCP may institute an administrative enforcement proceeding to enjoin the violations, to seek appropriate relief (which may include affected class and back pay relief), and to impose appropriate sanctions, or any of the above. However, if the contractor refuses to submit an affirmative action program, or refuses to supply records or other requested information, or refuses to allow the compliance agency access to its premises for an on-site review; and if conciliation efforts under this chapter are unsuccessful, OFCCP, notwithstanding the requirements of this chapter, may go directly to administrative enforcement proceedings to enjoin the violations, to seek appropriate relief, and to impose appropriate sanctions, or any of the above. Whenever the Director has reason to believe that there is substantial or material violation or the threat of substantial or material violation of the contractual provisions of the order or of the rules, regulations or orders issued pursuant thereto, he/she may refer the matter to the Solicitor of Labor to institute administrative enforcement proceedings as set forth in this section or refer the matter to the Department of Justice to enforce the contractual provisions of the order, to seek injunctive relief (including relief against noncontractors, including labor unions, who seek to thwart implementation of the order and regulations) and to seek such additional relief, including back pay, as may be appropriate. There are no procedural prerequisites to a referral to the Department of Justice by the Director, and such referrals may be accomplished without proceeding through the conciliation procedures in this chapter, and a referral may be made at any stage in the procedures under this chapter: *Provided,* That no order for debarment from further contracts or subcontracts pursuant to section 209(a)

(6) of the order shall be made without affording the contractor an opportunity for a hearing, either administrative or judicial.

(b) [Reserved]

(c) *Administrative enforcement proceedings.* Administrative enforcement proceedings shall be conducted under the control and supervision of the Solicitor of Labor and under the Rules of Practice for Administrative Proceedings to Enforce Equal Opportunity Under Executive Order 11246 contained in Part 60–30 of this chapter.

(d) *Decision following administrative proceeding.* If it is determined after a hearing (or after the contractor waives a hearing) that the contractor is violating the order or the regulations issued thereunder, the Secretary (in accordance with 41 CFR 60–30.30(a)) shall issue an Administrative order enjoining the violations and requiring the contractor to provide whatever remedies are appropriate, and imposing whatever sanctions are appropriate, or any of the above. In any event, failure to comply with the Administrative order shall result in the imposition of the sanctions contained in section 209(a)(5) or (a)(6) of the Executive order.

(e) *Referrals to the Department of Justice.* (1) Whenever a matter has been referred to the Department of Justice for consideration of judicial proceedings pursuant to § 60–1.26(a)(2) of these regulations, the Attorney General may bring a civil action in the appropriate district court of the United States requesting a temporary restraining order, preliminary or permanent injunction, and an order for such additional equitable relief, including back pay, deemed necessary or appropriate to ensure the full enjoyment of the rights secured by the order, or any of the above.

(2) The Attorney General is authorized to conduct such investigation of the facts as he may deem necessary or appropriate to carry out his responsibilities under these regulations.

(3) Prior to the institution of any judicial proceedings, the Attorney General, on behalf of the Director, is authorized to make reasonable efforts to secure compliance with the contract provisions of the order. He may do so by providing the contractor and any other respondent with reasonable notice of his findings, his intent to file suit, and the actions he believes necessary to obtain compliance with the contract provisions of the order without contested litigation, and by offering the contractor and any other respondent a reasonable opportunity for conference and conciliation, in an effort to obtain such compliance without contested litigation.

(4) As defined in these regulations, the Attorney General shall mean the Attorney General, the Assistant Attorney General for Civil Rights, or any other person authorized by regulations or practice to act for the Attorney General with respect to the enforcement of equal employment opportunity laws, orders and regulations generally, or in a particular matter or case.

(5) The Director or his/her designee, and representatives of the Attorney General may consult from time to time to determine what investigations should be conducted to determine whether contractors or groups of contractors or other persons may be engaged in patterns or practices in violation of the Executive order or these regulations, or of resistance to or interference with the full enjoyment of any of the rights secured by them, warranting judicial proceedings.

(f) *Initiation of lawsuits by the Attorney General without referral from the Director.* In addition to initiating lawsuits upon referral under 41 CFR 60–1.26, the Attorney General may, subject to approval by the Director, initiate independent investigations of contractors which he/she has reason to believe may be in violation of the order or the rules and regulations issued pursuant thereto. If, upon completion of such an investigation, the Attorney General determines that the contractor has in fact violated the order or the rules and regulations issued thereunder, he shall make reasonable efforts to secure compliance with the contract provisions of the order. He may do so by providing the contractor and any other respondent with reasonable notice of the Department's findings, its intent to file suit, and the actions that the Attorney General believes are necessary to obtain compliance with the contract provisions of the order without contested litigation, and by offering the contractor and any other respondent a reasonable opportunity for conference and conciliation in an effort to obtain such compliance without contested litigation. If these efforts are unsuccessful, the Attorney General may, upon approval by the Director, bring a civil action in the appropriate district court of the United States requesting a temporary restraining order, preliminary or permanent injunction, and an order for such additional equitable relief, including back pay, deemed necessary or appropriate to ensure the full enjoyment of the rights secured by the order or any of the above.

(g) To the extent applicable, this section and Part 60–30 of this chapter shall govern proceedings resulting from the Director's determination under § 60–2.2(b) that there are substantial issues of law or fact as to the contractor/bidder's responsibility.

(E.O. 11246 (30 FR 12319) as amended by E.O. 11375 and 12086; sec. 503, Pub.L. 93–112, 87 Stat. 393 (29 U.S.C. 793), as amended by sec. 111, Pub.L. 93–516, 88 Stat. 1619 (29 U.S.C. 706) and E.O. 11758; sec. 503(a), Pub.L. 92–540, 86 Stat. 1097 (38 U.S.C. 2012), as amended by sec. 402, Pub.L. 93–508, 88 Stat. 1593 (38 U.S.C. 2012))

[43 FR 49240, Oct. 20, 1978, as amended at 45 FR 9272, Feb. 12, 1980]

§ 60–1.27 Sanctions and penalties

The sanctions described in subsections (1), (5), and (6) of section 209(a) of the order may be exercised only by or with the approval of the Director. Referral of any matter arising under the order to the Department of Justice or to the Equal Employment Opportunity Commission shall be made by the Director.

§ 60–1.28 Show cause notices

When the director has reasonable cause to believe that a contractor has violated the equal opportunity clause he may issue a notice requiring the contractor to show cause, within 30 days, why monitoring, enforcement proceedings or other appropriate action to ensure compliance should not be instituted.

§ 60–1.29 Preaward notices

(a) *Preaward compliance reviews.* Upon the request of the Director, agencies shall not enter into contracts or approve the entry into contracts or subcontracts with any bidder, prospective prime contractor, or proposed subcontractor named by the Director until a preaward compliance review has been conducted and the Director or his designee has approved a determination that the bidder, prospective prime contractor or proposed subcontractor will be able to comply with the provisions of the equal opportunity clause.

(b) *Other special preaward procedures.* Upon the request of the Director, agencies shall not enter into contracts or approve the entry into subcontracts with any bidder; prospective prime contractor or proposed subcontractor specified by the Director until the agency has complied with the directions contained in the request.

§ 60–1.30 Contract ineligibility list

The Director shall distribute periodically a list to all executive departments and agencies giving the names of prime contractors and subcontractors who have been declared ineligible under the regulations in this part and the order.

§ 60–1.31 Reinstatement of ineligible prime contractors and sub-contractors

Any prime contractor or subcontractor declared ineligible for further contracts or subcontracts under the order may request reinstatement in a letter directed to the Director. In connection with the reinstatement proceedings, the prime contractor or subcontractor shall be required to show that it has established and will carry out employment policies and practices in compliance with the equal opportunity clause.

§ 60–1.32 Intimidation and interference

The sanctions and penalties contained in Subpart D of the order may be exercised by the Director against any prime contractor, subcontractor or applicant who fails to take all necessary steps to ensure that no person intimidates, threatens, coerces, or discriminates against any individual for the purpose of interfering with the filing of a complaint, furnishing information, or assisting or participating in any manner in an investigation, compliance review, hearing, or any other activity related to the administration of the order or any other Federal, State, or local laws requiring equal employment opportunity.

§ 60–1.33 Conciliation agreements

(a) If a compliance review, complaint investigation or other review by OFCCP or its representative indicates a material violation of the equal opportunity clause, and (1) if the contractor, subcontractor or bidder is willing to correct the violations and/or deficiencies, and (2) if OFCCP or its representative determines that settlement (rather than referral for consideration of formal enforcement) is appropriate, a written agreement shall be required. The agreement shall provide for such remedial action as may be necessary to correct the violations and/or deficiencies noted, including, where appropriate (but not necessarily limited to), remedies such as back pay and retroactive seniority.

(b) The term "conciliation agreement" does not include "letters of commitment" which are appropriate for resolving minor technical deficiencies.

(E.O. 11246 (30 FR 12319) as amended by E.O. 11375 and 12086)

[44 FR 77002, Dec. 28, 1979]

§ 60–1.34 Violation of a conciliation agreement or letter of commitment

(a) When a conciliation agreement has been violated, the following procedures are applicable:

(1) A written notice shall be sent to the contractor setting forth the violations alleged and summarizing the supporting evidence. The contractor shall have 15 days from receipt of the notice to respond, except in those cases in which such a delay would result in irreparable injury to the employment rights of affected employees or applicants.

(2) During the 15-day period the contractor may demonstrate in writing that it has not violated its commitments.

(3) If the contractor is unable to demonstrate that it has not violated its commitments, or if the complaint alleges irreparable injury, enforcement proceedings may be initiated immediately without issuing a show cause notice or proceeding through any other requirement contained in this chapter.

(b) If the contractor has violated a letter of commitment, the matter shall be handled, where appropriate, pursuant to 41 CFR 60–2.2(c) or 60–4.8. The violation may be corrected through a conciliation agreement, or an enforcement proceeding may be initiated.

(E.O. 11246 (30 FR 12319) as amended by EO 11375 and 12086)

[44 FR 77002, Dec. 28, 1979]

SUBPART C. ANCILLARY MATTERS

§ 60–1.40 Affirmative action compliance programs

(a) *Requirements of programs.* Each contractor who has 50 or more employees and (1) has a contract of $50,000 or more; or (2) has Government bills of lading which in any 12-month period, total or can reasonably be expected to total $50,000 or more; or (3) serves as a depository of Government funds in any amount; or (4) is a financial institution which is an issuing and paying agent for U.S. savings bonds and savings notes in any amount, shall develop a written affirmative action compliance program for each of it's establishments. Each contractor and subcontractor shall require each subcontractor who has 50 or more employees and (i) has a subcontract of $50,000 or more; or (ii) has Government bills of lading which in any 12-month period, total or can reasonably be expected to total $50,000 or more; or (iii) serves as a depository of Government funds in any amount; or (iv) is a financial institution which is an issuing and paying agent for U.S. savings bonds and savings notes in any amount, to develop a written affirmative action compliance program for each of its establishments. A necessary prerequisite to the development of a satisfactory affirmative action program is the identification and analysis of problem areas inherent in minority employment and an evaluation of opportunities for utilization of minority group personnel. The contractor's program shall provide in detail for specific steps to guarantee equal employment opportunity keyed to the problems and needs of members of minority groups, including, when there are deficiencies, the development of specific goals and time tables for the prompt achievement of full and equal employment opportunity. Each contractor shall include in its affirmative action compliance program a table of job classifications. This table should include but need not be limited to job titles, principal duties (and auxiliary duties, if any), rates of pay, and where more than one rate of pay applied (because of length of time in the job or other factors), the applicable rates. The affirmative action compliance program shall be signed by an executive official of the contractor.

(b) *Utilization evaluation.* The evaluation of utilization of minority group personnel shall include the following:

(1) An analysis of minority group representation in all job categories.

(2) An analysis of hiring practices for the past year, including recruitment sources and testing, to determine whether equal employment opportunity is being afforded in all job categories.

(3) An analysis of upgrading, transfer and promotion for the past year to determine whether equal employment opportunity is being afforded.

(c) *Maintenance of programs.* Within 120 days from the commencement of the contract, each contractor shall maintain a copy of separate affirmative action compliance programs for each establishment, including evaluations of utilization of minority group personnel and the job classification tables, at each local office responsible for the personnel matters of such establishment. An affirmative action compliance program shall be part of the manpower and training plans for each new establishment and shall be developed and made available prior to the staffing of such establishment. A report of the results of such program shall be compiled annually and the program shall be updated at that time. This information shall be made available to representatives of the Director upon request and the contractor's affirmative action program and the result it produces shall be evaluated as part of compliance review activities.

[43 FR 49240, Oct. 20, 1978; 43 FR 51400, Nov. 3, 1978]

§ 60–1.41 Solicitations or advertisements for employees

In solicitations or advertisements for employees placed by or on behalf of a prime contractor or subcontractor, the requirements of paragraph (2) of the equal opportunity clause shall be satisfied whenever the prime contractor or subcontractor complies with any of the following:

(a) States expressly in the solicitations or advertising that all qualified applicants will receive consideration for employment without regard to race, color, religion, sex, or national origin;

(b) Uses display or other advertising, and the advertising includes an appropriate insignia prescribed by the Director. The use of the insignia is considered subject to the provisions of 18 U.S.C. 701;

(c) Uses a single advertisement, and the advertisement is grouped with other advertisements under a caption which clearly states that all employers in the group assure all qualified applicants equal consideration for employment without regard to race, color, religion, sex, or national origin;

(d) Uses a single advertisement in which appears in clearly distinguishable type the phrase "an equal opportunity employer."

§ 60–1.42 Notices to be posted

(a) Unless alternative notices are prescribed by the Director, the notices which prime contractors and subcontractors are required to post by paragraphs (1) and (3) of the equal opportunity clause will contain the following language and will be provided by the contracting or administering agencies:

EQUAL EMPLOYMENT OPPORTUNITY IS THE LAW—DISCRIMINATION IS
PROHIBITED BY THE CIVIL RIGHTS ACT OF 1964
AND BY EXECUTIVE ORDER NO. 11246

Title VII of the Civil Rights Act of 1964—*Administered by:*

THE EQUAL EMPLOYMENT OPPORTUNITY COMMISSION

Prohibits discrimination because of Race, Color, Religion, Sex, or National Origin by Employers with 75 or more employees, by Labor Organizations with a hiring hall of 75 or more members, by Employment Agencies, and by Joint Labor-Management Committees for Apprenticeship or Training. After July 1, 1967, employers and labor organizations with 50 or more employees or members will be covered; after July 1, 1968, those with 25 or more will be covered.

ANY PERSON

Who believes he or she has been discriminated against

SHOULD CONTACT

THE EQUAL EMPLOYMENT OPPORTUNITY COMMISSION

2401 E Street NW, Washington, D.C. 20506
Executive Order No. 11246—*Administered by:*

THE OFFICE OF FEDERAL CONTRACT COMPLIANCE PROGRAMS

Prohibits discrimination because of Race, Color, Religion, Sex, or National Origin, and requires affirmative action to ensure equality of opportunity in all aspects of employment.

By all Federal Government Contractors and Subcontractors, and by Contractors Performing Work Under a Federal Assisted Construction Contract, regardless of the number of employees in either case.

ANY PERSON

Who believes he or she has been discriminated against

SHOULD CONTACT

THE OFFICE OF FEDERAL CONTRACT COMPLIANCE PROGRAMS

U.S. Department of Labor Washington, D.C. 20210

(b) The requirements of paragraph (3) of the equal opportunity clause will be satisfied whenever the prime contractor or subcontractor posts copies of the notification prescribed by or pursuant to paragraph (a) of this section in conspicuous places available to employees, applicants for employment, and representatives of each labor union or other organization representing his employees with which he has a collective-bargaining agreement or other contract or understanding.

§ 60–1.43 Access to records and site of employment

Each prime contractor and subcontractor shall permit access during normal business hours to its premises for the purpose of conducting on-site compliance reviews and inspecting and copying such books, records, accounts, and other material as may be relevant to the matter

under investigation and pertinent to compliance with the order, and
the rules and regulations promulgated pursuant thereto by the agency,
or the Director. Information obtained in this manner shall be used
only in connection with the administration of the order, the administration of the Civil Rights Act of 1964 (as amended) and in furtherance of
the purposes of the order and that Act. (See 41 CFR Part 60–60,
Contractor Evaluation Procedures for Nonconstruction Contractors; 41
CFR Part 60–40, Examination and Copying of OFCCP Documents.)
(Sec. 201. E.O. 11246, 30 FR 12319, and E.O. 11375, 32 FR 14303)

§ 60–1.44 Rulings and interpretations

Rulings under or interpretations of the order or the regulations
contained in this part shall be made by the Secretary or his designee.

§ 60–1.45 Existing contracts and subcontracts

All contracts and subcontracts in effect prior to October 24, 1965,
which are not subsequently modified shall be administered in accordance with the nondiscrimination provisions of any prior applicable
Executive orders. Any contract or subcontract modified on or after
October 24, 1965, shall be subject to Executive Order 11246. Complaints received by and violations coming to the attention of agencies
regarding contracts and subcontracts which were subject to Executive
Orders 10925 and 11114 shall be processed as if they were complaints
regarding violations of this order.

§ 60–1.46 Delegation of authority by the Director

The Director is authorized to redelegate the authority given to him
by the regulations in this part. The authority redelegated by the
Director pursuant to the regulations in this part shall be exercised
under his general direction and control.

§ 60–1.47 Effective date

The regulations contained in this part shall become effective July
1, 1968, for all contracts, the solicitations, invitations for bids, or
requests for proposals which were sent by the Government or an
applicant on or after said effective date, and for all negotiated contracts
which have not been executed as of said effective date. Notwithstanding the foregoing, the regulations in this part shall become effective as
to all contracts executed on and after the 120th day following said
effective date. Subject to any prior approval of the Secretary, any
agency may defer the effective date of the regulations in this part, for
such period of time as the Secretary finds to be reasonably necessary.
Contracts executed prior to the effective date of the regulations in this
part shall be governed by the regulations promulgated by the former
President's Committee on Equal Employment Opportunity which appear at 28 FR 9812, September 2, 1963, and at 28 FR 11305, October 23,
1963, the temporary regulations which appear at 30 FR 13441, October

22, 1965, and the orders at 31 FR 6881, May 10, 1966, and 32 FR 7439, May 19, 1967.

OFCCP—REVISED ORDER NO. 14
(41 CFR 60–60)

Contractor Evaluation Procedures for Contractors for Supplies and Services

SUBPART A. GENERAL

§ 60–60.1 Purpose and scope

This part shall be known as "Revised Order No. 14" and is intended to establish standardized contractor evaluation procedures for conducting compliance reviews of contractors for supplies and services subject to the Equal Employment Opportunity Requirements of 41 CFR 60–1.40 and 41 CFR Part 60–2 (Revised Order No. 4) for the development of written affirmative action programs.

§ 60–60.2 Background

(a) Each prime contractor or subcontractor with 50 or more employees and a contract of $50,000 or more is required to develop a written affirmative action program for each of its establishments (§ 60–1.40 of this chapter). If a contractor fails to submit an affirmative action program and supporting documents, including the workforce analysis within 30 days of a request therefor, the enforcement procedures specified in OFCCP Order No. 4 (§ 60–2.2(c) of this chapter) shall be applicable.

(b) Required affirmative action programs must contain a utilization analysis and goals and timetables as required in §§ 60–2.11 and 60–2.12 of this chapter.

[43 FR 49266, Oct. 20, 1978; 43 FR 51401, Nov. 3, 1978]

SUBPART B. PROCEDURES FOR CONTRACTOR EVALUATION

§ 60–60.3 Agency actions

(a) *Basic steps.* A contractor evaluation should proceed as follows:

(1) A desk audit of the contractor's affirmative action program with special attention directed to the included workforce analysis, using the format set forth in the Standard Compliance Review Report.

(2) An on-site review of those matters which still are not fully or satisfactorily addressed in the affirmative action program and workforce analysis, using the format set forth in the Standard Compliance Review Report and

(3) Where necessary, an off-site analysis of information supplied by the contractor during or pursuant to the on-site review. Contractors

may reach agreement with OFCCP on nationwide AAP formats or on frequency of updating statistics.

(b) *Desk Audit.* Using its approved methods of priority selection, OFCCP shall routinely request from among the Federal contractors within their jurisdiction affirmative action programs and supporting documentation, including the workforce analysis and support data for audit. As used throughout this part, the term "Affirmative Action Program (AAP) and supporting documentation" means the Required Contents of Affirmative Action Programs, as set forth in Subpart B of 41 CFR Part 60–2 and Methods of Implementing the Requirements of Subpart B, set forth in Subpart C of 41 CFR Part 60–2. "Workforce analysis" is defined as a listing of each job title as appears in applicable collective bargaining agreements or payroll records (not job groups) ranked from the lowest paid to the highest paid within each department or other similar organizational unit including departmental or unit supervision. If there are separate work units or lines of progression within a department a separate list must be provided for each such work unit, or line, including unit supervisors. For lines of progression there must be indicated the order of jobs in the line through which an employee could move to the top of the line. Where there are no formal progression lines or usual promotional sequences, job titles should be listed by department, job families, or disciplines, in order of wage rates or salary ranges. For each job title, the total number of incumbents, the total number of male and female incumbents, and the total number of male and female incumbents in each of the following groups must be given: Blacks, Spanish-surnamed Americans, American Indians, and Orientals. The wage rate or salary range for each job title must be given. All job titles, including all managerial job titles, must be listed.

(1) *Exceptions to the desk audit requirements.* For preaward reviews and for complaint investigations, the desk audit need not be carried out or an abbreviated desk audit may be performed and an immediate on-site review performed. Special reports that meet the criteria in paragraph (b)(1) of this section may be requested from contractors, as required, for submission to the OFCCP for complaint investigations and follow-up reviews performed within 1 year of a full compliance review. The Director may approve other special compliance reviews when the circumstances require an immediate on-site review.

(c) *On-site review.* If upon selection of an AAP and included workforce analysis for desk audit, the OFCCP finds that the material submitted does not demonstrate a reasonable effort by the contractor to meet all the requirements of Subparts B and C of Order No. 4 (Part 60–2 of this chapter) the on-site review need not be carried out and the enforcement procedures specified in Order 4 shall be applicable. Otherwise following a desk audit of the affirmative action program and supporting documentation the OFCCP will schedule an on-site review of the establishment, provided, that an on-site review need not be carried out when OFCCP can determine that the contractor's affirmative action program is acceptable. This determination must be based on the current desk audit and an on-site review conducted within the preceding 24 months and also must include an affirmative determination that the circumstances of the previous on-site review have not substantially changed.

(1) OFCCP is to request from those contractors scheduled for on-site reviews that information necessary to perform the review be made available on-site. Specifically, this includes (i) information necessary to conduct an indepth analysis of apparent deficiencies in the contractors utilization of women or minorities, (ii) information required for a complete and thorough understanding of data contained in or offered as support for the affirmative action program, and (iii) information concerning matters relevant to a determination of compliance with the requirements of Executive Order 11246 (as amended), but not adequately, addressed in the affirmative action program. However, the contractor should be requested to furnish only the specific items of information which the compliance officer determines are:

(a) Necessary for conducting the review and completing the standard compliance review report, and

(b) Not contained in or able to be derived from the material submitted by the contractor.

(2) In order to pursue certain issues uncovered in the compliance review, it may be necessary for the compliance officer to request certain additional information on-site even though such data have not been previously identified. Such additional information must also meet the above criteria.

(d) *Off-site analysis.* Where necessary, the compliance officer may take information made available during the on-site review off-site for further analysis. An off-site analysis should be conducted where issues have arisen concerning deficiencies or an apparent violation which, in the judgment of the compliance officer, should be more thoroughly analyzed off-site before a determination of compliance is made.

[43 FR 49266, Oct. 20, 1978; 43 FR 51401, Nov. 3, 1978]

SUBPART C. DISCLOSURE AND REVIEW OF CONTRACTOR DATA

§ 60–60.4 Confidentiality and relevancy of information

(a) *Desk audit data.* If the contractor is concerned with the confidentiality of such information as lists of employees, employee names, reasons for termination and pay data then alphabetic or numeric coding or the use of an index of pay and pay ranges are acceptable for desk audit purposes.

(b) *On-site data.* The contractor must provide full access to all relevant data on-site as required by § 60–1.43 of this chapter.

(c) *Data required for off-site analysis.* The contractor must provide all data determined by the compliance officer to be necessary for off-site analysis pursuant to § 60–60.3(c) of this part. Such data may only be coded if the contractor makes the code available to the compliance officer. If the contractor believes that particular information which is to be taken off-site is not relevant to compliance with the Executive order, the contractor may request a ruling by the OFCCP Area Director. The OFCCP Area Director shall issue a ruling within 10 days. The contractor may appeal that ruling to the OFCCP Assistant Regional Administrator within 10 days. The Assistant Regional Administrator shall issue a final ruling within 10 days. Pending a final ruling, the information in question must be made available to the compliance officer off-site, but shall be considered a part of the investigatory file and subject to the provisions of paragraph (d) of this section. The agency shall take all necessary precautions to safeguard all confidentiality of such information until a final determination is made. Such information may not be copied and access to the information shall be limited to the compliance officer and personnel involved in the determination of relevancy. Data determined to be not relevant to the investigation will be returned to the contractor immediately.

(d) *Public access to information.* Information obtained from a contractor under Subpart B will be subject to the public inspection and copying provisions of the Freedom of Information Act, 5 U.S.C. 552. Contractors should identify any information which they believe is not subject to disclosure under 5 U.S.C. 552, and should specify the reasons why such information is not disclosable. The OFCCP Assistant Regional Administrator will consider the contractor's claim and make a determination, within 10 days, as to whether the material in question is exempt from disclosure. The OFCCP Assistant Regional Administrator will inform the contractor of such a determination. The contractor may appeal that ruling to the Director of OFCCP within 10 days. The Director of OFCCP shall make a final determination within 10 days of the filing of the appeal. However, during the conduct of a compliance review or while enforcement action against the contractor is in progress or contemplated within a reasonable time, all information obtained from a contractor under Subpart B except information disclosable under §§ 60–40.2 and 60–40.3 of this chapter is to be considered part of an investigatory file compiled for law enforcement purposes within the meaning of 5 U.S.C. 552(b)(7), and such information obtained from a contractor under Subpart B shall be treated as exempt from mandatory disclosure under the Freedom of Information Act during the compliance review.

(e) *Examination and copying of documents.* Nothing contained herein is intended to supersede or otherwise limit the provisions contained in Part 60–40 of this chapter for public access to information from records of the OFCC or its various compliance agencies.

[43 FR 49266, Oct. 20, 1978; 43 FR 51401, Nov. 3, 1978]

§ 60–60.5 Employee interviews

The compliance officer should contact, where appropriate, a reasonable number of employees for interviews as part of the on-site review of the contractors' employment practices. The number, scope and manner of conducting such interviews should be discussed in advance with the contractor.

§ 60–60.6   Exit conference

(a) Upon completion of the on-site review (and off-site analysis, if one is undertaken) the compliance officer should schedule an exit conference with contractor officials to review the findings of the review. This exit conference should itemize the apparent violations that lend themselves to immediate correction, and solicit the contractor's agreement to take adequate corrective action by specified dates. The contractor's commitments should be contained in a written conciliation agreement signed at the exit conference. However, in cases where the apparent deficiencies require further analysis subsequent to the on-site review, the compliance officer will advise the contractor of the areas of concern, secure the data necessary to his ultimate compliance determination, complete the review later by notifying the contractor in writing of all apparent violations found, and obtain the contractor's commitments in a written conciliation agreement to correct such deficiencies.

(b) The contractor may at any time avail himself of the provisions of § 60–1.24(c)(4) of this chapter which provides as follows:

(1) When a prime contractor or subcontractor, without a hearing, shall have complied with the recommendations or orders of the Director and believes such recommendations or orders to be erroneous, he shall, upon filing a request therefor within 10 days of such compliance, be afforded an opportunity for a hearing and review of the alleged erroneous action.

§ 60–60.7   Time schedule for completion

(a) With the exception of extensions of time granted by the Director of OFCCP for good cause shown, within 60 days from the date the affirmative action program including the workforce analysis is received, the contractor must have been found in compliance and notified of that fact, or must have been issued a 30-day show cause notice as required under the rules and regulations pursuant to the Executive order.

(b) During this period the compliance officer shall:

(1) Complete the desk audit.

(2) Schedule the on-site review.

(3) Complete the on-site review.

(4) Complete the off-site analysis, if conducted.

(5) Give notice of compliance or issue show cause notice.

(c) Failure to give the contractor a notice of compliance or issue a show cause notice within the time period set forth in paragraph (a) shall not be deemed a finding of compliance or acceptance of the contractor's affirmative action program.

[43 FR 49266, Oct. 20, 1978; 43 FR 51401, Nov. 3, 1978]

§ 60–60.8 Supersedure

The requirements of this Part 60–60 supersede the prior version of Revised Order No. 14 published at 38 FR 13376, May 21, 1973.

EEOC—AFFIRMATIVE ACTION GUIDELINES
(29 CFR 1608)

Affirmative Action Appropriate Under Title VII of the Civil Rights Act of 1964, as Amended

§ 1608.1 Statement of purpose

(a) *Need for Guidelines.* Since the passage of Title VII in 1964, many employers, labor organizations, and other persons subject to Title VII have changed their employment practices and systems to improve employment opportunities for minorities and women, and this must continue. These changes have been undertaken either on the initiative of the employer, labor organization, or other person subject to Title VII, or as a result of conciliation efforts under Title VII, action under Executive Order No. 11246, as amended, or under other Federal, state, or local laws, or litigation. Many decisions taken pursuant to affirmative action plans or programs have been race, sex, or national origin conscious in order to achieve the Congressional purpose of providing equal employment opportunity. Occasionally, these actions have been challenged as inconsistent with Title VII, because they took into account race, sex, or national origin. This is the so-called "reverse discrimination" claim. In such a situation, both the affirmative action undertaken to improve the conditions of minorities and women, and the objection to that action, are based upon the principles of Title VII. Any uncertainty as to the meaning and application of Title VII in such situations threatens the accomplishment of the clear Congressional intent to encourage voluntary affirmative action. The Commission believes that by the enactment of Title VII Congress did not intend to expose those who comply with the Act to charges that they are violating the very statute they are seeking to implement. Such a result would immobilize or reduce the efforts of many who would otherwise take action to improve the opportunities of minorities and women without litigation, thus frustrating the Congressional intent to encourage voluntary action and increasing the prospect of Title VII litigation. The Commission believes that it is now necessary to clarify and harmonize the principles of Title VII in order to achieve these Congressional objectives and protect those employers, labor organizations, and other persons who comply with the principles of Title VII.

(b) *Purposes of Title VII.* Congress enacted Title VII in order to improve the economic and social conditions of minorities and women by providing equality of opportunity in the work place. These conditions were part of a larger pattern of restriction, exclusion, discrimination, segregation, and inferior treatment of minorities and women in many areas of life.[2] The Legislative Histories of Title VII, the Equal Pay Act, and the Equal Employment Opportunity Act of 1972 contain extensive analyses of the higher unemployment rate, the lesser occupational status, and the consequent lower income levels of minorities and women.[3] The purpose of Executive Order No. 11246, as amended, is similar to the purpose of Title VII. In response to these economic and social conditions, Congress, by passage of Title VII, established a national policy against discrimination in employment on grounds of race, color, religion, sex, and national origin. In addition, Congress strongly encouraged employers, labor organizations, and other persons subject to Title VII (hereinafter referred to as "persons," see section 701(a) of the Act) to act on a voluntary basis to modify employment practices and systems which constituted barriers to equal employment opportunity, without awaiting litigation or formal government action. Conference, conciliation, and persuasion were the primary processes adopted by Congress in 1964, and reaffirmed in 1972, to achieve these objectives, with enforcement action through the courts or agencies as a supporting procedure where voluntary action did not take place and conciliation failed. See § 706 of Title VII.

(c) *Interpretation in furtherance of legislative purpose.* The principle of nondiscrimination in employment because of race, color, religion, sex, or national origin, and the principle that each person subject to Title VII should take voluntary action to correct the effects of past discrimination and to prevent present and future discrimination without awaiting litigation, are mutually consistent and interdependent methods of addressing social and economic conditions which precipitated the enactment of Title VII. Voluntary affirmative action to improve opportunities for minorities and women must be encouraged and protected in order to carry out the Congressional intent embodied in Title VII.[4] Affirmative action under these principles means those actions

---

2. Congress has also addressed these conditions in other laws, including the Equal Pay Act of 1963, Pub.L. 88–38, 77 Stat. 56 (1963), as amended; the other Titles of the Civil Rights Act of 1964, Pub.L. 88–352, 78 Stat. 241 (1964), as amended; the Voting Rights Act of 1965, Pub.L. 89–110, 79 Stat. 437 (1965), as amended; the Fair Housing Act of 1968, Pub.L. 90–284, Title VII, 82 Stat. 73, 81 (1968), as amended; the Educational Opportunity Act (Title IX), Pub.L. 92–318, 86 Stat. 373 (1972), as amended; and the Equal Employment Opportunity Act of 1972, Pub.L. 92–261, 86 Stat. 103 (1972), as amended.

3. Equal Pay Act of 1963: S.Rep. No. 176, 88th Cong., 1st Sess., 1–2 (1963). Civil Rights Act of 1964: H.R.Rep. No. 914, pt. 2, 88th Cong., 1st Sess. (1971). Equal Employment Opportunity Act of 1972: H.R. Rep. No. 92–238, 92d Cong., 1st Sess.

(1971); S.Rep. No. 92–415, 92d Cong., 1st Sess. (1971). See also, Equal Employment Opportunity Commission, Equal Employment Opportunity Report—1975, Job Patterns for Women in Private Industry (1977); Equal Employment Opportunity Commission, Minorities and Women in State and Local Government—1975 (1977); United States Commission on Civil Rights, Social Indicators of Equality for Minorities and Women (1978).

4. Affirmative action often improves opportunities for all members of the workforce, as where affirmative action includes the posting of notices of job vacancies. Similarly, the integration of previously segregated jobs means that all workers will be provided opportunities to enter jobs previously restricted. See, e.g., EEOC v. AT&T, 419 F.Supp. 1022 (E.D.Pa.

appropriate to overcome the effects of past or present practices, policies, or other barriers to equal employment opportunity. Such voluntary affirmative action cannot be measured by the standard of whether it would have been required had there been litigation, for this standard would undermine the legislative purpose of first encouraging voluntary action without litigation. Rather, persons subject to Title VII must be allowed flexibility in modifying employment systems and practices to comport with the purposes of Title VII. Correspondingly, Title VII must be construed to permit such voluntary action, and those taking such action should be afforded the protection against Title VII liability which the Commission is authorized to provide under section 713(b)(1).

(d) *Guidelines interpret Title VII and authorize use of Section 713(b)(1).* These Guidelines describe the circumstances in which persons subject to Title VII may take or agree upon action to improve employment opportunities of minorities and women, and describe the kinds of actions they may take which are consistent with Title VII. These Guidelines constitute the Commission's interpretation of Title VII and will be applied in the processing of claims of discrimination which involve voluntary affirmative action plans and programs. In addition, these Guidelines state the circumstances under which the Commission will recognize that a person subject to Title VII is entitled to assert that actions were taken "in good faith, in conformity with, and in reliance upon a written interpretation or opinion of the Commission," including reliance upon the interpretation and opinion contained in these Guidelines, and thereby invoke the protection of section 713(b)(1) of Title VII.

(e) *Review of existing plans recommended.* Only affirmative action plans or programs adopted in good faith, in conformity with, and in reliance upon these Guidelines can receive the full protection of these Guidelines, including the section 713(b)(1) defense. See § 1608.10. Therefore, persons subject to Title VII who have existing affirmative action plans, programs, or agreements are encouraged to review them in light of these Guidelines, to modify them to the extent necessary to comply with these Guidelines, and to readopt or reaffirm them.

§ 1608.2 Written interpretation and opinion

These Guidelines constitute "a written interpretation and opinion" of the Equal Employment Opportunity Commission as that term is used in section 713(b)(1) of Title VII of the Civil Rights Act of 1964, as amended, 42 U.S.C. 2000e–12(b)(1), and section 1601.33 of the Procedural Regulations of the Equal Employment Opportunity Commission (29 CFR 1601.30; 42 FR 55,394 (October 14, 1977)). Section 713(b)(1) provides:

In any action or proceeding based on any alleged unlawful employment practice, no person shall be subject to any liability or punish-

1976), aff'd, 556 F.2d 167 (3rd Cir.1977),
cert. denied, 98 S.Ct. 3145 (1978).

ment for or on account of (1) the commission by such person of an unlawful employment practice if he pleads and proves that the act or omission complained of was in good faith, in conformity with, and in reliance on any written interpretation or opinion of the Commission * * *. Such a defense, if established, shall be a bar to the action or proceeding, notwithstanding that * * * after such act or omission, such interpretation or opinion is modified or rescinded or is determined by judicial authority to be invalid or of no legal effect * * *.

The applicability of these Guidelines is subject to the limitations on use set forth in § 1608.11.

§ 1608.3 Circumstances under which voluntary affirmative action is appropriate

(a) *Adverse effect.* Title VII prohibits practices, procedures, or policies which have an adverse impact unless they are justified by business necessity. In addition, Title VII proscribes practices which "tend to deprive" persons of equal employment opportunities. Employers, labor organizations and other persons subject to Title VII may take affirmative action based on an analysis which reveals facts constituting actual or potential adverse impact, if such adverse impact is likely to result from existing or contemplated practices.

(b) *Effects of prior discriminatory practices.* Employers, labor organizations, or other persons subject to Title VII may also take affirmative action to correct the effects of prior discriminatory practices. The effects of prior discriminatory practices can be initially identified by a comparison between the employer's work force, or a part thereof, and an appropriate segment of the labor force.

(c) *Limited labor pool.* Because of historic restrictions by employers, labor organizations, and others, there are circumstances in which the available pool, particularly of qualified minorities and women, for employment or promotional opportunities is artificially limited. Employers, labor organizations, and other persons subject to Title VII may, and are encouraged to take affirmative action in such circumstances, including, but not limited to, the following:

(1) Training plans and programs, including on-the-job training, which emphasize providing minorities and women with the opportunity, skill, and experience necessary to perform the functions of skilled trades, crafts, or professions;

(2) Extensive and focused recruiting activity;

(3) Elimination of the adverse impact caused by unvalidated selection criteria (see sections 3 and 6, Uniform Guidelines on Employee Selection Procedures (1978), 43 FR 30,290; 38,297; 38,299 (August 25, 1978));

(4) Modification through collective bargaining where a labor organization represents employees, or unilaterally where one does not, of promotion and layoff procedures.

§ 1608.4 Establishing affirmative action plans

An affirmative action plan or program under this section shall contain three elements: a reasonable self analysis; a reasonable basis for concluding action is appropriate; and reasonable action.

(a) *Reasonable self analysis.* The objective of a self analysis is to determine whether employment practices do, or tend to, exclude, disadvantage, restrict, or result in adverse impact or disparate treatment of previously excluded or restricted groups or leave uncorrected the effects of prior discrimination, and if so, to attempt to determine why. There is no mandatory method of conducting a self analysis. The employer may utilize techniques used in order to comply with Executive Order No. 11246, as amended, and its implementing regulations, including 41 CFR Part 60–2 (known as Revised Order 4), or related orders issued by the Office of Federal Contract Compliance Programs or its authorized agencies, or may use an analysis similar to that required under other Federal, state, or local laws or regulations prohibiting employment discrimination. In conducting a self analysis, the employer, labor organization, or other person subject to Title VII should be concerned with the effect on its employment practices of circumstances which may be the result of discrimination by other persons or institutions. See *Griggs v. Duke Power Co.,* 401 U.S. 424 (1971).

(b) *Reasonable basis.* If the self analysis shows that one or more employment practices: (1) Have or tend to have an adverse effect on employment opportunities of members of previously excluded groups, or groups whose employment or promotional opportunities have been artificially limited, (2) leave uncorrected the effects of prior discrimination, or (3) result in disparate treatment, the person making the self analysis has a reasonable basis for concluding that action is appropriate. It is not necessary that the self analysis establish a violation of Title VII. This reasonable basis exists without any admission or formal finding that the person has violated Title VII, and without regard to whether there exists arguable defenses to a Title VII action.

(c) *Reasonable action.* The action taken pursuant to an affirmative action plan or program must be reasonable in relation to the problems disclosed by the self analysis. Such reasonable action may include goals and timetables or other appropriate employment tools which recognize the race, sex, or national origin of applicants or employees. It may include the adoption of practices which will eliminate the actual or potential adverse impact, disparate treatment, or effect or past discrimination by providing opportunities for members of groups which have been excluded, regardless of whether the persons benefited were themselves the victims of prior policies or procedures which produced the adverse impact or disparate treatment or which perpetuated past discrimination.

(1) *Illustrations of appropriate affirmative action.* Affirmative action plans or programs may include, but are not limited to, those described in the Equal Employment Opportunity Coordinating Council

"Policy Statement on Affirmative Action Programs for State and Local Government Agencies," 41 FR 38,814 (September 13, 1976), reaffirmed and extended to all persons subject to Federal equal employment opportunity laws and orders, in the Uniform Guidelines on Employee Selection Procedures (1978) 43 FR 38,290; 38,300 (Aug. 25, 1978). That statement reads, in relevant part:

> When an employer has reason to believe that its selection procedures have * * * exclusionary effect * * *, it should initiate affirmative steps to remedy the situation. Such steps, which in design and execution may be race, color, sex or ethnic 'conscious,' include, but are not limited to, the following:

> The establishment of a long term goal and short range, interim goals and timetables for the specific job classifications, all of which should take into account the availability of basically qualified persons in the relevant job market;

> A recruitment program designed to attract qualified members of the group in question;

> A systematic effort to organize work and re-design jobs in ways that provide opportunities for persons lacking 'journeyman' level knowledge or skills to enter and, with appropriate training, to progress in a career field;

> Revamping selection instruments or procedures which have not yet been validated in order to reduce or eliminate exclusionary effects on particular groups in particular job classifications;

> The initiation of measures designed to assure that members of the affected group who are qualified to perform the job are included within the pool of persons from which the selecting official makes the selection;

> A systematic effort to provide career advancement training, both classroom and on-the-job, to employees locked into dead end jobs; and

> The establishment of a system for regularly monitoring the effectiveness of the particular affirmative action program, and procedures for making timely adjustments in this program where effectiveness is not demonstrated.

(2) *Standards of reasonable action.* In considering the reasonableness of a particular affirmative action plan or program, the Commission will generally apply the following standards:

(i) The plan should be tailored to solve the problems which were identified in the self analysis, see § 1608.4(a), supra, and to ensure that employment systems operate fairly in the future, while avoiding unnecessary restrictions on opportunities for the workforce as a whole. The race, sex, and national origin conscious provisions of the plan or program should be maintained only so long as is necessary to achieve these objectives.

(ii) Goals and timetables should be reasonably related to such considerations as the effects of past discrimination, the need for prompt elimination of adverse impact or disparate treatment, the availability of basically qualified or qualifiable applicants, and the number of employment opportunities expected to be available.

(d) *Written or unwritten plans or programs*—(1) *Written plans required for 713(b)(1) Protection.* The protection of section 713(b) of Title VII will be accorded by the Commission to a person subject to Title VII only if the self analysis and the affirmative action plan are dated and in writing, and the plan otherwise meets the requirements of Section 713(b)(1). The Commission will not require that there be any written statement concluding that a Title VII violation exists.

(2) *Reasonable cause determinations.* Where an affirmative action plan or program is alleged to violate Title VII, or is asserted as a defense to a charge of discrimination, the Commission will investigate the charge in accordance with its usual procedures and pursuant to the standards set forth in these Guidelines, whether or not the analysis and plan are in writing. However, the absence of a written self analysis and a written affirmative action plan or program may make it more difficult to provide credible evidence that the analysis was conducted, and that action was taken pursuant to a plan or program based on the analysis. Therefore, the Commission recommends that such analyses and plans be in writing.

§ 1608.5 Affirmative action compliance programs under Executive Order No. 11246, as amended

Under Title VII, affirmative action compliance programs adopted pursuant to Executive Order No. 11246, as amended, and its implementing regulations, including 41 CFR Part 60–2 (Revised Order 4), will be considered by the Commission in light of the similar purposes of Title VII and the Executive Order, and the Commission's responsibility under Executive Order No. 12067 to avoid potential conflict among Federal equal employment opportunity programs. Accordingly, the Commission will process Title VII complaints involving such affirmative action compliance programs under this section.

(a) *Procedures for review of Affirmative Action Compliance Programs.* If adherence to an affirmative action compliance program adopted pursuant to Executive Order No. 11246, as amended, and its implementing regulations, is the basis of a complaint filed under Title VII, or is alleged to be the justification for an action which is challenged under Title VII, the Commission will investigate to determine whether the affirmative action compliance program was adopted by a person subject to the Order and pursuant to the Order, and whether adherence to the program was the basis of the complaint or the justification.

(1) *Programs previously approved.* If the Commission makes the determination described in paragraph (a) of this section and also finds that the affirmative action program has been approved by an appropriate official of the Department of Labor or its authorized agencies, or is

part of a conciliation or settlement agreement or an order of an administrative agency, whether entered by consent or after contested proceedings brought to enforce Executive Order No. 11246, as amended, the Commission will issue a determination of no reasonable cause.

(2) *Program not previously approved.* If the Commission makes the determination described in paragraph (a), of this section but the program has not been approved by an appropriate official of the Department of Labor or its authorized agencies, the Commission will: (i) Follow the procedure in § 1608.10(a) and review the program, or (ii) refer the plan to the Department of Labor for a determination of whether it is to be approved under Executive Order No. 11246, as amended, and its implementing regulations. If, the Commission finds that the program does conform to these Guidelines, or the Department of Labor approves the affirmative action compliance program, the Commission will issue a determination of no reasonable cause under § 1608.10(a).

(b) *Reliance on these guidelines.* In addition, if the affirmative action compliance program has been adopted in good faith reliance on these Guidelines, the provisions of section 713(b)(1) of Title VII and of § 1608.10(b), below, may be asserted by the contractor.

§ 1608.6 Affirmative action plans which are part of Commission conciliation or settlement agreements

(a) *Procedures for review of plans.* If adherence to a conciliation or settlement agreement executed under Title VII and approved by a responsible official of the EEOC is the basis of a complaint filed under Title VII, or is alleged to be the justification for an action challenged under Title VII, the Commission will investigate to determine: (1) Whether the conciliation agreement or settlement agreement was approved by a responsible official of the EEOC, and (2) whether adherence to the agreement was the basis for the complaint or justification. If the Commission so finds, it will make a determination of no reasonable cause under § 1608.10(a) and will advise the respondent of its right under section 713(b)(1) of Title VII to rely on the conciliation agreement.

(b) *Reliance on these guidelines.* In addition, if the affirmative action plan or program has been adopted in good faith reliance on these Guidelines, the provisions of section 713(b)(1) of Title VII and of § 1608.10(b), below, may be asserted by the respondent.

§ 1608.7 Affirmative action plans or programs under State or local law

Affirmative action plans or programs executed by agreement with state or local government agencies, or by order of state or local government agencies, whether entered by consent or after contested proceedings, under statutes or ordinances described in Title VII, will be reviewed by the Commission in light of the similar purposes of Title VII and such statutes and ordinances. Accordingly, the Commission will process Title VII complaints involving such affirmative action plans or programs under this section.

(a) *Procedures for review of plans or programs.* If adherence to an affirmative action plan or program executed pursuant to a state statute or local ordinance described in Title VII is the basis of a complaint filed under Title VII or is alleged to be the justification for an action which is challenged under Title VII, the Commission will investigate to determine: (1) Whether the affirmative action plan or program was executed by an employer, labor organization, or person subject to the statute or ordinance, (2) whether the agreement was approved by an appropriate official of the state or local government, and (3) whether adherence to the plan or program was the basis of the complaint or justification.

(1) *Previously Approved Plans or Programs.* If the Commission finds the facts described in paragraph (a) of this section, the Commission will, in accordance with the "substantial weight" provisions of section 706 of the Act, find no reasonable cause where appropriate.

(2) *Plans or Programs not previously approved.* If the plan or program has not been approved by an appropriate official of the state or local government, the Commission will follow the procedure of § 1608.10 of these Guidelines. If the Commission finds that the plan or program does conform to these Guidelines, the Commission will make a determination of no reasonable cause as set forth in § 1608.10(a).

(b) *Reliance on these guidelines.* In addition, if the affirmative action plan or program has been adopted in good faith reliance on these Guidelines, the provisions of section 713(b)(1) and § 1608.10(b), below, may be asserted by the respondent.

§ 1608.8 Adherence to court order

Parties are entitled to rely on orders of courts of competent jurisdiction. If adherence to an Order of a United States District Court or other court of competent jurisdiction, whether entered by consent or after contested litigation, in a case brought to enforce a Federal, state, or local equal employment opportunity law or regulation, is the basis of a complaint filed under Title VII or is alleged to be the justification for an action which is challenged under Title VII, the Commission will investigate to determine: (a) Whether such an Order exists and (b) whether adherence to the affirmative action plan which is part of the Order was the basis of the complaint or justification. If the Commission so finds, it will issue a determination of no reasonable cause. The Commission interprets Title VII to mean that actions taken pursuant to the direction of a Court Order cannot give rise to liability under Title VII.

§ 1608.9 Reliance on directions of other government agencies

When a charge challenges an affirmative action plan or program, or when such a plan or program is raised as justification for an employment decision, and when the plan or program was developed pursuant to the requirements of a Federal or state law or regulation which in part seeks to ensure equal employment opportunity, the Commission will process the charge in accordance with § 1608.10(a). Other agencies with equal employment opportunity responsibilities may apply the principles of these Guidelines in the exercise of their authority.

§ 1608.10 Standard of review

(a) *Affirmative action plans or programs not specifically relying on these guidelines.* If, during the investigation of a charge of discrimination filed with the Commission, a respondent asserts that the action complained of was taken pursuant to an in accordance with a plan or program of the type described in these Guidelines, the Commission will determine whether the assertion is true, and if so, whether such a plan or program conforms to the requirements of these guidelines. If the Commission so finds, it will issue a determination of no reasonable cause and, where appropriate, will state that the determination constitutes a written interpretation or opinion of the Commission under section 713(b)(1). This interpretation may be relied upon by the respondent and asserted as a defense in the event that new charges involving similar facts and circumstances are thereafter filed against the respondent, which are based on actions taken pursuant to the affirmative action plan or program. If the Commission does not so find, it will proceed with the investigation in the usual manner.

(b) *Reliance on these guidelines.* If a respondent asserts that the action taken was pursuant to and in accordance with a plan or program which was adopted or implemented in good faith, in conformity with, and in reliance upon these Guidelines, and the self analysis and plan are in writing, the Commission will determine whether such assertion is true. If the Commission so finds, it will so state in the determination of no reasonable cause and will advise the respondent that:

(1) The Commission has found that the respondent is entitled to the protection of section 713(b)(1) of Title VII; and

(2) That the determination is itself an additional written interpretation or opinion of the Commission pursuant to section 713(b)(1).

§ 1608.11 Limitations on the application of these guidelines

(a) *No determination of adequacy of plan or program.* These Guidelines are applicable only with respect to the circumstances described in § 1608.1(d), above. They do not apply to, and the section 713(b)(1) defense is not available for the purpose of, determining the adequacy of an affirmative action plan or program to eliminate discrimination. Whether an employer who takes such affirmative action has done enough to remedy such discrimination will remain a question of fact in each case.

(b) *Guidelines inapplicable in absence of affirmative action.* Where an affirmative action plan or program does not exist, or where the plan or program is not the basis of the action complained of, these Guidelines are inapplicable.

(c) *Currency of plan or program.* Under section 713(b)(1), persons may rely on the plan or program only during the time when it is current. Currency is related to such factors as progress in correcting the conditions disclosed by the self analysis. The currency of the plan or program is a question of fact to be determined on a case by case basis. Programs developed under Executive Order No. 11246, as amended, will be deemed current in accordance with Department of Labor regulations at 41 CFR Chapter 60, or successor orders or regulations.

§ 1608.12 Equal employment opportunity plans adopted pursuant to section 717 of Title VII

If adherence to an Equal Employment Opportunity Plan, adopted pursuant to Section 717 of Title VII, and approved by an appropriate official of the U.S. Civil Service Commission, is the basis of a complaint filed under Title VII, or is alleged to be the justification for an action under Title VII, these Guidelines will apply in a manner similar to that set forth in § 1608.5. The Commission will issue regulations setting forth the procedure for processing such complaints.

OFCCP—AFFIRMATIVE ACTION GUIDELINES: REVISED ORDER NO. 4 (41 CFR 60–2)

Affirmative Action Programs

SUBPART A. GENERAL

§ 60–2.1 Title, purpose and scope

(a) This part shall also be known as "Revised Order No. 4," and shall cover nonconstruction contractors. Section 60–1.40 of this chapter, affirmative action compliance programs, requires that within 120 days from the commencement of a contract each prime contractor or subcontractor with 50 or more employees and (1) a contract of $50,000 or more; or (2) Government bills of lading which, in any 12-month period, total or can reasonably be expected to total $50,000 or more; or (3) who serves as a depository of Government funds in any amount; or (4) who is a financial institution which is an issuing and paying agent for U.S. savings bonds and savings notes in any amount, develop a written affirmative action compliance program for each of its establishments. A review of compliance surveys indicates that many contractors do not have affirmative action programs on file at the time an establishment is visited by a compliance investigator. This part details the review procedure and the results of a contractor's failure to develop and maintain an affirmative action program and then sets forth detailed guidelines to be used by contractors and the Government in developing and judging these programs as well as the good faith effort required to transform the programs from paper commitments to equal employment opportunity. Subparts B and C of this part are concerned with affirmative action plans only.

(b) Relief, including back pay where appropriate, for members of an affected class who by virtue of past discrimination continue to suffer the present effects of that discrimination, shall be provided in the conciliation agreement entered into pursuant to § 60–60.6 of this title. An "affected class" problem must be remedied in order for a contractor to be considered in compliance. Section 60–2.2 herein pertaining to an acceptable affirmative action program is also applicable to the failure to remedy discrimination against members of an "affected class."

§ 60–2.2 Agency action

(a) Any contractor required by § 60–1.40 of this chapter to develop an affirmative action program at each of its establishments who has not complied fully with that section is not in compliance with Executive Order 11246, as amended (30 FR 12319). Until such programs are developed and found to be acceptable in accordance with the standards and guidelines set forth in §§ 60–2.10 through 60–2.32, the contractor is unable to comply with the equal employment opportunity clause. An affirmative action plan shall be deemed to have been accepted by the Government at the time the appropriate OFCCP field, area, regional, or national office has accepted such plan unless within 45 days thereafter the Director has disapproved such plan.

(b) If, in determining such contractor's responsibility for an award of a contract it comes to the contracting officer's attention, through sources within his agency or through the Office of Federal Contract Compliance Programs or other Government agencies, that the contractor has no affirmative action program at each of its establishments, or has substantially deviated from such an approved affirmative action program, or has failed to develop or implement an affirmative action program which complies with the regulations in this chapter, the contracting officer shall declare the contractor/bidder nonresponsible and so notify the contractor and the Director, unless he can otherwise affirmatively determine that the contractor is able to comply with his equal employment obligations. Any contractor/bidder which has been declared nonresponsible in accordance with the provisions of this section may request the Director to determine that the responsibility of the contractor/bidder raises substantial issues of law or fact to the extent that a hearing is required. Such request shall set forth the basis upon which the contractor/bidder seeks such a determination. If the Director, in his/her sole discretion, determines that substantial issues of law or fact exist, an administrative or judicial proceeding may be commenced in accordance with the regulations contained in § 60–1.26; or the Director may require the investigation or compliance review be developed further or additional conciliation be conducted: Provided, That during any pre-award conferences, every effort shall be made through the processes of conciliation, mediation, and persuasion to develop an acceptable affirmative action program meeting the standards and guidelines set forth in §§ 60–2.10 through 60–2.32 so that, in the performance of his contract, the contractor is able to meet its equal employment obligations in accordance with the equal opportunity clause and applicable rules, regulations, and orders: Provided further, That a contractor/bidder may not be declared nonresponsible more than twice due to past noncompliance with the equal opportunity clause at a particular establishment or facility without receiving prior notice and an opportunity for a hearing.

(c)(1) Immediately upon finding that a contractor has no affirmative action program, or has deviated substantially from an approved affirmative action program, or has failed to develop or implement an affirmative action program which complies with the requirements of the regulations in this chapter, that fact shall be recorded in the investigation file. Whenever administrative enforcement is contemplated, the notice to the contractor shall be issued giving him 30 days to show cause why enforcement proceedings under section 209(a) of Executive Order 11246, as amended, should not be instituted. The notice to show cause should contain:

(i) An itemization of the sections of the Executive order and of the regulations with which the contractor has been found in apparent violation, and a summary of the conditions, practices, facts, or circumstances which give rise to each apparent violation;

(ii) The corrective actions necessary to achieve compliance or, as may be appropriate, the concepts and principles of an acceptable remedy and/or the corrective action results anticipated;

(iii) A request for a written response to the findings, including commitments to corrective action or the presentation of opposing facts and evidence; and

(iv) A suggested date for the conciliation conference.

(2) If the contractor fails to show good cause for his failure or fails to remedy that failure by developing and implementing an acceptable affirmative action program within 30 days, the case file shall be processed for enforcement proceedings pursuant to § 60–1.26 of this chapter. If an administrative complaint is filed, the contractor shall have 20 days to request a hearing. If a request for hearing has not been received within 20 days from the filing of the administrative complaint, the matter shall proceed in accordance with Part 60–30 of this chapter.

(3) During the "show cause" period of 30 days, every effort will be made through conciliation, mediation, and persuasion to resolve the deficiencies which led to the determination of nonresponsibility. If satisfactory adjustments designed to bring the contractor into compliance are not concluded, the case shall be processed for enforcement proceedings pursuant to § 60–1.26 of this chapter.

(d) During the "show cause" period and formal proceedings, each contracting agency must continue to determine the contractor's responsibility in considering whether or not to award a new or additional contract.

[43 FR 49249, Oct. 20, 1978; 43 FR 51400, Nov. 3, 1978]

SUBPART B. REQUIRED CONTENTS OF AFFIRMATIVE ACTION
PROGRAMS

§ 60–2.10 Purpose of affirmative action program

An affirmative action program is a set of specific and result-oriented procedures to which a contractor commits itself to apply every good faith effort. The objective of those procedures plus such efforts is equal employment opportunity. Procedures without effort to make them work are meaningless; and effort, undirected by specific and meaningful procedures, is inadequate. An acceptable affirmative action program must include an analysis of areas within which the contractor is deficient in the utilization of minority groups and women, and further, goals and timetables to which the contractor's good faith efforts must be directed to correct the deficiencies and, thus to achieve prompt and full utilization of minorities and women, at all levels and in all segments of its work force where deficiencies exist.

[43 FR 49249, Oct. 20, 1978; 43 FR 51400, Nov. 3, 1978]

§ 60–2.11 Required utilization analysis

Based upon the Government's experience with compliance reviews under the Executive order program and the contractor reporting system, minority groups are most likely to be underutilized in departments and jobs within departments that fall within the following Employer's Information Report (EEO–1) designations: Officials and managers, professionals, technicians, sales workers, office and clerical and craftsmen (skilled). As categorized by the EEO–1 designations, women are likely to be underutilized in departments and jobs within departments as follows: Officials and managers, professionals, technicians, sales workers (except over-the-counter sales in certain retail establishments), craftsmen (skilled and semi-skilled). Therefore, the contractor shall direct special attention to such jobs in its analysis and goal setting for minorities and women. Affirmative action programs must contain the following information:

(a) Workforce analysis which is defined as a listing of each job title as appears in applicable collective bargaining agreements or payroll records (not job group) ranked from the lowest paid to the highest paid within each department or other similar organizational unit including departmental or unit supervision. If there are separate work units or lines of progression within a department a separate list must be provided for each such work unit, or line, including unit supervisors. For lines of progression there must be indicated the order of jobs in the line through which an employee could move to the top of the line. Where there are no formal progression lines or usual promotional sequences, job titles should be listed by department, job families, or disciplines, in order of wage rates or salary ranges. For each job title, the total number of incumbents, the total number of male and female incumbents, and the total number of male and female incumbents in each of the following groups must be given: Blacks, Spanish-surnamed Americans, American Indians, and Orientals. The wage rate or salary range for each job title must be given. All job titles, including all managerial job titles, must be listed.

(b) An analysis of all major job groups at the facility, with explanation if minorities or women are currently being underutilized in any one or more job groups ("job groups" herein meaning one or a group of jobs having similar content, wage rates and opportunities). "Underutilization" is defined as having fewer minorities or women in a particular job group than would reasonably be expected by their availability. In making the utilization analysis, the contractor shall conduct such analysis separately for minorities and women.

(1) In determining whether minorities are being underutilized in any job group, the contractor will consider at least all of the following factors:

(i) The minority population of the labor area surrounding the facility;

(ii) The size of the minority unemployment force in the labor area surrounding the facility;

(iii) The percentage of the minority work force as compared with the total work force in the immediate labor area;

(iv) The general availability of minorities having requisite skills in the immediate labor area;

(v) The availability of minorities having requisite skills in an area in which the contractor can reasonably recruit;

(vi) The availability of promotable and transferable minorities within the contractor's organization;

(vii) The existence of training institutions capable of training persons in the requisite skills; and

(viii) The degree of training which the contractor is reasonably able to undertake as a means of making all job classes available to minorities.

(2) In determining whether women are being underutilized in any job group, the contractor will consider at least all of the following factors:

(i) The size of the female unemployment force in the labor area surrounding the facility;

(ii) The percentage of the female workforce as compared with the total workforce in the immediate labor area;

(iii) The general availability of women having requisite skills in the immediate labor area;

(iv) The availability of women having requisite skills in an area in which the contractor can reasonably recruit;

(v) The availability of women seeking employment in the labor or recruitment area of the contractor;

(vi) The availability of promotable and transferable female employees within the contractor's organization;

(vii) The existence of training institutions capable of training persons in the requisite skills; and

(viii) The degree of training which the contractor is reasonably able to undertake as a means of making all job classes available to women.

[43 FR 49249, Oct. 20, 1978; 43 FR 51400, Nov. 3, 1978]

§ 60–2.12 Establishment of goals and timetables

(a) The goals and timetables developed by the contractor should be attainable in terms of the contractor's analysis of its deficiencies and its entire affirmative action program. Thus, in establishing the size of its goals and the length of its timetables, the contractor should consider the results which could reasonably be expected from its putting forth every good faith effort to make its overall affirmative action program work. In determining levels of goals, the contractor should consider at least the factors listed in § 60–2.11.

(b) Involve personnel relations staff, department and division heads, and local and unit managers in the goalsetting process.

(c) Goals should be significant, measurable, and attainable.

(d) Goals should be specific for planned results, with timetables for completion.

(e) Goals may not be rigid and inflexible quotas which must be met, but must be targets reasonably attainable by means of applying every good faith effort to make all aspects of the entire affirmative action program work.

(f) In establishing timetables to meet goals and commitments, the contractor will consider the anticipated expansion, contraction, and turnover of and in the work force.

(g) Goals, timetables, and affirmative action commitments must be designed to correct any identifiable deficiencies.

(h) Where deficiencies exist and where numbers or percentages are relevant in developing corrective action, the contractor shall establish and set forth specific goals and timetables separately for minorities and women.

(i) Such goals and timetables, with supporting data and the analysis thereof shall be a part of the contractor's written affirmative action program and shall be maintained at each establishment of the contractor.

(j) A contractor or subcontractor extending a publicly announced preference for Indians as authorized in 41 CFR 60–1.5(a)(6) may reflect in its goals and timetables the permissive employment preference for Indians living on or near an Indian reservation.

(k) Where the contractor has not established a goal, its written affirmative action program must specifically analyze each of the factors listed in § 60–2.11 and must detail its reason for a lack of a goal.

(*l*) In the event it comes to the attention of the Office of Federal Contract Compliance Programs that there is a substantial disparity in the utilization of a particular minority group or men or women of a particular minority group, OFCCP may require separate goals and timetables for such minority group and may further require, where appropriate, such goals and timetables by sex for such group for such job classifications and organizational units specified by the OFCCP.

(m) Support data for the required analysis and program shall be compiled and maintained as part of the contractor's affirmative action program. This data will include but not be limited to progression line charts, seniority rosters, applicant flow data, and applicant rejection ratios indicating minority and sex status.

(n) Copies of affirmative action programs and/or copies of support data shall be made available to the Office of Federal Contract Compliance Programs, upon request, for such purposes as may be appropriate to the fulfillment of its responsibilities under Executive Order 11246, as amended.

[43 FR 49249, Oct. 20, 1978; 43 FR 51400, Nov. 3, 1978]

§ 60–2.13 Additional required ingredients of affirmative action programs

Effective affirmative action programs shall contain, but not necessarily be limited to, the following ingredients:

(a) Development or reaffirmation of the contractor's equal employment opportunity policy in all personnel actions.

(b) Formal internal and external dissemination of the contractor's policy.

(c) Establishment of responsibilities for implementation of the contractor's affirmative action program.

(d) Identification of problem areas (deficiencies) by organizational units and job group.

(e) Establishment of goals and objectives by organizational units and job groups, including timetables for completion.

(f) Development and execution of action-oriented programs designed to eliminate problems and further designed to attain established goals and objectives.

(g) Design and implementation of internal audit and reporting systems to measure effectiveness of the total program.

(h) Compliance of personnel policies and practices with the Sex Discrimination Guidelines (41 CFR Part 60–20).

(i) Active support of local and national community action programs and community service programs, designed to improve the employment opportunities of minorities and women.

(j) Consideration of minorities and women not currently in the work force having requisite skills who can be recruited through affirmative action measures.

§ 60–2.14   Program summary

The affirmative action program shall be summarized and updated annually. The program summary shall be prepared in a format which shall be prescribed by the Director and published in the Federal Register as a notice before becoming effective. Contractors and subcontractors shall submit the program summary to OFCCP each year on the anniversary date of the affirmative action program.

[44 FR 77003, Dec. 28, 1979]

§ 60–2.15   Compliance status

No contractor's compliance status shall be judged alone by whether or not it reaches its goals and meets its timetables. Rather, each contractor's compliance posture shall be reviewed and determined by reviewing the contents of its program, the extent of its adherence to this program, and its good faith efforts to make its program work toward the realization of the program's goals within the timetables set for completion. There follows an outline of examples of procedures that contractors and Federal agencies should use as a guideline for establishing, implementing, and judging an acceptable affirmative action program.

[43 FR 49249, Oct. 20, 1978; 43 FR 51400, Nov. 3, 1978. Redesignated at 44 FR 77003, Dec. 28, 1979]

SUBPART C. METHODS OF IMPLEMENTING THE REQUIREMENTS OF
SUBPART B

§ 60–2.20 Development or reaffirmation of the equal employment opportunity policy

(a) The contractor's policy statement should indicate the chief executive officer's attitude on the subject matter, assign overall responsibility and provide for a reporting and monitoring procedure. Specific items to be mentioned should include, but not be limited to:

(1) Recruit, hire, train, and promote persons in all job titles, without regard to race, color, religion, sex, or national origin, except where sex is a bona fide occupational qualification. (The term "bona fide occupational qualification" has been construed very narrowly under the Civil Rights Act of 1964. Under Executive Order 11246 as amended and this part, this term will be construed in the same manner.)

(2) Base decisions on employment so as to further the principle of equal employment opportunity.

(3) Insure that promotion decisions are in accord with principles of equal employment opportunity by imposing only valid requirements for promotional opportunities.

(4) Insure that all personnel actions such as compensation, benefits, transfers, layoffs, return from layoff, company sponsored training, education, tuition assistance, social and recreation programs, will be administered without regard to race, color, religion, sex, or national origin.

[43 FR 49249, Oct. 30, 1978; 43 FR 51400, Nov. 3, 1978]

§ 60–2.21 Dissemination of the policy

(a) The contractor should disseminate its policy internally as follows:

(1) Include it in contractor's policy manual.

(2) Publicize it in company newspaper, magazine, annual report, and other media.

(3) Conduct special meetings with executive, management, and supervisory personnel to explain intent of policy and individual responsibility for effective implementation, making clear the chief executive officer's attitude.

(4) Schedule special meetings with all other employees to discuss policy and explain individual employee responsibilities.

(5) Discuss the policy thoroughly in both employee orientation and management training programs.

(6) Meet with union officials to inform them of policy, and request their cooperation.

(7) Include nondiscrimination clauses in all union agreements, and review all contractual provisions to insure they are nondiscriminatory.

(8) Publish articles covering EEO programs, progress reports, promotions, etc., of minority and female employees, in company publications.

(9) Post the policy on company bulletin boards.

(10) When employees are featured in product or consumer advertising, employee handbooks or similar publications both minority and nonminority, men and women should be pictured.

(11) Communicate to employees the existence of the contractor's affirmative action program and make available such elements of its program as will enable such employees to know of and avail themselves of its benefits.

(b) The contractor should disseminate its policy externally as follows:

(1) Inform all recruiting sources verbally and in writing of company policy, stipulating that these sources actively recruit and refer minorities and women for all positions listed.

(2) Incorporate the equal opportunity clause in all purchase orders, leases, contracts, etc., covered by Executive Order 11246, as amended, and its implementing regulations.

(3) Notify minority and women's organizations, community agencies, community leaders, secondary schools, and colleges, of company policy, preferably in writing.

(4) Communicate to prospective employees the existence of the contractor's affirmative action program and make available such elements of its program as will enable such prospective employees to know of and avail themselves of its benefits.

(5) When employees are pictured in consumer or help wanted advertising, both minorities and nonminority men and women should be shown.

(6) Send written notification of company policy to all subcontractors, vendors, and suppliers requesting appropriate action on their part.

[43 FR 49249, Oct. 30, 1978; 43 FR 51400, Nov. 3, 1978]

§ 60–2.22 Responsibility for implementation

(a) An executive of the contractor should be appointed as director or manager of company equal opportunity programs. Depending upon the size and geographical alignment of the company, this may be his or her sole responsibility. He or she should be given the necessary top management support and staffing to execute the assignment. His or her identity should appear on all internal and external communications on the company's equal opportunity programs. His or her responsibilities should include, but not necessarily be limited to:

(1) Developing policy statements, affirmative action programs, internal and external communication techniques.

(2) Assisting in the identification of problem areas.

(3) Assisting line management in arriving at solutions to problems.

(4) Designing and implementing audit and reporting systems that will:

(i) Measure effectiveness of the contractor's programs.

(ii) Indicate need for remedial action.

(iii) Determine the degree to which the contractor's goals and objectives have been attained.

(5) Serve as liaison between the contractor and enforcement agencies.

(6) Serve as liaison between the contractor and minority organizations, women's organizations and community action groups concerned with employment opportunities of minorities and women.

(7) Keep management informed of latest developments in the entire equal opportunity area.

(b) Line responsibilities should include, but not be limited to the following:

(1) Assistance in the identification of problem areas and establishment of local and unit goals and objectives.

(2) Active involvement with local minority organizations, women's organizations, community action groups and community service programs.

(3) Periodic audit of training programs, hiring and promotion patterns to remove impediments to the attainment of goals and objectives.

(4) Regular discussions with local managers, supervisors, and employees to be certain the contractor's policies are being followed.

(5) Review of the qualifications of all employees to insure that minorities and women are given full opportunities for transfers and promotions.

(6) Career counseling for all employees.

(7) Periodic audit to insure that each location is in compliance in areas such as:

(i) Posters are properly displayed.

(ii) All facilities, including company housing, which the contractor maintains for the use and benefit of its employees, are in fact desegregated, both in policy and use. If the contractor provides facilities such as dormitories, locker rooms and rest rooms, they must be comparable for both sexes.

(iii) Minority and female employees are afforded a full opportunity and are encouraged to participate in all company sponsored educational, training, recreational, and social activities.

(8) Supervisors should be made to understand that their work performance is being evaluated on the basis of their equal employment opportunity efforts and results, as well as other criteria.

(9) It shall be a responsibility of supervisors to take actions to prevent harassment of employees placed through affirmative action efforts.

[43 FR 49249, Oct. 30, 1978; 43 FR 51401, Nov. 3, 1978]

§ 60–2.23 Identification of problem areas by organizational units and job groups

(a) An in-depth analysis of the following should be made, paying particular attention to trainees and those categories listed in § 60–2.11(b).

(1) Composition of the work force by minority group status and sex.

(2) Composition of applicant flow by minority group status and sex.

(3) The total selection process including position descriptions, position titles, worker specifications, application forms, interview procedures, test administration, test validity, referral procedures, final selection process, and similar factors.

(4) Transfer and promotion practices.

(5) Facilities, company sponsored recreation and social events, and special programs such as educational assistance.

(6) Seniority practices and seniority provisions of union contracts.

(7) Apprenticeship programs.

(8) All company training programs, formal and informal.

(9) Work force attitude.

(10) Technical phases of compliance, such as poster and notification to labor unions, retention of applications, notification to subcontractors, etc.

(b) If any of the following items are found in the analysis, special corrective action should be appropriate.

(1) An "underutilization" of minorities or women in specific job groups.

(2) Lateral and/or vertical movement of minority or female employees occurring at a lesser rate (compared to work force mix) than that of nonminority or male employees.

(3) The selection process eliminates a significantly higher percentage of minorities or women than nonminorities or men.

(4) Application and related preemployment forms not in compliance with Federal legislation.

(5) Position descriptions inaccurate in relation to actual functions and duties.

(6) Formal or scored selection procedures not validated as required by the OFCCP Uniform Guidelines on Employee Selection Procedures.

(7) Test forms not validated by location, work performance and inclusion of minorities and women in sample.

(8) Referral ratio of minorities or women to the hiring supervisor or manager indicates a significantly higher percentage are being rejected as compared to nonminority and male applicants.

(9) Minorities or women are excluded from or are not participating in company sponsored activities or programs.

(10) De facto segregation still exists at some facilities.

(11) Seniority provisions contribute to overt or inadvertent discrimination, i.e., a disparity by minority group status or sex exists between length of service and types of job held.

(12) Nonsupport of company policy by managers, supervisors or employees.

(13) Minorities or women underutilized or significantly under-represented in training or career improvement programs.

(14) No formal techniques established for evaluating effectiveness of EEO programs.

(15) Lack of access to suitable housing inhibits recruitment efforts and employment of qualified minorities.

(16) Lack of suitable transportation (public or private) to the work place inhibits minority employment.

(17) Labor unions and subcontractors not notified of their responsibilities.

(18) Purchase orders do not contain EEO clause.

(19) Posters not on display.

§ 60–2.24 Development and execution of programs

(a) The contractor should conduct detailed analyses of position descriptions to insure that they accurately reflect position functions, and are consistent for the same position from one location to another.

(b) The contractor should validate worker specifications by division, department, location or other organizational unit and by job title using job performance criteria. Special attention should be given to academic, experience and skill requirements to insure that the requirements in themselves do not constitute inadvertent discrimination. Specifications should be consistent for the same job title in all locations and should be free from bias as regards to race, color, religion, sex or national origin, except where sex is a bona fide occupational qualification. Where requirements screen out a disproportionate number of minorities or women, such requirements should be professionally validated to job performance.

(c) Approved position descriptions and worker specifications, when used by the contractor, should be made available to all members of management involved in the recruiting, screening, selection, and promotion process. Copies should also be distributed to all recruiting sources.

(d) The contractor should evaluate the total selection process to insure freedom from bias and, thus, aid the attainment of goals and objectives.

(1) All personnel involved in the recruiting, screening, selection, promotion, disciplinary, and related processes should be carefully selected and trained to insure elimination of bias in all personnel actions.

(2) The contractor shall observe the requirements of the OFCCP Uniform Guidelines on Employee Selection Procedures.

(3) Selection techniques other than tests may also be improperly used so as to have the effect of discriminating against minority groups and women. Such techniques include but are not restricted to, unscored interviews, unscored or casual application forms, arrest records, credit checks, considerations of marital status or dependency or minor children. Where there exist data suggesting that such unfair discrimination or exclusion of minorities or women exists, the contractor should analyze his unscored procedures and eliminate them if they are not objectively valid.

(e) Suggested techniques to improve recruitment and increase the flow of minority or female applicants follow:

(1) Certain organizations such as the Urban League, Job Corps, Equal Opportunity Programs, Inc., Concentrated Employment programs, Neighborhood Youth Corps, Secondary Schools, Colleges, and City Colleges with high minority enrollment, the State Employment Service, specialized employment agencies, Aspira, LULAC, SER, the G.I. Forum, the Commonwealth of Puerto Rico are normally prepared to refer minority applicants. Organizations prepared to refer women with specific skills are: National Organization for Women, Welfare Rights organizations, Women's Equity Action League, Talent Bank from Business and Professional Women (including 26 women's organizations), Professional Women's Caucus, Intercollegiate Association of University Women, Negro Women's sororities and service groups such as Delta Sigma Theta, Alpha Kappa Alpha, and Zeta Phi Beta; National Council of Negro Women, American Association of University Women, YWCA, and sectarian groups such as Jewish Women's Groups, Catholic Women's Groups and Protestant Women's Groups, and women's colleges. In addition, community leaders as individuals shall be added to recruiting sources.

(2) Formal briefing sessions should be held, preferably on company premises, with representatives from these recruiting sources. Plant tours, presentations by minority and female employees, clear and concise explanations of current and future job openings, position de-

scriptions, worker specifications, explanations of the company's selection process, and recruiting literature should be an integral part of the briefings. Formal arrangements should be made for referral of applicants, followup with sources, and feedback on disposition of applicants.

(3) Minority and female employees, using procedures similar to subparagraph (2) of this paragraph, should be actively encouraged to refer applicants.

(4) A special effort should be made to include minorities and women on the Personnel Relations staff.

(5) Minority and female employees should be made available for participation in Career Days, Youth Motivation Programs, and related activities in their communities.

(6) Active participation in "Job Fairs" is desirable. Company representative so participating should be given authority to make on-the-spot commitments.

(7) Active recruiting programs should be carried out at secondary schools, junior colleges, and colleges with predominant minority or female enrollments.

(8) Recruiting efforts at all schools should incorporate special efforts to reach minorities and women.

(9) Special employment programs should be undertaken whenever possible. Some possible programs are:

(i) Technical and nontechnical co-op programs with predominately Negro and women's colleges.

(ii) "After school" and/or work-study jobs for minority youths, male and female.

(iii) Summer jobs for underprivileged youth, male and female.

(iv) Summer work-study programs for male and female faculty members of the predominantly minority schools and colleges.

(v) Motivation, training and employment programs for the hardcore unemployed, male and female.

(10) When recruiting brochures pictorially present work situations, the minority and female members of the work force should be included, especially when such brochures are used in school and career programs.

(11) Help wanted advertising should be expanded to include the minority news media and women's interest media on a regular basis.

(f) The contractor should insure that minority and female employees are given equal opportunity for promotion. Suggestions for achieving this result include:

(1) Post or otherwise announce promotional opportunities.

(2) Make an inventory of current minority and female employees to determine academic, skill and experience level of individual employees.

(3) Initiate necessary remedial, job training and workstudy programs.

(4) Develop and implement formal employee evaluation programs.

(5) Make certain "worker specifications" have been validated on job performance related criteria. (Neither minority nor female employees should be required to possess higher qualifications than those of the lowest qualified incumbent.)

(6) When apparently qualified minority or female employees are passed over for upgrading, require supervisory personnel to submit written justification.

(7) Establish formal career counseling programs to include attitude development, education aid, job rotation, buddy system and similar programs.

(8) Review seniority practices and seniority clauses in union contracts to insure such practices or clauses are nondiscriminatory and do not have a discriminatory effect.

(g) Make certain facilities and company-sponsored social and recreation activities are desegregated. Actively encourage all employees to participate.

(h) Encourage child care, housing and transportation programs appropriately designed to improve the employment opportunities for minorities and women.

[43 FR 49249, Oct. 30, 1978; 43 FR 51401, Nov. 3, 1978]

§ 60–2.25 Internal audit and reporting systems

(a) The contractor should monitor records of referrals, placements, transfers, promotions and terminations at all levels to insure nondiscriminatory policy is carried out.

(b) The contractor should require formal reports from unit managers on a schedule basis as to degree to which corporate or unit goals are attained and timetables met.

(c) The contractor should review report results with all levels of management.

(d) The contractor should advise top management of program effectiveness and submit recommendations to improve unsatisfactory performance.

§ 60–2.26 Support of action programs

(a) The contractor should appoint key members of management to serve on merit employment councils, community relations boards and similar organizations.

(b) The contractor should encourage minority and female employees to participate actively in National Alliance of Businessmen programs for youth motivation.

(c) The contractor should support vocational guidance institutes, vestibule training programs and similar activities.

(d) The contractor should assist secondary schools and colleges in programs designed to enable minority and female graduates of these institutions to compete in the open employment market on a more equitable basis.

(e) The contractor should publicize achievements of minority and female employees in local and minority news media.

(f) The contractor should support programs developed by such organizations as National Alliance of Businessmen, the Urban Coalition and other organizations concerned with employment opportunities for minorities or women.

[43 FR 49249, Oct. 30, 1978; 43 FR 51401, Nov. 3, 1978]

SUBPART D. MISCELLANEOUS

§ 60–2.30 Use of goals

The purpose of a contractor's establishment and use of goals is to insure that it meet its affirmative action obligation. It is not intended and should not be used to discriminate against any applicant or employee because of race, color, religion, sex, or national origin.

[43 FR 49249, Oct. 30, 1978; 43 FR 51401, Nov. 3, 1978]

§ 60–2.31 Preemption

To the extent that any State or local laws, regulations or ordinances, including those which grant special benefits to persons on account of sex, are in conflict with Executive Order 11246, as amended, or with the requirements of this part, we will regard them as preempted under the Executive order.

§ 60–2.32 Supersedure

All orders, instructions, regulations, and memoranda of the Secretary of Labor, other officials of the Department of Labor and contracting agencies are hereby superseded to the extent that they are inconsistent herewith, including a previous "Order No. 4" from this office dated January 30, 1970. Nothing in this part is intended to amend 41 CFR Part 60–3 or 41 CFR 60–20.

EQUAL PAY ACT OF 1963

P.L. 88–38, codified as 29 U.S.C. Section 206(d)

An Act to prohibit discrimination on account of sex in the payment of wages by employers engaged in commerce or in the production of goods for commerce.

Be it enacted by the Senate and House of Representatives of the United States of America in Congress assembled, That:

This Act may be cited as the "Equal Pay Act of 1963".

Declaration of Purpose

Sec. 2. (a) The Congress hereby finds that the existence in industries engaged in commerce or in the production of goods for commerce of wage differentials based on sex—

(1) depresses wages and living standards for employees necessary for their health and efficiency;

(2) prevents the maximum utilization of the available labor resources;

(3) tends to cause labor disputes, thereby burdening, affecting, and obstructing commerce;

(4) burdens commerce and the free flow of goods in commerce; and

(5) constitutes an unfair method of competition.

(b) It is hereby declared to be the policy of this Act, through exercise by Congress of its power to regulate commerce among the several States and with foreign nations, to correct the conditions above referred to in such industries.

Sec. 3. Section 6 of the Fair Labor Standards Act of 1938, as amended (29 U.S.C. et seq.),[1] is amended by adding thereto a new subsection (d) as follows:

"(d)(1) No employer having employees subject to any provisions of this section shall discriminate, within any establishment in which such employees are employed, between employees on the basis of sex by paying wages to employees in such establishment at a rate less than the rate at which he pays wages to employees of the opposite sex in such establishment for equal work on jobs the performance of which requires equal skill, effort, and responsibility, and which are performed under similar working conditions, except where such payment is made pursuant to (i) a seniority system; (ii) a merit system; (iii) a system which measures earnings by quantity or quality of production; or (iv) a differential based on any other factor other than sex: Provided, That an employer who is paying a wage rate differential in violation of this subsection shall not, in order to comply with the provisions of this subsection, reduce the wage rate of any employee.

"(2) No labor organization, or its agents, representing employees of an employer having employees subject to any provisions of this section shall cause or attempt to cause such an employer to discriminate against an employee in violation of paragraph (1) of this subsection.

"(3) For purposes of administration and enforcement, any amounts owing to any employee which have been withheld in violation of this subsection shall be deemed to be unpaid minimum wages or unpaid overtime compensation under this Act.

1. 29 U.S.C.A. § 206.

"(4) As used in this subsection, the term 'labor organization' means any organization of any kind, or any agency or employee representation committee or plan, in which employees participate and which exists for the purpose, in whole or in part, of dealing with employers concerning grievances, labor disputes, wages, rates of pay, hours of employment, or conditions of work."

Sec. 4. The amendments made by this Act shall take effect upon the expiration of one year from the date of its enactment: Provided, That in the case of employees covered by a bona fide collective bargaining agreement in effect at least thirty days prior to the date of enactment of this Act, entered into by a labor organization (as defined in section 6(d)(4) of the Fair Labor Standards Act of 1938, as amended), the amendments made by this Act shall take effect upon the termination of such collective bargaining agreement or upon the expiration of two years from the date of enactment of this Act, whichever shall first occur.

Approved June 10, 1963.

AGE DISCRIMINATION IN EMPLOYMENT ACT OF 1967, AS AMENDED

§ 621. Congressional statement of findings and purpose

(a) The Congress hereby finds and declares that—

(1) in the face of rising productivity and affluence, older workers find themselves disadvantaged in their efforts to retain employment, and especially to regain employment when displaced from jobs;

(2) the setting of arbitrary age limits regardless of potential for job performance has become a common practice, and certain otherwise desirable practices may work to the disadvantage of older persons;

(3) the incidence of unemployment, especially long-term unemployment with resultant deterioration of skill, morale, and employer acceptability is, relative to the younger ages, high among older workers; their numbers are great and growing; and their employment problems grave;

(4) the existence in industries affecting commerce, of arbitrary discrimination in employment because of age, burdens commerce and the free flow of goods in commerce.

(b) It is therefore the purpose of this chapter to promote employment of older persons based on their ability rather than age; to prohibit arbitrary age discrimination in employment; to help employers and workers find ways of meeting problems arising from the impact of age on employment.

(Pub.L. 90–202, § 2, Dec. 15, 1967, 81 Stat. 602.)

§ 622. Education and research program; recommendation to Congress

(a) The Secretary of Labor shall undertake studies and provide information to labor unions, management, and the general public concerning the needs and abilities of older workers, and their potentials for continued employment and contribution to the economy. In order to achieve the purposes of this chapter, the Secretary of Labor shall carry on a continuing program of education and information, under which he may, among other measures—

(1) undertake research, and promote research, with a view to reducing barriers to the employment of older persons, and the promotion of measures for utilizing their skills;

(2) publish and otherwise make available to employers, professional societies, the various media of communication, and other interested persons the findings of studies and other materials for the promotion of employment;

(3) foster through the public employment service system and through cooperative effort the development of facilities of public and private agencies for expanding the opportunities and potentials of older persons;

(4) sponsor and assist State and community informational and educational programs.

(b) Not later than six months after the effective date of this chapter [1], the Secretary shall recommend to the Congress any measures he may deem desirable to change the lower or upper age limits set forth in section 631 of this title.

(Pub.L. 90–202, § 3, Dec. 15, 1967, 81 Stat. 602.)

Federal Jury Practice and Instructions

Jury instructions, see § 92.25 and Notes thereunder.

§ 623. Prohibition of age discrimination

(a) Employer practices

It shall be unlawful for an employer—

(1) to fail or refuse to hire or to discharge any individual or otherwise discriminate against any individual with respect to his compensation, terms, conditions, or privileges of employment, because of such individual's age;

(2) to limit, segregate, or classify his employees in any way which would deprive or tend to deprive any individual of employment opportu-

---

1. See Pub.L. 90–202, § 16.

nities or otherwise adversely affect his status as an employee, because of such individual's age; or

(3) to reduce the wage rate of any employee in order to comply with this chapter.

(b) Employment agency practices

It shall be unlawful for an employment agency to fail or refuse to refer for employment, or otherwise to discriminate against, any individual because of such individual's age, or to classify or refer for employment any individual on the basis of such individual's age.

(c) Labor organization practices

It shall be unlawful for a labor organization—

(1) to exclude or to expel from its membership, or otherwise to discriminate against, any individual because of his age;

(2) to limit, segregate, or classify its membership, or to classify or fail or refuse to refer for employment any individual, in any way which would deprive or tend to deprive any individual of employment opportunities, or would limit such employment opportunities or otherwise adversely affect his status as an employee or as an applicant for employment, because of such individual's age;

(3) to cause or attempt to cause an employer to discriminate against an individual in violation of this section.

(d) Opposition to unlawful practices; participation in investigations, proceedings, or litigation

It shall be unlawful for an employer to discriminate against any of his employees or applicants for employment, for an employment agency to discriminate against any individual, or for a labor organization to discriminate against any member thereof or applicant for membership, because such individual, member or applicant for membership has opposed any practice made unlawful by this section, or because such individual, member or applicant for membership has made a charge, testified, assisted, or participated in any manner in an investigation, proceeding, or litigation under this chapter.

(e) Printing or publication of notice or advertisement indicating preference, limitation, etc.

It shall be unlawful for an employer, labor organization, or employment agency to print or publish, or cause to be printed or published, any notice or advertisement relating to employment by such an employer or membership in or any classification or referral for employment by such a labor organization, or relating to any classification or referral for employment by such an employment agency, indicating any preference, limitation, specification, or discrimination, based on age.

(f) Lawful practices; age an occupational qualification; other reasonable factors; laws of foreign workplace; seniority system; employee benefit plans; discharge or discipline for good cause

It shall not be unlawful for an employer, employment agency, or labor organization—

(1) to take any action otherwise prohibited under subsections (a), (b), (c), or (e) of this section where age is a bona fide occupational qualification reasonably necessary to the normal operation of the particular business, or where the differentiation is based on reasonable factors other than age, or where such practices involve an employee in a workplace in a foreign country, and compliance with such subsections would cause such employer, or a corporation controlled by such employer, to violate the laws of the country in which such workplace is located;

(2) to observe the terms of a bona fide seniority system or any bona fide employee benefit plan such as a retirement, pension, or insurance plan, which is not a subterfuge to evade the purposes of this chapter, except that no such employee benefit plan shall excuse the failure to hire any individual, and no such seniority system or employee benefit plan shall require or permit the involuntary retirement of any individual specified by section 631(a) of this title because of the age of such individual; or

(3) to discharge or otherwise discipline an individual for good cause.

(g) Entitlement to coverage under group health plan

(1) For purposes of this section, any employer must provide that any employee aged 65 through 69, and any employee's spouse aged 65 through 69, shall be entitled to coverage under any group health plan offered to such employees under the same conditions as any employee, and the spouse of such employee, under age 65.

(2) For purposes of paragraph (1), the term "group health plan" has the meaning given to such term in section 162(i)(2) of Title 26.

(g)[1] Practices of foreign corporations controlled by American employers; foreign persons not controlled by American employers; factors determining control

(1) If an employer controls a corporation whose place of incorporation is in a foreign country, any practice by such corporation prohibited under this section shall be presumed to be such practice by such employer.

(2) The prohibitions of this section shall not apply where the employer is a foreign person not controlled by an American employer.

---

1. So in original. Another subsec. (g) is set out above.

(3) For the purpose of this subsection the determination of whether an employer controls a corporation shall be based upon the—

    (A) interrelation of operations,

    (B) common management,

    (C) centralized control of labor relations, and

    (D) common ownership or financial control,

of the employer and the corporation.

(Pub.L. 90–202, § 4, Dec. 15, 1967, 81 Stat. 603; Pub.L. 95–256, § 2(a), Apr. 6, 1978, 92 Stat. 189; Pub.L. 97–248, Title I, § 116(a), Sept. 3, 1982, 96 Stat. 353; Pub.L. 98–369, Title III, § 2301(b), July 18, 1984, 98 Stat. 1063; Pub.L. 98–459, Title VIII, § 802(b), Oct. 9, 1984, 98 Stat. 1792.)

Federal Practice and Procedure

Class actions maintainable, see Wright & Miller: Civil § 1772 et seq.

Propriety of summary judgment in complicated and important litigation, see Wright, Miller & Kane: Civil 2d § 2732.2.

Federal Jury Practice and Instructions

Jury instructions, see § 92.25 and Notes thereunder.

West's Federal Practice Manual

Damage awards, see § 16409.

Pre-arranged mandatory retirement plans, see § 15435.

Private sector employees,

    Permitted acts, see § 15390.

    Prohibited acts, see § 15389.

Recovery of back pay, distinctions between different statutes and regulations, see § 16392.

Specific problem areas in retirements, see § 16981.

Code of Federal Regulations

Employment requirements, see 29 CFR 860.1 et seq.

Selected Court Decisions

Congress did not intend wholesale invalidation of retirement plans instituted in good faith before passage of the Age Discrimination in Employment Act of 1967 [this chapter], nor did it intend to require employers to bear the burden of showing a business or economic purpose to justify bona fide preexisting plans. United Air Lines Inc. v. McMann, Va.1977, 98 S.Ct. 444, 434 U.S. 192, 54 L.Ed.2d 402.

§ 624. Study by Secretary of Labor; reports to President and Congress; scope of study; implementation of study; transmittal date of reports

(a)(1) The Secretary of Labor is directed to undertake an appropriate study of institutional and other arrangements giving rise to involuntary retirement, and report his findings and any appropriate legislative recommendations to the President and to the Congress. Such study shall include—

(A) an examination of the effect of the amendment made by section 3(a) of the Age Discrimination in Employment Act Amendments of 1978 [1] in raising the upper age limitation established by section 631(a) of this title to 70 years of age;

(B) a determination of the feasibility of eliminating such limitation;

(C) a determination of the feasibility of raising such limitation above 70 years of age; and

(D) an examination of the effect of the exemption contained in section 631(c) of this title, relating to certain executive employees, and the exemption contained in section 631(d) of this title, relating to tenured teaching personnel.

(2) The Secretary may undertake the study required by paragraph (1) of this subsection directly or by contract or other arrangement.

(b) The report required by subsection (a) of this section shall be transmitted to the President and to the Congress as an interim report not later than January 1, 1981, and in final form not later than January 1, 1982.

(Pub.L. 90–202, § 5, Dec. 15, 1967, 81 Stat. 604; Pub.L. 95–256, § 6, Apr. 6, 1978, 92 Stat. 192.)

§ 625. Administration

The Secretary [1] shall have the power—

(a) Delegation of functions; appointment of personnel; technical assistance

to make delegations, to appoint such agents and employees, and to pay for technical assistance on a fee for service basis, as he deems necessary to assist him in the performance of his functions under this chapter;

(b) Cooperation with other agencies, employers, labor organizations, and employment agencies

to cooperate with regional, State, local, and other agencies, and to cooperate with and furnish technical assistance to employers, labor

1. Pub.L. 95–256, § 3(a). See section 631 of this title.

1. See 1978 Reorg. Plan No. 1, § 2, eff. Jan. 1, 1979, 43 F.R. 19807, 92 Stat. 3781.

organizations, and employment agencies to aid in effectuating the purposes of this chapter.

(Pub.L. 90–202, § 6, Dec. 15, 1967, 81 Stat. 604.)

§ 626. Recordkeeping, investigation, and enforcement

(a) Attendance of witnesses; investigations, inspections, records, and homework regulations

The Equal Employment Opportunity Commission shall have the power to make investigations and require the keeping of records necessary or appropriate for the administration of this chapter in accordance with the powers and procedures provided in sections 209 and 211 of this title.

(b) Enforcement; prohibition of age discrimination under fair labor standards; unpaid minimum wages and unpaid overtime compensation; liquidated damages; judicial relief; conciliation, conference, and persuasion

The provisions of this chapter shall be enforced in accordance with the powers, remedies, and procedures provided in sections 211(b), 216 (except for subsection (a) thereof), and 217 of this title, and subsection (c) of this section. Any act prohibited under section 623 of this title shall be deemed to be a prohibited act under section 215 of this title. Amounts owing to a person as a result of a violation of this chapter shall be deemed to be unpaid minimum wages or unpaid overtime compensation for purposes of sections 216 and 217 of this title: *Provided,* That liquidated damages shall be payable only in cases of willful violations of this chapter. In any action brought to enforce this chapter the court shall have jurisdiction to grant such legal or equitable relief as may be appropriate to effectuate the purposes of this chapter, including without limitation judgments compelling employment, reinstatement or promotion, or enforcing the liability for amounts deemed to be unpaid minimum wages or unpaid overtime compensation under this section. Before instituting any action under this section, the Equal Employment Opportunity Commission shall attempt to eliminate the discriminatory practice or practices alleged, and to effect voluntary compliance with the requirements of this chapter through informal methods of conciliation, conference, and persuasion.

(c) Civil actions; persons aggrieved; jurisdiction; judicial relief; termination of individual action upon commencement of action by Commission; jury trial

(1) Any person aggrieved may bring a civil action in any court of competent jurisdiction for such legal or equitable relief as will effectuate the purposes of this chapter: *Provided,* That the right of any person to bring such action shall terminate upon the commencement of an action by the Equal Employment Opportunity Commission to enforce the right of such employee under this chapter.

(2) In an action brought under paragraph (1), a person shall be entitled to a trial by jury of any issue of fact in any such action for recovery of amounts owing as a result of a violation of this chapter, regardless of whether equitable relief is sought by any party in such action.

(d) Filing of charge with Commission; timeliness; conciliation, conference, and persuasion

No civil action may be commenced by an individual under this section until 60 days after a charge alleging unlawful discrimination has been filed with the Equal Employment Opportunity Commission. Such a charge shall be filed—

(1) within 180 days after the alleged unlawful practice occurred; or

(2) in a case to which section 633(b) of this title applies, within 300 days after the alleged unlawful practice occurred, or within 30 days after receipt by the individual of notice of termination of proceedings under State law, whichever is earlier.

Upon receiving such a charge, the Commission shall promptly notify all persons named in such charge as prospective defendants in the action and shall promptly seek to eliminate any alleged unlawful practice by informal methods of conciliation, conference, and persuasion.

(e) Statute of limitations; reliance in future on administrative ruling, etc.; tolling

(1) Sections 255 and 259 of this title shall apply to actions under this chapter.

(2) For the period during which the Equal Employment Opportunity Commission is attempting to effect voluntary compliance with requirements of this chapter through informal methods of conciliation, conference, and persuasion pursuant to subsection (b) of this section, the statute of limitations as provided in section 255 of this title shall be tolled, but in no event for a period in excess of one year.

(Pub.L. 90–202, § 7, Dec. 15, 1967, 81 Stat. 604; Pub.L. 95–256, § 4(a), (b)(1), (c)(1), Apr. 6, 1978, 92 Stat. 190, 191; 1978 Reorg. Plan No. 1, § 2, eff. Jan. 1, 1979, 43 F.R. 19807, 92 Stat. 3781.)

§ 627. Notices to be posted

Every employer, employment agency, and labor organization shall post and keep posted in conspicuous places upon its premises a notice to be prepared or approved by the Equal Employment Opportunity Commission setting forth information as the Commission deems appropriate to effectuate the purposes of this chapter.

(Pub.L. 90–202, § 8, Dec. 15, 1967, 81 Stat. 605; 1978 Reorg.Plan No. 1, § 2, eff. Jan. 1, 1979, 43 F.R. 19807, 92 Stat. 3781.)

§ 628. Rules and regulations; exemptions

In accordance with the provisions of subchapter II of chapter 5 of Title 5, the Equal Employment Opportunity Commission may issue such rules and regulations as it may consider necessary or appropriate for carrying out this chapter, and may establish such reasonable exemptions to and from any or all provisions of this chapter as it may find necessary and proper in the public interest.

(Pub.L. 90-202, § 9, Dec. 15, 1967, 81 Stat. 605; 1978 Reorg.Plan No. 1, § 2, eff. Jan. 1, 1979, 43 F.R. 19807, 92 Stat. 3781.)

§ 629. Criminal penalties

Whoever shall forcibly resist, oppose, impede, intimidate or interfere with a duly authorized representative of the Equal Employment Opportunity Commission while it is engaged in the performance of duties under this chapter shall be punished by a fine of not more than $500 or by imprisonment for not more than one year, or by both: *Provided, however,* That no person shall be imprisoned under this section except when there has been a prior conviction hereunder.

(Pub.L. 90–202, § 10, Dec. 15, 1967, 81 Stat. 605; 1978 Reorg.Plan No. 1, § 2, eff. Jan. 1, 1979, 43 F.R. 19807, 92 Stat. 3781.)

§ 630. Definitions

For the purposes of this chapter—

(a) The term "person" means one or more individuals, partnerships, associations, labor organizations, corporations, business trust, legal representatives, or any organized groups of persons.

(b) The term "employer" means a person engaged in an industry affecting commerce who has twenty or more employees for each working day in each of twenty or more calendar weeks in the current or preceding calendar year: *Provided,* That prior to June 30, 1968, employers having fewer than fifty employees shall not be considered employers. The term also means (1) any agent of such a person, and (2) a State or political subdivision of a State and any agency or instrumentality of a State or a political subdivision of a State, and any interstate agency, but such term does not include the United States, or a corporation wholly owned by the Government of the United States.

(c) The term "employment agency" means any person regularly undertaking with or without compensation to procure employees for an employer and includes an agent of such a person; but shall not include an agency of the United States.

(d) The term "labor organization" means a labor organization engaged in an industry affecting commerce, and any agent of such an organization, and includes any organization of any kind, any agency, or employee representation committee, group, association, or plan so engaged in which employees participate and which exists for the purpose, in whole or in part, of dealing with employers concerning grievances, labor disputes, wages, rates of pay, hours, or other terms or conditions of employment, and any conference, general committee, joint or system board, or joint council so engaged which is subordinate to a national or international labor organization.

(e) A labor organization shall be deemed to be engaged in an industry affecting commerce if (1) it maintains or operates a hiring hall or hiring office which procures employees for an employer or procures for employees opportunities to work for an employer, or (2) the number of its members (or, where it is a labor organization composed of other labor organizations or their representatives, if the aggregate number of the members of such other labor organization) is fifty or more prior to July 1, 1968, or twenty-five or more on or after July 1, 1968, and such labor organization—

(1) is the certified representative of employees under the provisions of the National Labor Relations Act, as amended [29 U.S.C.A. § 151 et seq.], or the Railway Labor Act, as amended [45 U.S.C.A. § 151 et seq.]; or

(2) although not certified, is a national or international labor organization or a local labor organization recognized or acting as the representative of employees of an employer or employers engaged in an industry affecting commerce; or

(3) has chartered a local labor organization or subsidiary body which is representing or actively seeking to represent employees of employers within the meaning of paragraph (1) or (2); or

(4) has been chartered by a labor organization representing or actively seeking to represent employees within the meaning of paragraph (1) or (2) as the local or subordinate body through which such employees may enjoy membership or become affiliated with such labor organization; or

(5) is a conference, general committee, joint or system board, or joint council subordinate to a national or international labor organization, which includes a labor organization engaged in an industry affecting commerce within the meaning of any of the preceding paragraphs of this subsection.

(f) The term "employee" means an individual employed by any employer except that the term "employee" shall not include any person elected to public office in any State or political subdivision of any State by the qualified voters thereof, or any person chosen by such officer to be on such officer's personal staff, or an appointee on the policy-making level or an immediate adviser with respect to the exercise of the constitutional or legal powers of the office. The exemption set forth in the preceding sentence shall not include employees subject to the civil service laws of a State government, governmental agency, or political subdivision. The term "employee" includes any individual who is a citizen of the United States employed by an employer in a workplace in a foreign country.

(g) The term "commerce" means trade, traffic, commerce, transportation, transmission, or communication among the several States; or between a State and any place outside thereof; or within the District of Columbia, or a possession of the United States; or between points in the same State but through a point outside thereof.

(h) The term "industry affecting commerce" means any activity, business, or industry in commerce or in which a labor dispute would hinder or osbtruct commerce or the free flow of commerce and includes any activity or industry "affecting commerce" within the meaning of the Labor Management Reporting and Disclosure Act of 1959 [29 U.S.C.A. § 401 et seq.].

(i) The term "State" includes a State of the United States, the District of Columbia, Puerto Rico, the Virgin Islands, American Samoa, Guam, Wake Island, the Canal Zone, and Outer Continental Shelf lands defined in the Outer Continental Shelf Lands Act [43 U.S.C.A. § 1331 et seq.].

(Pub.L. 90–202, § 11, Dec. 15, 1967, 81 Stat. 605; Pub.L. 93–259, § 28(a)(1)–(4), Apr. 8, 1974, 88 Stat. 74; Pub.L. 98–459, Title VIII, § 802(a), Oct. 9, 1984, 98 Stat. 1792.)

§ 631. Age limits

(a) Individuals at least 40 but less than 70 years of age

The prohibitions in this chapter shall be limited to individuals who are at least 40 years of age but less than 70 years of age.

(b) Employees or applicants for employment in Federal Government

In the case of any personnel action affecting employees or applicants for employment which is subject to the provisions of section 633a of this title, the prohibitions established in section 633a of this title shall be limited to individuals who are at least 40 years of age.

(c) Bona fide executives or high policymakers

(1) Nothing in this chapter shall be construed to prohibit compulsory retirement of any employee who has attained 65 years of age but not 70 years of age, and who, for the 2-year period immediately before retirement, is employed in a bona fide executive or a high policymaking position, if such employee is entitled to an immediate nonforfeitable annual retirement benefit from a pension, profit-sharing, savings, or deferred compensation plan, or any combination of such plans, of the employer of such employee, which equals, in the aggregate, at least $44,000.

(2) In applying the retirement benefit test of paragraph (1) of this subsection, if any such retirement benefit is in a form other than a straight life annuity (with no ancillary benefits), or if employees contribute to any such plan or make rollover contributions, such benefit shall be adjusted in accordance with regulations prescribed by the Equal Employment Opportunity Commission, after consultation with

the Secretary of the Treasury, so that the benefit is the equivalent of a straight life annuity (with no ancillary benefits) under a plan to which employees do not contribute and under which no rollover contributions are made.

(Pub.L. 90–202, § 12, Dec. 15, 1967, 81 Stat. 607; Pub.L. 95–256, § 3(a), (b)(3), Apr. 6, 1978, 92 Stat. 189, 190; 1978 Reorg.Plan No. 1, § 2, eff. Jan. 1, 1979, 43 F.R. 19807, 92 Stat. 3781; Pub.L. 98–459, Title VIII, § 802(c)(1), Oct. 9, 1984, 98 Stat. 1792.)

§ 632. Annual report to Congress

The Equal Employment Opportunity Commission shall submit annually in January a report to the Congress covering its activities for the preceding year and including such information, data and recommendations for further legislation in connection with the matters covered by this chapter as it may find advisable. Such report shall contain an evaluation and appraisal by the Commission of the effect of the minimum and maximum ages established by this chapter, together with its recommendations to the Congress. In making such evaluation and appraisal, the Commission shall take into consideration any changes which may have occurred in the general age level of the population, the effect of the chapter upon workers not covered by its provisions, and such other factors as it may deem pertinent.

(Pub.L. 90–202, § 13, Dec. 15, 1967, 81 Stat. 607; 1978 Reorg.Plan No. 1, § 2, eff. Jan. 1, 1979, 43 F.R. 19807, 92 Stat. 3781.)

§ 633. Federal-State relationship

(a) Federal action superseding State action

Nothing in this chapter shall affect the jurisdiction of any agency of any State performing like functions with regard to discriminatory employment practices on account of age except that upon commencement of action under this chapter such action shall supersede any State action.

(b) Limitation of Federal action upon commencement of State proceedings

In the case of an alleged unlawful practice occurring in a State which has a law prohibiting discrimination in employment because of age and establishing or authorizing a State authority to grant or seek relief from such discriminatory practice, no suit may be brought under section 626 of this title before the expiration of sixty days after proceedings have been commenced under the State law, unless such proceedings have been earlier terminated: *Provided,* That such sixty-day period shall be extended to one hundred and twenty days during the first year after the effective date of such State law. If any requirement for the commencement of such proceedings is imposed by a State authority other than a requirement of the filing of a written and signed statement of the facts upon which the proceeding is based, the proceeding shall be deemed to have been commenced for the purposes of this subsection at the time such statement is sent by registered mail to the appropriate State authority.

(Pub.L. 90–202, § 14, Dec. 15, 1967, 81 Stat. 607.)

§ 633a. Nondiscrimination on account of age in Federal Government employment

(a) Federal agencies affected

All personnel actions affecting employees or applicants for employment who are at least 40 years of age (except personnel actions with regard to aliens employed outside the limits of the United States) in military departments as defined in section 102 of Title 5, in executive agencies as defined in section 105 of Title 5 (including employees and applicants for employment who are paid from nonappropriated funds), in the United States Postal Service and the Postal Rate Commission, in those units in the government of the District of Columbia having positions in the competitive service, and in those units of the legislative and judicial branches of the Federal Government having positions in the competitive service, and in the Library of Congress shall be made free from any discrimination based on age.

(b) Enforcement by Equal Employment Opportunity Commission and by Librarian of Congress in the Library of Congress; remedies; rules, regulations, orders, and instructions of Commission; compliance by Federal agencies; powers and duties of Commission; notification of final action on complaint of discrimination; exemptions; bona fide occupational qualification

Except as otherwise provided in this subsection, the Equal Employment Opportunity Commission is authorized to enforce the provisions of subsection (a) of this section through appropriate remedies, including reinstatement or hiring of employees with or without backpay, as will effectuate the policies of this section. The Equal Employment Opportunity Commission shall issue such rules, regulations, orders, and instructions as it deems necessary and appropriate to carry out its responsibilities under this section. The Equal Employment Opportunity Commission shall—

(1) be responsible for the review and evaluation of the operation of all agency programs designed to carry out the policy of this section, periodically obtaining and publishing (on at least a semiannual basis) progress reports from each department, agency, or unit referred to in subsection (a) of this section;

(2) consult with and solicit the recommendations of interested individuals, groups, and organizations relating to nondiscrimination in employment on account of age; and

(3) provide for the acceptance and processing of complaints of discrimination in Federal employment on account of age.

The head of each such department, agency, or unit shall comply with such rules, regulations, orders, and instructions of the Equal Employment Opportunity Commission which shall include a provision that an employee or applicant for employment shall be notified of any final action taken on any complaint of discrimination filed by him thereunder. Reasonable exemptions to the provisions of this section may be established by the Commission but only when the Commission has established a maximum age requirement on the basis of a determination that age is a bona fide occupational qualification necessary to the performance of the duties of the position. With respect to employment in the Library of Congress, authorities granted in this subsection to the Equal Employment Opportunity Commission shall be exercised by the Librarian of Congress.

(c) Civil actions; jurisdiction; relief

Any person aggrieved may bring a civil action in any Federal district court of competent jurisdiction for such legal or equitable relief as will effectuate the purposes of this chapter.

(d) Notice to Commission; time of notice; Commission notification of prospective defendants; Commission elimination of unlawful practices

When the individual has not filed a complaint concerning age discrimination with the Commission, no civil action may be commenced by any individual under this section until the individual has given the Commission not less than thirty days' notice of an intent to file such action. Such notice shall be filed within one hundred and eighty days after the alleged unlawful practice occurred. Upon receiving a notice of intent to sue, the Commission shall promptly notify all persons named therein as prospective defendants in the action and take any appropriate action to assure the elimination of any unlawful practice.

(e) Duty of Government agency or official

Nothing contained in this section shall relieve any Government agency or official of the responsibility to assure nondiscrimination on account of age in employment as required under any provision of Federal law.

(f) Applicability of statutory provisions to personnel action of Federal departments, etc.

Any personnel action of any department, agency, or other entity referred to in subsection (a) of this section shall not be subject to, or affected by, any provision of this chapter, other than the provisions of section 631(b) of this title and the provisions of this section.

(g) Study and report to President and Congress by Equal Employment Opportunity Commission; scope

(1) The Equal Employment Opportunity Commission shall undertake a study relating to the effects of the amendments made to this section by the Age Discrimination in Employment Act Amendments of 1978, and the effects of section 631(b) of this title.

(2) The Equal Employment Opportunity Commission shall transmit a report to the President and to the Congress containing the findings of the Commission resulting from the study of the Commission under paragraph (1) of this subsection. Such report shall be transmitted no later than January 1, 1980.

(Pub.L. 90–202, § 15, as added Pub.L. 93–259, § 28(b)(2), Apr. 8, 1974, 88 Stat. 74, and amended Pub.L. 95–256, § 5(a), (e), Apr. 6, 1978, 92 Stat. 191; 1978 Reorg.Plan No. 1, eff. Jan. 1, 1979, § 2, 43 F.R. 19807, 92 Stat. 3781.)

VETERANS READJUSTMENT ACT OF 1974 (38 U.S.C., CH. 42, SECTIONS 2012 AND 2014)

§ 2012. Veterans' employment emphasis under Federal contracts

(a) Any contract in the amount of $10,000 or more entered into by any department or agency for the procurement of personal property and non-personal services (including construction) for the United States, shall contain a provision requiring that the party contracting with the United States shall take affirmative action to employ and advance in employment qualified special disabled veterans and veterans of the Vietnam era. The provisions of this section shall apply to any subcontract entered into by a prime contractor in carrying out any contract for the procurement of personal property and non-personal services (including construction) for the United States. In addition to requiring affirmative action to employ such veterans under such contracts and subcontracts and in order to promote the implementation of such requirement, the President shall implement the provisions of this section by promulgating regulations which shall require that (1) each such contractor undertake in such contract to list immediately with the appropriate local employment service office all of its suitable employment openings, and (2) each such local office shall give such veterans priority in referral to such employment openings.

(b) If any special disabled veteran or veteran of the Vietnam era believes any contractor of the United States has failed to comply or refuses to comply with the provisions of the contractor's contract relating to the employment of veterans, the veteran may file a complaint with the Secretary of Labor, who shall promptly investigate such complaint and take appropriate action in accordance with the terms of the contract and applicable laws and regulations.

(c) The Secretary shall include as part of the annual report required by section 2007(c) of this title the number of complaints filed pursuant to subsection (b) of this section, the actions taken thereon and the resolutions thereof. Such report shall also include the number of contractors listing suitable employment openings, the nature, types, and number of positions listed and the number of veterans receiving priority pursuant to subsection (a)(2) of this section.

Added Pub.L. 92–540, Title V, § 503(a), Oct. 24, 1972, 86 Stat. 1097, and amended Pub.L. 93–508, Title IV, § 402, Dec. 3, 1974, 88 Stat. 1593; Pub.L. 94–502, Title VI, §§ 605, 607(2), Oct. 15, 1976, 90 Stat. 2405; Pub.L. 95–520, § 6(a), Oct. 26, 1978, 92 Stat. 1821.

(d)(1) Each contractor to whom subsection (a) of this section applies shall, in accordance with regulations which the Secretary shall prescribe, report at least annually to the Secretary on—

(A) the number of employees in the work force of such contractor, by job category and hiring location, who are veterans of the Vietnam era or special disabled veterans; and

(B) the total number of new employees hired by the contractor during the period covered by the report and the number of such employees who are veterans of the Vietnam era or special disabled veterans.

(2) The Secretary shall ensure that the administration of the reporting requirement under paragraph (1) of this subsection is coordinated with respect to any requirement for the contractor to make any other report to the Secretary.

(As amended Pub.L. 96–466, Title V, § 509, Title VIII, § 801(j), Oct. 17, 1980, 94 Stat. 2206, 2217; Pub.L. 97–306, Title III, § 310(a), Oct. 14, 1982, 96 Stat. 1442.)

1982 Amendment. Subsec. (d). Pub.L. 97–306 added subsec. (d).

§ 2014. Employment within the Federal Government

(a)(1) It is the policy of the United States and the purpose of this section to promote the maximum of employment and job advancement opportunities within the Federal Government for qualified disabled veterans and veterans of the Vietnam era.

(2) For the purposes of this section, the term "agency" means a department, agency, or instrumentality in the executive branch.

(b)(1) To further the policy stated in subsection (a) of this section, veterans of the Vietnam era shall be eligible, in accordance with regulations which the Office of Personnel Management shall prescribe, for veterans readjustment appointments, and for subsequent career-conditional appointments, under the terms and conditions specified in Executive Order Numbered 11521 (March 26, 1970), except that—

(A) such an appointment may be made up to and including the level GS–9 or its equivalent;

(B) a veteran of the Vietnam era shall be eligible for such an appointment without any time limitation with respect to eligibility for such an appointment;

(C) a veteran of the Vietnam era who is entitled to disability compensation under the laws administered by the Veterans' Administration or whose discharge or release from active duty was for a disability incurred or aggravated in line of duty shall be eligible for such an appointment without regard to the number of years of education completed by such veteran; and

(D) a veteran given an appointment under the authority of this subsection whose employment under the appointment is terminated within one year after the date of such appointed shall have the same right to appeal that termination to the Merit Systems Protection Board as a career or career-conditional employee has during the first year of employment.

(2) No veterans readjustment appointment may be made under authority of this subsection after September 30, 1986.

[(3) Redesignated (2).]

(c) Each agency shall include in its affirmative action plan for the hiring, placement, and advancement of handicapped individuals in such agency as required by section 501(b) of the Rehabilitation Act of 1973 (29 U.S.C. 791(b)), a separate specification of plans (in accordance with regulations which the Office of Personnel Management shall prescribe in consultation with the Administrator, the Secretary of Labor, and the Secretary of Health and Human Services, consistent with the purposes, provisions, and priorities of such Act) to promote and carry out such affirmative action with respect to disabled veterans in order to achieve the purpose of this section.

(d) The Office of Personnel Management shall be responsible for the review and evaluation of the implementation of this section and the activities of each agency to carry out the purpose and provisions of this section. The Office shall periodically obtain (on at least an annual basis) information on the implementation of this section by each agency and on the activities of each agency to carry out the purpose and provisions of this section. The information obtained shall include specification of the use and extent of appointments made by each agency under subsection (b) of this section and the results of the plans required under subsection (c) of this section.

(e)(1) The Office of Personnel Management shall submit to the Congress annually a report on activities carried out under this section. Each such report shall include the following information with respect to each agency:

(A) The number of appointments made under subsection (b) of this section since the last such report and the grade levels in which such appointments were made.

(B) The number of individuals receiving appointments under such subsection whose appointments were converted to career or career-conditional appointments, or whose employment under such an appointment has terminated, since the last such report, together with a complete listing of categories of causes of appointment terminations and the number of such individuals whose employment has terminated falling into each such category.

(C) The number of such terminations since the last such report that were initiated by the agency involved and the number of such terminations since the last such report that were initiated by the individual involved.

(D) A description of the education and training programs in which individuals appointed under such subsection are participating at the time of such report.

(2) Information shown for an agency under clauses (A) through (D) of paragraph (1) of this subsection—

(A) shall be shown for all veterans; and

(B) shall be shown separately (i) for veterans of the Vietnam era who are entitled to disability compensation under the laws administered by the Veterans' Administration or whose discharge or release from active duty was for a disability incurred or aggravated in line of duty, and (ii) for other veterans.

(f) Notwithstanding section 2011 of this title, the terms "veteran" and "disabled veteran" as used in subsection (a) of this section shall have the meaning provided for under generally applicable civil service law and regulations.

Added Pub.L. 93–508, Title IV, § 403(a), Dec. 3, 1974, 88 Stat. 1593, and amended Pub.L. 95–202, Title III, § 308, Nov. 23, 1977, 91 Stat. 1445; Pub.L. 95–520, § 6(b), Oct. 26, 1978, 92 Stat. 1821.

(g) To further the policy stated in subsection (a) of this section, the Administrator may give preference to qualified special disabled veterans and qualified veterans of the Vietnam era for employment in the Veterans' Administration as veterans' benefits counselors and veterans' claims examiners and in positions to provide the outreach services required under section 241 of this title, to serve as veterans' representatives at certain educational institutions as provided in section 243 of this title, or to provide readjustment counseling under section 612A of this title to veterans of the Vietnam era.

(As amended Pub.L. 96–466, Title V, § 510, Title VIII, § 801(*l*), Oct. 17, 1980, 94 Stat. 2207, 2217; Pub.L. 97–72, Title II, § 202(a), Nov. 3, 1981, 95 Stat. 1054; Pub.L. 97–295, § 4(95)(A), Oct. 12, 1982, 96 Stat. 1313; Pub.L. 98–543, Title II, § 211, Oct. 24, 1984, 98 Stat. 2743.)

VOCATIONAL REHABILITATION ACT OF 1973
(29 U.S.C. SECTIONS 701 ET SEQ.)

§ 790. Existing law affected; references in other provisions; availability of unexpended appropriations; savings provision; extension of appropriations

(a) The Vocational Rehabilitation Act [1] is repealed ninety days after September 26, 1973, and references to such Vocational Rehabilitation Act in any other provision of law shall, ninety days after such date,

1. Act June 2, 1920, c. 219, 41 Stat. 735.

be deemed to be references to the Rehabilitation Act of 1973.[2] Unexpended appropriations for carrying out the Vocational Rehabilitation Act may be made available to carry out this chapter, as directed by the President. Approved State plans for vocational rehabilitation, approved projects, and contractual arrangements authorized under the Vocational Rehabilitation Act will be recognized under comparable provisions of this chapter so that there is no disruption of ongoing activities for which there is continuing authority.

(b) The authorizations of appropriations in the Vocational Rehabilitation Act are hereby extended at the level specified for the fiscal year 1972 for the fiscal year 1973.

(Pub.L. 93–112, Title V, § 500, Sept. 26, 1973, 87 Stat. 390.)

§ 791. Employment of handicapped individuals

(a) Interagency Committee on Handicapped Employees; establishment; membership; co-chairmen; availability of other Committee resources; purpose and functions

There is established within the Federal Government an Interagency Committee on Handicapped Employees (hereinafter in this section referred to as the "Committee"), comprised of such members as the President may select, including the following (or their designees whose positions are Executive Level IV or higher): the Chairman [1] of the Office of Personnel Management, the Administrator of Veterans' Affairs, and the Secretaries of Labor and Education and Health and Human Services. The Secretary of Education and the Chairman of the Office of Personnel Management shall serve as co-chairmen of the Committee. The resources of the President's Committees on Employment of the Handicapped and on Mental Retardation shall be made fully available to the Committee. It shall be the purpose and function of the Committee (1) to provide a focus for Federal and other employment of handicapped individuals, and to review, on a periodic basis, in cooperation with the Office of Personnel Management, the adequacy of hiring, placement, and advancement practices with respect to handicapped individuals, by each department, agency, and instrumentality in the executive branch of Government, and to insure that the special needs of such individuals are being met; and (2) to consult with the Office of Personnel Management to assist the Office to carry out its responsibilities under subsections (b), (c), and (d) of this section. On the basis of such review and consultation, the Committee shall periodically make to the Office of Personnel Management such recommendations for legislative and administrative changes as it deems necessary or desirable. The Office of Personnel Management shall timely transmit to the appropriate committees of Congress any such recommendations.

2. This chapter.

1. So in original. Probably should be "Director".

(b) Federal agencies; affirmative action program plans

Each department, agency, and instrumentality (including the United States Postal Service and the Postal Rate Commission) in the executive branch shall, within one hundred and eighty days after September 26, 1973, submit to the Office of Personnel Management and to the Committee an affirmative action program plan for the hiring, placement, and advancement of handicapped individuals in such department, agency, or instrumentality. Such plan shall include a description of the extent to which and methods whereby the special needs of handicapped employees are being met. Such plan shall be updated annually, and shall be reviewed annually and approved by the Office, if the Office determines, after consultation with the Committee, that such plan provides sufficient assurances, procedures and commitments to provide adequate hiring, placement, and advancement opportunities for handicapped individuals.

(c) State agencies; rehabilitated individuals, employment

The Office of Personnel Management, after consultation with the Committee, shall develop and recommend to the Secretary for referral to the appropriate State agencies, policies and procedures which will facilitate the hiring, placement, and advancement in employment of individuals who have received rehabilitation services under State vocational rehabilitation programs, veterans' programs, or any other program for handicapped individuals, including the promotion of job opportunities for such individuals. The Secretary shall encourage such State agencies to adopt and implement such policies and procedures.

(d) Report to Congressional committees

The Office of Personnel Management, after consultation with the Committee, shall, on June 30, 1974, and at the end of each subsequent fiscal year, make a complete report to the appropriate committees of the Congress with respect to the practices of and achievements in hiring, placement, and advancement of handicapped individuals by each department, agency, and instrumentality and the effectiveness of the affirmative action programs required by subsection (b) of this section, together with recommendations as to legislation which have been submitted to the Office of Personnel Management under subsection (a) of this section, or other appropriate action to insure the adequacy of such practices. Such report shall also include an evaluation by the Committee of the effectiveness of the activities of the Office of Personnel Management under subsections (b) and (c) of this section.

(e) Federal work experience without pay; non-Federal status

An individual who, as a part of his individualized written rehabilitation program under a State plan approved under this chapter, participates in a program of unpaid work experience in a Federal agency, shall not, by reason thereof, be considered to be a Federal employee or to be subject to the provisions of law relating to Federal employment, including those relating to hours of work, rates of compensation, leave, unemployment compensation, and Federal employee benefits.

(f) Federal agency cooperation; special consideration for positions on President's Committee on Employment of the Handicapped

(1) The Secretary of Labor and the Secretary of Education are authorized and directed to cooperate with the President's Committee on Employment of the Handicapped in carrying out its functions.

(2) In selecting personnel to fill all positions on the President's Committee on Employment of the Handicapped, special consideration shall be given to qualified handicapped individuals.

(Pub.L. 93–112, Title V, § 501, Sept. 26, 1973, 87 Stat. 390; Pub.L. 98–221, Title I, § 104(b)(3), Feb. 22, 1984, 98 Stat. 18.)

§ 793. Employment under Federal contracts

(a) Amount of contracts or subcontracts; provision for employment and advancement of qualified handicapped individuals; regulations

Any contract in excess of $2,500 entered into by any Federal department or agency for the procurement of personal property and nonpersonal services (including construction) for the United States shall contain a provision requiring that, in employing persons to carry out such contract the party contracting with the United States shall take affirmative action to employ and advance in employment qualified handicapped individuals as defined in section 706(7) of this title. The provisions of this section shall apply to any subcontract in excess of $2,500 entered into by a prime contractor in carrying out any contract for the procurement of personal property and nonpersonal services (including construction) for the United States. The President shall implement the provisions of this section by promulgating regulations within ninety days after September 26, 1973.

(b) Administrative enforcement; complaints; investigations; departmental action

If any handicapped individual believes any contractor has failed or refuses to comply with the provisions of his contract with the United States, relating to employment of handicapped individuals, such individual may file a complaint with the Department of Labor. The Department shall promptly investigate such complaint and shall take such action thereon as the facts and circumstances warrant, consistent with the terms of such contract and the laws and regulations applicable thereto.

(c) Waiver by President; national interest special circumstances for waiver of particular agreements

The requirements of this section may be waived, in whole or in part, by the President with respect to a particular contract or subcontract, in accordance with guidelines set forth in regulations which he shall prescribe, when he determines that special circumstances in the national interest so require and states in writing his reasons for such determination.

(Pub.L. 93–112, Title V, § 503, Sept. 26, 1973, 87 Stat. 393; Pub.L. 95–602, Title I, § 122(d)(1), Nov. 6, 1978, 92 Stat. 2987.

§ 794. Nondiscrimination under federal grants and programs; promulgation of rules and regulations

No otherwise qualified handicapped individual in the United States, as defined in section 706(7) of this title, shall, solely by reason of his handicap, be excluded from the participation in, be denied the benefits of, or be subjected to discrimination under any program or activity receiving Federal financial assistance or under any program or activity conducted by any Executive agency or by the United States Postal Service. The head of each such agency shall promulgate such regulations as may be necessary to carry out the amendments to this section made by the Rehabilitation, Comprehensive Services, and Developmental Disabilities Act of 1978.[1] Copies of any proposed regulation shall be submitted to appropriate authorizing committees of the Congress, and such regulation may take effect no earlier than the thirtieth day after the date on which such regulation is so submitted to such committees.

(Pub.L. 93–112, Title V, § 504, Sept. 26, 1973, 87 Stat. 394; Pub.L. 95–602, Title I, §§ 119, 122(d)(2), Nov. 6, 1978, 92 Stat. 2982, 2987.)

§ 794a. Remedies and attorney fees

(a)(1) The remedies, procedures, and rights set forth in section 717 of the Civil Rights Act of 1964 (42 U.S.C. 2000e–16), including the application of sections 706(f) through 706(k) (42 U.S.C. 2000e–5(f) through (k)), shall be available, with respect to any complaint under section 791 of this title, to any employee or applicant for employment aggrieved by the final disposition of such complaint, or by the failure to take final action on such complaint. In fashioning an equitable or affirmative action remedy under such section, a court may take into account the reasonableness of the cost of any necessary work place accommodation, and the availability of alternatives therefor or other appropriate relief in order to achieve an equitable and appropriate remedy.

(2) The remedies, procedures, and rights set forth in title VI of the Civil Rights Act of 1964 [42 U.S.C.A. § 2000d et seq.] shall be available

1. Pub.L. 95–602, Nov. 6, 1978, 92 Stat. 2955.

to any person aggrieved by any act or failure to act by any recipient of Federal assistance or Federal provider of such assistance under section 794 of this title.

(b) In any action or proceeding to enforce or charge a violation of a provision of this subchapter, the court, in its discretion, may allow the prevailing party, other than the United States, a reasonable attorney's fee as part of the costs.

(Pub.L. 93–112, Title V, § 505, as added Pub.L. 95–602, Title I, § 120, Nov. 6, 1978, 92 Stat. 2982.)

OTHER REFERENCE MATERIALS

Civil Rights Act of 1968, Title I—Interference with Federally Protected Activities (P.L. 90–284)

Age Discrimination Act of 1975 (42 U.S.C. Sections 6101–6107)

EEOC:

Procedural Regulations (29 CFR 1601)

Records and Reports (29 CFR 1602)

Guidelines on Discrimination Because of Sex (29 CFR 1604)

Guidelines on Discrimination Because of Religion (29 CFR 1605)

Guidelines on Discrimination Because of National Origin (29 CFR 1606)

Availability of Records (29 CFR 1610)

Privacy Act Regulations (29 CFR 1611)

Government in the Sunshine Act Regulations (29 CFR 1612)

Equal Employment Opportunity in the Federal Government (29 CFR 1613)

Records to be Made or Kept Relating to Age; Notices to be Posted; Administrative Exemptions (29 CFR 1627)

OFCCP:

Construction Contractors—Affirmative Action Requirements (41 CFR 60–4)

Sex Discrimination Guidelines (41 CFR 60–20)

Rules of Practice for Administrative Proceedings to Enforce Equal Opportunity Under Executive Order 11246 (41 CFR 60–30)

Examination and Copying of OFCCP Documents (41 CFR 60–40)

Guidelines on Discrimination Because of Religion or National Origin (41 CFR 60–50)

Affirmative Action Obligations of Contractors and Subcontractors for Disabled Veterans and Veterans of the Vietnam Era (41 CFR 60–250)

Affirmative Action Obligations of Contractors and Subcontractors for Handicapped Workers (41 CFR 60–741)

Uniform Guidelines on Employee Selection Procedures (29 CFR 1607)

Questions and Answers on Employee Selection Guidelines (Federal Register, March 2, 1979)

OFCCP–EEOC Memorandum of Understanding (46 FR 7435)

Department of Health and Human Services: Nondiscrimination on the Basis of Age in Programs or Activities Receiving Federal Financial Assistance (45 CFR 90)

Labor Department:

Equal Employment Opportunity in Apprenticeship and Training (29 CFR 30)

Age Discrimination in Employment (29 CFR 860)

Office of Personnel Management: Affirmative Employment Programs (5 CFR 720)

Department of the Treasury: Nondiscrimination by States and Local Governments Receiving Entitlement Funds (31 CFR 51.50)

Export Administrative Act (P.L. 95–52, Sec. 201)

Executive Orders:

Equal Employment Opportunity in the Federal Government: E.O. 11478 (1969) as last amended by E.O. 12106 (1979)

Prescribing Additional Arrangements for Developing and Coordinating a National Program for Minority Business Enterprise: E.O. 11625 (1971)

Providing for Coordination of Federal Equal Employment Opportunity Programs: E.O. 12067 (1978) last amended by Sec. 2 of E.O. 12107 (1979)

Declaring a Public Policy Against Discrimination on the Basis of Age: E.O. 11141 (1964)

Citizenship Requirements for Federal Employment: E.O. 11935 (1976)

Competitive Status for Handicapped Federal Employees: E.O. 12125 (1979)

Employment of Veterans by Federal Agencies and Government Contractors and Subcontractors: E.O. 11701 (1973)

*

Index

References are to Pages

†